Revit® Architecture 2012

A Comprehensive Guide

H. Edward Goldberg

AIA, NCARB

WITHDRAWN

Boston Columbus Indianapolis New York San Francisco Upper Saddle River
Amsterdam Cape Town Dubai London Madrid Milan Munich Paris Montreal Toronto
Delhi Mexico City São Paulo Sydney Hong Kong Seoul Singapore Taipei Tokyo

Editorial Director: Vernon R. Anthony
Acquisitions Editor: Sara Eilert
Assistant Editor: Laura Weaver
Editorial Assistant: Doug Greive
Director of Marketing: David Gesell
Senior Marketing Manager: Alicia Wozniak
Marketing Assistant: Les Roberts
Associate Managing Editor: Alexandrina Benedicto Wolf
Production Project Manager: Alicia Ritchey
Operations Specialist: Deidra Skahill
Art Director: Jayne Conte
Cover Designer: Suzanne Duda
Cover Art: Courtesy of Hord Coplan Macht
Lead Media Project Manager: Karen Bretz
Full-Service Project Management: Mohinder Singh/Aptara®, Inc.
Composition: Aptara® Inc.
Printer/Binder: Edwards Brothers Malloy
Cover Printer: Lehigh-Phoenix Color
Text Font: Times New Roman PS MT

Certain images and materials contained in this publication were reproduced with the permission of Autodesk, Inc. © 2013. All rights reserved. Autodesk, AutoCAD, Revit, DWG, and the DWG logo are registered trademarks of Autodesk, Inc., in the U.S.A. and certain other countries.

Disclaimer
The publication is designed to provide tutorial information about AutoCAD® and/or other Autodesk computer programs. Every effort has been made to make this publication complete and as accurate as possible. The reader is expressly cautioned to use any and all precautions necessary, and to take appropriate steps to avoid hazards, when engaging in the activities described herein.

Neither the author nor the publisher makes any representations or warranties of any kind, with respect to the materials set forth in this publication, express or implied, including without limitation any warranties of fitness for a particular purpose or merchantability. Nor shall the author or the publisher be liable for any special, consequential or exemplary damages resulting, in whole or in part, directly or indirectly, from the reader's use of, or reliance upon, this material or subsequent revisions of this material.

Credits and acknowledgments borrowed from other sources and reproduced, with permission, in this textbook appear on appropriate page within text.

Copyright © 2013 by Pearson Education, Inc., publishing as Prentice Hall. All rights reserved. Manufactured in the United States of America. This publication is protected by Copyright, and permission should be obtained from the publisher prior to any prohibited reproduction, storage in a retrieval system, or transmission in any form or by any means, electronic, mechanical, photocopying, recording, or likewise. To obtain permission(s) to use material from this work, please submit a written request to Pearson Education, Inc., Permissions Department, One Lake Street, Upper Saddle River, New Jersey 07458, or you may fax your request to 201-236-3290.

Many of the designations by manufacturers and sellers to distinguish their products are claimed as trademarks. Where those designations appear in this book, and the publisher was aware of a trademark claim, the designations have been printed in initial caps or all caps.

Library of Congress Cataloging-in-Publication Data
Goldberg, H. Edward.
Revit Architecture 2012: A Comprehensive Guide/H. Edward Goldberg, AIA. —First [edition].
pages cm
ISBN-13: 978-0-13-295510-2
ISBN-10: 0-13-295510-5
1. Architectural drawing—Computer-aided design. 2. Architectural design—Data processing. I. Title.
NA2728.G683 2013
720.28'40285536—dc23

2012002184

10 9 8 7 6 5 4 3 2 1

ISBN 10: 0-13-295510-5
ISBN 13: 978-0-13-295510-2

I dedicate this book to the women I love:
my 99-year-old mother, Lillian,
my wife of 40 years, Judith Ellen,
and my daughter, Allison Julia.

Features of *Revit® Architecture 2012*

This text presents a modern approach to using Revit Architecture. That is, it addresses advances in technology and software evolution and introduces commands and procedures that reflect a modern, efficient use of Revit Architecture 2012. Features include:

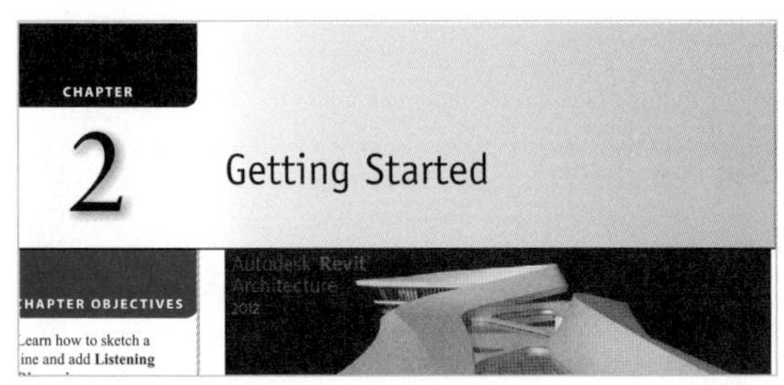

A **Getting Started** chapter at the beginning of the book allows users to get up to speed in no time to create Revit Architecture drawings.

Chapter Objectives with a bulleted list of learning objectives for each chapter provide users with a roadmap of important concepts and practices that will be introduced in the chapter.

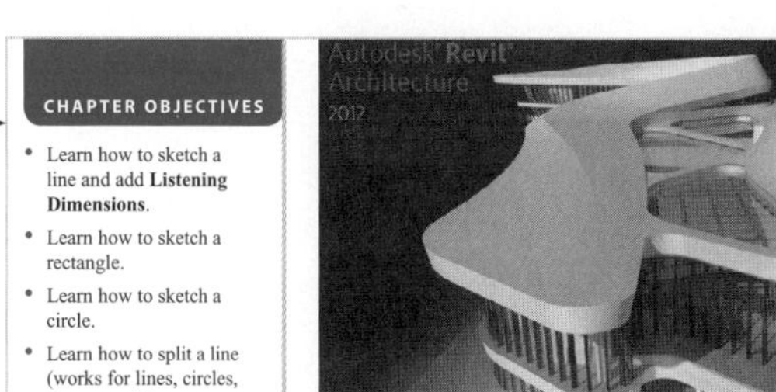

7. Click in the **Drawing Editor** to specify the start point of the line.
8. Move the cursor and click to specify the endpoint of the line.

You can also use **Listening Dimensions** to specify the length of the line.

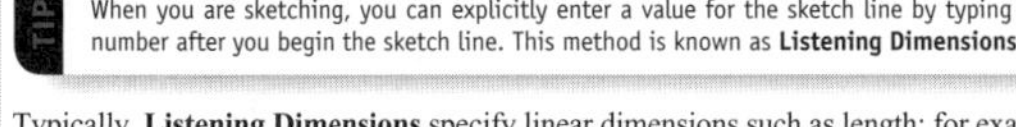

Typically, **Listening Dimensions** specify linear dimensions such as length; for exam the length of a line (when drawing a line), length of a chord (when drawing the se point of a 3-point arc), or length of a radius (when drawing an arc, circle, or polygo

9. Again, in the **Home** toolbar, select the **Model Line** button to bring up the **Mo**

Tips relate the authors' experiences to specific chapter content. These will enhance the student's success in the workplace and provide real-life tips and tricks for the problems.

Notes present hints, tips, and tricks to enhance productivity.

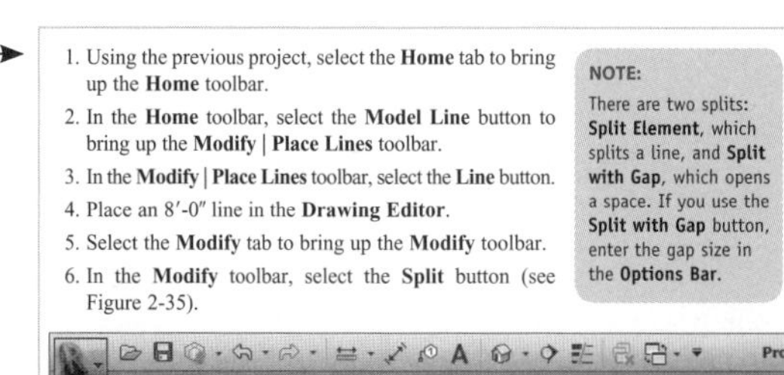
1. Using the previous project, select the **Home** tab to bring up the **Home** toolbar.
2. In the **Home** toolbar, select the **Model Line** button to bring up the **Modify | Place Lines** toolbar.
3. In the **Modify | Place Lines** toolbar, select the **Line** button.
4. Place an 8′-0″ line in the **Drawing Editor**.
5. Select the **Modify** tab to bring up the **Modify** toolbar.
6. In the **Modify** toolbar, select the **Split** button (see Figure 2-35).

NOTE:
There are two splits: **Split Element**, which splits a line, and **Split with Gap**, which opens a space. If you use the **Split with Gap** button, enter the gap size in the **Options Bar**.

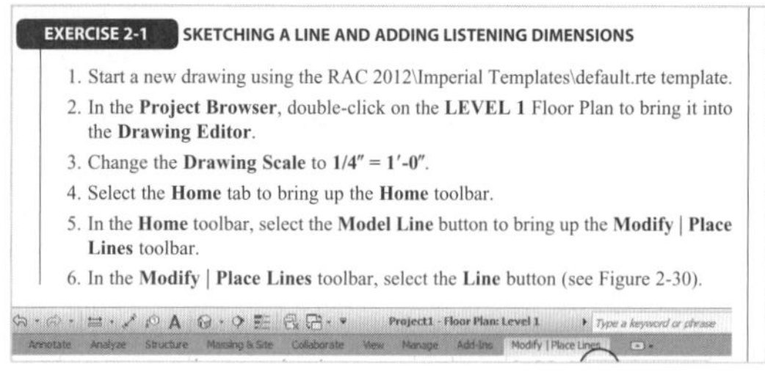

EXERCISE 2-1 SKETCHING A LINE AND ADDING LISTENING DIMENSIONS

1. Start a new drawing using the RAC 2012\Imperial Templates\default.rte template.
2. In the **Project Browser**, double-click on the **LEVEL 1** Floor Plan to bring it into the **Drawing Editor**.
3. Change the **Drawing Scale** to **1/4″ = 1′-0″**.
4. Select the **Home** tab to bring up the **Home** toolbar.
5. In the **Home** toolbar, select the **Model Line** button to bring up the **Modify | Place Lines** toolbar.
6. In the **Modify | Place Lines** toolbar, select the **Line** button (see Figure 2-30).

Exercises throughout the chapters provide step-by-step walk-through activities for the student, allowing immediate practice and reinforcement of newly learned skills.

End-of-Chapter material, easily located by shaded bars on page edges, includes:

- Chapter Summary
- Chapter Test Questions
  - Multiple Choice
  - True or False
  - Questions
  - Exercises

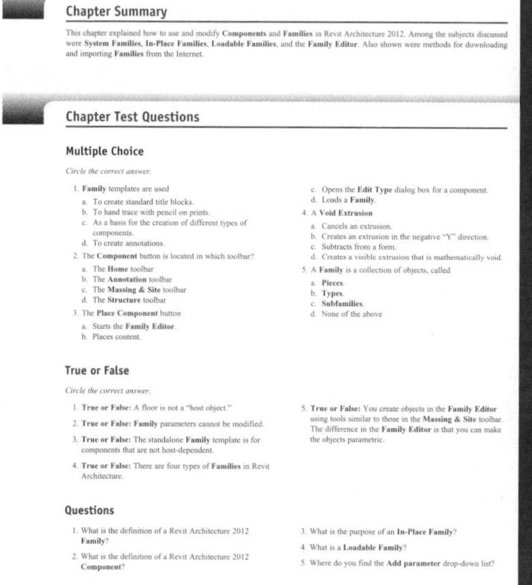

Chapter Summary

This chapter explained how to use and modify **Components** and **Families** in Revit Architecture 2012. Among the subjects discussed were **System Families**, **In-Place Families**, **Loadable Families**, and the **Family Editor**. Also shown were methods for downloading and importing **Families** from the Internet.

Chapter Test Questions

Multiple Choice

Circle the correct answer.

1. **Family** templates are used
   a. To create standard title blocks.
   b. To hand trace with pencil on prints.
   c. As a basis for the creation of different types of components.
   d. To create annotations.
2. The **Component** button is located in which toolbar?
   a. The **Home** toolbar
   b. The **Annotation** toolbar
   c. The **Massing & Site** toolbar
   d. The **Structure** toolbar
3. The **Place Component** button
   a. Starts the **Family Editor**.
   b. Places content.
   c. Opens the **Edit Type** dialog box for a component.
   d. Loads a **Family**.
4. A **Void Extrusion**
   a. Cancels an extrusion.
   b. Creates an extrusion in the negative "Y" direction.
   c. Subtracts from a form.
   d. Creates a visible extrusion that is mathematically void.
5. A **Family** is a collection of objects, called
   a. **Pieces**.
   b. **Types**.
   c. **Subfamilies**.
   d. None of the above

True or False

Circle the correct answer.

1. **True or False:** A floor is not a "host object."
2. **True or False: Family** parameters cannot be modified.
3. **True or False:** The standalone **Family** template is for components that are not host-dependent.
4. **True or False:** There are four types of **Families** in Revit Architecture.
5. **True or False:** You create objects in the **Family Editor** using tools similar to those in the **Massing & Site** toolbar. The difference in the **Family Editor** is that you can make the objects parametric.

Questions

1. What is the definition of a Revit Architecture 2012 **Family**?
2. What is the definition of a Revit Architecture 2012 **Component**?
3. What is the purpose of an **In-Place Family**?
4. What is a **Loadable Family**?
5. Where do you find the **Add parameter** drop-down list?

CHAPTER

20 Tutorial Project

HAPTER OBJECTIVES

Place a JPG logo in a emplate file.

Create a plot sheet family rom scratch

The **Tutorial Project** at the end of this text illustrates the methodology for creating a set of construction documents in Revit Architecture 2012 while giving practical practice in using Revit Architecture 2012 tools.

Style Conventions in *Revit® Architecture 2012*

Text Element	Example
Toolbar and panel names, palette names, menu items, and dialog box names—Bold and follow capitalization convention in Revit toolbar or pull-down menu (generally first letter cap).	The **Section** button in the **View** toolbar The **File** menu
Toolbar names, tool buttons, and dialog box controls/input items—Bold and follow the name of the item or the name shown in the Revit tooltip.	Choose the **Line** tool from the **Draw** panel. Choose the **Symbols and Arrows** button in the **Modify Dimension Style** dialog box. Choose the **Wall** button in the **Home** toolbar palette. In the **Lines and Arrows** toolbar set the **Arrow size**: to **.125.**
Revit prompts—Dynamic input prompts are set in a different font to distinguish them from the text. Command window prompts are set to look like the text in the command window, including capitalization, brackets, and punctuation. Text following the colon of the prompts specifies user input in bold.	Revit prompts you to *Specify first point*: *Specify center point for circle or [3P/2P/Ttr (tan tan radius)]:* **3.5**
Keyboard Input—Bold with special keys in brackets.	Type **3.5 <Enter>**

Instructor Resources

The **Online Instructor's Manual** provides answers to chapter exercises and tests and solutions to end-of-chapter problems; drawing files to get users started; and lecture-supporting PowerPoint slides.

To access supplementary materials online, instructors need to request an instructor access code. Go to **www.pearsonhighered.com/irc**, where you can register for an instructor access code. Within 48 hours after registering you will receive a confirming e-mail including an instructor access code. Once you have received your code, go to the site and log on for full instructions on downloading the materials you wish to use.

Student Resources

Pearson Design Central—Pearson has created an online community where students can share examples of their drawings and obtain resources for their drawing projects. Student data files needed for certain projects in this book can be obtained at **www.pearsondesigncentral.com**. URLs in the margin direct students to the online student data files.

About the Author

H. Edward Goldberg, AIA, NCARB, is a prominent AEC/O (Architecture/Engineering/Construction/Owner) industry analyst, Industrial Designer, and practicing licensed architect. With over 40 years experience in the field, he has been an Industrial Designer, project architect, construction project manager, owner of a design/build firm, author, and educator. Ed lives and works in both Washington, DC and Baltimore, Maryland, where he is currently principal of his own firm, HEGRA Architects Inc. (www.hegra.org). Ed specializes in commercial and residential rehabilitation, reuse, and new mid-range commercial and multistory buildings.

Mr. Goldberg is considered a leading authority on Building Information Modeling (BIM) and digital technology for the practice of architecture. He has lectured and conducted workshops at the AIA National Convention, Design DC, Autodesk University, Architecture East, AEC Systems Expos, Design Build Institute, and Associated General Contractors, among other venues.

Ed was a contributing editor for *CADALYST* Magazine, the top AEC industry publication, for ten years. He has authored thirteen books on Architectural Desktop (now AutoCAD Architecture), Revit, and Bentley Architecture. His Revit 2009/2010 book has been translated into Russian for use by the Russian state schools.

As an educator, he was the first professor of Industrial Design in the state of Israel, Coordinator of CAD and Multi-Media at Carroll Community College in 1994–2000, Coordinator of the Industrial Design Program at Towson University in 2000–2003, and now teaches the Revit course at the ITT Technical Institute in Owings Mills, Maryland.

Michael Anonuevo is an Autodesk® Revit® Architecture 2011 Certified Professional. He runs www.littledetailscount.com, a website specializing in detailed Revit families created in native Revit geometry. Since 2006, he has been using Revit to produce construction documents used in large-scale casino and entertainment projects. Prior to Revit, he has done 3D modeling work for other firms using DesignWorkshop, Form Z, and Sketchup. Michael's passion is creating unique Revit families, some of which are showcased in his website. He is also a contributing author for ClubRevit.com and AUGI AEC EDGE ezine. When not in front of the computer, he plays his keyboard synthesizer and figures out chords of R & B and jazz tunes from his collection of MP3s. He currently lives in Las Vegas.

Preface

In the ten years since it was conceived, Revit has radically changed the architectural design and documentation industry. Not only does this purpose-built solution for Building Information Modeling (BIM), building design, and authoring help architects and designers capture and analyze early concepts, but it automatically maintains the coordination of the construction documents.

With the release of Revit Architecture 2012, users have access to a robust collection of easy-to-use modeling tools for quick and precise design conceptualization, visualization, and communication. This release supports several new modeling paradigms, including intuitive direct manipulation, robust free-form modeling, and bidirectional parametric control. In addition, some highly specialized patterning and penalization techniques are now more readily accessible. New to this release is the Analyze feature to analyze energy use by structures. In building design, visualizing forms in their earliest stages enhances a designer's ability to communicate ideas; the ability to analyze and evaluate these forms yields an advantage in predicting and optimizing the real-world performance of the built project. These attributes form a core value of the Building Information Modeling (BIM) process, which Autodesk® Revit® Architecture software is purpose-built to support.

This book is based on the "tutorial" method, starting with the basic tools and finally working up to a complete building project. As with all well-designed software solutions, there is a methodology behind the operation of the interface, and that methodology is explained through simple exercises. It is the author's intent in these exercises to provide the reader with a particular routine necessary to operate the program professionally.

The topics are presented and discussed in a production-based order. Once the user has successfully completed the basic exercises, he/she can then move on to the final project, which puts all the exercises together and illustrates the development of a real-world project from start to finish. With the exception of the final project, this book deliberately discourages independent design. The author, through many years of experience as an architect and professor, has found that allowing students to design while learning a software program is counterproductive. It is therefore recommended that this book be used in the order that it has been written. This is not to discourage design, but rather to get students "up and running" with the basic program before they move on to more exploratory visions. Please try to become familiar with each exercise before moving on to the next one. You must be open to different ways of operating Revit Architecture. After completing a series of tutorials, it is often helpful to go back and experiment with settings to see what changes happen. Although Revit Architecture is relatively easy to understand, it is a very deep and complex program, and different operators choose to operate it in different ways.

An Instructor's Resource website is available including PowerPoint® presentations and an Instructors' Manual with a proposed curriculum.

About This Book

This book can serve as a reference for architects and designers or as a guide. The text traverses, chapter by chapter, through the complete and advanced usage of each of the software's capabilities. Each chapter ends with problems, with answers given in the Instructor's Manual. These problems can be used as test questions, additional exercises, or homework assignments.

Features New to This Edition

1. New, comprehensive tutorials explaining the Massing and Modeling features of Revit 2012.
2. New Energy Model and Energy Analysis tutorials.
3. New True or False and Multiple Choice questions at the end of each chapter.
4. Rearrangement of chapters to facilitate a more logical learning method.
5. New Truss exercises.

Acknowledgments

I want to thank all the people at Autodesk for their help on this book. I especially want to thank Michael Anonuevo for his excellent tutorials on massing and modeling. I also want to thank the following whose contributions helped shape the final text:

Reviewers

Patrick E. Connolly
Purdue University

Clark Cory
Purdue University

Frank Heitzman
Trito College

Alex Lepeska
Renton Technical College

Brief Contents

Contents

Revit® Architecture 2012

CHAPTER

1

The BIM and Revit Architecture

The Building Information Model and BIM Software

Autodesk® Revit®
Architecture
2012
Image courtesy of CCDI Group
Autodesk®

CHAPTER OBJECTIVES

- Understand the history and concept of **Building Information Modeling (BIM)**.
- Understand the concept of parametric modeling.
- Understand why parametric building modeling matters.
- Understand the one-model **BIM** concept.

Introduction

Twenty-five years ago, Autodesk created AutoCAD and revolutionized architectural drafting for the masses. With the introduction of AutoCAD, production time decreased significantly. Regardless, AutoCAD was only electronic drawing—quicker perhaps, but it still followed the concept of 2D plan, elevation, section, and detail that had been in use for hundreds of years. Today, with Revit Architecture, which is Building Information Model (BIM) authoring software, designers are creating buildings in a new way. Instead of depending on 2D views, they are designing buildings virtually. This has several benefits. The first benefit of the virtual building is its ability to allow easy visual examination of the building from any direction. This allows the designer to better visualize his/her design. The next benefit is the ability to test, analyze, and quantify the building. Because the virtual building acts like its real-world counterpart, it is possible to analyze such things as energy usage, shading, and component clashes. Another benefit of the BIM is that it allows the contractors to price and simulate the construction of the building while checking different construction scenarios. This last capability (simulation), often called *4D,* has been used by many of the large construction companies to schedule when and where material should be delivered. Programs such as NavisWorks combine a Microsoft® Project or Primavera schedule with a BIM model, allowing you to construct a simulation based on these scheduling programs. Finally, because the components of the BIM model are 3D digital models, they are often prime candidates for automated manufacturing. It is becoming quite common for the steel beams and stairs designed in BIM models to be sent directly to computerized steel cutting and assembly machines. All of this BIM capability, though, does have drawbacks. BIM operators are often no longer just draftspersons; they are also licensed professionals. This is because operators of BIM software must have a much better understanding of how buildings go together. The BIM is opening up new opportunities for those who understand how to build and analyze models. As the BIM and Revit Architecture become an industry standard, new operator definitions such as Virtual Contractor or Virtual Architect may be created.

Big BIM, Little Bim

Much has been written about the BIM, but few people really understand its meaning and its impact. The book *BIG BIM, little bim* by Finith E. Jernigan does a good job in explaining the difference between the concept of the BIM (the Big BIM) and the software utilized to create it (the little bim) and is highly recommended reading.

Basically, the Big BIM is defined by Jernigan as "all the information about a project within its property lines to the center of the earth and infinitely to the sky from its inception through construction and use until its final decommission and elimination." This includes the structures and associated information, weather history, taxes, ground compaction, utilities, manufactures, equipment, and more. Eventually the BIM will include all of the available digital databases of information available through the Internet.

The little bim, as this author interprets Jernigan, is the software used to create the Big BIM. To be truly viable, a BIM software solution must contain a modeler capable of quickly and easily modeling a 3D model. If it takes longer to create the 3D model than it would take to draw the model in three views, much of the design benefit of the BIM is lost. To this end, the major BIM software player, Revit Architecture, includes routines that allow for ease of modeling. Since the BIM mimics a real project, some of the real benefits on the design side can be fully realized only when the architect or designer is the computer operator. This issue demands thoughtful attention from many of the large architectural firms that have traditionally used CAD as an electronic drafting tool. They have structured their practices with a hierarchy in which a project architect sketches a concept, and the CAD operator merely acts as a scribe. One of the greatest values of using Revit Architecture at the design stage is the ability for the designer to understand the relationships between the building and its systems virtually instantaneously. This understanding may involve aesthetic, special, performance, or program issues. Until recently, the modeling of virtual buildings has focused primarily on improving drawing productivity in creating construction documents. One of the great productivity features of Revit Architecture software is its ability to generate elevations and sections automatically from the model and have them coordinated and updated whenever a change has been made to the model. Another productivity feature is the ability to create and maintain schedules for objects such as doors, windows, walls, and so on.

Autodesk Defines the BIM

According to Autodesk, "(BIM) refers to the creation and use of coordinated, consistent, computable information about a building project in design—information used for design decision making, production of high-quality construction documents, predicting performance, cost-estimating and construction planning, and, eventually, for managing and operating the facility."

Parametric Building Modeling: BIM's Foundation

What Is Parametric Modeling?

Original CAD engines used explicit, coordinate-based geometry to create graphic entities. Editing these "dumb graphics" was cumbersome and extremely error prone. Documentation was created by extracting coordinates from the model and generating standalone 2D drawings. As graphic engines matured, graphical entities were combined to represent a design element (a wall, a hole, etc.). Depending on the software, the models became "smarter" and were a bit easier to edit. Surface and solid modelers added more intelligence to the elements and enabled the creation of complex forms. However, the result was still an explicit (coordinate-based) geometric model, which was inherently difficult to edit and had a tenuous relationship to extracted drawings that easily fell out of sync with the model. Then parametric modeling engines that used parameters (numbers or characteristics) to determine the behavior of a graphical entity and define relationships between model components arrived. For example, "the diameter of this hole is one inch" or "the center of this hole is midway between these edges." This meant that the design criteria or intent could be captured during the modeling process. Editing the model became much easier and preserved the original design intent. This was the breakthrough that gave credibility to the concept of a digital design model. The mechanical design world (at the forefront of parametric modeling) made MCAD parametric modeling the status quo for mechanical design. (For more information, refer to the Autodesk Technical White Paper, *Parametric Building Modeling: BIM's Foundation,* 2007.)

What about Buildings?

Unfortunately, MCAD parametric modelers do not scale to a building project. They usually rely on two basic technologies to propagate change: history-based (which plays back the design steps for the model each time a change is made) or variational (which attempts to solve all conditions simultaneously with each change). Using these change engines to resolve even a small building is prohibitively slow. MCAD modelers also generally require the user to embed a lot of constraints (such as Relationships) so that the change technologies described above can recalculate the result. These "fully constrained" models are suitable for the mechanical design world because the product (manufactured from raw chunks of material) has to be precisely defined—unlike a building, which is generally a collection of prefabricated components with relatively few constraints that really matter to a building designer. The technology that made parametric modeling work for building design, and therefore enabled parametric building modeling, is the context-driven change engine used in the Revit platform for building information modeling.

Why Parametric Building Modeling Matters

Why is parametric building modeling so vital to BIM? BIM is an approach to building design that is characterized by the creation and use of coordinated, internally consistent, computable information about a building project. Reliable building information is the essential feature of BIM and its digital design processes. BIM solutions that use parametric building modelers provide building information that is more coordinated, more reliable, of better quality, and more internally consistent than that provided by object CAD software that has been repurposed for BIM.

Purpose-Built for Architecture

Purpose-built BIM applications that use a parametric building modeler, like Revit, deliver this kind of information by design, through the natural operation of the software. When using a CAD solution, the graphical presentation of information (such as drawings or renderings) may look similar to the output of a purpose-built parametric building modeler, but is it coordinated, internally consistent, and reliable? CAD-based technology is rarely used for BIM, due to the extremely high level of effort required to include and coordinate actionable building information such as schedule, cost, design scope, building performance, and so on. More sophisticated, object CAD systems store some (nongraphical) data about a building in a logical structure with the 3D building graphics. Users can extract this data to provide information about quantities and attributes, just as they can extract 2D drawings from 3D graphics. However, object CAD systems remain anchored to graphics. Because of this, additional tools (and effort) are required to keep the graphical and nongraphical data in sync to assure the integrity and coordination of object CAD models and to deliver the benefits of BIM. One example of such a tool is Solibri Model Checker®, which is designed to identify inconsistencies and errors in data produced from object CAD models before the data are used for other purposes. The larger the project, the greater the effort required to keep the data coordinated, and the greater the likelihood of inconsistencies. A parametric building model combines a design model (geometry and data) with a behavioral model (change management). The entire building model and complete set of design documents is in an integrated database, where everything is parametric and interconnected. The analogy of a spreadsheet is often used to describe parametric building modeling. A change made anywhere in a spreadsheet is expected to update everywhere automatically. The same is true for a parametric building modeler—real-time self-coordination of the information in every view of the model. No one expects to have to update a spreadsheet manually. Similarly, no one has to revise a document or schedule manually from a parametric building modeler. This bidirectional associativity and immediate, comprehensive change propagation results in the high-quality, consistent, reliable model output that is key to BIM, facilitating digital-based processes for design, analysis, and documentation.

Documentation

It is Autodesk's opinion that only a purpose-built data architecture built around a parametric building model can provide an immediate and fully coordinated set of accurate and reliable conventional documents. A BIM solution that can coordinate changes and maintain consistency at all times lets users focus on building design versus change management. This built-in change-management capability is critical to the disconnected building process—which is still heavily dependent on construction documentation—providing confidence in drawing deliverables.

The BIM and the One-Model Concept

The BIM is also about collaboration, often real-time, with other resources such as owners, engineers, contractors, manufacturers, and so on. This collaboration should increase productivity because more information will be available at the earlier stages of a project, rather than later as is presently done. When informed decisions are made early in a project design, mistakes are reduced, and costs are lowered. Part of this collaboration can also be attributed to the *one-model concept*. In this concept, all of the engineers contribute their part of the model to create a "virtual" whole. For example, the structural engineer creates the structure, such as a steel frame, and it is integrated into the model being created by the architect. Some contractors have a problem with the one-model concept, preferring to create a model specifically tailored to their own needs. Other contractors prefer to work with the architect or designer during the design process to incorporate their needs into the one-model concept. Regardless how it is done, BIM is the direction in which building design and documentation is going.

The following figures show examples of buildings being built using BIM software. As of today, though, very few of the buildings designed using BIM software are being designed utilizing the Big BIM concept (see Figures 1-1 through 1-7).

Figure 1-1

Office building
(Hord | Coplan | Macht)

Figure 1-2

Lobby
(Hord | Coplan | Macht)

Figure 1-3

Building framework
(BIM model created by EYP Architecture & Engineering P.C. Used with permission.)

Figure 1-4

Office complex

Figure 1-5

Storage facility
(Courtesy of HEGRA Architects)

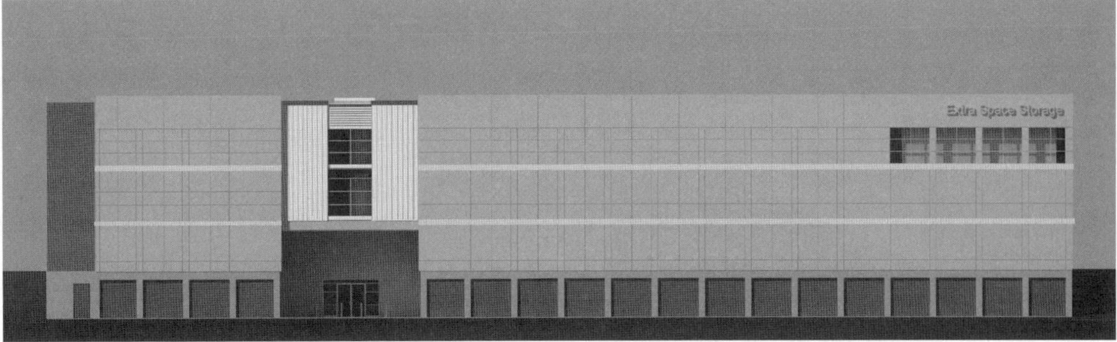

Figure 1-6

Storage facility
(Courtesy of HEGRA Architects)

Additional Software and Services

Although Revit has features that speed construction documentation, new values have been found in utilizing the information contained in the BIM model. With Revit Architecture as the base modeling product, you can analyze, estimate, construct, and then finally manage the operation of a project. The following are some of the additional software and services that extend the viability of Revit Architecture.

e-SPECS® Automated Specifications

http://www.e-specs.com

e-SPECS automates the preparation of construction specifications by extracting the product and material requirements directly from the project's model (see Figure 1-8). e-SPECS solutions integrate the entire project team into the specification development process, streamlining the document coordination process and reducing reliance on inefficient and nonintegrated word processing systems.

Green Building Studio®

http://www.greenbuildingstudio.com

Green Building Studio, now owned by Autodesk, is a Web service that assists in the energy analysis of buildings in the design stages as well as the selection of energy-efficient green building products and materials. The Green Building Studio Web service was developed by Green Building Studio, Inc., and funded through grants from the California Energy Commission Public Interest Energy Research (PIER) Program, Pacific Gas & Electric Company, U.S. Environmental Protection Agency, Northwest Energy Efficiency Alliance, and other organizations. Some of the data that can be generated from the BIM model by Green Building Studio V3.0 are as follows:

- **Carbon Neutral Building Check**—Automatically estimates the feasibility for each building to achieve carbon neutral status using local grid emission data.
- **U.S. EPA ENERGY STAR Score**—Computes each building's U.S. EPA ENERGY STAR score or Architecture 2030's targets.
- **Water Use Analysis**—Estimates the water needs, savings associated with efficiency measures, rain capture potential, and LEED credits for the building.

Figure 1-7

One World Trade Center
(Courtesy of Skidmore, Owings & Merrill)

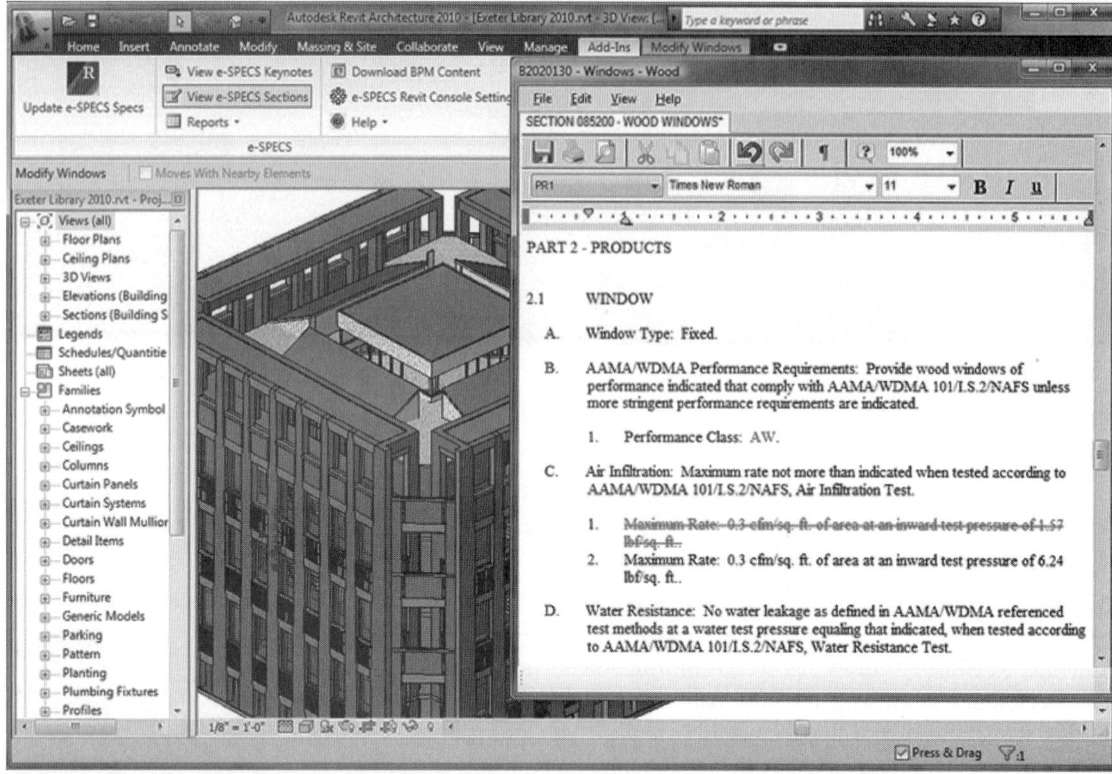

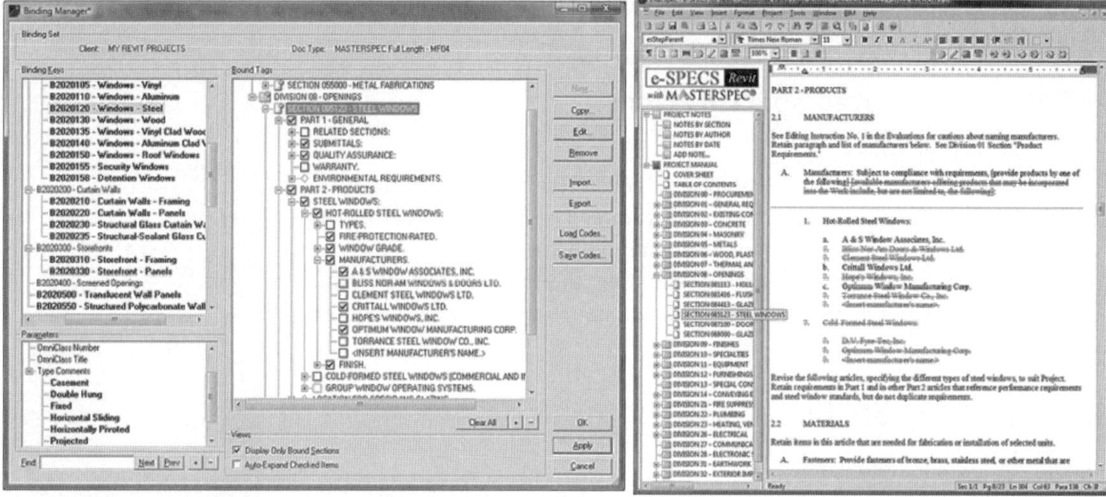

Figure 1-8

e-SPECS software

(e-SPECS is a product of InterSpec, Inc. Used with permission.)

- **Day Lighting with Energy Savings**—Automatically determines the LEED Glaze factor for each room with lighting control energy savings.
- **Natural Ventilation Potential**—Automatically determines whether the building location and loads are well suited for naturally ventilating the building.
- **Local Weather Data**—Provides access to over 60,000 weather locations, ensuring that the design team uses local hourly weather data obtained within 14 km of a building rather than from the typical 230 airport locations.
- **Corporate Accounts**—Provides firmwide management of users, building designs, building templates, and review of corporatewide CO_2 emissions, energy, and water use analyses. Leverages key staff on every project no matter which office they are in (see Figures 1-9 and 1-10).

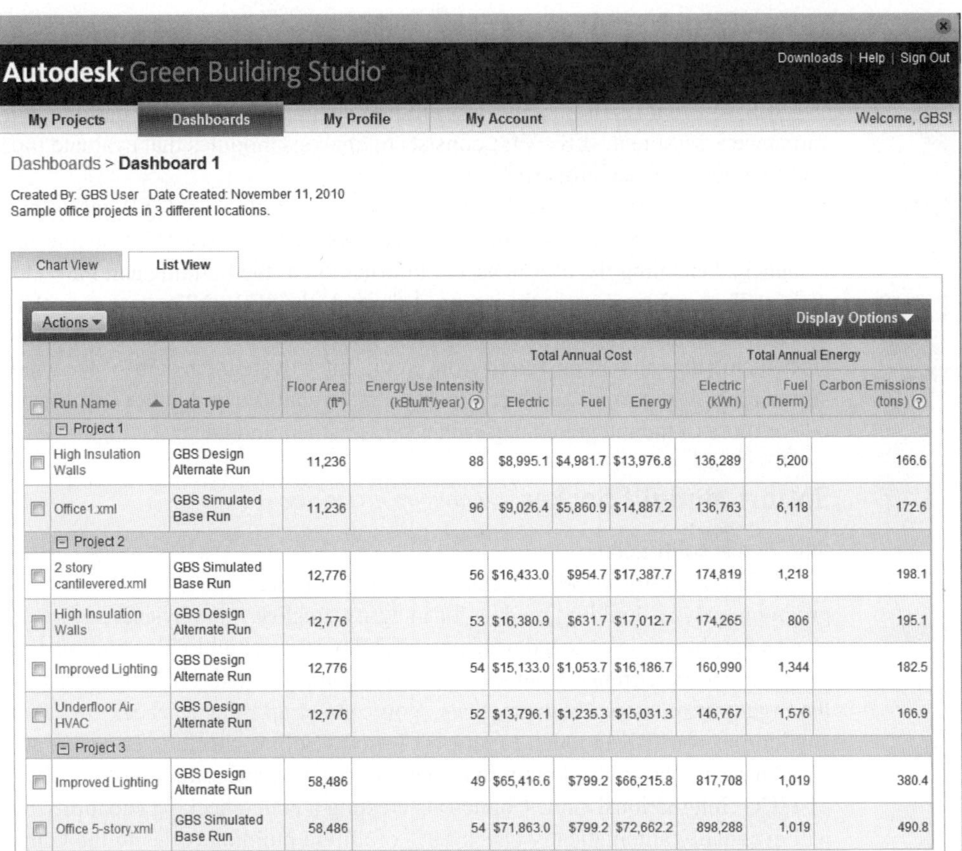

Run Name	Data Type	Floor Area (ft²)	Energy Use Intensity (kBtu/ft²/year)	Total Annual Cost: Electric	Fuel	Energy	Total Annual Energy: Electric (kWh)	Fuel (Therm)	Carbon Emissions (tons)
Project 1									
High Insulation Walls	GBS Design Alternate Run	11,236	88	$8,995.1	$4,981.7	$13,976.8	136,289	5,200	166.6
Office1.xml	GBS Simulated Base Run	11,236	96	$9,026.4	$5,860.9	$14,887.2	136,763	6,118	172.6
Project 2									
2 story cantilevered.xml	GBS Simulated Base Run	12,776	56	$16,433.0	$954.7	$17,387.7	174,819	1,218	198.1
High Insulation Walls	GBS Design Alternate Run	12,776	53	$16,380.9	$631.7	$17,012.7	174,265	806	195.1
Improved Lighting	GBS Design Alternate Run	12,776	54	$15,133.0	$1,053.7	$16,186.7	160,990	1,344	182.5
Underfloor Air HVAC	GBS Design Alternate Run	12,776	52	$13,796.1	$1,235.3	$15,031.3	146,767	1,576	166.9
Project 3									
Improved Lighting	GBS Design Alternate Run	58,486	49	$65,416.6	$799.2	$66,215.8	817,708	1,019	380.4
Office 5-story.xml	GBS Simulated Base Run	58,486	54	$71,863.0	$799.2	$72,662.2	898,288	1,019	490.8

Figure 1-9

Green Building Studio general information

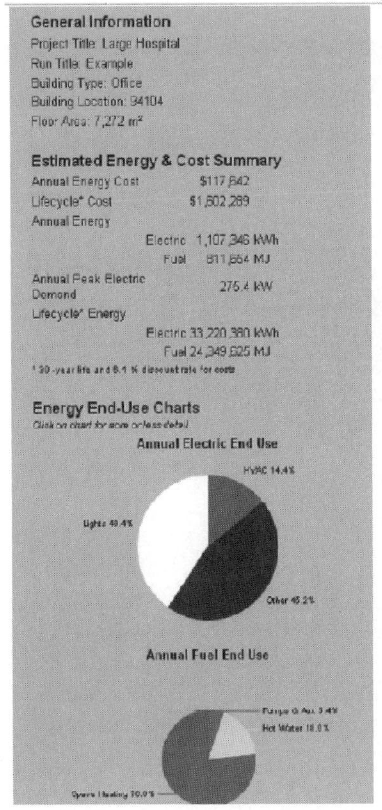

General Information: The General Building information section at the top of the page describes the project scenario, building type, geographic location, and gross floor area.

Estimated Energy & Cost Summary: Most building energy cost comparisons and early compliance decisions can be made using annualized energy cost and consumption information. Costs are estimated using local utilities rates. The following information is provided:

- Annual Energy Cost
- Lifecycle Energy Costs (30 year)
- Annual Energy Consumption (electric and gas)
- Peak Electric Energy Demand (kW)
- Lifecycle Energy Consumption (electric and gas)

Energy End-Use Charts: Further breakdowns of energy use for major electric and gas end uses like lighting, HVAC, and space heating are provided in graphical format. Numbers associated with each category can be seen by clicking on the pie charts with your mouse.

Figure 1-10

Green Building Studio energy information

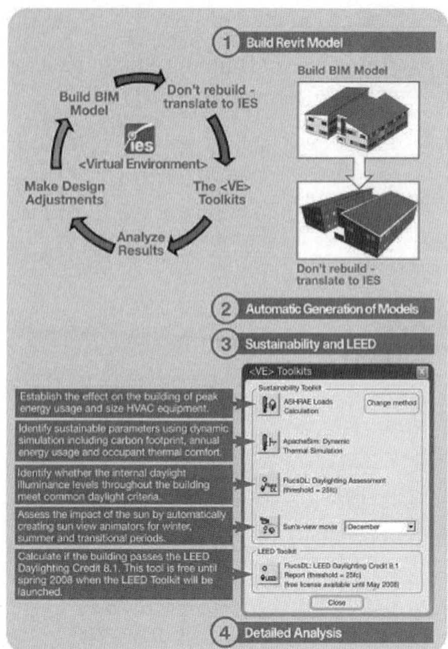

Figure 1-11

<Virtual Environment> Sustainability Toolkit
(Courtesy of IES VE Software)

IES <Virtual Environment>®

http://www.iesve.com

IES <Virtual Environment> is a unique, integrated system for building performance assessment. IES <VE> consists of analysis modules that evaluate most building performance properties.

The <VE> Sustainability Toolkit makes it extremely easy for Revit users to undertake a range of building simulation analyses. Within Revit MEP, an interface is launched enabling the user to assign information to the building and individual rooms. This information is then passed through the IES <VE>, and the <VE> Toolkit is displayed. Select any button, and the Toolkit will run the chosen analysis by using the model transferred from Revit. Interrogate the results of the analysis via an html report, or conduct a more detailed analysis within the <VE> using one or more of the integrated performance assessment modules (see Figure 1-11).

Solibri Model Checker®

http://www.solibri.com

Think of Solibri Model Checker as a spell checker for virtual models. The program analyzes building models for integrity, quality, and physical security. It checks for potential flaws and weaknesses in the design, highlights clashing components, and determines whether the model complies with building codes and the organization's own best practices. You can set up rules to check just about anything in your BIM model. Figure 1-12 shows Solibri checking escape routes.

Automatic code checking will be a boon to the architectural design industry. The ICC (International Code Council) is creating a code-checking capability that will eventually automatically check 80% of all the building codes in the United States. You can try the Smart Codes Instant Code Compliance Checking demonstration using the Solibri Model Viewer at http://www.iccsafe.org/Pages/default.aspx.

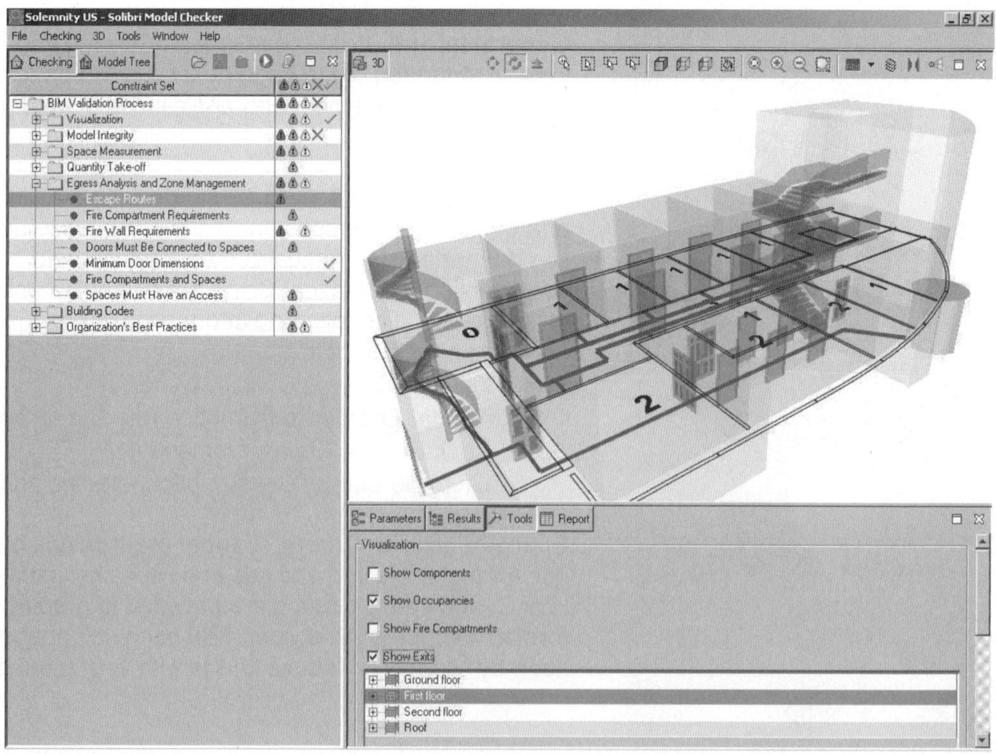

Figure 1-12

Solibri Model Checker
(Courtesy of Solibri Inc.)

Ecotect®

http://www.autodesk.com/ecotect-analysis

Ecotect is a fully featured building performance analysis and design solution. It combines an interactive building design interface and 3D modeler with a wide range of environmental analysis tools for a detailed assessment of solar, thermal, lighting, shadows and shading design, energy and building regulations, acoustics, airflow, cost, and resource performance of buildings at any scale. Even more importantly, this has been written and developed by designers for designers to be as useful at the concept stage as it is during final design development (see Figures 1-13 and 1-14).

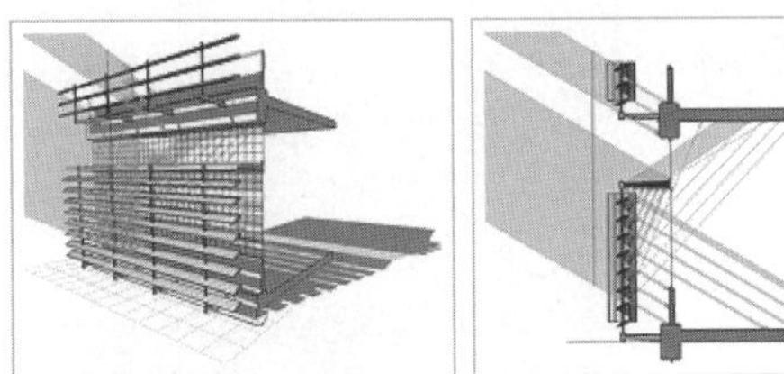

Alternatively, by tracking solar rays you can quickly see how your own more complex shading and light redirection systems are likely to work under different conditions throughout the year.

Figure 1-13

Ecotect tracking solar rays

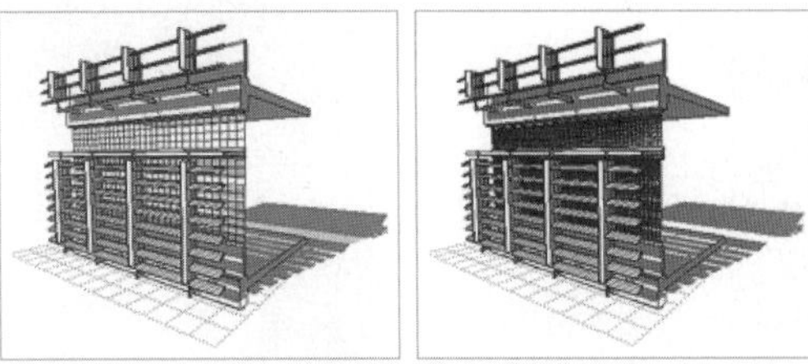

Once a complex shading system has been modelled, you can quickly calculate how much solar radiation actually hits any part of the window, either instantaneously or over any date and time range.

Figure 1-14

Ecotect calculating solar radiation

NavisWorks JetStream V5®

http://usa.autodesk.com/navisworks

This company was recently purchased by Autodesk. The software is capable of importing file formats and models from most of the different BIM software vendors. Using NavisWorks, you can bring together models from different disciplines and analyze the entire model (see Figure 1-15).

Roamer—Smooth real-time walkthrough of all major native 3D design and laser scan file formats to combine models produced in different applications for review.

Publisher—Share 3D models faithful to the original design data with anyone using the free JetStream Freedom viewing software.

Freedom—Free .nwd viewing software.

Presenter—Easily create compelling images and animations to convey design ideas and intent accurately and effectively.

Clash Detective—Effective identification, inspection, and reporting of interferences in a 3D project model.

TimeLiner—Visual simulation of work processes by linking 3D model data to project schedules.

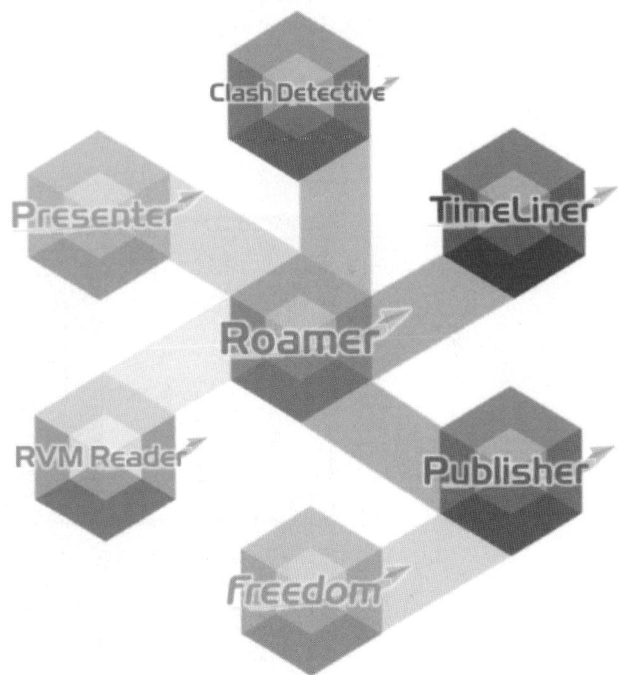

Figure 1-15

NavisWorks analyzes models from different disciplines

Innovaya Visual Estimating®

http://www.innovaya.com

Innovaya Visual Estimating 9.4 is a true BIM-based estimating solution that integrates Revit applications with Microsoft Excel, MC2 ICE, and Sage Timberline Estimating, and it integrates with 4D scheduling through Innovaya 4D Visual Simulation supporting MS Project and Primavera. This program is used by many of the large construction companies for estimating (see Figures 1-16 and 1-17).

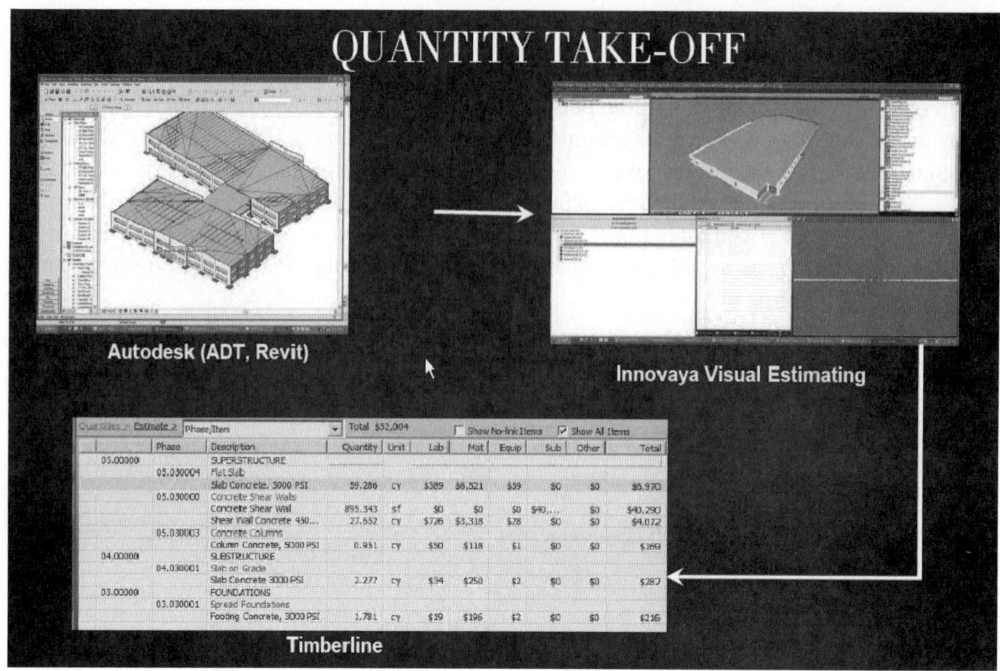

Figure 1-16

Innovaya Visual Estimating integrates with other applications
(Courtesy of Innovaya, LLC)

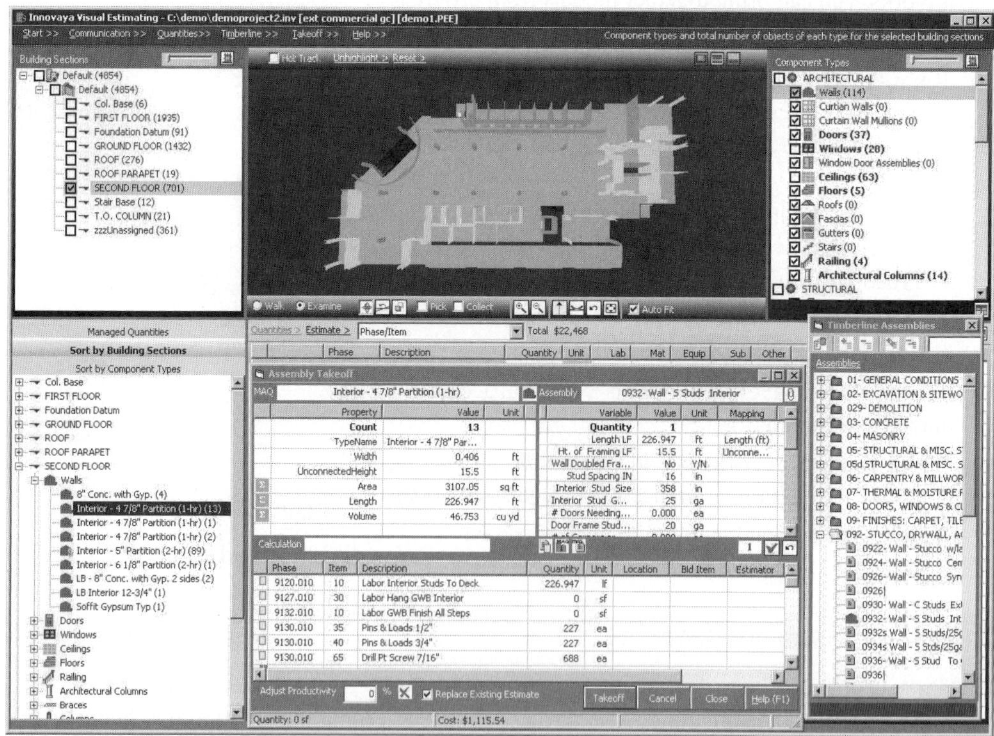

Figure 1-17

Innovaya Visual Estimating program
(Courtesy of Innovaya, LLC)

Additional Resources

Presently, most of the large architecture firms such as SOM, HOK, HNTB, RTKL, and so on are using Revit Architecture, and the small-firm user base is growing exponentially. In the near future, the BIM and Revit Architecture (BIM software) may well become standard for the design, analysis, construction, and operation of buildings.

The following resources may be helpful in understanding the role that the BIM and Autodesk Revit Architecture play in the Architecture, Engineering, and Construction (AEC) industry.

Books

- Eastman, Chuck, Teicholz, Paul, Sacks, Rafael, Liston, Kathleen, et al. *BIM Handbook: A Guide to Building Information Modeling for Owners, Managers, Designers, Engineers, and Contractors*. Hoboken, NJ: John Wiley and Sons, 2008.
- Jernigan, Finith E. *BIG BIM, little bim*, 2nd ed. Salisbury, MD: 4Site Press, 2008.

Websites

- TenLinks

  http://www.tenlinks.com

  This CAD electronic daily magazine includes information about the CAD industry as well as tutorials, tips, and tricks.
- 123 Revit

  http://aec.cadalyst.com

  This site has various links to the *Cadalyst* online magazine, as well as tips and tricks for architectural design.
- AECbytes

  http://www.aecbytes.com

  This is the home page for a monthly newsletter containing BIM information, software reviews, and tips and tricks for the AEC industry.
- Architectural Record

  http://archrecord.construction.com

  This online monthly magazine provides articles on topics related to design ideas and trends, building science, business and professional strategies, exploration of key issues, new products, and computer-aided practice.
- CADinfo.net

  http://www.cadinfo.net

  This site offers information on computer-aided design, computer-aided manufacturing, computer-aided engineering, design, technical drawing, drafting, delineation, visualization, and manufacturing.
- Ed's Independent Voice

  http://www.hegra.org

  Monthly newsletter aimed at the digital AEC industry. This newsletter discusses the BIM, and all the new and important BIM software products.
- National BIM Standard

  http://www.buildingsmartalliance.org/nbims

  This website has information about the National Institute of Building Sciences (NIBS).

Chapter Summary

This chapter discussed the concepts behind the BIM (Building Information Model), BIM software (BIM authoring tools), and the benefits of the BIM.

Chapter Test Questions

True or False

Circle the correct answer.

1. **True or False:** The BIM is an evolution of CAD.
2. **True or False:** BIM software can be used as traditional 2D CAD.
3. **True or False:** One of the values of the BIM is the ability for the designer to understand the relationships of the building and its systems.
4. **True or False:** The BIM model can be used for manufacturing.
5. **True or False:** Eventually the BIM will include all the available digital databases of information available through the Internet.

Questions

1. What is the difference between the BIM and BIM authoring software?
2. How does BIM software differ from traditional 2D CAD?
3. What does "4D" mean in relationship to BIM software?
4. How can the BIM be used for analysis?
5. What is your interpretation of the Virtual Contractor or Virtual Architect?

CHAPTER

2 Getting Started

CHAPTER OBJECTIVES

- Learn how to sketch a line and add **Listening Dimensions**.
- Learn how to sketch a rectangle.
- Learn how to sketch a circle.
- Learn how to split a line (works for lines, circles, arcs, or walls).
- Understand families.
- Understand levels.
- Understand check boxes.
- Understand radio buttons.
- Use and understand contextual menus.
- Use and understand constraints.
- Understand dialog boxes and context-sensitive menus.
- Understand object snaps.
- Understand and use the **Application** menu.

Autodesk® Revit®
Architecture
2012
Image courtesy of CCDI Group
Autodesk®

Introduction

Autodesk Revit® Architecture 2012 is the latest iteration of Autodesk's purpose-built BIM software running on Windows-based computers. In this version, Autodesk has refined its Toolbar interface, and improved its conceptual creation tools. The program can be run as either a 32-bit or a 64-bit version. (Both version options are included upon installation.)

A Note from the Author

There is a philosophy behind the tutorial method used in this book. These tutorials have been designed to give the student an experience of the operation methodology that I feel is effective in learning Revit Architecture. In my opinion, the operation of any architectural design and documentation software can be analogized both to driving an automobile with a manual transmission and to playing a game of chess.

First, I often remind students how difficult it seemed when they first tried to drive an automobile, especially with a manual transmission. Then I ask them to remember any of the actions they made while driving to class. If they had a manual transmission, did they remember changing gears? The point is, when you practice using the tools on simple tasks, they become routine. As you add more tasks, you build a repertoire of solutions. Operating Revit Architecture effectively depends on picking the correct tool for a particular task.

Second, chess is a game of strategy, and operating Revit Architecture is similar to playing chess. The goal in Revit Architecture is to get the most result with the least effort (keystrokes). In order to do this, you must think several moves ahead with a clear goal in mind. As with chess, your building project will always be opposing you (as all projects do). Don't be afraid of trying a new strategy (unless you are on deadline), and practice, practice, practice.

Finally, you must be open to learning different ways to operate Revit Architecture. After you have completed a series of tutorials, go back and experiment with settings to see what changes happen. Although Revit Architecture is relatively easy to understand, it is a very deep and complex program, and different operators use it in different ways.

Let's get started!

Creating a Project

Following is the process for creating a new project in Revit Architecture.

1. Whenever you start Revit Architecture 2012, the **Recent Files** screen appears.
2. Select the **New** button (under **Projects**) to bring up the **Autodesk Revit Architecture Workspace** (see Figure 2-1).

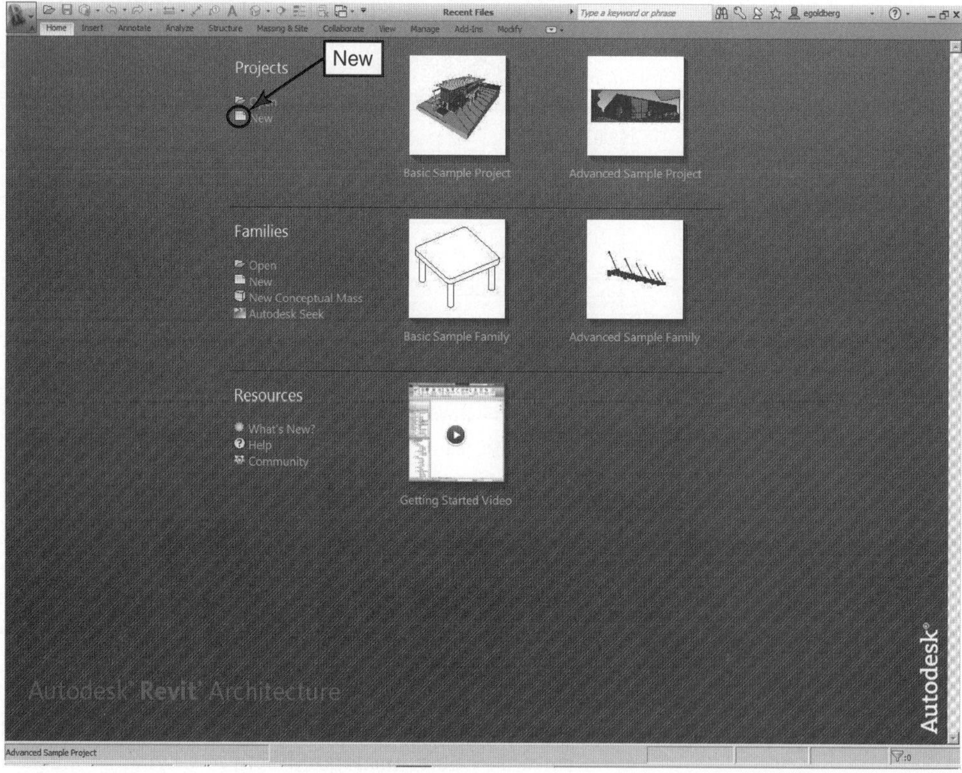

Figure 2-1

The **Revit Architecture Workspace**

3. The **Revit Architecture** interface will appear, and you will be ready to work (see Figure 2-2).
4. Once inside a Revit project, more projects can be created or opened from the **Application** menu.
5. Select **Application menu** > **New** > **Project** to bring up the **New Project** dialog box.
6. In the **New Project** dialog box, select the C:\ProgramData\Autodesk\RAC 2012\Imperial Templates\default.rte from the **Template file**, select the **Project** radio button, and then press the **OK** button to create a new project (see Figure 2-3).

NOTE:

You can open existing projects from either the **Recent Files** screen or the **Application** menu by selecting the **Open** button.

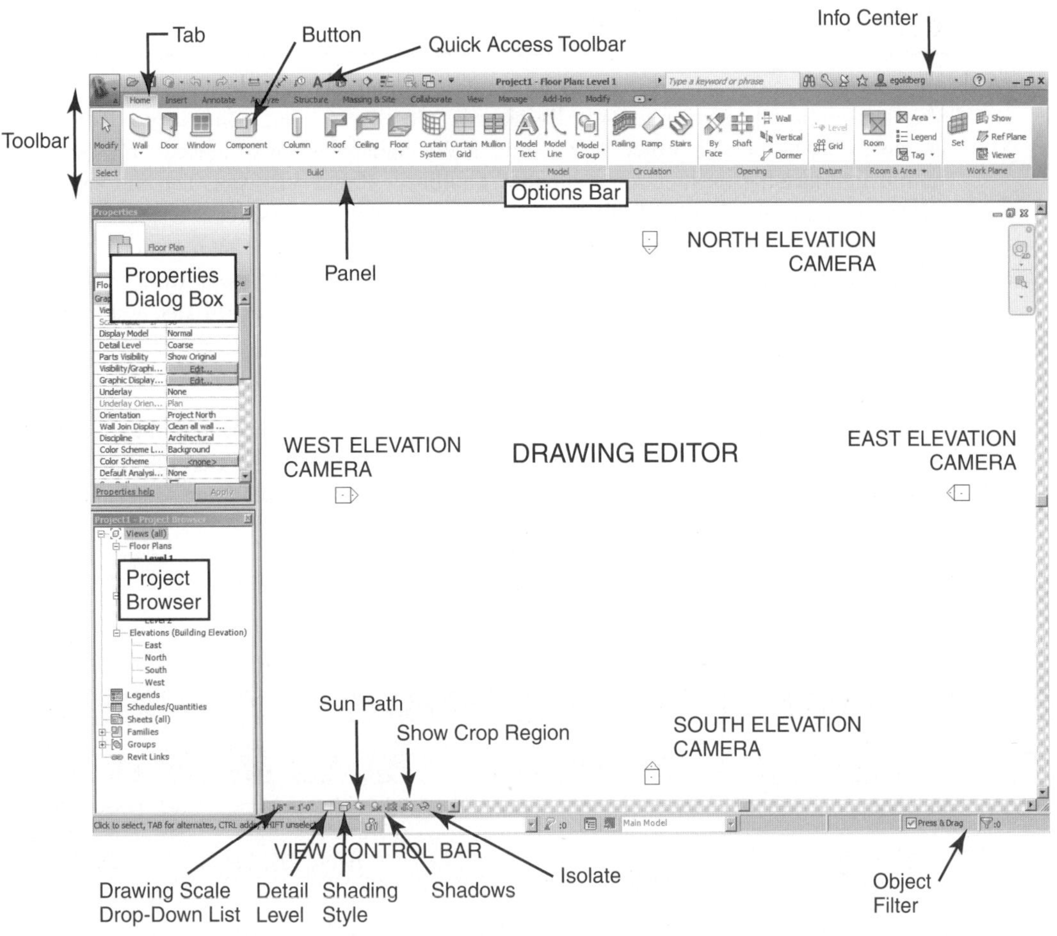

Figure 2-2

The **Revit Architecture** interface

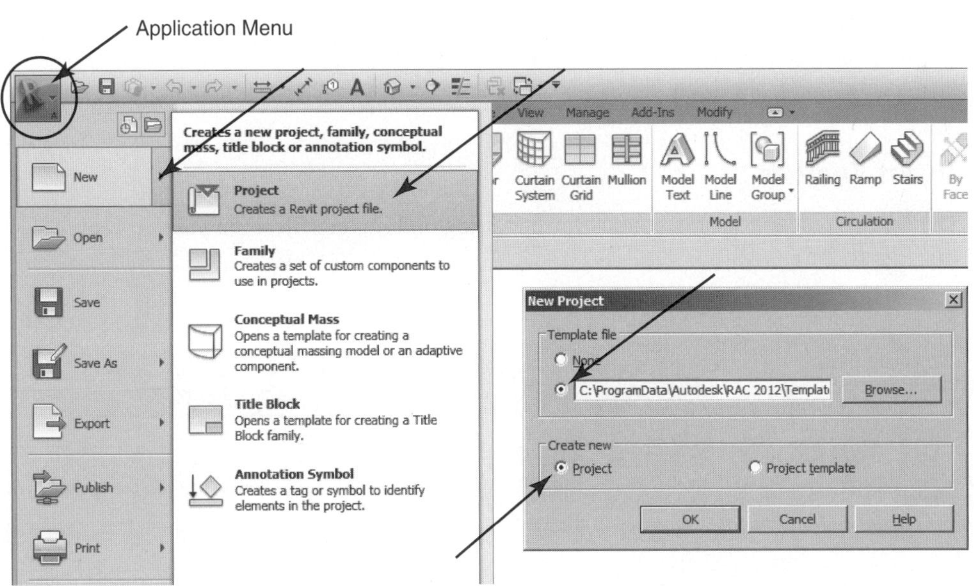

Figure 2-3

New Project dialog box

Toolbar Menu Interface

The **Toolbar** menu interface was new to Revit 2010 and has been further refined in Revit 2012. The toolbar displays automatically when you create or open a file. It provides all the tools necessary to create a project and automatically changes when you select an object. The **Toolbar** interface has the hierarchy of **Tab** > **Toolbar** > **Panel** > **Button**. The buttons are the tools that you use, and they are located in panels that are placed on toolbars. The toolbar can be customized by changing its **View** state and by rearranging the panels that contain the buttons. The Revit 2012 **Toolbar** menu contains eleven tabs. These tabs are **Home**, **Insert**, **Annotate, Analyze**, **Structure**, **Massing & Site**, **Collaborate**, **View**, **Manage**, **Add-Ins**, and **Modify**.

Home Toolbar

The **Home** toolbar contains buttons for creating the building model. Among these are **Build** buttons for creating walls, windows, doors, components (objects such as furniture), roofs, stairs, structural, rooms, and area objects. Also included in this toolbar are **Grid** and **Work Plane** buttons for placing objects (see Figure 2-4).

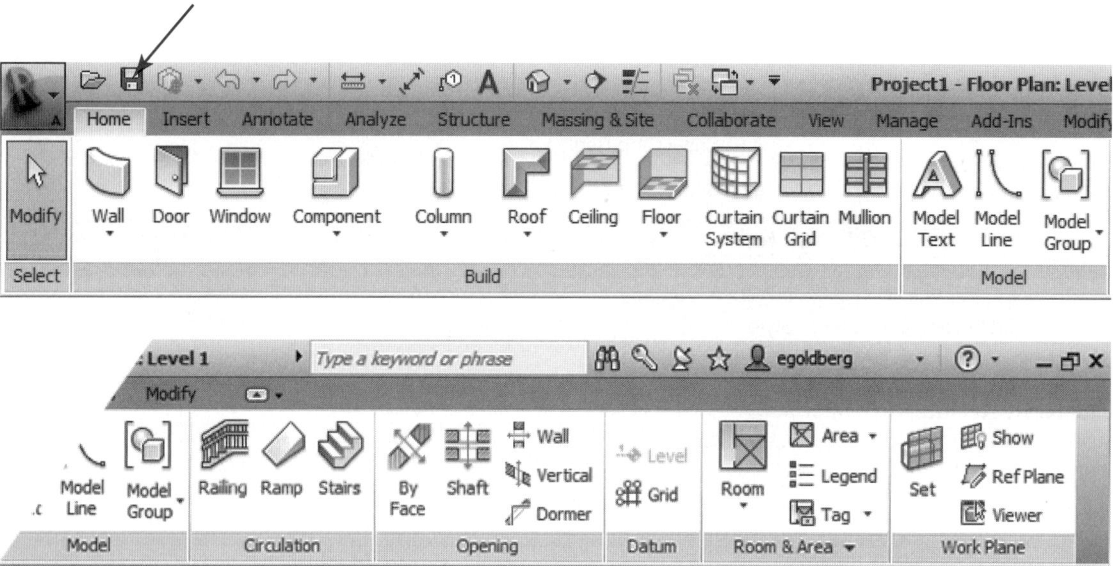

Figure 2-4

Home toolbar

Insert Toolbar

The **Insert** toolbar contains buttons for importing and linking files into your current project (see Figure 2-5).

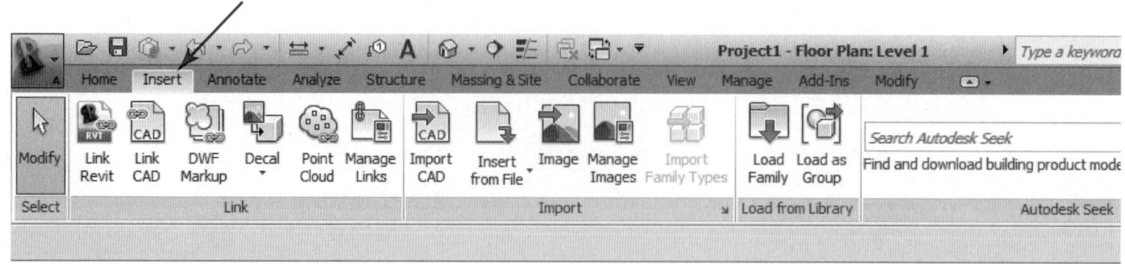

Figure 2-5

Insert toolbar

Annotate Toolbar

The **Annotate** toolbar contains buttons for adding 2D information to your drawings. These annotation objects are *View specific,* which means that they are used only in plan elevation or drafting views (see Figure 2-6).

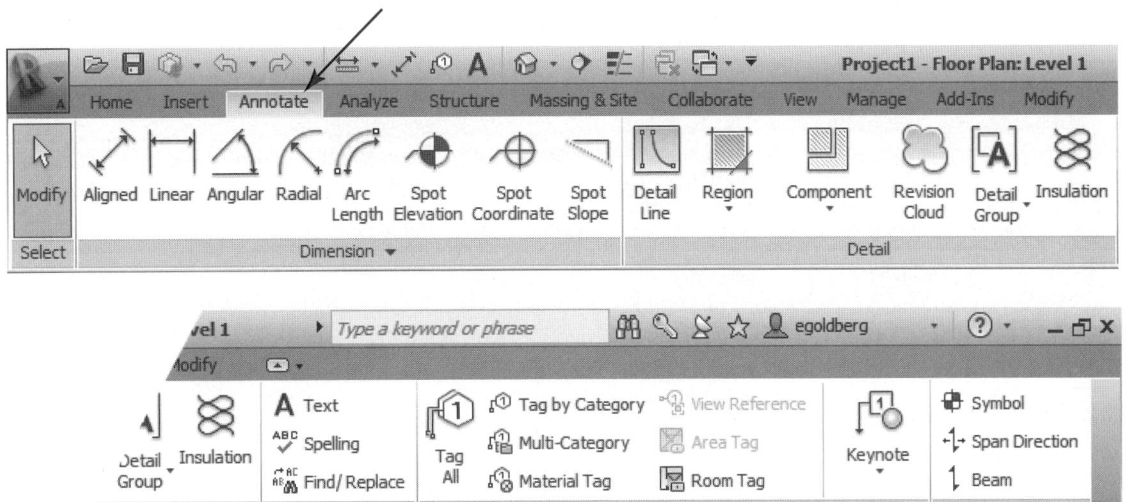

Figure 2-6

Annotate toolbar

Analyze Toolbar

The **Analyze** toolbar contains buttons used for setting and analyzing Energy Models (see Figure 2-7).

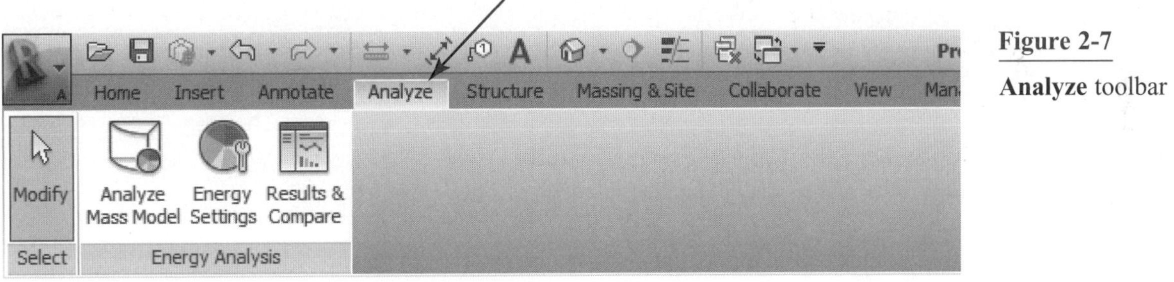

Figure 2-7

Analyze toolbar

Structure Toolbar

The **Structure** toolbar contains buttons used for creating, placing, and modifying structural elements and foundations (see Figure 2-8).

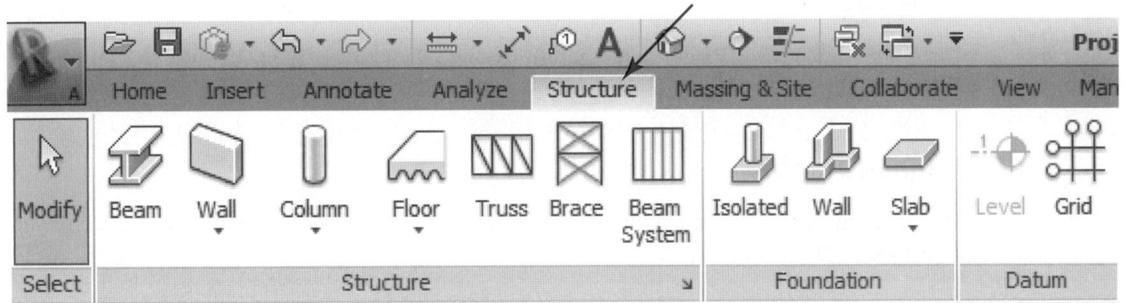

Figure 2-8

Structure toolbar

Massing & Site Toolbar

The **Massing & Site** toolbar contains buttons for modeling and modifying conceptual mass families and site elements (see Figure 2-9).

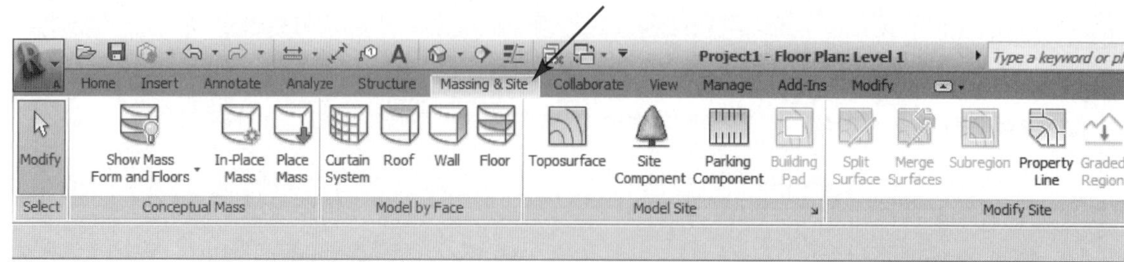

Figure 2-9

Massing & Site toolbar

Collaborate Toolbar

The **Collaborate** toolbar contains buttons for collaboration with internal and external project team members (see Figure 2-10).

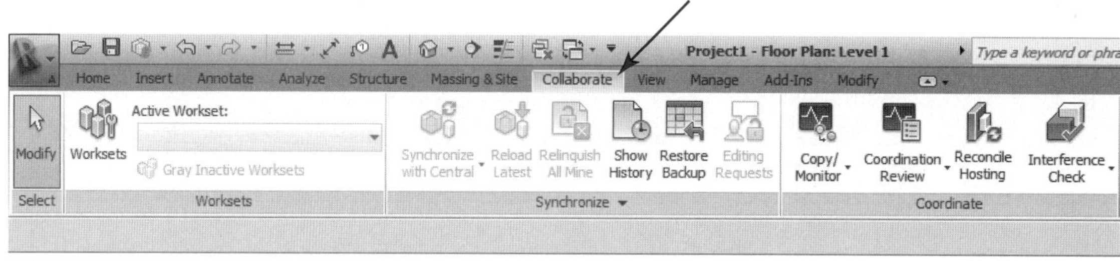

Figure 2-10

Collaborate toolbar

View Toolbar

The **View** toolbar contains buttons used for managing and modifying the current view and for switching views (see Figure 2-11).

Manage Toolbar

The **Manage** toolbar contains buttons for managing project and system parameters and settings (see Figure 2-12).

Add-Ins Toolbar

The **Add-Ins** toolbar allows access to external and third-party tools (see Figure 2-13).

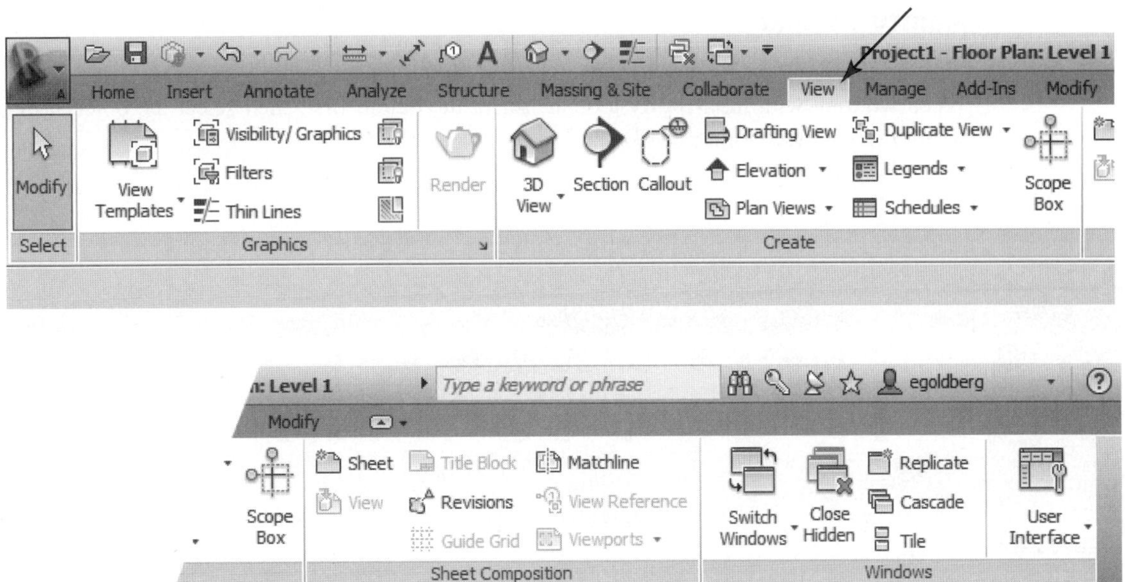

Figure 2-11

View toolbar

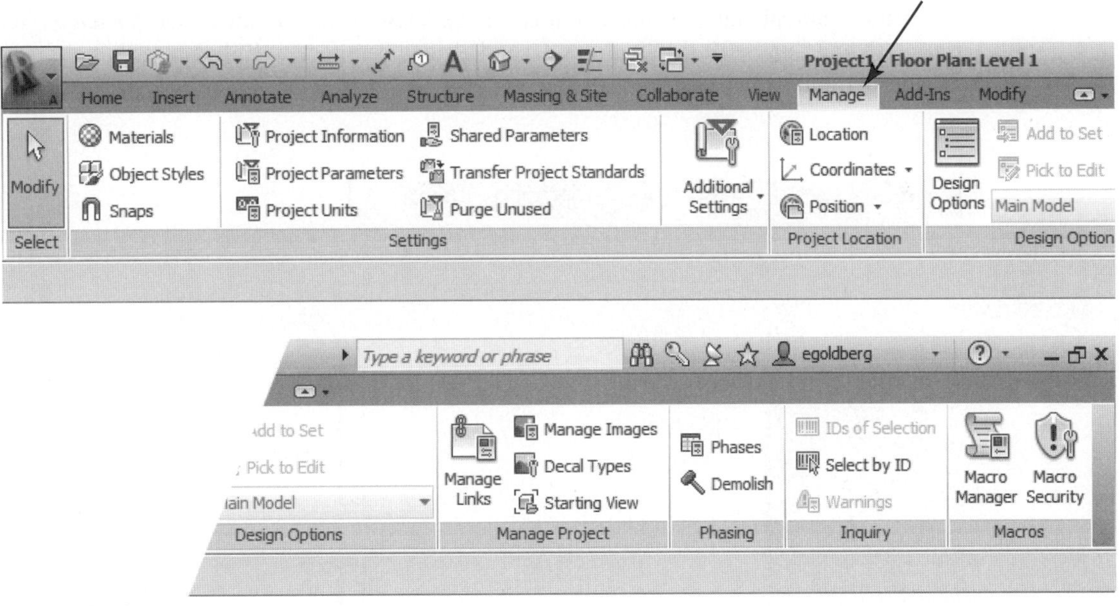

Figure 2-12

Manage toolbar

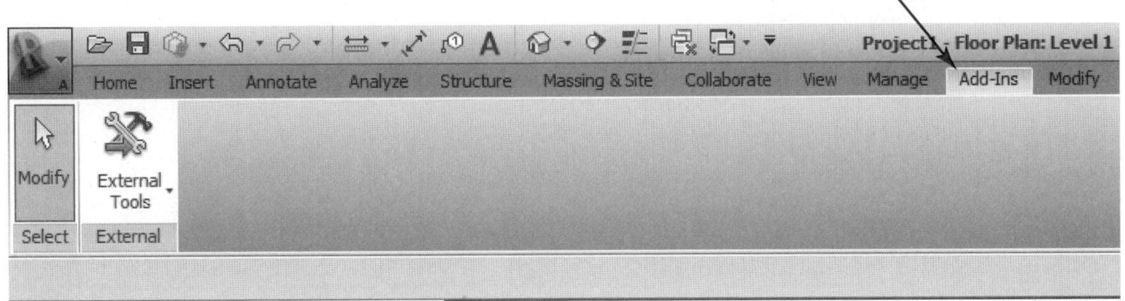

Figure 2-13

Add-Ins toolbar

Modify Toolbar

The **Modify** toolbar contains buttons used for editing existing elements, data, and systems. When working with the **Modify** toolbar, select the button first; then select the objects you want to modify (see Figure 2-14).

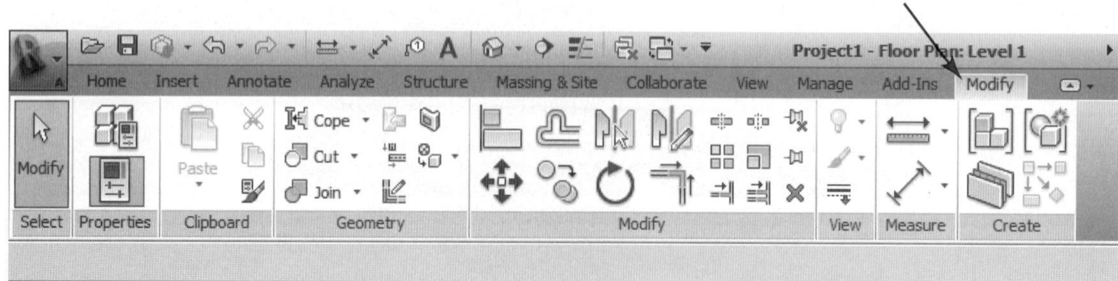

Figure 2-14

Modify toolbar

View Control Bar

The **View Control Bar** contains controls for the **View Scale**, **Detail Level**, **Visual Style**, **Sun Path and Sun Settings**, **Shadows**, **Crop Region**, **Temporary Hide/Isolate** buttons (see Figures 2-15 through 2-22).

Figure 2-15

View Control Bar

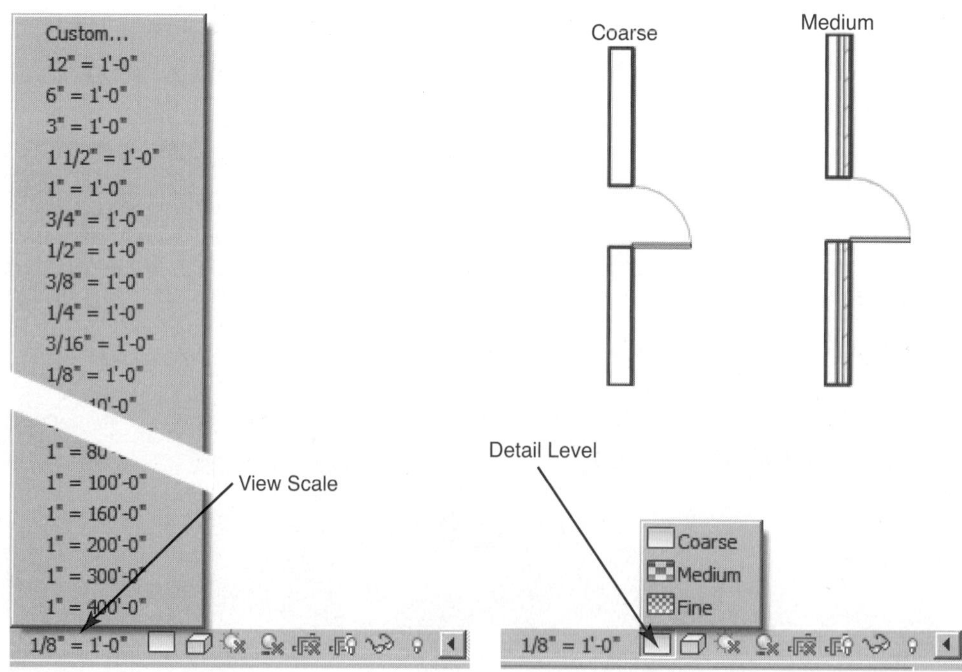

Figure 2-16

View Scale button

Figure 2-17

Detail Level button

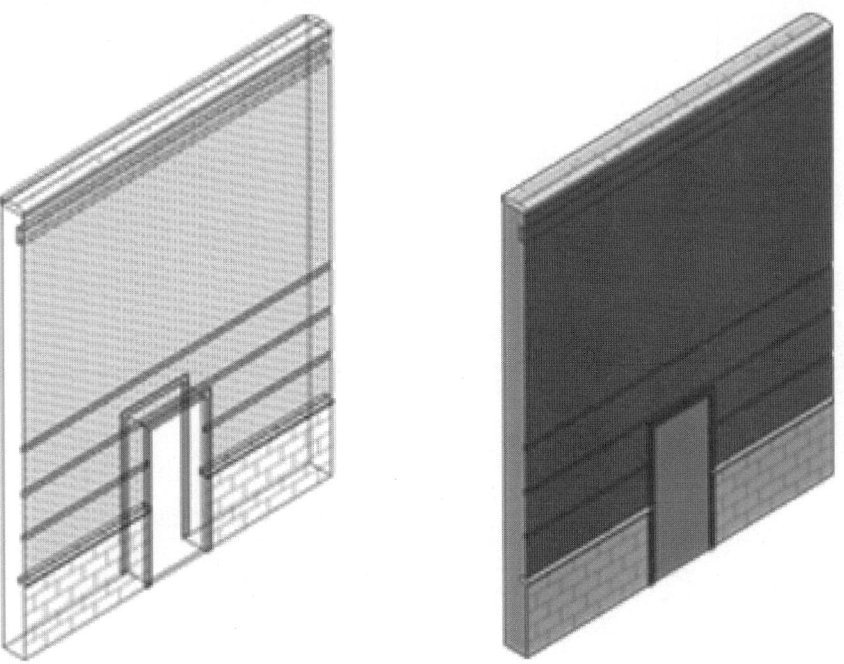

Figure 2-18

Visual Style button

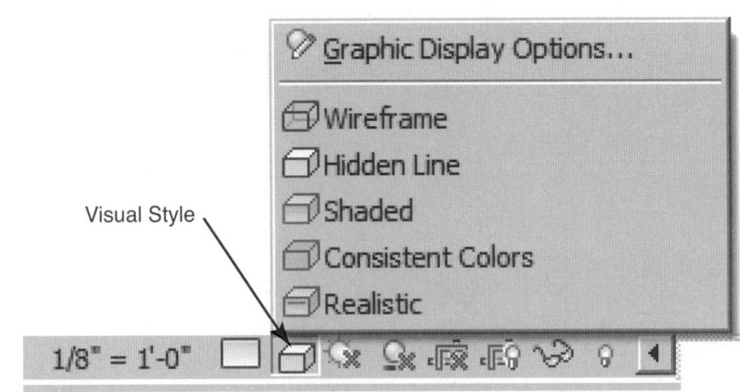

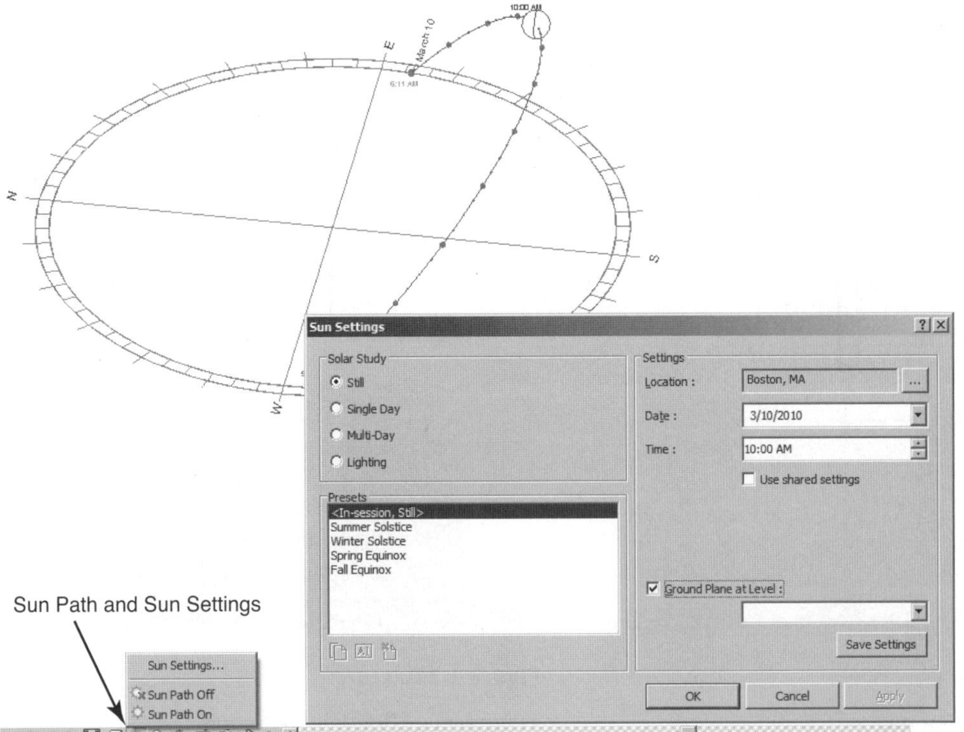

Figure 2-19

Sun Path and Sun Settings button

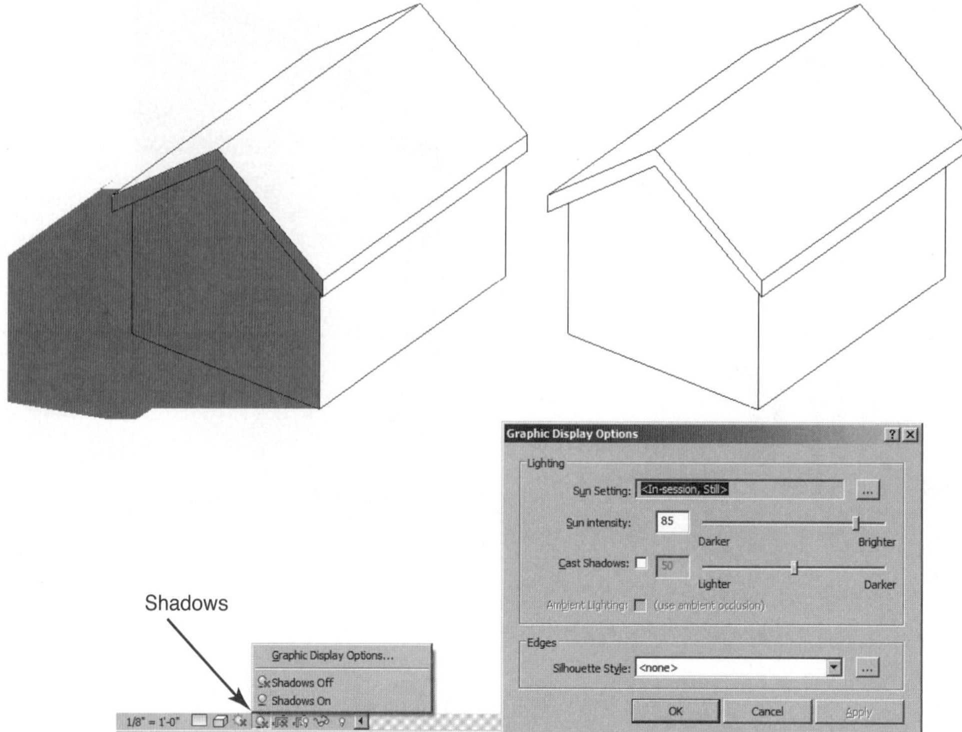

Figure 2-20

Shadows button

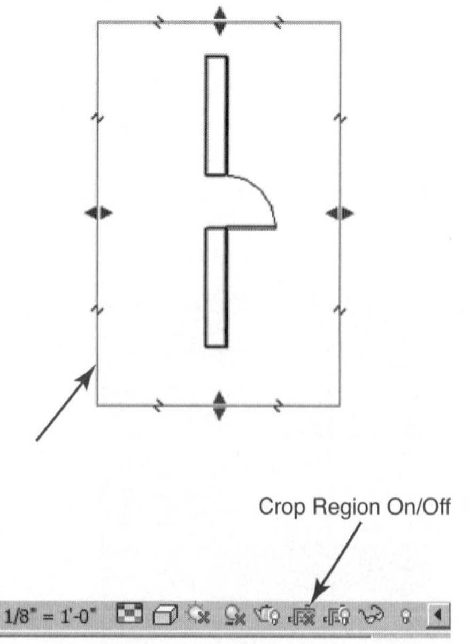

Figure 2-21

Crop Region button

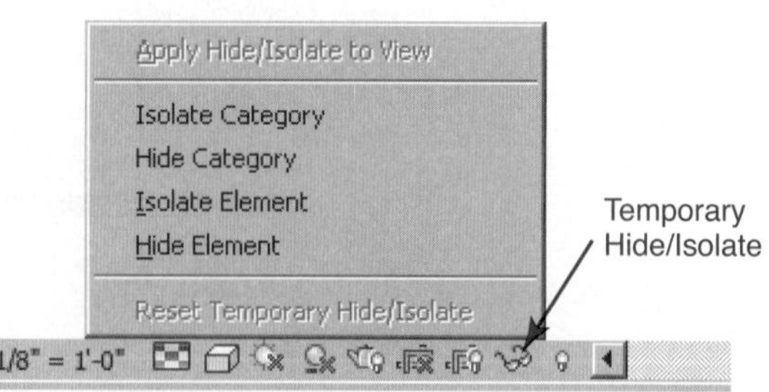

Figure 2-22

Temporary Hide/Isolate button

SteeringWheels

If you are in a **2D** view, the **Navigation Bar** will appear when you select the **Navigation Bar** check box at the right end of the **View** tab under the **User Interface** button (see Figure 2-23).

Click on the **Magnifier** icon shown in Figure 2-24 to bring up the **2D SteeringWheel**.

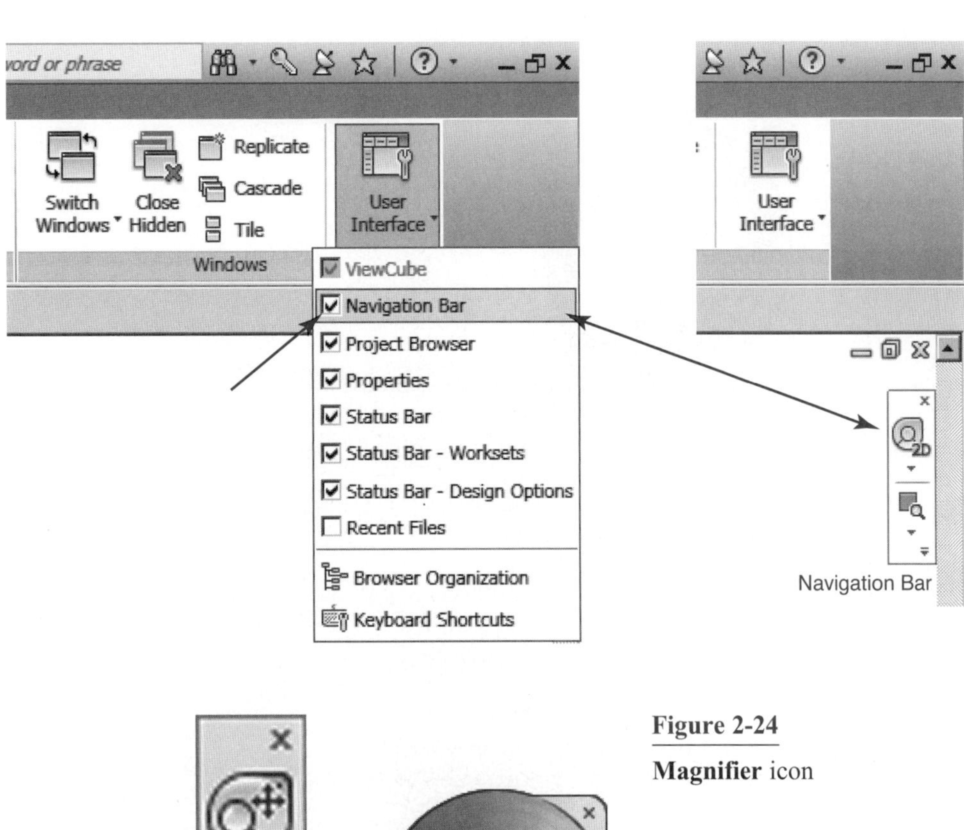

Figure 2-23

Navigation Bar

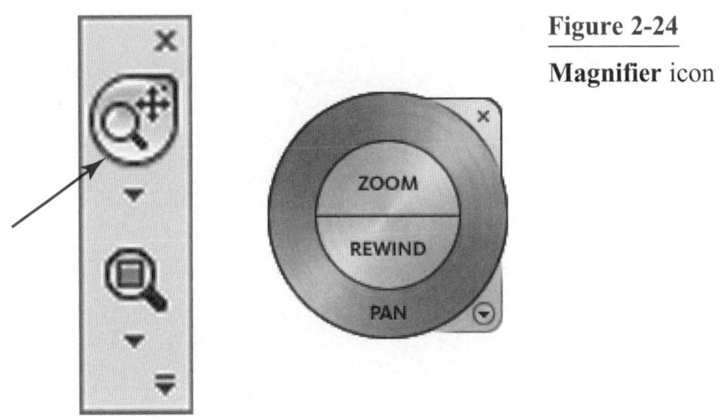

Figure 2-24

Magnifier icon

Drag your **SteeringWheel** to the center of your drawing by moving your cursor (the **SteeringWheel** will follow your cursor), and then click, hold, and move your cursor over the word **ZOOM**. The workspace will then zoom in toward the center of the **SteeringWheel**. Repeat for the word **PAN**.

The **Rewind** option in the **SteeringWheel** allows you to retrack to any previous view (see Figure 2-25).

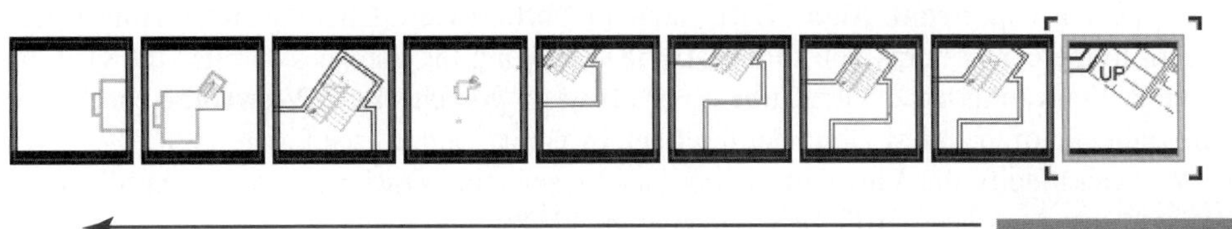

Figure 2-25

Rewind option in **SteeringWheel**

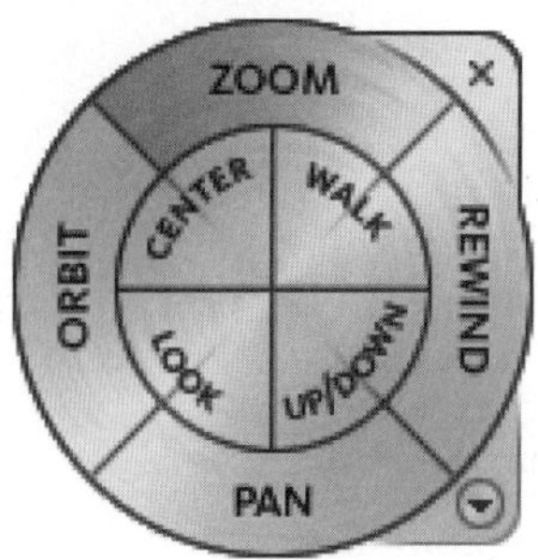

Figure 2-26

3D SteeringWheel

If you are in a **3D** view, clicking on the **Magnifier** icon will bring up the **3D SteeringWheel**. Experiment with **ZOOM**, **CENTER**, **ORBIT**, and other options, as you did with the **2D SteeringWheel** (see Figure 2-26).

As in Figure 2-27, click to show the **3D SteeringWheel** options. Experiment with the different settings.

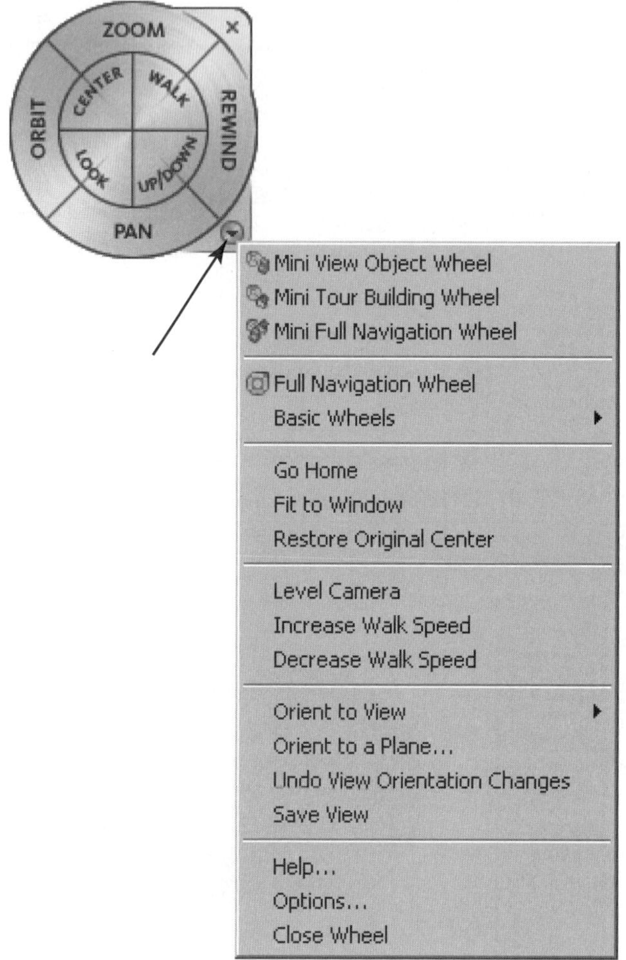

Figure 2-27

3D SteeringWheel options

ViewCube

The **ViewCube** appears only when you are in a **3D** or **Camera** view. Clicking on the cube places you in a **Top**, **Front**, **Right**, **Left**, **Back**, or **Bottom** view. Clicking on the **House** icon adjacent to the cube returns you to the **3D** view. Moving the compass "orbits" the view in real-time. You can turn the **ViewCube** on or off when you check the **ViewCube** check box at the right end of the **View** tab under the **User Interface** button (see Figure 2-28).

You can modify the **ViewCube** properties by selecting **Options** from the **Application** menu and selecting the **ViewCube** tab (see Figure 2-29).

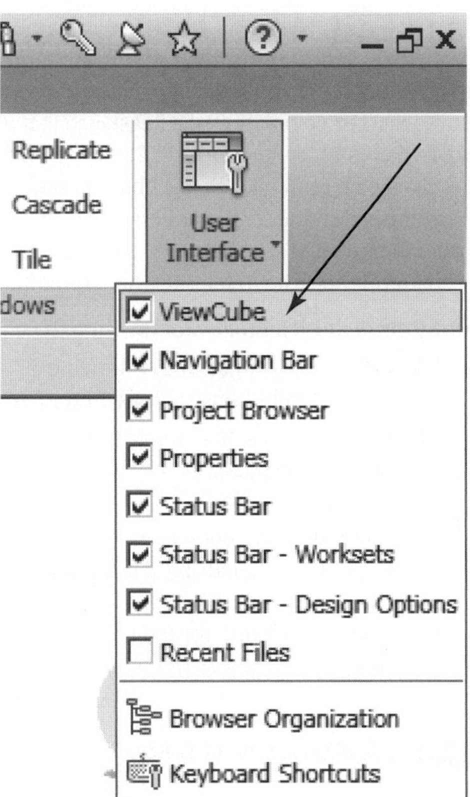

Figure 2-28
ViewCube

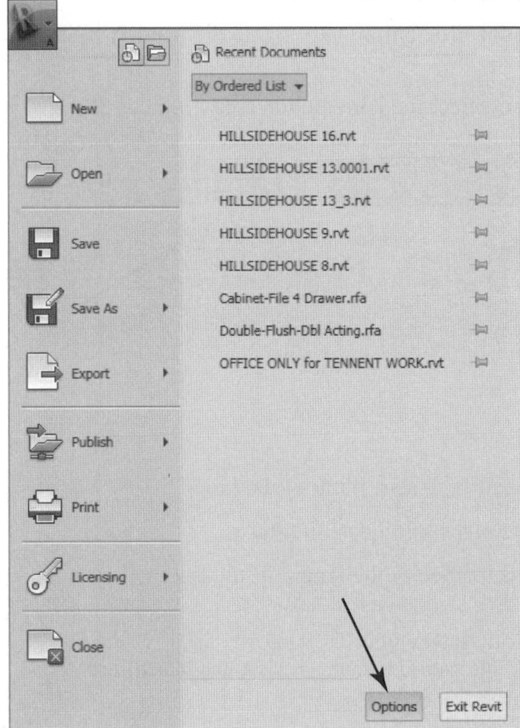

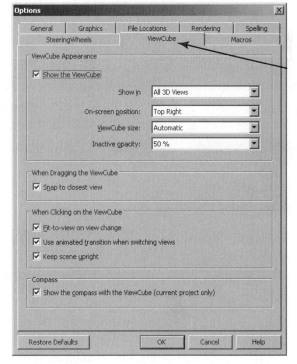

Figure 2-29
Modify **ViewCube** properties

Sketching and Edit Mode

In earlier releases of Revit Architecture, the term ***Sketch** mode* was used to refer to the drawing of lines, circles, and so on. The completion of a 2D sketch that resulted in a change in a 3D object was termed as **Finish Sketch** mode. In Revit 2012, the term ***Edit** mode* is used more often. Now, when a 3D object is changed by a 2D sketch, the object is said to be in **Edit** mode, and its completion is referred to as **Finish Edit** mode. Regardless, the terms refer to the same process. Because older users often refer to drawing as "sketching," these two terms can be used interchangeably.

There are several terms specific to the sketching or editing process in Revit Architecture:

- **Sketching and Edit** mode is a process of drawing 2D elements in Revit Architecture.
- **Sketching and Edit** mode is similar to 2D drawing in **AutoCAD**, and much of the 2D detailing is done with **Sketch** buttons such as **Line**, **Circle**, **Arc**, **Rectangle**, and so on.
- **Sketch-based elements** are those that are typically created using **Edit** mode (for example, floors, ceilings, and extrusions). Other elements, such as walls, are sketched but do not require the use of **Sketch** mode.
- **Sketch and Edit** mode is the environment in Revit Architecture that allows you to sketch elements whose size or shape cannot be determined automatically; for example, when you create or edit a sketch of a roof or a floor. When you enter **Edit** mode, the toolbar displays only the buttons applicable for the type of sketch you are creating or editing.
- All of the elements that comprise a sketch-based element (such as a roof) are known as the *sketch.*

EXERCISE 2-1 **SKETCHING A LINE AND ADDING LISTENING DIMENSIONS**

1. Start a new drawing using the RAC 2012\Imperial Templates\default.rte template.
2. In the **Project Browser**, double-click on the **LEVEL 1** Floor Plan to bring it into the **Drawing Editor**.
3. Change the **Drawing Scale** to **1/4″ = 1′-0″**.
4. Select the **Home** tab to bring up the **Home** toolbar.
5. In the **Home** toolbar, select the **Model Line** button to bring up the **Modify | Place Lines** toolbar.
6. In the **Modify | Place Lines** toolbar, select the **Line** button (see Figure 2-30).

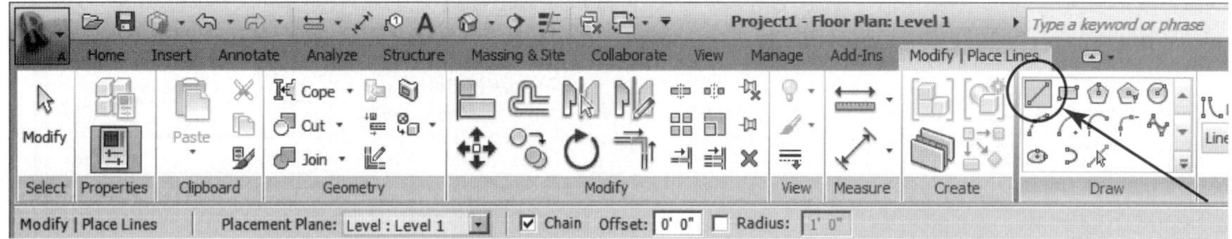

Figure 2-30

Modify | Place Lines toolbar

7. Click in the **Drawing Editor** to specify the start point of the line.
8. Move the cursor and click to specify the endpoint of the line.

You can also use **Listening Dimensions** to specify the length of the line.

When you are sketching, you can explicitly enter a value for the sketch line by typing a number after you begin the sketch line. This method is known as **Listening Dimensions**.

Typically, **Listening Dimensions** specify linear dimensions such as length; for example, the length of a line (when drawing a line), length of a chord (when drawing the second point of a 3-point arc), or length of a radius (when drawing an arc, circle, or polygon).

9. Again, in the **Home** toolbar, select the **Model Line** button to bring up the **Modify | Place Lines** toolbar.

10. Click in the **Drawing Editor** to specify the start point of the line.
11. Type the length value. When you type a number, a text box appears. If you need a line that is 8 feet 6 inches long, type the value as **8 6**, and press the <**Enter**> key. The sketch line is drawn the specified length.
12. Press the <**Esc**> key to finish the command, or move your cursor to a new direction and repeat with another value (see Figure 2-31).

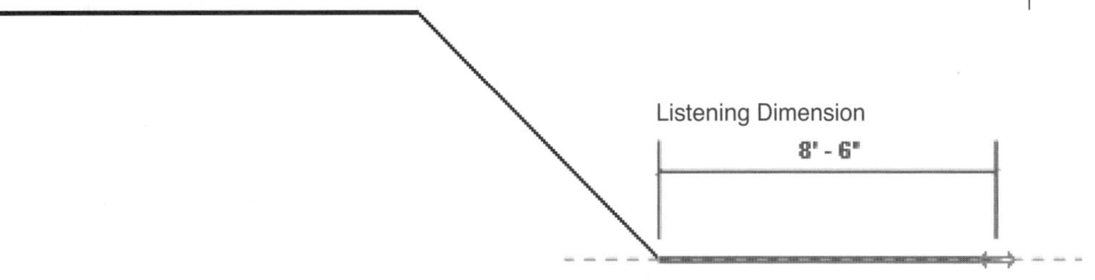

Figure 2-31

Sketching a line

EXERCISE 2-2 **SKETCHING A RECTANGLE**

1. Using the previous project, select the **Home** tab to bring up the **Home** toolbar.
2. In the **Home** toolbar, select the **Model Line** button to bring up the **Modify | Place Lines** toolbar.
3. In the **Modify | Place Lines** toolbar, select the **Rectangle** button.
4. On the **Options Bar**, check the **Radius** check box, and enter **1′-0″** in the **Radius** field.
5. Click to place the rectangle, then drag its corner, and click to place a rectangle with radius corners (see Figure 2-32).

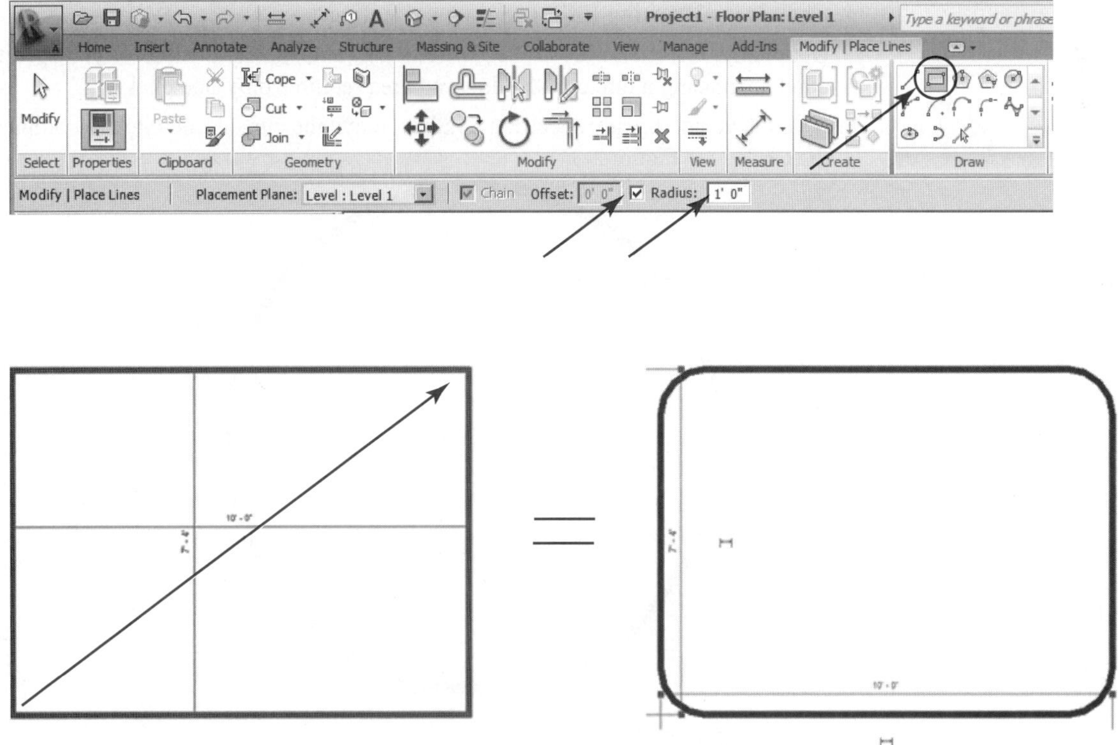

Figure 2-32

Sketching a rectangle

6. Adjust the rectangle by selecting an edge and dragging it or by entering a new dimension in **Listening Dimensions** (see Figure 2-33).

NOTE:
Don't check the **Radius** check box if you want square corners.

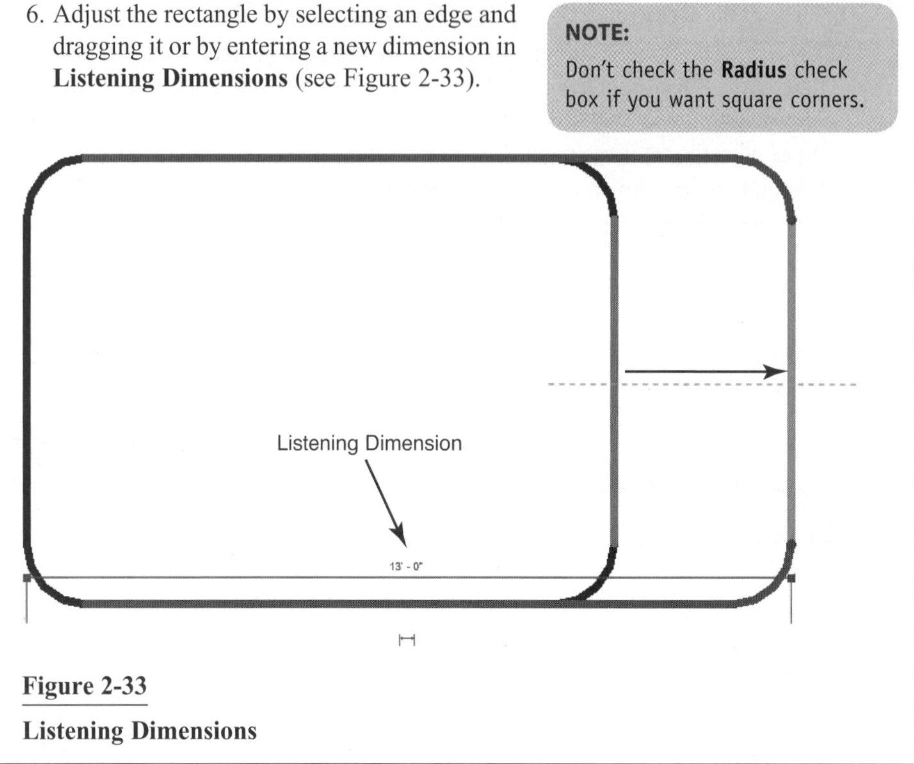

Figure 2-33

Listening Dimensions

EXERCISE 2-3 **SKETCHING A CIRCLE**

1. Using the previous project, select the **Home** tab to bring up the **Home** toolbar.
2. In the **Home** toolbar, select the **Model Line** button to bring up the **Modify | Place Lines** toolbar.
3. In the **Modify | Place Lines** toolbar, select the **Circle** button.
4. Click in the **Drawing Editor** to set a center point.
5. Optionally, select **Radius** in the **Options Bar** and specify a value. If you specify a radius, placing a circle in the drawing area requires only one click.
6. If you have not already specified a radius, move the cursor, and click to complete the circle (see Figure 2-34).

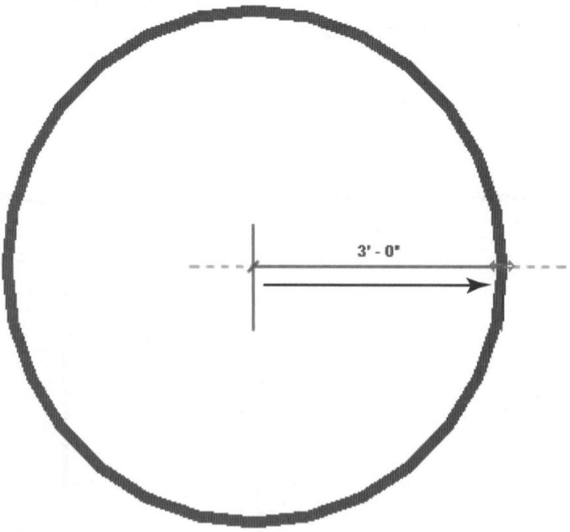

Figure 2-34

Sketching a circle

EXERCISE 2-4 SPLITTING A LINE (WORKS FOR LINES, CIRCLES, ARCS, OR WALLS)

1. Using the previous project, select the **Home** tab to bring up the **Home** toolbar.
2. In the **Home** toolbar, select the **Model Line** button to bring up the **Modify | Place Lines** toolbar.
3. In the **Modify | Place Lines** toolbar, select the **Line** button.
4. Place an 8′-0″ line in the **Drawing Editor**.
5. Select the **Modify** tab to bring up the **Modify** toolbar.
6. In the **Modify** toolbar, select the **Split** button (see Figure 2-35).

NOTE:
There are two splits: **Split Element**, which splits a line, and **Split with Gap**, which opens a space. If you use the **Split with Gap** button, enter the gap size in the **Options Bar**.

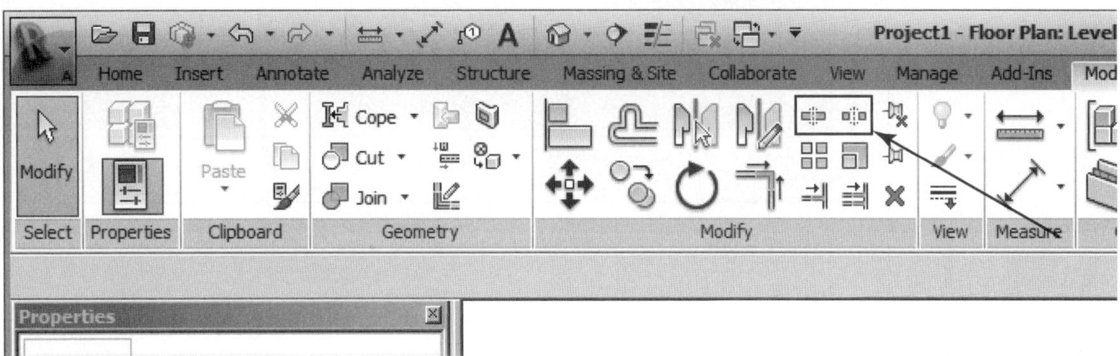

Figure 2-35

Splitting a line

7. Click on two places and delete the midsection of the line (see Figure 2-36).

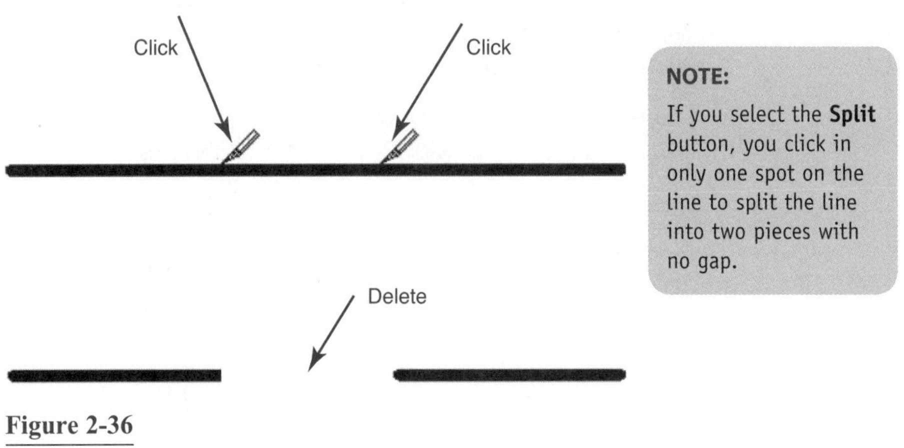

NOTE:
If you select the **Split** button, you click in only one spot on the line to split the line into two pieces with no gap.

Figure 2-36

Deleting the midsection of a line

8. Try splitting other sketch lines (see Figure 2-37).

Figure 2-37

Splitting other sketch lines

9. You can get more information on **Sketching**, **Editing**, and **Edit** modes in the Revit Help file.
10. Select the **Question Mark** shown in Figure 2-38 to bring up the Revit Architecture **Help** dialog box.

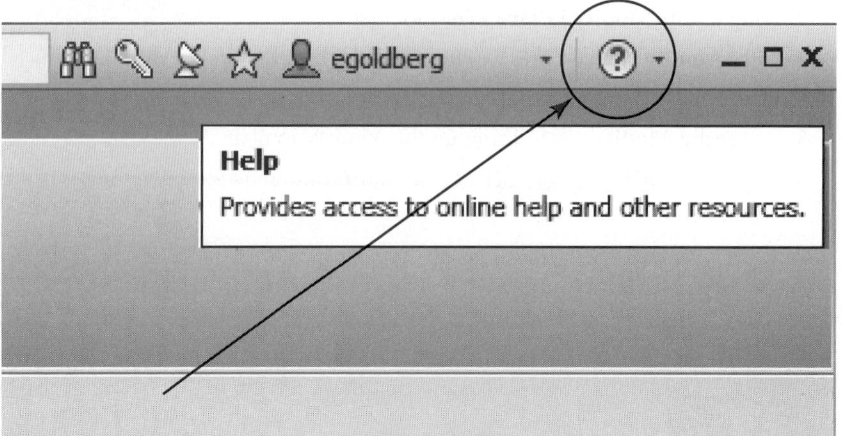

Figure 2-38

Selecting the Help file

11. In the Revit Architecture **Help** dialog box, enter **Sketch Mode** in the **Search** tab, and press the **List Topics** button to see information on related subjects (see Figure 2-39).

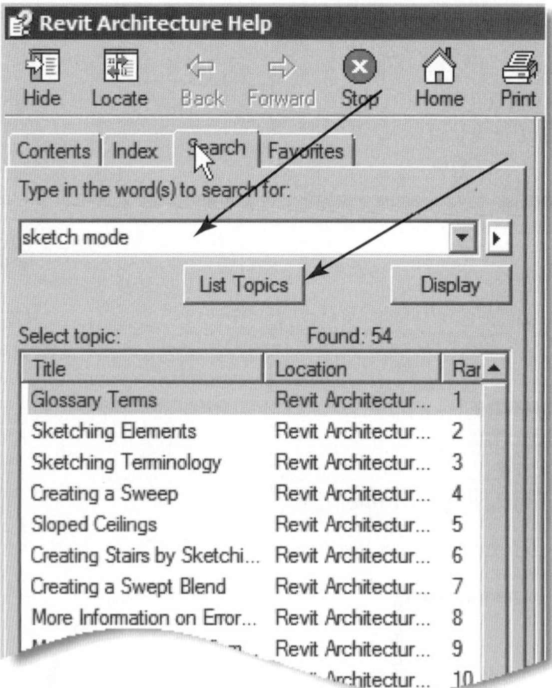

Figure 2-39

Searching in the **Help** dialog box

By practicing with **Sketch** and **Edit** tools, you will be able to create 2D details, profiles, and so on for creating and modifying 3D objects.

Families

All objects in Revit Building are "Family based." The term *Family* describes a concept used throughout Revit Building to help you manage your data and make changes easily. Each **Family** element can have multiple types defined within it, each with a different size, shape, material set, or other parameter variables as designed by the **Family** creator. Changes to a **Family**-type definition propagate through a project and are automatically reflected in every instance of that **Family** type within the project. This keeps objects coordinated and saves you the time and effort of updating components and schedules manually (see Figure 2-40).

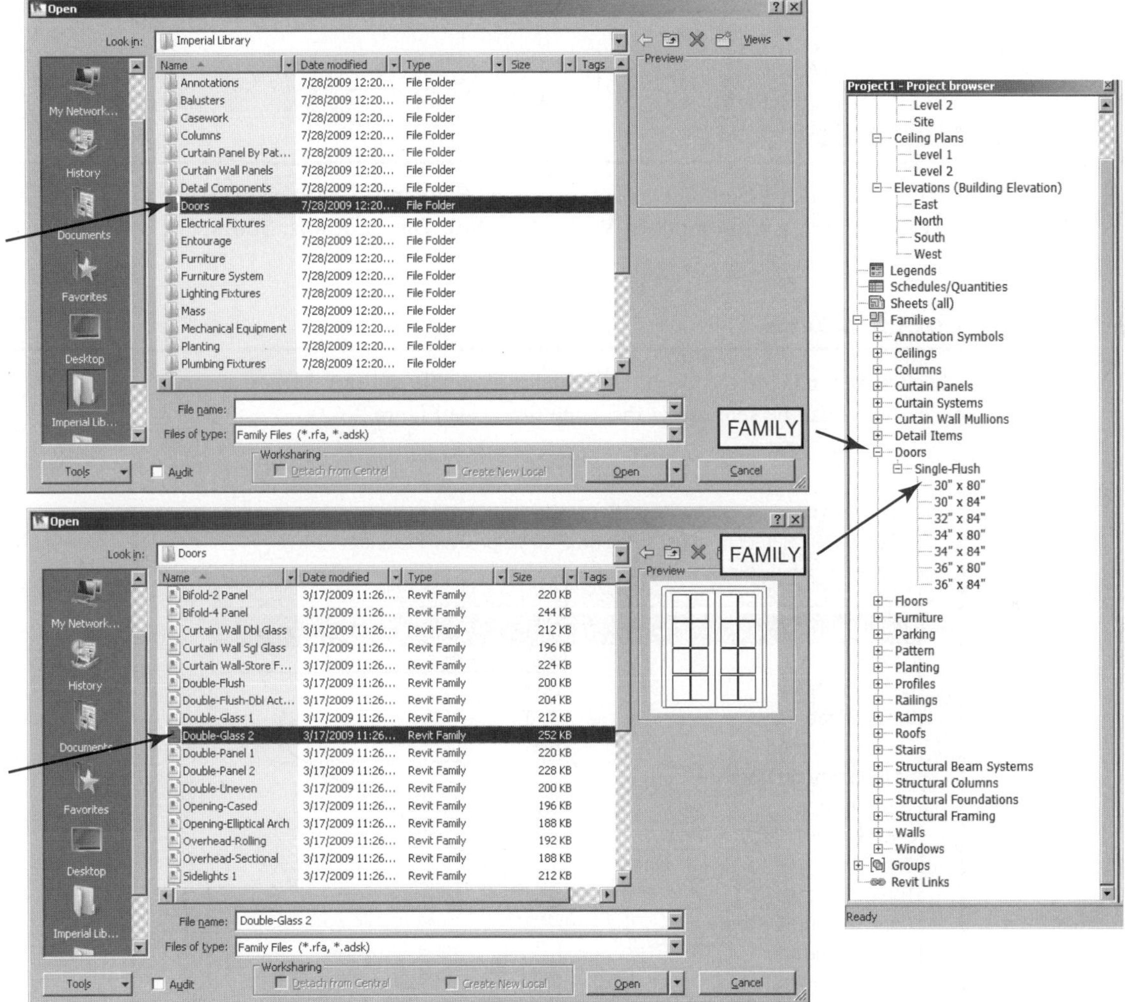

Figure 2-40

Using the **Family** element to update objects automatically

Levels

Levels are horizontal planes that act as a reference for elements, such as roofs, floors, ceilings, and so on. These levels, which are seen only in the elevations, correspond to levels in the **Project Browser**. Adding new levels in any elevation will add corresponding levels in the **Project Browser** (see Figure 2-41).

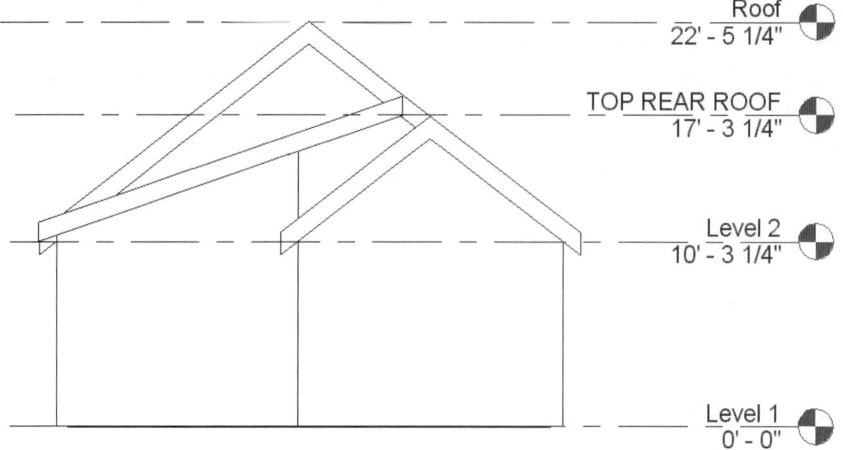

Figure 2-41
Levels

Elements

All objects in Revit Building are referred to as **Elements**. These include, but are not limited to, **Lines**, **Circles**, **Components**, **Walls**, **Window**, **Doors**, **Roofs**, **Stairs**, and so on.

Check Boxes

Check boxes indicate the On or Off state of available options. If they are in a group, several check boxes can be selected at the same time (see Figure 2-42).

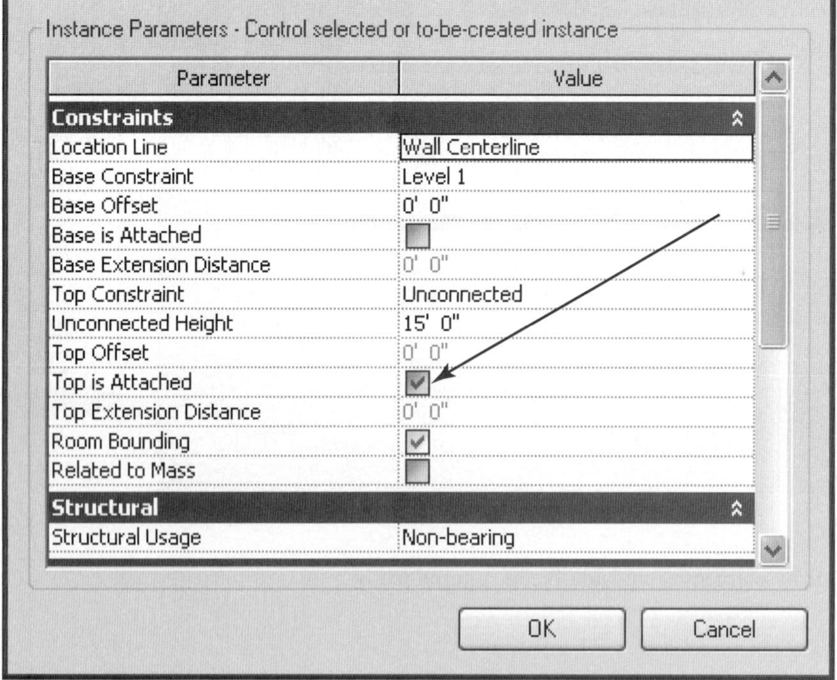

Figure 2-42
Check boxes

Radio Buttons

Radio buttons (the name comes from the button selectors on car radios) indicate the On or Off state of available options. Only one button in a group of buttons can be chosen (see Figure 2-43).

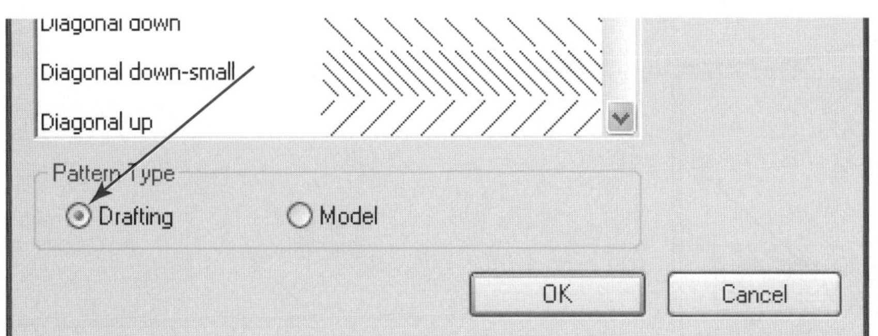

Figure 2-43

Radio buttons

Contextual Menus

Contextual (context-sensitive) menus became popular when Microsoft introduced Windows 95. Revit Building uses these menus to control options and subcommands of various components. Contextual menus typically are summoned by clicking the right mouse button on a specific object, entity, or spot in the interface. Through programming, the appropriate menu or "context" will appear for that object at that point in its command structure. As an example, clicking the right mouse button on a door within a wall will provide all the commands available for the door and its relationship to the wall (see Figure 2-44).

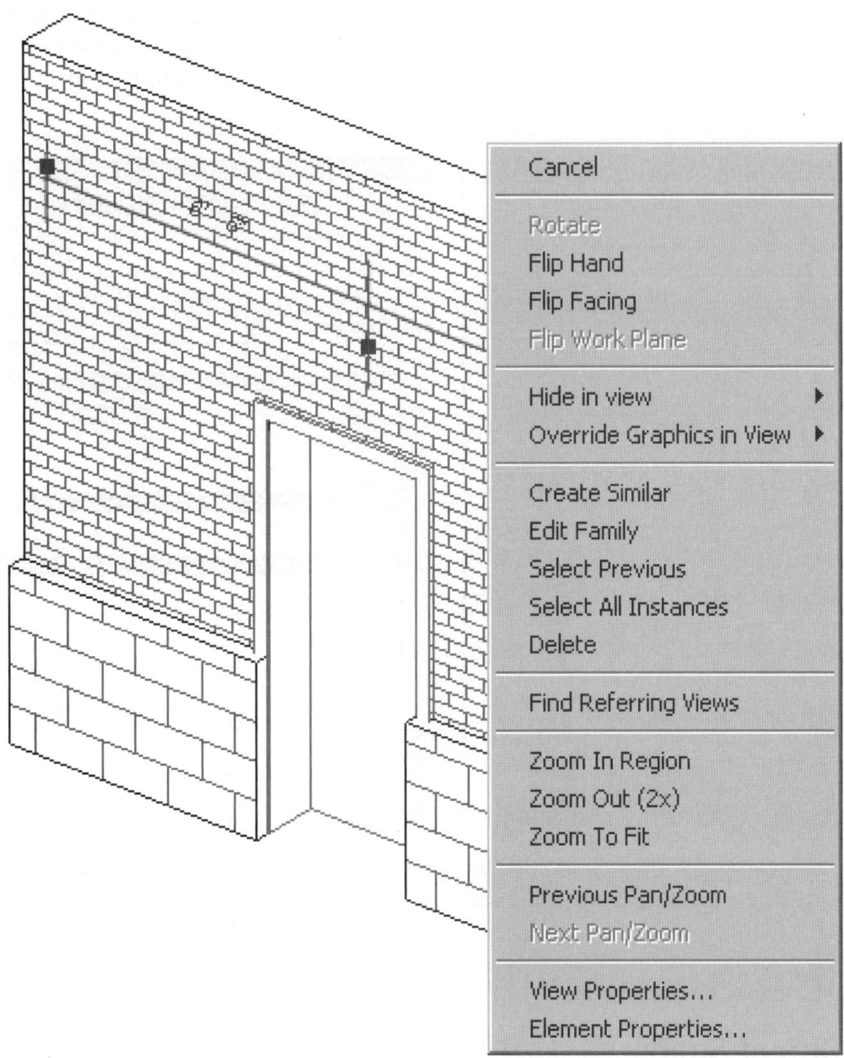

Figure 2-44

Contextual menu for a door in a wall

Constraints

Constraints are created either by placing dimensions and locking them or by creating equality constraints. Constraints are very helpful when you wish to hold a wall in place while changing the dimension of an adjacent wall (see Figures 2-45 and 2-46).

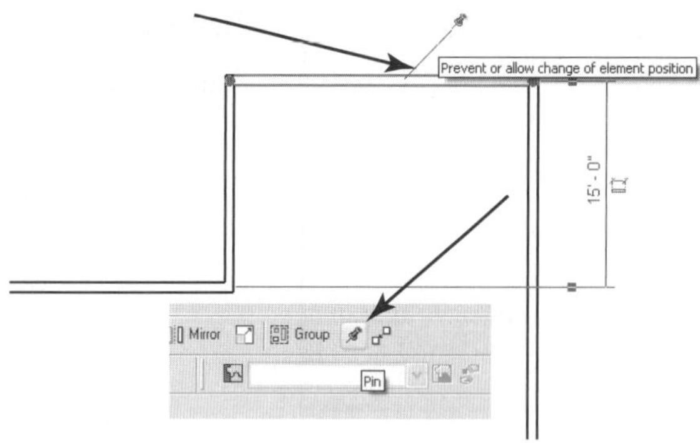

Figure 2-45

Using constraints to hold one wall while changing an adjacent wall

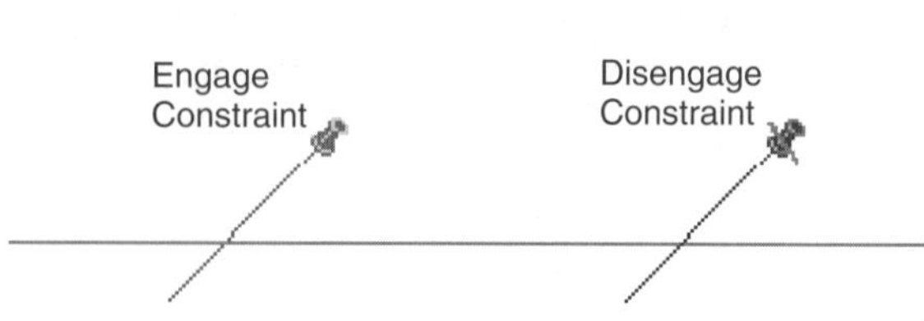

Figure 2-46

Creating constraints

Dialog Boxes and Context-Sensitive Menus

Dialog boxes contain fields, drop-down lists, and so on, that you fill in to change settings. Contextual (context-sensitive) menus became popular when Microsoft introduced Windows 95. In Revit Architecture, right mouse clicking on an object will bring up a menu with commands that can be given for that particular object in that particular situation. Right mouse clicking in the **Drawing Editor** (drawing area) will also bring up a contextual menu with controls for that editor (see Figure 2-47).

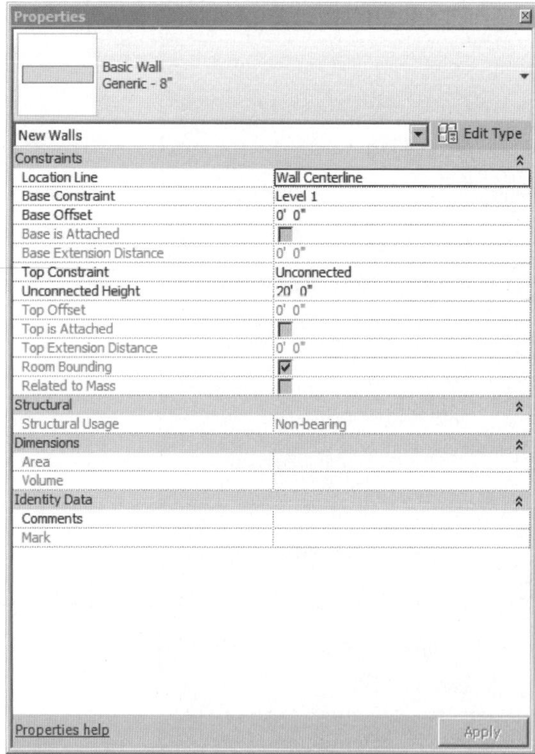

Figure 2-47

Dialog boxes and context-sensitive menus

Object Snaps

Object Snaps allow you to grab onto objects and lines at predetermined locations, automatically, when doing operations such as **Move**, **Copy**, **Rotate**, and so on. This concept comes to Revit Architecture from the 2D CAD programs. The **Snaps** dialog box can be reached by clicking on the **Snaps** button in the **Manage** toolbar. With the **Snaps On**, Revit Architecture displays snap points and snap lines to assist in lining up elements, components, or lines with existing geometry. Snap points depend on the type of snap and are represented in the drawing area as shapes (triangles, squares, diamonds, and so on). Snap lines are represented as dashed green lines in the drawing area.

In the **Snaps** dialog box, you can check which snaps you wish to appear automatically when you make an operation. You can enable or disable object snaps and specify dimension snap increments. You can also override snap settings using keyboard shortcuts (see **keyboard shortcuts** in the Help file). Settings are held for the duration of the Revit Architecture session. **Snap** settings apply to all files open in the session but are not saved with a project (see Figure 2-48).

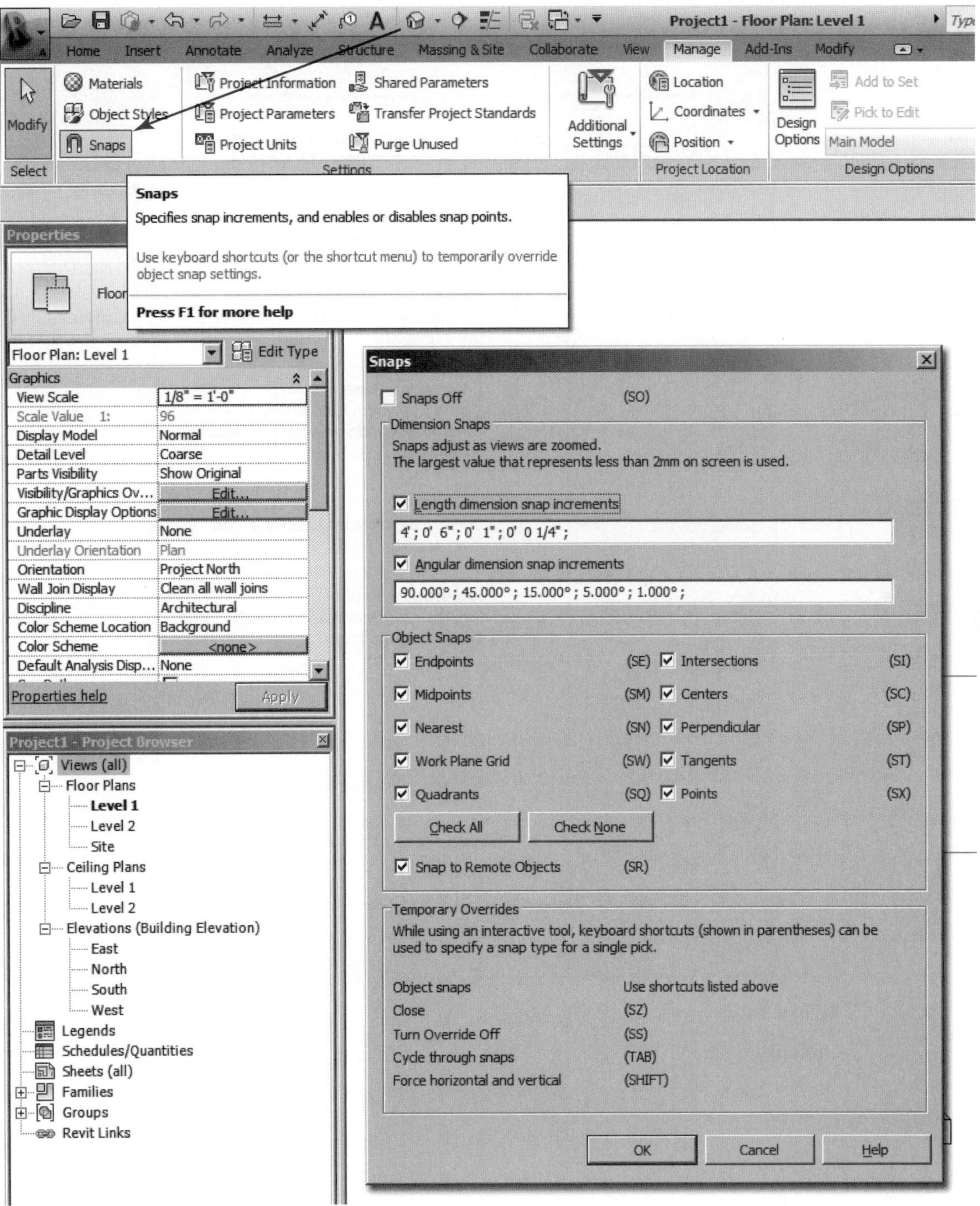

Figure 2-48

Using object snaps

Application Menu

The **Application** menu appears at the very top of the Revit Architecture interface. It contains drop-down menus with names. When a horizontal triangle appears after a name, clicking on that name will bring up more menu names. Picking one of these names will take you to a dialog box. If you select the **Options** button at the bottom of the **Application** menu, you will get access to nine tabs that contain interface, graphics, and general controls. It is important for the operator to become familiar with these controls (see Figures 2-49 through 2-54).

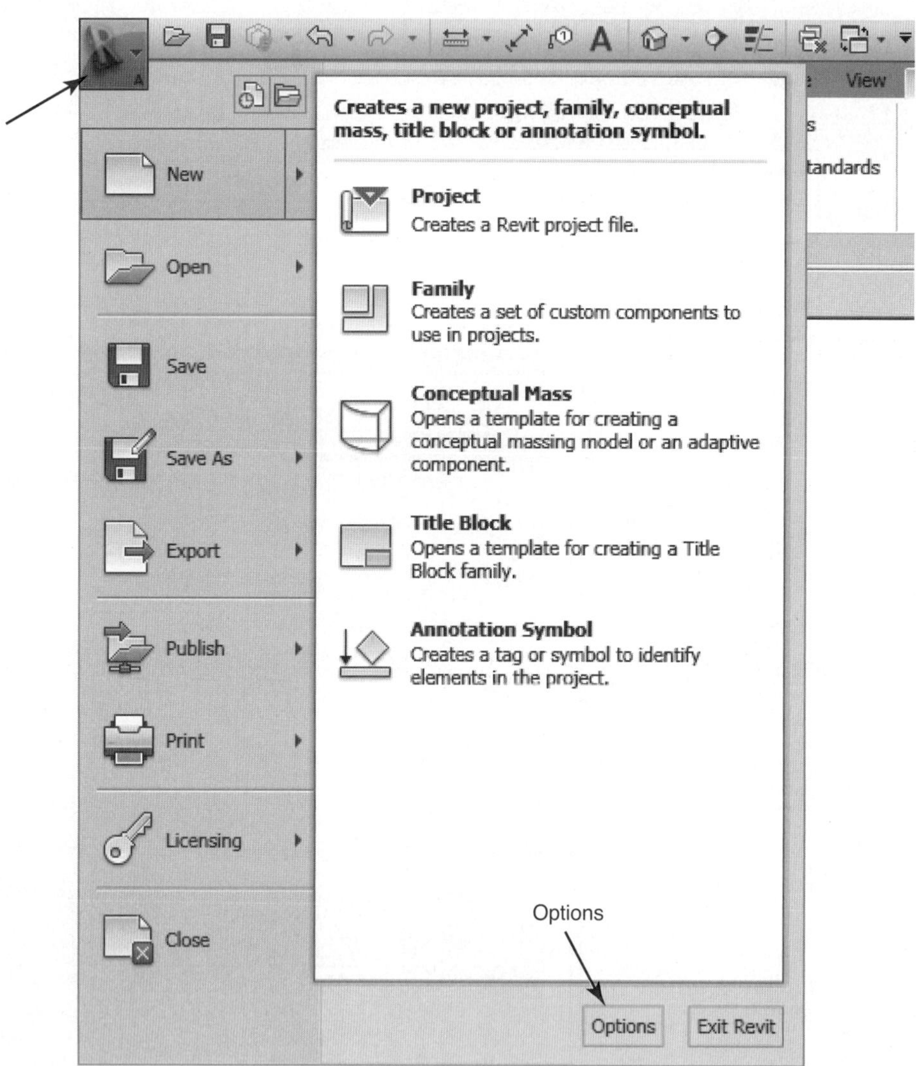

Figure 2-49

Options button

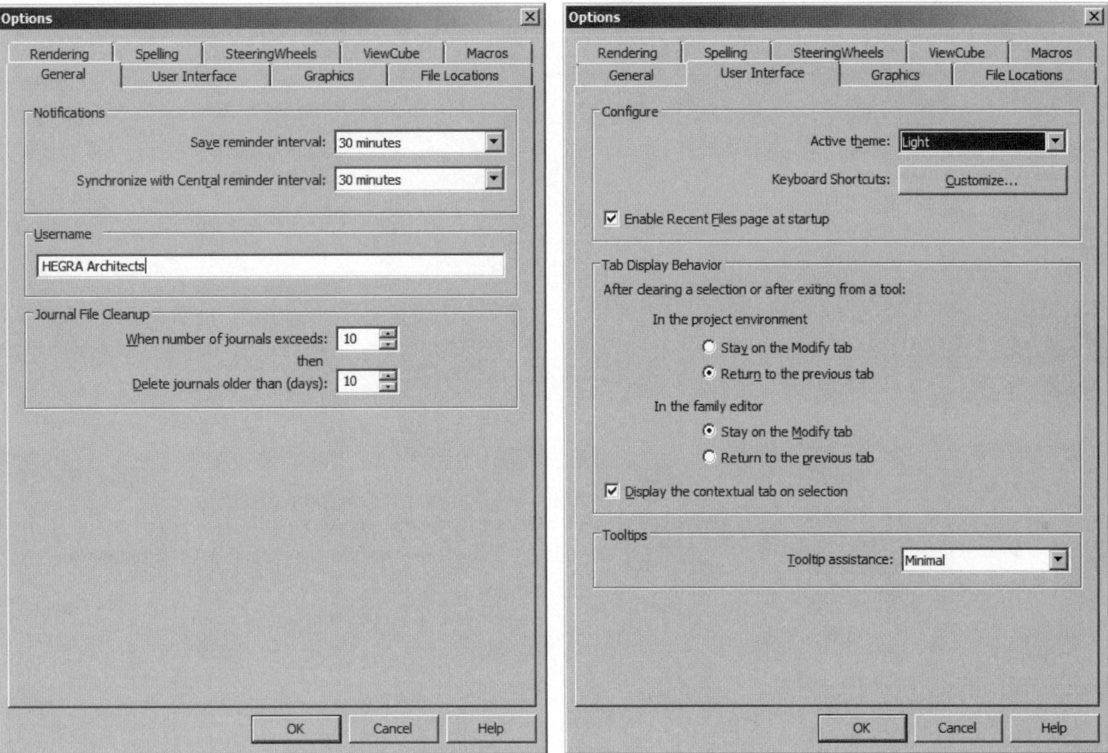

Figure 2-50

General and **User Interface** tabs in **Options** dialog box

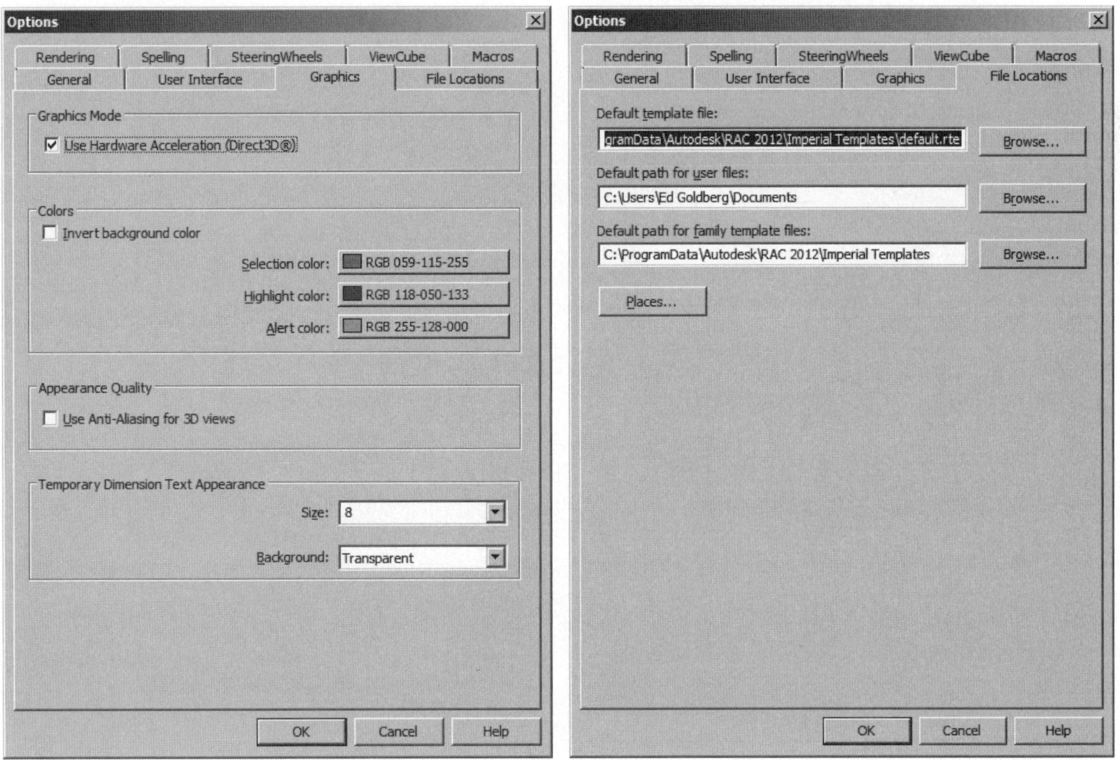

Figure 2-51

Graphics and **File Locations** tabs in **Options** dialog box

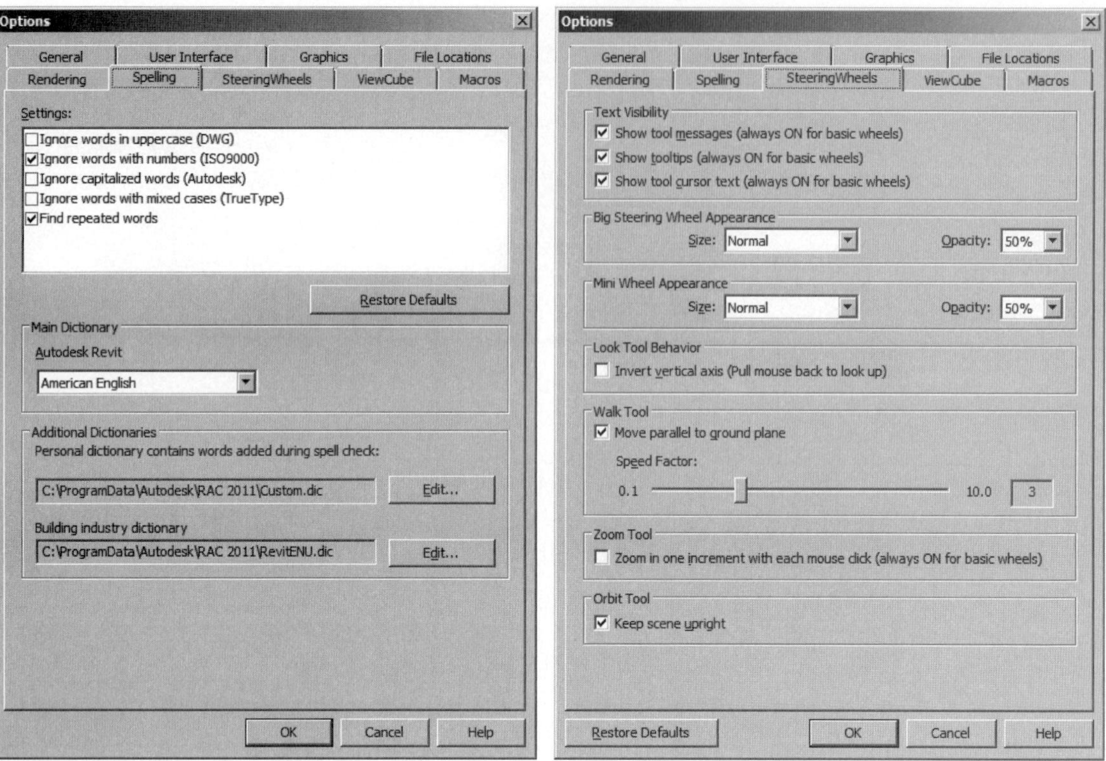

Figure 2-52

Spelling and **SteeringWheels** tabs in **Options** dialog box

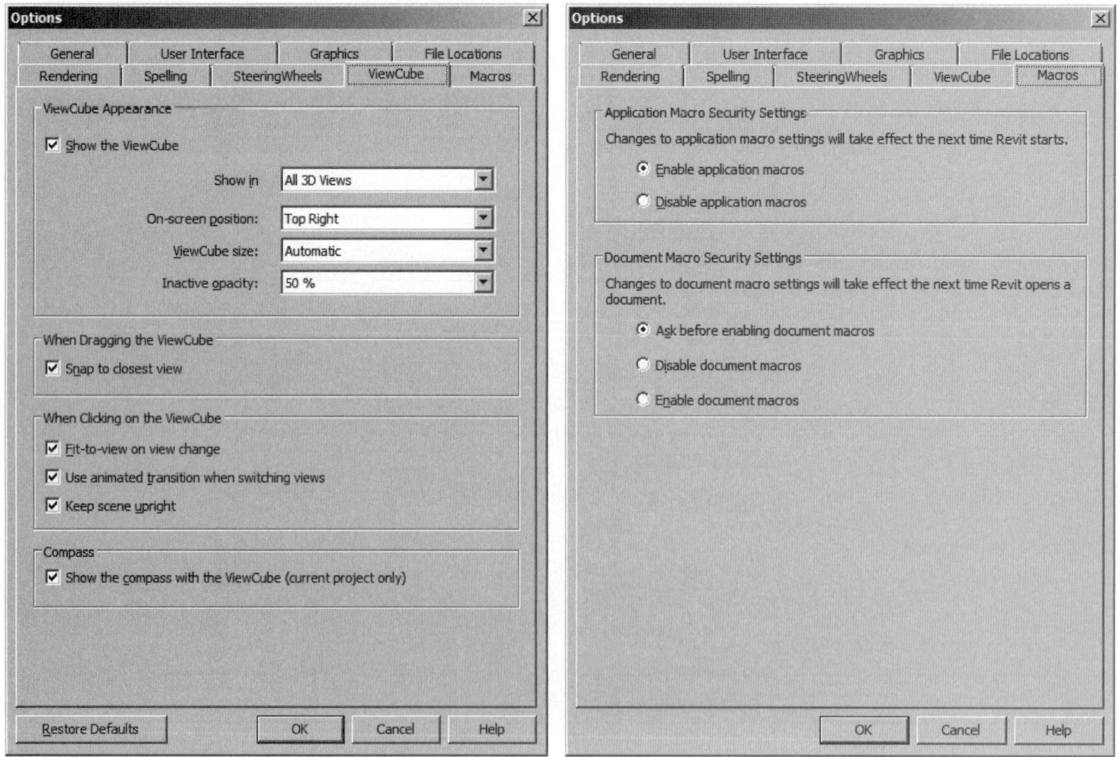

Figure 2-53

ViewCube and **Macros** tabs in **Options** dialog box

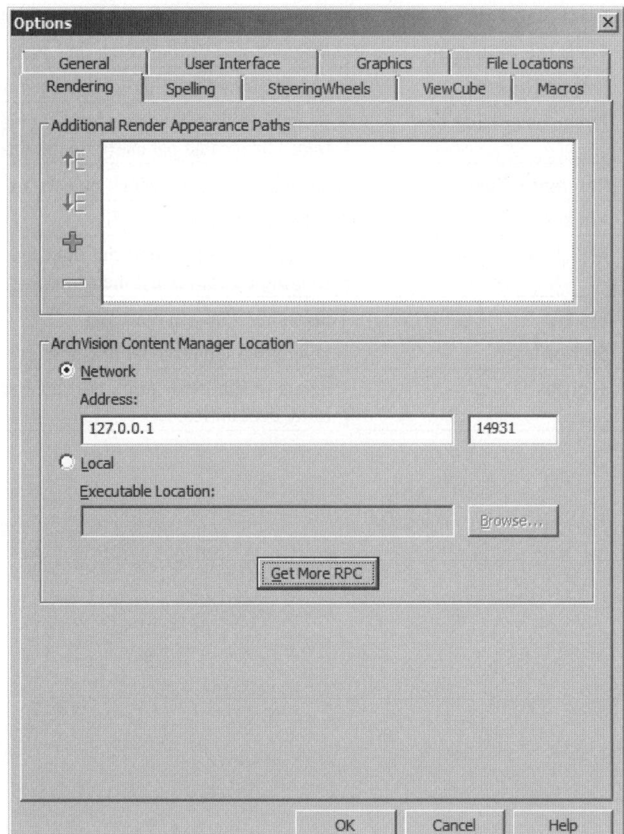

Figure 2-54

Rendering tab in **Options** dialog box

Abbreviations

In order to make this book easier to understand, shortcut abbreviations are often used. The following list codifies those abbreviations.

Please Read Before Proceeding

Revit or Revit Architecture	Refers to Autodesk Revit Architecture 2012.
Browse	Refers to searching through the file folders and files.
Contextual menu	Refers to any menu that appears when an object or entity is selected with a right mouse button (**RMB**).
Cut Plane	Height at which a plan view is displayed; usually 3′– 4′.
Dialog box	Refers to any menu containing parameters or input fields.
Display tree	Refers to Microsoft Windows folder listing consisting of + and – signs. If a + sign appears, then the listing is compressed with more folders available
Drawing Editor	Refers to the drawing area where drawings and 3D models are created.
Drop-down list	Refers to the typical Windows operating system list. When selected, a series of options appears in a vertical list.
DWG	Refers to an AutoCAD Drawing.
Elevation View	Refers to **Front**, **Back**, **Right**, or **Left View**, perpendicular to the ground plane.
<Esc> key	Refers to the **<Esc>** key on the keyboard.
Floor Plan View	Refers to looking at a plan from the **Top View**.
Model, Virtual model	Refers to a 3D representation of a real building or component.
Press the Enter button	Refers to any **Enter** button in any dialog box on the screen.

(continued)

Press the <Enter> key	Refers to the **<Enter>** key on the keyboard.
Press the OK button	Refers to any **OK** button in any dialog box on the screen.
Project Browser	Refers to the list of views contained in the project.
Properties dialog box	Dialog box that appears when an object is selected. This dialog box contains changeable parametric data about the selected object.
Reference Plane	Custom plane upon which objects are placed.
Rfa file	Refers to a Revit Family file.
RMB	Refers to clicking using the right mouse button. This is most often used to bring up contextual menus.
Rvt file	Refers to a Revit project file.
Section View	Refers to a longitudinal or transverse cut through the model.
Tooltips	Refers to the information that appears when the cursor is held momentarily over an icon.

CHAPTER

3 Walls

CHAPTER OBJECTIVES

- Learn three ways to place a **Wall** object.
- Use **Pick Lines** on an imported **2D CAD** file.
- Create wall sweeps and reveals.
- Learn how to use **Join Geometry**, **Cut Geometry**, and **Wall Joins**.
- Modify vertically-compound walls.
- Create a profile for a **Wall Sweep**.
- Create a compound wall with the **SWEEP** command.
- Modify **End Caps** and **Insert** conditions.
- Create embedded walls.

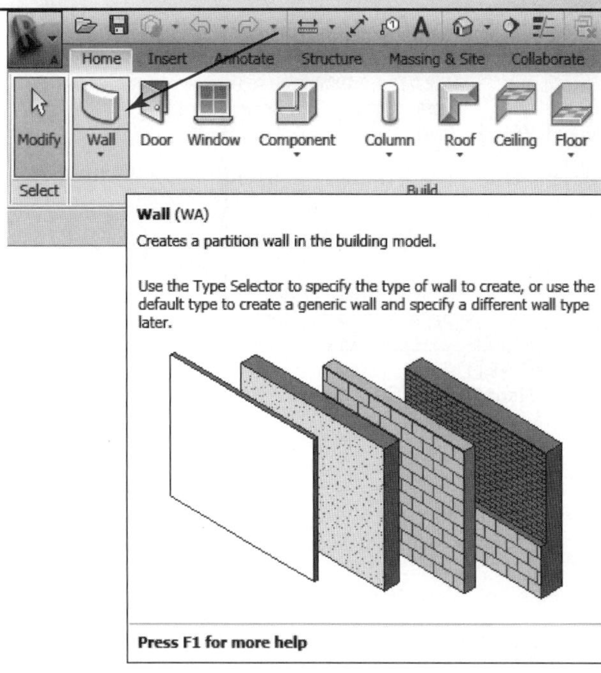

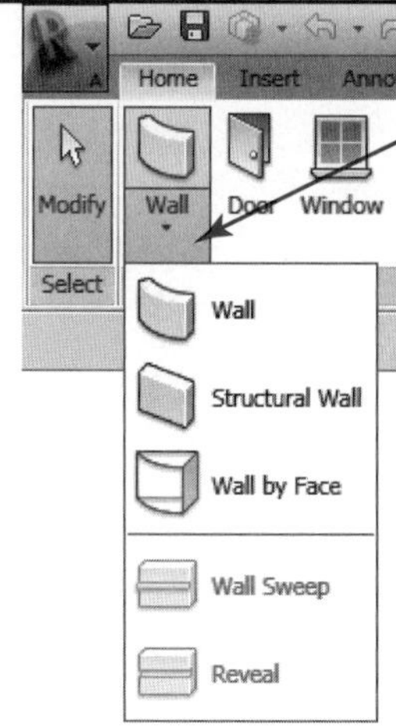

Introduction

Wall objects are the basis of all buildings; they enclose space and give the building its character. Because buildings require a vast variety of wall types and configurations, these objects have become very sophisticated in Revit Building. Walls can function as interior, exterior, foundation, and retaining. All walls have a structure that can be defined through the type properties of the wall. In addition, various instance and type properties can be specified to define the appearance of the wall.

Creating a Wall

You create a wall by sketching the location line of the wall in a Plan view or a 3D view. Revit Architecture applies the thickness, height, and other properties of the wall around the location line of the wall. The location line is a plane in the wall that does not change, even if the wall type changes. For example, if you draw a wall and specify its location line as Core Centerline, the location line remains there, even if you select that wall and change it to another type or change its structure.

EXERCISE 3-1 **PLACING A WALL OBJECT BY LINE**

1. Start a new drawing using the RAC 2012\Imperial Templates\default.rte template.
2. In the **Project Browser**, double-click **Floor Plans** > **Level 1**.
3. Set the **Detail** to **Medium** (see Figure 3-1 so that you can see the wall components in Plan view).

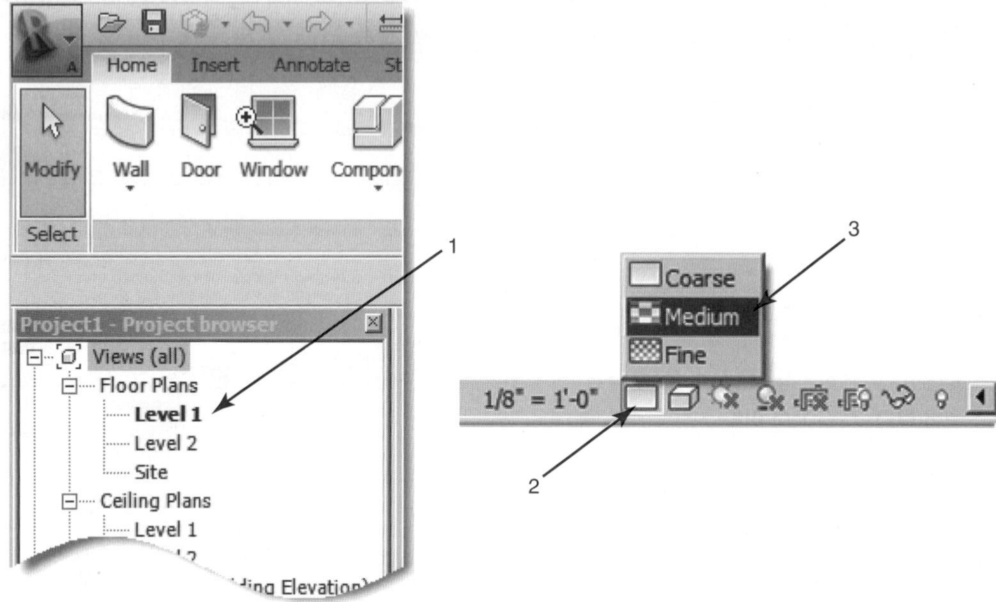

Figure 3-1

Creating a new drawing

4. In the **Home** toolbar, select the **Wall** button.
5. The **Wall** toolbar will change to the **Modify | Place Wall** toolbar.
6. Pick the **Line** button from the **Draw** panel.
7. In the **Place Wall** toolbar, select **Basic Wall: Exterior – Brick on CMU** from the **Properties** drop-down list. In the **Options Bar**, set the **Height** to **Unconnected**, then set the height to **10′-0″**, set the **Location Line** to **Finish Face: Exterior**, and check the **Chain** check box (see Figure 3-2).

> **NOTE:**
> When you set the **Height** to **Unconnected**, you are not connected to a **Level**; thus, you must set its height.

8. Place the wall horizontally by clicking a spot in the **Drawing Editor**, releasing the mouse button, moving the mouse to the right, and clicking again when the number above the wall reads **28′-0″**. Press the **<Esc>** key on the keyboard or select the **Modify** arrow in the upper left of the **Modify | Place Wall** toolbar to finish the command.

Notice that the wall is being drawn in relation to the face of the wall; this is the **Location Line**.

9. Again, select the **Wall** button from the **Home** toolbar.
10. Change the **Location Line** to **Core Face: Exterior**, and place another wall **28′-0″** long.

Notice that the wall is now being drawn in relation to the face of the CMU core. Repeat Steps 5 and 6 with all the different **Location Lines** (see Figure 3-3).

11. Delete the walls you placed.
12. Again, in the **Place Wall** toolbar, select **Basic Wall: Exterior – Brick on CMU** from the **Properties** drop-down list. In the **Options Bar**, set the **Height** to **Unconnected**,

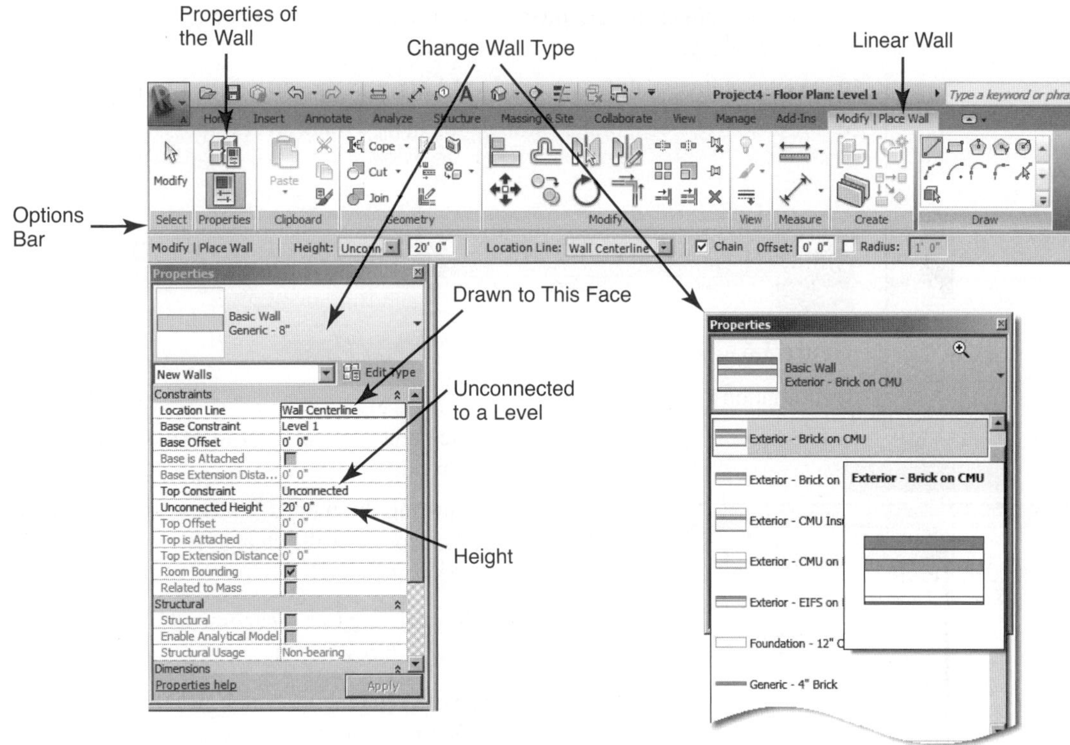

Figure 3-2

Setting **Wall** properties

then set the height to **10′-0″**, set the **Location Line** to **Finish Face: Exterior**, check the **Chain** check box, and pick the **Line** button.

13. Click a spot, move your cursor vertically, enter **11** (11′-0″), and press <**Enter**> to create an 11′-0″ long wall.
14. Repeat this process, moving your cursor horizontally, entering **28′-6′** (28′-6″).
15. Move your cursor vertically downward until you see a dashed line appear that shows you are aligned with the bottom of the first wall you placed.
16. Click at this spot, and then press the <**Esc**> key twice, or select the **Modify** arrow in the upper left of the **Modify | Place Wall** toolbar to finish the command (see Figure 3-4).
17. Select the left vertical wall to expose the temporary dimension lines. If the temporary dimensions are not from face to face, double-click the **Witness Line** node as shown in Figure 3-5 until the **Witness Line** is in the correct position. Repeat for both sides.

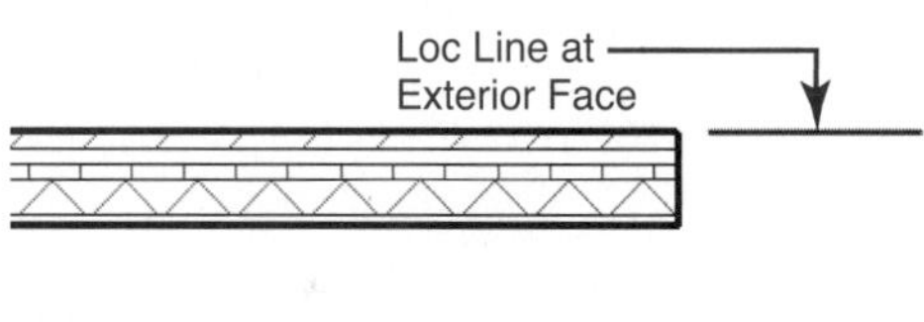

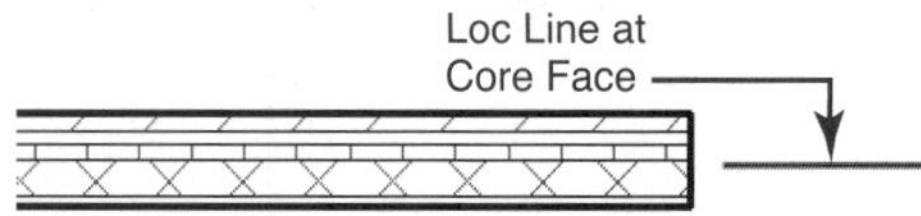

Figure 3-3

Setting **Location Lines**

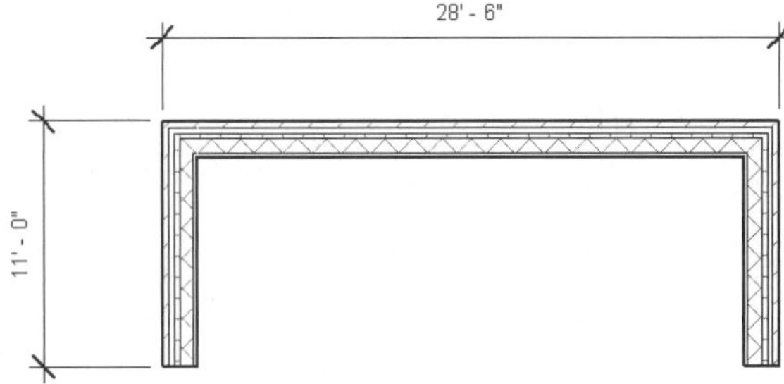

Figure 3-4

Creating a wall

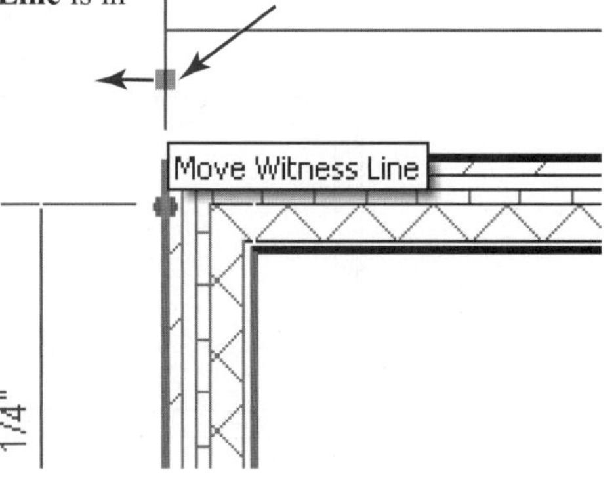

Figure 3-5

Moving a witness line

18. Select the dimension for the horizontal wall, change it to **35** (35′-0″), and press the <**Enter**> key.
19. The horizontal wall becomes 35′-0″ long, and the left vertical wall moves left.
20. Press <**Ctrl**>+<**Z**>, or the **Undo** button in the **Quick Access** toolbar (see Figure 3-6).

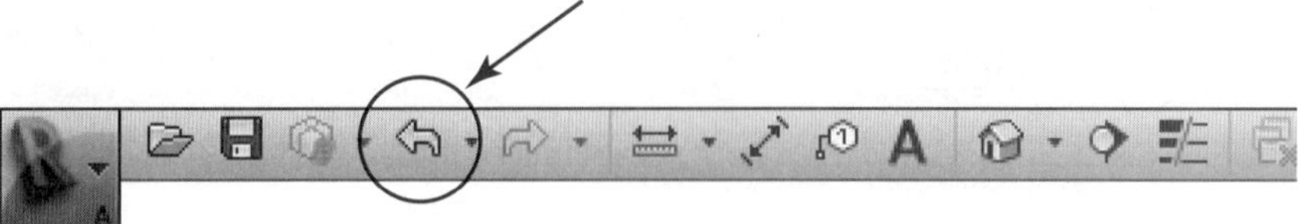

Figure 3-6

Undo button

21. Select the right vertical wall to expose the temporary dimension lines.
22. After adjusting the witness lines, select the dimension for the horizontal wall, change it to **35** (35′-0″), and press the <**Enter**> key.

This time, the horizontal wall becomes 35′-0″ long, and the right vertical wall moves right.

23. Select a wall, right mouse button **(RMB)** click, and select **Create Similar** from the contextual menu that appears.
24. Add and adjust walls to create the enclosure shown in Figure 3-7.
25. Select the wall shown in Figure 3-8.

By entering numbers in the temporary dimension area, you can move the selected wall.

26. Save this file as **PLACING WALLS**.

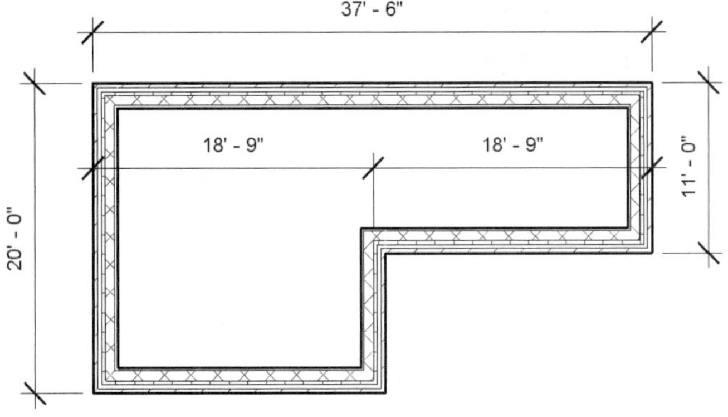

Figure 3-7

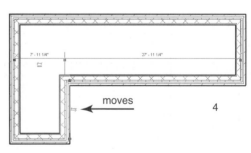

Adding and adjusting walls

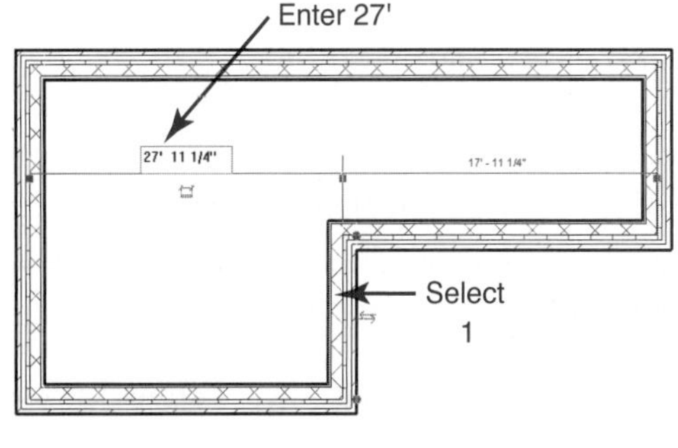

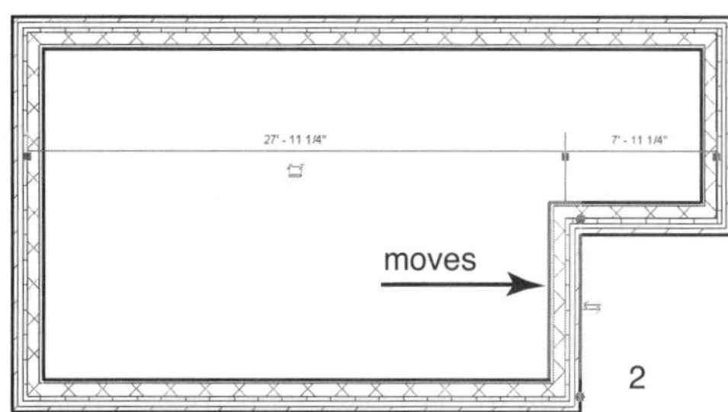

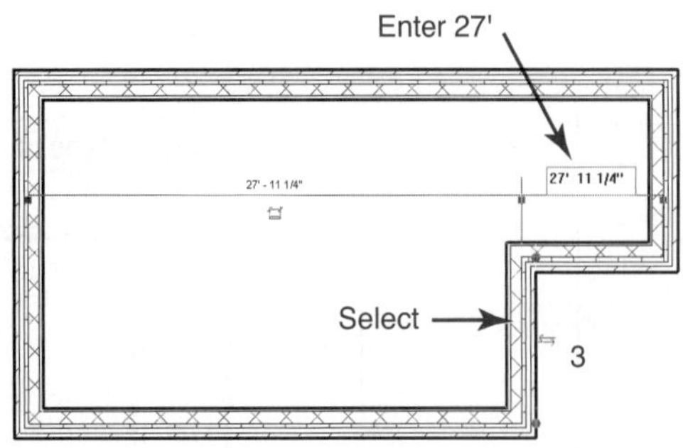

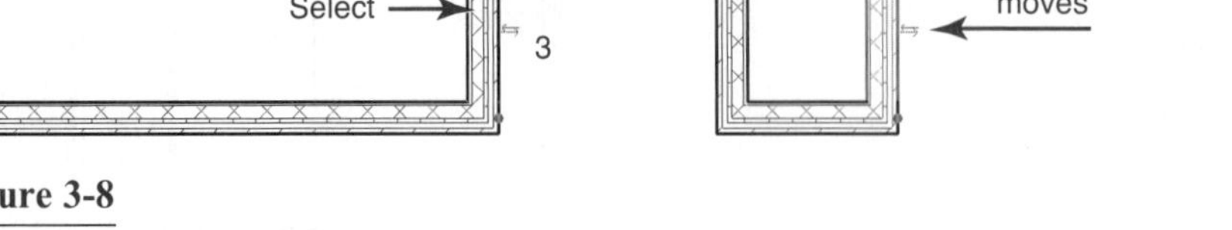

Figure 3-8

Selecting and moving a wall

Using Pick Lines on an Imported 2D CAD File

Using the **Pick Lines** option for creating walls allows you to pick any 2D CAD or line drawing. This is especially useful when you import a DWG, DXF, or MicroStation DGN file.

EXERCISE 3-2 USING PICK LINES ON AN IMPORTED 2D CAD FILE

To access student data files, go to **www.pearsondesigncentral.com.**

1. Download the **CARRIAGE HOUSE WALLS** CAD file from **www.pearsondesigncentral.com** and place it in a new directory named **WALLS**.
2. Start a new drawing using the RAC 2012\Imperial Templates\default.rte template.
3. In the **Project Browser**, double-click **Floor Plans > Level 1**.
4. Select **Link CAD** from the **Insert** tab to bring up the **Link CAD Formats** dialog box.
5. In the **Link CAD Formats** dialog box, select the **CARRIAGE HOUSE WALLS** file from the **WALLS** directory.

The 2D CAD drawing will now appear in the **Drawing Editor** (see Figure 3-9).

6. Select **Visibility/Graphics** from the **View** toolbar, or type **VG** to bring up the **Visibility/Graphics Overrides** dialog box (see Figure 3-10).

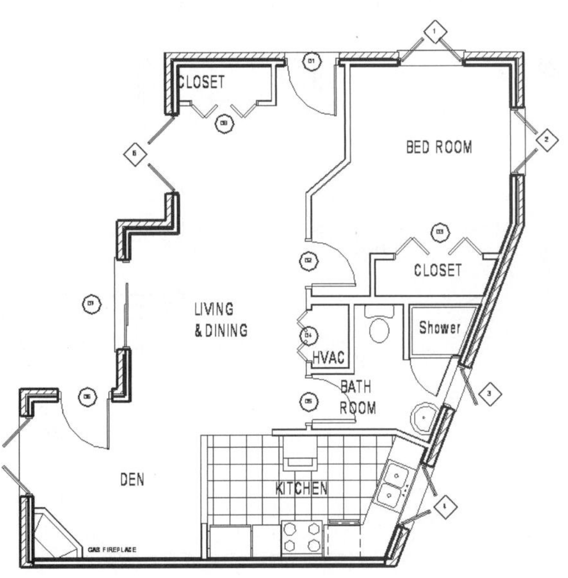

Figure 3-9

2D CAD drawing

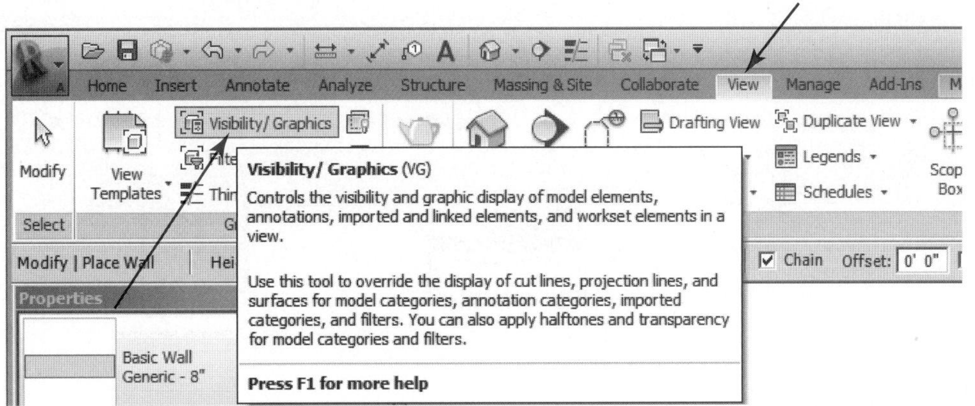

Figure 3-10

Visibility/Graphics Overrides dialog box

7. In the **Visibility/Graphics Overrides** dialog box, change to the **Imported Categories** tab.
8. In the **Imported Categories** tab, check the **Halftone** check box for the **CARRIAGE HOUSE WALLS** drawing.
9. In the **Imported Categories** tab, expand the **CARRIAGE HOUSE WALLS** drawing, uncheck all the layers except **A-Wall** and **B-Wall**, and press the **OK** button to close the dialog box.

This will turn off all the walls except those on layers **A-Wall** and **B-Wall**, and give them a halftone appearance (see Figure 3-11).

10. Select the **Wall** button from the **Home** toolbar to bring up the **Place Wall** toolbar.
11. In the **Properties** drop-down list, select the Basic Wall: Generic 8″ wall type.
12. In the **Modify | Place Wall** toolbar, select the **Pick Lines** button and **Finish Face Exterior** from the **Options Bar** drop-down list. Set the **Height** to **10′-0″** (see Figure 3-12).
13. Move the cursor over the lines in the **Linked.DWG** file as shown in Figure 3-13.

Be sure that the blue dashed line that appears is inside the wall, not outside, and then click on each line.

14. Select the **Trim** button from the **Modify** toolbar (see Figure 3-14).
15. Trim all the corners to complete the exterior walls (see Figure 3-15).

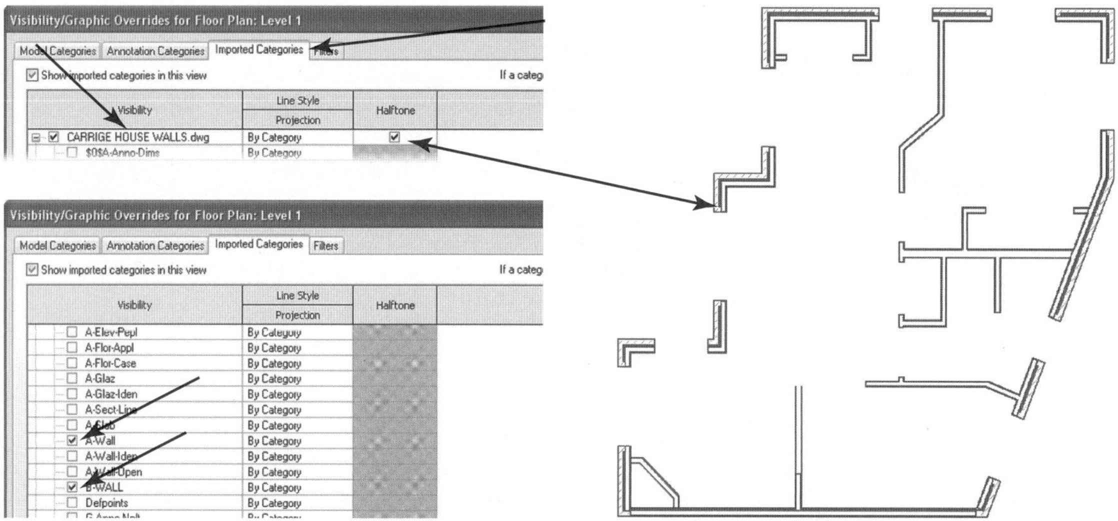

Figure 3-11

Imported Categories tab

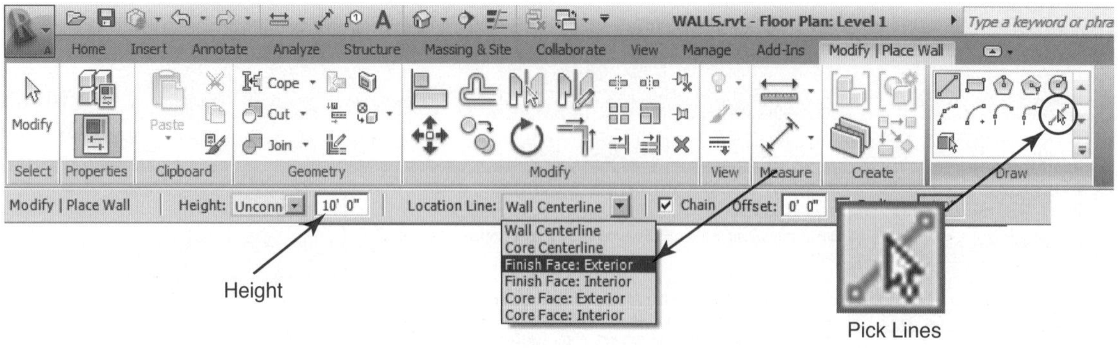

Figure 3-12

Modify | Place Wall toolbar

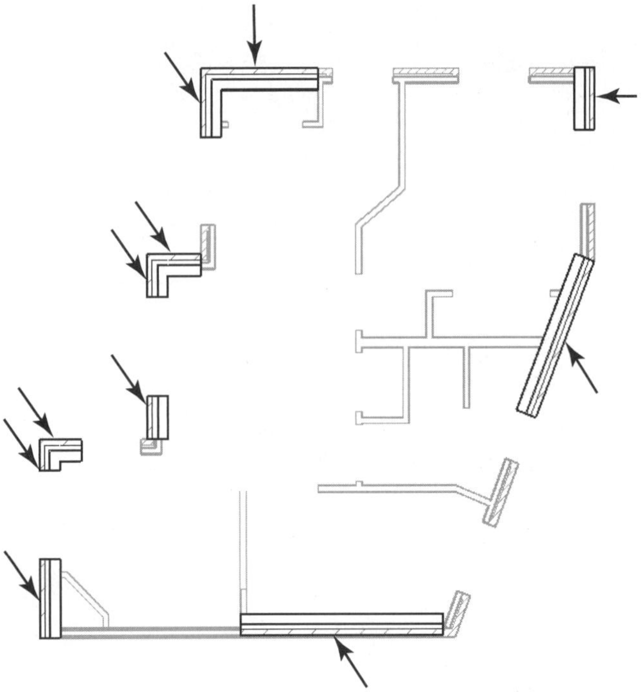

Figure 3-13

Picked lines

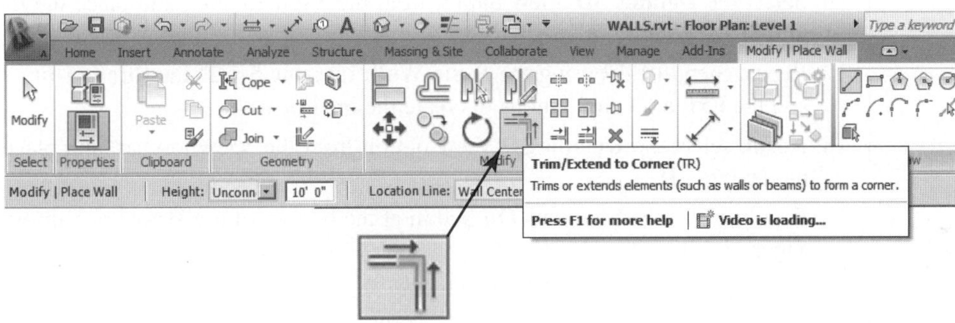

Figure 3-14

Trim button

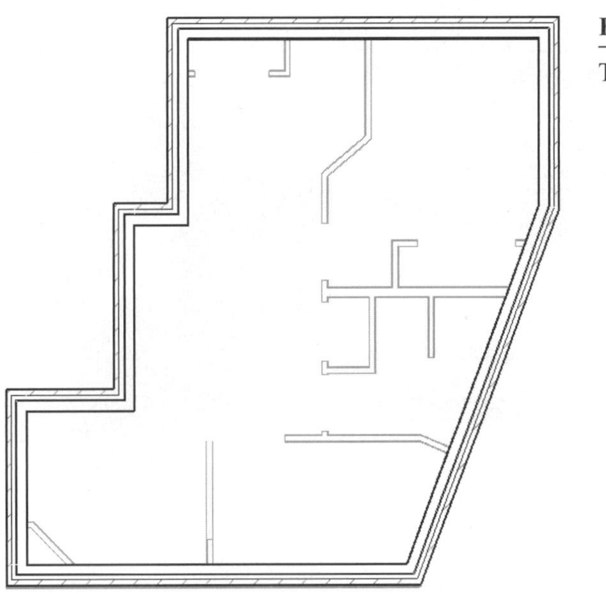

Figure 3-15

Trimmed corners

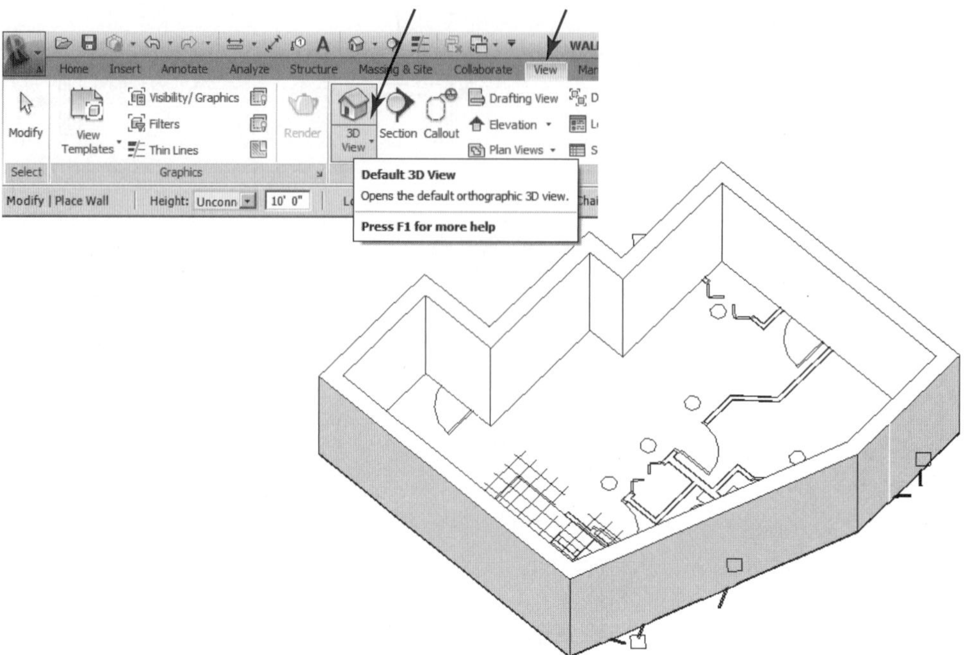

Figure 3-16

Default 3D View button

16. Select the **Default 3D View** button from the **View** toolbar, and place the model into **3D** (see Figure 3-16).
17. Repeat Steps 10–12 using the **Basic Wall: interior 5-1/2″ Partition (1-hr)** wall, and the **Extend/Trim** buttons to create the interior walls.
18. Again, select the **Default 3D View** button from the **View** toolbar, and place the model into **3D**.
19. Finally, press the **Shadows On** button at the bottom of the **Drawing Editor** (see Figure 3-17).

You have now traced your 2D CAD drawing, and converted it into a 3D Revit model.

20. Save this file as **WALLS by PICK LINES**.

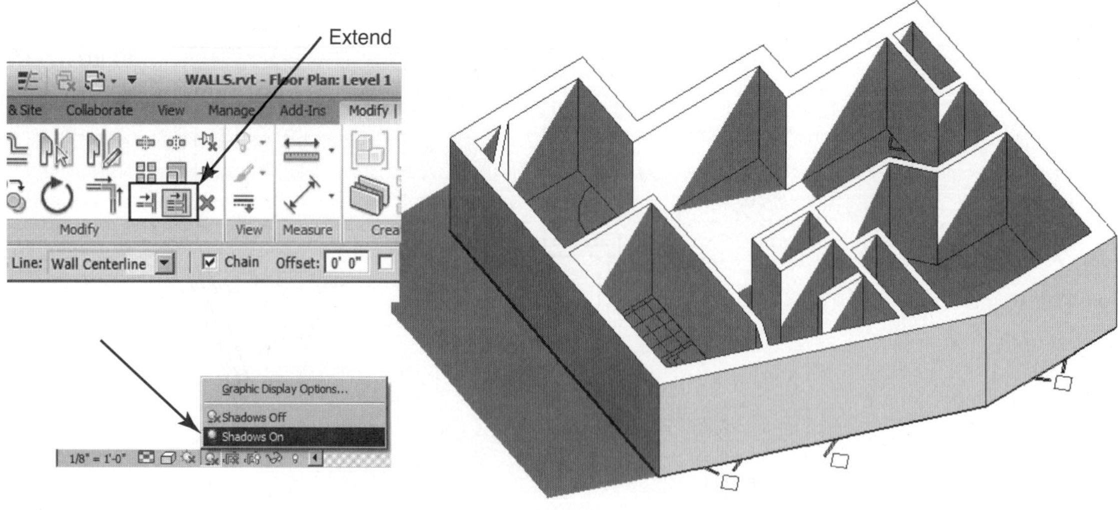

Figure 3-17

3D drawing

EXERCISE 3-3 **USING THE WALL BY FACES BUTTON**

The **Wall by Faces** button is used to place walls on a **Massing** object. This is covered in detail in the Massing & Site chapter.

EXERCISE 3-4 **WALL SWEEPS AND WALL REVEALS**

Wall sweeps and reveals are used to add details such as moldings, handrails, indentations, and so on, to walls without adding extra objects. Although you could create separate moldings, for instance, it is quicker to have them as part of the walls so that they are created at the same time as the walls.

1. Start a new drawing using the RAC 2012\Imperial Templates\default.rte template.
2. In the **Project Browser**, double-click **Floor Plans > Level 1**.
3. Set the **Detail** to **Medium** so that you can see the wall components in Plan view.
4. In the **Home** toolbar, select the **Wall** button.
5. Select the **Line** button from the **Draw** panel.
6. Select **Basic Wall: Generic - 12** from the **Properties** drop-down list. In the **Options Bar**, set the **Height** to **Unconnected**, the **height** to **8′-0″**, and then set the **Location Line** to **Finish Face: Exterior**.
7. Place a **16′-0″** long wall, press the **<Esc>** key on the keyboard or select the **Modify** arrow in the upper left of the **Modify | Place Wall** toolbar to finish the command, and then press the **3D** button in the **View** toolbar to place the wall in **3D**.

Loading the Profile

Profiles are **2D** lines that create the cross sections (**Profiles**) of Revit's **Sweeps** and **Reveals**.

1. Select **Load Family** from the **Insert** toolbar to bring up the **Imperial Library** folder in the **Load Family** dialog box (see Figure 3-18).

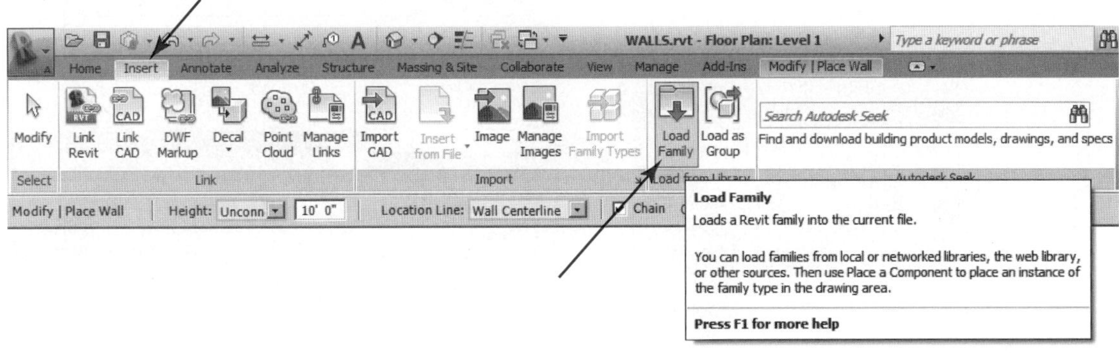

Figure 3-18

Select **Load Family** from the **Insert** toolbar

2. In the **Imperial Library** folder, open the **Profiles** folder.
3. In the **Profiles** folder, select the **Base 1** family, and then press the **Open** button to load the family (see Figure 3-19).

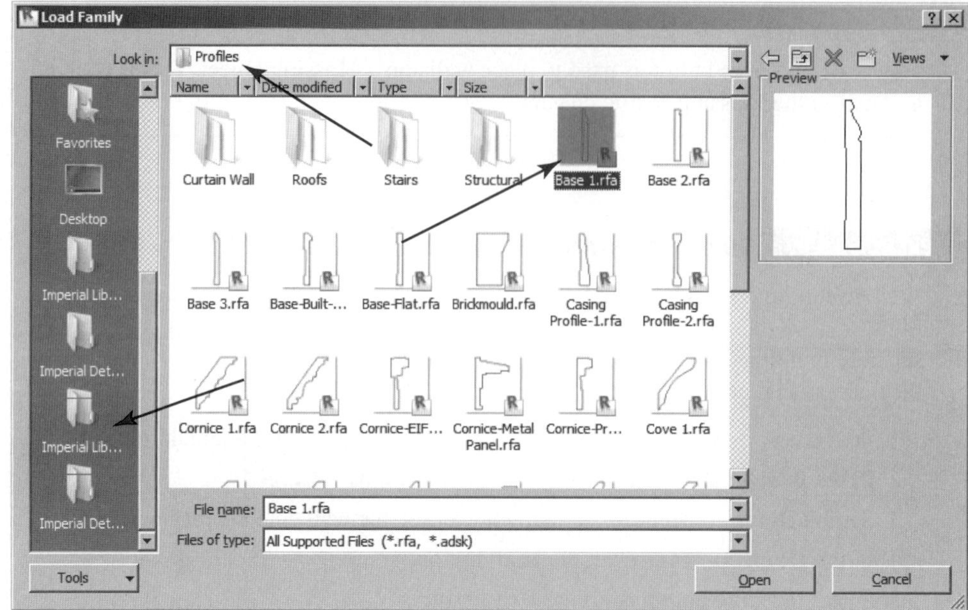

Figure 3-19

Open the **Base 1** family from the **Profiles** folder

4. Select the wall you placed**,** and then select the **Type Properties** button from the **Modify | Walls** toolbar to bring up the **Type Properties** dialog box.
5. In the **Type Properties** dialog box, press the **Duplicate** button at the top right to bring up the **Name** dialog box.
6. In the **Name** dialog box, enter **TEST WALL SWEEP**, and press the **OK** button to return to the **Type Properties** dialog box **(**see Figure 3-20).

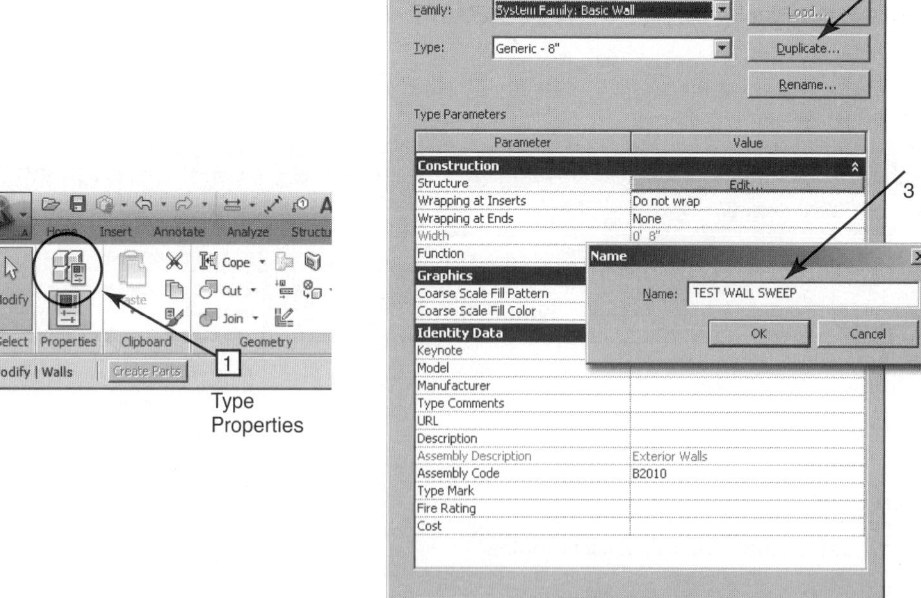

Figure 3-20

Type Properties dialog box

7. In the **Type Properties** dialog box, press the **Edit** button to bring up the **Edit Assembly** dialog box (see Figure 3-21).
8. In the **Edit Assembly** dialog box, set the **Sample Height** to **8′-0″**.
9. Press the **Preview** button at the bottom left of the **Edit Assembly** dialog box.
10. In the **Edit Assembly** dialog box, select **Section: Modify type attributes** from the **View** drop-down list as shown in Figure 3-22.

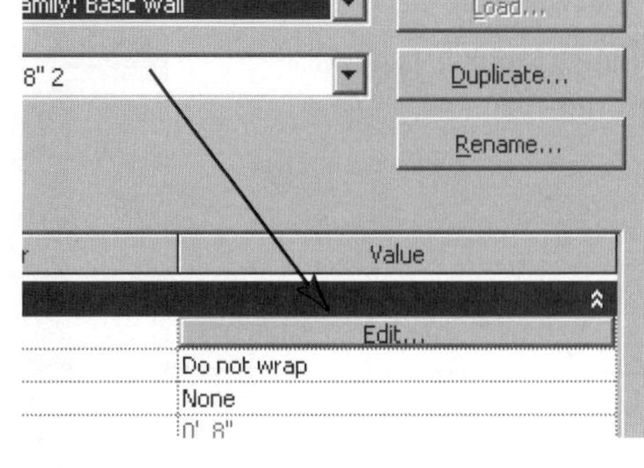

Figure 3-21

Edit Assembly dialog box

Notice that the **Sweeps** button, as well as the **Reveals**, **Merge Regions**, **Split Region** buttons, and so on, are lit. This is because you can only modify these in Section view, not in Plan view.

11. In the **Edit Assembly** dialog box, press the **Sweeps** button to bring up the **Wall Sweeps** dialog box.
12. In the **Wall Sweeps** dialog box, press the **Add** button to add a **Default** profile.
13. Press the **Default Profile** drop-down list, select **Base 1: 7 1/4″ × 5/8″**, and press the **OK** button.

NOTE:
7 1/4″ × 5/8″ is one of the profiles you loaded when you loaded the **Base 1** family (see Figure 3-23).

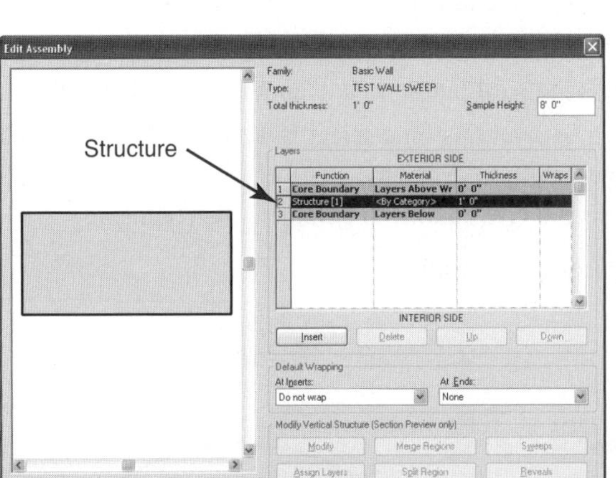

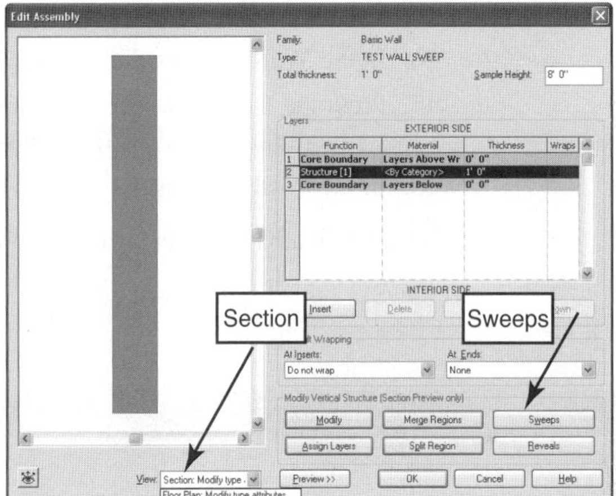

Figure 3-22

Select **Section: Modify type attributes** from the **View** list

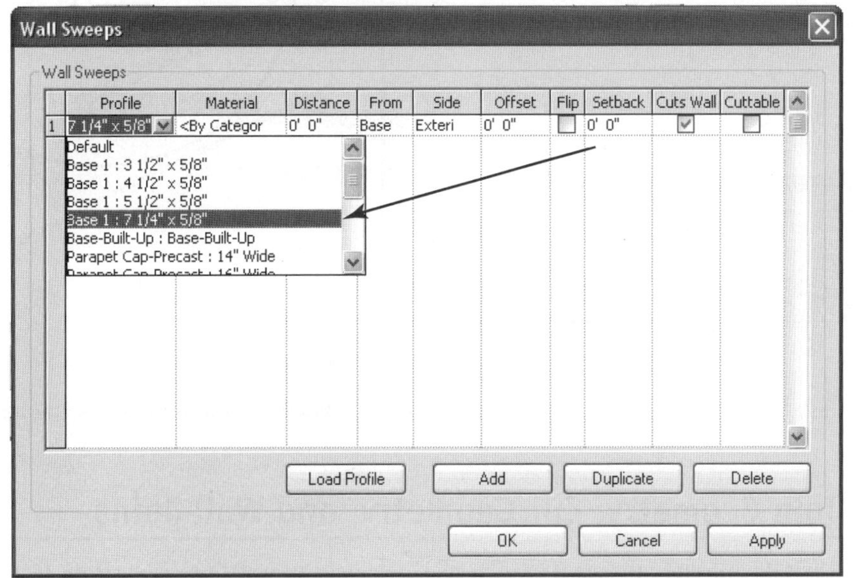

Figure 3-23

Profile selections in **Wall Sweeps** dialog box

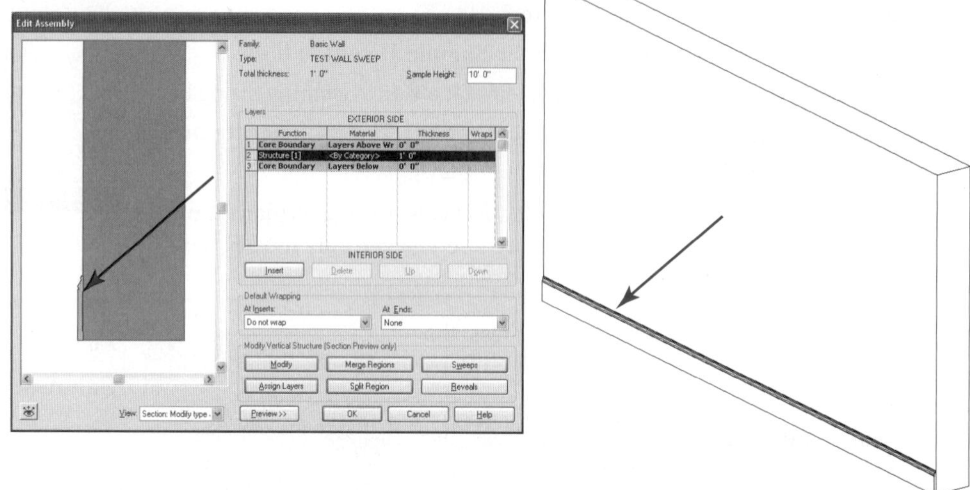

Figure 3-24

Adding another **Default** profile

14. The wall will now have a **Wall Sweep** profile assigned to it (see Figure 3-24).
15. Press the **Sweeps** button again to bring up the **Wall Sweeps** dialog box.
16. In the **Wall Sweeps** dialog box, press the **Add** button to add another **Default Profile**.
17. Press the **Default Profile** drop-down list, but this time select **Base 1: 3 1/2″** × **5/8″**, and set its distance to **3′-0″** from **Base** (see Figures 3-25 and 3-26).
18. In the **Wall Sweeps** dialog box, press the **OK** buttons to complete the command.

Notice that a base and chair molding appear on the wall.

19. Save this file as **WALL SWEEPS**.

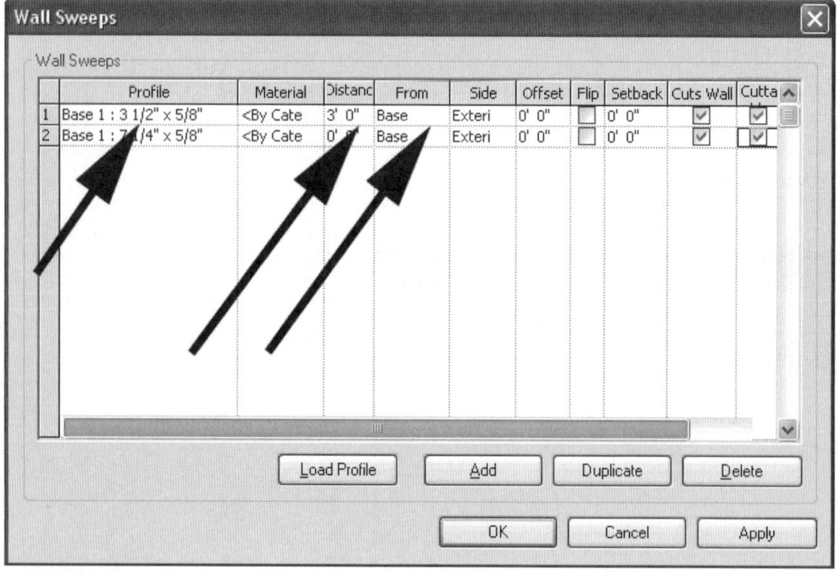

Figure 3-25

Wall Sweeps dialog box

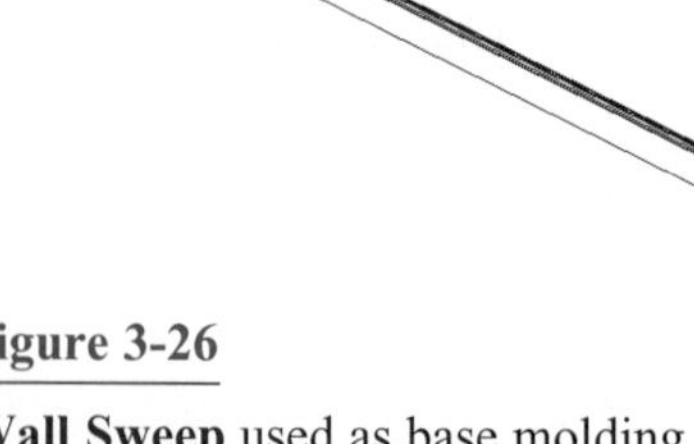

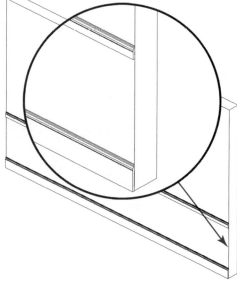

Figure 3-26

Wall Sweep used as base molding

Join Geometry, Cut Geometry, and Wall Joins

Revit Architecture makes it easy to make changes to walls using the **Join Geometry**, **Cut Geometry**, and **Wall Joins** tools.

EXERCISE 3-5 **USING JOIN GEOMETRY, CUT GEOMETRY, AND WALL JOINS**

Join Geometry

1. Place a **Basic Wall: Generic - 12″** in the **Drawing Editor**. Make it **12′-0″** long and **8′-0″** high.
2. Place a **Basic Wall: Generic - 6″** in the **Drawing Editor**. Make it **8′-0″** long and **8′-0″** high.
3. Place the **8″** wall intersecting the **12″** wall, ignore the warning, and click in an empty space in the **Drawing Editor** to end the command.
4. Select the **Join Geometry** button in the **Modify** toolbar.
5. Select the **12″** wall, and then select the **6″** wall to join them (see Figure 3-27).

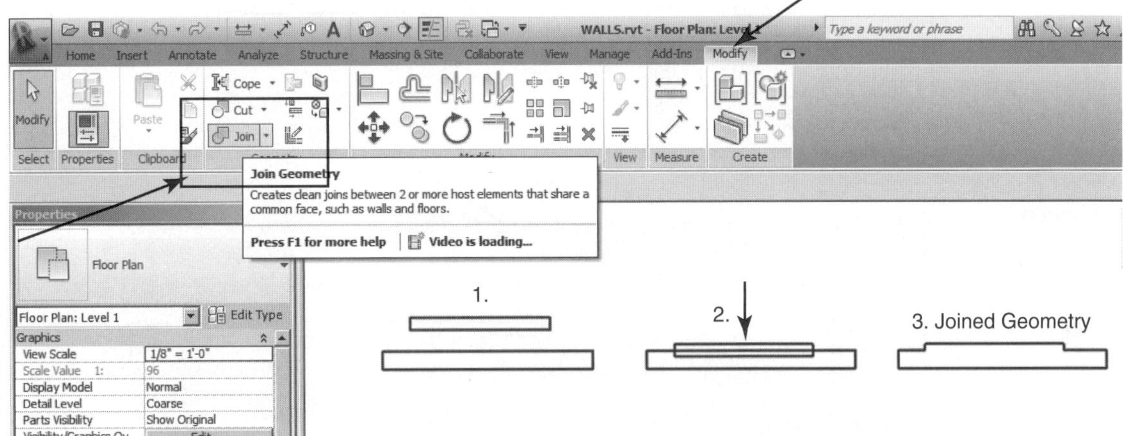

Figure 3-27

Join Geometry command

6. Select both of the joined walls, and make a copy by pressing <**Ctrl**> and moving the wall.
7. Select the copied set of joined walls, and select **Basic Wall: Generic - 12″ Masonry** from the **Properties** drop-down list (see Figure 3-28).

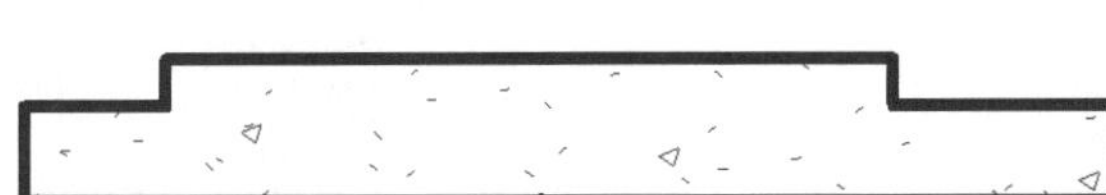

Figure 3-28

Joined walls

Cut Geometry

8. Place a **Basic Wall: Generic - 12″** in the **Drawing Editor**. Make it **12′-0″** long and **8′-0″** high.
9. Place a **Basic Wall: Generic - 6″** in the **Drawing Editor**. Make it **8′-0″** long and **8′-0″** high.
10. Place the **6″** wall inside the **12″** wall.
11. Select the **Cut Geometry** button from the **Modify** toolbar.
12. Select the **12″** wall, and then select the **6″** wall.
13. Select the **Join Geometry** button to join the two walls again.
14. Select the **Basic Wall: Generic - 6″** wall, and change it to **Basic Wall: Generic - 6″ Masonry** (see Figure 3-29).
15. Select the **Default 3D View** button in the **Quick Access** toolbar to change to the **Default 3D View**. Press **Z**, and then **A** on the keyboard (**Zoom All**) (see Figure 3-30).

NOTE:

Again, you will get a warning. Just click in an empty space and proceed.

Wall Joins

16. Place a **Basic Wall: Generic - 12″ Masonry** in the **Drawing Editor** as shown in Figure 3-31.

Figure 3-29

Cut Geometry button in the **Modify** toolbar

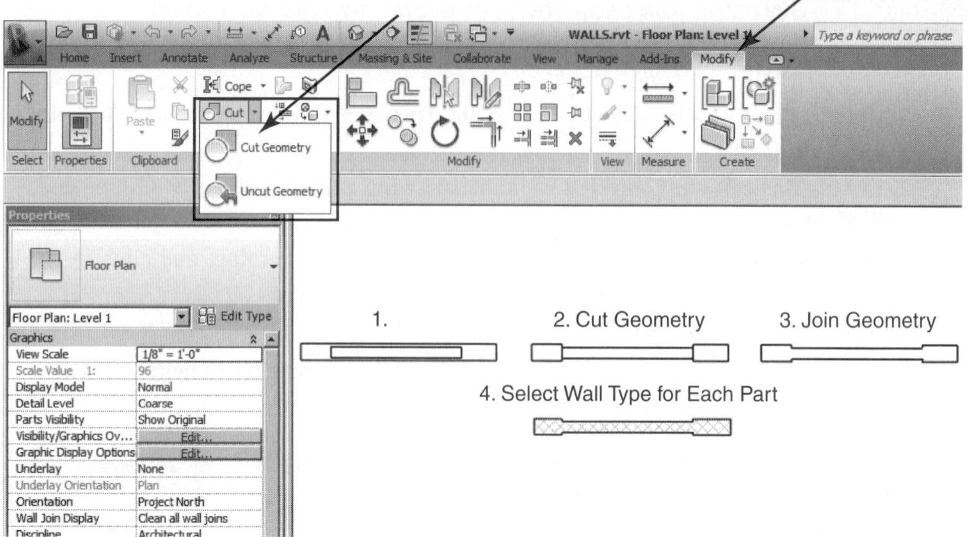

Figure 3-30

Default 3D View button

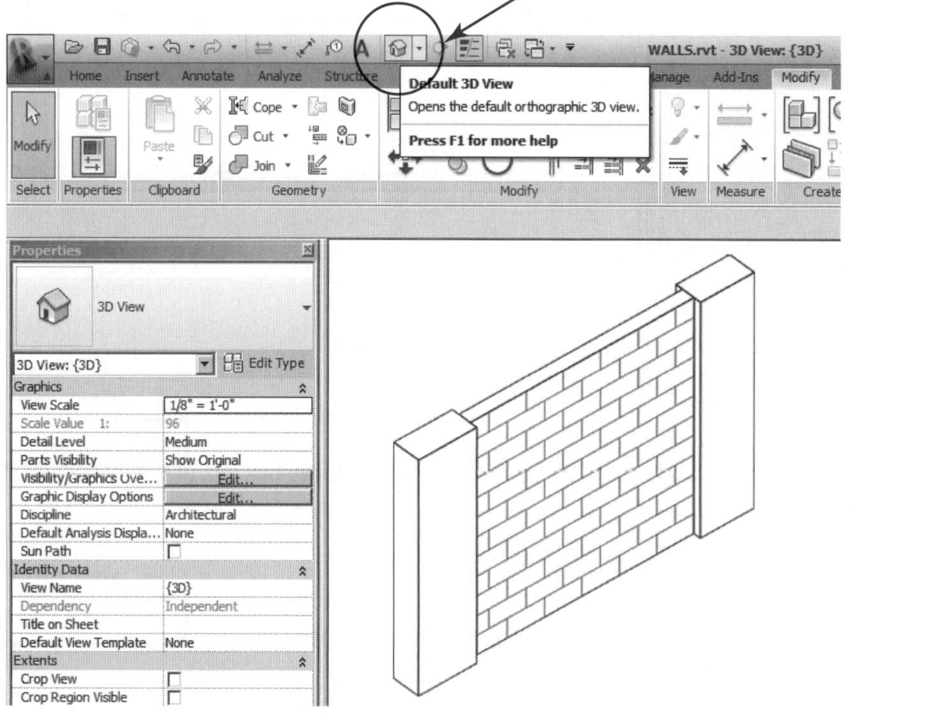

Figure 3-31

A basic wall inserted in the **Drawing Editor**

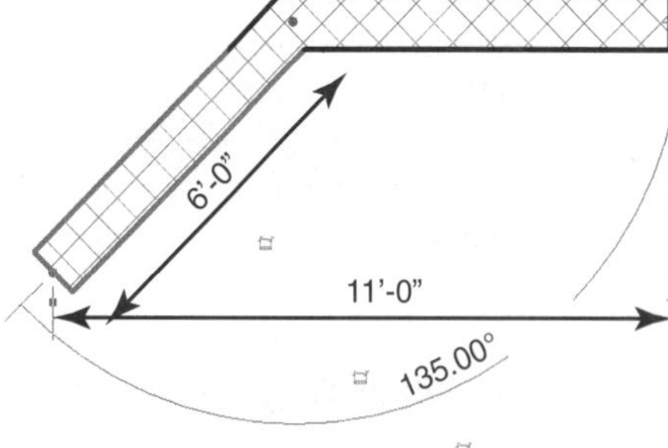

17. Select the **Wall Joins** button from the **Modify** toolbar.
18. Select a junction point of two walls, and click. A rectangle will appear at the junction (see Figure 3-32).
19. Select **Don't Clean Join** from the **Display** drop-down list.

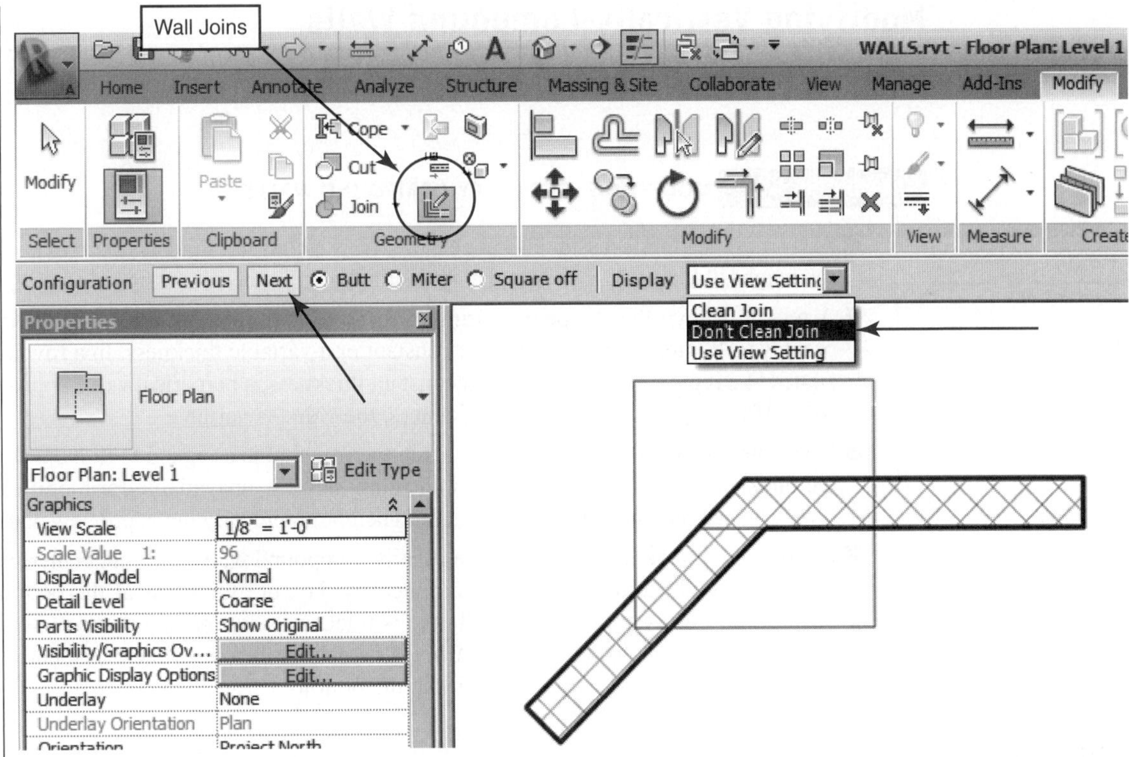

Figure 3-32

Wall Joins button

20. In the **Options Bar**, select the **Butt**, **Miter**, and **Square off** radio buttons, and watch the changes.
21. Select the **Butt** radio button, then press the **Next** button, and watch the changes.
22. Select the **Square off** radio button, then press the **Next** button, and watch the changes (see Figure 3-33).
23. Save this file as **JOIN GEOMETRY_CUT GEOMETRY_WALL JOINS**.

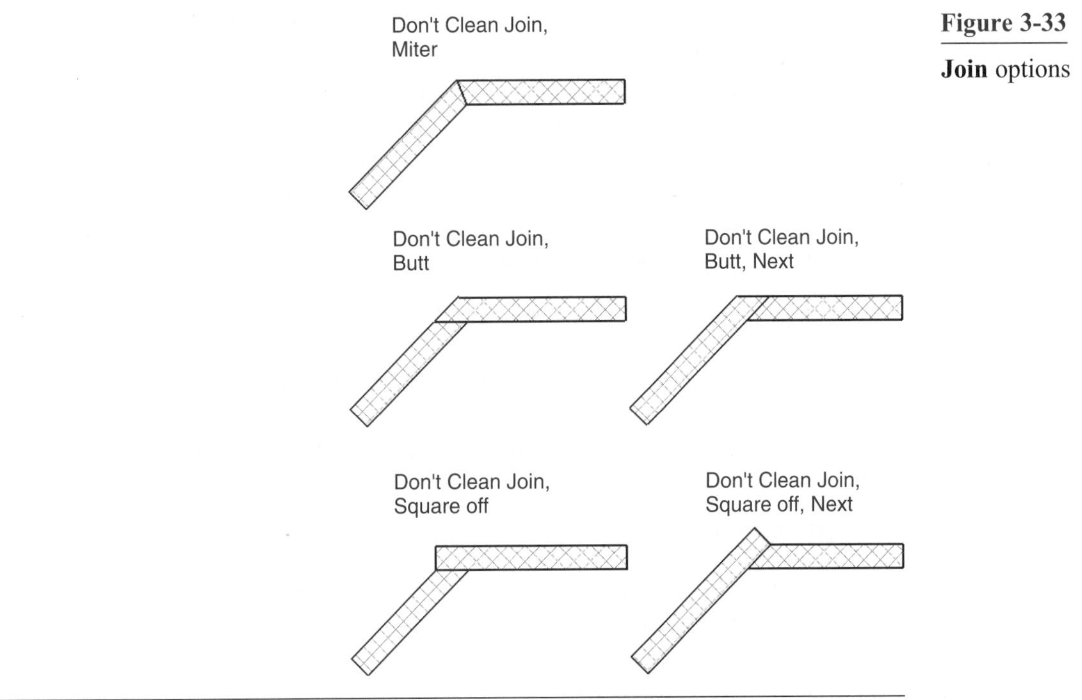

Figure 3-33

Join options

Modifying Vertically-Compound Walls

You define the structure of vertically-compound walls using either layers or regions.

EXERCISE 3-6 MODIFYING VERTICALLY-COMPOUND WALLS

- A layer is a rectangle assigned to one row. It has a constant thickness and extends the height of the wall. You can change its thickness in the row assigned to it.
- A region is any other shape appearing in the wall that does not meet the criteria of a layer. Regions can have either a constant or a variable thickness. In a row assigned to a region, if the region has a constant thickness, a numerical value appears for it. If the region has a variable thickness, the value is variable.
- You cannot change a region's thickness in the row that is assigned to it. Note that the thickness value appears shaded, indicating that it is unavailable for modification. You can only change its thickness and height graphically in the preview pane.
- Because core thickness can vary in vertically-compound walls, the core centerline and core face location lines are determined by the core thickness at the bottom of the wall. For example, if the wall core is thicker at the top than at the bottom, and you specify the location line as **Core Centerline**, the centerline of the core is measured between the core boundaries at the bottom.

The following graphics visualize the concepts of rows, layers, and regions.

Layer Rows—Correspond to layers or regions.

Wall Layer—Constant thickness and extends the height of the wall.

Regions—Neither region extends the full height of the wall.

1. Place a **Basic Wall: Exterior – Brick on CMU** in the **Drawing Editor**. Make it **12′-0″** long and **8′-0″** high. Press the **<Esc>** key on the keyboard to end the command.
2. Change to the **Default 3D View**.
3. Select **Realistic Visual Style** from the **Visual Control Bar** at the bottom of the **Drawing Editor** (see Figure 3-34).
4. Select the wall you placed to bring up the **Modify | Walls** toolbar.
5. In the **Modify | Walls** toolbar, select the **Type Properties** button to bring up the **Type Properties** dialog box.
6. In the **Type Properties** dialog box, press the **Duplicate** button at the top right to bring up the **Name** dialog box.
7. In the **Name** dialog box, enter **TEST COMPOUND WALL**, and press the **OK** button to return to the **Type Properties** dialog box.
8. In the **Type Properties** dialog box, press the **Edit** button in the **Structure** field to bring up the **Edit Assembly** dialog box.
9. In the **Edit Assembly** dialog box, press the **Preview** button at the bottom left of the dialog box.
10. In the **Edit Assembly** dialog box, select **Section: Modify type attributes** from the **View** drop-down list.
11. Zoom with your center mouse roller so that you can see the lower portion of the wall section more clearly.

Split Regions

12. In the **Edit Assembly** dialog box, select **Layer 1 (Finish 1[4] – Masonry Brick)**.
13. Select the **Split Region** button at the bottom of the **Edit Assembly** dialog box, and click on the exterior brick twice as shown in Figure 3-35. Press the **Split Region** button again to turn it off.

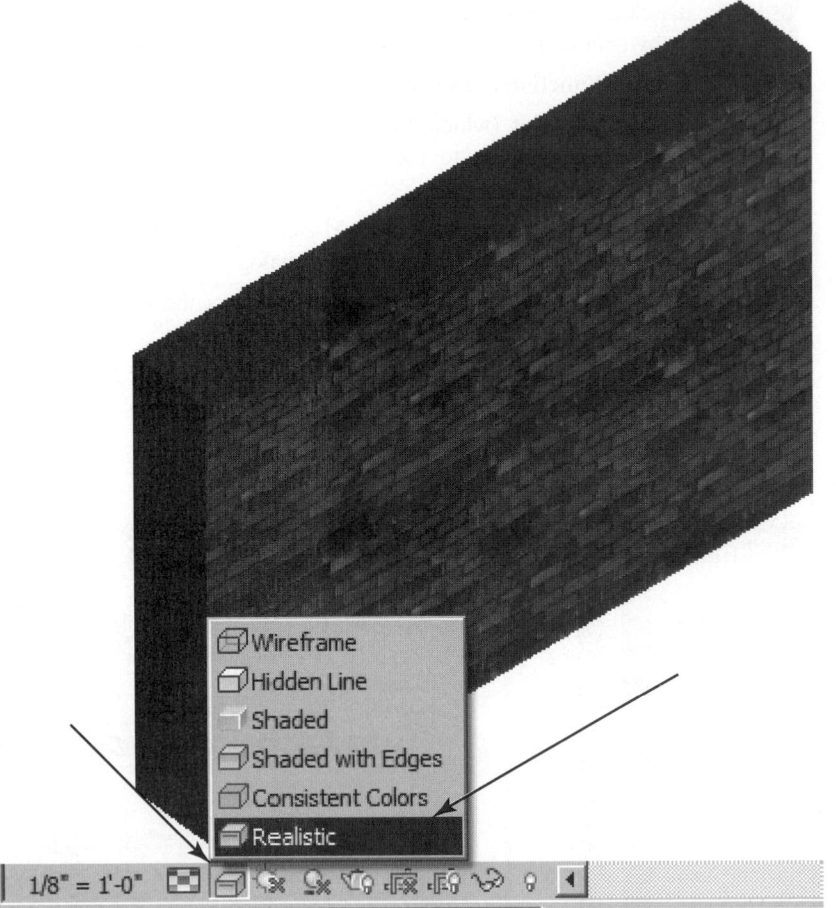

Figure 3-34

Realistic Visual Style

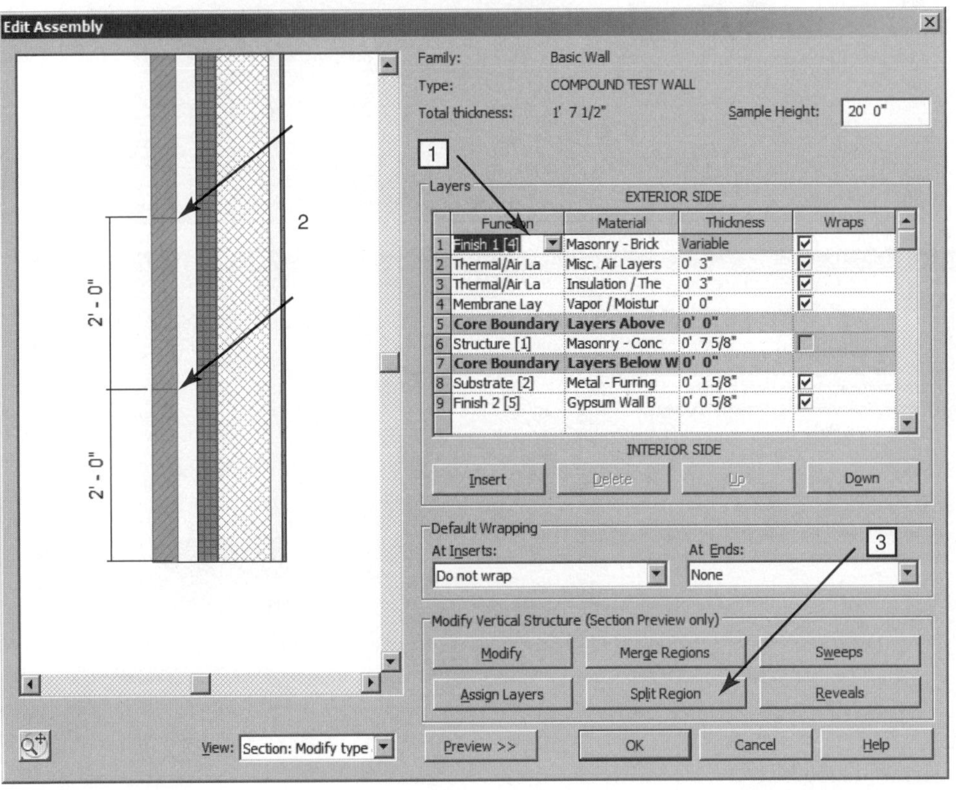

Figure 3-35

Split Region button

14. Next, select the **Insert** button to add a new layer (by default it will be **Structure [1]**).
15. Change the **Function** to **Finish 1 [4]**.
16. Select the **Material** (which by default is **<By Category>**) to go to the **Materials** dialog box.

> **NOTE:**
> The number **[4]** in **Finish 1 [4]** signifies the line weight surrounding that finish.

17. In the **Materials** dialog box, select **Masonry – Concrete Masonry Units**, and press the **OK** button at the bottom of the dialog box (see Figure 3-36).
18. Select the **Assign Layers** button, and then select the **2′-0″** region you created. Press the **OK** buttons to return to the **Drawing Editor**.
19. You have now added concrete block to the brick wall (see Figure 3-37).
20. Save this file as **COMPOUND WALL**.

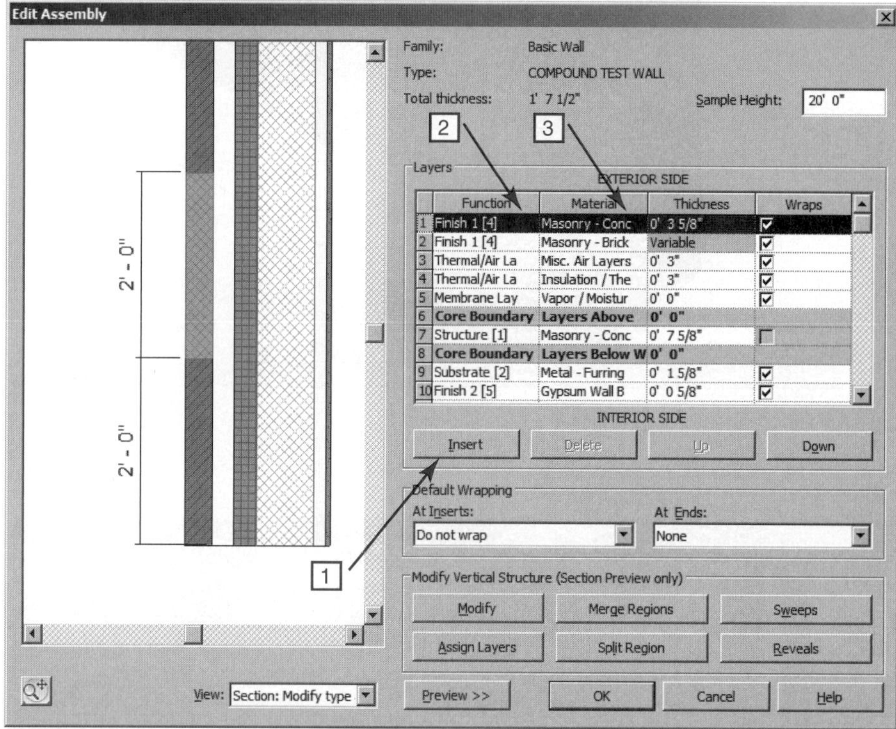

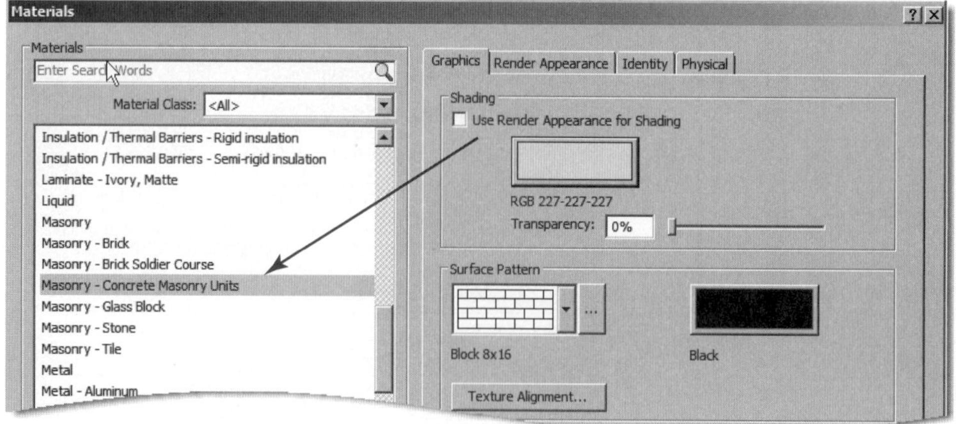

Figure 3-36

Materials dialog box

Figure 3-37

Concrete block added to brick wall

EXERCISE 3-7 CREATING A PROFILE FOR A WALL SWEEP

1. Open the **COMPOUND WALL** file.
2. In the **Project Browser**, double-click **Floor Plans** > **Level 1**.
3. Select **File** > **New** > **Family** from the **Application** menu to bring up the **New Family – Select Template File** dialog box in the **Imperial Templates** folder.
4. In the **Imperial Templates**, select the **Profile.rft** template.

The **Home** toolbar will now appear.

5. Select the **Line** button to bring up the **Modify | Place Lines** toolbar.
6. Create the 2D figure *exactly* as shown in Figure 3-38.

NOTE:

The **Profile** template has preset dashed lines to indicate the face of walls.

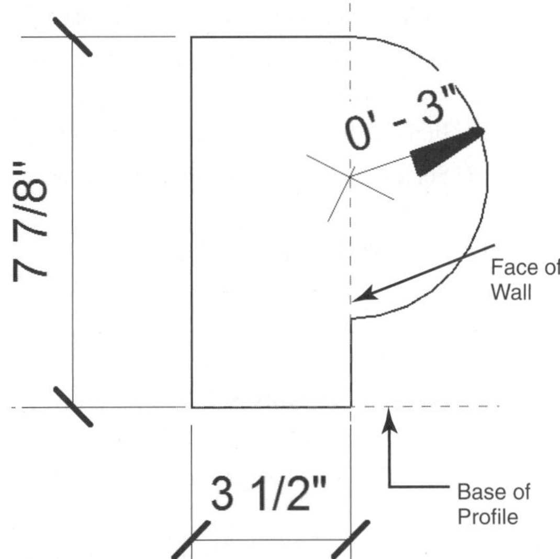

Figure 3-38

Creating a **Wall Sweep** profile

7. Select **Save As > Family** from the **Application** menu, save the profile you just created in the **Local Disc (C:) / ProgramData / Autodesk / RAC 2012 / Libraries / US Imperial / Profiles** folder as **TEST PROFILE.rfa**, and close the file.
8. Select the **Insert** tab to bring up the **Insert** toolbar.
9. In the **Insert** toolbar, select the **Load Family** button to bring up the **Load Family** dialog box.

> **NOTE:**
> Optionally, you can place the **TEST PROFILE.rfa** file in a new folder that you create.

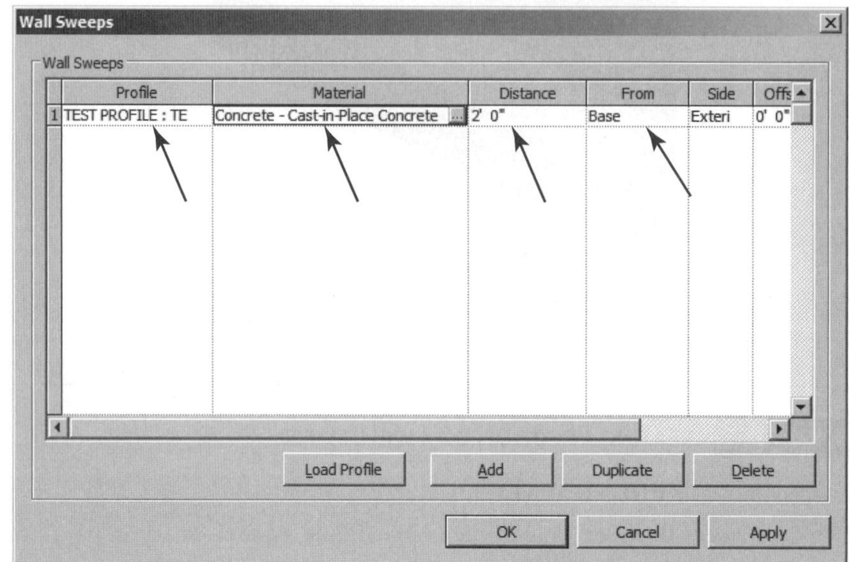

Figure 3-39

Wall Sweeps dialog box

Figure 3-40

Wall with profile added

10. In the **Load Family** dialog box, select and open the **TEST PROFILE.rfa** file from the **Profiles** folder.
11. Select the compound wall you created in the previous exercise to bring up the **Modify | Walls** toolbar.
12. In the **Modify | Walls** toolbar, select the **Type Properties** button to bring up the **Type Properties** dialog box.
13. In the **Type Properties** dialog box, press the **Edit** button in the **Structure** field to bring up the **Edit Assembly** dialog box.
14. In the **Edit Assembly** dialog box, press the **Preview** button.
15. Select the **Sweeps** button to bring up the **Wall Sweeps** dialog box.
16. In the **Wall Sweeps** dialog box, press the **Load Profile** button, then locate and open the **TEST PROFILE** you just created.
17. In the **Wall Sweeps** dialog box, press the **Add** button to add a **Default** profile on the **Exterior**.
18. Press the **Default** profile drop-down list, select the **TEST PROFILE**, and press the **OK** button.
19. In the **Wall Sweeps** dialog box, set the settings shown in Figure 3-39.
20. Finally, press the **OK** buttons to return to the **Drawing Editor** (see Figure 3-40).
21. Save this file as **COMPOUND WALL WITH SWEEP**.

EXERCISE 3-8 MODIFYING END CAPS AND INSERT CONDITIONS

1. Start a new drawing using the RAC 2012\Imperial Templates\default.rte template.
2. In the **Project Browser**, double-click **Floor Plans > Level 1**.
3. Set the **Scale** to **1″ = 1′-0″**.
4. Set the **Detail Level** to **Medium** so you can see all the detail.
5. Place an **8′-0″** long **Basic Wall: Exterior – Brick on CMU** in the **Drawing Editor**.
6. Select the **Window** button in the **Home** toolbar.
7. Place a **36″** × **48″** window centered on the wall (see Figure 3-41).

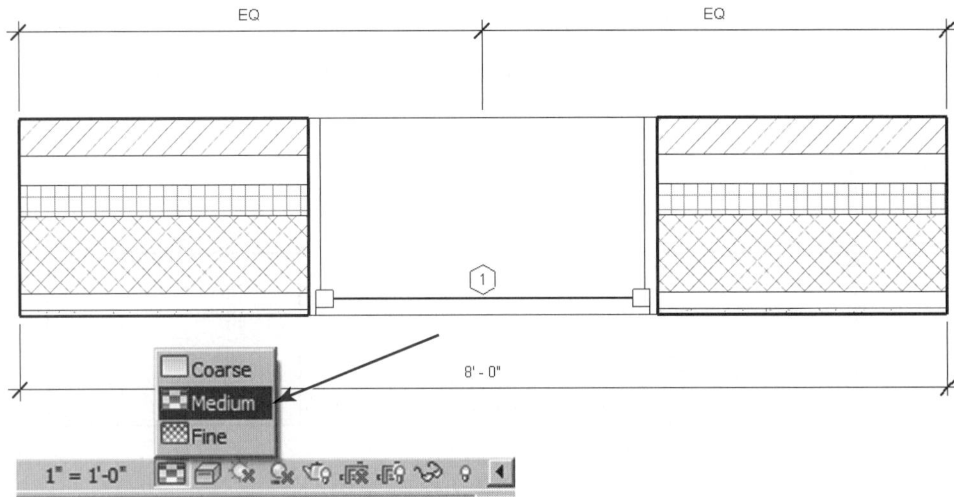

Figure 3-41

Detail Level setting

8. Select the wall to bring up the **Properties** dialog box.
9. In the **Properties** dialog box, press the **Edit Type** button to bring up the **Type Properties** dialog box.
10. In the **Type Properties** dialog box, press the **Wrapping at Inserts** field drop-down list, and select **Exterior**. Press the **OK** buttons to return to the **Drawing Editor** (see Figure 3-42).

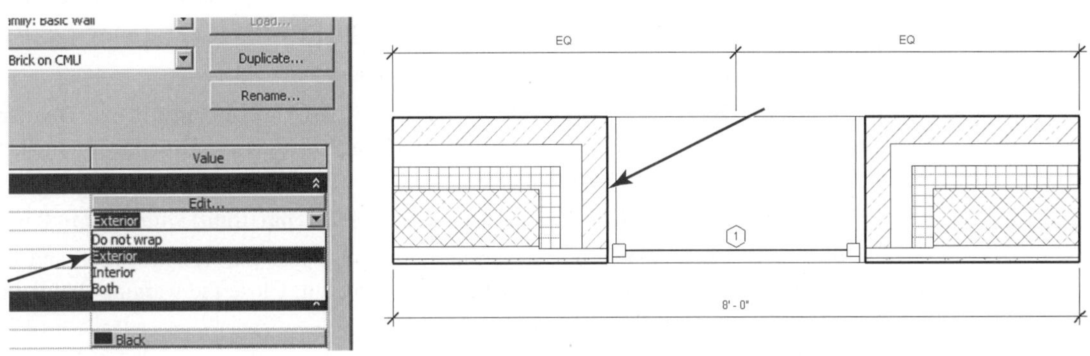

Figure 3-42

Exterior setting

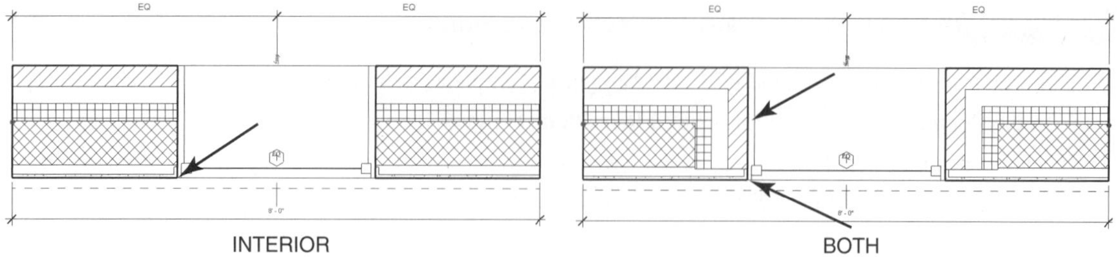

Figure 3-43

Interior setting

11. Repeat this process, selecting the **Interior** and then the **Both** option from the drop-down list (see Figure 3-43).
12. Repeat this process for the **Wrapping at Ends** option (see Figure 3-44).
13. Save this file as **END CAPS_INSERTS**.

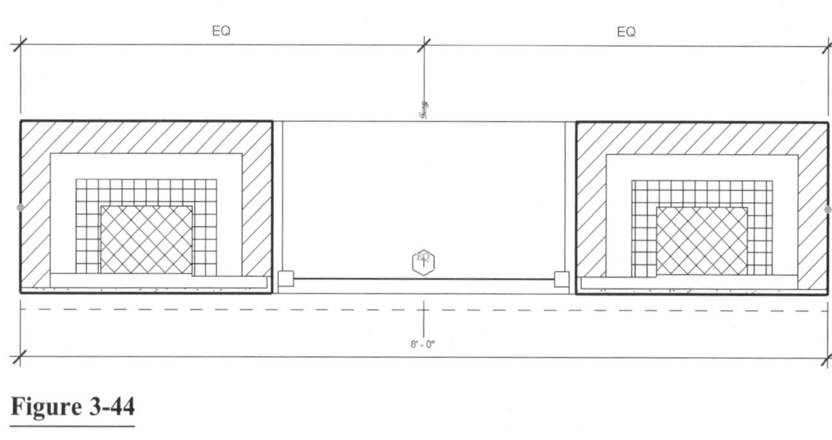

Figure 3-44

Wrapping at Ends option

Embedded Curtain Walls and Storefront

You can enhance and modify walls using the **Embedded Curtain Walls** and **Storefront** tools.

EXERCISE 3-9 EMBEDDED WALLS

1. Start a new drawing using the RAC 2012\Imperial Templates\default.rte template.
2. In the **Project Browser**, double-click **Floor Plans > Level 1**.
3. Select the **Wall** button from the **Home** toolbar.
4. Place a **Basic Wall: Exterior – Brick on CMU** horizontally in the **Drawing Editor**; and make it **22′-0″** long and **10′-0″** high. Press the **<Esc>** key on the keyboard to complete the command.
5. Place a second wall, **8′-0″** high (use **Interior 4-7/8″ partition)** within the first wall.
6. You will immediately get a warning telling you that the walls overlap, and you need to use the **Cut Geometry** button to embed it. Close the warning dialog box (see Figure 3-45).
7. Change to the **Default 3D View**.
8. Select the **Cut Geometry** button from the **Modify** toolbar (see Figure 3-46).
9. Select the **Brick on CMU wall**, and then select the **Interior 4-7/8″ partition** wall.

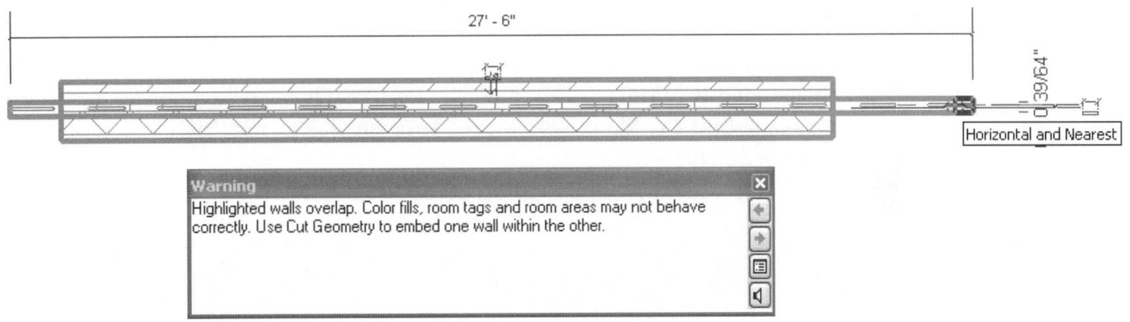

Figure 3-45

Walls overlap warning

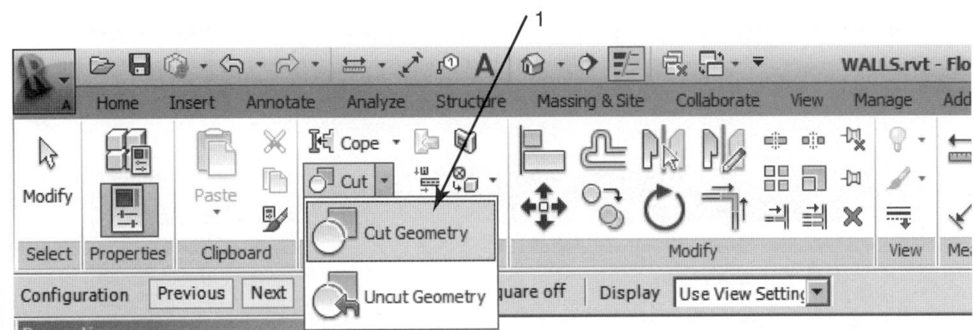

Figure 3-46

Cut Geometry button

The **Interior 4-7/8″ partition** wall now cuts through the **Brick on CMU** wall (see Figure 3-47). You may have to rotate the view to match this figure.

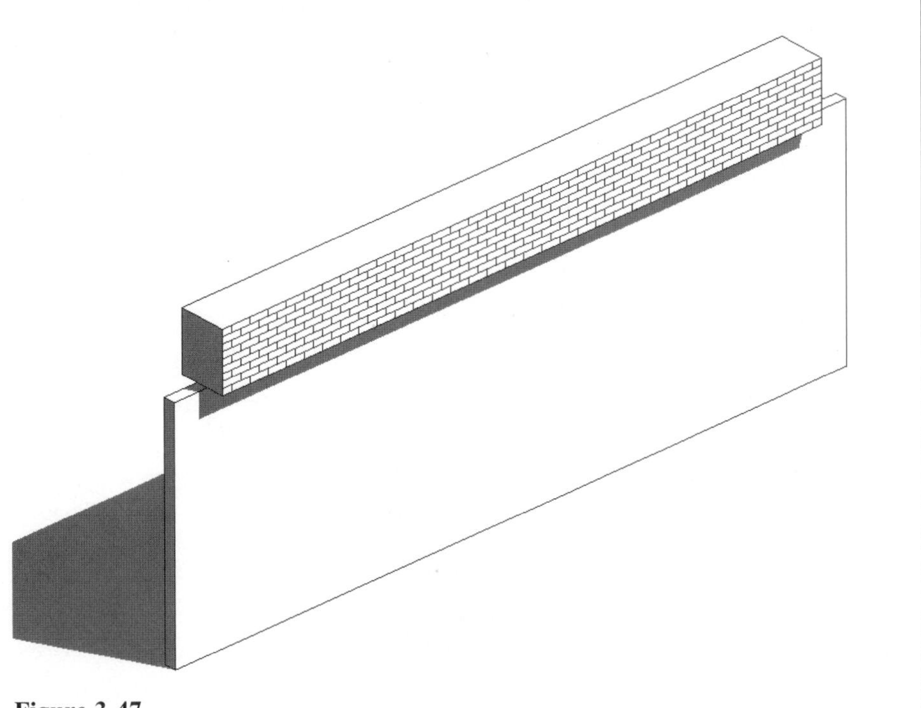

Figure 3-47

Embedded wall

10. Select the **Interior 4-7/8″ partition** wall, and the **Modify | Walls** toolbar will appear.
11. In the **Modify | Walls** toolbar, press the **Edit Profile** button to bring up the **Modify | Walls > Edit Profile** toolbar for the **Interior 4–7/8″ partition** wall (see Figures 3-48 and 3-49).

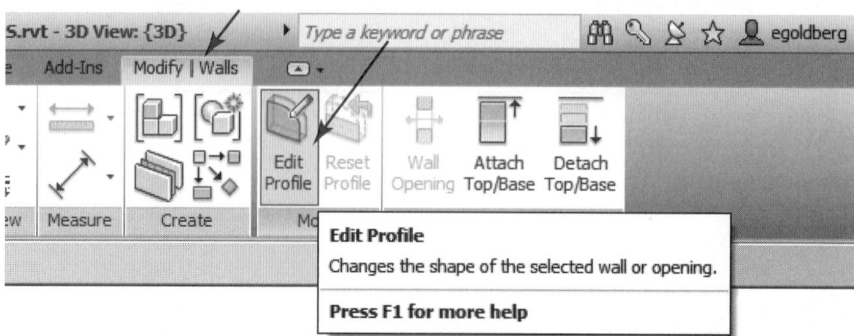

Figure 3-48

Modify | Walls toolbar

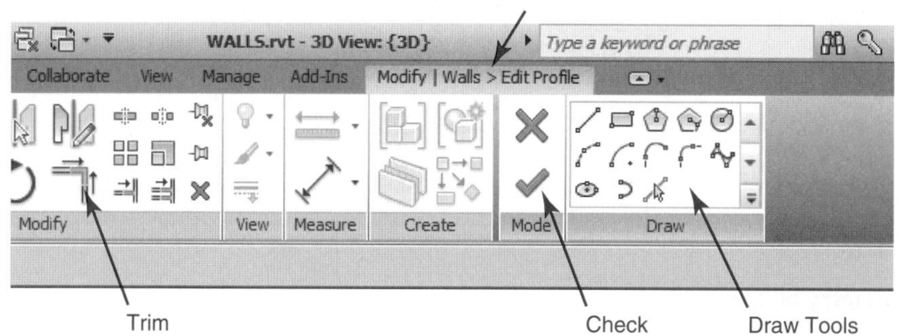

Figure 3-49

Edit Profile button

12. Using the **Draw** and **Trim** Tools in the **Modify | Walls** toolbar, change the wall profile. When you are finished, press the **Check Mark** in the **Mode** panel to complete the command (see Figure 3-50).

NOTE:

When you try to adjust the profile, you will get the warning, *"Constraints are not satisfied"*; press the **Remove Constraints** button. This allows you to change the shape of the wall.

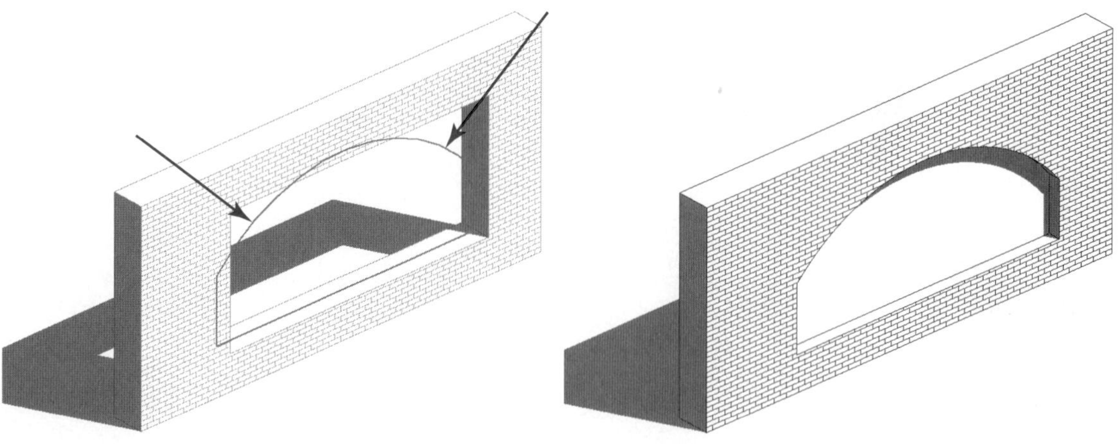

Figure 3-50

Wall profile changed

13. Select the **Interior 4-7/8″ partition** wall, and then select **Generic - 8″ Masonry** from the drop-down list from the **Element** panel in the **Modify | Walls** toolbar (see Figure 3-51).
14. Save this file as **EMBEDDED WALLS**.

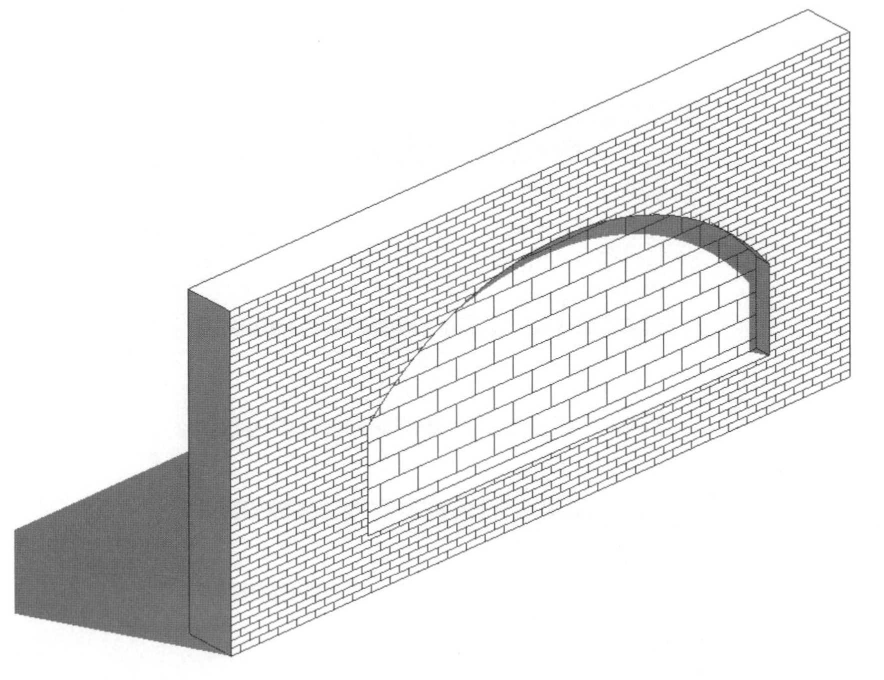

Figure 3-51

Completed embedded wall

EXERCISE 3-10 EMBEDDED CURTAIN WALLS AND STOREFRONT

Because **Storefront** is often embedded into walls, **Storefront** and **Curtain Walls** have a dedicated embedding capability.

1. Start a new drawing using the RAC 2012\Imperial Templates\default.rte template.
2. Select the **Wall** button from the **Home** toolbar.
3. Place a **Basic Wall: Exterior – Brick on CMU** horizontally in the **Drawing Editor**; make it **22′-0″** long and **10′-0″** high.
4. Select the **Wall** button again.
5. Place a **Curtain Wall: Storefront** wall in the **Brick on CMU** wall; make it **18′-0″** long and **8′-0″** high.

NOTE:
Notice that the **Curtain Wall: Storefront** wall automatically cuts the geometry of the **Brick on CMU** wall (see Figure 3-52).

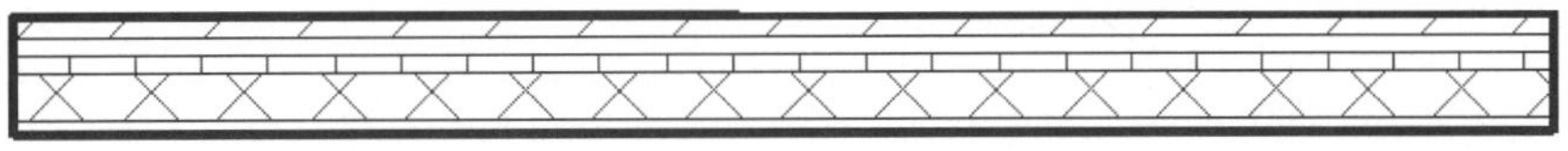

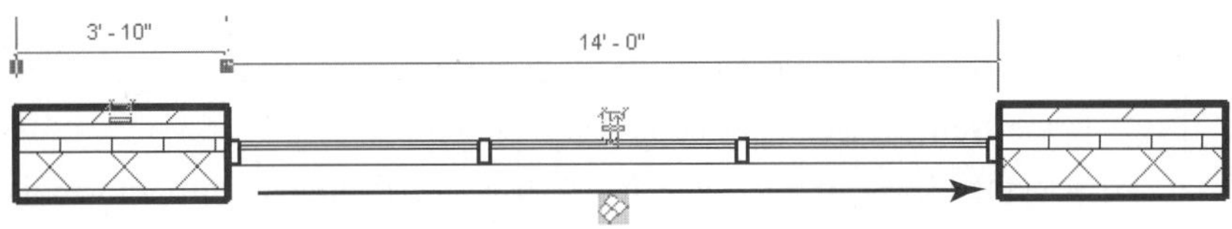

Figure 3-52

Curtain Wall: Storefront option

6. Select the **Curtain Wall: Storefront** wall you just placed to bring up the **Modify | Walls** toolbar.
7. In the **Modify | Walls** toolbar, press the **Type Properties** button to bring up the **Type Properties** dialog box.
8. In the **Type Properties** dialog box, notice the **Automatically Embed** check box (see Figure 3-53).

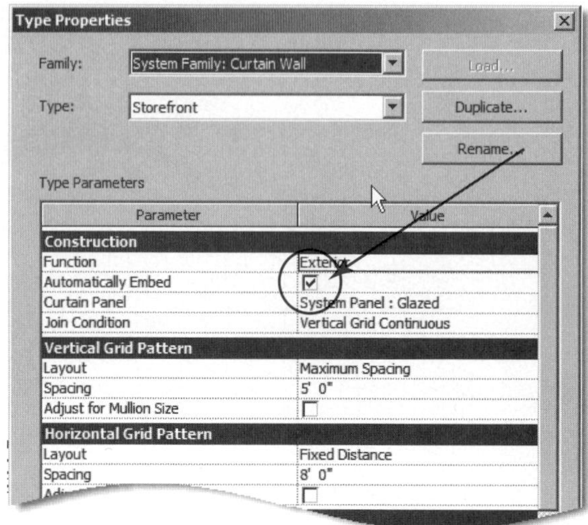

Figure 3-53

Automatically Embed check box

9. Once you have placed the **Storefront** wall, you can modify its profile as you did in the previous exercise (see Figure 3-54).
10. Save this file as **EMBEDDED STOREFRONT**.

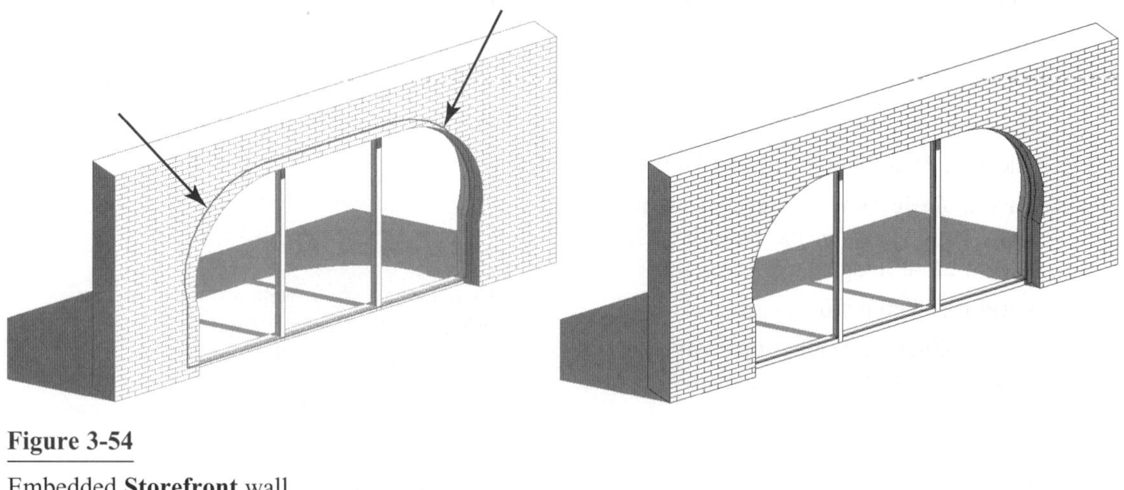

Figure 3-54

Embedded **Storefront** wall

EXERCISE 3-11 CREATING A NEW WALL TYPE—BRICK AND CMU WALL WITH STEEL STUD AND GYPSUM BOARD

1. Start a new drawing using the RAC 2012\Imperial Templates\default.rte template.
2. In the **Home** toolbar, select the **Wall** button.
3. Select the **Basic Wall: Generic - 8″** from the **Properties** drop-down list.

The **Modify | Place Wall** toolbar will now appear.

4. In the **Modify | Place Wall** toolbar, select the **Type Properties** button in the **Properties** panel to bring up the **Type Properties** dialog box (see Figure 3-55).

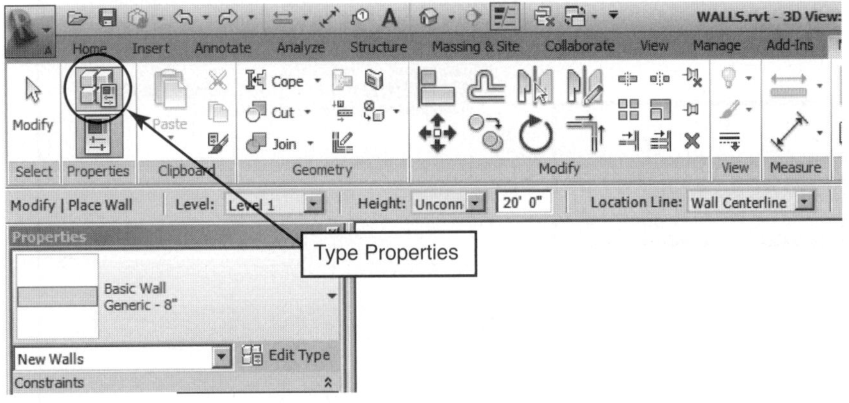

Figure 3-55

Modify | Place Wall toolbar

5. In the **Type Properties** dialog box, select the **Duplicate** button at the top right of the dialog box to bring up the **Name** dialog box.
6. In the **Name** dialog box, enter **NEW BRICK and CMU WALL**, and press the **OK** button to return to the **Type Properties** dialog box.
7. In the **Type Properties** dialog box, press the **Preview** >> button to open the preview pane.
8. In the **Type Properties** dialog box, select **Floor Plan: Modify type attributes** from the **View** drop-down list.
9. Press the **Edit** button in the **Structure** field to bring up the **Edit Assembly** dialog box (see Figures 3-56 and 3-57).

NOTE:

Floor Plan: Modify type attributes allows you to see and check the wall in Plan view.

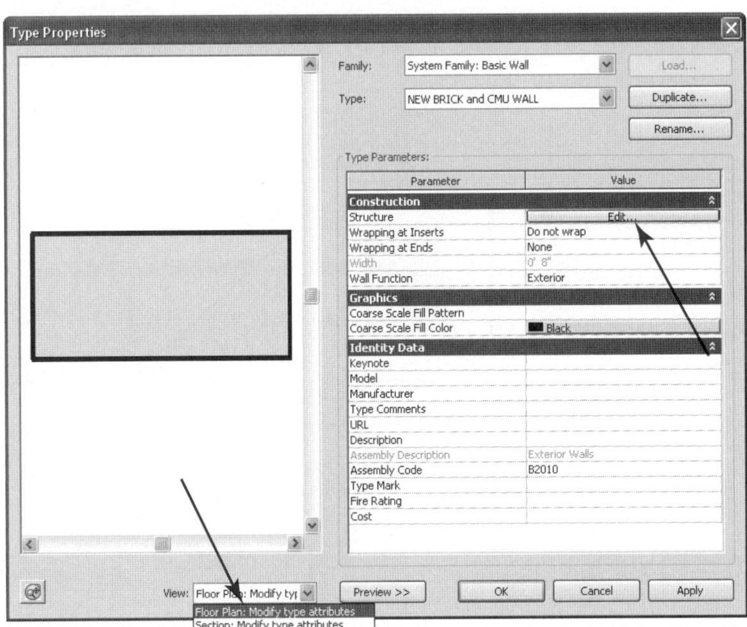

Figure 3-56

Type Properties dialog box

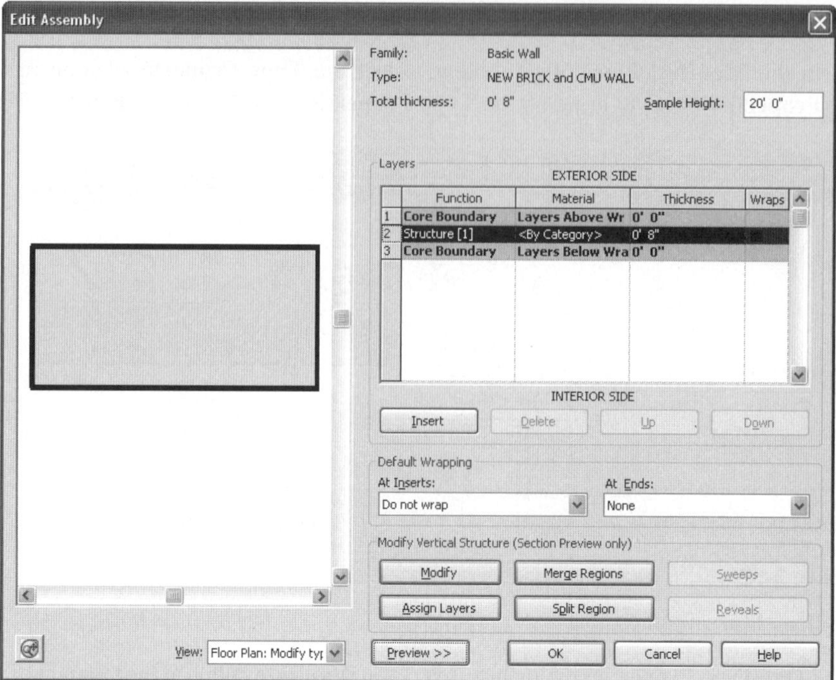

Figure 3-57

Edit Assembly dialog box

10. In the **Edit Assembly** dialog box, change the **Sample Height** to **10′-0″**.
11. Press the **Insert** button, and insert five structures between the **Core Boundary** objects (see Figure 3-58).

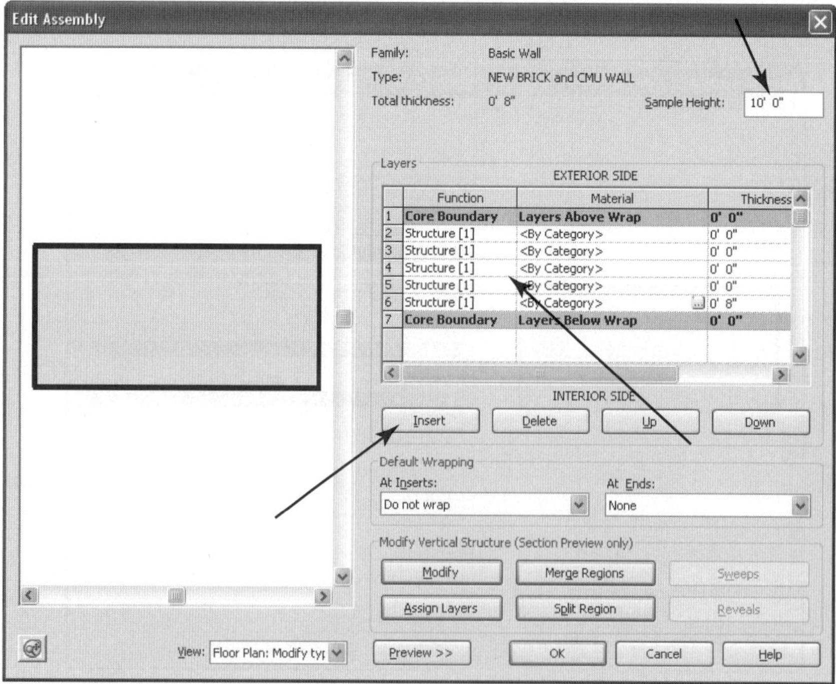

Figure 3-58

Inserting structures between the **Core Boundary** objects

12. Select the number **2 <By Category>** field to activate it, and click the three dots that appear to its right to bring up the **Materials** dialog box (see Figure 3-59).
13. In the **Materials** dialog box, select **Masonry – Brick**, and press the **OK** button to return to the **Edit Assembly** dialog box (see Figure 3-60).
14. Repeat the previous process, assigning materials to each of the layers between the **Core Boundary** objects.
15. Assign Layers **3–6** to **Air Barrier – Air Infiltration Barrier**, **Masonry – Concrete Masonry Units**, **Metal – Stud Layer**, and **Gypsum Wall Board**, respectively.

Layers

EXTERIOR SIDE

	Function	Material	Thick
1	Core Boundary	Layers Above Wrap	0' 0"
2	Structure [1]	<By Category>	0' 0"
3	Structure [1]	<By Category>	0' 0"
4	Structure [1]	<By Category>	0' 0"
5	Structure [1]	<By Category>	0' 0"
6	Structure [1]	<By Category>	0' 8"
7	Core Boundary	Layers Below Wrap	0' 0"

Figure 3-59

Layers <By Category> field

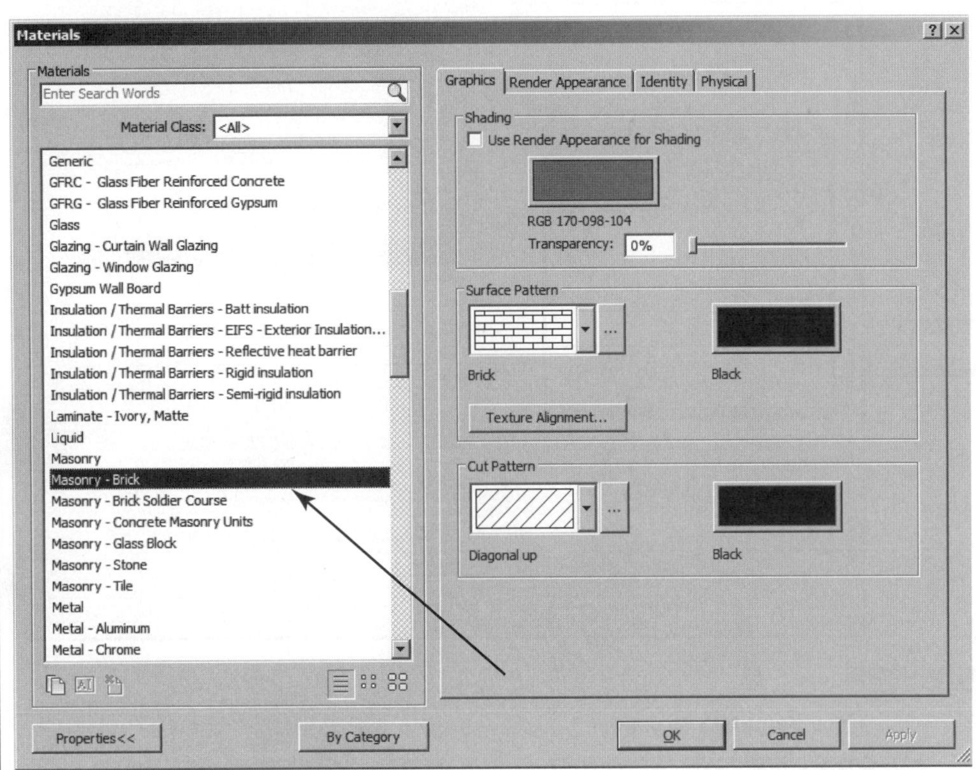

Figure 3-60

Materials dialog box

16. Click on **Structure [1]** on Layer **2**, and select **Finish 1 [4]** from the drop-down list.
17. Set the width of each material in the **Thickness** column.
18. Press the **Up** and **Down** buttons to move the **Brick** and **Air Infiltration Barrier** to the **Exterior Side** of the **Core Boundary**, and move the **Metal - Stud Layer** and **Gypsum Wall Board** to the **Interior Side** of the **Core Boundary**.
19. In the **Edit Assembly** dialog box, select **Section: Modify type attributes** from the **View** drop-down list.
20. Press the **OK** buttons in the dialog boxes to return to the **Drawing Editor**.

NOTE:

Finishes are used outside the **Core Boundary;** Structure is used within the **Core Boundary.** The number within the square brackets represents the line thickness surrounding the material (see Figure 3-61).

NOTE:

The **Masonry – Concrete Masonry Units** are the core of the wall and are thus inside the **Core Boundary** structure (see Figure 3-62).

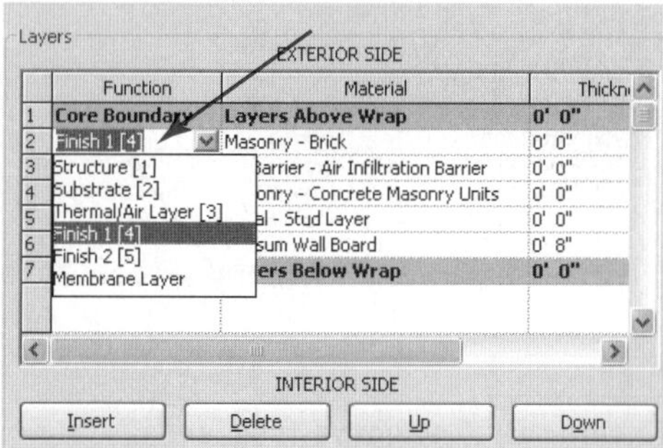

Figure 3-61

Finish fields

To test the wall, change to the **Floor Plan** view, select the **Wall** button from the **Home** toolbar, choose **NEW BRICK and CMU WALL** from the **Change Element Type** drop-down list, and place the wall.

21. Save this file as **CREATING NEW WALL TYPES**.

> **NOTE:**
>
> **Section: Modify type attributes** allow you to see and check the wall in Section view (see Figure 3-63).

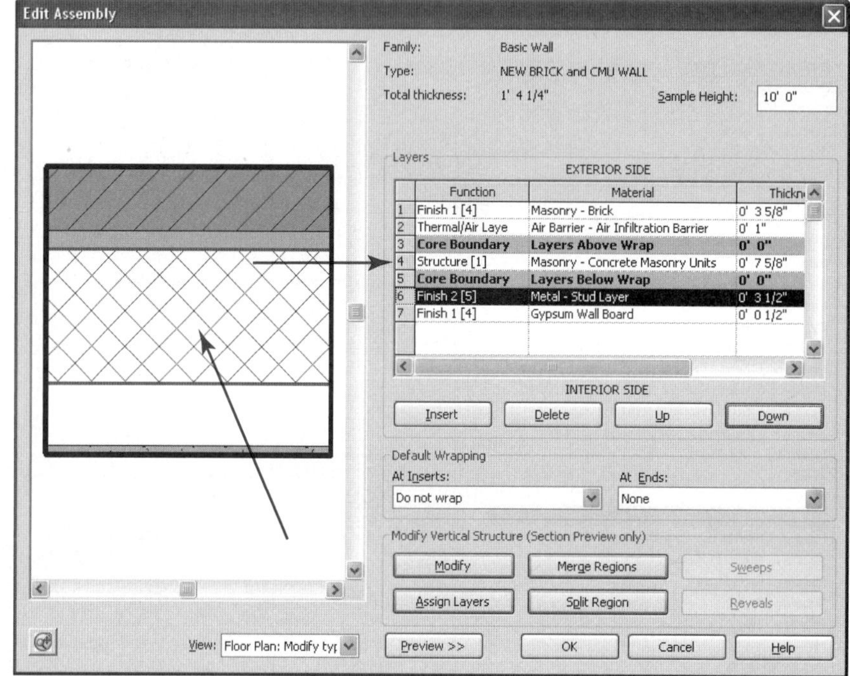

Figure 3-62

Core Boundary structure

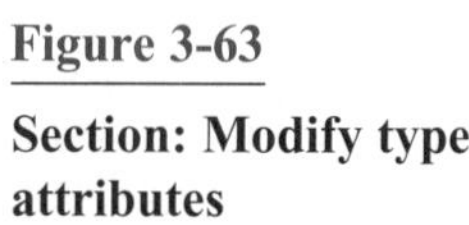

Figure 3-63

Section: Modify type attributes

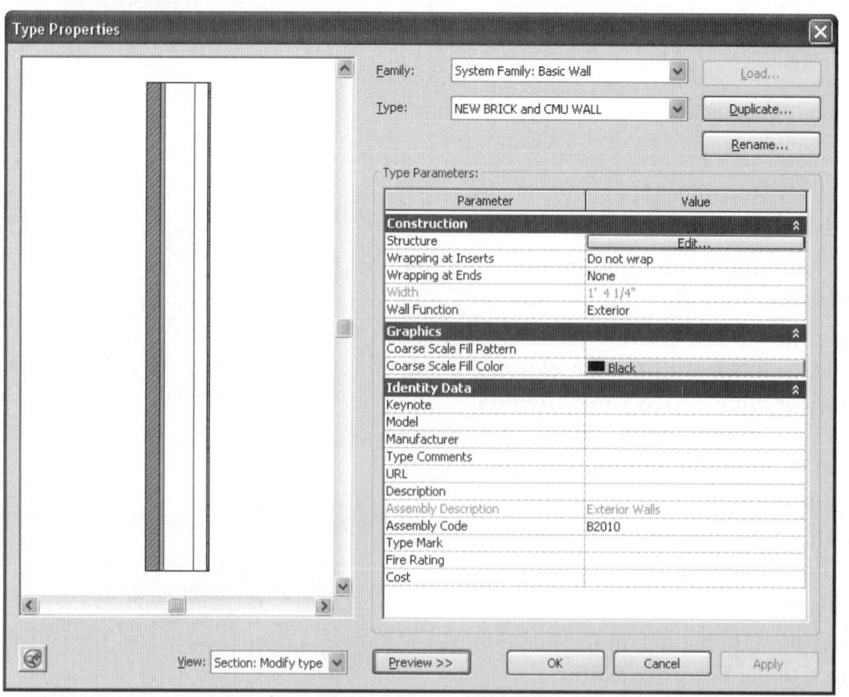

Chapter Summary

This chapter gives the basics needed to create, modify, and place most wall types in Revit Architecture. It is a good idea to create a library of custom wall types and profiles that you can easily load into your project.

Chapter Test Questions

Multiple Choice

Circle the correct answer.

1. There are how many wall location lines?
   a. 3
   b. 5
   c. 5
   d. 6
2. The wall height is set
   a. In the **Wall** button.
   b. In the **Properties** dialog box.
   c. In the **Wall Height** button.
   d. On the **Options Bar**.
3. The ________ button brings an AutoCAD file into the Revit project.
   a. **Open CAD**
   b. **Link AutoCAD**
   c. **Link CAD**
   d. **Link Revit**
4. The **Wall** button is found in the ________ toolbar.
   a. **Insert Wall**
   b. **Structure**
   c. **Modify | Place Wall**
   d. **Home**
5. There are ________ **Wrapping at Inserts** options.
   a. 1
   b. 2
   c. 3
   d. 4

True or False

Circle the correct answer.

1. **True or False:** Revit walls can be directly imported from AutoCAD Architecture or AutoCAD.
2. **True or False:** Revit walls cannot be placed on an angle.
3. **True or False:** Vertically-Compound walls are used to join two walls together.
4. **True or False: Wall Sweeps** are used to create curved walls.
5. **True or False: Storefront** and **Curtain Walls** have a dedicated embedding capability.

Questions

1. How does the **Detail** button at the bottom of the screen affect the wall display?
2. What is the difference between the **Draw** and **Pick Lines** buttons in relation to walls?
3. What is the purpose of a **Profile**?
4. How many **End Cap** and **Insert** conditions are there?
5. What is the purpose of the embedded wall?

CHAPTER

4 Doors

CHAPTER OBJECTIVES

- Learn how to place and control doors.
- Learn how to **Tag** doors.
- Understand **Wall Closure**.
- Learn how to modify doors.
- Learn how to change door sizes.
- Learn how to change door materials.
- Learn how to edit **Doors** in place.
- Understand **Head** and **Sill** locations.
- Learn how to place different door styles.

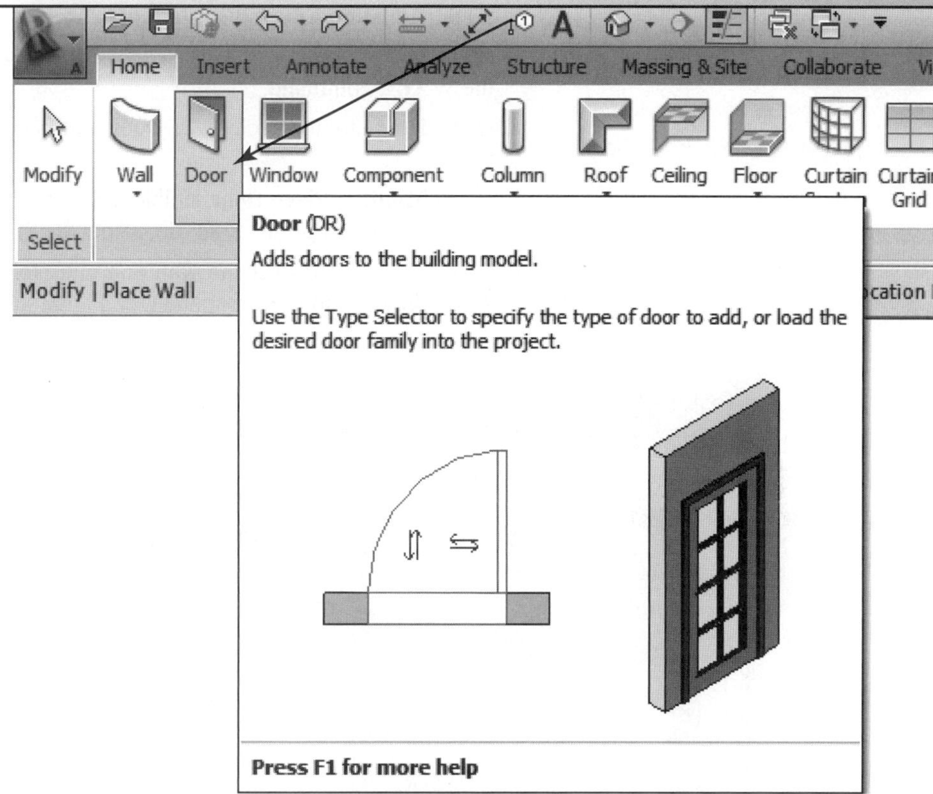

Introduction

In Revit Architecture 2012, door objects are totally customizable. All is possible in this program—from customizing the size and shape of the door or the size and shape of the jamb to including side lights, mullions, and/or a sill. As with other features of this program, a premade library of door styles greatly enhances productivity. Websites such as Autodesk Seek currently offer content from many manufacturers.

Customizing Doors

Revit Architecture has a variety of tools that make it easy to create, modify, place, and number all types of doors.

EXERCISE 4-1 PLACING AND CONTROLLING DOORS

1. Start a new drawing using the RAC 2012\Imperial Templates\default.rte template.
2. In the **Project Browser**, double-click **Floor Plans > Level 1**.

3. Change the **Drawing Scale** to **1/4″ = 1′-0″**.
4. In the **Home** toolbar, select the **Wall > Wall** button to bring up the **Modify | Place Wall** toolbar.
5. In the **Modify | Place Wall** toolbar, select the **Line** button from the **Draw** panel.
6. In the **Properties** drop-down list, select **Basic wall: Exterior – Brick on CMU**. In the **Options Bar**, set the **Height** to **Unconnected**, then set the **Height** to **10′-0″**, set the **Location Line** to **Finish Face: Exterior**, and uncheck the **Chain** check box.
7. Place a **20′-0″** long wall in the **Drawing Editor**, and press the **<Esc>** key to end the **WALL** command.
8. In the **Home** toolbar, select the **Door** button to bring up the **Modify | Place Door** toolbar.
9. In the **Modify | Place Door** toolbar, select the **Tag on Placement** button, and then select **Single-Flush: 36″ × 84″** door from the **Properties** dialog box (see Figure 4-1).
10. Move your cursor over the wall and click to place the door, and then press the <**Esc**> key to end the command (see Figure 4-2).

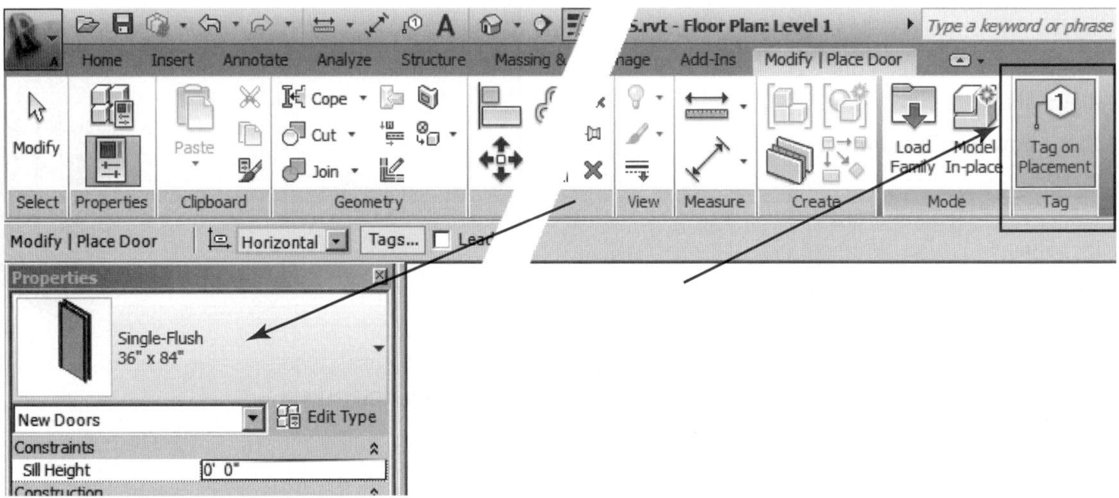

Figure 4-1

Modify | Place Door toolbar

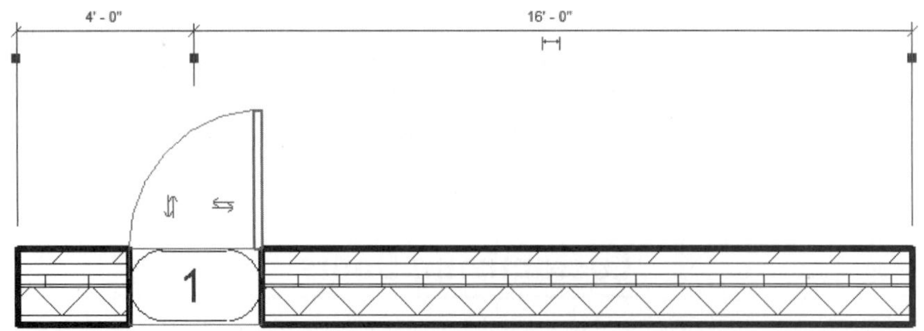

Figure 4-2

Create a door

11. If the number in the door is not **1**, select it and enter **1** from the keyboard.

Subsequent doors will follow numerically.

12. Click the grip shown in Figure 4-3 to move the witness line to the center or edges of the door. Drag the grip to place the witness line at the front of the door panel.

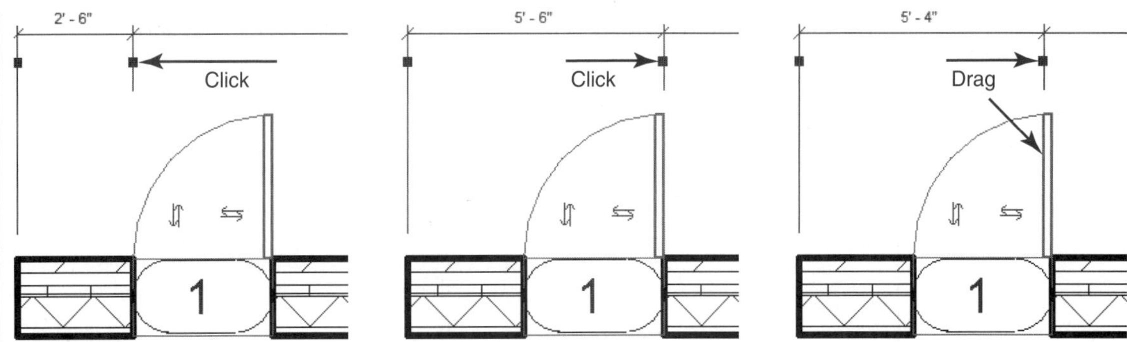

Figure 4-3

Place a witness line

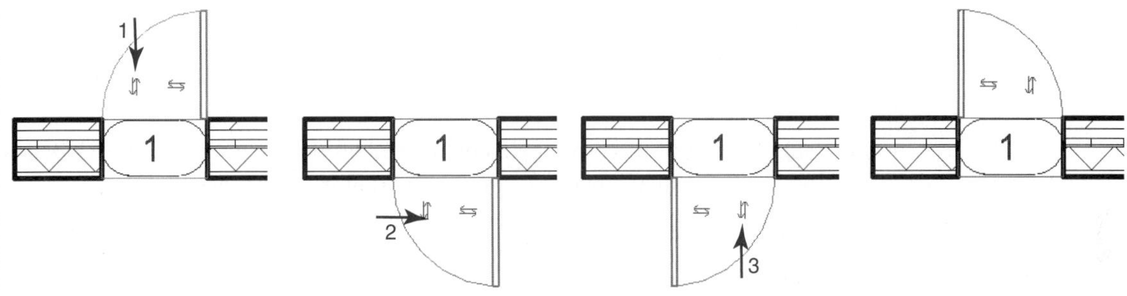

Figure 4-4

Flip door swings

13. Select the door, and click the double arrows to flip the door swings (see Figure 4-4).
14. Select the door, Right Mouse Button click (**RMB**), and select **Create Similar** from the contextual menu that appears to create a new similar door.
15. Place two more doors by moving your cursor over the wall and clicking to place the doors.
16. Select the **Linear** button from the **Annotate Toolbar** to bring up the **Modify | Place Dimensions** toolbar.
17. Select the left corner of the wall, then the top corner of the first door. Continue placing dimensions as shown in Figure 4-5, and then move your cursor upward and click to place the dimensions. (Dimensions are covered in detail in the Dimensions chapter.)

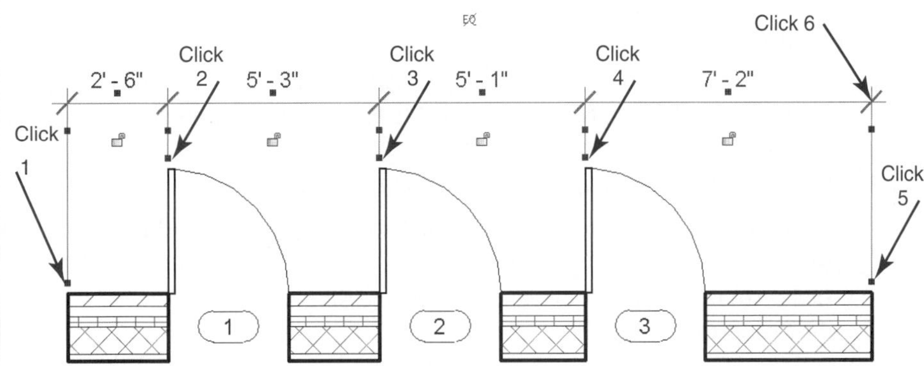

Figure 4-5

Place dimensions

18. Click the **EQ** symbol to space all the doors equally (see Figure 4-6).

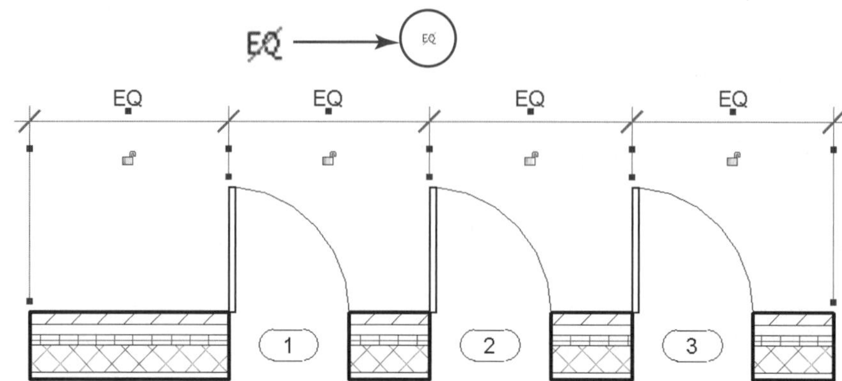

Figure 4-6

Space doors equally

19. Right Mouse Button click **(RMB)** on the dimension string, and select **EQ Display** from the contextual menu that appears to bring back dimensions.

The dimensions will then show, and they will all be the same (see Figure 4-7).

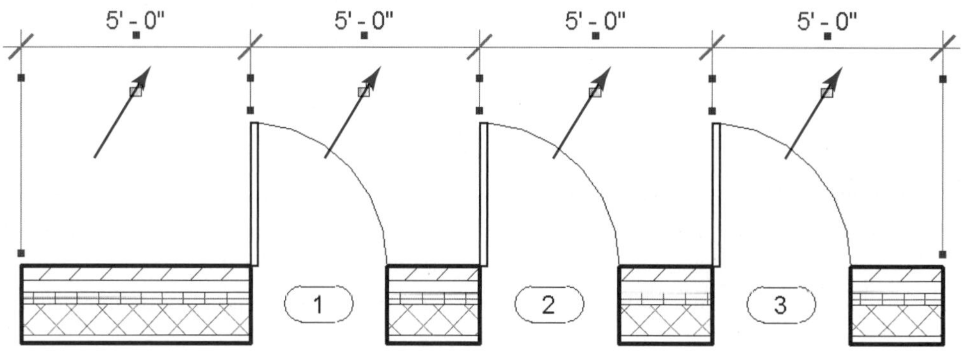

Figure 4-7

Equal dimensions

EXERCISE 4-2 **TAGGING DOORS**

Doors can be inserted with number tags as you place the doors, or after you place them.

Tagging After Insertion

1. Using the previous exercise, select one of the doors, Right Mouse Button click **(RMB)**, and select **All Instances > Visible in View** from the contextual menu that appears. All the doors will be selected.
2. Press the **<Del>** key to delete the doors and their annotations.
3. In the **Home** toolbar, select the **Door** button to bring up the **Modify | Place Door** toolbar.
4. In the **Modify | Place Door** toolbar, select the **Single-Flush: 36″ × 84″** door from the **Properties** dialog box.
5. Click on the **Tag on Placement** button until it is *not* lit (light blue color).
6. Place three doors in the wall. They will not have door numbers.
7. Select the **Annotation** toolbar.

8. In the **Annotation** toolbar, click on the **Tag by Category** button to bring up the **Modify | Tag** toolbar.
9. In the **Modify | Tag** toolbar, uncheck the **Leader** check box (see Figure 4-8).

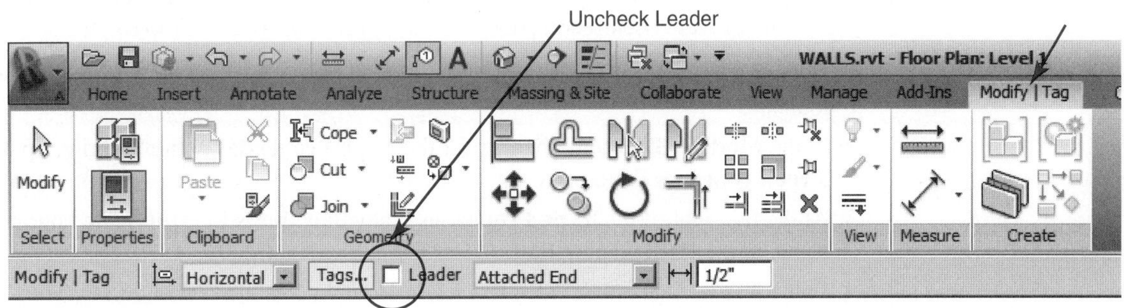

Figure 4-8

Modify | Tag toolbar

10. Click on the first door to place the number tag.
11. Once again, the number may be wrong. If so, change it to the number **1**.
12. Select **Tag All** from the **Annotation** toolbar to bring up the **Tag All Not Tagged** dialog box.
13. In the **Tag All Not Tagged** dialog box, select **Horizontal** from the **Orientation** drop-down list, and press the **Apply** button to add number tags to the other doors. You may have to renumber the new door tags (see Figure 4-9).

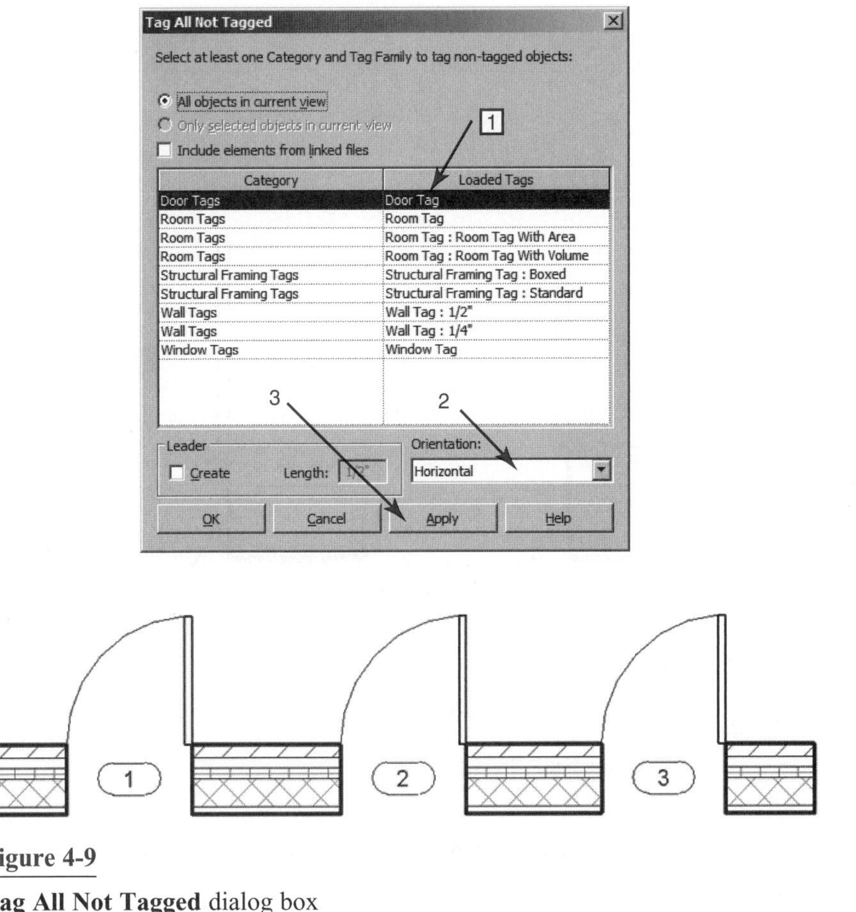

Figure 4-9

Tag All Not Tagged dialog box

EXERCISE 4-3 WALL CLOSURE

In Chapter 3, we discussed **Wall Wrapping at Inserts**. They were labeled **Do not wrap**, **Exterior**, **Interior**, and **Both**. This controls how the wall finishes will wrap at these conditions. Sometimes you may want a wall to wrap differently at individual doors. To take care of these occurrences, doors are equipped with **Wall Closure** options.

1. Using the previous exercise, select one of the doors to bring up the **Modify | Doors** toolbar.
2. In the **Modify | Doors** toolbar, select the **Type Properties** button to bring up the **Type Properties** dialog box.
3. At the top right of the **Type Properties** dialog box, press the **Duplicate** button to bring up the **Name** dialog box.
4. In the **Name** dialog box, enter **INTERIOR**, and press the **OK** button to return to the **Type Properties** dialog box.
5. In the **Type Properties** dialog box, select **Interior** from the **Wall Closure** drop-down list (see Figure 4-10).
6. Press the **OK** buttons to return to the **Drawing Editor**.

Notice that the **Wrapping at Insert** or **Wall Closure** at the door has changed, but the other **Wall Closures** have not because they are either **By host** or **Neither** (see Figure 4-11).

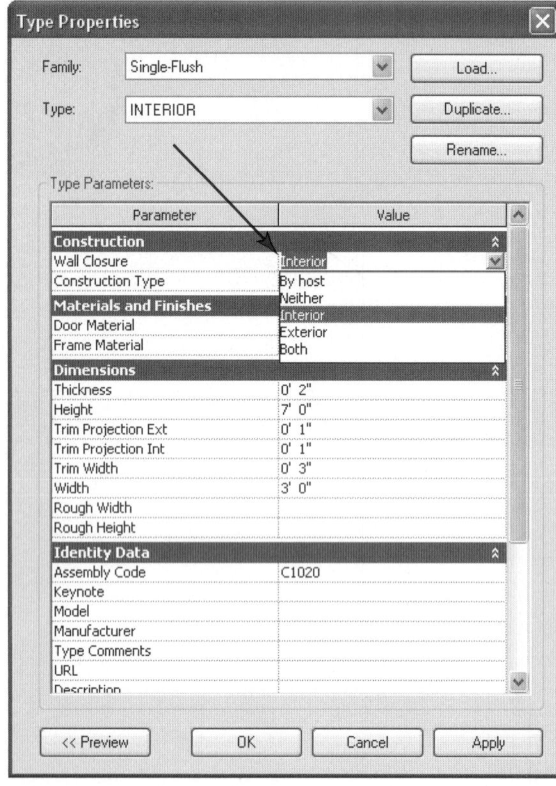

Figure 4-10

Type Properties dialog box

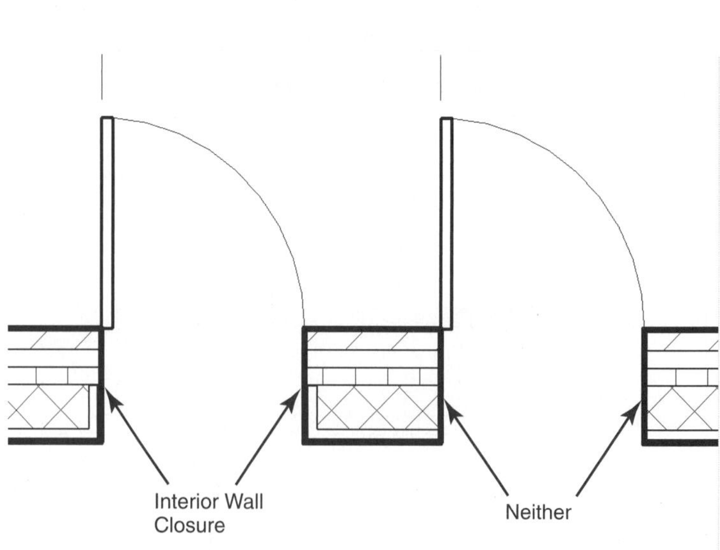

Figure 4-11

Interior wall closure

7. Repeat Steps 1–6 creating **EXTERIOR** and **BOTH** doors and see their **Wall Closure** effects (see Figure 4-12).
8. Save the file as **WALL CLOSURE AT DOORS**.

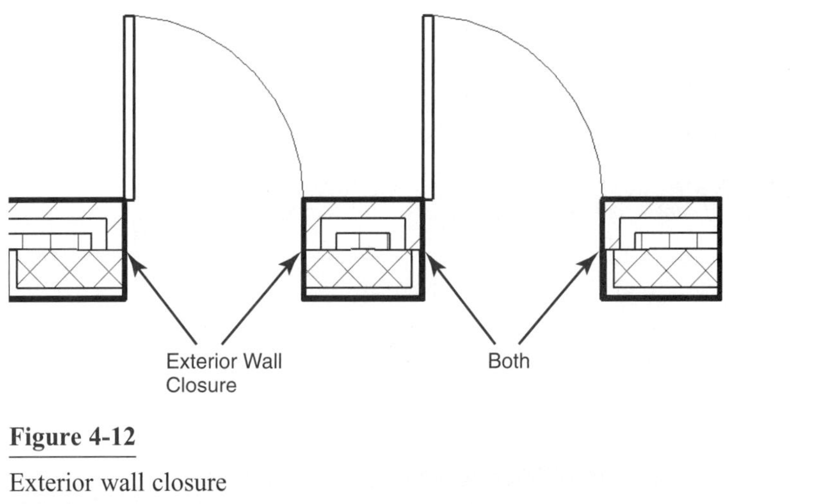

Figure 4-12

Exterior wall closure

EXERCISE 4-4 **MODIFYING DOORS**

Changing Door Sizes

1. Using the previous exercise, select one of the doors to bring up the **Modify | Doors** toolbar.
2. In the **Modify | Doors** toolbar, select the **Type Properties** button to bring up the **Type Properties** dialog box.
3. At the top right of the **Type Properties** dialog box, press the **Duplicate** button to bring up the **Name** dialog box.
4. In the **Name** dialog box, enter **TEST 24″ × 80″ DOOR**, and press the **OK** button to return to the **Type Properties** dialog box (see Figure 4-13).

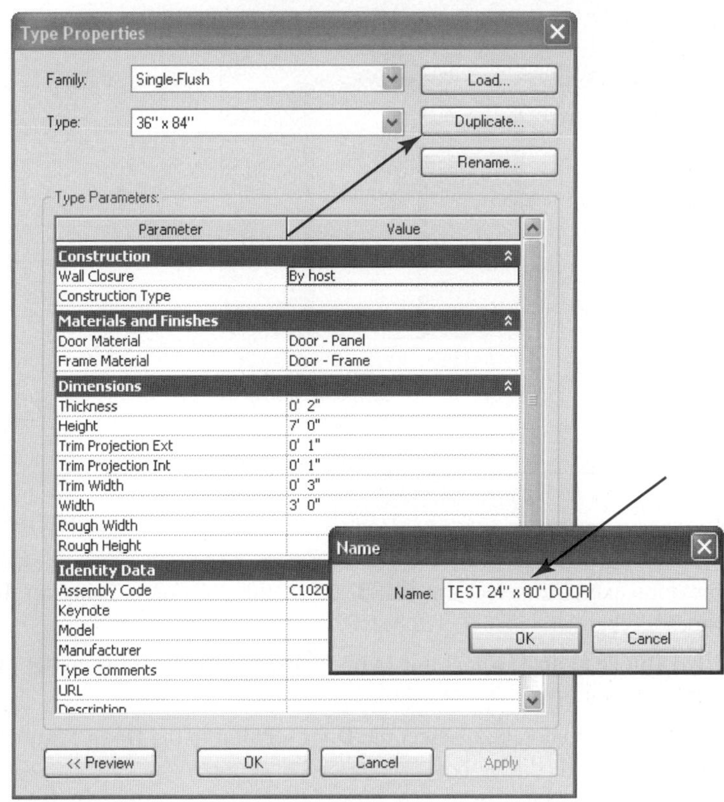

Figure 4-13

Create TEST 24″ × 80″ DOOR

5. In the **Type Properties** dialog box, enter the sizes shown in Figure 4-14, and press the **OK** buttons to return to the **Drawing Editor**.
6. In the **Project Browser**, double-click on the **South Elevation** to bring it up in the **Drawing Editor** (see Figure 4-15).

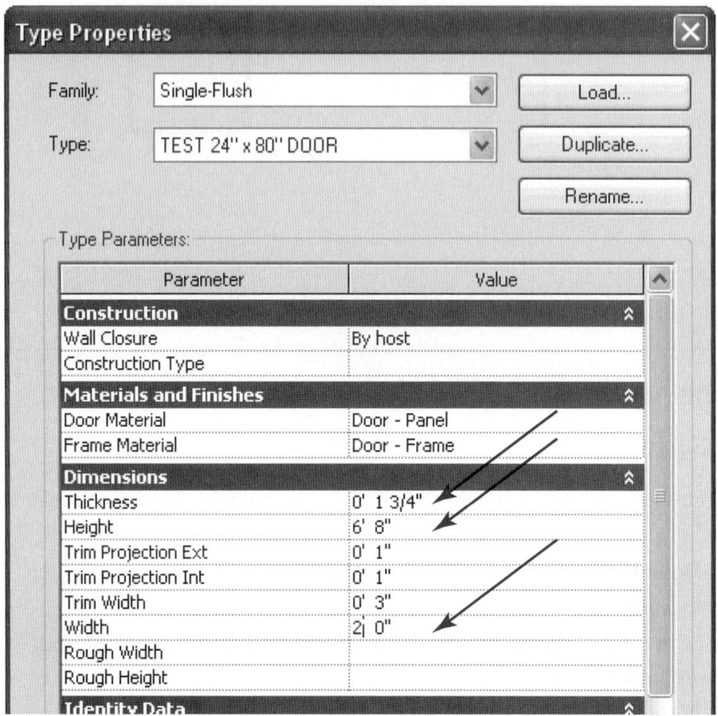

Figure 4-14

Add sizes to TEST 24″ × 80″ DOOR

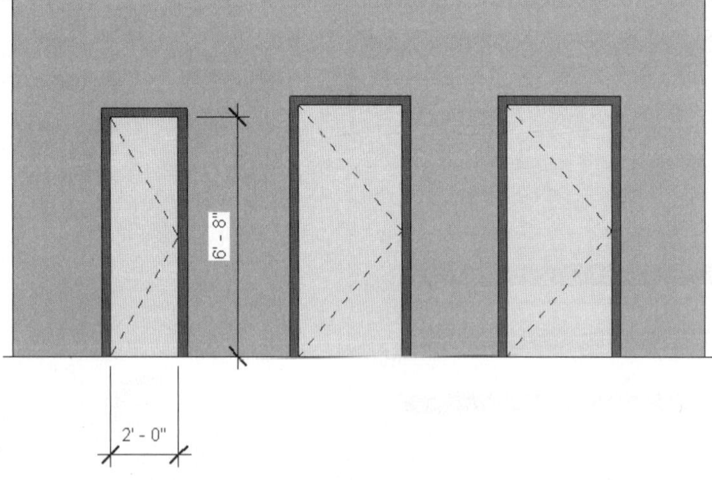

Figure 4-15

South Elevation in **Drawing Editor**

EXERCISE 4-5 **CHANGING DOOR MATERIALS**

1. Using the previous exercise, select the **TEST 24″ × 80″ DOOR** to bring up the **Modify | Doors** toolbar.
2. In the **Modify | Doors** toolbar, select the **Type Properties** button to bring up the **Type Properties** dialog box.
3. In the **Type Properties** dialog box, select the **Door - Panel** in the **Door Material** field to open the **Materials** dialog box.
4. At the bottom left of the **Materials** dialog box, select the **Duplicate** button to bring up the **Duplicate Revit Material** dialog box.
5. In the **Duplicate Revit Material** dialog box, enter **TEST DOOR PANEL**, and press the **OK** button to return to the **Materials** dialog box (see Figure 4-16).

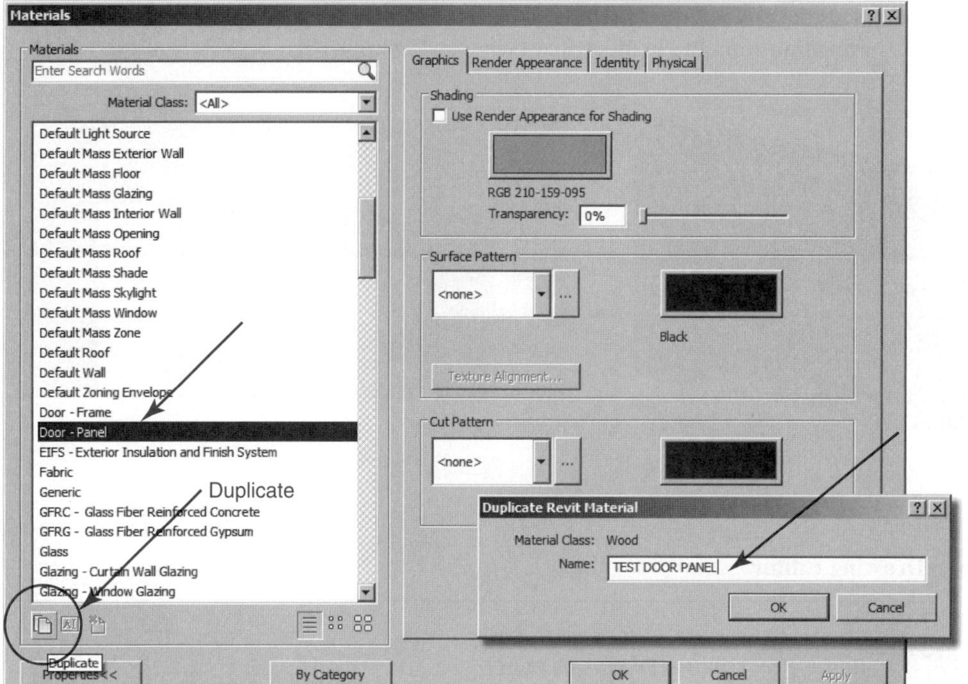

Figure 4-16

Materials dialog box

6. In the **Materials** dialog box, select the **TEST DOOR PANEL**, and select the **Graphics** tab.
7. In the **Graphics** tab, change the **Shading Color** to **Black**, the **Surface Pattern** to **Wood 3**, and the **Surface Pattern Color** to **White** (see Figure 4-17).

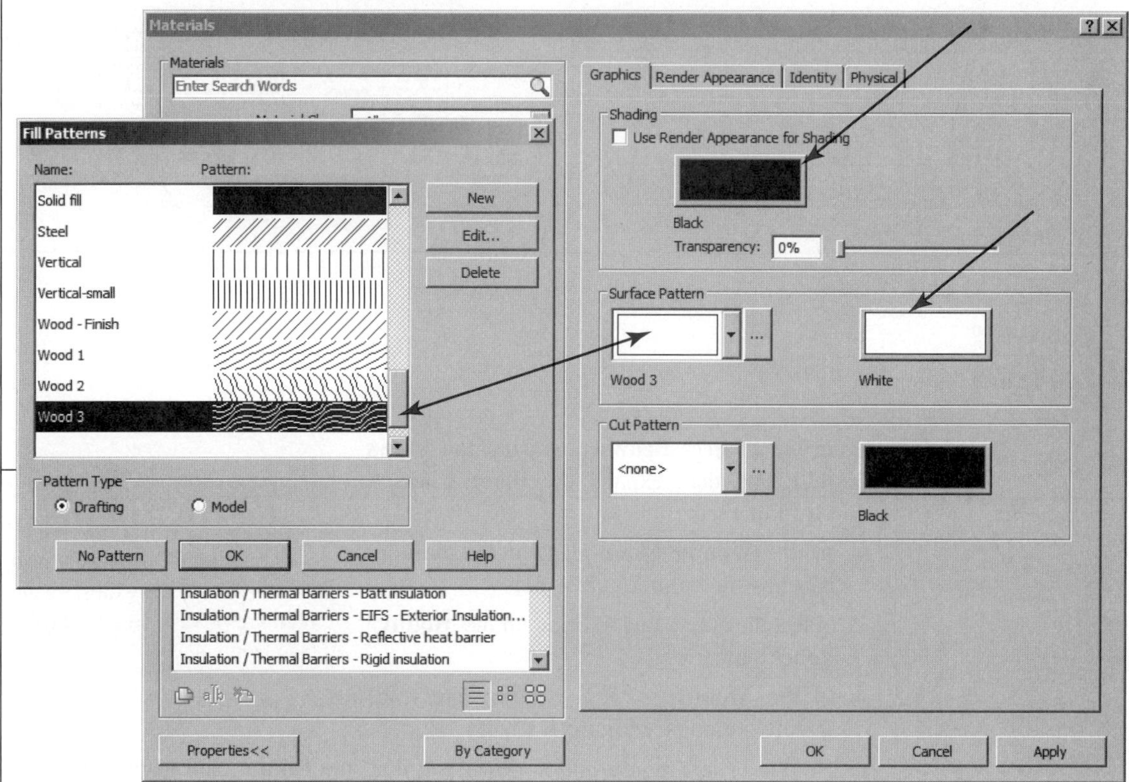

Figure 4-17

TEST DOOR PANEL

8. Press the **OK** buttons to return to the **Drawing Editor**, and again select the **South Elevation** from the **Project Browser** (see Figure 4-18).

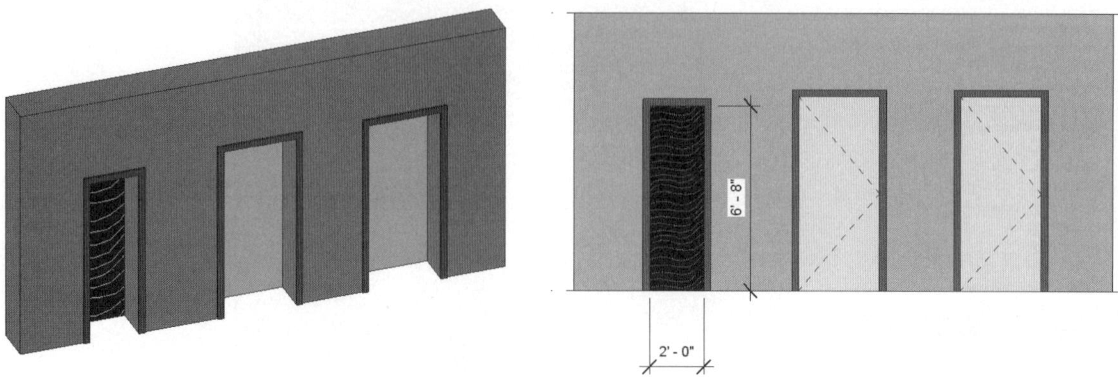

Figure 4-18

South Elevation in **Drawing Editor**

EXERCISE 4-6 **EDITING DOORS IN PLACE**

Opening a Door

1. Using the previous exercise, select the **TEST 24″ × 80″ DOOR** to bring up the **Modify | Doors** toolbar.
2. In the **Modify | Doors** toolbar, select the **Edit Family** button to bring up the **Family Editor** (see Figure 4-19).

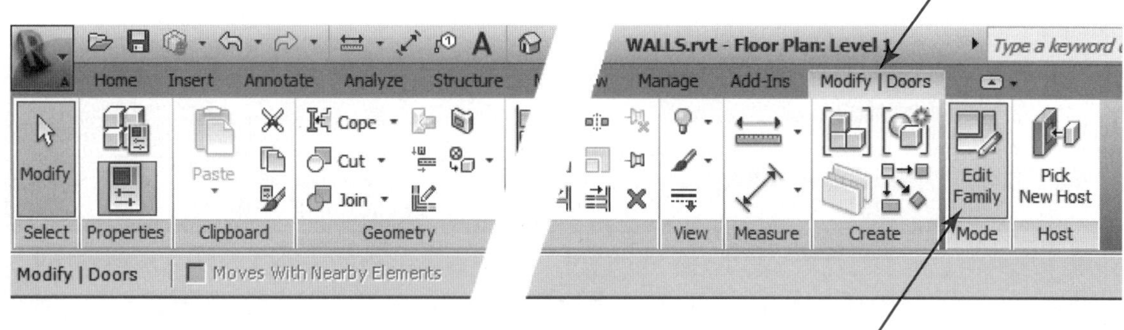

Figure 4-19

Edit Family button

3. In the **Project Browser**, expand the **Views [all]**, and then expand the **Floor Plans > Ground Floor**.
4. In the **Ground Floor** plan, locate the door panel as shown in Figure 4-21.
5. Select the door panel to bring up the **Modify | Panel** toolbar.
6. In the **Modify | Panel** toolbar, press the **Rotate** button (see Figure 4-22).
7. Hold your left mouse button down and drag the **Rotate** icon to the upper right corner of the door panel to set the rotation axis, and release the mouse button.
8. Drag your mouse horizontally to the far left, and click the left mouse button.

> **NOTE:**
>
> You will recognize that you are in the **Family Editor** if you open the **Home** toolbar because it will contain **Extrusion**, **Blend**, and **Revolve** buttons (see Figure 4-20).

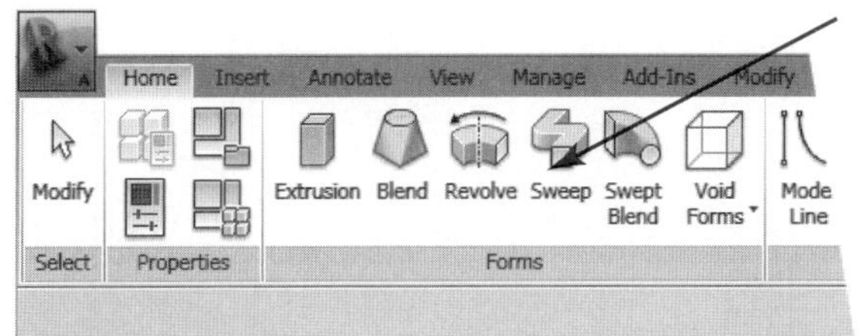

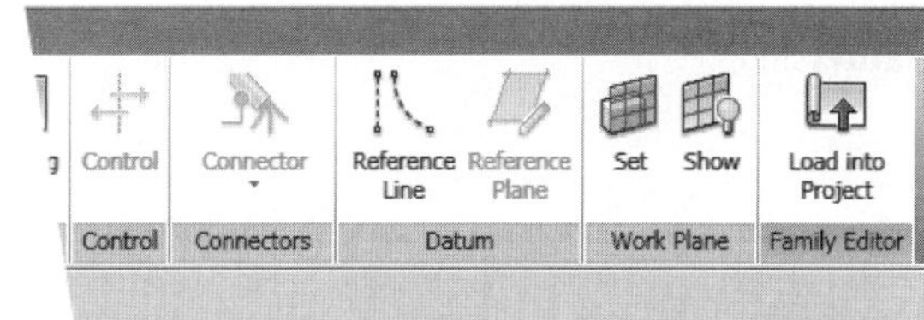

Figure 4-20

Family Editor

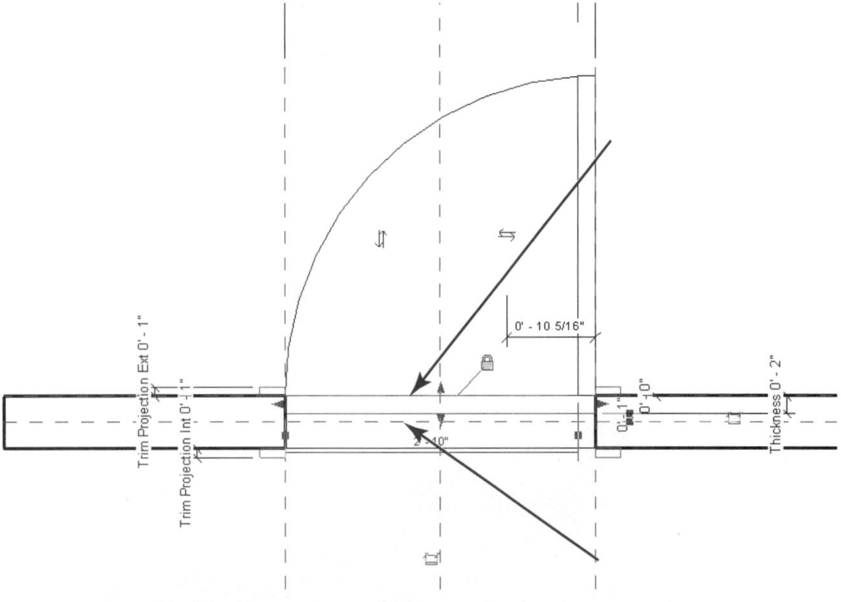

Figure 4-21

Door panel

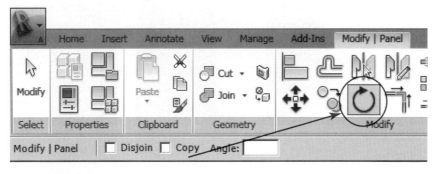

Figure 4-22

Rotate button

9. Finally drag your mouse vertically, and then click the left mouse to complete the rotation.
10. You will get a **Revit error** warning; press the **Remove Constraints** button to remove the **Constraints** and **Dimensions** (see Figure 4-23).

The reason that you have to remove the **Constraints** is because they are linked to parameters and no longer apply to the rotated door.

> **NOTE:**
>
> The rotation technique may take a couple of practices to get it right. This system is used for all rotations, and dragging the **Rotate** icon sets the center of rotation.

11. Select **Save As** from the **Application** menu, save the **New Family** file as **Single Flush Open**, and close the file.

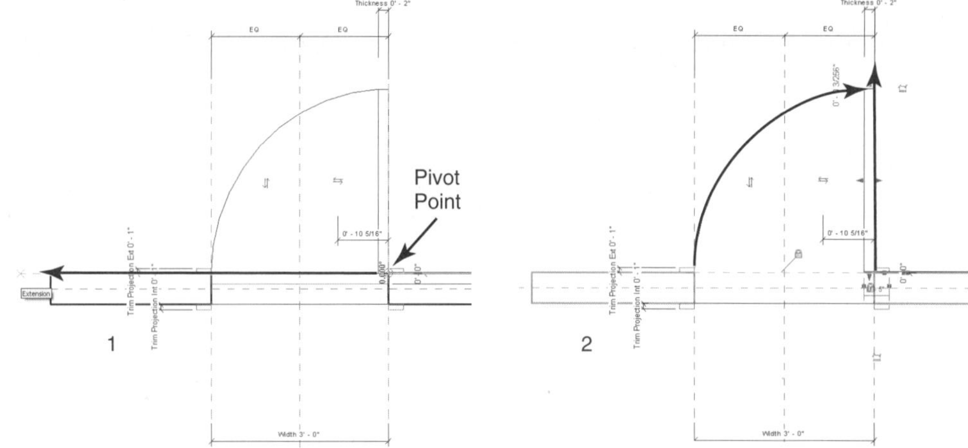

Figure 4-23

Remove **Constraints** and **Dimensions**

12. Finally, return to your **3D** view of the doors, and select the **TEST 24″ × 80″ Door** to bring up its **Properties** dialog box. In the **Properties** dialog box, select the **Edit Type** button to bring up the **Type Properties** dialog box.
13. At the top right of the **Type Properties** dialog box, select the **Load** button, locate the **Single Flush Open** door you just created, and then press the **OK** button to return to the **Drawing Editor**.

The door will now be open (see Figure 4-24).

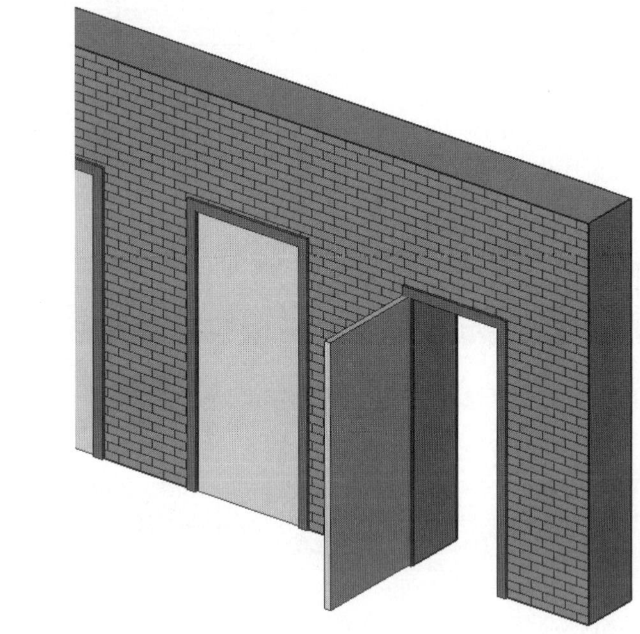

Figure 4-24

Single Flush Open door drawing

EXERCISE 4-7 HEAD AND SILL LOCATION

1. Using the previous exercise, select the **Single Flush Open** door you just created, Right Mouse Button click (**RMB**), and again select **Element Properties** from the contextual menu that appears to bring up the **Properties** dialog box.
2. Select the **Value** in the **Sill Height** field, and change it to **8″**.

Notice that the head height changes to 7′-4″. This is because the door height has been set to 6′-8″. You can set either the **Sill Height** or the **Head Height**. They are related to the door panel height (see Figure 4-25).

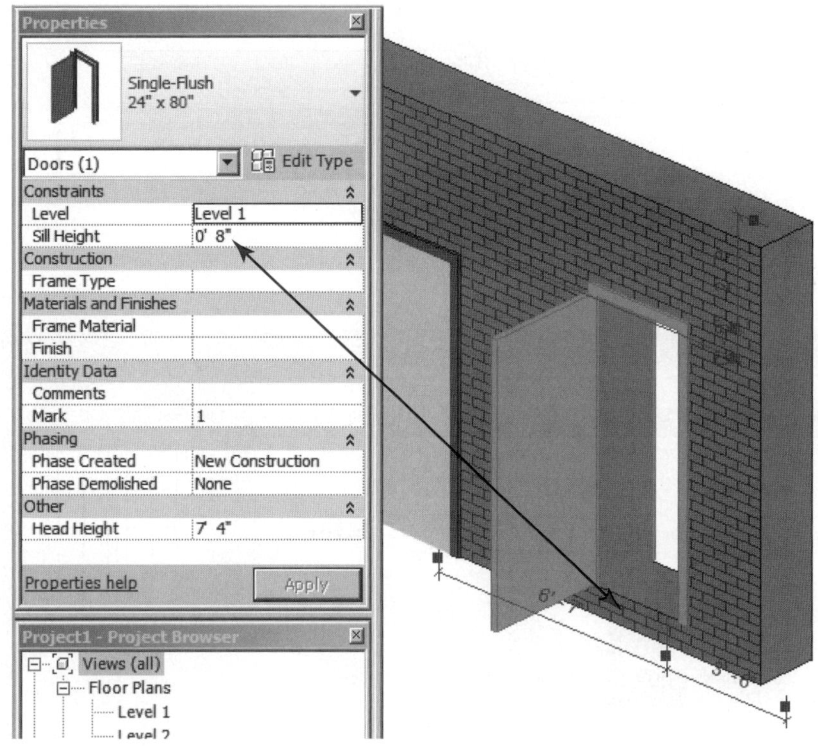

Figure 4-25

Sill and head height are related to the door height

EXERCISE 4-8 PLACING DIFFERENT DOOR STYLES

Revit Architecture 2012 has a library of different door families, and you can download more families from the Internet. All Revit doors are parametric and modifiable.

1. Start a new drawing using the RAC 2012\Imperial Templates\default.rte template.
2. In the **Project Browser**, double-click **Floor Plans > Level 1**.
3. Change the **Drawing Scale** to **1/4″ = 1′-0″**.
4. In the **Home** toolbar, select the **Wall** button to bring up the **Modify | Place Wall** toolbar.
5. In the **Modify | Place Wall** toolbar, select the **Line** button from the **Draw** panel.
6. In the **Properties** dialog box, select **Basic Wall: Generic-8″** from the drop-down list. In the **Options Bar**, set the **Height** to **Unconnected**, then set the height to **10′-0″**, set the **Location Line** to **Finish Face: Exterior**, and check the **Chain** check box.
7. Place a **10′** long, **10′** high wall in the **Drawing Editor**.
8. Select the **Insert** tab to bring up the **Insert** toolbar.
9. In the **Insert** toolbar, select the **Load Family** button to bring up the **Load Family** dialog box (see Figure 4-26).
10. In the **Load Family** dialog box, select the **Doors** folder from the **Program Data > Autodesk > RAC 2012 > Imperial Library** folder.
11. In the **Doors** folder, select the **Double-Glass 2** door, and press the **Open** button to return to the **Drawing Editor** (see Figure 4-27).

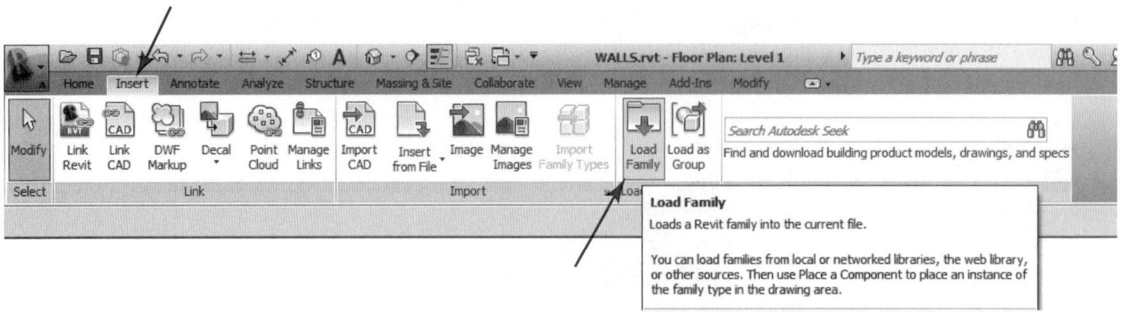

Figure 4-26

Load Family dialog box

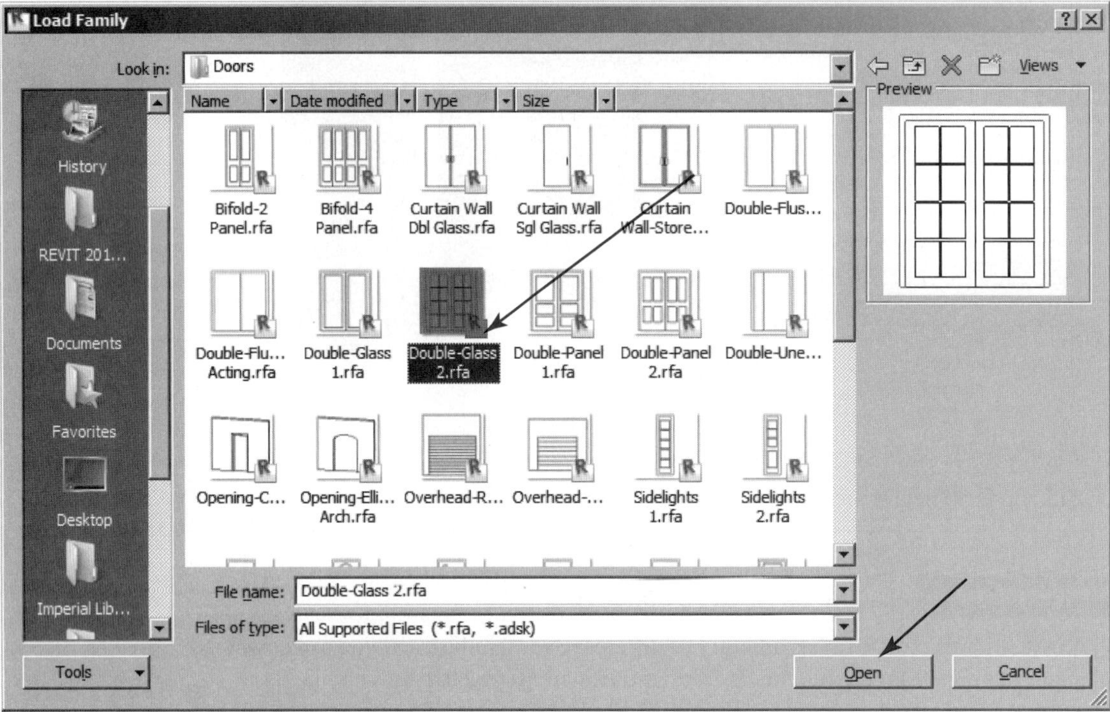

Figure 4-27

Doors folder

12. In the **Project Browser**, expand the **Doors**, and then expand the **Double-Glass 2**.
13. Under **Double-Glass 2**, drag the **68″ × 80″** door into the wall you placed in the **Drawing Editor** (see Figure 4-28).

Figure 4-28

Insert **Double-Glass 2** door option into a **Wall** drawing

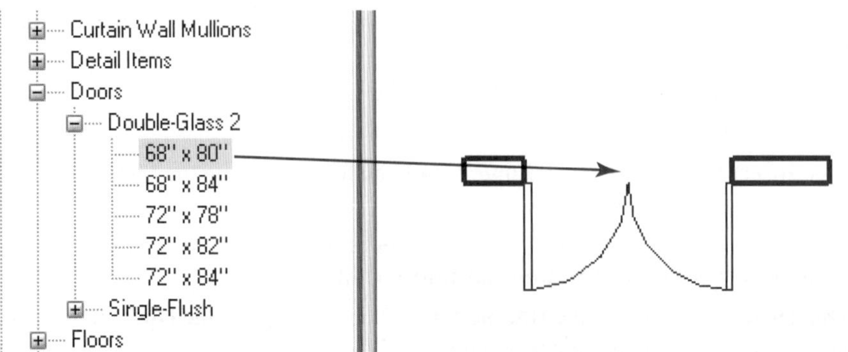

14. Change to the **Default 3D View** (see Figure 4-29).

As mentioned previously, there are many places on the Internet to locate practically any door you need. If you cannot find what you want, you can always modify an existing **Door Family** to suit your needs—see the Components and Families chapter.

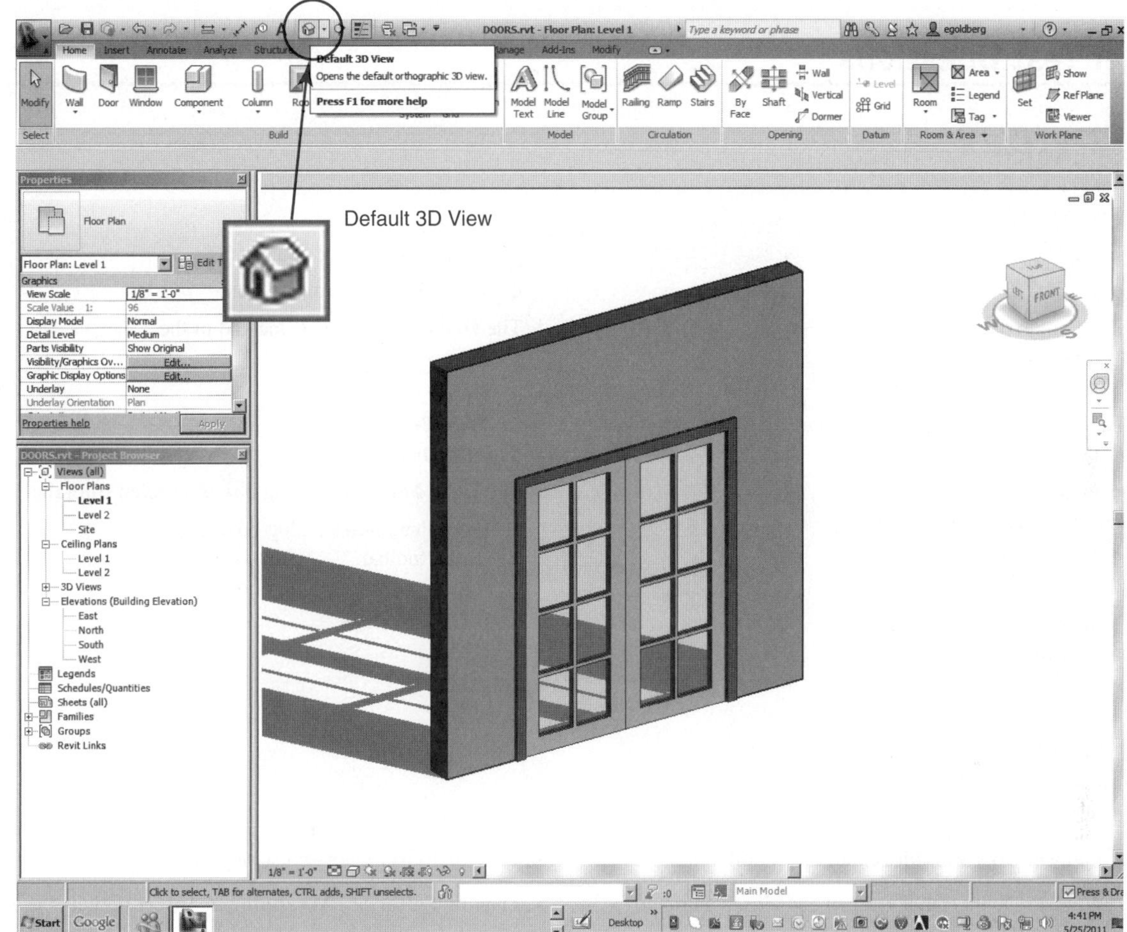

Figure 4-29

Default 3D View

Chapter Summary

This chapter discussed the methods for placing, numbering, creating, and modifying all types of doors in Revit Architecture 2012.

Chapter Test Questions

Multiple Choice

Circle the correct answer.

1. Door tag families are set from the
   a. **Home** toolbar.
   b. **Door Properties** dialog box.
   c. **Options Bar**.
   d. All of the above
2. The **Tag on Placement** button is located on the
   a. **Home** button.
   b. **Options Bar**.
   c. **Modify | Place Door** toolbar.
   d. All of the above
3. The door sill height is located in the
   a. **Home** toolbar.
   b. **Door Properties** dialog box.
   c. **Options Bar**.
   d. **Type Properties** dialog box.
4. The **Default 3D View** is located in the
   a. **View Control Bar**.
   b. **Quick Access** toolbar.
   c. **Type Properties** dialog box.
   d. **Options Bar**.
5. The **Door Materials** dialog box is selected from the
   a. **Door Properties** dialog box.
   b. **Home** toolbar.
   c. **Type Properties** dialog box.
   d. All of the above

True or False

Circle the correct answer.

1. **True or False:** Door **Families** cannot be modified.
2. **True or False:** Doors can be opened and closed automatically in 3D.
3. **True or False: Door Frame** materials cannot be changed.
4. **True or False:** Doors must be placed in walls.
5. **True or False:** The **Wrapping at Insert** option is used to wrap doors around curved walls.

Questions

1. What is the difference between a door Family and a door Type?
2. How do you place several doors an equal distance apart in a wall?
3. What are door grips used for?
4. Where do you control door tag placement?
5. How do you tag all doors that are not tagged?

CHAPTER

5 Windows

CHAPTER OBJECTIVES

- Understand the difference between Revit's **Windows** and Revit's **Doors**.
- Learn how to place a **Window** object.
- Learn how to place and use **Window** tags.
- Learn how to apply the **View Range** option.
- Understand how to **Array** and **Group** windows.

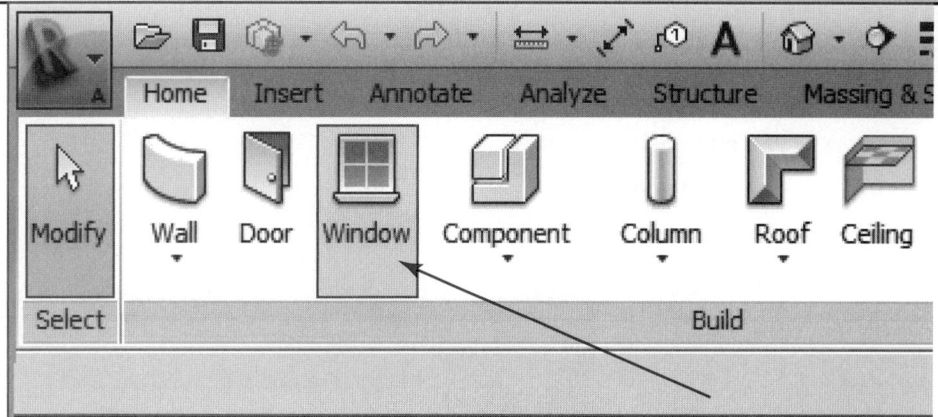

Introduction

In Revit Architecture 2012, **Window** objects are totally customizable. All is possible in this program—from customizing the size and shape of the window. As with other features of this program, a premade library of window styles greatly enhances productivity. Websites such as Autodesk Seek (http://seek.autodesk.com) are currently offering content from many major manufacturers.

Window Options

Windows can be created from a variety of styles available in Revit's **Window Families**.

NOTE:

Because **Windows** are so similar to **Doors**, this chapter should be studied in combination with **Doors**. The **Array** routine, the **View Range** routine, the Web Library, and so on, apply to both of these subjects.

EXERCISE 5-1 LOADING WINDOWS

1. Start a new drawing using the RAC 2012\Imperial Templates\default.rte template.
2. In the **Project Browser**, double-click **Floor Plans > Level 1**.
3. Change the **Drawing Scale** to **1/4″ = 1′-0″**.
4. Set the **Detail Level** to **Medium**.
5. Place a **Basic Wall: Exterior – Brick on CMU 20′-0″** high and **20′-0″** long.
6. Select the **Load Family** button from the **Insert** tab to bring up the **Load Family** dialog box (see Figure 5-1).
7. In the **Load Family** dialog box, press the **Imperial Library** icon on the left, and then locate the **Windows** folder (see Figure 5-2).

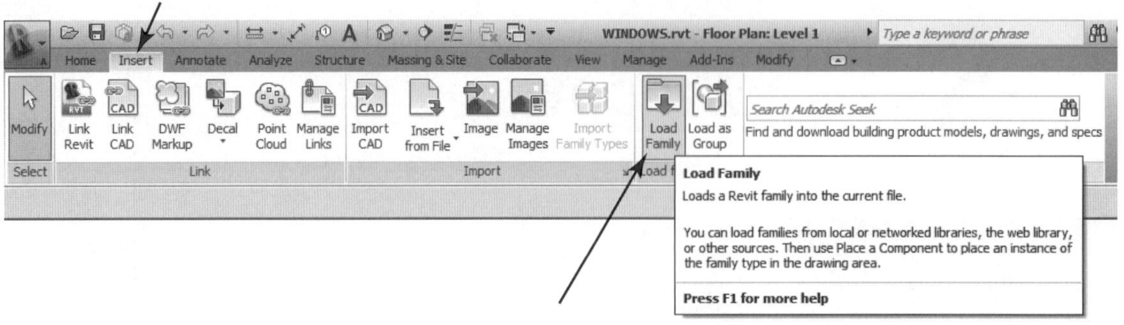

Figure 5-1

Load Family button

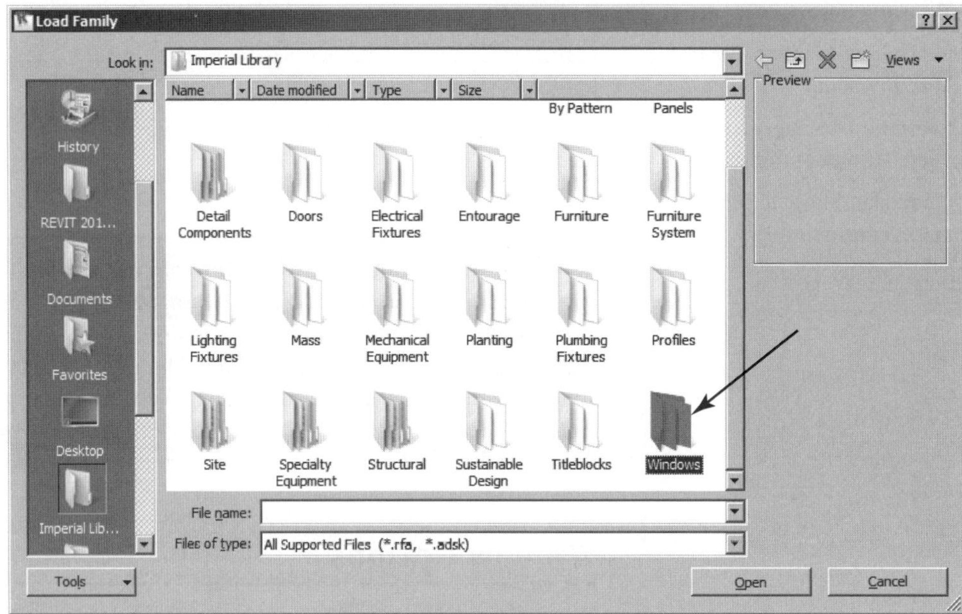

Figure 5-2

Windows folder in **Imperial Library** directory

8. Double-click on the **Windows** folder, select all the windows, and then press the **Open** button at the lower right of the **Load Family** dialog box.

You have now loaded all the **Window Families** that are included with Revit Architecture 2012. To see which **Windows** have been loaded and are now available, do the following:

9. Go to the **Project Browser**, and locate **Families**.
10. Expand **Families**, and locate **Windows**.
11. Expand **Windows** to see all the **Window** families.
12. Expand **Double Hung** to see the sizes available (see Figure 5-3).
13. Select the **Insert** tab to bring up the **Insert** toolbar.

NOTE:

You must have a working Internet connection for the following exercise.

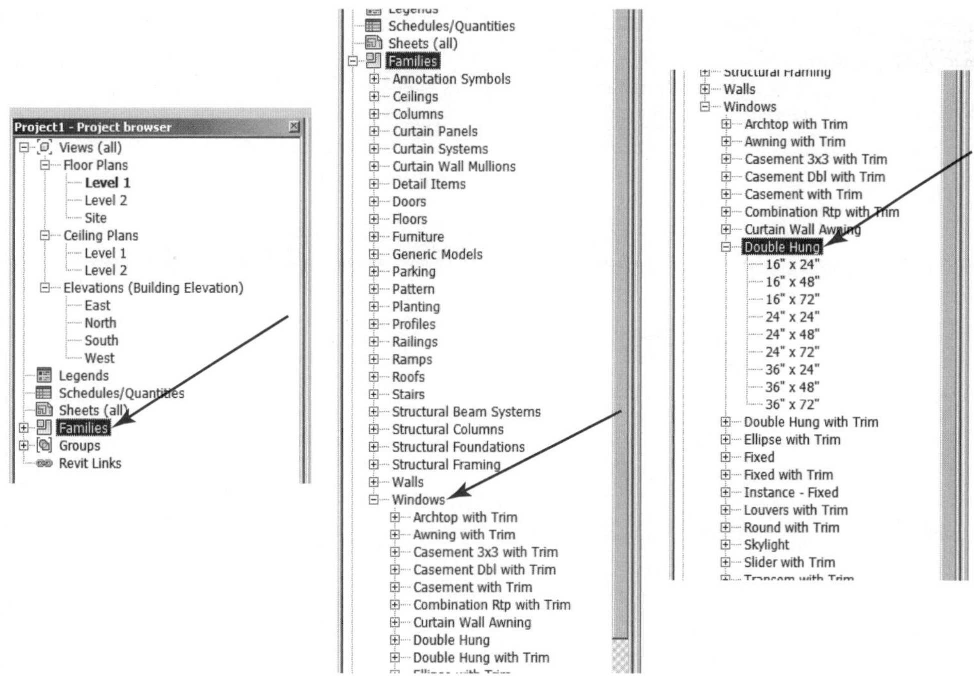

Figure 5-3

View **Double Hung Windows** choices

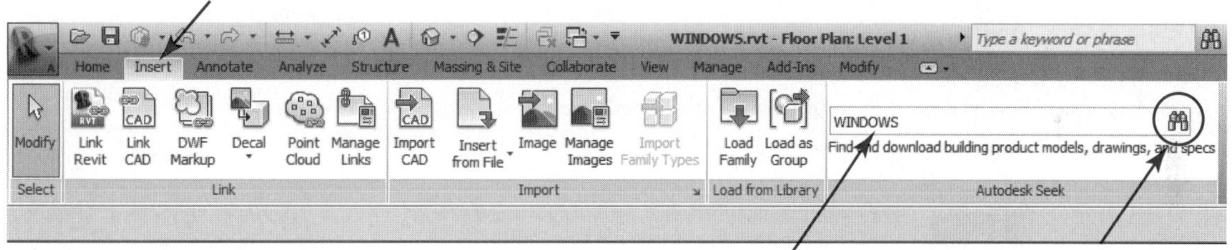

Figure 5-4

Autodesk Seek panel on the **Insert** toolbar

14. In the **Insert** toolbar, enter **WINDOWS** in the **Autodesk Seek** panel (see Figure 5-4).
15. Press the **Binoculars** icon to the right of the word **WINDOWS** you just entered to bring up the Autodesk Seek website (see Figure 5-5).
16. In the Autodesk Seek web page**,** click on the **RFA** icon for the Andersen 400 Series Casement window to bring up the Revit options for these windows (see Figure 5-6).
17. In the **Revit** options for the Andersen 400 Series Casement windows, check the **Casement CR13 CW135** check box, and press the **Download** button to add it to your **Windows Library** folder. Optionally, if you have a wall in your workspace, you can drag a window from the Autodesk Seek website and place it directly in your wall (see Figure 5-7).
18. Save this file as **LOADING WINDOWS**.

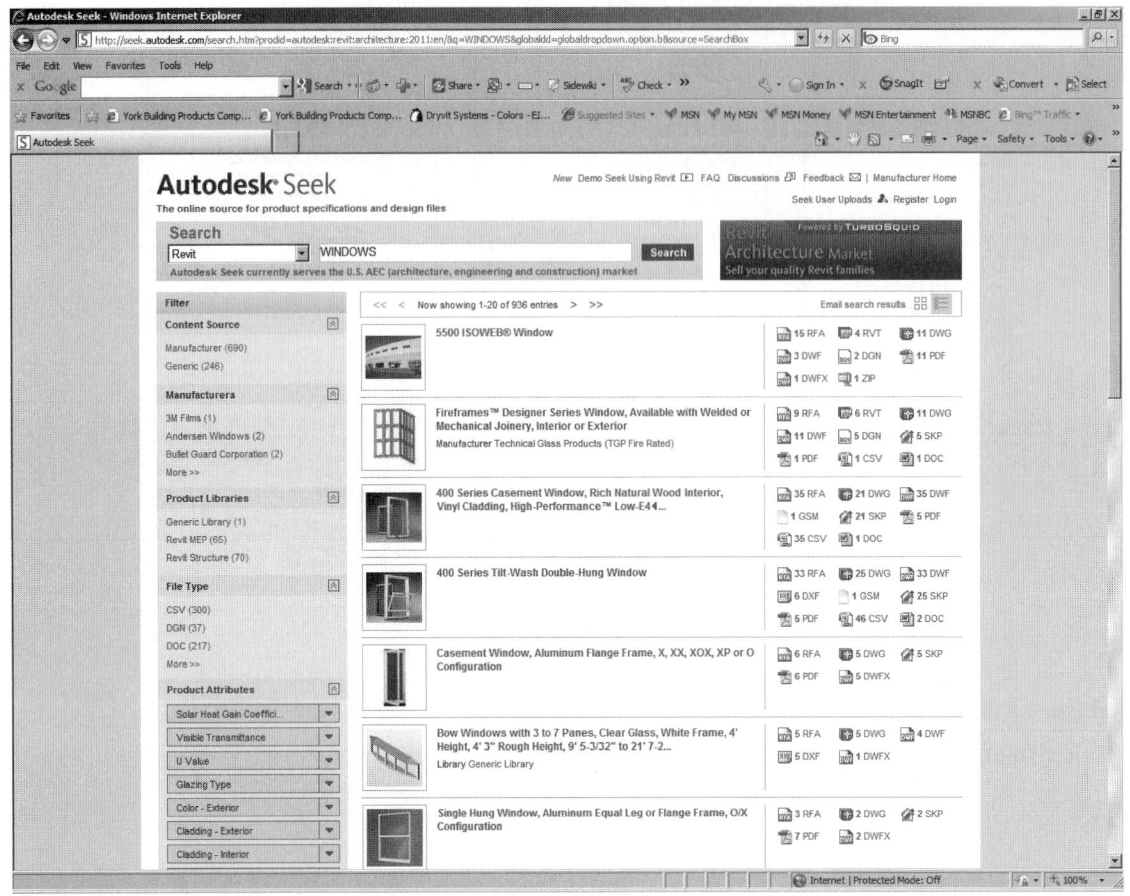

Figure 5-5

Autodesk Seek website
(Autodesk screen shots reprinted with the permission of Autodesk, Inc.)

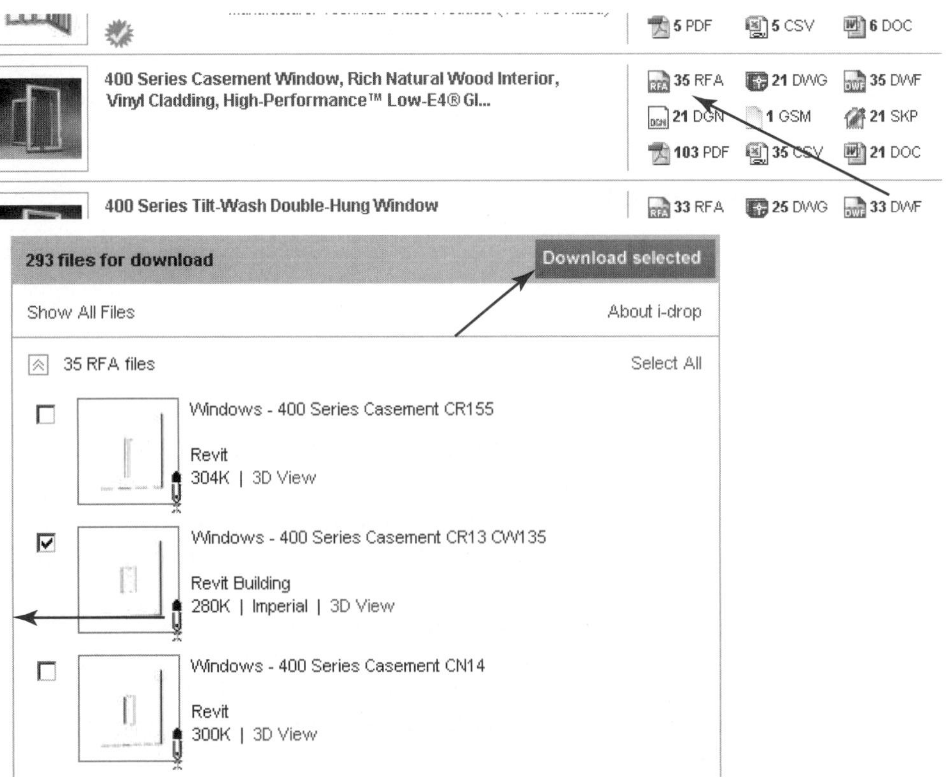

Figure 5-6

RFA icon on Autodesk Seek web page

Figure 5-7

Download manufacturers' window specifications and graphics from the Autodesk Seek website

EXERCISE 5-2 THE VIEW RANGE

NOTE:
The **View Range** works only in Plan view.

1. Using the previous exercise, select the **Window** button in the **Home** toolbar to bring up the **Modify | Place Window** toolbar.
2. In the **Properties** dialog box, select **Andersen_Windows_400_Series_Casement_CW135** from the drop-down list.
3. In the **Modify | Place Window** toolbar, unselect the **Tag on Placement** button, and move your cursor over the wall you placed in the previous exercise.
4. Click the wall to place the window.
5. Click the window to enable the **Listening Dimensions**. Click on the left dimension, change it to **4′-8″**, and click it again to make it permanent (see Figure 5-8).

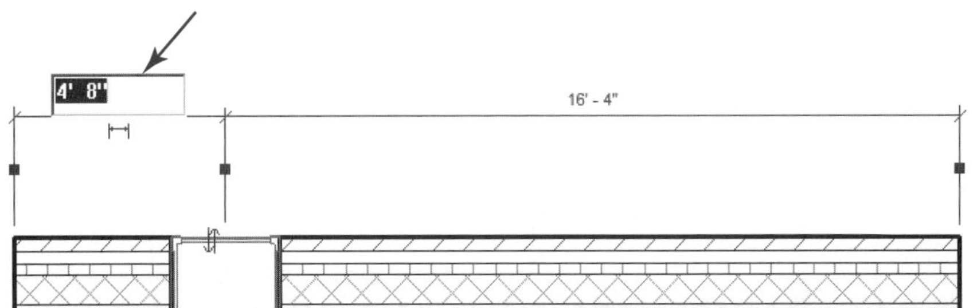

Figure 5-8

Enable **Listening Dimensions** to change dimensions

6. Double-click the **South Elevation** in the **Project Browser** to bring it up in the **Drawing Editor**.
7. Select the **View** tab to bring up the **View** toolbar.
8. In the **View** toolbar, select the **Tile** button in the **Windows** panel to tile the **South Elevation** and **Floor Plan** (see Figure 5-9).

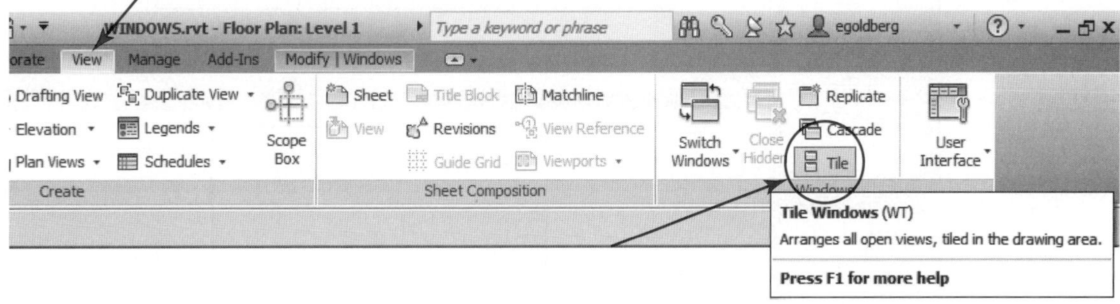

Figure 5-9

Tile button

9. Set the scale of **Floor Plan: Level 1** to **1/2″ = 1′-0″** and **Elevation: South** to **1/4″ = 1′-0″**.
10. Adjust the tiled modeling areas as shown in Figure 5-10.

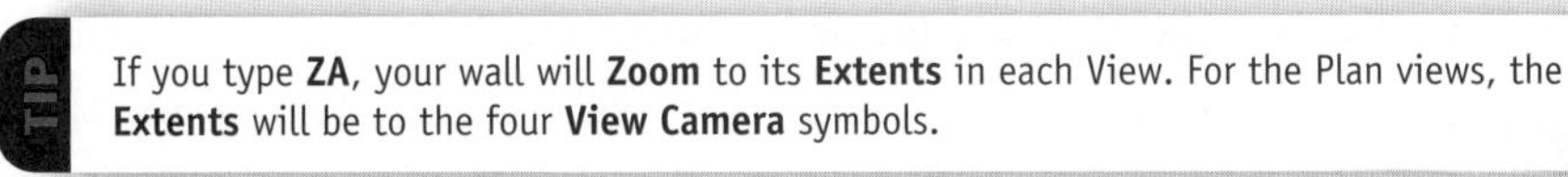

TIP If you type **ZA**, your wall will **Zoom** to its **Extents** in each View. For the Plan views, the **Extents** will be to the four **View Camera** symbols.

11. Select the window in the **South Elevation** to bring up its **Properties** dialog box.
12. In the **Properties** dialog box, change the **Sill Height** to **5′-0″**, and press the **OK** button.

Notice that the window appears as only an outline in **Level 1** view. This is because the **Cut Plane** of the **View Range** is set lower than the window (see Figure 5-11).

Figure 5-10

Adjust tiled modeling areas

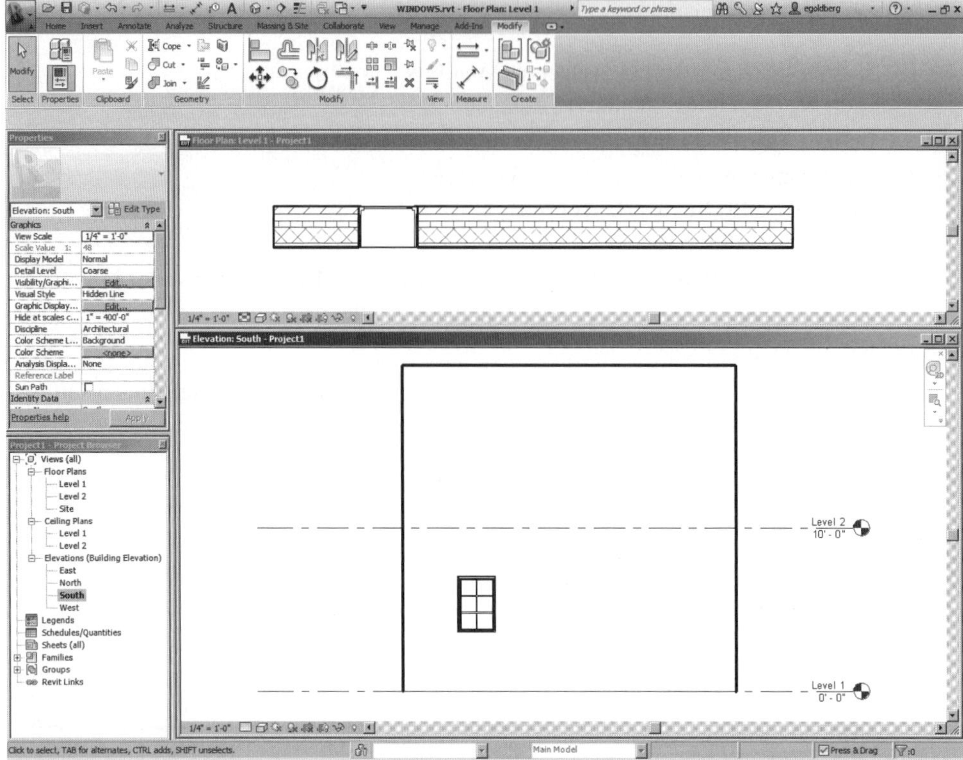

Figure 5-11

South Elevation Properties dialog box

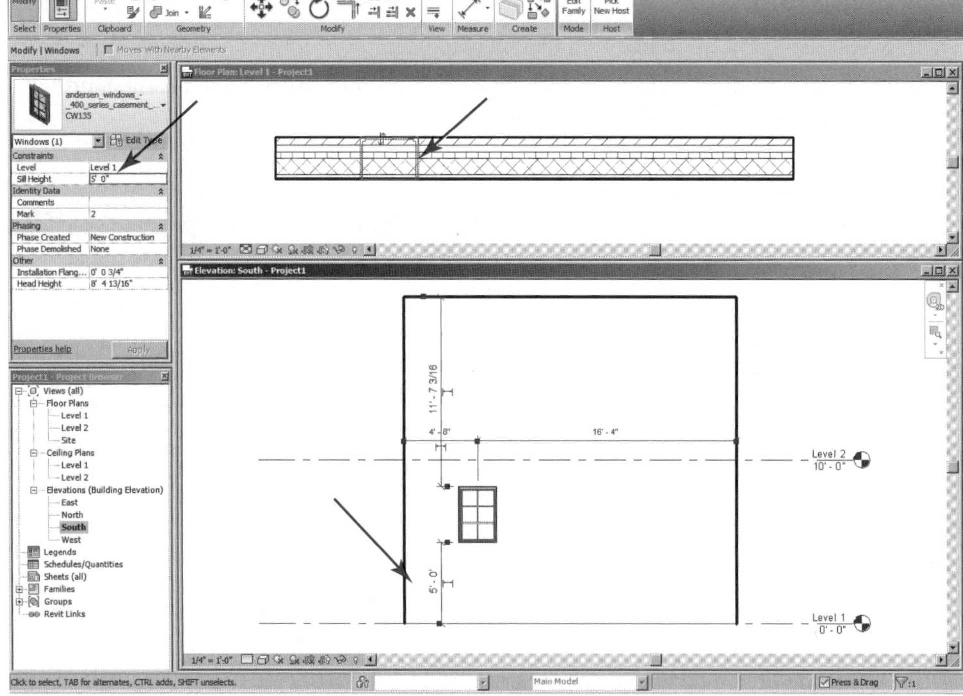

The cut plane is the height above the floor at which the floor plan is displayed.

TIP If you select the window and move it above the cut plane, you will not see it in the floor plan.

13. Click in the **Level 1** view to bring up its **Properties** dialog box.
14. In the **Properties** dialog box, select the **Edit** button in the **View Range** field to bring up the **View Range** dialog box.

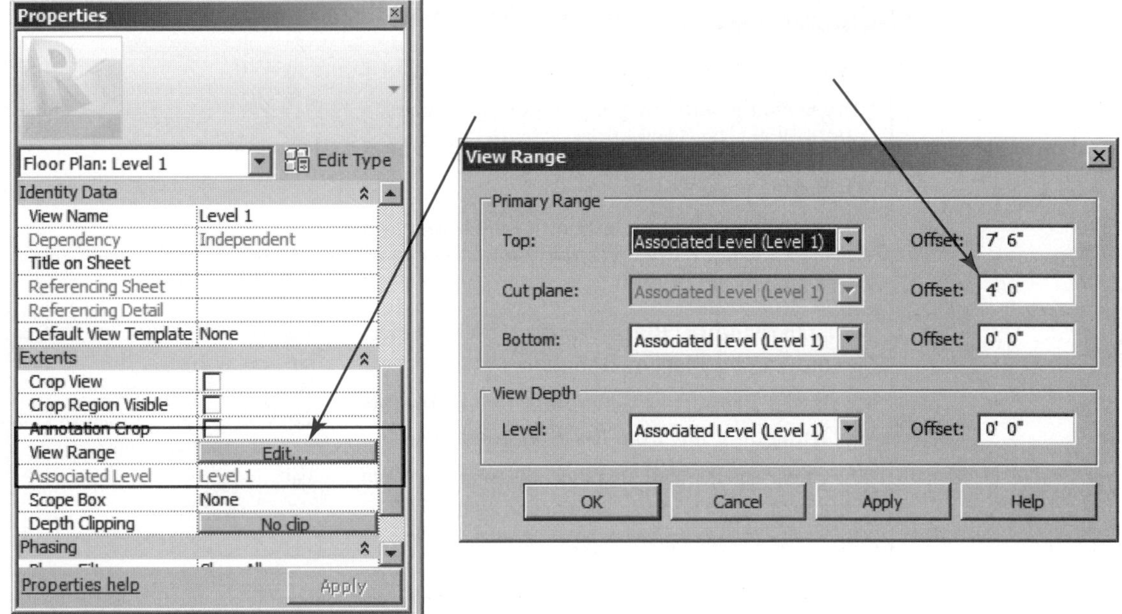

Figure 5-12

View Range dialog box

15. In the **View Range** dialog box, the **Cut plane: Offset** sets the height from the level for the cut plane (see Figure 5-12).
16. Change the **Cut plane** to **6′-0″**, and press the **Apply** button.

Notice that the window again appears fully in the Plan view. That is because the cut plane is higher than the sill height of the window.

17. In the **South Elevation**, move the window up and down the wall. Watch as the window crosses the cut plane and appears and disappears from the Plan view.
18. Save this file as **VIEW RANGE**.

View Range Options

Name	Description
Top	Sets the upper boundary of the primary range. The upper boundary is defined as a level and an offset from that level. Elements display as defined by their object styles. Elements above the offset value do not display.
Cut Plane	Sets a height at which elements in a Plan view are cut, such that building components below the cut plane display in projection, and others that intersect it display as cut. Building components that display as cut include walls, roofs, ceilings, floors, and stairs. A cut plane does not cut components, such as desks, tables, and beds.
Bottom	Sets the level of the Primary Range's lower boundary. If you access **View Range** while viewing the lowest level of your project and set this property to a level below, you must specify a value for **Offset.** You must also set **View Depth** to a level below it.
View Depth	Sets a vertical range for the visibility of elements between specified levels. In a floor plan, it should be below the cut plane. In a reflected ceiling plan (RCP), it should be above. For example, if you are designing a multistory building, you might have a floor plan for the 10th floor that had a depth to the first level. Specifying view depth lets you display visible objects below the current level; such objects include stairs, balconies, and objects visible through holes in a floor.

EXERCISE 5-3 **ARRAYING AND GROUPING WINDOWS**

1. Using the previous exercise, return the **Cut plane** to **4′-0″**.
2. Delete the window you previously placed.
3. Close the **Level 1** view, and expand the **South Elevation**.
4. Set the scale to **1/4″ = 1′-0″**.
5. Select the **Window** button in the **Home** toolbar to bring up the **Modify | Place Window** toolbar.
6. In the **Modify | Place Window** toolbar, select the **Tag on Placement** button.
7. In the **Properties** dialog box, select **Double Hung 36″× 48″** from the drop-down list.
8. Click on the wall to place the window, and adjust its location as shown in Figure 5-13.

NOTE:

Windows can be automatically labeled in Plan or Elevation view. Be sure to change the label annotation. Windows are usually labeled by letters, and all windows of the same type will automatically have the same letter.

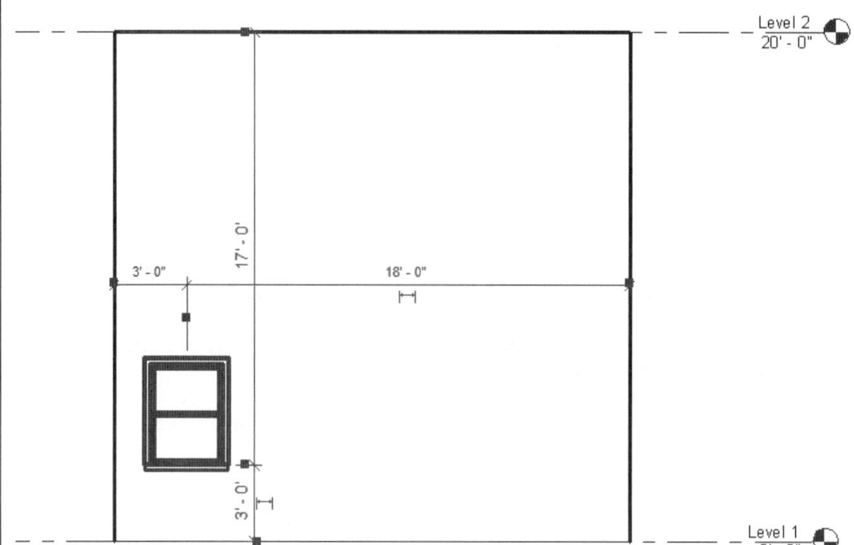

Figure 5-13

Place a window in a wall

9. Select the window to bring up the **Modify Windows** toolbar.
10. In the **Modify Windows** toolbar**,** select the **Array** button in the **Modify** panel (see Figure 5-14).

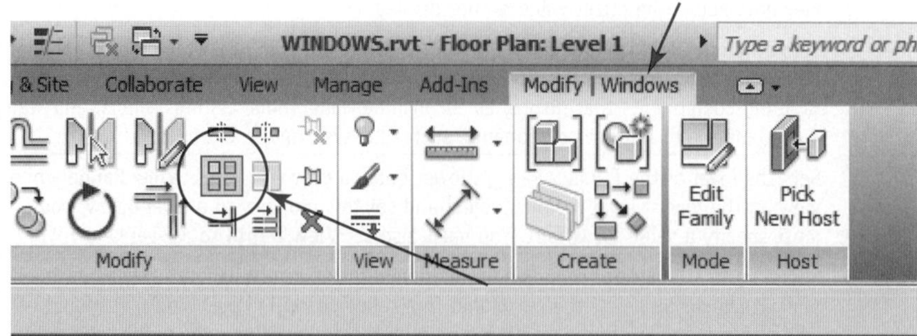

Figure 5-14

Array button

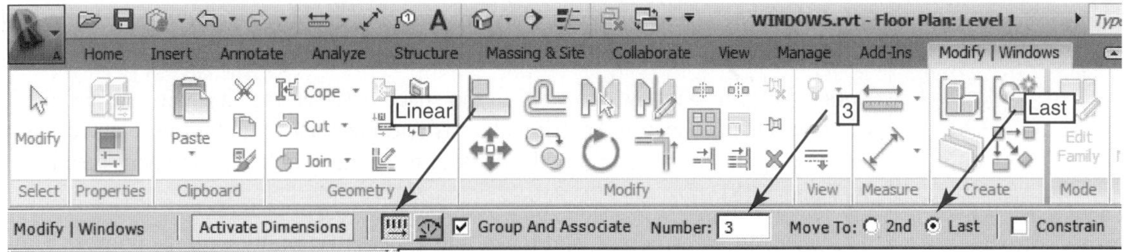

Figure 5-15

Linear array icon

11. In the **Options Bar**, select the **Linear Array** button, check the **Group And Associate** check box, enter **3** in the **Number** field, and select the **Last** radio button (see Figure 5-15).

NOTE:

- **Group And Associate:** Includes each member of the array in a group. If not selected, Revit Architecture creates the specified number of copies and does not group them. Once placed, each copy acts independently of the others.
- **Number:** Specifies the total number of copies (of the selected elements) in the array.
- **Move To:**
  - **2nd:** Specifies the spacing between each member of the array. Additional array members appear after the second member.
  - **Last:** Specifies the entire span of the array. Array members are evenly spaced between the first member and the last member.
- **Constrain:** Restricts movement of array members along horizontal or vertical direction only.

12. Grab the window at its top center (make sure **Midpoint Snap** is on), drag the window to the right, enter **14′** in the **Listening Dimension**, and press the <**Enter**> key to set the last window location and create three windows (see Figure 5-16).

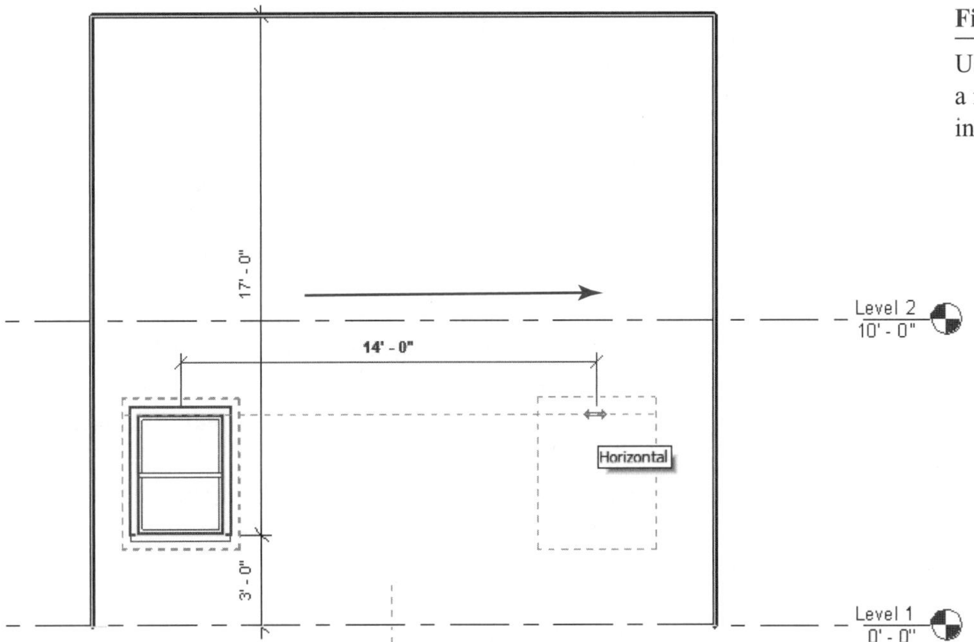

Figure 5-16

Using **Linear** array to create a new window from an existing one

13. Select one of the windows (they are now all part of a group), change the number to **4**, and press the **<Enter>** key.

Notice that four windows now fill in the space between the first window and the last window. This is because the original array had the **Last** radio button selected when it was first applied. Try changing the number to **2**, and watch what happens (see Figures 5-17 and 5-18).

14. Select all the windows, and repeat this process vertically with the number being **3** and the **Constrain** check box checked (see Figures 5-19, 5-20, and 5-21).

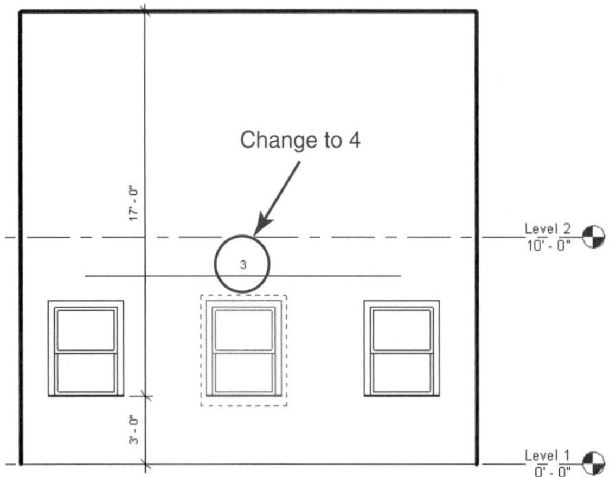

Figure 5-17

Create four windows horizontally

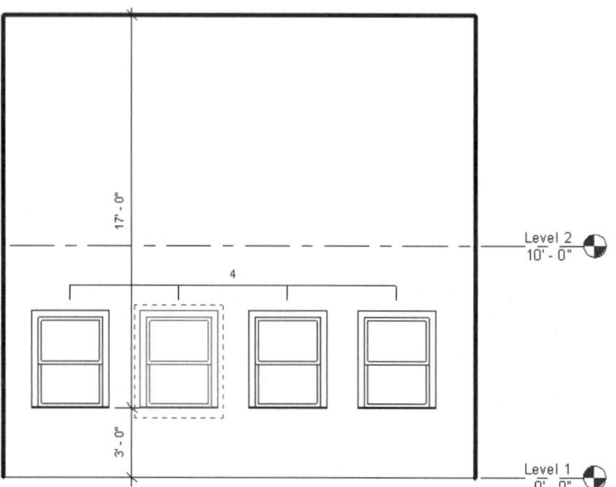

Figure 5-18

Create two windows horizontally

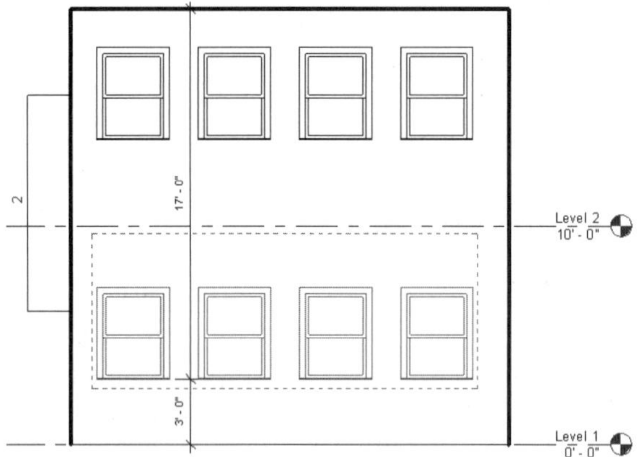

Figure 5-19

Create four windows vertically

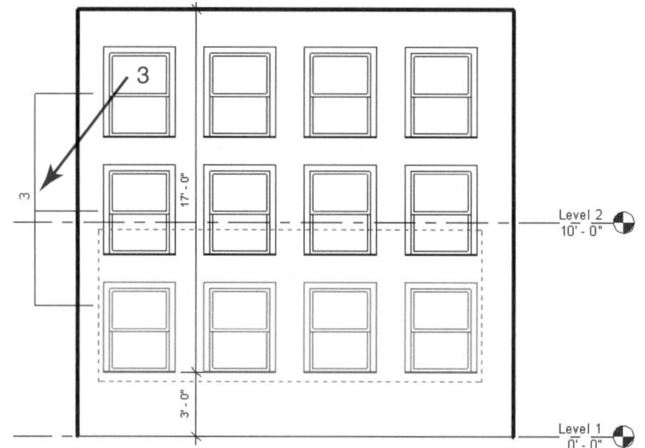

Figure 5-20

Create four more windows vertically

15. Move the lower left window vertically up and down, and watch how the windows automatically space themselves.
16. Select the lower left window again to bring up the **Modify | Model Groups** toolbar.
17. In the **Modify | Model Groups** toolbar, select the **Ungroup** button to separate the window completely from all window groups (see Figure 5-22).
18. Now when you select the left window and move it, it moves separately from the other windows.
19. Save this file as **ARRAYING AND GROUPING WINDOWS**.

Figure 5-21

Wall with 12 windows added

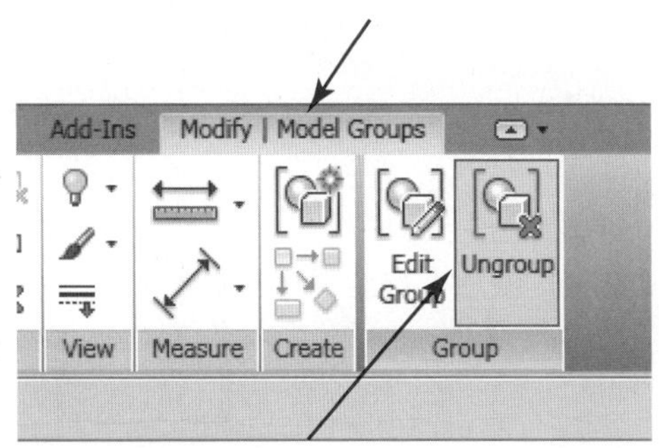

Figure 5-22

Use **Ungroup** to separate a window from a group

EXERCISE 5-4 **TAGGING THE WINDOWS**

1. Using the previous file, change to the **Annotate** tab to bring up the **Annotate** toolbar.
2. In the **Annotate** toolbar, select the **Tag All Not Tagged** button in the **Tag** panel to bring up the **Tag All Not Tagged** dialog box.
3. In the **Tag All Not Tagged** dialog box, select the **All objects in current view** radio button. Select the **Window Tags** field, and uncheck the **Leader > Create** check box (you don't want a leader on the tag).
4. Press the **Apply** button to apply all the tags, and then press the **OK** button to close the **Tag All Not Tagged** dialog box and return to the **Drawing Editor** (see Figure 5-23).
5. Open the **Level 1** floor plan.
6. Change the **Scale** to **1/4″ = 1′-0**.
7. Select the **Annotate** tab to bring up the **Annotate** toolbar.
8. In the **Annotate** toolbar, select the **Tag All** button from the **Tag** panel to again bring up the **Tag All Not Tagged** dialog box.
9. In the **Tag All Not Tagged** dialog box, select the **All objects in current view** radio button. Select the **Window Tags** field, and uncheck the **Leader > Create** check box (you don't want a leader on the tag).
10. Press the **Apply** button to apply all the tags, and then press the **OK** button to close the **Tag All Not Tagged** dialog box and return to the **Drawing Editor** (see Figure 5-24).
11. Save this file as **TAGGING WINDOWS**.

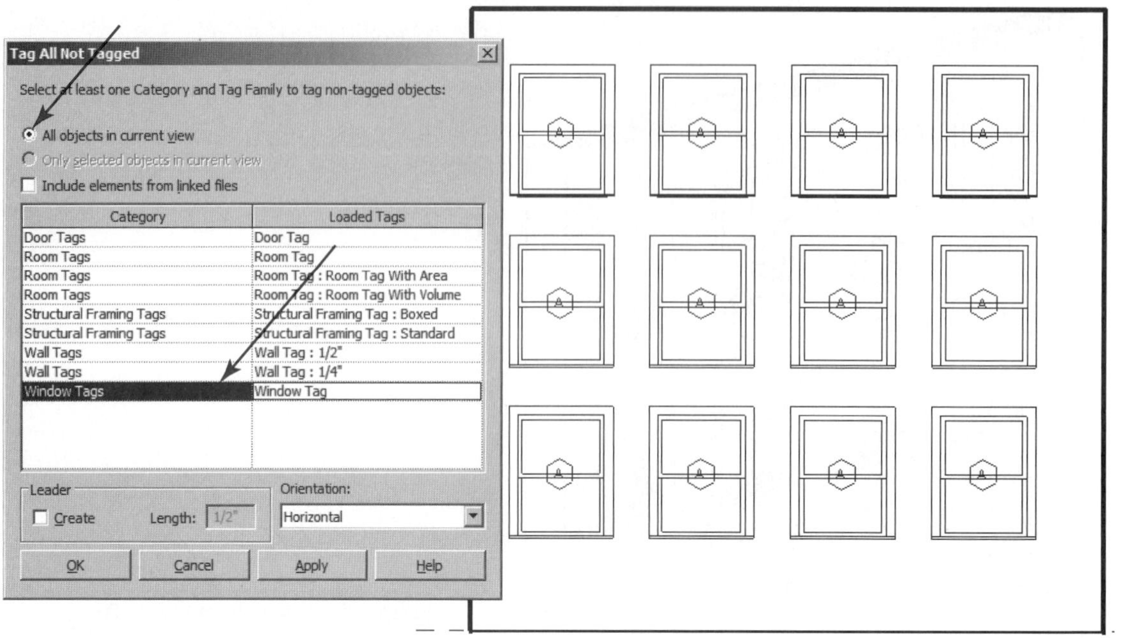

Figure 5-23

Tag All Not Tagged dialog box

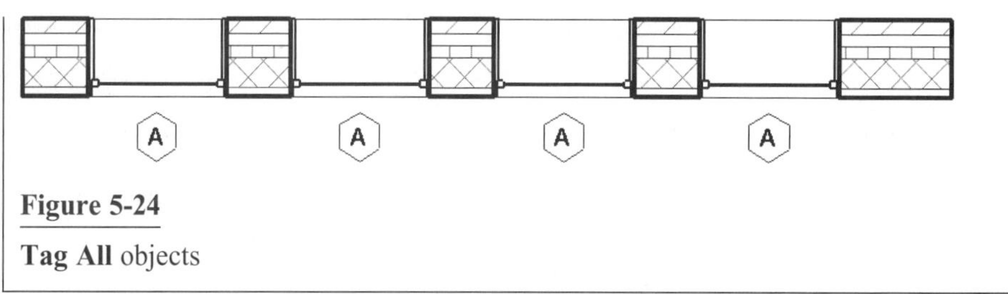

Figure 5-24

Tag All objects

As mentioned previously, there are many places on the Internet to locate practically any window you need. If this is not enough, you can always modify an existing **Window Family** to suit your needs. See the chapter on Components and Families.

Chapter Summary

This chapter discussed the methods for loading, arraying, grouping, and tagging all types of windows in Revit Architecture 2012.

Chapter Test Questions

True or False

Circle the correct answer.

1. **True or False:** Revit windows and doors are similar objects.
2. **True or False:** The **cut plane** is the height above the **floor** at which the floor plan is displayed.

3. **True or False:** Revit's windows must be created by content creation companies.
4. **True or False:** The **Tile** button in the **Modify** toolbar creates a new tile material.
5. **True or False:** The **Window Properties** dialog appears when you press the **Edit Type** button.

Questions

1. How do you access the **Family Editor**?
2. How do you know that you are in the **Family Editor**?
3. Which toolbar do you access to place **Window Tags**?
4. What is the purpose of the **View Range**?
5. What is the purpose of the binoculars in the **Autodesk Seek** panel on the **Insert** toolbar?

Exercise

1. Go to http://seek.autodesk.com on the Internet.
2. In the Autodesk Seek website, select the **Windows** link (see Figure 5-25).

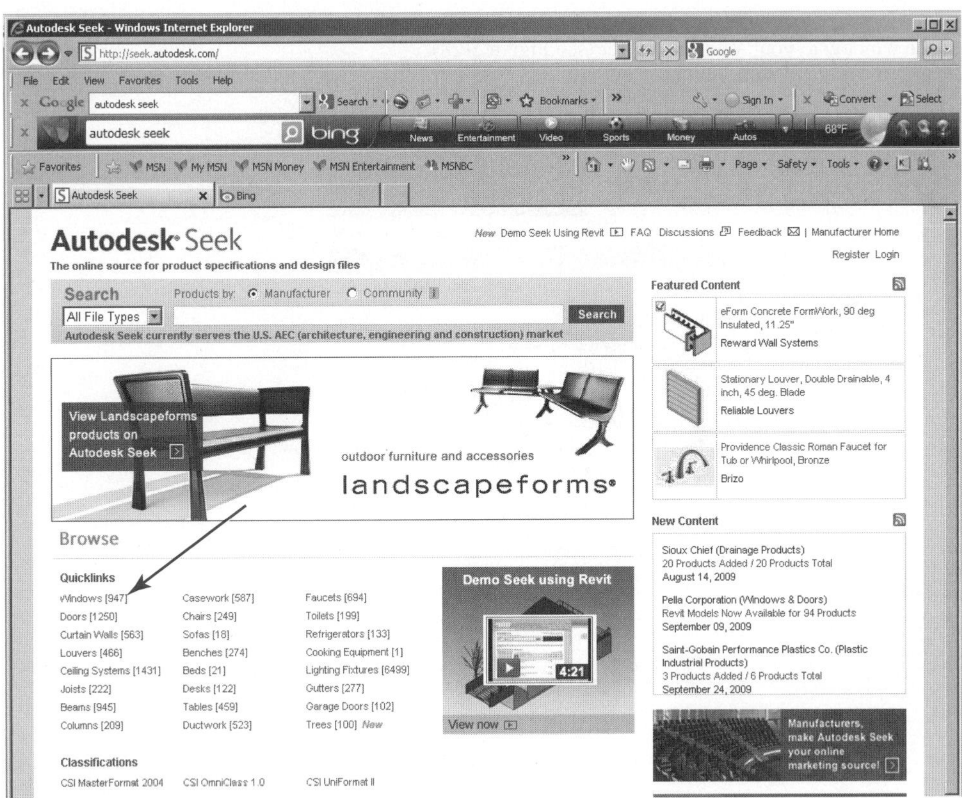

Figure 5-25

Autodesk Seek website
(Autodesk screen shots reprinted with the permission of Autodesk, Inc.)

3. In the next screen, select **Revit** from the **Search** drop-down list, click on the **Manufacturer** radio button, enter **Marvin** in the name field, and then press the **Search** button at the right of the **Name** field (see Figure 5-26).

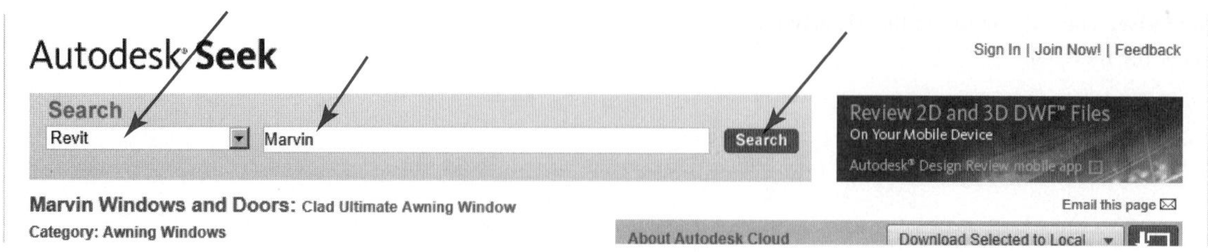

Figure 5-26

RFA search
(Autodesk screen shots reprinted with the permission of Autodesk, Inc.)

4. In the next screen, click on the **Clad Awning Ultimate Window,** picture or the **RFA** icon to take you to the next screen (see Figure 5-27).

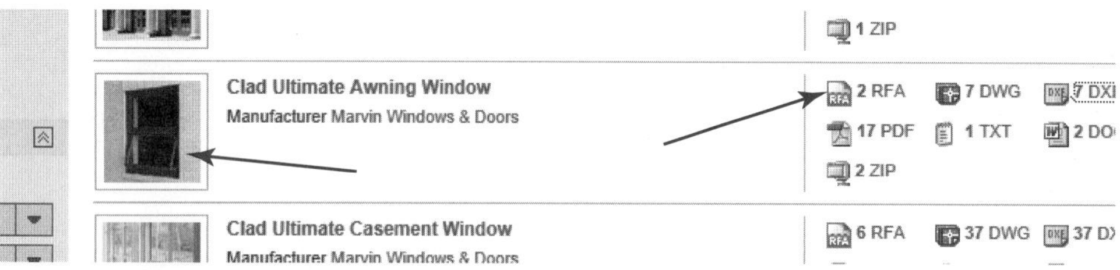

Figure 5-27

Select a window from the Autodesk Seek website

5. In the next screen, download the window to your **Window** folder (see Figure 5-28).

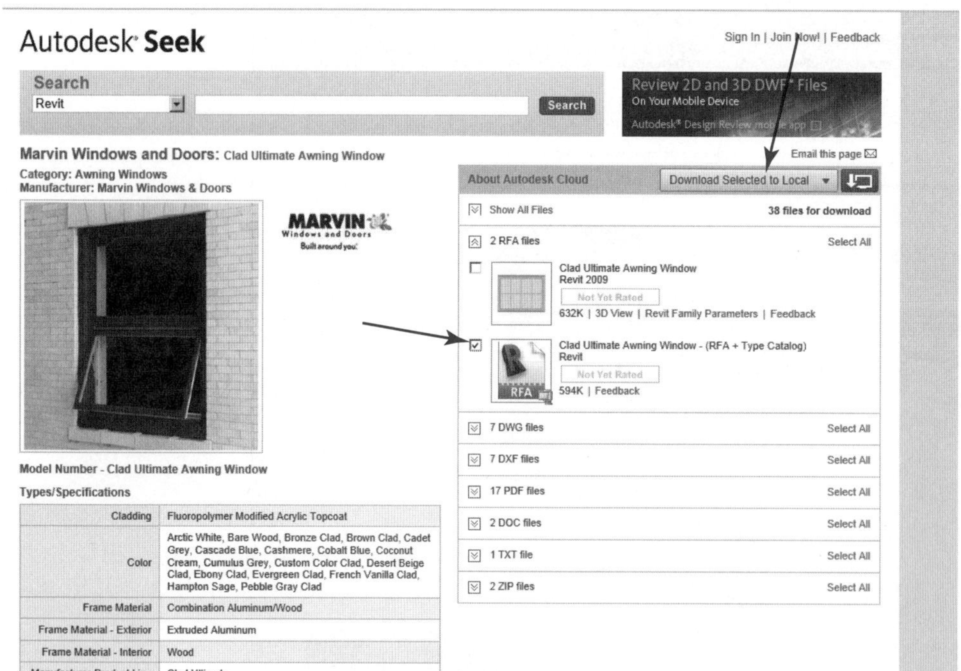

Figure 5-28

Download a window from the Autodesk Seek website
(Autodesk screen shots reprinted with the permission of Autodesk, Inc.)

6. Load the window into a new project file, and place the window in a wall as shown in Exercise 5-1.

CHAPTER

6 Components and Families

CHAPTER OBJECTIVES

- Learn how to add and modify **Components** in your project.
- Understand and use **System Families**.
- Understand and use **In-Place Families**.
- Understand and use **Loadable Families** and the **Family Editor**.

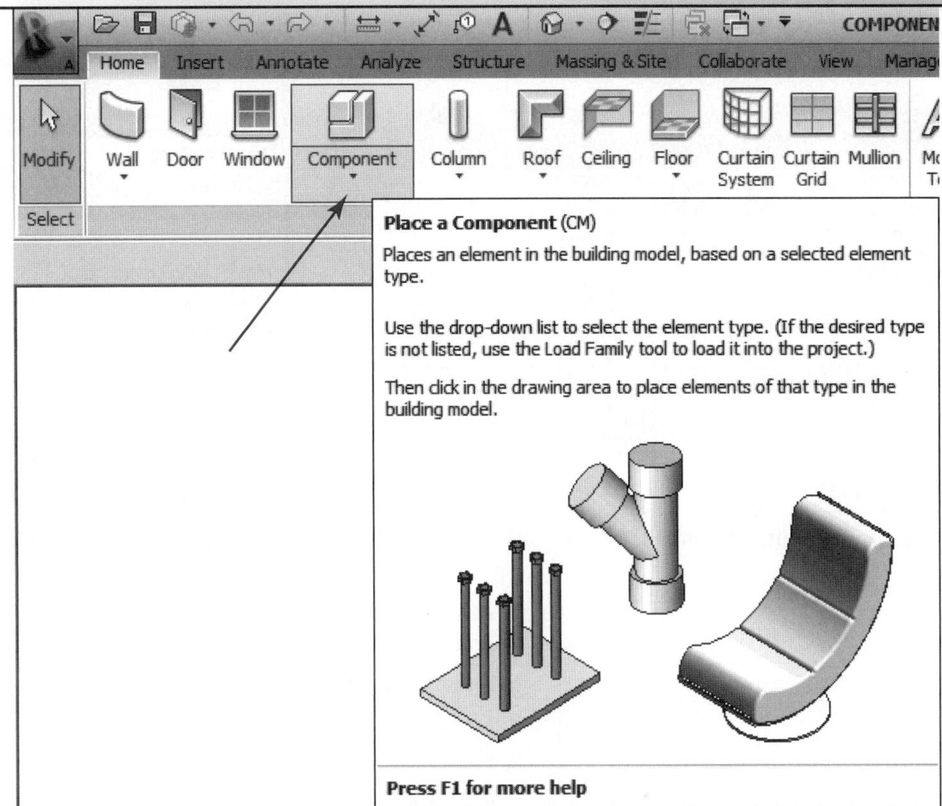
Home
Insert
Annotate
Analyze
Structure
Massing & Site
Collaborate
View
Modify
Wall
Door
Window
Component
Column
Roof
Ceiling
Floor
Curtain System
Curtain Grid
Mullion
Select
Place a Component (CM)
Places an element in the building model, based on a selected element type.
Use the drop-down list to select the element type. (If the desired type is not listed, use the Load Family tool to load it into the project.)
Then click in the drawing area to place elements of that type in the building model.
Press F1 for more help

Introduction

Components and **Families** are Revit Architecture 2012's method for creating and adding parametric (adjustable) content.

Components

Revit has a variety of **Components**, such as different types of furniture, which can be added to a drawing or modified to fit design needs. **Components** can also be downloaded from the Internet.

EXERCISE 6-1 ADDING AND MODIFYING COMPONENTS

1. Start a new drawing using the RAC 2012\Imperial Templates\default.rte template.
2. In the **Project Browser**, double-click on the **Level 1** floor plan to bring it into the **Drawing Editor**.
3. Change the **Drawing Scale** to **1/4″ = 1′-0″**.
4. Set the **Detail Level** to **Medium**.

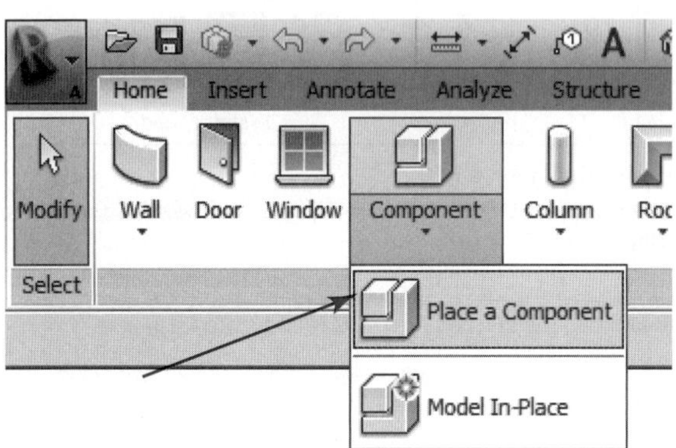

Figure 6-1

Place a Component button

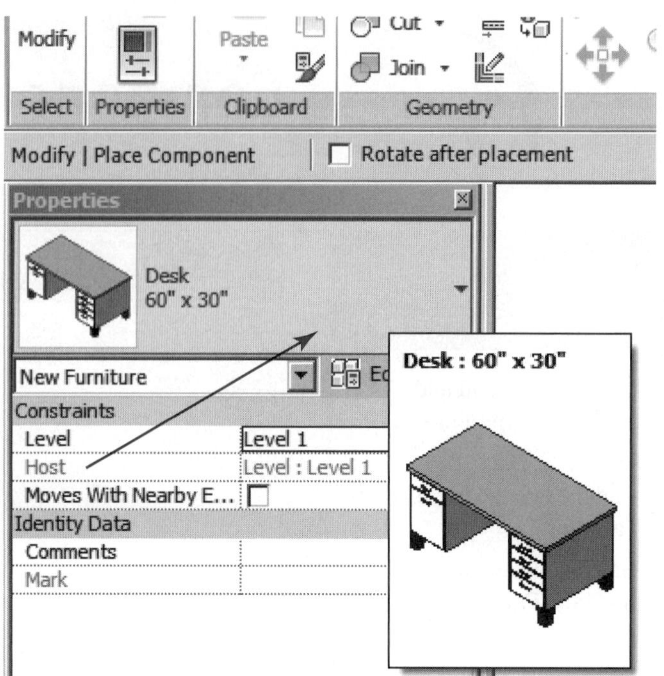

Figure 6-2

Component Properties drop-down list

5. In the **Home** toolbar, select the **Component > Place a Component** button to bring up the **Modify | Place Component** toolbar (see Figure 6-1).
6. Select **Desk: 60″ × 30″** from the **Properties** drop-down list, and click (see Figure 6-2).
7. Move your cursor into your **Level 1** view.
8. Press the <**Space bar**> on your keyboard to rotate the desk, click in the **Drawing Editor** to place the desk, and then press the <**Esc**> key twice to end the command.
9. Change to the **Default 3D View** (see Figure 6-3).
10. Double-click on the **Level 1** floor plan view in the **Project Browser** to bring it up in the **Drawing Editor**.

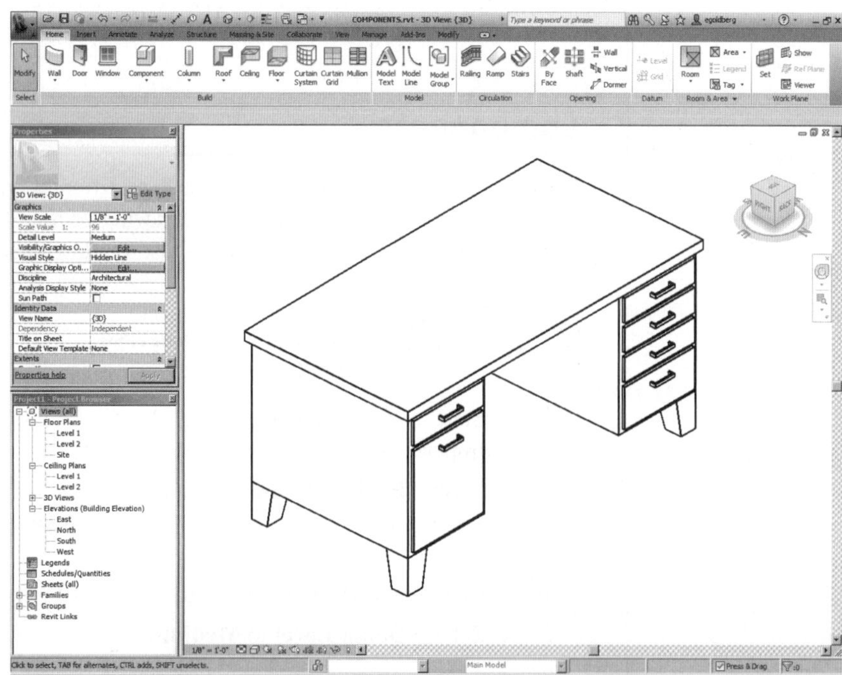

Figure 6-3

Desk in **Default 3D View**

11. Again, select the **Component > Place a Component** button in the **Home** toolbar to bring up the **Modify | Place Component** toolbar.
12. In the **Modify | Place Component** toolbar, press the **Load Family** button to bring up the **Load Family** dialog box for the **Imperial Library**.
13. In the **Load Family** dialog box, open the **Furniture** folder.
14. In the **Furniture** folder, select the **Chair-Breuer**, and press the **Open** button to return to the **Drawing Editor**.
15. Press the <**Space bar**> to rotate the chair, and then click in the **Drawing Editor** to place the chair.
16. Change to the **Default 3D View** (see Figure 6-4).
17. Select the desk to bring up the **Modify | Furniture** toolbar.
18. In the **Modify | Furniture** toolbar, select the **Type Properties** button to bring up the **Type Properties** dialog box.
19. In the **Type Properties** dialog, press the **Duplicate** button to bring up the **Name** dialog box.
20. In the **Name** dialog box, enter **TEST DESK**, and press the **OK** button to return to the **Type Properties** dialog box.
21. In the **Type Properties** dialog box, enter **4′-0″** in the **Depth** field and **8′-0″** in the **Width** field. Then press the **OK** buttons to return to the **Drawing Editor** (see Figure 6-5).

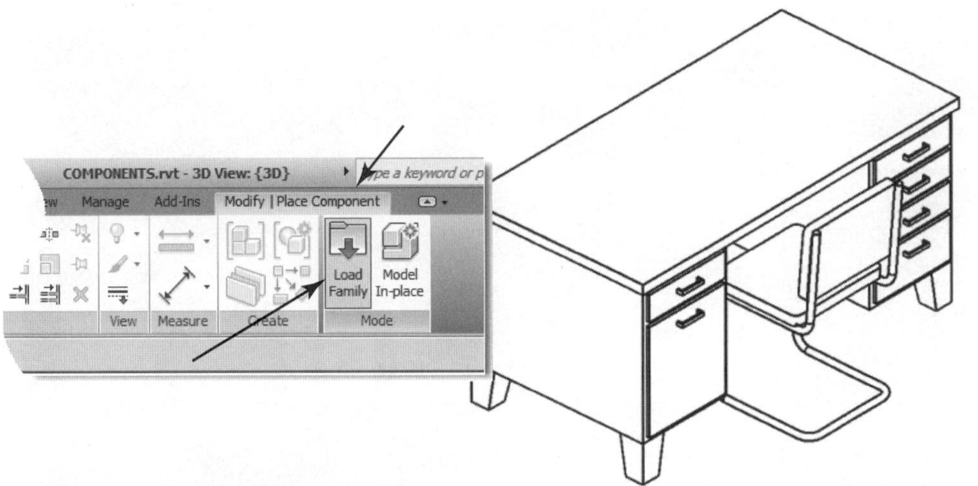

Figure 6-4

Load Family button

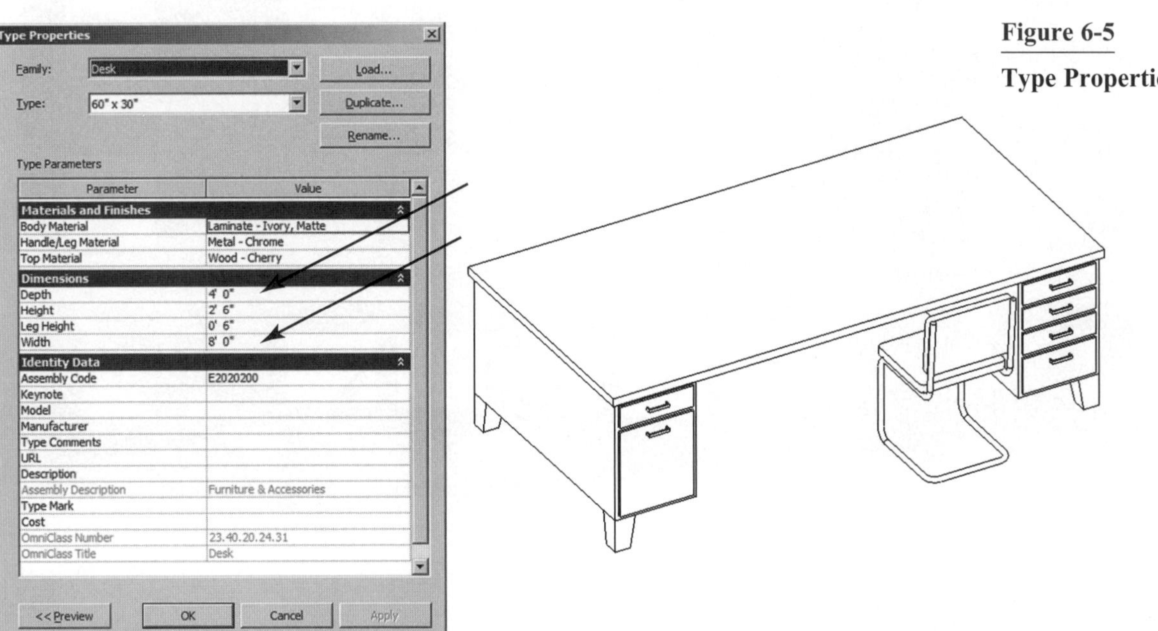

Figure 6-5

Type Properties dialog box

NOTE:

Components have usually been created with parameters that can be changed. Experiment by changing their **Type** parameters.

You can create your own components with parameters (see Exercise 6-2 on **In-Place Families**).

TIP

You can locate components on the Internet by Googling on "Revit Components" or "Revit Component Families."

Some of the sites you will find will offer components for sale, and others will offer free components.

Revit Architecture Market (http://www.turbosquid.com/Revit-market) is an excellent source for content (see Figure 6-6).

You can also download **Components** from Autodesk Seek by clicking on the down arrow at the right of the **Help** icon and selecting **Additional Resources > Revit Web Content Library** (see Figure 6-7).

Figure 6-6

Revit Architecture Market website

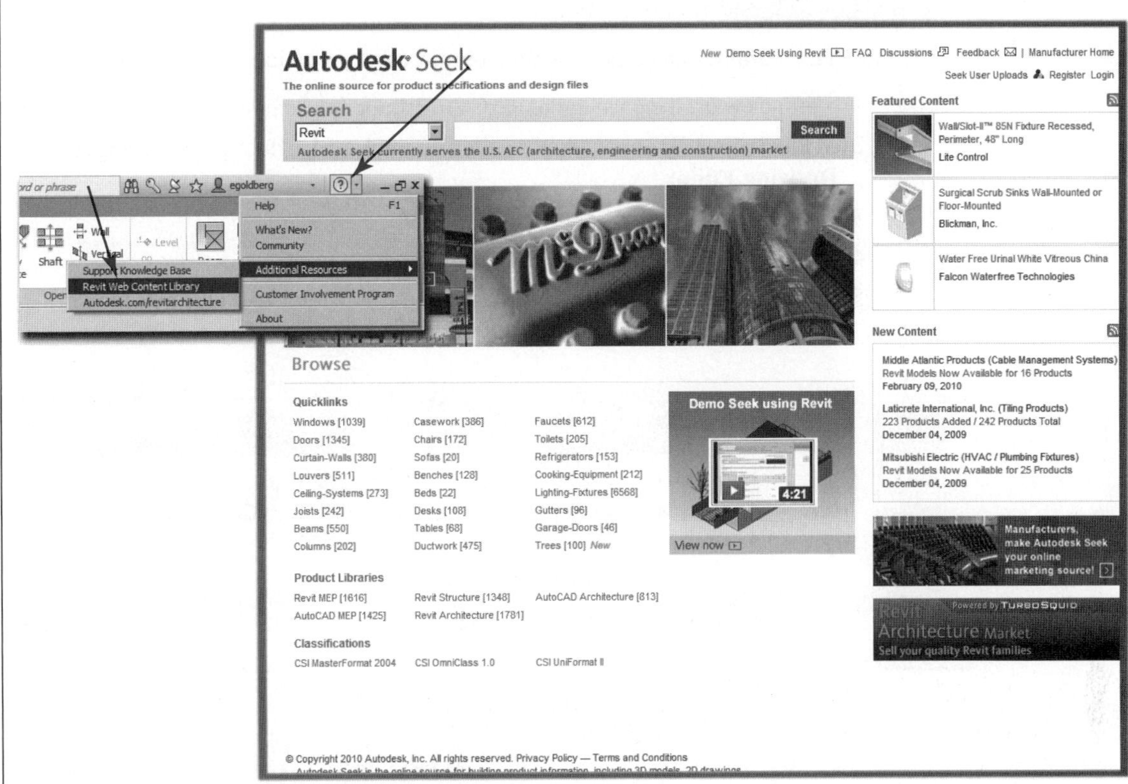

Figure 6-7

Autodesk Seek website
(Autodesk screen shots reprinted with the permission of Autodesk, Inc.)

Families

A *family* is a collection of objects, called *types*. A family groups elements with a common set of parameters, identical use, and similar graphical representation. Different types within a family may have different values of some or all parameters, but the set of parameters—their names and their meanings—are the same. All elements in Revit Architecture are family-based.

Type

A *type* is a member of a family. Each type has specific parameters, or **Type Parameters**, that are constant for all instances of the type that exist in a model. Types also have **Instance Parameters**, which may vary for each instance of a type in the model.

Revit Architecture provides a large number of predefined families for use in your project. If you need to create families for a certain project, Revit Architecture gives you that facility. Creating a new family is easy, because Revit Architecture provides many templates, including templates for doors, structural members, windows, furniture, and electrical fixtures, and lets you graphically draw the new family.

There are three types of families in Revit Architecture. They are **System Families**, **In-Place Families**, and **Loadable Families**.

System Families

System Families are the basic building blocks of Revit Architecture. Among these are **Curtain Systems**, **Curtain Wall Mullions**, **Detail Items**, **Floors**, **Model Text**, **Railings**, **Ramps**, **Roofs**, **Site (Pad)**, **Stairs**, **Structural Columns**, **Structural Foundations**, **Structural Framing**, and **Walls**. Unlike the other two family types, **System Families** are "hardwired" into the system. They cannot be created or deleted, but they can be modified.

EXERCISE 6-2 **IN-PLACE FAMILIES**

In-Place Families are created within a project and are unique to that project.

1. Start a new drawing using the RAC 2012\Imperial Templates\default.rte template.
2. In the **Project Browser**, double-click on the **Level 1** floor plan to bring it into the **Drawing Editor**.
3. Change the **Drawing Scale** to **1/4″ = 1′-0″**.
4. Set the **Detail Level** to **Medium**.
5. In the **Home** toolbar, select the **Component > Model In-Place** button to bring up the **Family Category and Parameters** dialog box (see Figure 6-8).

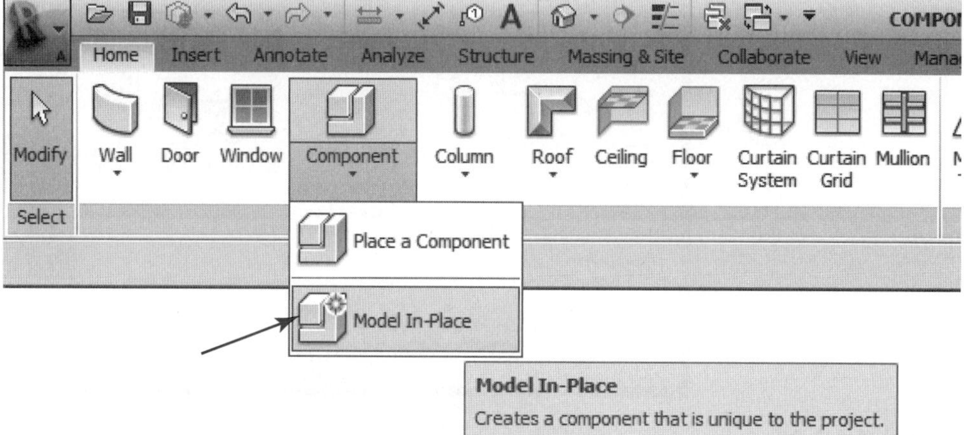

Figure 6-8

Model In-Place button

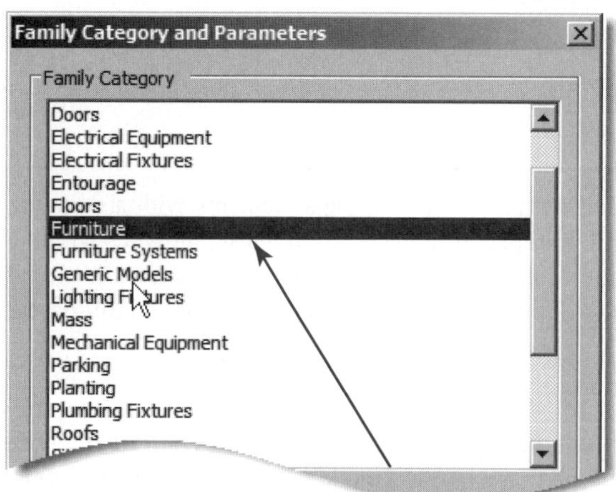

Figure 6-9

Family Category and Parameters dialog box

6. In the **Family Category and Parameters** dialog box, select **Furniture**, and press the **OK** button to bring up the **Name** dialog box (see Figure 6-9).
7. In the **Name** dialog box, enter **IN PLACE FAMILY TEST**, and press the **OK** button to return to the **Drawing Editor** and bring up the **Model In-Place Editor**.

NOTE:

The **Model In-Place Editor** is really just another set of toolbars dedicated specifically to building models inside a project.

You can tell when you are in a **Model In-Place Editor** or a **Family Editor** because the **Home** toolbar will include **Form** creation tools such as **Extrusion**, **Blend**, **Sweep**, **Void Forms**, and so on.

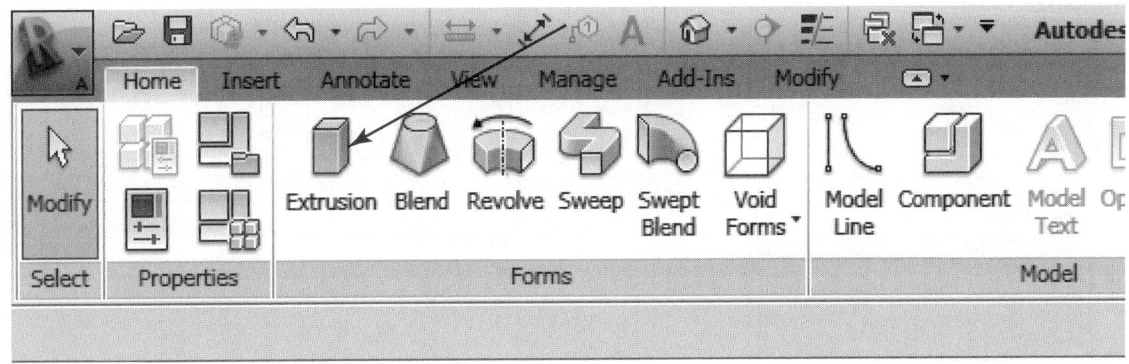

Figure 6-10

Model In-Place toolbar

8. In the **Model In-Place** toolbar, select the **Solid > Extrusion** button to bring up the **Modify | Create Extrusion** toolbar (see Figure 6-10).
9. In the **Modify | Create Extrusion** toolbar, select the **Rectangle** button from the **Draw** panel.
10. Place a **4′ × 8′** rectangle in the **Drawing Editor** (see Figure 6-11).
11. In the **Modify | Create Extrusion** toolbar, press the **Finish Edit Mode** button to bring up the **Modify Extrusion** toolbar (see Figure 6-12).
12. Change to the **Default 3D View**.

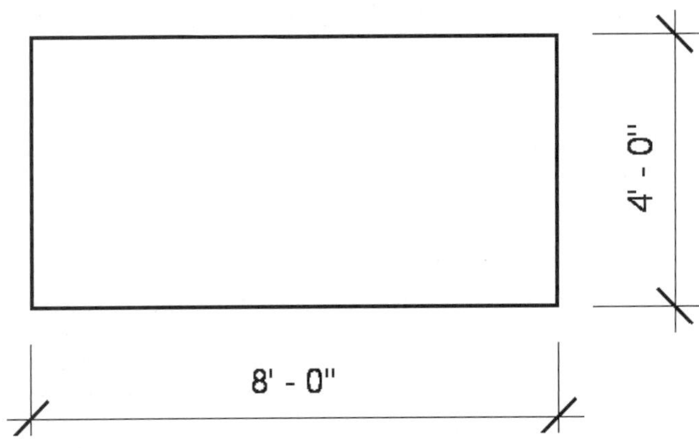

Figure 6-11

Drawing Editor

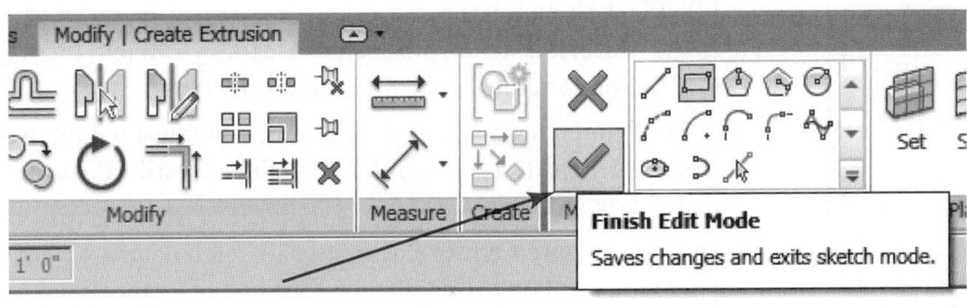

Figure 6-12

Modify Extrusion toolbar

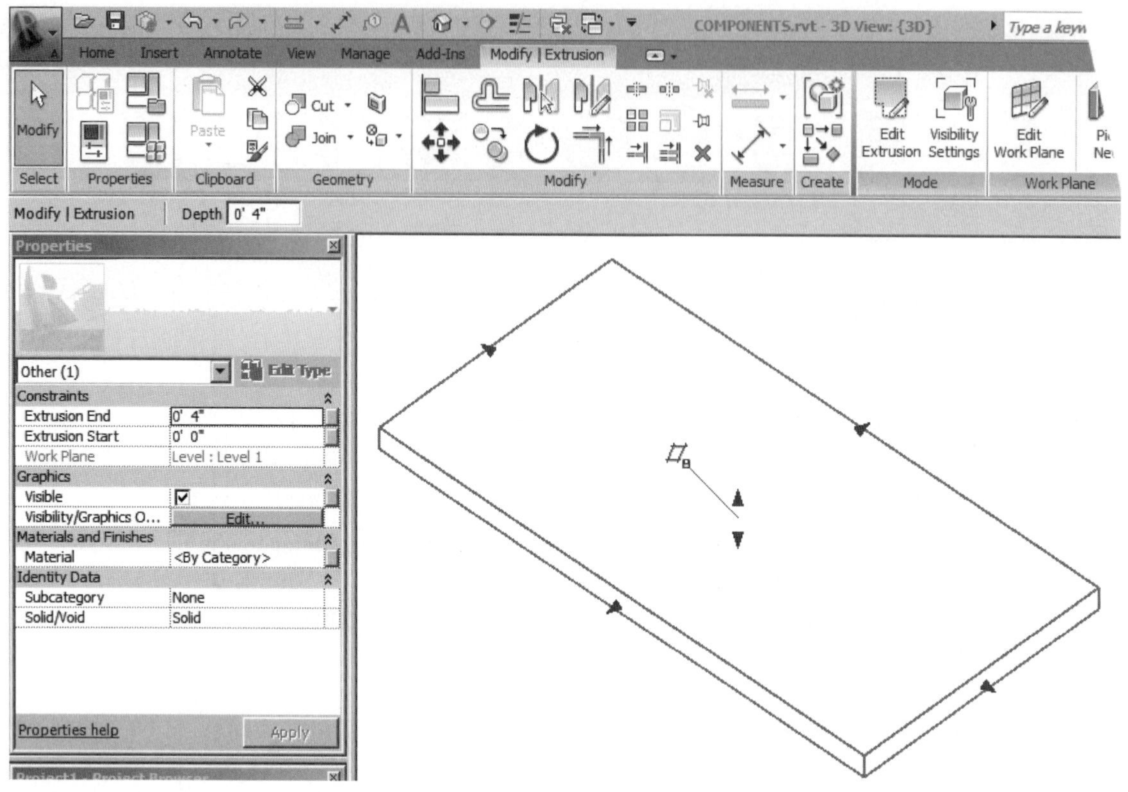

Figure 6-13

Options Bar

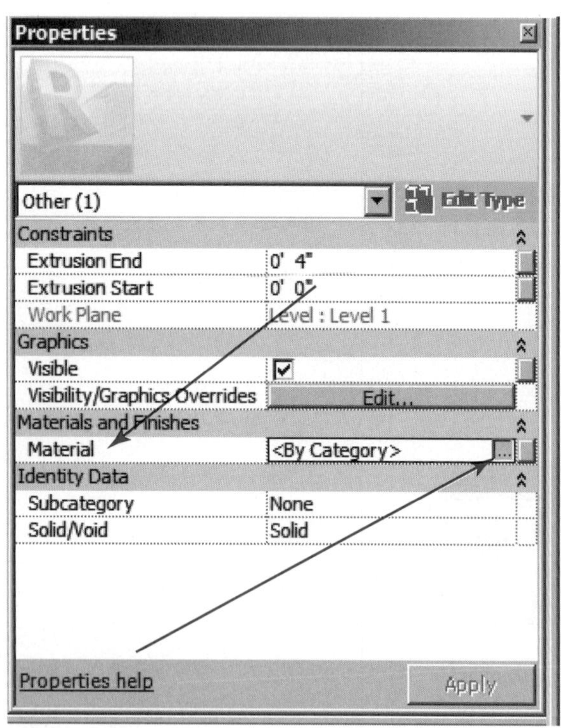

Figure 6-14

Material field

13. In the **Modify Extrusion** toolbar, in the **Options Bar**, enter **0′-4″** in the **Depth** field (see Figure 6-13).
14. Make sure the object is still selected (if not, select it).
15. In the **Properties** dialog box, select the **<By Category>** button in the **Material** field to create a button at the end of the field.

> **NOTE:**
>
> There will already be a button at the end of the field, but when you select **<By Category>**, another button will appear. Thus, you will have two buttons.

16. Pick the leftmost button that appears in the **Material** field to bring up the **Materials** dialog box (see Figures 6-14 and 6-15).
17. In the **Materials** dialog box, select **Masonry - Brick**; press the **OK** button to return to the **Properties** dialog box.
18. In the **Properties** dialog box, select the rightmost button in the **Material** field to bring up the **Associate Family Parameter** dialog box (see Figure 6-16).
19. In the **Associate Family Parameter** dialog box, press the **Add parameter** button to bring up the **Parameter Properties** dialog box.
20. In the **Parameter Properties** dialog box, select the **Family parameter** radio button, enter **TABLE TOP MATERIAL** in the

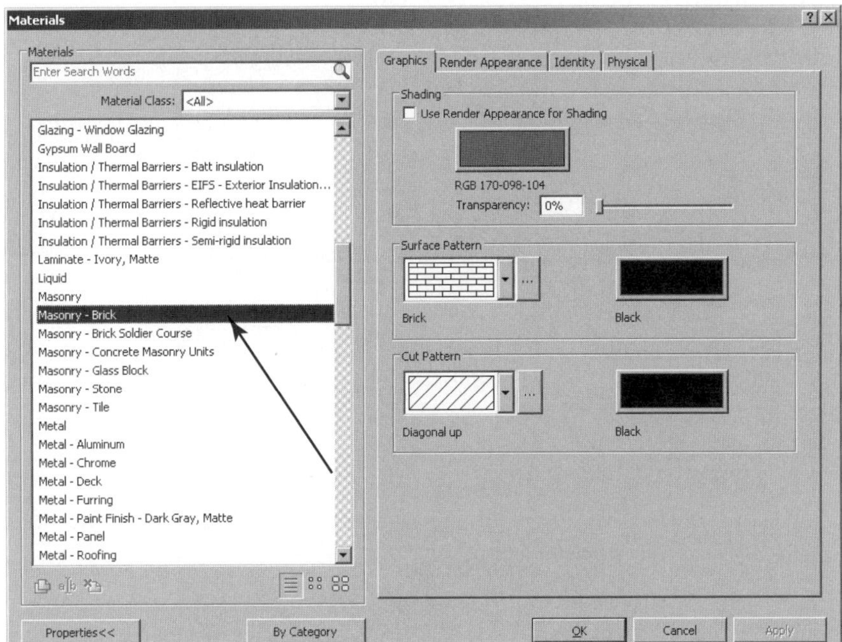

Figure 6-15

Materials dialog box

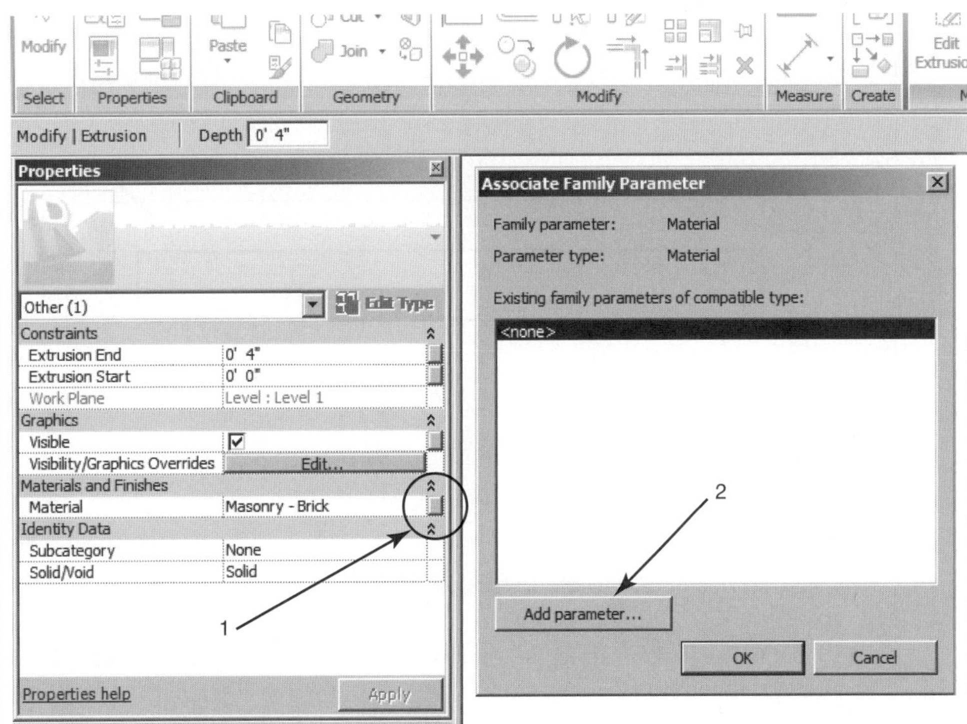

Figure 6-16

Associate Family Parameter dialog box

Name field, select **Materials and Finishes** from **Group parameters under:**, and select the **Type** radio button (see Figure 6-17).

21. Press the **OK** buttons to return to the **Drawing Editor**.
22. Change to the **Level 1** floor plan.
23. Select the **Home** tab to open the **Home** toolbar (remember, you are still in the **Model In-Place Editor**).

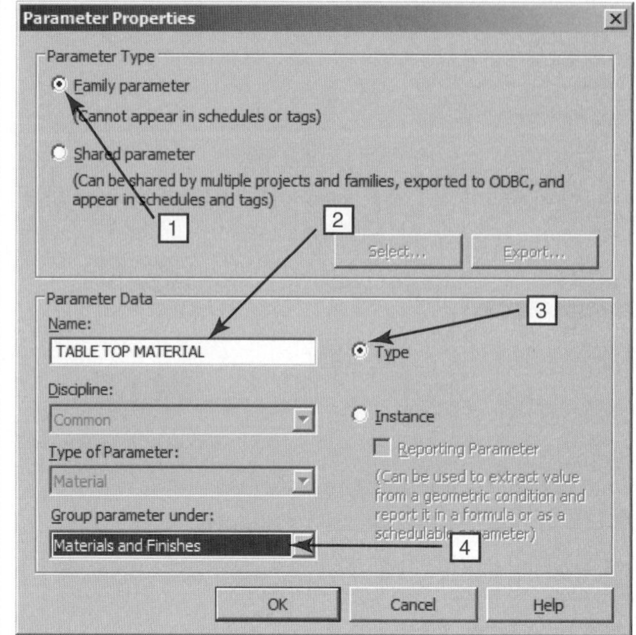

Figure 6-17

Parameter Properties dialog box

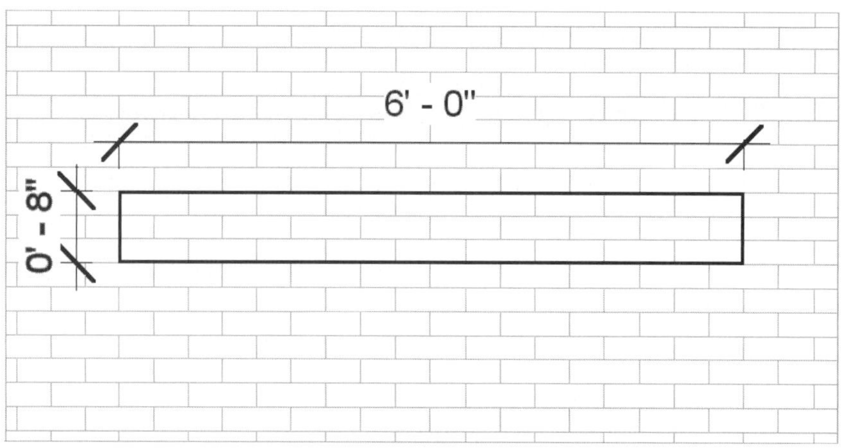

Figure 6-18

Rectangle created in the **Create Extrusion** toolbar

24. In the **Home** toolbar, select the **Extrusion** button to bring up the **Modify | Create Extrusion** toolbar.
25. In the **Modify | Create Extrusion** toolbar, select the **Rectangle** button from the **Draw** panel.
26. Place a **6′ × 8″** rectangle in the center of the table top (see Figure 6-18).
27. In the **Modify | Create Extrusion** toolbar, press the **Finish Edit Mode** button to create the object.
28. Change to the **Default 3D View**.
29. Select the extrusion you just created to bring up the **Properties** dialog box.
30. In the **Properties** dialog box, select the **Masonry – Brick** button in the **Material** field to create a button at the end of the field.

NOTE:

A button will already be at the end of the field, but when you select **Masonry – Brick**, another button will appear. Thus, you will have two buttons.

31. Pick the leftmost button that appears in the **Material** field to bring up the **Materials** dialog box.
32. In the **Materials** dialog box, select **Siding – Clapboard**, and press the **OK** button to return to the **Properties** dialog box.
33. In the **Instance Properties** dialog box, select the rightmost button in the **Material** field to bring up the **Associate Family Parameter** dialog box.
34. In the **Associate Family Parameter** dialog box, press the **Add parameter** button to bring up the **Parameter Properties** dialog box.
35. In the **Parameter Properties** dialog box, select the **Family parameter** radio button, enter **TABLE LEG** in the **Name** field, select **Materials and Finishes** from **Group parameters under:**, and select the **Type** radio button.
36. Press the **OK** buttons to return to the **Model In-Place Editor**.
37. In any toolbar, press the **Finish Model** button to create the table.
38. Select the table to bring up the **Modify | Furniture** toolbar.
39. In the **Modify | Furniture** toolbar, select the **Type Properties** button to bring up the **Type Properties** dialog box.
40. In the **Type Properties** dialog box, select the buttons at the right side of the **TABLE TOP** and **TABLE LEG Materials and Finishes** to bring up the **Materials** dialog box.
41. Change the **Materials** for the **TABLE TOP** and **TABLE LEG** (see Figures 6-19 and 6-20).

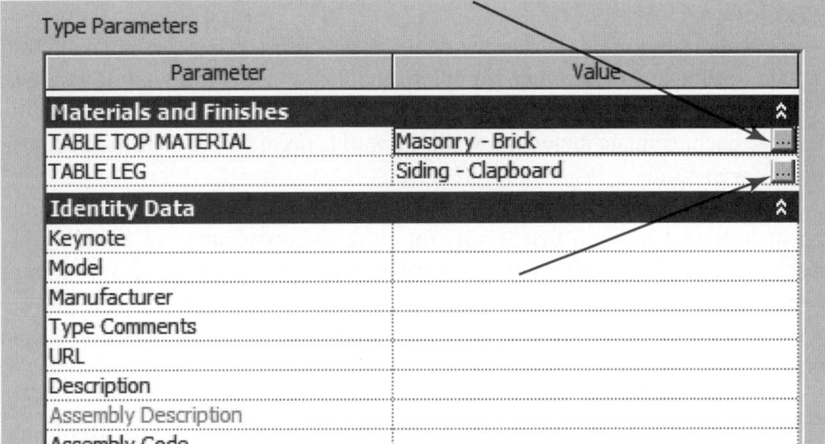

Figure 6-19

Type Parameters for **Materials and Finishes**

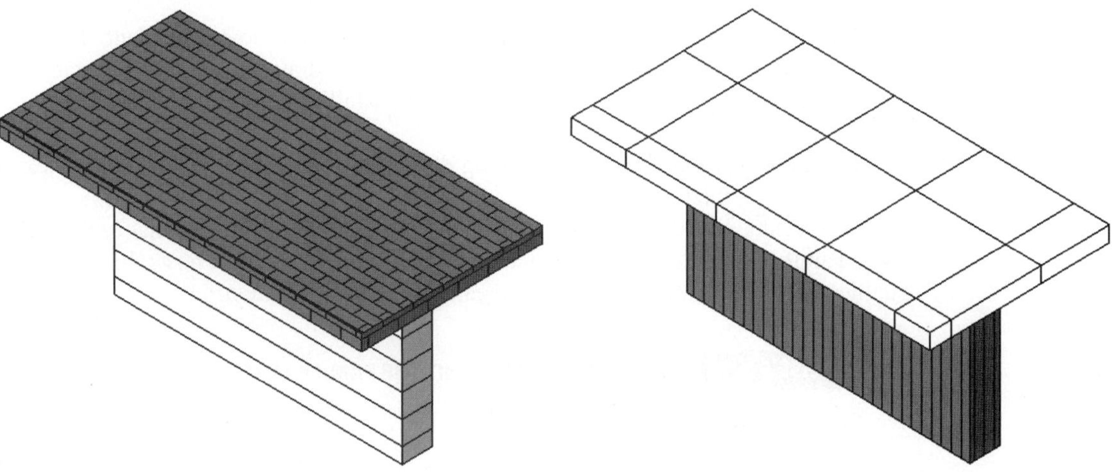

Figure 6-20

Table Top and **Table Leg** drawings

You have just created an **In-Place Family** with material parameters that you can change. Try creating your own family with different parameters.

42. Save the file as **IN PLACE FAMILIES**.

Creating Families

When you create a family, Revit Architecture provides you with a template that serves as a building block and contains most of the information needed by Revit Architecture to place the family in the project. Among other elements, the template can include reference planes, dimensions, and predefined geometry, such as window trim.

Following are the basic kinds of family templates:

- Wall-based
- Ceiling-based
- Floor-based
- Roof-based
- Standalone
- Line-based
- Face-based

Wall-based, ceiling-based, floor-based, and roof-based templates are known as *host-based templates*. A host-based family can be placed in a project only if an element of its host type is present.

The wall-based template is for components inserted into walls. Wall components can include openings, so that when you place the component on a wall, it also cuts an opening in the wall. Some examples of wall-based components include doors, windows, and lighting fixtures. Each template includes a wall; the wall is necessary for showing how the component fits in a wall.

The ceiling-based template is for components inserted into ceilings. Ceiling components can include openings, so that when you place the component on a ceiling, it also cuts an opening in the ceiling. Examples of ceiling-based families include sprinklers and recessed lighting fixtures.

The floor-based template is for components inserted into floors. Floor components can include openings, so that when you place the component on a floor, it also cuts an opening in the floor. An example of a floor-based family is a heating register.

The roof-based template is for components inserted into roofs. Roof components can include openings, so that when you place the component on a roof, it also cuts an opening in the roof. Examples of roof-based families include soffits and fans.

The standalone template is for components that are not host-dependent. A standalone component can appear anywhere in a model and can be dimensioned to other standalone or host-based components. Examples of standalone families include columns, furniture, and appliances.

The line-based template is for creating detail and model families that use 2-pick placement similar to structural beams.

The face-based template is for creating work plane–based families that can modify their hosts. Families created from the template can make complex cuts in hosts. Instances of these families can be placed on any surface, regardless of its orientation.

EXERCISE 6-3 **LOADABLE FAMILIES AND THE FAMILY EDITOR**

Creating a Door

1. Start a new drawing using the RAC 2012\Imperial Templates\default.rte template.
2. Select **File > New > Family** from the **Application** main menu to bring up the **New Family – Select Template File** dialog box (see Figure 6-21).

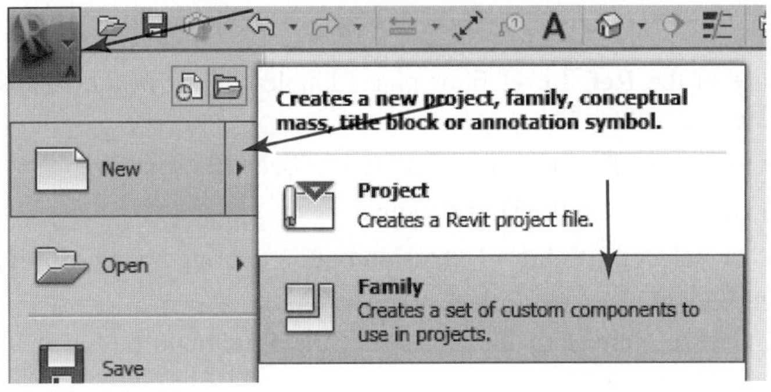

Figure 6-21

Select > New > Family option

3. In the **New Family – Select Template File** dialog box, select **Door.rft**, and press the **Open** button (see Figure 6-22).

You are now in the **Family Editor**. In the **Family Editor**, you can make an object "parametric." This means that you can make the object modifiable through the **Instance Properties** dialog box.

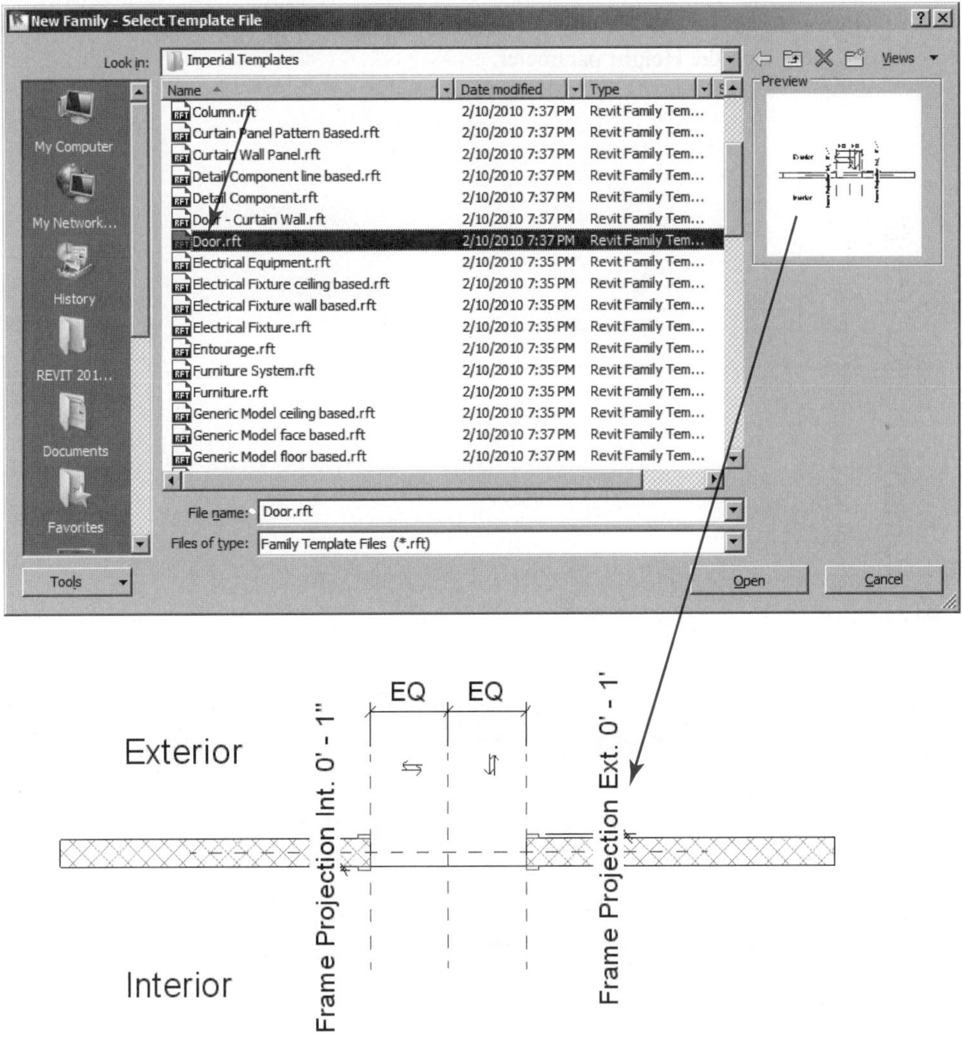

Figure 6-22

New Family – Select Template File dialog box

The Door

4. Make sure you are in the **Ref. Level** floor plan (double-click it in the **Project Browser** if you are not).
5. Change the scale to **1″ = 1′-0″** so that the working text becomes smaller.
6. Select the **Home** tab to bring up the **Home** toolbar.
7. In the **Home** toolbar, select the **Solid > Extrusion** button to bring up the **Modify | Create Extrusion** toolbar.
8. In the **Modify | Create Extrusion** toolbar, select the **Rectangle** button in the **Draw** panel.
9. Place a **3′-0″** × **1 3/4″** rectangle as shown in Figure 6-23.
10. In the **Project Browser**, change to the **Exterior Elevation**, and notice that the door height is dimensioned to **7′-0″** and labeled **Height**.
11. Press the **OK** button to close the **Family Types** dialog box.
12. In the **Properties** dialog box, select the right button in the **Extrusion End** field to bring up the **Associate Family Parameter** dialog box.
13. In the **Associate Family Parameter** dialog box, pick the **Height** parameter.

> **NOTE:**
> **Height** is a parametric dimension in this template. To see all the parametric dimensions, select the **Family Types** button in the **Modify | Create Extrusion** toolbar to open the **Family Types** dialog box. Notice that the **Height** and **Width** for the **Door** template have been preset to **7′-0″** and **3′-0″** (see Figures 6-24 and 6-25).

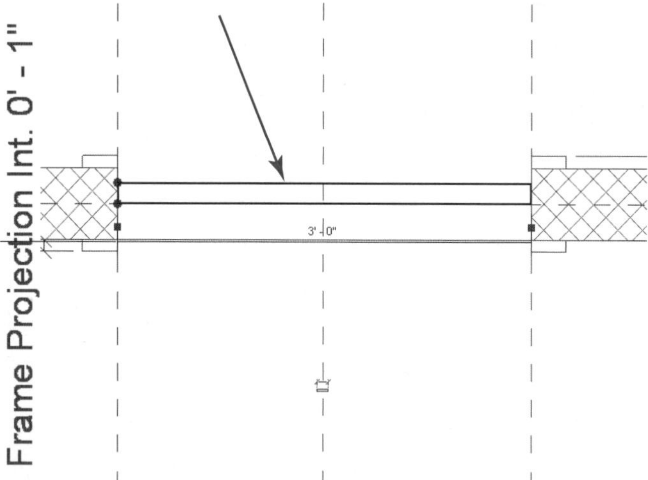

Figure 6-23

Rectangle created in the **Modify | Create Extrusion** toolbar

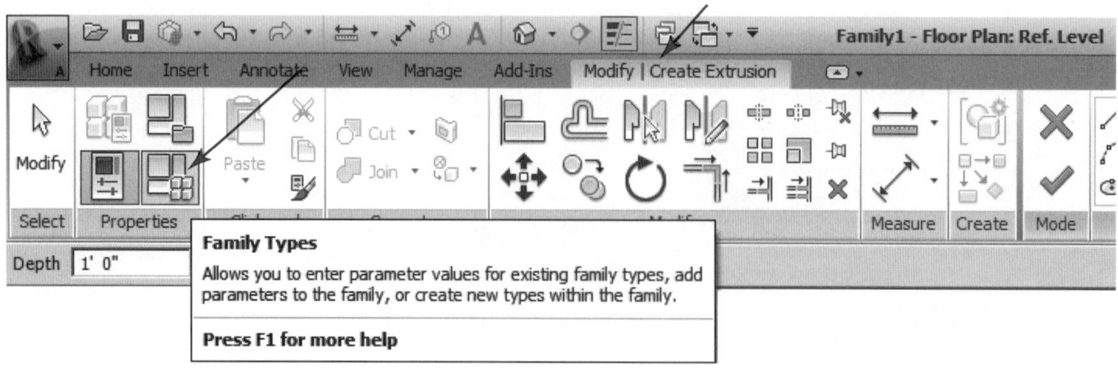

Figure 6-24

Parameter values in **Family Types**

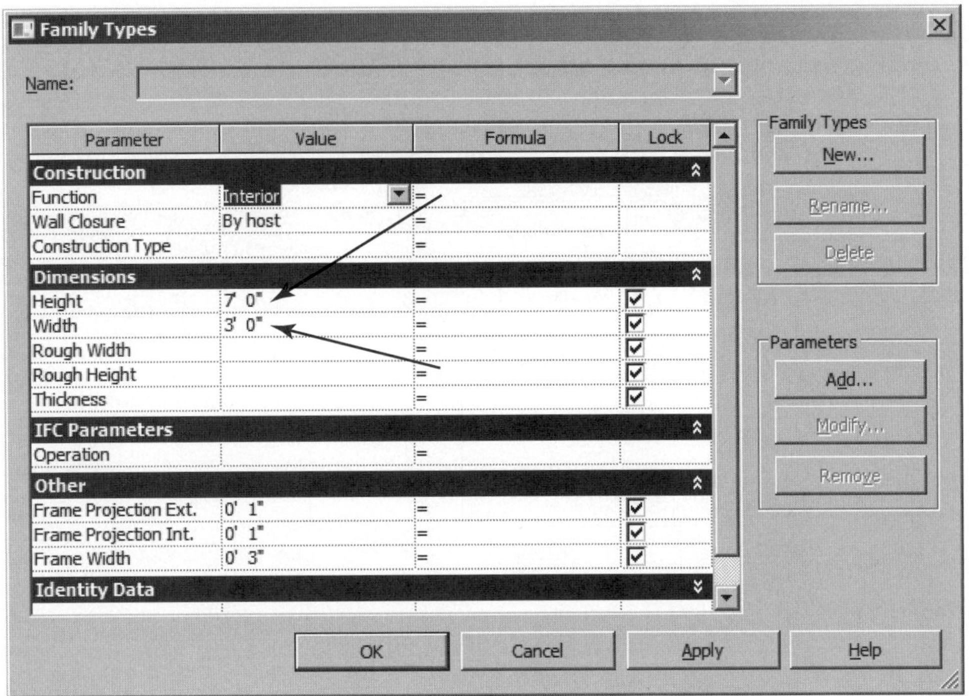

Figure 6-25

Family Types dialog box

This will make the height of the **Extrusion** (door you are creating) match the height of the door opening (see Figure 6-26).

14. Press the **OK** buttons to return to the **Drawing Editor**.
15. In the **Modify | Create Extrusion** toolbar, press the **Finish Extrusion** button to finish the extrusion.

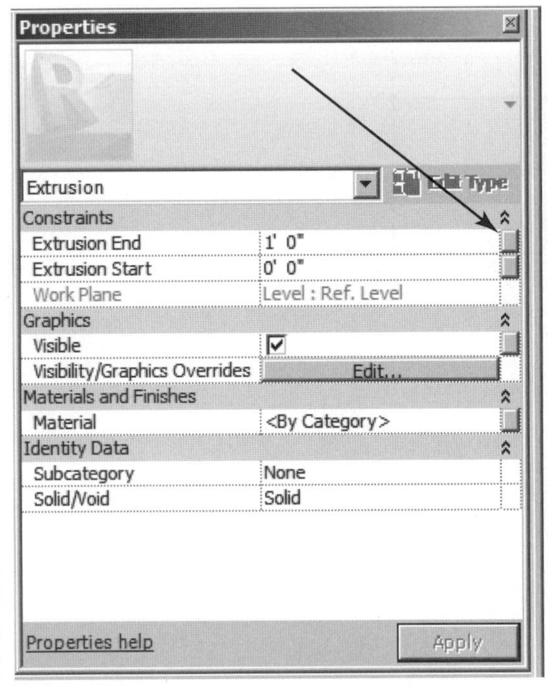

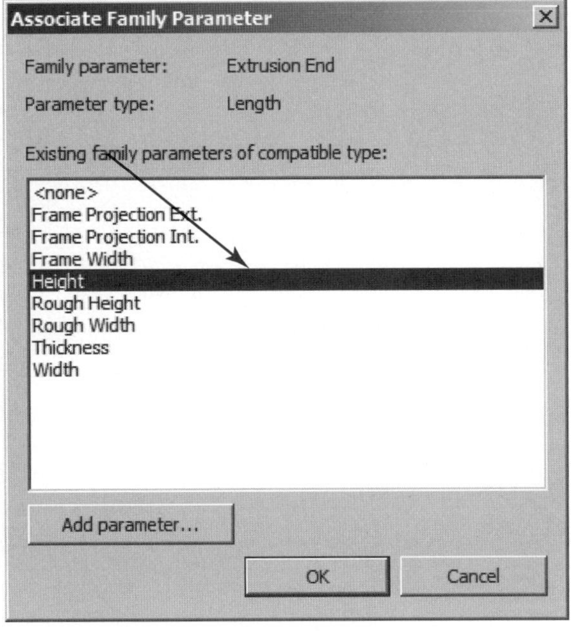

Figure 6-26

Associate Family Parameter dialog box

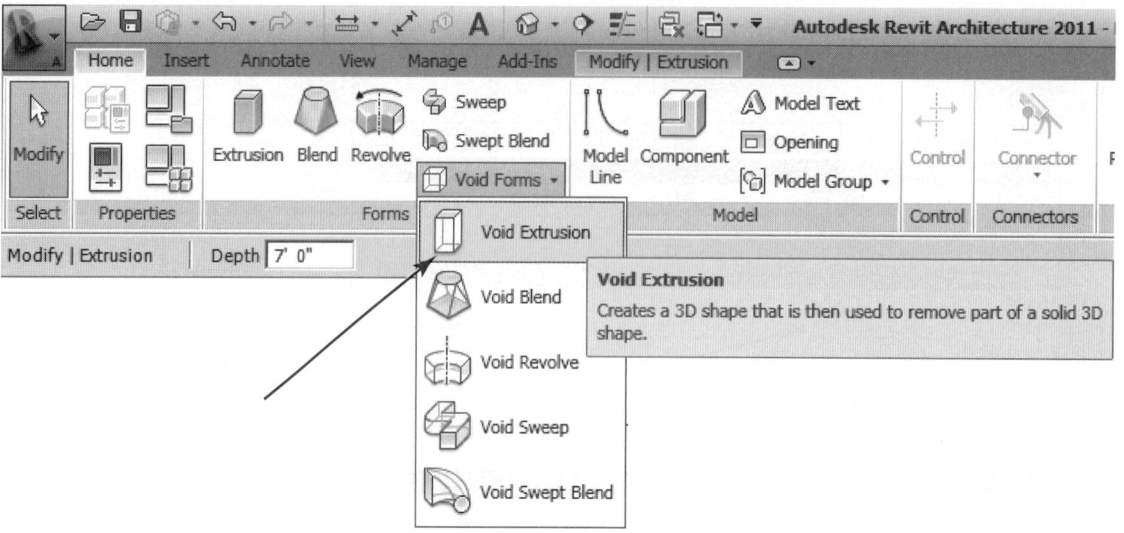

Figure 6-27

Void Extrusion button

You have now extruded a 3D door and opening whose heights are controlled by the **Height** parameter.

16. In the **Home** toolbar, select the **Void Forms > Void Extrusion** button to bring up the **Modify | Create Void Extrusion** toolbar (see Figure 6-27).
17. In the **Modify | Create Void Extrusion** toolbar, select the **Rectangle** button in the **Draw** panel.
18. Place a **2′-0″** × **2′-0″** rectangle as shown in Figure 6-28.
19. Change to the **Default 3D View**.
20. Change the **Drawing Scale** to **1″ = 1′-0″**.

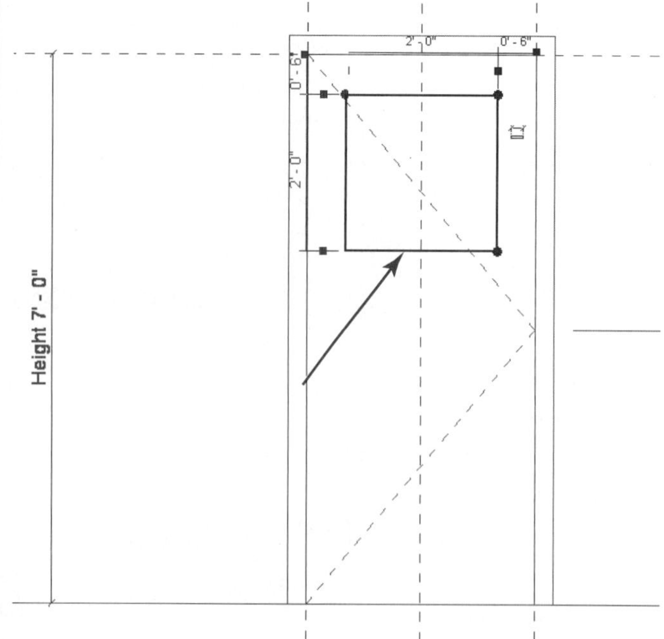

Figure 6-28

Rectangle created in the **Modify | Create Void Extrusion** toolbar

21. In the **Options Bar**, enter **-1′-0″** in the **Depth** field (this will extrude the **Void Extrusion** in the negative direction).
22. In the **Modify | Create Void Extrusion** toolbar, press the **Finish Edit Mode** button (green check mark) to complete the void extrusion, and return to the **Family Editor**.

Notice that the door now has a 2′ × 2′ opening (see Figure 6-29).

23. Return to the **Exterior Elevation**, and deselect the door by pressing the <**Esc**> key.
24. Select the **Annotate** tab to bring up the **Annotate** toolbar.
25. In the **Annotate** toolbar, select the **Aligned** button in the **Dimensions** panel.
26. Select the places shown in Figure 6-30 to dimension the opening.
27. Select the **2′-0″** dimension at the right side of the opening to bring up the **Modify | Dimensions** toolbar.

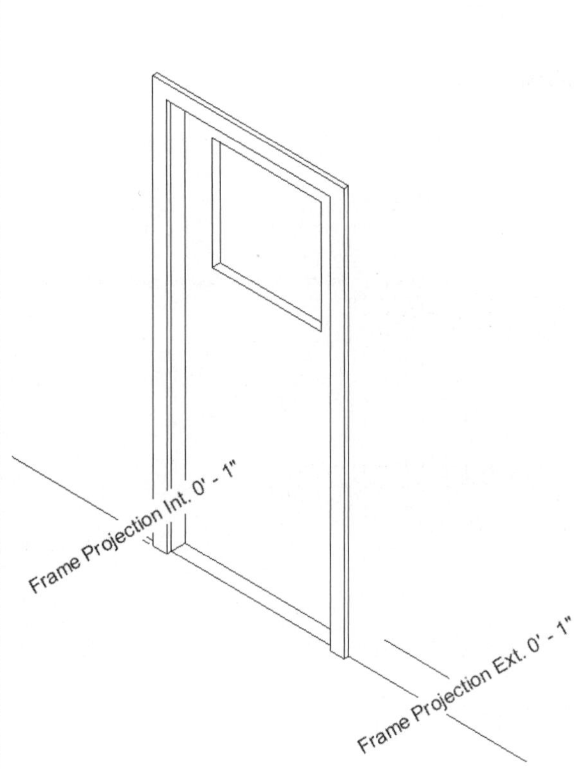

Figure 6-29

Opening in door created using **Extrusion**

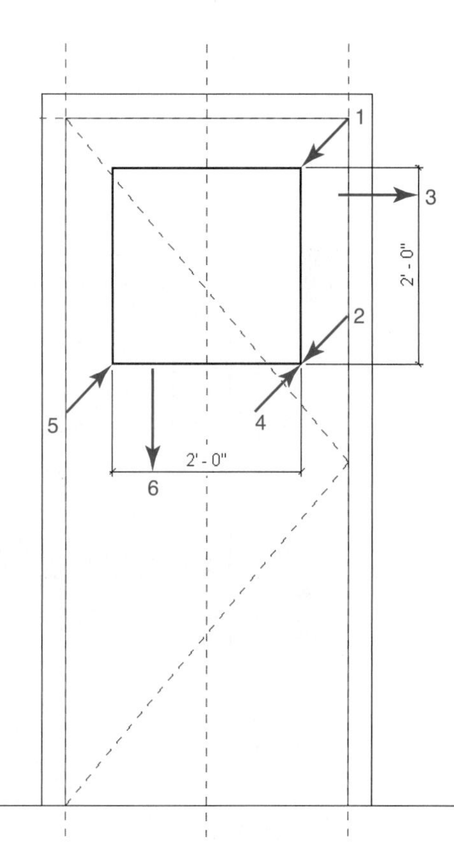

Figure 6-30

Dimensioned opening

Adding a New Parameter

28. In the **Options Bar**, select **<Add parameter...>** from the **Label** drop-down list to bring up the **Parameter Properties** dialog box (see Figure 6-31).
29. In the **Parameter Properties** dialog box, select the **Family parameter** radio button, enter **OPENING HEIGHT** in the **Name** field, select **Dimensions** from **Group parameters under:**, select the **Type** radio button, and then press the **OK** button (see Figure 6-32).

NOTE:

The other parameters you see in the **Label** list control different dimensions in the **Family**, thus controlling the size of different components in the **Family** object. You will be adding a new controllable parameter to the object.

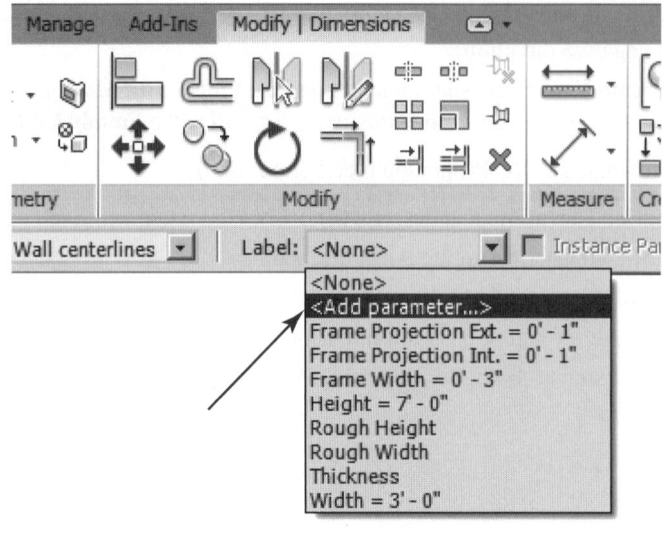

Figure 6-31

Parameter Properties dialog box

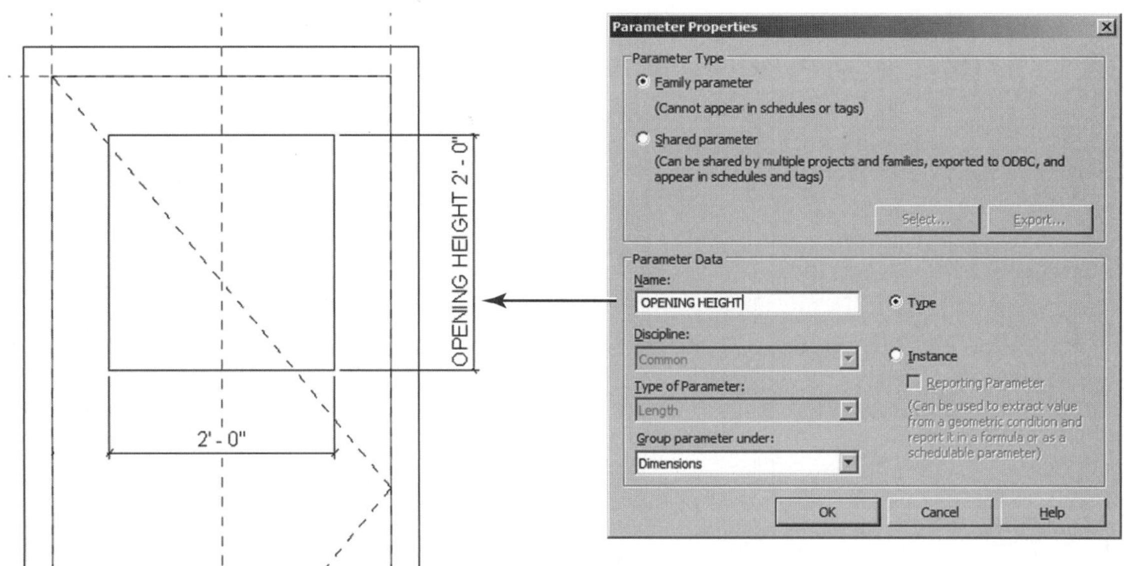

Figure 6-32

OPENING HEIGHT parameters

30. Repeat Step 29 creating the **OPENING WIDTH**, **LEFT STILE**, and **TOP STILE** parameters.
31. Select the **Types** button in the **Create Extrusion** toolbar to open the **Family Types** dialog box.

Notice that the new parameters you just created are in the **Family Types** dialog box (see Figure 6-33).

32. Select **File > Save As > Family** from the **Application** menu, and save the **TEST DOOR** family in your **Imperial Library** folder.

EXERCISE 6-4 USING THE NEW TEST DOOR FAMILY

1. Start a new drawing using the RAC 2012\Imperial Templates\default.rte template.
2. In the **Project Browser**, double-click **Floor Plans > Level 1**.

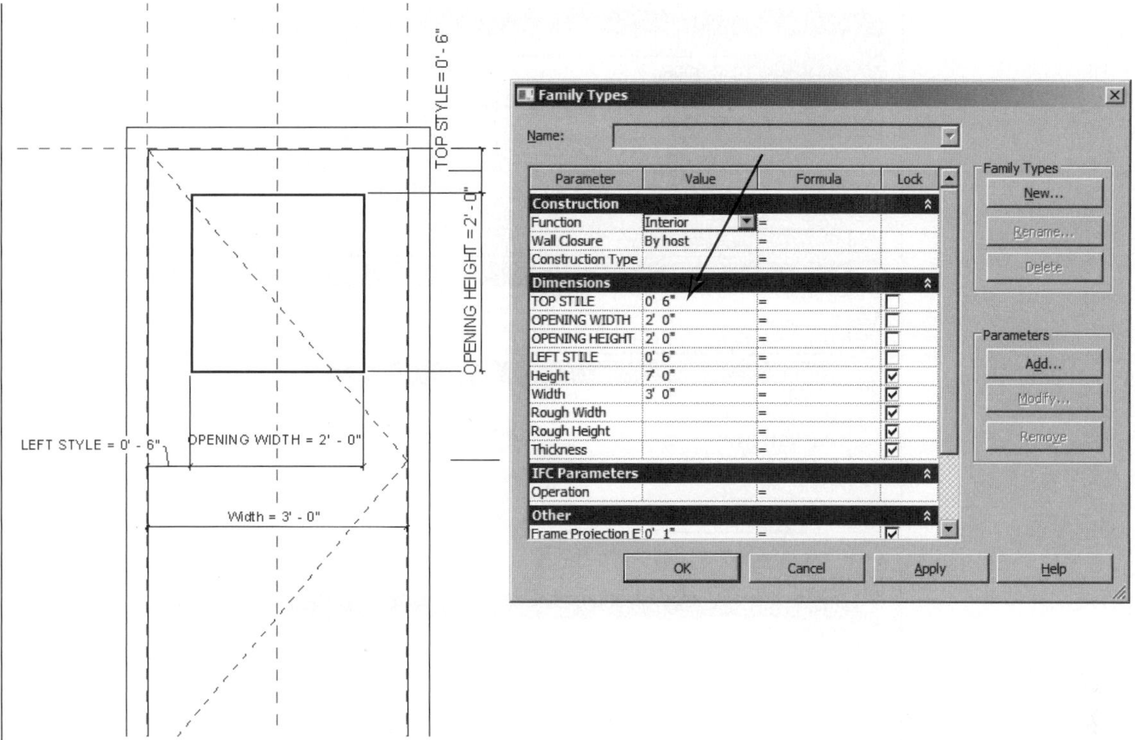

Figure 6-33

Options in **Family Types** dialog box

3. Change the **Drawing Scale** to **1/4″** = **1′-0″**.
4. Set the **Detail Level** to **Medium**.
5. Select the **Wall** button in the **Home** toolbar.
6. Place a **Basic Wall: Generic - 8″** wall **10′-0″** high and **10′-0″** long in the **Drawing Editor**.
7. Select the **Insert** tab to bring up the **Insert** toolbar.
8. In the **Insert** toolbar, select the **Load Family** button to open the **Load Family** dialog box.
9. In the **Load Family** dialog box, locate the **TEST DOOR** family you created in the previous exercise.
10. In the **Home** toolbar, select the **Door** button.
11. From the **Properties** dialog box, select the **TEST DOOR**.
12. Place the **TEST DOOR** into the wall.
13. Change to the **Default 3D View**.
14. Select the door to bring up the **Properties** dialog box.
15. In the **Properties** dialog box, select the **Edit Type** button near the top right to bring up the **Type Properties** dialog box.
16. In the **Type Properties** dialog box, change the **OPENING WIDTH** to **2′-6″**, **OPENING HEIGHT** to **5′-0″**, the **LEFT STILE** to **3″**, and then press the **OK** button to return to the **Drawing Editor** (see Figure 6-34).

The door opening changes because it is parametrically controlled from the **Type Properties** dialog box (see Figure 6-35).

17. Save the file as **FAMILY EDITOR**.

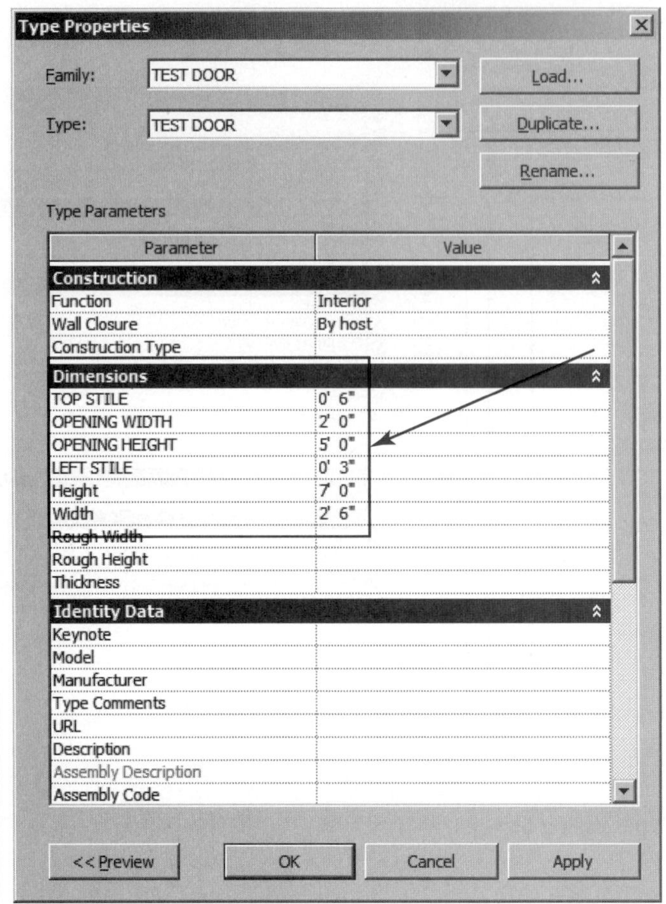

Figure 6-34

Type Properties dialog box

Figure 6-35

Door opening changes

Chapter Summary

This chapter explained how to use and modify **Components** and **Families** in Revit Architecture 2012. Among the subjects discussed were **System Families, In-Place Families, Loadable Families**, and the **Family Editor**. Also shown were methods for downloading and importing **Families** from the Internet.

Chapter Test Questions

Multiple Choice

Circle the correct answer.

1. **Family** templates are used
   a. To create standard title blocks.
   b. To hand trace with pencil on prints.
   c. As a basis for the creation of different types of components.
   d. To create annotations.
2. The **Component** button is located in which toolbar?
   a. The **Home** toolbar
   b. The **Annotation** toolbar
   c. The **Massing & Site** toolbar
   d. The **Structure** toolbar
3. The **Place Component** button
   a. Starts the **Family Editor**.
   b. Places content.
   c. Opens the **Edit Type** dialog box for a component.
   d. Loads a **Family**.
4. A **Void Extrusion**
   a. Cancels an extrusion.
   b. Creates an extrusion in the negative "Y" direction.
   c. Subtracts from a form.
   d. Creates a visible extrusion that is mathematically void.
5. A **Family** is a collection of objects, called
   a. **Pieces**.
   b. **Types**.
   c. **Subfamilies**.
   d. None of the above

True or False

Circle the correct answer.

1. **True or False:** A floor is not a "host object."
2. **True or False: Family** parameters cannot be modified.
3. **True or False:** The standalone **Family** template is for components that are not host-dependent.
4. **True or False:** There are four types of **Families** in Revit Architecture.
5. **True or False:** You create objects in the **Family Editor** using tools similar to those in the **Massing & Site** toolbar. The difference in the **Family Editor** is that you can make the objects parametric.

Questions

1. What is the definition of a Revit Architecture 2012 **Family**?
2. What is the definition of a Revit Architecture 2012 **Component**?
3. What is the purpose of an **In-Place Family**?
4. What is a **Loadable Family**?
5. Where do you find the **Add parameter** drop-down list?

CHAPTER

7 Roofs and Ceilings

CHAPTER OBJECTIVES

- Learn how to place a **Roof by Footprint**.
- Learn how to make a wall meet a roof.
- Learn how to change the **Rafter Cut**.
- Learn how to modify a roof slope with the **Slope Arrow**.
- Learn how to create a hole in a roof.
- Learn how to modify a flat roof slab by adding and moving vertices.
- Learn how to create a roof by **Extrusion**.
- Learn how to use the **Join/ Unjoin Roof** button.
- Learn how to create dormers.
- Learn how to place gutters.
- Learn how to create a **Roof Family**.
- Learn how to place and modify **Ceilings**.

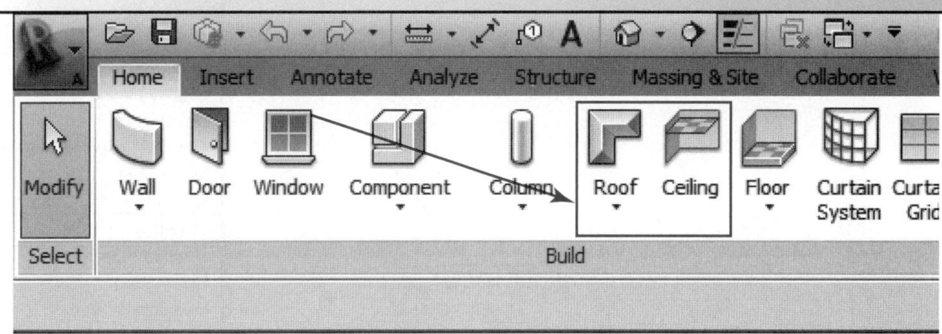

Introduction

In Revit Architecture, roofs can be placed by three methods: **Roof by Footprint**, **Roof by Extrusion**, and **Roof by Face**. **Roof by Footprint** and **Roof by Extrusion** are explained in this chapter, along with instructions on modifying and creating roofs and placing ceilings.

> **NOTE:**
> **Roof by Face** is used to place a roof on any surface of a **Mass** model. Instructions on how to use this feature are covered in Chapter 15 on Massing & Site.

EXERCISE 7-1 ROOF BY FOOTPRINT

1. Start a new drawing using the RAC 2012\Imperial Templates\default.rte template.
2. In the **Project Browser**, double-click on the **LEVEL 1** floor plan to bring it into the **Drawing Editor**.
3. Change the **Drawing Scale** to **1/4″ = 1′-0″**.
4. Set the **Detail Level** to **Medium**.
5. Select the **Home** tab to bring up the **Home** toolbar.
6. In the **Home** toolbar, select the **Wall** button to bring up the **Modify | Place Wall** toolbar.
7. In the **Modify | Place Wall** toolbar, select the **Rectangle** button in the **Draw** panel.
8. Place a **15′-0″** × **30′-0″** rectangular enclosure using a **10′-0″** high **Generic - 8″** wall.
9. Double-click the **South Elevation** in the **Project Browser** to bring it into your workspace.
10. In the **South Elevation**, double-click on the **Level 2** name, and change it to **ROOF BASE**.

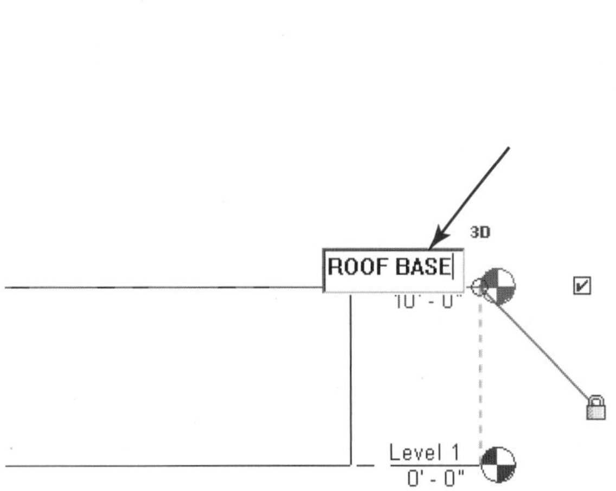

Figure 7-1

Changing a name of an element in a drawing

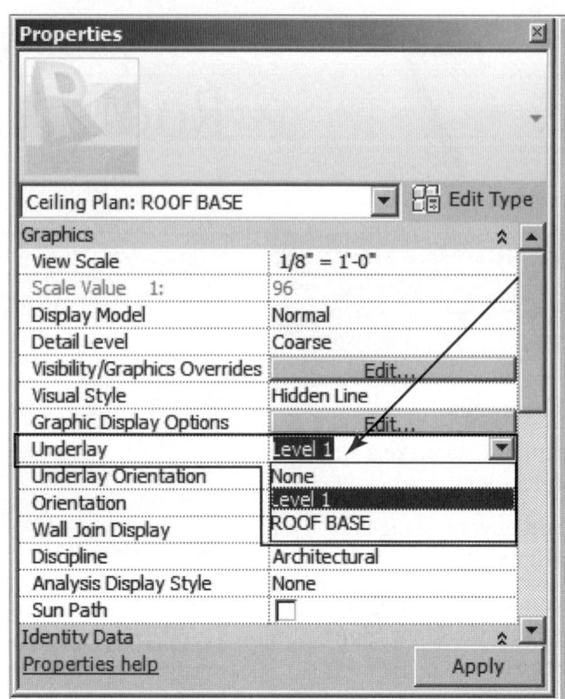

Figure 7-2

Underlay drop-down list in **Properties** dialog box

You can do this by clicking on and entering **ROOF BASE** from the keyboard (see Figure 7-1).

11. Press the **Yes** button at the **Revit** dialog box asking whether you would like to rename corresponding views (**Ceiling Views**).
12. Make sure the **ROOF BASE** height is 10′-0″ by clicking on it on an elevation view and entering **10′-0″** from the keyboard.
13. In the **Project Browser**, double-click on **ROOF BASE** to bring it into the **Drawing Editor**.

You should see **Level 1** in halftone.

a. If you do not see an underlay of **Level 1**, click in an empty area in the **Drawing Editor** to bring up the **Properties** dialog box.
b. In the **Properties** dialog box, select **Level 1** from the **Underlay** drop-down list (see Figure 7-2).

14. Select the **Home** tab again to bring up the **Home** toolbar.
15. In the **Home** toolbar, select the **Roof > Roof by Footprint** button to bring up the **Modify | Create Roof Footprint** toolbar (see Figure 7-3).
16. In the **Modify | Create Roof Footprint** toolbar, select the **Pick Walls** button in the **Draw** panel.
17. In the **Options Bar**, select the **Defines Slope** check box, and enter **1′-0″** in the **Overhang** field (see Figure 7-4).
18. Move your cursor above and below the northmost wall, and notice the dashed line that appears. This is the overhang location.
19. Again move your cursor above the northmost wall, and click the left mouse button.

A blue line and open angle with a number will appear above the wall. The line is the edge of the overhang, and the angle number represents the roof rise per foot of roof run.

20. Repeat Steps 12–13 for the rest of the walls (see Figure 7-5).
21. In the **Properties** dialog box, select the **Edit Type** button to bring up the **Type Properties** dialog box.

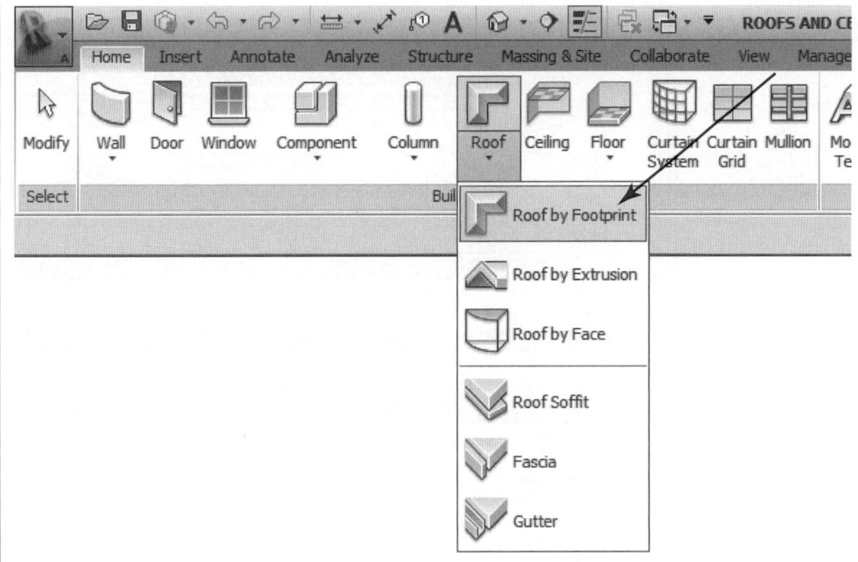

Figure 7-3

Roof by Footprint button

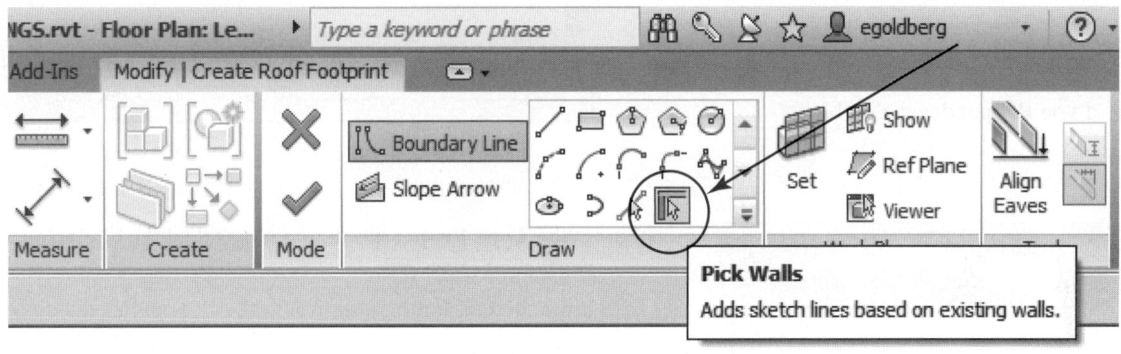

Figure 7-4

Defines Slope check box

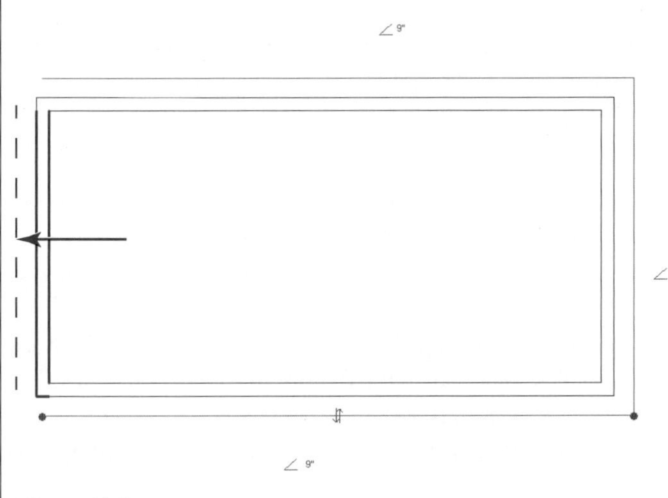

Figure 7-5

Overhang location

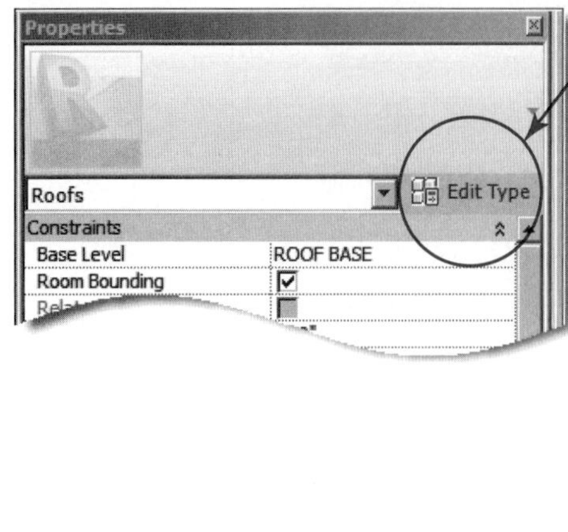

Figure 7-6

Type Properties dialog box

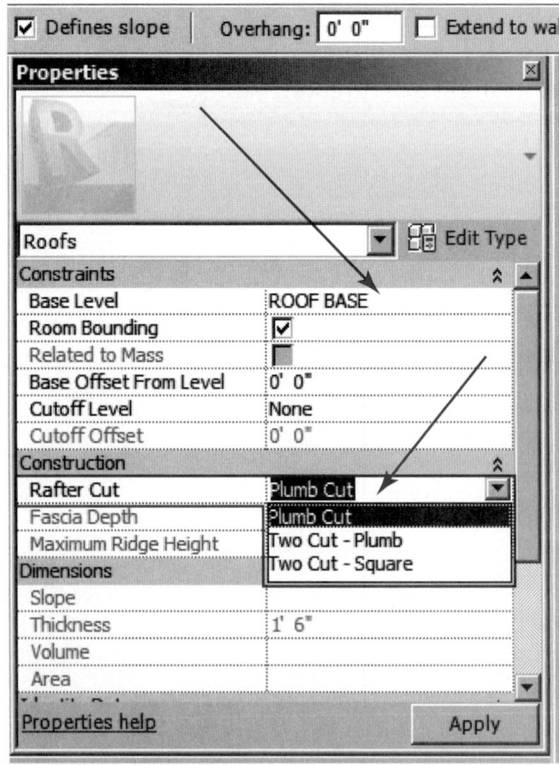

Figure 7-7

Select **ROOF** settings in the **Properties** dialog box

22. In the **Type Properties** dialog box, select the **Generic - 12″ roof** (see Figure 7-6).
23. Press the **OK** button to return to the **Properties** dialog box.
24. In the **Properties** dialog box, set the settings shown in Figure 7-7.

NOTE:

If you click on any of the blue lines, the **Rise** number **(9/)** will appear. You can change the rise there or in the **Slope** field of the **Properties** dialog box (see Figure 7-8).

25. Press the **Finish Edit Mode** button in the **Modify | Create Roof Footprint** toolbar (see Figure 7-9).
26. Select **No** when the **Revit** dialog box asks whether you would like to attach the highlighted walls to the roof.
27. Press the **Default 3D View** button on the **Quick Access** toolbar to change to the **Default 3D View** (see Figure 7-10).
28. Select the **Shadows** button in the **View Control Bar** at the bottom of the **Drawing Editor**, and select the **Shadows On** button (see Figure 7-11).
29. Next, select the **Sun Settings** button in the **Sun Path** button to bring up the **Sun Settings** dialog box (see Figure 7-12).

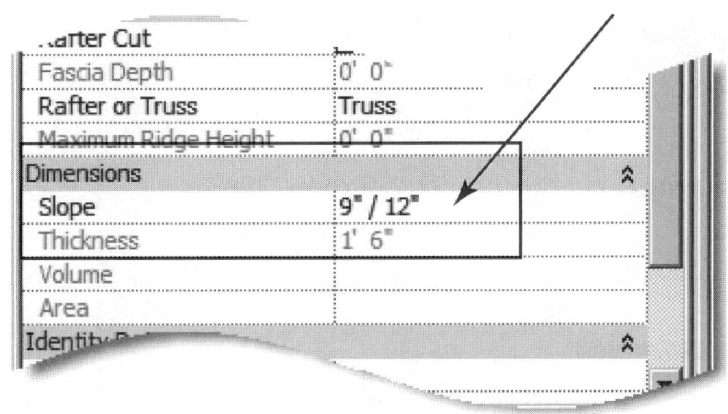

Figure 7-8

Slope field

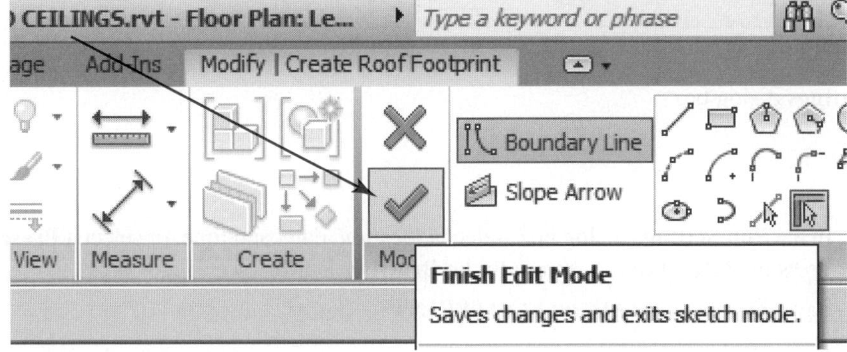

Figure 7-9

Finish Edit Mode button

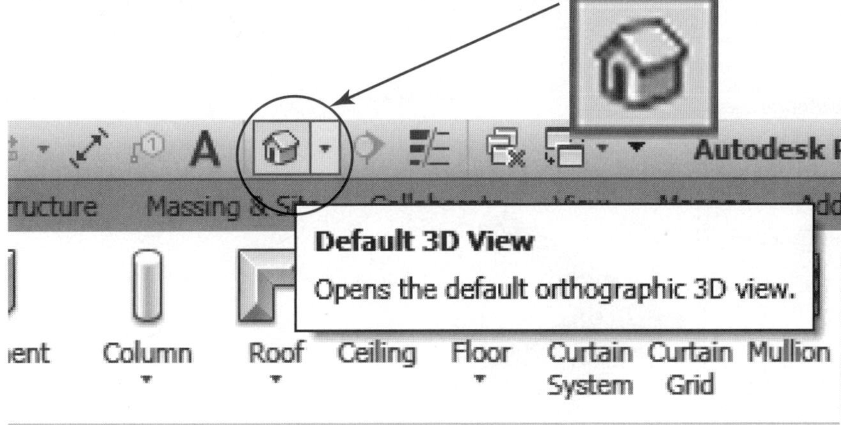

Figure 7-10

Default 3D View button

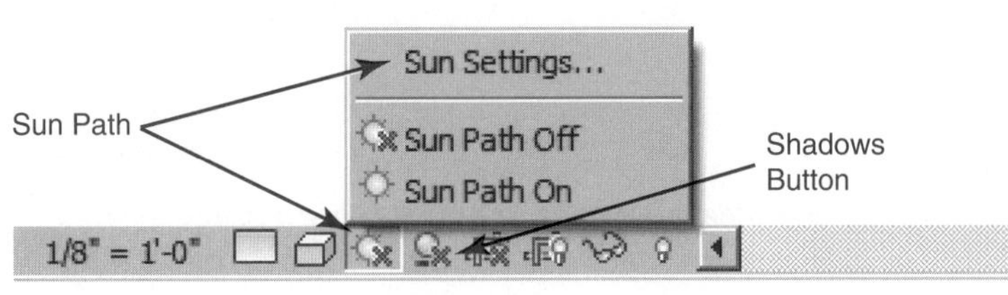

Figure 7-11

Shadows button

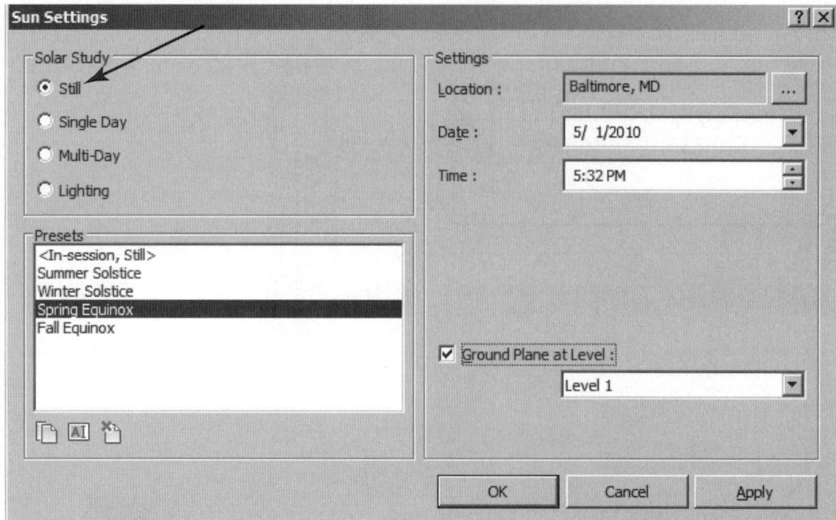

Figure 7-12

Sun Settings dialog box

30. In the **Sun Settings** dialog box, select a location, date, and time, or select a **Preset**. Press the **OK** buttons to return to the **Drawing Editor** (see Figure 7-13).
31. Save this file as **ROOF by FOOTPRINT.**

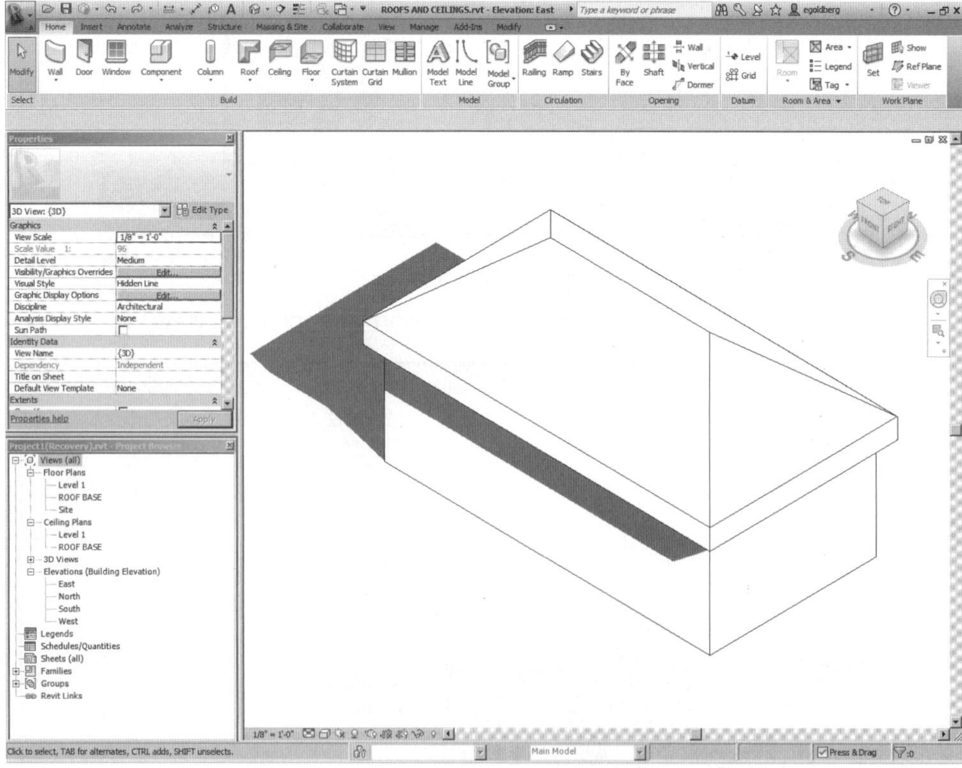

Figure 7-13

Roof by Footprint

EXERCISE 7-2 MODIFYING A ROOF BY FOOTPRINT

1. Using the previous exercise, double-click on the **East Elevation** in the **Project Browser** to bring it into your workspace.
2. Select the **ROOF BASE** level line, **RMB**, and select **Create Similar** from the contextual menu that appears.
3. Drag a new level from the **ROOF BASE** to the top of the roof, and name it **TOP of ROOF** (see Figure 7-14).

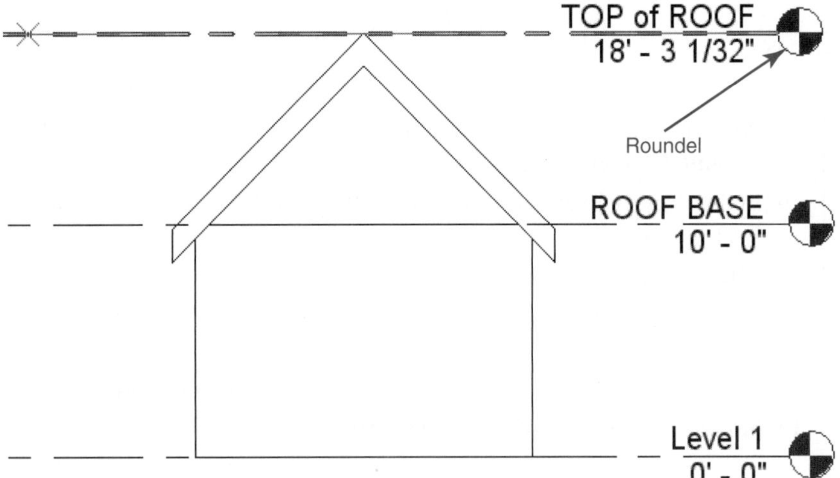

Figure 7-14

Create **TOP of ROOF**

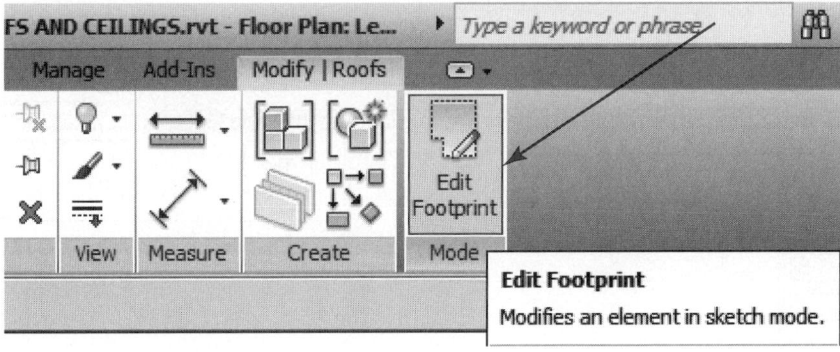

Figure 7-15

Edit Footprint toolbar

4. Double-click on the **TOP of ROOF roundel** or **TOP of ROOF** in the **Project Browser** to bring the **TOP of ROOF** view into your **Drawing Editor**.
5. In the **Drawing Editor**, select the roof to bring up the **Modify | Roofs** toolbar.
6. In the **Modify | Roofs** toolbar, select the **Edit Footprint** button to bring up the **Modify | Roofs > Edit Footprint** toolbar (see Figure 7-15).

The **Roof** will now be in its **Sketch Mode** and will return to an outline.

7. Select the **Right** roof line, and then *uncheck* the **Defines Slope** check box in the **Options Bar** that appears (see Figure 7-16).

NOTE:

The **Defines Slope** check box determines whether you have a roof slope or not. If the check box is *checked*, you will see an angle and slope rise number. If the check box is *unchecked*, you will not see an angle and slope number next to a roof line.

8. In the **Modify | Roofs > Edit Footprint** toolbar, press the **Finish Edit Mode** button, and select **No** when the **Revit** dialog box asks whether you would like to attach the highlighted walls to the roof.

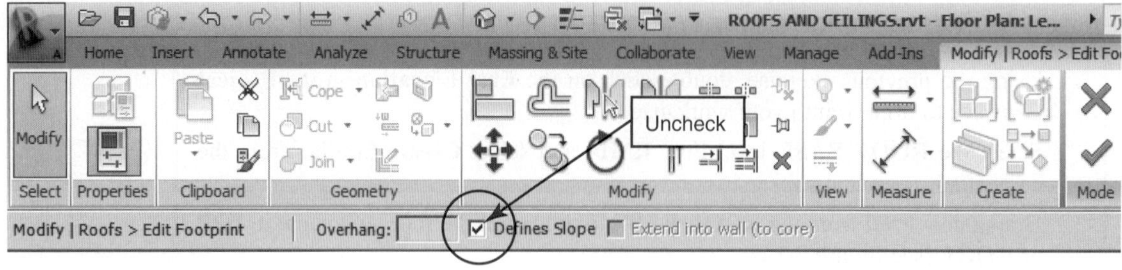

Figure 7-16

Defines Slope check box

9. Press the **Default 3D View** tool on the **Quick Access** toolbar to change to the **Default 3D View**.
10. In the **Project Browser**, select the **TOP of ROOF**, **Elevation South**, **Elevation East**, and **3D View**.
11. Select the **View** tab to bring up the **View** toolbar.
12. In the **View** toolbar, select the **Tile** button from the **Windows** panel to tile the **Drawing Editor**.
13. In each viewport, type **ZE** on the keyboard to **Zoom** to **Extents** (see Figure 7-17).
14. Save this file as **ROOF by FOOTPRINT**.

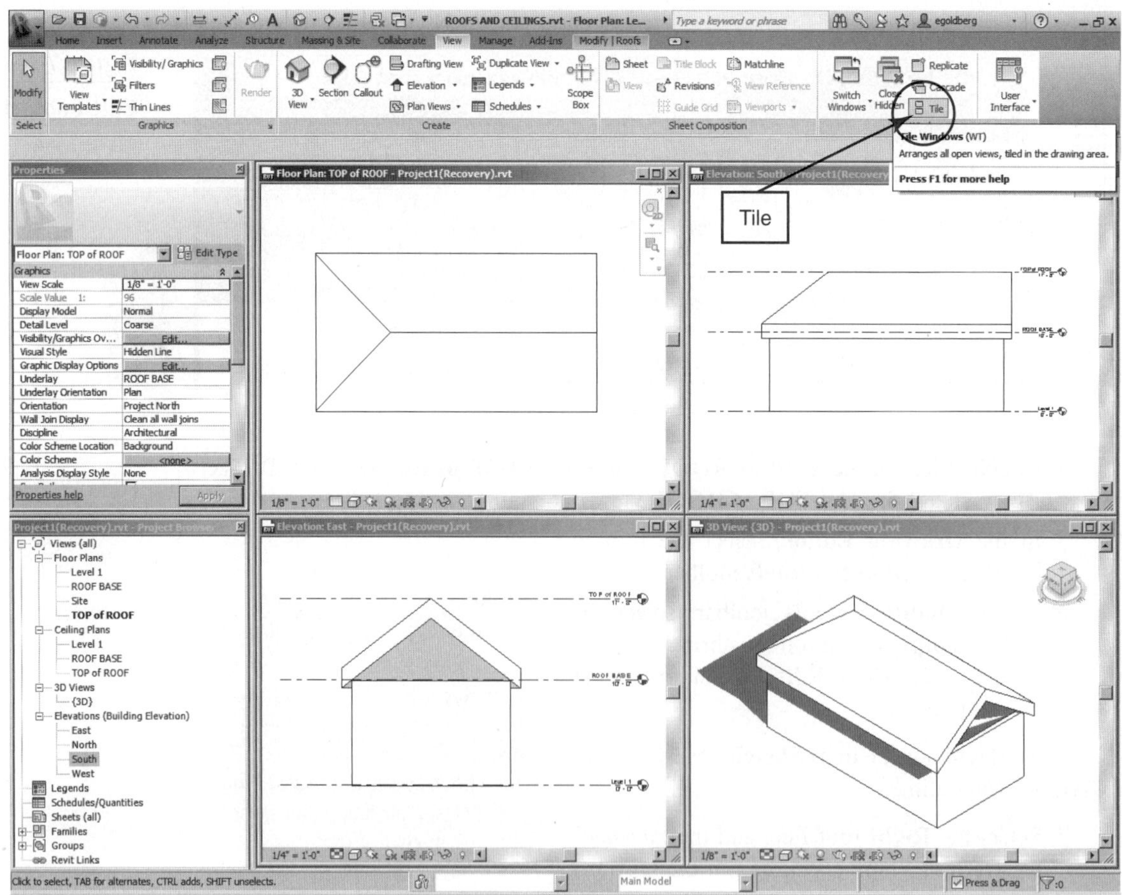

Figure 7-17

Tile button

EXERCISE 7-3 MAKING A WALL MEET A ROOF

1. Using the previous exercise, stay in the **Default 3D View**.
2. Select the right wall below the roof to bring up the **Modify | Walls** toolbar.
3. In the **Modify | Walls** toolbar, press the **Attach Top/Base** button (see Figure 7-18).
4. Select the roof of the building.

The wall attaches to the roof (see Figure 7-19).

5. Save the file as **WALL MEETS ROOF**.

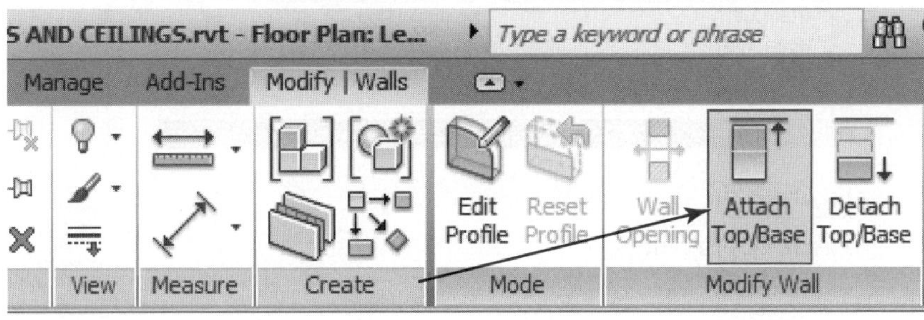

Figure 7-18

Attach Top/Base button

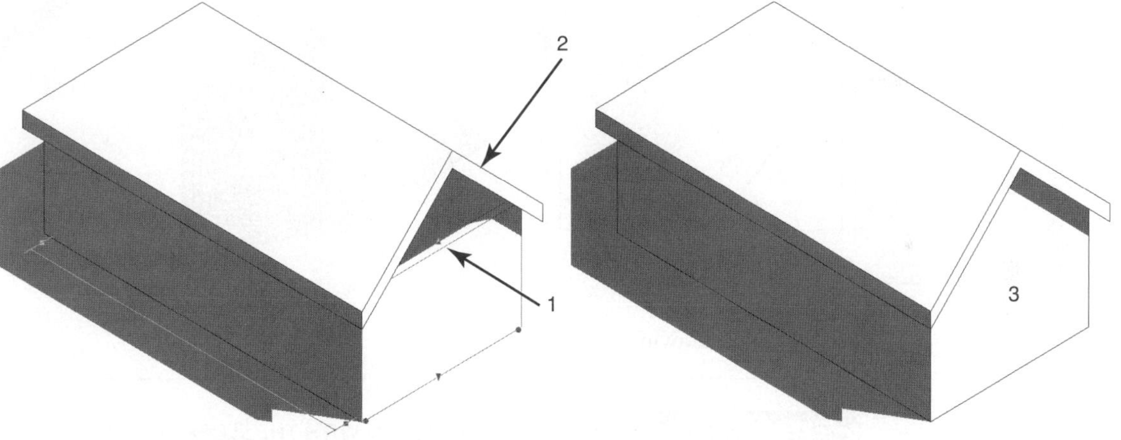

Figure 7-19

Wall attached to the roof

EXERCISE 7-4 CHANGING THE RAFTER CUT

1. Using the previous exercise, bring the **TOP of ROOF** plan view into your **Drawing Editor**.
2. In the **Drawing Editor**, select the roof to bring up the **Modify | Roofs** toolbar.
3. In the **Modify | Roofs** toolbar, select the **Edit Footprint** button to bring up the **Modify | Roofs > Edit Footprint** toolbar.

The **Roof** will now be in its **Sketch Mode** state and will return to an outline.

4. Select the **Left** roof line, and then uncheck the **Defines Slope** check box in the **Options Bar**.
5. In the **Modify | Roofs > Edit Footprint** toolbar, press the **Finish Edit Mode** button, and select **Yes** when the **Revit** dialog box asks whether you would like to attach the highlighted walls to the roof.

The left wall attaches to the roof.

6. Bring the **East Elevation** into the **Drawing Editor**.
7. Select the roof. In the **Properties** dialog box, select **Two Cut – Plumb** from the **Rafter Cut** field, and set the **Fascia Depth** to **6″** (see Figures 7-20 and 7-21).
8. Experiment with the other **Rafter Cut** options and different **Fascia Depths**.
9. Save the file as **RAFTER CUT OPTIONS**.

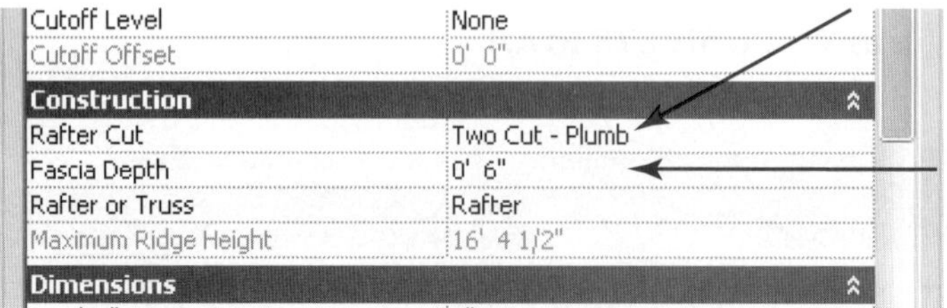

Figure 7-20

Fascia Depth field

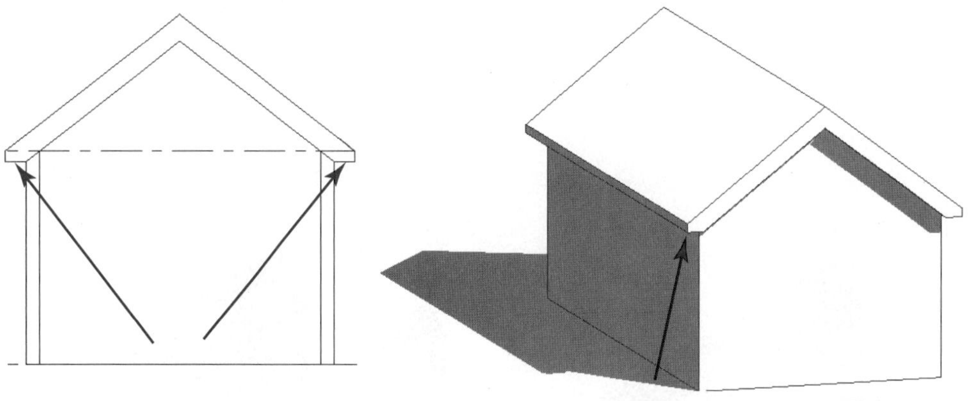

Figure 7-21

East Elevation drawing

EXERCISE 7-5 **MODIFYING A ROOF SLOPE WITH THE SLOPE ARROW**

1. Using the previous exercise, change to the **ROOF BASE** floor plan view.
2. Delete the **Roof**.
3. In the **Home** toolbar, select the **Roof > Roof by Footprint** button to bring up the **Modify | Create Roof Footprint** toolbar.
4. In the **Modify | Create Roof Footprint** toolbar, select the **Pick Walls** button from the **Draw** panel.
5. In the **Options Bar**, uncheck the **Defines Slope** check box, and enter **1′-0″** in the **Overhang** field.
6. Select all the walls as you have in a previous exercise.
7. Select the lower south line, and move it back to the wall so there will be no overhang.
8. In the **Modify | Roofs > Edit Footprint** toolbar, select the **Slope Arrow** button (see Figure 7-22).
9. Place a **Slope Arrow** as shown in Figure 7-23.
10. Change to the **Default 3D View**.
11. Select the arrow to bring up the **Properties** dialog box for the arrow.

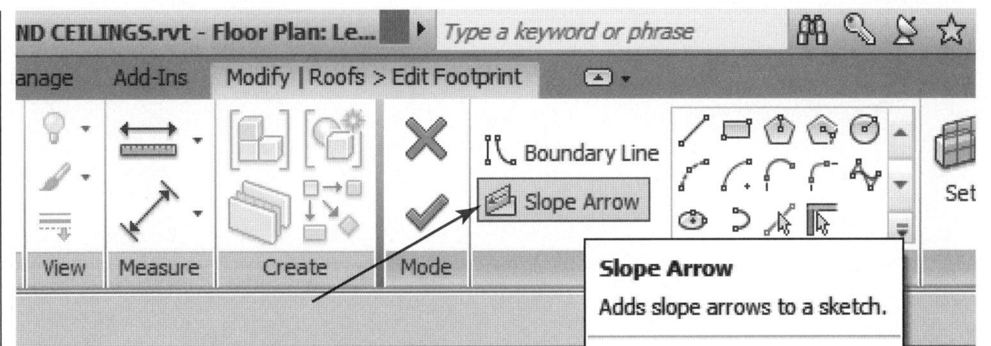

Figure 7-22

Slope Arrow button

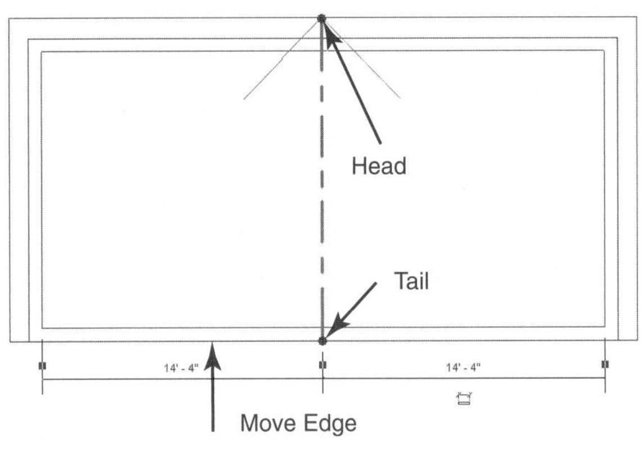

Figure 7-23

Slope Arrow in drawing

In the **Properties** dialog box, you can set the height of the arrow at its head and tail. Since the **Slope Arrow** controls the roof slope, you can parametrically control the roof slope.

12. In the **Properties** dialog box, set the **Level at Tail** to **ROOF BASE**, and **Level at Head** to **TOP of ROOF**, and then press the **Apply** button.
13. Press the **Finish Edit Mode** button in the **Modify | Create Roof Footprint** toolbar, and select **Yes** when the **Revit** dialog box asks whether you would like to attach the highlighted walls to the roof.

You have now set the slope of the roof by adjusting the **Slope Arrow** (see Figures 7-24 and 7-25).

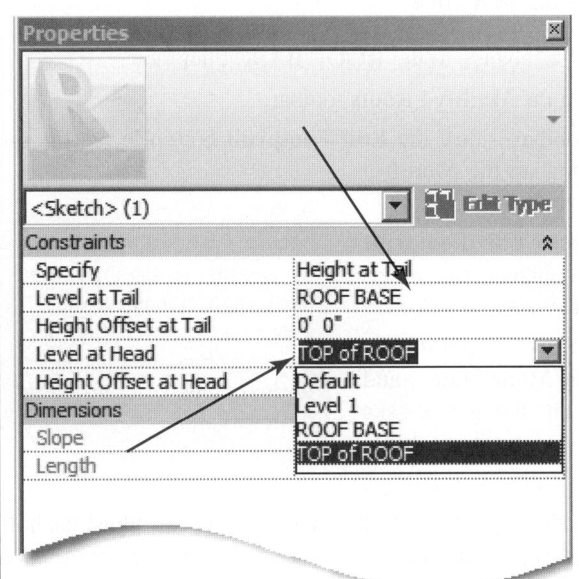

Figure 7-24

Arrow Properties options

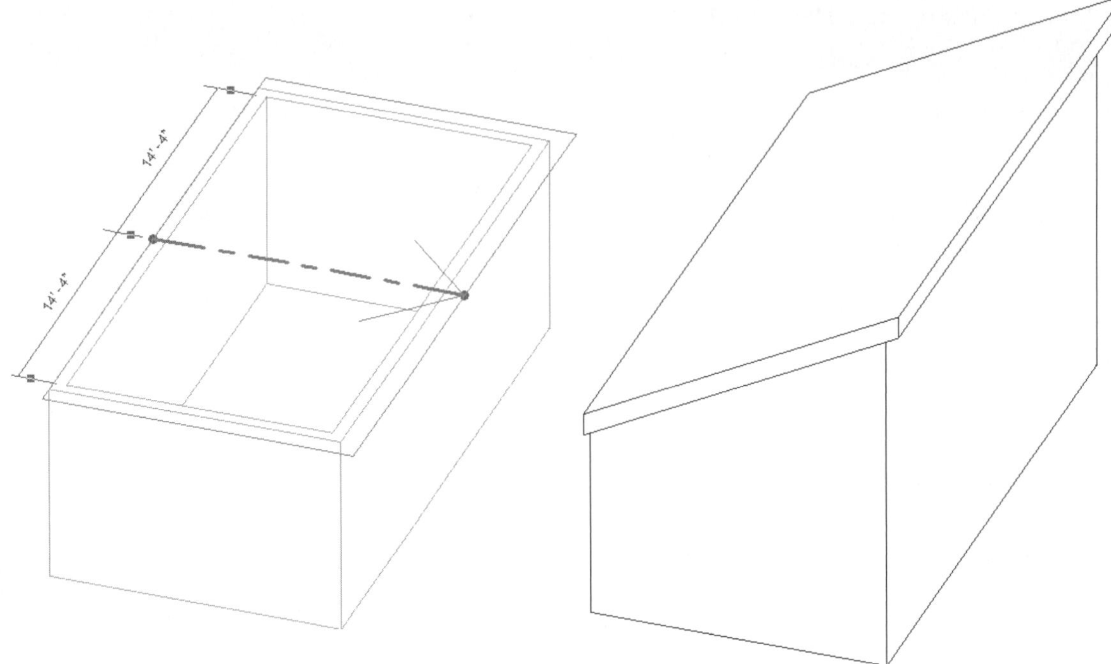

Figure 7-25

Slope of roof adjusted

14. Select the roof to again bring up the **Modify | Roofs** toolbar.
15. In the **Modify | Roofs** toolbar, again select the **Edit Footprint** button to put the roof in **Sketch Mode**.
16. Select the **Slope Arrow** again to bring up the **Properties** dialog box.
17. Experiment with all the settings in the **Properties** dialog box, press the **Finish Edit Mode** button, and notice the changes that happen to the roof.
18. Experiment with moving the arrow head and tail to different locations, and notice the changes that happen to the roof.
19. Save the file as **SLOPE ARROW**.

EXERCISE 7-6 **CREATING A HOLE IN A ROOF**

1. Using the previous exercise, change to the **ROOF BASE** Plan view.
2. Select the roof to bring up the **Modify | Roofs** toolbar.
3. In the **Modify | Roofs** toolbar, select the **Edit Footprint** button to put the roof in **Sketch Mode** and bring up the **Modify | Roofs > Edit Footprint** toolbar.
4. From the **Modify | Roofs > Edit Footprint** toolbar, place a circle, a rectangle, and an ellipse in the **ROOF BASE** view.
5. In the **Modify | Roofs > Edit Footprint** toolbar, press the **Finish Edit Mode** button, and select **Yes** when the **Revit** dialog box asks whether you would like to attach the highlighted walls to the roof.

NOTE:

Be sure that all the lines in the circle and rectangles do not have slope angles. If they do, select the lines, and uncheck the **Defines Slope** check box in the **Options Bar.**

You have now placed holes in the roof. If you select the holes, you can adjust the holes with arrow grips that appear, or repeat Steps 2–3 of this exercise and change the shape of the holes there (see Figure 7-26).

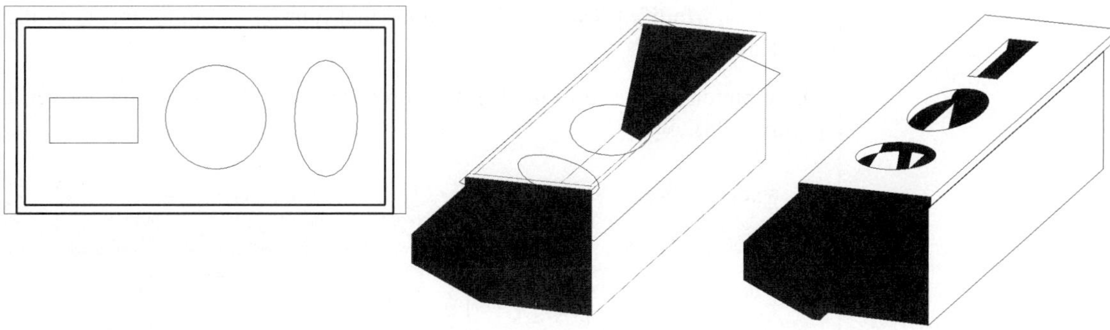

Figure 7-26

Shape of holes can be changed using arrow grips

6. Open the **ROOF by FOOTPRINT** file.
7. Repeat Steps 2–5 of this exercise on that file (see Figure 7-27).
8. Save this file as **ROOF HOLES**.

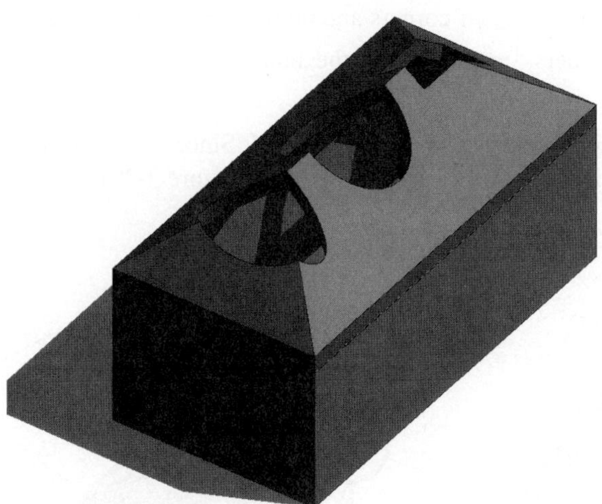

Figure 7-27

Drawing with holes in roof

EXERCISE 7-7 MODIFYING A ROOF SLAB BY MOVING VERTICES

1. Open the **ROOF by FOOTPRINT** file.
2. Change to the **ROOF BASE** plan view.
3. Select the roof to bring up the **Modify | Roofs** toolbar.
4. In the **Modify | Roofs** toolbar, select the **Edit Footprint** button to put the roof in **Sketch Mode** and bring up the **Modify | Roofs > Edit Footprint** toolbar.
5. In the **Modify | Roofs > Edit Footprint** toolbar, select all the roof edge lines and uncheck the **Defines Slope** check box in the **Options Bar**.
6. In the **Modify | Roofs > Edit Footprint** toolbar, press the **Finish Edit Mode** button, and select **Yes** when the Revit dialog box asks whether you would like to attach the highlighted walls to the roof.

This will create a flat roof.

7. Change to the **Default 3D View**.
8. Select the flat roof to bring up the **Modify | Roofs** toolbar.

9. In the **Modify | Roofs** toolbar, notice that four new buttons appear in the **Shape Editing** panel.

These buttons are used to modify flat roofs (not extruded flat roofs) by vertices (see Figure 7-28).

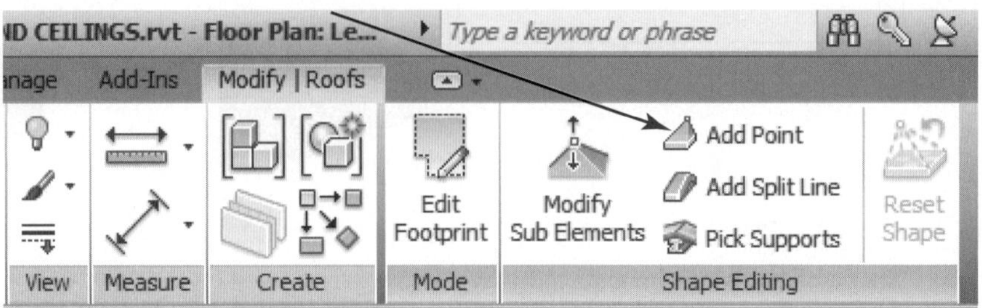

Figure 7-28

Modify | Roofs toolbar

10. In the **Modify | Roofs** toolbar, select the **Modify Sub Elements** button, and notice that green grips appear at all four corners and on the top surface of the roof.
11. Select one of the corners, enter **6′-0″** in the number field, and then press the **<Enter>** key.

The corner of the roof moves upward (Z direction) **6′-0″**. Since the walls are attached to the roof, they automatically move upward as well (see Figure 7-29).

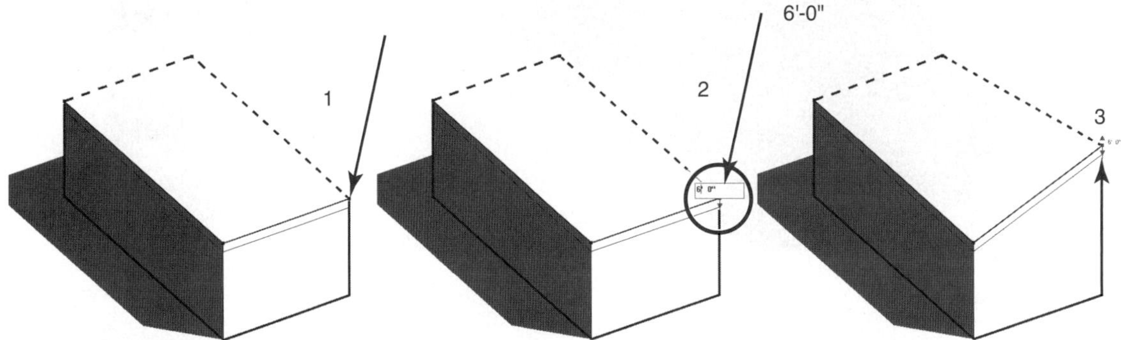

Figure 7-29

Corner of roof moves upward

12. Experiment by moving the other vertices.
13. Select the roof again, and press the **Reset Shape** button in the **Modify | Roofs** toolbar to revert back to the roof's original flat shape.
14. Change to the **ROOF BASE** Plan view.
15. In the **Modify | Roofs** toolbar, select the **Add Point** button, and place three points.
16. Change to the **Default 3D View**.
17. Select the **Modify Sub Elements** button again, and lift the three points **6′-0″** vertically. Press the **<Esc>** key to end the operation (see Figure 7-30).
18. Change to the **ROOF BASE** Plan view.
19. Select the roof again, and press the **Reset Shape** button in the **Modify | Roofs** toolbar to revert back to the roof's original flat shape.
20. Select the roof again to bring up the **Modify | Roofs** toolbar.
21. In the **Modify | Roofs** toolbar, select the **Add Split Line** button.
22. Click at the top left corner, and then click on the diagonal corner to add the **Split Line**.

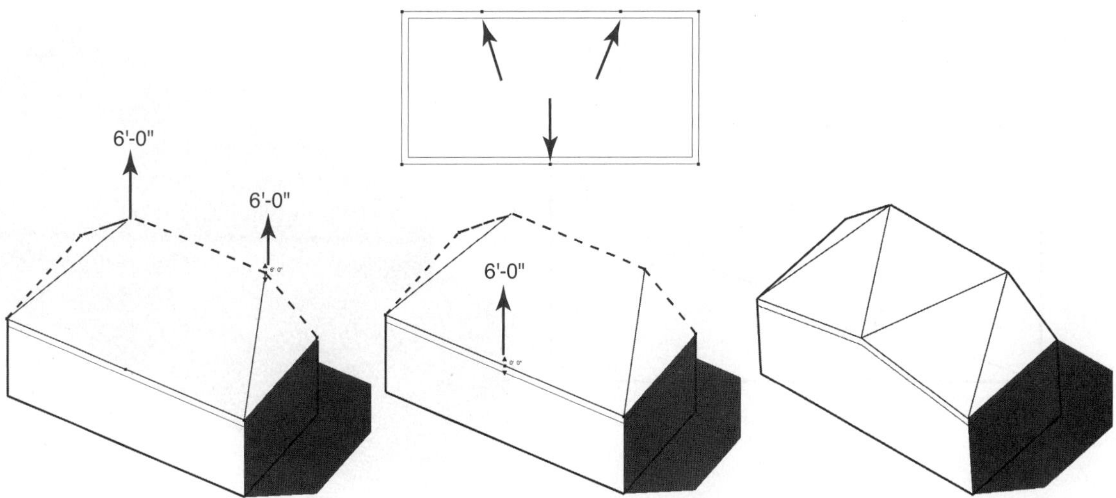

Figure 7-30

Shape of roofs changed

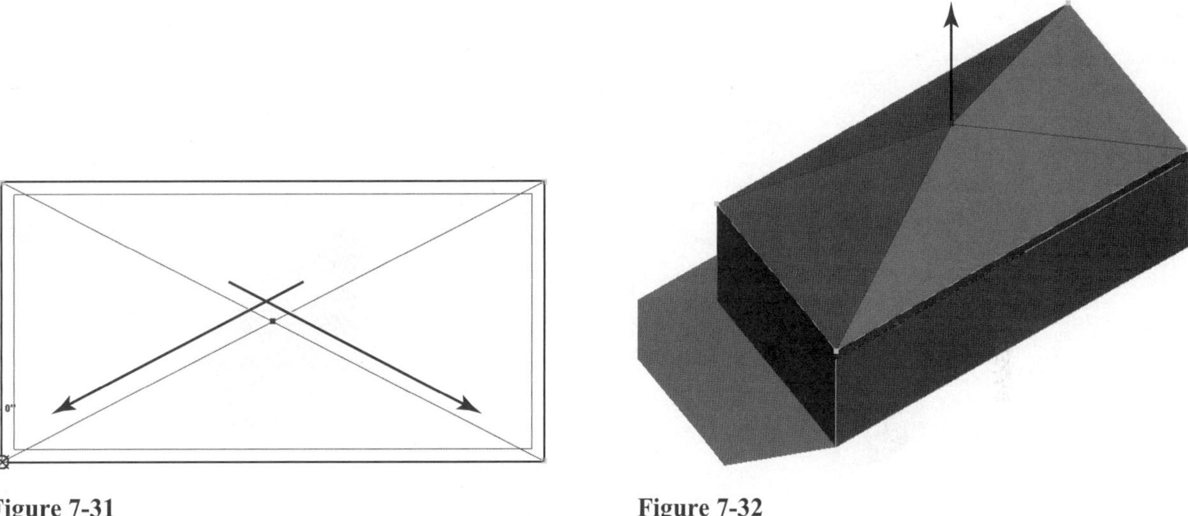

Figure 7-31

Split Line drawing

Figure 7-32

Modified roof

23. Repeat for the other diagonal (see Figure 7-31).
24. Change to the **Default 3D View**.
25. Select the roof again to bring up the **Modify | Roofs** toolbar.
26. In the **Modify | Roofs** toolbar, select the **Modify Sub Elements** button, and then lift the crossing point **6′-0″** vertically, and press the **<Esc>** key to end the operation (see Figure 7-32).
27. Change to the **ROOF BASE** Plan view again.
28. Select the roof again to bring up the **Modify | Roofs** toolbar.
29. In the **Modify | Roofs** toolbar, select the **Modify Sub Elements** button, and then move the crossing point **6′-0″** horizontally.
30. Press the **<Esc>** key to end the operation (see Figure 7-33).
31. Change to the **ROOF BASE** Plan view, and repeat adding and moving **Split Lines** (see Figure 7-34).

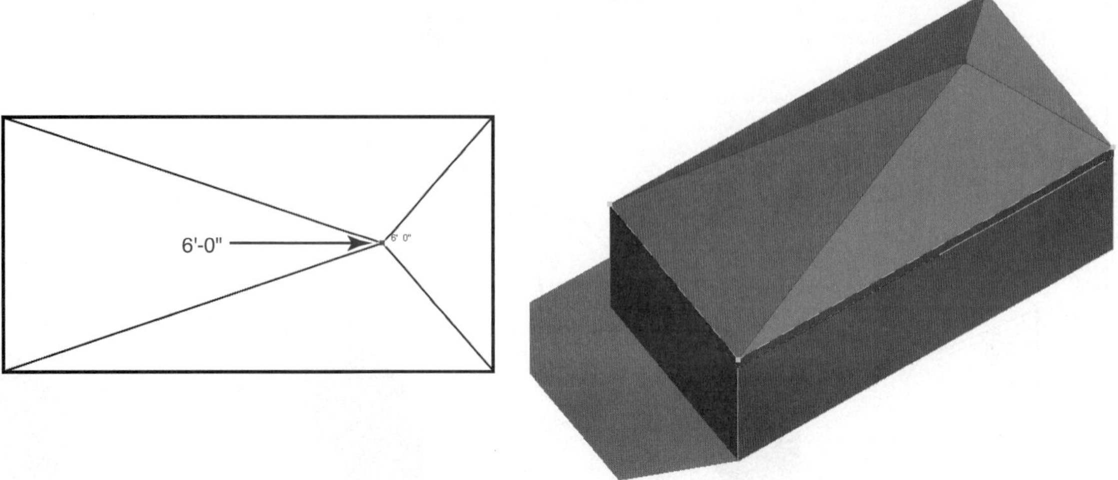

Figure 7-33

Modified roof with crossing point moved

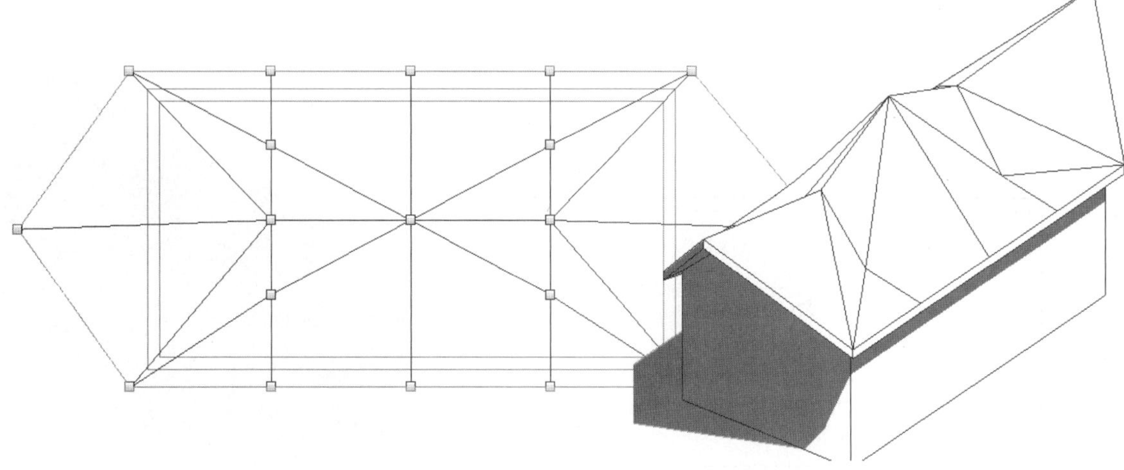

Figure 7-34

Multiple roof line changes

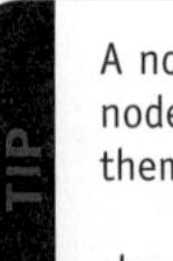

A node is formed everywhere that one **Split Line** crosses another. You can move these nodes in Plan view with your keyboard arrow keys; change their height by clicking on them and entering a dimension.

You can also go back into **Edit** (**Sketch Mode**), and change the exterior perimeter shape of the roof.

32. Select the roof again to bring up the **Modify | Roofs** toolbar.
33. In the **Modify | Roofs** toolbar, press the **Reset Shape** button to revert back to the roof's original flat shape.
34. Change to the **ROOF BASE** plan view.
35. Select the **Structure** tab to bring up the **Structure** toolbar.
36. In the **Structure** toolbar, press the **Beam** button to bring up the **Modify | Place Beam** toolbar (see Figure 7-35).
37. In the **Properties** dialog box, select the **W-Wide Flange: W12×26** from the **Properties** drop-down list, and place the beam as shown in Figure 7-36.
38. Select the roof to bring up the **Modify | Roofs** toolbar.

39. In the **Modify | Roofs** toolbar, in the **Shape Editing** panel, select the **Pick Supports** button, and select the **W-Wide Flange: W12×26** you just placed.
40. In the **Modify | Roofs** toolbar, in the **Shape Editing** panel, select the **Modify Sub Elements** button again, and lift the endpoints **6′-0″** vertically as shown in Figure 7-37.
41. Save this file as **MOVING ROOF VERTICES**.

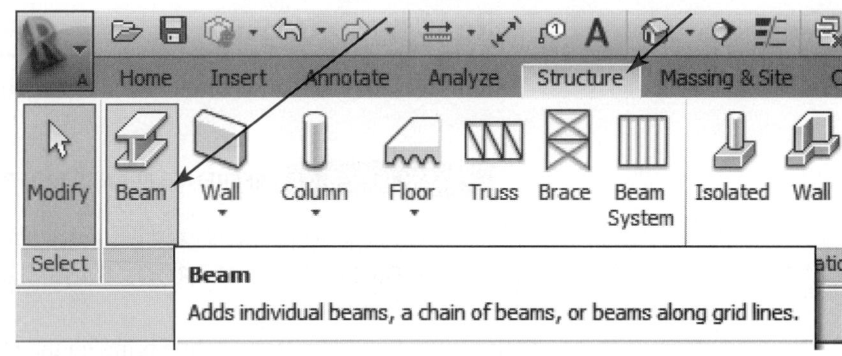

Figure 7-35
Beam button

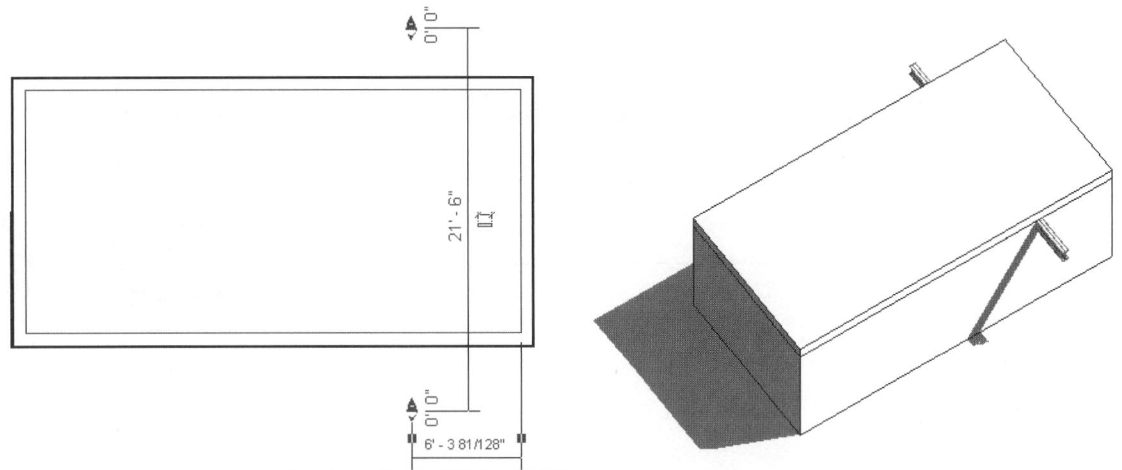

Figure 7-36

Beam placement

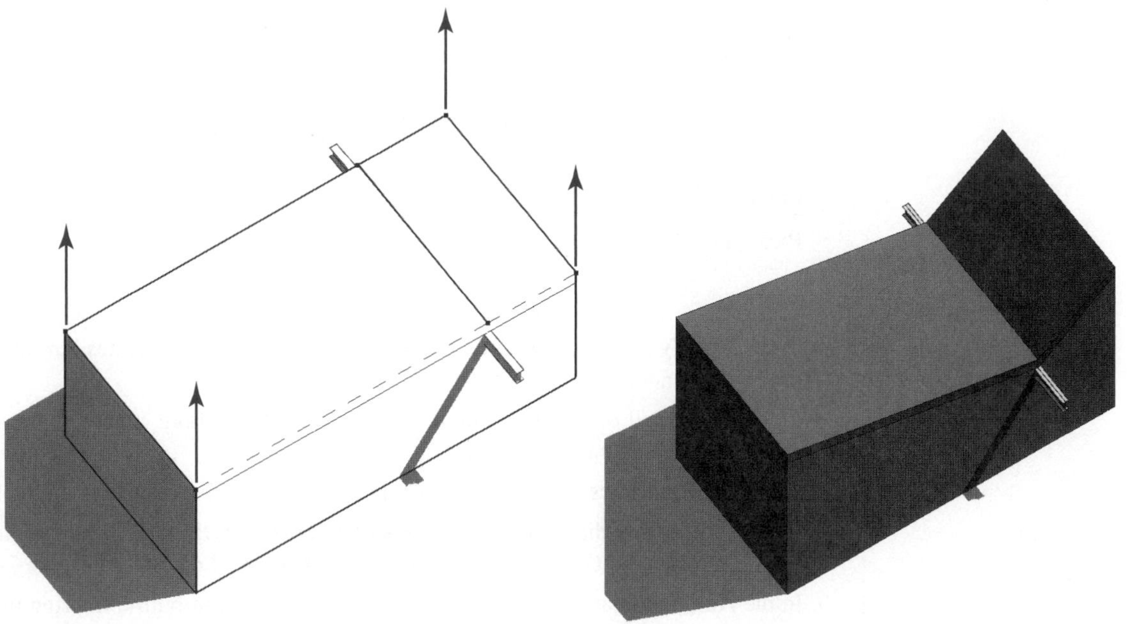

Figure 7-37

End of roof lifted

Roof by Extrusion

Roof by Extrusion allows you to add items, such as gutters, to a roof.

EXERCISE 7-8 REFERENCE PLANES AND ROOF BY EXTRUSION

1. Using the previous exercise, delete the roof.
2. Double-click on the **ROOF BASE** plan in the **Project Browser** to bring it into the **Drawing Editor**.
3. Select the **Home** tab to bring up the **Home** toolbar.
4. In the **Home** toolbar, select the **Ref Plane** button from the **Work Plane** panel to bring up the **Modify | Place Reference Plane** toolbar (see Figure 7-38).

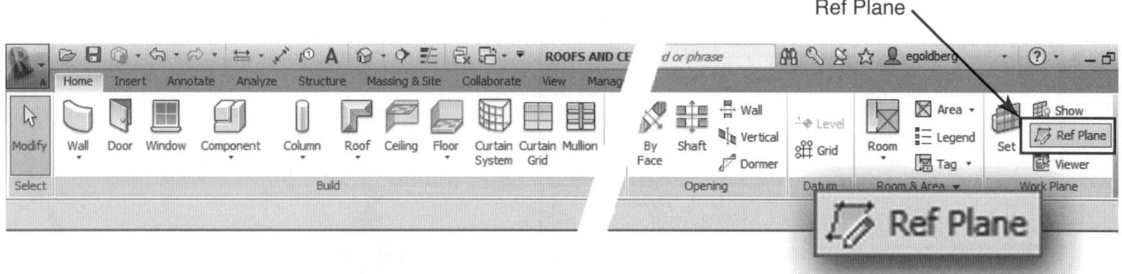

Figure 7-38

Ref Plane button

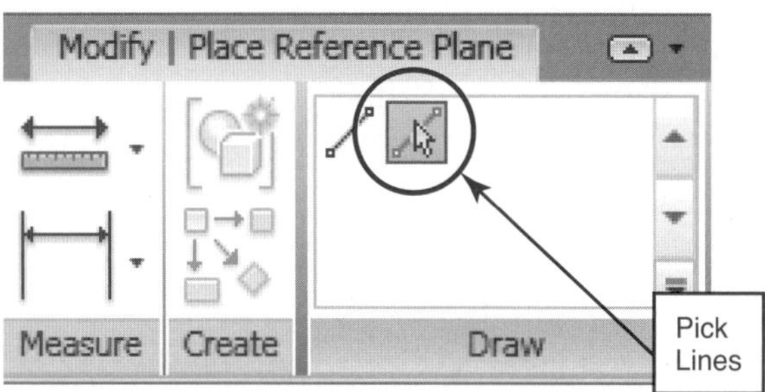

Figure 7-39

Pick Lines button

5. In the **Modify | Place Reference Plane** toolbar, select the **Pick Lines** button from the **Draw** panel (see Figure 7-39).
6. Pick the left wall of the enclosure to place a **Reference Plane**, and then press the **<Esc>** key to end the command.
7. Select the **Reference Plane** you just created to bring up its **Properties** dialog box.
8. In the **Properties** dialog box, enter **EXTRUDED ROOF EDGE** in the **Name** field, and press the **OK** button to return to the **Drawing Editor** (see Figure 7-40).
9. In the **Home** toolbar, select the **Roof > Roof by Extrusion** button to bring up the **Work Plane** dialog box (see Figure 7-41).
10. In the **Work Plane** dialog box, select the **Pick a plane** radio button and **Reference Plane: EXTRUDED ROOF EDGE** from the **Specify a new Work Plane** drop-down list. Finally, press the **OK** button.

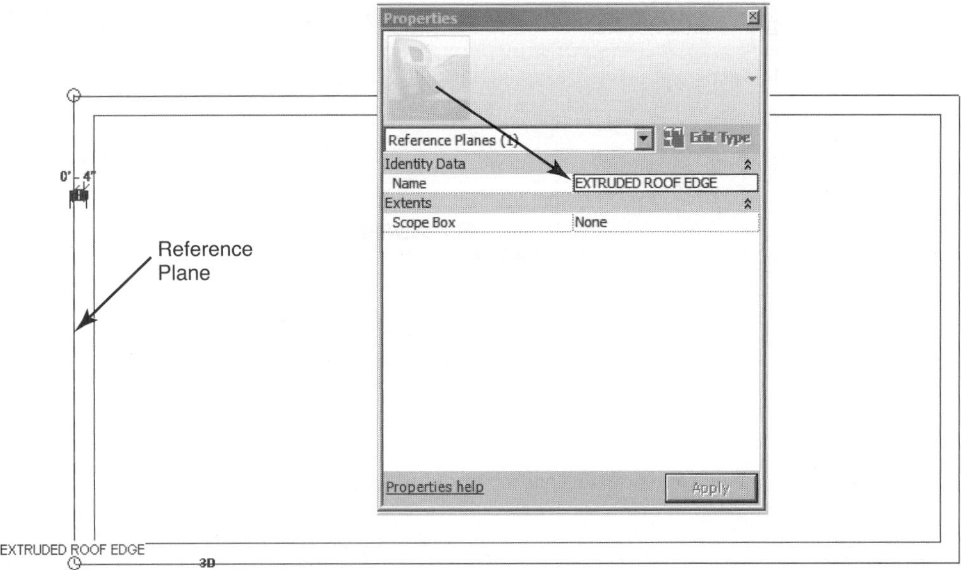

Figure 7-40

Save drawing as **EXTRUDED ROOF EDGE**

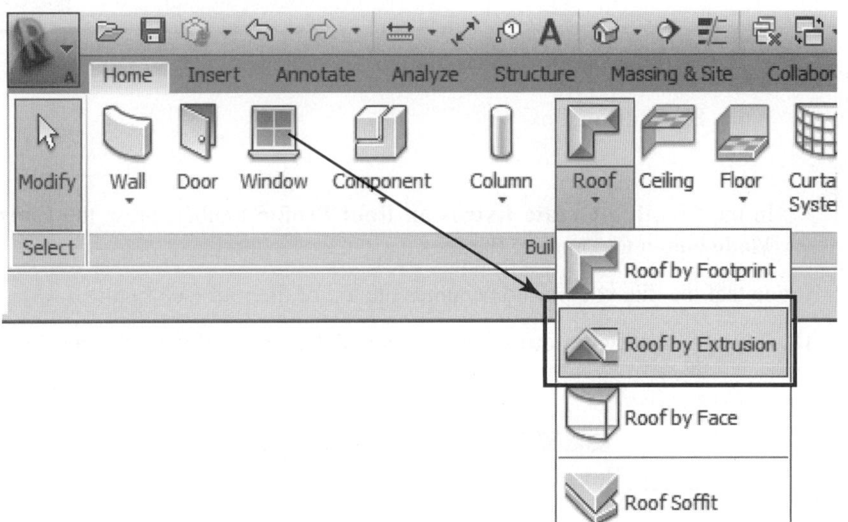

Figure 7-41

Roof by Extrusion button

11. Since you are in a Plan view, the **Go To View** dialog box will now appear.
12. In the **Go To View** dialog box, select **Elevation: East**, and press the **Open View** button.
13. The view will now change to the **East Elevation**, and the **Roof Reference Level and Offset** dialog box will appear.
14. In the **Roof Reference Level and Offset** dialog box, change to **ROOF BASE** from the **Level** drop-down list, and press the **OK** button to change to the **East Elevation** (see Figure 7-42).
15. From the **Modify | Create Extrusion Roof Profile** toolbar, select the **Start-End-Radius Arc** in the **Draw** panel.
16. With the **Snaps (On)**, click on the top of the left wall, then the top of the right wall. Drag your mouse upward, and click again to place an arc between the left and right walls.

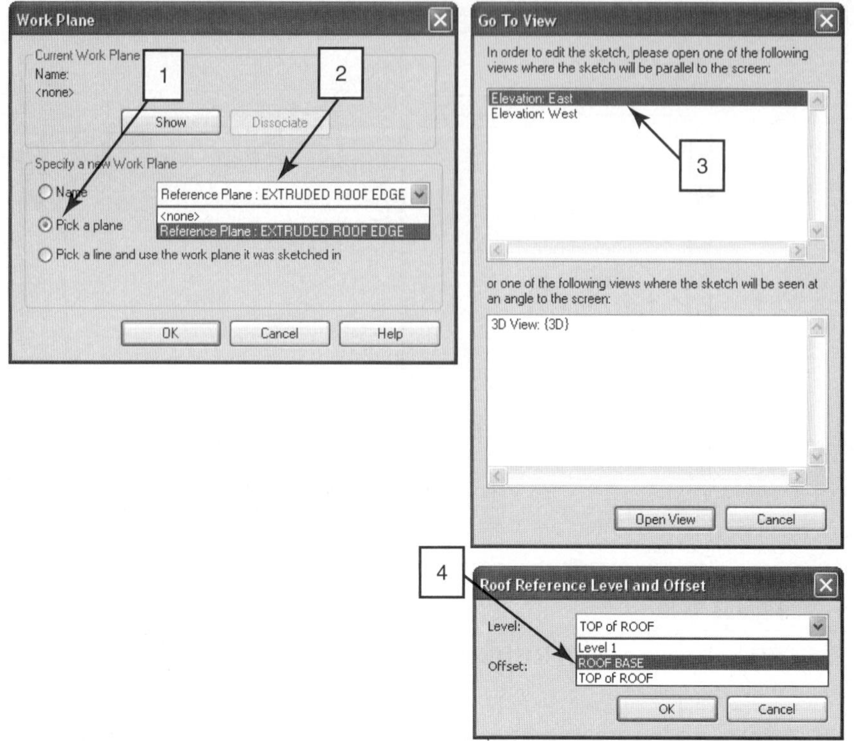

Figure 7-42

Work Plane dialog box

17. In the **Modify | Create Extrusion Roof Profile** toolbar, press the **Finish Edit Mode** button to complete the roof.

Notice that the line you placed becomes the top of the roof (see Figure 7-43).

18. Return to the **Elevation: East** view, and delete the roof you just created.

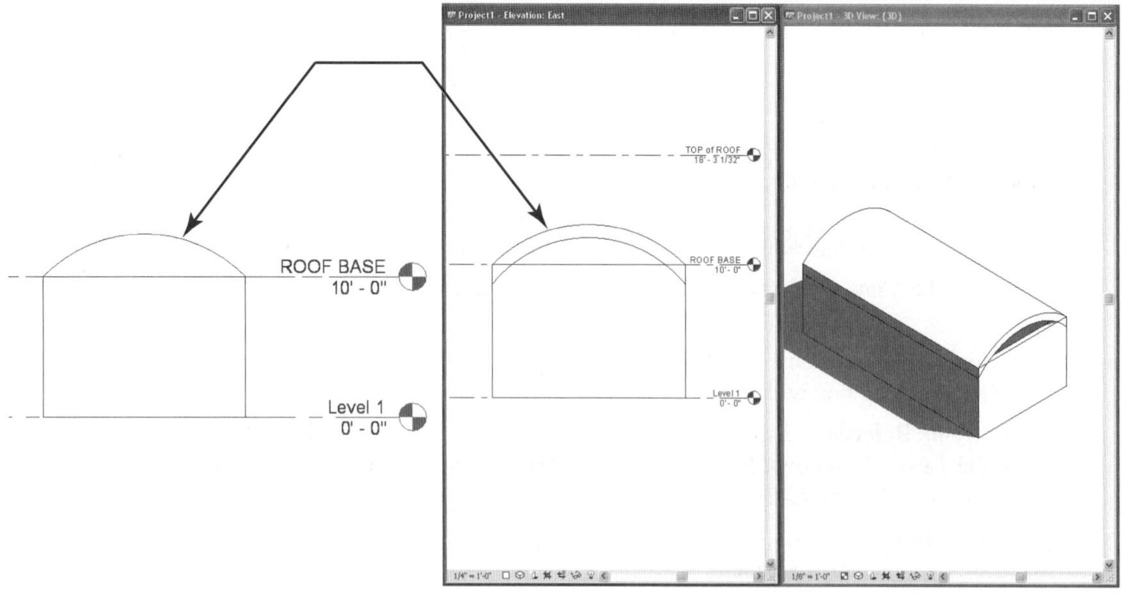

Figure 7-43

Line placed becomes the top of the roof

Figure 7-44

Create a roof using the **Spline** button

Repeat Steps 15–18 using the **Spline** button (see Figure 7-44).

19. Select the roof you placed again, to bring up the **Modify | Roofs** toolbar.
20. In the **Modify | Roofs** toolbar, select the **Edit Profile** button from the **Modify Roof Panel** to bring up the **Modify Roofs | Edit Profile** toolbar, and change the roof back to a spline (see Figure 7-45).

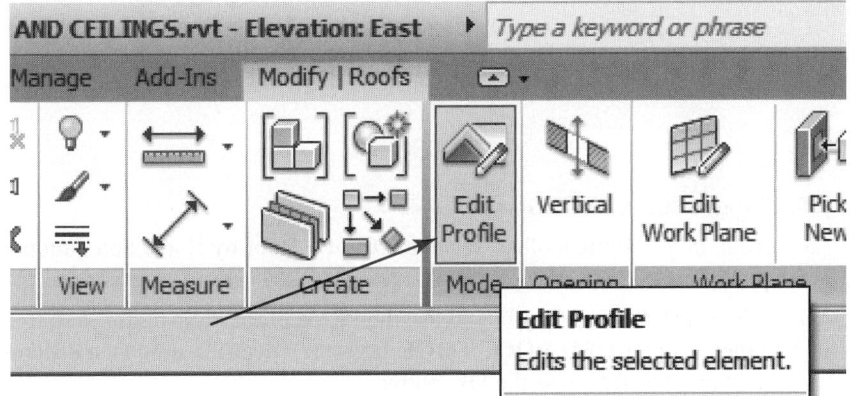

Figure 7-45

Edit Profile button

21. Move the vertices in the spline to change its shape, and then press the **Finish Edit Mode** button in the **Modify Roofs | Edit Profile** toolbar to modify the roof.
22. Delete the roof again, and return to the **Default 3D View**.
23. In the **Home** toolbar, select the **Set Work Plane** button to bring up the **Work Plane** dialog box.
24. In the **Work Plane** dialog box, press the **Show** button (to show the **Work Plane**), select the **Name** radio button, and select **EXTRUDED ROOF EDGE** from the drop-down list (see Figure 7-46).

NOTE:

This will display your work planes as a rectangle in the **Default 3D View.** If you select the **Show Work Plane** button in the **Work Plane** panel of the **Home** toolbar, you will see the **Work Plane** with a grid.

If you select different **Work Planes** from the **Work Plane** dialog box, you can cycle through and see all the **Work Planes.**

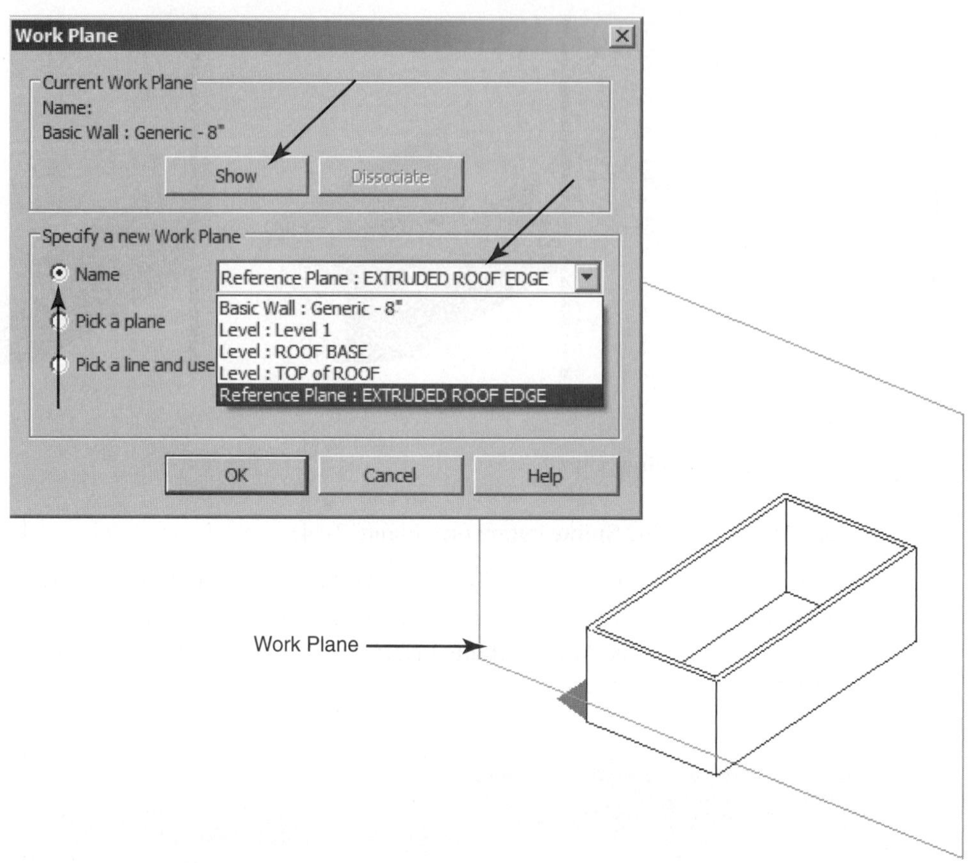

Figure 7-46

Show Work Plane button

25. Change to the **LEVEL 1** view.
26. Again, in the **Home** toolbar, select the **Roof > Roof by Extrusion** button to bring up the **Work Plane** dialog box.
27. In the **Work Plane** dialog box, select the **Pick a plane** radio button, and **Reference Plane: EXTRUDED ROOF EDGE** from the **Specify a new Work Plane** drop-down list. Finally, press the **OK** button.
28. In the **Go To View** dialog box, select **Elevation: East**, and press the **Open View** button.

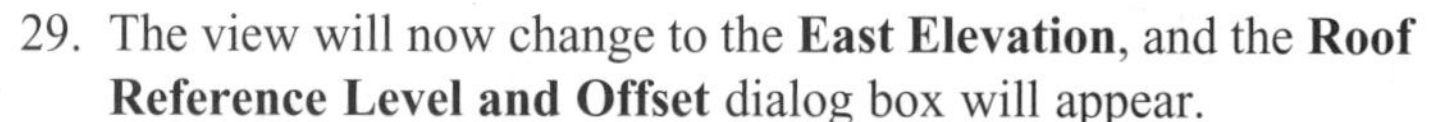

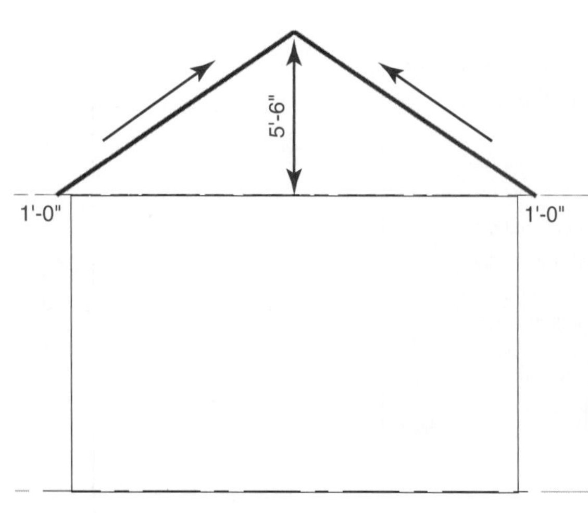

Figure 7-47

Use the **Create Extrusion Roof Profile** to create the roof drawing

29. The view will now change to the **East Elevation**, and the **Roof Reference Level and Offset** dialog box will appear.
30. In the **Roof Reference Level and Offset** dialog box, change to **ROOF BASE** from the **Level** drop-down list, and press the **OK** button to change to the **East Elevation**.
31. From the **Modify | Create Extrusion Roof Profile** toolbar, select the **Line** button in the **Draw** panel, and draw the lines shown in Figure 7-47.
32. In the **Modify | Create Extrusion Roof Profile** toolbar, press the **Finish Edit Mode** button to complete the roof.
33. Change to the **Default 3D View**.
34. Select the roof to bring up its **Properties** dialog box.
35. In the **Properties** dialog box, change the **Level Offset** to **1′-6″**, and press the **Apply** button to move the roof upward.
36. Grab on the grips and stretch the roof (see Figure 7-48).
37. Save this file as **REFERENCE PLANES and ROOF by EXTRUSION**.

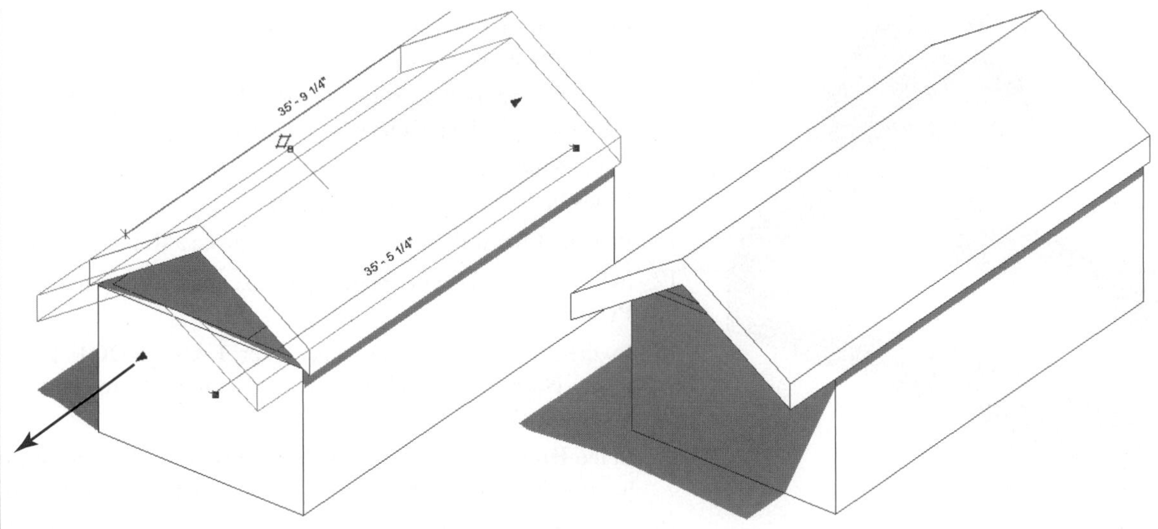

Figure 7-48

Use the grips to stretch the roof

EXERCISE 7-9 **THE JOIN/UNJOIN ROOF TOOL**

1. Start a new drawing using the RAC 2012\Imperial Templates\default.rte template.
2. In the **Project Browser**, double-click on the **LEVEL 1** floor plan to bring it into the **Drawing Editor**.
3. Change the **Drawing Scale** to **1/4″ = 1′-0″**.
4. Set the **Detail Level** to **Medium**.
5. Select the **Home** tab to bring up the **Home** toolbar.
6. In the **Home** toolbar, select the **Wall** button to bring up the **Modify | Place Wall** toolbar.
7. In the **Modify | Place Wall** toolbar, select the **Line** button in the **Draw** panel.
8. Place **10′** high **Generic - 8″** walls as shown in Figure 7-49.
9. In the **Home** toolbar, select the **Roof > Roof by Footprint** button to bring up the **Modify | Create Roof Footprint** toolbar.
10. Select **Yes** when asked whether you want to move the **Roof** to **Level 2**.
11. In the **Modify | Create Roof Footprint** toolbar, select the **Line** button in the **Draw** panel, and create the lines shown in Figure 7-50.

Be sure that only the **East** wall has a **Slope Angle**, and that the **Slope Angle** is 6″ (click on the line to expose the **Slope Angle** icon, change it by clicking on the numeric field, and enter **6″** from the keyboard).

12. In the **Modify | Create Roof Footprint** toolbar, press the **Finish Edit Mode** button, and select **No** when the **Revit** dialog box asks whether you would like to attach the highlighted walls to the roof (see Figure 7-51).

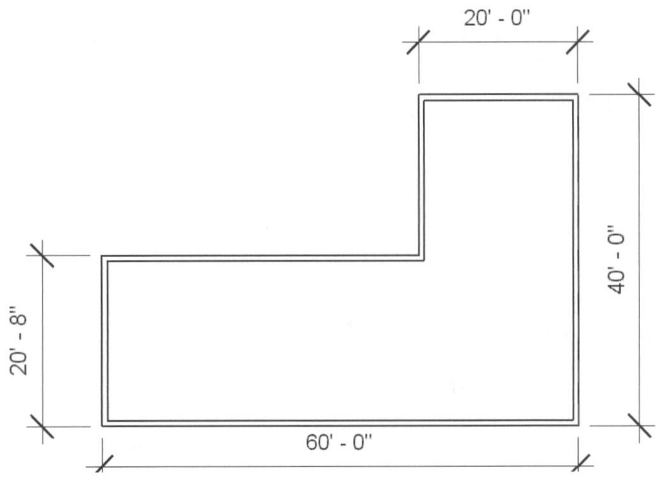

Figure 7-49

Create **Generic - 8″** walls

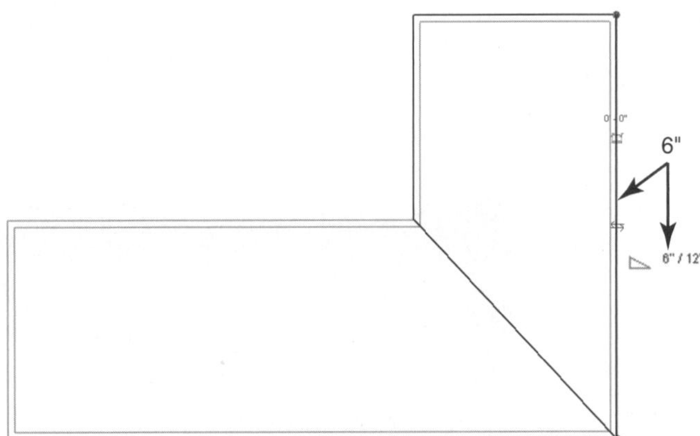

Figure 7-50

Use the **Line** tool to modify the wall

13. In the **LEVEL 1** Plan view, select the **Home** tab to bring up the **Home** toolbar.
14. In the **Home** toolbar, select the **Ref Plane** button to bring up the **Modify | Place Reference Plane** toolbar.
15. In the **Modify | Place Reference Plane** toolbar, pick the **Pick Lines** button from the **Draw** panel.
16. Pick the **East** wall of the enclosure to place a **Reference Plane**.
17. Select the **Reference Plane** you just placed to bring up its **Properties** dialog box.
18. In the **Properties** dialog box, enter **EAST ROOF EDGE** in the **Name** field, and press the **OK** button to return to the **Drawing Editor**.
19. In the **Home** toolbar, select the **Roof > Roof by Extrusion** button from the **Build** panel to bring up the **Work Plane** dialog box.
20. In the **Work Plane** dialog box, select the **Pick a plane** radio button and **Reference Plane: EAST ROOF EDGE** from the **Specify a new Work Plan** drop-down list. Finally, press the **OK** button.

Figure 7-51

Finish Edit Mode

21. Since you are in a Plan view, the **Go To View** dialog box will now appear.
22. In the **Go To View** dialog box, select **Elevation: East**, and press the **Open View** button.
23. The view will now change to the **East Elevation**, and the **Roof Reference Level and Offset** dialog box will appear.
24. In the **Roof Reference Level and Offset** dialog box, change to **Level 2** from the **Level** drop-down list, and press the **OK** button.

You will now be in the **Modify | Create Extrusion Roof Profile** toolbar.

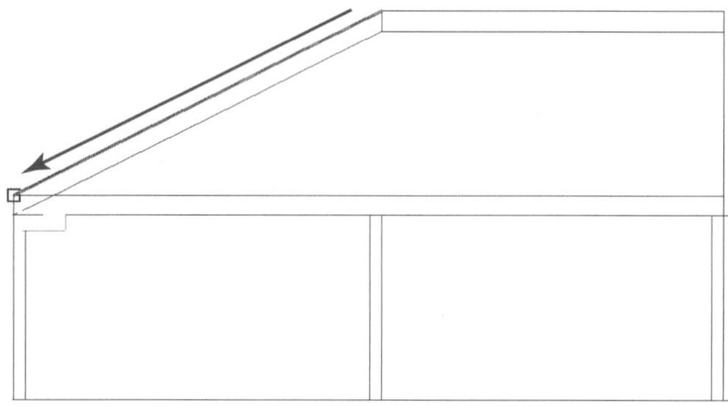

Figure 7-52

Place a **line** with **Snaps (On)**

25. In the **Modify | Create Extrusion Roof Profile** toolbar, select the **Line** button in the **Draw** panel.
26. With the **Snaps (On)**, place a line as shown in Figure 7-52, and press the **<Esc>** key to end the command.
27. Press the **Finish Edit Mode** button in the **Roof** panel, and select **No** when the **Revit** dialog box asks whether you would like to attach the highlighted walls to the roof.
28. Change to the **Default 3D View**.
29. Select the **Modify** tab to bring up the **Modify** toolbar.
30. In the **Modify** toolbar, select the **Join/Unjoin Roof** button from the **Geometry** panel (see Figure 7-53).

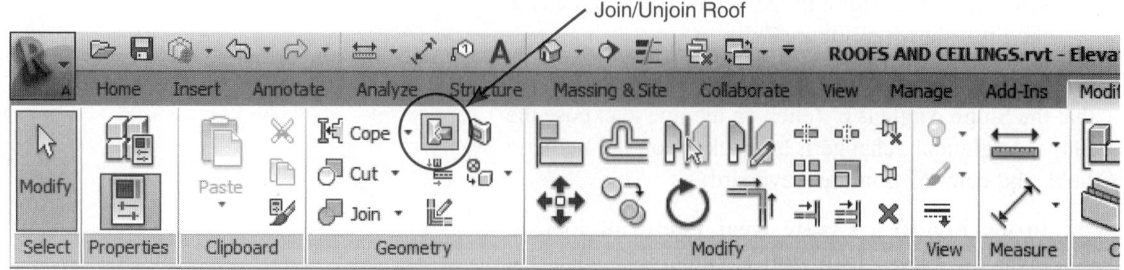

Figure 7-53

Join/Unjoin Roof button

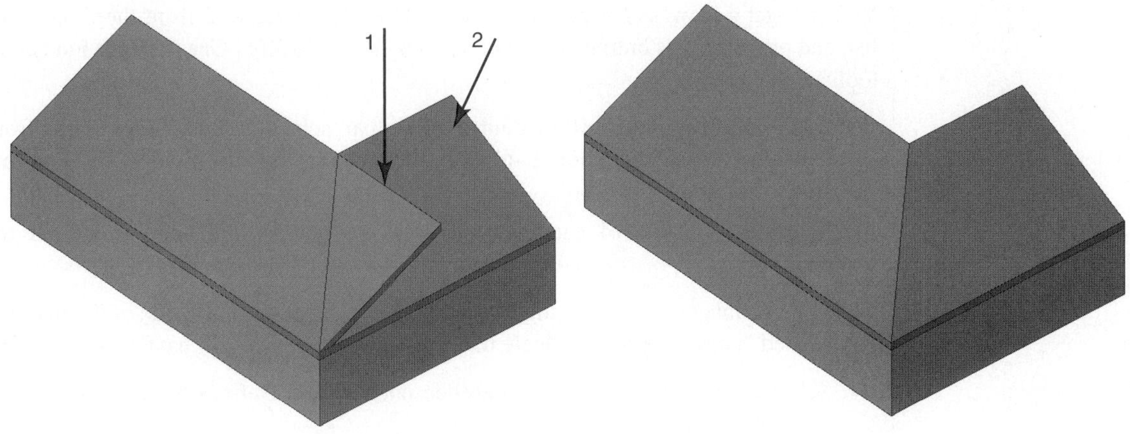

Figure 7-54

Select the roofs you want to join

31. Select the edge of the roof you want to join, and then the existing roof you want to join with it (see Figure 7-54).
32. Save this file as **JOIN_UNJOIN ROOF**.

EXERCISE 7-10 **CREATING A DORMER**

1. Start a new drawing using the RAC 2012\Imperial Templates\default.rte template.
2. In the **Project Browser**, double-click on the **LEVEL 1** floor plan to bring it into the **Drawing Editor**.
3. Change the **Drawing Scale** to **1/4″ = 1′-0″**.
4. Set the **Detail Level** to **Medium**.
5. Select the **Home** tab to bring up the **Home** toolbar.
6. In the **Home** toolbar, select the **Wall** button to bring up the **Modify | Place Wall** toolbar.
7. In the **Modify | Place Wall** toolbar, select the **Rectangle** button from the **Draw** panel, and create an enclosure **50′-0″** long by **30′-0″** wide and **10′-0″** high using the **Generic - 8″** wall (see Figure 7-55).
8. In the **Home** toolbar, select the **Roof > Roof by Footprint** button.

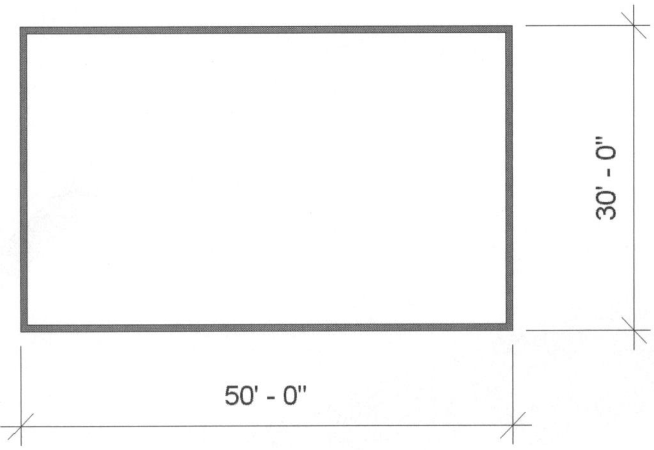

Figure 7-55

Create an enclosure

You will get a **Lowest Level Notice** dialog box. Select **Level 2** from the drop-down list, and press the **Yes** button. You will now enter the **Modify | Create Roof Footprint** toolbar.

9. In the **Modify | Create Roof Footprint** toolbar, select the **Pick Lines** button from the **Draw** panel, and enter **2′-0″** in the **Overhang** numeric field of the **Options Bar**.
10. Select the outside of each wall until a continuous line appears around the enclosure.

Notice that a magenta-colored angle symbol appears opposite each side of the line you just created. These symbols indicate that this side of the roof will have a slope.

11. Select the left and right lines, and then uncheck the **Defines Slope** check box in the **Options Bar**.
12. Select the top and bottom lines, and enter **12** in the numeric field next to the angle symbol. This will create a **12″/12″** or **45 degree** slope (see Figure 7-56).

Figure 7-56

Create a slope

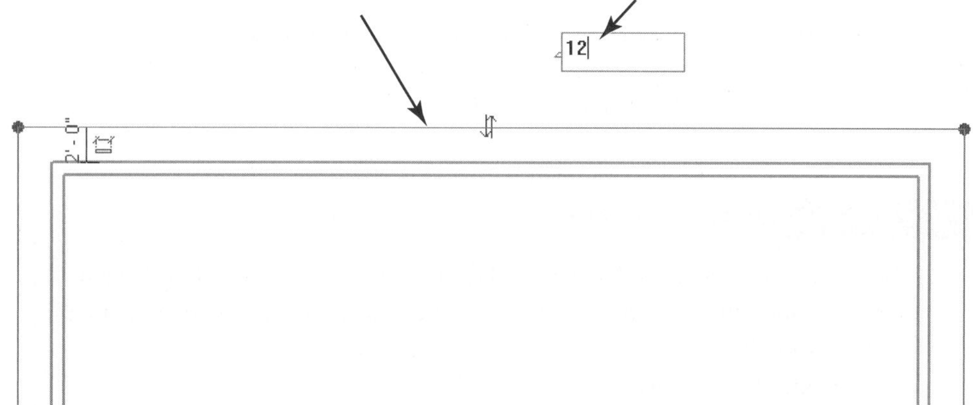

13. In the **Modify | Create Roof Footprint** toolbar, press the **Finish Edit Mode** button to create the roof.

A **Revit** dialog box will appear asking whether you would like to attach the highlighted walls to the roof. Press the **Yes** button, and select the **3D** button in the **View** toolbar to bring up a **Default 3D View** (see Figure 7-57).

Figure 7-57

Change to **Default 3D View**

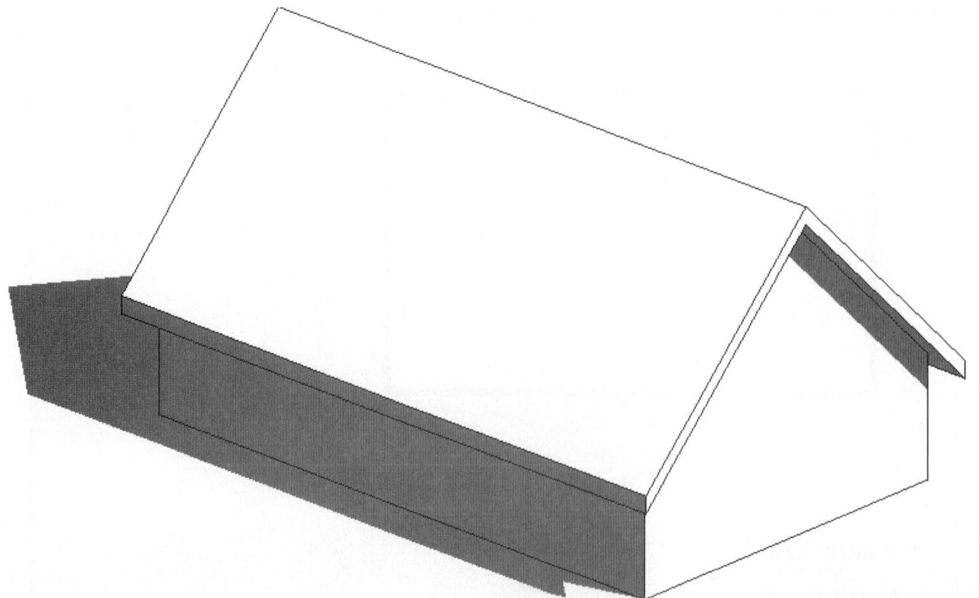

14. Double-click on the **LEVEL 2** floor plan in the **Project Browser** to bring it into the **Drawing Editor**.
15. In the **LEVEL 2** floor plan, select the roof, and then select the **Temporary Hide/Isolate** button at the bottom of the **Drawing Editor**. Select **Hide Element** to hide the roof (see Figure 7-58).

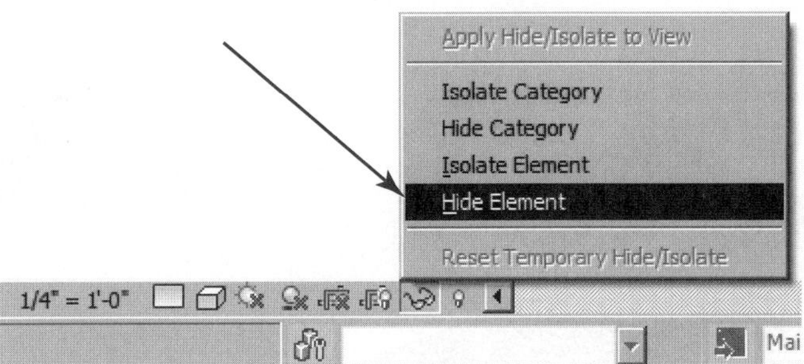

Figure 7-58

Select **Hide Element** to hide the roof

16. Select one of the walls of the enclosure, **RMB**, and select **Create Similar** from the contextual menu that appears.
17. In the **Options Bar**, select **Unconnected** from the **Height** drop-down list, and enter **6′-0″** in the adjacent numerical field, and then select **Location Line = Finish Face Exterior** to create **6′-0″** high dormer walls.
18. Place walls as shown in Figure 7-59.

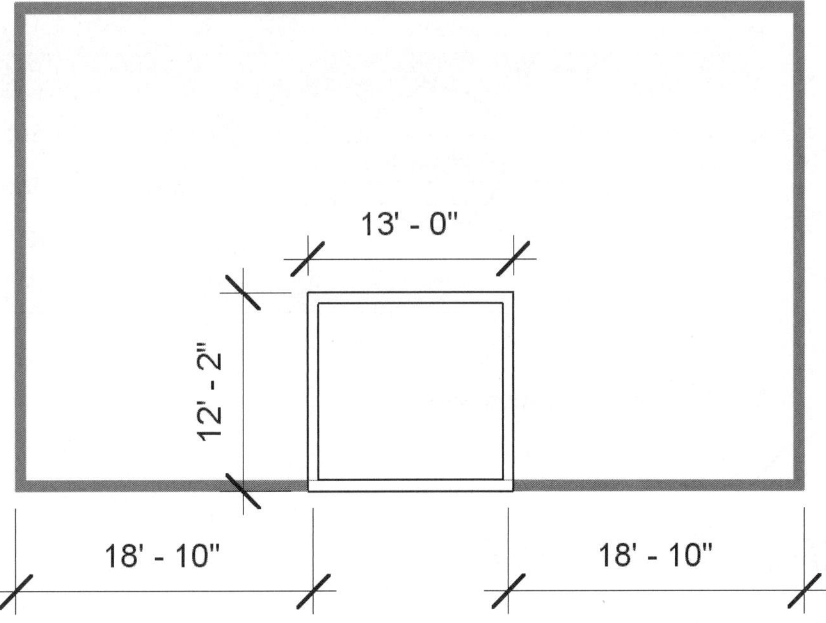

Figure 7-59

Walls in place

19. Again, select the **3D** button in the **Quick Access** toolbar to bring up a **Default 3D View** (see Figure 7-60).
20. Select the **Temporary Hide/Isolate** button at the bottom of the **Drawing Editor**, and select **Reset Temporary Hide/Isolate** to unhide the roof.
21. Double-click on the **East Elevation** in the **Project Browser** to bring it into the **Drawing Editor**.

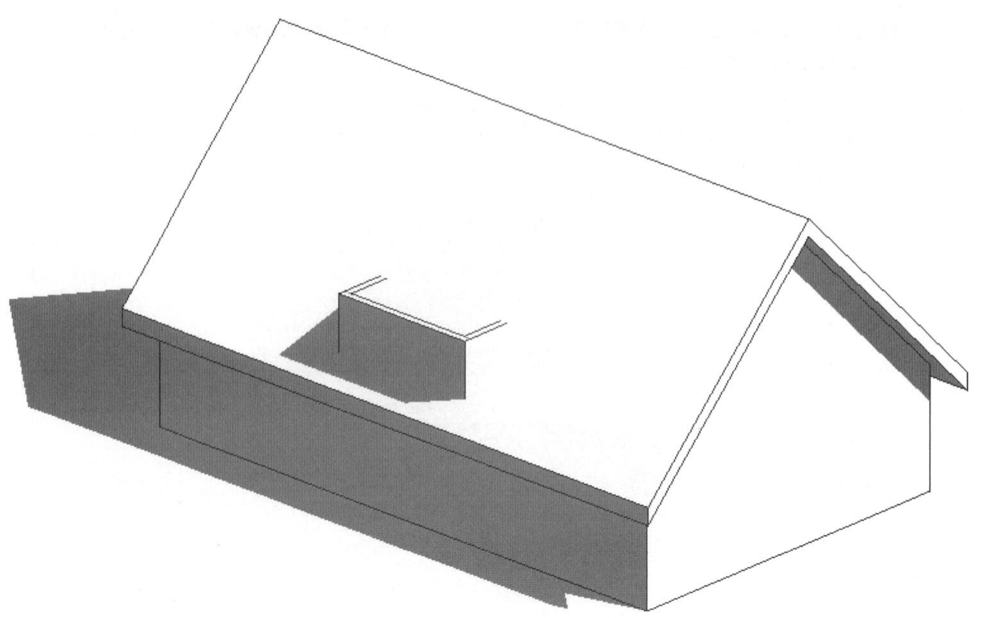

Figure 7-60

Open a **Default 3D View**

22. In the **Home** toolbar, select the **Level** button in the **Datum** panel, and place a new level called **Level 3** at the top of the dormer wall you just created (see Figures 7-61 and 7-62).

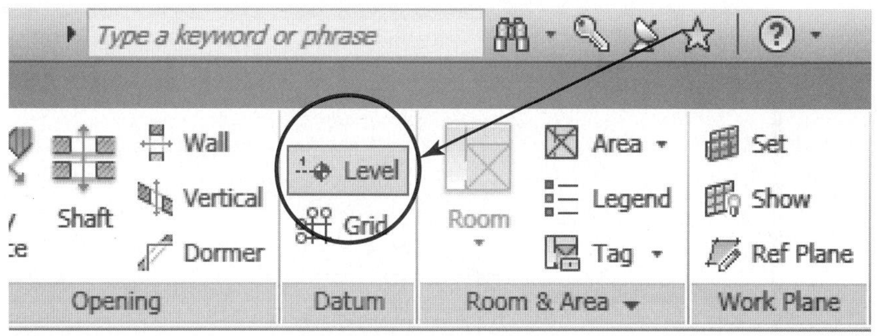

Figure 7-61

Level button in the **Datum** panel

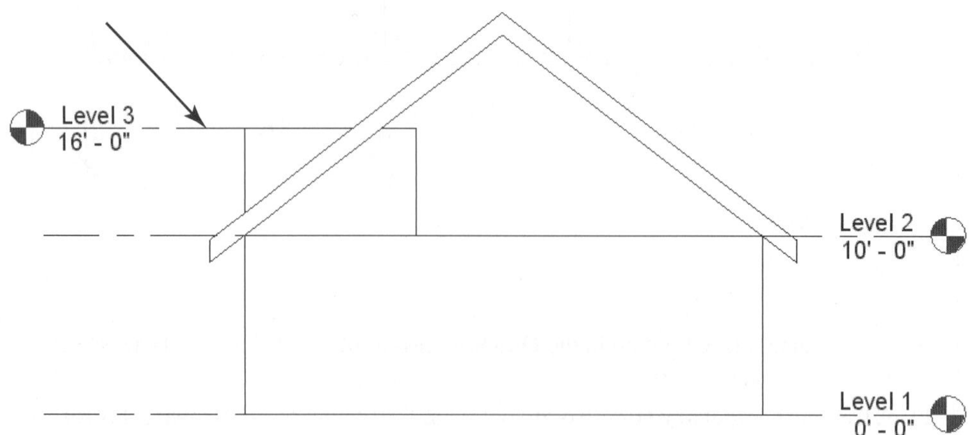

Figure 7-62

New **Level 3**

23. In the **Project Browser**, double-click on the **LEVEL 3** floor plan you created to bring that view into the **Drawing Editor**.
24. In the **Home** toolbar, select the **Roof > Roof by Footprint** button to bring up the **Modify | Create Roof Footprint** toolbar.
25. In the **Modify | Create Roof Footprint** toolbar, select the **Pick Lines** button, and enter **2′-0″** in the **Overhang** numeric field of the **Options Bar**.
26. Select the outside of each of the **6′-0″** high walls until a continuous line appears around the enclosure.

Notice that a magenta-colored angle symbol appears opposite each side of the line you just created. These symbols indicate that this side of the roof will have a slope.

27. Select the top and bottom lines, and then uncheck the **Defines Slope** check box in the **Options Bar**.
28. Select the top and bottom lines, and enter **9** in the numeric field next to the angle symbol. This will create a **9″/12″** slope.
29. Press the **Finish Edit Mode** button to create the dormer roof.
30. Select the **3D** button in the **Quick Access** toolbar to bring up a **Default 3D View** (see Figure 7-63).

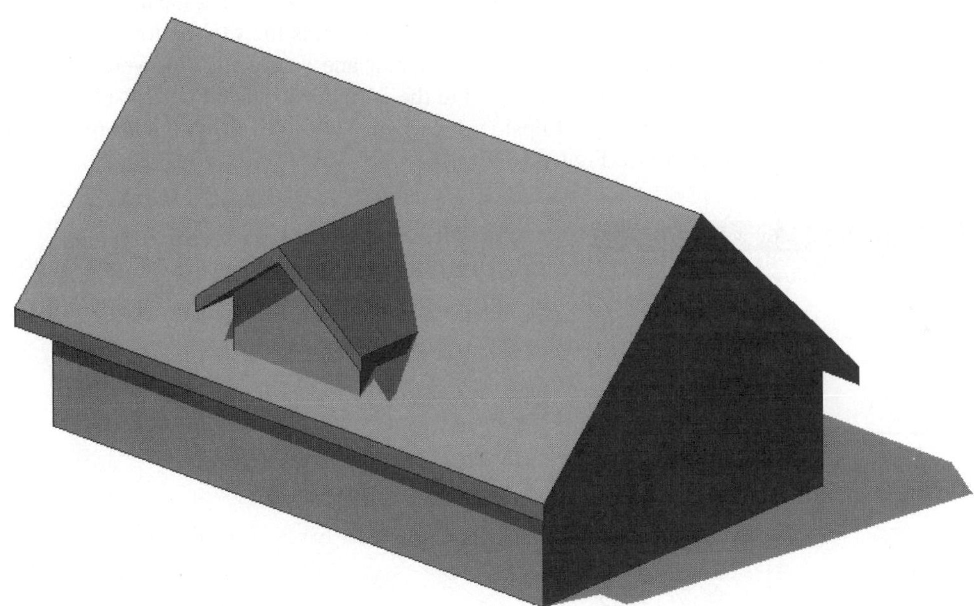

Figure 7-63

Default 3D View of dormer

Now you must now join the dormer roof to the main roof.

31. Select the **Model Graphics Style** button at the bottom of the **Drawing Editor**, and then select **Wireframe** (see Figure 7-64).
32. Select the **Modify** tab to bring up the **Modify** toolbar.
33. In the **Modify** toolbar, select the **Join/Unjoin Roof** button from the **Geometry** panel.
34. Select an edge of the dormer roof that touches the main roof, and then touch an edge of the roof that touches the dormer roof (see Figure 7-65).

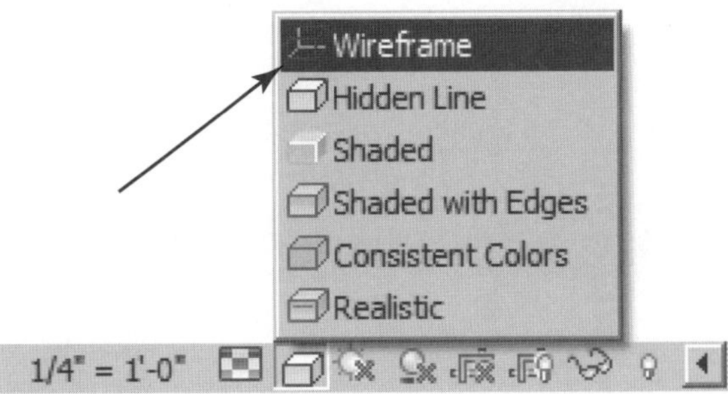

Figure 7-64

Select **Wireframe**

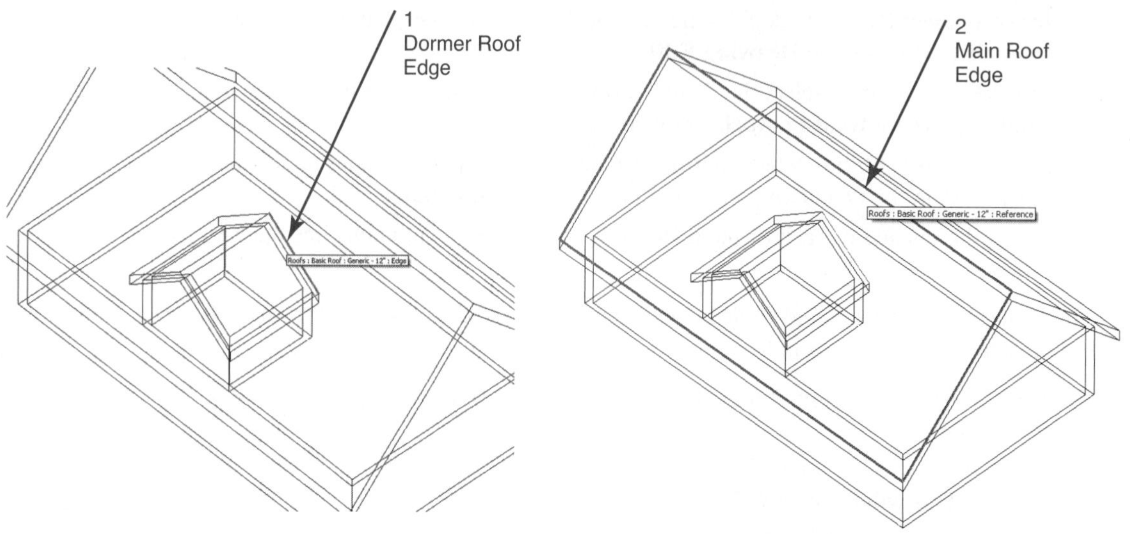

Figure 7-65

Select edges of the dormer and main roofs

You will get a **Revit Architecture** dialog box telling you that the highlighted walls are attached to, but miss, the highlighted targets. Press the **OK** button. The dormer roof will be cut to fit the main roof, and the rear and side walls that were attached to the dormer no longer are fully attached to the dormer roof (see Figure 7-66).

If you turn the model upside down, you will notice that the dormer has not cut through the roof (see Figure 7-67).

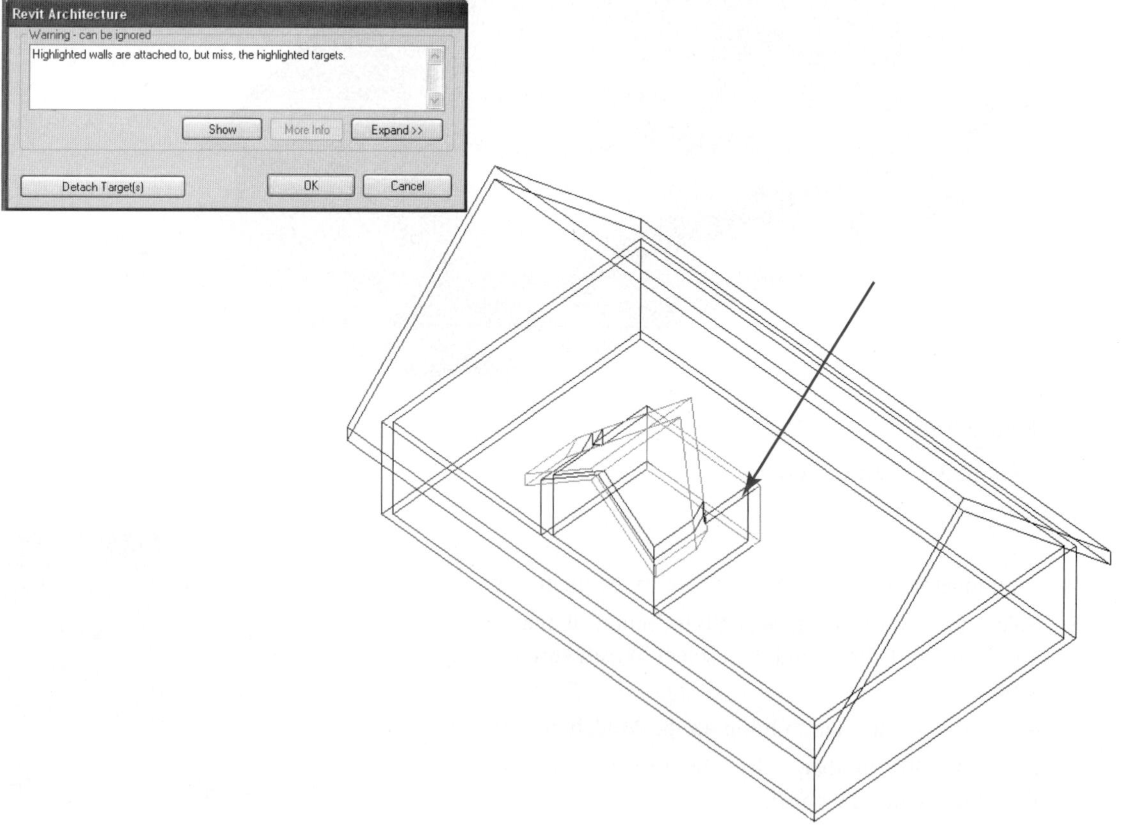

Figure 7-66

Dormer rear and side walls are no longer attached to dormer

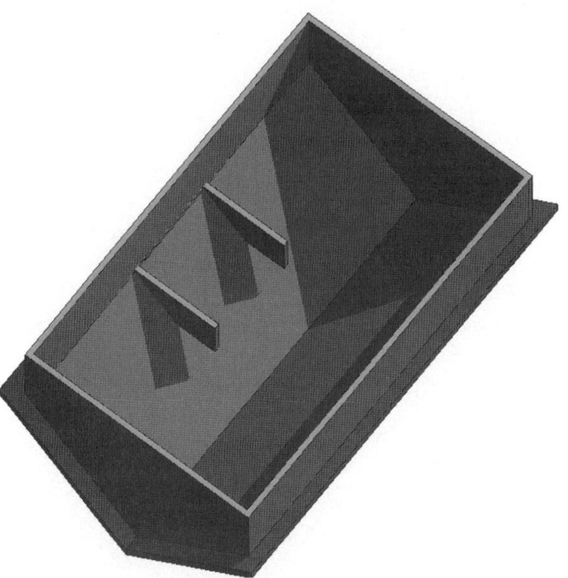

Figure 7-67

Turn the model upside down to see that dormer has not cut through the roof

35. Return the model to its normal position.
36. In the **Home** toolbar, select the **Dormer** button in the **Opening** panel (see Figure 7-68).

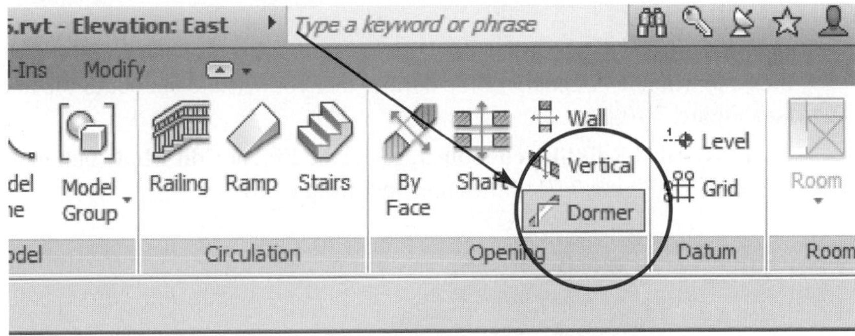

Figure 7-68

Select the **Dormer** button

37. Select the main roof to bring up the **Modify | Edit Sketch** toolbar.
38. In the **Modify | Edit Sketch** toolbar, select the **Pick Roof/Wall Edges** button (see Figure 7-69).

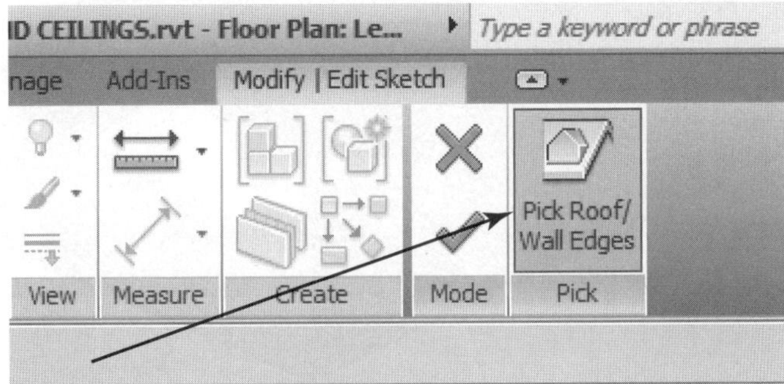

Figure 7-69

Pick Roof/Wall Edges button

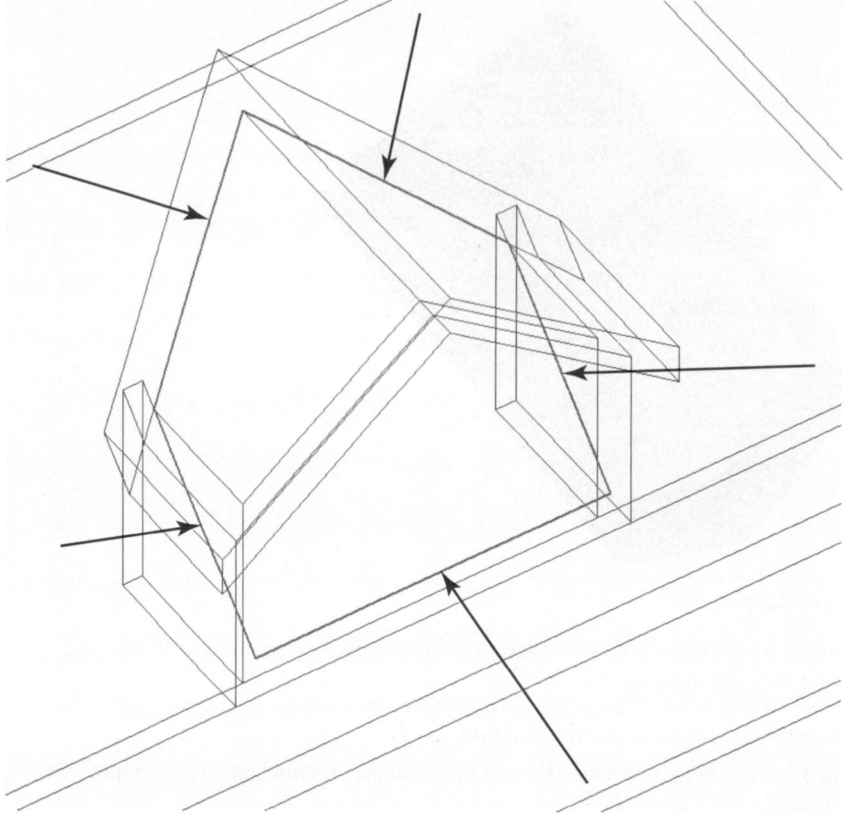

Figure 7-70

Pick and trim the boundary of the dormer to be cut out

39. Pick and trim the boundary of the dormer that you wish to cut out of the main roof (see Figure 7-70).
40. In the **Modify | Edit Sketch** toolbar, select the **Finish Edit Mode** button to create the opening. Figure 7-71 shows the view from below.

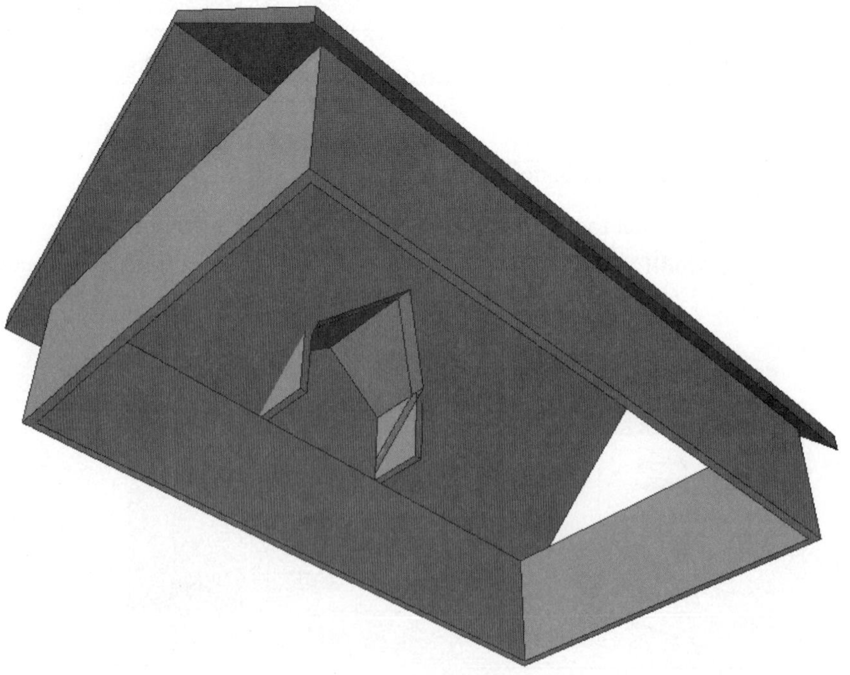

Figure 7-71

View showing the cut-out dormer from below

41. Select the **Home** tab to bring up the **Home** toolbar.
42. In the **Home** toolbar, select the **Window** button to bring up the **Modify | Place Window** toolbar.
43. From the **Modify | Place Window** toolbar, add a window (see Figure 7-72).

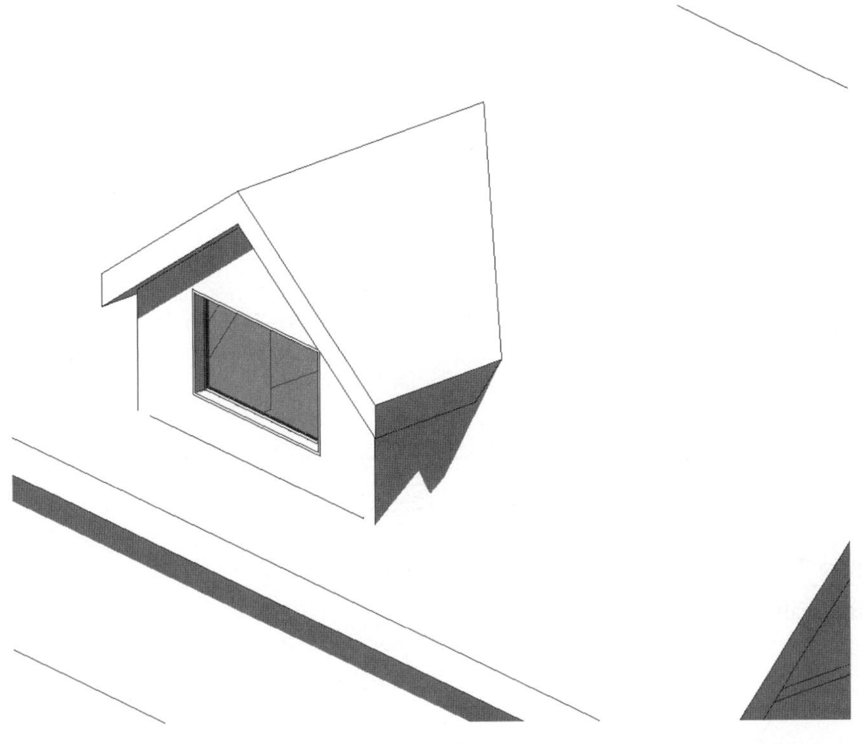

Figure 7-72

Add a window

44. Double-click on the **LEVEL 3** floor plan to bring up the **Level 3** view in the **Drawing Editor**.
45. Select the dormer walls, roof, and window (hold down the **<CTRL>** key while selecting each object) to bring up the **Modify | Multi-Select** toolbar.
46. In the **Modify | Multi-Select** toolbar, select the **Move** button and move them to the left.
47. Select the dormer walls, roof, and window again, and then select **Mirror - Draw Axis** from the **Modify | Multi-Select** toolbar. In the **Options Bar**, check the **Copy** check box (see Figure 7-73).

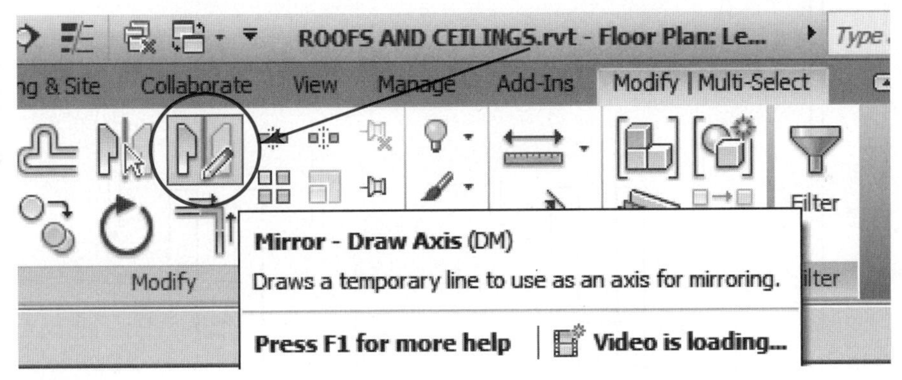

Figure 7-73

Modify | Multi-Select toolbar

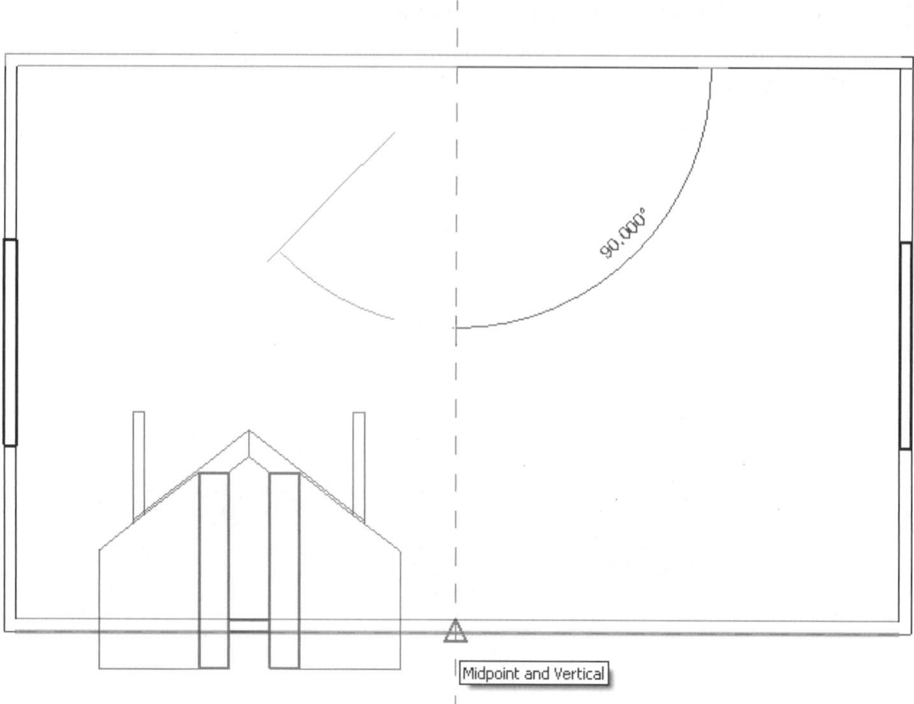

Figure 7-74

South wall

48. With the **Midpoint Snap (On)**, select the **South** wall, as shown in Figure 7-74.
49. Click the second point of the axis to make a copy of the dormer (see Figures 7-75 and 7-76).
50. Save this file as **DORMERS**.

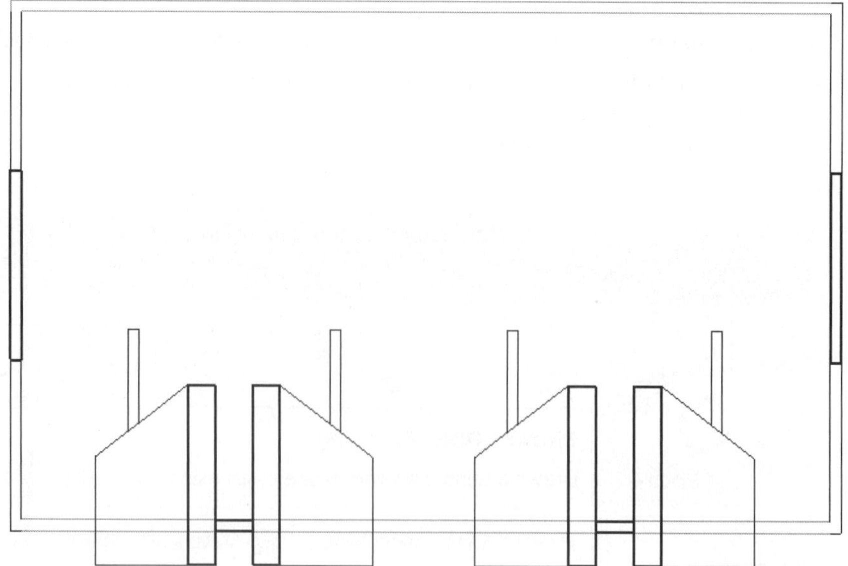

Figure 7-75

Make a copy of the dormer

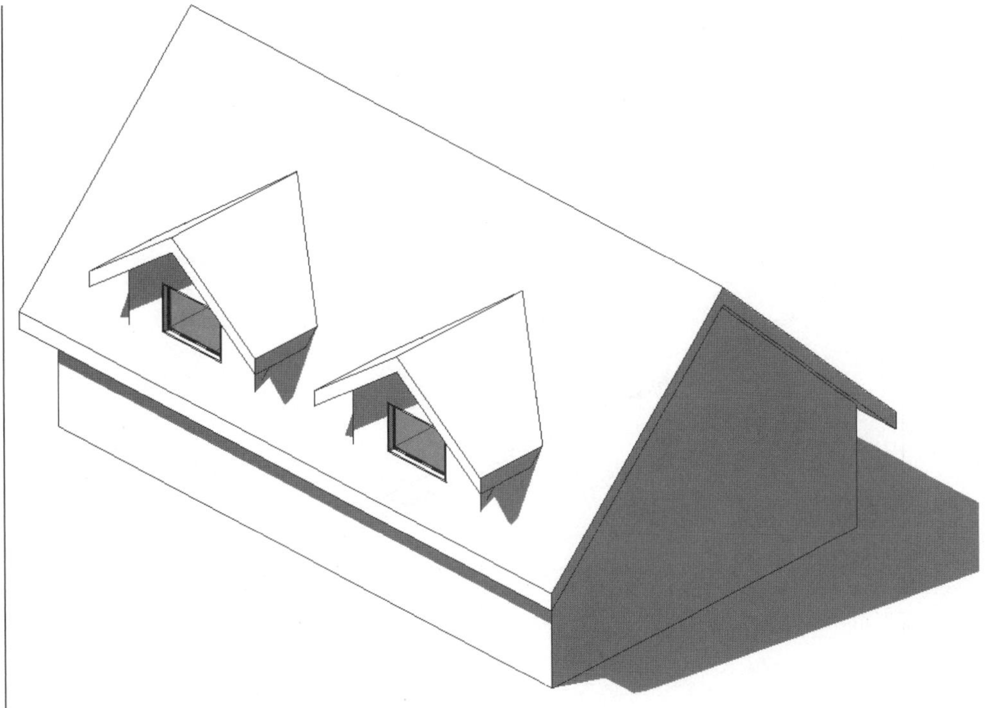

Figure 7-76
Dormer drawing

EXERCISE 7-11 ADDING GUTTERS

1. Use the **JOIN/UNJOIN ROOF** file.
2. Change to the **Default 3D View**.
3. Select the **Home** tab to bring up the **Home** toolbar.
4. In the **Home** toolbar, select the **Roof > Gutter** button in the **Build** panel to bring up the **Modify | Place Gutter** toolbar (see Figure 7-77).

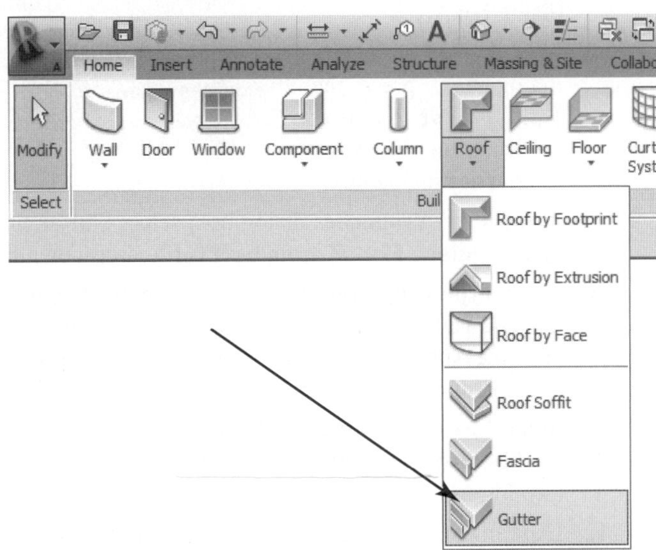

Figure 7-77
Roof > Gutter button

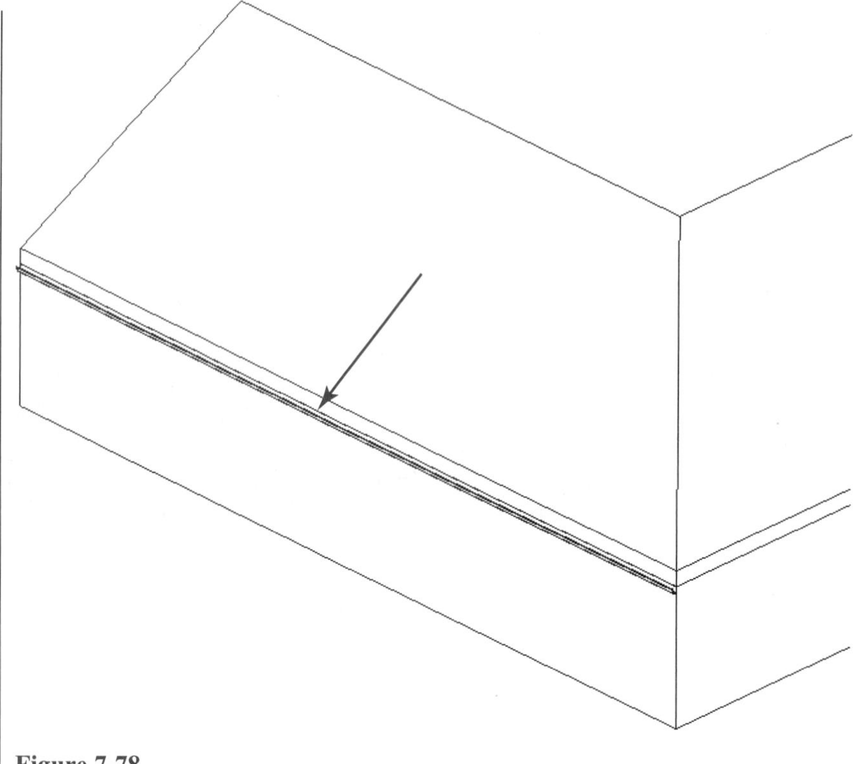

Figure 7-78

Place a gutter on the edge of the roof

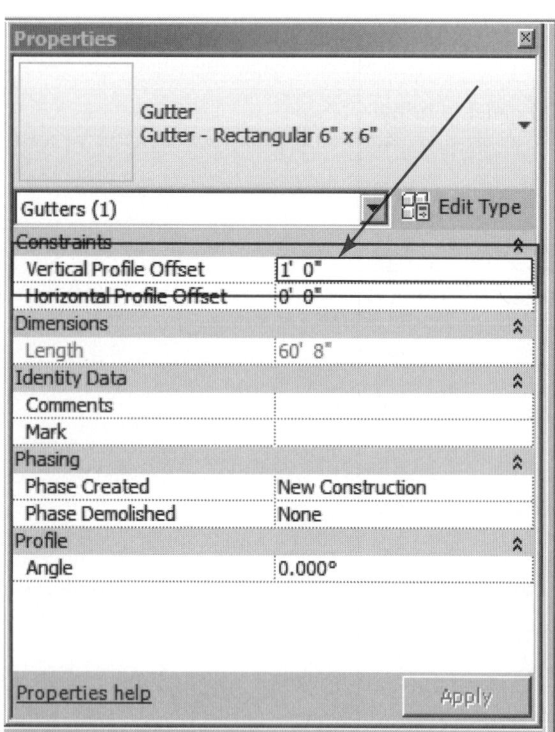

Figure 7-79

Instance Properties dialog box

5. Select the edge of the roof, and a gutter will appear (see Figure 7-78).
6. Change to the **East** view so that you can see the gutter in profile.
7. Select the gutter to bring up its **Properties** dialog box.
8. In the **Properties** dialog box, press the **Edit Type** button to bring up the **Type Properties** dialog box.

> **NOTE:**
>
> The default gutter is **Bevel 5′ × 5′**, but you can change the type of gutter by selecting the gutter to bring up the **Modify Gutters** toolbar and selecting a different gutter from the **Change Element** drop-down list.
>
> Gutters are created from profiles, and the profiles are located in the **Imperial Library > Families > Roofs** folder.

9. In the **Type Properties** dialog box, select **Gutter profile – Rectangular : 5″ × 5″** from the **Profile** drop-down list.
10. In the **Type Properties** dialog box, select the **Duplicate** button, and name the duplicate **Gutter – Rectangular 6″ × 6″**, press the **Apply** button, and then press the **OK** button to return to the **Properties** dialog box.
11. In the **Instance Properties** dialog box, change the **Vertical Profile Offset** to **1′-0″**, and watch the gutter move upward (see Figure 7-79).
12. Experiment by changing profiles and adjusting the **Vertical** and **Horizontal Profile Offsets**.
13. Save this file as **ROOF GUTTERS**.

EXERCISE 7-12 CREATING A ROOF FAMILY

Revit ships with seven default Roofs. Roof type structures are created in the same manner as you create Wall types.

1. Open the **ROOF by FOOTPRINT** file.
2. Change to the **South Elevation** view.
3. Select the roof to bring up its **Properties** dialog box.
4. In the **Properties** dialog box, select **Steel Truss – Insulation on Metal deck – EPDM** from the **Type** drop-down list.
5. In the **Properties** dialog box, press the **Edit Type** button to bring up the **Type Properties** dialog box.
6. In the **Type Properties** dialog box, press the **Edit** button in the **Structure** field to bring up the **Edit Assembly** dialog box.
7. In the **Edit Assembly** dialog box, at the lower left, press the **Preview** button to see a preview of the roof structure.

You can now see how the **Steel Truss – Insulation on Metal deck – EPDM** is structured. The method for changing the structure is identical to that shown in Chapter 3 on Wall structures.

8. Experiment by changing the roof structure, and observe how the roof changes.

EXERCISE 7-13 SHAPE EDITING

1. Start a new drawing using the RAC 2012\Imperial Templates\default.rte template.
2. In the **Project Browser**, double-click on the **LEVEL 1** floor plan to bring it into the **Drawing Editor**.
3. Change the **Drawing Scale** to **1/4″ = 1′-0″**.
4. Set the **Detail Level** to **Medium**.
5. Select the **Home** tab to bring up the **Home** toolbar.
6. In the **Home** toolbar, select the **Wall** button to bring up the **Modify | Place Wall** toolbar.
7. Place **Generic - 8″** walls **10′-0″** high as shown in Figure 7-80.

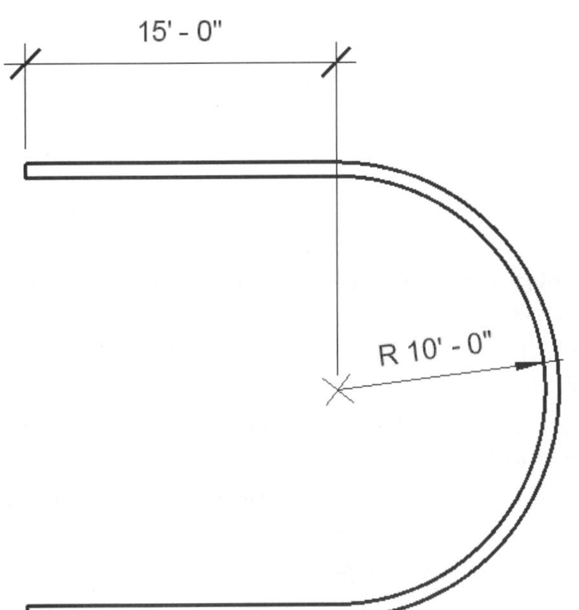

Figure 7-80

Create **Generic - 8″** walls

8. Change to the **Default 3D View**.
9. Select the arc wall to bring up its **Properties** dialog box.
10. In the **Properties** dialog box, change the arc wall to **16′-0″** high (see Figure 7-81).

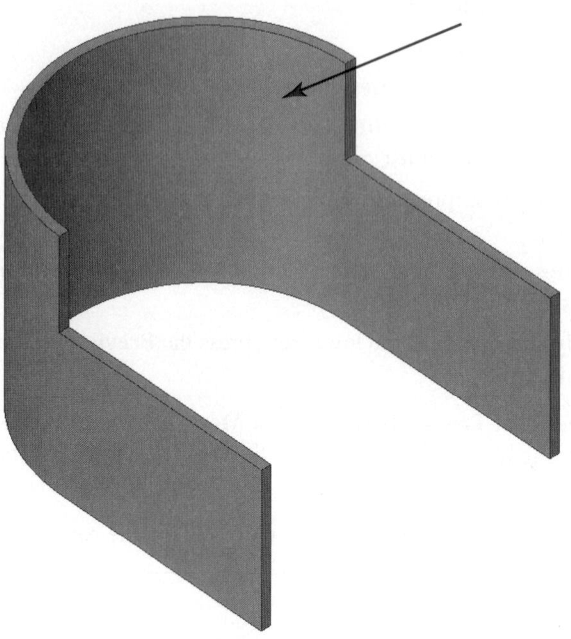

Figure 7-81

Arc wall

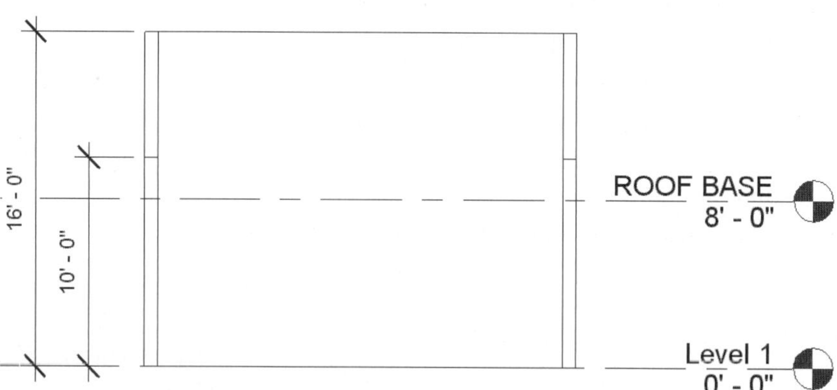

Figure 7-82

Change height of **East Elevation**

11. Change to the **East Elevation**, rename **Level 2** to **ROOF BASE**, and change its height to **8′-0″** (see Figure 7-82).
12. Double-click on the **ROOF BASE** floor plan in the **Project Browser** to bring it into the **Drawing Editor**.
13. In the **Home** toolbar, select the **Roof > Roof by Footprint** button to bring up the **Modify | Create Roof Footprint** toolbar.
14. In the **Modify | Create Roof Footprint** toolbar in the **Draw** panel, select the **Pick Walls** button.
15. In the **Options Bar**, uncheck the **Defines Slope** check box.
16. Pick the inside of the three walls.

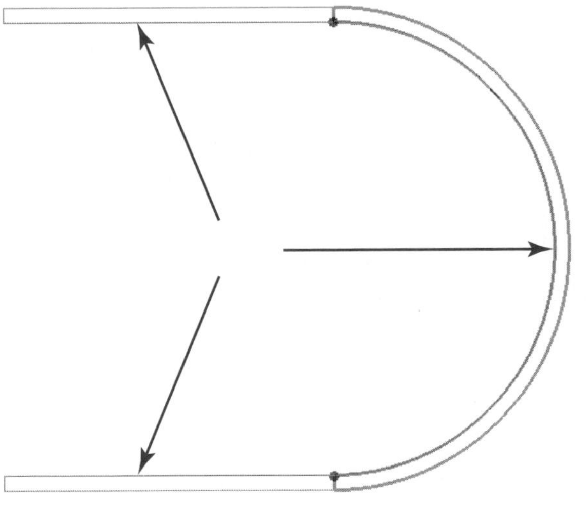

Figure 7-83

Complete the roof lines

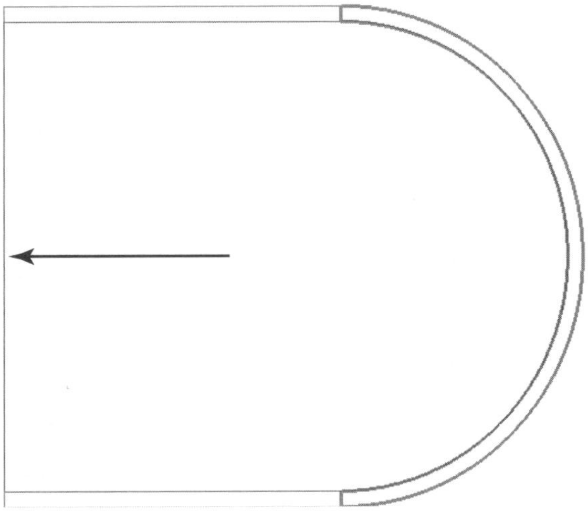

Figure 7-84

Complete the roof lines

17. Next, in the **Modify | Create Roof Footprint** toolbar, select the **Pick Lines** button, and complete the roof lines (see Figures 7-83 and 7-84).
18. In the **Properties** dialog box, select the **Edit Type** button to bring up the **Type Properties** dialog box (see Figure 7-85).
19. In the **Type Properties** dialog box, select **Generic - 12″** for the **Type**, and press the **OK** button to return to the **Properties** dialog box.
20. In the **Properties** dialog box, select **ROOF BASE** for the **Base Level,** and press the **OK** button to return to the **Drawing Editor**.
21. Next, in the **Modify | Create Roof Footprint** toolbar, select the **Finish Edit Mode** button to create the roof.
22. Change to the **Default 3D View** (see Figure 7-86).
23. Select the roof you just placed to bring up the **Modify | Roofs** toolbar.

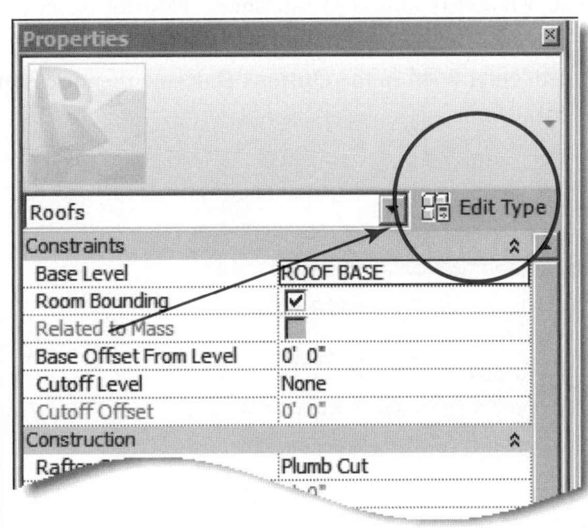

Figure 7-85

Type Properties dialog box

Figure 7-86

Default 3D View

24. In the **Modify | Roofs** toolbar, select the **Add Point** button (see Figure 7-87).
25. Select the middle of the curved section of the roof to place a point (see Figure 7-88).

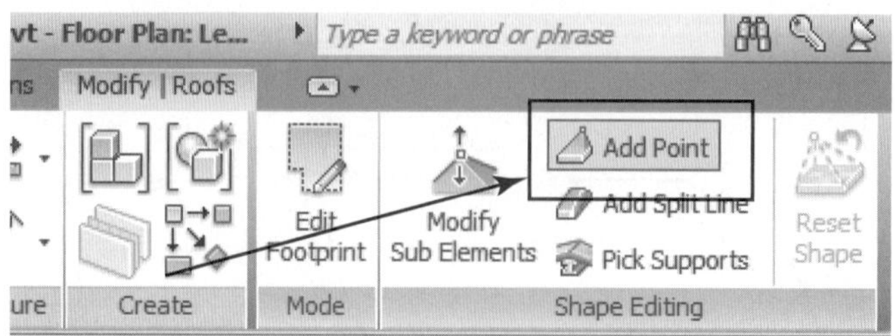

Figure 7-87

Add Point button

Figure 7-88

Curved section of roof

26. Next, select the **Modify Sub Elements** button in the **Shape Editing** panel (see Figure 7-89).
27. Select the point you just added, enter **3′-0″** in the **Options Bar**, and then press the **<Enter>** key (see Figure 7-90).

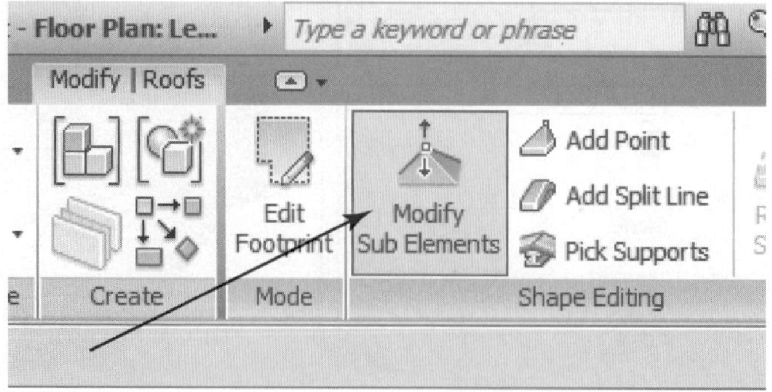

Figure 7-89

Modify Sub Elements button in the **Shape Editing** panel

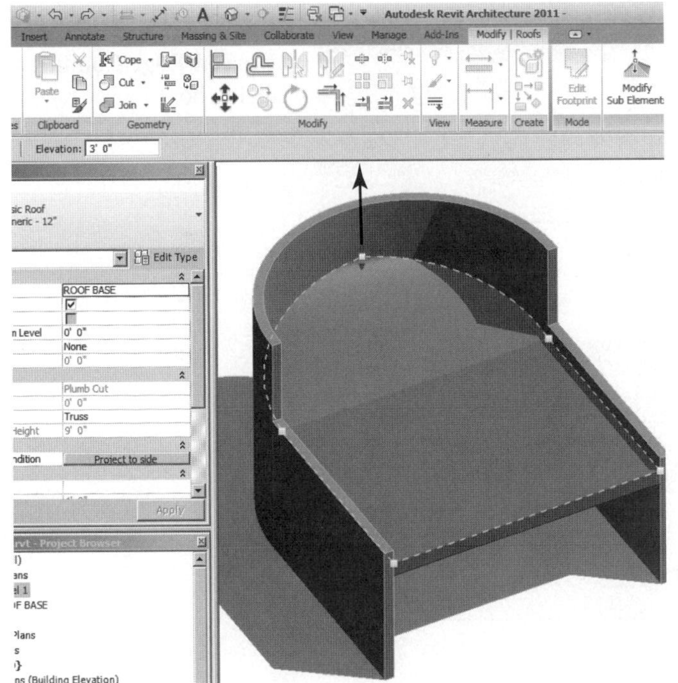

Figure 7-90

Change the value of the point just added

28. Take notice of the warning, and then press the <**Esc**> key on your keyboard to complete the command (see Figure 7-91).
29. Again, select the roof, to bring up its **Properties** dialog box.
30. In the **Properties** dialog box, select the button opposite the **Curved Edge Condition** field to bring up the **Curved Edge Condition** dialog box.

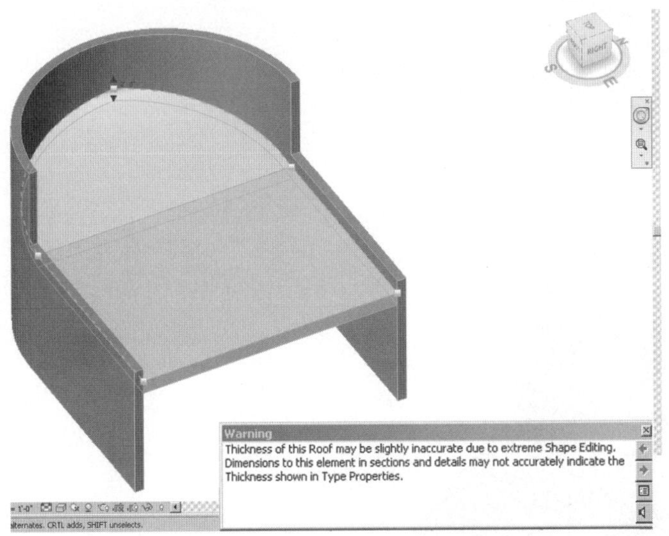

Figure 7-91

Notice the warning, then finish the command

31. In the **Curved Edge Condition** dialog box, select the **Project to side** radio button, and press the **OK** button to return to the **Drawing Editor** (see Figure 7-92).
32. In the **Modify | Roofs** toolbar, again select the **Add Point** button, and add a point at the midpoint of the slab.
33. Again, select the **Modify Sub Elements** button in the **Shape Editing** panel.
34. Select the point you just placed, and enter **-0′-4″** in the **Elevation** field in the **Options Bar** to move the point downward (see Figure 7-93).
35. Double-click on the **Site** view in the **Project Browser** to bring it into the **Drawing Editor**.

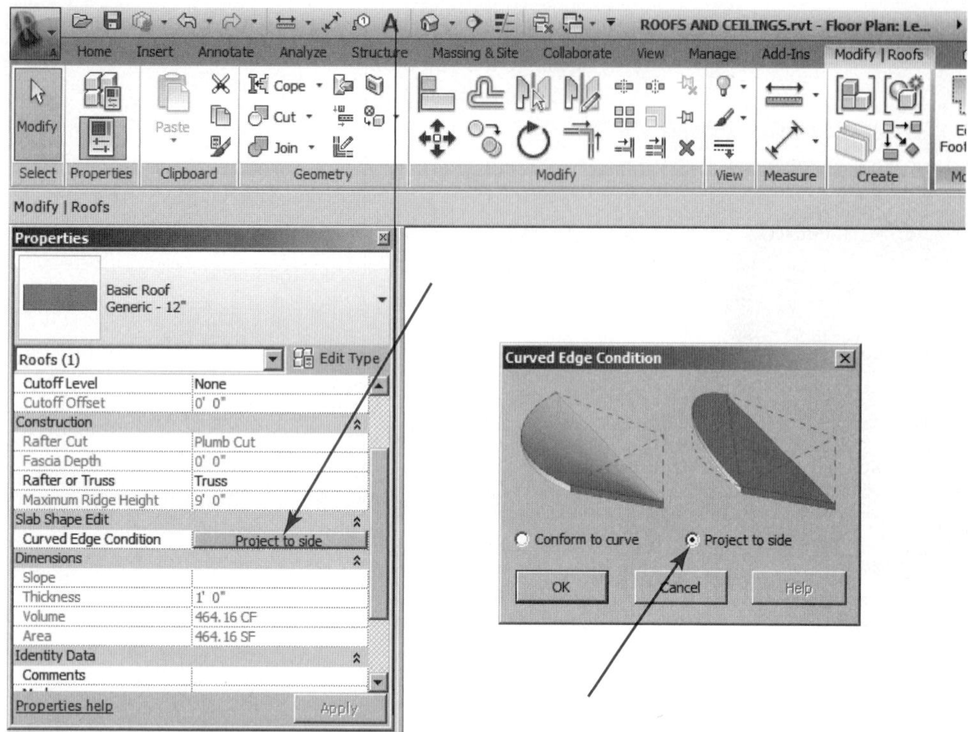

Figure 7-92

Curved Edge Condition dialog box

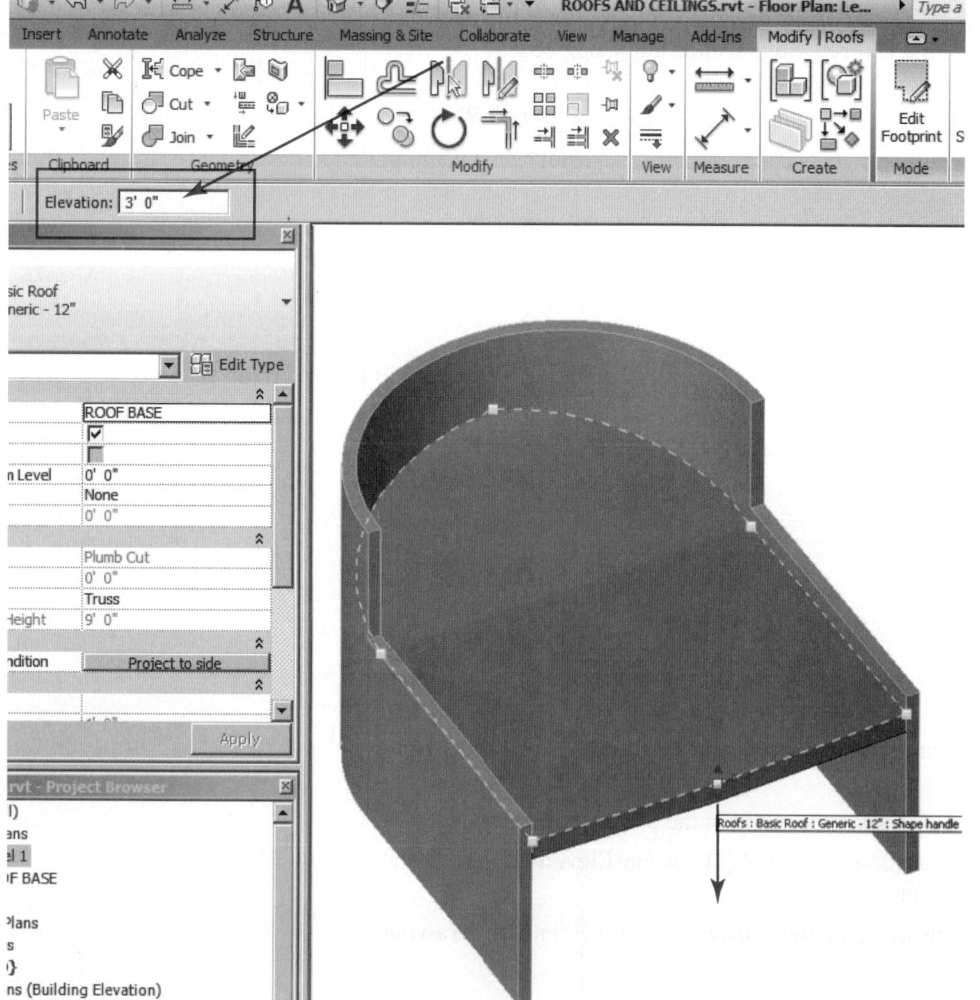

Figure 7-93

Move the point downward

36. Select the walls and roof to bring up the **Modify | Multi-Select** toolbar.
37. In the **Modify | Multi-Select** toolbar, select the **Mirror - Draw Mirror Axis** button in the **Modify** panel.
38. In the **Options Bar**, check the **Copy** check box, and drag an axis as shown in Figure 7-94.

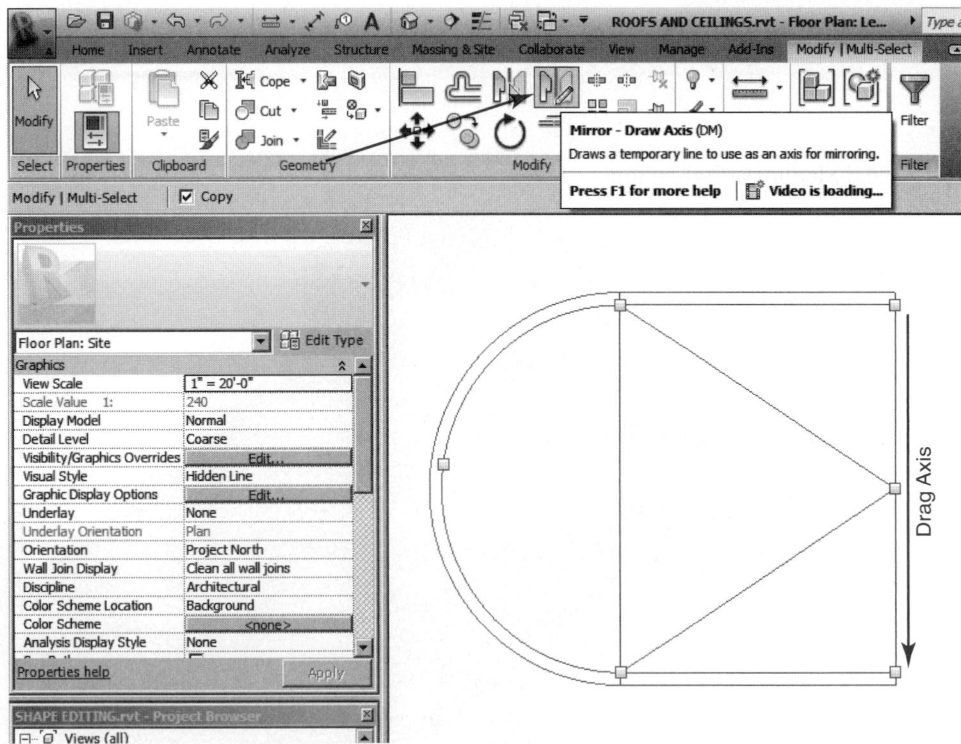

Figure 7-94

Drag an axis

You will now have mirrored both sides of the building. Observe the warning, and then press the **<Esc>** key to finish the command (see Figure 7-95).

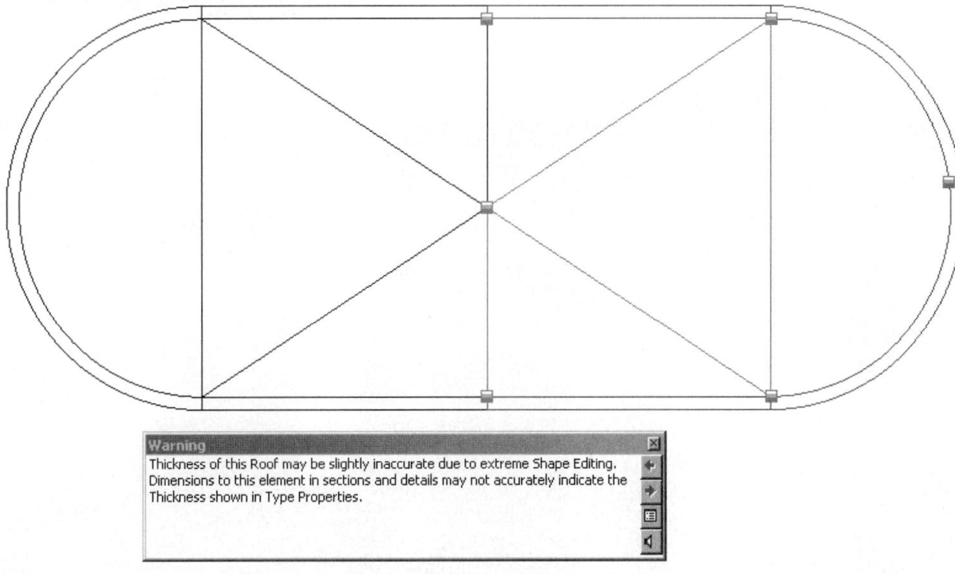

Figure 7-95

Notice the warning, then finish the command

39. Change to the **Default 3D View**, select **Shaded with Edges,** and turn **Shadows (On)** in the **View Control Bar** at the bottom of your workspace (see Figures 7-96 and 7-97).
40. Adjust the wall heights, add windows, and you have a building with a Shape Edited roof (see Figure 7-98).
41. Save this file as **ROOF SHAPE EDITING**.

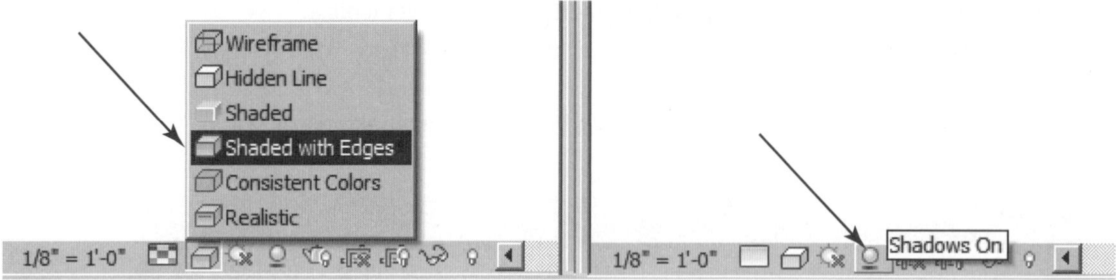

Figure 7-96

Shaded with Edges and **Shadows (On)** options

Figure 7-97

Shape Edited roof

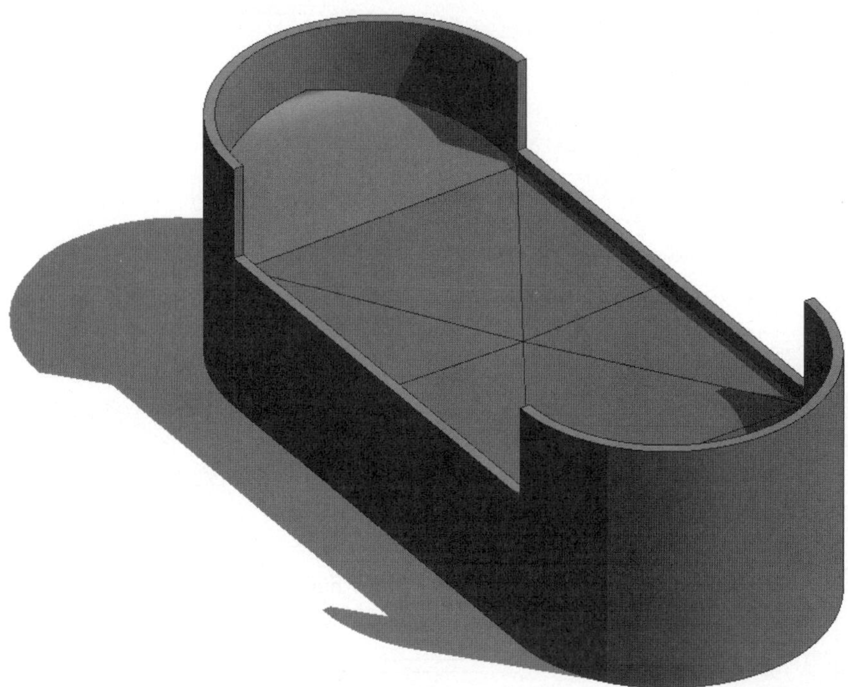

Figure 7-98

Building with a Shaped Edited roof

Placing Ceilings

There are two ways to place a **Ceiling Grid**. The first creates an automated boundary by walls, and the second creates a boundary by manual sketching.

EXERCISE 7-14 PLACING CEILINGS

Automated Placement of a Ceiling

1. Open the **ROOF BY FOOTPRINT** file you previously created.
2. Double-click on **Ceiling Plans > Level 1** in the **Project Browser** to bring it into the **Drawing Editor**.

Ceiling plans are often called *Reflected Ceiling Plans* (RCP). Except for the Site plan, when creating a new layer, **Revit** automatically will ask whether you want to create a corresponding RCP.

3. Select the **Home** tab to bring up the **Home** toolbar.
4. In the **Home** toolbar, select the **Ceiling** button to bring up the **Modify | Place Ceiling** toolbar.
5. The **Automatic Ceiling** button in the **Modify | Place Ceiling** toolbar will be selected.
6. In the **Properties** dialog box, select the **Compound Ceiling 2′ × 4′ ACT System** (acoustical ceiling tile) from the drop-down list.
7. In the **Properties** dialog box, make sure the level is set to **Level 1,** the **Height Offset From Level** is **8′-0″** (this is the height above the floor), and check the **Room Bounding** check box.
8. Click in the center of the enclosure (you will see a red interior perimeter line appear) to place the ceiling (see Figure 7-99).

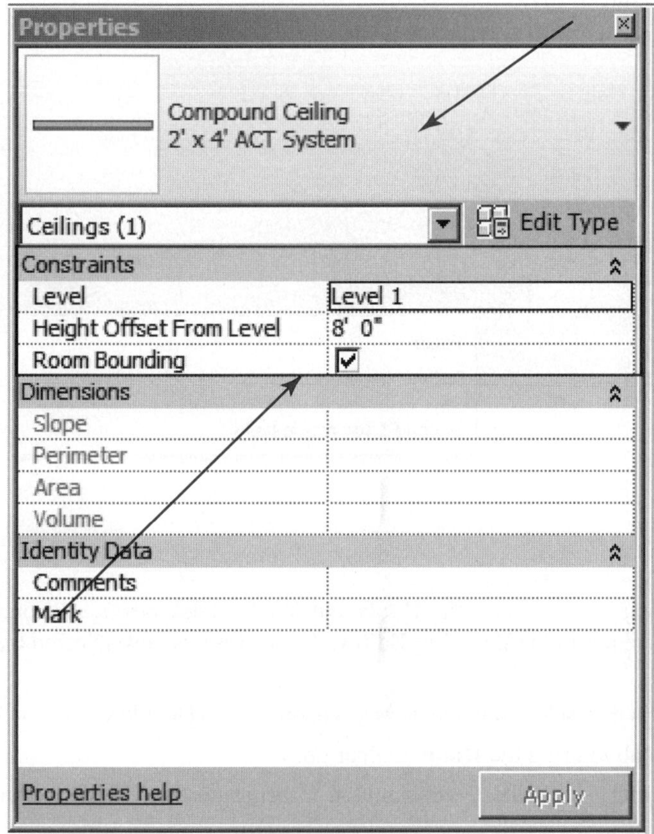

Figure 7-99

Compound Ceiling Properties dialog box

9. Click on one of the ceiling grid lines to bring up the **Modify | Ceilings** toolbar.
10. In the **Modify | Ceilings** toolbar, select the **Rotate** button in the **Modify** panel.
11. Move your cursor northward (beyond the walls), and click.
12. Move your cursor eastward beyond the walls, and click again.

You have rotated the grid (see Figure 7-100).

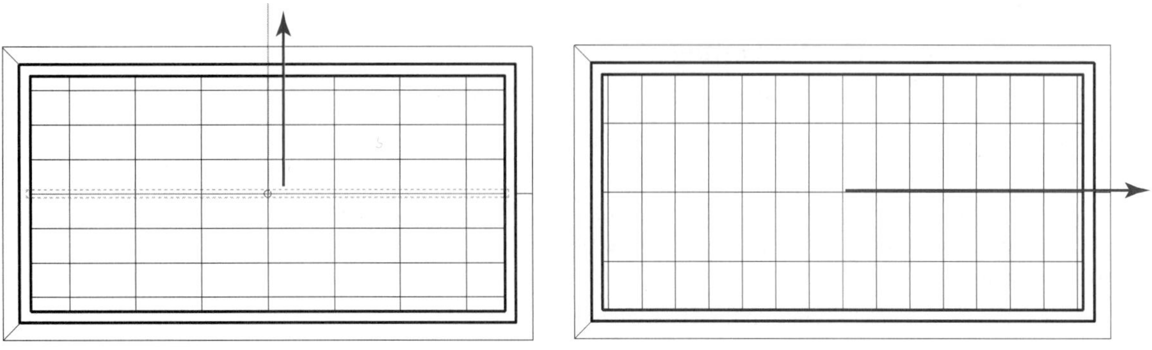

Figure 7-100

Rotate a ceiling grid

13. Click on any ceiling grid line.
14. In the **Modify | Ceilings** toolbar, select the **Move** button in the **Modify** panel.
15. Move your cursor in any direction to move the grid.

Placement of a Ceiling by Sketching

16. Select everything on the screen to bring up the **Modify | Multi-Select** toolbar.
17. In the **Modify | Multi-Select** toolbar, select the **Filter** button to bring up the **Filter** dialog box (see Figure 7-101).

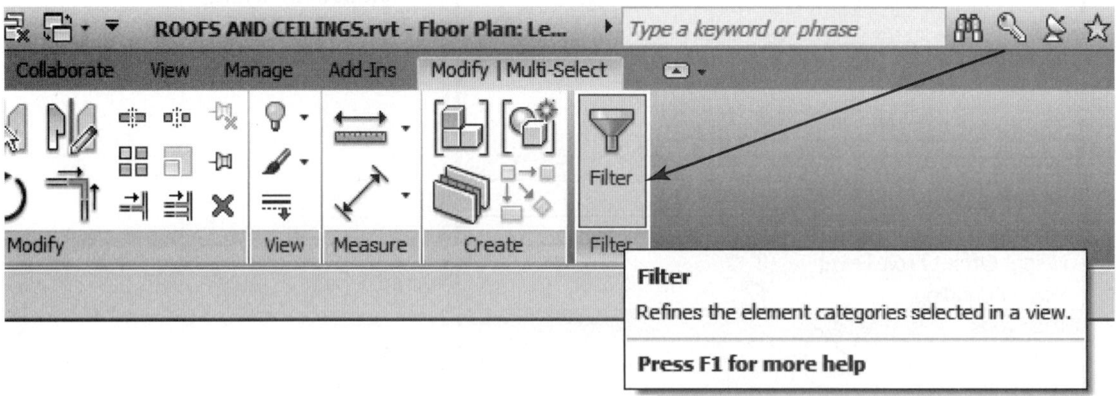

Figure 7-101

Filter button

18. In the **Filter** dialog box, uncheck the **Roofs** and **Walls** check boxes, and press the **OK** button to return to the **Drawing Editor**. The **Ceiling** is now selected (see Figure 7-102).
19. Since the **Ceiling** is now selected in the workspace, press the **<Del>** key to delete it.
20. Select the **Home** tab to bring the **Home** toolbar up.
21. In the **Home** toolbar, select the **Ceiling** button to bring up the **Modify | Place Ceiling** toolbar.

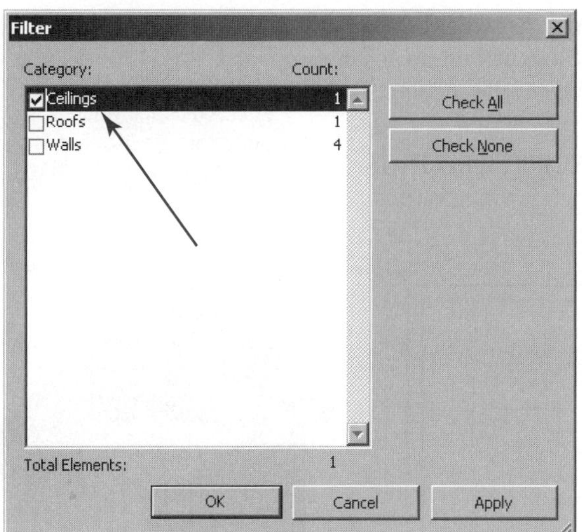

Figure 7-102

Filter dialog box

22. In the **Modify | Place Ceiling** toolbar, select the **Sketch Ceiling** button to bring up the **Modify | Create Ceiling Boundary** toolbar.
23. In the **Modify | Create Ceiling Boundary** toolbar, select the **Rectangle** button in the **Draw** panel (see Figure 7-103).
24. Place a **24′-0″ × 9′-0″** rectangle as shown in Figure 7-104.

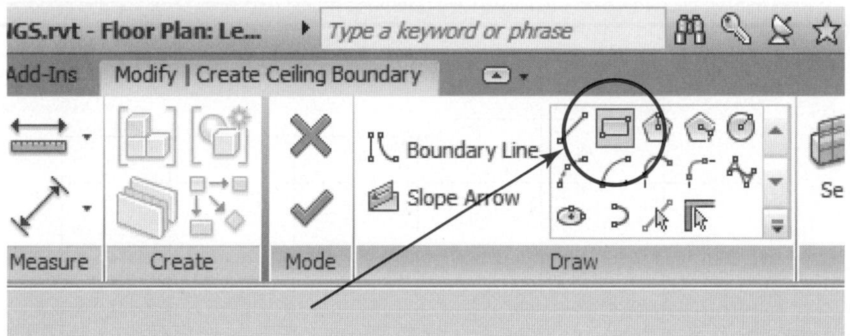

Figure 7-103

Create Ceiling Boundary toolbar

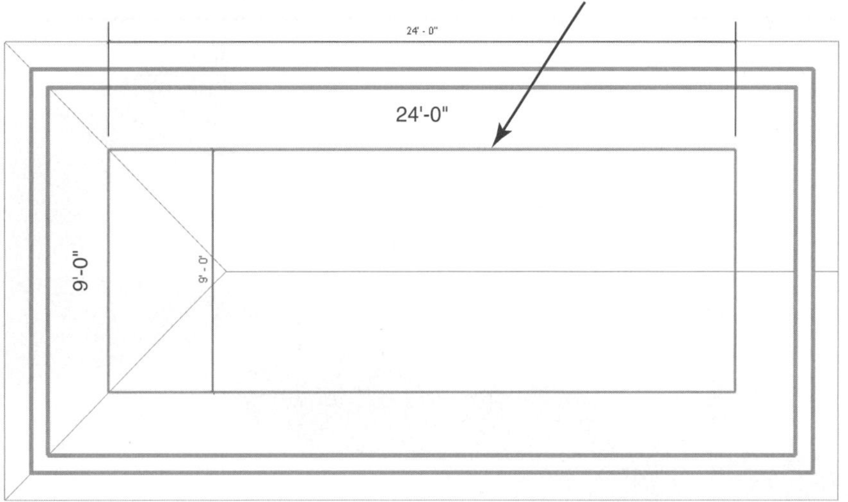

Figure 7-104

Place a rectangle

25. In the **Create Ceiling Boundary** toolbar, select the **Finish Sketch** button in the **Ceiling** panel to create the ceiling (see Figure 7-105).
26. Save this file as **PLACING CEILINGS**.

NOTE:

You can use any of the **Draw** tools when sketching ceilings, so you can create practically any shape of ceiling (see Figure 7-106).

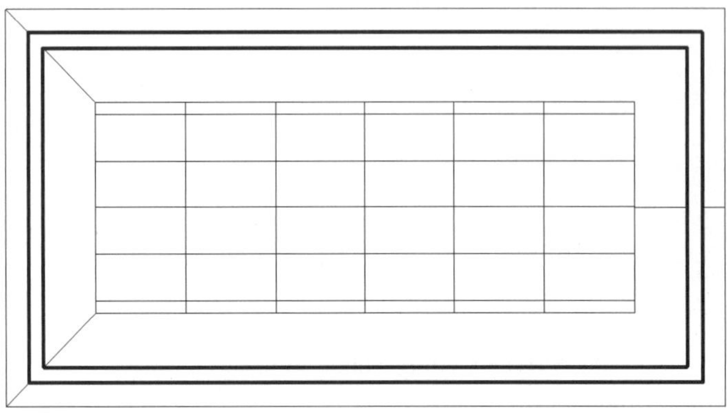

Figure 7-105

Created ceiling

Figure 7-106

Any shape of ceiling can be created using the **Draw** tools

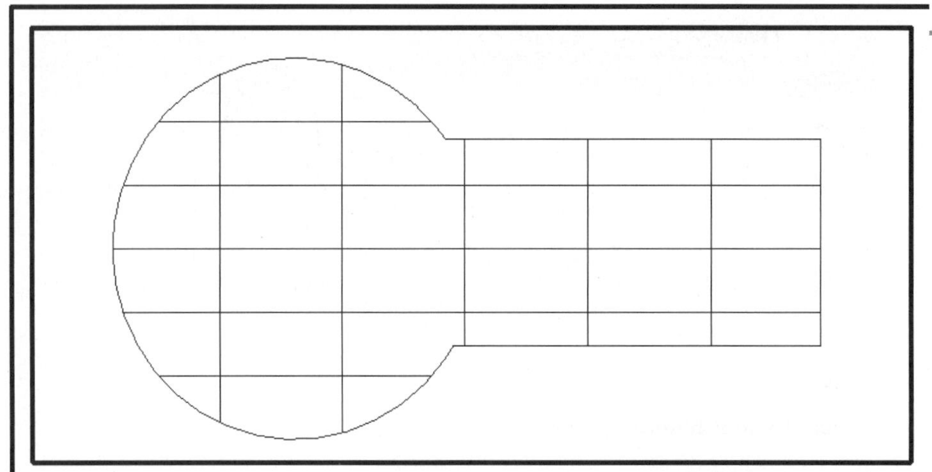

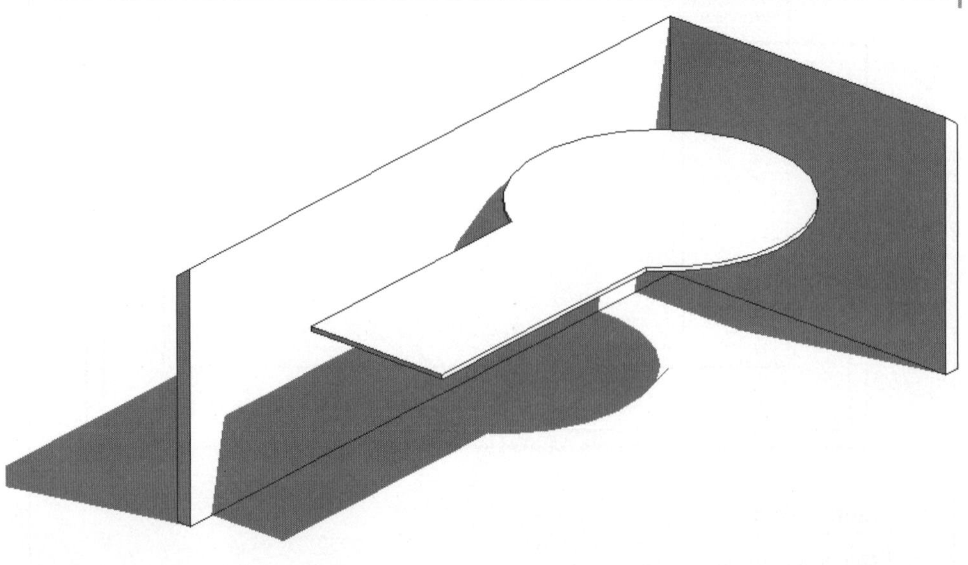

Chapter Summary

This chapter discussed the methods for creating and modifying roofs, dormers and ceilings in Revit Architecture 2012.

Chapter Test Questions

Multiple Choice

Circle the correct answer.

1. **Roof Shape Editing** is available
   a. Only for roofs.
   b. Only for flat roofs.
   c. For both pitched and flat roofs.
   d. For extruded roofs.
2. The **Sketch Ceiling** button is located
   a. In the **Home** toolbar.
   b. In the **Modify** toolbar.
   c. In the **Modify | Place Ceiling** toolbar.
   d. All of the above
3. The **Dormer** button is located in the
   a. **Home** toolbar.
   b. **Modify | Place Roof** toolbar.
   c. **Modify | Create Footprint** toolbar.
   d. **Modify | Edit Sketch** toolbar.
4. The **Defines Slope** check box is located in the
   a. **Home** toolbar.
   b. **Modify | Roof** toolbar.
   c. **Modify | Roof** toolbar, **Options Bar**.
   d. **Modify | Create Roof Footprint** toolbar, **Options Bar**.
5. The **Ref Plane** button for Roofs is located
   a. In the **Home** toolbar.
   b. In the **Modify | Place Roof** toolbar.
   c. In the **Modify | Create Roof Footprint** toolbar.
   d. None of the above

True or False

Circle the correct answer.

1. **True or False:** Organic-shaped roofs can be created in Revit.
2. **True or False:** Only rectangular openings can be created in Revit roofs.
3. **True or False:** Revit allows you to change the materials and colors of roofs.
4. **True or False:** Revit has a button for creating dormer openings in roofs.
5. **True or False:** Shape Editing points move vertically and horizontally.

Questions

1. What are the three methods for placing a roof?
2. What are the two methods for placing a ceiling?
3. What is the **Slope Arrow** used for?
4. When do you use a **Roof by Extrusion**?
5. What does the **Join/Unjoin Roof** button do?

CHAPTER

8 Floors

CHAPTER OBJECTIVES

- Learn how to create a floor by **Face**.
- Learn how to place a floor by **Walls**.
- Learn how to create a **Floor Family**.
- Learn how to add a **Floor Slab Edge**.
- Learn how to use the **Edit Cut Profile** tool.

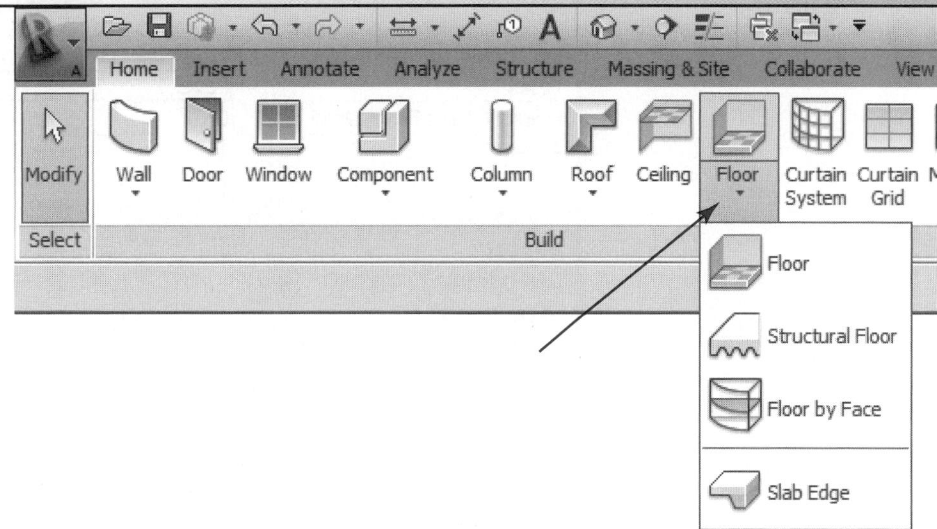

Introduction

In Revit Architecture, **Floor** objects are horizontal slabs that are very similar to Roofs. These slabs can be used for any horizontal purpose such as countertops, ceilings, and so on. As with Walls and Roofs, Floors can be configured with components such as structure, floor finishes, carpet, and so on.

You typically want to create a floor in a floor plan view. Floors are, by default, offset downward from the level on which they are placed.

The **Floor Properties** dialog box contains the **Instance Properties** (properties of the floor object) (see Figure 8-1).

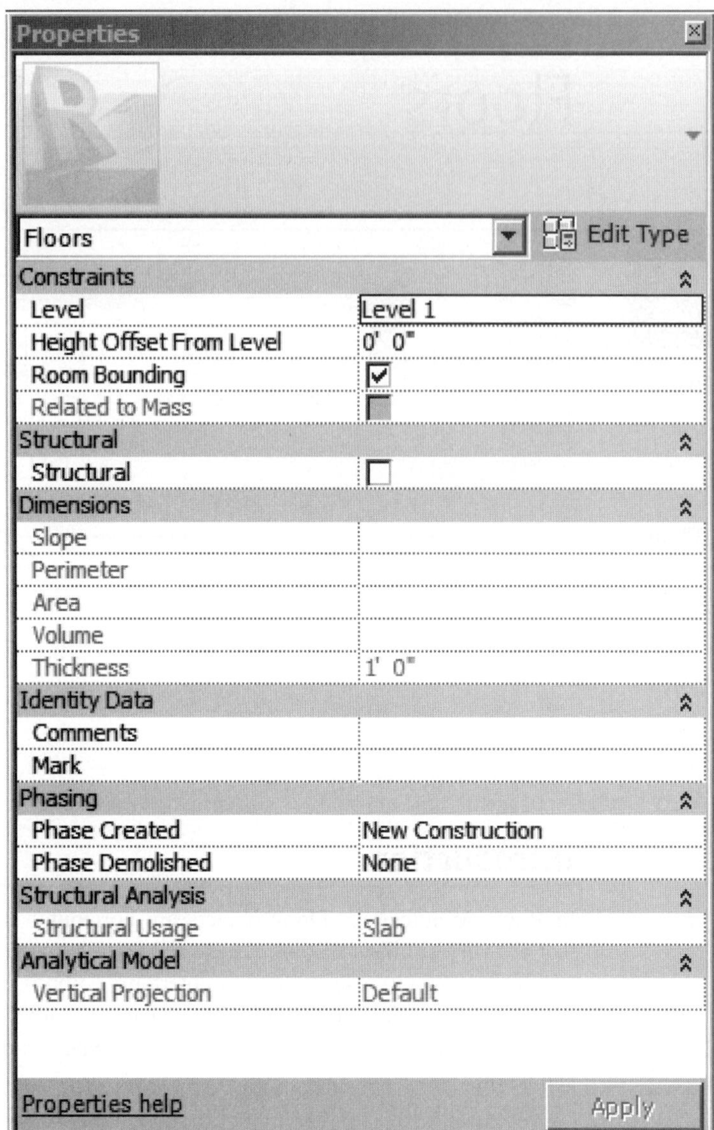

Figure 8-1

Instance Properties in the **Floor Properties** dialog box

Name	**Description**
Constraints	
Level	The level with which the floor is associated.
Height Offset From Level	The height at which the floor is offset from the level.
Room Bounding	Indicates that the floor is a room-bounding element.
Related to Mass	Indicates that the element was created from a mass element. This is a read-only value.
Structural	
Structural	Indicates that the element has an analytical model. This is a read-only value.
Dimensions	
Slope (Slope Angle; Rise/12″ for Imperial; Rise/1000 for Metric)	Changes the value of slope-defining lines to the specified value without the need to edit the sketch. The parameter initially displays a value if there is a slope-defining line. If there is no slope-defining line, the parameter is blank and disabled.

Name	Description
Perimeter	The perimeter of the floor. This is a read-only value.
Area	The area of the floor. This is a read-only value.
Volume	The volume of the floor. This is a read-only value.
Thickness	Indicates the thickness of the floor. This is a read-only value.
Identity Data	
Comments	Specific comments related to the floor that are not already covered in the description or type comments.
Mark	A user-specified label for the floor. This value must be unique for each floor in a project. Revit Architecture warns you if the number is already used but allows you to continue using it. You can see the warning using the **REVIEW WARNINGS** command.
Phasing	
Phase Created	The phase when the floor was created.
Phase Demolished	The phase when the floor was demolished.
Structural Analysis	
Structural Usage	Sets the structural usage of the floor. This property is read-only before creating a floor. After you draw the floor, you can select it and then modify this property.
Analytical Model	
Vertical Projection	The plane of the floor used for analysis and design.

As with Roofs, Floors can be created by three methods: by **Picking Walls**, by **Sketching with Lines**, or by selecting **Mass** faces.

Floor by Face

Floor by Face is used to place a floor on any horizontal face of a **Mass** model. Instructions on how to use this feature are covered in Chapter 15 on Massing & Site.

EXERCISE 8-1 FLOOR BY PICKING WALLS

1. Start a new drawing using the RAC 2012\Imperial Templates\default.rte template.
2. In the **Project Browser**, double-click on the **LEVEL 1** floor plan to bring it into the **Drawing Editor**.
3. Change the **Drawing Scale** to **1/4″ = 1′-0″**.
4. Set the **Detail Level** to **Medium**.
5. Select the **Home** tab to bring up the **Home** toolbar.
6. In the **Home** toolbar, select the **Wall** button to bring up the **Modify | Place Wall** toolbar.
7. In the **Modify | Place Wall** toolbar, select the **Rectangle** button in the **Draw** panel.
8. Place a **15′-0″ × 30′-0″** rectangular enclosure using a **10′-0″** high **Exterior – Brick on CMU** wall with the **Location Line** in the **Options Bar** set to **Finish Face: Exterior**.
9. Select the **Home** tab to bring up the **Home** toolbar.
10. In the **Home** toolbar, select the **Floor > Floor** buttons to bring up the **Modify | Create Floor Boundary** toolbar.

11. In the **Modify | Create Floor Boundary** toolbar, select the **Pick Walls** button from the **Draw** panel.
12. In the **Options Bar**, check the **Extend into wall (to core)** check box.
13. Click on the north wall and notice the sketch line appears at the outer face of the wall core.
14. Repeat, clicking on the remaining walls (see Figure 8-2).

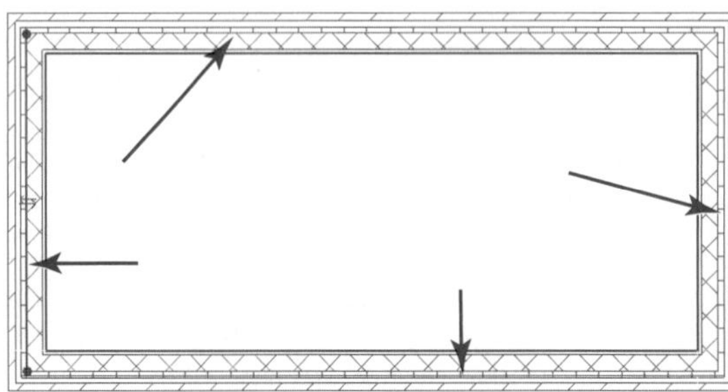

Figure 8-2

Pick Walls sketch

15. In the **Properties** dialog box, select the **Edit Type** button to bring up the **Type Properties** dialog box.
16. In the **Type Properties** dialog box, select **Generic - 12″** from the **Type** drop-down list, and press the **OK** button to return to the **Properties** dialog box.
17. In the **Properties** dialog box, set the settings shown in Figure 8-3. (Make sure that the **Height Offset From Level** is set to **3′-0″**.)

NOTE:
This will place the floor 3′-0″ above **Level 1**.

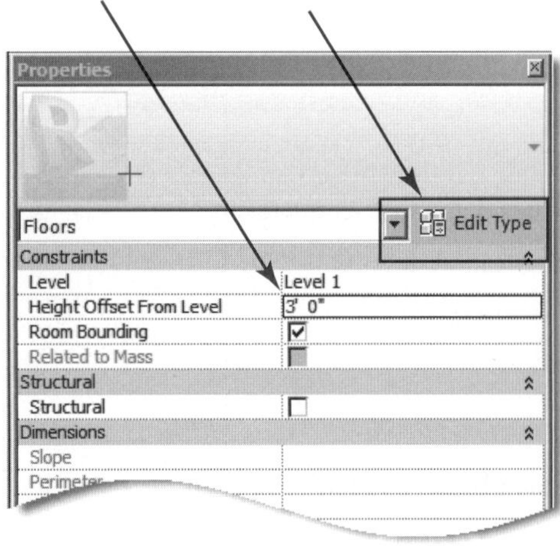

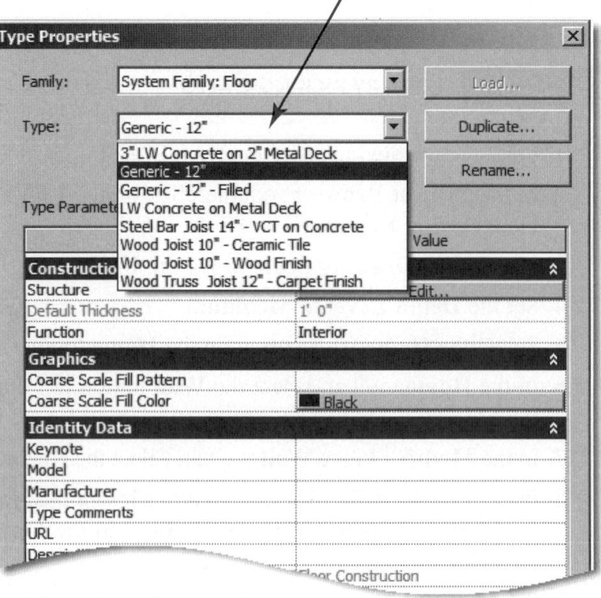

Figure 8-3

Type Properties dialog box

18. In the **Modify | Create Floor Boundary** toolbar, press the **Finish Edit Mode** button, and select **Yes** when the **Revit** dialog box asks, *The floor/roof overlaps the highlighted wall(s). Would you like to join geometry and cut the overlapping volume out of the wall(s)?* (see Figure 8-4).

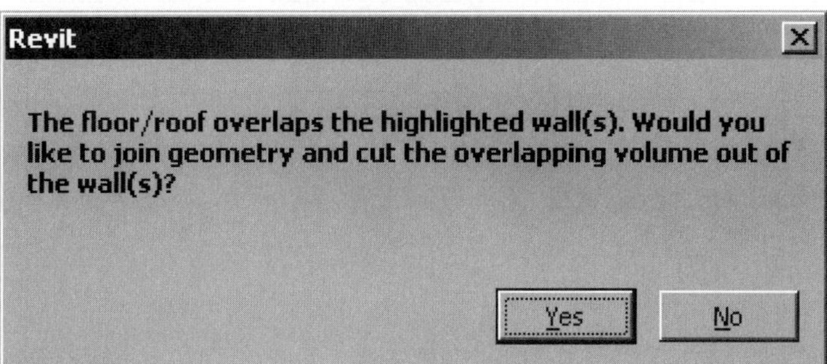

Figure 8-4

Revit dialog box

19. Select the **View** tab to bring up the **View** toolbar.
20. In the **View** toolbar, select the **Section** button to bring up the **Modify | Section** toolbar (see Figure 8-5).

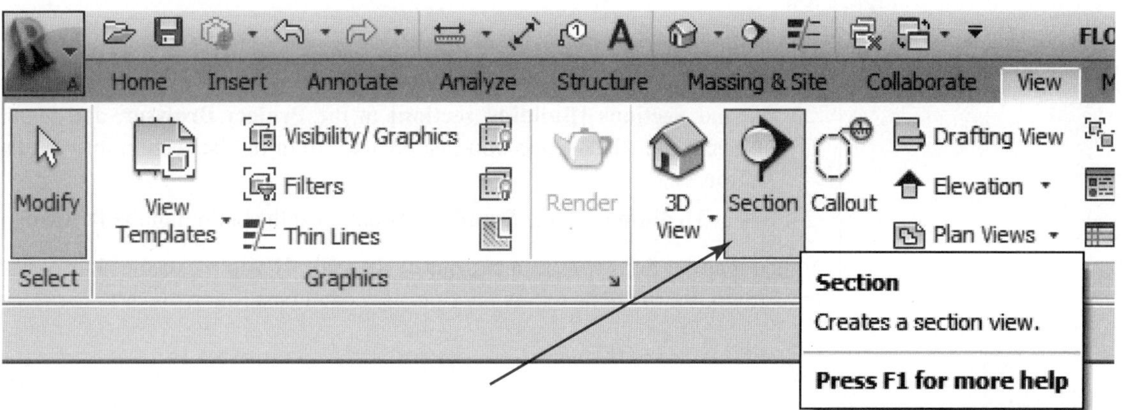

Figure 8-5

Modify | Section toolbar

21. In the **Properties** dialog box, select **Building Section** from the **Properties** drop-down list.
22. Place a section by first clicking north of the **North** wall, and then clicking again south of the **South** wall as shown in Figure 8-6 to create a building section.

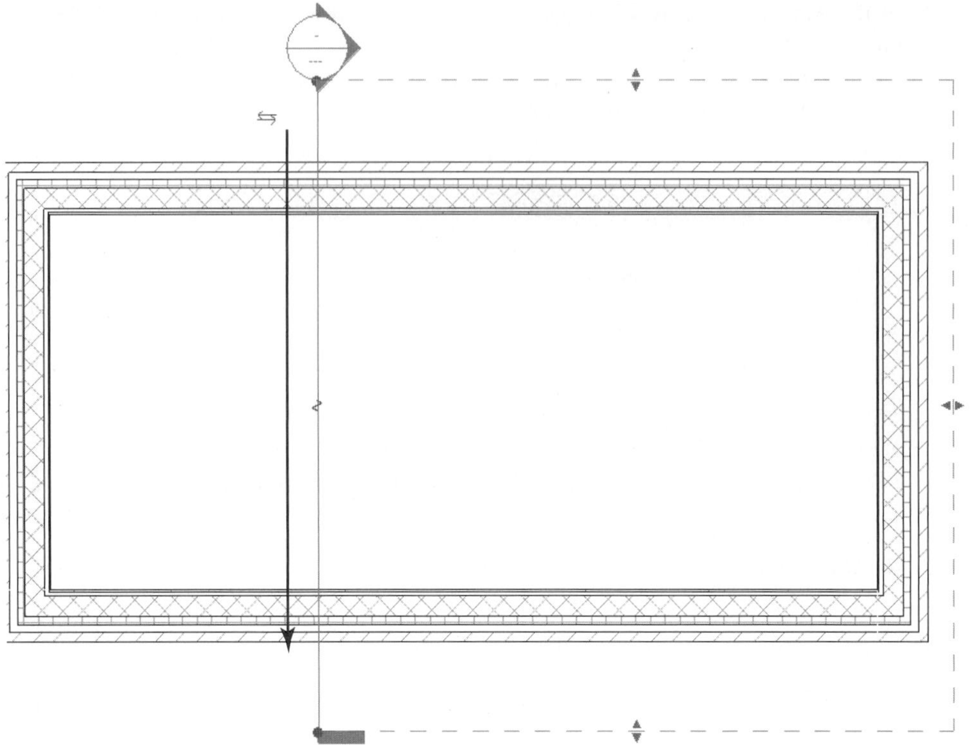

Figure 8-6

Creating a building section

23. Expand **Sections [Building section]** in the **Project Browser**, and double-click on **Section 1** (the section you just created) to bring the section into the **Drawing Editor**.
24. Select **Medium** from the **Detail Level** button at the bottom of the **Drawing Editor**.

Notice that the floor has been cut out of the wall. If you move the floor vertically in the section, the wall "heals" as the floor is moved (see Figure 8-7).

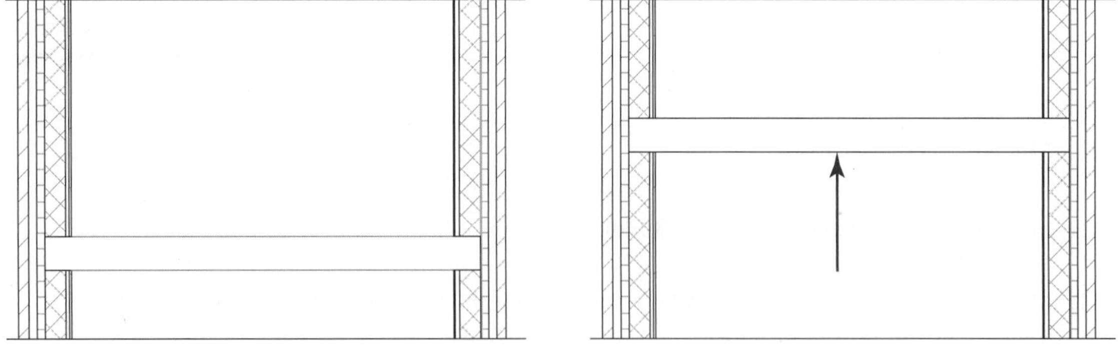

Figure 8-7

A wall heals as the floor is moved

25. Save this file as **FLOOR by FOOTPRINT**.

Floor Families

Revit ships with eight default **Floors**. A Floor type structure is created in the same manner as you create Wall and Roof types.

EXERCISE 8-2 CREATING AND MODIFYING A FLOOR FAMILY

1. Using the previous exercise, make sure you are still in **Section 1**.
2. Select the floor to bring up the **Properties** dialog box.
3. In the **Properties** dialog box, select the **Edit Type** button to bring up the **Type Properties** dialog box.
4. In the **Type Properties** dialog box, select **Wood Joist 10″ – Wood Finish** from the **Type** drop-down list, and press the **OK** button to return to the **Properties** dialog box.
5. In the **Properties** dialog box, set the **Level** to **1** and the **Height Offset From Level** to **0′-0″**, and press the **OK** button.
6. Set the **Detail Level** to **Medium**.
7. Select the **View** tab to bring up the **View** toolbar.
8. In the **View** toolbar, press the **Thin Lines** button (see Figure 8-8).

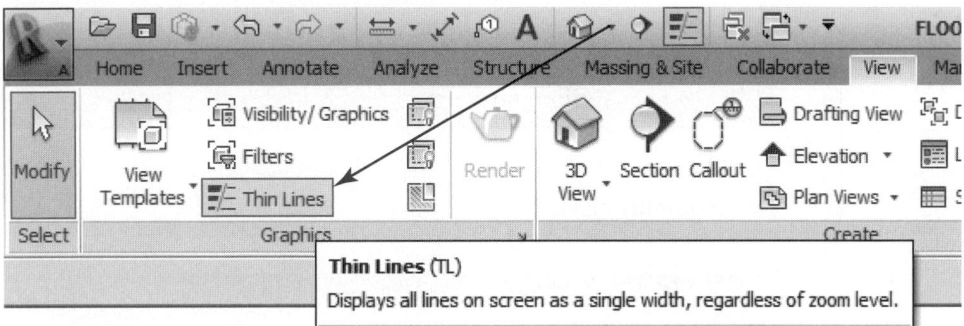

Figure 8-8

Thin Lines button

9. In the **View Control Bar**, set the scale to **1/2″ = 1′-0″**.
10. Again, select the floor, to bring up the **Properties** dialog box.
11. In the **Properties** dialog box, press the **Edit Type** button to open the **Type Properties** dialog box.
12. In the **Type Properties** dialog box, press the **Duplicate** button, and name the new floor **CONCRETE 12″ – Wood Finish**. Press the **OK** button to return to the **Type Properties** dialog box.
13. In the **Type Properties** dialog box, press the **Edit** button in the **Structure** field to bring up the **Edit Assembly** dialog box.
14. In the **Edit Assembly** dialog box, at the lower left, press the **Preview** button to see a preview of the floor structure.
15. In the **Edit Assembly** dialog box, change the thickness of **Layer 4 – Structure [1]** to **10 1/2″**.
16. In the **Material** column, click on **Structure – Wood**, and then click the small button that appears next to it to bring up the **Materials** dialog box.
17. In the **Edit Assembly** dialog box, select **Layer 4 – Structure [1]**, change its **Material** from **Structure: Wood joist/Rafter Layer** to **Concrete – Cast-in-Place Concrete**, and press the **OK** buttons to return to the **Drawing Editor** (see Figures 8-9 and 8-10).

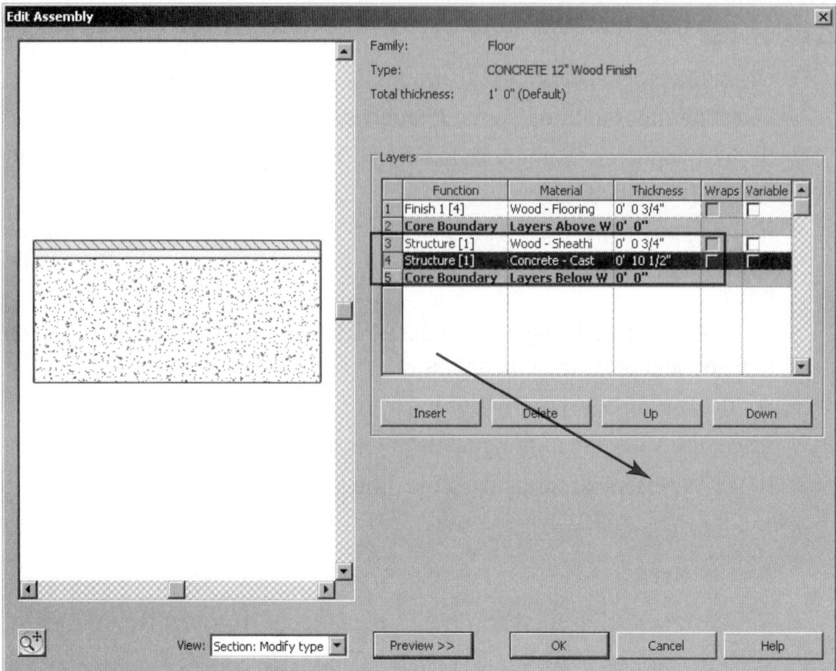

Figure 8-9

Edit Assembly dialog box

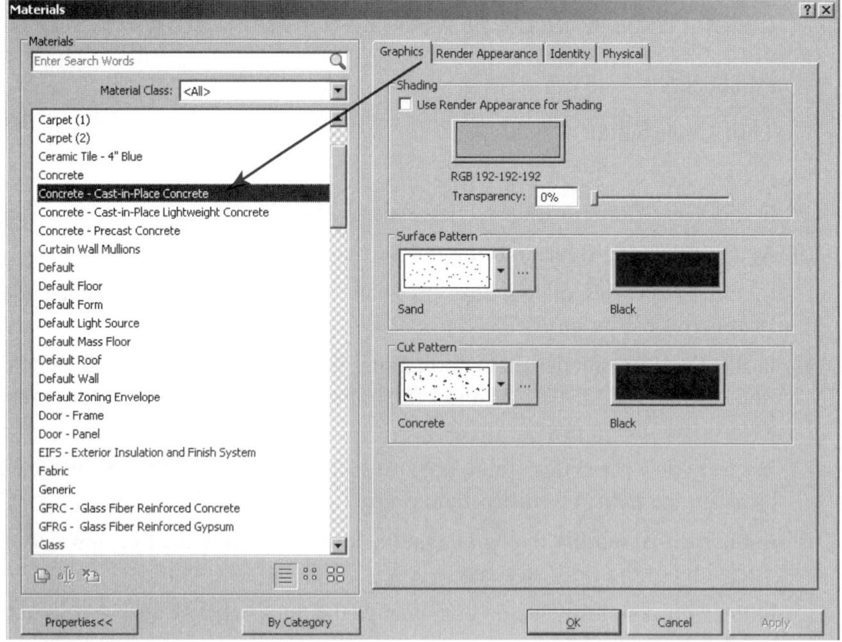

Figure 8-10

Materials dialog box

Floors by default automatically change their thickness from the level they are on downward (see Figure 8-11).

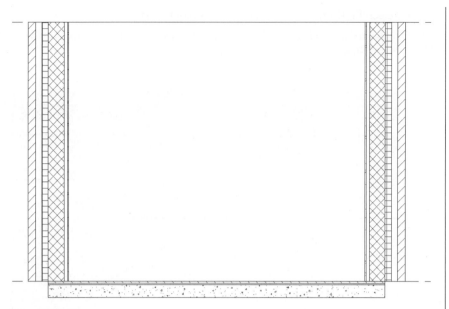

Figure 8-11

Floors change thickness downward

18. Experiment making new floors by duplicating existing floors and making changes in floor layer sizes and materials.
19. Save this file as **FLOOR FAMILIES**.

EXERCISE 8-3 CHANGING AND MODIFYING A FLOOR SLAB EDGE

1. Using the previous exercise, make sure both the **Section 1** and **Default 3D Views** are open in the **Drawing Editor**.
2. Select the **South** wall, and select **Temporary Hide/Isolate > Hide Element** from the **View Control Bar** to hide the **South** wall (see Figure 8-12).

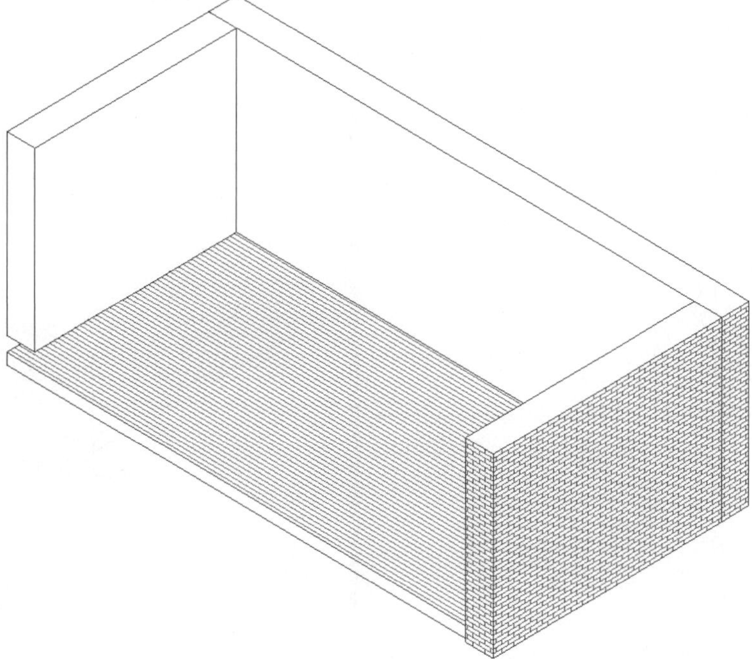

Figure 8-12

Hide the **South** wall

3. Select the **Home** tab to bring up the **Home** toolbar.
4. In the **Home** toolbar, select the **Floor > Slab Edge** button to bring up the **Modify | Place Slab Edge** toolbar (see Figure 8-13).

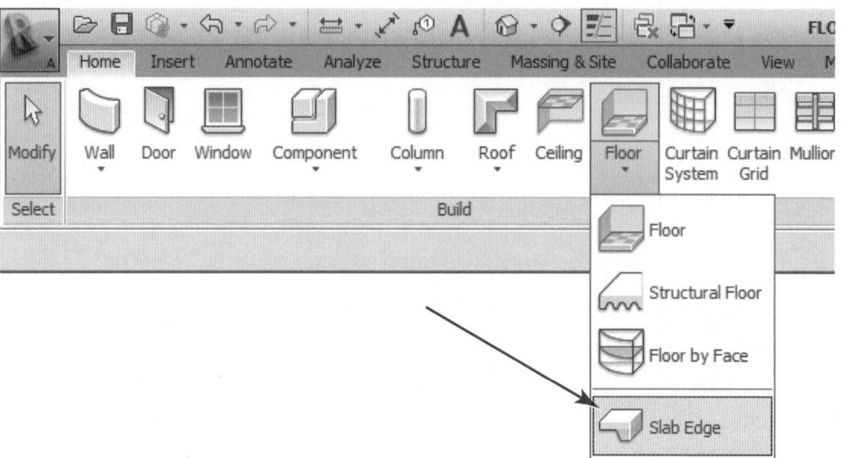

Figure 8-13

Floor Slab Edge button

5. In the **Modify | Place Slab Edge** toolbar, select the **Slab Edge: Thickened 24″ × 12″ Properties** drop-down list.
6. Select the lower edge of the floor (slab) in the **Default 3D View** or the lower left edge of the floor (slab) in the **Section 1** view.

The thickened slab edge will appear. This edge is created from a profile (see Figure 8-14).

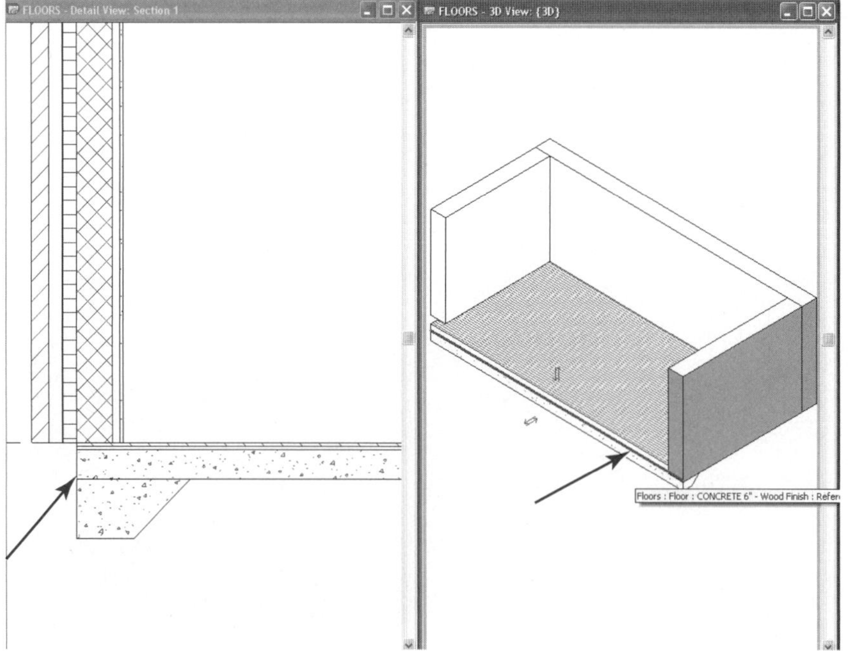

Figure 8-14

Thickened slab edge

To change the shape of the edge, you will need to change the profile. The **Slab Edge** profiles are located in the **Imperial** or **Metric Library**.

7. Select **File** > **Open** > **Family** from the **Application** menu to bring up the **Open** dialog box.
8. In the **Open** dialog box, select the **Imperial** (or **Metric**) **Library** at the left side of the dialog box to bring up the **Imperial Library**.
9. In the **Imperial Library**, open the **Profiles** > **Structural** folder.
10. In the **Structural** folder, you will find the default **Slab Edge** profiles.
11. Double-click the **Slab Edge – Thickened** profile to bring it into the **Drawing Editor**.

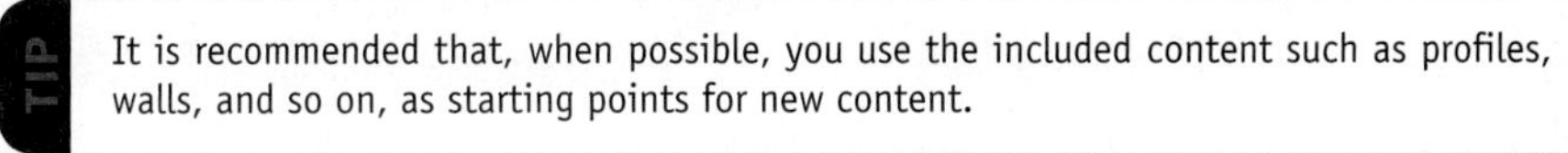

TIP: It is recommended that, when possible, you use the included content such as profiles, walls, and so on, as starting points for new content.

12. An abbreviated toolbar will now appear because you are in a 2D drawing view.
13. In the **Home** toolbar, select the **Line** button to bring up the **Modify | Place Lines** toolbar.
14. In the **Modify | Place Lines** toolbar, select the **Line** button in the **Draw** panel. Using this tool and the **Split** and **Trim** tools in the **Modify** panel, change the **Slab Edge - Thickened** profile to that shown in Figure 8-15.

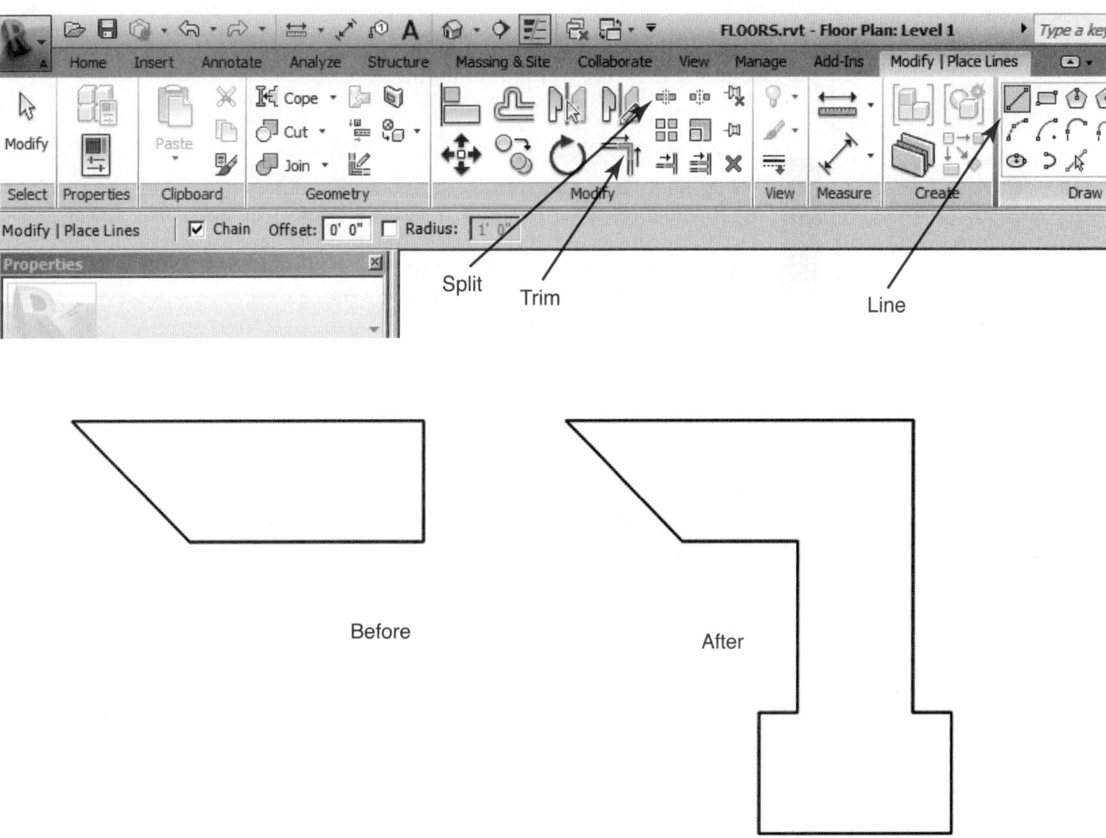

Figure 8-15
Modify | Place Lines toolbar

15. Select **File** > **Save As** > **Family** from the **Application** menu.
16. Save the file as **Slab Edge – TEST** in the **Imperial Library** > **Profiles** > **Structural** folder, and close the file.

You will now be returning to the **FLOOR FAMILIES** file.

17. In the **FLOOR FAMILIES** file, double-click on **Section 1** in the **Project Browser** to bring it into the **Drawing Editor**.
18. Select the **Insert** tab to bring up the **Insert** toolbar.
19. In the **Insert** toolbar, select the **Load Family** button, and locate the **Imperial Library** > **Profiles** > **Structural** folder (see Figure 8-16).

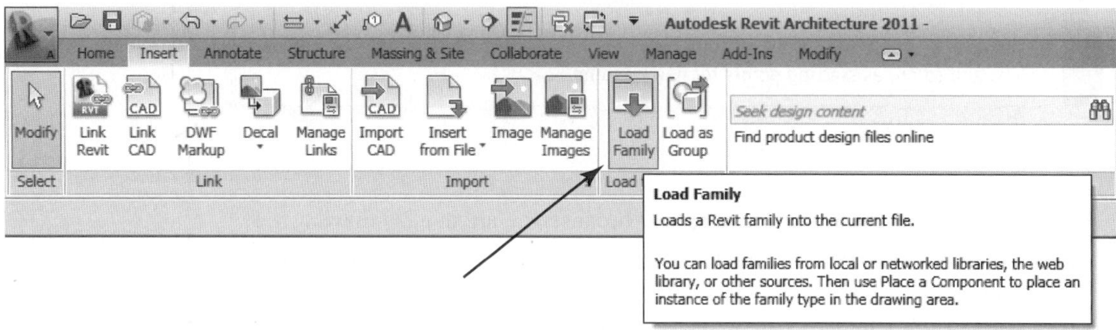

Figure 8-16

Load Family button

20. In the **Imperial Library** > **Profiles** > **Structural** folder, double-click the **Slab Edge – TEST** file to load it into the session.

TIP

All the lines for profiles must be continuous from intersection to intersection in order for a profile to work. If you get a message saying that the profile cannot be made, reopen the profile, and check to make sure that you have not placed a line on top of a line or that the line is split into two parts.

21. In the **Section 1** view, select the slab edge you previously placed to bring up its **Properties** dialog box.
22. In the **Properties** dialog box, press the **Edit Type** button to open the **Type Properties** dialog box.
23. In the **Type Properties** dialog box, press the **Duplicate** button, name it **TEST EDGE with FOOTING**, and press the **OK** button to return to the **Type Properties** dialog box.
24. In the **Type Properties** dialog box, change the profile to **Slab Edge – TEST: 36″ × 12″**, and press the **OK** buttons to return to the **Drawing Editor** (see Figure 8-17).

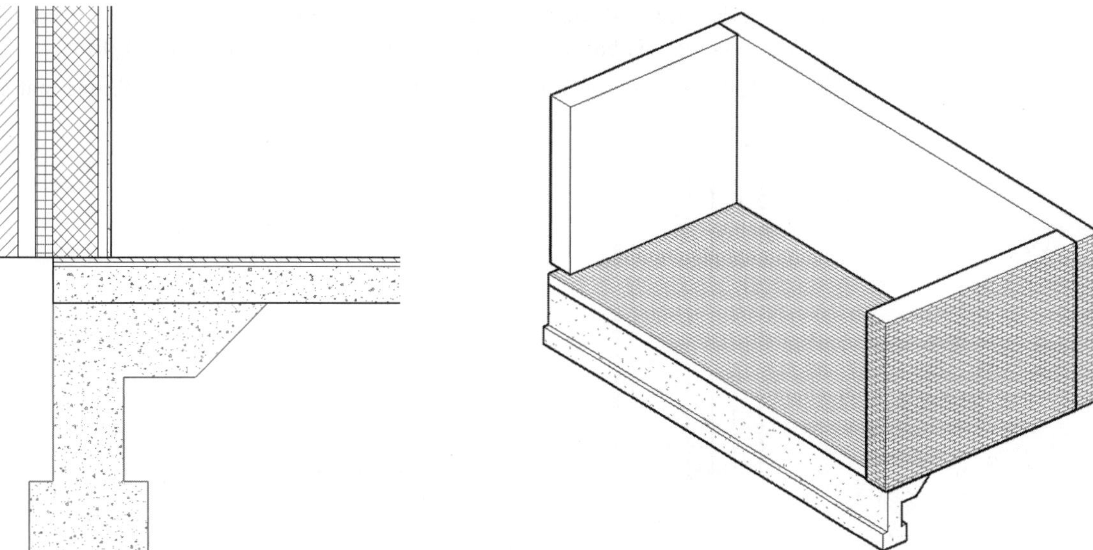

Figure 8-17

Slab Edge drawing

25. Bring **Section 1** into the **Drawing Editor**.
26. Select the floor slab to bring up the **Modify | Floors** toolbar.
27. In the **Properties** dialog box, select **Floor Generic - 12″ – Filled** from the **Properties** drop-down list.
28. Notice that the floor and floor edge now join. This is because both the floor and the floor edge are the same material (see Figure 8-18).

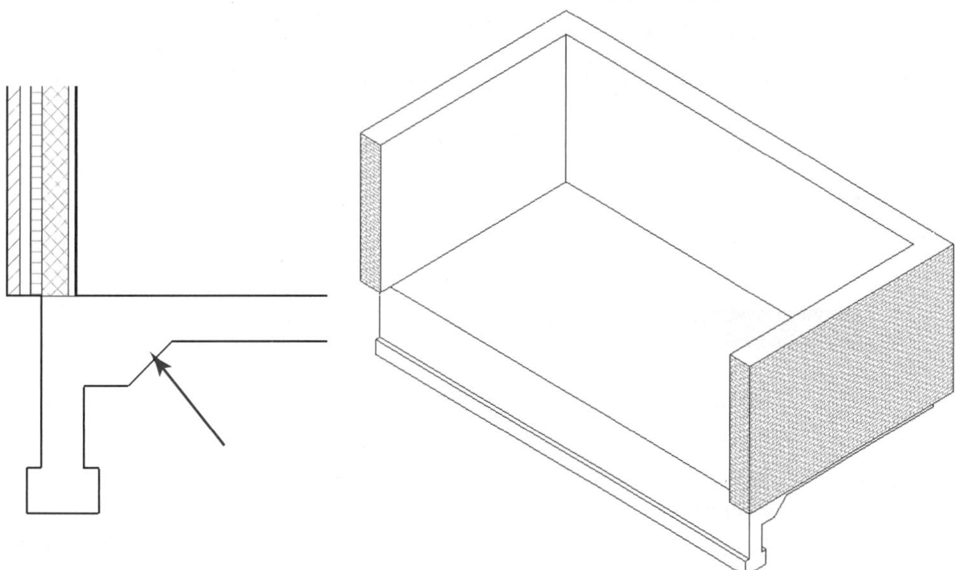

Figure 8-18

Floor and floor edge are joined because they are the same material

29. Select the floor edge to bring up the **Properties** dialog box.
30. In the **Properties** dialog box, select the **Edit Type** button to bring up the **Type Properties** dialog box.
31. In the **Type Properties** dialog box, press the **Materials** button to bring up the **Materials** dialog box.

32. In the **Materials** dialog box, select **Concrete – Cast-in-Place Concrete**, and then press the **OK** buttons to return to **Section 1** in the **Drawing Editor**.
33. The slab edge is now a separate part because it is a different material (see Figure 8-19).

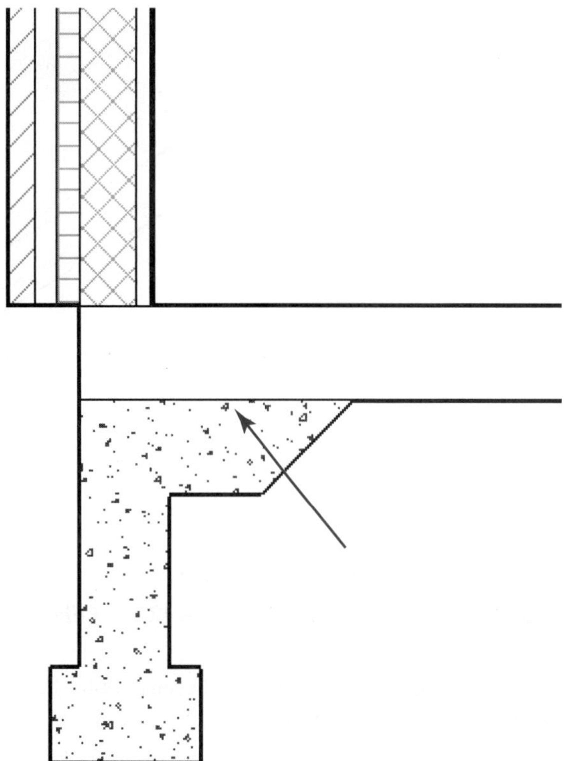

Figure 8-19

Floor and floor edge are separate because they are different materials

34. Save this file as **FLOOR SLAB EDGES**.

EXERCISE 8-4 USING THE EDIT CUT PROFILE TOOL

1. Bring the **Section 1** view into the **Drawing Editor**.
2. Select the floor to bring up its **Properties** dialog box.
3. In the **Properties** dialog box, select the **Edit Type** button to bring up the **Type Properties** dialog box.
4. In the **Type Properties** dialog box, press the **Edit** button in the **Structure** field to bring up the **Edit Assembly** dialog box.
5. In the **Edit Assembly** dialog box, select the button for **Materials** in the **Structure [1]** field to bring up the **Materials** dialog box.
6. In the **Materials** dialog box, select **Concrete – Cast-in-Place Concrete**, and then press the **OK** buttons to return to **Section 1** in the **Drawing Editor**.
7. In the **Modify | Floors** toolbar, select the **Join > Unjoin Geometry** button.
8. Select and touch the floor slab edge to unjoin it from the floor (see Figure 8-20).

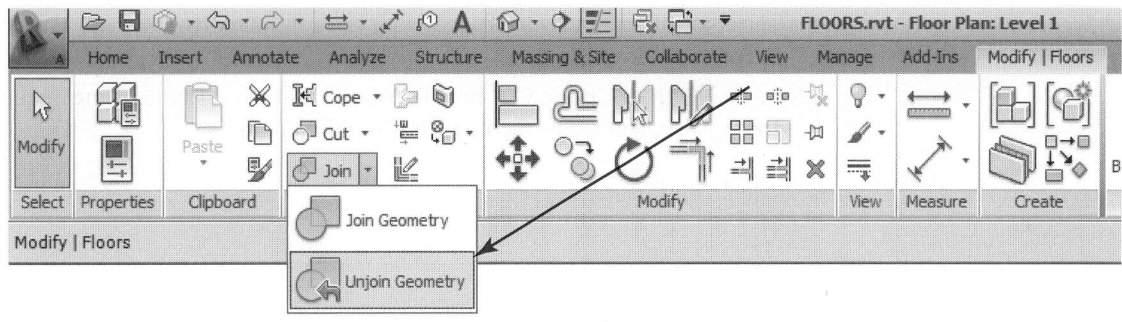

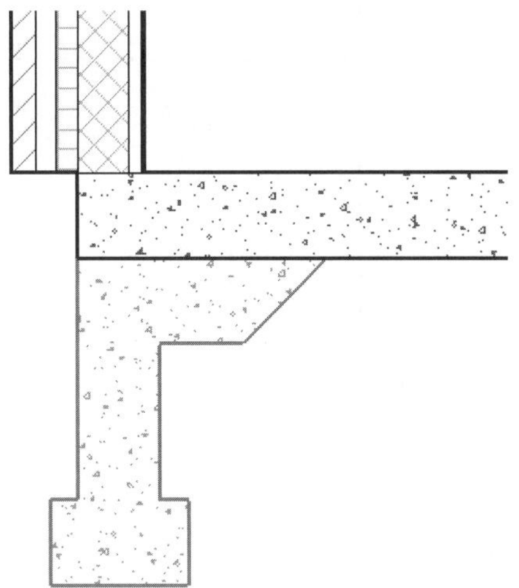

Figure 8-20

Unjoin Geometry button

9. Select the **View** tab to bring up the **View** toolbar.
10. In the **View** toolbar, select the **Cut Profile** button from the **Graphics** panel, select the **Boundary between faces** radio button, and select the border between the slab edge and the slab (see Figure 8-21).

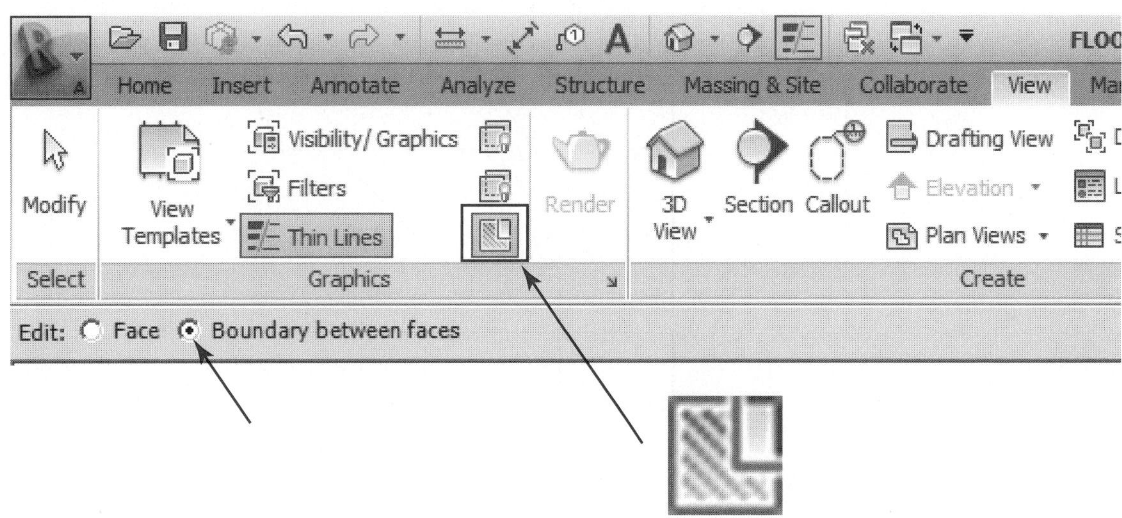

Figure 8-21

Cut Profile button

11. The floor slab edge will change color, and the **Modify | Create Cut Profile, Sketch** toolbar will appear.
12. In the **Modify | Create Cut Profile, Sketch** toolbar, select the **Line** button in the **Draw** panel, and create the lines shown in Figure 8-22.

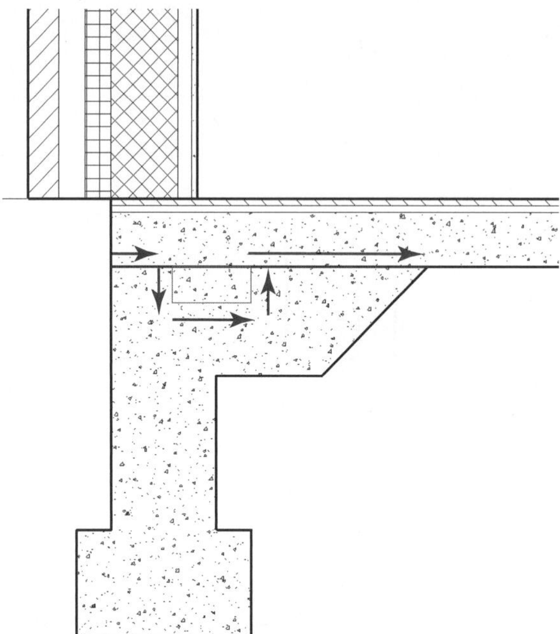

Figure 8-22

Use the **Line** button to create lines

NOTE:

This changes only the **Section** view, not the model itself (see Figure 8-23).

13. In the **Modify | Create Cut Profile, Sketch** toolbar, select and press the **Finish Edit Mode** button to complete the profile cut.

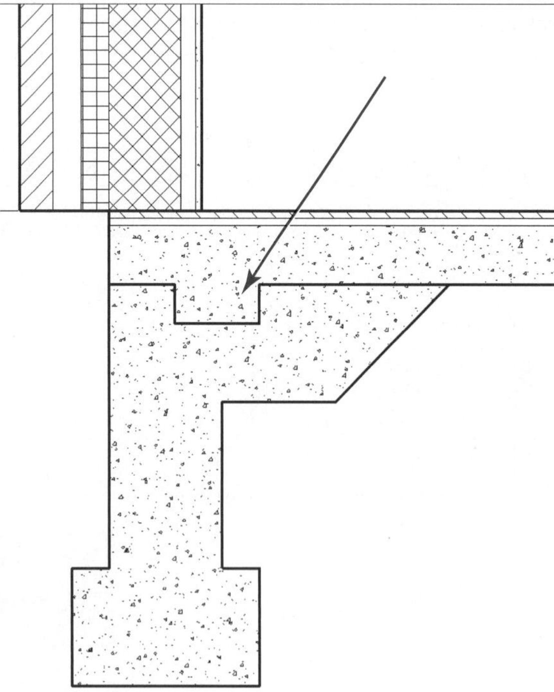

Figure 8-23

Only the **Section** view is changed

14. Save this file as **EDIT CUT PROFILE**.

NOTE:

Modifying a **Floor** slope with the **Slope Arrow**, creating a hole in a **Floor Slab**, and modifying a **Floor Slab** by **Shape Editing** are all done in the same manner as those shown in the Roofs chapter. Please refer to those sections, and make sure you can use those commands.

Chapter Summary

This chapter discussed the methods for creating and modifying **Floor Slabs**. Included were methods for adding and modifying floor slab edges and using the **Edit Cut Profile** button.

Chapter Test Questions

Multiple Choice

Circle the correct answer.

1. **Floor Structures** are edited
   a. In the **Properties** dialog box.
   b. In the **Type Properties** dialog box.
   c. In the **Edit Assembly** dialog box.
   d. None of the above
2. The **Thin Lines** button is located in the
   a. **Home** toolbar.
   b. **Modify | Create Floor** toolbar.
   c. **View** toolbar.
   d. **Annotate** toolbar.
3. The **Create Cut Profile** tool affects
   a. The **Model** only.
   b. The **Section** drawing only.
   c. Both the **Model** and the **Section**.
4. The **Floor Material** field is changed from the
   a. **Options Bar**.
   b. **Properties** dialog box.
   c. **Type Properties** dialog box.
   d. **Edit Assembly** dialog box.
5. The **Section** button is located
   a. In the **Home** toolbar.
   b. In the **View** toolbar.
   c. In the **Quick Access** toolbar.
   d. All of the above

True or False

Circle the correct answer.

1. **True or False**: Holes cannot be created in **Floors**.
2. **True or False**: **Floor Slab Edges** are profiles.
3. **True or False**: **Floors** can be edited with **Shape Editing**.
4. **True or False: Revit** floors are offset downward from the level on which they are placed by default.
5. **True or False:** Floor overlaps into walls must be manually cut to display correctly in **Section** view.

Questions

1. What controls the shape of **Floor Slab Edges**?
2. What is the difference between **Floor Slabs** and **Roof Slabs** in Revit Architecture?
3. Under what conditions can you create floors by **Face**?
4. Explain how you create floors by picking walls.
5. What does the **Extend into wall** check box do?

CHAPTER

9 Curtain Walls and Glazing

CHAPTER OBJECTIVES

- Learn how to use **Curtain Wall 1**.
- Learn how to create **Curtain Walls by Face**.
- Learn how to configure the **Curtain Wall Grid**.
- Learn how to create sloped glazing.
- Learn how to create curved **Curtain Walls**.
- Learn how to add **doors** and panels to **Curtain Walls**.

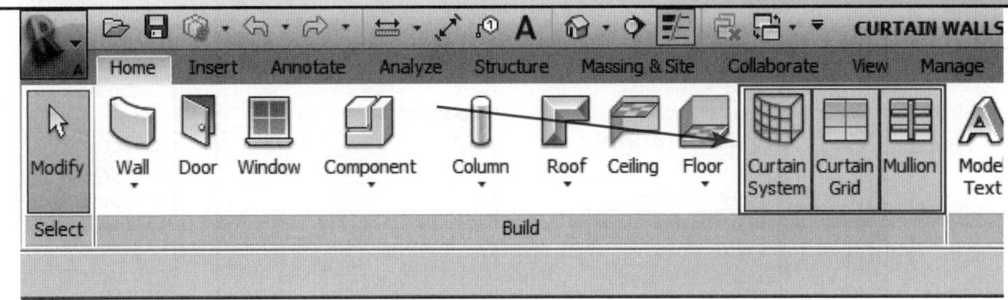

Introduction

Curtain Walls are very popular in contemporary commercial buildings. They are often called "storefronts" when used as entrance windows in malls and stores and are never used as bearing components. In Revit Architecture, **Curtain Wall** objects are specialized versions of walls. Revit Architecture also contains several tools to create the curtain systems, create and change the curtain wall grids, and place and modify curtain wall mullions.

Curtain Wall Properties

Figure 9-1 shows the **Curtain Wall Properties** dialog box. The following table describes the features of this dialog box.

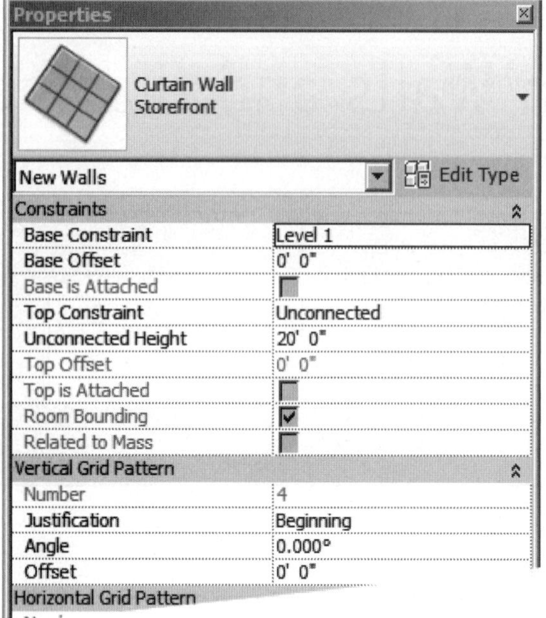

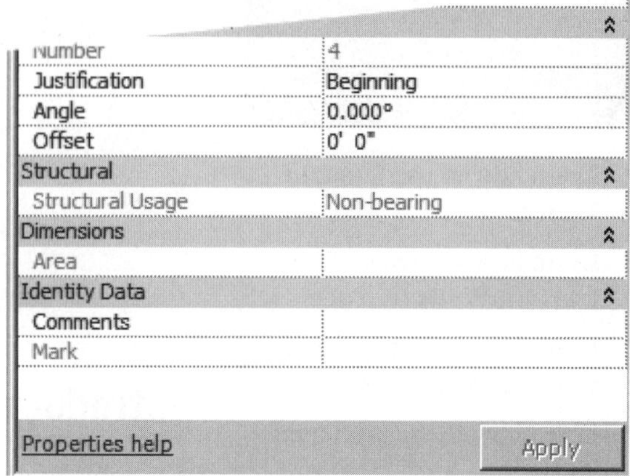

Figure 9-1

Curtain Wall Properties dialog box

Name	Description
Constraints	
Base Constraint	The base level of the curtain wall. For example, **Level 1**.
Base Offset	Sets the curtain wall's height from its base constraint. This property is available only when the **Base Constraint** is set to a level.
Base is Attached	Indicates whether the base of the curtain wall is attached to another model component, such as a floor. This is a read-only value.
Top Constraint	Curtain wall height extends to the value specified in **Unconnected Height**.
Unconnected Height	The height of the curtain wall when it is sketched.
Top Offset	Sets the curtain wall's offset from the top level.
Top is Attached	Indicates whether the curtain wall top is attached to another model component, such as a roof or ceiling. This is a read-only value.
Room Bounding	If selected, the curtain wall is part of a room boundary. If not selected, the curtain wall is not part of a room boundary. This property is read-only before creating a curtain wall. After you draw the wall, you can select it and then modify this property.
Related to Mass	Indicates that the element was created from a mass element. This is a read-only value.
Vertical/Horizontal Grid Pattern	
Number	If **Layout** (under **Vertical/Horizontal Grid Pattern**) is set to **Fixed Number**, enter a value here for the number of curtain grids on the curtain instance. The maximum value is 200.
Justification	Determines how Revit Architecture adjusts the spacing of grids along the curtain element face, when the grid spacing does not divide evenly into the length of the face. **Justification** also determines which grid lines are first removed or added when grid lines are added or removed because of parameter changes or changes to the size of the face. **Beginning** adds space to the end of the face before placing the first grid. **Center** adds an even amount of space at both the beginning and end of the face. **End** adds space from the beginning of the face before placing the first grid.

Name	Description
Angle	Rotates the curtain wall grids to the specified angle. You can also specify this value for individual faces. If you specify this parameter for a face, no value displays in this field. Valid values are between **89** and **-89**.
Offset	Starts grid placement at the specified distance from the justification point of the grids. For example, if **Justification** is specified as **Beginning** and you enter a value of **5′** here, Revit Architecture places the first grid 5′ from the beginning of the face. Note that you can also set this value for individual faces. If you specify this parameter for a face, no value displays in this field.
Structural	
Structural Usage	Sets the structural usage of the curtain wall. This property is read-only before creating a curtain wall. After you draw the curtain wall, you can select it and then modify this property.
Dimensions	
Area	The area of the curtain wall. This is a read-only value.
Identity Data	
Comments	Specific comments about the curtain wall.
Mark	Sets a label for the curtain wall. This value must be unique for each curtain wall in a project. Revit Architecture warns you if the number is already used but allows you to continue using it.

Figure 9-2 shows the **Curtain Wall Type Properties** dialog box. The following table describes the features of this dialog box.

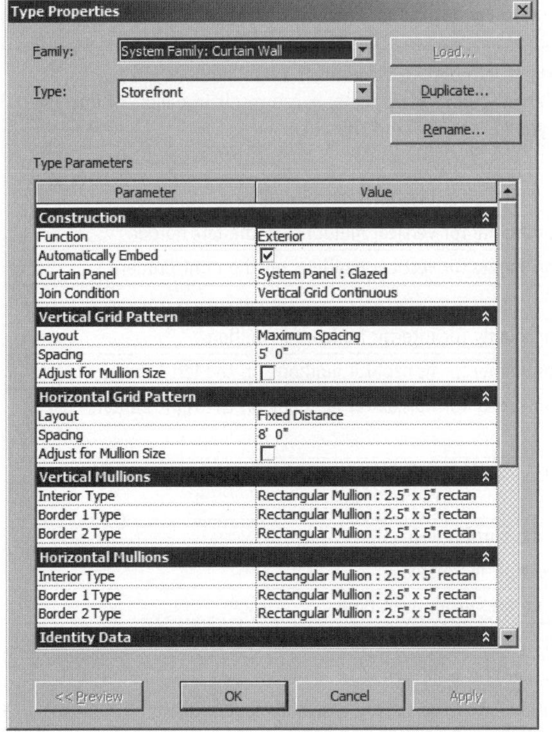

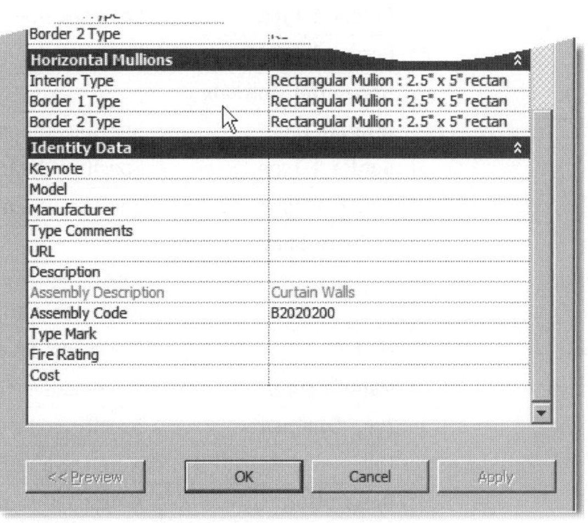

Figure 9-2

Curtain Wall Type Properties dialog box

Name	Description
Construction	
Function	Indicates the wall function.
Automatically Embed	Indicates whether the curtain wall automatically embeds into the wall.
Curtain Panel	Sets the curtain panel family type for the curtain element.
Join Condition	Controls which mullions break at intersections on a curtain element type. For example, this parameter makes all horizontal or vertical mullions on a curtain wall continuous, or it can make mullions on **Grid 1** or **Grid 2** continuous on a curtain system or sloped glazing.
Vertical/Horizontal Grid Pattern	
Layout	Sets an automatic vertical/horizontal layout for curtain grid lines along the length of a curtain wall. When set to a value other than **None**, Revit Architecture automatically adds vertical/horizontal grid lines to a curtain wall. **Fixed Distance** indicates that the curtain wall grids are placed at the exact value specified for **Vertical/Horizontal Spacing**. If the spacing is not an even factor of the wall's length, Revit Architecture inserts space at one or both ends of the wall, depending on the **Justification** parameter. For example, if the wall is 46′, the vertical spacing is 5′, and the **Justification** is set to **Beginning,** Revit Architecture adds 1′ from the beginning of the wall before placing the first grid. See the **Vertical/Horizontal Justification Instance Property** description for more information on justification. **Fixed Number** indicates that you can set different numbers of curtain grids for different curtain wall instances. See the **Vertical/Horizontal Number Instance Property** description for more information. **Maximum Spacing** indicates that the curtain grids are placed at even intervals along the length of the curtain wall at a distance up to the value specified for **Vertical/Horizontal Spacing.**
Spacing	Enabled when **Layout** is set to **Fixed Distance** or **Maximum Spacing.** When the layout is set to a fixed distance, Revit Architecture uses the exact value for **Spacing.** When the layout is at a maximum spacing, Revit Architecture uses up to the specified value to lay out the grids.
Adjust for Mullion Size	Adjusts the position of type-driven grid lines to ensure that curtain wall panels are of equal size, whenever possible. Sometimes when mullions are placed, particularly on borders of curtain wall hosts, it can result in panels of unequal size, even if the **Layout** is set to **Fixed Distance.**
Vertical Mullions	
Interior Type	Specifies the mullion family for interior vertical mullions.
Border 1 Type	Specifies the mullion family for vertical mullions on the left border.
Border 2 Type	Specifies the mullion family for vertical mullions on the right border.
Horizontal Mullions	
Interior Type	Specifies the mullion family for interior horizontal mullions.
Border 1 Type	Specifies the mullion family for horizontal mullions on the left border.
Border 2 Type	Specifies the mullion family for horizontal mullions on the right border.
Identity Data	
Keynote	Add or edit the curtain wall keynote. Click in the **Value** box to open the **Keynotes** dialog box.
Model	The model type for the curtain wall.
Manufacturer	Manufacturer for the stair materials.
Type Comments	Specific comments on the curtain wall type.
URL	A link to a web page for the manufacturer or other appropriate link.
Description	A description for the curtain wall.
Assembly Description	Description of the assembly based on the assembly code selection.
Assembly Code	Uniformat assembly code selected from hierarchical list.
Type Mark	A value to designate the particular curtain wall. Useful if you need to identify more than one curtain wall. This value must be unique for each curtain wall in a project. Revit Architecture warns you if the number is already used but allows you to continue using it.
Fire Rating	The fire rating of the curtain wall.
Cost	Material cost.

EXERCISE 9-1 **USING CURTAIN WALL 1**

Curtain Walls are specialized walls. Revit Architecture ships with a default curtain wall labeled **Curtain Wall 1**.

1. Start a new drawing using the RAC 2012\Imperial Templates\default.rte template.
2. In the **Project Browser**, double-click on the **LEVEL 1** floor plan to bring it into the **Drawing Editor**.
3. Change the **Drawing Scale** to **1/4″ = 1′-0″**.
4. Set the **Detail Level** to **Medium**.
5. Select the **Home** tab to bring up the **Home** toolbar.
6. In the **Home** toolbar, select the **Wall** button to bring up the **Modify | Place Wall** toolbar.
7. In the **Modify | Place Wall** toolbar, select the **Line** button in the **Draw** panel.
8. In the **Properties** dialog box, select **Curtain Wall 1** from the **Properties** drop-down list (see Figure 9-3).
9. Place a **15′** long, **10′-0″** high curtain wall in the **Drawing Editor**.
10. Change to the **Default 3D View**.

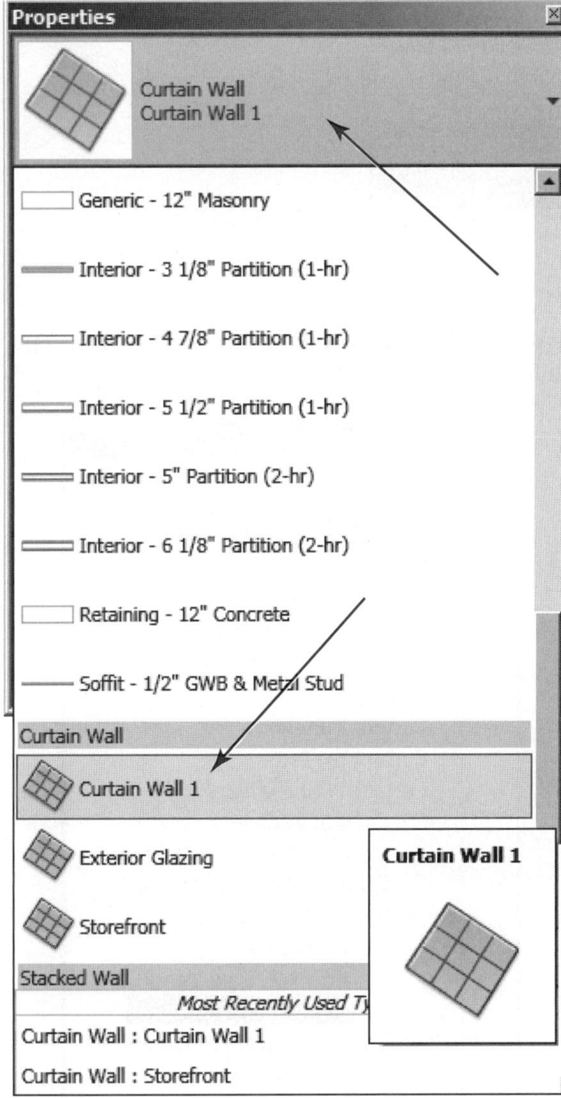

Figure 9-3

Select **Curtain Wall 1**

Notice that **Curtain Wall 1** does not contain a grid or mullions, just glass.

11. Select the curtain wall you just placed to bring up its **Properties** dialog box.
12. In the **Properties** dialog box, press the **Edit Type** button to bring up the **Type Properties** dialog box.
13. In the **Type Properties** dialog box, set the **Vertical Mullions > Border 1 Type** to **Rectangular Mullion: 2.5″ × 5″**, and press the **OK** buttons to return to the **Drawing Editor** (see Figure 9-4).

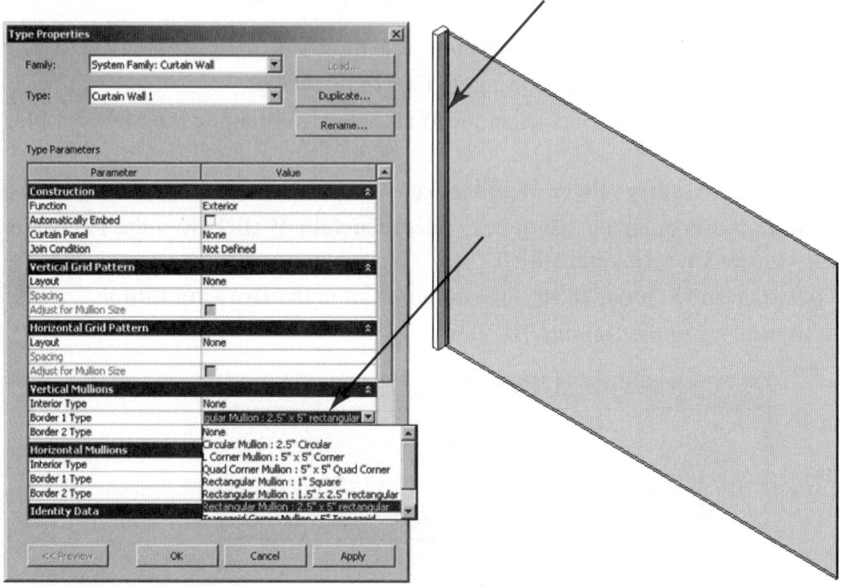

Figure 9-4

Set **Vertical Mullions**

14. In the **Project Browser**, expand the **Families > Curtain Wall Mullions > Rectangular Mullion** folder (see Figure 9-5).

Figure 9-5

Expand **Families**

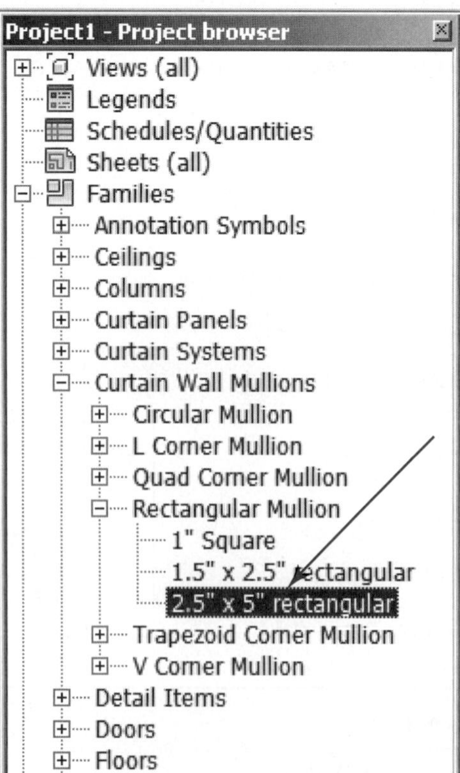

15. Select the **2.5″ × 5″ Rectangular Mullion**, **RMB**, and select **Properties** from the contextual menu that appears to bring up the **Type Properties** dialog box.
16. In the **Type Properties** dialog box, at the top right, press the **Duplicate** button, enter **8″ × 5″ Rectangular** in the **Name** dialog box, and then press the **OK** button.
17. In the **Type Properties** dialog box, under **Dimensions**, set the **Width on side 2** to **8″**, **Width on side 1** to **5″**, and press the **OK** button to return to the **Drawing Editor**.
18. Select the curtain wall again to bring up the **Properties** dialog box.
19. In the **Properties** dialog box, press the **Edit Type** button to bring up the **Type Properties** dialog box.
20. In the **Type Properties** dialog box, set the **Vertical Mullions > Border 2 Type** and **Horizontal Mullions > Border 2 Type** to **Rectangular Mullion: 2.5″ × 5″**.
21. In the **Type Properties** dialog box, set the **Horizontal Mullions > Border 1 Type** to **Rectangular Mullion: 8″ × 5″** (the **Mullion Type** you just created), and press the **OK** buttons to return to the **Drawing Editor** (see Figure 9-6).

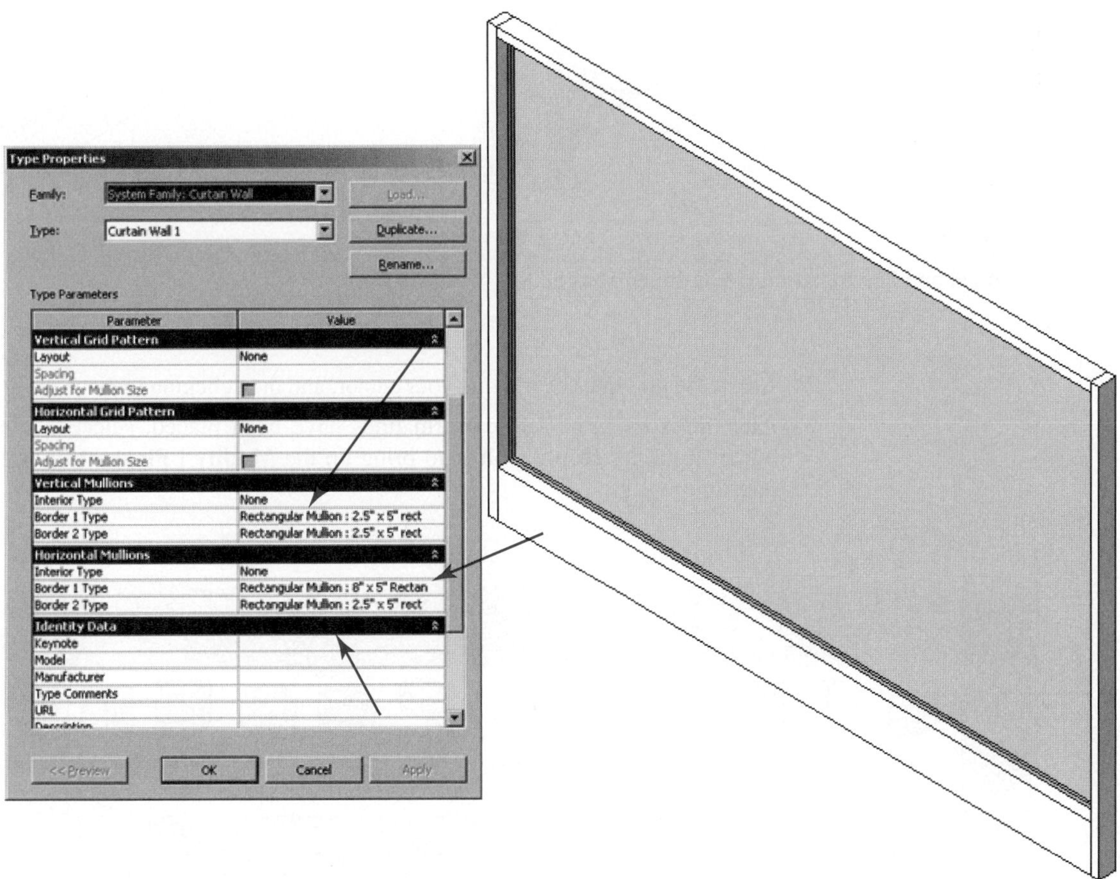

Figure 9-6

Set **Vertical** and **Horizontal Mullions**

22. In the **Home** toolbar, select the **Curtain Grid** button to bring up the **Modify | Place Curtain Grid** toolbar.

23. Move your cursor over the top mullion, and a vertical line and dimensions will appear on the glass. Move your cursor over the side mullion, and a horizontal line will appear (see Figure 9-7).

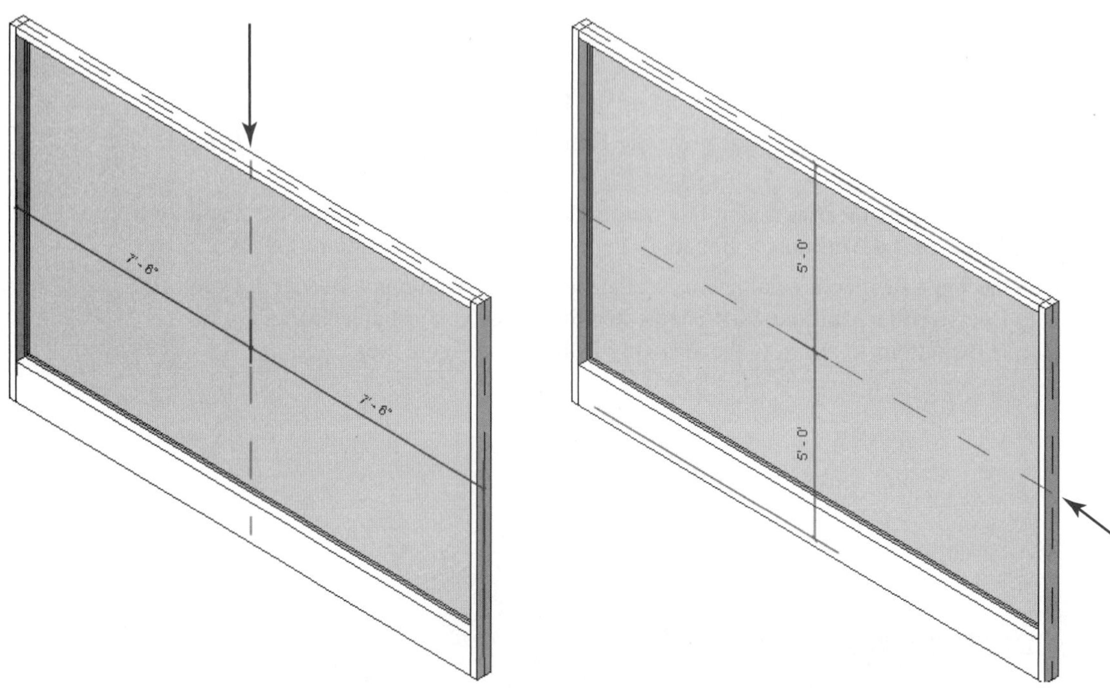

Figure 9-7

Vertical and horizontal lines and dimensions added

24. Adjust the grid lines by moving your cursor, and then clicking to place the grid line.
25. After horizontal and vertical grid lines have been placed, select the **Mullion** button from the **Home** toolbar to bring up the **Modify | Place Mullion** toolbar (see Figure 9-8).

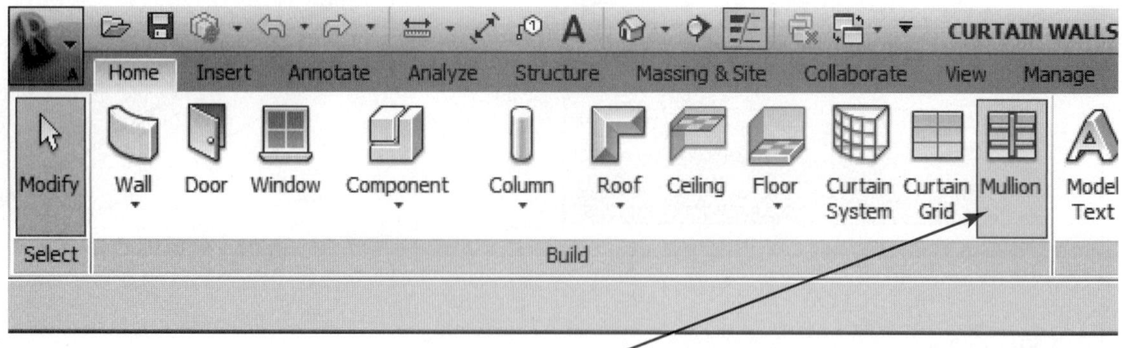

Figure 9-8

Modify | Place Mullion toolbar

26. In the **Modify | Place Mullion** toolbar, select the **2.5″ × 5″ Rectangular Mullion** from the **Properties** drop-down list. Select the **Grid Line** button, and then click on the vertical and horizontal curtain grid lines you just placed to create mullions (see Figure 9-9).

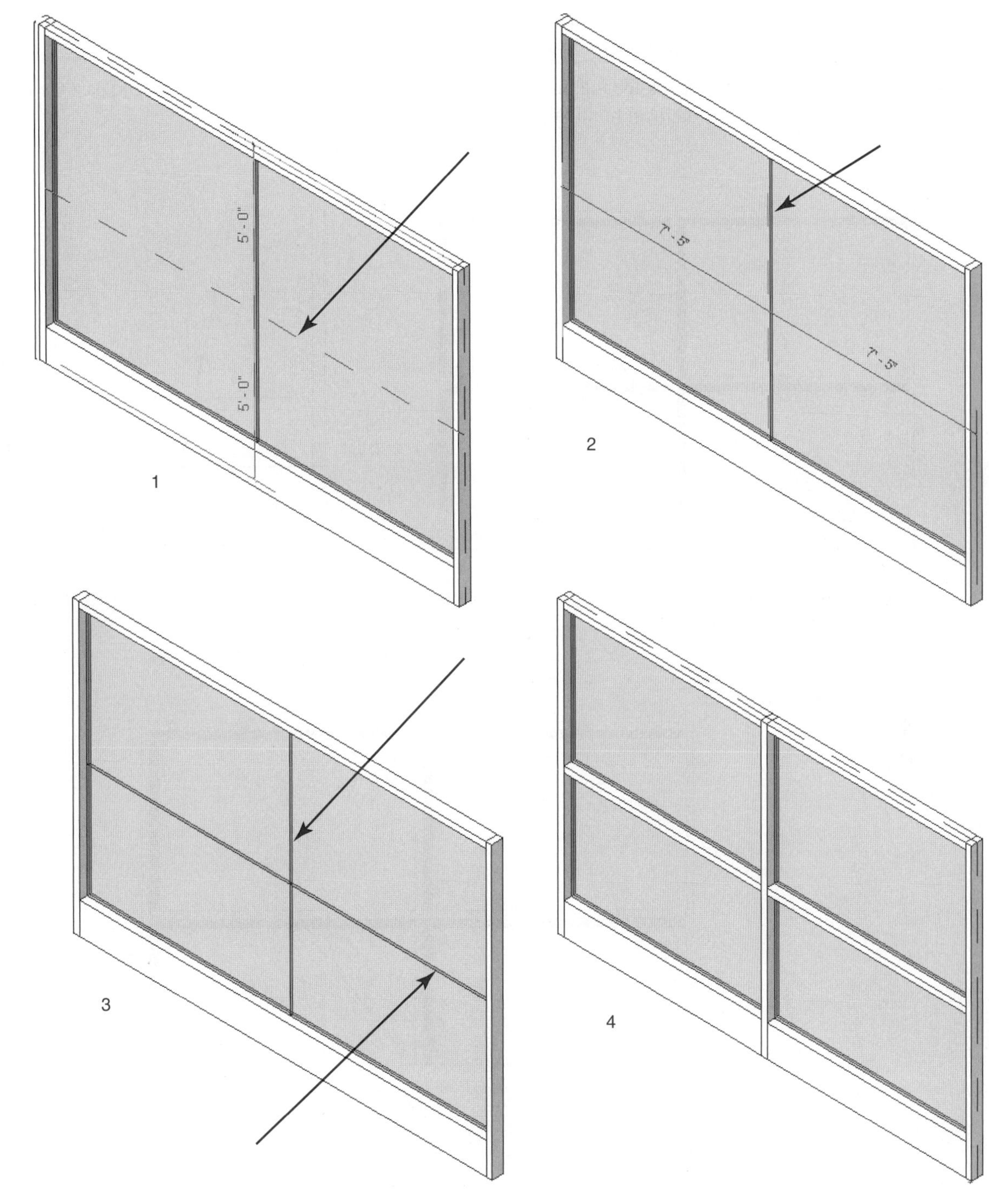

Figure 9-9

Add grid lines

27. Change to the **South Elevation**.
28. Notice that the vertical mullions do not meet the horizontal mullions correctly.
29. Select a mullion, and notice the two blue hatch marks that appear at the ends of the mullion.

The blue hatch marks are toggles to change the way one mullion meets another.

> **NOTE:**
> You may have to tap the **<Tab>** key as you select the curtain wall in order to cycle through all the mullions.

30. Click the toggle shown to make the bottom border mullion extend past the middle vertical mullion (see Figures 9-10 and 9-11).

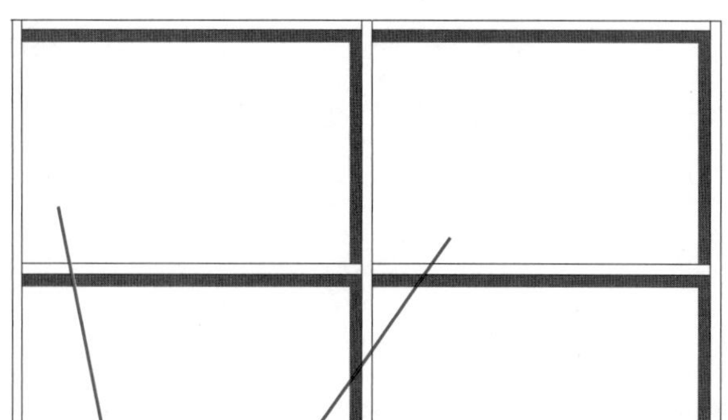
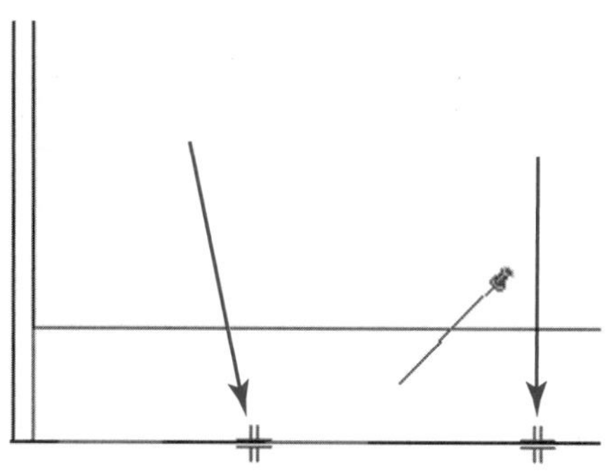

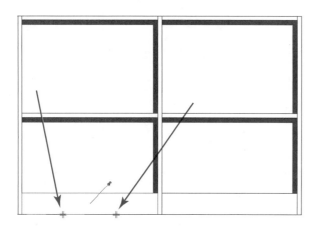

Figure 9-10

Extend mullion borders

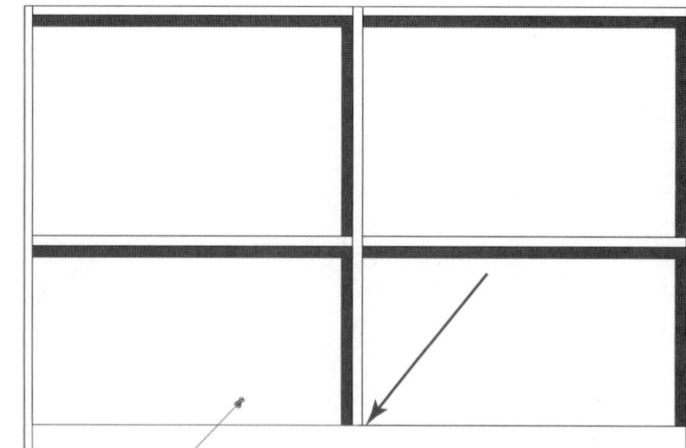

Figure 9-11

Extend mullion borders

31. Continue to individually select all the mullions and click their toggles to see the results (see Figure 9-12).

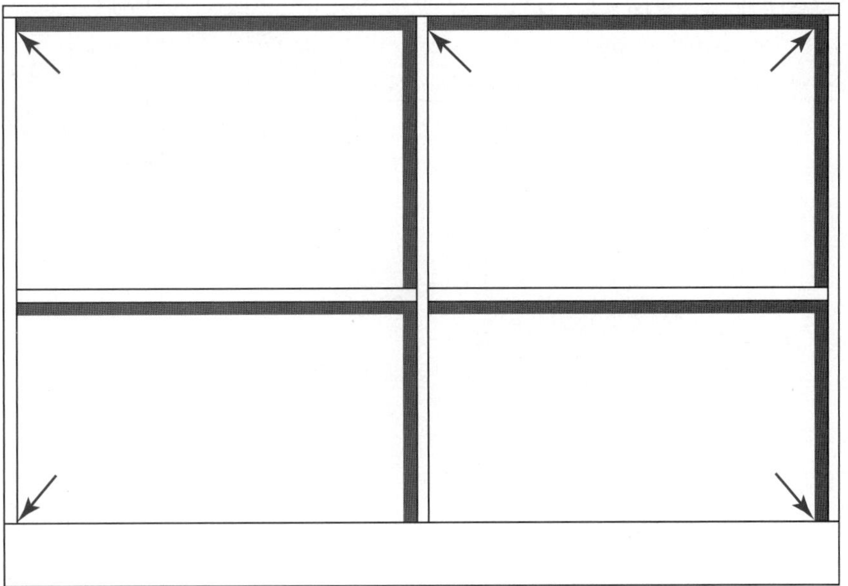

Figure 9-12

Results of mullion changes

32. Save this file as **USING CURTAIN WALL 1**.

EXERCISE 9-2 CURTAIN WALLS BY FACE ON A MASS OBJECT

In Revit Architecture 2012, you have the ability to place the **Curtain System by Face** on a **Mass** model.

1. Start a new drawing using the RAC 2012\Imperial Templates\default.rte template.
2. In the **Project Browser**, double-click on the **LEVEL 1** floor plan to bring it into the **Drawing Editor**.
3. Change the **Drawing Scale** to **1/4″ = 1′-0″**.
4. Set the **Detail Level** to **Medium**.
5. Select the **Massing & Site** tab to bring up the **Massing & Site** toolbar.
6. In the **Massing & Site** toolbar, select the **In-Place Mass** button. You will get a **Revit** warning; just read it, and press the **Close** button to bring up the **Name** dialog box.
7. In the **Name** dialog box, enter **TEST MASS**, and press the **OK** button to return to the **Drawing Editor**.
8. In the **Home** toolbar, select the **Rectangle** button in the **Draw** panel to bring up the **Modify | Place Lines** toolbar.
9. Place a **30′ × 30′-0″** rectangle in the **Drawing Editor**, and press the **Modify** button to end the command.
10. Select the **3D** button in the **Quick Access** toolbar to change to the **Default 3D View**.
11. Select all the lines of the rectangle you just created.

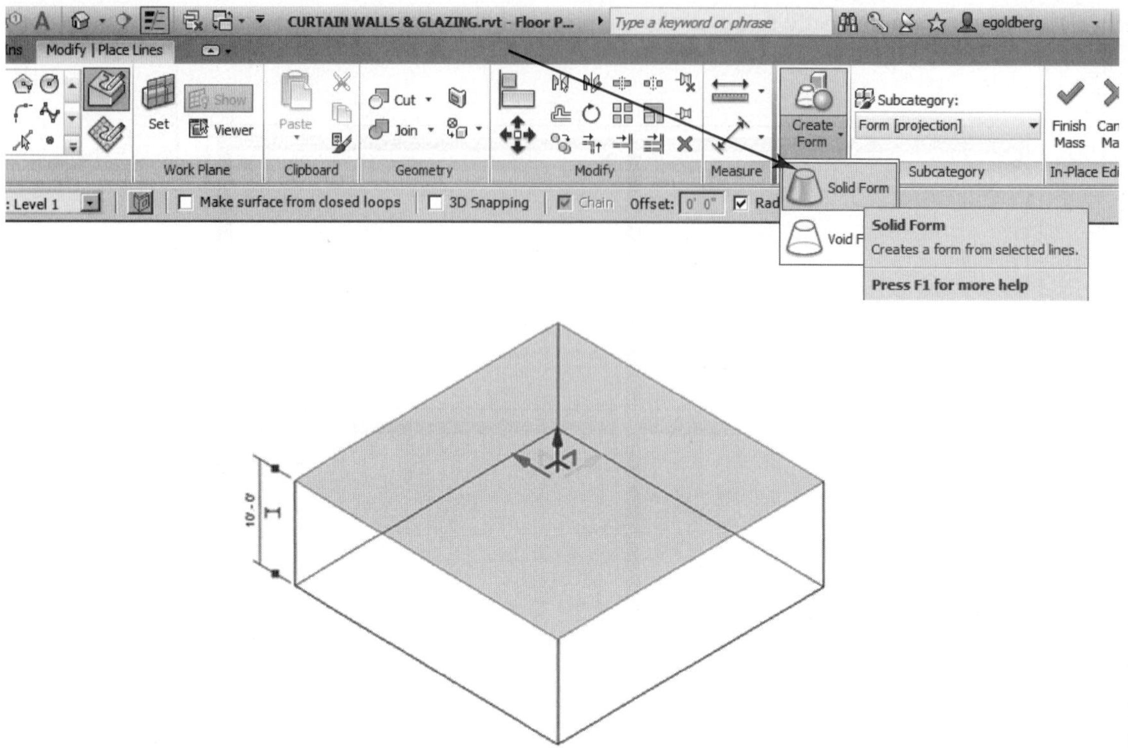

Figure 9-13

Change the **Rectangle** into a **Mass** form

12. In the **Modify | Place Lines** toolbar, select the **Create Form > Solid Form** button to change the **Rectangle** into a **Mass** form (see Figure 9-13).

By default, the new form will be created 10′-0″ high.

13. Select the top center of the form to bring up the change arrows (you will now be in the **Modify | Form** toolbar). Click on the **10′-0″** dimension, enter **15′-0″**, and press the **<Enter>** key to change the form's height (see Figure 9-14).

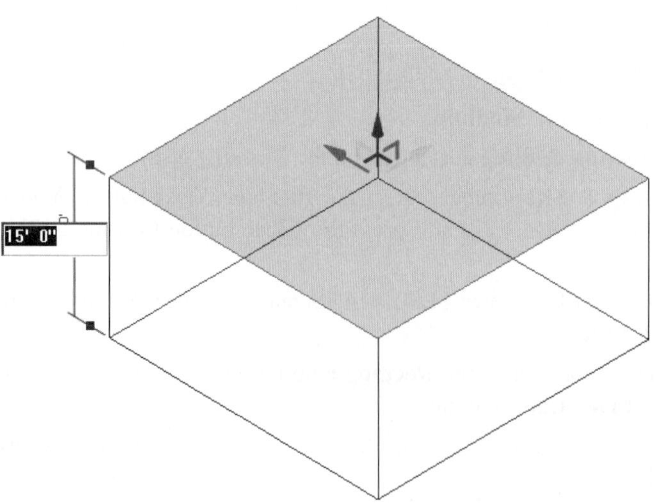

Figure 9-14

Change the height of the form

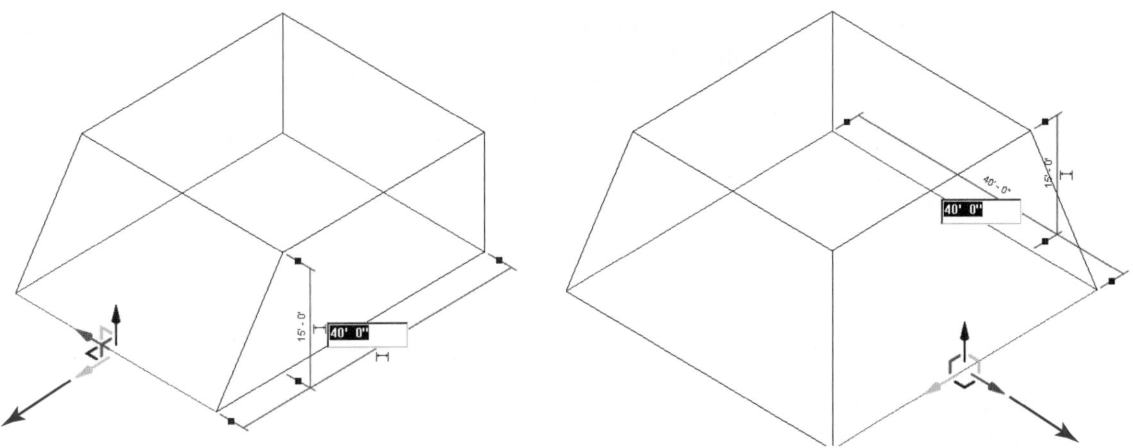

Figure 9-15

Change the **West** and **South** edges of the form

14. Select the lower **West** edge of the form to bring up the change arrows. Click on the **30′-0″** dimension, enter **40′-0″**, and press the **<Enter>** key to change the form.
15. Select the lower **South** edge of the form to bring up the change arrows. Click on the **30′-0″** dimension, enter **40′-0″**, and press the **<Enter>** key to change the form (see Figure 9-15).
16. In the **Modify | Form** toolbar, press the **Finish Mass** button in the **In-Place Editor** panel to complete the command, and return to the **Drawing Editor**.
17. In the **Home** toolbar, select the **Curtain System** button in the **Build** panel to bring up the **Modify | Place Curtain System by Face** toolbar.
18. Select the **5′ × 10′** from the **Properties** drop-down list.
19. In the **Modify | Place Curtain System by Face** toolbar, select the **Select Multiple** button in the **Multiple** selection panel.
20. Select the two sides of the mass to create the curtain system as shown in Figure 9-16.
21. Press the **<Esc>** key twice to end the command.

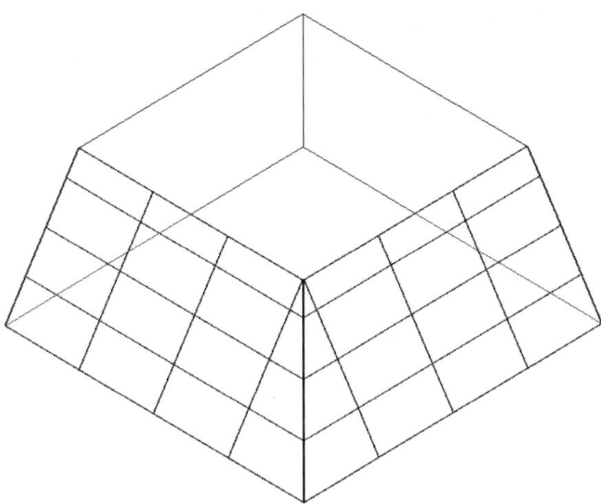

Figure 9-16

Create a curtain system

22. In the **Home** toolbar, select the **Mullion** button in the **Build** panel to bring up the **Modify | Place Mullion** toolbar.
23. Select the **2.5″ × 5″ Rectangular** mullion from the **Properties** drop-down list.
24. In the **Modify | Place Mullion** toolbar, select the **All Grid Lines** button, and touch one of the grid lines in each curtain system to place the mullions (see Figure 9-17).

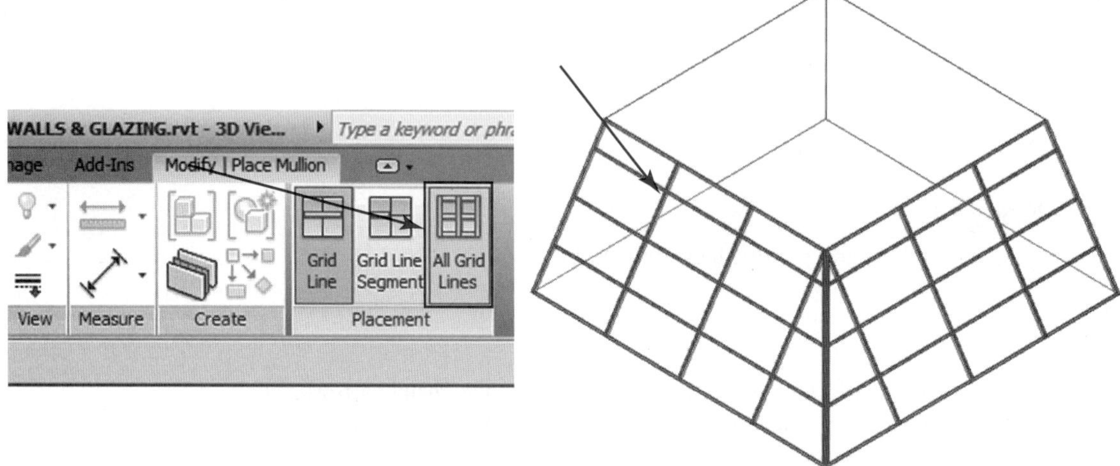

Figure 9-17

Place the mullions in each curtain system

If you want to create a different **Curtain Wall System**, do the following:

25. In the **Project Browser**, expand the **Families > Curtain Wall System > 5′ × 10′** folder.
26. **RMB** (**R**ight **M**ouse **B**utton click) on the > **5′ × 10′**, and select **Properties** from the contextual menu that appears to bring up the **Type Properties** dialog box.
27. Duplicate the **5′ × 10′ Curtain Wall System**, and modify the mullions in a similar manner to that shown in Steps 17–21 of Exercise 9-1.
28. If you need to hide the **Mass** object, type **VG** to bring up the **Visibility/Graphic Overrides** dialog box for the view you are in.
29. In the **Visibility/Graphic Overrides** dialog box, select the **Model Categories** tab.
30. In the **Model Categories** tab, uncheck the **Mass** check box, and press the **OK** button (see Figure 9-18).

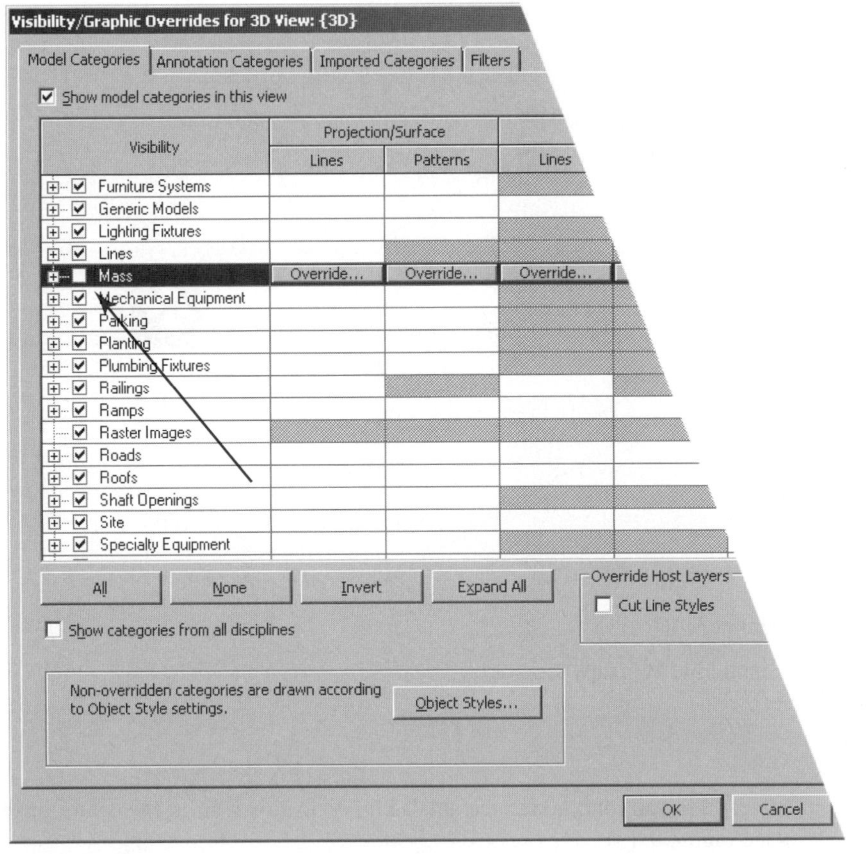

Figure 9-18

Model Categories tab

31. Save this file as **CURTAIN WALLS BY FACE**.

EXERCISE 9-3 CONFIGURING THE CURTAIN WALL GRID

You may want to have a curtain wall grid that is not horizontal and vertical, but rather at an angle. This is controlled by the **Curtain Wall Grid** icon on the face of the curtain wall.

1. Start a new drawing using the RAC 2012\Imperial Templates\default.rte template.
2. In the **Project Browser**, double-click on the **LEVEL 1** floor plan to bring it into the **Drawing Editor**.
3. Change the **Drawing Scale** to **1/4″ = 1′-0″**.
4. Set the **Detail Level** to **Medium**.
5. Select the **Home** tab to bring up the **Home** toolbar.
6. In the **Home** toolbar, select the **Wall** button to bring up the **Modify | Place Wall** toolbar.
7. In the **Modify | Place Wall** toolbar, select the **Line** button in the **Draw** panel.
8. Select **Curtain Wall 1** from the **Properties** dialog box.
9. Place a **20′** long, **15′-0″** high curtain wall in the **Drawing Editor**.
10. Change to the **Default 3D View**, and press the <Esc> key twice to clear all commands.

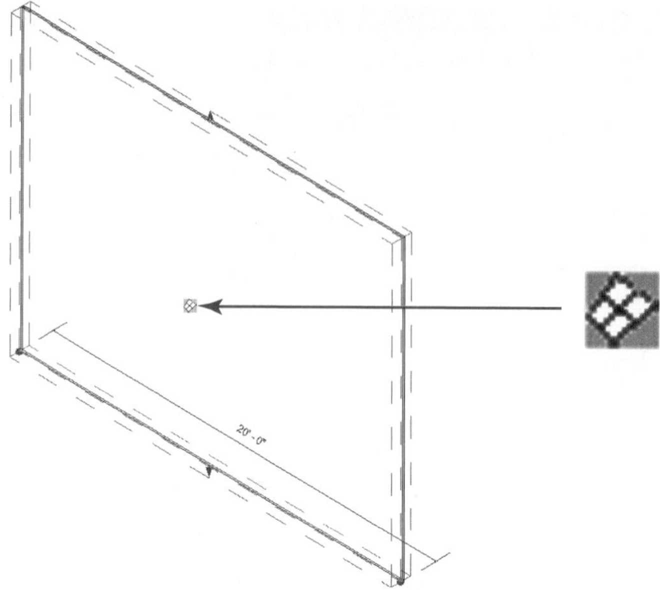

Figure 9-19

Small blue **Window** icon

11. Select the wall, and notice the small blue **Window** icon in the center of the wall (see Figure 9-19).
12. Select the icon, and a grid will appear with numbers at the top and right quadrants.

The first numbers represent the vertical and horizontal grid offset, and the other numbers represent the degree of rotation of the grid.

13. Select the degree number, enter **25** (percent), and then press the **<Enter>** key (see Figure 9-20).

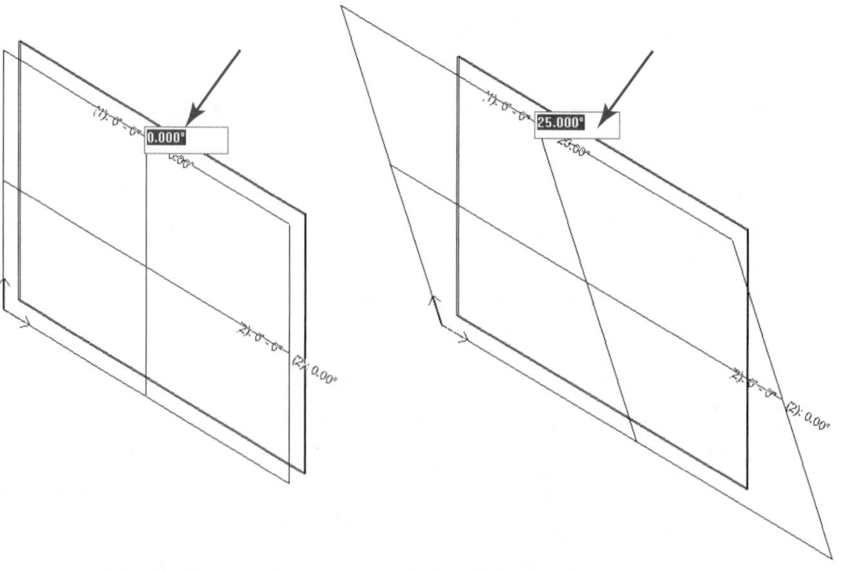

Figure 9-20

Add degree number

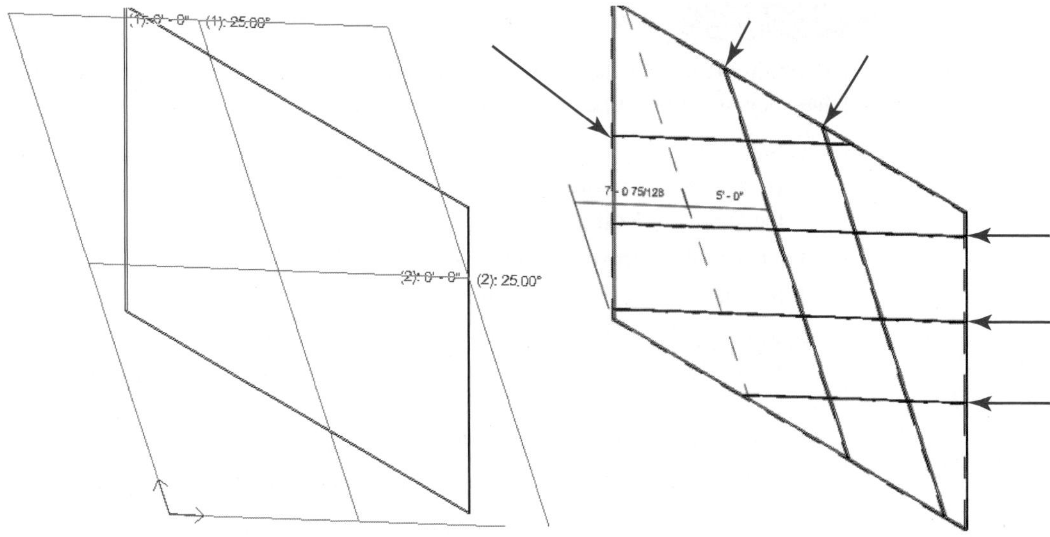

Figure 9-21

Place grids

14. Repeat this process with the right side numbers.
15. In the **Home** toolbar, select the **Curtain Grid** button, and place grids (see Figure 9-21).
16. In the **Home** toolbar, select the **Mullion** button to bring up the **Modify | Place Mullion** toolbar.
17. In the **Properties** dialog box, select **Rectangular Mullion 2.5″ × 5″**.
18. In the **Modify | Place Mullion** toolbar, select the **All Grid Lines** button, and select the outside of the **Curtain System** and the grid lines you rotated to place mullions (see Figure 9-22).
19. Save this file as **CONFIGURING THE CURTAIN GRID**.

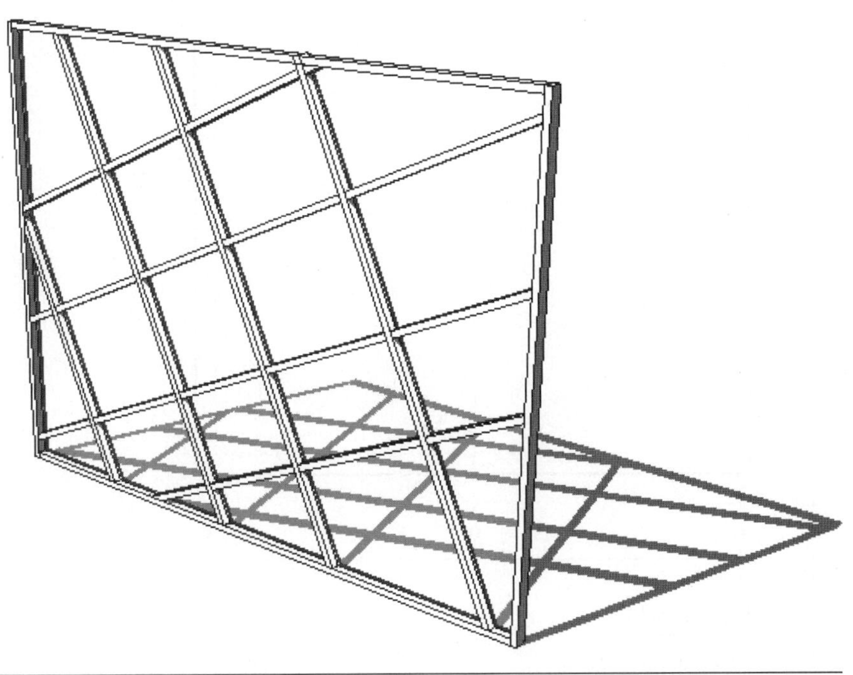

Figure 9-22

Select all grid lines

EXERCISE 9-4 CREATING SLOPED GLAZING

Curtain Walls can also be used for canopies and sloped glass roofs. Revit Architecture has tools that make this process quick and painless.

1. Start a new drawing using the RAC 2012\Imperial Templates\default.rte template.
2. In the **Project Browser**, double-click on the **LEVEL 1** floor plan to bring it into the **Drawing Editor**.
3. Change the **Drawing Scale** to **1/4″ = 1′-0″**.
4. Set the **Detail Level** to **Medium**.
5. Select the **Home** tab to bring up the **Home** toolbar.
6. In the **Home** toolbar, select the **Wall** button to bring up the **Modify | Place Wall** toolbar.
7. In the **Modify | Place Wall** toolbar, select the **Rectangle** button in the **Draw** panel.
8. In the **Modify | Place Wall** toolbar, select **Generic – 8″** from the **Change Element Type** dialog box.
9. Place an **18′-0″ × 18′-0″** enclosure **10′-0″** high in the **Drawing Editor**.
10. Change to the **South Elevation** view, and change the height of **Level 2** to **20′-0″**.
11. In the **Home** toolbar, select the **Roof > Roof by Footprint** button.

Because you can only use the **Roof by Footprint** button in a **floor plan** view, you will get a **"Go to View"** dialog warning. Select **Floor Plan: Level 2**, press the **Open View** button to bring **Level 2** into the **Drawing Editor**, and bring up the **Modify | Create Roof Footprint** toolbar.

12. In the **Modify | Create Roof Footprint** toolbar, select the **Pick Walls** button in the **Draw** panel.
13. In the **Options Bar**, uncheck the **Defines Slope** check box.
14. Pick all the walls, and then select the **Slope Arrow** button from the **Modify | Create Roof Footprint** toolbar.
15. Place an arrow as shown in Figure 9-23.

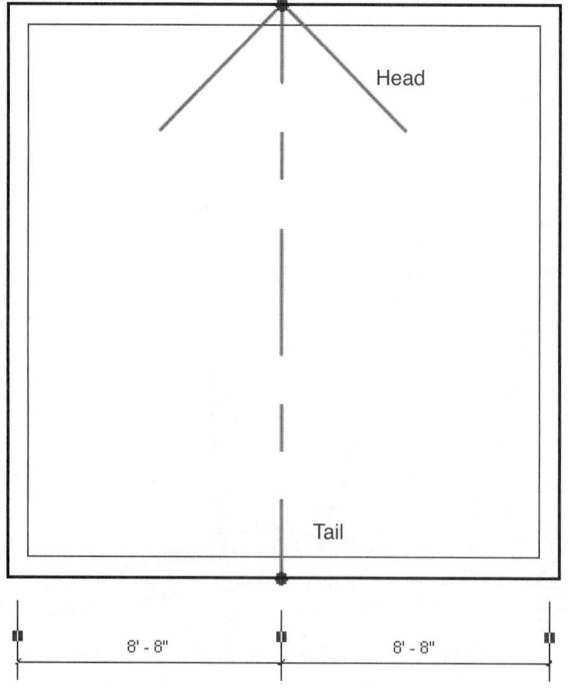

Figure 9-23

Place an arrow

16. Select the arrow to bring up the **Properties** dialog box.
17. In the **Properties** dialog box, set the **Level at Tail** to **Level 1**.
18. In the **Properties** dialog box, set the **Height Offset at Tail** to **15′-0″** (the height of the wall at the tail).
19. Set the **Level at Head** to **Level 2**.
20. In the **Properties** dialog box, set the **Height Offset at Head** to **0′-0″**, and press the **Apply** button to return to the **Drawing Editor**.
21. In the **Modify | Create Roof Footprint** toolbar, press the **Finish Edit Mode** button to create the roof.

A **Revit** dialog box will ask whether you would like to attach the highlighted walls to the roof. Press the **Yes** button.

22. Change to the **Default 3D View**.
23. Select the roof to bring up the **Modify | Roofs** toolbar.
24. Choose **Sloped Glazing** from the **Properties** drop-down list to create the sloped-glazed roof (see Figures 9-24 and 9-25).

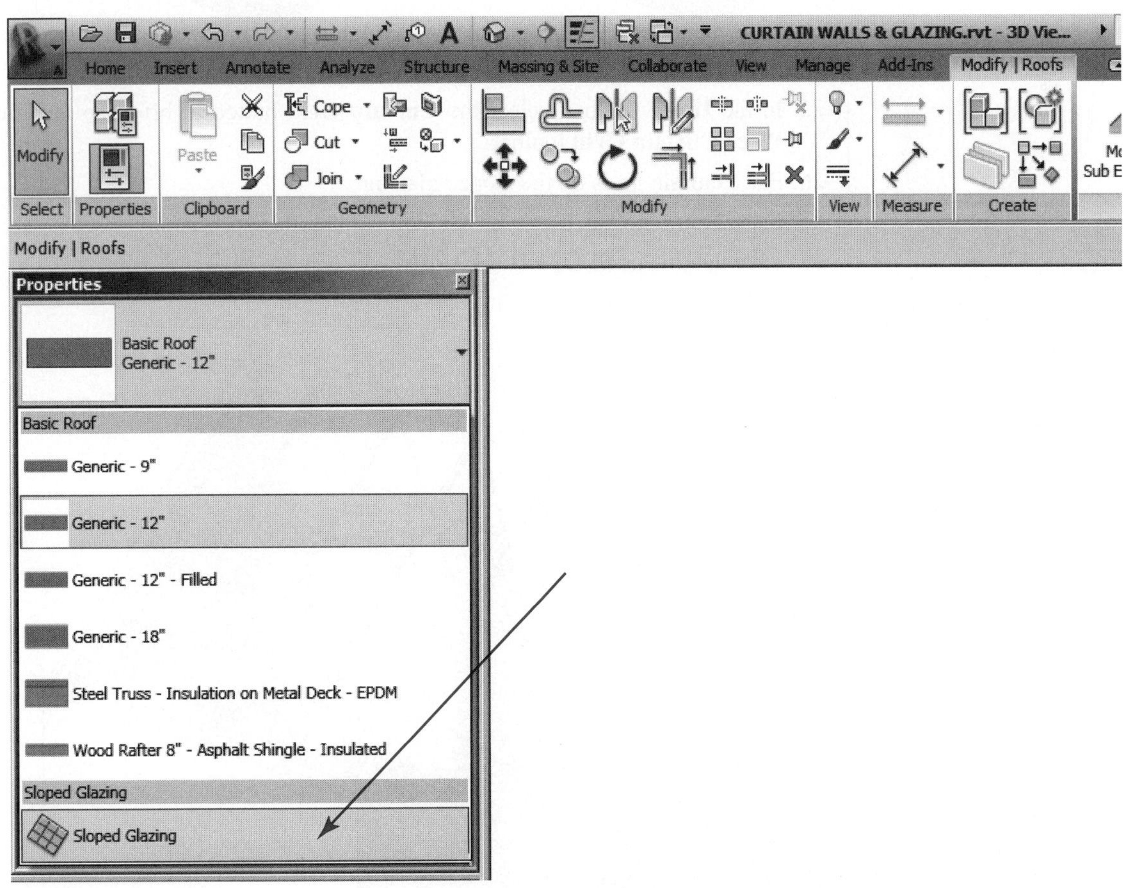

Figure 9-24

Modify | Roofs toolbar

Figure 9-25

Sloped-glazed roof

25. In the **Home** toolbar, select the **Curtain Grid** button to bring up the **Modify | Place Curtain Grid** toolbar.
26. Place curtain grids on the sloped glazing.
27. In the **Home** toolbar, select the **Mullion** button, and apply mullions (see Figure 9-26).
28. Save this file as **SLOPED GLAZING**.

Figure 9-26

Apply mullions

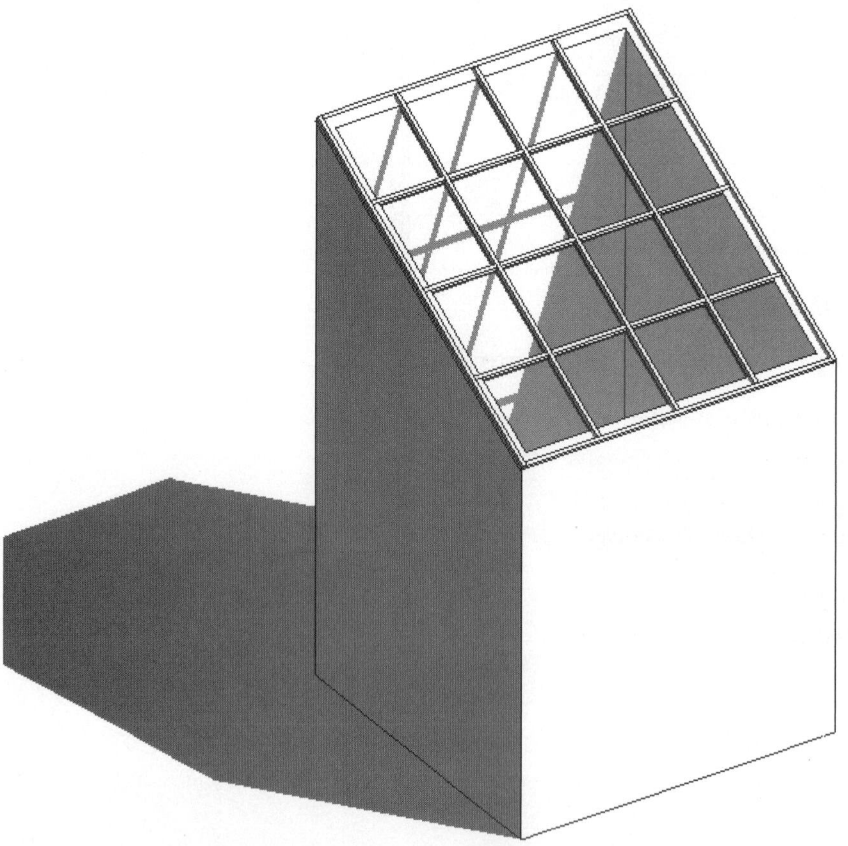

EXERCISE 9-5 CURVED CURTAIN WALLS

Any curved wall can be changed into a curtain wall by selecting it and choosing **Curtain Wall 1** from the **Change Element Type** drop-down list. When you do this with **Curtain Wall 1**, the curved wall will become flat but will automatically curve as you add grid segments. The more grid segments you add, the smoother the curve becomes (see Figure 9-27).

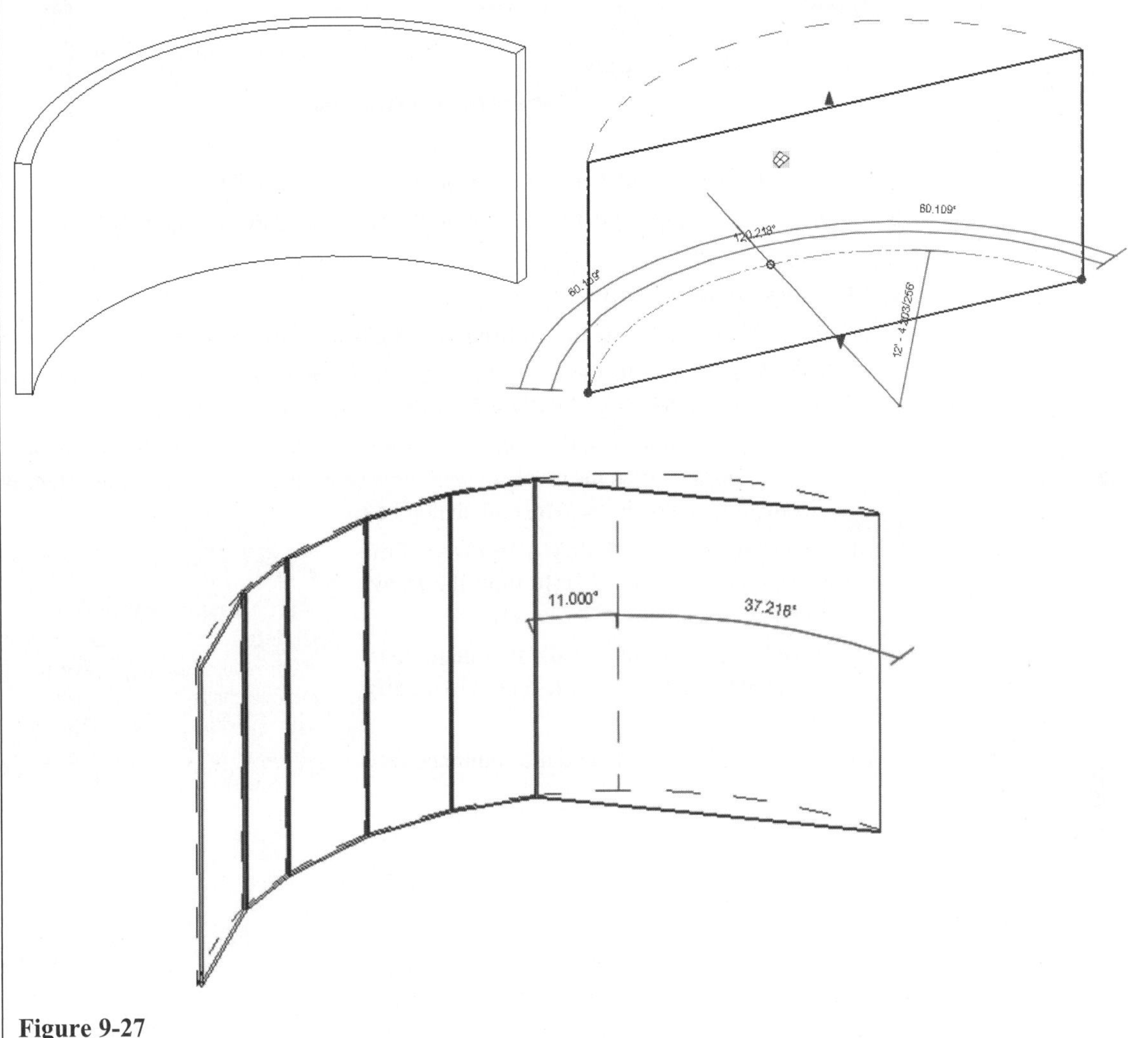

Figure 9-27

Curved curtain walls

EXERCISE 9-6 MAKING ODD-SHAPED CURTAIN WALLS

1. Start a new drawing using the RAC 2012\Imperial Templates\default.rte template.
2. In the **Project Browser**, double-click on the **LEVEL 1** floor plan to bring it into the **Drawing Editor**.
3. Change the **Drawing Scale** to **1/4″ = 1′-0″**.
4. Set the **Detail Level** to **Medium**.
5. Select the **Home** tab to bring up the **Home** toolbar.
6. In the **Home** toolbar, select the **Wall** button to bring up the **Modify | Place Wall** toolbar.
7. In the **Modify | Place Wall** toolbar, select the **Line** button in the **Draw** panel.

Figure 9-28

Modify | Walls > Edit Profile toolbar

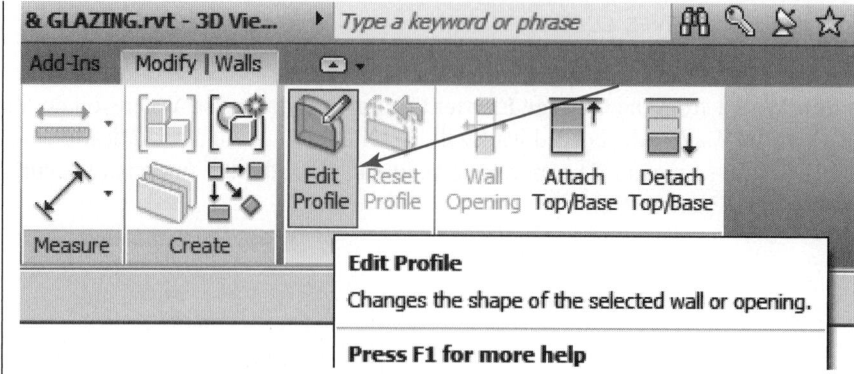

8. Select **Curtain Wall 1** from the **Properties** drop-down list.
9. Place a **40′-0″** long, **20′-0″** high wall in the **Drawing Editor**—starting from left to right.
10. Change to the **South Elevation** view.
11. Select the wall to bring up the **Modify | Walls** toolbar.
12. In the **Modify | Walls** toolbar, select the **Edit Profile** button from the **Mode** panel to bring up the **Modify | Walls > Edit Profile** toolbar (see Figure 9-28).
13. Adjust the sketch lines of the wall that appear. You will get a message, "*Constraints are not satisfied*" (this means these wall dimensions are locked). Press the **Remove Constraints** button in the **Message** dialog box.
14. While still in the **Modify | Walls > Edit Profile** toolbar, select **Circle** from the **Draw** panel, and add a circle to the wall.
15. In the **Modify | Walls > Edit Profile** toolbar, select the **Finish Edit Mode** button to modify the curtain wall.
16. Press the <**Esc**> key to end the command (see Figure 9-29).

NOTE:

Walls always have their constraints set when you create them. You will always have to remove these constraints before you can change the profile shape of a wall for the first time.

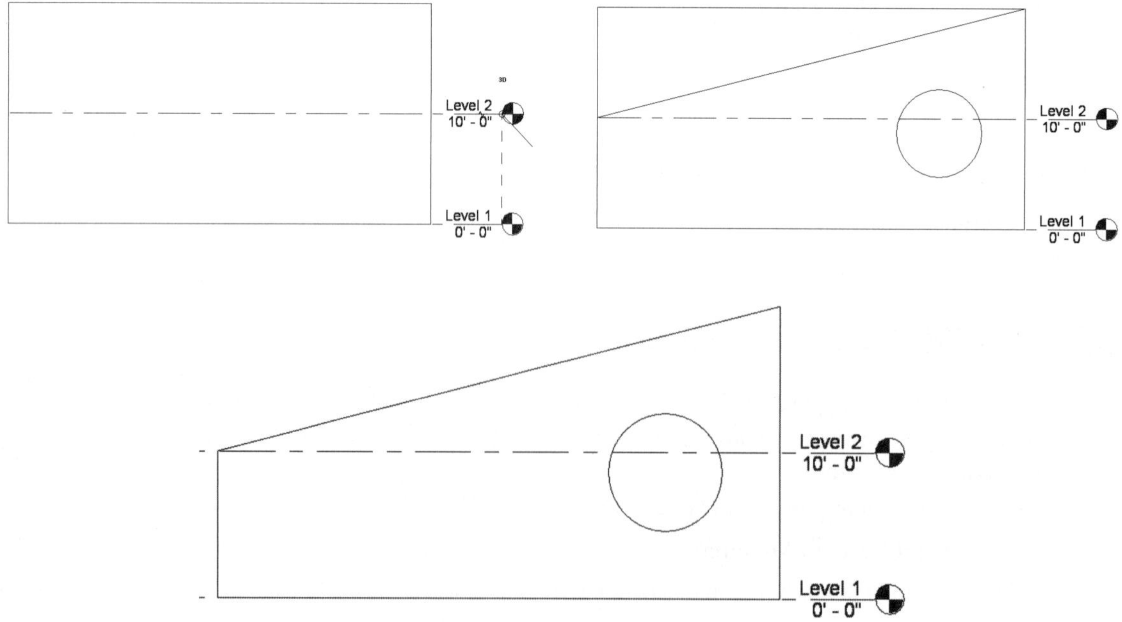

Figure 9-29

Circle added to drawing

17. Change to the **Default 3D View**.
18. In the **Home** toolbar, select the **Curtain Grid** button, and add grids.
19. In the **Home** toolbar, select the **Mullion** button to bring up the **Modify | Place Mullion** toolbar.
20. In the **Properties** dialog box, select **Rectangular Mullion 2.5″ × 5″**.
21. In the **Modify | Place Mullion** toolbar, select the **All Grid Lines** button, and select the outside of the curtain system and grid lines to place mullions (see Figure 9-30).
22. Save this file as **ODD SHAPED CURTAIN WALLS**.

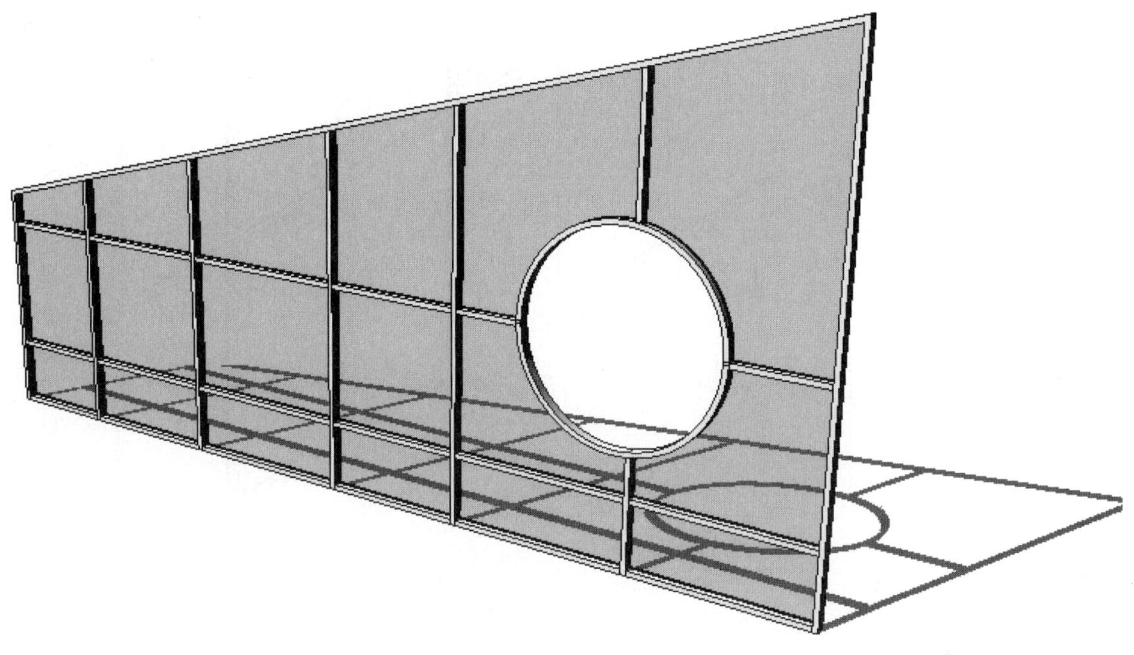

Figure 9-30
Place mullions

EXERCISE 9-7 ADDING DOORS AND PANELS TO CURTAIN WALLS

1. Start a new drawing using the RAC 2012\Imperial Templates\default.rte template.
2. In the **Project Browser**, double-click on the **LEVEL 1** floor plan to bring it into the **Drawing Editor**.
3. Change the **Drawing Scale** to **1/4″ = 1′-0″**.
4. Set the **Detail Level** to **Medium**.
5. Select the **Home** tab to bring up the **Home** toolbar.
6. In the **Home** toolbar, select the **Wall** button to bring up the **Modify | Place Wall** toolbar.
7. In the **Modify | Place Wall** toolbar, select the **Line** button in the **Draw** panel.
8. In the **Properties** dialog box, select **Exterior Glazing** from the **Properties** drop-down list.
9. Place a **40′-0″** long, **20′-0″** high wall in the **Drawing Editor**—starting from left to right.
10. Apply mullions to all the grid lines in the **Exterior Glazing** wall you just created, and press the **<Esc>** key to end the command.

11. Change to the **Default 3D View** (see Figure 9-31).

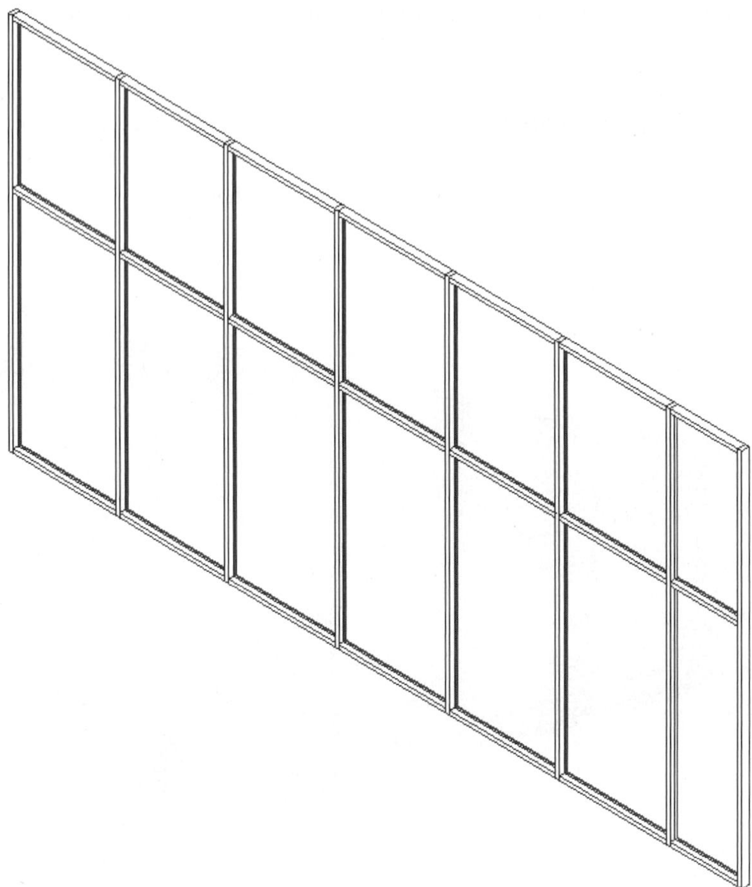

Figure 9-31

Mullions added to all grid lines

12. Place your cursor near one of the mullions, tap the <**Tab**> key until a glazing panel is selected, and then click your left mouse button to select it.
13. With the panel still selected, press the **Edit Type** button in the **Properties** dialog box to bring up the **Type Properties** dialog box.

> **NOTE:**
> When you have selected a glazing panel, the **Modify | Curtain Panels** toolbar will appear.

14. In the **Type Properties** dialog box, select the **Load** button (at the very top of the dialog box) to bring up the **Open** menu in the **Imperial** or **Metric Library**.
15. In the **Imperial** or **Metric Library**, open the **Doors** folder.
16. In the **Doors** folder, select the **Curtain Wall Dbl Glass** door, press the **Open** button to load the **Family** into the program, and return to the **Type Properties** dialog box.
17. Repeat the previous step, and load the **Curtain Wall Sgl Glass** door.
18. In the **Type Properties** dialog box, press the **OK** button to return to the **Drawing Editor**.
19. Now that the door is loaded, select the panel again to bring up its **Properties** dialog box.
20. In the **Properties** dialog box, change the **Family** to **Curtain Wall Dbl Glass** (see Figure 9-32).

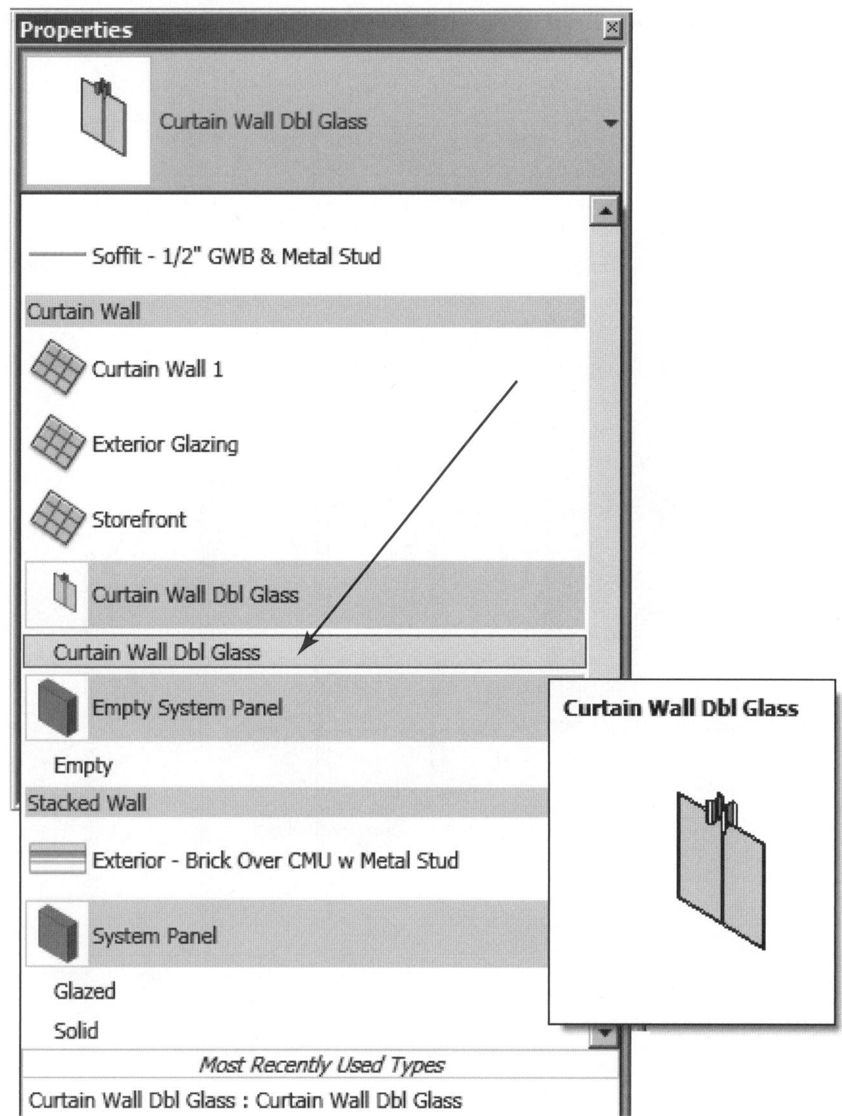

Figure 9-32

Properties | **Curtain Wall Dbl Glass** dialog box

21. Repeat this process, and place the **Curtain Wall Sgl Glass** door.

You have now placed three doors into the curtain wall.

22. Again, with the <**Tab**> key, select the **Curtain Wall Dbl Glass** door you placed.
23. With the door selected, press the **Edit Type** button in its **Properties** dialog box to bring up the **Type Properties** dialog box.
24. In the **Type Properties** dialog box, select the **Duplicate** button, enter **WOOD CURTAIN WALL DOOR** in the **Name** field, and press the **OK** button to return to the **Type Properties** dialog box.
25. In the **Type Properties** dialog box, select the **Glazing Material** field to open the **Materials** dialog box.

NOTE:

You can now either create a new sill profile for the door sill mullions or just delete the mullions below the doors. The base of the doors will elongate downward to meet the **Level** if you delete the sill mullions.

26. In the **Materials** dialog box, select **Wood – Flooring**, and press the **OK** buttons to return to the **Drawing Editor** (see Figure 9-33).

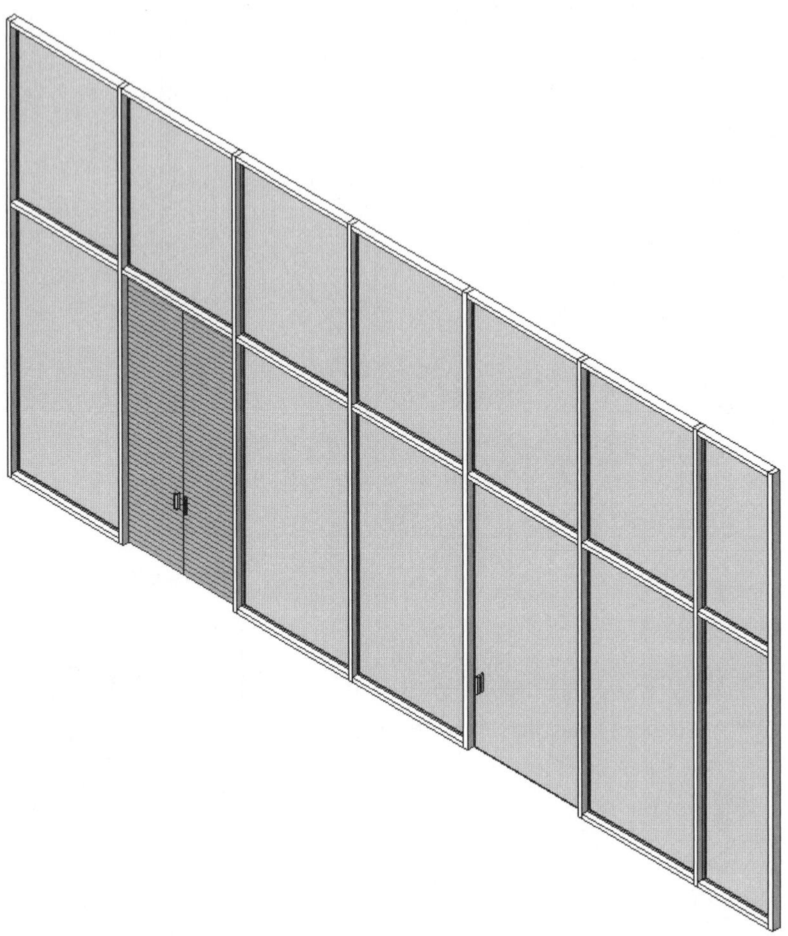

Figure 9-33

Door material changed to wood

27. Using the <**Tab**> key, select the panel above the wood door you just created.
28. With the panel selected, select **Generic – 4″ Brick** from the **Properties** dialog box drop-down list.

NOTE:

Curtain Wall panels will accept any wall but only doors based on **Curtain Wall** doors.

29. Delete one of the horizontal mullions.
30. Select the horizontal curtain wall grid where the deleted mullion existed.
31. Click the **Push Pin** icon to turn off the **Constraint**, select the **Add or Remove Segments** button from the **Modify | Curtain Wall Grids** toolbar, and click the grid again to join the two glazing panels into one panel. Press the <**Esc**> key to end the command (see Figure 9-34).

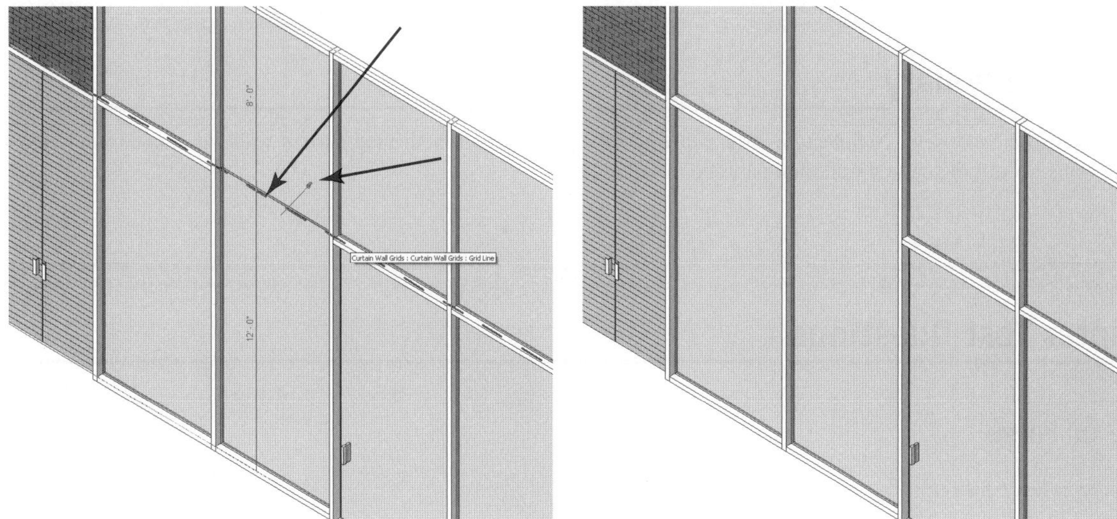

Figure 9-34

Two glazing panels joined into one panel

32. Using the <**Tab**> key, select the single panel you just created, and again select **Generic – 4″ Brick** from the **Properties** dialog box drop-down list (see Figure 9-35).
33. Save this file as **CURTAIN WALL DOORS AND PANELS**.

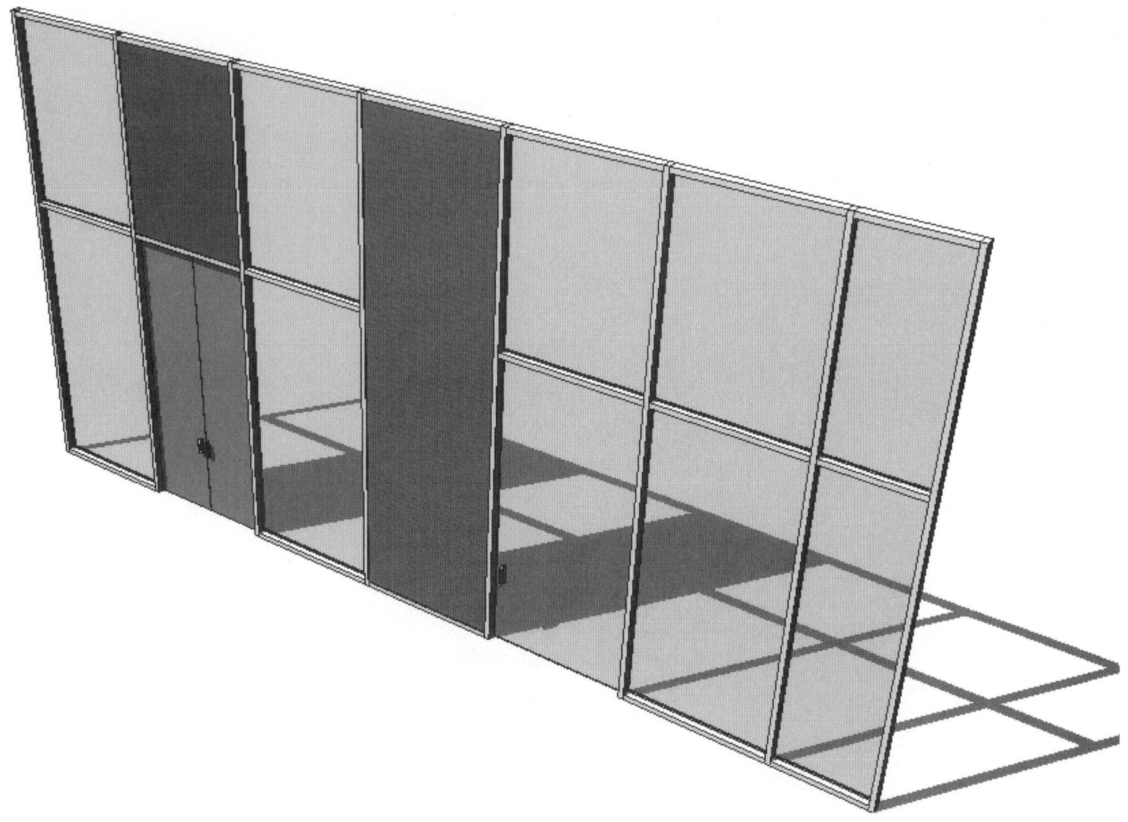

Figure 9-35

Generic – 4″ Brick selected from the **Properties** dialog box

Chapter Summary

This chapter discussed Revit Architecture 2012's methods for creating and modifying curtain walls. It also covered creating sloped glazing walls, modifying curtain wall mullions, and inserting doors.

Chapter Test Questions

True or False

Circle the correct answer.

1. **True or False:** Any door can be placed in a **Curtain Wall** panel.
2. **True or False:** A wall cannot be changed into glazing.
3. **True or False: Curtain Grids** can only be placed horizontally and vertically.
4. **True or False: Curtain Wall** mullions can only be created from profiles.
5. **True or False:** Mullions can be placed without having previously placed a **Curtain Grid**.

Questions

1. Where are the mullion families located?
2. What is a **Curtain Wall**?
3. What is the **Default Layer**?
4. What is **Curtain Grid** used for?
5. What is **Edit Profile** used for?

Exercise

Create a flat-topped 20′ × 20′ × 15′ high pyramid with curtain walls for sides (see Figure 9-36).

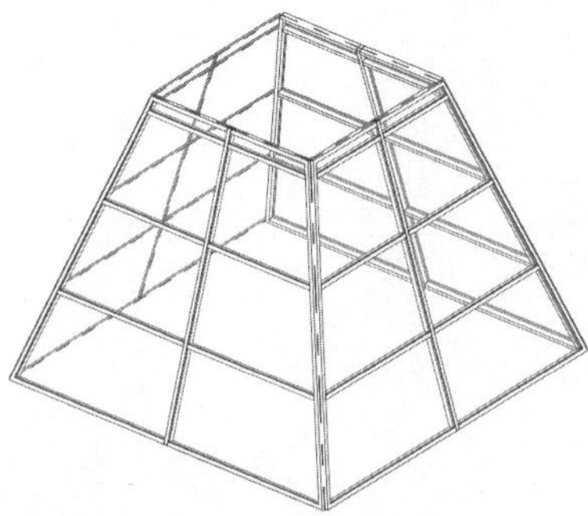

Figure 9-36

Pyramid with curtain walls

CHAPTER

10 Stairs, Railings, and Ramps (Circulation)

CHAPTER OBJECTIVES

- Learn how to create and modify **Straight** stairs using the **Run** tool.
- Learn how to create and modify **U-shaped** stairs using the **Run** tool.
- Learn how to add and delete risers.
- Learn how to create and modify stairs using the **Boundary** tool.
- Learn how to create **Multistory** stairs.
- Learn how to create **Monolithic** stairs.
- Learn how to modify and host **Rail** objects.
- Learn how to create **Ramps**.

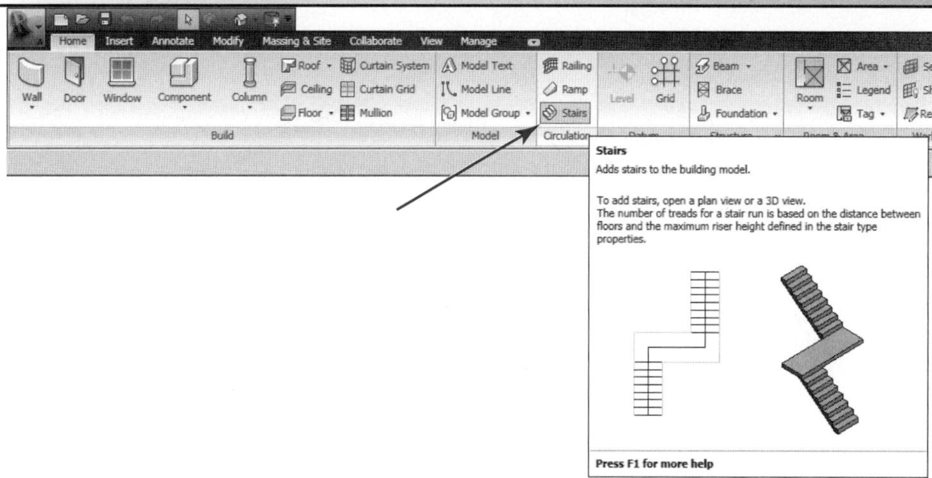

Introduction

Stairs, railings, and ramps are an important part of almost every project and where designers often make mistakes. Revit Architecture 2012's stair and railing systems aid in the productivity and accuracy of these objects. Because of the complexity and variance of stairs, there are many settings. Once these are understood and preset, placing and modifying stairs is quite easy. By creating your own Revit **Families**, stairs, railings, and ramps can be placed into a project quickly and efficiently.

Before you start these exercises, it is a good idea to understand some basic stair terms. Among these are **Rise** and **Run, Tread, Riser, Nosing,** and **Stringer** (see Figures 10-1 and 10-2).

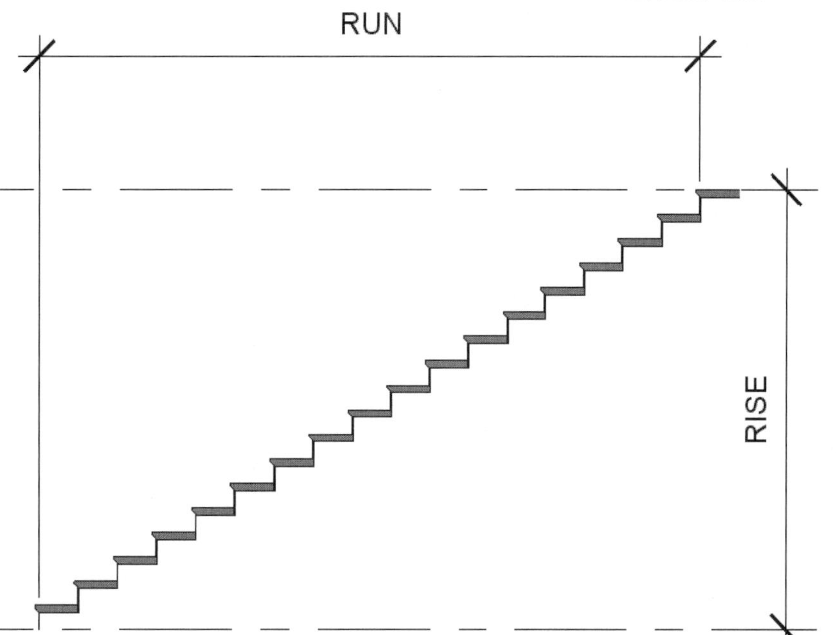

Figure 10-1
Rise and **Run**

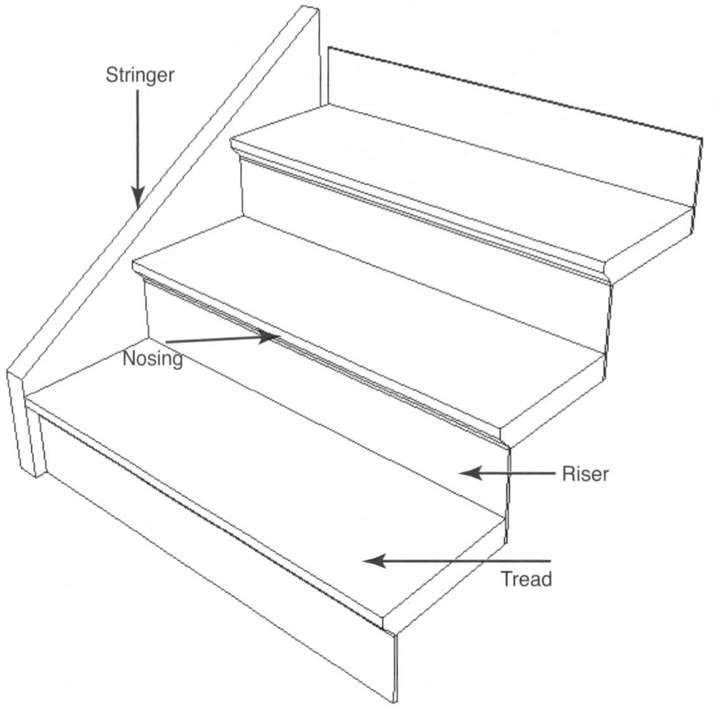

Figure 10-2

Tread, **Riser**, **Nosing**, and **Stringer**

Stair Properties Dialog Box

The **Stair Properties** dialog box is where you can view and modify the parameters that define the properties of stairs (see Figure 10-3).

Name	Description
Constraints	
Base Level	Sets the base of the stairs.
Base Offset	Sets the stair's height from its base level.
Top Level	Sets the top of the stairs.
Top Offset	Sets the stair's offset from the top level.
Multistory Top Level	Sets the top of the stairs in a multistory building. The advantage to using this parameter (as opposed to sketching individual runs) is that if you change the railing on one run, that railing is changed on all the runs. Also, if you use this parameter, the Revit Architecture project file size does not change as significantly as it would if you sketched individual runs. **Note:** The levels in the multistory building should be a uniform distance apart.
Graphics	
Up Text	Sets the text for the **Up** symbol in plan. The default value is **UP**.
Down Text	Sets the text for the **Down** symbol in plan. The default value is **DN**.
Up Label	Displays or hides the **Up** label in plan.
Up Arrow	Displays or hides the **Up** arrow in plan.
Down Label	Displays or hides the **Down** label in plan.
Down Arrow	Displays or hides the **Down** arrow in plan.
Show Up Arrow in All Views	Displays the **Up** arrow in all project views.

Name	Description
Dimensions	
Width	Width of the stairs.
Desired Number of Risers	The number of risers is calculated based on the height between levels.
Actual Number of Risers	Normally, the same as **Desired Number of Risers**. However, it may be different if you do not complete adding the correct number of risers for the given run of the stairs. This is a read-only value.
Actual Riser Height	Displays the actual riser height. The value is equal to or less than the value specified in **Maximum Riser Height**. This is a read-only value.
Actual Tread Depth	You can set this value to change the tread depth without having to create a new stair type. Also, the **Stair Calculator** can change this value to satisfy the stair equation.
Identity Data	
Comments	Specific comments on the staircase.
Mark	A label created for the stairs. This value must be unique for each stairway in a project. Revit Architecture warns you if the number is already used but allows you to continue using it. You can see the warning using the **REVIEW WARNINGS** command.
Phasing	
Phase Created	The phase when the stairs were created.
Phase Demolished	The phase when the stairs were demolished.

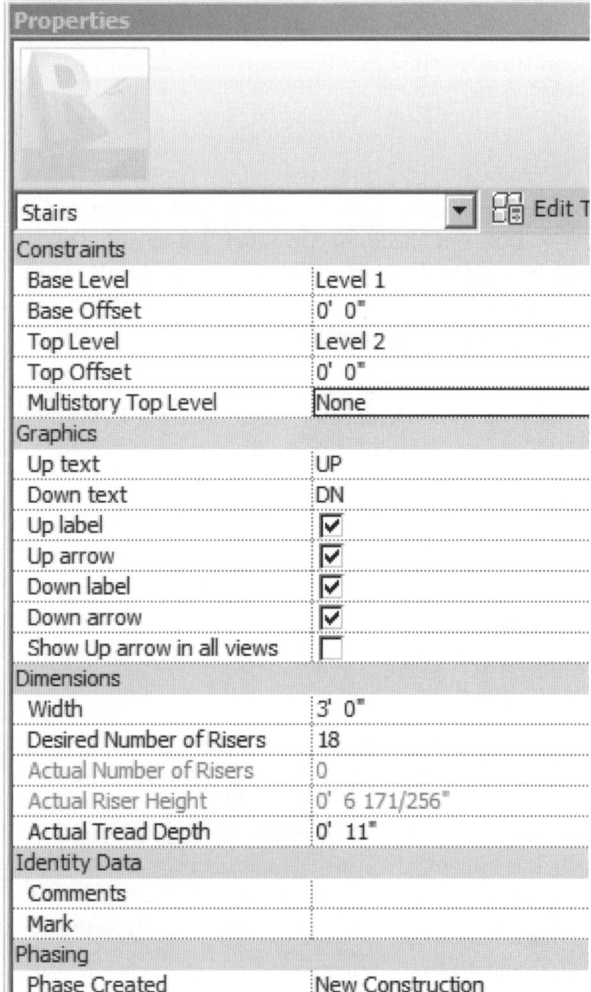

Figure 10-3

Stair Properties dialog box

Creating and Modifying Stairs

There are basically two ways to create stairs: by **Run** or by **Boundary**. Both of these methods ultimately are similar when you edit them.

EXERCISE 10-1 **CREATING AND MODIFYING STAIRS BY THE RUN METHOD**

Straight Stairs

1. Start a new project using the RAC 2012\Imperial Templates\default.rte template.
2. In the **Project Browser**, double-click **Floor Plans > Level 1** to bring it into the **Drawing Editor**.
3. In the **Home** toolbar, select the **Stairs** button to bring up the **Modify | Create Stairs Sketch** toolbar.
4. In the **Modify | Create Stairs Sketch** toolbar, select the **Run** button (see Figure 10-4).

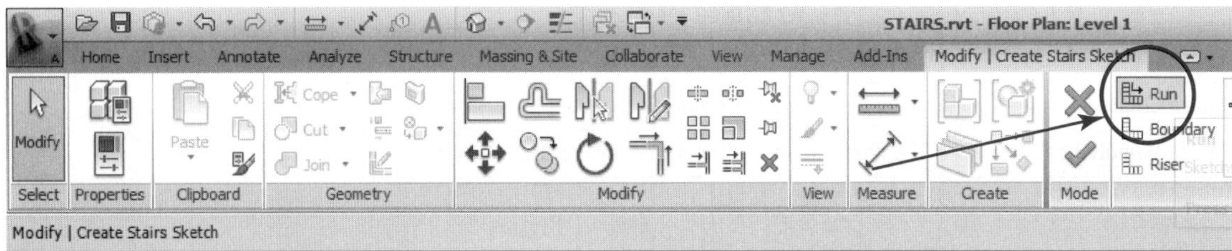

Figure 10-4
Run button

5. In the **Properties** dialog box, set the **Base Level** to **Level 1**, **Top Level** to **Level 2**, **Up text** to **UP**, **Down text** to **DN**, and check the **Up label, Up arrow**, **Down label**, and **Down arrow** check boxes. Uncheck the **Show Up arrow in all views** check box (you only want to see **Up** arrows in the Plan views). Set the **Width** to **4′-0″**, and set the **Phase Created** to **New Construction**.

You can change the **Desired Number of Risers**, but there is no need as Revit automatically calculates this for you based on the difference between the **Base Level** and **Top Level**.

If you are creating "as built" drawings, set the **Phase Created** to **Existing**, and press the **OK** button to return to the **Drawing Editor**.

6. A cross-shaped cursor will now appear. Click, drag your cursor to the right until you see **15″-7′** appear, and then click again.
7. In the **Modify | Create Stairs Sketch** toolbar, press the **Finish Edit Mode** button to create the stair (see Figures 10-5 and 10-6).

NOTE:
The break mark indicates that the stair is going upward and is being cut at the cut plane. When the stair is shown going down, no break mark is shown.

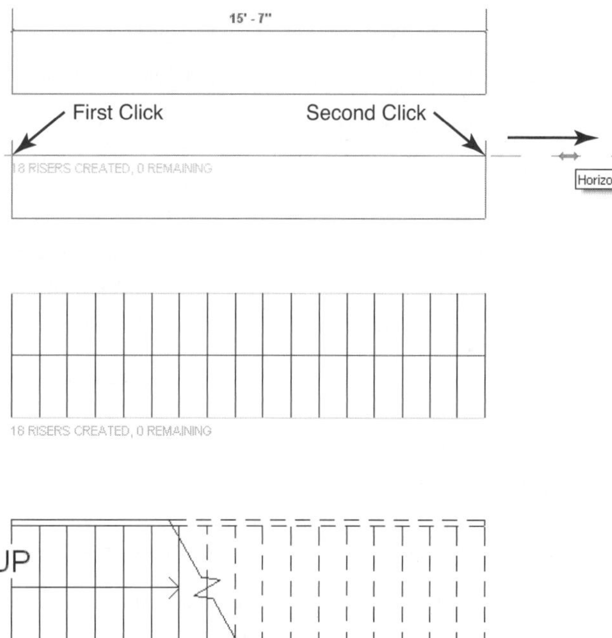

Figure 10-5

Modify | Create Stairs Sketch toolbar to create the stair

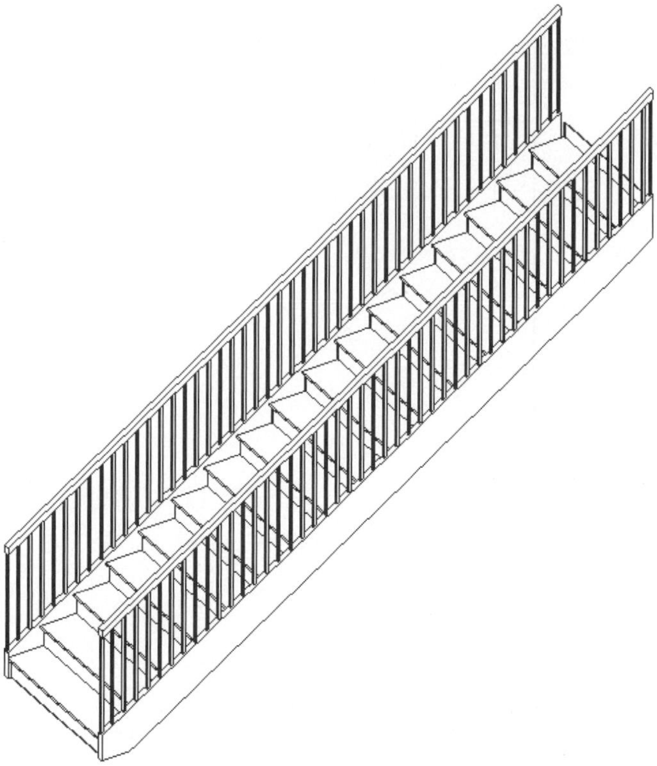

Figure 10-6

Drawing of stairs

8. Be sure you are in the **Level 1** floor plan.
9. Select the stair to bring up the **Modify | Stairs** toolbar.
10. In the **Modify | Stairs** toolbar, select the **Edit Sketch** button to bring up the **Modify | Stairs > Edit Sketch** toolbar.

NOTE:

Notice that a railing appears on the stair. You can remove or change the railing, but the railings appear when you create a stair.

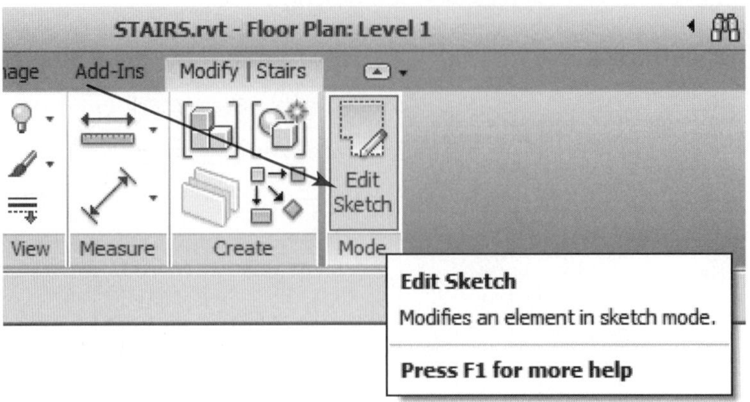

Figure 10-7

Edit Sketch Mode toolbar

The stair will enter **Sketch Mode (Edit Mode)** (see Figure 10-7).

11. Select the bottom left grip of the stair, and drag it downward.
12. In the **Modify | Stairs > Edit Sketch** toolbar, again press the **Finish Edit Mode** button to create the changed stair.
13. Click in an empty place in the **Drawing Editor** to end the command (see Figures 10-8 and 10-9).

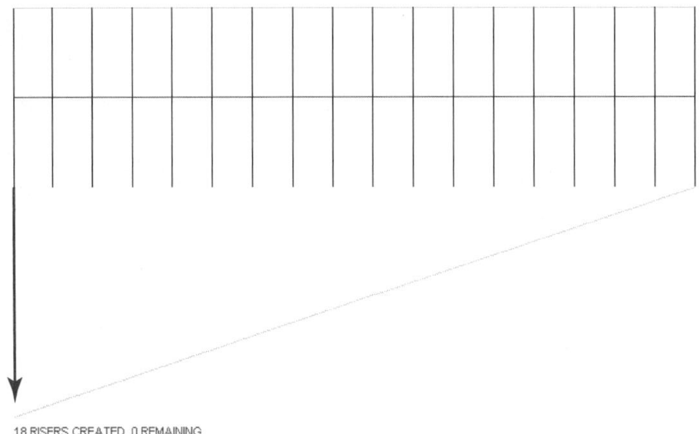

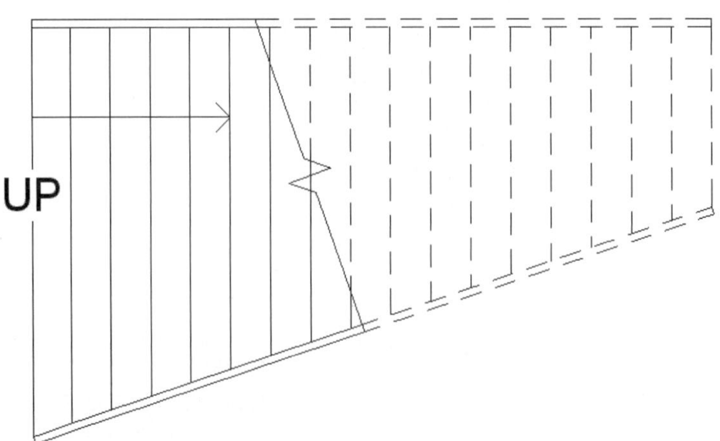

Figure 10-8

Drag the bottom left grip of the stair downward

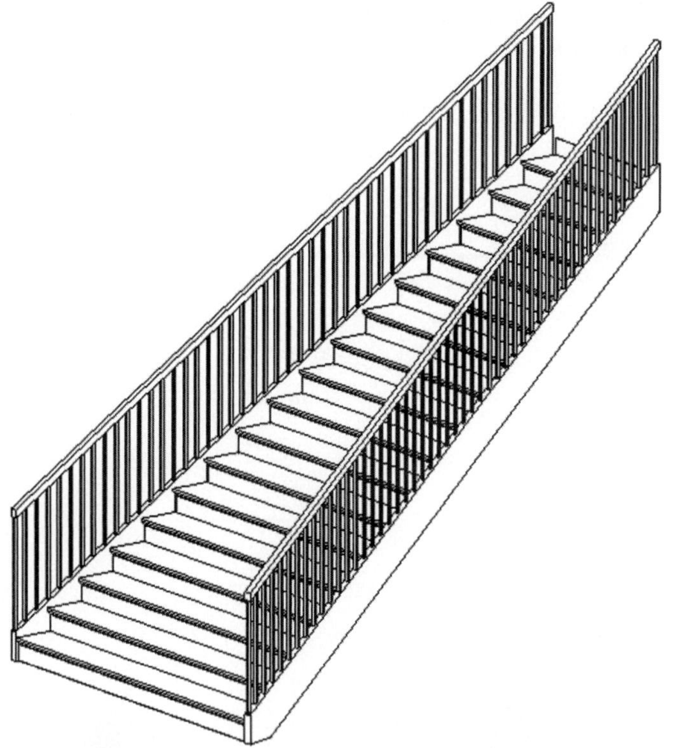

Figure 10-9

Completed stair

14. In the **Level 1** floor plan, select the stair again.
15. Select the stair to bring up the **Modify | Stairs** toolbar.
16. In the **Modify | Stairs** toolbar, select the **Edit Sketch** button to bring up the **Modify | Stairs > Edit Sketch** toolbar.
17. Delete the line you moved in Step 11 of this exercise.
18. Select the **Boundary** button in the **Modify | Stairs > Edit Sketch** toolbar (see Figure 10-10).

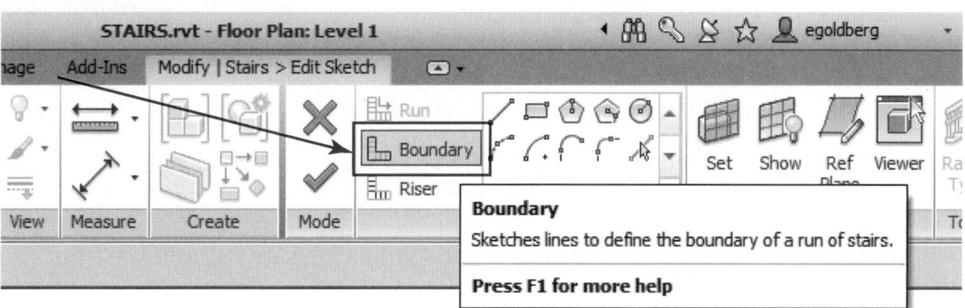

Figure 10-10

Boundary button

19. In the **Modify | Stairs > Edit Sketch** toolbar, select the **Start-End-Radius Arc** button.
20. Replace the line you just deleted with an arc.
21. In the **Modify | Stairs > Edit Sketch** toolbar, press the **Finish Edit Mode** button to create the changed stair.

22. Click in an empty place in the **Drawing Editor** to end the command (see Figures 10-11 and 10-12).

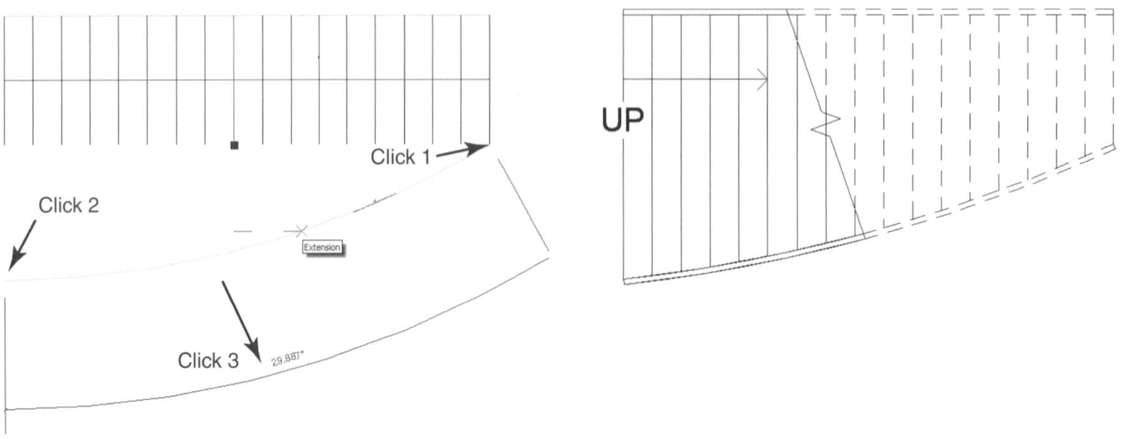

Figure 10-11

Replace a line with an arc

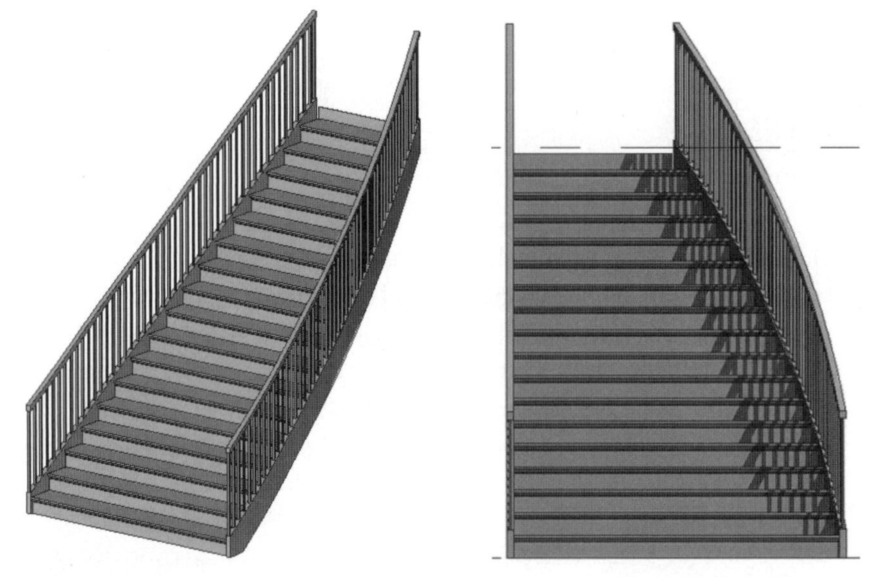

Figure 10-12

Stair with an arc

23. Save this file as **STRAIGHT STAIRS**.

EXERCISE 10-2 **CREATING AND MODIFYING STAIRS BY THE RUN METHOD**

U-Shaped Stairs

1. Start a new drawing using the RAC 2012\Imperial Templates\default.rte template.
2. In the **Project Browser**, double-click **Floor Plans > Level 1** to bring it into the **Drawing Editor**.
3. In the **Home** toolbar, select the **Stairs** button to bring up the **Modify | Create Stairs Sketch** toolbar.
4. In the **Properties** dialog box, set the parameters to be the same as in the previous exercise.
5. In the **Modify | Create Stairs Sketch** toolbar, select the **Run** button.

6. Click, then drag your cursor to the right until the wording "*6 RISERS CREATED, 12 REMAINING*" appears, and click again.
7. Drag your cursor downward, and click again.
8. Drag your cursor to the left, and click again to create the stair lines (see Figures 10-13 and 10-14).
9. In the **Modify | Create Stairs Sketch** toolbar, press the **Finish Edit Mode** button to create the stair.

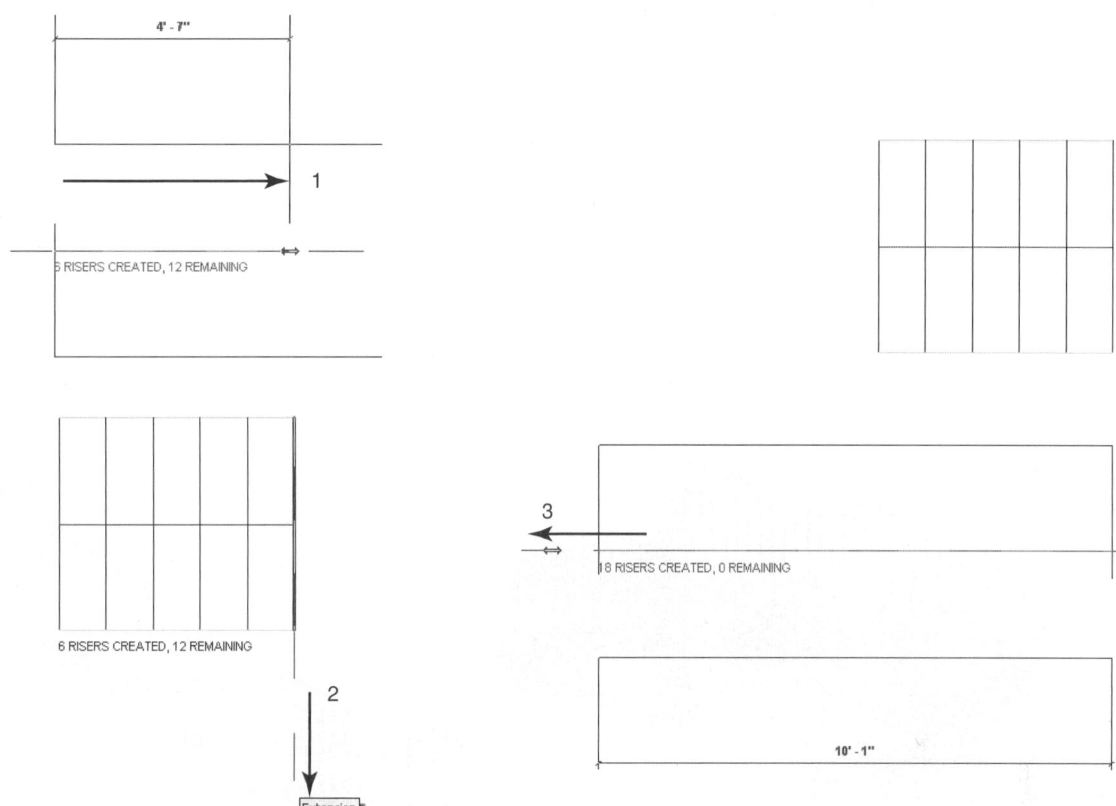

Figure 10-13

Use the **Run** method to create and modify stair lines

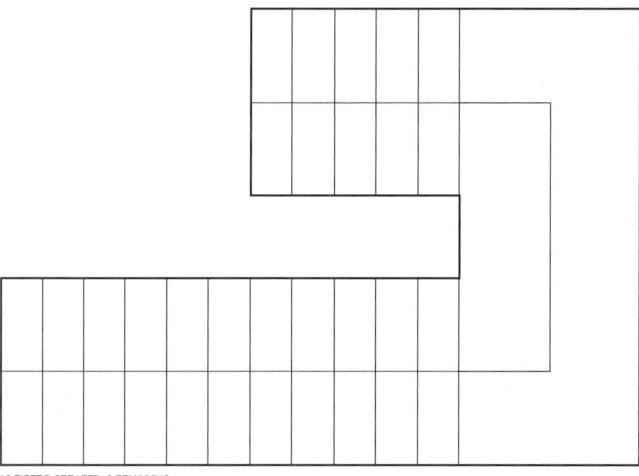

Figure 10-14

18 risers created

10. Click in an empty place in the **Drawing Editor** to end the command (see Figures 10-15 and 10-16).
11. Return to the **Level 1** floor plan, and select the stair. Notice the small arrow shown in Figure 10-17.

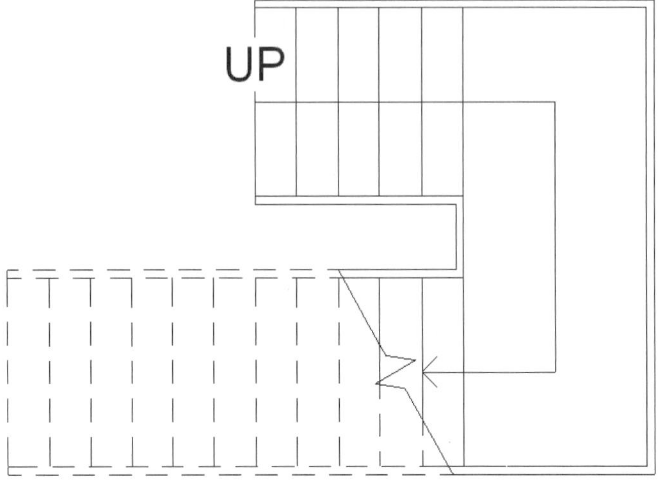

Figure 10-15

Use the **Finish Edit Mode** button to complete the stair

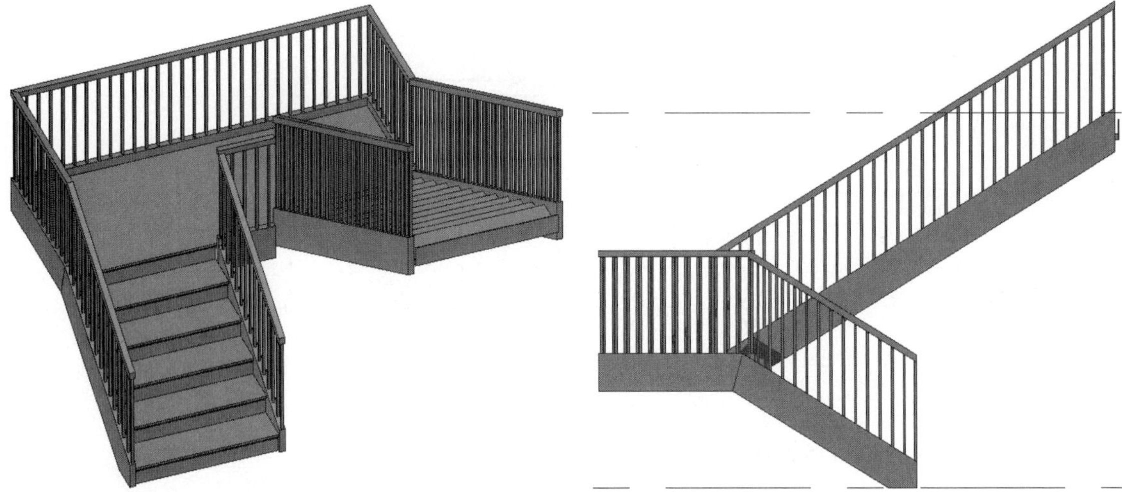

Figure 10-16

3D drawing of stair

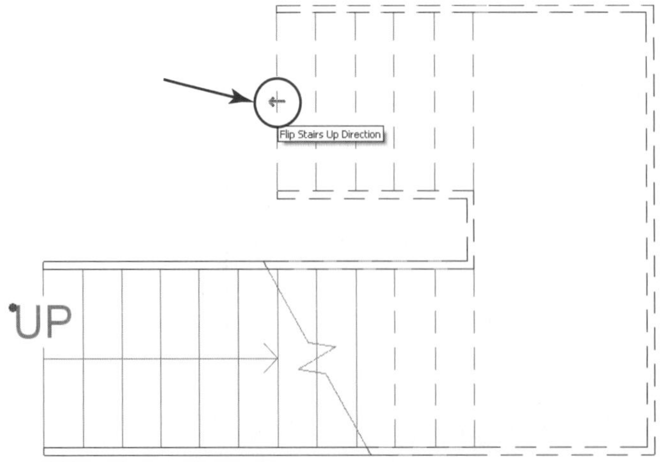

Figure 10-17

Small arrow on drawing

12. Click the arrow to change the **Up/Down** direction of the stair, and change to the **Default 3D View** to see the change (see Figure 10-18).

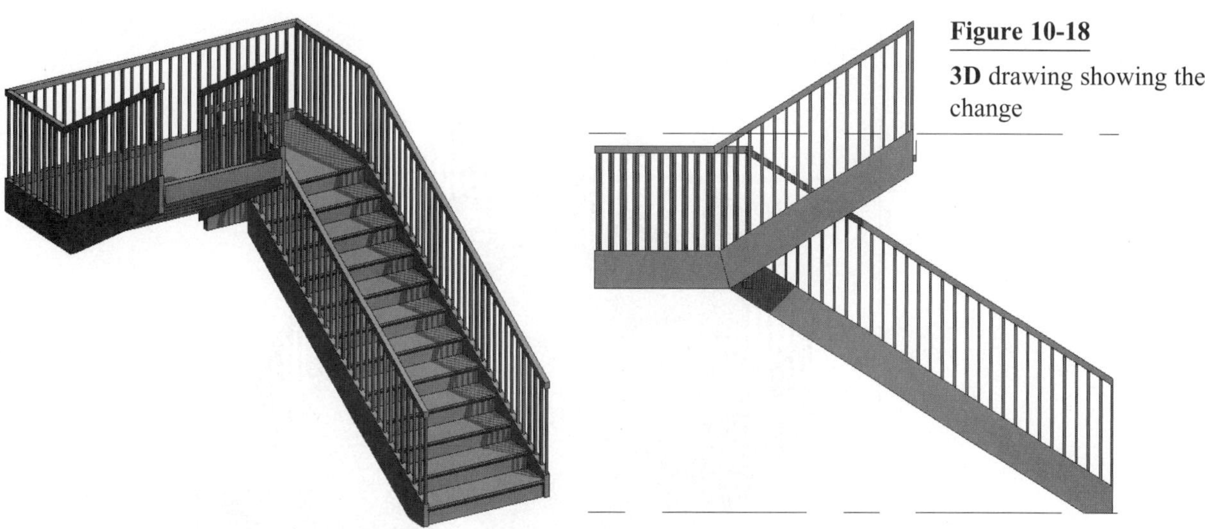

Figure 10-18

3D drawing showing the change

13. Change to the **Level 1** view, and again select the stair.
14. Select the stair to bring up the **Modify | Stairs** toolbar.
15. In the **Modify | Stairs** toolbar, select the **Edit Sketch** button to bring up the **Modify | Stairs > Edit Sketch** toolbar.
16. In the **Modify | Stairs > Edit Sketch** toolbar, select the **Boundary** button, and then the **Rectangle** button in the **Draw** panel (see Figure 10-19).
17. Place a rectangle over the landing, and adjust the landing using the **Split** and **Trim** buttons as shown in Figure 10-20.

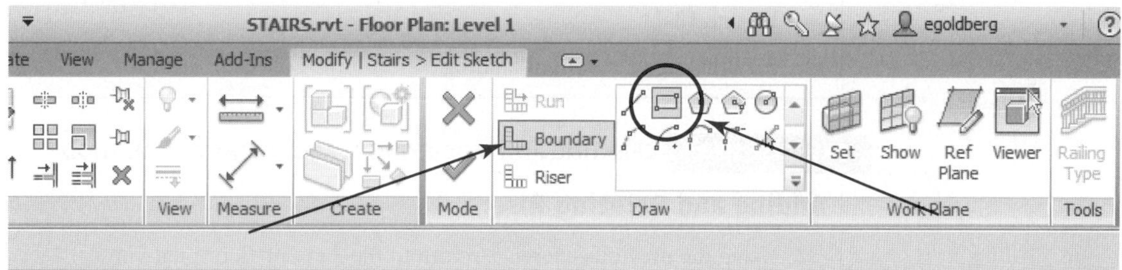

Figure 10-19

Draw panel

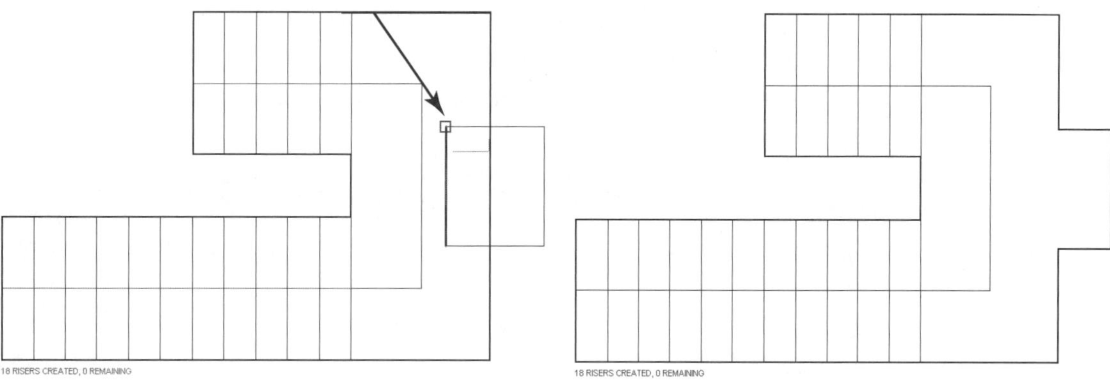

Figure 10-20

Landing changed

18. Again press the **Finish Edit Mode** button to create the changed stair.
19. Click in an empty place in the **Drawing Editor** to end the operation (see Figure 10-21).
20. Save this file as **U-SHAPED STAIRS**.

Figure 10-21

3D drawing of modified landing

EXERCISE 10-3 **CREATING AND MODIFYING STAIRS BY THE RUN METHOD**

Adding and Deleting Risers

1. Using the previous exercise, return to the **Level 1** floor plan view.
2. Select the stair to bring up the **Modify | Stairs** toolbar.
3. In the **Modify | Stairs** toolbar, select the **Edit Sketch** button to bring up the **Modify | Stairs > Edit Sketch** toolbar.
4. Delete a riser from the long run (see Figure 10-23, Arrow 1).
5. Drag the stringer lines backwards (see Figure 10-23, Arrows 2 and 3).
6. In the **Modify | Stairs > Edit Sketch** toolbar, select the **Riser** button (see Figure 10-22).

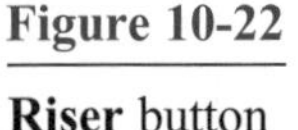

Figure 10-22

Riser button

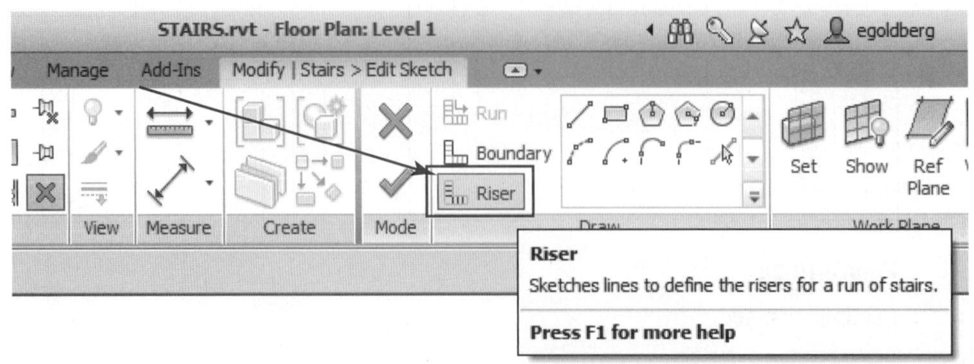

7. Draw a riser and add to the shorter stair (see Figure 10-23, Arrow 4).
8. Drag the shorter stringer line to meet the new riser (see Figure 10-23, Arrows 5 and 6).
9. In the **Modify | Stairs > Edit Sketch** toolbar, again select the **Finish Edit Mode** button to create the changed stair.

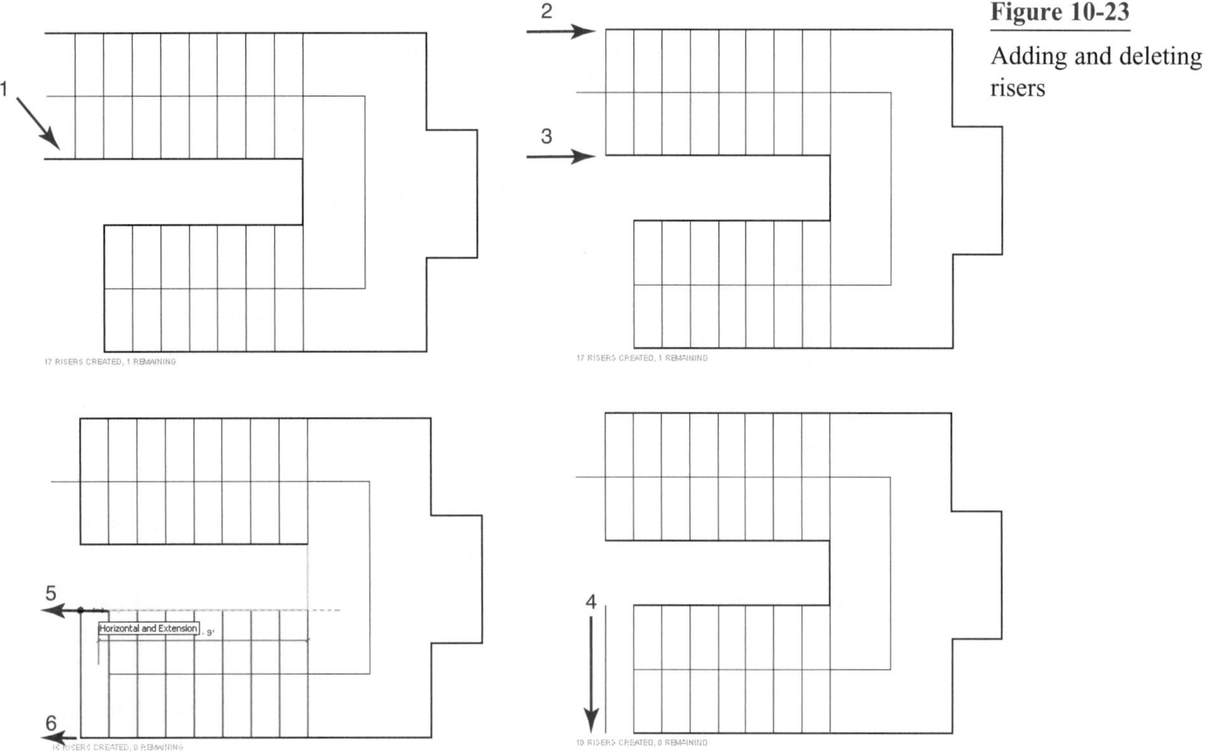

Figure 10-23

Adding and deleting risers

10. Click in an empty place in the **Drawing Editor** to end the command (see Figure 10-24).
11. Experiment with changing the stairs by returning to the **Edit Sketch** button, and using the **Boundary** button.
12. Save this file as **ADDING and REPLACING RISERS**.

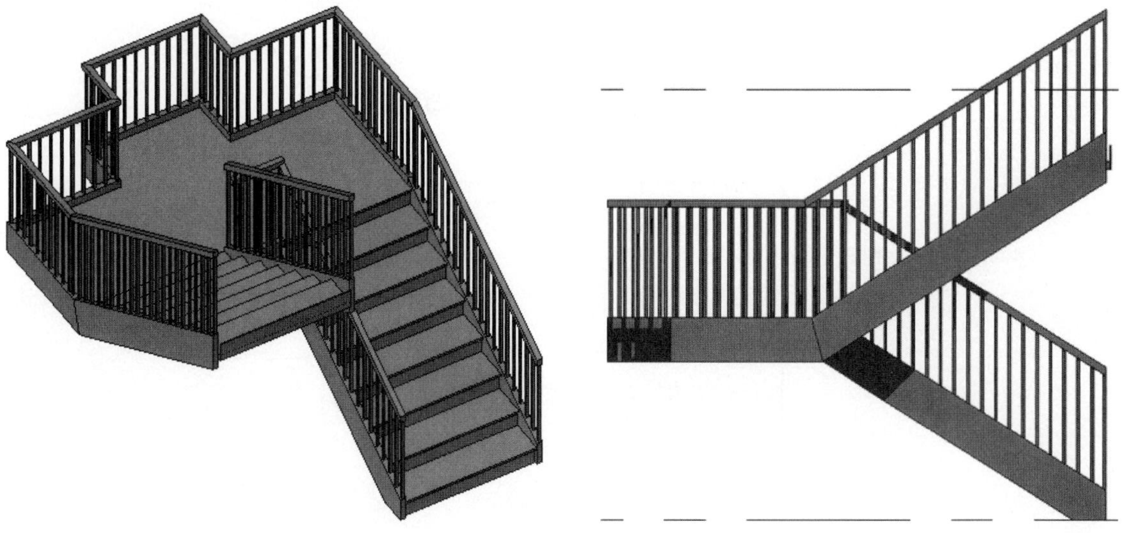

Figure 10-24

3D drawing of modified risers

EXERCISE 10-4 CREATING AND MODIFYING STAIRS USING THE BOUNDARY METHOD

1. Start a new drawing using the RAC 2012\Imperial Templates\default.rte template.
2. In the **Project Browser**, double-click **Floor Plans > Level 1** to bring it into the **Drawing Editor**.
3. In the **Home** toolbar, select the **Stairs** button to bring up the **Modify | Create Stairs Sketch** toolbar.
4. In the **Modify | Create Stairs Sketch** toolbar, select the **Run** button.
5. Set the parameters in the **Properties** dialog box to be the same as in the previous exercises.
6. In the **Properties** dialog box, also notice that the **Desired Number of Risers** is **18** (automatically calculated by the stair calculator).

> **TIP**
>
> If you want to see or change the way the stair calculator calculates, do the following:
>
> 1. In the **Properties** dialog box, press the **Edit Type** button to open the **Type Properties** dialog box.
> 2. In the **Type Properties** dialog box, press the **Edit** button in the **Calculation Rules** field to bring up the **Stair Calculator** dialog box.
> 3. The calculator has been set for **IBC** and **BOCA** codes, so leave it alone.
> 4. Press the **OK** buttons to return to the **Drawing Editor**.

7. In the **Modify | Create Stairs Sketch** toolbar, select the **Boundary** button, select the **Line** button from the **Draw** panel, and place a line **10′-0″** long.

Notice that the statement below the lines reads, *"0 RISERS CREATED, 18 REMAINING."*

8. Select the **Boundary** button again, and select the **Start-End-Radius Arc** button from the **Draw** panel.
9. Select the **Riser** button, and place a riser joining the two **Boundary** lines (see Figure 10-25).

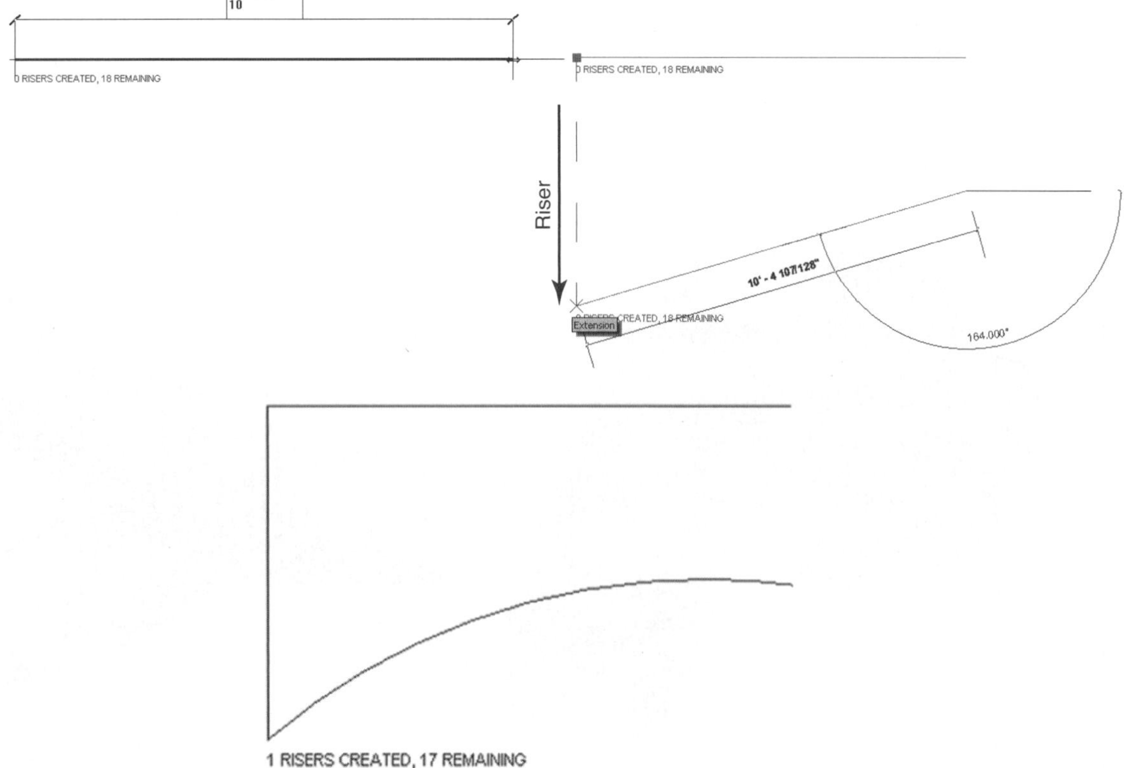

Figure 10-25

Riser joining two **Boundary** lines

Notice that the readout below the bottom boundary tells you how many risers you have placed and how many more need to be offset.

10. In the **Modify | Create Stairs Sketch** toolbar, select the **Offset** button.
11. In the **Options Bar**, set the **Offset** to **0′-11″**, and check the **Copy** check box.
12. Select the riser you placed to offset and copy it (see Figure 10-26).

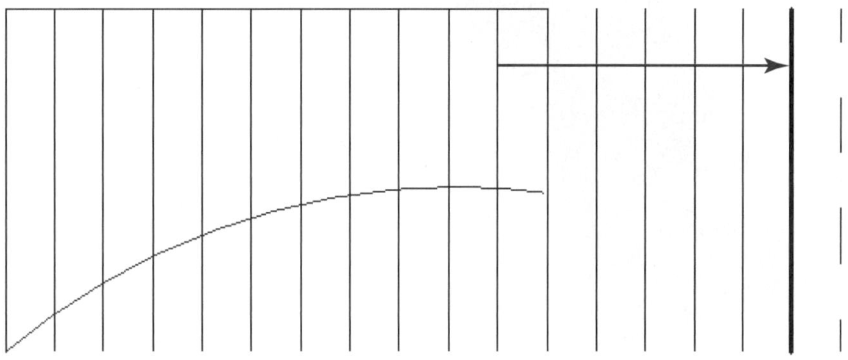

Figure 10-26

Offset and copy a riser

13. Continue until all the risers have been offset, and drag the top boundary line to meet the last riser.
14. In the **Modify | Create Stairs Sketch** toolbar, select the **Boundary** button again, and again select the **Start-End-Radius Arc** button from the **Draw** panel.
15. Add an additional arc line from the first arc to the last riser.
16. In the **Modify | Create Stairs Sketch** toolbar, select the **Finish Edit Mode** button to create the stair (see Figures 10-27 and 10-28).
17. Experiment changing the stairs by returning to the **Edit Sketch** and **Boundary** buttons.
18. Save this file as **BOUNDARY STAIRS**.

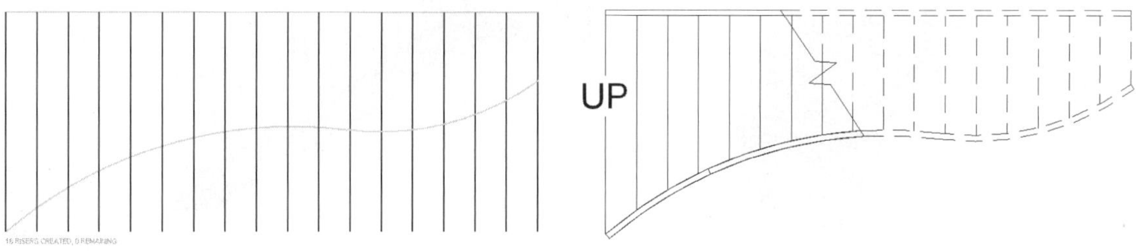

Figure 10-27

Add an arc line

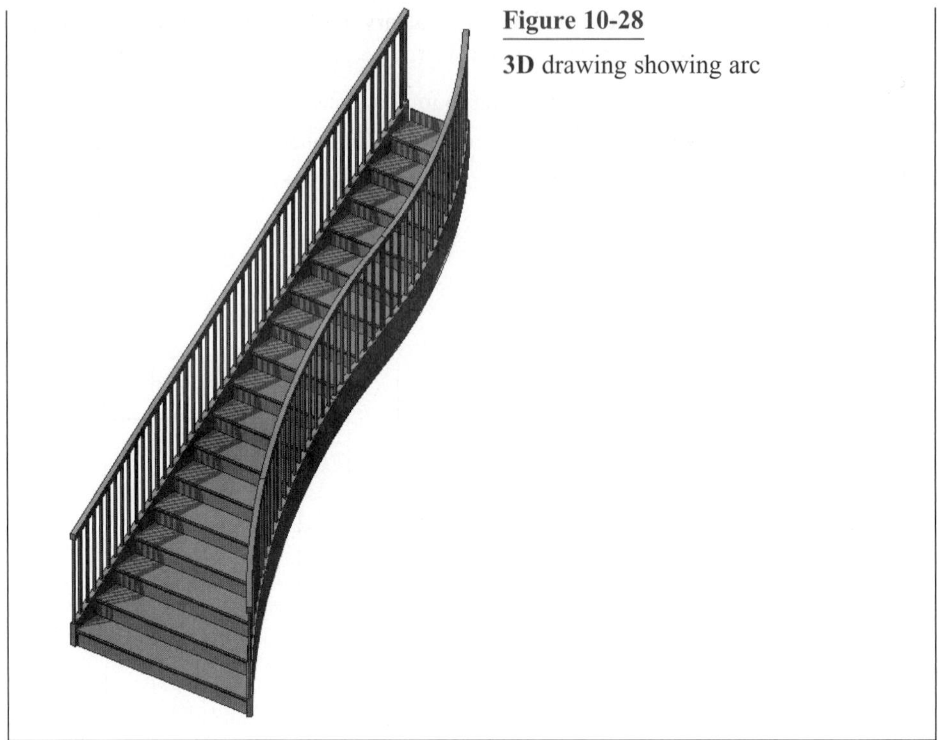

Figure 10-28

3D drawing showing arc

EXERCISE 10-5 **CREATING MULTISTORY STAIRS**

Multistory Stairs

Multistory buildings need repeating stairs or **Stair Towers**. Revit Architecture makes this process easy.

1. Start a new drawing using the RAC 2012\Imperial Templates\default.rte template.
2. In the **Project Browser**, double-click **Floor Plans > Level 1** to bring it into the **Drawing Editor**.
3. Using the information you have learned in the previous exercises, create a **3′-0″** wide **U-Shaped** stair with even runs up and down (see Figure 10-29).

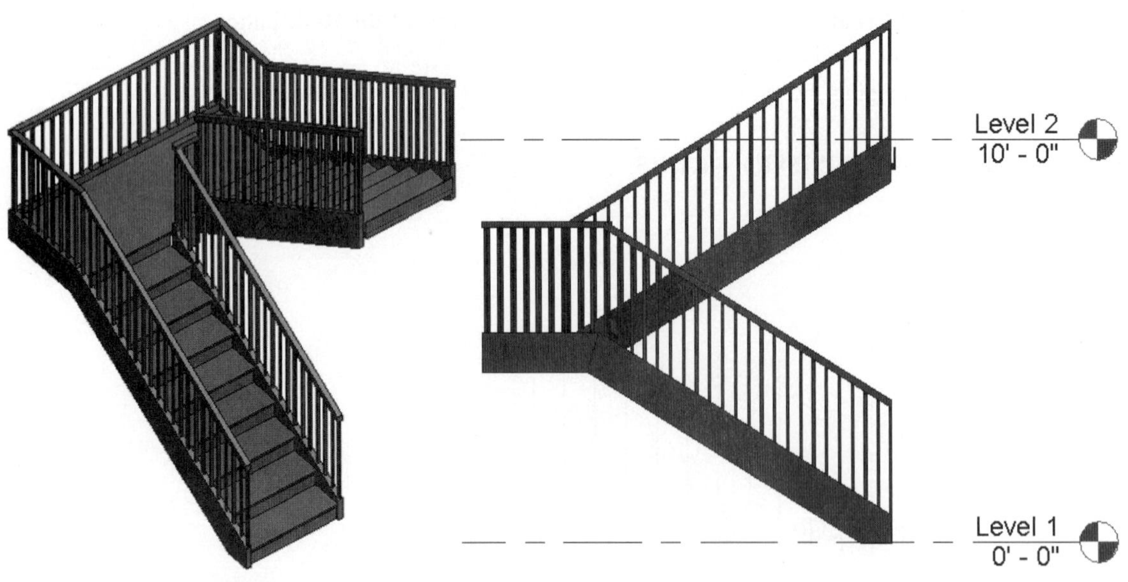

Figure 10-29

3D drawing of multistory stairs

4. Change to the **North Elevation**, and add three more levels—**10′-0″** from level to level (see Figure 10-30).
5. Select the stair to bring up its **Properties** dialog box.
6. In the **Properties** dialog box, select **Level 5** from the **Multistory Top Level** drop-down list (see Figure 10-31).
7. The stair will repeat until it reaches **Level 5** (see Figure 10-32).
8. Save this file as **MULTISTORY STAIRS**.

NOTE:

The **Multistory** operation only works between equal height levels.

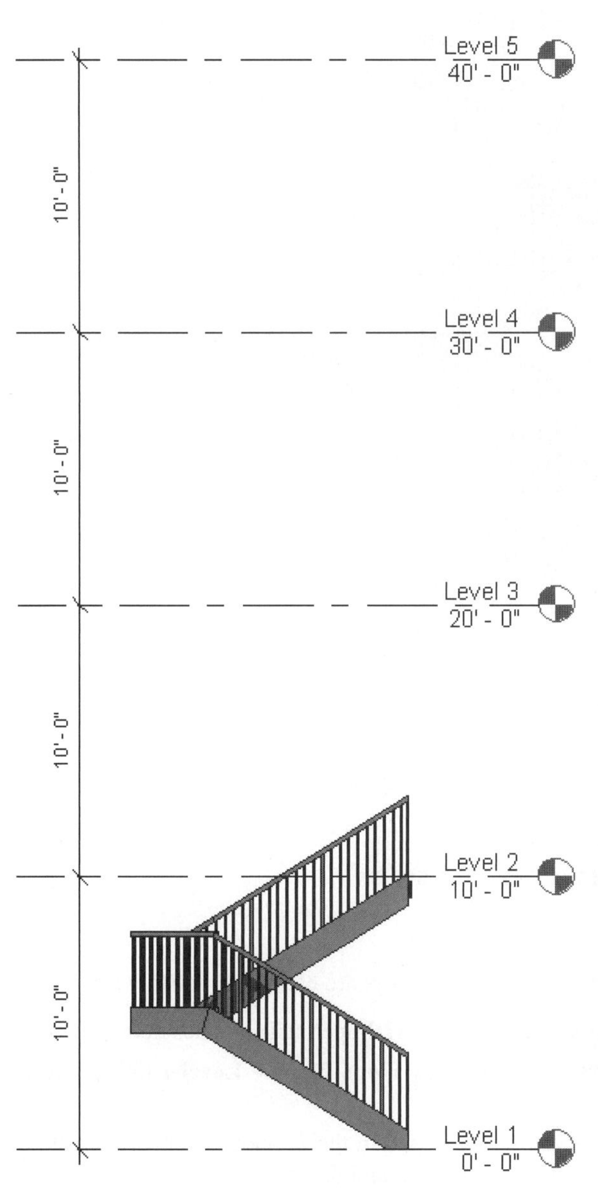

Figure 10-30

Add three more levels

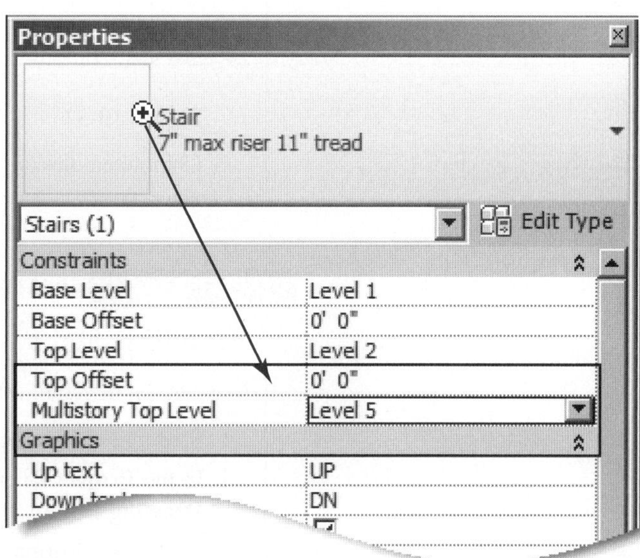

Figure 10-31

Multistory Top Level drop-down list

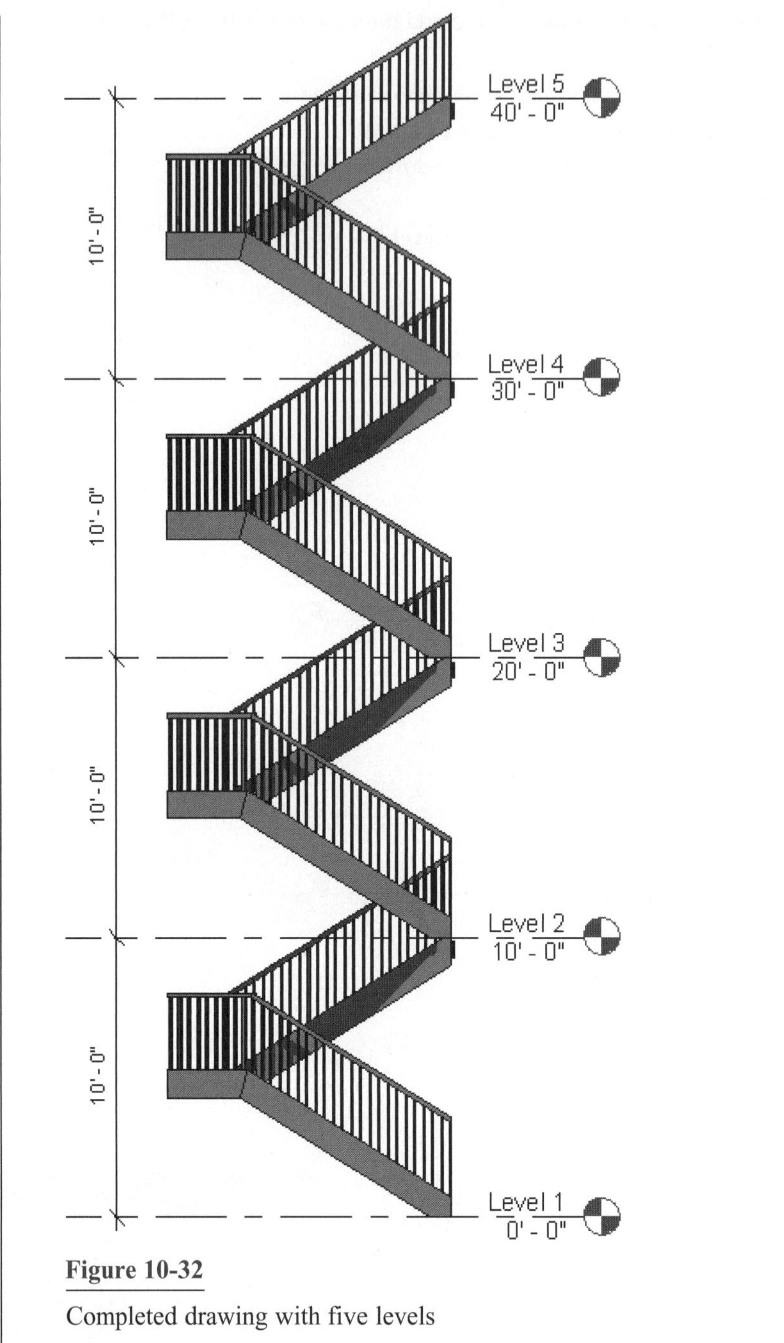

Figure 10-32

Completed drawing with five levels

EXERCISE 10-6 **CREATING MONOLITHIC STAIRS**

Monolithic Stairs

In Revit Architecture 2012, cast concrete stairs are called **Monolithic** stairs.

1. Start a new drawing using the RAC 2012\Imperial Templates\default.rte template.
2. In the **Project Browser**, double-click **Floor Plans > Level 1** to bring it into the **Drawing Editor**.
3. Using the information you have learned in the previous exercises, create a **3′-0″** wide **U-Shaped** stair with even runs up and down.
4. Change to the **Default 3D View**.
5. Select the stair to bring up its **Properties** dialog box.

6. In the **Properties** dialog box, select the **Edit Type** button to bring up the **Type Properties** dialog box.
7. In the **Type Properties** dialog box, check the **Monolithic Stairs** check box, set the **Tread** and **Riser Thickness** to **1/4″**, select **Slanted** from the **Riser Type** drop-down list, and then press the **OK** buttons to return to the **Drawing Editor** (see Figures 10-33 and 10-34).

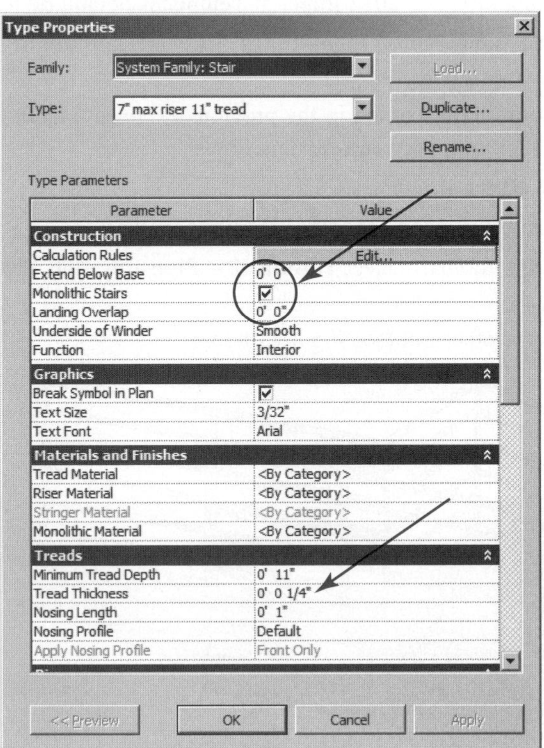

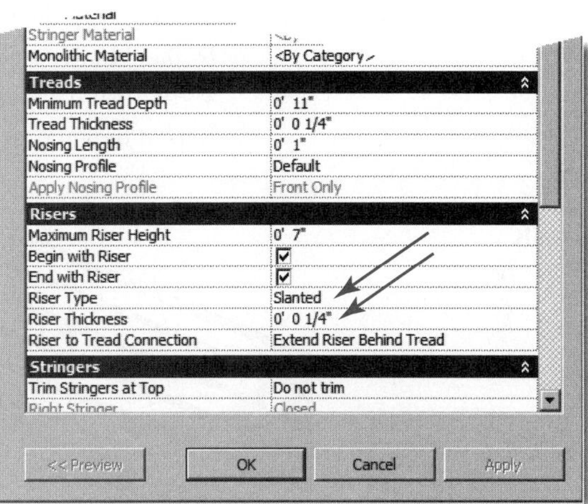

Figure 10-33

Stair Type Properties dialog box

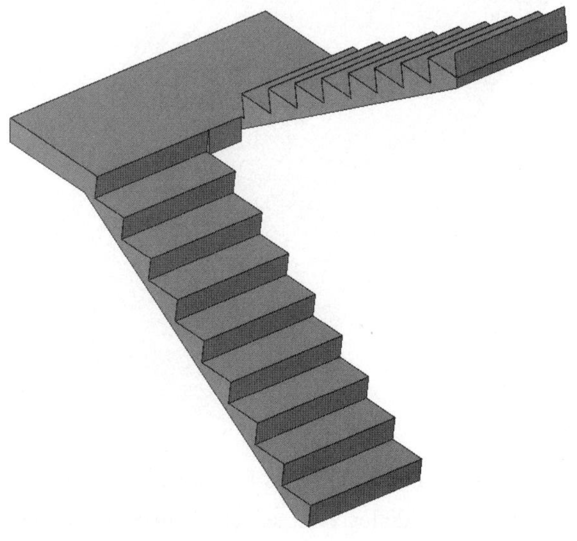

Figure 10-34

Monolithic Stairs drawing

8. Save this file as **MONOLITHIC STAIRS**.

Railings

You can add railings as freestanding components to levels or attach them to hosts (such as floors, ramps, or stairs).

EXERCISE 10-7 MODIFYING RAILINGS

1. Start a new drawing using the RAC 2012\Imperial Templates\default.rte template.
2. In the **Project Browser**, double-click **Floor Plans > Level 1** to bring it into the **Drawing Editor**.
3. Using the information you have learned in the previous exercises, again create a **3′-0″** wide **U-Shaped** stair with even runs up and down.
4. Change to the **Default 3D View**.
5. Select one of the rails to bring up the **Modify | Railings** toolbar.
6. In the **Modify | Railings** toolbar, select **Handrail – Pipe** from the **Properties** drop-down list.
7. Repeat the process for the other rail (see Figure 10-35).

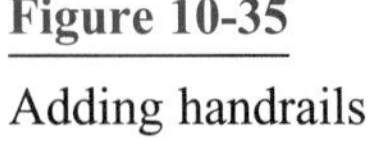

Figure 10-35
Adding handrails

8. Select a rail again to bring up its **Properties** dialog box.
9. In the **Properties** dialog box, select the **Edit Type** button to bring up the **Type Properties** dialog box.
10. In the **Type Properties** dialog box, select the **Edit** button in the **Rail Structure** field to bring up the **Edit Rails** dialog box (see Figure 10-36).
11. In the **Edit Rails** dialog box, click on **Rail 1 Profile**, change the **Rail 1 Profile** to **Rectangular Handrail: 2″ × 3″** from the **Profile** drop-down list, and then press the **OK** buttons to return to the **Drawing Editor** (see Figure 10-37).

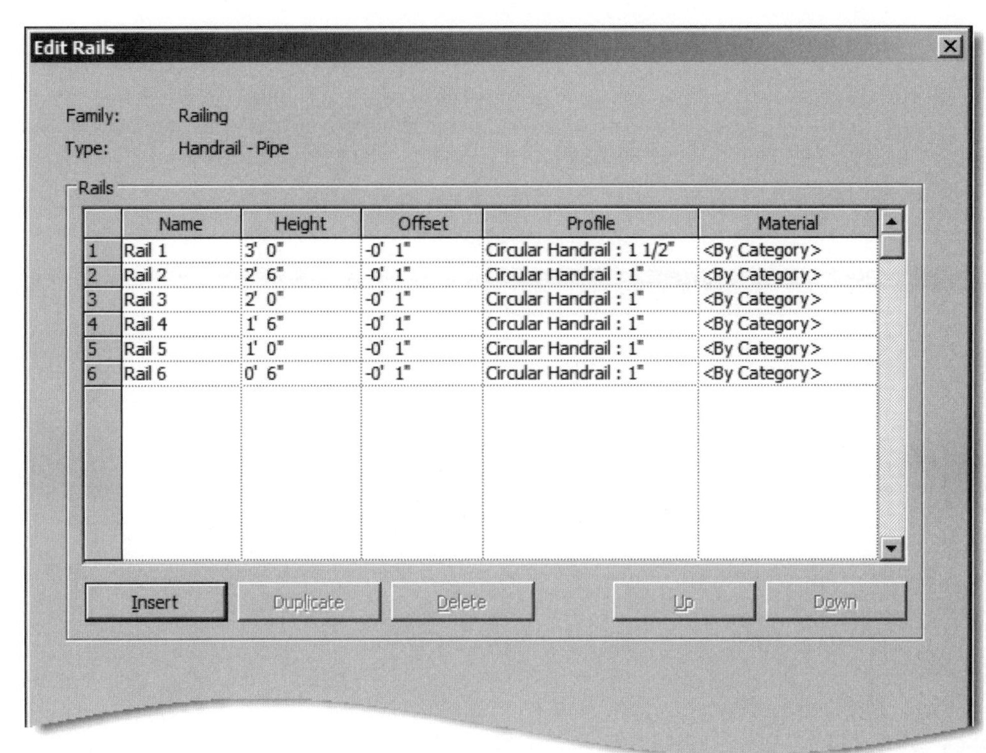

Figure 10-36

Edit Rails dialog box

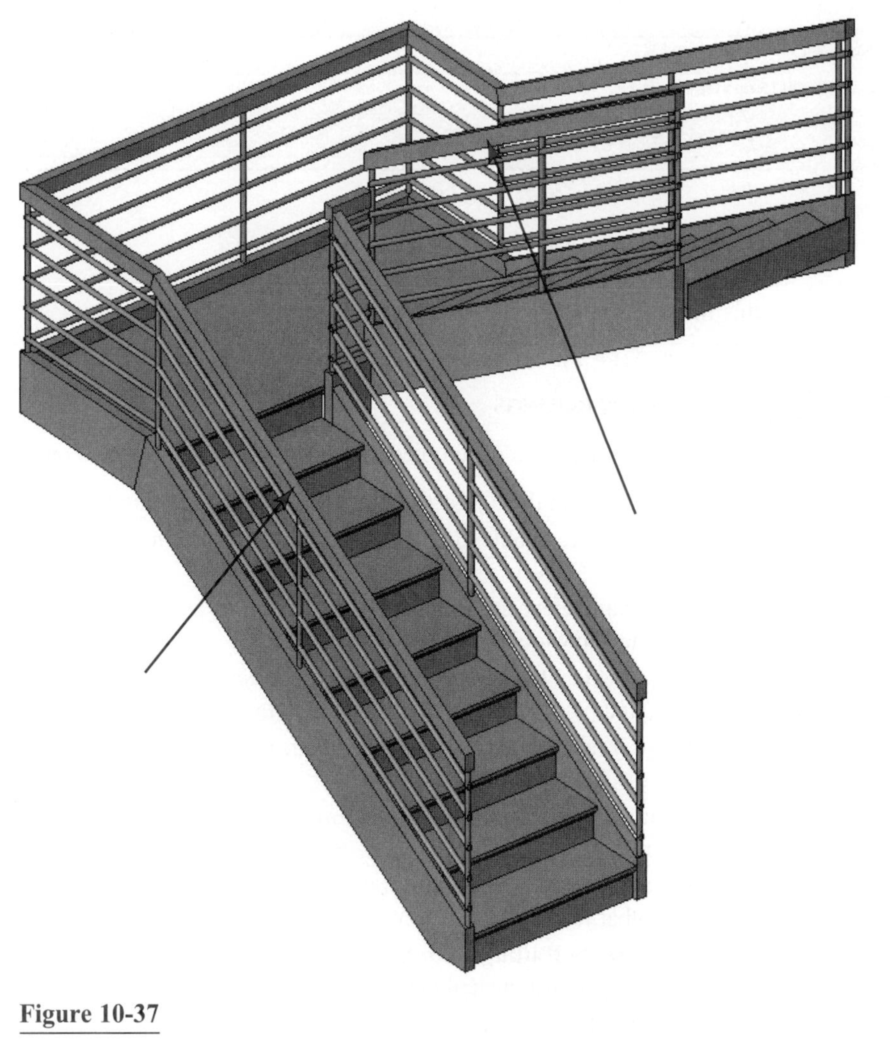

Figure 10-37

Changed handrails

NOTE:

The rails and baluster shapes are controlled by profiles. As shown in previous chapters, you can start with the default profiles and modify them to create new profiles. The rail profiles are contained in the **Profiles > Stairs** folder in either the **Imperial** or **Metric Library** (see Figure 10-38).

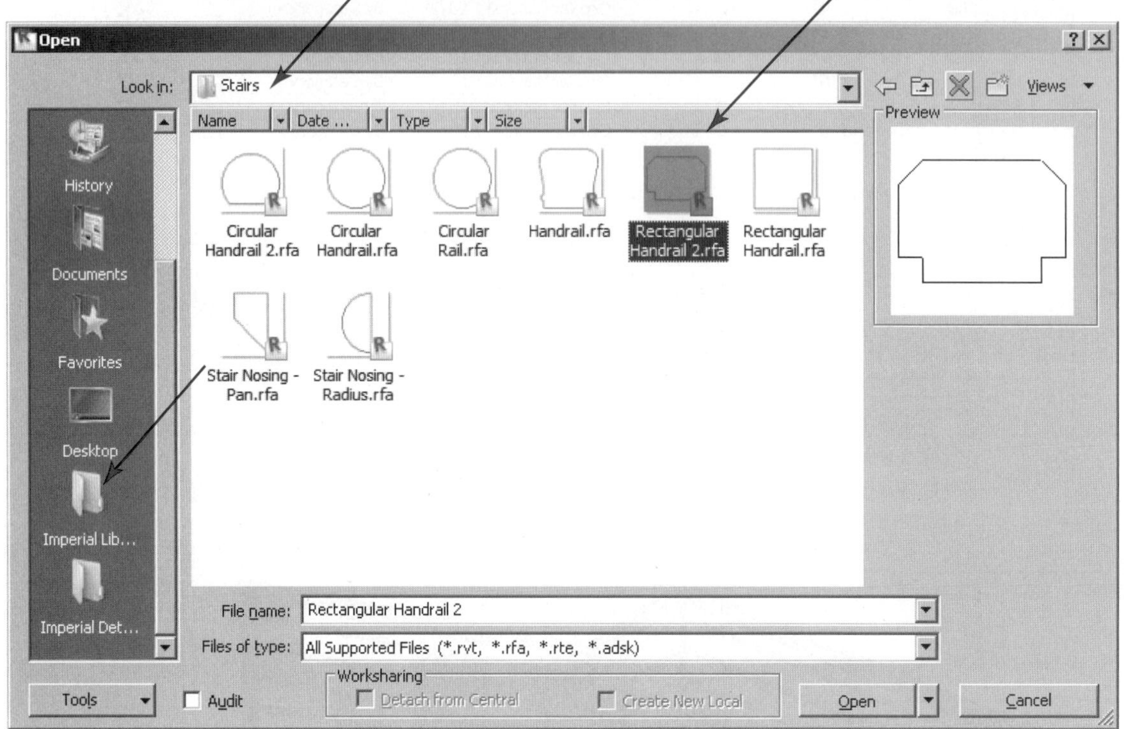

Figure 10-38

Rail profiles

12. Save this file as **MODIFYING RAILINGS**.

EXERCISE 10-8 HOSTING RAILINGS

Hosting allows you to attach railings to objects such as floors, slabs, and so on.

1. Start a new drawing using the RAC 2012\Imperial Templates\default.rte template.
2. In the **Project Browser**, double-click **Floor Plans > Level 1** to bring it into the **Drawing Editor**.
3. In the **Home** toolbar, select the **Floor > Floor** button to bring up the **Modify | Create Floor Boundary** toolbar.
4. In the **Modify | Create Floor Boundary** toolbar, select the **Rectangle** button in the **Draw** panel, and place a **10′ × 15′** rectangle in the **Drawing Editor**.
5. In the **Modify | Create Floor Boundary** toolbar, press the **Finish Edit Mode** button to create the floor.
6. Click in an empty space in the **Drawing Editor** to end the command, and return to the **Home** toolbar.
7. In the **Home** toolbar, select the **Railing** button to bring up the **Modify | Create Railing Path** toolbar (see Figure 10-39).
8. In the **Modify | Create Railing Path** toolbar, select the **Pick New Host** button, and select the floor you just created (see Figure 10-40).
9. Change to the **Level 1** floor plan.
10. In the **Modify | Create Railing Path** toolbar, select **Line** from the **Draw** panel.

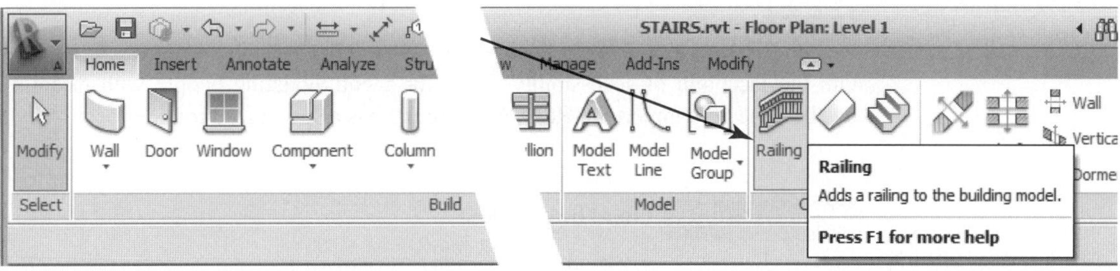

Figure 10-39

Railing button

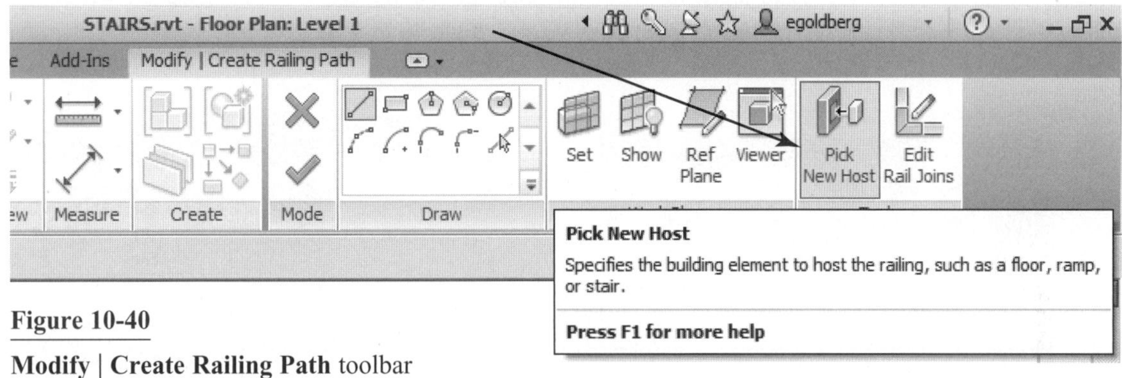

Figure 10-40

Modify | Create Railing Path toolbar

11. Place lines where you want a rail, and press the **Finish Edit Mode** button to create the railing.
12. Click in an empty place in the **Drawing Editor** to complete the command, and return to the **Home** toolbar (see Figure 10-41).
13. Save this file as **HOSTED RAILINGS**.

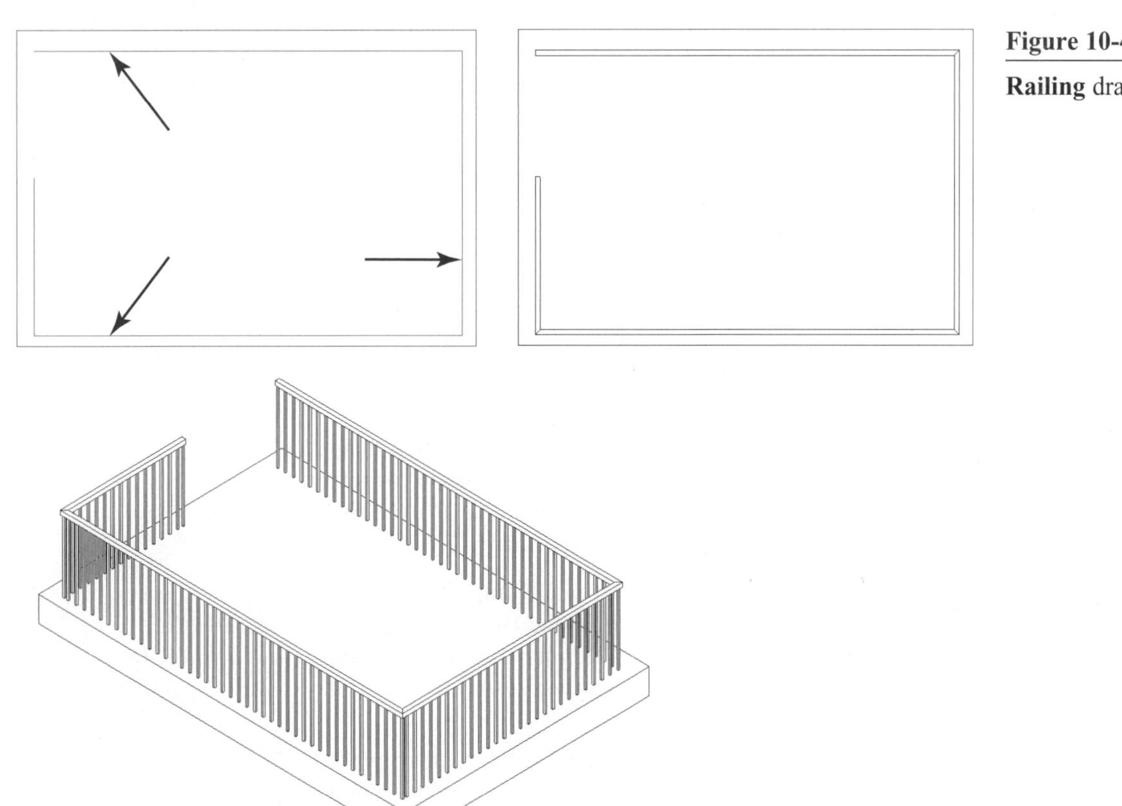

Figure 10-41

Railing drawing

Ramps

With the inception of accessibility codes for accommodating people with disabilities, ramps have become very important. Revit Architecture has a specialized routine specifically for ramps.

EXERCISE 10-9 CREATING RAMPS

1. Start a new drawing using the RAC 2012\Imperial Templates\default.rte template.
2. In the **Project Browser**, double-click **Floor Plans > Level 1** to bring it into the **Drawing Editor**.
3. In the **Home** toolbar, select the **Ramp** button to bring up the **Modify | Create Ramp Sketch** toolbar (see Figure 10-42).

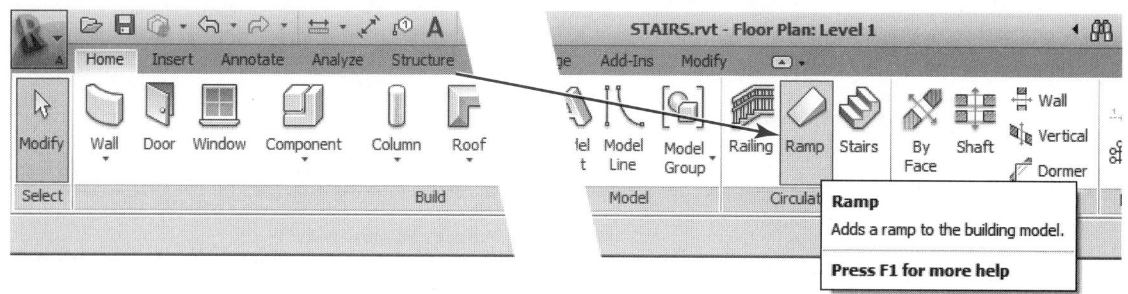

Figure 10-42
Ramp button

4. In the **Ramp Properties** dialog box, set the **Top Level** to **None** and **Width** to **3′-0″**.

You can alternately set the **Top Level** of the ramp to a level. If you prefer this method, be sure to name the level **TOP OF RAMP**, and set its height appropriately.

5. In the **Properties** dialog box, select the **Edit Type** button to bring up the **Type Properties** dialog box.
6. In the **Type Properties** dialog box, set the **Thickness** to **4″**, **Maximum Incline Length** to **18′-0″**, and **Ramp Max Slope (1/x)** to **6.0000** (you will have to scroll down to the bottom of the list to see this).

This means that you will create a **3″** thick ramp starting at **Level 1**, rising 1″ for every 6″ of run. Since you have set the run to **18′** (216″), the rise will then be **3′-0″**. Let's check it.

7. In the **Modify | Create Ramp Sketch** toolbar, select **Run** from the **Draw** panel, click in the **Drawing Editor**, drag to the right until the measurement reads **18′-0″**, and click again.
8. In the **Create Ramp Sketch** toolbar, press the **Finish Ramp** button to create the ramp (see Figure 10-43).

NOTE:
You will see *"18′ of inclined ramp created, 0″ remaining"* below the ramp. This means that you have placed the sketch correctly.

NOTE:
As with stairs, you can change the **Up/Down** direction of the ramp by clicking on the arrow that appears in the **Level 1** floor plan (see Figure 10-44).

NOTE:
A ramp incline of 1″ per 6″ does not meet the accessibility code but was used for visual clarity in the **Ramps** exercise. The Americans with Disabilities Act (ADA) requires 1″ per 12″ if the change in height of the ramp is over 6″.

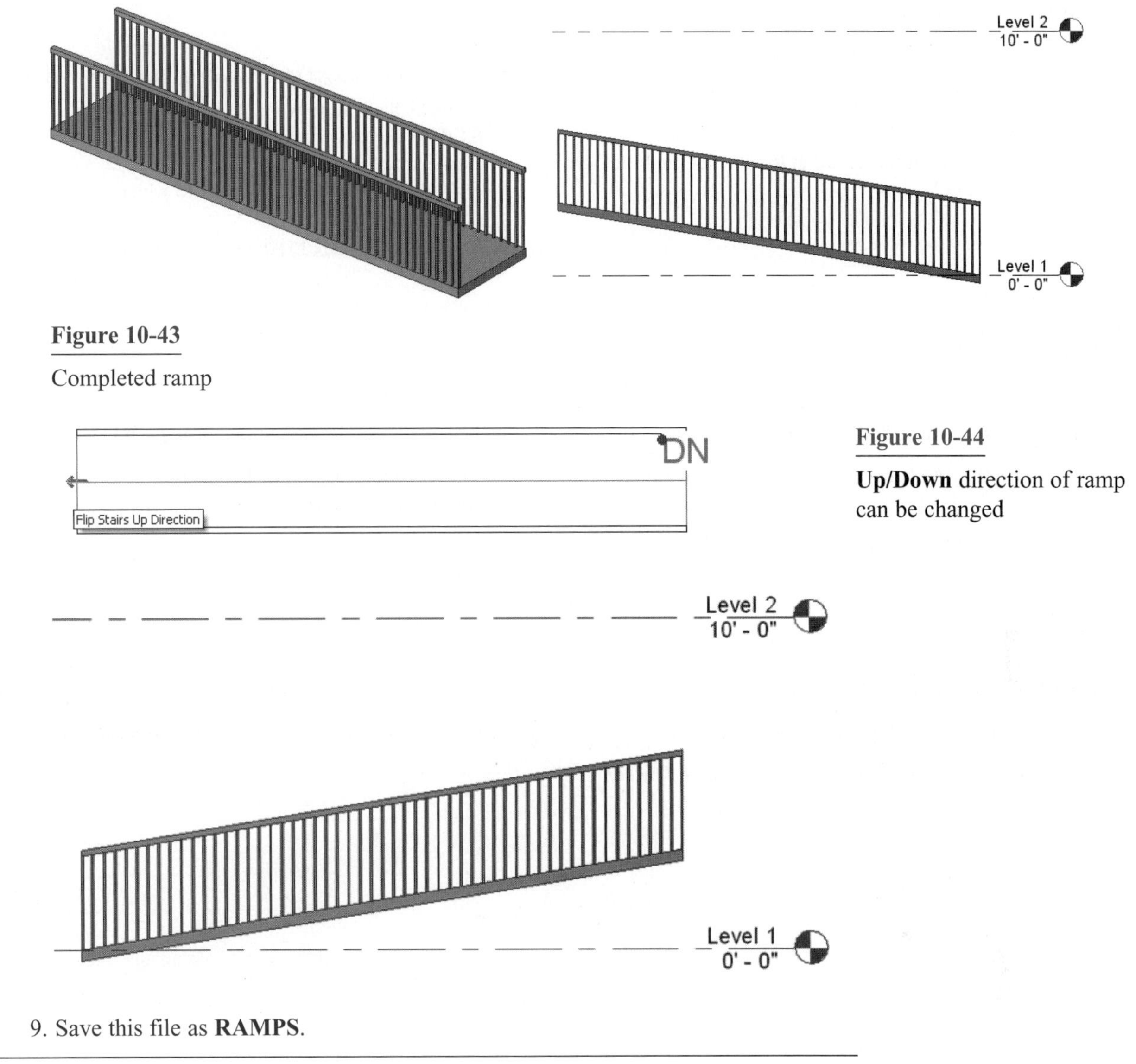

Figure 10-43

Completed ramp

Figure 10-44

Up/Down direction of ramp can be changed

9. Save this file as **RAMPS**.

Chapter Summary

This chapter discussed the methods for creating and modifying **Stairs**, **Railings**, and **Ramps** in Revit Architecture 2012.

Chapter Test Questions

Multiple Choice

Circle the correct answer.

1. The **Stairs** button is located in the ________ toolbar.
   a. **Home**
   b. **Structure**
   c. **Massing**
   d. **Create Stairs**

2. **Stairs** contain all the following except
   a. **Risers**.
   b. **Treads**.
   c. **Carriers**.
   d. All of the above

3. By code, ramps must not exceed
   a. 1″ per 3″.
   b. 1″ per 6″.
   c. 1″ per 8″.
   d. 1″ per 1′.
4. What is the depth of the **Tread** in Revit's IBC and BOCA codes calculator?
   a. 9″
   b. 10″
   c. 11″
   d. 12″
5. What is the purpose of the **Railing Pick New Host** tool?
   a. Picks the wall to which to attach the railing.
   b. Picks the person to host the next Revit Users Group meeting.
   c. Picks the floor, ramp, or stair to which to attach the railing.
   d. Picks the railing to which to attach the top handrail.

True or False

Circle the correct answer.

1. **True or False:** Revit **Stairs** can only be straight stairs.
2. **True or False:** A stair rise is the distance between the treads.
3. **True or False:** Revit **Stairs** can be created without railings.
4. **True or False:** Revit's **Stair Nosing** can be modified.
5. **True or False:** The **Stair Properties** dialog box is where you set **Stair Materials**.

Questions

1. What are Revit's **Monolithic Stairs** used for?
2. What is the purpose of Revit's **Hosted Railings**?
3. What type of Revit **Stair** do you use in a **Stair Tower**?
4. What is the purpose of the break mark in stairs going up?
5. Why do the stairs going down have no break mark?

CHAPTER

11 Room and Area

CHAPTER OBJECTIVES

- Understand and create **Rooms** and **Room Volumes**.
- Understand and create **Gross Building** and **Areas**.
- Understand **Rentable Areas**.
- Learn how to create **Area Schedules**.
- Learn how to create **Color Scheme Legends**.
- Learn how to create **Area Reports**.

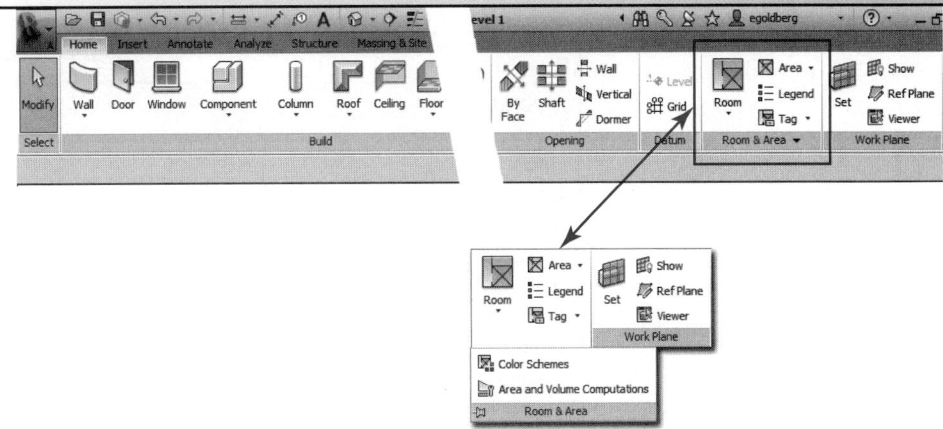

Introduction

Volume and area are important pieces of information for architects, engineers, contractors, and owners. In Autodesk Revit 2012, this type of information is handled by the **Room** and **Area** tools found in the **Home** toolbar.

Room Area and Volume

The **Room** object is a 3D volumetric object.

The following elements are considered to be bounding elements for room area and volume calculations:

- Walls (curtain, standard, in-place, face-based)
- Roofs (standard, in-place, face-based)
- Floors (standard, in-place, face-based)
- Ceilings (standard, in-place, face-based)
- Columns (architectural, structural with material set to concrete)
- Curtain systems
- Room separation lines

Below is the **Properties** dialog box for **Room** objects (see Figure 11-1).

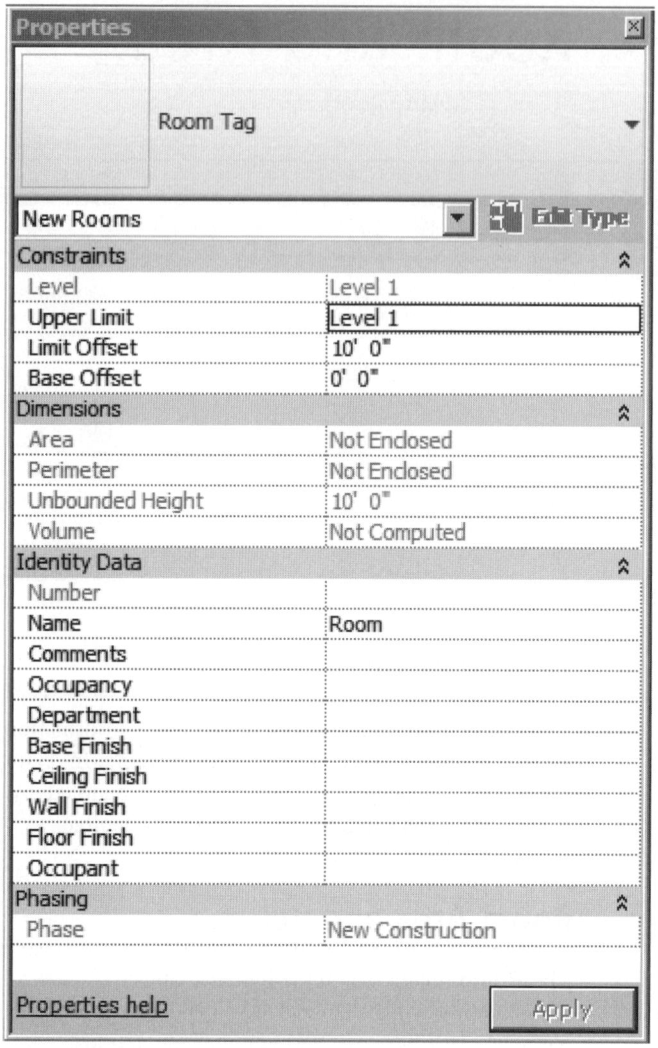

Figure 11-1

Room Properties dialog box

Name	Description
Constraints	
Level	The base level the room is on. This is a read-only value.
Upper Limit	The level specified in **Upper Limit** plus the value in **Limit Offset** define the upper boundary of the room.
Limit Offset	May be negative. The **Limit Offset** plus the **Upper Limit** define the upper boundary of the room.
Base Offset	The distance at which the lower boundary of the room occurs, measuring from the base level (defined by the **Level** parameter). Enter a positive number to go above the base level, or enter a negative number to go below it. Enter 0 (zero) to use the base level. The default is 0.
Dimensions	
Area	The net area calculated from the room-bounding elements. This is a read-only value.
Perimeter	The perimeter of the room. This is a read-only value.

Name	Description
Unbounded Height	The height of the room as defined by the distance between the room's base level and the **Upper Limit** plus the **Limit Offset**. This is a read-only value.
Volume	The volume of the room if volume computations are enabled. This is a read-only value.
Identity Data	
Number	Sets the room number, such as **1**. This value must be unique for each room in a project. Revit Architecture warns you if the number is already used but allows you to continue using it. You can see the warning using the **REVIEW WARNINGS** command. Room numbers are assigned sequentially.
Name	Sets the room name, such as **Conference Room**.
Comments	Specific comments about the room.
Occupancy	Type of occupancy for structure, such as **Retail**.
Department	Department name.
Base Finish	Finish for the base.
Ceiling Finish	Finish for the ceiling, such as stucco.
Wall Finish	Finish for the wall, such as painted.
Floor Finish	Finish for the floor, such as carpeting.
Occupant	Occupant name.
Phasing	
Phase	Stage or time period in the construction process.

EXERCISE 11-1 ROOMS AND ROOM VOLUMES

1. Start a new project using the RAC 2012\Imperial Templates\default.rte template.
2. In the **Project Browser**, double-click **Floor Plans > Level 1** to bring it into the **Drawing Editor**.
3. In the **Home** toolbar, select the **Wall** button to bring up the **Modify | Place Wall** toolbar.
4. In the **Modify | Place Wall** toolbar, select the **Rectangle** button in the **Draw** panel.
5. In the **Options Bar**, select **Finish Face Interior** for the **Location Line**.
6. Place a **Generic - 8″** wall enclosure **10′-0″** long, **10′-0″** wide, and **10′-0″** high. Make sure that the interior of the enclosure is **10′-0″ × 10′-0″** (see Figure 11-2).

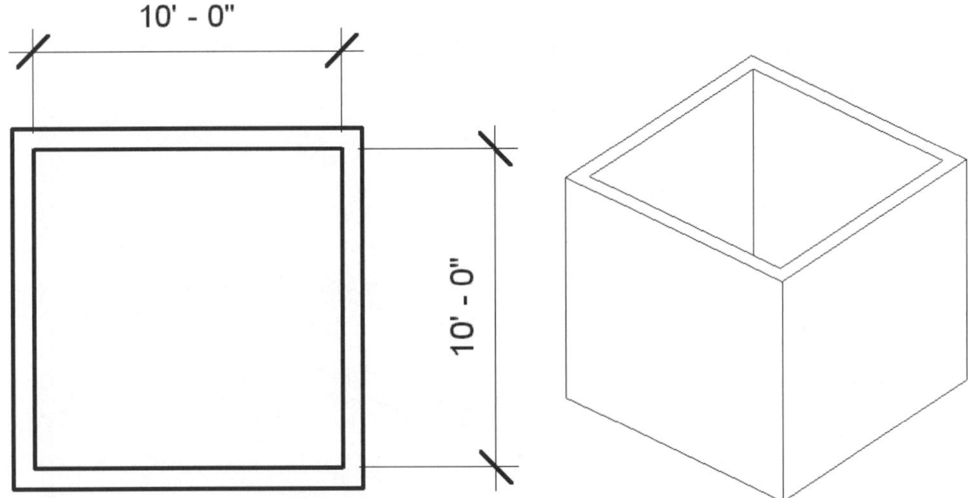

Figure 11-2

Create a wall enclosure

7. Using the **Floor** and **Roof** buttons from the **Home** toolbar, place a flat roof (no slope) and floor to bound (enclose) the enclosure. Make sure the walls are attached to the roof (see Figure 11-3).

Figure 11-3

Attach a roof to the enclosure

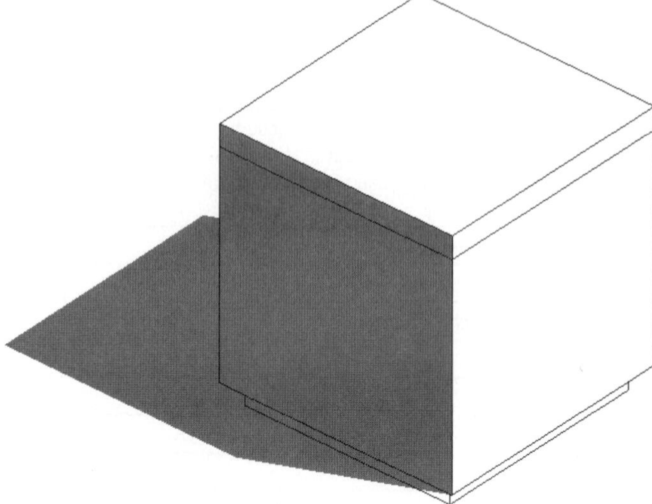

8. In the **Home** toolbar, select the **Area and Volume Computations** button from the **Room & Area** panel to bring up the **Area and Volume Computations** dialog box (see Figure 11-4).

Figure 11-4

Room & Area panel

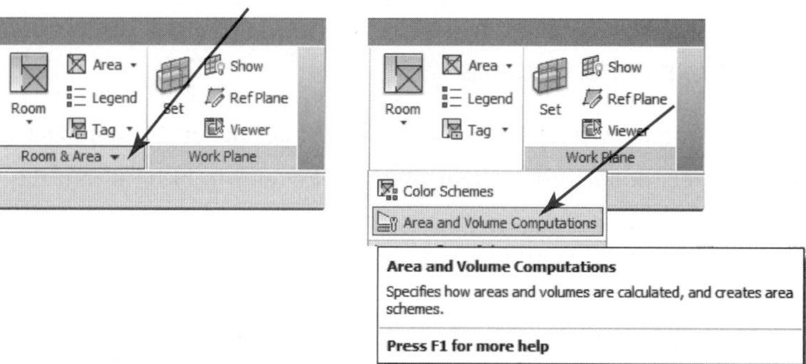

9. In the **Area and Volume Computations** dialog box, select the **Areas and Volumes** and **At wall finish** radio buttons, and press the **OK** button to return to the **Drawing Editor** (see Figure 11-5).

Figure 11-5

Area and Volume Computations dialog box

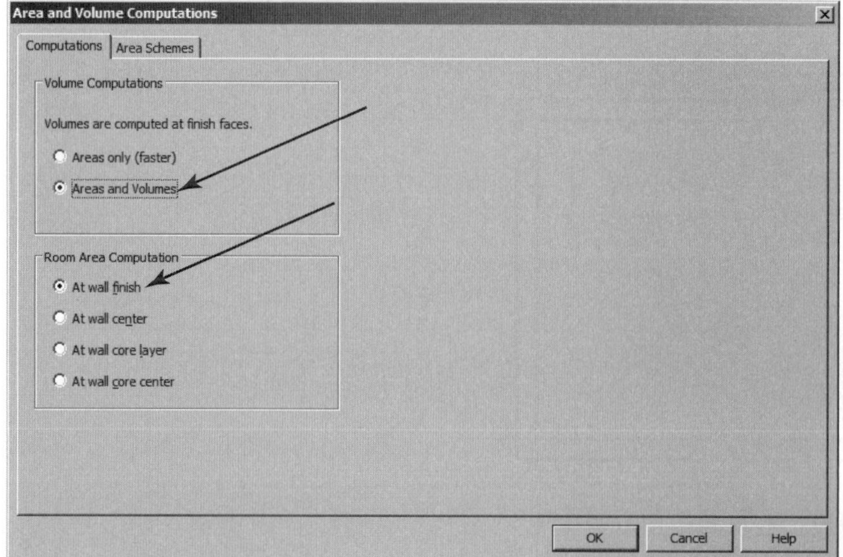

10. In the **Home** toolbar, select the **Room > Room** button to bring up the **Modify | Place Room** toolbar.
11. In the **Modify | Place Room** toolbar, select the **Type Properties** button to bring up the **Type Properties** dialog box (see Figure 11-6).

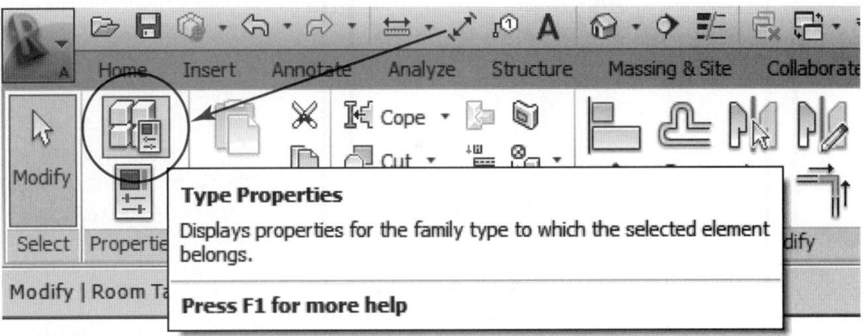

Figure 11-6

Type Properties button

12. In the **Type Properties** dialog box, select **Room Tag With Volume** from the **Type** drop-down list, and press the **OK** button to return to the **Drawing Editor** (see Figure 11-7).

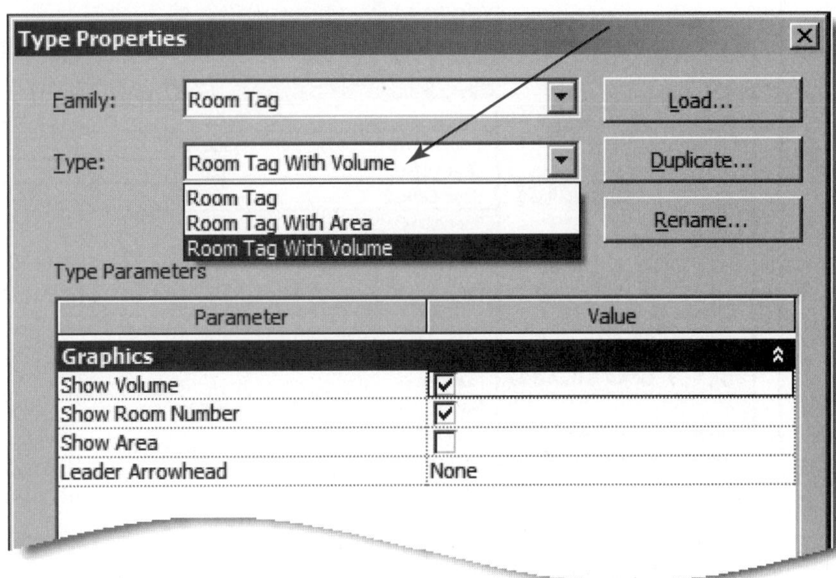

Figure 11-7

Room Tag With Volume Type

13. In the **Level 1** floor plan, move your cursor over the enclosure to place the room, and click to complete the command.

14. Notice that the **Room Tag** reads **1000.00 CF** (see Figure 11-8).

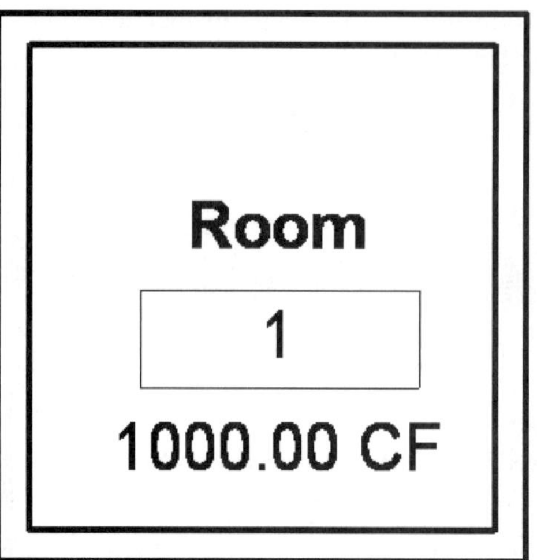

Figure 11-8

Room tag

NOTE: (FROM THE REVIT HELP FILE)

The volume calculation uses room area multiplied by upper limit only when the default height is lower than the ceiling or floor or roof. If it is higher than those elements, then Revit Architecture calculates the room volume based on the room-bounding elements, regardless of their shape. Therefore, for rooms under roofs, such as attic spaces, specify a room height (upper limit) that is greater than the height of the roof. This will ensure that the volume will be calculated up to the roof pitch. Note that the graphical representation in section does not reflect the actual boundaries used by the calculation.

15. To select a room, move your cursor over the room until the crosshairs graphic is displayed, and then click to bring up the room's **Properties** dialog box.
16. In the **Properties** dialog box, change the **Limit Offset** to **20′-0″** (this now allows you to calculate the volume for a room with a pitched roof) (see Figure 11-9).

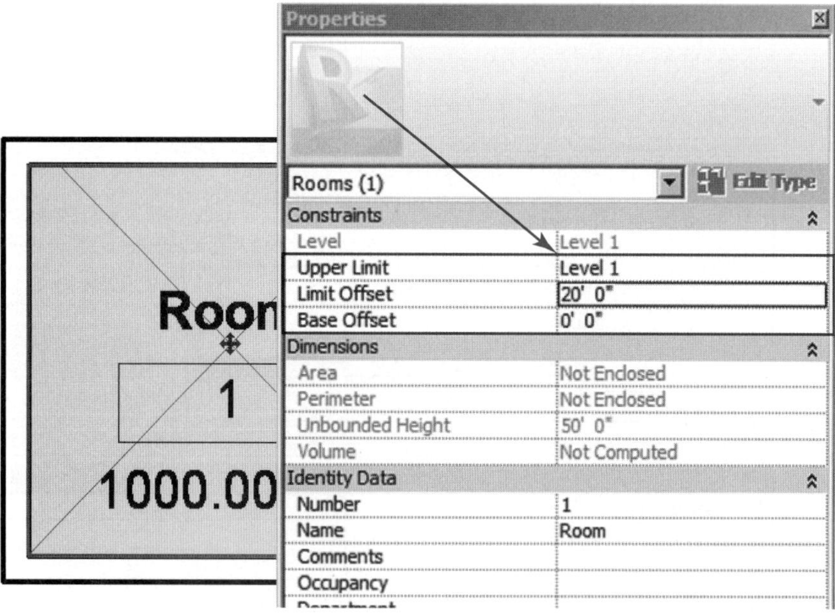

Figure 11-9

Change the **Limit Offset** value

17. Change to **Level 2**.
18. Select the roof to bring up the **Modify | Roofs** toolbar.
19. In the **Modify | Roofs** toolbar, select the **Edit Footprint** button to bring up the **Modify | Roofs > Edit Footprint** toolbar, and enter **Sketch or Edit Mode**.

NOTE:

Although you have changed the **Limit Offset**, the **Room Tag** still reads **1000.00 CF.** If you change to a pitched roof, the volume will change.

20. Select the **South** sketch line to bring up its **Properties** dialog box.
21. In the **Properties** dialog box, check the **Defines Roof Slope** check box, and change the **Slope** to **6″ / 12″** (see Figure 11-10).

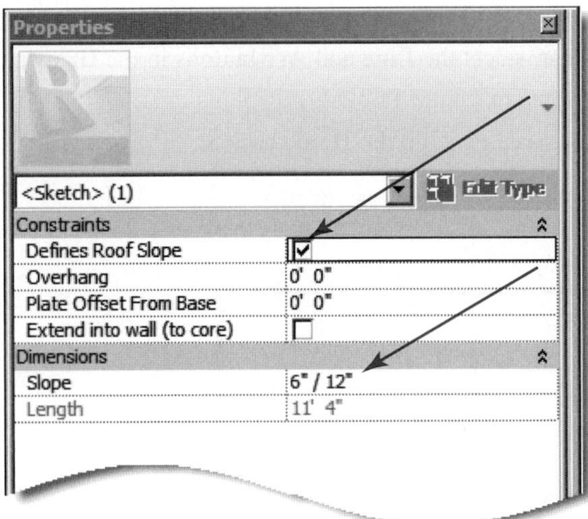

Figure 11-10

Properties dialog box for **South** line

22. In the **Modify | Roofs > Edit Footprint** toolbar, select the **Finish Edit Mode** button to complete the roof.
23. Press the **Yes** button in the **Revit Alert** dialog box to attach the walls to the roof.
24. Return to **Level 1** where you placed the **Room Tag**.

The **Room Tag** now reads **1283.33 CF** because it is reading the pitched roof volume (see Figure 11-11).

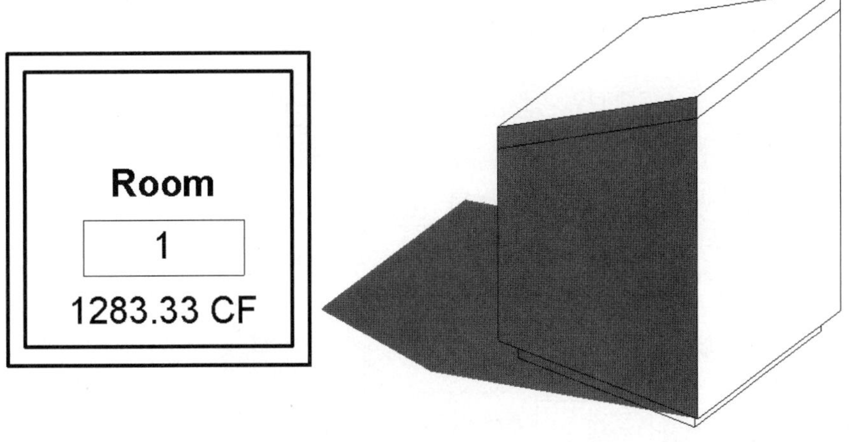

Figure 11-11

Pitched roof volume

25. Save this file as **ROOM VOLUMES**.

EXERCISE 11-2 **GROSS BUILDING AND AREAS**

1. Start a new project using the RAC 2012\Imperial Templates\default.rte template.
2. In the **Project Browser**, double-click **Floor Plans > Level 1** to bring it into the **Drawing Editor**.
3. In the **Home** toolbar, select the **Wall** button to bring up the **Place Wall** toolbar.
4. In the **Place Wall** toolbar, select the **Line** and **Arc** buttons in the **Draw** panel.
5. Create the enclosure shown in Figure 11-12.
6. Change to the **Room & Area** panel in the **Home** toolbar.

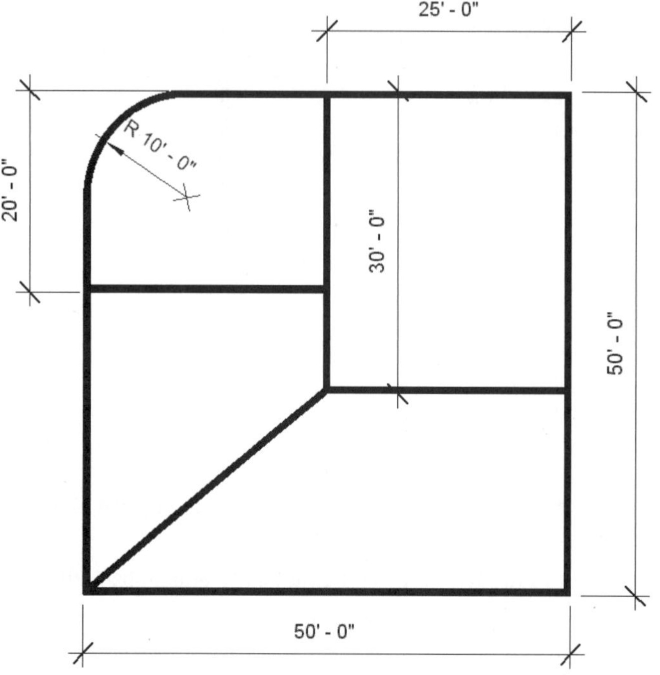

Figure 11-12

Create an enclosure

7. In the **Room & Area** panel, select the **Area Plan** button to bring up the **New Area Plan** dialog box (see Figure 11-13).

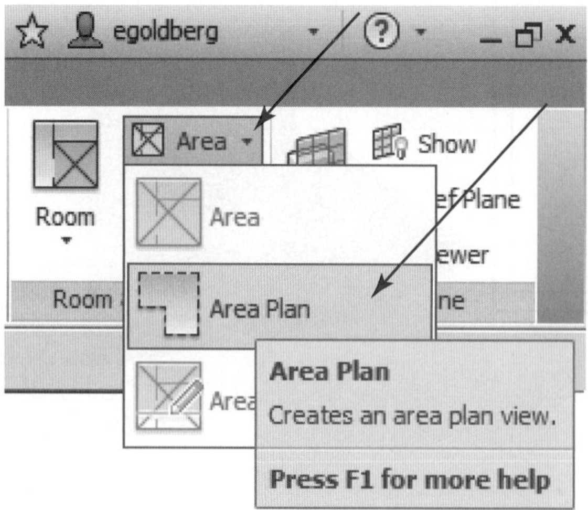

Figure 11-13

Area Plan button

8. In the **New Area Plan** dialog box, select **Gross Building** from the **Type** drop-down list, **Level 1** from the **Area Plan views**, and then press the **OK** button to create the **New Area Plan** (see Figure 11-14).

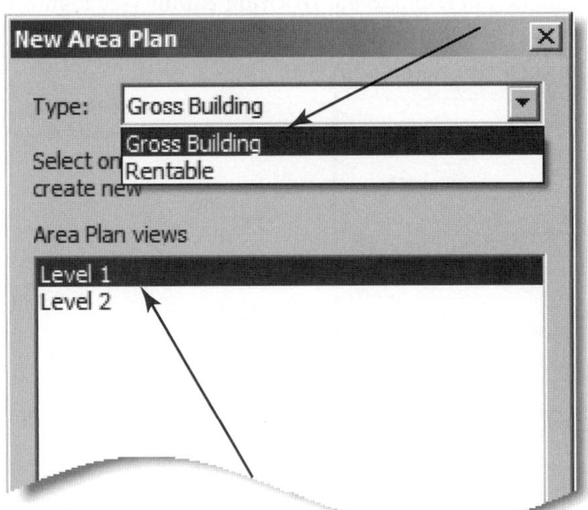

Figure 11-14

New Area Plan dialog box

9. Press the **Yes** button on the **Revit** dialog box that asks, *"Automatically create boundary lines associated with all external walls?"*

Area Plans [Gross Building] > Level 1 will now appear in the **Project Browser**.

10. Double-click **Area Plans [Gross Building] > Level 1** from the **Project Browser** to bring it into the **Drawing Editor**.

Blue boundary lines will appear around the entire enclosure.

11. Select the word **Area** in the tag you just placed, enter **GROSS BUILDING** in the text field, and then click in an empty area in the **Drawing Editor** to complete the tag (see Figure 11-15).

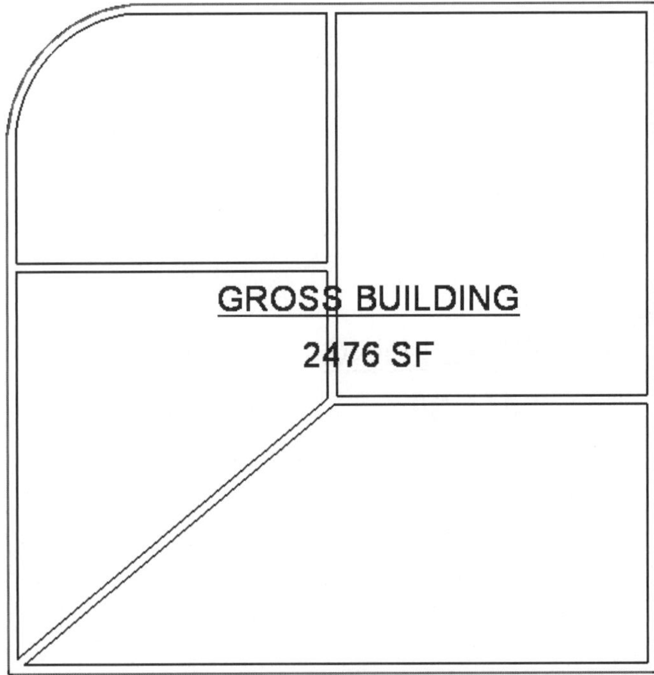

Figure 11-15

GROSS BUILDING Tag

12. Move your cursor over the area until the crosshairs graphic is displayed.
13. Select the crosshairs to bring up the **Properties** dialog box.
14. In the **Properties** dialog box, select **Exterior Area** from the **Area Type** drop-down list, and press the **Apply** button to return to the **Drawing Editor** (see Figure 11-16).

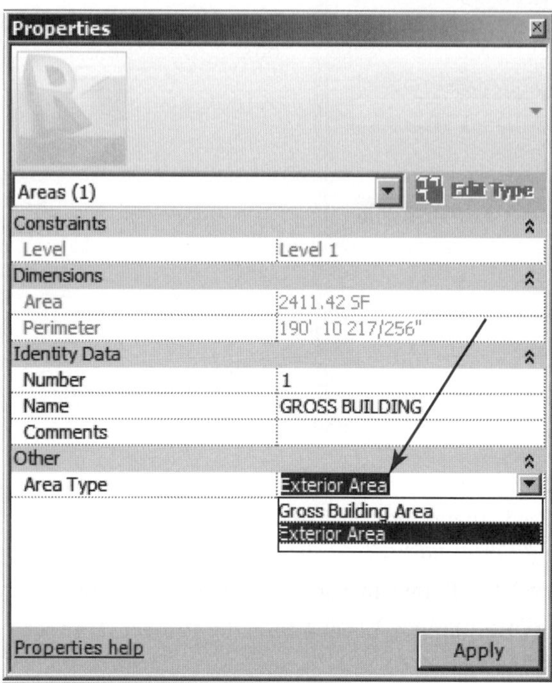

Figure 11-16

Area Type drop-down list

Notice that the blue boundary lines now appear around the entire enclosure, but in the center of the walls. Notice also that the **Area** square foot number has changed (see Figure 11-17).

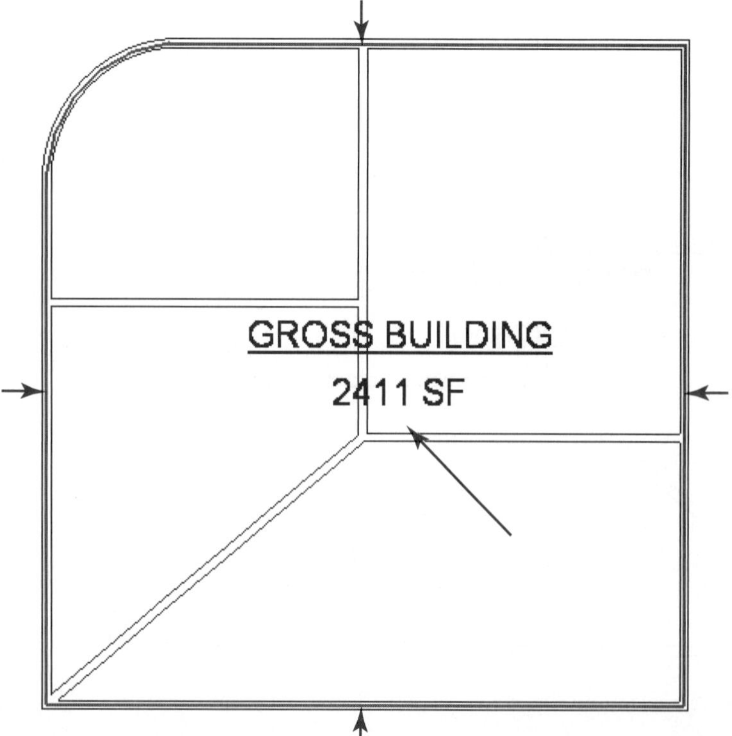

Figure 11-17

Blue boundary lines

Revit Architecture 2012 uses **Area** rules to control the area calculation. The following are the rules for **Gross Building** and **Exterior Area** calculations.

Area Types

Gross Building Area Scheme Types		
Area Type Selected	**Bordering Area Type**	**Measurement Rule**
Gross Building Area		
Gross Building Area	None	**Area Boundary** measured to the outside surface of the building.
Gross Building Area	**Exterior Area**	**Area Boundary** measured from the outside surface of the building.
Exterior Area		
Exterior Area	**Exterior Area**	**Area Boundary** measured from the wall centerline.
Exterior Area	**Gross Building Area**	**Area Boundary** measured from the outside surface of the building.

15. Save this file as **GROSS AND EXTERIOR AREAS**.

EXERCISE 11-3 RENTABLE AREAS

1. Use the previous exercise.
2. In the **Home** toolbar, select the **Area Plan** button to bring up the **New Area Plan** dialog box.
3. In the **New Area Plan** dialog box, select **Rentable** from the **Type** drop-down list, **Level 1** from the **Area Plan views**, and then press the **OK** button to create the **New Area Plan**.
4. Press the **No** button on the **Revit** dialog box that asks, "*Automatically create boundary lines associated with all external walls?*"
5. Double-click **Area Plans [Rentable] > Level 1** from the **Project Browser** to bring it into the **Drawing Editor**.
6. In the **Home** toolbar, select the **Area > Area Boundary Line** button to bring up the **Modify | Place Area Boundary** toolbar.
7. In the **Modify | Place Area Boundary** toolbar, select the **Pick Lines** button in the **Draw** panel, and check the **Apply Area Rules** check box in the **Options Bar**.

Checking the **Apply Area Rules** check box before applying an area boundary will allow you to calculate the area based on the type of area you are selecting. The following are **Rentable Area Scheme Types** that are included in Revit Architecture 2012.

NOTE:

Windows in Rentable Area Scheme Types: If you place windows within the exterior walls, Revit Architecture places the area boundary lines according to the following rules based on the height of the windows. If the window height is greater than 50% of the wall height, the area boundary lines go to the face of the glass. If the window height is less than 50% of wall height, the area boundary lines go to the interior face of the exterior walls.

Gross Building Area Scheme Types		
Area Type Selected	**Bordering Area Type**	**Measurement Rule**
Building Common Area		
Building Common Area	**Building Common Area, Office, Store**	**Area Boundary** measured from the wall centerline.
Building Common Area	**Exterior, Major Vertical Penetration**	**Area Boundary** measured from the wall face bordering the **Building Common Area.**
Office Area		
Office Area	**Building Common Area, Office, Store**	**Area Boundary** measured from the wall centerline.
Office Area	**Exterior, Major Vertical Penetration**	**Area Boundary** measured from the wall face bordering the **Office Area.**
Exterior Area		
Exterior Area	**Exterior**	**Area Boundary** measured from the wall centerline.
Exterior Area	**Store**	**Area Boundary** measured from the wall face bordering **Exterior Area.**
Exterior Area	Any other areas	**Area Boundary** measured from the wall face bordering the other area.
Floor Area		
Floor Area	**Office, Store or Building Common Area**	**Area Boundary** measured from the wall face bordering the other area.
Floor Area	**Exterior, Major Vertical Penetration**	**Area Boundary** measured from the wall face bordering the **Floor Area.**
Floor Area	**Floor Area**	**Area Boundary** measured from the wall centerline.
Major Vertical Penetration		
Major Vertical Penetration	**Major Vertical Penetration**	**Area Boundary** measured from the wall centerline.
Major Vertical Penetration	**Exterior**	**Area Boundary** measured from the wall face bordering the **Major Vertical Penetration** area.
Major Vertical Penetration	Any other area (except **Exterior**)	**Area Boundary** measured from the wall face bordering the other area.
Store Area		
Store Area	**Major Vertical Penetration, Floor**	**Area Boundary** measured from the wall face bordering the **Store Area.**
Store Area	**Exterior**	**Area Boundary** measured from the wall face bordering the **Exterior Area.**
Store Area	**Building Common Area, Office, Store**	**Area Boundary** measured from the wall centerline.

8. With the **Area Boundary** button selected and **Pick Lines** and **Apply Area Rules** applied, select the boundaries of the area you want to calculate.
9. Select the **Area** button from the **Room & Area** panel, move it over the enclosed area you just created, and click your mouse to place the **Area Tag** (see Figure 11-19).
10. Select the area by moving your cursor over the room until the crosshairs graphic is displayed, and then click.
11. Select the crosshairs to bring up the **Properties** dialog box.

NOTE:

As you pick boundaries, the boundary lines will first appear in the center of the walls. After you have selected all the enclosing walls, the lines will automatically enclose the inner walls of the area (see Figure 11-18).

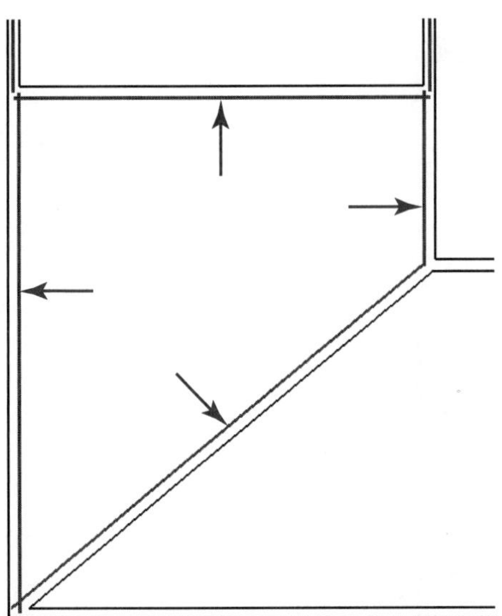

Figure 11-18

Boundary lines enclose the selected area

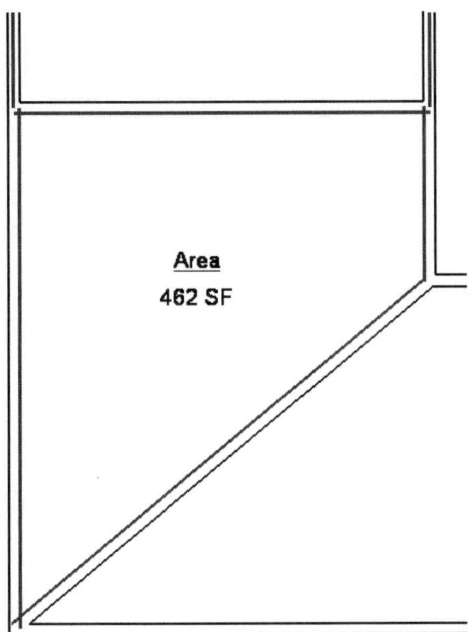

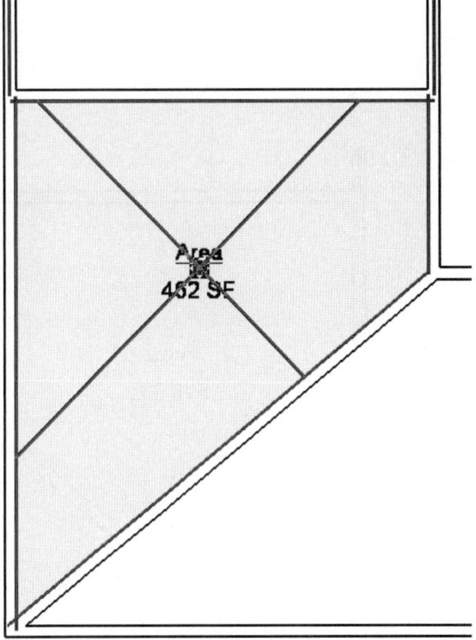

Figure 11-19

Place the **Area Tag**

12. In the **Properties** dialog box, change the **Area Type** to **Store Area**, and then press the **OK** button to return to the **Drawing Editor** (see Figure 11-20).

Notice that the **Area Boundary** has automatically changed location and that the area calculated has increased. This is because the rule for **Store Area** has been automatically applied when you change the **Area Type** in the **Instance Properties** dialog box to **Store Area** (see Figure 11-21).

13. Again, select the area crosshairs to bring up the **Properties** dialog box.
14. In the **Properties** dialog box, change the **Area Type** to **Office Area**, and then press the **OK** button to return to the **Drawing Editor**.

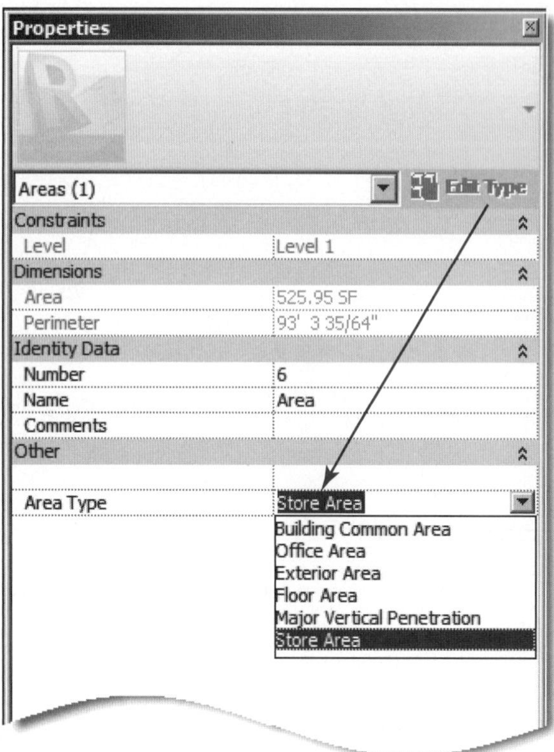

Figure 11-20

Change the **Area Type**

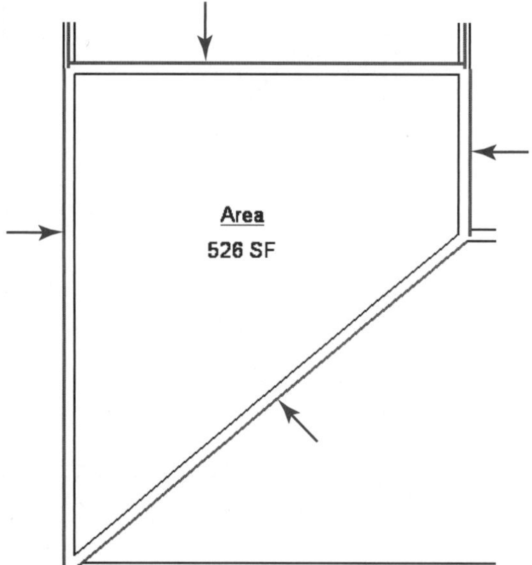

Figure 11-21

Instance Properties dialog box

Notice that the **Area Boundary** has automatically changed location to the inside face of the walls, and the area has changed to **462 SF**.

15. In the **Home** toolbar, select the **Window** button to bring up the **Modify | Place Window** toolbar.
16. In the **Modify | Place Window** toolbar, select the **Load Family** button to bring up the **Load Family** dialog box.
17. In the **Load Family** dialog box, load the **Slider with Trim** from the **Windows** folder.
18. Place windows in the wall.

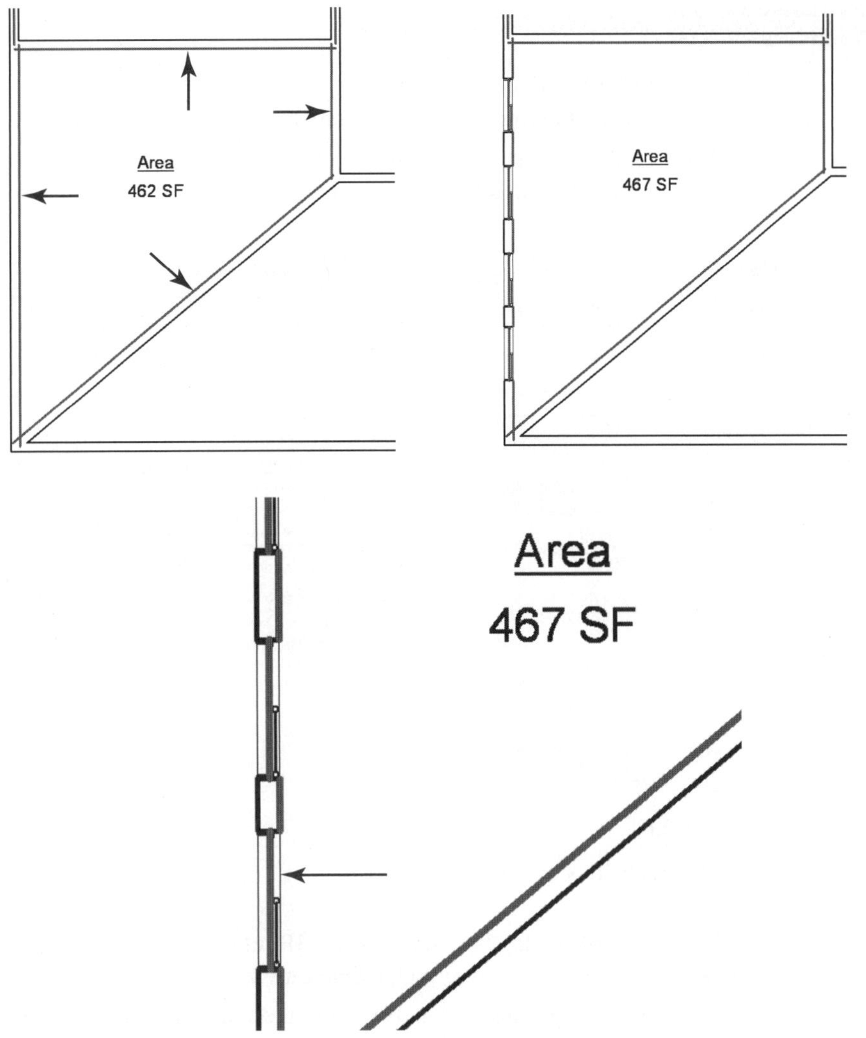

Figure 11-22

Area of window glass changed

Notice that the area has changed to **467 SF**. This is because Revit calculates an **Office Area** to the face of the window glass (see Figure 11-22).

19. Change the windows to **Slider with Trim: 48″ × 48″**.

Notice that the boundary no longer calculates to the face of the glass. If the window height is less than 50% of the wall height, Revit calculates the area boundary lines to the interior face of the exterior walls.

20. Again, select the **Area > Area Boundary Line** button from the **Home** toolbar, and create area boundaries for the other enclosures.
21. Select the area names, and change them to numbers.
22. Save this file as **RENTABLE AREAS**.

Area Schedules

With Revit Architecture, you can create a key schedule or a schedule of building components. A key schedule lets you define keys to automatically fill in some information for the schedule.

EXERCISE 11-4 **CREATING AREA SCHEDULES**

1. Use the previous exercise.
2. Select the **View** tab to bring up the **View** toolbar.
3. In the **View** toolbar, select the **Schedules > Schedule/Quantities** button to bring up the **New Schedule** dialog box (see Figure 11-23).

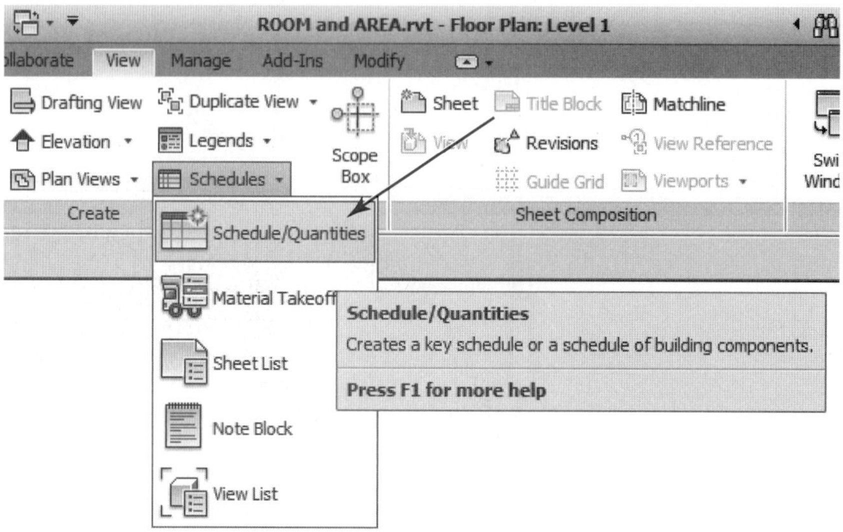

Figure 11-23

Schedule/Quantities button

4. In the **New Schedule** dialog box, select **Areas [Rentable]** from the **Category** list, and press the **OK** button to bring up the **Schedule Properties** dialog box.
5. In the **Schedule Properties** dialog box, select **Area**, **Area Type**, **Name**, and **Perimeter** from the **Available fields**: list, and press the **Add** button (see Figure 11-24).

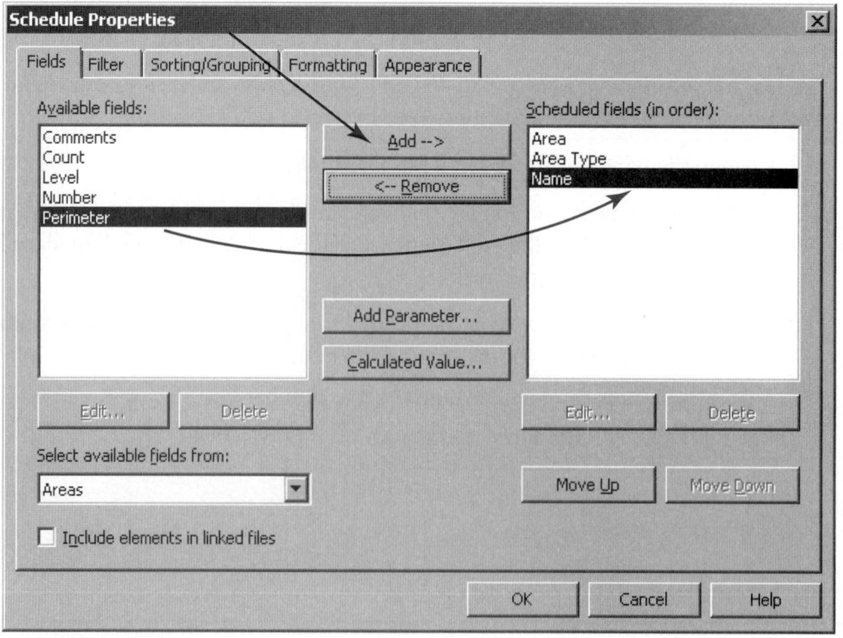

Figure 11-24

Schedule Properties dialog box

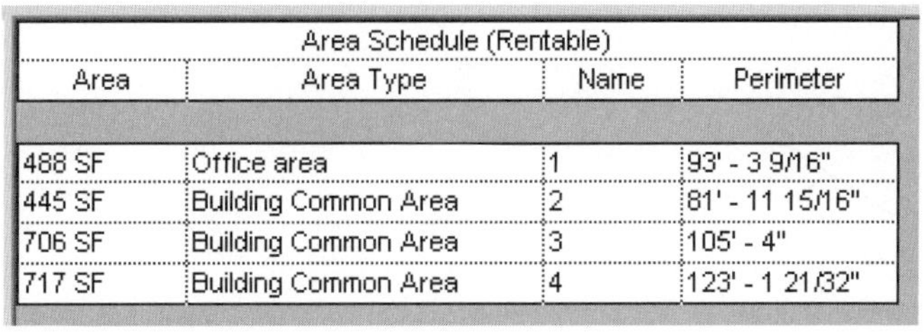

Area Schedule (Rentable)			
Area	Area Type	Name	Perimeter
488 SF	Office area	1	93' - 3 9/16"
445 SF	Building Common Area	2	81' - 11 15/16"
706 SF	Building Common Area	3	105' - 4"
717 SF	Building Common Area	4	123' - 1 21/32"

Figure 11-25

Area (Rentable) Schedule

6. Press the **OK** button to create the schedule (see Figure 11-25).
7. Select new area types from the **Area Type** drop-down list, and notice that the **Area SF** changes (see Figure 11-26).
8. Save this file as **AREA SCHEDULES**.

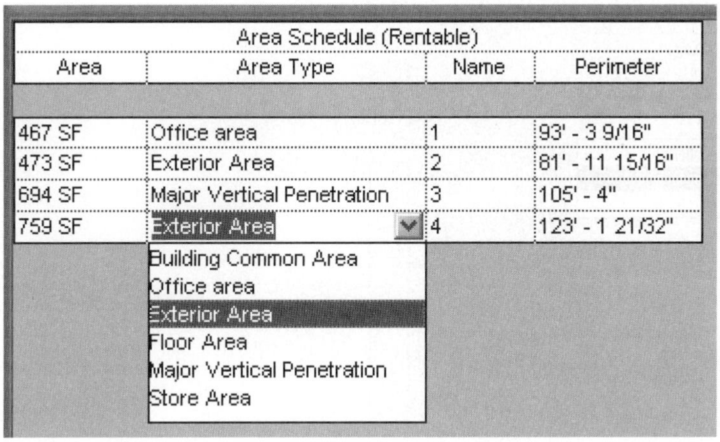

Area Schedule (Rentable)			
Area	Area Type	Name	Perimeter
467 SF	Office area	1	93' - 3 9/16"
473 SF	Exterior Area	2	81' - 11 15/16"
694 SF	Major Vertical Penetration	3	105' - 4"
759 SF	Exterior Area	4	123' - 1 21/32"

Building Common Area
Office area
Exterior Area
Floor Area
Major Vertical Penetration
Store Area

Figure 11-26

Area Type drop-down list

Color Schemes

Revit Architecture uses **Color Schemes** to create or modify a color fill scheme for rooms and areas.

EXERCISE 11-5 **CREATING COLOR SCHEME LEGENDS**

1. Use the previous exercise.
2. Double-click on **Area plans [Rentable] > Level 1** in the **Project Browser** to bring it into the **Drawing Editor**.
3. In the **Home** toolbar, select the **Color Schemes** button from the **Room & Area** panel to bring up the **Edit Color Scheme** dialog box (see Figure 11-27).
4. In the **Edit Color Scheme** dialog box, select **Areas (Rentable)** from the **Category** drop-down list (see Figure 11-28).
5. In the **Scheme Definition** area, select **Color:** by **Area**, **Area Type**, **Name**, **Number**, or **Perimeter** (see Figure 11-29).

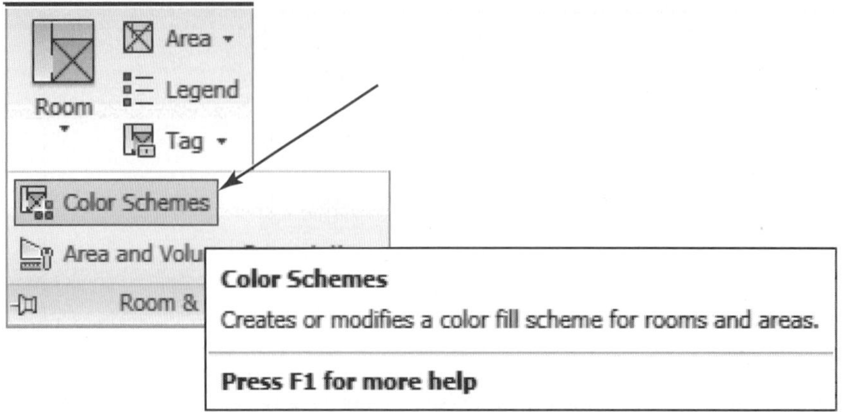

Figure 11-27

Color Schemes button

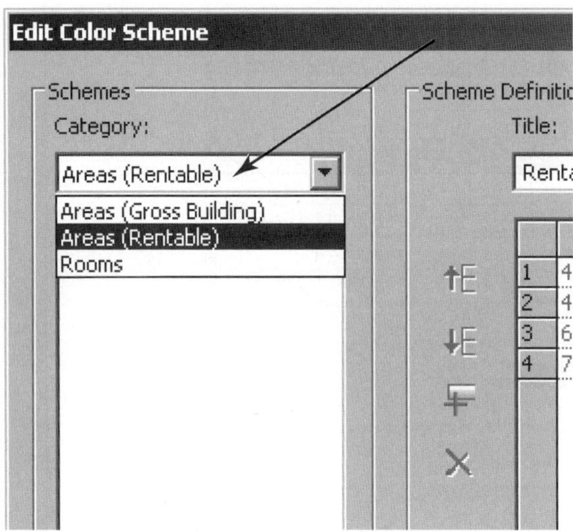

Figure 11-28

Edit Color Scheme dialog box

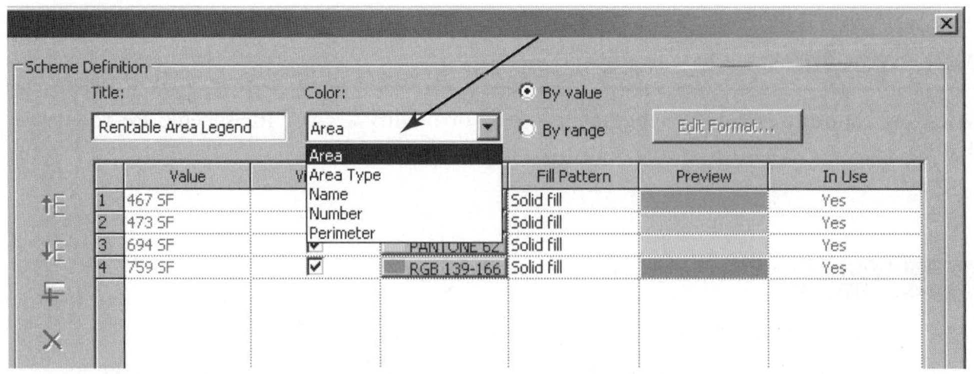

Figure 11-29

Scheme Definition area

6. In the **Scheme Definition** area, select the **Color:** and **Fill Pattern** of your choice. In the **Options** section of the **Edit Color Scheme** dialog box, check the **Include elements from linked files** check box.
7. Press the **OK** button to return to the **Drawing Editor**.

8. In the **Home** toolbar, select **Legend** from the **Room & Area** panel to bring up the **Modify | Place Color Scheme Legend** toolbar.
9. Click in the **Area plans [Rentable] > Level 1** that is in the **Drawing Editor** to place the **Color Legend**.

NOTE:
If the wrong legend appears or if you wish to change the legend, repeat Steps 3–5 of this exercise, and edit the **Color Scheme.**

The room areas will now fill with color to match the legend (see Figure 11-30).

10. Save this file as **COLOR SCHEME LEGENDS**.

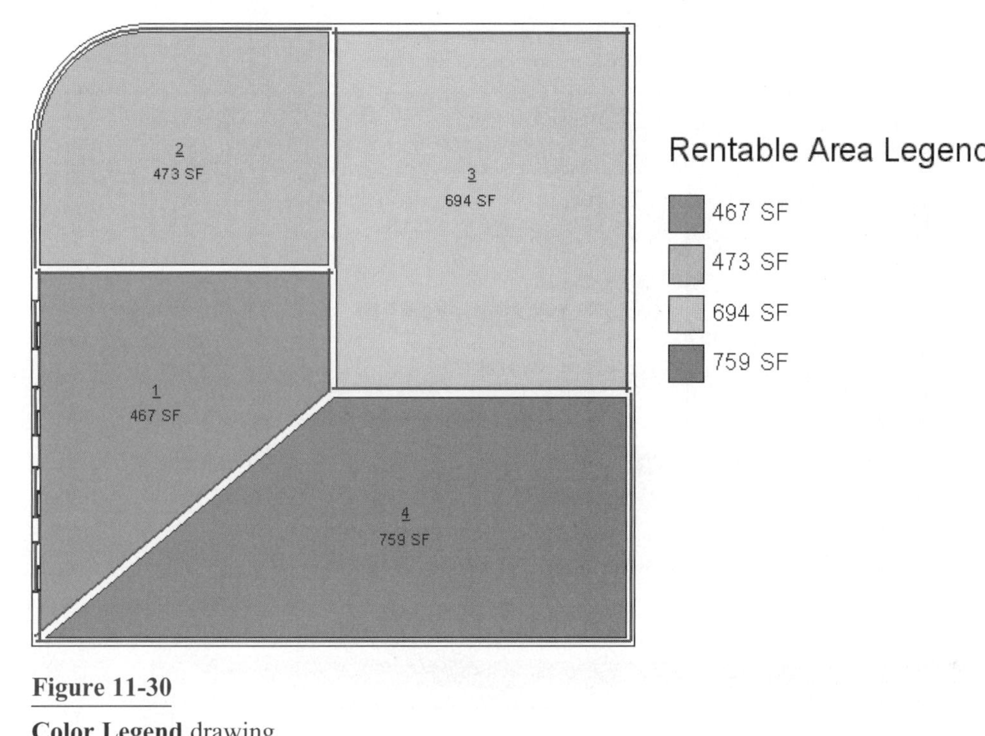

Figure 11-30

Color Legend drawing

Area Reports

Revit Architecture enables you to create and export room and area reports.

EXERCISE 11-6 **EXPORTING A ROOM/AREA REPORT**

1. Use the previous exercise.
2. Select **File > Export > Room/Area Report** from the **Application** menu to bring up the **Export Room Area Report** dialog box (see Figure 11-31).
3. In the **Export Room Area Report** dialog box, select **Current View** from the **Range:** drop-down list (see Figure 11-32).
4. Browse to a convenient folder to save the file, and press the **Save** button.
5. Using the Windows Explorer, browse to the folder where you saved the file.

NOTE:
You can pick **Select Views** from the **Range:** drop-down list, and select several floors (views) to report.

The folder where you saved your file contains a new subfolder with images from the **AREA REPORT** file you created and an **AREA REPORT.html** file (see Figure 11-33).

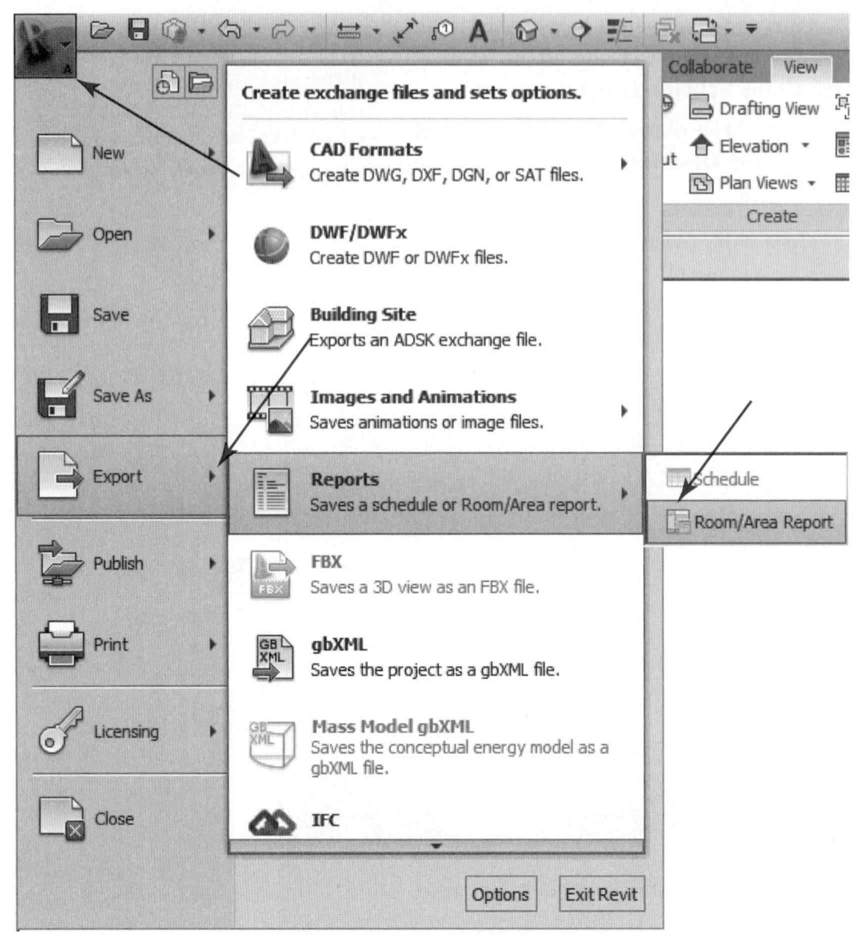

Figure 11-31

Export Room/Area Report option

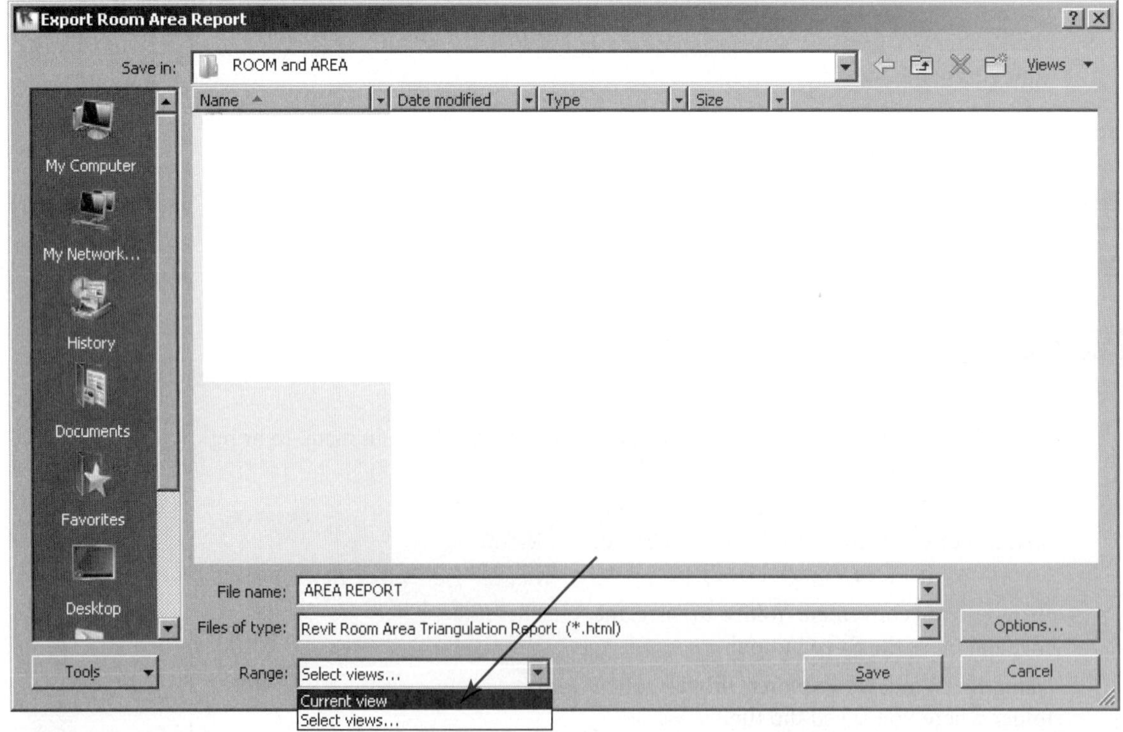

Figure 11-32

Export Room Area Report dialog box

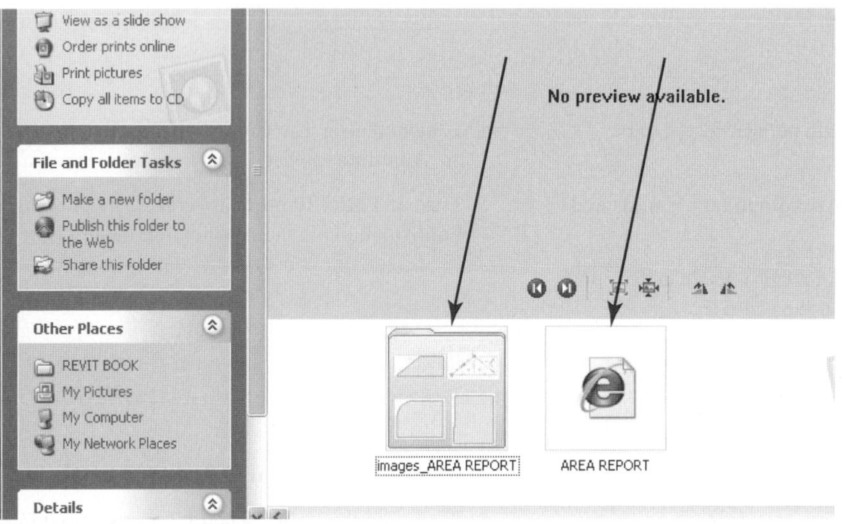

Figure 11-33

Subfolders in **AREA REPORT** file

6. Double-click on the **AREA REPORT.html** file to open it in your Internet browser.
7. Save this file as **AREA REPORT**.

Chapter Summary

This chapter explained and demonstrated Revit Architecture 2012's **Room** and **Area** tools. These tools are used to analyze area and volumes in buildings. Among the tools demonstrated were the **Volume**, **Gross Building**, **Rentable Areas**, **Area Schedules**, **Color Scheme**, and **Area Reports** tools.

Chapter Test Questions

Multiple Choice

Circle the correct answer.

1. Schedule tools are located in the ________ toolbar.
   a. **Home**
   b. **Annotate**
   c. **View**
   d. **Add-Ins**
2. The **Area Plan** button is located in the ________ toolbar.
   a. **Home**
   b. **Annotate**
   c. **View**
   d. **Add-Ins**
3. The **Area and Volume Computations** dialog box controls ________
   a. Only the **Areas**.
   b. **Areas** and **Volumes**.
   c. The mathematical formulas for **Area**.
   d. All of the above
4. The **Export Room Area Report** is exported in ________ file format.
   a. .TXT
   b. .XML
   c. .HTML
   d. .DOC
5. The **Area Type** field is located in the ________
   a. **Type Properties** dialog box.
   b. **Properties** dialog box.
   c. **Options Bar**.
   d. **Room & Area** panel drop-down list.

True or False

Circle the correct answer.

1. **True or False:** Curtain walls are not considered to be bounding objects.
2. **True or False:** In Revit, the **Area Boundary** is measured from wall centerline.
3. **True or False:** As you pick boundaries, the boundary lines will first appear in the center of the walls.
4. **True or False:** The **Color Schemes** button is located in the **Annotate** toolbar.
5. **True or False: Reports** are created by pressing the **Publish** button in the **Application** menu.

Questions

1. Name three **Bounding** objects.
2. What is an **Area Boundary Line** used for?
3. Name three **Area Types**.
4. Where is the **Room/Area Report** located?
5. What does the **Color Scheme Legend** tool do?

CHAPTER

12 Annotations, Dimensions, and Detailing

CHAPTER OBJECTIVES

- Know how to set the **Dimension Style** variables and place dimension strings.
- Know how to use the **Spot Dimensions** tool.
- Learn how to use the **Text** tool.
- Learn how to use the **Grid** tool.
- Learn how to use the **Tag** and **Tag All Not Tagged** tools.
- Learn how to use the **Symbol** tool.
- Know how to set **Line Styles, Line Weights**, and **Line Patterns**.
- Learn how to use the **Detail Group** tool.
- Know how to **Create Details**.
- Learn how to use the **Repeating Detail** tool.
- Learn how to use the **Detail Component** tool.
- Learn how to use the **Masking Region** tool.
- Learn how to use the **Insulation** tool.
- Know how to use the **Break Line** tool.

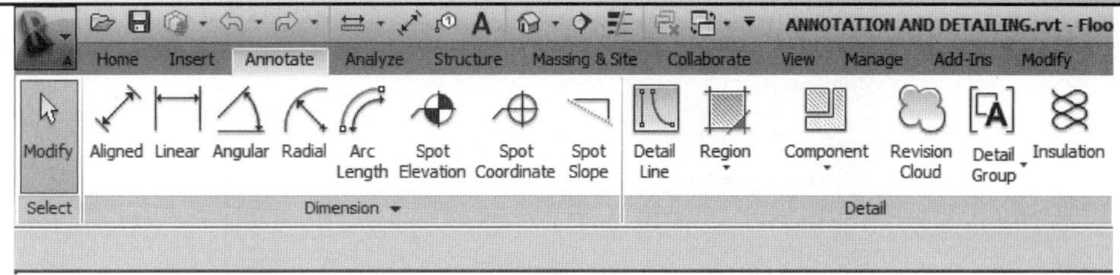

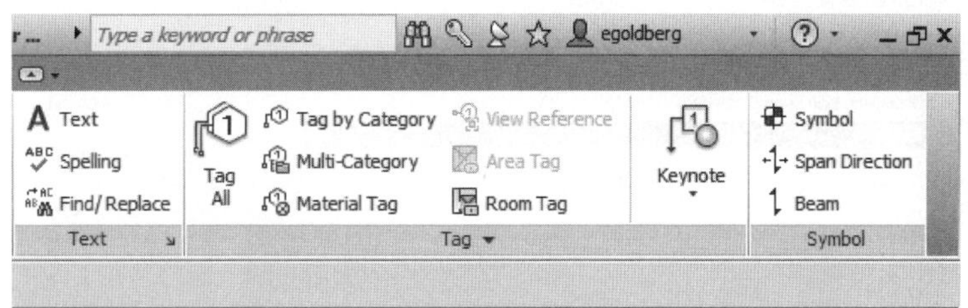

Introduction

Dimensioning, annotation, and 2D drafting compose a large component of the architectural documentation process. Revit Architecture 2012 utilizes standard electronic drafting tools plus automated **2D Detail Components** to aid in this documentation.

Annotate, Dimension, and Details Tools

The best way to understand how **Dimension** variables work is to place a dimension string, change the variables, and observe their effect. This is also true for learning how the **Annotate** and **Details** options work. A variety of tools are available in Revit Architecture to make changes to a drawing faster and easier.

The **Type Properties** dialog box for **Dimensions** is shown in Figure 12-1.

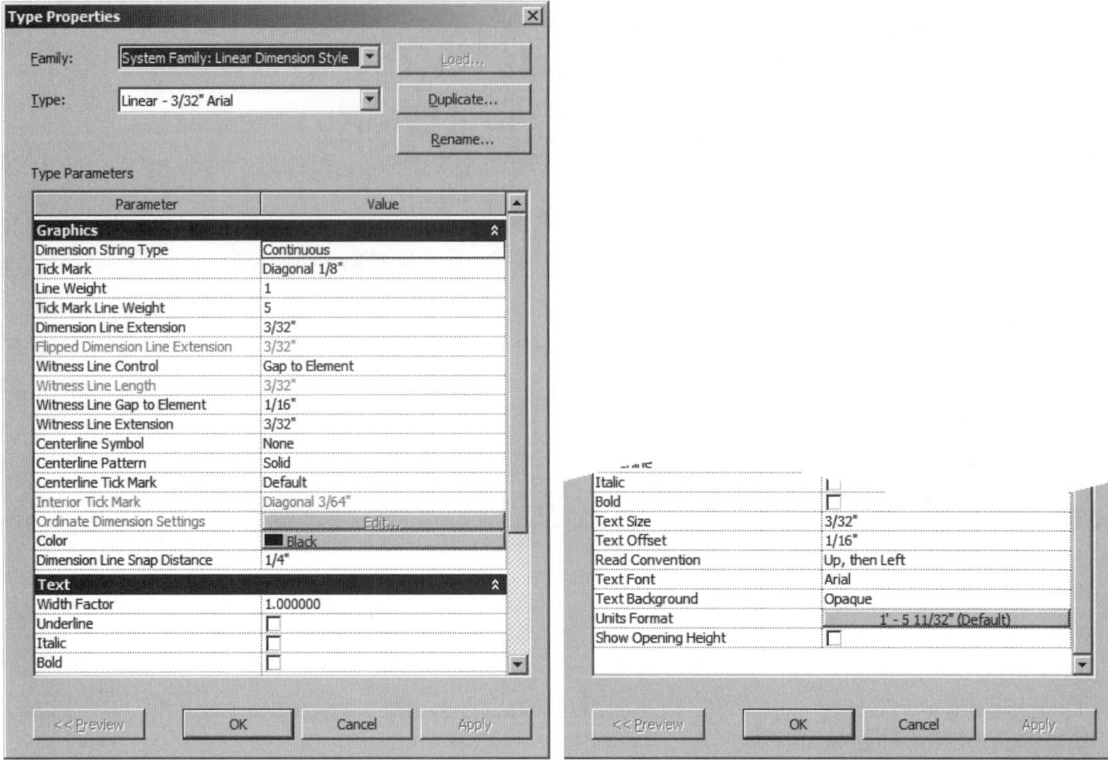

Figure 12-1

Dimensions Type Properties dialog box

Name	**Description**
Graphics	
Dimension String Type	**Continuous, Baseline, Ordinate**
Tick Mark	The name of the tick mark style.
Line Weight	Sets the line weight number that designates the thickness of the dimension line. You can choose from a list of values defined in Revit Architecture or define your own. You can change the definition of the line weights using the **LINE WEIGHTS** command in the **Settings** menu.
Tick Mark Line Weight	Sets the line weight that designates thickness of the tick mark. You can choose from a list of values defined in Revit Architecture or define your own.
Dimension Line Extension	Extends the dimension line beyond the intersection of the witness lines to the specified value. When you set this value, this is the size at which the dimension line plots if you are printing at 100%.
Flipped Dimension Line Extension	Controls the extent of the dimension line beyond the flipped arrow if the arrow flips on the ends of the dimension string. This parameter is enabled only when the **Tick Mark Type** parameter is set to an arrow type.
Witness Line Control	Switches between the fixed gap functionality and the fixed dimension line functionality.
Witness Line Length	If **Witness Line Control** is set to **Fixed to Dimension Line**, this parameter becomes available. Specifies the length of all witness lines in the dimensions. When you set this value, this is the size at which the witness line plots if you are printing at 100%.
Witness Line Gap to Element	If **Witness Line Control** is set to **Gap to Element**, this parameter sets the distance between the witness line and the element being dimensioned.

Name	Description
Graphics Cont'd.	
Witness Line Extension	Sets the extension of a witness line beyond the tick mark. When you set this value, this is the size at which the witness line plots if you are printing at 100%.
Centerline Symbol	You can select any of the **Annotation** symbols loaded in the project. The **Centerline** symbol appears above the witness lines that reference the centerlines of family instances and walls. If the witness line does not reference a center plane, you cannot place a **Centerline** symbol above it.
Centerline Pattern	Changes the line pattern of the witness lines of the dimension if the dimension references are the centerlines of family instances and walls. If the references are not at the centerline, this parameter does not affect the witness line pattern.
Centerline Tick Mark	Changes the tick mark at the ends of the centerline of a dimension.
Interior Tick Mark	Designates the tick mark display for inner witness lines when adjacent segments of a dimension line are too small for arrows to fit. When this occurs, the ends of the short-segment string flip, and the inner witness lines display the designated interior tick mark. This parameter is enabled only when the **Tick Mark Type** parameter is set to an arrow type.
Color	Sets the color of dimension lines. You can choose from a list of colors defined in Revit Architecture or define your own. The default value is black.
Dimension Line Snap Distance	To use this parameter, set the **Witness Line Control** parameter to **Fixed to Dimension Line**. With these parameters set, additional snapping is available that aids in stacking linear dimensions at even intervals. This value should be greater than the distance between the text and the dimension line, plus the height of the text. This parameter is used primarily in the European market.
Text	
Width Factor	1.0 is the default for regular text width. The font width is scaled proportionately to the **Width Factor**. Height is not affected.
Underline	Specifies that the text will be underlined.
Italic	Specifies that the text will be set in *italics*.
Bold	Specifies that the text will be set in **bold**.
Text Size	Specifies the size of the typeface for the dimension.
Text Offset	Specifies the offset of the text from the dimension line.
Read Convention	Specifies the read convention for the dimension text.
Text Font	Sets the Microsoft® TrueType fonts for the dimensions.
Text Background	If you set the value to opaque, the dimension text is surrounded by a box that overlaps any geometry or text behind it in the view. If you set the value to transparent, the box disappears, and everything not overlapped by the dimension text is visible.
Units Format	Click the button to open the **Format** dialog box. You can then set the format of the units with the dimension.
Show Opening Height	Places a dimension whose witness lines reference the same insert (window, door, or opening) in a Plan view. If you select this parameter, the dimension includes a label that shows the height of the opening for the instance. The value appears below the dimension value you initially placed. **Note**: This parameter is used primarily in the German market.
Other	
Center Marks	Shows or hides the arc dimension center mark.
Center Mark Size	Sets the size of the arc dimension center mark. This property is enabled when **Center Marks** is selected.
Radius Prefix	Shows or hides **Prefix (R)** for radial dimensions.

EXERCISE 12-1 **SETTING THE DIMENSION STYLE VARIABLES**

1. Start a new project using the RAC 2012\Imperial Templates\default.rte template.
2. In the **Project Browser**, double-click **Floor Plans > Level 1** to bring it into the **Drawing Editor**.
3. Set the **Scale** to **1/8″ = 1′-0″**.
4. Change the **Detail Level** to **Medium**.
5. In the **Home** toolbar, select the **Wall** button to bring up the **Modify | Place Wall** toolbar.
6. In the **Modify | Place Wall** toolbar, select the **Rectangle** button in the **Draw** panel.
7. In the **Options Bar**, select **Finish Face Exterior** for the **Location Line**.
8. Place a **Basic Wall: Exterior – Brick on CMU** wall **25′-0″** long, **25′-0″** wide, and **10′-0″** high for the enclosure.
9. Select the **Annotate** tab to bring up the **Annotate** toolbar.
10. In the **Annotate** toolbar, select the **Aligned** button to bring up the **Modify | Place Dimensions** toolbar (see Figure 12-2).

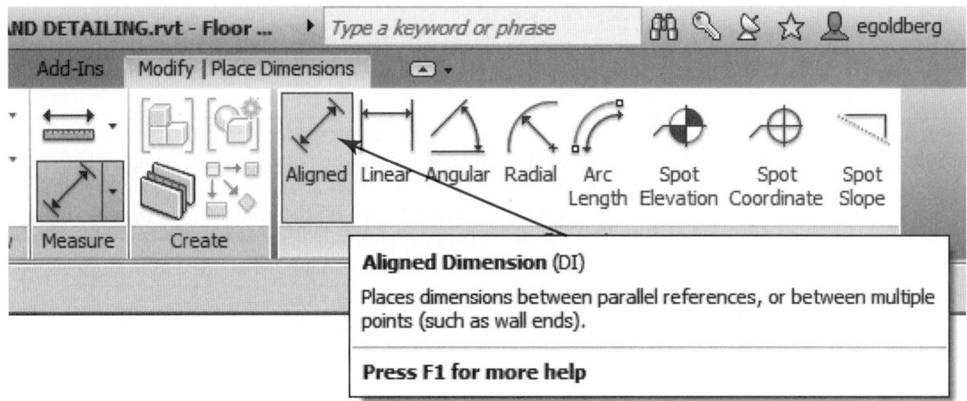

Figure 12-2
Aligned button

11. In the **Properties** dialog box, select the **Linear Dimension Style: Linear-3/32″ Arial** from the **Properties** drop-down list.
12. In the **Options Bar**, select **Wall faces** from the **Prefer** field, and **Individual References** from the **Pick** field (see Figure 12-3).

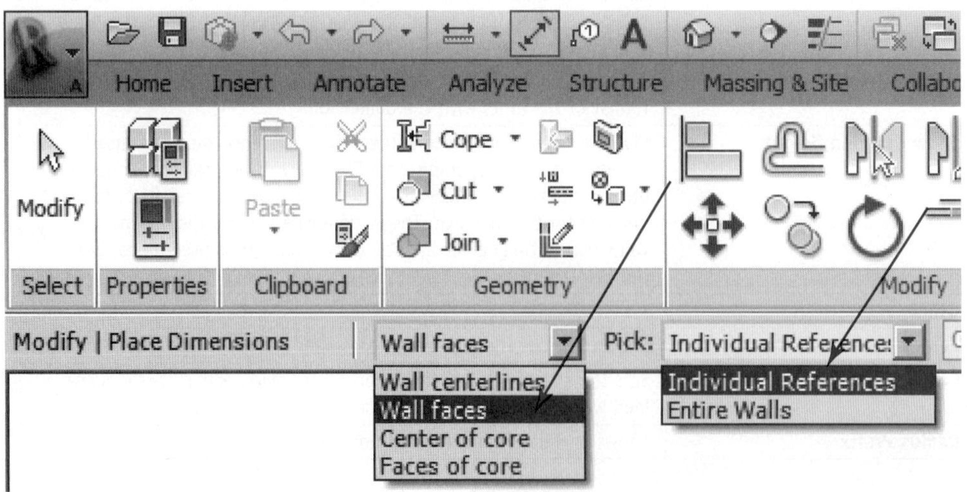

Figure 12-3
Options Bar

13. Select the left wall of the enclosure, then select the right wall, drag your cursor upward to locate the dimension string, and click to place the dimension (see Figure 12-4).
14. In the **Modify | Place Dimensions** toolbar, select the **Element Properties > Type Properties** button from the **Properties** panel to bring up the **Type Properties** dialog box (see Figure 12-5).

> **NOTE:**
> The **Place Dimensions** options allow you to place the dimensions at **Wall centerlines, Wall faces, Center of core,** and **Faces of core.** You can also select placement by tapping the **<Tab>** key when selecting walls. This is very handy if you need to dimension from the studs.

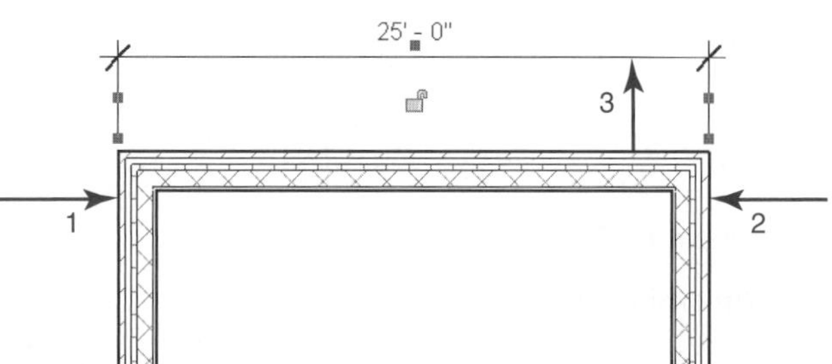

Figure 12-4
Place a dimension

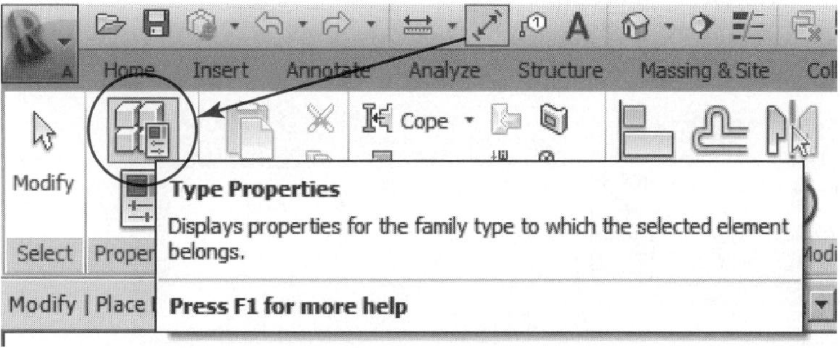

Figure 12-5
Type Properties dialog box

15. In the **Type Properties** dialog box, change each of the settings, and observe the changes to the dimension string (see Figures 12-6 and 12-7).

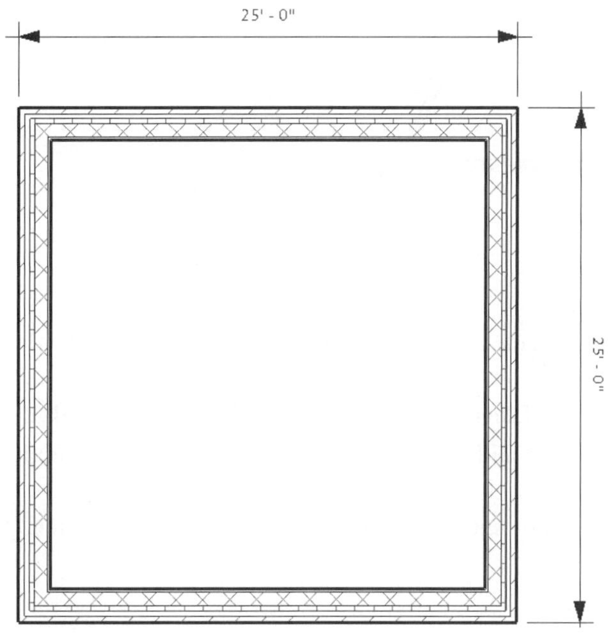

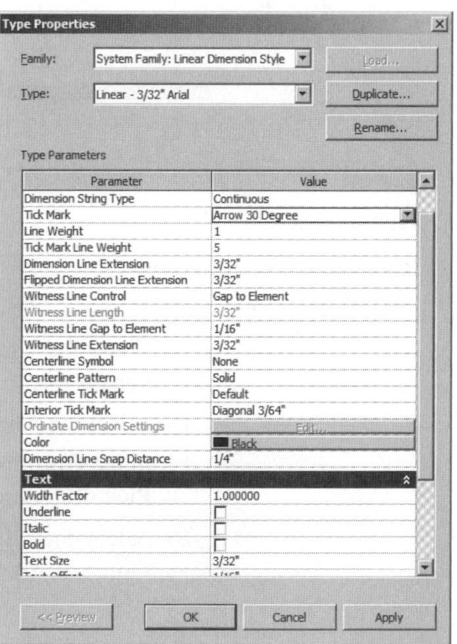

Figure 12-6
Change settings in the **Type Properties** dialog box and observe the changes

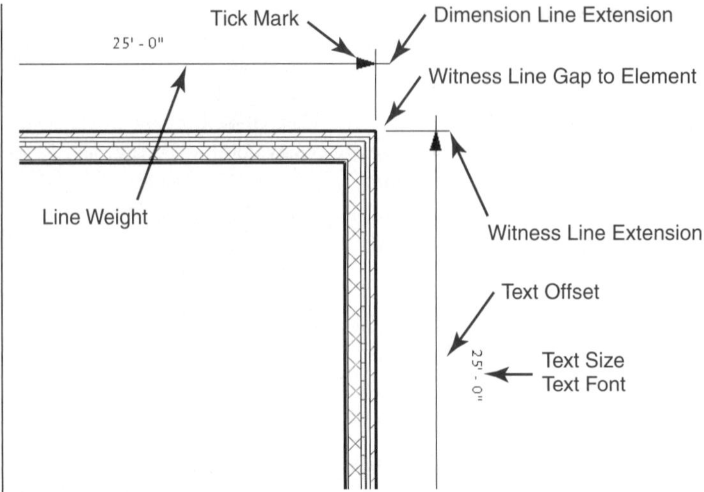

Figure 12-7

Dimension elements

16. Place walls, and select the different dimension placement options as shown in Figure 12-8.

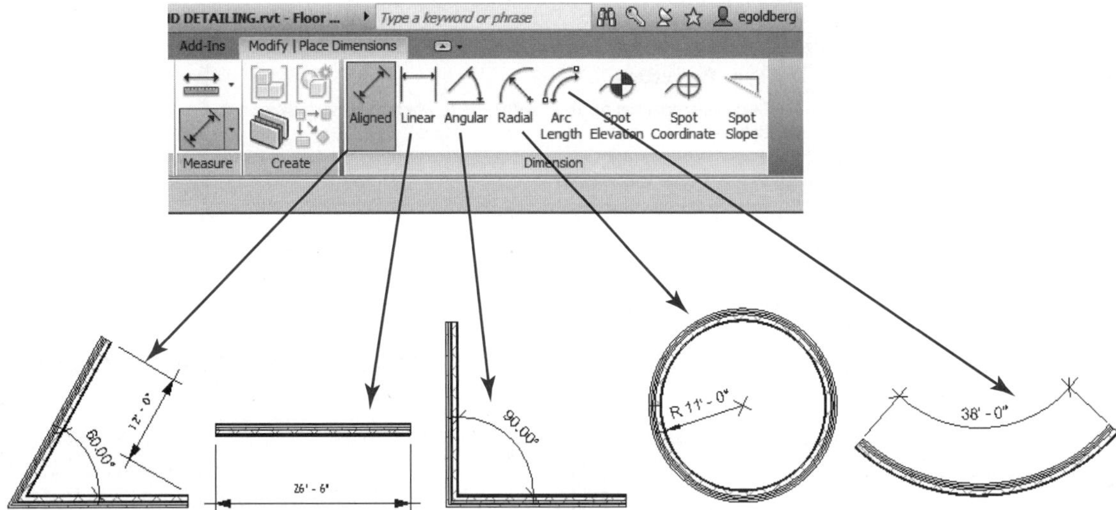

Figure 12-8

Dimension placement options

17. Using the enclosure you made at the beginning of this exercise, delete all the dimensions.
18. Select the **Align** button and **Linear Dimension Style: Linear-3/32″ Arial**.
19. In the **Options Bar**, select **Wall faces**, but this time select **Entire Walls** from the **Pick** drop-down list.
20. Select the edge of the wall, and click and drag to place the dimension (see Figure 12-9).

You might find that the **Entire Walls** placement method is often simpler and faster than the **Individual References** method because you use fewer mouse clicks.

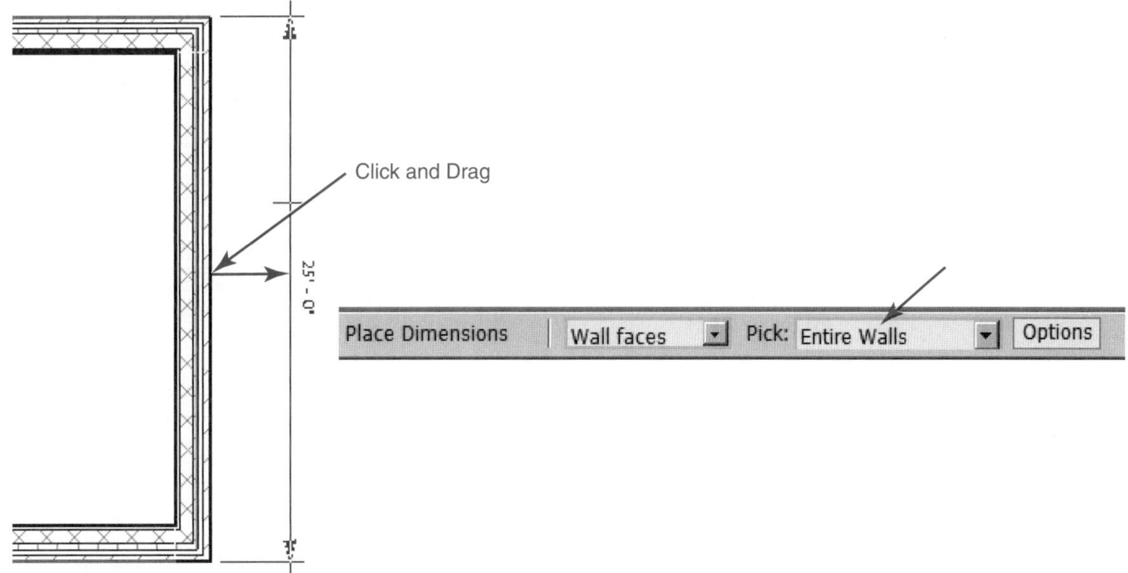

Figure 12-9

Click and drag to place dimensions

21. In the **Options Bar**, with the **Entire Walls** pick still chosen, press the **Options** button to bring up the **Auto Dimension Options** dialog box (see Figure 12-10).
22. In the **Auto Dimension Options** dialog box, select the **Centers** radio button.
23. Add a door to your enclosure, and place a dimension in the wall.
24. Add another door, select the **Options** button, select the **Widths** radio button this time, and place a dimension (see Figure 12-11).

> **NOTE:**
> The **Dimension Options** button on the **Options Bar** appears only when **Entire Walls** is selected from the **Pick** drop-down list.

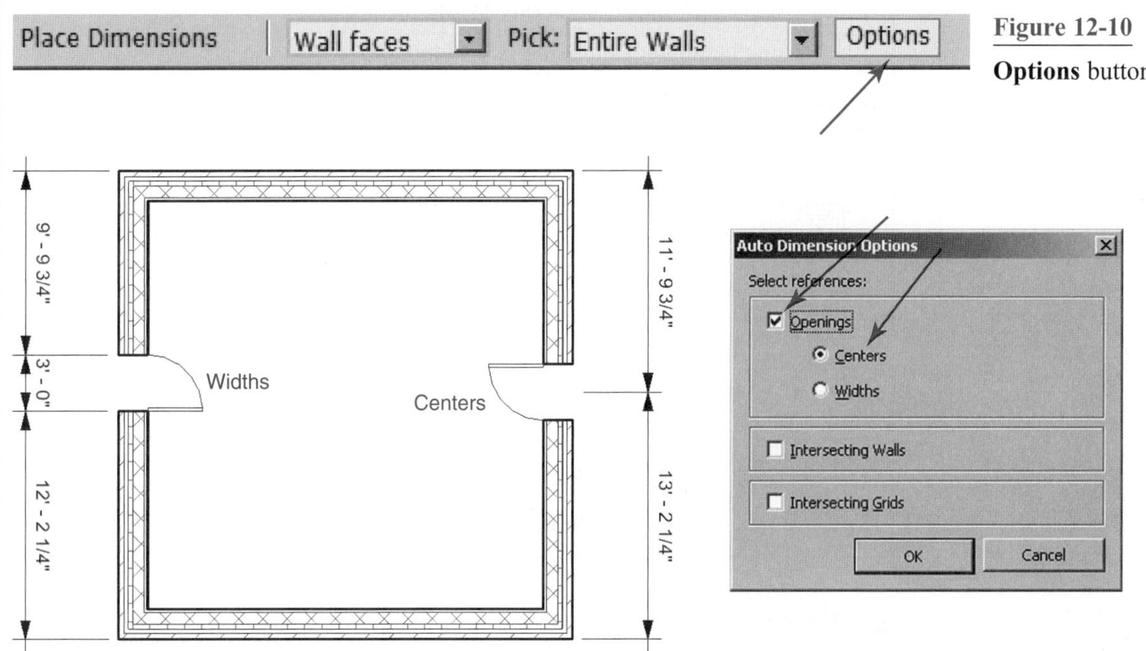

Figure 12-10

Options button

Figure 12-11

Auto Dimension options

25. Select the dimension string you just placed for the **Openings Centers** of a door.
26. Notice the blue **EQ** symbol that has been crossed out.
27. Select the symbol to activate it. The door will become equally spaced between the end walls, and the dimension string will read **EQ** on both sides.
28. Select the blue **EQ** symbol again to deactivate it (remove the constraints); the dimension string will now read as dimensions (see Figure 12-12).

NOTE:

When you deactivate the **EQ**, you remove the automatic constraint. If you move the walls, the equality will no longer work.

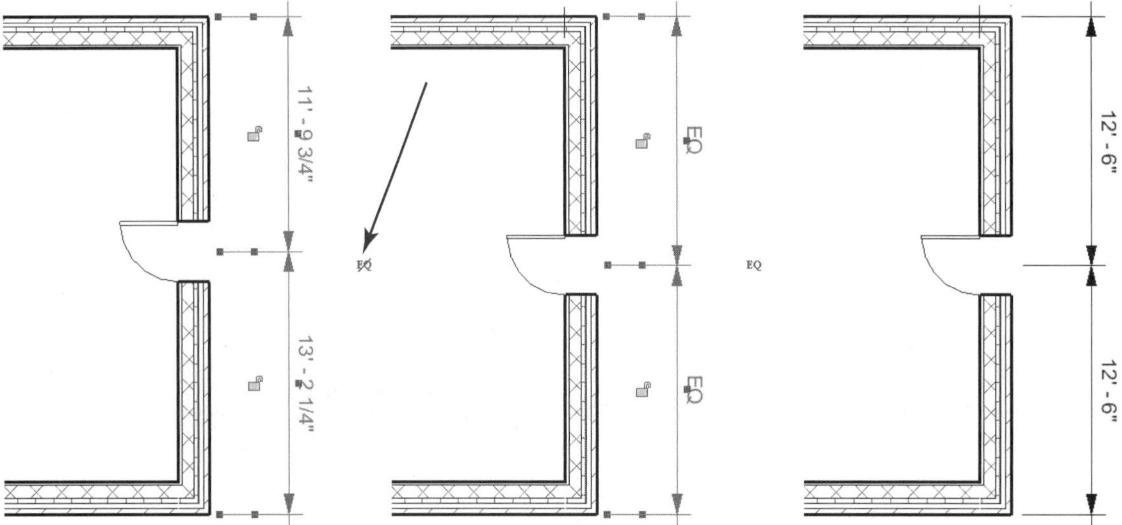

Figure 12-12

Dimension strings

29. Select the **Options** button again, activate the **Auto Dimension Options** dialog box, and check the **Intersecting Walls** check box.
30. Add another dimension string (see Figure 12-13).

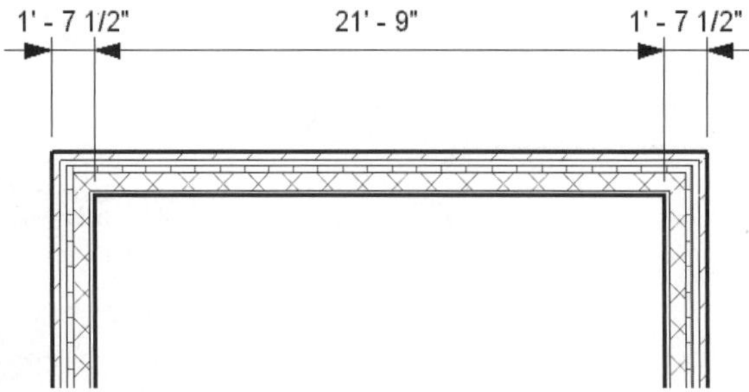

Figure 12-13

Add another dimension string

31. Save this file as **DIMENSIONS**.

Spot Dimensions Tool

Spot dimensions display the elevation of a selected point. You can place them in **Plan**, **Elevation**, and **3D** views. They are typically used to obtain a point of elevation for ramps, roads, Toposurfaces, and stair landings.

EXERCISE 12-2 **USING THE SPOT DIMENSIONS TOOL**

1. Start a new project using the RAC 2012\Imperial Templates\default.rte template.
2. In the **Project Browser**, double-click **Floor Plans > Level 1** to bring it into the **Drawing Editor**.
3. Set the **Scale** to **1/8″ = 1′-0″**.
4. In the **View Control Bar**, select the **Model Graphics Style > Wireframe** button (see Figure 12-14).

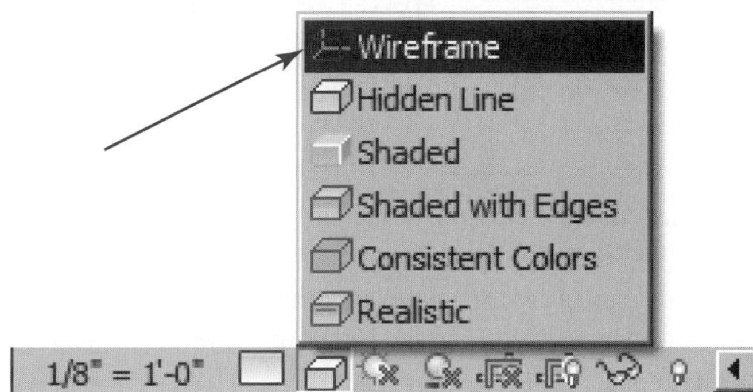

Figure 12-14
Wireframe button

5. In the **Home** toolbar, select the **Wall** button to bring up the **Modify | Place Wall** toolbar.
6. In the **Modify | Place Wall** toolbar, select the **Line** button in the **Draw** panel.
7. Place a **15′-0″** long, **20′-0″** high **Basic Wall: Generic - 8″** wall from left to right horizontally.
8. Add a stair run (settings do not matter), and delete the railing.
9. Change to the **South Elevation** view.
10. Add windows and doors as shown in Figure 12-15.

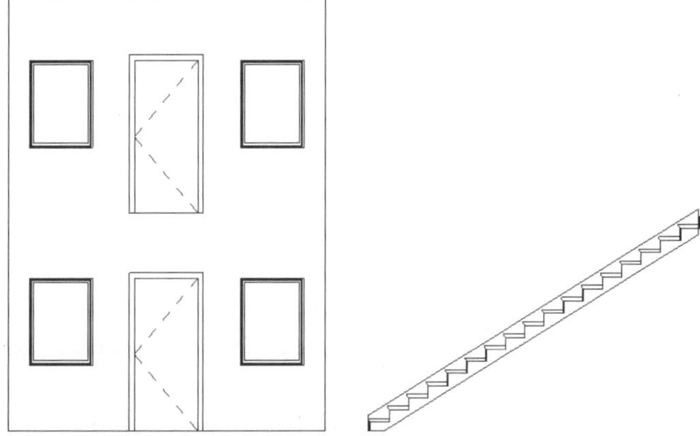

Figure 12-15
Add windows and doors

11. Select the **Annotate** tab to bring up the **Annotate** toolbar.
12. In the **Annotate** toolbar, select the **Spot Elevation** button to bring up the **Spot Elevation** toolbar (see Figure 12-16).

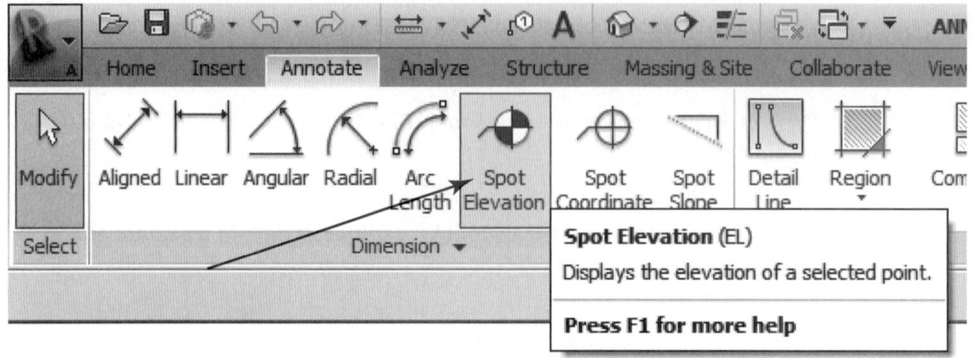

Figure 12-16

Spot Elevation button

13. Select the top of the lower door, click, drag to the left, click again, drag horizontally, and click to place the **Spot Elevation**.
14. In the **Spot Elevation** toolbar, select the **Spot Coordinate** button.
15. Select the top of the upper left window, click, drag to the left, click again, drag horizontally, and click to place the **Spot Coordinate**.
16. In the **Spot Coordinate** toolbar, select the **Spot Elevation** button.
17. Select one of the stair treads, click, drag to the left, click again, drag horizontally, and click to place the **Spot Elevation** (see Figure 12-17).

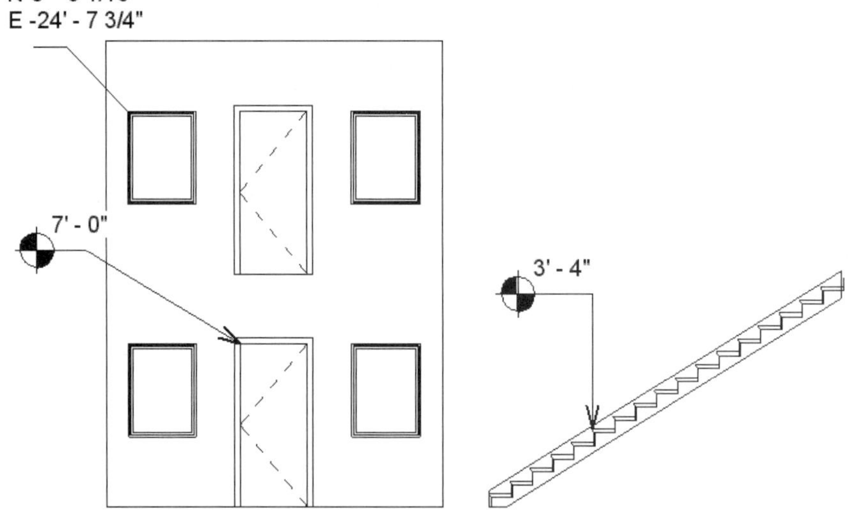

Figure 12-17

Click and drag to move elements

18. Select the spot elevation you placed for the door to bring up the **Properties** dialog box.
19. In the **Properties** dialog box, press the **Edit Type** button at the top right of the dialog box to bring up the **Type Properties** dialog box.
20. In the **Type Properties** dialog box, put your name in the **Elevation Indicator** field, and press the **OK** buttons to return to the **Drawing Editor**. Notice that your name precedes the **Spot Dimension** (you may have to select the dimension itself and move it upward if it blocks the **Spot Elevation** symbol).
21. Again, select the spot elevation you placed, and bring up the **Type Properties** dialog box.

22. This time, change the **Indicator as Prefix / Suffix** field to **Suffix**, and press the **OK** buttons to return to the **Drawing Editor**. Again, notice that your name comes after the **Spot Elevation**.
23. Select the **3D** button from the **Quick Access** toolbar to change to the **Default 3D View**.
24. Select the wall to bring up the **Modify | Walls** toolbar.
25. In the **Modify | Walls** toolbar, select the **Rotate** button.
26. Click on the wall, and rotate it. Notice that the **Spot Elevation > Coordinate** for the window changes (see Figure 12-18).

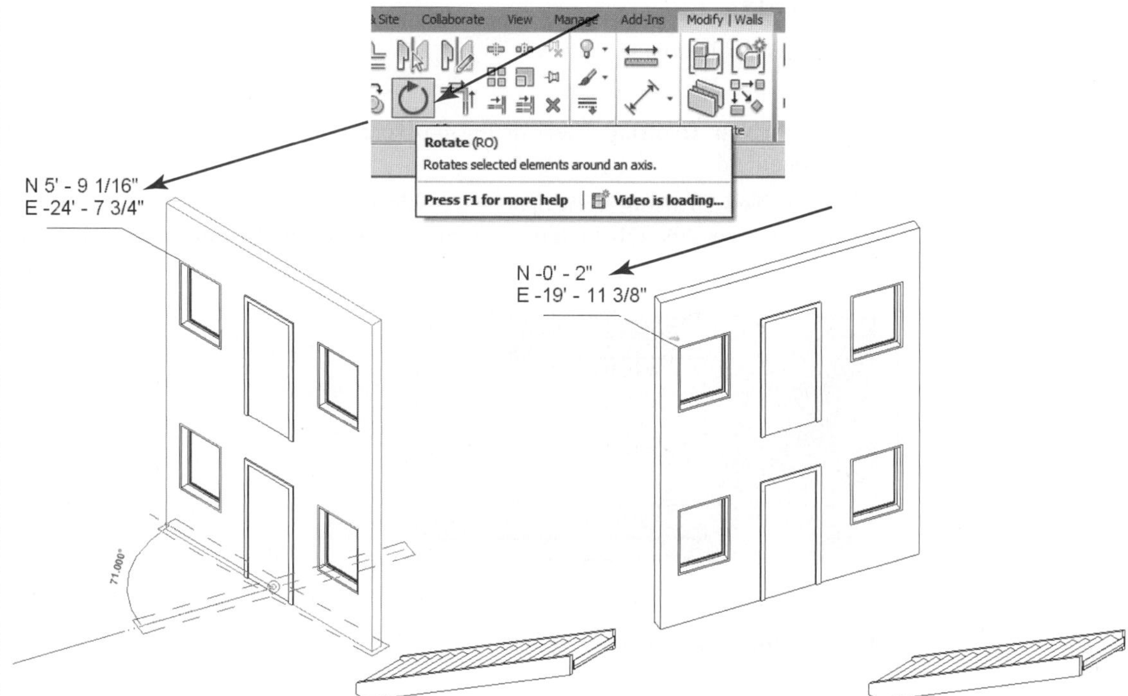

Figure 12-18

Rotate the wall

27. Continue to select the spot dimensions you placed, and change their **Type Properties** to see their effects.
28. Save this file as **SPOT DIMENSIONS**.

Text Tool

If you use a word processor such as Microsoft Word, Revit Architecture's **Text** tool should be quite easy to learn.

EXERCISE 12-3 USING THE TEXT TOOL

1. Start a new project using the RAC 2012\Imperial Templates\default.rte template.
2. Select the **View** tab to bring up the **View** toolbar.
3. In the **View** toolbar, select the **Drafting View** button to bring up the **New Drafting View** dialog box (see Figure 12-19).

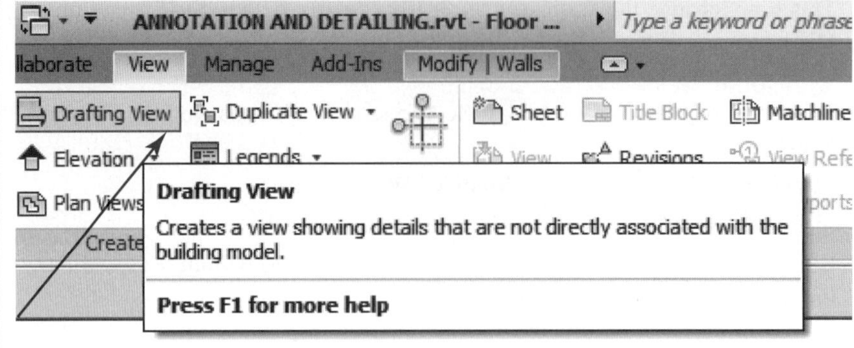

Figure 12-19

Drafting View button

4. In the **New Drafting View** dialog box, enter **TEST ANNOTATIONS** in the **Name** field.
5. In the **New Drafting View** dialog box, select **1″ = 1′-0″** from the **Scale** drop-down list, and press the **OK** button to return to the **Drawing Editor** (see Figure 12-20).

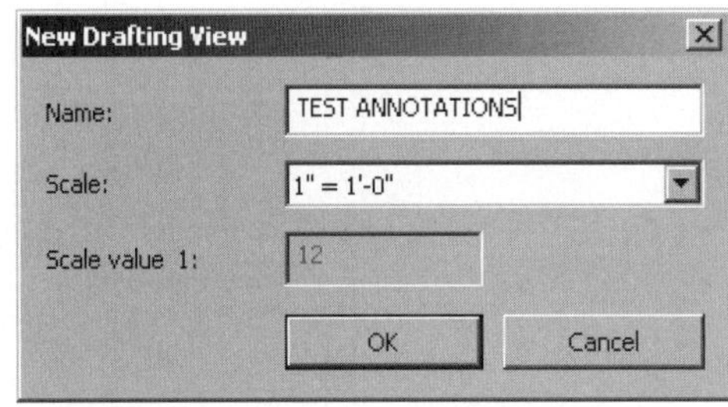

Figure 12-20

New Drafting View dialog box

6. Select the **Annotate** tab to bring up the **Annotate** toolbar.
7. In the **Annotate** toolbar, select the **Text** button in the **Text** panel to bring up the **Modify | Place Text** toolbar (see Figure 12-21).

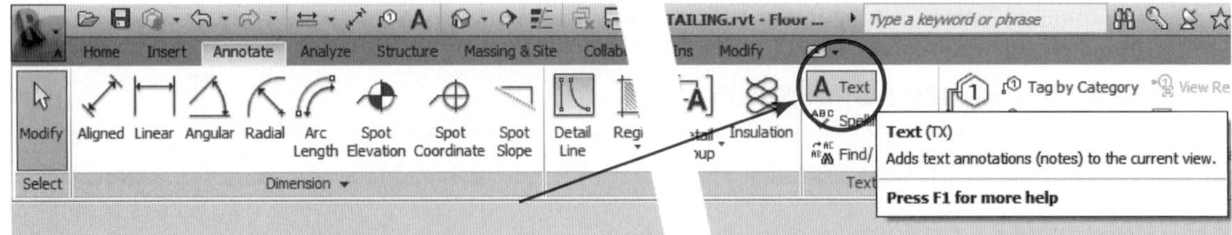

Figure 12-21

Text button

8. Select **Text 3/32″ Arial** from the **Properties** drop-down list in the **Properties** dialog box.
9. In the **Modify | Place Text** toolbar, select the **Align Left** button in the **Format** panel, and then select the **No Leader** button in the **Format** panel (see Figure 12-22).
10. Click in the drafting view, drag diagonally to the right, and click again to create a word field.

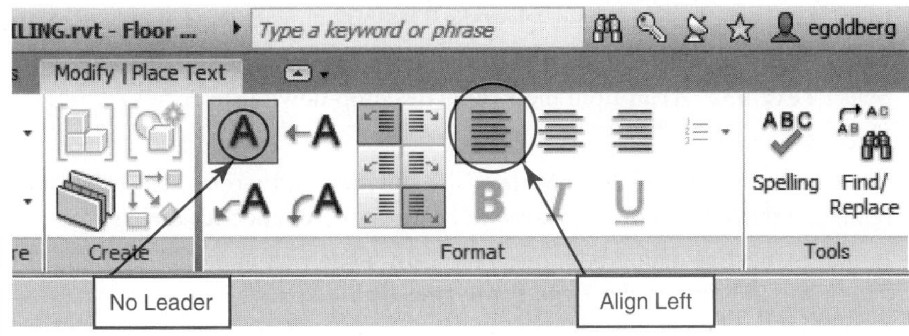

Figure 12-22

Align Left and **No Leader** buttons

11. Enter **Now is the time for all good drafts people to use Revit** in the text field. If this takes two lines, the field needs to be stretched.
12. Drag the **Text** field until your statement is on two lines (see Figure 12-23).
13. With the **Text** field still selected, select the **Rotate** icon and rotate the **Text** field (see Figure 12-24).

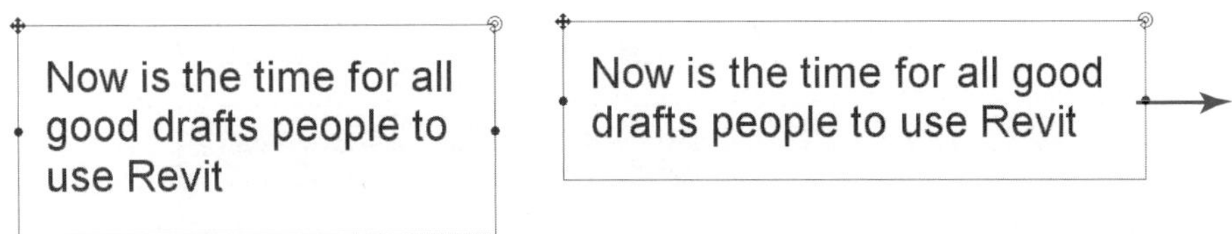

Figure 12-23

Enter text in the **Text** field

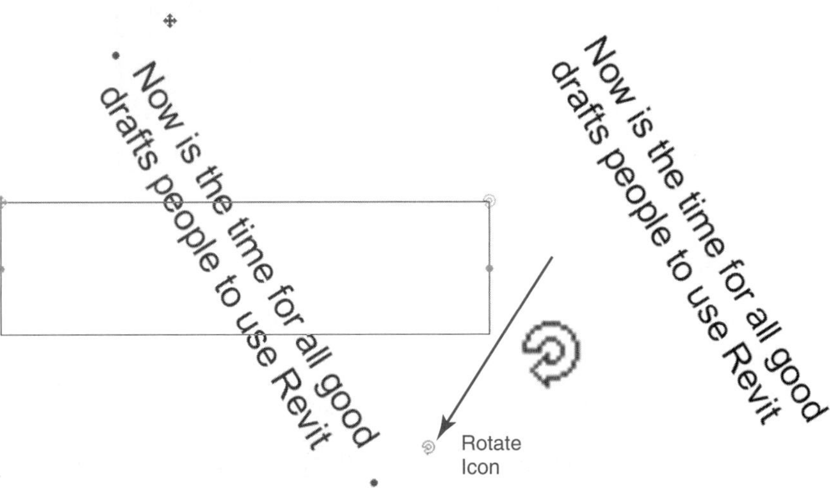

Figure 12-24

Rotate text

14. Select the text field to bring up the **Modify | Text Notes** toolbar.
15. In the **Modify | Text Notes** toolbar, select all the text, and then select the **B** (bold) button in the **Format** panel.

> **NOTE:**
> The **Text** field is the text you just placed.

16. With the **Text** field still selected, select the ***I*** (italic) and **U** (underline) tools.
17. Click twice in an empty space in the drafting view to end the command and return to the **Annotate** toolbar.

18. In the **Annotate** toolbar, again select the **Text** button from the **Text** panel to bring up the **Modify | Place Text** toolbar.
19. Select **Text 3/32″ Arial** from the **Properties** drop-down list.
20. Place text again.
21. If you want to change the font, text size, arrows, and so on, select the outside outline of the **Text** field you placed to bring up the **Properties** dialog box.
22. In the **Properties** dialog box, press the **Edit Type** button at the top right of the dialog box to bring up the **Type Properties** dialog box.
23. In the **Type Properties** dialog box, select **Arrow Filled 30 Degree** from the **Leader Arrowhead** drop-down list, and press the **OK** buttons to return to the **Modify | Text Notes** toolbar (see Figure 12-25).

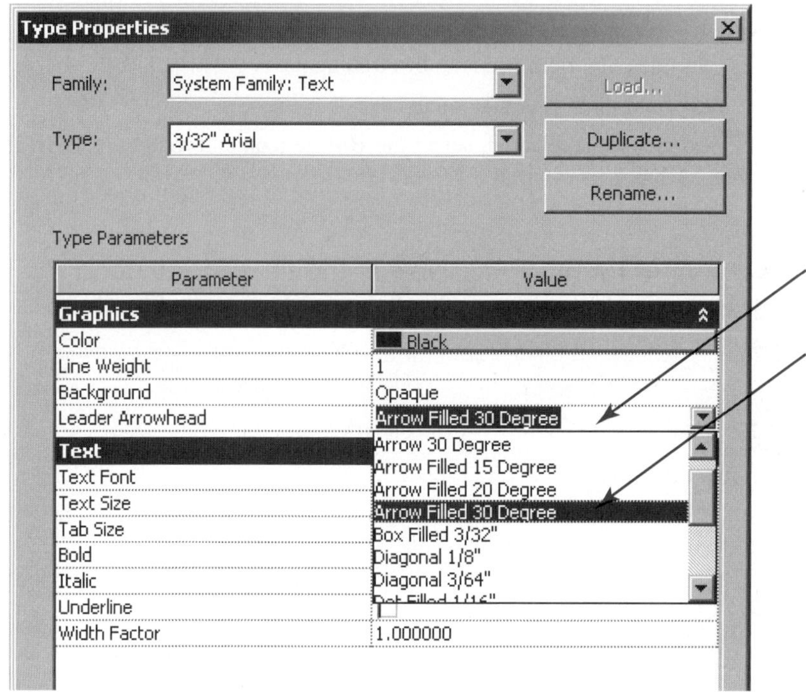

Figure 12-25

Type Properties dialog box

24. In the **Modify | Text Notes** toolbar, select the **Add Left Side Straight Leader** button (see Figure 12-26).

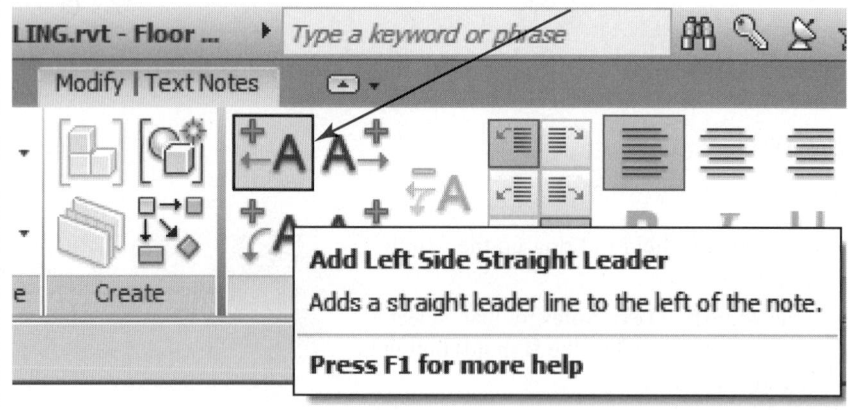

Figure 12-26

Add Left Side Straight Leader button

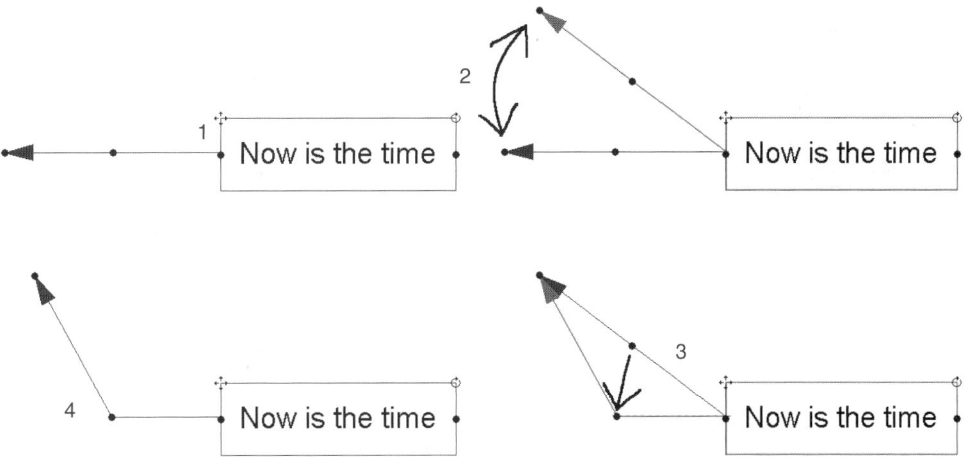

Figure 12-27
Adjust leaders

25. A leader and an arrow will appear at the left of the text field.
26. Select the points shown in Figure 12-27 to adjust the leader.
27. In the **Modify | Text Notes** toolbar, select the **Remove Last Leader** button in the **Leader** panel to remove the last leader you placed from the selected **Text** field (see Figure 12-28).
28. Save this file as **USING TEXT**.

NOTE:
You can place multiple arrows from any side, and drag any leader 360 degrees around the **Text** field. The **Arc Leaders** work in a similar manner to the **Straight Leaders**. You cannot have both **Straight** and **Arc Leaders** from a **Text** field (see Figure 12-29).

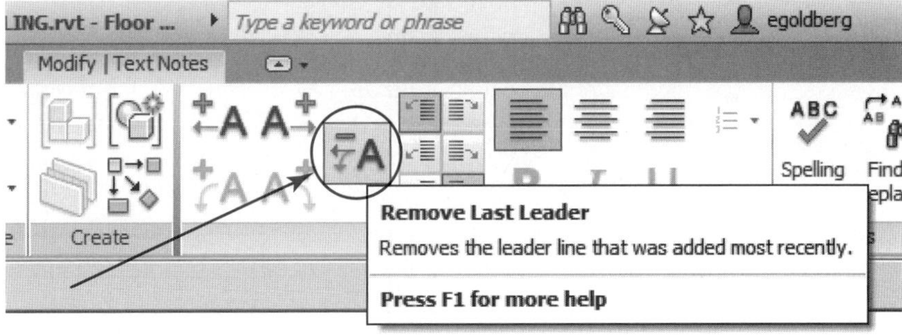

Figure 12-28
Remove Last Leader button

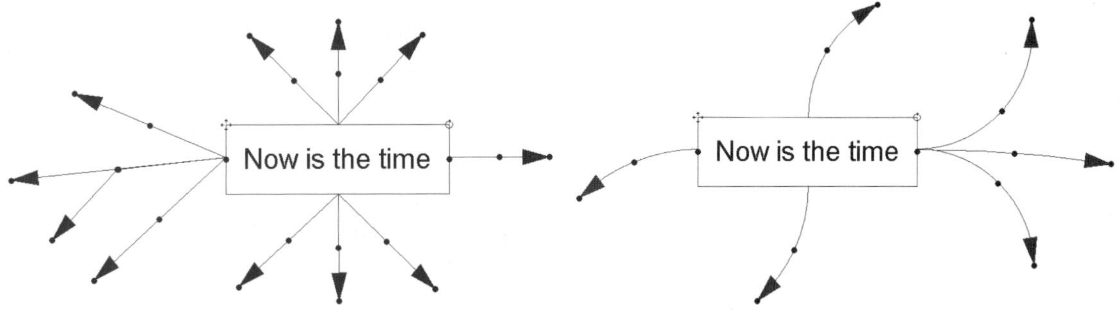

Figure 12-29
Straight and **Arc Leaders**

Tag Tool

Tags can be attached to an element based on the element category or the type of material and can be used on multiple elements in one operation.

EXERCISE 12-4 HOW TO USE THE TAG BY CATEGORY TOOL

1. Start a new project using the RAC 2012\Imperial Templates\default.rte template.
2. In the **Project Browser**, double-click **Floor Plans > Level 1** to bring it into the **Drawing Editor**.
3. Set the **Scale** to **1/4″ = 1′-0″**.
4. Change the **Detail Level** to **Medium**.
5. In the **Home** toolbar, select the **Wall** button to bring up the **Modify | Place Wall** toolbar.
6. In the **Modify | Place Wall** toolbar, select the **Rectangle** button in the **Draw** panel.
7. Place an **Exterior – Brick on CMU** wall **25′-0″** long, **25′-0″** wide, and **10′-0″** high.
8. Select the **Door** and **Window** buttons to bring up their respective **Modify | Place** toolbars.
9. In their respective **Modify | Place** toolbars, unselect the **Tag on Placement** button.
10. Place doors and windows as shown (with no tags) in Figure 12-30.

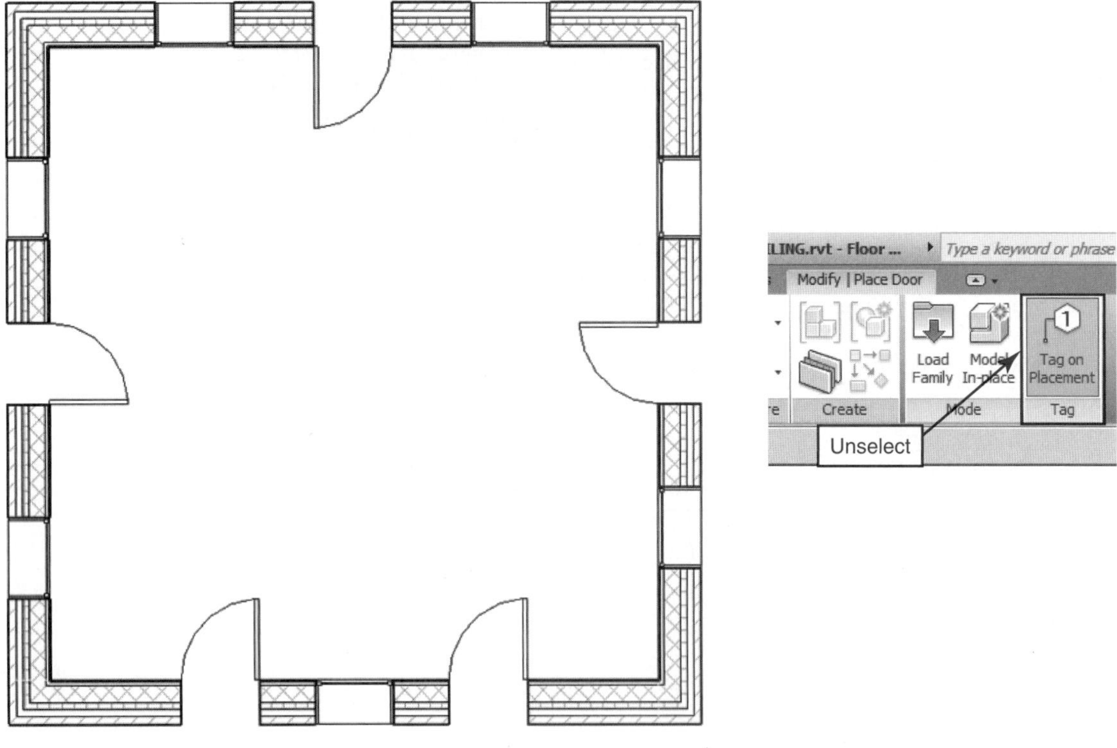

Figure 12-30

Unselect all tags

11. Select the **Annotate** tab to bring up the **Annotate** toolbar.
12. In the **Annotate** toolbar, select the **Tag by Category** button (Figure 12-31).
13. In the **Options Bar**, select **Horizontal** from the drop-down list, and uncheck the **Leader** check box.
14. Click on a window and then a door to place their tags.
15. Select the **Tag by Category** button again.

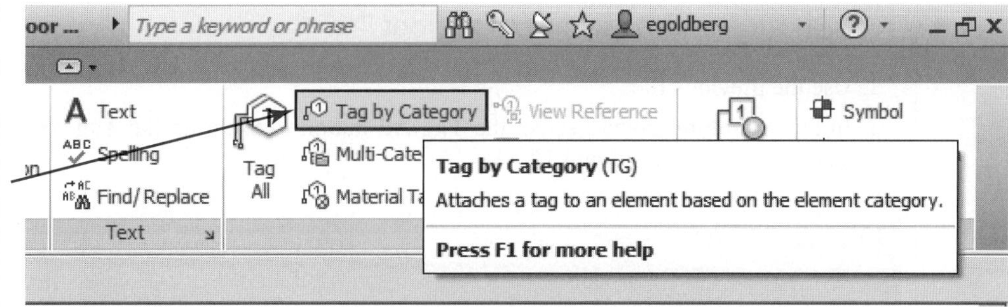

Figure 12-31

Tag by Category button

16. In the **Options Bar**, select the **Tags** button to bring up the **Tags** dialog box.
17. In the **Tags** dialog box, press the **Load** button, load the **Wall** tag from the **Annotations** > **Architectural** folder of the **Imperial Library**, and press the **OK** button to return to the **Drawing Editor**.
18. In the **Options Bar**, check the **Leader** check box, select **Attached End** from the drop-down list, and enter **1/2″** in the **Number** field.
19. Select each wall, and place a **Wall** tag.
20. Select a wall to bring up its **Properties** dialog box.
21. In the **Properties** dialog box, press the **Edit Type** button to bring up the **Type Properties** dialog box.
22. In the **Type Properties** dialog box, enter **A** in the **Type Mark** field, and press the **OK** buttons to return to the **Drawing Editor**.
23. Move over a wall, and the **Wall** tag will appear; click to place the tag (see Figure 12-32).
24. Save this file as **TAG BY CATEGORY**.

NOTE:

The tag will be empty. This is because the walls have not been given a type letter or number.

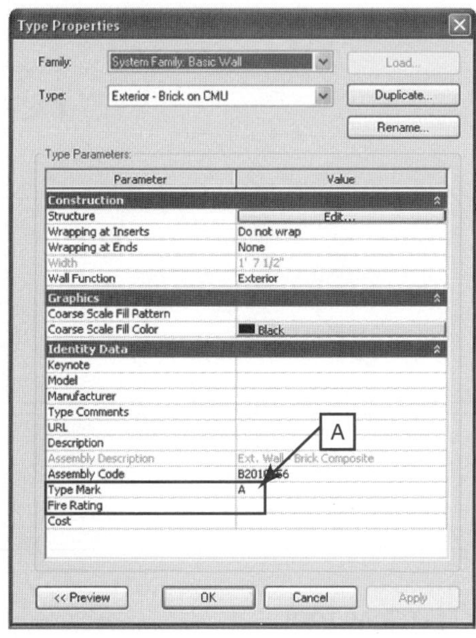

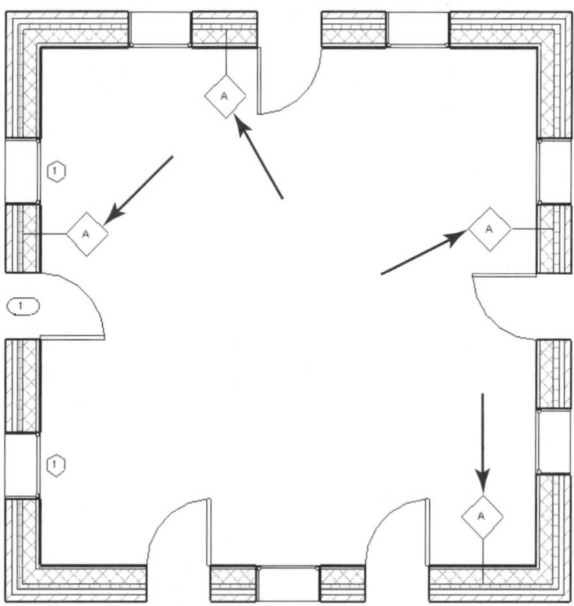

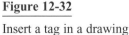

Figure 12-32

Insert a tag in a drawing

EXERCISE 12-5 **HOW TO USE THE TAG ALL TOOL**

1. Use the previous file.
2. In the **Annotate** toolbar, select the **Tag All** button to bring up the **Tag All Not Tagged** dialog box (Figure 12-33).

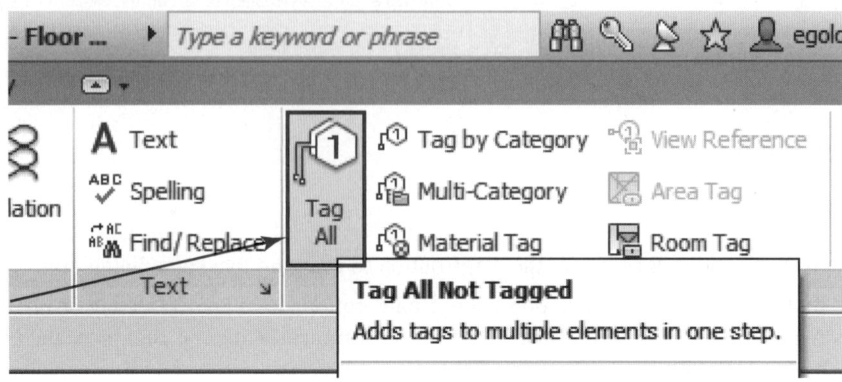

Figure 12-33

Tag All button

3. In the **Tag All Not Tagged** dialog box, select the **All objects in current view** radio button and the **Door Tag** field, and press the **Apply** button.
4. Repeat the process for the **Window Tag**, press the **Apply** button again, and then press the **OK** button to return to the **Drawing Editor** (see Figure 12-34).

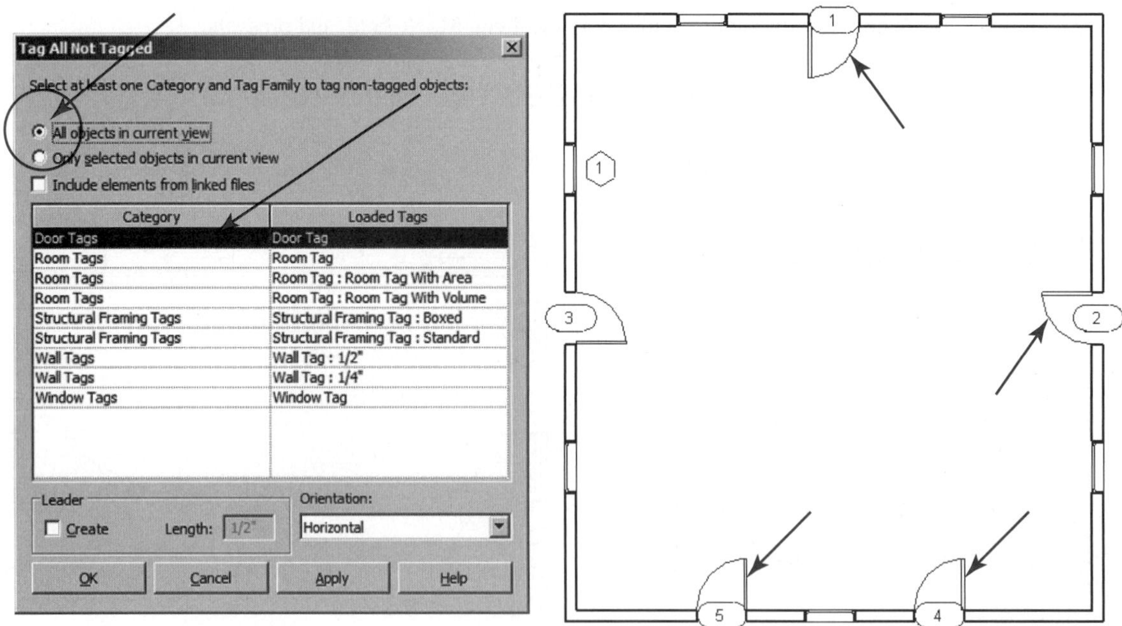

Figure 12-34

Apply **Tag All Not Tagged** option

EXERCISE 12-6 **HOW TO USE THE TAG BY MATERIAL TOOL**

1. Select the **Manage** tab to bring up the **Manage** toolbar.
2. In the **Manage** toolbar, select the **Materials** button to bring up the **Materials** dialog box (see Figure 12-35).

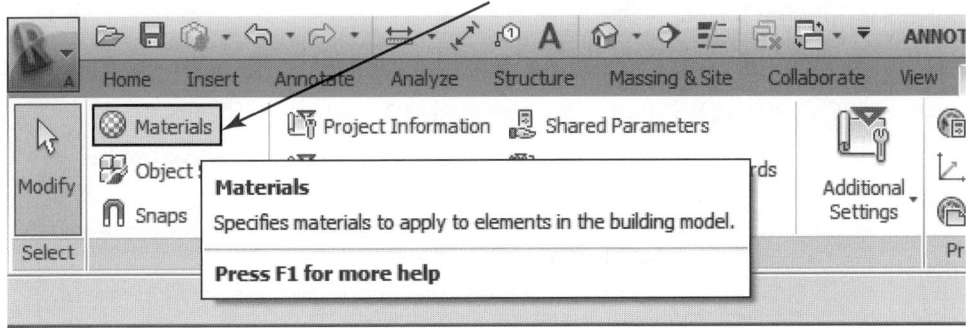

Figure 12-35

Materials button

3. In the **Materials** dialog box, select **Masonry – Brick**.
4. In the **Materials** dialog box, select the **Identity** tab.
5. In the **Identity** tab, enter **BRICK WALL** in the **Description Information** field (see Figure 12-36).

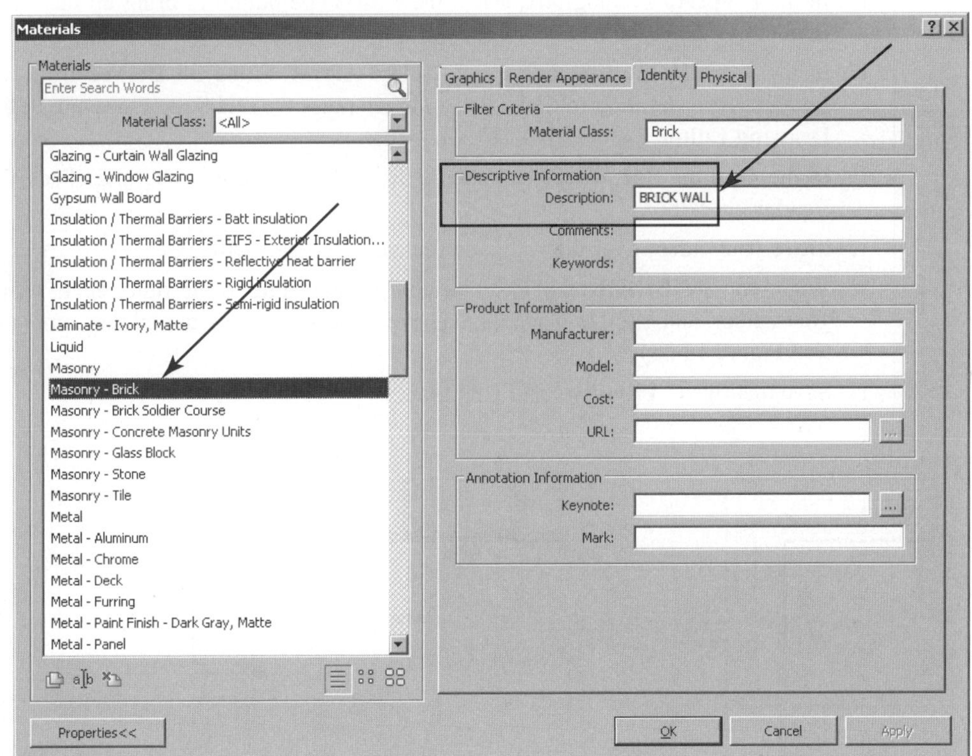

Figure 12-36

Materials dialog box

6. Repeat this process for **Masonry – Concrete Masonry Units**, entering **CMU** in the **Description** field.
7. Repeat this process for **Insulation / Thermal Barriers – Rigid Insulation**, entering **Rigid Insulation** in the **Description** field.
8. Repeat this process for **Metal – Furring**, entering **Metal Furring** in the **Description** field.
9. Press the **OK** button to return to the **Drawing Editor**.
10. Select the **Annotate** tab to bring up the **Annotate** toolbar.

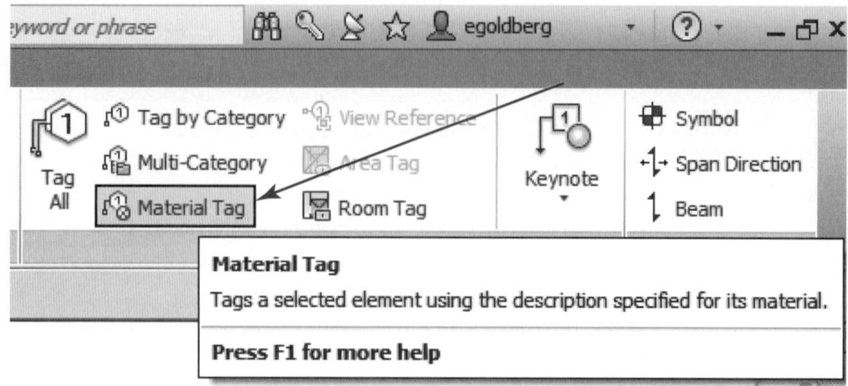

Figure 12-37

Material Tag button

11. In the **Annotate** toolbar, select the **Material Tag** button in the **Tag** panel to bring up the **Modify | Tag Material** toolbar (see Figure 12-37).
12. In the **Properties** dialog box, select the **Edit Type** button to bring up the **Type Properties** dialog box.
13. In the **Type Properties** dialog box, select **Arrow Filled 30 Degree** from the **Leader Arrowhead** drop-down list, and then press the **OK** button to return to the **Drawing Editor**.
14. In the **Options Bar**, select **Horizontal** from the drop-down list, and check the **Leader** check box.
15. Move your cursor over the wall, and the wall materials will appear.
16. When you see **BRICK** appear, click your mouse, drag to the right, click, move your cursor, and click to place the tag. Press the **<Esc>** key to end the command (see Figure 12-38).
17. Save this file as **TAG by MATERIAL**.

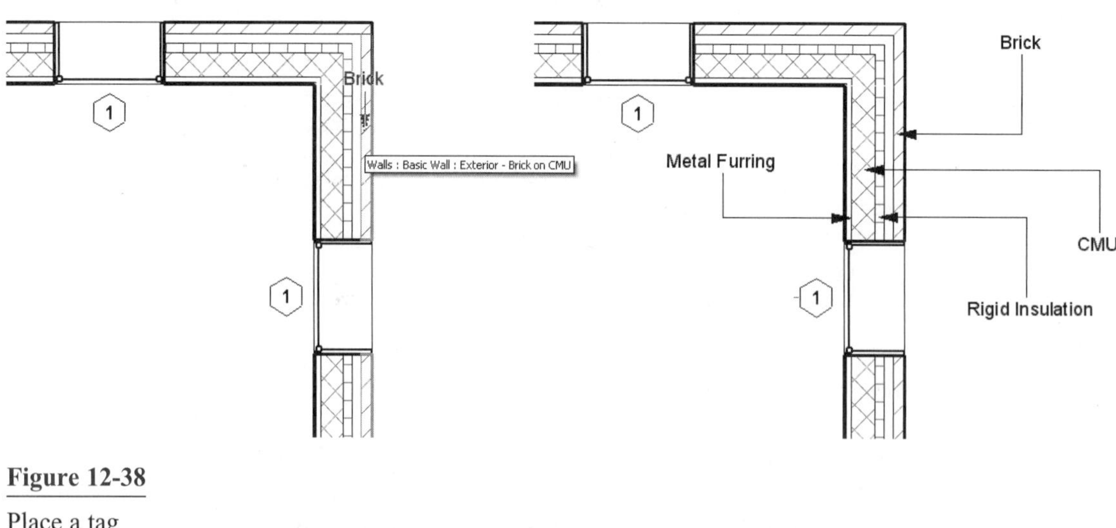

Figure 12-38

Place a tag

Symbol Tool

The **Symbol** tool places 2D annotation drawing symbols into the project.

EXERCISE 12-7 HOW TO USE THE SYMBOL TOOL

1. Start a new project using the RAC 2012\Imperial Templates\default.rte template.
2. Save the project as **REVIT SYMBOLS**.
3. Select the **View** tab to bring up the **View** toolbar.
4. In the **View** toolbar, select the **Drafting View** button to bring up the **New Drafting View** dialog box.
5. In the **New Drafting View** dialog box, select **1/4″ = 1′-0″** from the **Scale** drop-down list, and press the **OK** button to bring the **Drafting View** into the **Drawing Editor**.
6. Select the **Annotate** tab to bring up the **Annotate** toolbar.
7. In the **Annotate** toolbar, select the **Symbol** button to bring up the **Modify | Place Symbol** toolbar (see Figure 12-39).

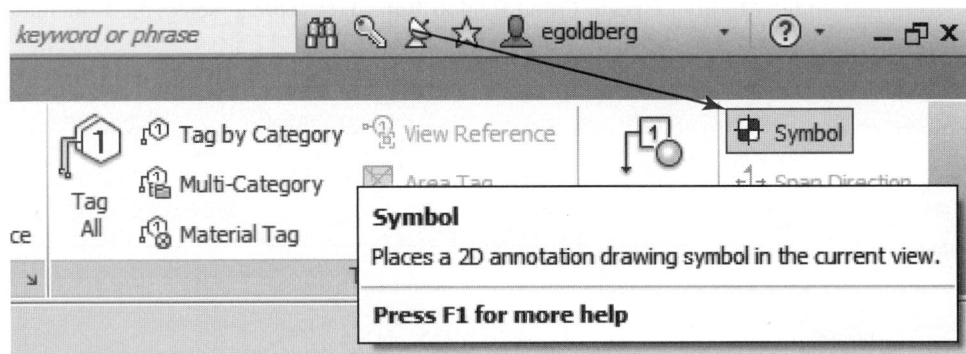

Figure 12-39
Symbol button

8. In the **Modify | Place Symbol** toolbar, press the **Load Family** button to bring up the **Load Family** dialog box.
9. In the **Load Family** dialog box, select **North Arrow 1** from the **Annotations** folder in the **Imperial Library**, and press the **Open** button to return to the **Drawing Editor**.
10. In the **Properties** dialog box, select the **Type Properties** button to bring up the **Type Properties** dialog box.
11. In the **Type Properties** dialog box, select **Arrow Filled 30 Degree** from the **Leader Arrowhead** drop-down list, and then press the **OK** buttons to return to the **Drawing Editor**.
12. In the **Options Bar**, select **3** from the **Number of Leaders** field, and check the **Rotate after placement** check box.
13. Click in the **Drafting View** to place the **North Arrow 1** symbol.
14. Because you selected **3** leaders in the **Options Bar**, three leaders appear with the symbol.
15. Rotate the symbol, and adjust the leaders.
16. If you want to add or remove a leader, select the symbol to bring up the **Modify | Generic Annotations** toolbar.
17. In the **Modify | Generic Annotations** toolbar, select the **Add or Remove Leader** button in the **Leader** panel.
18. In the **Modify | Generic Annotations** toolbar, select the **Edit Family** button.

NOTE:
You are now in the **Family Editor** for the **North Arrow 1** symbol.

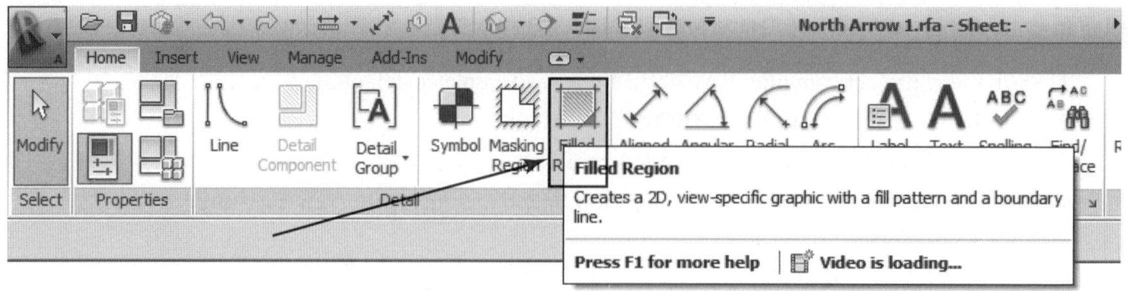

Figure 12-40

Filled Region button

19. In the **Home** toolbar, select the **Filled Region** button to bring up the **Modify | Create Filled Region Boundary** toolbar (see Figure 12-40).
20. In the **Modify | Create Filled Region Boundary** toolbar, select the **Line** button, and trace the arrowhead (see Figure 12-41).

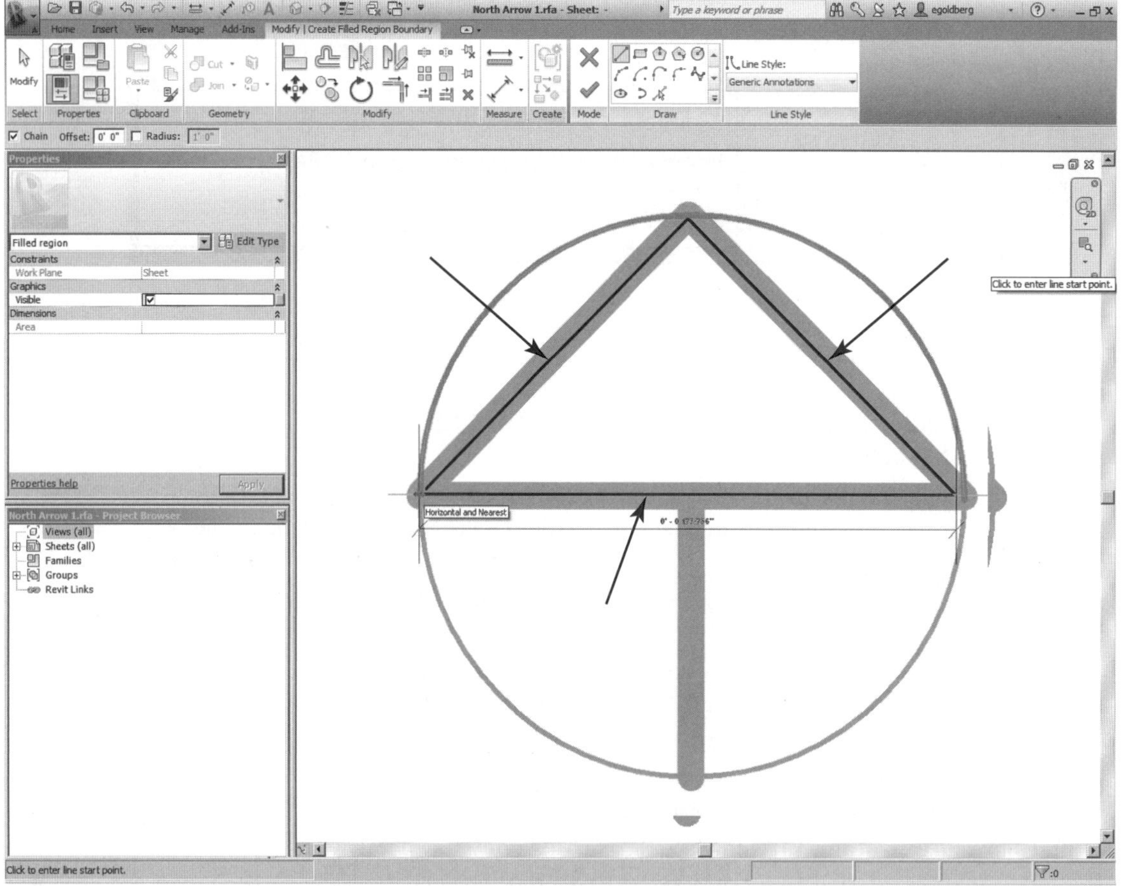

Figure 12-41

Trace the arrowhead

21. In the **Properties** dialog box, select the **Edit Type** button to bring up the **Type Properties** dialog box.
22. In the **Type Properties** dialog box, select the button to the right of **Diagonal crosshatch** in the **Cut fill pattern** field to open the **Fill Patterns** dialog box.
23. In the **Fill Patterns** dialog box, select the **Solid fill** pattern and press the **OK** buttons to return to the **Drawing Editor** (see Figure 12-42).

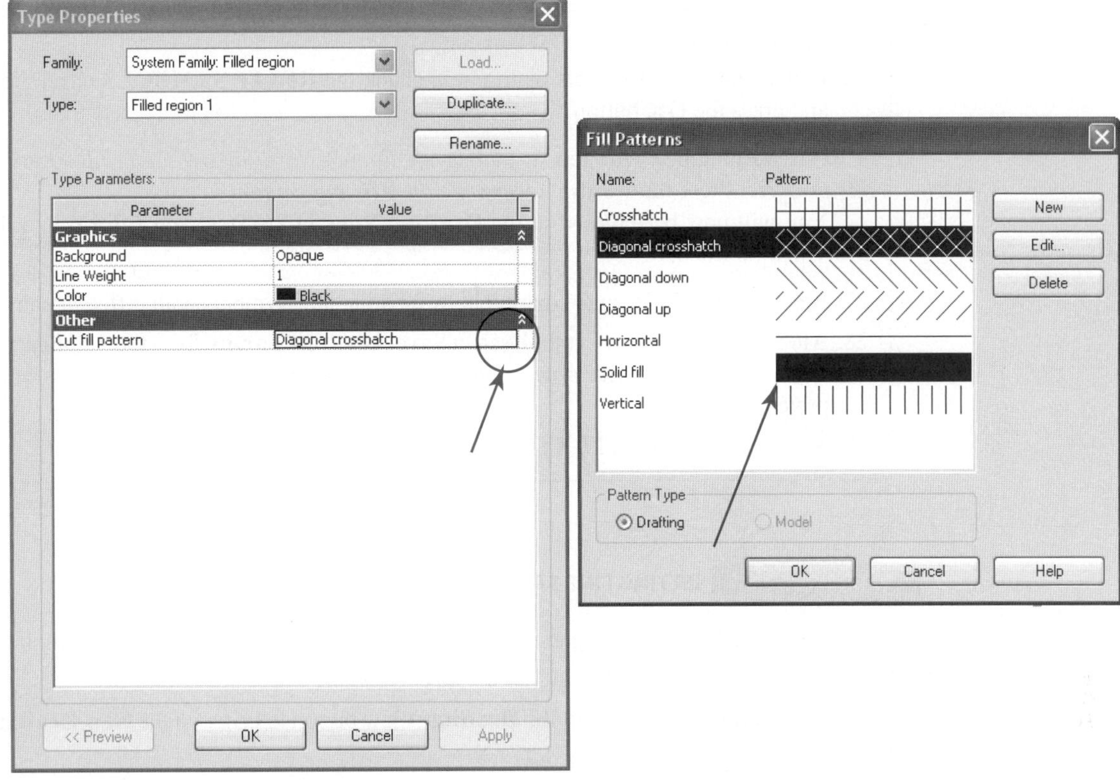

Figure 12-42

Fill Patterns dialog box

24. In the **Create Filled Region Boundary** toolbar, select the **Finish Edit Mode** button, and click in an empty place in the **Drawing Editor** to complete the command (see Figure 12-43).

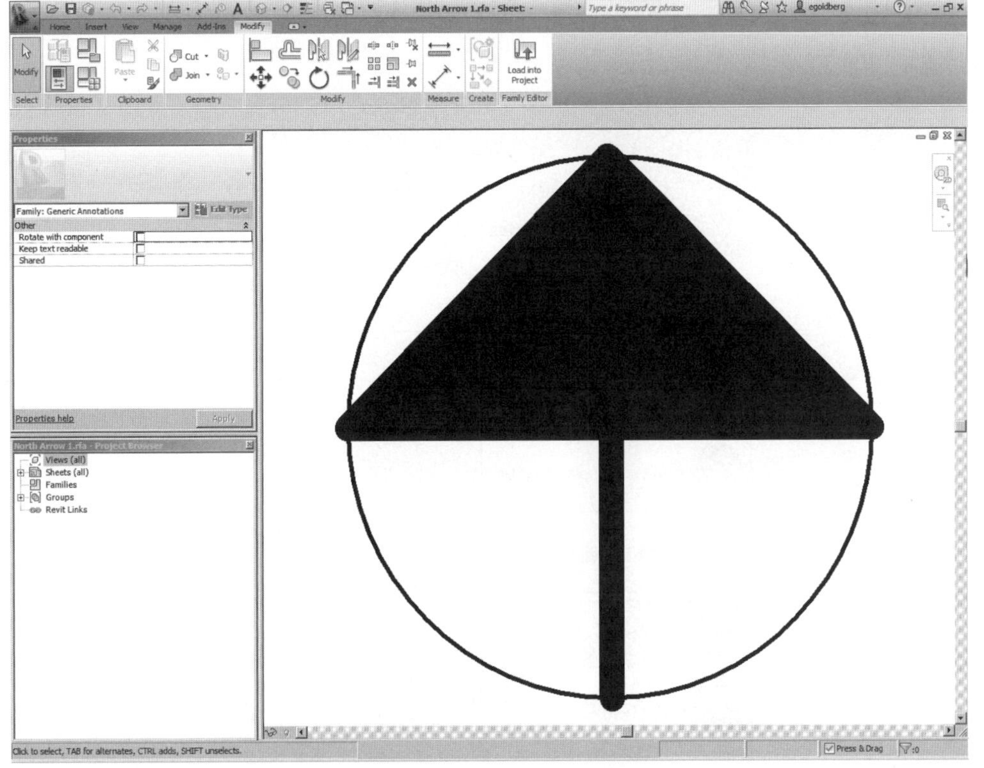

Figure 12-43

Filled arrowhead

25. Select the **Load into Project** button in the **Family Editor** panel to bring up the **Load into Projects** dialog box.
26. In the **Load into Projects** dialog box, check the **REVIT SYMBOLS** check box, and press the **OK** button.

A **Revit** warning box will appear that says, "*Family North arrow 1 already exists in this project.*" Press the words, "*Overwrite the existing version.*"

You will now be returned to the **Drafting View** in the **Drawing Editor**, and the arrow will be filled.

27. Repeat Steps 17–26, and experiment by creating new symbols with different names.
28. After you create a new symbol, select **Save As > New Family** from the **Application** menu, and save it with a new family name so that you can use it later on other projects.
29. Save this file as **REVIT SYMBOLS**.

EXERCISE 12-8 SETTING LINE STYLES, LINE WEIGHTS, AND LINE PATTERNS

1. Start a new project using the RAC 2012\Imperial Templates\default.rte template.
2. Select the **View** tab to bring up the **View** toolbar.
3. In the **View** toolbar, select the **Drafting View** button to bring up the **New Drafting View** dialog box.
4. In the **New Drafting View** dialog box, select **1/4″ = 1′-0″** from the **Scale** drop-down list, and press the **OK** button to bring the **Drafting View** into the **Drawing Editor**.
5. Select the **Manage** tab to bring up the **Manage** toolbar.
6. In the **Manage** toolbar, select the **Additional Settings > Line Styles** button to bring up the **Line Styles** dialog box (see Figure 12-44).

NOTE:
The **Line Styles** dialog box is where you create named line styles and set their colors and weights (width) (see Figure 12-45).

Figure 12-44
Additional Settings button

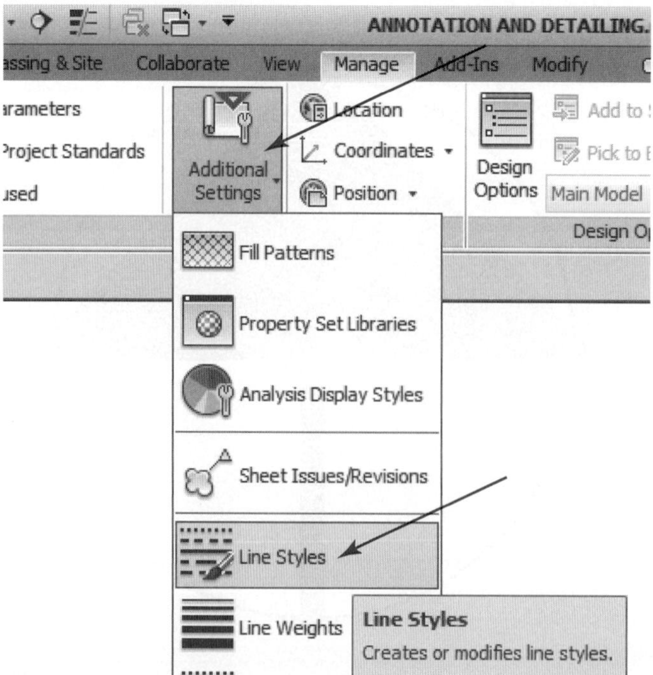

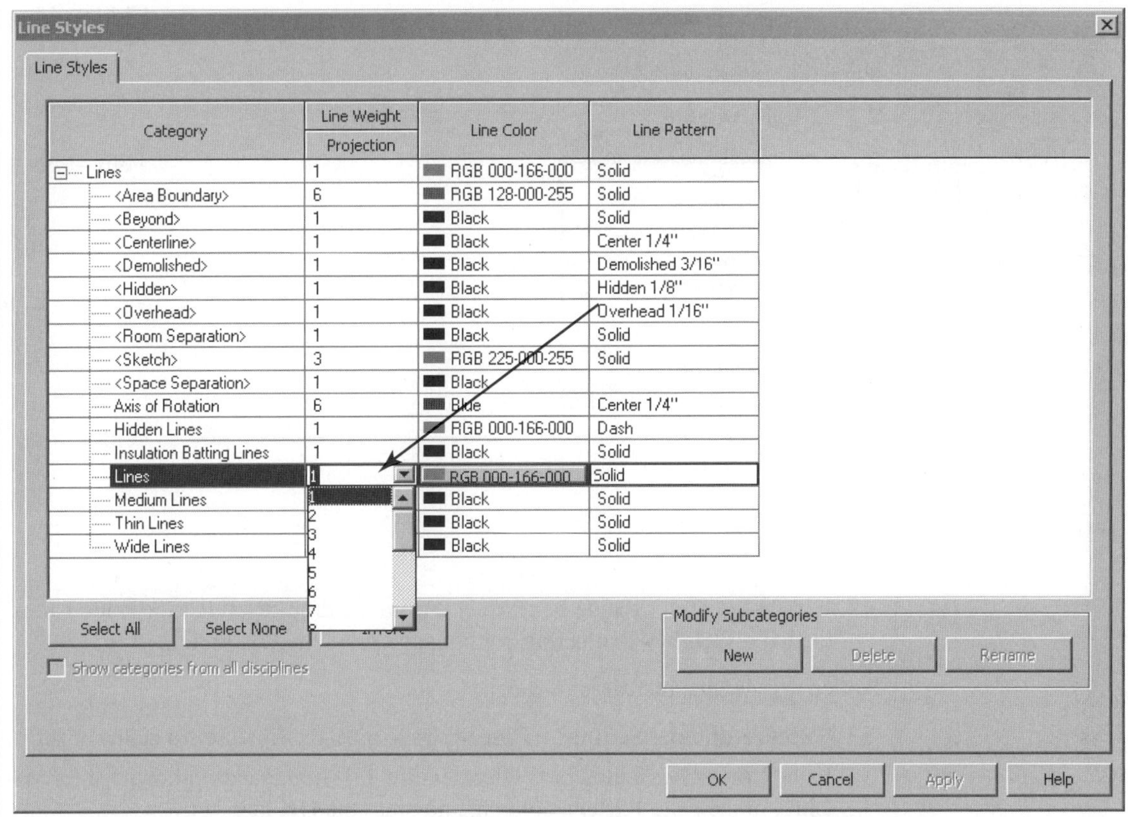

Category	Line Weight Projection	Line Color	Line Pattern
Lines	1	RGB 000-166-000	Solid
<Area Boundary>	6	RGB 128-000-255	Solid
<Beyond>	1	Black	Solid
<Centerline>	1	Black	Center 1/4"
<Demolished>	1	Black	Demolished 3/16"
<Hidden>	1	Black	Hidden 1/8"
<Overhead>	1	Black	Overhead 1/16"
<Room Separation>	1	Black	Solid
<Sketch>	3	RGB 225-000-255	Solid
<Space Separation>	1	Black	
Axis of Rotation	6	Blue	Center 1/4"
Hidden Lines	1	RGB 000-166-000	Dash
Insulation Batting Lines	1	Black	Solid
Lines	1	RGB 000-166-000	Solid
Medium Lines	1	Black	Solid
Thin Lines	2	Black	Solid
Wide Lines	3	Black	Solid

Figure 12-45

Line Styles dialog box

7. Select the **Annotate** tab to bring up the **Annotate** toolbar.
8. In the **Annotate** toolbar, select the **Detail Line** button in the **Detail** panel to bring up the **Modify | Place Detail Lines** toolbar (see Figure 12-46).
9. In the **Modify | Place Detail Lines** toolbar, select lines from the **Line Style** drop-down list.
10. Place four **1′-0″** long lines with the **Line Styles** shown in Figure 12-47.
11. Select additional **Settings > Line Styles** to open the **Line Styles** dialog box again.

> **NOTE:**
> Detail lines are not 3D but are used as you would use typical 2D CAD drawing lines.

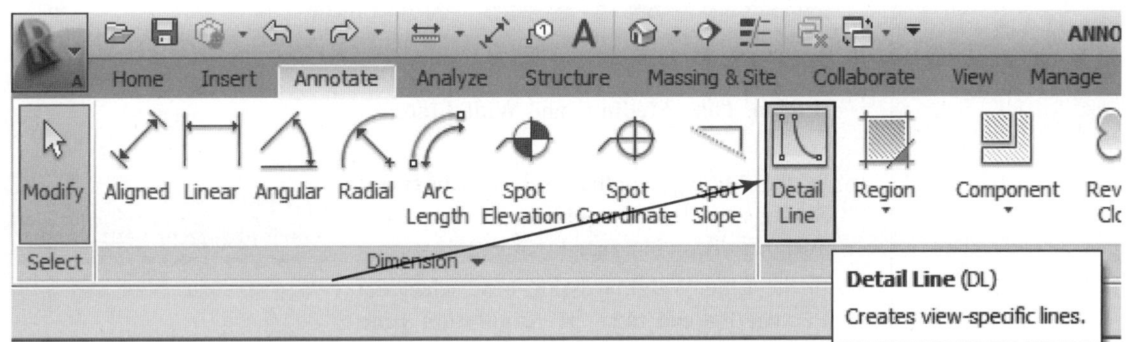

Figure 12-46

Detail Line button

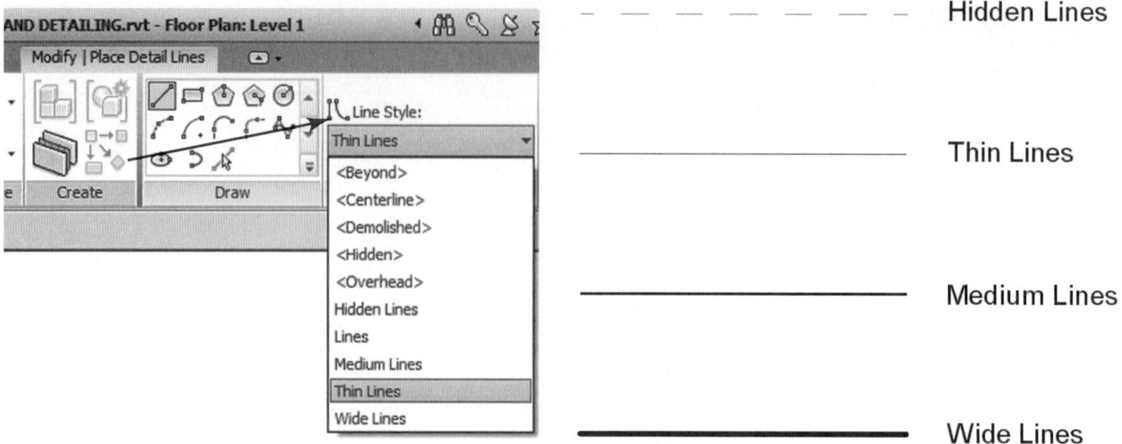

Figure 12-47

Detail Lines styles

12. In the **Line Styles** dialog box, select **8** from the drop-down list for **Wide Lines** in the **Line Weight / Projection** column, and press the **OK** button.

Notice that the line increases in weight.

13. Select **Additional Settings > Line Styles** to open the **Line Styles** dialog box again.
14. In the **Line Styles** dialog box, select **Center 1/4″** from the drop-down list for **Wide Lines** in the **Line Pattern** column, and press the **OK** button.
15. Repeat this process, changing the various settings for the **Hidden**, **Thin**, and **Medium Lines** (see Figure 12-48).

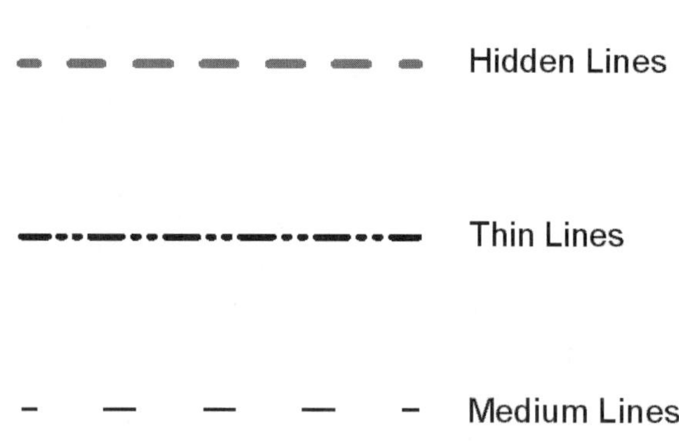

Figure 12-48

Hidden, **Thin**, **Medium,** and **Wide Lines**

16. In the **Manage** toolbar, select **Additional Settings > Line Weights** to open the **Line Weights** dialog box (see Figure 12-49).
17. In the **Line Weights** dialog box, select the **Perspective** and then the **Annotation Line Weights** tabs.

> **NOTE:**
> Revit Architecture 2012 ships with 16 line weights.

These tabs allow you to have unlimited line weight control over different types of views and annotations.

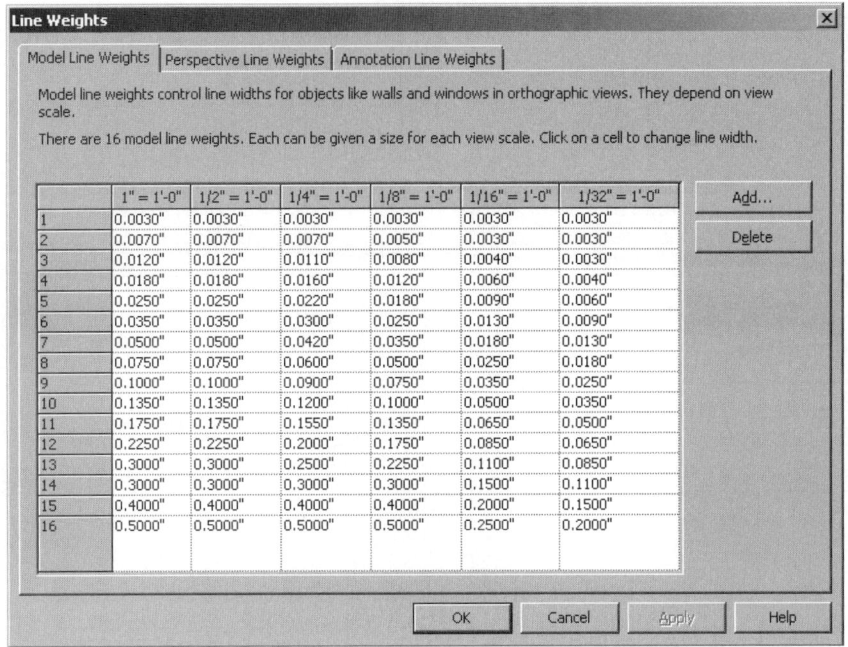

	1" = 1'-0"	1/2" = 1'-0"	1/4" = 1'-0"	1/8" = 1'-0"	1/16" = 1'-0"	1/32" = 1'-0"
1	0.0030"	0.0030"	0.0030"	0.0030"	0.0030"	0.0030"
2	0.0070"	0.0070"	0.0070"	0.0050"	0.0030"	0.0030"
3	0.0120"	0.0120"	0.0110"	0.0080"	0.0040"	0.0030"
4	0.0180"	0.0180"	0.0160"	0.0120"	0.0060"	0.0040"
5	0.0250"	0.0250"	0.0220"	0.0180"	0.0090"	0.0060"
6	0.0350"	0.0350"	0.0300"	0.0250"	0.0130"	0.0090"
7	0.0500"	0.0500"	0.0420"	0.0350"	0.0180"	0.0130"
8	0.0750"	0.0750"	0.0600"	0.0500"	0.0250"	0.0180"
9	0.1000"	0.1000"	0.0900"	0.0750"	0.0350"	0.0250"
10	0.1350"	0.1350"	0.1200"	0.1000"	0.0500"	0.0350"
11	0.1750"	0.1750"	0.1550"	0.1350"	0.0650"	0.0500"
12	0.2250"	0.2250"	0.2000"	0.1750"	0.0850"	0.0650"
13	0.3000"	0.3000"	0.2500"	0.2250"	0.1100"	0.0850"
14	0.3000"	0.3000"	0.3000"	0.3000"	0.1500"	0.1100"
15	0.4000"	0.4000"	0.4000"	0.4000"	0.2000"	0.1500"
16	0.5000"	0.5000"	0.5000"	0.5000"	0.2500"	0.2000"

Figure 12-49

Line Weights dialog box

18. In the **Line Weights** dialog box, select the **Model Line Weights** tab.
19. Select the **Add** button at the top right of the dialog box to bring up the **Add Scale** dialog box.
20. In the **Add Scale** dialog box, select **1 1/2″ = 1′-0″** from the drop-down list, and press the **OK** button to return to the **Line Weights** dialog box.

Here you can change the line weight for each of the 16 numbered lines, specifically for the **1 1/2″ = 1′-0″** scale.

21. In the **Manage** toolbar, select **Additional Settings > Line patterns** to bring up the **Line Patterns** dialog box (see Figure 12-50).
22. In the **Line Patterns** dialog box, select the **New** button to bring up the **Line Pattern Properties** dialog box.
23. In the **Line Pattern Properties** dialog box, enter **TEST LINE PATTERN**.

NOTE:

Line patterns are a series of dashes or dots alternating with blank spaces.

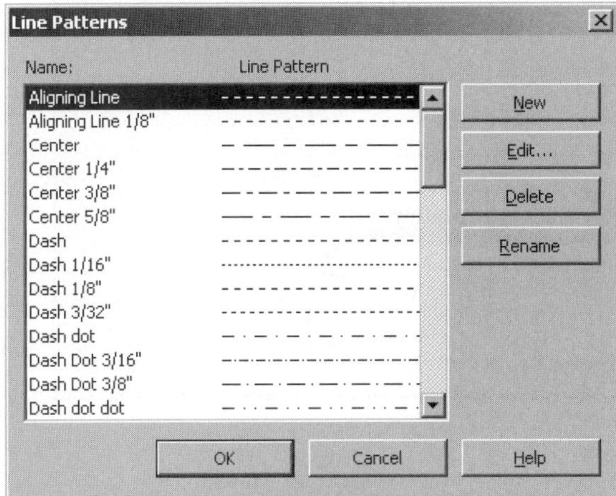

Figure 12-50

Line Patterns dialog box

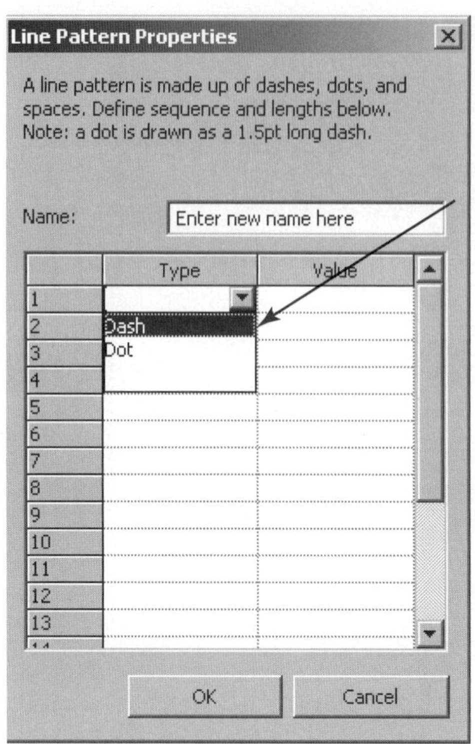

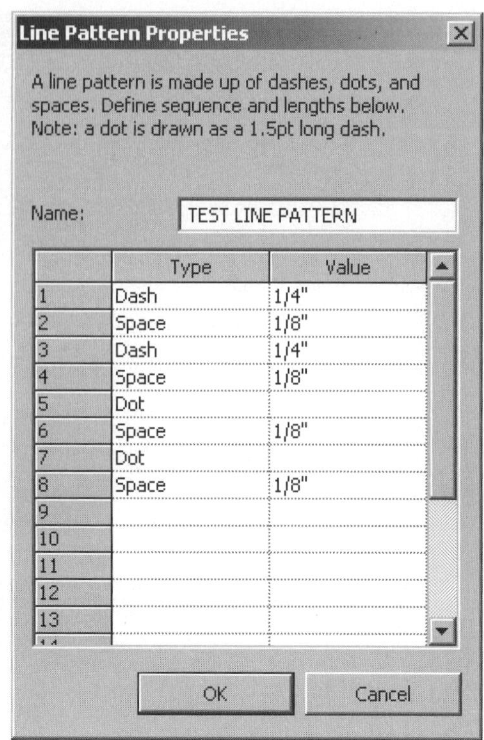

Figure 12-51

Line Pattern Properties dialog box

24. Enter the **Dash/Dot Type** and **Values** shown in Figure 12-51.
25. Press the **OK** button in the **Line Pattern Properties** dialog box to return to the **Line Patterns** dialog box (see Figure 12-52).

NOTE:

Dots do not need a value, **Spaces** will be the only **Type** option after a **Dash** or **Dot**, and a **Space** must be selected as the last **Type.**

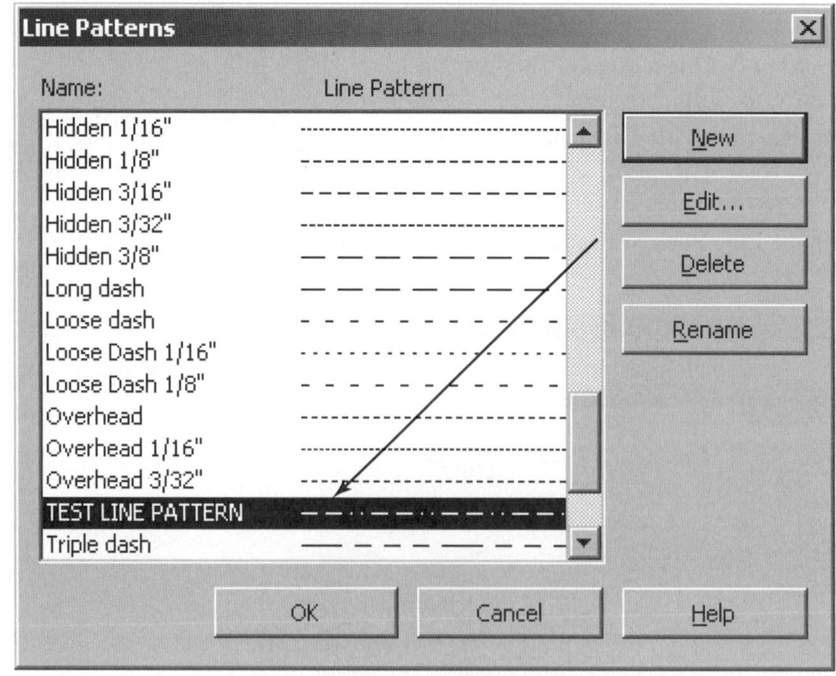

Figure 12-52

Line Patterns dialog box

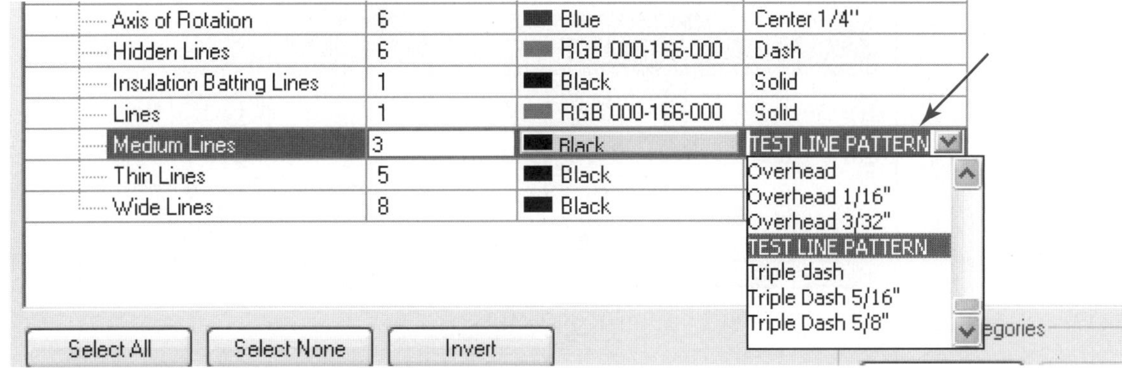

Figure 12-53

Set **Medium Lines** to **TEST LINE PATTERN**

26. In the **Manage** toolbar, select **Additional Settings > Line Styles** again, and set the **Line Pattern** for the **Medium Lines** to **TEST LINE PATTERN** (that you just created) (see Figure 12-53).
27. Press the **OK** button in the **Line Styles** dialog box to return to the **Drawing Editor**, and then place a **2′-0″ Medium Line** (see Figure 12-54).
28. Save this file as **LINE SETTINGS**.

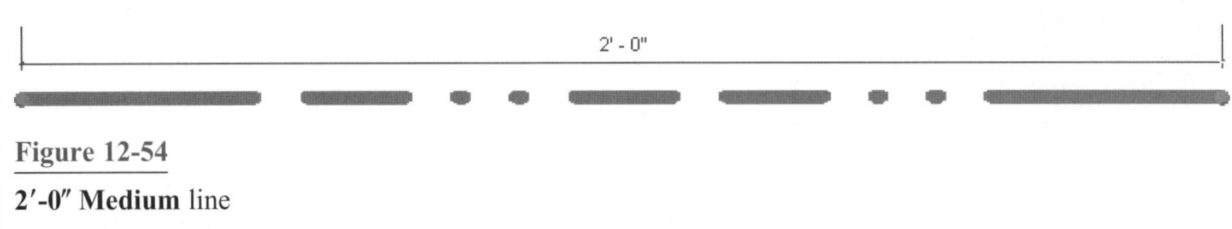

Figure 12-54

2′-0″ Medium line

Detail Group Tool

Detail Groups are collections of elements such as detail lines that can be placed as copies in the **Drawing Editor**. Because groups are linked copies, changes to one of the elements in a group affect all the copies in that group. **Detail Groups** are particularly useful for automatically making changes over copies such as windows.

EXERCISE 12-9 USING THE DETAIL GROUP TOOL

1. Use the **Drafting view** you created in the previous exercise.
2. In the **Annotate** toolbar, select the **Detail Line** button to bring up the **Modify | Place Detail Lines** toolbar.
3. In the **Modify | Place Detail Lines** toolbar, select the **Circle** and **Rectangle** buttons from the **Draw** panel.
4. Place the circle and rectangle in the **Drafting View** (see Figure 12-55).
5. In the **Annotate** toolbar, select the **Detail Group > Create Group** button to bring up the **Create Group** dialog box (see Figure 12-56).

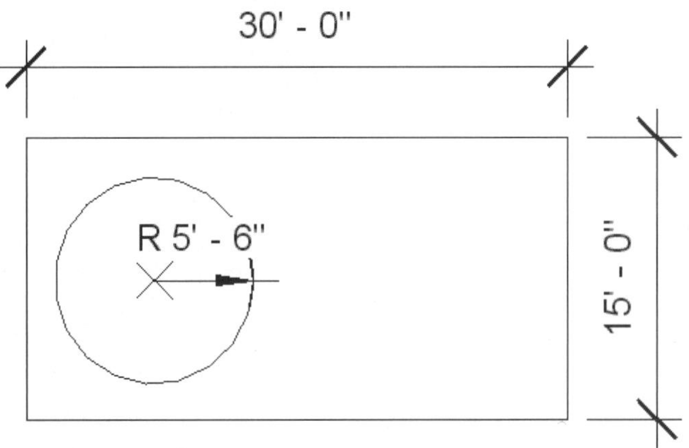

Figure 12-55

Place a circle and a rectangle in a drawing

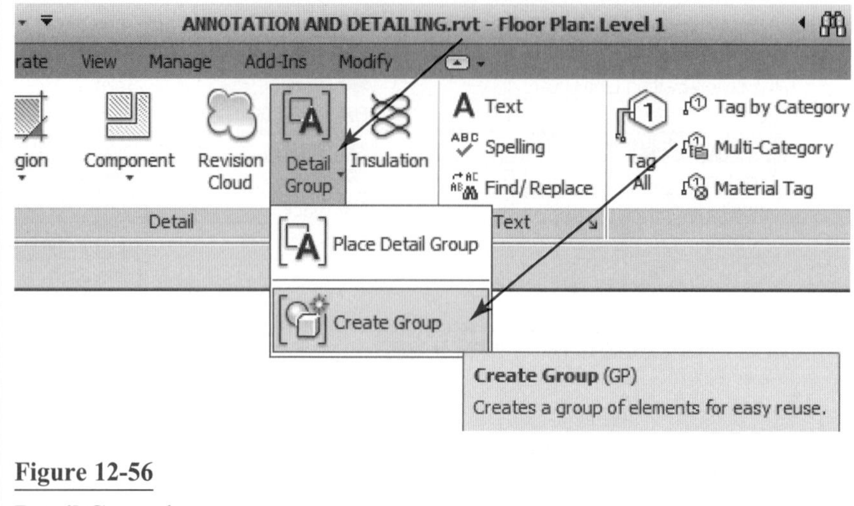

Figure 12-56

Detail Group button

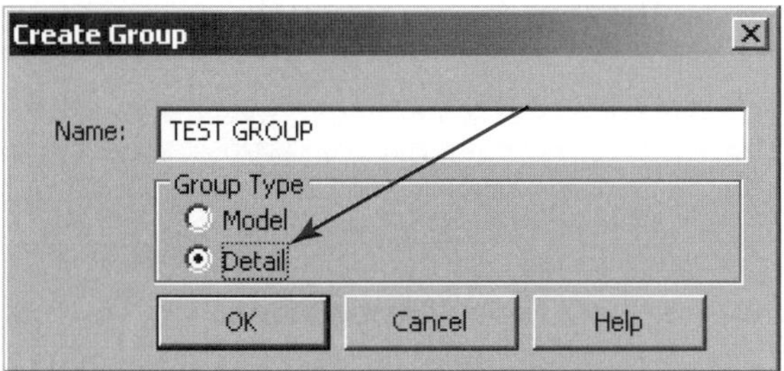

Figure 12-57

Create Group dialog box

6. In the **Create Group** dialog box, enter **TEST GROUP**, select the **Detail** radio button, and press the **OK** button to "yellow" the screen (see Figure 12-57).
7. Select the **Add** button in the **Edit Group** panel to bring up the **Add to Group** toolbar.
8. Select all the detail lines you created, and then select the **Finish** button to create the group and return to the **Drawing Editor** (see Figure 12-58).
9. Select the group and move it.
10. Select the group in the **Drawing Editor** that you just created to bring up the **Modify | Detail Groups** toolbar.
11. In the **Modify | Detail Groups** toolbar, select the **Edit Group** button in the **Group** panel to bring up the **Edit Group** panel.
12. In the **Edit Group** panel, select the **Remove** button, select the circle to remove it from the group, and then select the **Finish** button.

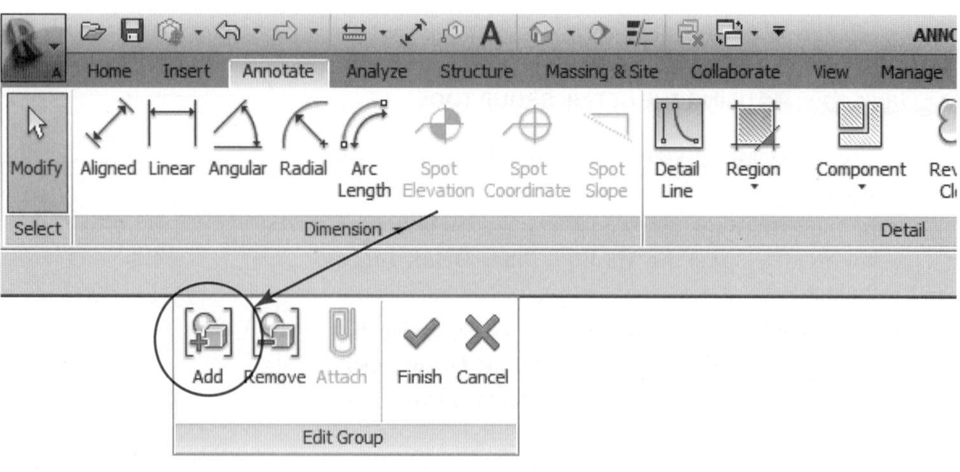

Figure 12-58

Add button

13. Select the group, and move it again. The circle should not move with the group because it has been removed from the group.
14. To ungroup, select the group you made to bring up the **Modify | Detail Groups** toolbar.
15. In the **Modify | Detail Groups** toolbar, select the **Ungroup** button to ungroup the lines, and then press the **<Esc>** key to end the command.
16. Regroup the lines and circle, and re-create the **TEST GROUP** you created in the **Drawing Editor**.
17. Select the group to bring up the **Modify | Detail Groups** toolbar.
18. In the **Modify | Detail Groups** toolbar, select the **Copy** button in the **Modify** panel.
19. In the **Options Bar**, check the **Constrain** check box.
20. Click in a spot in the workspace, move to another spot, and click again.

You will have created a copy of the group constrained to horizontal and vertical.

NOTE:
In the **Options Bar**, *checking* the **Detail Group Constrain** check box constrains the group copies to horizontal and vertical. With the **Detail Group Constrain** check box *unchecked*, your group copies will be placed at any angle (see Figure 12-59).

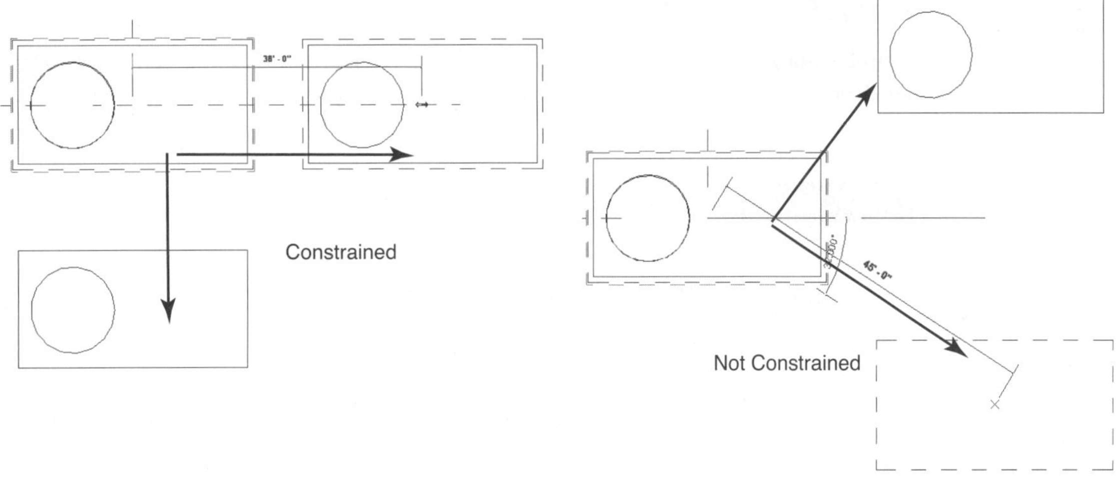

Figure 12-59

Constrained and not constrained groups

21. Select the first group object used to create the group (the left-hand object) to bring up the **Modify | Detail Groups** toolbar.
22. In the **Modify | Detail Groups** toolbar, select the **Edit Group** button to "yellow" the screen, and return to the **Annotate** toolbar.
23. Remove the circle from the group, and delete it.
24. Using the **Detail Line** button, place a rectangle inside the original rectangle you created.
25. Select the **Annotate** tab to bring up the **Annotate** toolbar.
26. In the **Annotate** toolbar, select the **Text** button, add the word **TEXT**, and then press the **Finish** button.

All the copies of the original group change to match the first group (see Figure 12-60).

27. Experiment creating, editing, adding, and deleting groups.
28. Save this file as **DETAIL GROUPS**.

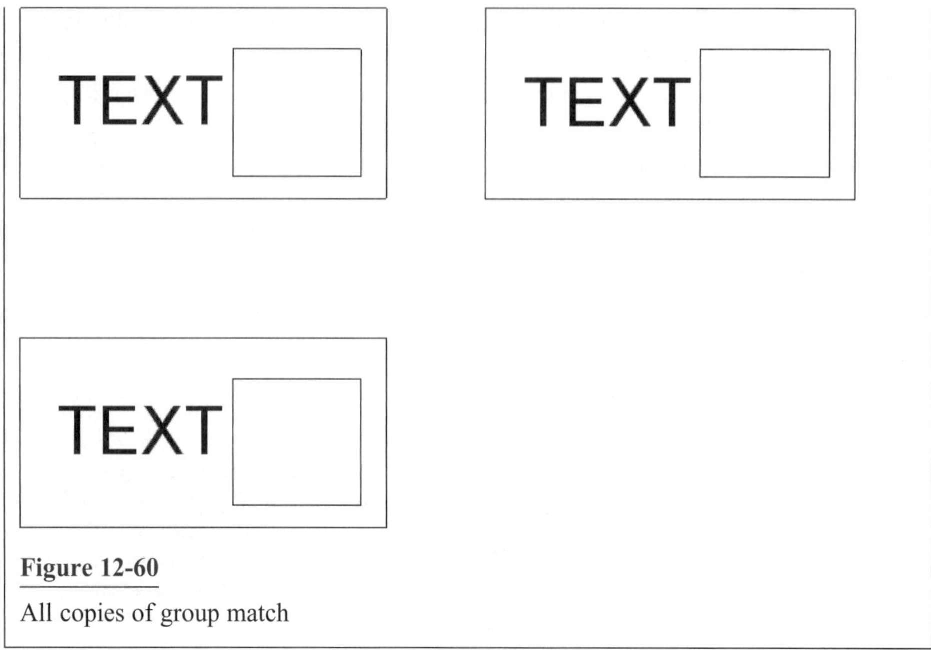

Figure 12-60

All copies of group match

Detail Component Tool

Detail Components are predrawn, line-based, 2D elements that you can add to **Detail** or **Drafting** views. They are visible only in those views. They scale with the model rather than the sheet.

EXERCISE 12-10 **USING THE DETAIL COMPONENT TOOL**

1. Create a new drafting view as shown in the previous exercises.
2. Name it **DETAIL COMPONENTS VIEW**.
3. Set the scale to **1 1/2″ = 1′-0″**.
4. Select the **Annotate** toolbar to bring up the **Annotate** toolbar.
5. In the **Annotate** toolbar, select the **Component** > **Detail Component** button to bring up the **Modify | Place Detail Component** toolbar (see Figure 12-61).
6. In the **Modify | Place Detail Component** toolbar, select the **Load Family** button to bring up the **Load Family** dialog box in the **Library** (**Imperial** or **Metric**).
7. In the **Library**, locate and open the **Detail Components** folder.

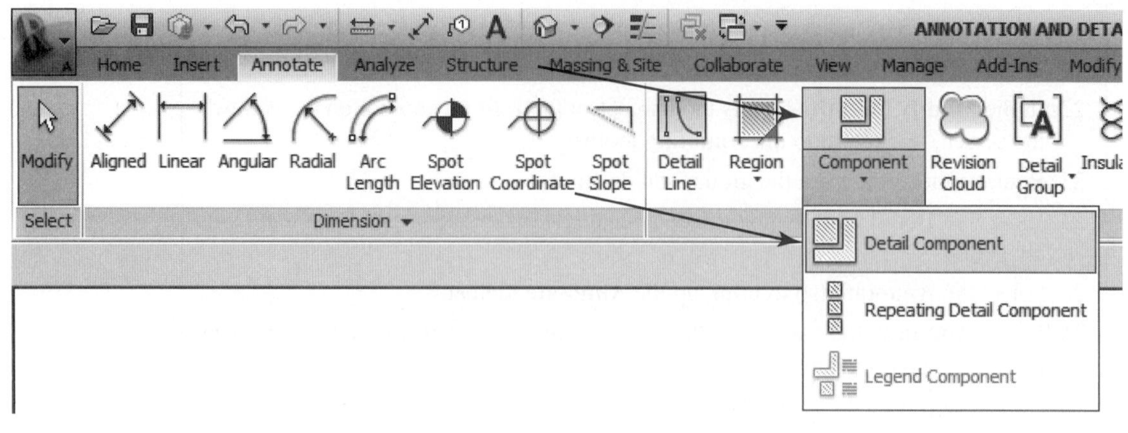

Figure 12-61

Detail Component button

The **Detail Components** folder contains folders corresponding to the Construction Specification Institute (CSI) MasterFormat Division list (see Figure 12-62).

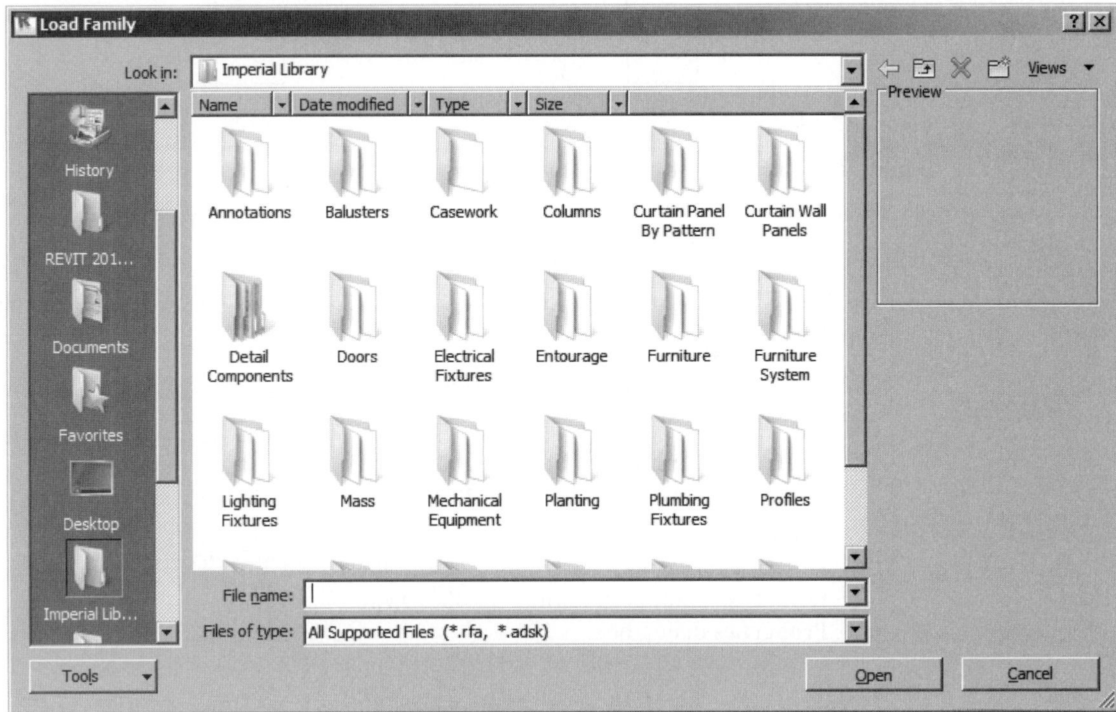

Figure 12-62

Load Family folder

8. In the **Detail Components** folder, open the **Div 03-Concrete** folder.
9. In the **Div 03-Concrete** folder, open the **033100-Structural Concrete** folder.
10. In the **033100-Structural Concrete** folder, select the **Double Tee Joist-Section**, and press the **Open** button to load the family and return to the **Drawing Editor** (see Figure 12-63).

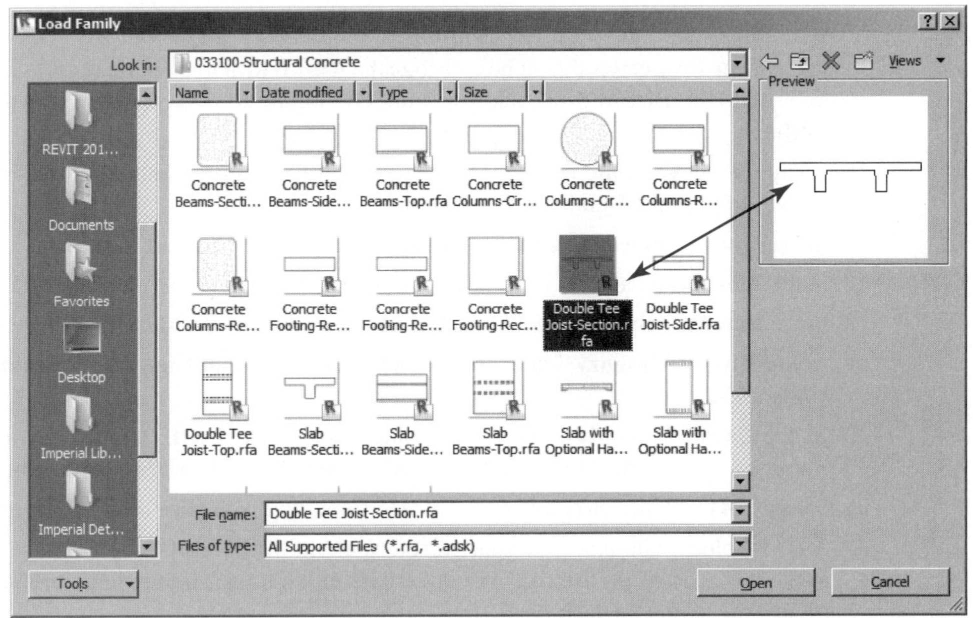

Figure 12-63

Load the **Double Tee Joist-Section** component

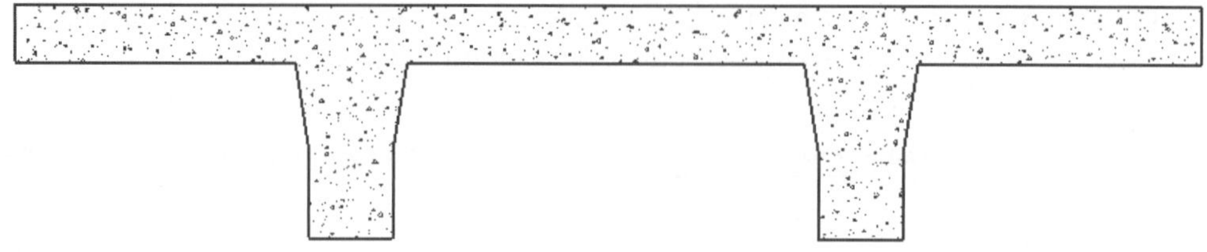

Figure 12-64

Double Tee Joist-Section component

11. Click in the **Drawing Editor** to place the **Double Tee Joist-Section** (see Figure 12-64).

As with all **Detail Components**, the **Double Tee Joist-Section** is parametric.

12. Select the **Double Tee Joist-Section** component you placed to open its **Properties** dialog box.
13. In the **Properties** dialog box, select the **Edit Type** button to bring up the **Type Properties** dialog box.

NOTE:

By pressing the **Preview** button, you can see the results of your changes before returning to the **Drawing Editor** (see Figure 12-65).

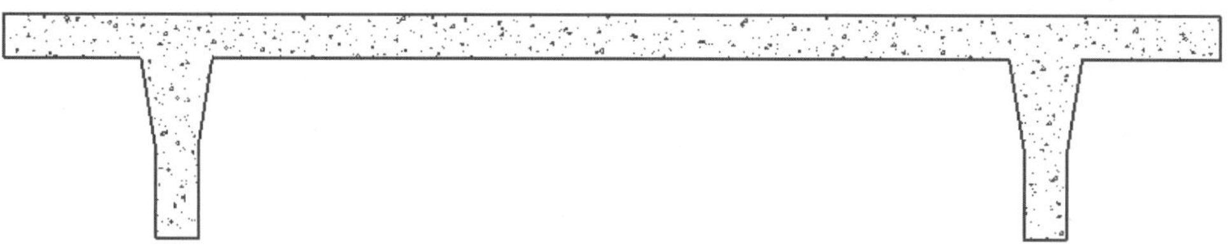

Figure 12-65

Preview of changes to the **Double Tee Joist-Section**

14. In the **Type Properties** dialog box, change the **Rib_Width** to **3″**, **Thickness** (slab) to **3″** and **Rib_Dist** to **5′-0″**, and press the **OK** button to return to the **Drawing Editor**.
15. Again, in the **Annotate** toolbar, select the **Detail Component** button to bring up the **Modify | Place Detail Component** toolbar.
16. In the **Modify | Place Detail Component** toolbar, select the **Load Family** button.
17. In the **Library**, locate and open the **Detail Components** folder.
18. In the **Detail Components** folder, select and open the **Div 04-Masonry** folder.
19. In the **Div 04-Masonry** folder, select and open the **04220-Concrete Masonry Units** folder.
20. In the **04200-Clay Masonry Units** folder, select the **CMU-2 Core-Section Family**, and press the **Open** button to load it and return to the **Drawing Editor**.
21. Select **CMU-2 Core-Section: 8″ × 8″ × 16″** from the **Properties** drop-down list.
22. A **CMU** block will appear at your cursor. With the **End Point Snap (On)**, snap to the left edge of the **Double Tee Joist-Section** you placed, and then press the **<Esc>** key to end the command.

NOTE:

You will now need to make 14 copies vertically of the CMU. This can be done in several ways. One way is to **Array** the CMU vertically, but the best way is to use the **Repeating Detail Component** button.

Using the **Array** button:

a. Select the **CMU** you placed to bring up the **Modify | Detail Items** toolbar.

b. In the **Modify | Detail Items** toolbar, select the **Array** button from the **Modify** panel (see Figure 12-66).

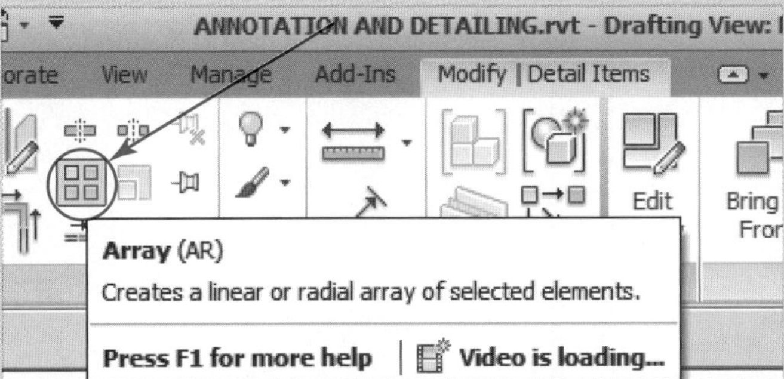

Figure 12-66

Array button

c. In the **Options Bar**, select the **Linear** button, uncheck **Group And Associate,** enter **14** in the **Number** field, check the **Constrain** check box, and press the **Activate Dimensions** button (see Figure 12-67).

d. Select the lower left corner of the **CMU**, and move your cursor upward until the dimension reads **8″**, and click again to create **14** vertical copies of the CMU (see Figures 12-68 and 12-69).

Using the **Repeating Detail Component** button:

a. In the **Annotate** toolbar, select the **Component > Repeating Detail Component** button to bring up the **Modify | Place Repeating Detail Component** toolbar (see Figure 12-70).

b. In the **Properties** dialog box, select the **Edit Type** button to bring up the **Type Properties** dialog box.

c. In the **Type Properties** dialog box, select the **Duplicate** button to bring up the **Name** dialog box.

d. Enter **REPEATING CMU** in the **Name** field, and press the **OK** button to return to the **Type Properties** dialog box.

e. In the **Type Properties** dialog box, select **CMU-2 Core-Section: 8″ × 8″ × 16″** from the **Detail** drop-down list.

f. In the **Type Properties** dialog box, select **Fixed Distance** from the **Layout** drop-down list, set the **Spacing** to **8″**, and press the **OK** buttons to return to the **Drawing Editor** (see Figure 12-71).

g. Click your cursor at the top of the **CMU** you placed in Step 22, drag your cursor upward, and enter **9′4** (9′-4″) in the **Number** field, and press the **<Enter>** key to create the 14 CMU copies (see Figure 12-72).

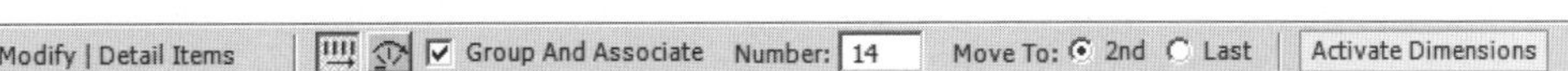

Figure 12-67

Activate Dimensions button

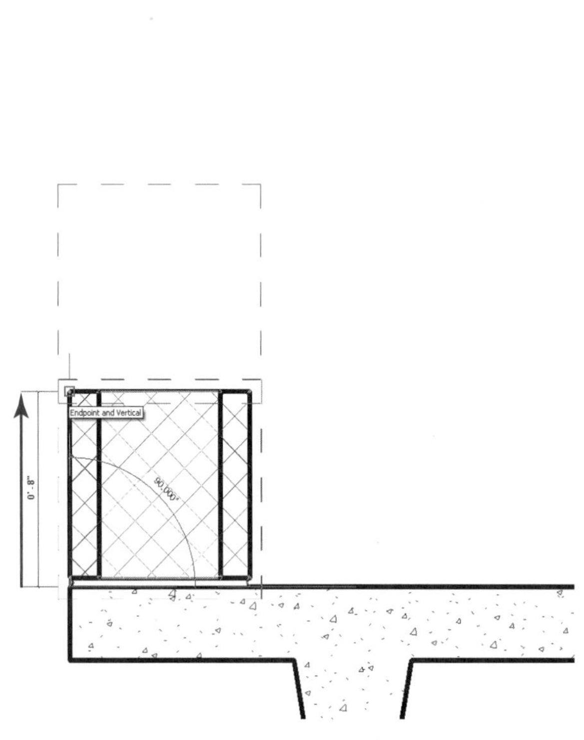

Figure 12-68

Array CMU vertically

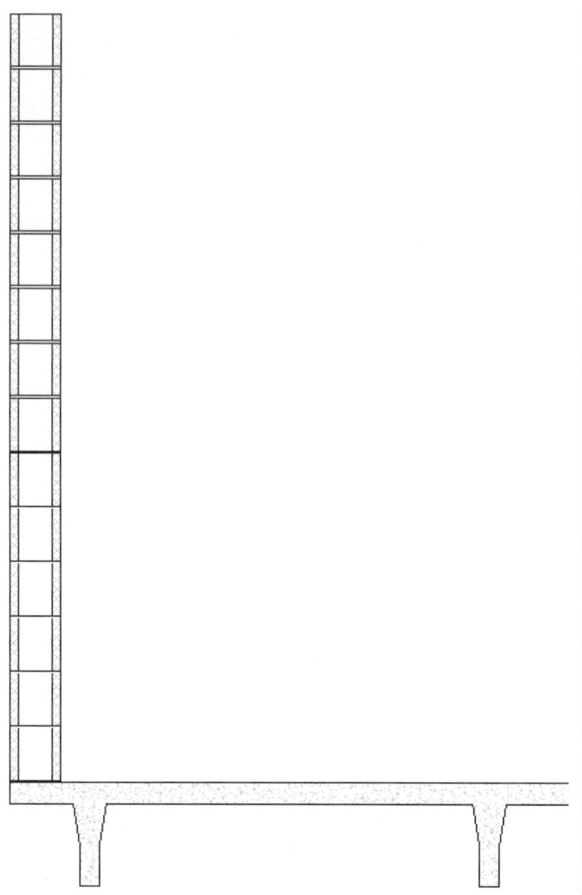

Figure 12-69

Create 14 copies of the **CMU** block

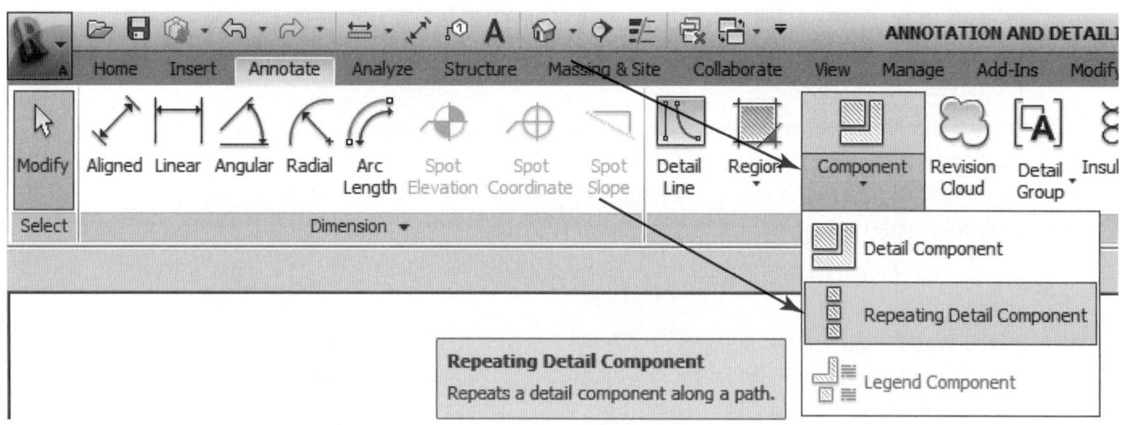

Figure 12-70

Repeating Detail Component toolbar

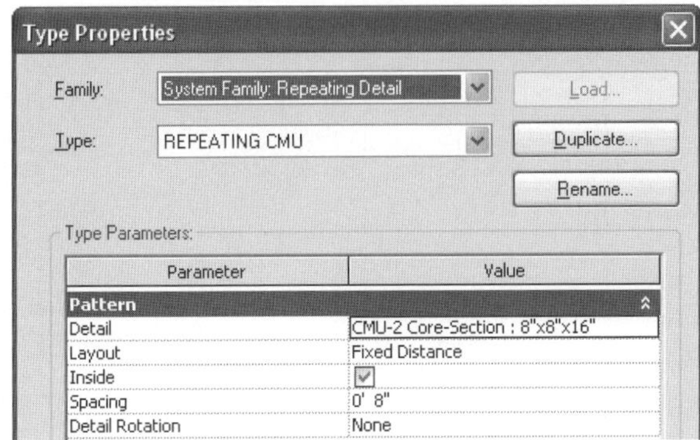

Figure 12-71

Type Properties dialog box

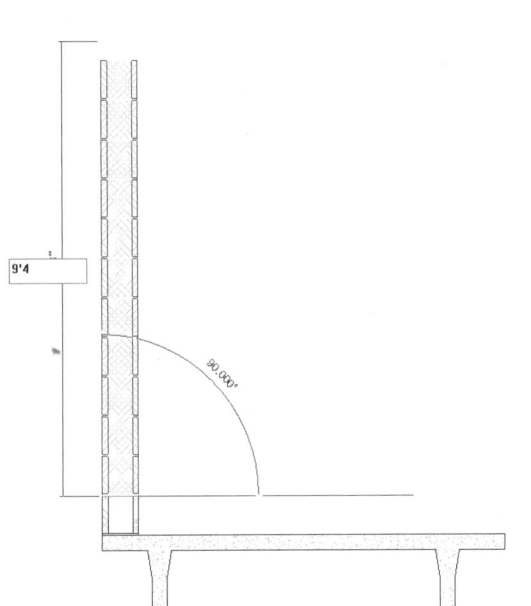

Figure 12-72

Create 14 **CMU** copies

23. Select the **Detail Component** button again, press the **Load Family** button, and select the **Div 05-Metals > 050500-Metal Fastenings** folder.
24. In the **050500-Metal Fastenings** folder, select the **Steel Base Plate-Side-Width** and **Anchor Bolts Hook-Side** families, and open them.
25. Again, select the **Detail Component** button to bring up the **Modify | Place Detail Component** toolbar.
26. Select **Steel Base Plate-Side-Width: 1″** from the **Properties** drop-down list, and place it on top of the **CMU**.
27. Select the **Detail Component** button to bring up the **Modify | Place Detail Component** toolbar.
28. Select the **Anchor Bolts Hook-Side: 3/4″** from the **Properties** drop-down list, and then place it in the base plate.

NOTE:

You will have to use the **Mirror** button (selecting the bolt and then selecting the **Mirror** button from the toolbar that appears). Adjust the length and hook length of the **J bolt** by selecting it and moving the small adjustment arrows that appear (see Figure 12-73).

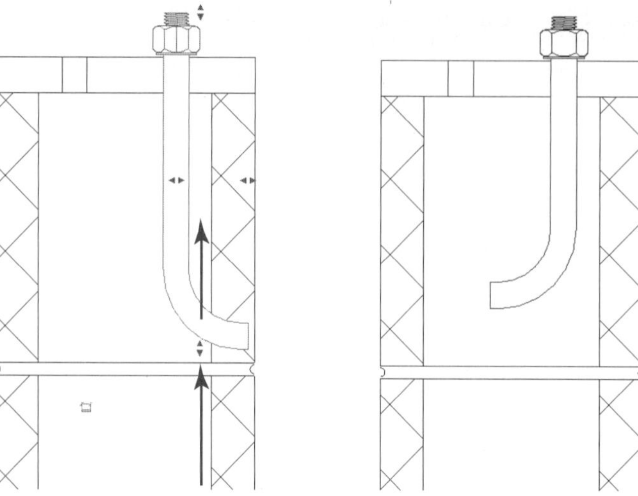

Figure 12-73

Adjust the length and the hook length of the **J bolt**

29. In the **Annotate** toolbar, select the **Component** > **Detail Component** button to bring up the **Modify | Place Detail Component** toolbar.
30. In the **Modify | Place Detail Component** toolbar, select the **Load Family** button, and locate the **Detail Components > Div 05-Metals > 052100-Steel Joists Framing** folder.
31. In the **052100-Steel Joists Framing** folder, select the **K-Series Bar Joist-Side Family**, select the **18K3 Joist** from the list, and then open it to bring up the **Specify Types** dialog box.
32. In the **Specify Types** dialog box, select the **K-Series Bar Joist-Side: 18K3 Joist**, press the **OK** button, and then place it on top of the base plate (see Figure 12-75).
33. Select the joist you just placed, and move the top and bottom **Joist Cord** adjustment arrows (see Figure 12-76).

NOTE:

If the **J bolt** body does not appear, it may be behind the CMU and plate. To correct this, select the **J bolt** head to bring up the **Modify | Detail Items** toolbar, and select the **Bring to Front** button from the **Arrange** panel (see Figure 12-74).

NOTE:

Some of the **Detail Components** will have a list of types in the folder. **Metal Joists** is an example of this.

NOTE:

Remember to press the **<Esc>** key to end commands.

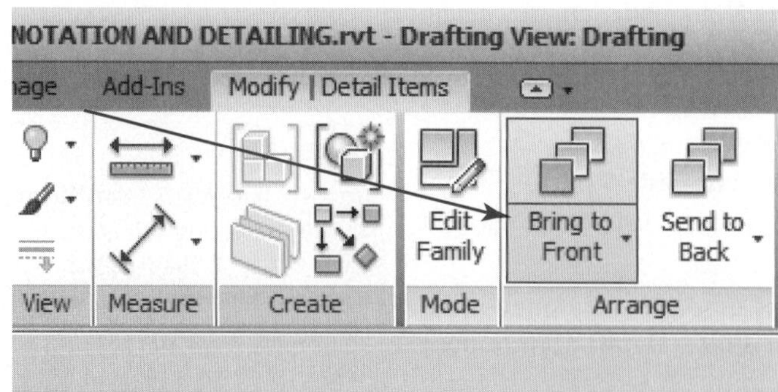

Figure 12-74

Bring to Front button

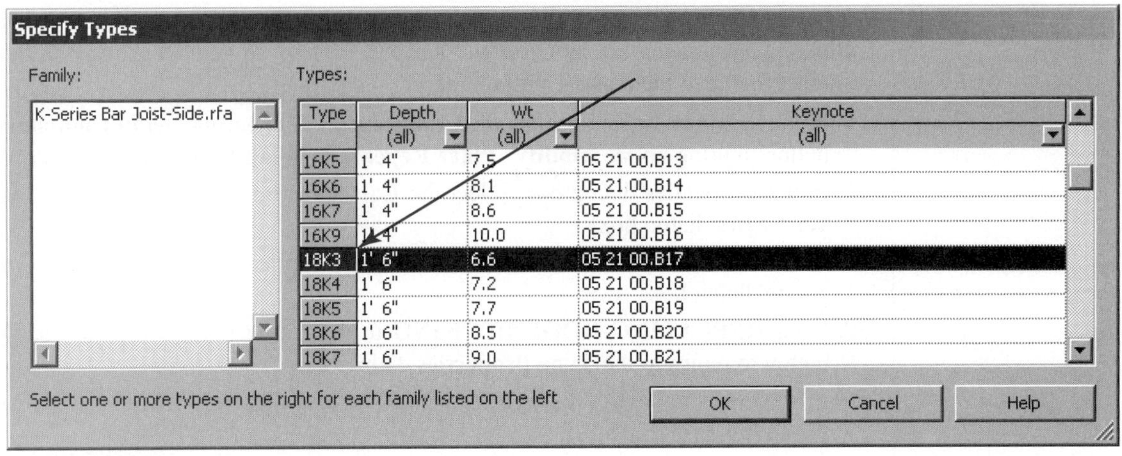

Figure 12-75

Specify Types dialog box

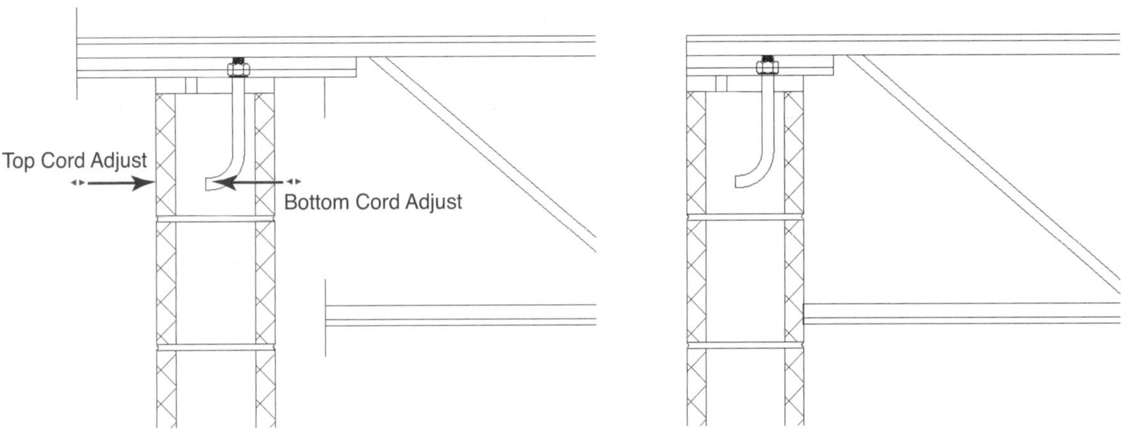

Figure 12-76

Adjust the top and bottom joist cords

34. Select the **Detail Component** button again, press the **Load Family** button, and select the **Div 05-Metals > 053100 - Steel Decking** folder.
35. In the **053100-Steel Decking** folder, select the **Roof Deck-Section Family**, and then open it.

> **NOTE:**
> The **J bolt** head may be behind the joist. To correct this, select the joist, and select the **Send to Back** button (see Figure 12-77).

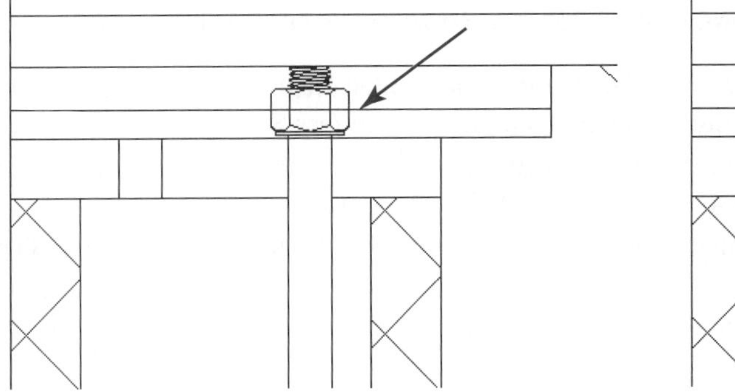

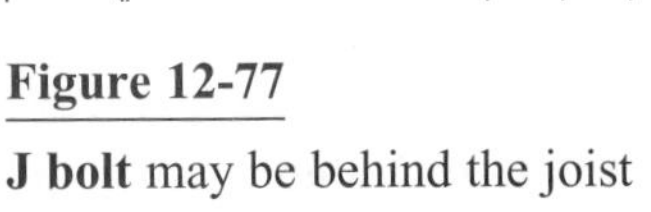

Figure 12-77

J bolt may be behind the joist

A section of the roofing will appear; click to place it in an empty space in the **Drawing Editor**. After inserting the roof section, delete it. In order to load **Repeating Details**, you must first load them as a **Component**.

36. In the **Annotate** toolbar, select the **Component** > **Repeating Detail Component** button to bring up the **Modify | Place Repeating Detail Component** toolbar.
37. In the **Properties** dialog box, select the **Edit Type** button to bring up the **Type Properties** dialog box.
38. In the **Type Properties** dialog box, select the **Duplicate** button to bring up the **Name** dialog box.
39. Enter **REPEATING ROOF DECKING** in the **Name** field, and press the **OK** button to return to the **Type Properties** dialog box.
40. In the **Type Properties** dialog box, select **Roof Decking Section: 1.5 NR 18** from the **Detail** drop-down list.
41. In the **Type Properties** dialog box, select **Fixed Distance** from the **Layout** drop-down list, set the **Spacing** to **6″**, **Detail Rotation** to **90 Counterclockwise**, and press the **OK** buttons to return to the **Drawing Editor**.
42. Click at the top left corner of the **Joist Top Cord**, drag your cursor to the right **5′-0″**, and then click again to create the roof decking detail (see Figure 12-78).

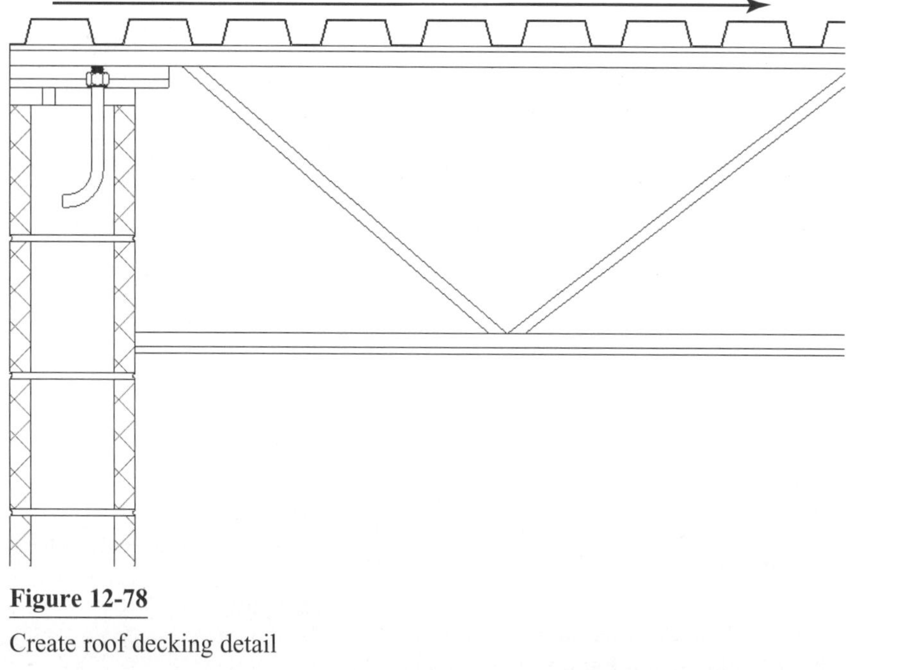

Figure 12-78

Create roof decking detail

EXERCISE 12-11 CREATING GRAVEL AND EARTH WITH THE FILLED REGION TOOL

1. In the **Annotate** toolbar, select the **Region** > **Filled Region** button to bring up the **Modify | Create Filled Region Boundary** toolbar (see Figure 12-79).
2. In the **Modify | Create Filled Region Boundary** toolbar, select the **Rectangle** button, and place a **4″** wide rectangle below the slab.
3. In the **Properties** dialog box, select the **Edit Type** button to bring up the **Type Properties** dialog box.
4. In the **Type Properties** dialog box, select the **Duplicate** button to bring up the **Name** dialog box.
5. Enter **GRAVEL PATTERN** in the **Name** field, and press the **OK** button to return to the **Type Properties** dialog box.
6. In the **Type Properties** dialog box, select the **Fill Pattern Value** to bring up the **Fill Patterns** dialog box.

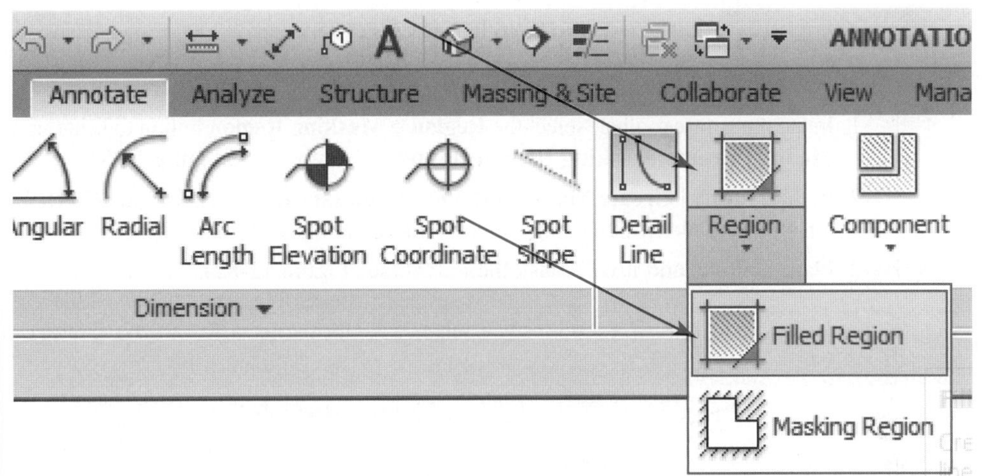

Figure 12-79

Filled Region button

NOTE:

Revit Architecture 2012 does not have a gravel pattern, but AutoCAD Architecture does. You can also search the Internet for patterns. The AutoCAD Architecture 2010 hatch patterns are located in **Documents and Settings > Administrator > Application Data > Autodesk > ACD-A 2010 > enu > Support > pats.** To load a new pattern into Revit, do the following:

a. In the **Fill Patterns** dialog box, select the **Edit** button to bring up the **Modify Pattern Properties** dialog box.

b. In the **Modify Pattern Properties** dialog box, select the **Custom** radio button.

c. Press the **Import** button, and locate the **(Hatch Patterns [*.pat])** files.

d. Select the **Sitework_Gravel** pattern, and press the **Open** button to return to the **Modify Pattern Properties** dialog box.

e. In the **Modify Pattern Properties** dialog box, set the **Import scale** to **.25**, and press the **OK** buttons to return to the **Drawing Editor.**

7. In the **Modify | Create Filled Region Boundary** toolbar, press the **Finish Edit Mode** button to create the **Filled Region** with **Gravel**. Remember to press the **Send to Back** button if the gravel is in front of the slab (see Figure 12-80).

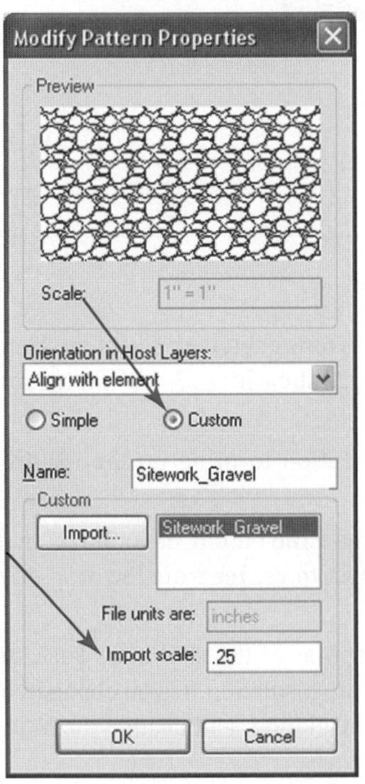

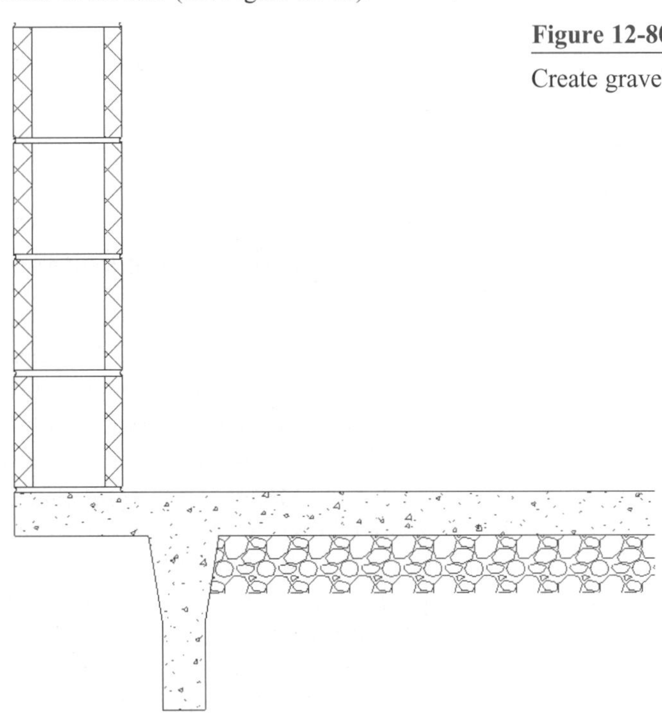

Figure 12-80

Create gravel

EXERCISE 12-12 USING THE MASKING REGION BUTTON

The **Masking Region** is used to cover or "mask" objects.

1. In the **Annotate** toolbar, select the **Region > Masking Region** button to bring up the **Modify | Create Masking Region Boundary** toolbar (see Figure 12-81).
2. In the **Modify | Create Masking Region Boundary** toolbar, select the **Circle** button from the **Draw** panel, and select **Wide** from the **Line Style** drop-down list.
3. Place a circle, and it will mask the gravel (see Figure 12-82).

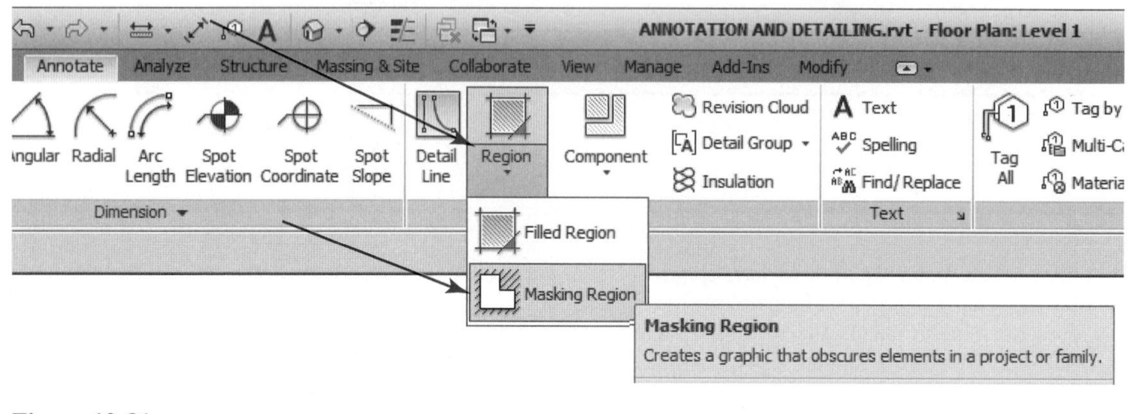

Figure 12-81

Masking Region button

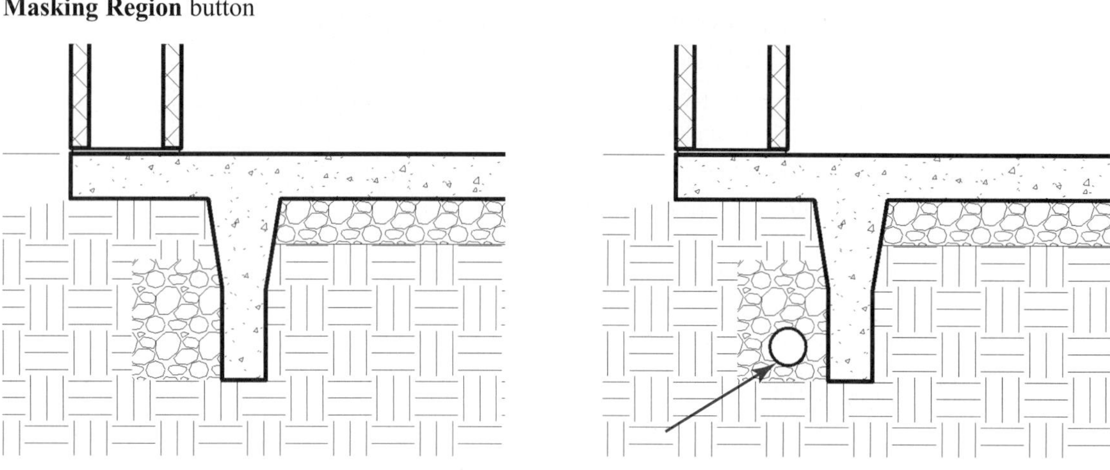

Figure 12-82

Mask the gravel

EXERCISE 12-13 USING THE INSULATION BUTTON

1. Using the information you have learned in the previous exercises, select the **Detail Component** button, and then select and place a **1/2″ sheathing**, **3-1/2″ metal stud**, and **1/2″ gypsum board** in your detail.
2. In the **Annotate** toolbar, select the **Insulation** button to bring up the **Modify | Place Insulation** toolbar (see Figure 12-83).
3. In the **Modify | Place Insulation** toolbar, select the **Line** button, enter **3-1/2″** in the **Width** field, check the **Chain** check box, and select **to center** from the drop-down list (see Figure 12-84).
4. With the **Midpoint Snap (On)**, click at the midpoint of the stud at its base, and then drag and snap to the top of the stud to place the insulation. If you change your mind about the size of the insulation, select the insulation, and change the **Width** field (see Figure 12-85).

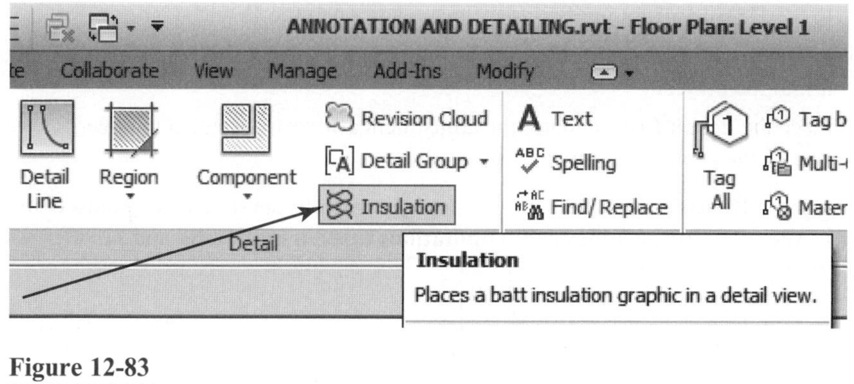

Figure 12-83

Insulation button

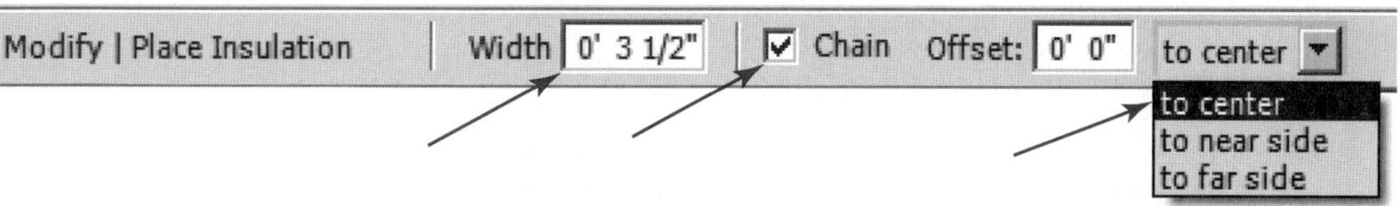

Figure 12-84

Modify | **Place Insulation** toolbar

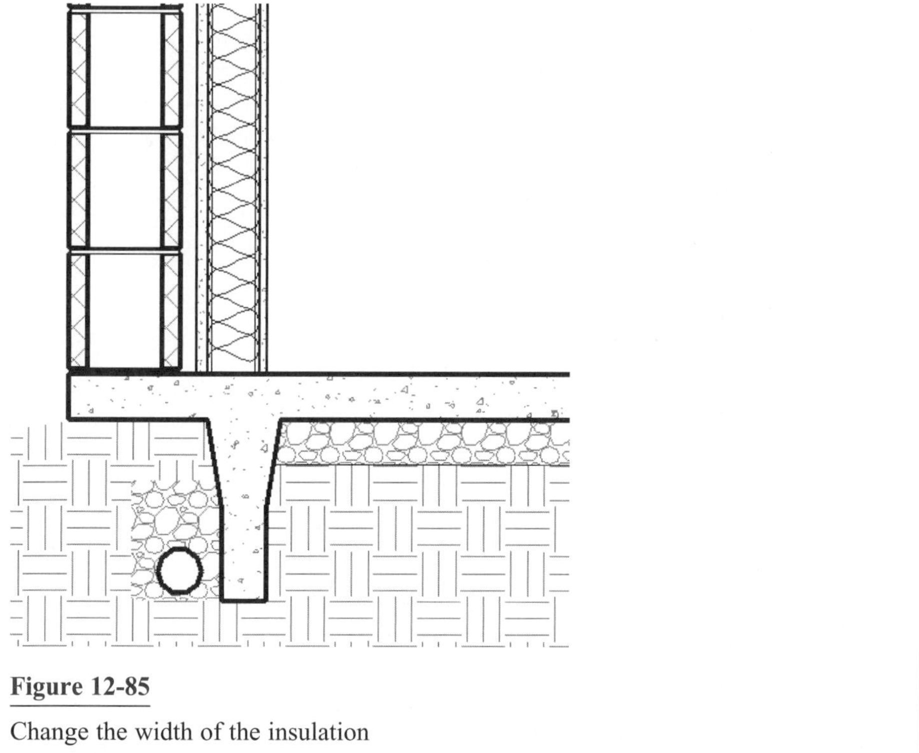

Figure 12-85

Change the width of the insulation

EXERCISE 12-14 **USING THE BREAK LINE**

Designers often make use of **Break Lines** to isolate parts of a drawing.

1. In the **Annotate** toolbar, select the **Component** > **Detail Component** button to bring up the **Modify** | **Place Detail Component** toolbar.
2. In the **Modify** | **Place Detail Component** toolbar, select the **Load Family** toolbar to bring up the **Library (Imperial or Metric)**.
3. In the **Library**, locate and open the **Detail Components** folder.

4. In the **Detail Components** folder, locate and open the **Div 01-General** folder.
5. In the **Div 01-General** folder, select the **Break Line Family** and **Open** it to load it into the project.
6. Place the **Break Line**, and use the adjustment arrows to stretch it to cover the right side of the detail (see Figure 12-86).

Using the information you have now learned, complete the detail by adding components. Add more **Break Lines** and **Annotations** (see Figures 12-87 and 12-88).

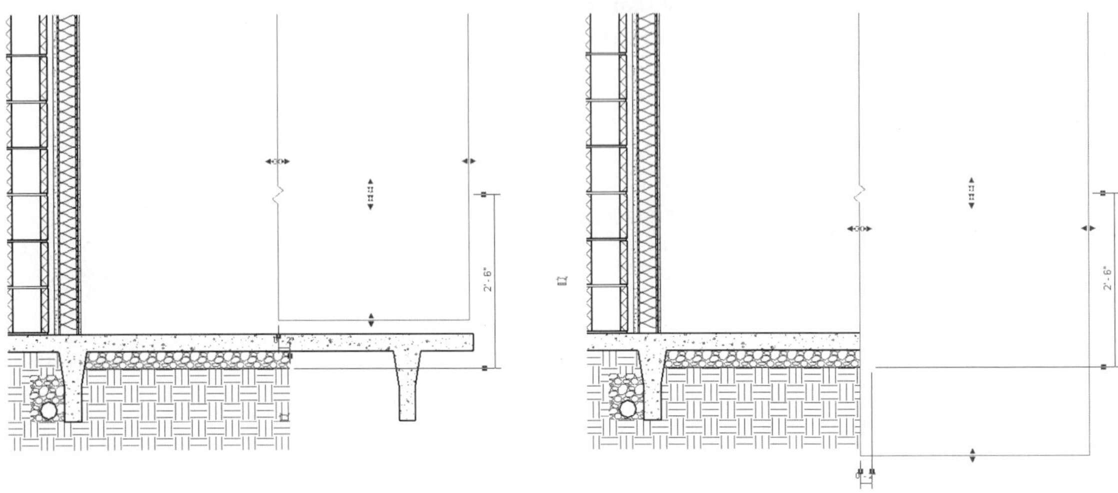

Figure 12-86

Break Lines

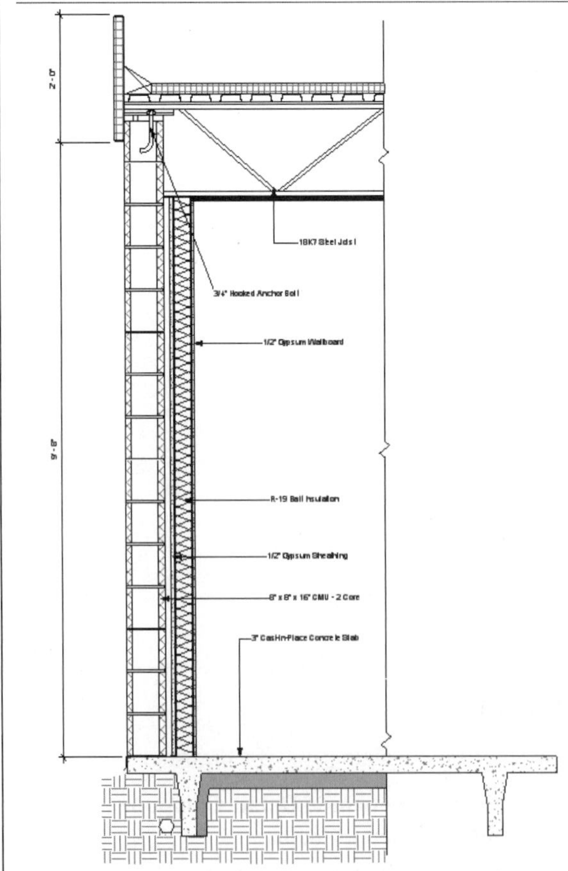

Figure 12-87

Add more **Break Lines** and **Annotations**

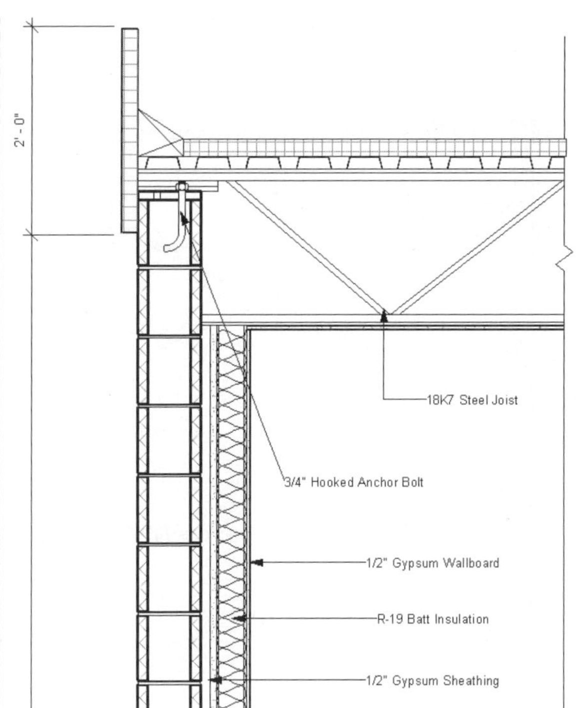

Figure 12-88

Add more **Break Lines** and **Annotations**

The following are examples of details created by the author for one of his projects (see Figures 12-89 through 12-94).

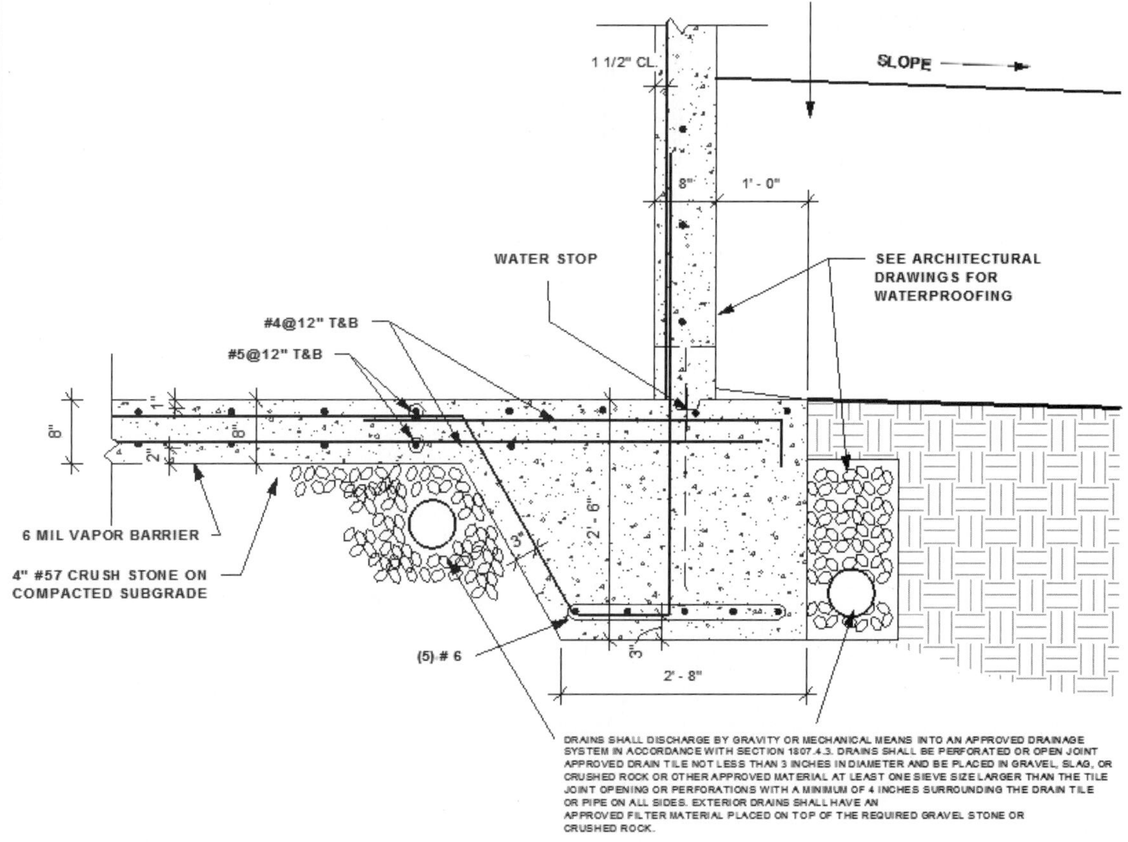

Figure 12-89

Drop Footing detail

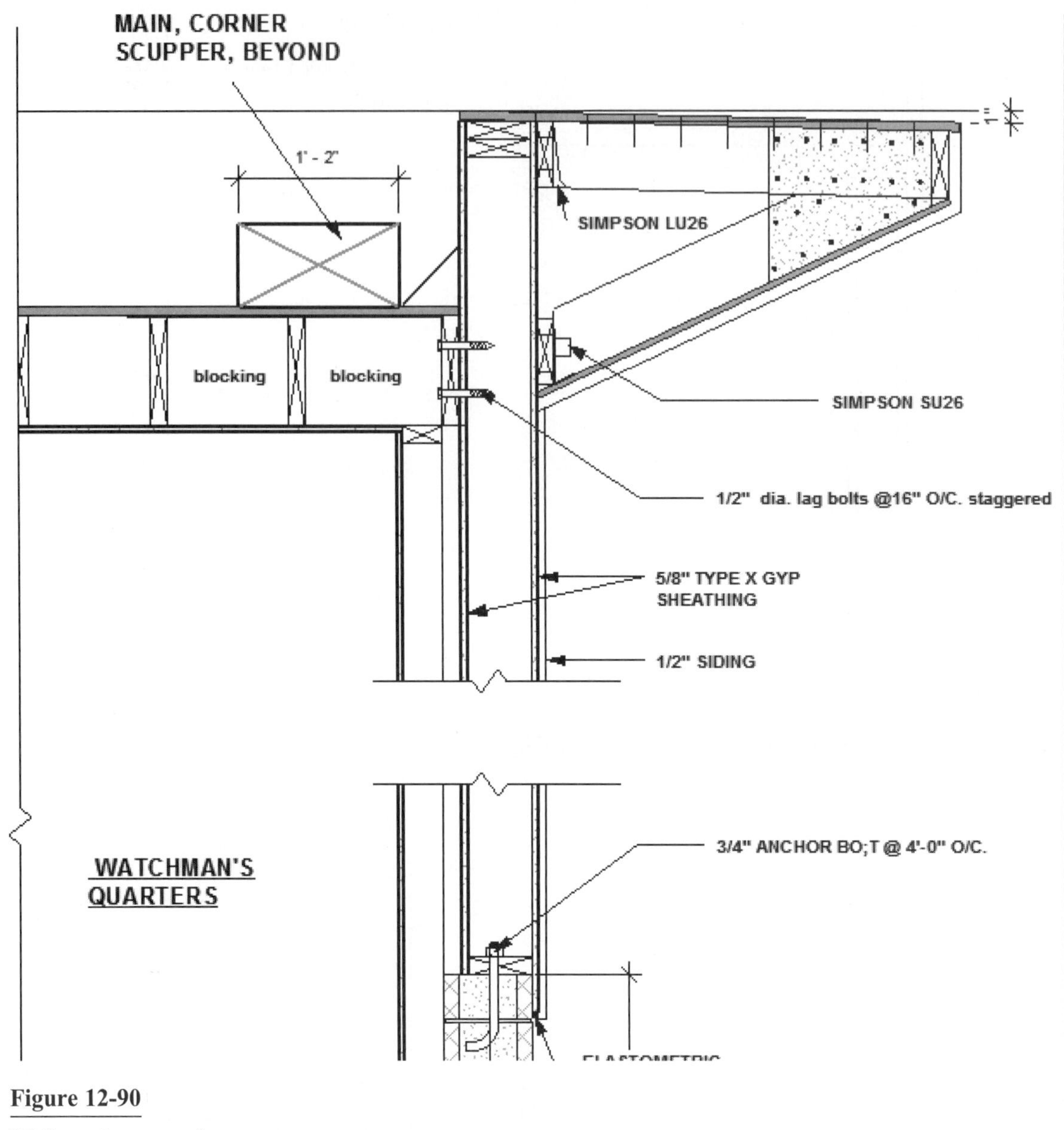

Figure 12-90

Wall section at roof

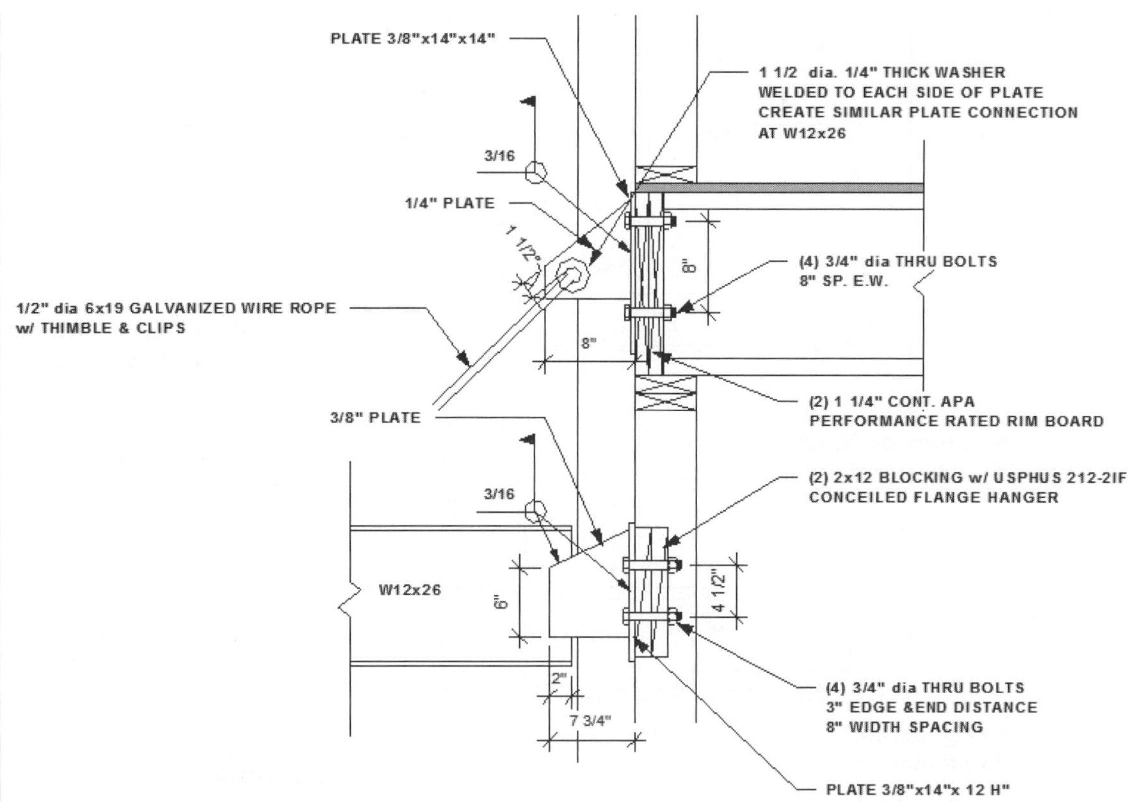

Figure 12-91

Connection detail at steel canopy

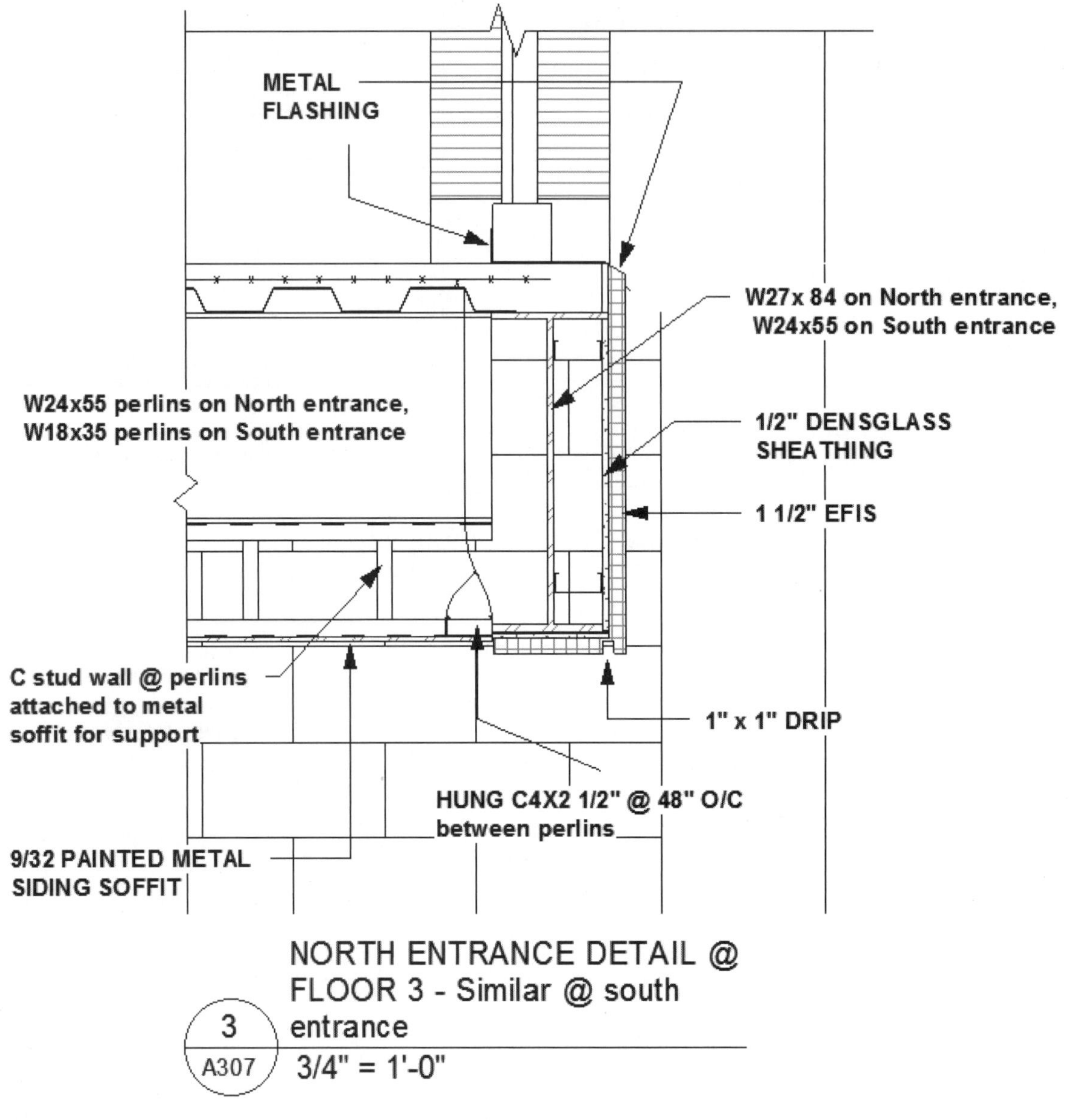
METAL
FLASHING
W27x 84 on North entrance,
W24x55 on South entrance
W24x55 perlins on North entrance,
W18x35 perlins on South entrance
1/2" DENSGLASS
SHEATHING
1 1/2" EFIS
C stud wall @ perlins
attached to metal
soffit for support
1" x 1" DRIP
HUNG C4X2 1/2" @ 48" O/C
between perlins
9/32 PAINTED METAL
SIDING SOFFIT
NORTH ENTRANCE DETAIL @
FLOOR 3 - Similar @ south
entrance
3
A307
3/4" = 1'-0"

Figure 12-92

Entrance detail

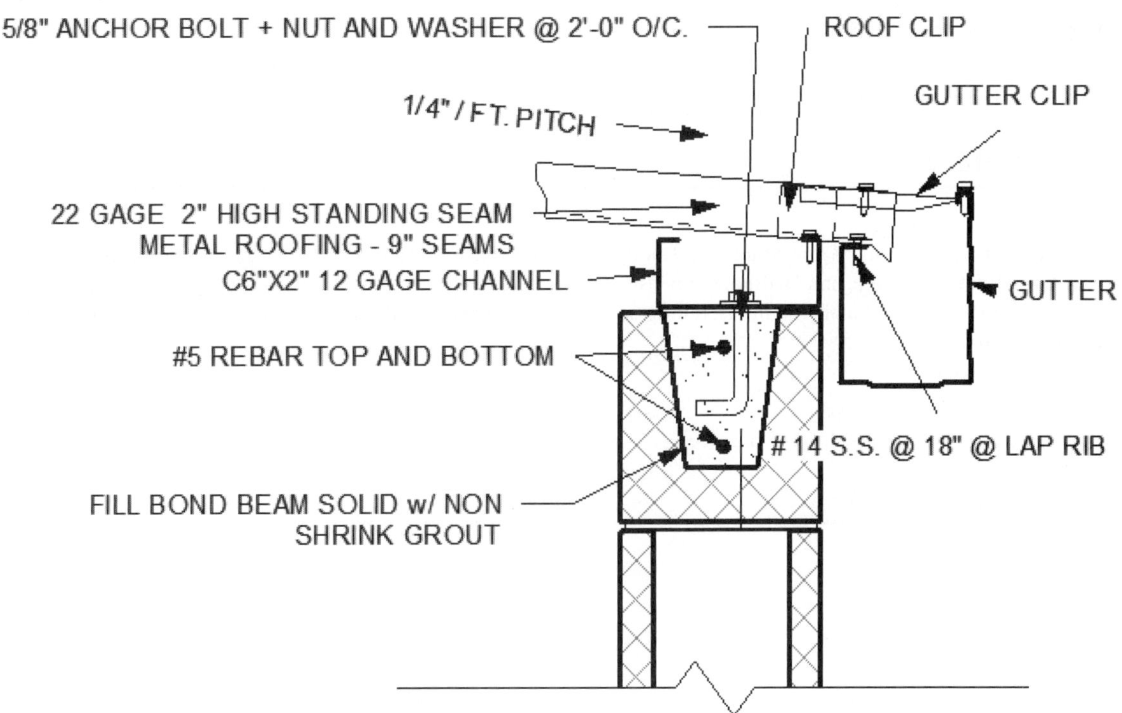

Figure 12-93

Gutter detail

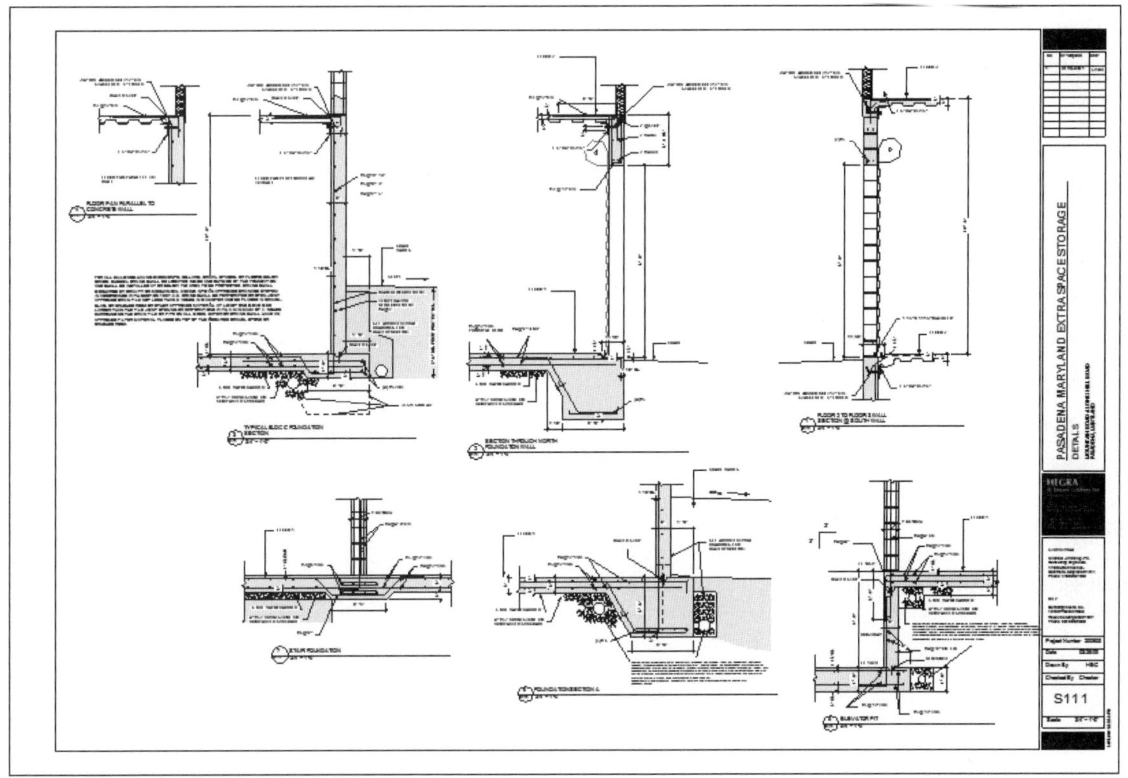

Figure 12-94

Structural Detail page

Chapter Summary

This chapter discussed **Dimensioning**, **Annotation**, and **Detailing** using Revit Architecture 2012. In the **Dimensioning** section, **Spot** dimensions and **Coordinate**, **Baseline**, and **Ordinate** dimensioning were covered. In the **Annotation** section, the methods for placing and modifying text were illustrated. Finally, in the **Detailing** section, creating and modifying details using Revit's **Detail Component Families** were examined.

Chapter Test Questions

Multiple Choice

Circle the correct answer.

1. The **Dimension** buttons are located in the ____________ toolbar.
   a. **Home**
   b. **Annotate**
   c. **View**
   d. **Add-Ins**
2. **Detail Components** are located in the
   a. **Doors** folder.
   b. **Detail Components** folder.
   c. **Annotations** folder.
   d. All of the above
3. **Detail Components** can be placed into
   a. Floor plans.
   b. Ceiling plans.
   c. Drafting views.
   d. All of the above
4. **Line Styles** are located from the _________ toolbar.
   a. **Home**
   b. **Annotate**
   c. **Manage**
   d. **Modify**
5. The **Tick Mark** size is located
   a. In the **Properties** dialog box.
   b. On the **Options Bar**.
   c. In the **Type Properties** dialog box.

Questions

1. What is the definition of **Ordinate** dimensioning?
2. What is the definition of **Baseline** dimensioning?
3. What is the purpose of the **Symbol** in the **Annotate** ribbon?
4. From where do you open the **Line Styles** dialog box?
5. What are **Detail Groups**?
6. What are **Detail Components**?
7. What is the purpose of the **Repeating** tool?
8. What is the purpose of the **Masking Region** tool?
9. What is the purpose of the **Filled Region** tool?
10. From where do you get the **Break Line** tool?

Exercise

Create a wall section of one floor of the building that you are in now.

CHAPTER

13 Analyze

CHAPTER OBJECTIVES

- Know how to set the geographic location.
- Know how to set the project position relative to **True North**.
- Learn how to use the **Sun Path** tool.
- Learn how to create the **Mass Model** for energy study.
- Know how to set the **Energy Settings** and perform an **Energy Analysis**.

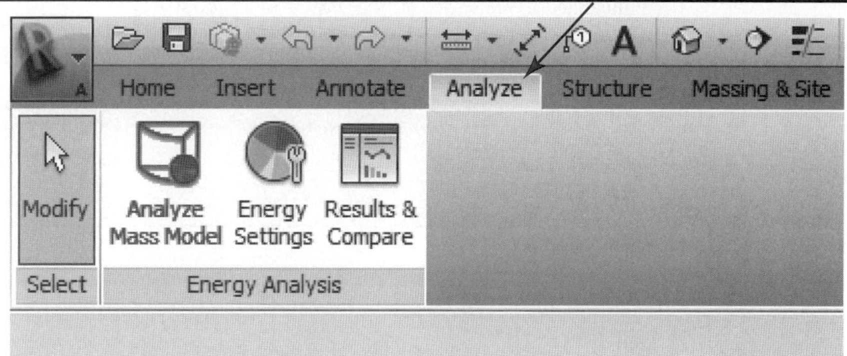

Introduction

In Revit 2012, the **Analyze** feature is now standard. This feature allows Conceptual Energy Analysis (CEA) of Revit **Mass Models**, which are 3D representations of the major mass of a building (creating **Mass Models** is described in depth in Chapter 15). Revit then uploads your project to Green Building Studio (GBS) to compile an analysis. It does this by analyzing the mass model based on parameters such as site location, construction type, percentage of glazing, and so on. Using this feature, one can predict and fine tune a structure to be optimally energy efficient at its location.

EXERCISE 13-1 SETTING THE GEOGRAPHIC LOCATION

1. Start a new project using the RAC 2012\Imperial Templates\default.rte template.
2. In the **Project Browser**, double click **Site** to bring it up into the **Drawing Editor**.
3. Set the **Scale** to **18″ = 1′-0″**.
4. Select the **Manage** tab to bring up the **Manage** toolbar.
5. In the **Manage** toolbar, select the **Location** button to bring up the **Location Weather and Site** dialog box.
6. In the **Location Weather and Site** dialog box, enter the location of the building in the **Project Address** field, and press the **Search** button to activate the **Location** (see Figure 13-1).

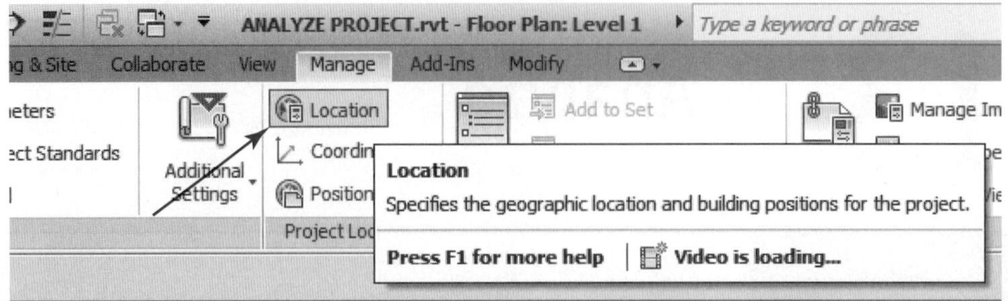

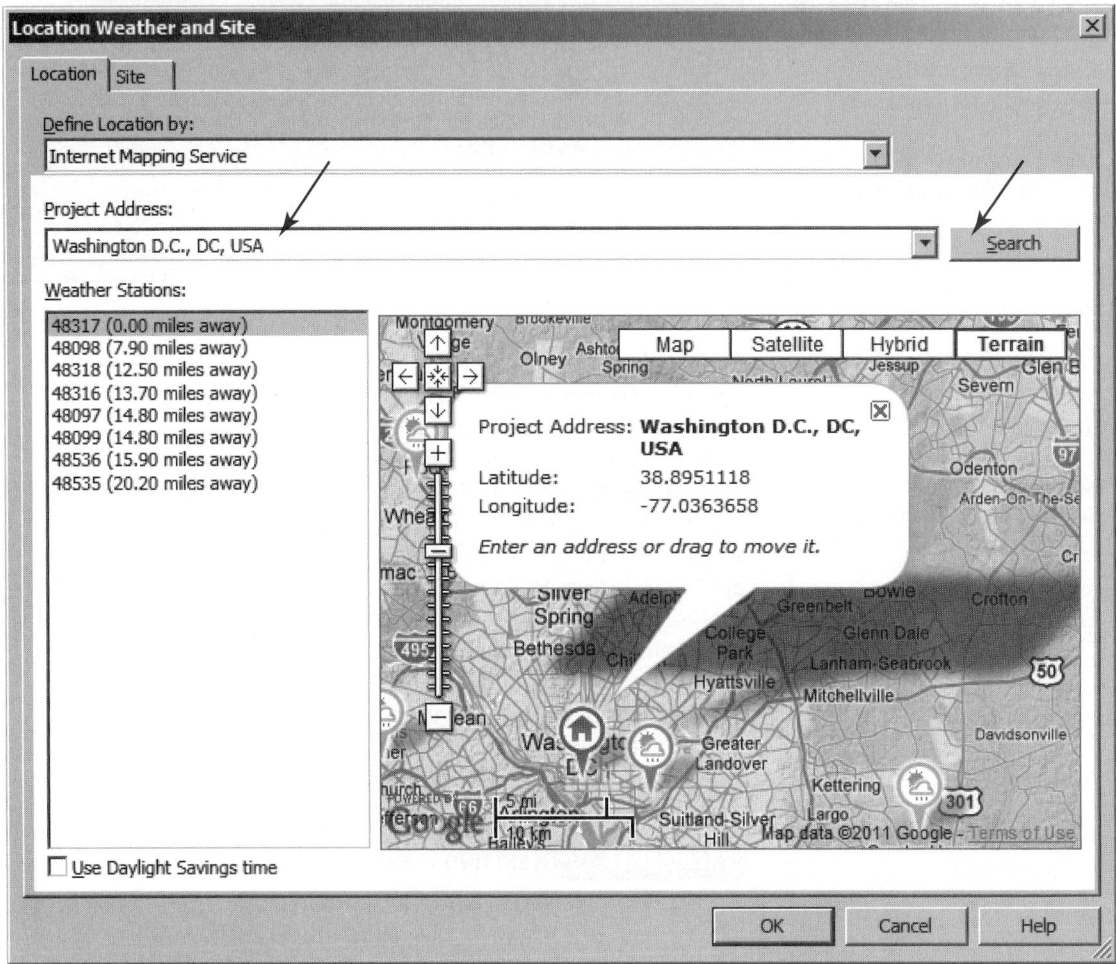

Figure 13-1

Location Weather and Site dialog box

7. Notice that the Google map changes to the building's location, and a red "house" icon appears showing the location of the building and its **Latitude** and **Longitude**.
8. The **Weather Stations** area will display the distance from the building to its most local stations.
9. In the Google map, the **Weather Stations** will also appear as orange icons (see Figure 13-2).
10. Press the **OK** button to close the dialog box.
11. Save the file as **GEOGRAPHIC LOCATION**.

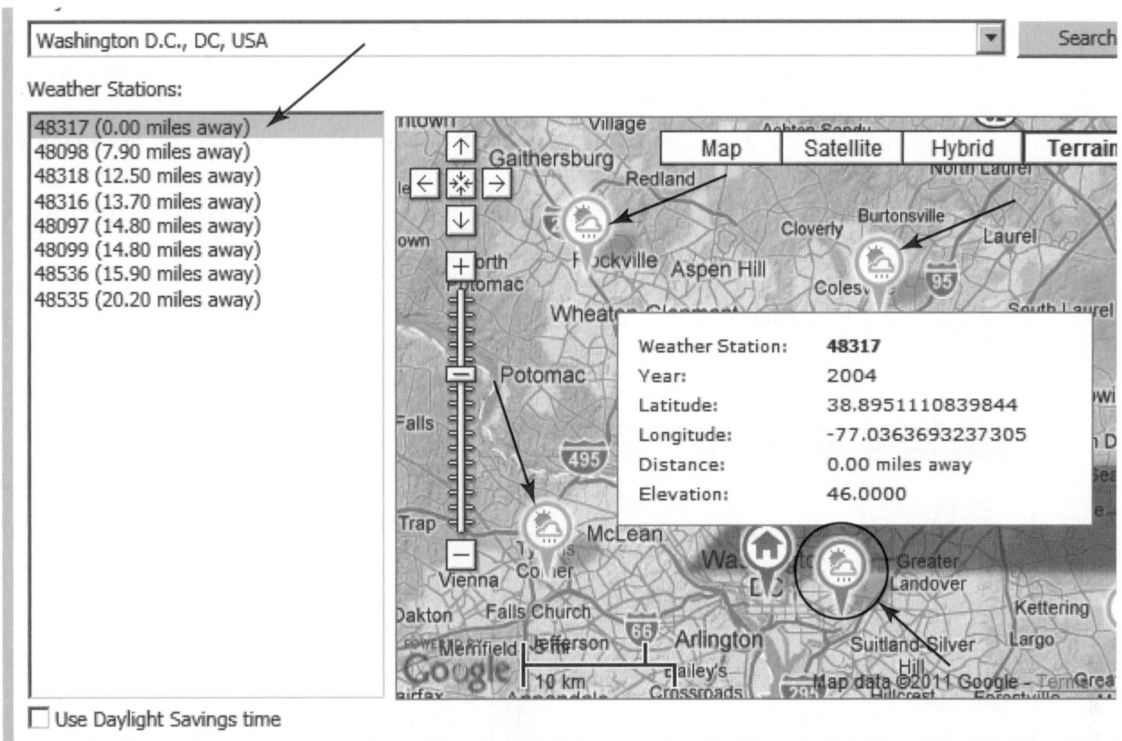

Figure 13-2

Weather Stations appear as orange icons

EXERCISE 13-2 **SETTING THE PROJECT POSITION RELATIVE TO TRUE NORTH**

In order to get true sun and shadow settings for the building's location, you will need to locate the building relative to True North. True North is a geographical direction represented on maps and globes by lines of longitude. Each line of longitude begins and ends at the Earth's poles and represents north and south travel (see Figure 13-3).

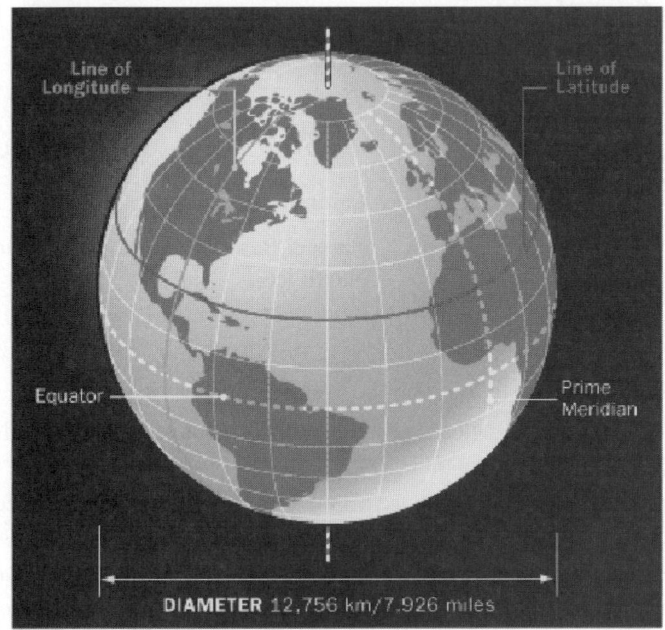

Figure 13-3

Line of longitude

Surveyors will always locate a site relative to True North.

1. Utilizing the previous file, in the **Project Browser**, select the **Site** to bring it into the **Drawing Editor.**
2. Click in an empty place in the **Drawing Editor** to bring up the **Floor Plan Properties** dialog box.
3. In the **Floor Plan Properties** dialog box, select **True North** from the **Orientation** field (see Figure 13-4).
4. Select the **Project Base Point**, **Angle to True North** icon and make sure it is set to **0.000** (see Figure 13-5).

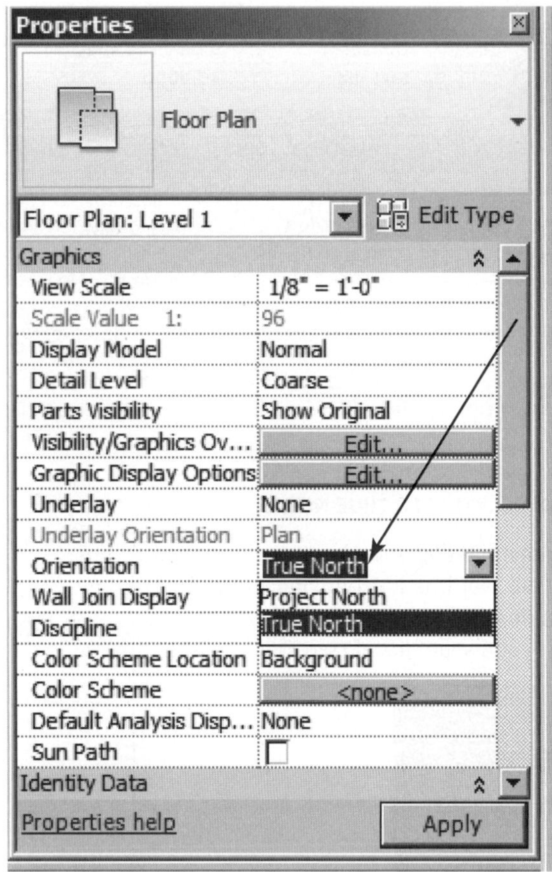

Figure 13-4

Select **True North**

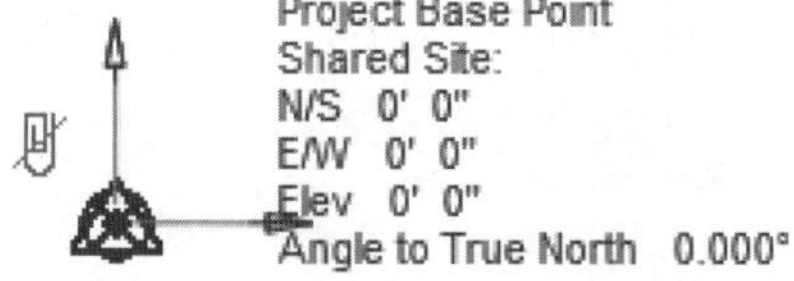

Figure 13-5

Project Base Point, **Angle to True North** icon

5. Select the **Massing & Site** tab to bring up the **Massing & Site** toolbar.
6. In the **Massing & Site** toolbar, select the **Property Line** button to bring up the **Create Property Line** dialog box.
7. In the **Create Property Line** dialog box, select the **Create by entering distances and bearings** option to bring up the **Property Lines** dialog box.
8. In the **Property Lines** dialog box, enter the information shown in Figure 13-6. Continue to insert data as shown until completed, and then select the **OK** button to make the property line appear.
9. Place the **Property Line** at the **Project Base Point** as shown in Figure 13-7.
10. Save the file as **TRUE NORTH.**

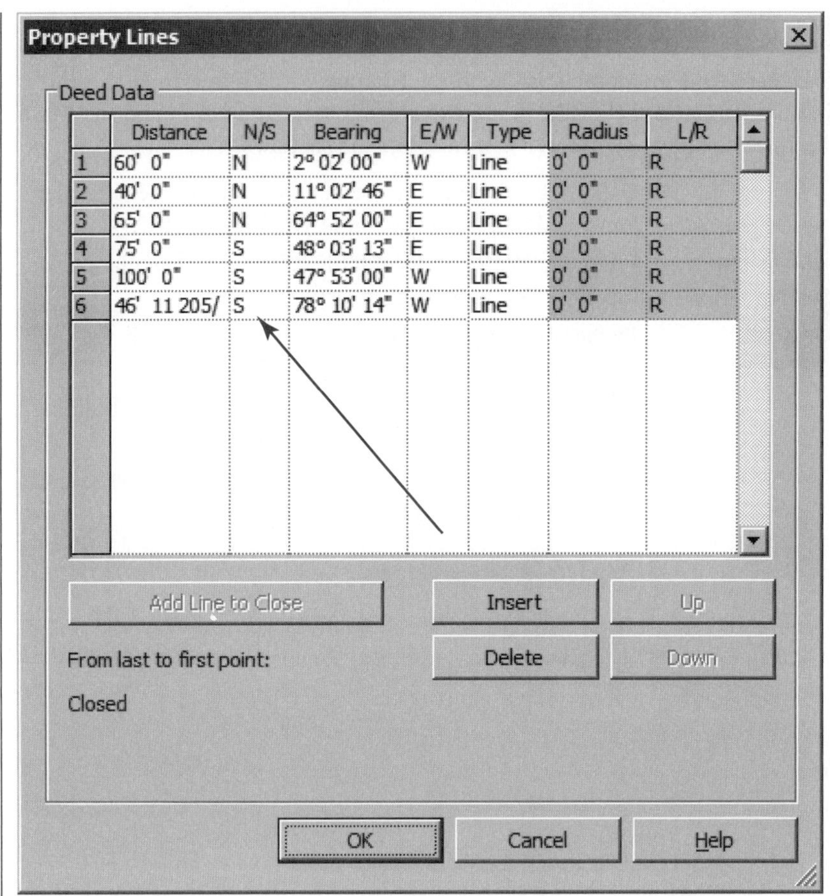

Figure 13-6

Property Lines dialog box

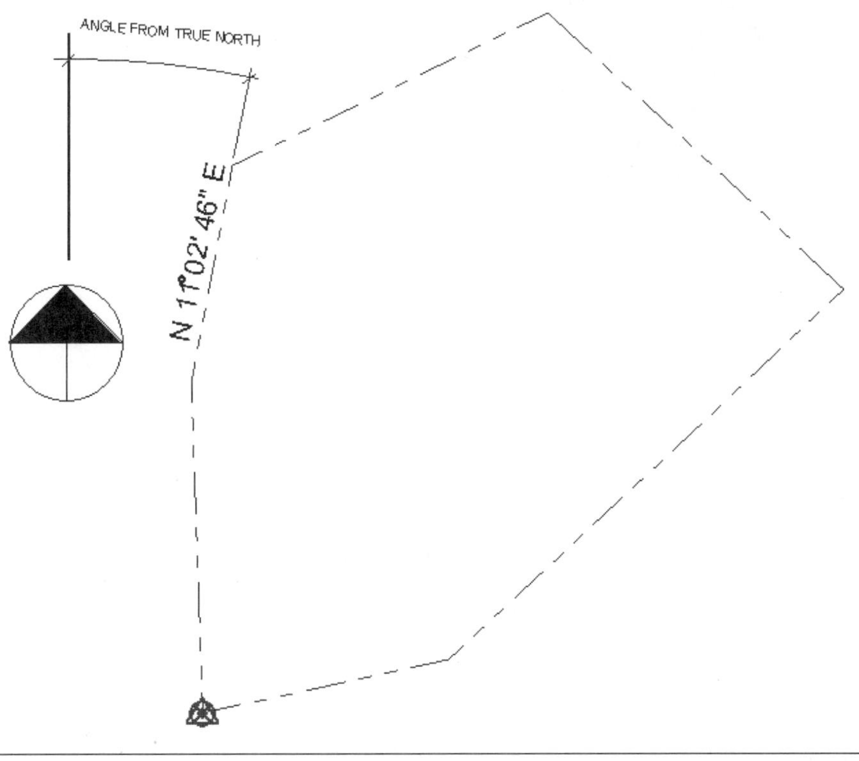

Figure 13-7

Place the **Property Line** at the **Project Base Point**

EXERCISE 13-3 USING THE SUN PATH TOOL

The **Sun Path** tool in combination with the **Shadows** tool allows one to adjust the building in relation to the shadows it creates. Now that True North and the location have been set for the project, Revit can calculate the shadows.

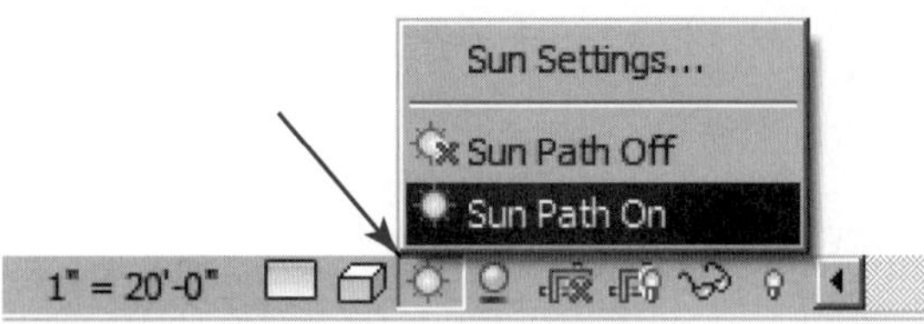

1. Using the previous file, be sure you are in the **Site** plan view, and that the **Location** is **Washington DC**.
2. Using the **Wall** and **Roof** tools, create a rectangular building **20′** × **50′** × **60′** high.
3. In the **View Control Bar**, select the **Sun Path On** and **Shadows On** buttons (see Figure 13-8).
4. The **Sun Path** compass will now appear, and the building will display its shadow (see Figure 13-9).
5. Selecting the date as shown in Figure 13-10 allows you to specify the month and day.

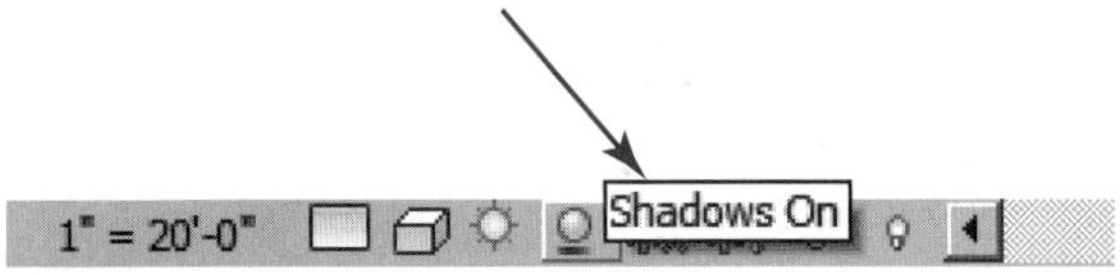

Figure 13-8

Sun Path On and **Shadows On** buttons

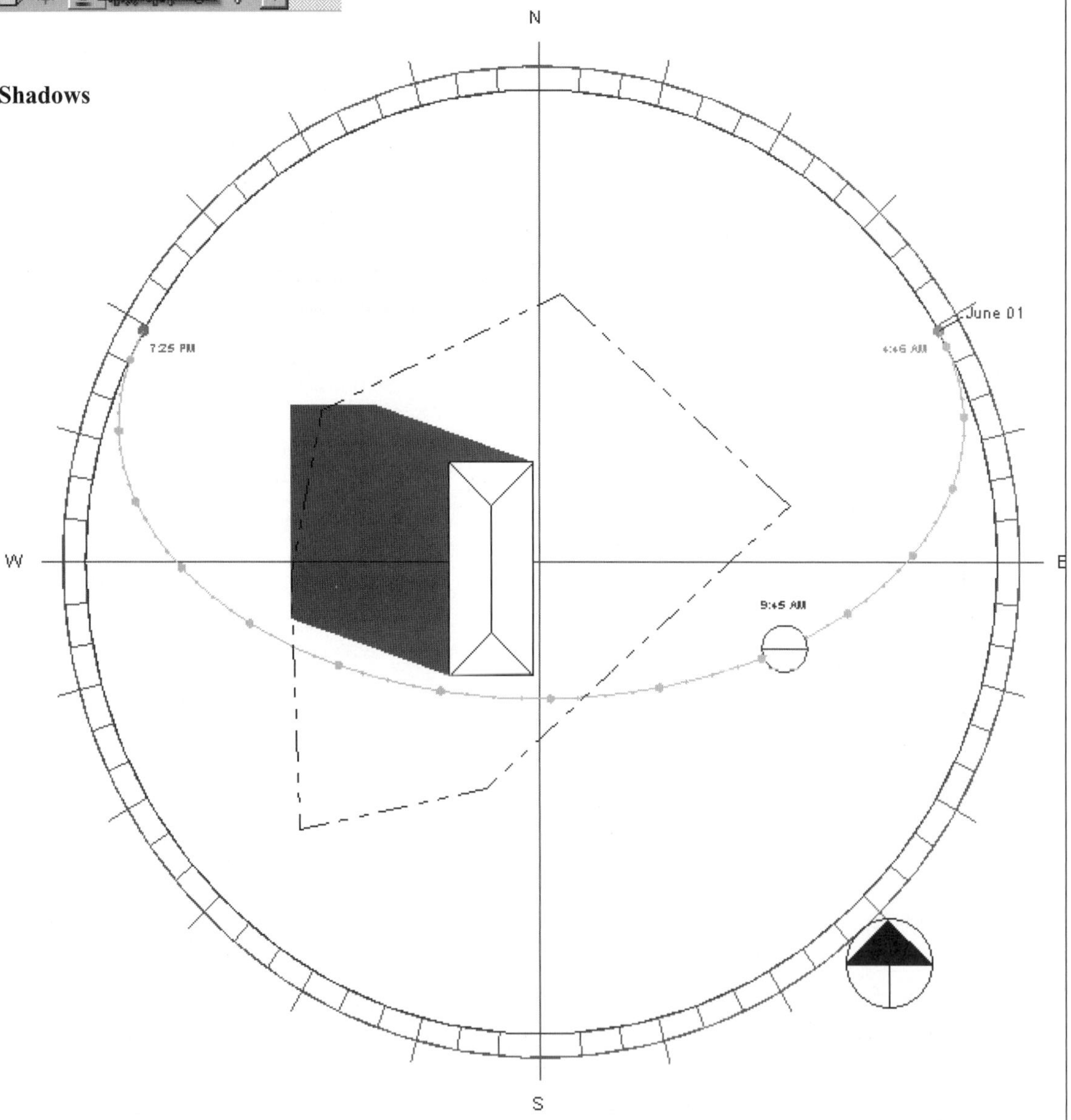

Figure 13-9

The building will display its shadow

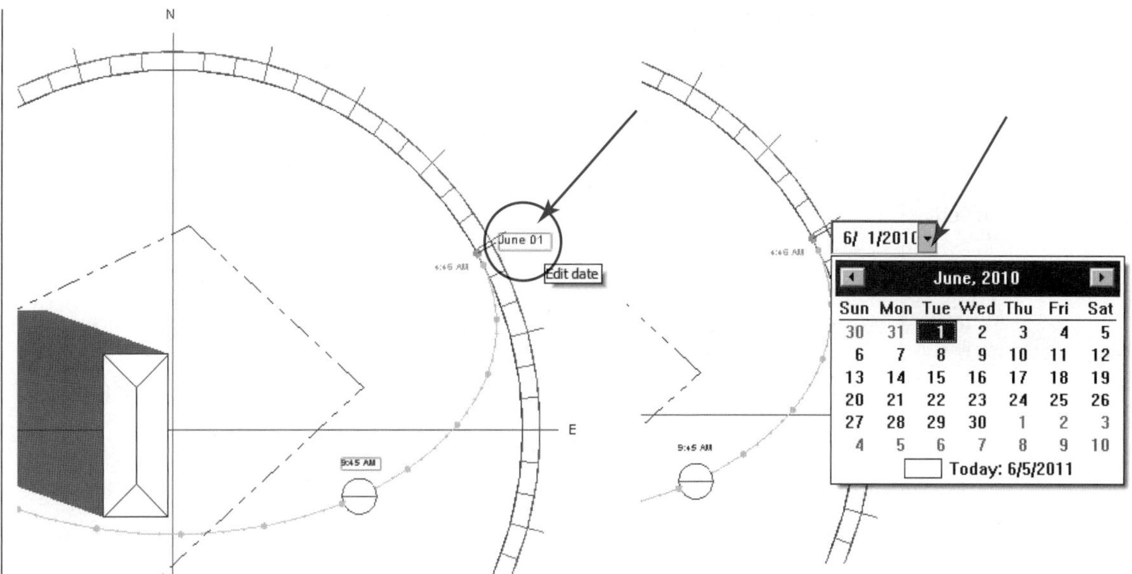

Figure 13-10

Selecting the date

6. Select the **Time** icon, and change the time. The shadow will reflect the time of day at that location (see Figure 13-11).
7. Save the file as **SUNPATH & SHADOWS.rvt**.

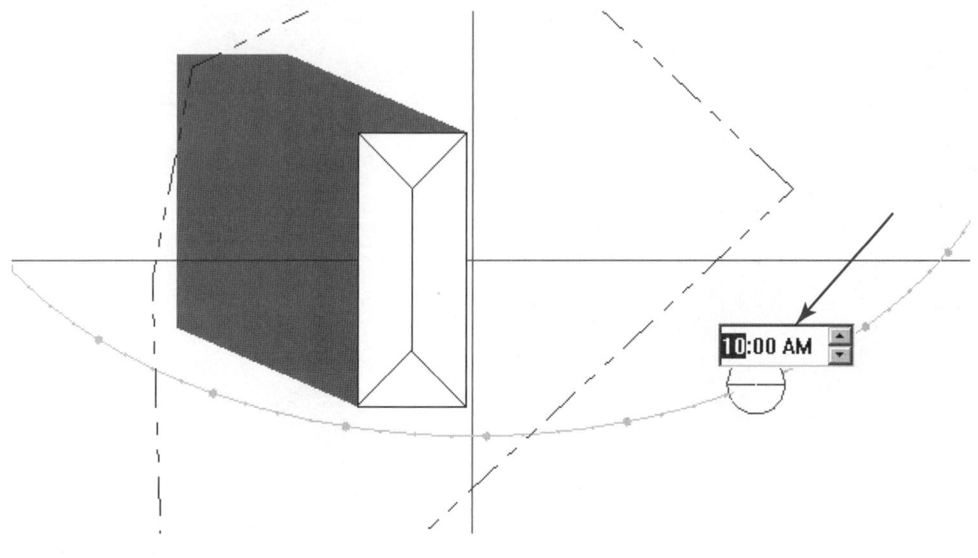

Figure 13-11

Changing the time

EXERCISE 13-4 CREATING THE MASS MODEL FOR ENERGY STUDY

1. Start a new project using the RAC 2012\Imperial Templates\default.rte template.
2. In the **Project Browser**, double click **Site** to bring it up into the **Drawing Editor**.
3. Select **Save As > Project** from the **Application** menu, and save it as **ANALYZE.rvt**.

NOTE:

Shadow studies can be done with any type of Revit model, but **Energy Analysis** can only be done to a **Mass Model**.

4. Set the **Location** to your school location (see Exercise 13-1).
5. Double click the **East Elevation** in the **Project Browser** to bring the **East Elevation** into the **Drawing Editor**.
6. In the **East Elevation**, create **six** levels **10′-0″** each for a total of **50′-0″.**
7. In the **Project Browser**, double click **Floor Plans > Level 1** to bring it up into the **Drawing Editor**.
8. Set the **Scale** to **1/8″ = 1′-0″**.
9. Select the **Massing & Site** tab to bring up the **Massing & Site** toolbar.
10. In the **Massing & Site** toolbar, select the **In-Place Mass** button to bring up the **Name** dialog box.
11. In the **Name** dialog box, enter **TEST BUILDING**, and press the **OK** button.

You will now be in the mass creation toolbars.

12. Select the **Rectangle** button in the **Draw** panel and place a **120′** × **50′** rectangle in **Level 1**.
13. Change to the **Default 3D** view, and select the rectangle you placed.
14. In the **Modify | Place Lines** toolbar, select the **Create Form > Solid Form** button to create the mass.
15. Click on the top surface of the form, and change its height to **50′-0″** (see Figure 13-12).

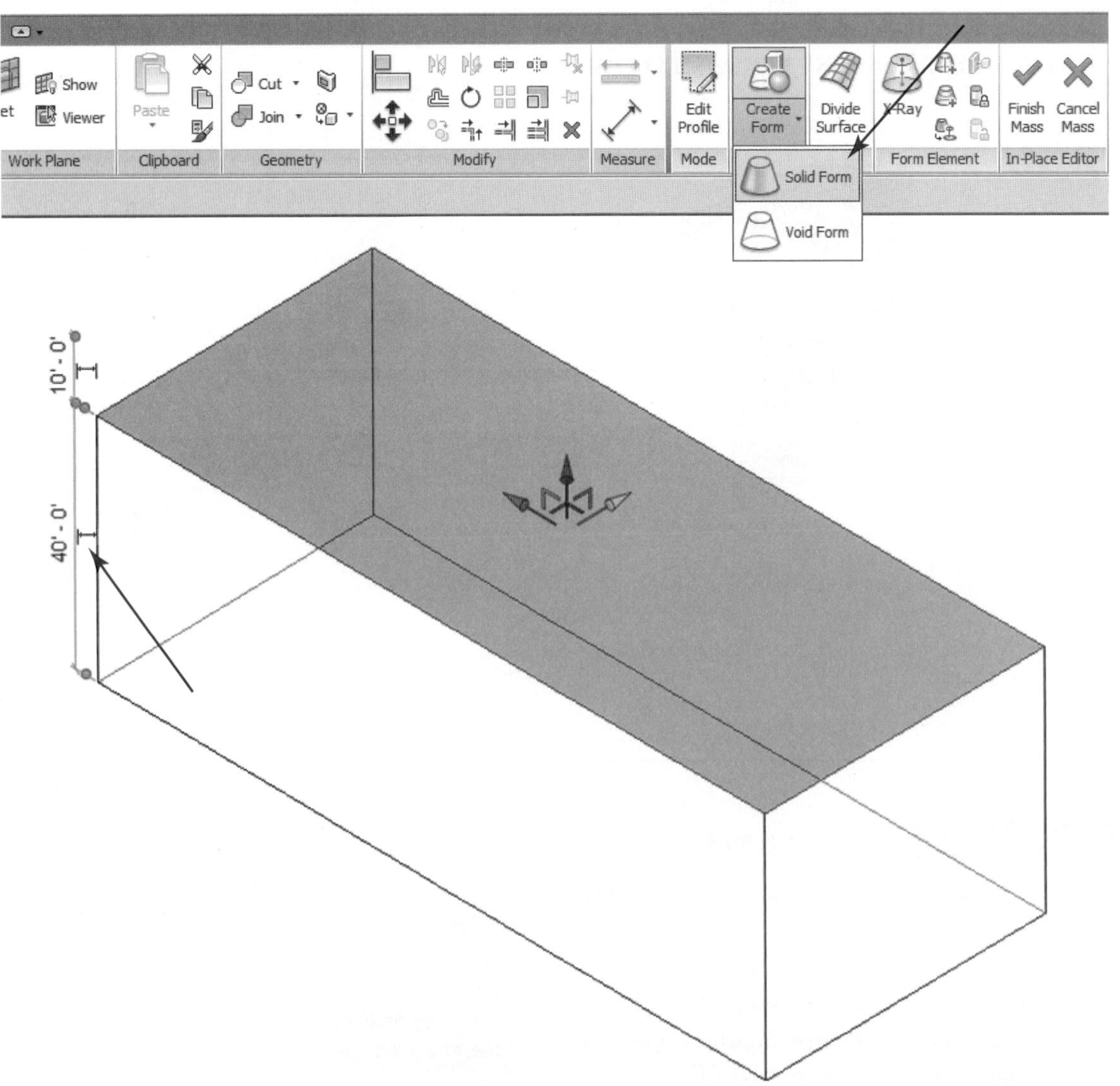

Figure 13-12

Change the form's height to **50′-0″**

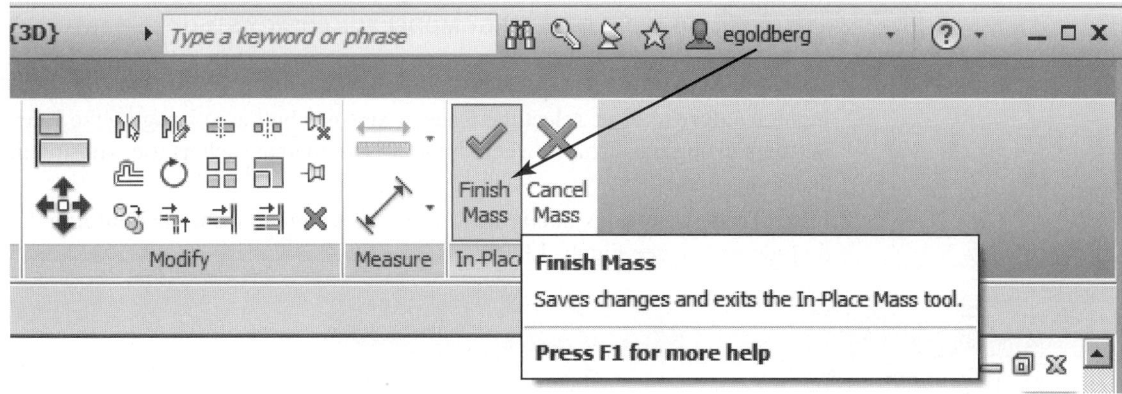

Figure 13-13

Select the **Finish Mass** button

16. Select the **Finish Mass** button to create the **TEST BUILDING** mass (see Figure 13-13).
17. Select the **TEST BUILDING** mass, and select the **Mass Floors** button in the **Modify | Mass** toolbar to bring up the **Mass Floors** dialog box.
18. In the **Mass Floors** dialog box, check all the **Level** check boxes (see Figure 13-14).
19. Save the file.

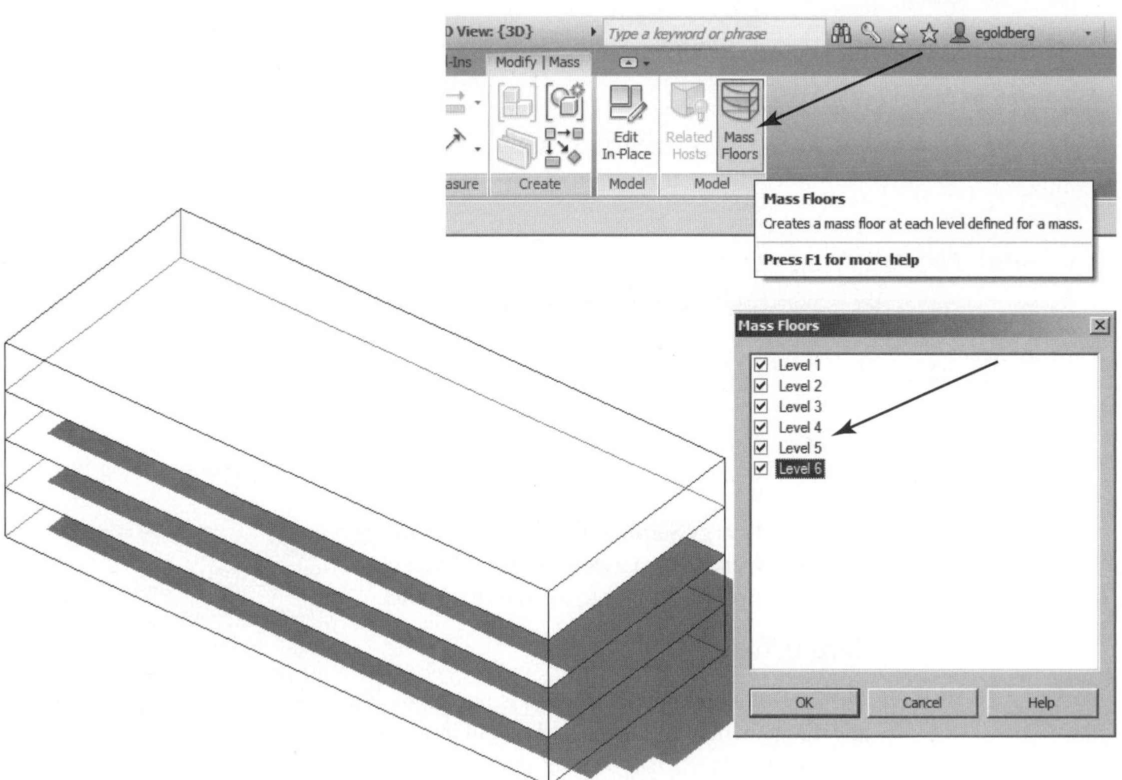

Figure 13-14

The **Mass Floors** dialog box

EXERCISE 13-5 **CREATING THE ENERGY MODEL FOR ENERGY STUDY**

1. Using the **ANALYZE.rvt**, select the **Analyze** tab to bring up the **Analyze** toolbar.
2. In the **Analyze** toolbar, select the **Energy Settings** button to bring up the **Energy Settings** dialog box. This is where building parameters such as use, construction, and so on are set.
3. In the **Energy Settings** dialog box, select **Warehouse** from the **Building Type** drop-down list (see Figure 13-15).

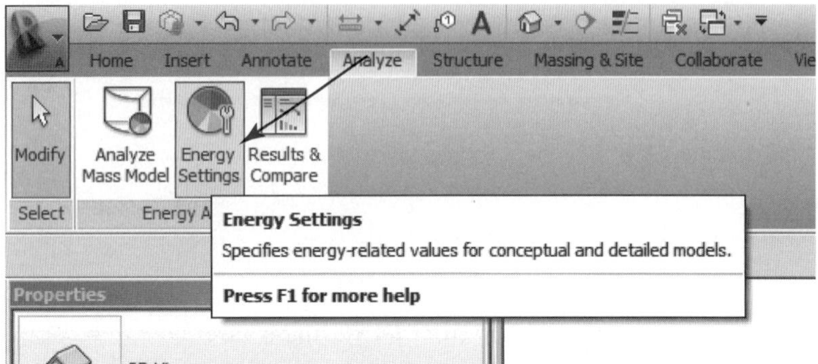

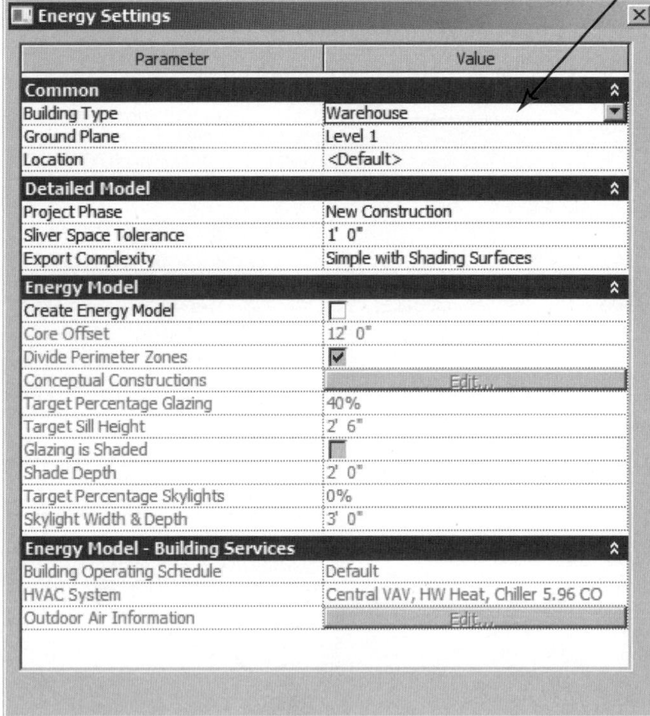

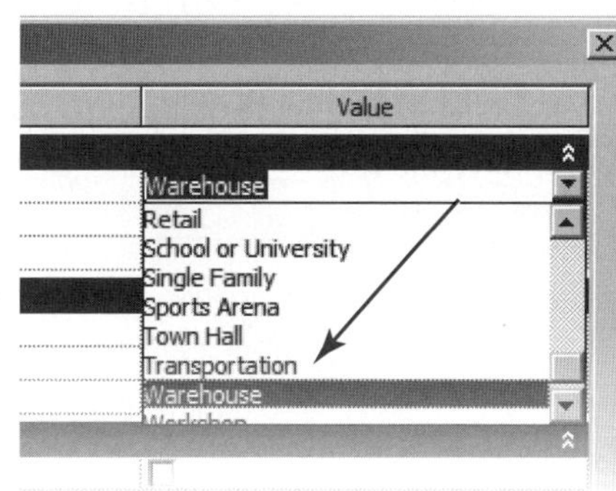

Figure 13-15

The **Energy Settings** dialog box

4. In the **Energy Settings** dialog box, under **Energy Model**, check the **Create Energy Model** check box to enable changes to the **Energy Model**.

NOTE:

Selecting the **Building Type** will automatically enable an approximate amount of occupants per square foot for that type of structure. Occupants add to the cooling load.

Core Offset

The core of a building, because it is not exposed to any direct thermal influence or daylight through the walls or windows, has heating and cooling loads that differ from those at the perimeter. A typical core offset is 12 to 15 feet.

Divide Perimeter Zones

Select this option to divide the perimeter of the building (excluding the core) into four thermal zones: northeast, southeast, northwest, and southwest. Perimeter zones often result in more accurate energy consumption estimates. For example, in late-summer afternoons, a west façade will encounter cooling loads from the sun. However, the east façade will not be exposed to the sun and may require simultaneous heating.

Target Percentage Glazing

This setting specifies the percentage of exterior walls to be glazed openings (windows). It is also known as the *window-to-wall ratio (WWR)*. The default is 40%; the maximum is 95% (which applies to curtain walls, taking into account framing area).

Target Sill Height

Specify the distance from the floor to the bottom of the window. Window areas below task height (typically 0.75 meter or 2.5 feet) contribute to heat gain and heat loss without contributing to effective daylighting.

The **Target Percentage Glazing** and **Target Sill Height** settings work together. If you specify a larger **Target Percentage Glazing**, Revit may use a sill height that is lower than specified to meet the requirement.

Glazing is Shaded

Select this setting if you want light shelves to shade windows and other glazing for conceptual energy analysis. Proper shading greatly reduces cooling energy spent on a space with large areas of unprotected glazing. In the conceptual model, automatic light shelves are external only, and they cannot be manipulated separately from their windows. However, you can manually create light shelves or other types of shades (such as awnings) for the conceptual model by using mass **Surfaces**.

Shade Depth

When you select **Glazing is Shaded**, use the **Shade Depth** setting to specify the depth of the shades. The recommended depth of an external shade is roughly equal to its height above task height (typically 0.75 meter or 2.5 feet in office and school environments).

Target Percentage Skylights

Specify the percentage of roofs that should be skylights. This value is also known as the *skylight-to-roof ratio (SRR)*. The default value is 0%. For 100% daylighting from traditional skylights, approximately 5% of the roof area should be skylights. However, the benefits of daylighting must be weighed against the unwanted effects of heat gain/loss through the skylights. The skylight specifications depend on climate. In all climates, use skylights with a high visible light transmittance (Tvis or VLT). Hot climates should have a low Solar Heat Gain Coefficient (SHGC). Cooler climates should have a low U-value. Tubular skylights require a skylight-to-roof ratio (SRR) approximately 1–2% lower than that of traditional skylights.

Skylight Width & Depth

When you specify a value for **Target Percentage Skylights**, use this setting to specify the size of the skylights.

5. Leave the **Core Offset** at **12′-0″** and click the **Edit** button in the **Conceptual Constructions** field to open the **Conceptual Constructions** dialog box.
6. In the **Conceptual Constructions** dialog box, select the drop-down lists and select the settings shown in Figure 13-16.
   a. Mass Exterior Wall – **Lightweight Construction – Typical Mild Climate Insulation**
   b. Mass Interior Wall – **Lightweight Construction – No Insulation**
   c. Mass Exterior Wall – Underground – **High Mass Construction – No Insulation**

> **NOTE:**
> The core is automatically calculated differently from the perimeter because the perimeter building construction buffers the effects of heat and cold. A core can be thought of as an internal corridor.

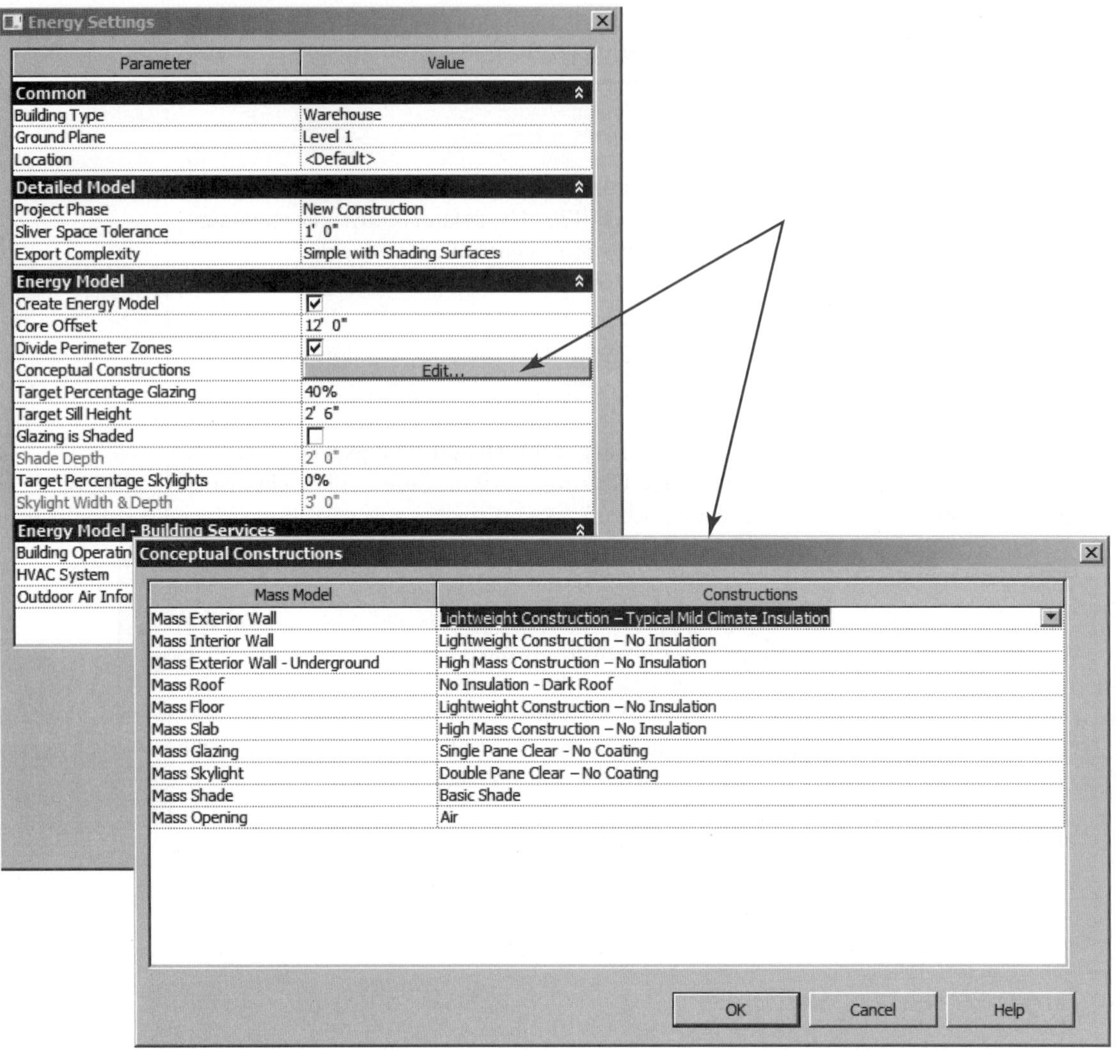

Figure 13-16

The **Conceptual Constructions** dialog box

d. Mass Roof – **No Insulation – Dark Roof**

e. Mass Floor – **Lightweight Construction – No Insulation**

f. Mass Slab – **High Mass Construction – No Insulation**

g. Mass Glazing – **Single Pane Clear – No Coating**

7. Press the **OK** button in the **Conceptual Constructions** dialog box to return to the **Energy Settings** dialog box.
8. In the **Energy Settings** dialog box, set the **Target Percentage Glazing** to **40%**, and the **Target Sill Height** to **2′-6″**.
9. In the **Energy Settings** dialog box, under **Energy Model – Building Services**, select:

   a. **Building Operating Schedule – 24/7 Facility** (24 hours a day, 7 days a week)

   b. **HVAC System – 12 SEER/7.7 HSPF Split Packaged Heat Pump**
10. In the **Energy Settings** dialog box, press the **OK** button to create the **Energy Model** and return to the **Drawing Editor** (see Figures 13-17 and 13-18).
11. Select **Save** from the **Application** menu, and save the file as **ANALYZE.rvt.**

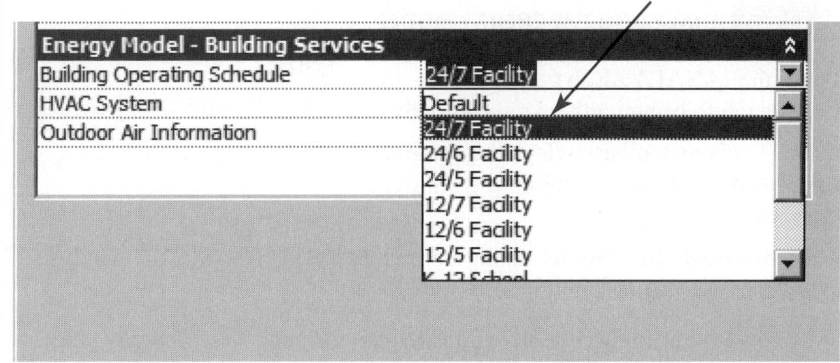

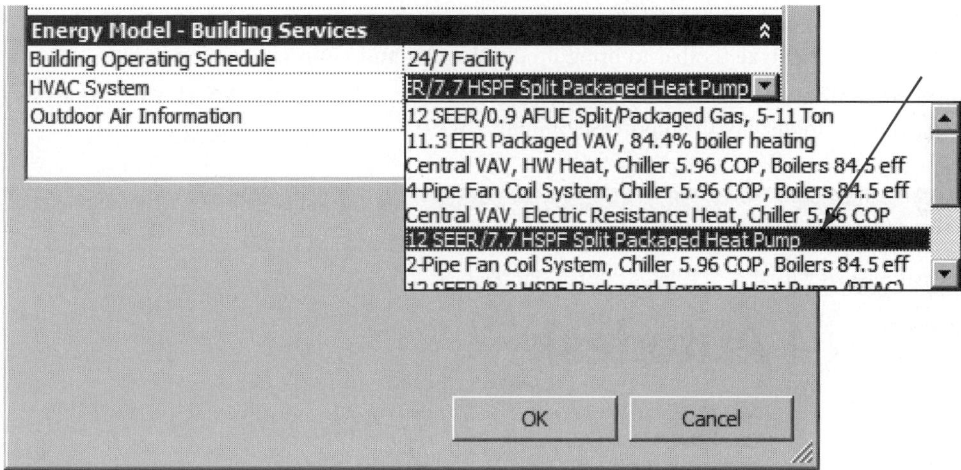

Figure 13-17

Create the **Energy Model**

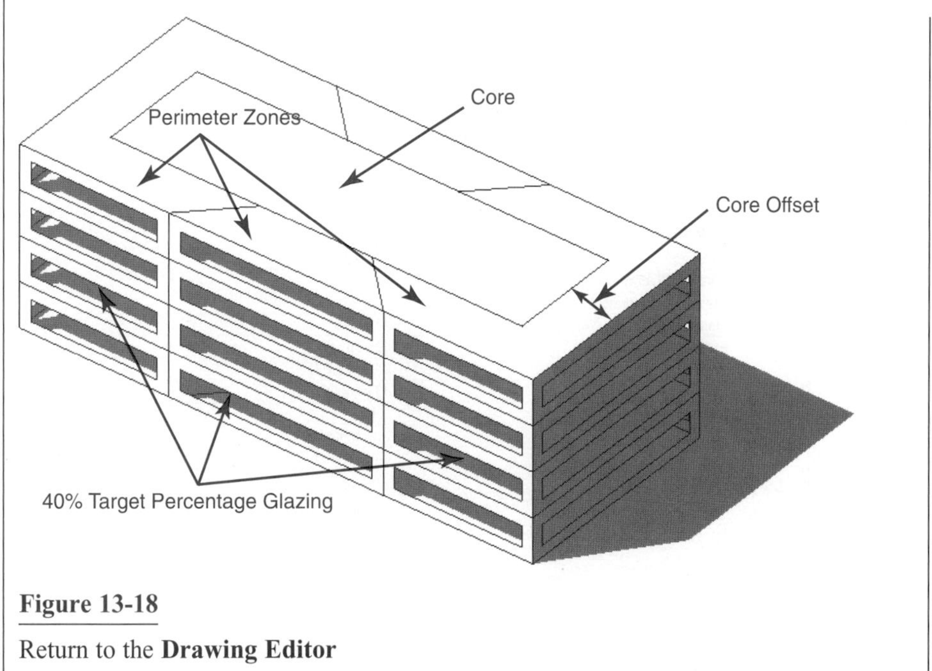

Figure 13-18

Return to the **Drawing Editor**

EXERCISE 13-6 ANALYZING THE ENERGY MODEL

> **NOTE:**
> For this **Analyze** operation you need an Internet connection.

1. Using the **ANALYZE.rvt** file, select the **Analyze** tab to bring up the **Analyze** toolbar.
2. In the **Analyze** toolbar, select the **Analyze Mass Model** button to bring up the **Analyze Mass Model** dialog box.
3. In the **Analyze Mass Model** dialog box, enter **TEST ANALYZE Analysis (1)**, and select the **Continue** button.

Revit will now go out to the Internet and calculate the analysis. This may take a few moments. When finished, Revit will post a notice at the lower right corner of the **Drawing Editor.**

4. When the analysis is finished, select the **Results & Compare** button in the **Analyze** toolbar to bring up the **Results and Compare** dialog box.
5. In the **Results and Compare** dialog box, select **TEST ANALYZE Analysis (1)** to display the report (see Figure 13-19).

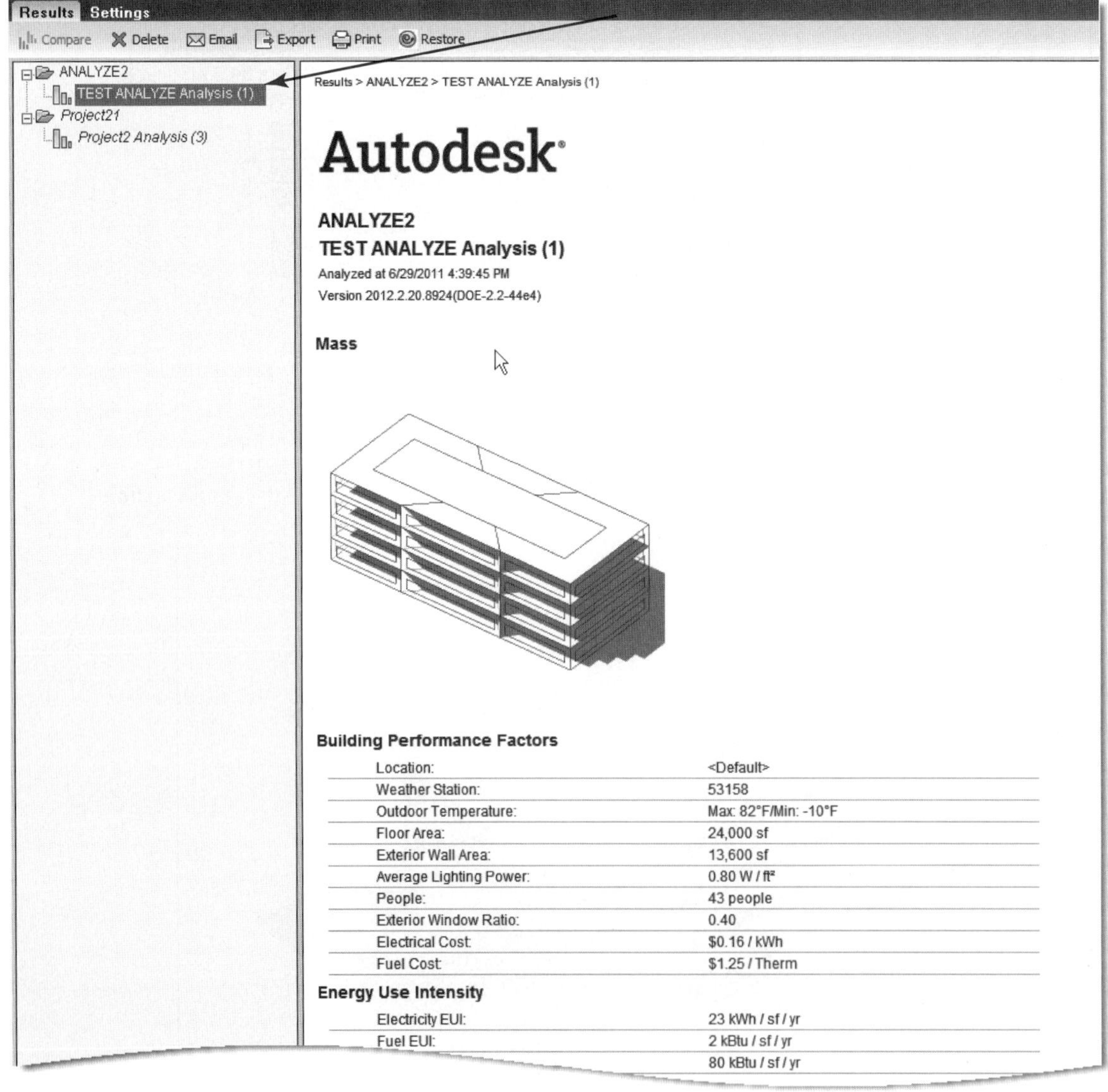

Figure 13-19

Display the **TEST ANALYZE Analysis (1)** report

The **Building Performance Factors** give general information about the Energy Model such as floor and wall areas, how many occupants, **Average Lighting Power** in **W/ft^2**, and **Electrical** and **Fuel** costs per **KWh** and **Therm** for the location of the Energy Model.

6. Scroll down the report to see the **Energy Use Intensity (EUI)**.

The **Energy Use Intensity** tells how many thousand Btu per square foot per year are consumed for this model. The fewer Btu per square foot per year, the more efficient the model.

7. Scroll down the report to see the **Life Cycle Energy Use/Cost**.

The **Life Cycle Energy Use/Cost** field predicts the cost of fuel and electricity for a 30-year life period.

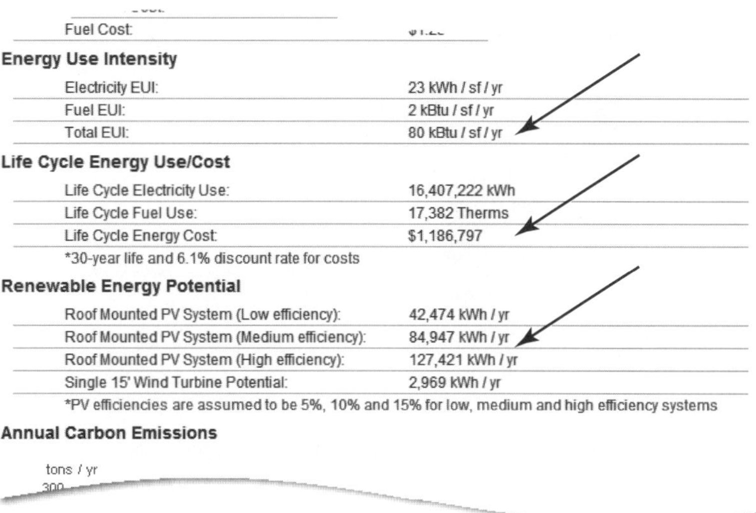

Fuel Cost:	
Energy Use Intensity	
Electricity EUI:	23 kWh / sf / yr
Fuel EUI:	2 kBtu / sf / yr
Total EUI:	80 kBtu / sf / yr
Life Cycle Energy Use/Cost	
Life Cycle Electricity Use:	16,407,222 kWh
Life Cycle Fuel Use:	17,382 Therms
Life Cycle Energy Cost:	$1,186,797
*30-year life and 6.1% discount rate for costs	
Renewable Energy Potential	
Roof Mounted PV System (Low efficiency):	42,474 kWh / yr
Roof Mounted PV System (Medium efficiency):	84,947 kWh / yr
Roof Mounted PV System (High efficiency):	127,421 kWh / yr
Single 15' Wind Turbine Potential:	2,969 kWh / yr
*PV efficiencies are assumed to be 5%, 10% and 15% for low, medium and high efficiency systems	
Annual Carbon Emissions	

Figure 13-20

The **Energy Use Intensity**, **Life Cycle Energy Use/Cost**, and **Renewable Energy Potential** fields

8. Scroll down the report to see the **Renewable Energy Potential**.

The **Renewable Energy Potential** fields predict the potential photovoltaic and wind power needed to create renewable electricity for the location of the Energy Model (see Figure 13-20).

9. Scroll down the report to see the **Annual Carbon Emissions**.

The **Annual Carbon Emissions** field predicts the amount of **Net CO_2** generated by the Energy Model. It also subtracts CO_2 for any potential **Renewable Energy Generation** (see Figure 13-21).

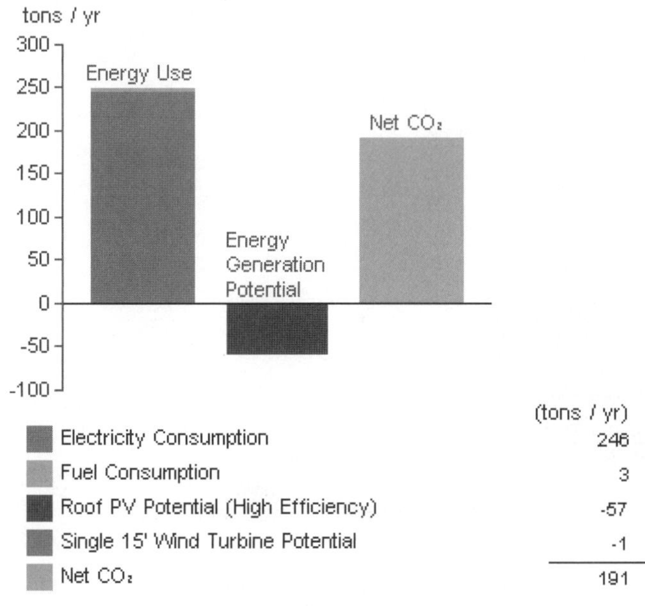

Figure 13-21

The **Annual Carbon Emissions** field

Annual Energy Use/Cost

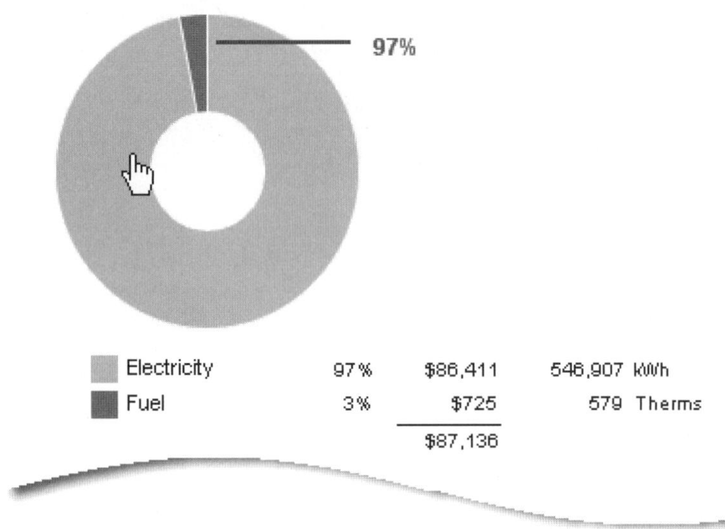

Figure 13-22

The **Annual Energy Use/Cost** diagram

Energy Use: Fuel

100%

			(Therms)
HVAC	0%	$0	0
Domestic Hot Water	100%	$724	579
		$724	579

Figure 13-23

The **Energy Use: Fuel** diagram

10. Scroll down the report to see the **Annual Energy Use/Cost.**

The **Annual Energy Use/Cost** diagram predicts the total yearly **Electricity** and **Fuel** costs for the Energy Model (see Figure 13-22).

11. Scroll down the report to see the **Energy Use: Fuel.**

The **Energy Use: Fuel** diagram predicts the yearly fuel costs for **HVAC** and **Domestic Hot Water** for the Energy Model (see Figure 13-23).

12. Scroll down the report to see the **Energy Use: Electricity.**

The **Energy Use: Electricity** diagram predicts the yearly electrical costs for **HVAC, Lighting,** and **Misc. Equipment** such as computers and other devices (see Figure 13-24).

Figure 13-24

The **Energy Use: Electricity** diagram

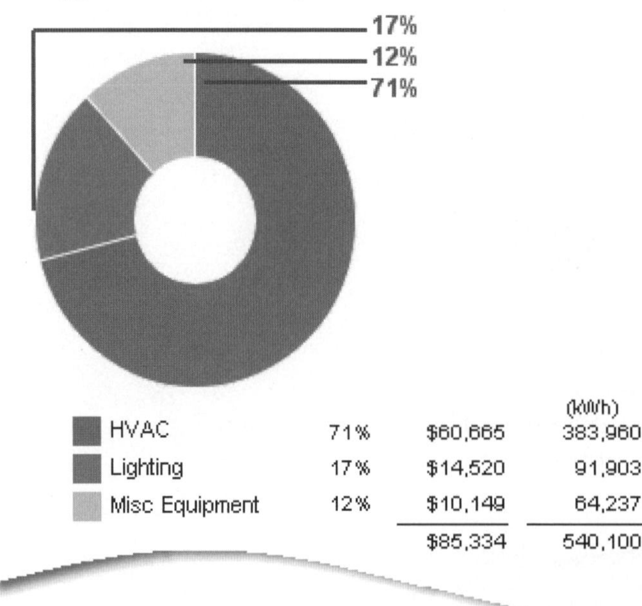

13. Scroll down the report to see the **Monthly Heating Load.**

The **Monthly Heating Load** diagram predicts how many million Btus are gained as heat from things such as **Misc. Equipment**, **Light Fixtures**, **Occupants**, and so on. The diagram also shows how many million Btus are lost through the **Windows**, **Roofs**, **Walls**, and other components (see Figure 13-25).

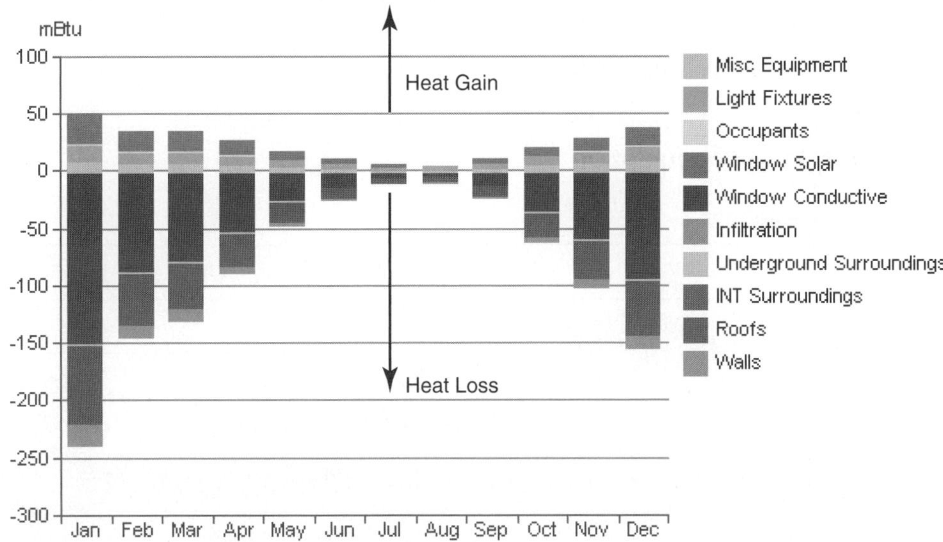

Figure 13-25

The **Monthly Heating Load** diagram

14. Scroll down the report to see the **Monthly Cooling Load.**

The **Monthly Cooling Load** diagram predicts how many million Btus are needed to cool the building, and how much things such as **Misc. Equipment**, **Light Fixtures**, **Occupants**, and so on are contributing to that cooling load (see Figure 13-26).

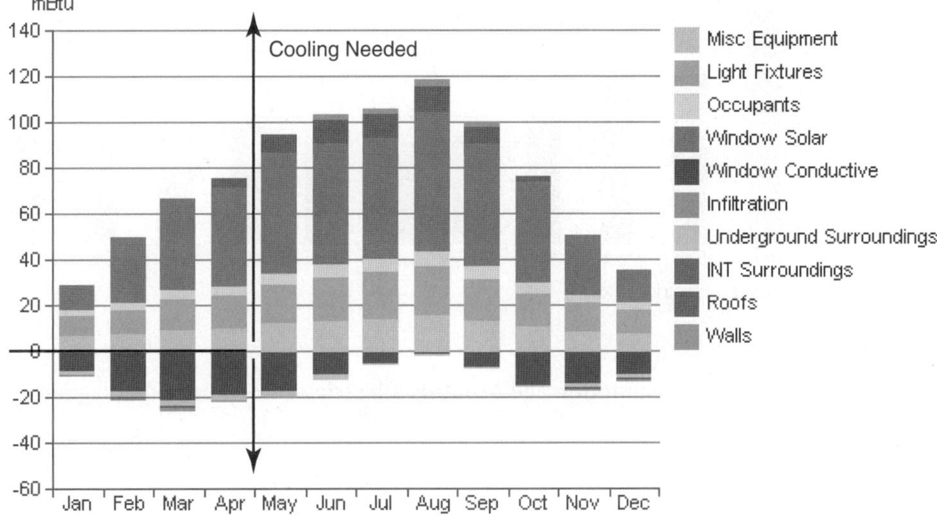

Figure 13-26

The **Monthly Cooling Load** diagram

15. Scroll down the report to see the **Monthly Fuel Consumption** and **Monthly Electricity Consumption** diagrams.

The **Monthly Fuel Consumption** and **Monthly Electricity Consumption** diagrams predict how many **Therms** and **kWh,** respectively, are consumed each month at the building's location (see Figure 13-27).

16. Scroll down the report to see the **Annual Wind Rose**.

The **Annual Wind Rose** illustrates the wind speed, direction, and frequency at the building's location (see Figure 13-28).

17. Save this file as **ENERGY MODEL**.

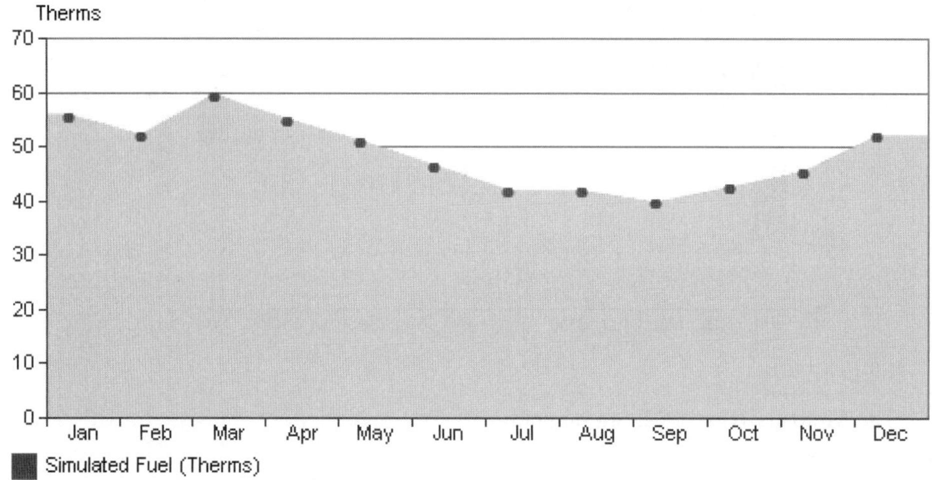

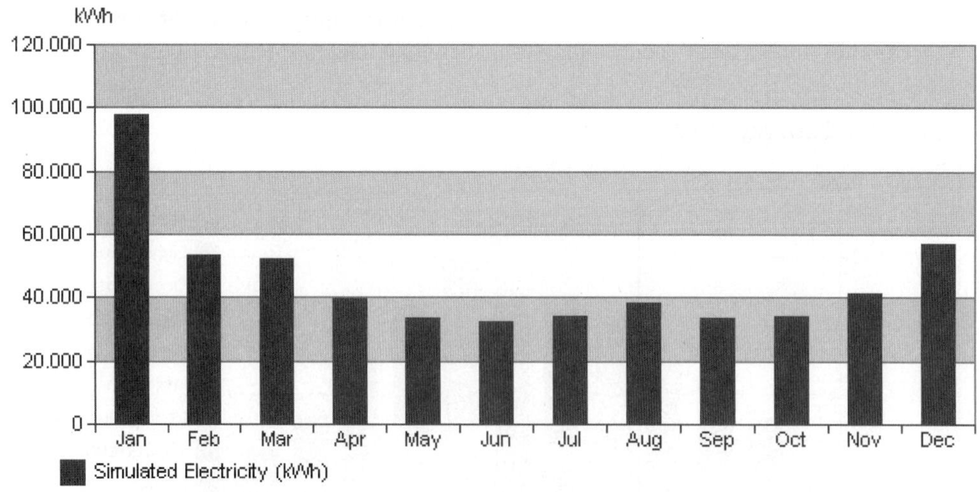

Figure 13-27

The **Monthly Fuel Consumption** and **Monthly Electricity Consumption** diagrams

Annual Wind Rose (Speed Distribution)

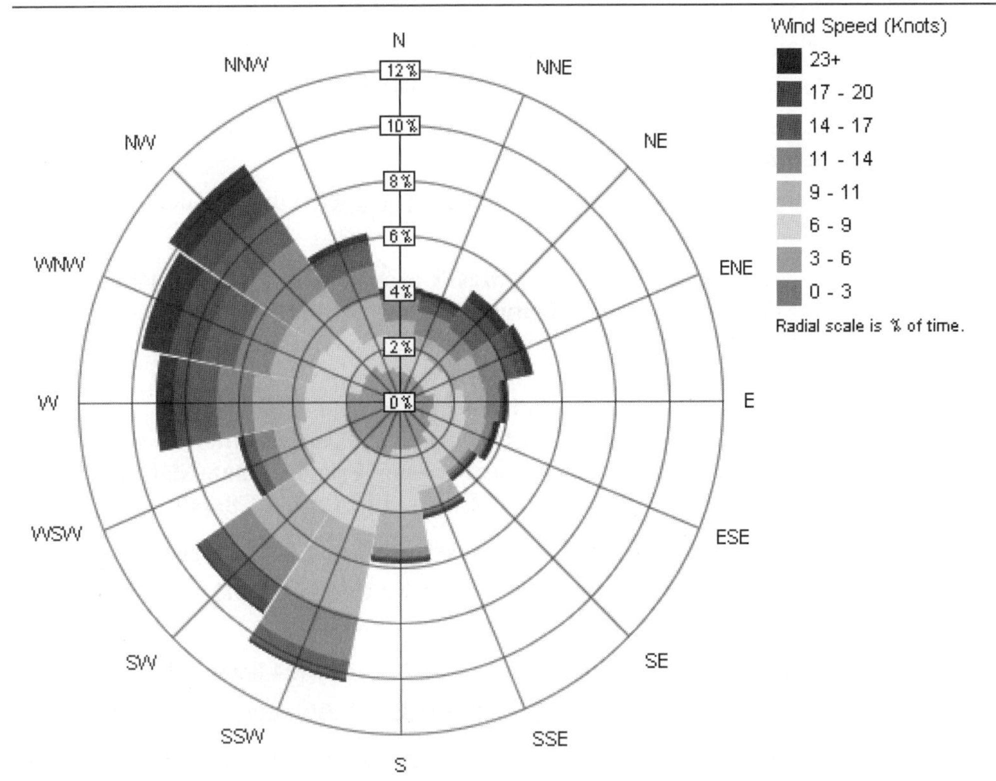

Annual Wind Rose (Frequency Distribution)

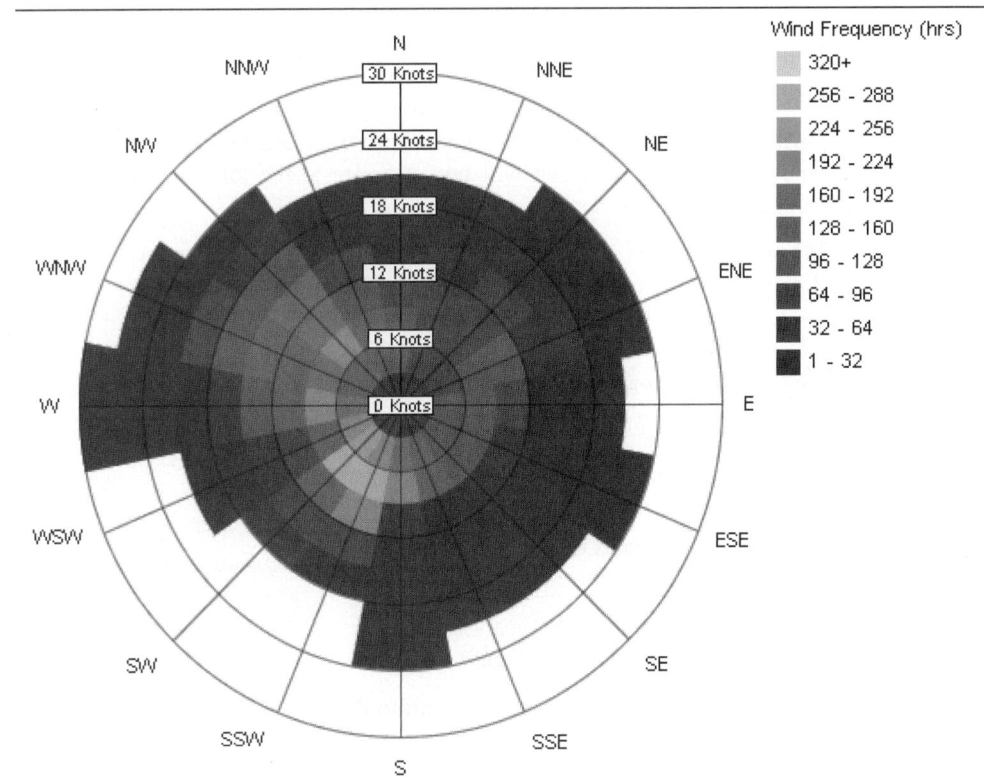

Figure 13-28

The **Annual Wind Rose**

EXERCISE 13-7 MODIFYING THE ENERGY MODEL

1. Minimize the report to reveal the Revit **Drawing Editor**.
2. Select the **Analyze** tab to bring up the **Analyze** toolbar.
3. In the **Analyze** toolbar, select the **Energy Settings** button to bring up the **Energy Settings** dialog box.
4. In the **Conceptual Constructions** dialog box, select the drop-down lists and select the following settings:

   a. Mass Exterior Wall – **High Mass Construction – High Insulation**
   b. Mass Interior Wall – **Lightweight Construction – No Insulation**
   c. Mass Exterior Wall – **Underground – High Mass Construction – High Insulation**
   d. Mass Roof – **High Insulation – Cool Roof**
   e. Mass Floor – **Lightweight Construction – No Insulation**
   f. Mass Slab – **High Mass Construction – Frigid Climate Slab Insulation**
   g. Mass Glazing – **Double Pane Clear – LowE Cold Climate, High SHGC**

5. In the **Energy Settings** dialog box, set the **Target Percentage Glazing** to **20%**.
6. In the **Energy Settings** dialog box, under **Energy Model – Building Services**, select:

   a. **Building Operating Schedule – 24/7 Facility** (24 hours a day, 7 days a week)
   b. **HVAC System – 12 SEER/0.9 AFUE Split/Packaged Gas, 5-11 Ton**

7. In the **Energy Settings** dialog box, select the **OK** button to return to the **Drawing Editor**.
8. In the **Analyze** toolbar, select the **Analyze Mass Model** button to bring up the **Analyze Mass Model** dialog box.
9. In the **Analyze Mass Model** dialog box, enter **TEST ANALYZE Analysis (2)** and select the **Continue** button.

Revit will now go out to the Internet and calculate the analysis. This may take a few moments. When finished, Revit will post a notice at the lower right corner of the **Drawing Editor.**

10. When the analysis is finished, select the **Results & Compare** button in the **Analyze** toolbar to bring up the **Results and Compare** dialog box.

EXERCISE 13-8 COMPARING THE ENERGY MODELS

1. Select both **TEST ANALYZE Analysis (1)** and **TEST ANALYZE Analysis (2)** and then select the **Compare** button to see the two analyses side by side (see Figure 13-29).
2. Scroll down the report to see the **Energy Use Intensity (EUI)**.

> **NOTE:**
> Hold down the **<Ctrl>** key on the keyboard while selecting multiple files.

Notice that the EUI for the second analysis uses less kBtu per square foot per year (see Figure 13-30).

3. Scroll down the report to see the **Annual Energy Use/Cost.**

Notice that the **Annual Energy Use/Cost** is lower for the second analysis. Also notice that less electricity, and more fuel, is used for the second analysis. This is because the heating plant for the second analysis was changed from electric to gas (see Figure 13-31).

4. Scroll down the report to see the **Energy Use: Fuel.**

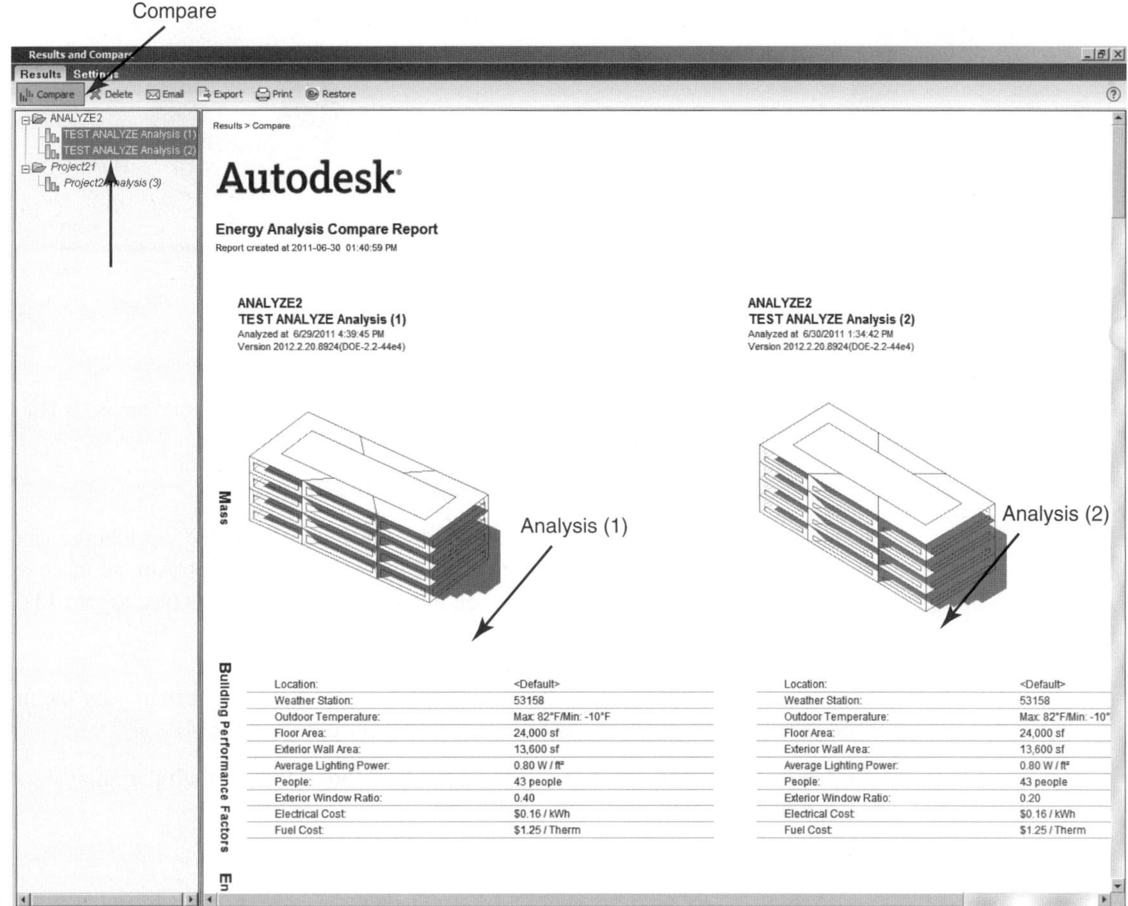

Figure 13-29

Comparing both **TEST ANALYZE Analysis (1)** and **TEST ANALYZE Analysis (2)** (Autodesk screen shots reprinted with the permission of Autodesk, Inc.)

Figure 13-30

The **Energy Use Intensity (EUI)**

Figure 13-31

The **Annual Energy Use/Cost**

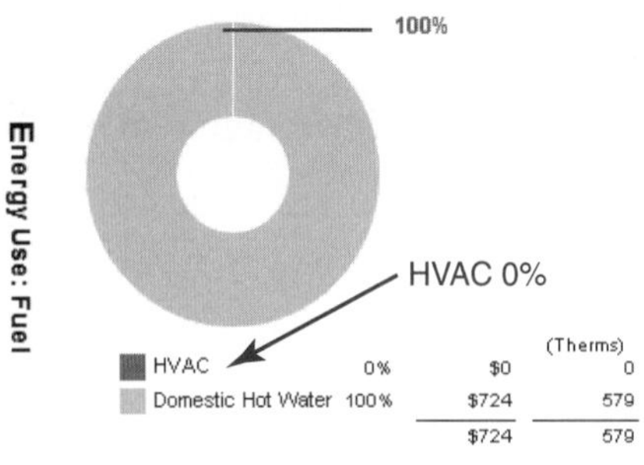

Figure 13-32

The **Energy Use: Fuel** diagram

Notice that the **Energy Use: Fuel** diagram now shows that the second analysis HVAC system is powered by fuel (gas) (see Figure 13-32).

5. Scroll down the report to see the **Monthly Heating Load.**

Notice that the second analysis has a much lower heat loss due to the fact that the second analysis used building constructions that were more energy efficient. Among these were a smaller glass area, a cool-insulated roof, and better insulated walls (see Figure 13-33).

6. Scroll down the report to see the **Monthly Cooling Load.**

Notice that the second analysis has a lower cooling load created primarily by the insulated roof, smaller windows, and insulated walls (see Figure 13-34).

7. Continue to make changes to the **Energy Model**. Create multiple analyses and **Compare** them.
8. Save this file as **ENERGY COMPARISON**.

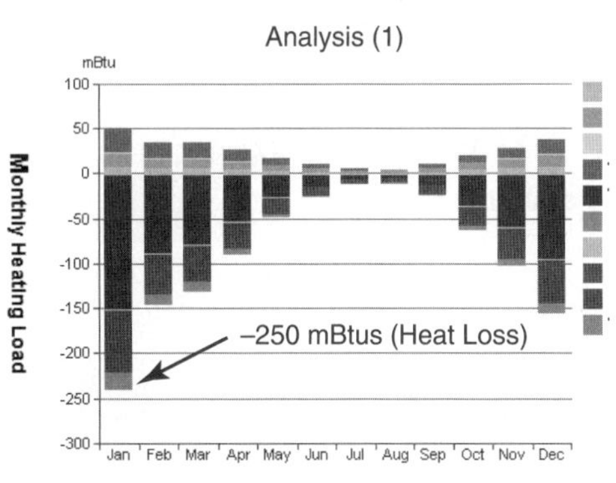

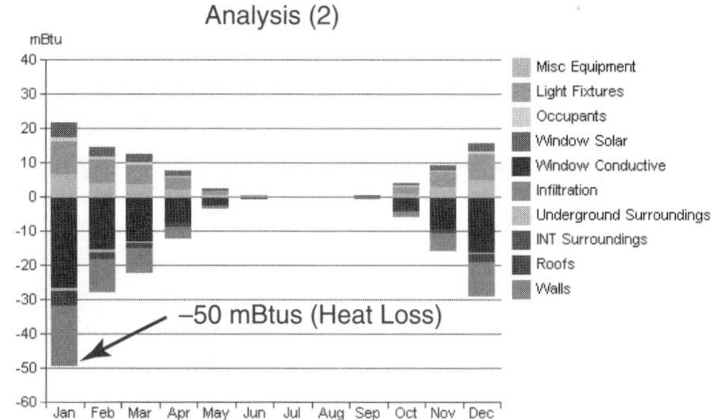

Figure 13-33

The **Monthly Heating Load**

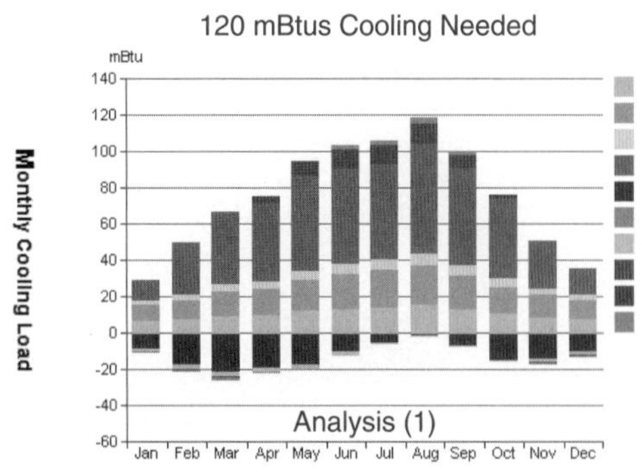

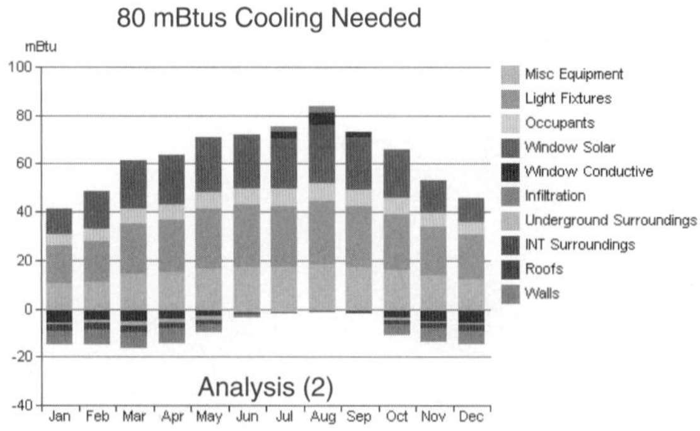

Figure 13-34

The **Monthly Cooling Load**

EXERCISE 13-9 MODIFYING MASS ZONES

Mass Zones are areas of the **Energy Model** that act like rooms or areas.

1. Using the previous file, select the **Massing & Site** tab to bring up the **Massing & Site** toolbar.
2. In the **Massing & Site** toolbar, select the **Show Mass Zones and Shades** button (see Figure 13-35).

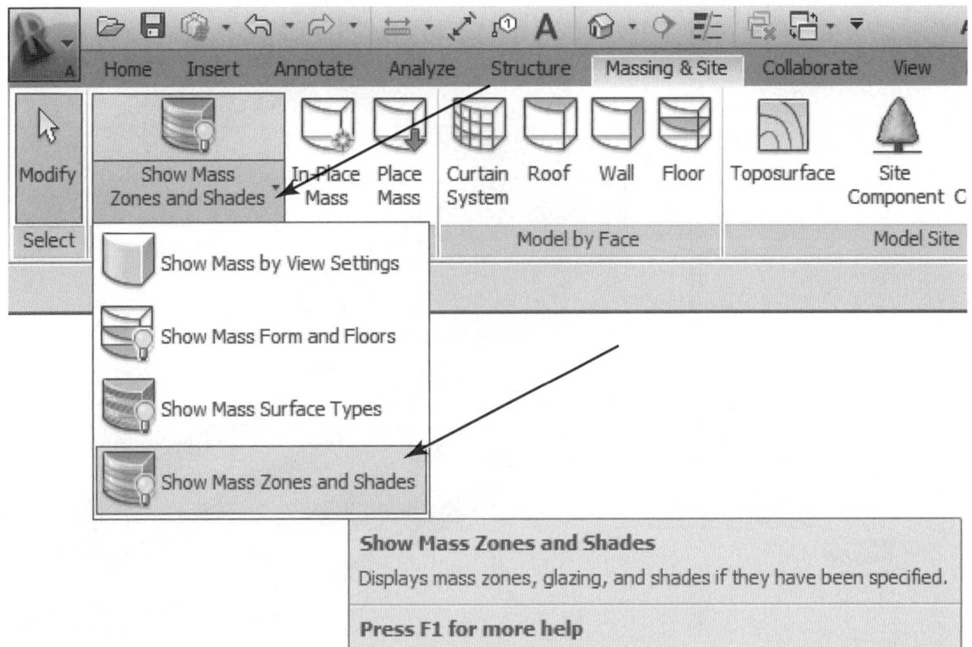

Figure 13-35

Select the **Show Mass Zones and Shades** button

3. In the **Drawing Editor**, move the cursor over the **Energy Model**, and the **Zones** will appear.
4. Click on a **Zone** to activate it.
5. In the **Properties** dialog box, select a different space type from the **Space Type** drop-down list.
6. Select **Heated and cooled** from the **Condition Type** drop-down list (see Figure 13-36).
7. Repeat, changing **Zones** and reanalyzing the **Energy Model**.
8. Save this file as **MODIFYING MASS ZONES**.

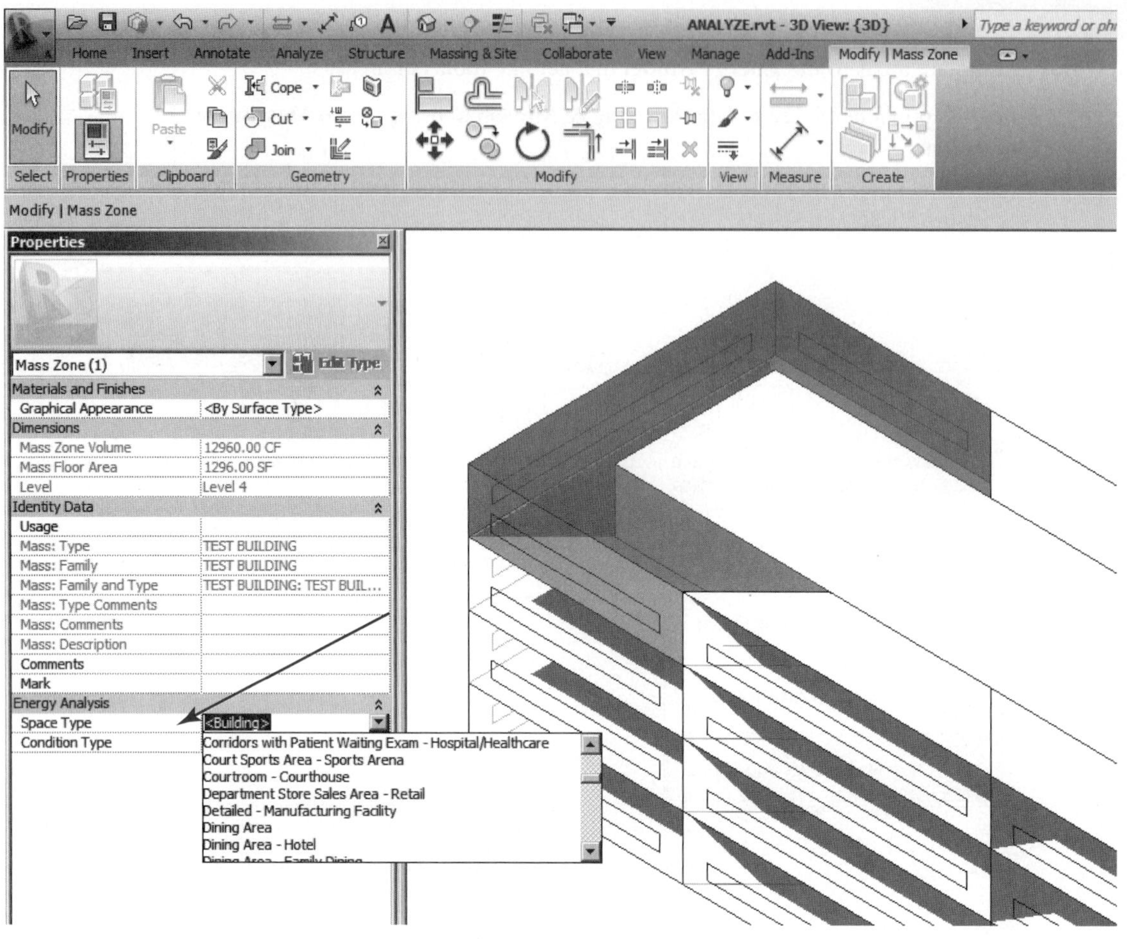

Figure 13-36

Select a different **Space Type** and **Condition Type** in the **Properties** dialog box

EXERCISE 13-10 MODIFYING ENERGY MODEL SURFACES

Modifying **Energy Model** surfaces gives one capability to change glazing, insulation, and mass wall construction for a surface.

1. Using the previous file, select the **Massing & Site** tab to bring up the **Massing & Site** toolbar.
2. In the **Massing & Site** toolbar, select the **Show Mass Surface Types** button (see Figure 13-37).
3. In the **Drawing Editor**, move the cursor over the **Energy Model** and press the **<Tab>** key on the keyboard until a surface "lights up" with a light aqua color.
4. Click to select the surface.
5. In the **Properties** dialog box, select **<By Surface>** from the **Values** field (see Figure 13-38).
6. Change the **Target Percentage Glazing** to **90%**.
7. Check the **Glazing is Shaded** check box.
8. Set the **Shade Depth** to **5′-0″** (see Figure 13-39).
9. Save the file as **MODIFYING ENERGY MODEL SURFACES**.

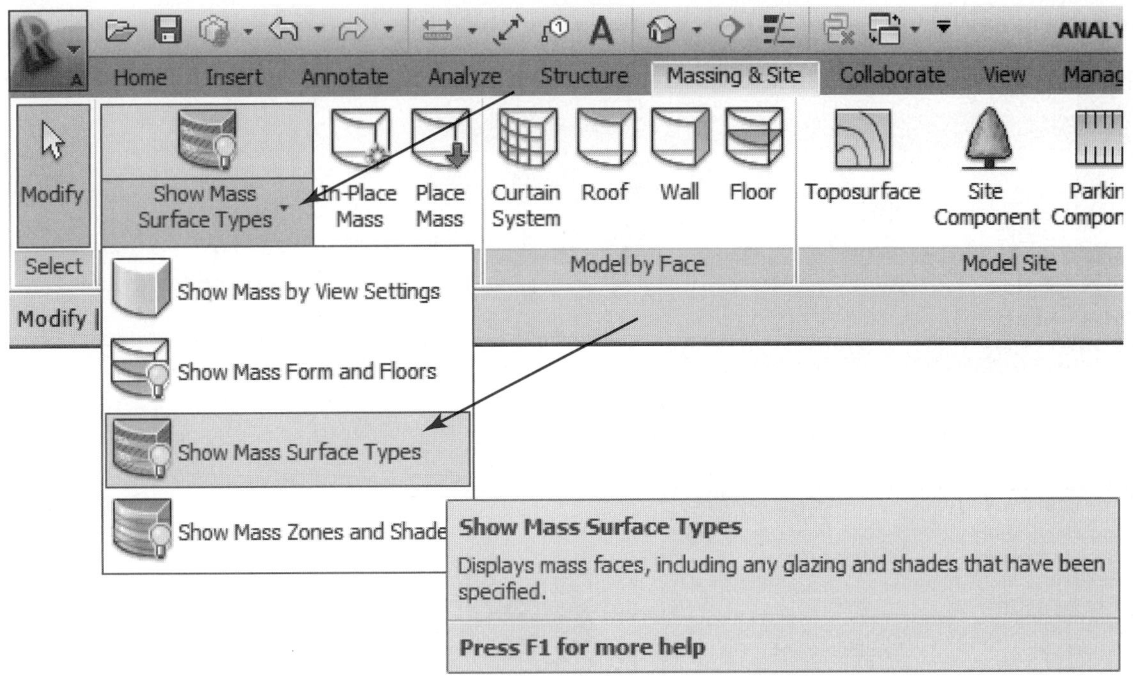

Figure 13-37

Select the **Show Mass Surface Types** button

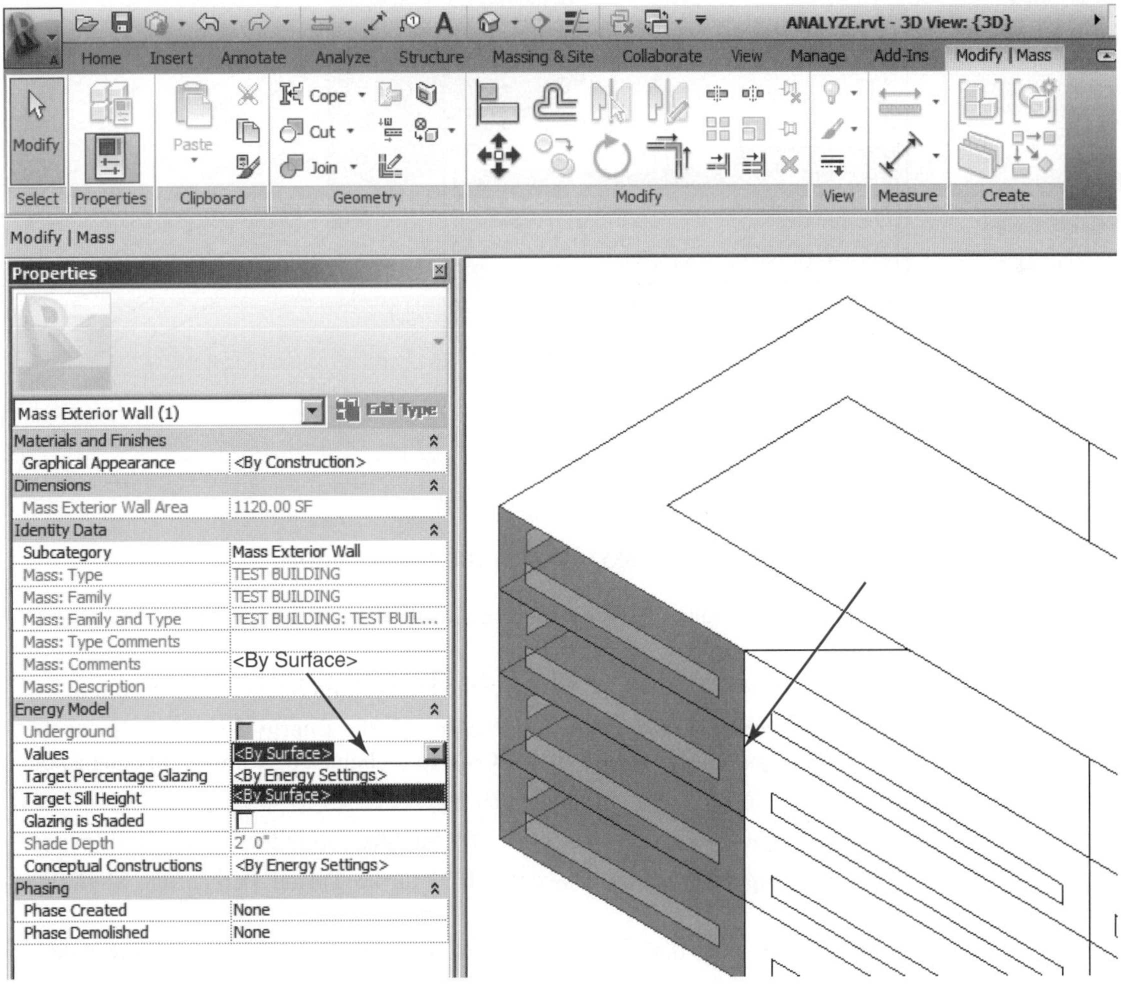

Figure 13-38

Select **<By Surface>** from the **Values** field

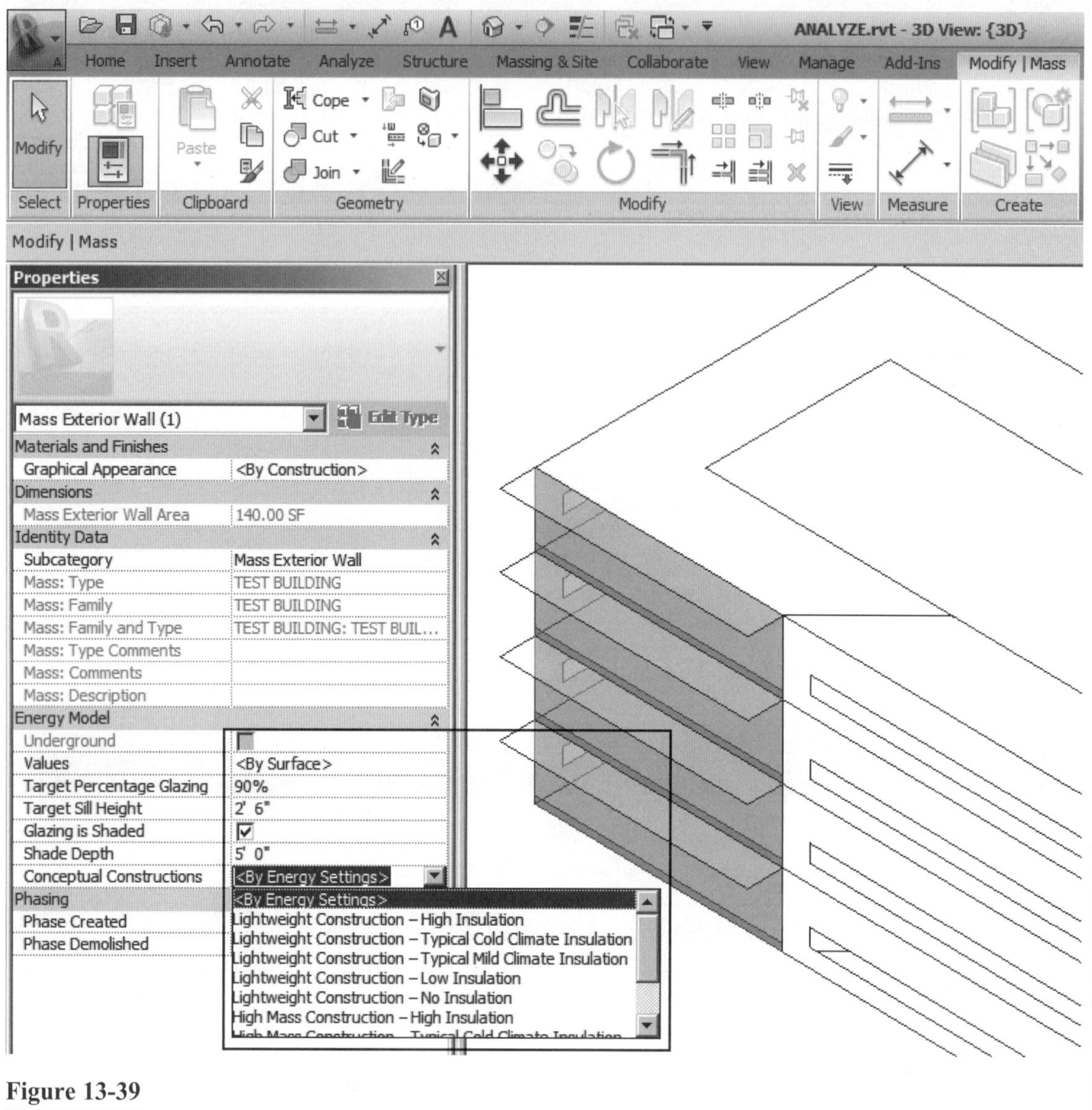

Figure 13-39

Set the **Shade Depth** to **5′-0″**

EXERCISE 13-11 CREATING SKYLIGHTS IN THE ENERGY MODEL

1. Using the previous file, select the **Massing & Site** tab to bring up the **Massing & Site** toolbar.
2. In the **Massing & Site** toolbar, select the **Show Mass Surface Types** button.
3. In the **Drawing Editor**, move the cursor over the **Energy Model** and press the **<Tab>** key on the keyboard until a **Core** roof "lights up" with a light aqua color.
4. Click to select the roof of the **Core** surface.
5. In the **Properties** dialog box, select **<By Surface>** from the **Values** field.
6. In the **Properties** dialog box, enter **25%** in the **Target Percentage Skylights** field.
7. In the **Properties** dialog box, enter **3′-0″** in the **Skylight Width & Depth** field.
8. Press the **Apply** button at the bottom of the **Properties** dialog box to make the changes to the **Energy Model** (see Figure 13-40).
9. Save the file as **CREATING SKYLIGHTS IN THE ENERGY MODEL**.

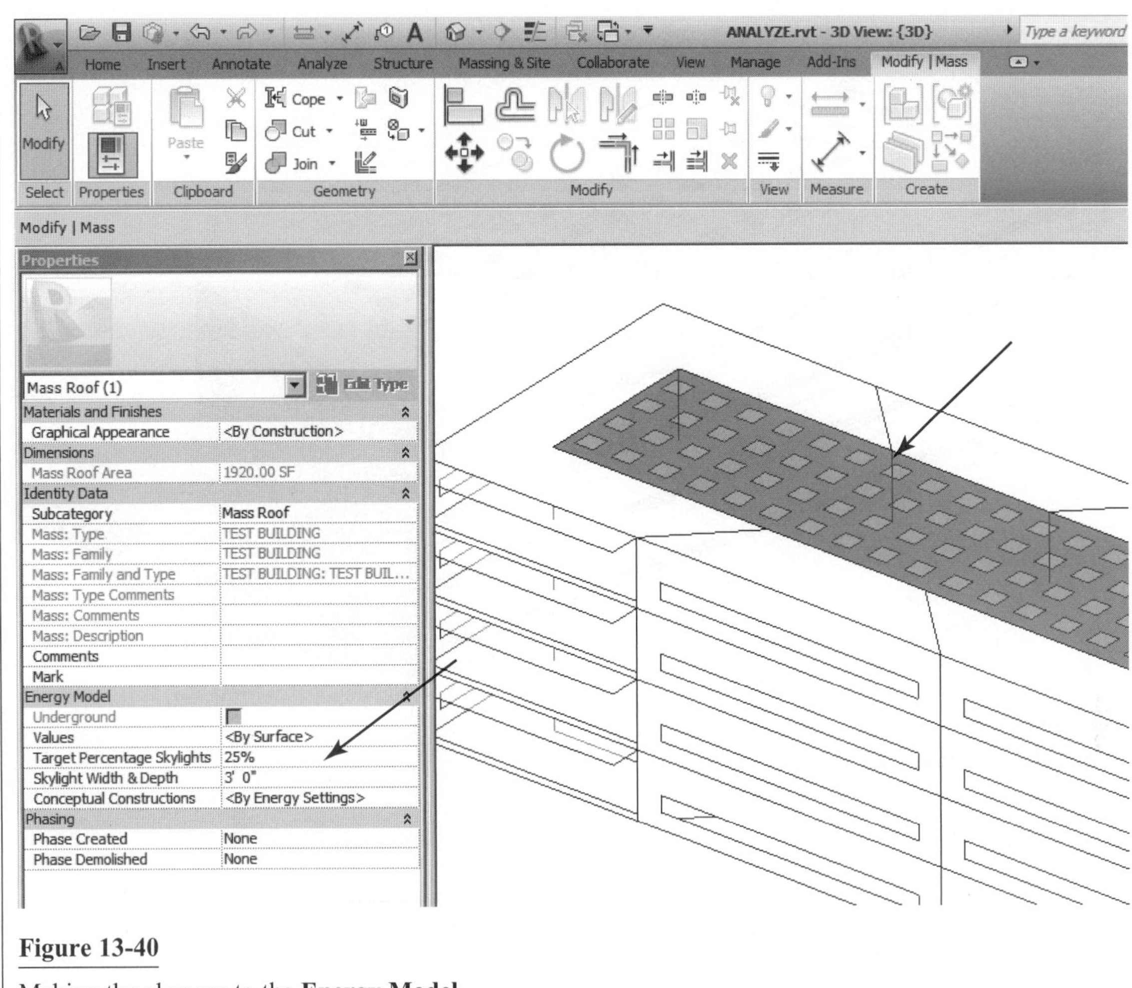

Figure 13-40

Making the changes to the **Energy Model**

EXERCISE 13-12 CREATING CUSTOM SURFACES AND ZONES IN THE ENERGY MODEL

1. Using the previous file, select the **Analyze** tab to bring up the **Analyze** toolbar.
2. In the **Analyze** toolbar, select the **Energy Settings** button to bring up the **Energy Settings** dialog box.
3. In the **Energy Settings** dialog box, uncheck the **Divide Perimeter Zones** check box and press the **OK** button to return to the **Drawing Editor** (see Figure 13-41).
4. Change to the **Level 1** floor plan.
5. Select the **Massing & Site** tab to bring up the **Massing & Site** toolbar.
6. In the **Massing & Site** toolbar, select the **In-Place Mass** button to bring up the **Name** dialog box.
7. In the **Name** dialog box, enter **TEST BUILDING ADDITION**, and press the **OK** button.
8. Place a line drawing as shown in Figure 13-42.
9. Change to the **Default 3D** view, and select the lines you placed.
10. In the **Modify | Place Lines** toolbar, select the **Create Form > Solid Form** button to create the Mass.
11. Click on the top surface of the form, and change its height to **20′-0″**.
12. In the **Modify | Form** toolbar, select the **Finish Mass** button to create the second mass.

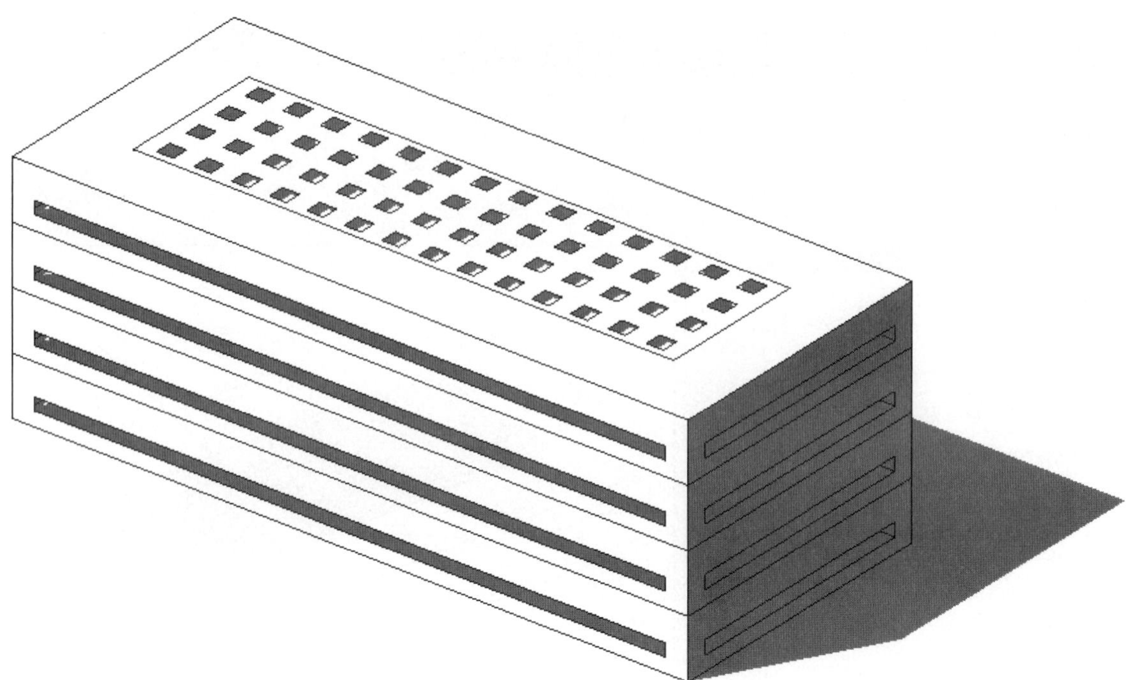

Figure 13-41

Return to the **Drawing Editor**

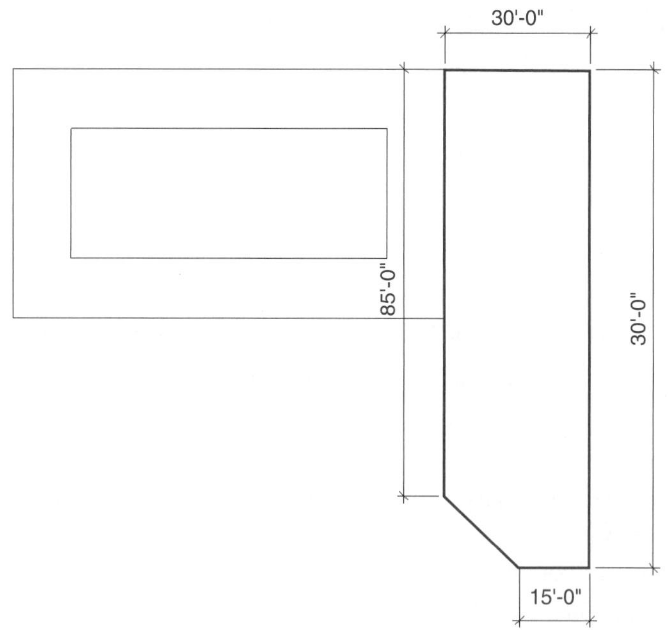

Figure 13-42

Place a line drawing

13. Select the **Modify** tab to bring up the **Modify** toolbar.
14. In the **Modify** toolbar, select the **Cut Geometry** button.
15. Click the original mass, and then select the new mass (see Figure 13-43).
16. Select the second **Mass** to bring up the **Modify | Mass** toolbar.
17. In the **Modify | Mass** toolbar, select the **Mass Floors** button to bring up the **Mass Floors** dialog box.

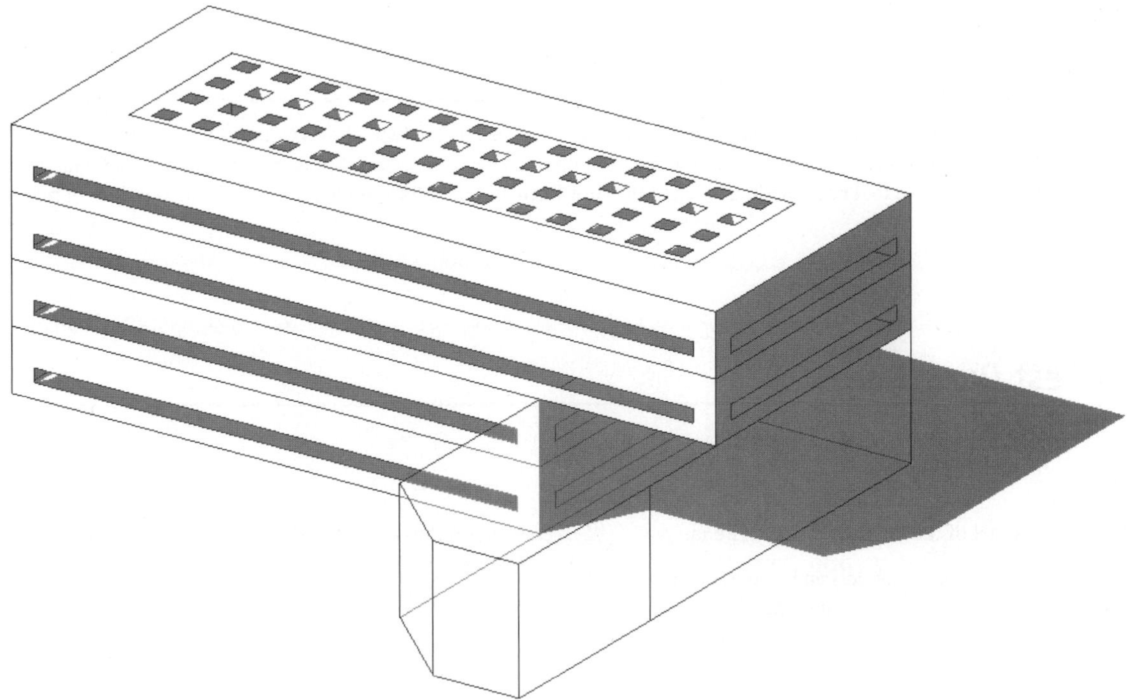

Figure 13-43

Select the new mass

18. In the **Mass Floors** dialog box, check the **Level 1** and **Level 2** check boxes, and press the **OK** button to create the new custom surfaces and custom zones (see Figure 13-44).
19. Using the concepts learned in the previous exercises, change the **Surfaces** and **Zones**.
20. Save this file as **CREATING CUSTOM SURFACES AND ZONES**.

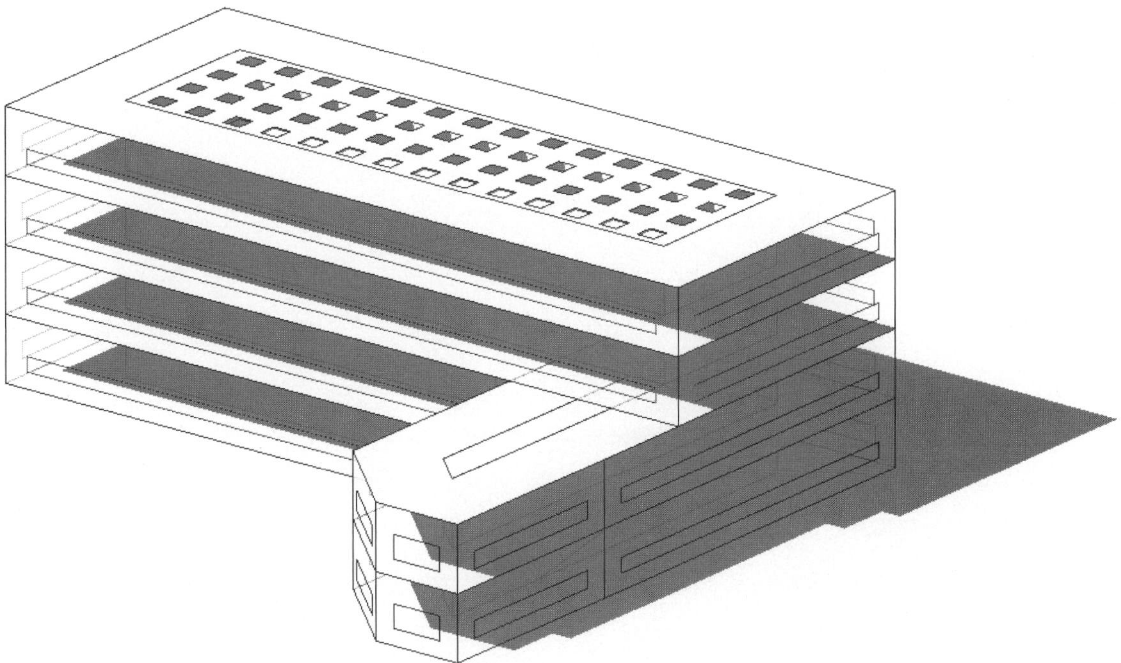

Figure 13-44

The new custom surfaces and custom zones

Chapter Summary

This chapter presented the **Analyze** feature, now standard in Revit Architecture 2012, which allows Conceptual Energy Analysis (CEA) of Revit **Mass Models**, 3D representations of the major mass of a building. The chapter also discussed setting the geographic location, setting the project position relative to **True North,** and using the **Sun Path** and the **Shadows** tools to adjust the building in relation to the shadows it creates.

Chapter Test Questions

Exercises

1. Create a Mass Model of the building that you are in.
2. Create three different energy models and analysis using different materials for walls, areas, and other structures.
3. Explain in writing the difference between the three results.

CHAPTER

14 Structure, Levels, Grids, Columns, Beams, and Trusses

CHAPTER OBJECTIVES

- Understand and use the **Grid** and **Level** tools.
- Understand and use the **Split Grid Lines** tool.
- Understand and use **Custom Grid Lines**.
- Understand and use **Structural Members—Columns**.
- Understand and use **Structural Members—Beams**.
- Understand and use **Architectural Columns**.
- Understand and use **Trusses**.
- Understand and use the **Beam System**.
- Understand and use the **Wall Foundation** tool.

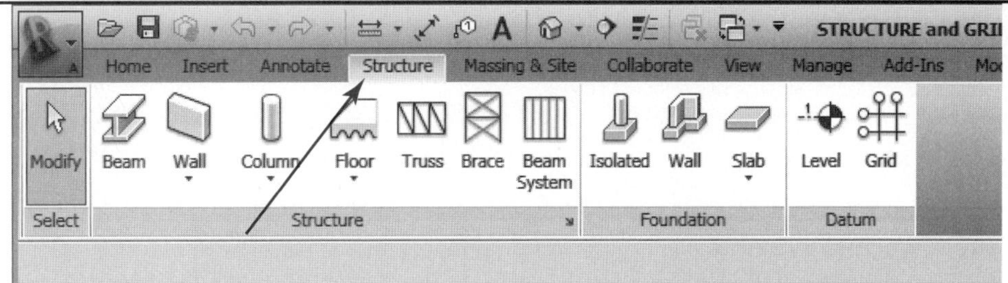

Introduction

This chapter covers the basics needed to create and modify custom grids and structural components such as columns, beams and the beam system, trusses, and wall foundation tools.

Levels and Grids

Level and **Grid** tools are used to create and modify levels and grids in a drawing.

EXERCISE 14-1 USING THE LEVEL AND GRID TOOLS

1. Start a new project using the RAC 2012\Imperial Templates\default.rte template.
2. In the **Project Browser**, double-click **East Elevation** to bring it into the **Drawing Editor**.
3. In the **Structure** toolbar, select the **Level** button to bring up the **Modify | Place Level** toolbar.
4. In the **Modify | Place Level** toolbar, select the **Line** button in the **Draw** panel.
5. Click your cursor in the **Drawing Editor**, move it to the right until the right point of the level datum line aligns with the right point of **Level 2**, and click to set the point.
6. Select the height number, and set it to **20′-0″**.
7. Repeat Steps 3–6, creating another level datum line at **30′-0″** (see Figure 14-1).
8. Select one of the level datum lines, and notice the check box at the end that does not have a bullet marker.
9. Check the check box to turn the level datum line markers **On** and **Off** (see Figure 14-2).

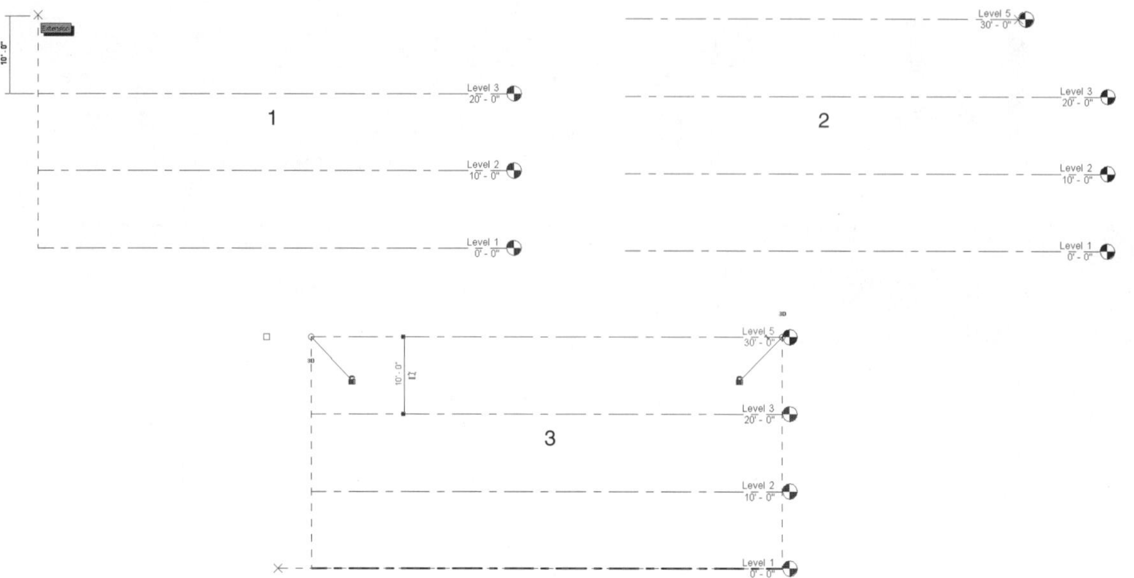

Figure 14-1

Create a **level** datum line

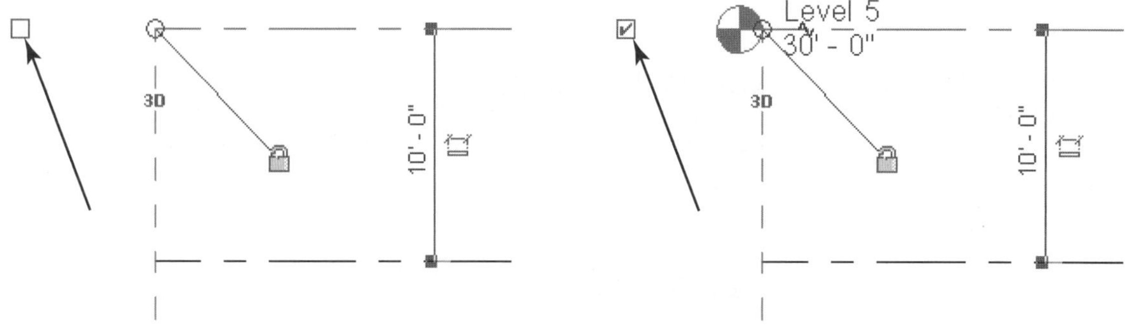

Figure 14-2

Turn **level** datum line markers **On** and **Off**

10. In the **Project Browser**, double-click the **Level 1** floor plan to bring it into the **Drawing Editor**.
11. In the **Structure** toolbar, select the **Grid** button to bring up the **Modify | Place Grid** toolbar.
12. In the **Modify | Place Grid** toolbar, select the **Line** button in the **Draw** panel.
13. Click in the **Drawing Editor**, drag upward, and click again to place the grid line and bubble.
14. Select the number in the grid bubble, and enter the letter **A**.
15. Select the bottom of the grid line, **RMB**, and select **Create Similar** from the contextual menu that appears.
16. Drag your cursor to the right **10′-0″**, and click to place a new grid line.
17. Drag your cursor upward until it aligns with the top of the previous grid bubble.

Notice that the new grid bubble is labeled **B**.

18. Repeat the previous steps, creating grid lines **C** and **D**.
19. Click in the **Drawing Editor**, drag right (horizontal), and click again to place the grid line and bubble.

20. This time, label the grid bubble **1**.
21. Create two more horizontal grids.

Notice that the new grid bubbles are labeled **2** and **3** (see Figure 14-3).

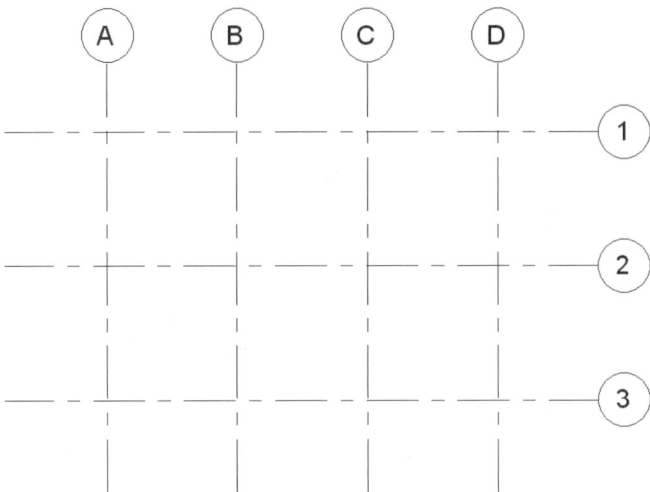

Figure 14-3

Create two new grid bubbles

As with level datum line markers, you can check and uncheck the grid bubbles to make them visible or invisible.

22. In the **Project Browser**, double-click on the rest of the floor plan levels to bring them into the **Drawing Editor**.
23. Close any other views.
24. Select **Window** > **Tile** from the **View** menu.
25. Select grid line **1**, drag it to the right, and notice that it moves in all the levels.
26. Click on the blue **3D** text to change it to **2D** (notice that the small circle near the **3D** mark fills in) (see Figure 14-4).

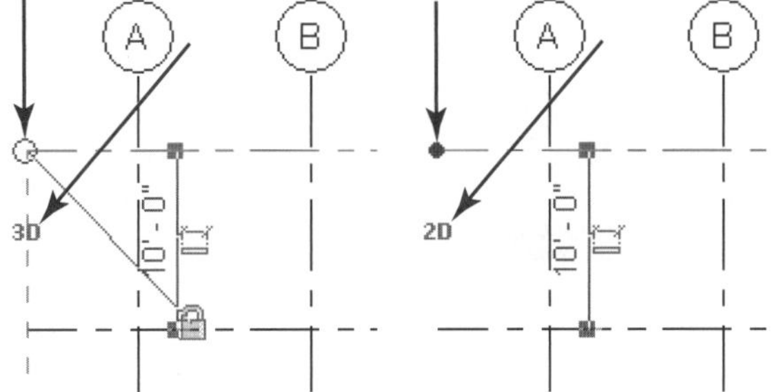

Figure 14-4

Change **3D** text to **2D**

27. With the **2D** activated, again drag grid line **1** to the right, and notice that the grid does not change in the other floor levels (see Figure 14-5).
28. Select the grid line you moved in **Level 1** to bring up the **Modify | Grids** toolbar.
29. In the **Modify | Grids** toolbar, press the **Propagate Extents** button to bring up the **Propagate datum extents** dialog box.

> **NOTE:**
>
> **3D Extents** (the **3D – 2D** text) allows you to have the grid lines linked in all floor plans or just one floor plan. Experiment in all the views by turning the **3D Extents On** and **Off** and moving grid lines.

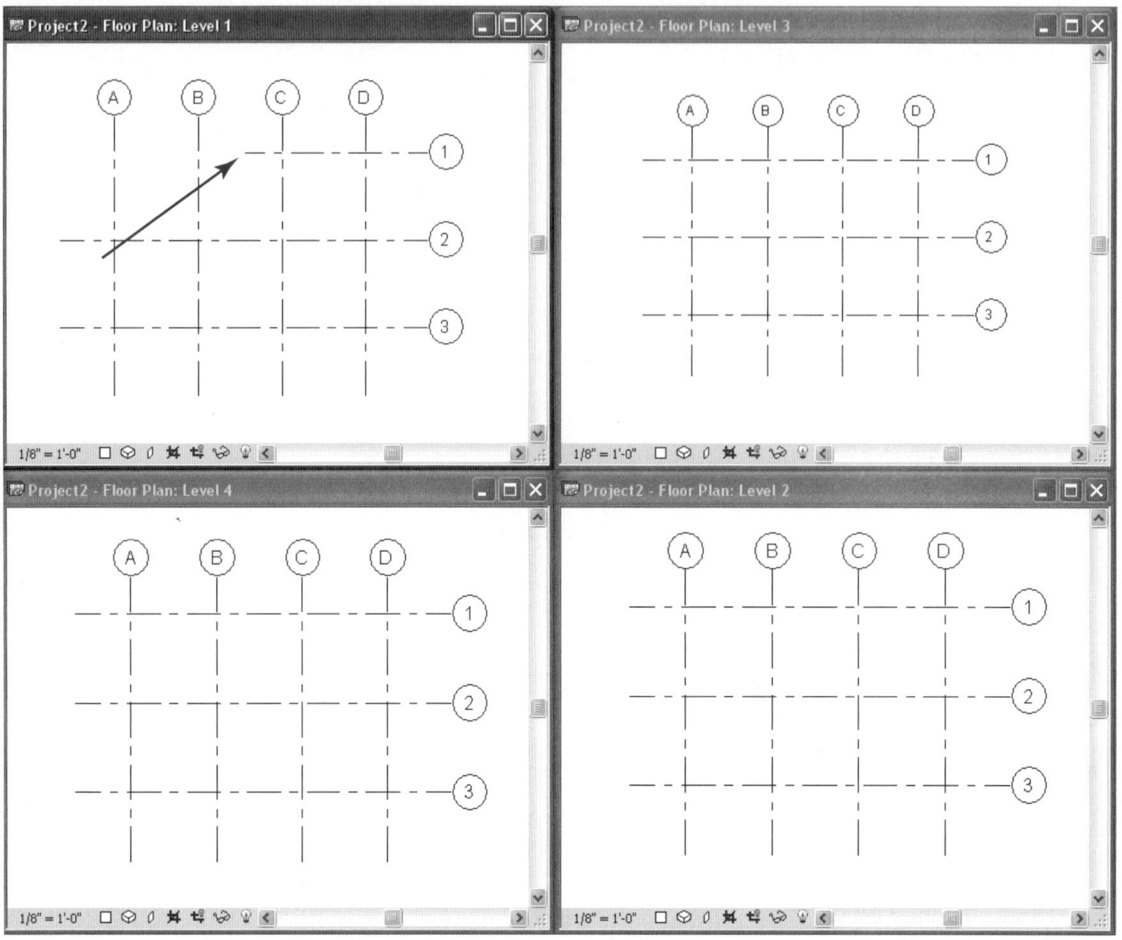

Figure 14-5

Grids in other floor levels do not change with **2D** activated

30. In the **Propagate datum extents** dialog box, check the **Floor Plan: Level 2** and **Floor Plan: Level 3** check boxes (see Figure 14-6).

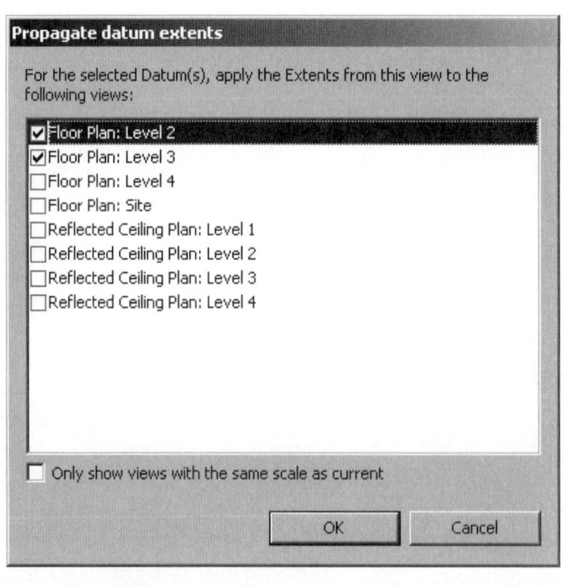

Figure 14-6

Propagate datum extents dialog box

Grid lines for **Floor Plan: Level 2** and **Floor Plan: Level 3** will now match the grid lines in **Floor Plan: Level 1,** but not in **Floor Plan: Level 4** (see Figure 14-7).

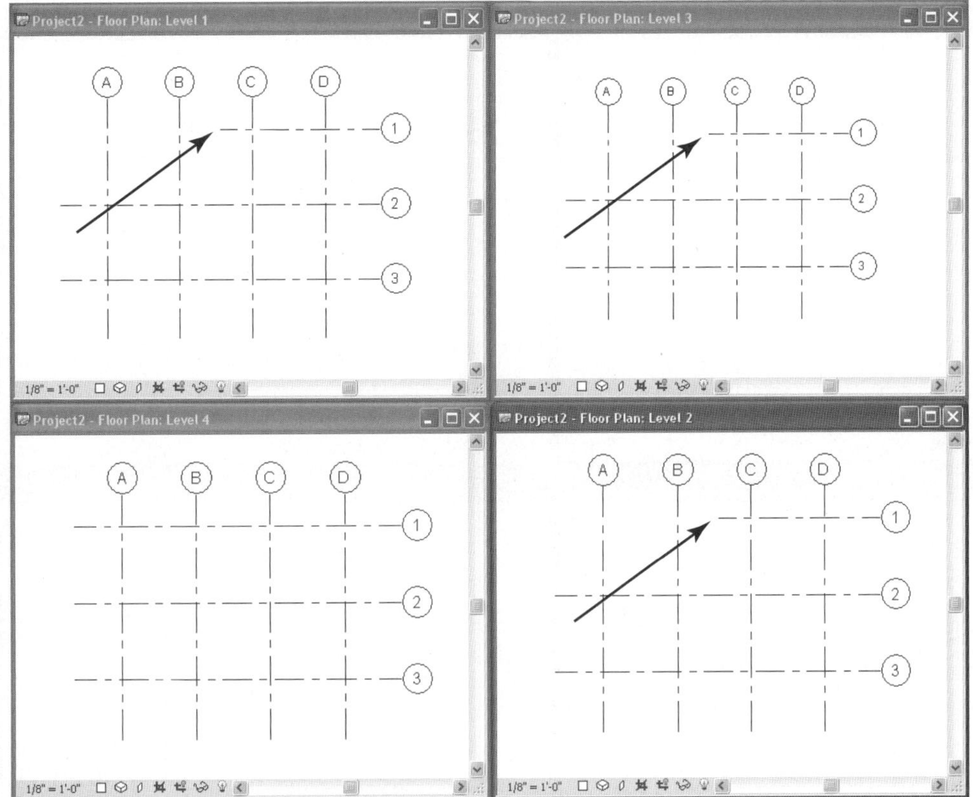

Figure 14-7

Grid lines do not match in **Floor Plan: Level 4**

31. In the **Project Browser**, double-click **East Elevation** to bring it into the **Drawing Editor**.
32. In the **East Elevation**, unlock and then move the grid bubble below the **Level 2** datum line (see Figure 14-8).

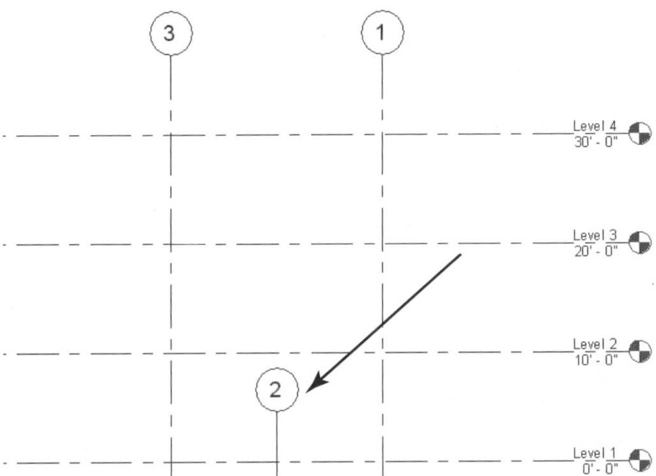

Figure 14-8

Unlock and move a grid bubble

Notice that the grid lines for **Floor Plan: Level 2, Floor Plan: Level 3,** and **Floor Plan: Level 4** do not display grid line **2** because it is below those levels in the **East Elevation** (see Figure 14-9).

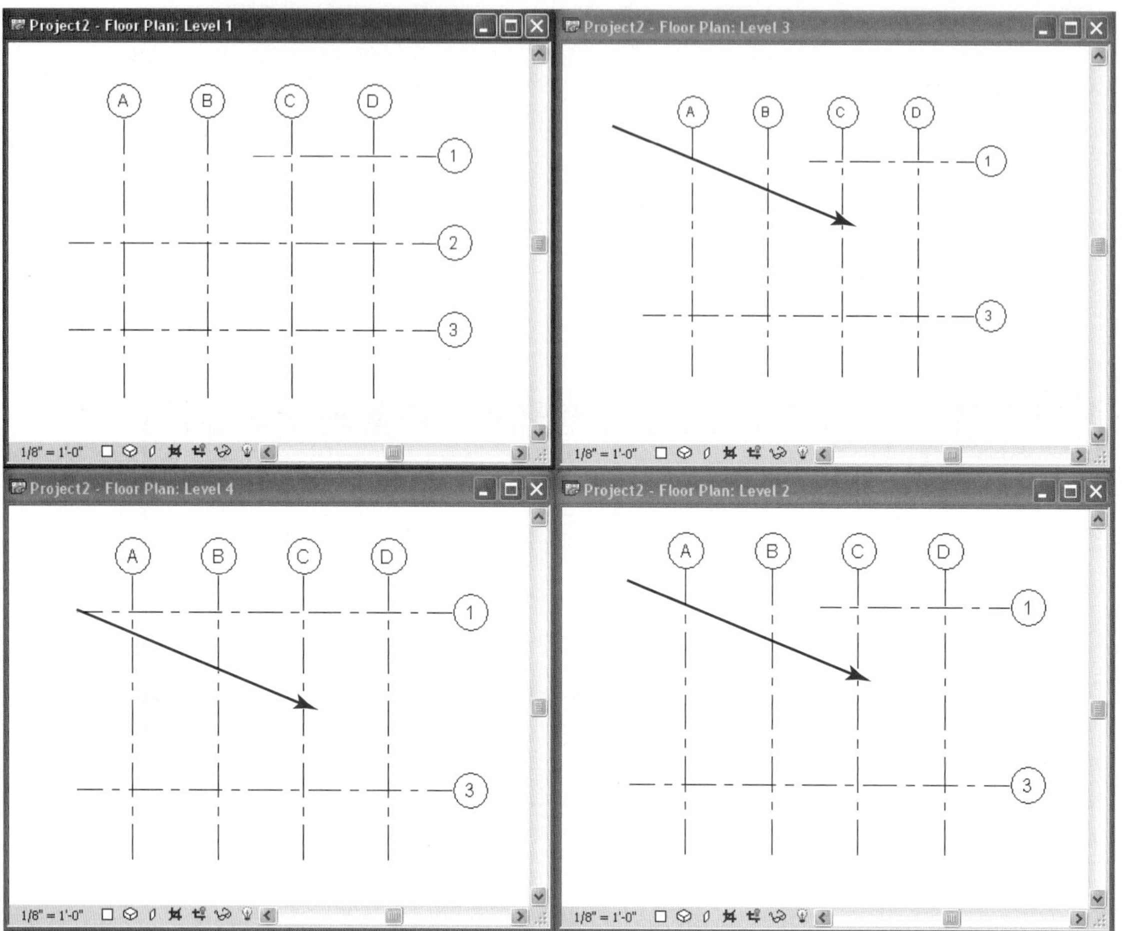

Figure 14-9

Grid line **2** does not display in **Levels 2, 3,** and **4**

33. In the **Floor Plan: Level 1**, select grid line **1**, and click the **Z** icon to allow you to move the grid bubble. This is important if you have many grid lines close to each other (see Figure 14-10).

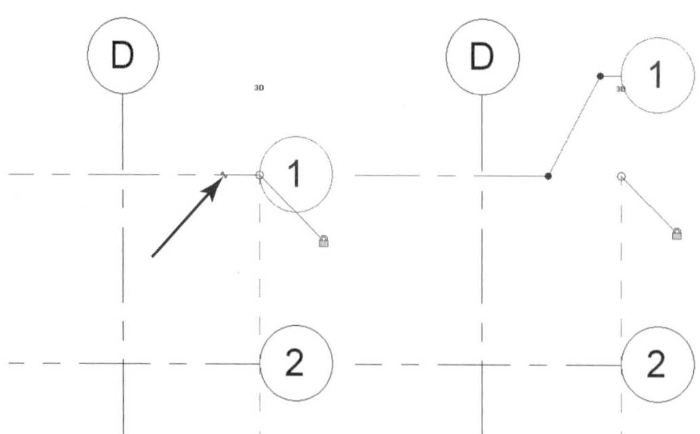

Figure 14-10

The **Z** icon allows you to move a bubble

34. Save this file as **GRID TOOL**.

EXERCISE 14-2 **SPLIT GRID LINES (NONE)**

1. Start a new project using the RAC 2012\Imperial Templates\default.rte template.
2. In the **Project Browser**, double-click **Floor Plans** > **Level 1** to bring it into the **Drawing Editor**.
3. In the **Structure** toolbar, select the **Grid** button to bring up the **Modify | Place Grid** toolbar.
4. In the **Modify | Place Grid** toolbar, select the **Line** button in the **Draw** panel.
5. In the **Properties** dialog box, select the **1/4″ Bubble** from the **Properties** drop-down list (see Figure 14-11).

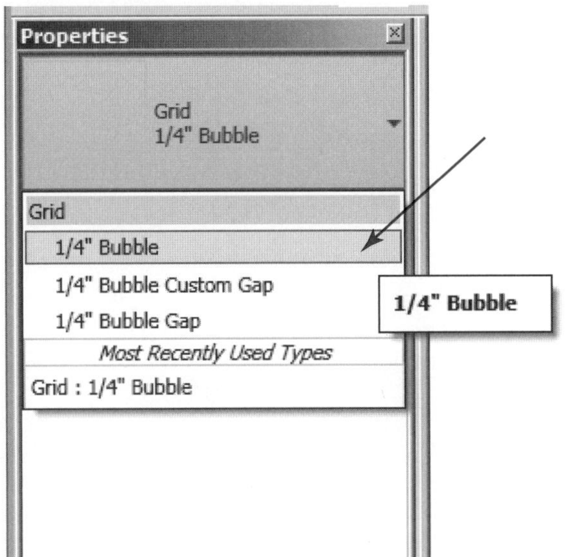

Figure 14-11

Properties dialog box

6. In the **Properties** dialog box, press the **Edit Type** button at the top right to bring up the **Type Properties** dialog box.
7. In the **Type Properties** dialog box, select **None** from the **Center Segment** field (see Figure 14-12).

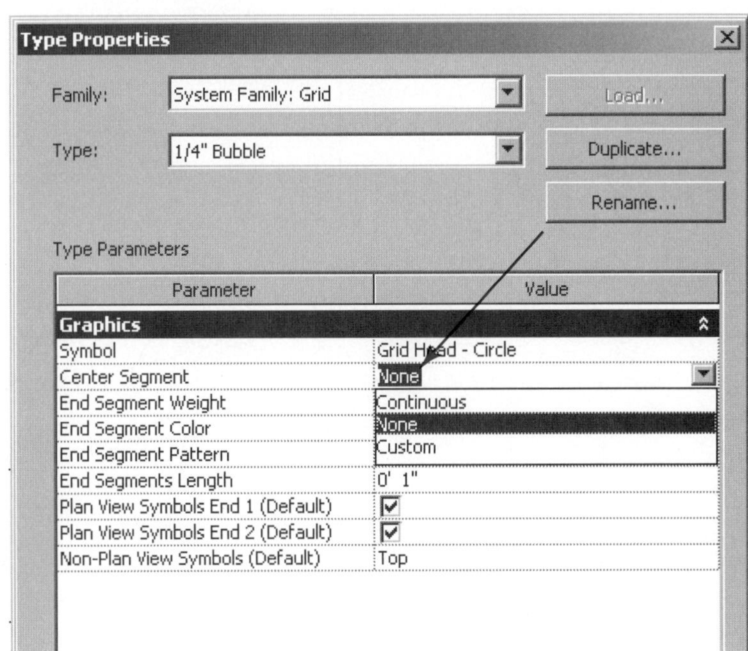

Figure 14-12

Type Properties dialog box

8. Place four grid lines, and notice that the grid lines are broken at their centers (see Figure 14-13).

Figure 14-13

Grid lines are broken at their centers

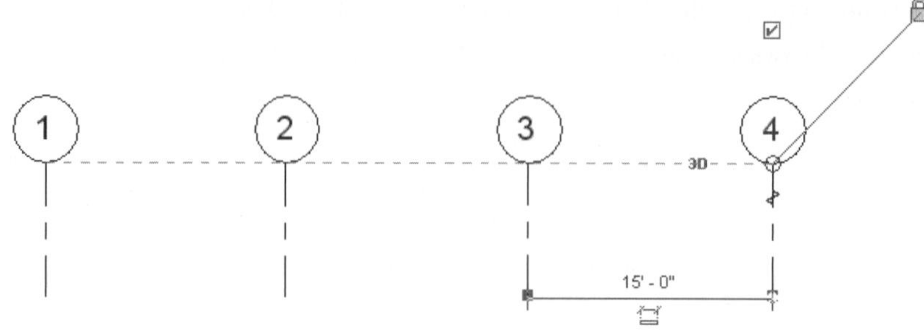

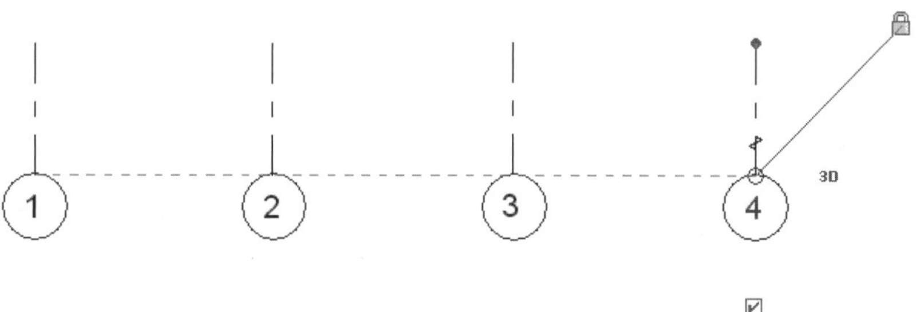

9. If you select a grid line and select the points shown, you can drag and adjust the opening for each grid line (see Figures 14-14 and 14-15).

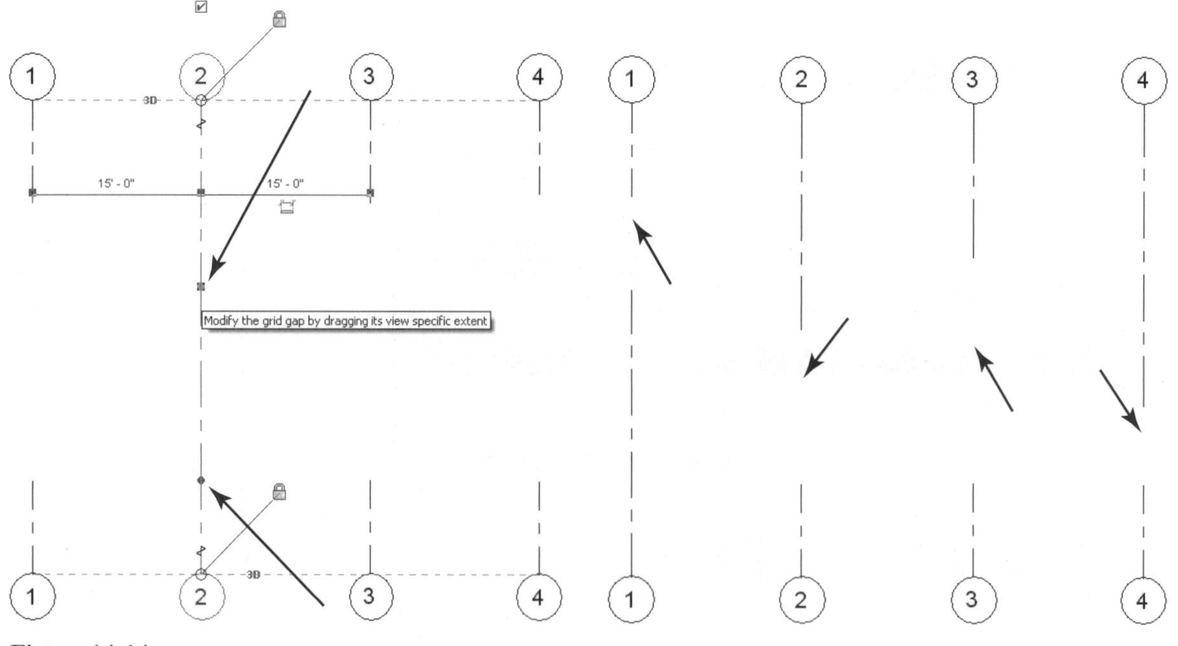

Figure 14-14

Select a grid line

Figure 14-15

Drag and adjust a grid line

10. Save this file as **SPLIT GRID LINES**.

EXERCISE 14-3 CUSTOM GRID LINES

1. Using the previous file, select one of the grid lines to bring up the **Modify | Grids** toolbar.
2. In the **Properties** dialog box, select the **Edit Type** button to bring up the **Type Properties** dialog box.
3. In the **Type Properties** dialog box, set the following:
   a. **Center Segment** to **Custom**
   b. **Center Segment Pattern** to **Hidden 1/8″**
   c. **Center Segment Weight** to **1**
   d. **End Segment Weight** to **8**
   e. **End Segment Pattern** to **Double Dash 5/8″** (see Figure 14-16).

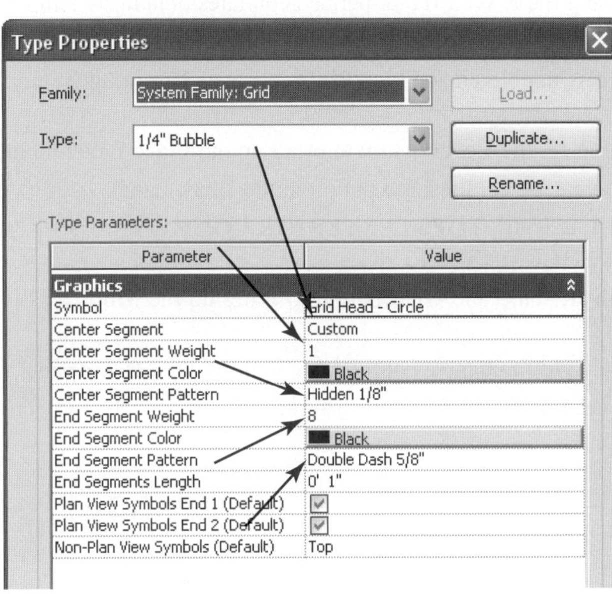

Figure 14-16

Change settings in the **Type Properties** dialog box

4. Press the **OK** buttons to return to the **Drawing Editor**.

Notice the changes that happen to the grid lines. If you select the points that you moved in the previous exercise, you can adjust the segments (see Figure 14-17).

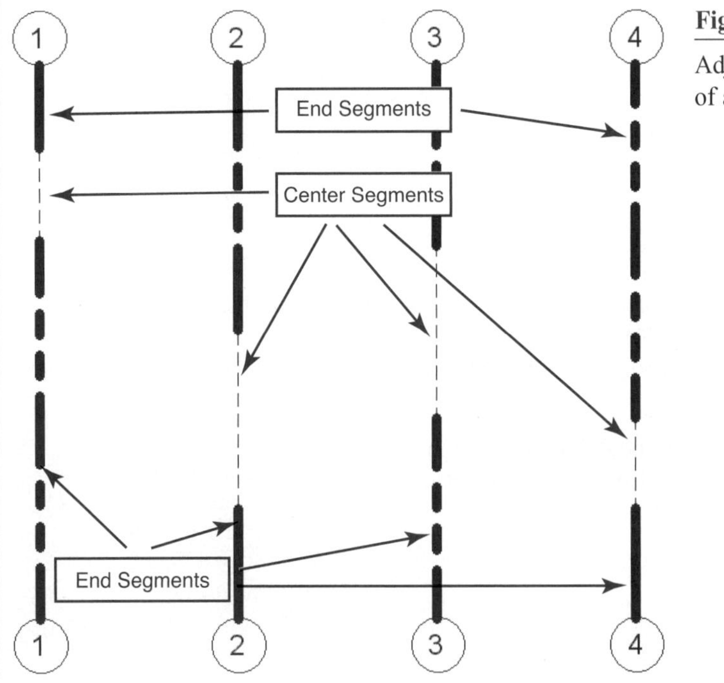

Figure 14-17

Adjust segments of a grid line

5. Continue making changes in the **Type Properties** dialog box, and observe the results.
6. Save this file as **CUSTOM GRID LINES**.

Structural Members, Columns, Trusses, and Beams

To maintain structural integrity, buildings require support in addition to the support provided by the walls. This is done with structural members, columns, trusses, and beams.

EXERCISE 14-4 STRUCTURAL MEMBERS—COLUMNS

You may want to repeat the following procedure several times to investigate all the structural members.

1. Start a new project using the RAC 2012\Imperial Templates\default.rte template.
2. Set the **Scale** to **1/8″ = 1′-0″**.
3. In the **Project Browser**, double-click **Floor Plans** > **Level 1** to bring it into the **Drawing Editor**.
4. In the **Home** toolbar, select the **Level** button to bring up the **Place Level** toolbar.
5. In the **Place Level** toolbar, select the **Line** button in the **Draw** panel.
6. Place **3** levels: **Level 1** @ **0′-0″**, **TOP of EXTERIOR COLUMNS** @ **9′-0″**, and **TOP of INTERIOR COLUMNS** @ **12′-0″**.
7. In the **Structure** toolbar, select the **Grid** button to bring up the **Modify | Place Grid** toolbar.
8. In the **Modify | Place Grid** toolbar, select the **Line** button in the **Draw** panel.
9. Place the grids in **Level 1** as shown in Figure 14-18.

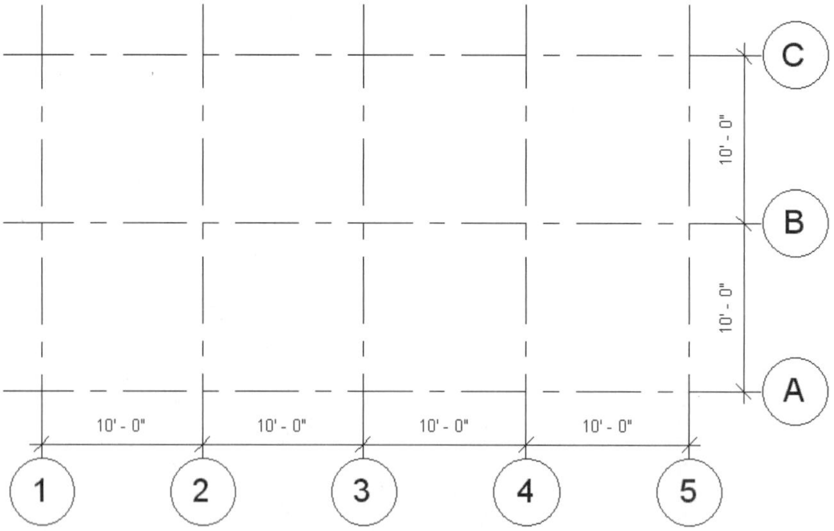

Figure 14-18

Place grids in **Level 1**

TIP: There is a **Column** button in both the **Home** and **Structure** toolbars; use whichever matches your workflow.

10. In the **Structure** toolbar, select the **Column** > **Structural Column** button to bring up the **Modify | Place Structural Column** toolbar (see Figure 14-19).

NOTE:

Structural Columns get their content from the **Structural** folder in the **Library. Architectural Columns** get their content from the **Columns** folder in the **Library.**

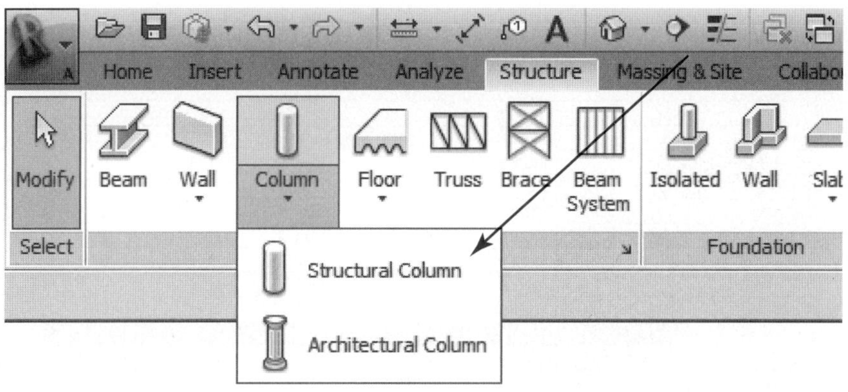

Figure 14-19

Column > **Structural Column** button

11. In the **Modify | Place Structural Column** toolbar, press the **Load Family** button to go to the **Imperial Library**.
12. In the **Imperial Library**, select the **Structural** folder.
13. In the **Structural** folder, select the **Columns** folder.
14. In the **Columns** folder, select the **Steel** folder.
15. In the **Steel** folder, double-click the **HSS-Hollow Structural Section-Column.rfa** column family (see Figure 14-20).

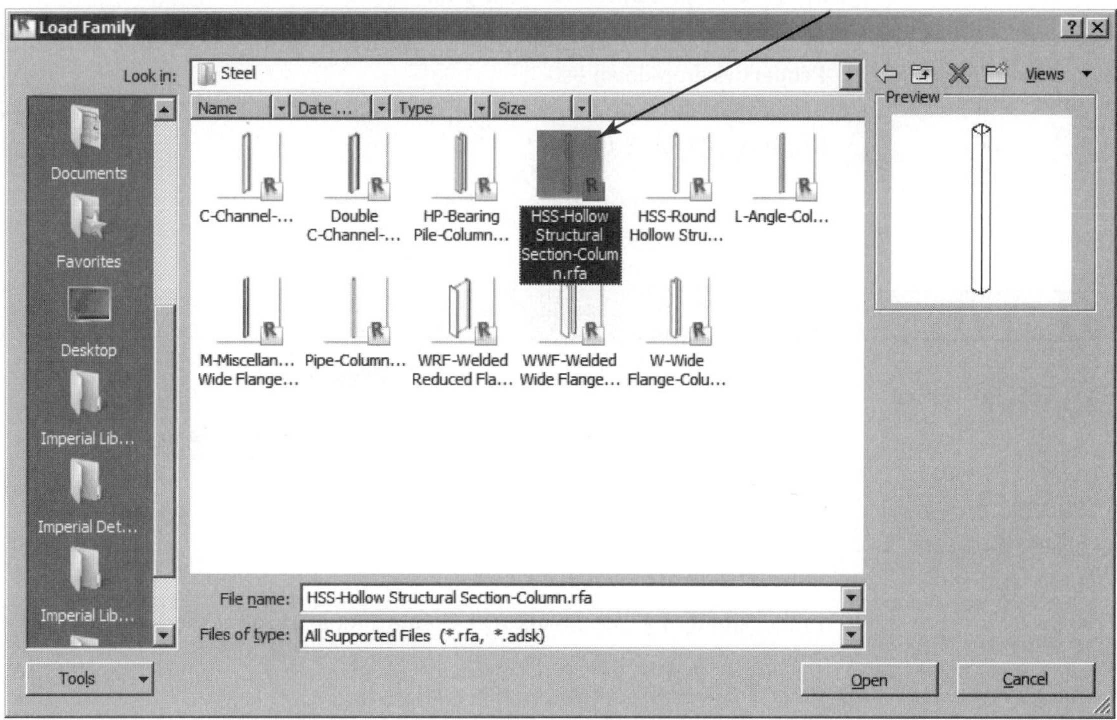

Figure 14-20

Select a column family in the **Steel** folder

16. In the **Specify Types** dialog box, select the **HSS4 × 4 × 5/16** column, and press the **OK** button to return to the **Drawing Editor** (see Figure 14-21).

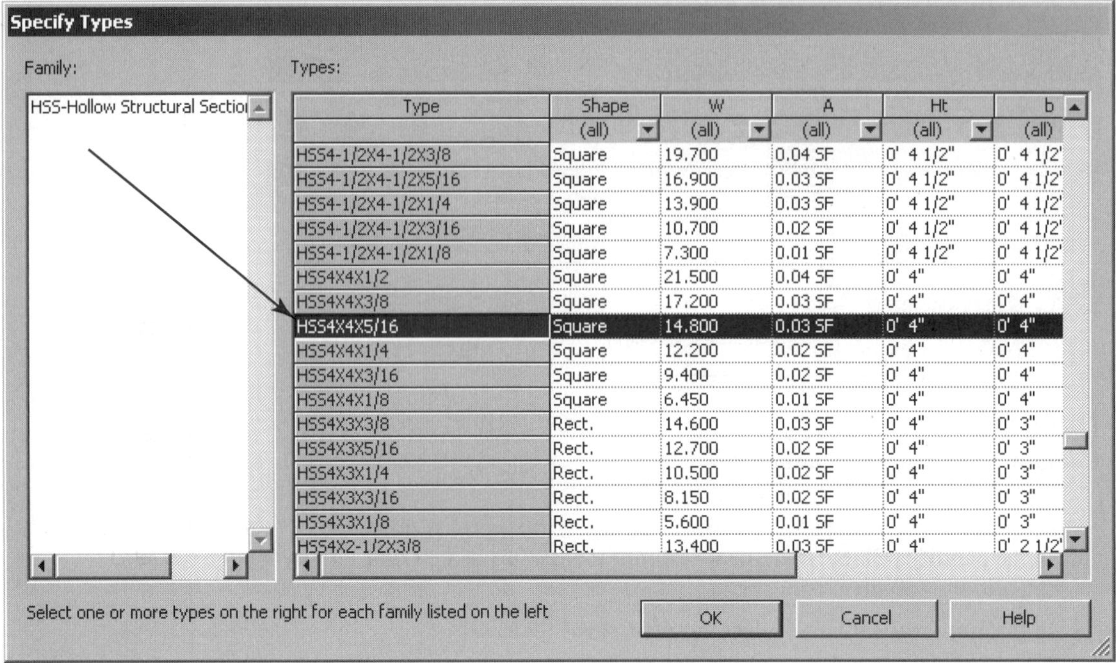

Figure 14-21

Specify Types dialog box

You have now loaded a new **Structural Column Family** into Revit Architecture, and it is available for placement into your grid.

17. In the **Properties** dialog box, select the **HSS4 × 4 × 5/16** column from the **Properties** drop-down list.
18. In the **Options Bar**, select **Height, Unconnected**, and **9′-0″** to set the column height (see Figure 14-22).

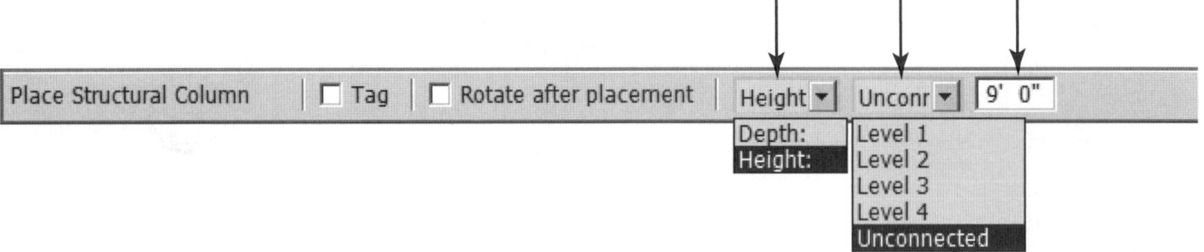

Figure 14-22

Options Bar

19. In the **Modify | Place Structural Column** toolbar, select the **Vertical Column** button.
20. Click at the intersections of the grid, and place columns at each intersection.
21. Select one of the columns you just placed, **RMB**, and select the **Select All Instances** > **Visible in View** option from the contextual menu that appears.

All the columns will be selected; press the **<Del>** key to delete them.

NOTE:

Placing columns at intersections is slow, especially when you have to place a lot of columns. By using the **At Grids** button, you can automate this process.

22. Returning to the **Structure** toolbar, again select the **Column** > **Structural Column** button to bring up the **Modify | Place Structural Column** toolbar.
23. As before, select the **HSS4 × 4 × 5/16** column from the **Change Element Type** drop-down list.
24. In the **Modify | Place Structural Column** toolbar, select the **At Grids** button to bring up the **Place Structural Column** > **At Grid Intersection** toolbar (see Figure 14-23).
25. Select all the grid lines from right to left (see Figure 14-24).

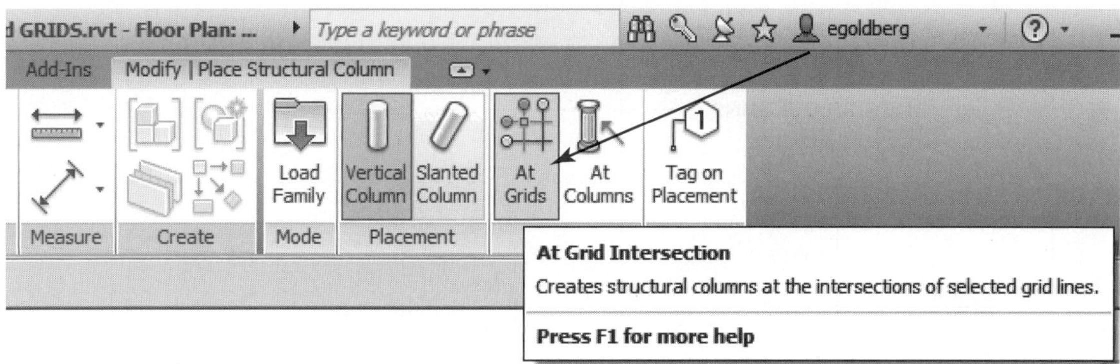

Figure 14-23

At Grids button

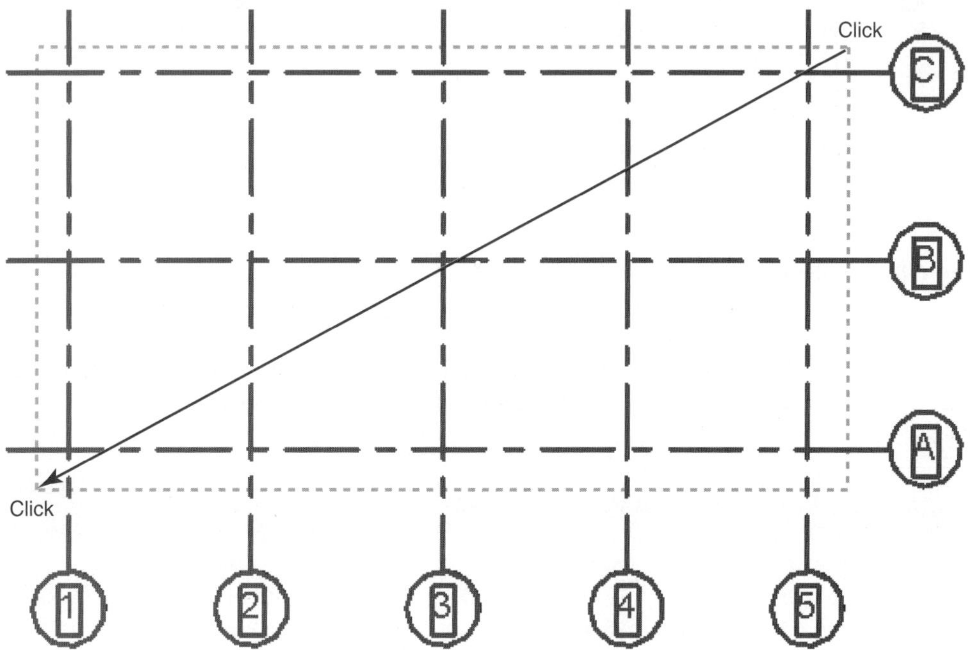

Figure 14-24

Select all grid lines from right to left

26. In the **Modify | Place Structural Column** > **At Grid Intersection** toolbar, press the **Finish** button to place the columns at all intersections.
27. Select all the columns on grid line **B** (**Interior Columns**) to bring up the **Modify | Structural Columns** toolbar.

> **NOTE:**
> While placing columns, you can use the **<Spacebar>** to change the column rotation before a column is placed. Each time you press the **<Spacebar>**, the column rotates to align with the intersecting grids at the selected location.

28. In the **Properties** dialog box, change the **Top Offset** to **3′-0″**, and press the **OK** button (see Figure 14-25).

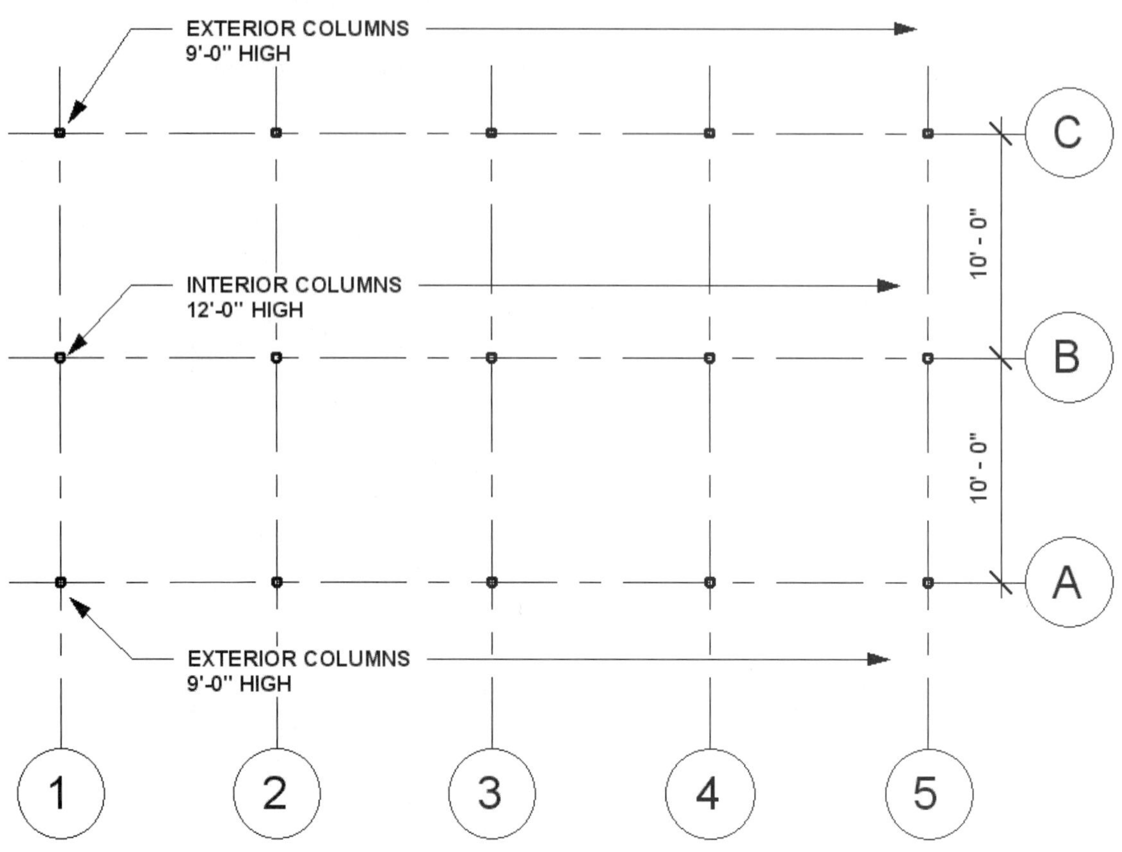

Figure 14-25

Change the **Top Offset** in the **Properties** dialog box

29. Select the **Structure** tab to bring up the **Structure** toolbar.
30. In the **Structure** toolbar, select the **Floor > Structural Floor** button to bring up the **Modify | Create Floor Boundary** toolbar (see Figure 14-26).

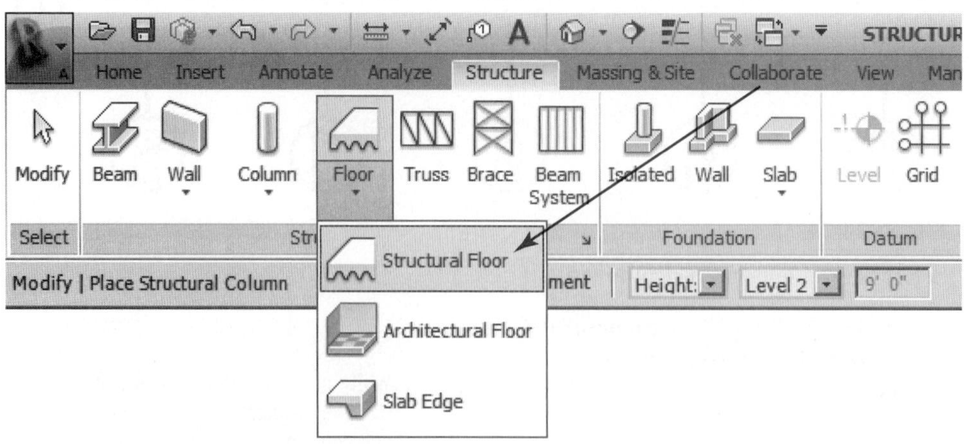

Figure 14-26

Floor > Structural Floor button

> **TIP** There is a **Floor** button in both the **Home** and **Structure** toolbars; use whichever matches your workflow.

31. In the **Modify | Create Floor Boundary** toolbar, select the **Rectangle** button in the **Draw** panel.
32. In the **Properties** dialog box, select the **Edit Type** button to bring up the **Type Properties** dialog box.
33. In the **Type Properties** dialog box, select the **Generic – 12″** floor, and press the **OK** button to return to the **Drawing Editor**.
34. In the **Drawing Editor**, place a rectangle surrounding all the columns on **Level 1** as shown in Figure 14-27.

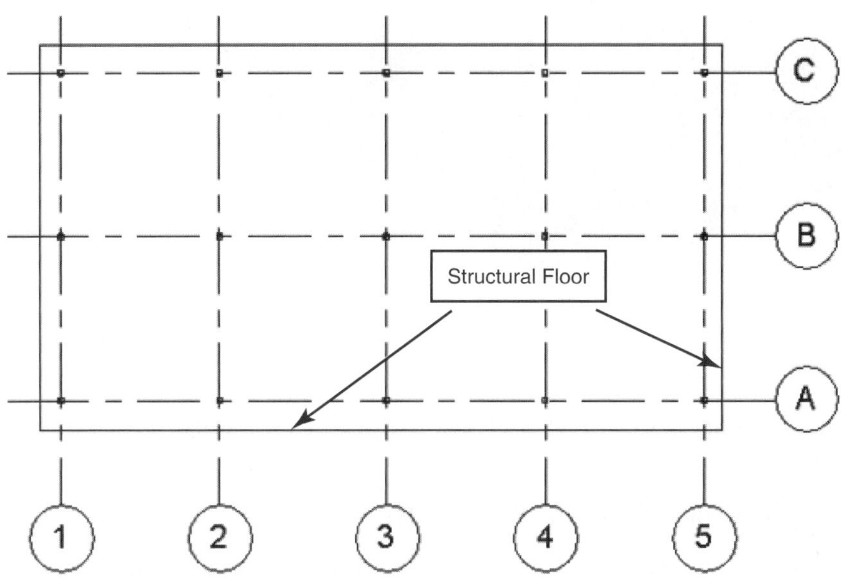

Figure 14-27

Place a rectangle surrounding all the columns

35. In the **Modify | Create Floor Boundary** toolbar, press the **Finish Edit Mode** button to create the structural floor.
36. Select the **Default 3D View** button from the **Quick Access** toolbar to change to the **Default 3D View** (see Figures 14-28 and 14-29).

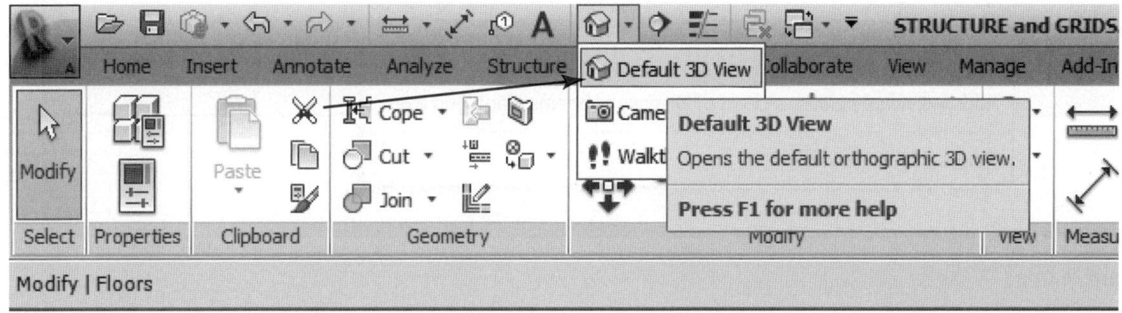

Figure 14-28

Default 3D View button

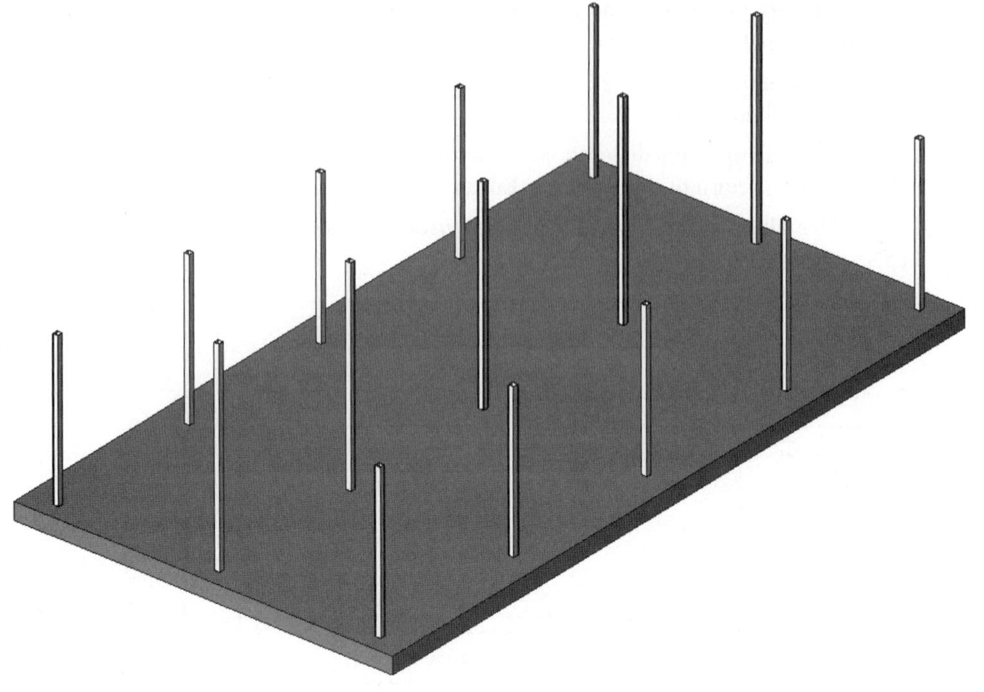

Figure 14-29

3D drawing

37. Save this file as **STRUCTURAL MEMBERS – COLUMNS**.

EXERCISE 14-5 **STRUCTURAL MEMBERS – BEAMS**

You may want to repeat this procedure several times to investigate all the structural members.

1. Use the **STRUCTURAL MEMBERS – COLUMNS** file.
2. Change to the **Default 3D View**.
3. In the **Structure** toolbar, select the **Beam** button to bring up the **Modify | Place Beam** toolbar (see Figure 14-30).

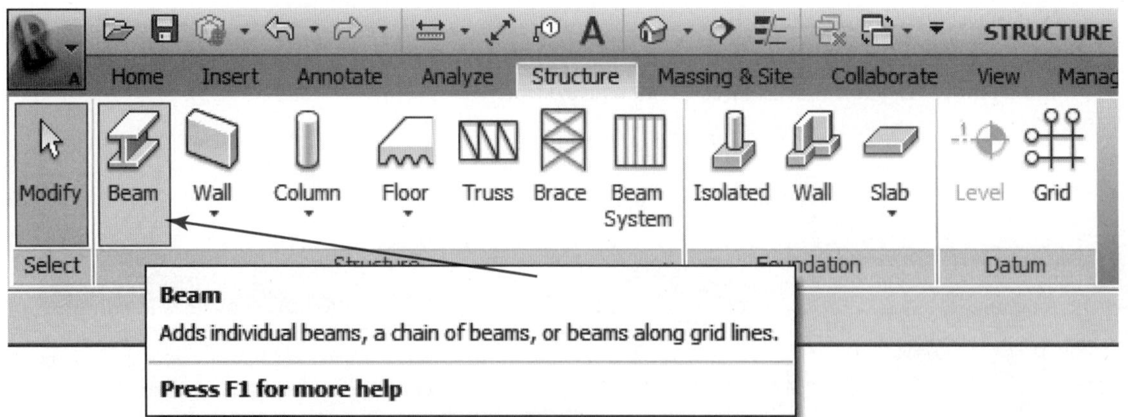

Figure 14-30

Beam button

4. In the **Modify | Place Beam** toolbar, select the **Load Family** button to go to the **Imperial Library**.
5. In the **Imperial Library**, select the **Structural** folder.

6. In the **Structural** folder, select the **Framing** folder.
7. In the **Framing** folder, select the **Steel** folder.
8. In the **Steel** folder, double-click the **K-Series Bar Joist-Angle Web.rfa Beam Family**, and the **Specify Types** dialog box will appear.
9. In the **Specify Types** dialog box, select the **14K6** beam, and press the **OK** button to return to the **Drawing Editor**.
10. In the **Properties** dialog box, set the **Reference Level** to **Level 1**, **z-Direction Justification** to **Other**, and **z-Direction Offset Value** to **0′-3″** so that the bottom of the joist "seat" will be at the level of placement.
11. In the **Instance Properties** dialog box, press the **OK** button to return to the **Modify | Place Beam** toolbar (see Figure 14-31).

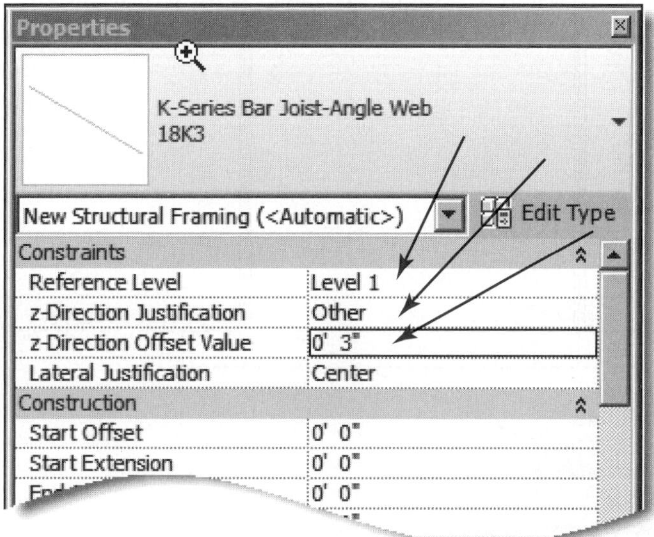

Figure 14-31

Instance Properties dialog box

12. In the **Options Bar**, check the **3D Snapping** check box.
13. Move your cursor to the top of the first exterior column until a vertical line appears in the column (see Figure 14-32).

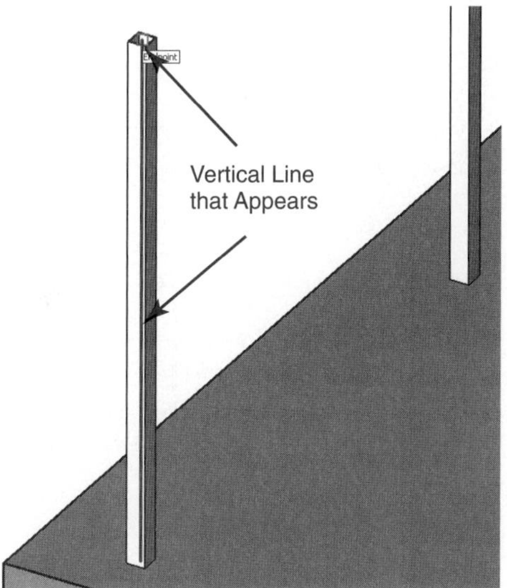

Figure 14-32

Vertical line at top of column

14. Click to place the start of the **Bar Joist**, and then click again to place the other end of the **Bar Joist** at the top of the **Interior** column.
15. Double-click on the **West Elevation** view in the **Project Browser** to bring it into the **Drawing Editor**.

16. Set the **Detail Level** to **Medium**, and you will see the **Bar Joist** in full detail (see Figure 14-33).

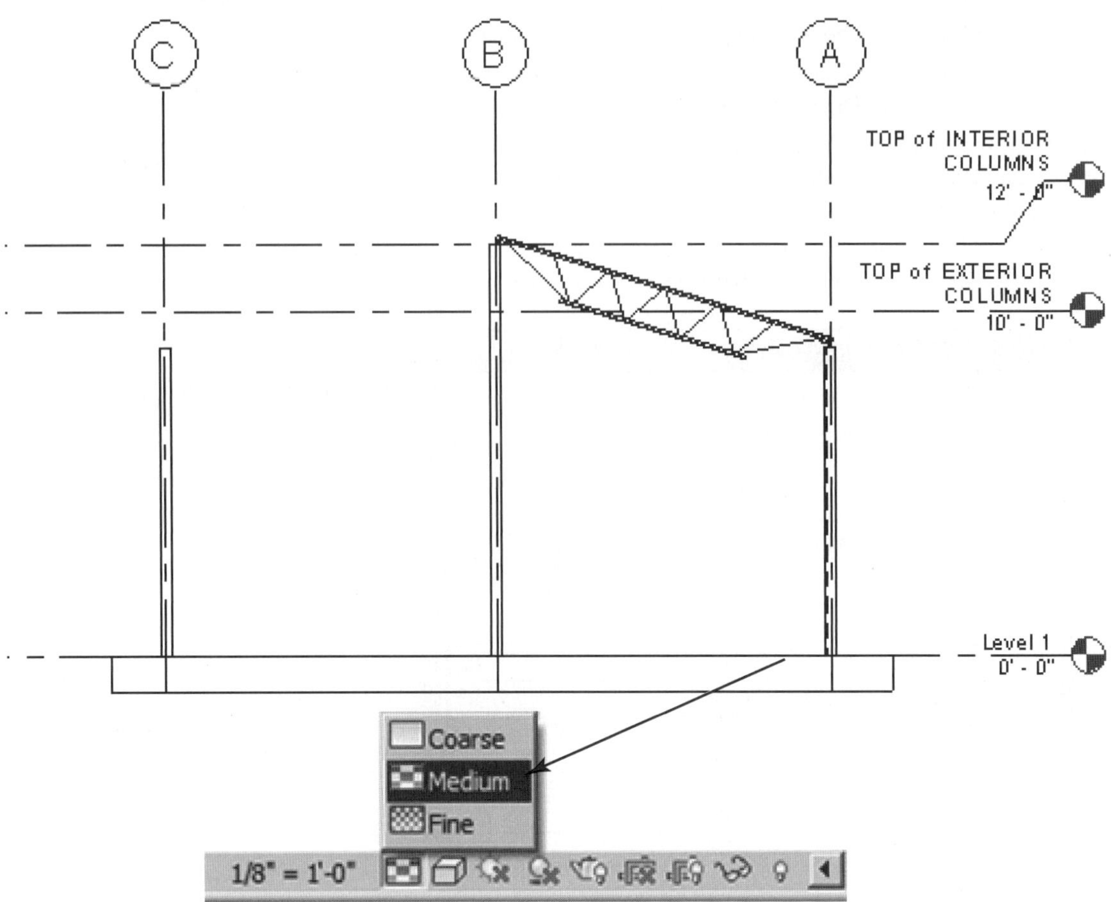

Figure 14-33

Bar Joist drawing

17. In the **West Elevation** view, select the **Bar Joist**, and click and drag the arrow grips to extend the end of the **Joist** (see Figure 14-34).

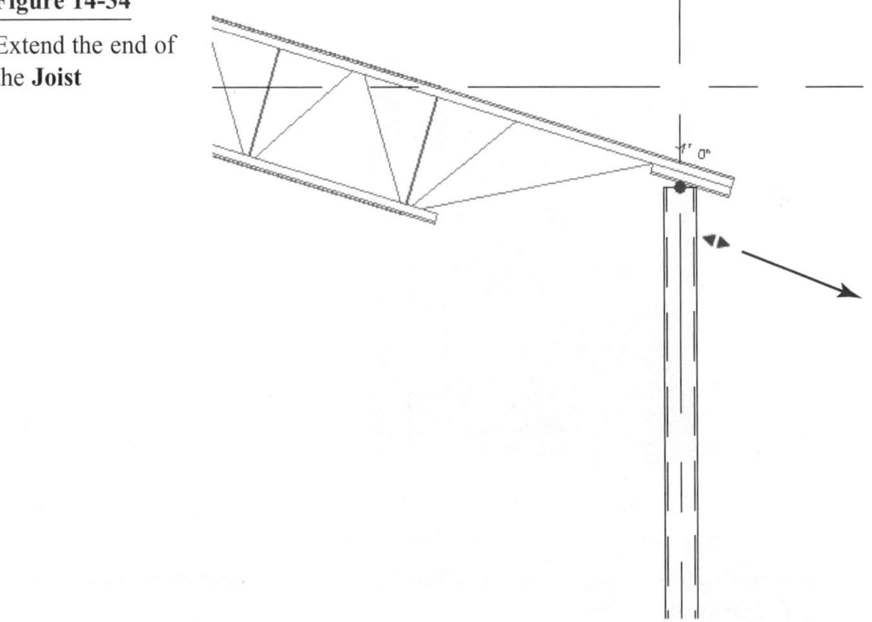

Figure 14-34

Extend the end of the **Joist**

18. Bring the **TOP of INTERIOR COLUMNS** view into the **Drawing Editor**.
19. Select the **Bar Joist** you just placed to bring up the **Modify | Structural Framing** toolbar.
20. In the **Modify | Structural Framing** toolbar, select the **Array** button (see Figure 14-35).

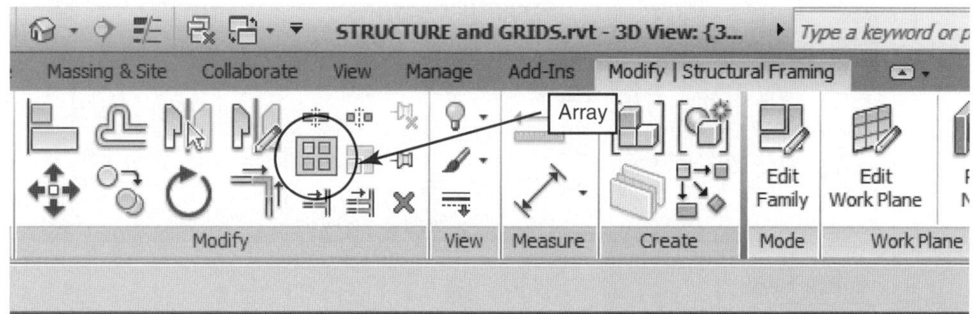

Figure 14-35

Array button

21. On the **Options Bar**, press the **Linear** button, check the **Group And Associate** check box, enter **2** in the **Number:** field, select the **Move To: 2nd** radio button, and check the **Constrain** check box (see Figure 14-36).

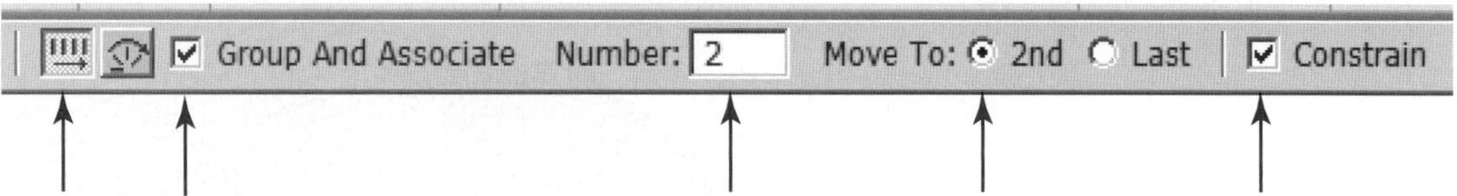

Figure 14-36

Group And Associate options

22. Drag the **Bar Joist** to the left **2′-0″**, and click to place.
23. Enter **21** in the **Number:** field that appears above the arrayed beams, and press the **<Enter>** key (see Figure 14-37).

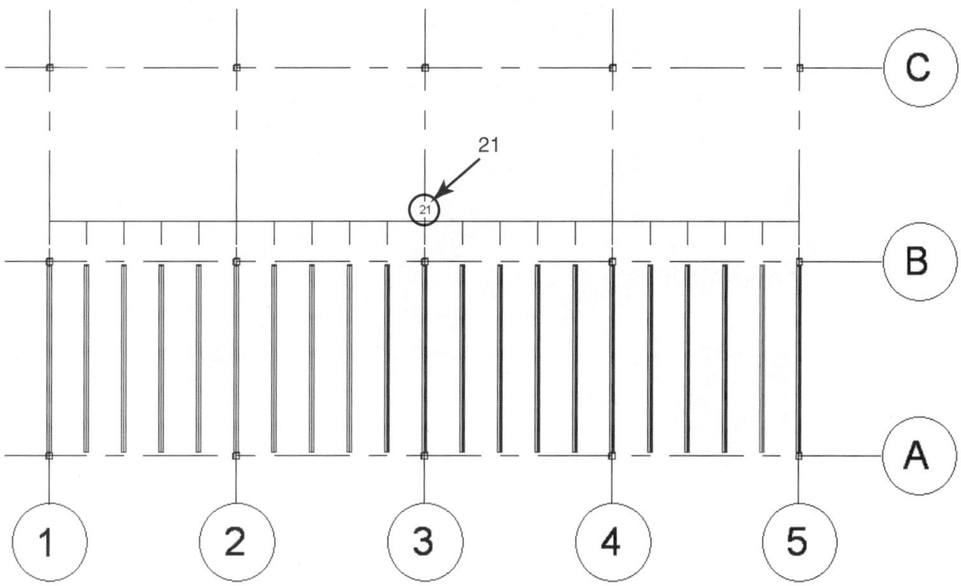

Figure 14-37

Arrayed beams

24. Select all the **Bar Joists** you just arrayed (hold down the **<Ctrl>** key while selecting) to bring up the **Modify | Model Groups** toolbar.
25. In the **Modify | Model Groups** toolbar, select the **Mirror > Pick Axis** button (see Figure 14-38).

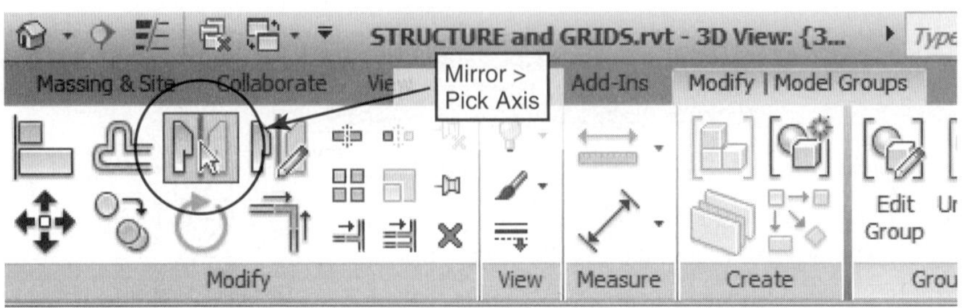

Figure 14-38

Mirror > Pick Axis button

26. Select the **B** grid line to mirror the **Bar Joists**.
27. Change to the **Default 3D View**, and select the **Fine** button from the **View Control Bar** (see Figure 14-39).

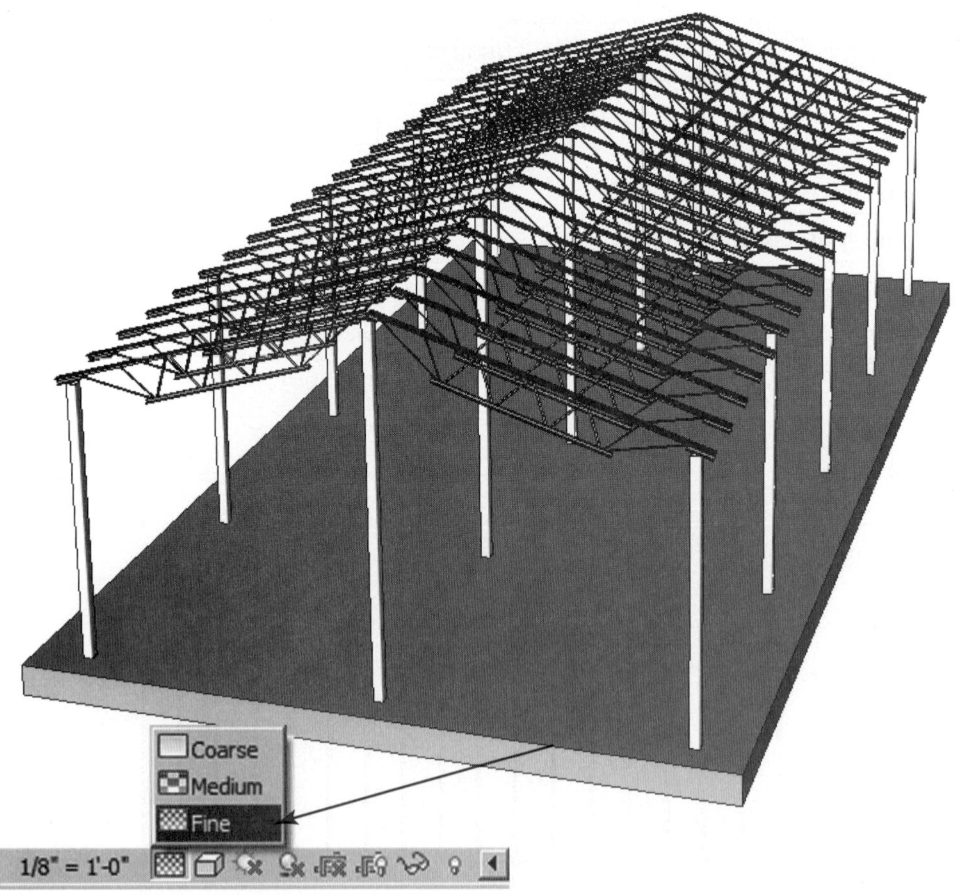

Figure 14-39

Beams drawing

28. Save this file as **STRUCTURAL MEMBERS – BEAMS**.

EXERCISE 14-6 ARCHITECTURAL COLUMNS

Architectural Columns are parametric 3D built-up units, unlike **Structural Columns,** which are actual structural shapes.

1. Use the previous file (**STRUCTURAL MEMBERS – BEAMS)**.
2. Delete the columns and beams, and change to the **East Elevation** view.
3. In the **East Elevation**, make sure that you have **TOP of EXTERIOR COLUMNS** and **TOP of INTERIOR COLUMNS** levels as shown in Figure 14-40.

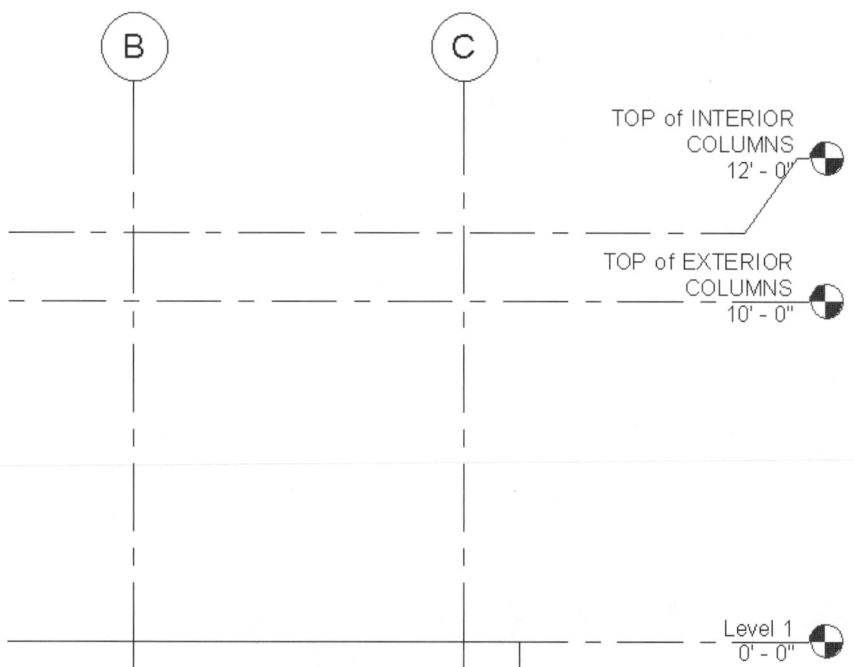

Figure 14-40

East Elevation view

4. In the **Project Browser**, double-click **Floor Plans** > **Level 1**.
5. In the **Structure** toolbar, select the **Column** > **Architectural Column** button to bring up the **Modify | Place Column** toolbar.
6. In the **Modify | Place Column** toolbar, select the **Load Family** button to bring up the **Load Family** dialog box.
7. In the **Load Family** dialog box, select the **Columns** folder.
8. In the **Columns** folder, you will find six different columns.
9. Select the **Doric Column,** and press the **Open** button to load it into your project.
10. In the **Options Bar**, select **Height** and **Unconnected**, and set the **Column Height** to **9′-0″**.
11. In the **Properties** dialog box, select the **Doric Column** from the **Properties** drop-down list.
12. In the **Properties** dialog box, select the **Edit Type** button to bring up its **Type Properties** dialog box.
13. In the **Type Properties** dialog box, you can change the **Diameter** and **Neck Diameter** of the column (see Figure 14-41).

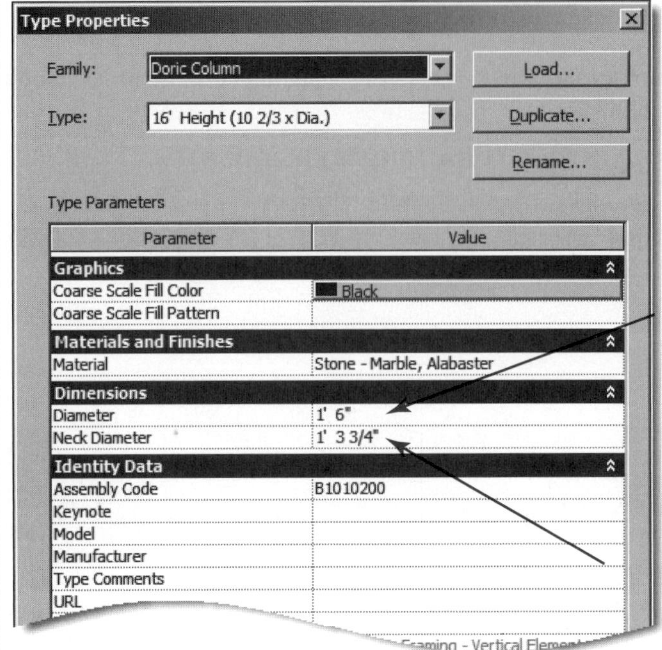

Figure 14-41

Type Properties dialog box

14. In the **Type Properties** dialog box, press the **Preview** button to expand the dialog box.
15. In the preview, select **Elevation: Front** from the drop-down list to see the **Doric Column** in **Elevation** view (see Figure 14-42).

NOTE:
In **Preview** mode, you will be able to see the changes to the column that you make in the **Dimensions** fields.

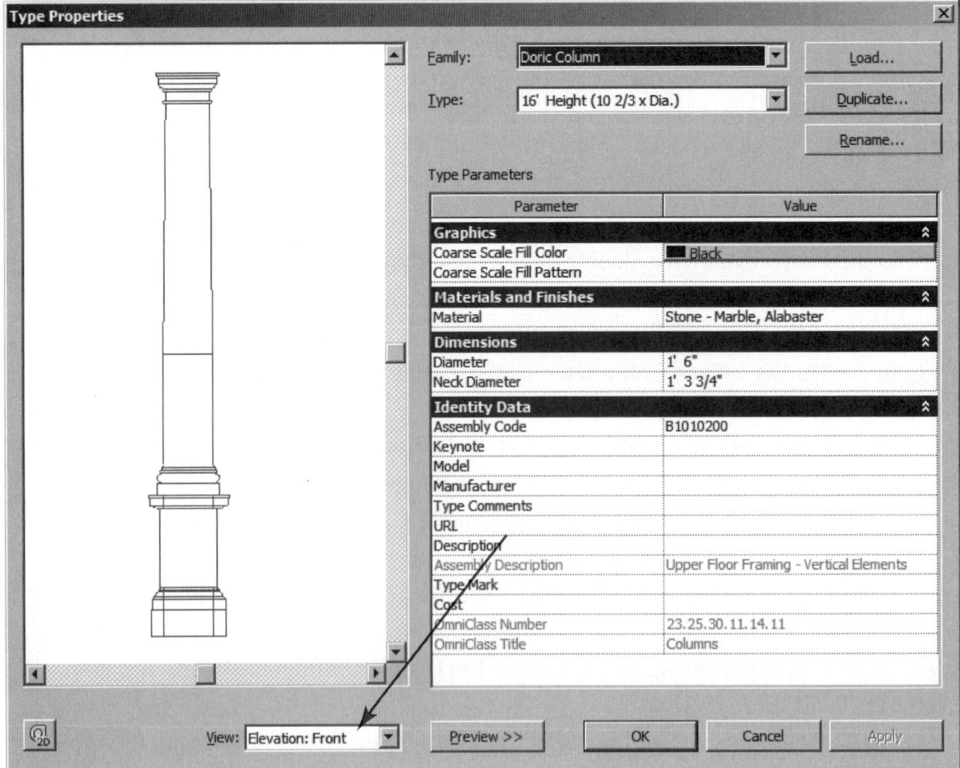

Figure 14-42

Doric Column dialog box

16. In the **Options Bar**, select **TOP of EXTERIOR COLUMNS** from the **Height** drop-down list (see Figure 14-43).

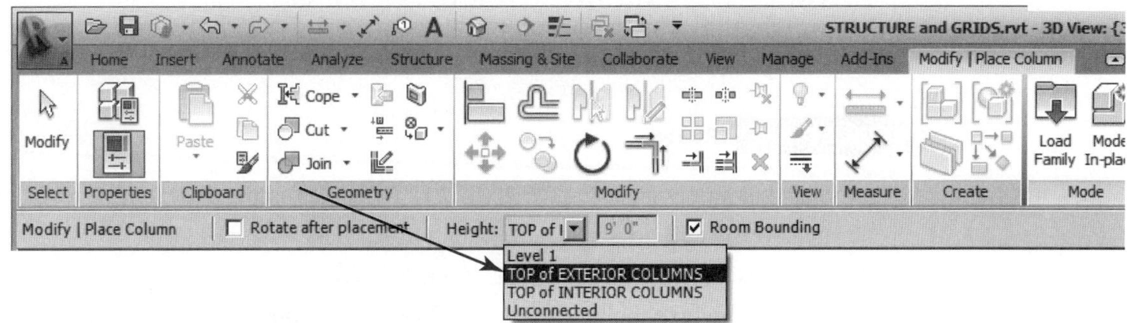

Figure 14-43

TOP of EXTERIOR COLUMNS option

17. Place the **Doric Column** at a grid intersection.
18. Change to the **West Elevation** view.
19. Notice that the column is as high as the **TOP of EXTERIOR COLUMNS** level (this is because its **Height** has been set to the **TOP of EXTERIOR COLUMNS** level).
20. Select the column, and set its **Height** to the **TOP of INTERIOR COLUMNS** level from the **Options Bar**.
21. Notice that the column is now as high as the **TOP of INTERIOR COLUMNS** level (this is because its **Height** has been set to the **TOP of INTERIOR COLUMNS** level).
22. If you now change the height of the **TOP of INTERIOR COLUMNS** level, the column will meet it.
23. If you select a column, you can change its **Top Level** by selecting it from the **Properties** dialog box (see Figure 14-44).

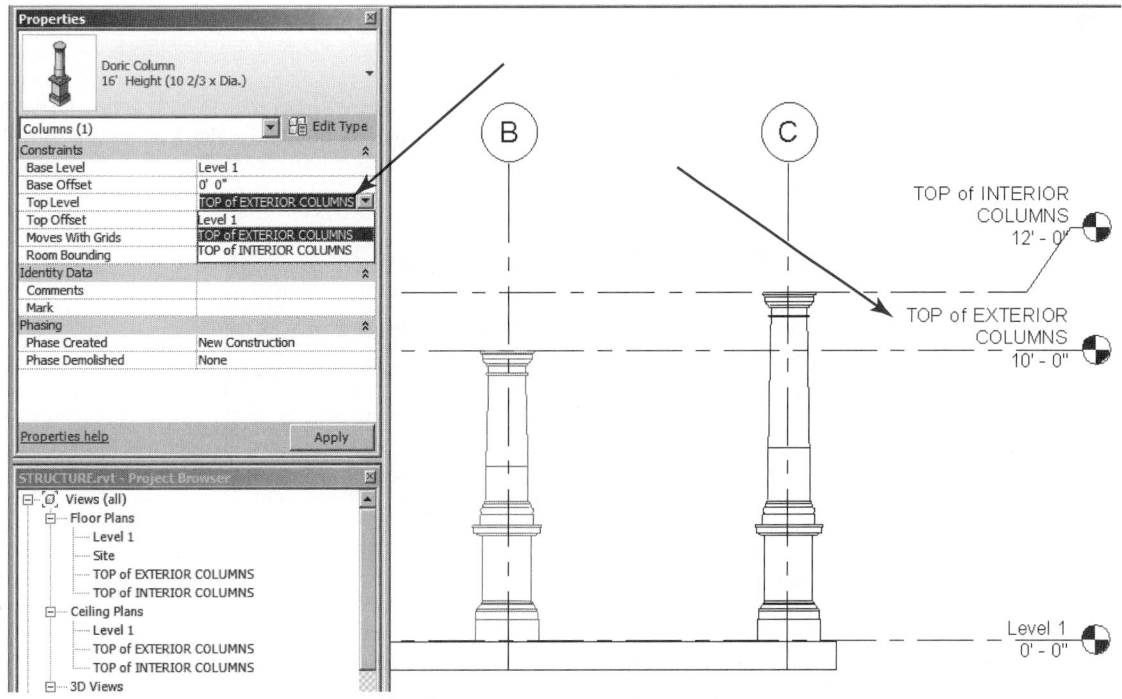

Figure 14-44

Properties dialog box

24. Experiment by placing all the different **Architectural** columns, and changing their parameters.
25. Save this file as **ARCHITECTURAL COLUMNS**.

EXERCISE 14-7 TRUSSES

1. Start a new drawing using the RAC 2012\Imperial Templates\default.rte template.
2. In the **Project Browser**, double-click **Floor Plans** > **Level 1**.
3. Select the **Structure** tab to bring up the **Structure** toolbar.
4. In the **Structure** toolbar, select the **Wall** > **Structural Wall** button, and create a **20′× 20′ Generic - 8″** enclosure **10′-0″** high (use the information you have learned from the Walls chapter to create this enclosure).
5. Make sure that **Level 2** is **10′-0″** above **Level 1**.
6. Change to **Level 2**.
7. In the **Structure** toolbar, select the **Truss** button (see Figure 14-45).

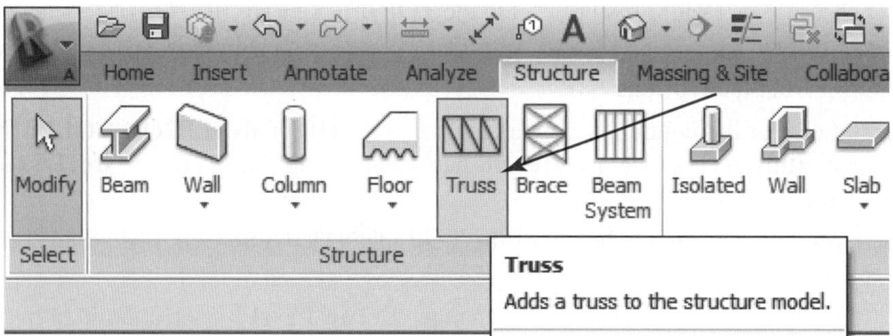

Figure 14-45

Truss button

8. If you have not loaded a **Truss Family**, you will get the *"No Structural Trusses Family is loaded. . . ."* message (see Figure 14-46); press the **Yes** button to bring up the **Load Family** dialog box.

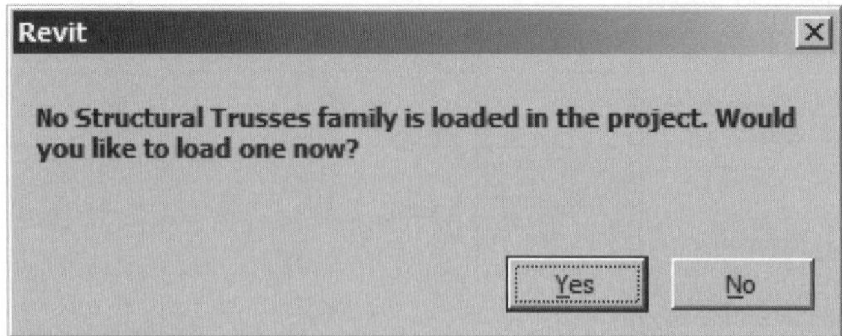

Figure 14-46

Revit message

9. In the **Load Family** dialog box, select the **Structural** folder.
10. In the **Structural** folder, select the **Trusses** folder.
11. In the **Trusses** folder, select the **Howe Gabled Truss-6 Panel.rfa**, and press the **Open** button to load it into the project (see Figure 14-47).

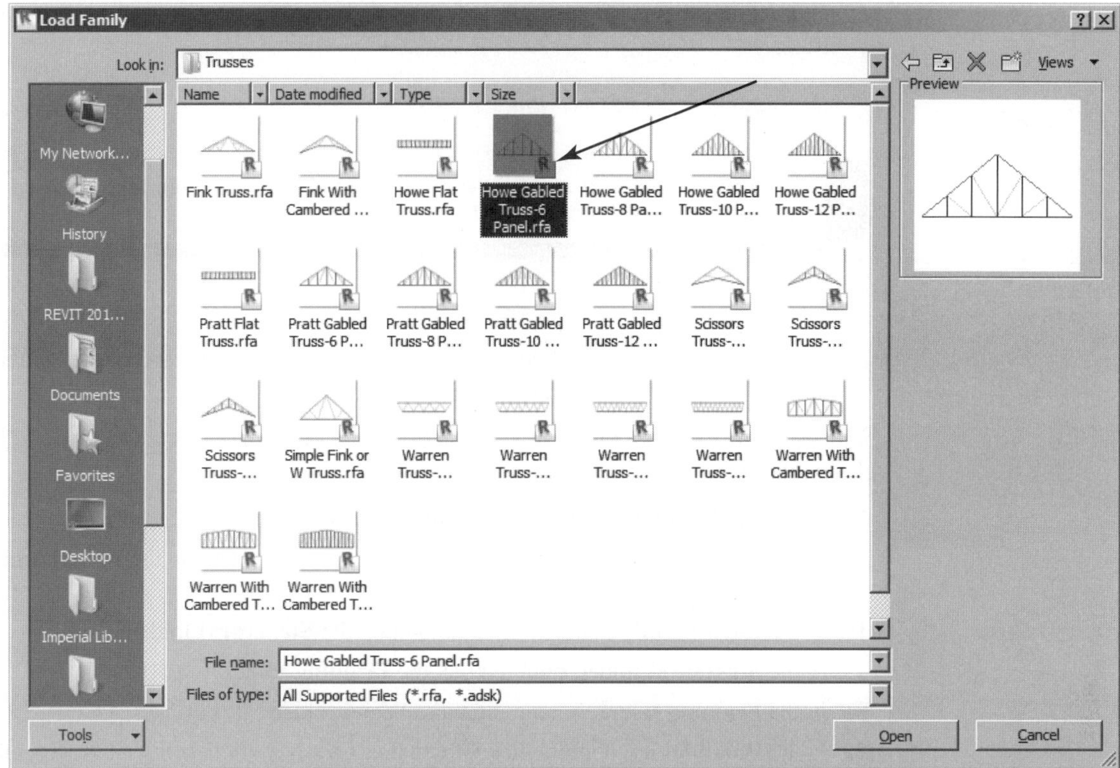

Figure 14-47

Trusses folder

12. Make sure that **Level 2** is **10′-0″** above **Level 1**.
13. Change to **Level 2**.
14. In the **Properties** dialog box, set the **Bearing Chord** to **Bottom** (see Figure 14-48).

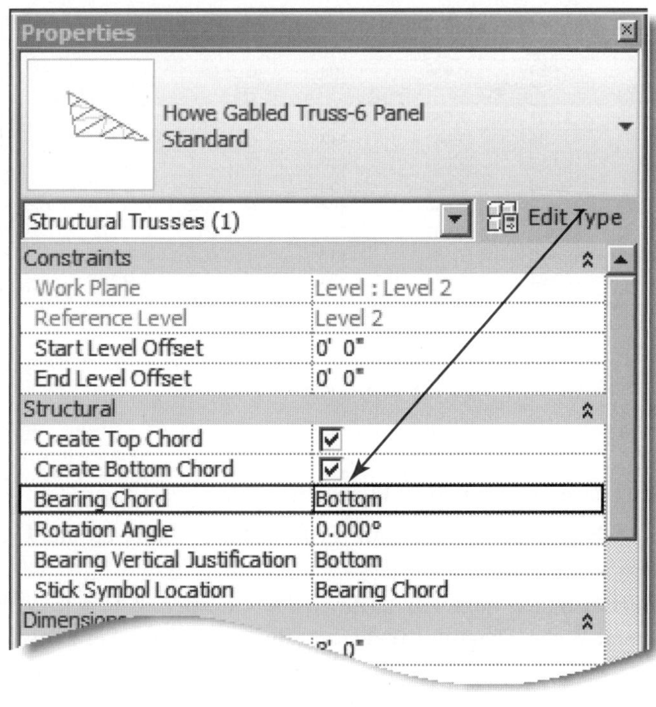

Figure 14-48

Properties dialog box

15. Click at the center of one wall, and then click on the opposite wall to place the truss.

If you only see a line, change the **Detail Level** to **Medium** in the **View Control Bar** to see the entire truss. Revit does this to save video resources.

16. Change to the **Default 3D View**; select the **Detail Level: Medium** button from the **View Control Bar** to see the truss in full detail.

Notice that it is a truss based on steel sections, but you may want a wood truss. To change the members to wood, do the following:

17. Select the **Insert** tab to bring up the **Insert** toolbar.
18. In the **Insert** toolbar, select the **Load Family** button to bring up the **Load Family** dialog box.
19. In the **Load Family** dialog box, double-click the **Structural** folder.
20. In the **Structural** folder, double-click the **Framing** folder.
21. In the **Framing** folder, double-click the **Wood** folder.
22. In the **Wood** folder, double-click **Dimension Lumber.rfa** to bring up the **Specify Types** dialog box.
23. Select **2 × 4** under **Type**, and press the **OK** button to load the **2 × 4** lumber into the project (see Figure 14-49).

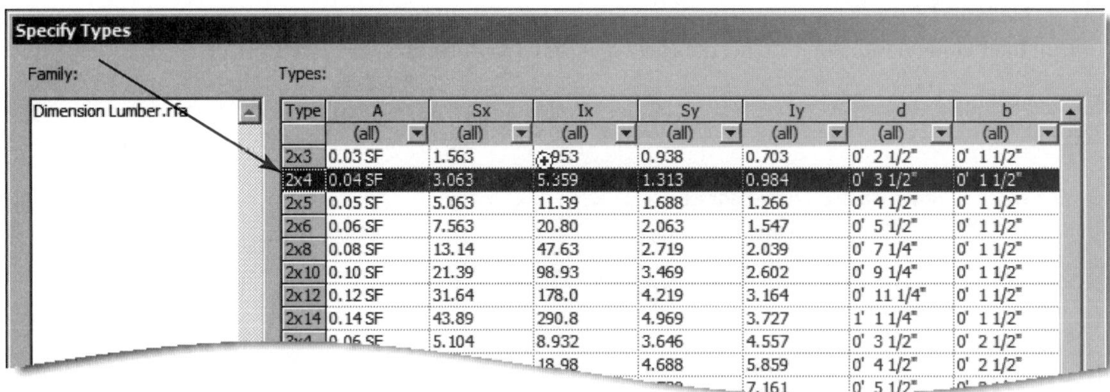

Type	A	Sx	Ix	Sy	Iy	d	b
	(all)	(all)	(all)	(all)	(all)	(all)	(all)
2x3	0.03 SF	1.563	1.953	0.938	0.703	0' 2 1/2"	0' 1 1/2"
2x4	0.04 SF	3.063	5.359	1.313	0.984	0' 3 1/2"	0' 1 1/2"
2x5	0.05 SF	5.063	11.39	1.688	1.266	0' 4 1/2"	0' 1 1/2"
2x6	0.06 SF	7.563	20.80	2.063	1.547	0' 5 1/2"	0' 1 1/2"
2x8	0.08 SF	13.14	47.63	2.719	2.039	0' 7 1/4"	0' 1 1/2"
2x10	0.10 SF	21.39	98.93	3.469	2.602	0' 9 1/4"	0' 1 1/2"
2x12	0.12 SF	31.64	178.0	4.219	3.164	0' 11 1/4"	0' 1 1/2"
2x14	0.14 SF	43.89	290.8	4.969	3.727	1' 1 1/4"	0' 1 1/2"
		5.104	8.932	3.646	4.557	0' 3 1/2"	0' 2 1/2"
			18.98	4.688	5.859	0' 4 1/2"	0' 2 1/2"

Figure 14-49

Specify Types dialog box

24. Select the truss you placed to bring up its **Properties** dialog box.
25. In the **Properties** dialog box, press the **Edit Type** button to bring up the **Type Properties** dialog box.
26. In the **Type Properties** dialog box, select **Dimension Lumber: 2 × 4** from the **Top Chords**, **Vertical Webs**, **Diagonal Webs**, and **Bottom Chords Set Framing** drop-down lists.
27. In the **Type Properties** dialog box, press the **OK** button to return to the **Drawing Editor**. The truss is now made of **Wood 2 × 4** members (see Figures 14-50 and 14-51).

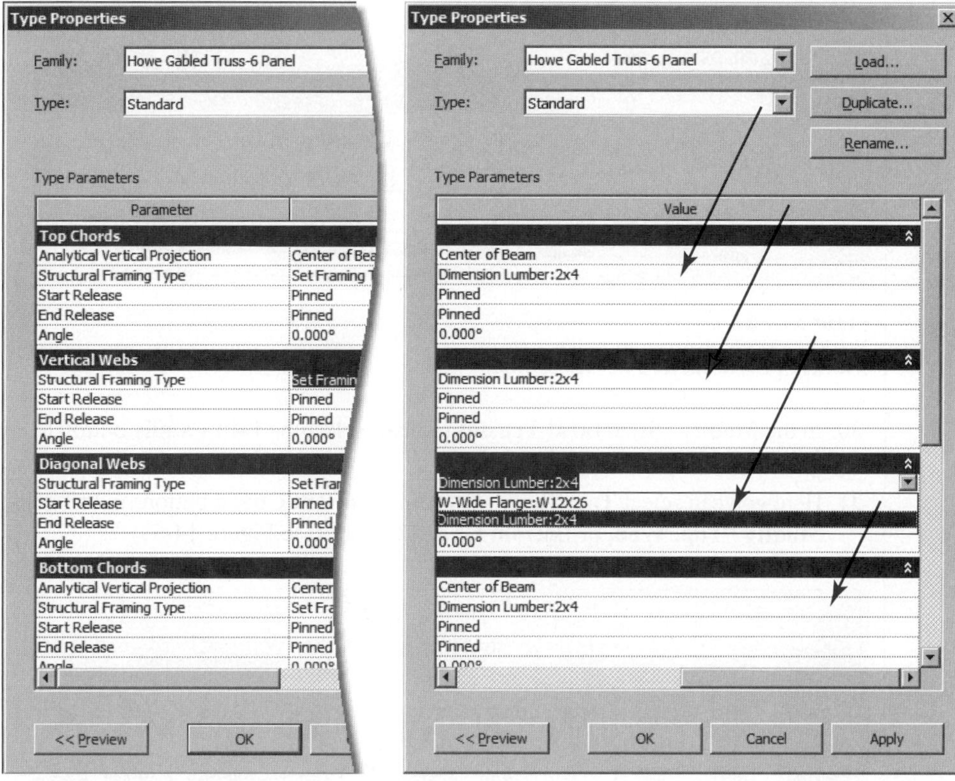

Figure 14-50

Type Properties dialog box

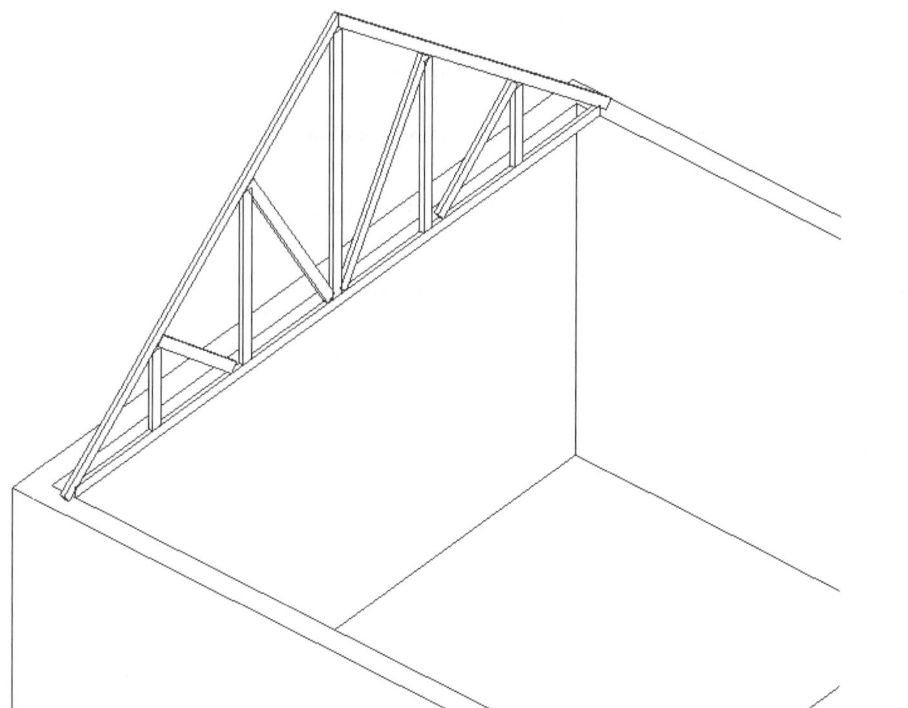

Figure 14-51

Drawing of a truss

28. Select the truss to bring up the **Modify | Structural Trusses** toolbar.
29. In the **Modify | Structural Trusses** toolbar, you have several buttons to edit the floors and roofs, similar to those shown in the Walls chapter (see Figure 14-52).

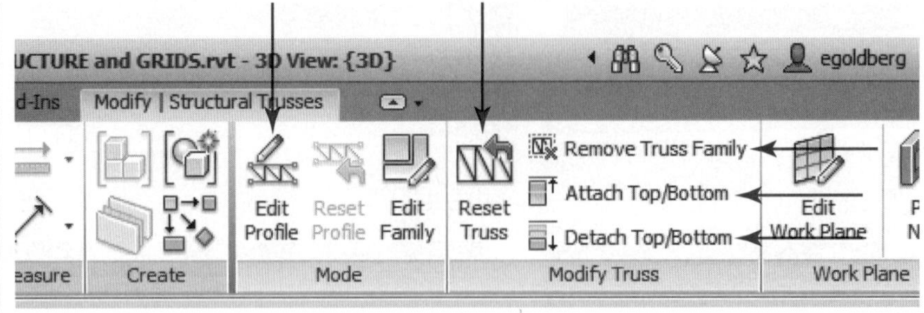

Figure 14-52

Modify | Structural Trusses toolbar

30. In the **Modify | Structural Trusses** toolbar, select the **Edit Family** button to enter the **Family Editor** for trusses.
31. Here you can select **Top Chord**, **Web**, and **Bottom Chord** buttons to bring up the **Modify | Top, Web,** or **Bottom Chord** toolbar (see Figure 14-53).

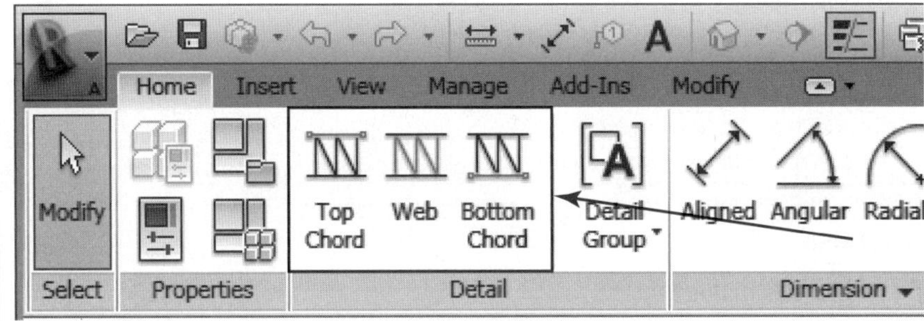

Figure 14-53

Top Chord, **Web**, and **Bottom Chord** buttons

32. In any of the **Modify | Top, Web,** or **Bottom Chord** toolbars, select buttons from the **Draw** panel, and change the truss.
33. In the **Modify | Top, Web, or Bottom Chord** toolbar, select the **Load into Project** button to load the changed truss (see Figure 14-54).

Figure 14-54

Modify | Top, **Web**, or **Bottom Chord** toolbars

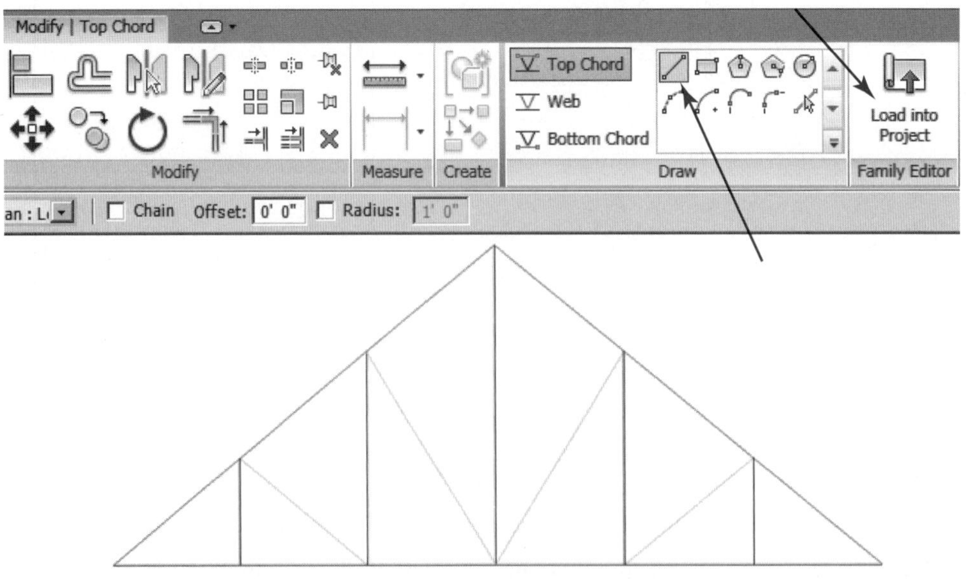

34. Save this file as **TRUSSES**.

EXERCISE 14-8 THE BEAM SYSTEM

This is an automated system for applying an entire area of beams.

1. Start a new drawing using the RAC 2012\Imperial Templates\default.rte template.
2. In the **Project Browser**, double-click **Floor Plans** > **Level 1**.
3. Set the **View Scale** to **1/4″ = 1′-0″**.
4. Select the **Insert** tab to bring up the **Insert** toolbar.
5. In the **Insert** toolbar, select the **Load Family** button to bring up the **Load Family** dialog box.
6. In the **Load Family** dialog box, double-click the **Structural** folder.
7. In the **Structural** folder, double-click the **Framing** folder.
8. In the **Framing** folder, double-click the **Wood** folder.
9. In the **Wood** folder, double-click **Plywood Web Joist.rfa** to load it into the project.
10. Select the **Structure** tab to bring up the **Structure** toolbar.
11. In the **Structure** toolbar, select the **Beam System** button to bring up the **Modify | Create Beam System Boundary** toolbar (see Figure 14-55).

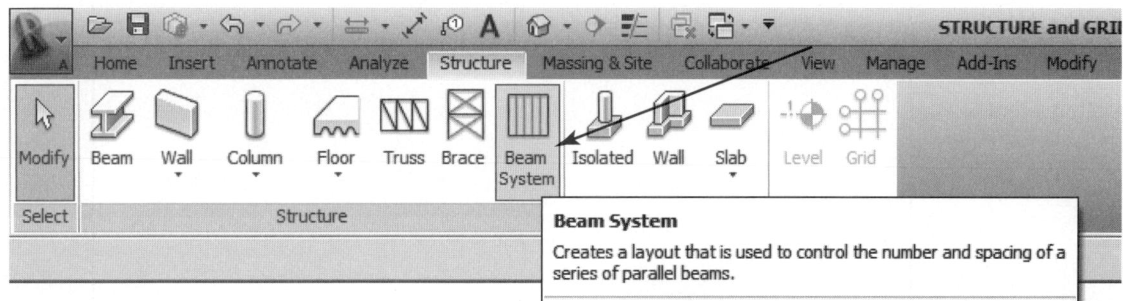

Figure 14-55

Beam System button

12. In the **Properties** dialog box (see Figure 14-56), set the following:
    a. Check the **3D** check box.
    b. **Elevation = 0′ - 11 7/8″**
    c. **Beam Type = Plywood Web Joist: 1 3/4 × 11 7/8**
    d. **Layout Rule = Fixed Distance**
    e. **Fixed Spacing = 2′-0″**
    f. **Tag New Members in View = Level 1**
13. In the **Modify | Create Beam System Boundary** toolbar, select the **Boundary Line** button and the **Rectangle** button in the **Draw** panel (see Figure 14-57).
14. Place a **30′ × 20′** rectangle in the **Drawing Editor**.

Notice the two short lines shown in Figure 14-58; they dictate the direction in which the joists will be placed.

15. In the **Modify | Create Beam System Boundary** toolbar, select the **Finish Edit Mode** button to create the system of **Plywood Web Joists**.
16. Change to the **Default 3D View**, and select **Medium** from the **Detail Level** button in the **View Control Bar** (see Figure 14-59).

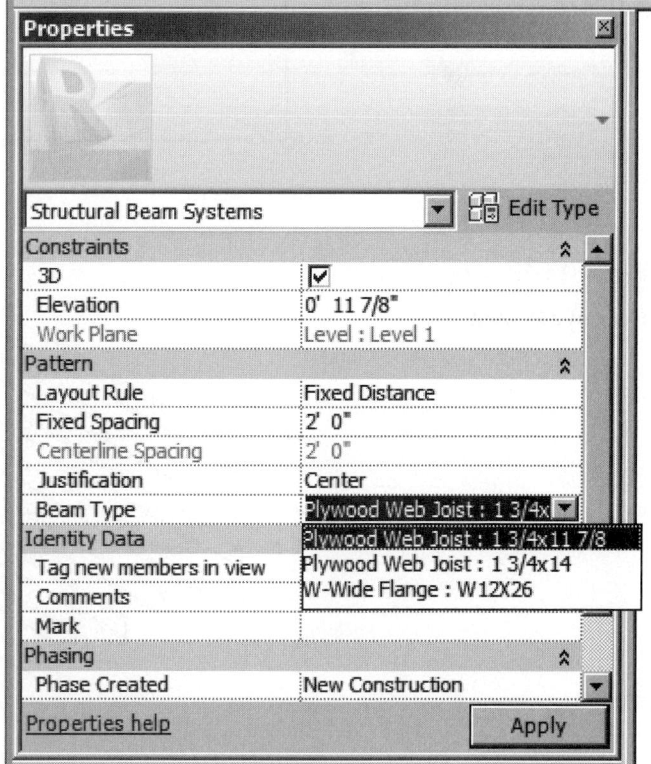

Figure 14-56

Properties dialog box

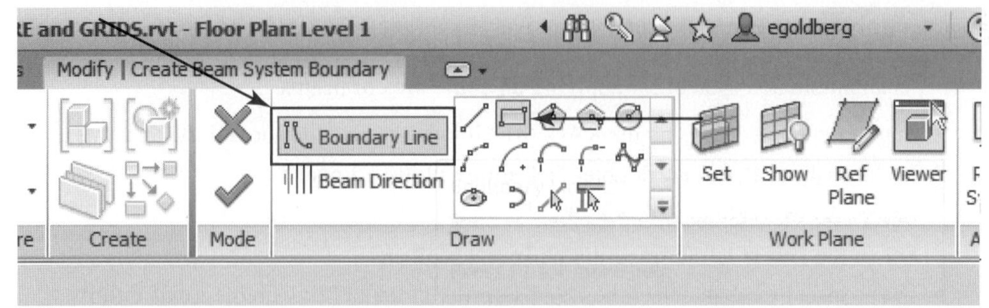

Figure 14-57

Boundary Line and **Rectangle** buttons

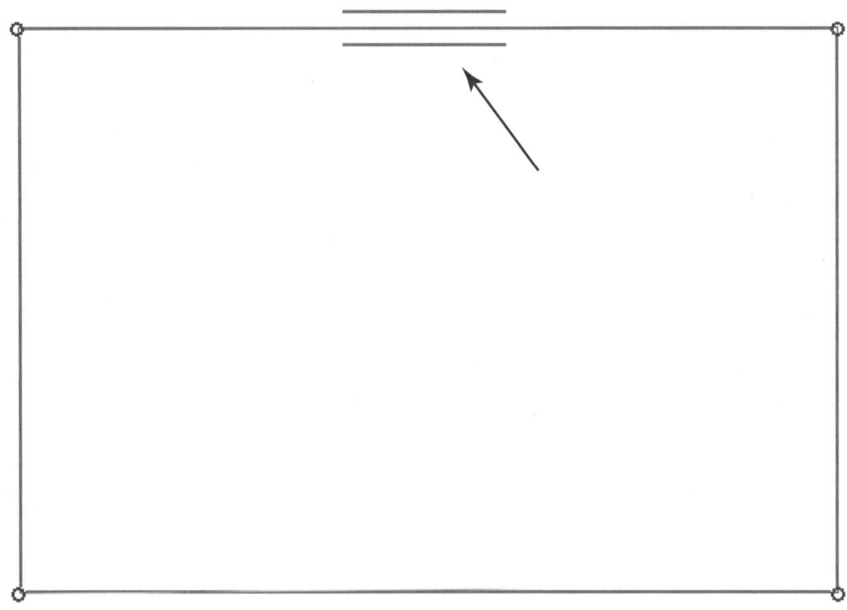

Figure 14-58

Two short lines indicate direction of joists

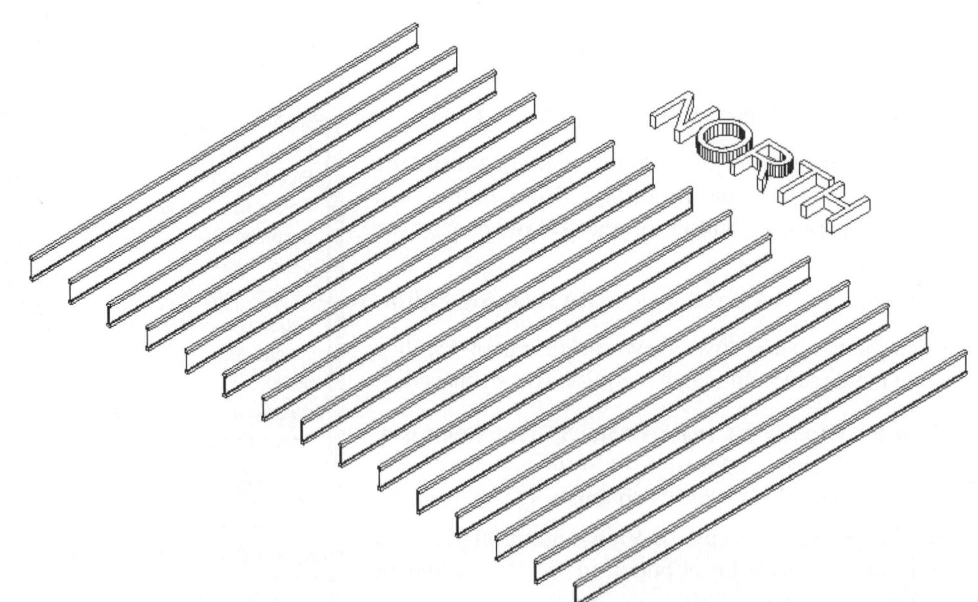

Figure 14-59

Default 3D View

17. Move your cursor over the joists until you see a dashed line, and then click to bring up the **Modify | Create Structural Beam System Boundary** toolbar (see Figure 14-60).

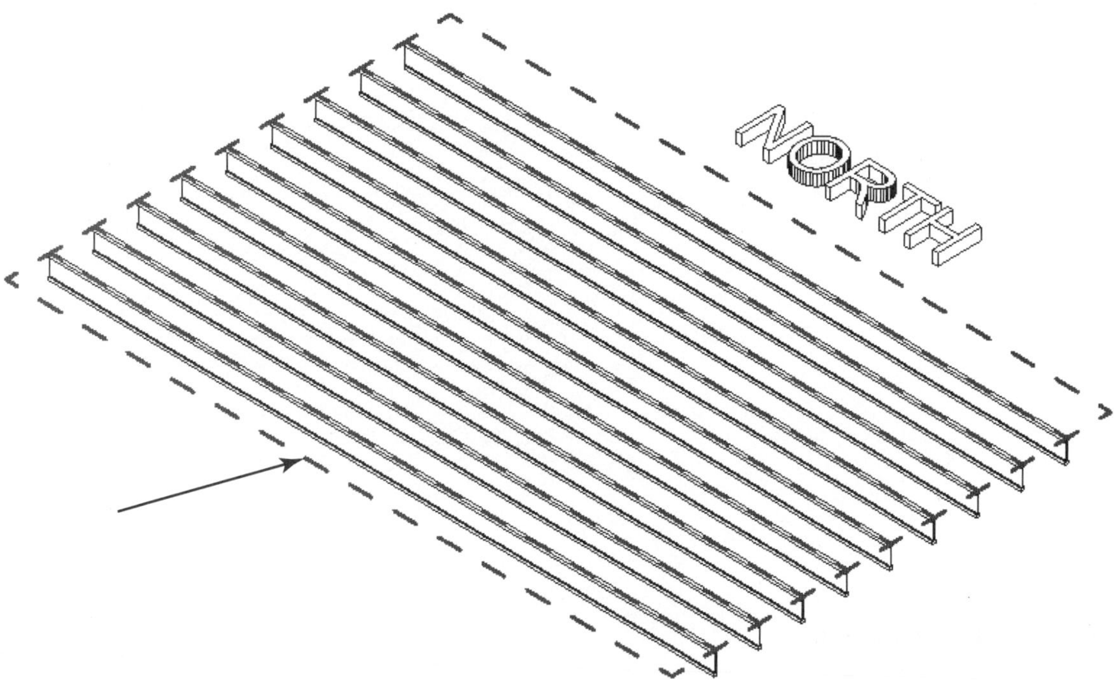

Figure 14-60

Dashed lines around joist

18. In the **Modify | Create Structural Beam System Boundary** toolbar, select the **Edit Boundary** button to bring up the **Modify | Structural Beam Systems** > **Edit Boundary** toolbar.
19. In the **Modify | Structural Beam Systems** > **Edit Boundary** toolbar, select the **Beam Direction** button, and select the **West Boundary Line** (see Figures 14-61 and 14-62).

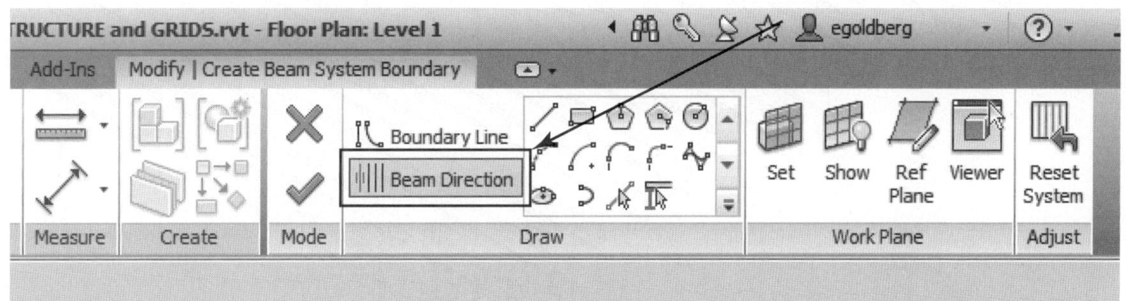

Figure 14-61

Beam Direction button

20. In the **Modify | Structural Beam Systems** > **Edit Boundary** toolbar, select the **Finish Edit Mode** button to create the changed system of **Plywood Web Joists** (see Figure 14-63).
21. If you select the **Edit Boundary** button again, you can modify the **Beam Systems** by modifying the boundary with the **Draw** tools.

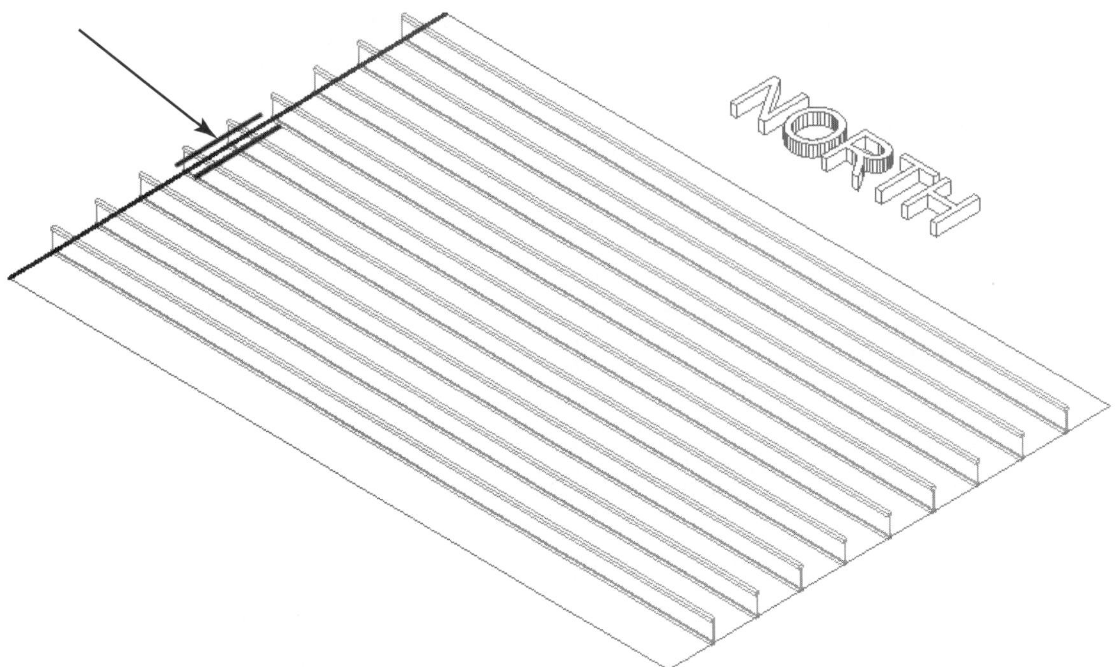

Figure 14-62

Select **West Boundary Line**

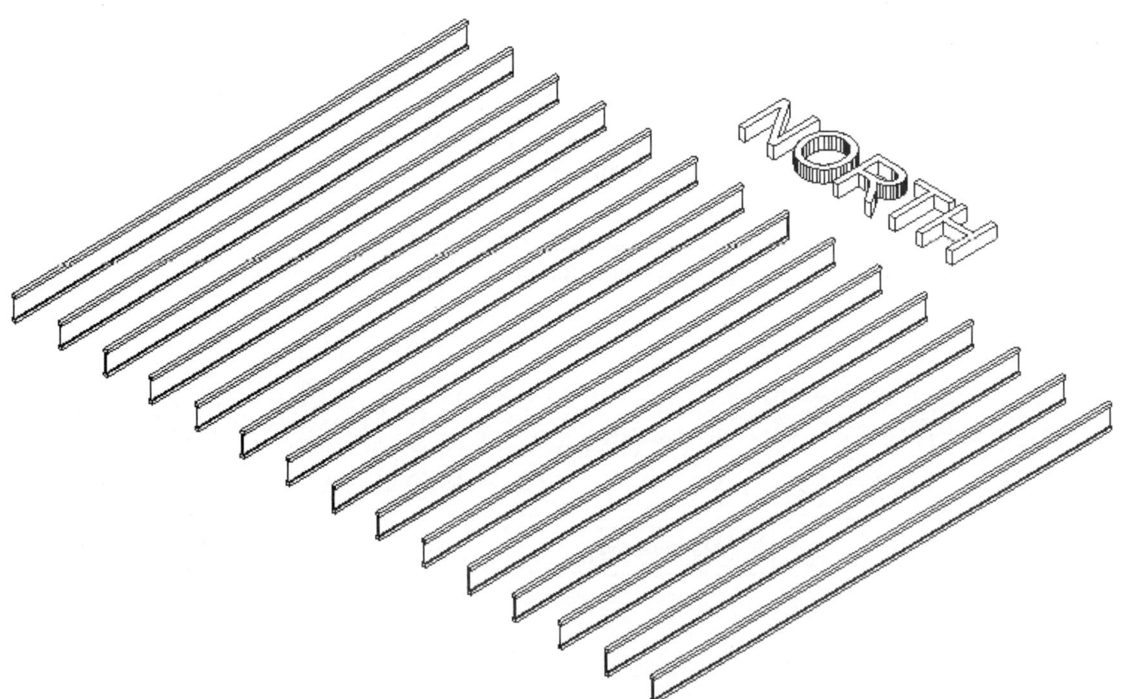

Figure 14-63

Completed **Plywood Web Joists** system

22. Experiment with this feature to see the full capability of this tool (see Figures 14-64 and 14-65).
23. Save this file as **BEAM SYSTEM**.

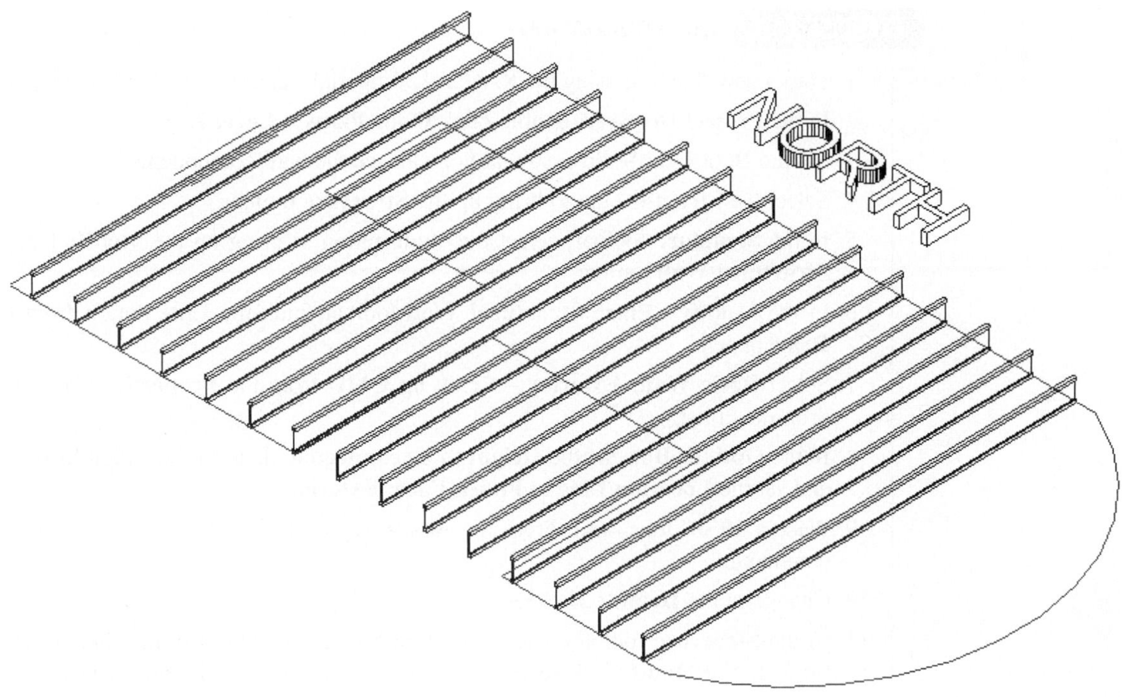

Figure 14-64

Beam System example

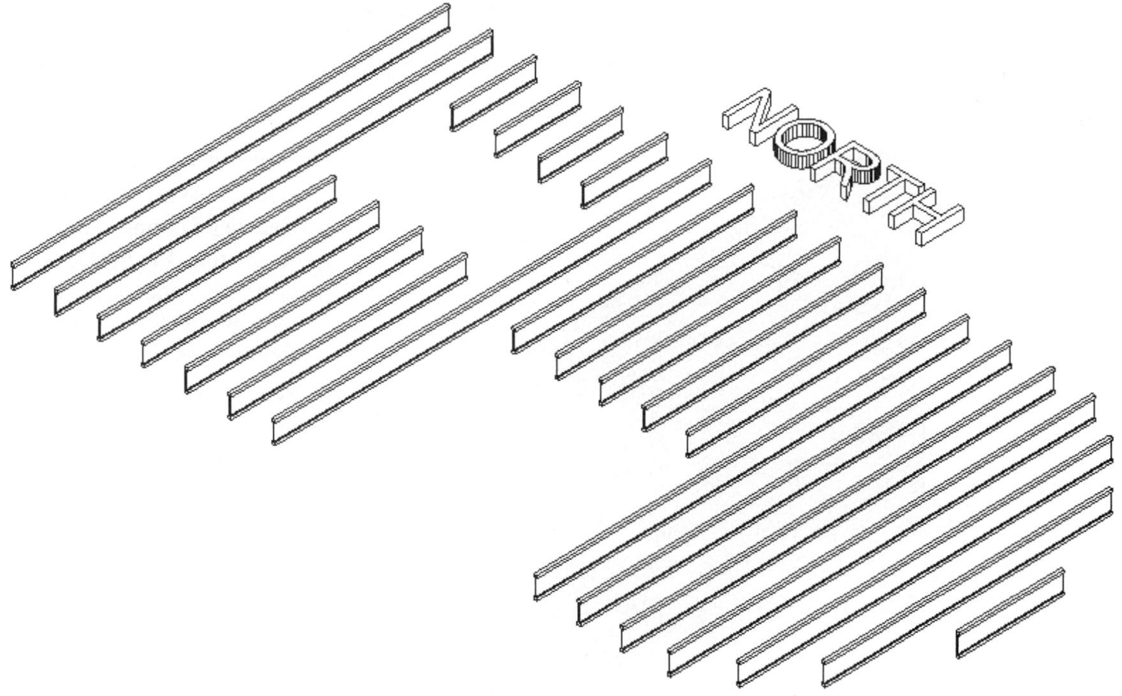

Figure 14-65

Beam System example

EXERCISE 14-9 WALL FOUNDATION

1. Start a new drawing using the RAC 2012\Imperial Templates\default.rte template.
2. In the **Project Browser**, double-click **Floor Plans** > **Level 1**.
3. Set the **Detail** to **Medium** so that you can see the wall components in Plan view.
4. Select the **Structure** tab to bring up the **Structure** toolbar.
5. In the **Structure** toolbar, select the **Wall** button to bring up the **Modify | Place Structural Wall** toolbar.
6. In the **Modify | Place Structural Wall** toolbar, pick the **Line** button from the **Draw** panel.
7. Select **Basic Wall: Exterior – Brick on CMU** from the **Properties** dialog box drop-down list.
8. In the **Options Bar**, set the **Height** to **Unconnected**, then set the height to **10′-0″**, and set the **Location Line** to **Finish Face: Exterior**.
9. Place a **10′-0″** long wall. Press the **<Esc>** key on the keyboard to complete the command.
10. Change to the **Default 3D View**.
11. In the **Structure** toolbar, select the **Wall** button from the **Foundation** panel to bring up the **Modify | Place Wall Foundation** toolbar (see Figure 14-66).

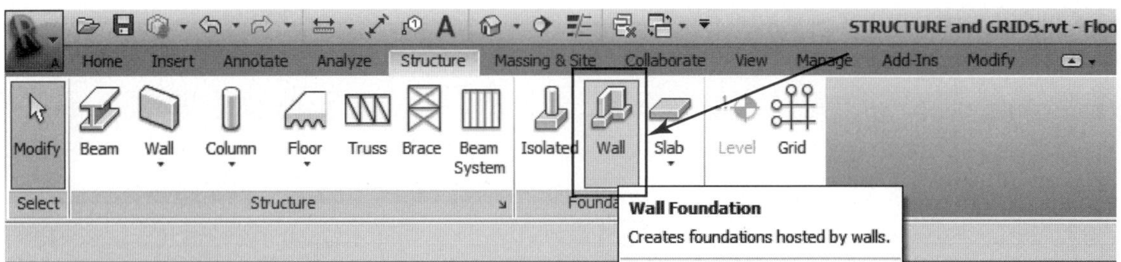

Figure 14-66

Wall Foundation button

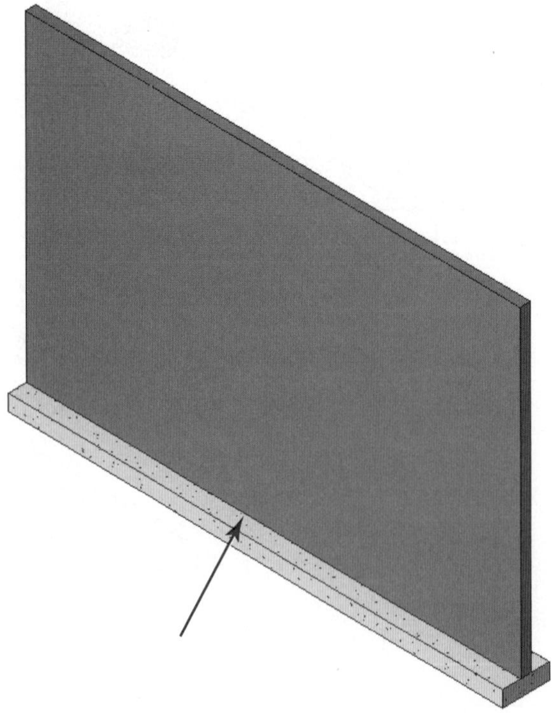

Figure 14-67

Select the bottom of the wall to place the footing

12. In the **Properties** dialog box, select **Wall Foundation Bearing Footing – 36″ × 12″** from the **Properties** drop-down list, and select the bottom of the wall to place the footing (see Figure 14-67).
13. Select the footing you just placed, and select **Retaining Footing - 24″ × 12″ × 12″** from the **Properties** drop-down list.
14. Select the footing, and then select the **Type Properties** button from the **Properties** dialog box to bring up the **Type Properties** dialog box.
15. In the **Type Properties** dialog box, change the **Heel Length** to **5′-0″**, and press the **OK** button to return to the **Drawing Editor** (see Figure 14-68).
16. Save this file as **WALL FOUNDATIONS**.

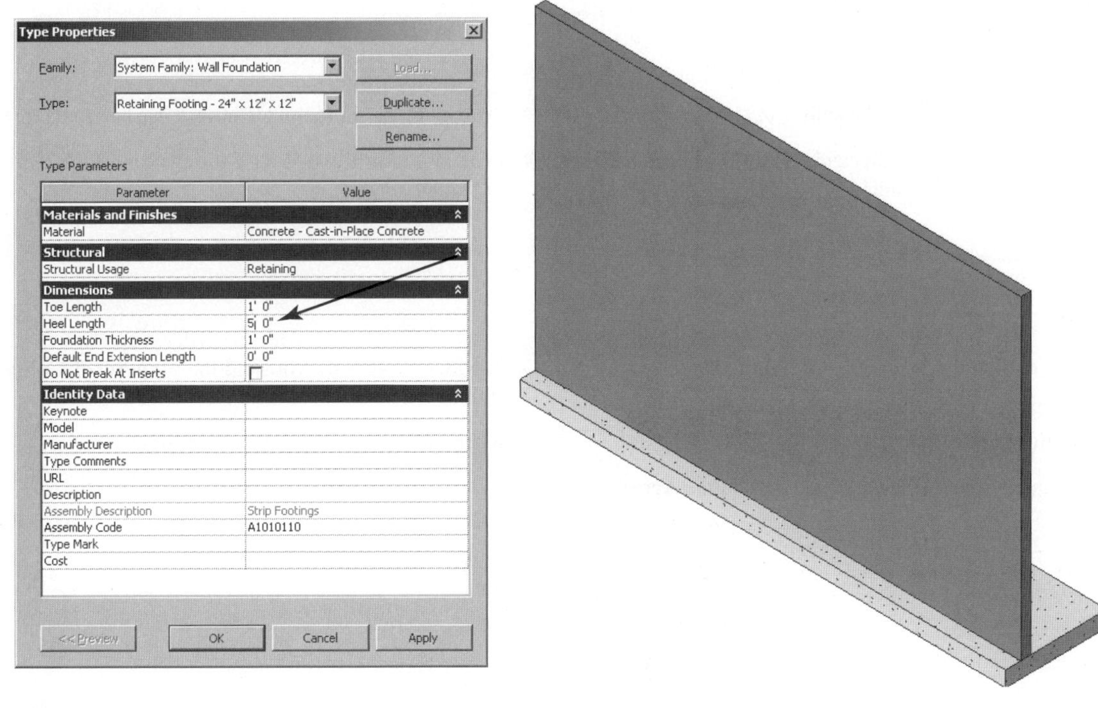

Figure 14-68

Type Properties dialog box

Chapter Summary

This chapter explained the basics needed to create, modify, and place column grids and structural components such as bar joists, trusses, and wall footings.

Chapter Test Questions

Multiple Choice

Circle the correct answer.

1. The **Wall** button can be found in
   a. The **Insert** toolbar.
   b. The **Home** toolbar only.
   c. The **Structure** toolbar.
   d. Both the **Home** and **Structure** toolbars.
2. The **System Grid** segment controls are found in the
   a. **Properties** dialog box.
   b. **Type Properties** dialog box.
   c. **Annotate** toolbar.
   d. **Structure** toolbar.
3. The **Beam Direction** button
   a. Controls the location of the **Beam** button.
   b. Controls which end of the beam is bearing.
   c. Controls which way the beam is oriented.
   d. None of the above
4. **Architectural Columns** and **Structural Columns** are similar, except
   a. Only the **Architectural Column** can have its height adjusted.
   b. **Structural Columns** are load bearing.
   c. Only **Structural Columns** width can vary.
   d. **Architectural Columns** can be load bearing.
5. There is a duplicate **Floor** button in which toolbars?
   a. **Structure** and **Home**
   b. **Structure** and **Insert**
   c. **Annotate** and **Home**
   d. **Structure** and **Annotate**

True or False

Circle the correct answer.

1. **True or False:** Grid lines can be split.
2. **True or False:** In Revit, **Beams** and **Columns** can use the same structural member families.
3. **True or False:** In Revit, a **Column** is a horizontal member.
4. **True or False:** Revit **Wall Footings** can be adjusted for width and height.

Questions

1. Where can you find the **Structural Members**?
2. What is the difference between a **Bearing Footing** and a **Retaining Footing**?
3. When creating a **Structure**, where do you find the **Array** button?
4. In which toolbar do you find the **Structural Column** button?
5. Where do you find the **Truss Families**?

CHAPTER

15 Massing & Site

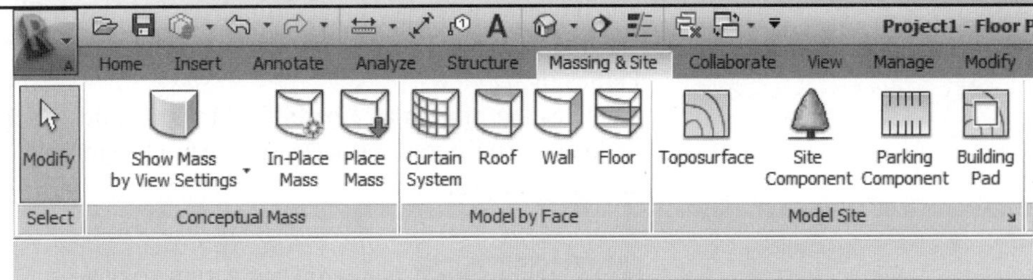

CHAPTER OBJECTIVES

- Understand the **In-Place Mass** family interface and **Work Planes**.
- Understand the **Conceptual Mass panel** and the **Model by Face panel**.
- Understand the **Loadable Mass Family** editor interface and **Work Planes**.
- Understand the **Draw** and **Form Element** panels.
- Understand how to use the **3D Site tools**.

Introduction

When creating a building in Revit 2012, you can use the building modeling tools and system to come up with design concepts. However, this can be limiting when attempting to create abstract mass forms. By using the massing tools, you can create flexible and organic shapes. These forms can then be assigned parameters that control shape and physical properties. When the values of the parameters change, the shapes update. Finally, the created mass forms can then be turned into Revit system components such as curtain walls, floors, and roofs.

Many architectural projects include site design. Revit Architecture 2012 has an excellent 3D site creation tool called the **Toposurface** tool. This tool allows you to develop the 3D site model manually by entering elevation points, or automatically by importing point data from your civil engineer's or surveyor's 3D files.

This extensive chapter deals with the basics of both Revit's **Massing** and **3D Site** tools.

Massing

In-Place and Loadable Mass Families

Creating mass objects can be approached in two ways. You can create them either inside or outside a project file. You have the choice of using **In-Place Mass** or **Loadable Mass** families. Let's see how they differ:

1. **In-Place Mass Families:** In this method, massing is done *inside* a project environment. If the object is a unique element that will be used only once, this may be the way to go. If you're designing a unique family that is directly related to the project, it will be more efficient to do it inside a project environment.
2. **Loadable Mass Families:** In this method, massing is done *outside* a project environment. When you're dealing with design concepts that may change from time

to time, creating them outside a project environment is the best way to do it. If the component will repeat several times, then creating this element as a loadable family is more effective. When the design changes and you reload the family back into a project, all instances update.

Although both methods share the same tools functionality, there is a difference. With **In-Place Mass** families, you will not see the **Levels** and **Reference Planes** in 3D views. You can, however, reference them through the **Set Work Plane** tool, which will be explained later on. In **Loadable Mass** families, you can create, select, and see the **Levels** and **Reference Planes** in 3D views.

Creating objects as **Loadable Mass** families offers better flexibility because they can be loaded to different projects. You can change your design as often as you want without affecting the project.

EXERCISE 15-1 THE MASSING & SITE TOOLBAR

In-Place Mass Family Interface

The **Massing & Site** tab contains two distinct tool sets. The first (the **Massing Tools**) are used for creating **Conceptual Masses** (see Figure 15-1).

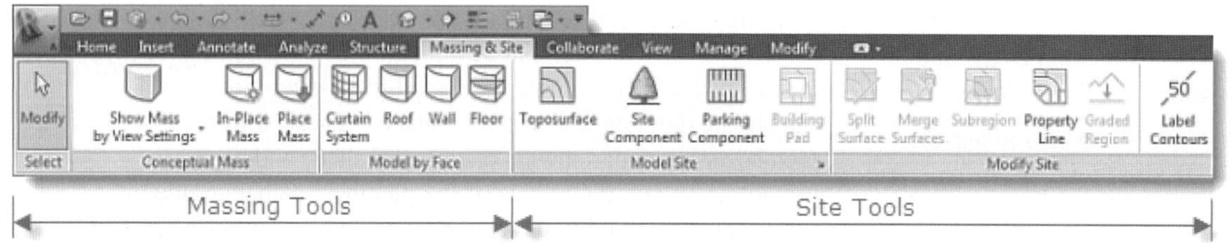

Figure 15-1

The **Massing & Site** toolbar

Creating a New Mass from the Massing & Site Toolbar

1. In the **Massing & Site** toolbar, select the **In-Place Mass** button (Figure 15-2).

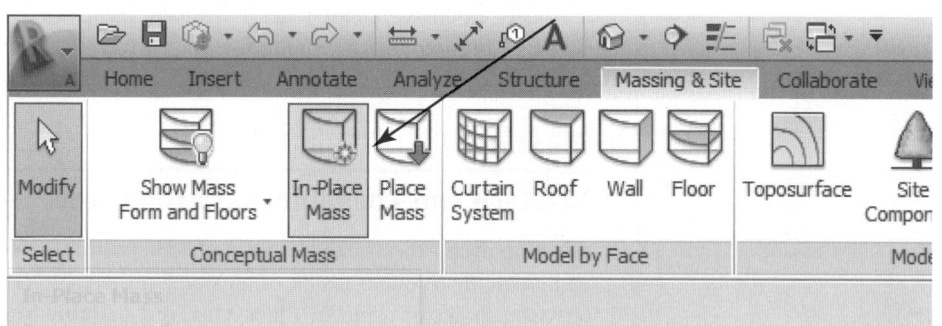

Figure 15-2

In-Place Mass button

2. The first time you click the **In-Place Mass** button, the **Massing - Show Mass Enabled** message will appear (see Figure 15-3).

This is a visibility reminder. After clicking **Close**, the **Name** dialog box will appear (see Figure 15-4).

3. In the **Name** dialog box, enter a name for the mass, and press the **OK** button to bring up the **In-Place Editor** (see Figure 15-5).

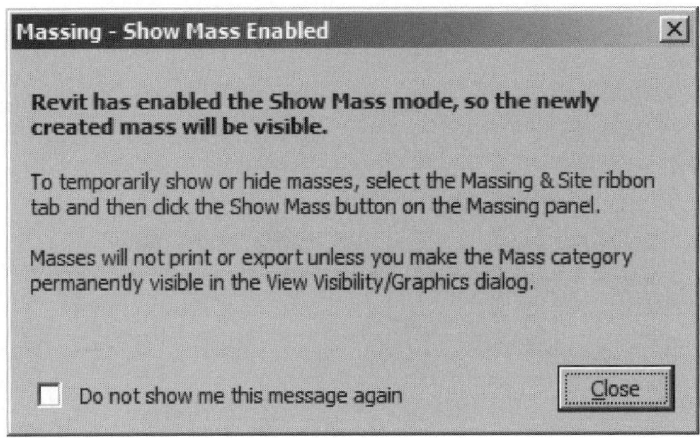

Figure 15-3

Massing - Show Mass Enabled message

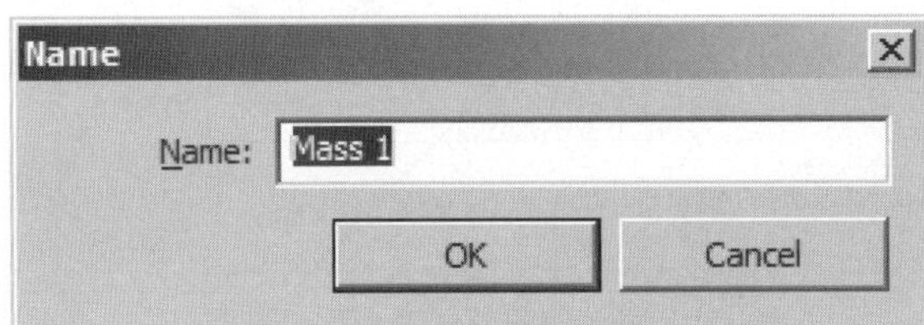

Figure 15-4

Name dialog box

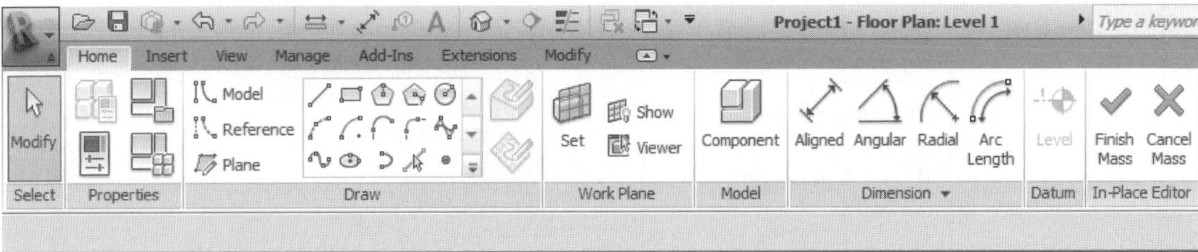

Figure 15-5

In-Place Editor interface

The Mass Visibility Settings

The **Massing - Show Mass Enabled** message that pops up the first time you click the **In-Place Mass** button (see Figure 15-3) is a reminder that the **Show Mass** mode is *enabled by default*. Later on, when you quit and open the file again, the mass you just created will not be visible. In order to see the mass permanently every time you open a project file, you must select it from the **Visibility/Graphic Overrides** dialog box. Open this dialog box by pressing **VG** on the keyboard (Figure 15-6). This setting affects only the view or views in which the mass is set to be visible.

Inside the **In-Place Mass Editor,** selecting the **Show Mass** button will hide the mass. Selecting the **Show Mass** button again will make the mass visible (see Figure 15-7).

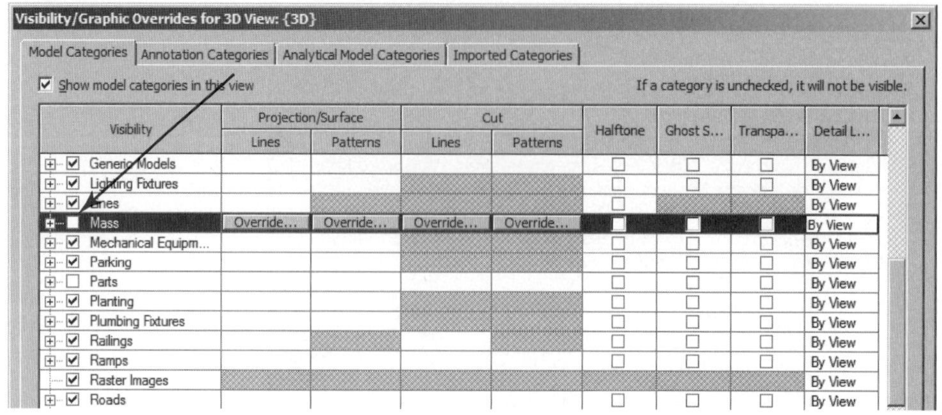

Figure 15-6

Visibility/Graphic Overrides for 3D View dialog box

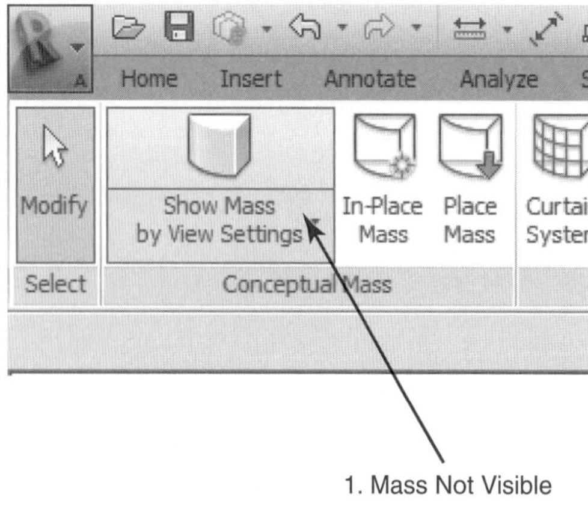

Figure 15-7

Show Mass button

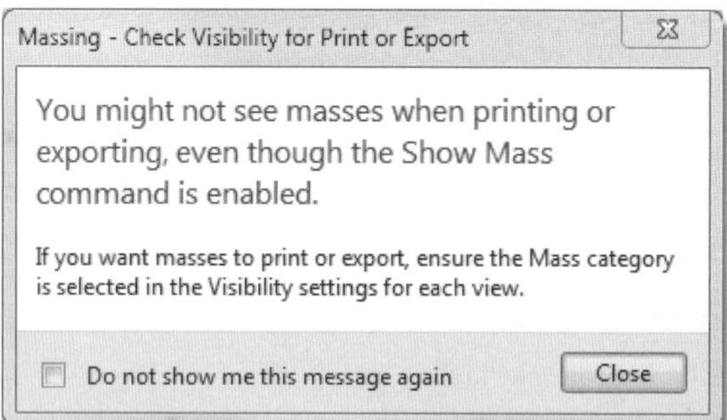
Massing - Check Visibility for Print or Export

You might not see masses when printing or exporting, even though the Show Mass command is enabled.

If you want masses to print or export, ensure the Mass category is selected in the Visibility settings for each view.

Do not show me this message again

Close

Figure 15-8

Massing - Check Visibility for Print or Export message

Placing an Existing Mass from the Massing & Site Toolbar

1. In the **Massing & Site** toolbar, select the **Place Mass** button (Figure 15-9).

If you have not loaded a family in your project yet, you will get the following Revit prompt (see Figure 15-10).

2. In the **Revit** prompt, click the **Yes** button to bring up the **Load Family** dialog box. This is where you locate and open the mass family you want to load in your project (see Figure 15-11).

> **NOTE:**
>
> **Show Mass** is a global switch that affects all views *temporarily*. Unless you change the **Visibility/Graphic Overrides** setting, all the massing views at this state will not be visible the next time you open the file. You also will not be able to print and export. If you attempt to print or export, you will get a message (see Figure 15-8).

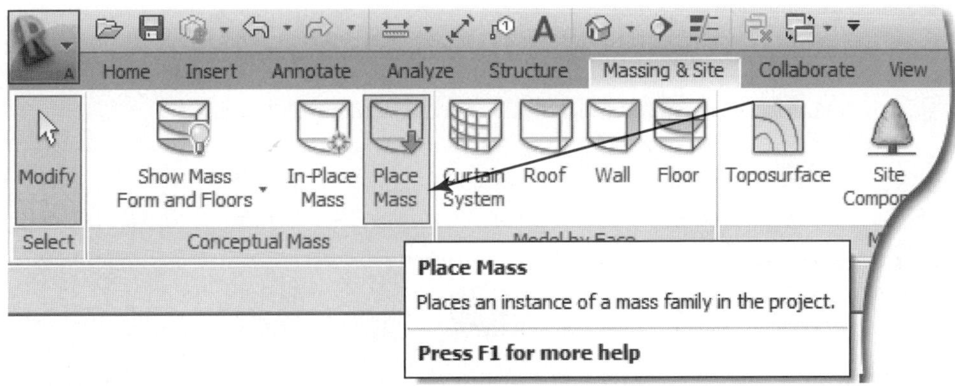

Figure 15-9

Place Mass button

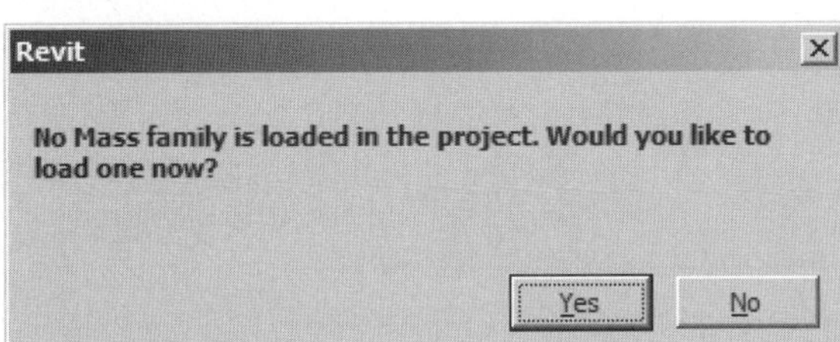

Figure 15-10

Revit reminder message

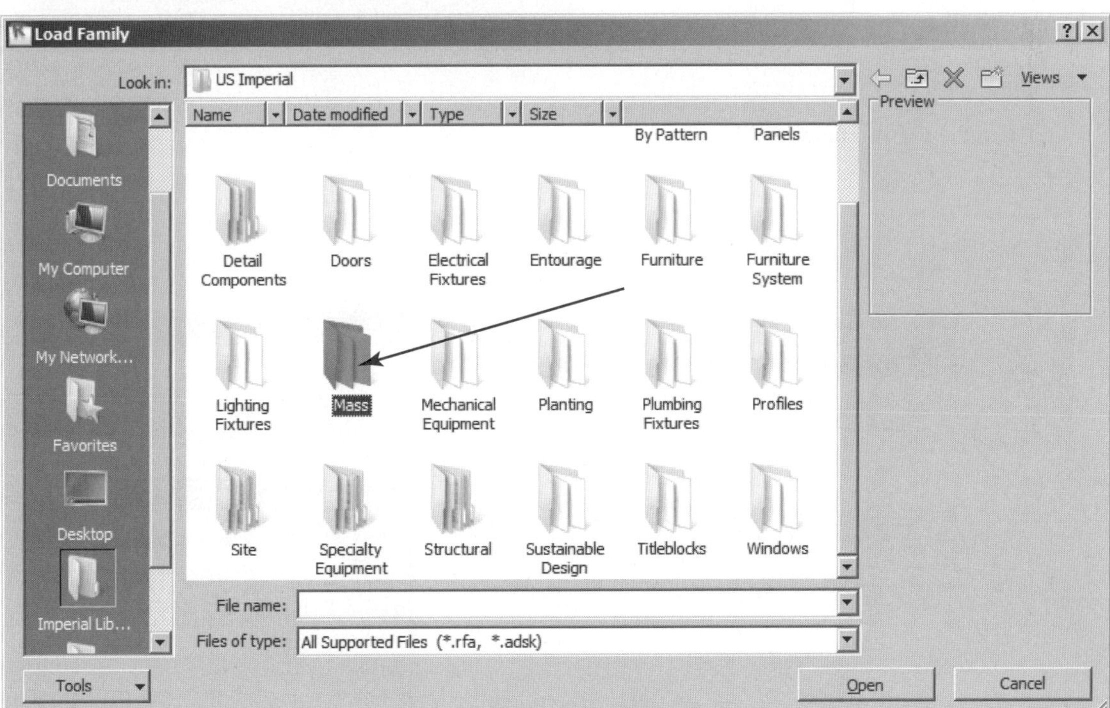

Figure 15-11

Load Family dialog box

3. In the **Mass** folder, double click the **Gable.rfa** file to load it into the program (see Figure 15-12).
4. In the **Modify | Place Mass** tab, select the **Place on Work Plane** button, and click in the **Drawing Editor** to place the **Gable Mass**.
5. Change to the **Default 3D view** to see the **Gable Mass** in 3D (see Figure 15-14).

NOTE:

Once a mass family is loaded, a *contextual menu* is added to the **Modify | Place Mass** tab showing the default placement method, which is **Place on Face.** The **Properties** dialog box will also show the mass family name in the type selector (Figure 15-13).

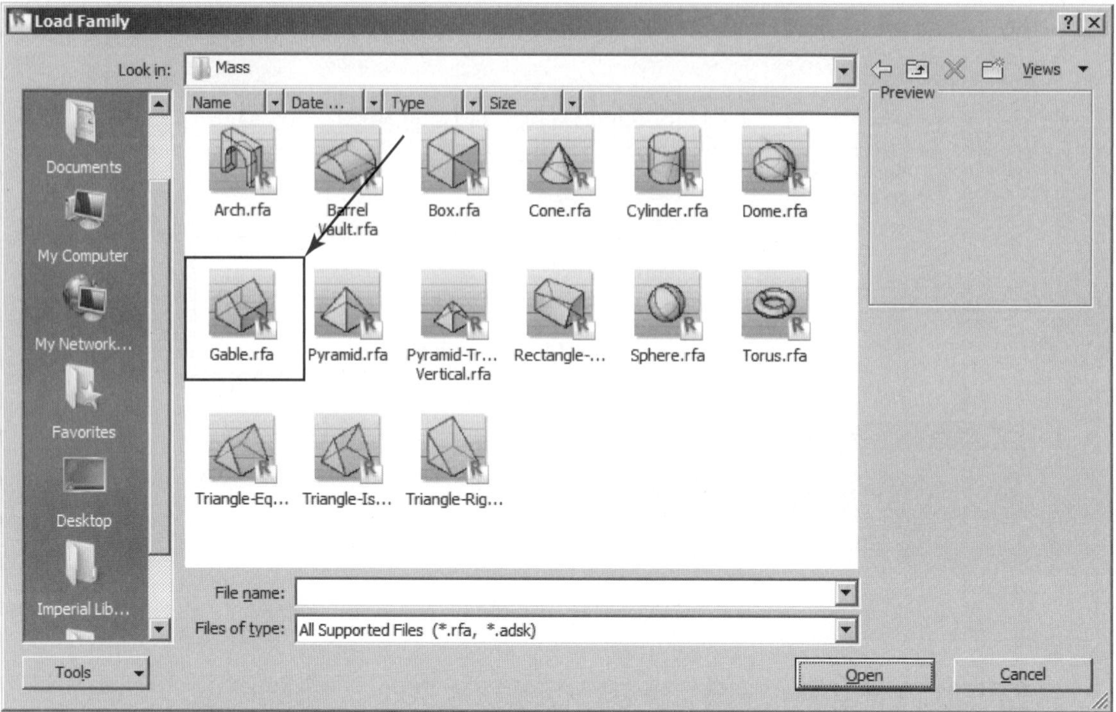

Figure 15-12

Click the **Gable.rfa** to load it.

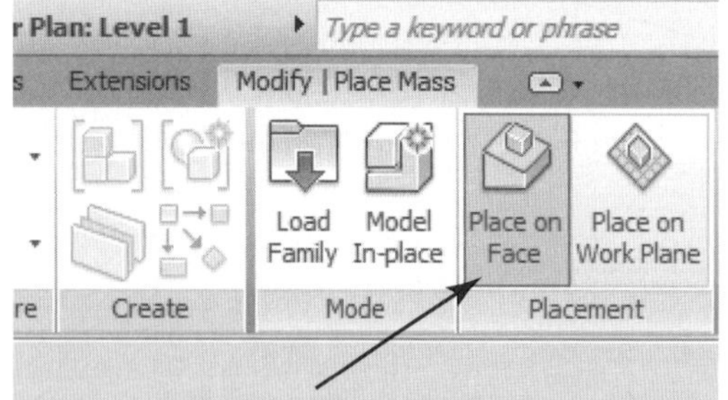

Properties	
Gable	
New Mass	Edit Type
Constraints	
Offset	0' 0"
Work Plane	<not associated>
Materials and Finishes	
Mass Material	Default Form
Dimensions	
Width	30' 0"
Height	30' 0"
Eave Height	15' 0"
Depth	30' 0"
Gross Floor Area	
Gross Surface Area	
Gross Volume	
Identity Data	
Comments	
Mark	
Other	
Schedule Level	
Properties help	Apply

Figure 15-13

Place on Face button and **Properties** palette

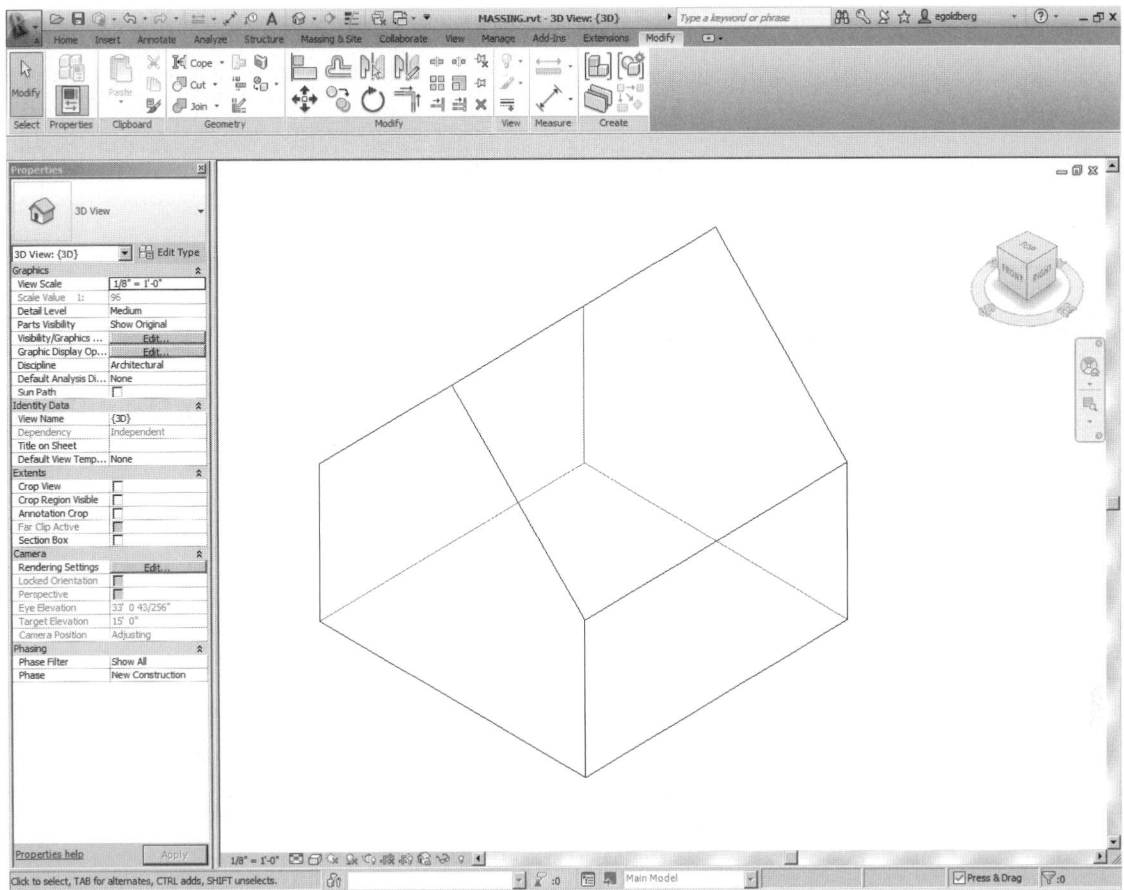

Figure 15-14

Default 3D view of **Gable Mass**

The Model by Face Panel

The **Model by Face** panel (see Figure 15-15) consists of tools that convert mass elements into model elements:

1. **Curtain System**: This tool converts the face of a mass element into a curtain wall.
2. **Roof**: This tool converts the roof of a mass into a typical roof family type.
3. **Wall**: This tool converts the faces of a mass element into a wall.
4. **Floor**: This tool converts floors created from **Modify | Mass>Model>Mass Floors** into floor family types.

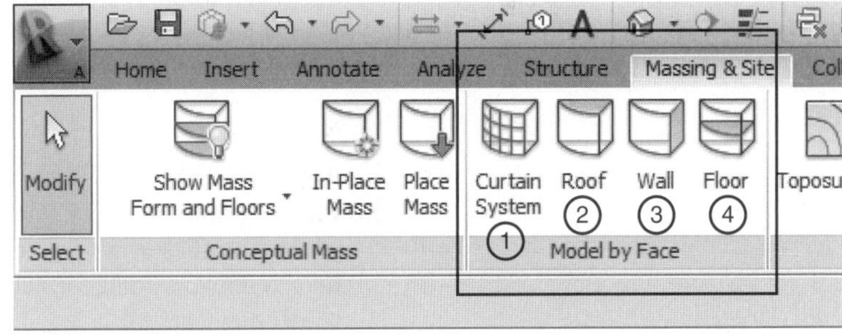

Figure 15-15

Model by Face panel

Work Planes

The Revit work plane in the massing environment is the surface on which you sketch or model. The work planes for an **In-Place Mass** family consist of **Levels** and **Reference Planes**.

There are two methods of selecting a particular work plane in an **In-Place Mass** family:

a. Select the **Modify** tab to bring up the **Modify** toolbar (see Figure 15-16).

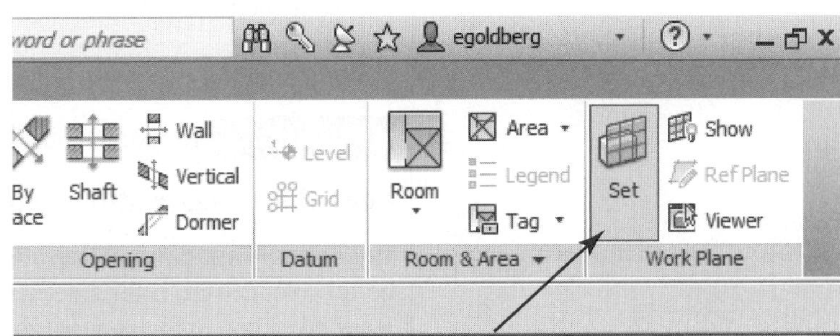

Figure 15-16

Set button

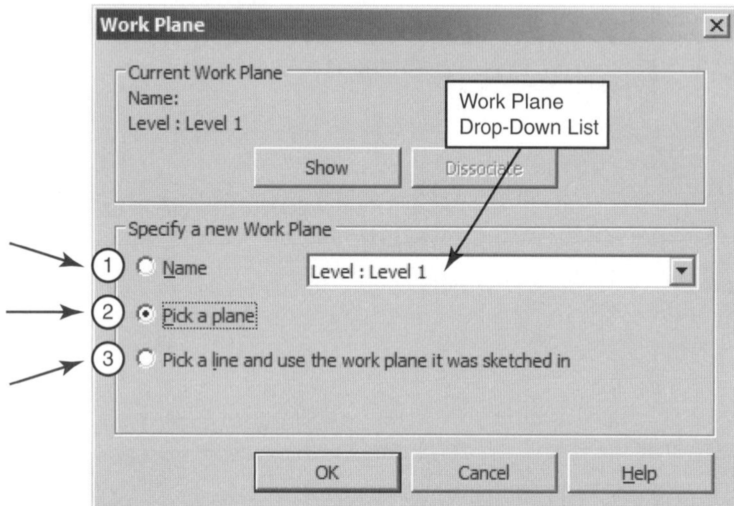

Figure 15-17

Work Plane dialog box

Go To View

In order to edit the sketch, please open one of the following views where the sketch will be parallel to the screen:

Floor Plan: Level 1
Floor Plan: Level 2
Floor Plan: Site
Reflected Ceiling Plan: Level 1
Reflected Ceiling Plan: Level 2

or one of the following views where the sketch will be seen at an angle to the screen:

3D View: {3D}

Open View | Cancel

Figure 15-18

Go To View dialog box

b. In the **Modify** toolbar, select the **Set** button in the **Work Plane** panel to bring up the **Work Plane** dialog box (see Figure 15-17).

In the **Work Plane** dialog box, you have three options to choose from:

a. **Name:** Click the drop-down list and choose a work plane from a list, which includes levels, grid lines, and user-named reference planes.

b. **Pick a plane:** A work plane is established when you click a reference plane, reference line, reference point, or face of an existing model element.

c. **Pick a line and use the work plane it was sketched in:** If you click a model line, the work plane that it was created from will become active.

> **NOTE:**
> If you select a view perpendicular to your current view, the **Go To View** dialog box will appear, where you are prompted to select an appropriate view from a list (see Figure 15-18).

EXERCISE 15-2 **THE MASS FAMILY EDITOR INTERFACE**

Loadable Mass Family Interface

Loadable Mass families are created in templates outside the project. They can also be downloaded from the Internet. Opening the **Mass** family template to create a new mass takes you to the **conceptual massing environment,** which is also referred as the **Mass Family Editor**.

Here is an exploded image showing the **Loadable Mass Family** editor's five default toolbars (see Figure 15-19).

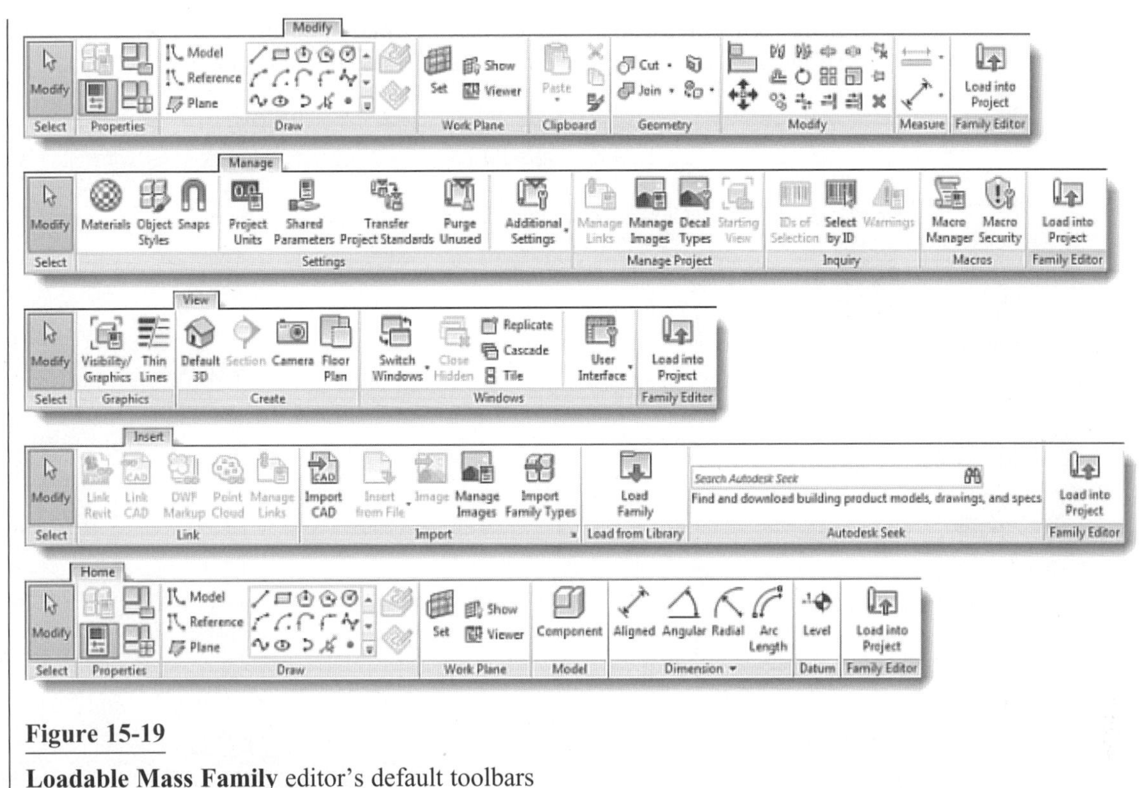

Figure 15-19

Loadable Mass Family editor's default toolbars

EXERCISE 15-3 STARTING A LOADABLE MASS FAMILY

1. From the **Application** menu, select **New** > **Conceptual Mass** to bring up the **New Conceptual Mass - Select Template File** dialog box (see Figure 15-20).

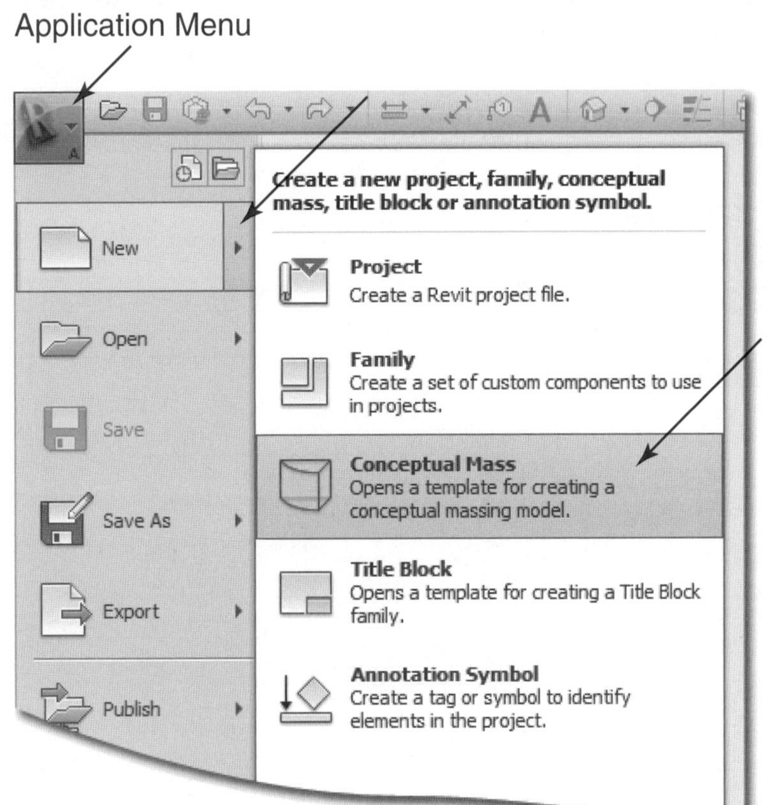

Figure 15-20

From the **Application** menu, select **New** > **Conceptual Mass**

2. In the **New Conceptual Mass - Select Template File** dialog box, select the **Mass.rft** template to bring up the **Conceptual Mass** editor (see Figure 15-21).

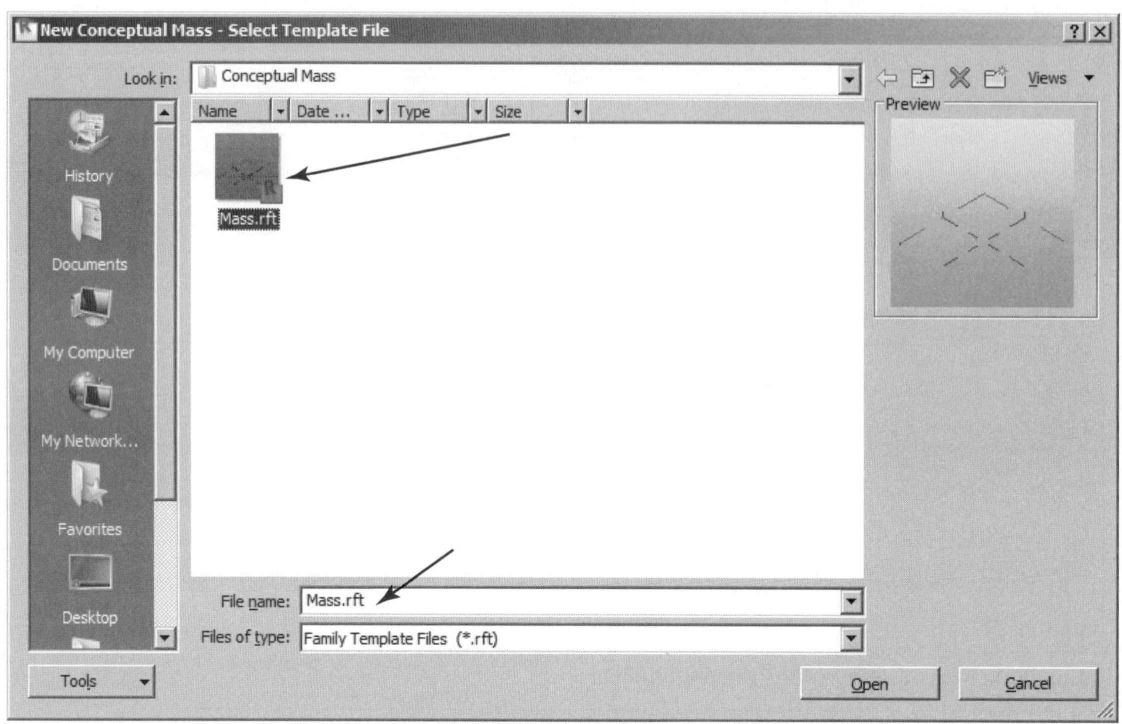

Figure 15-21

Select the **Mass.rft** template

3. In the **Conceptual Mass** editor, note that the default **Level** and **Reference Planes** are visible (see Figure 15-22).

Figure 15-22

Work Planes

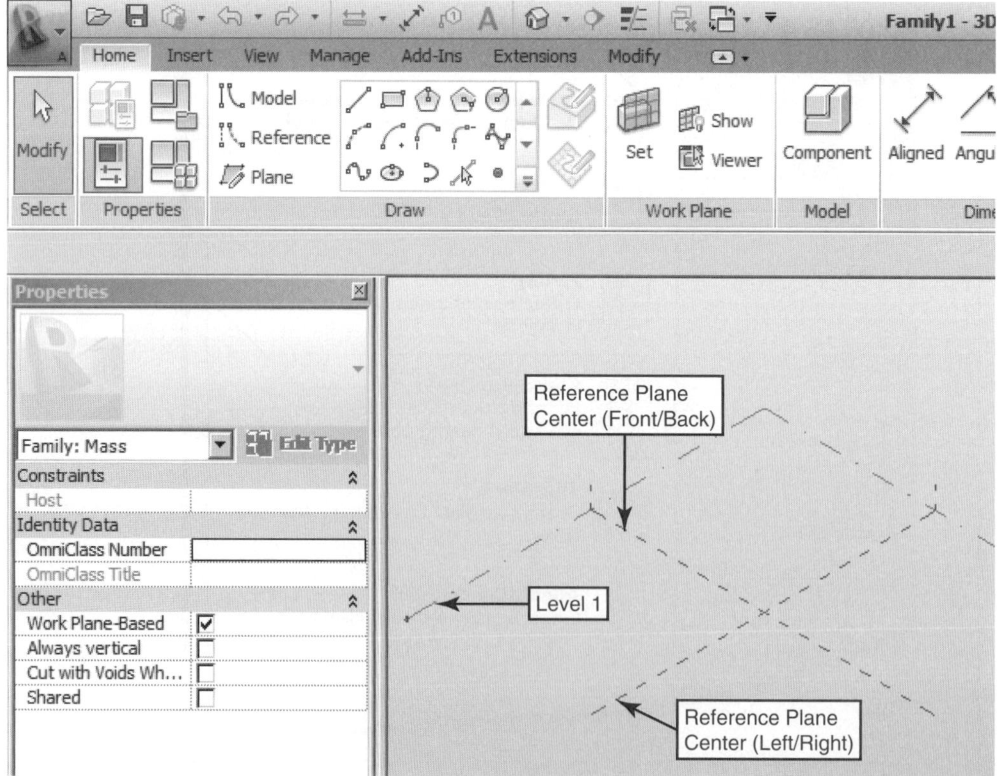

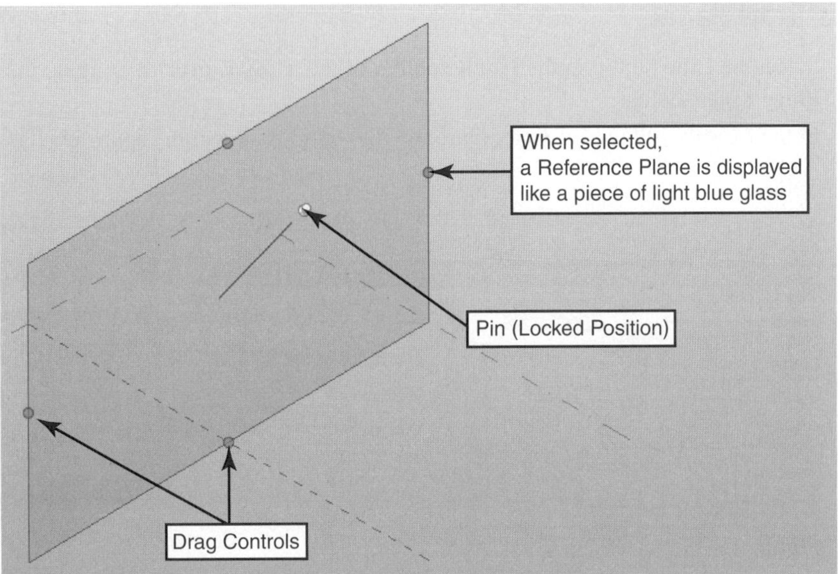

Figure 15-23

Work plane appearance when selected

When you click a **Work Plane**, a glass-like plane appears in a shade of blue (see Figure 15-23).

4. Select all the default **Reference** planes by holding down the **<Ctrl>** key while selecting. More **Reference** planes can be added (see Figure 15-24).

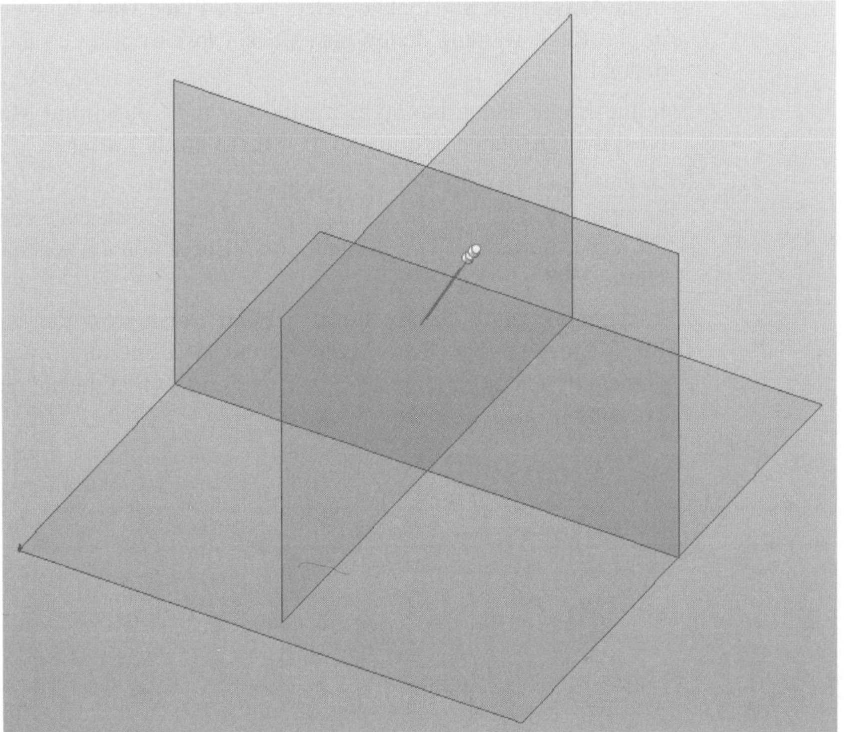

Figure 15-24

Select all the default **Reference** planes by holding down the **<Ctrl>** key while selecting

The Draw Panel

1. Select the **Line** button in the **Home** toolbar of the **Mass Editor** to bring up the **Modify | Place Lines** toolbar.
2. In the **Modify | Place Lines** toolbar, note the buttons shown in Figure 15-25.

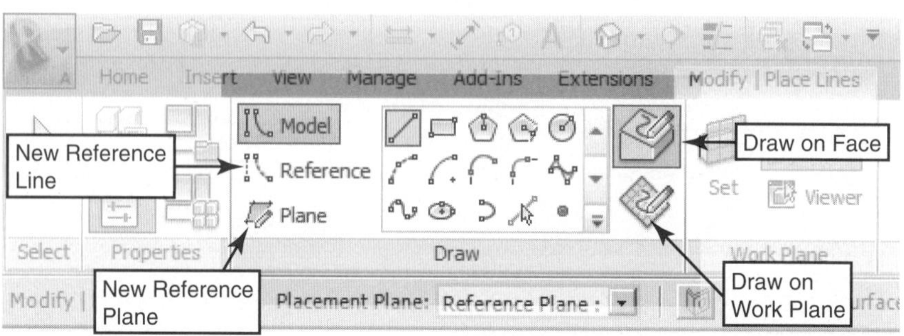

Figure 15-25

In the **Modify | Place Lines** toolbar, note the buttons

3. Resave the **Mass.rft** file with no changes.

EXERCISE 15-4 CREATING AN IN-PLACE MASS

1. Start a new drawing using the RAC 2012\Imperial Templates\default.rte template.
2. In the **Project Browser**, double click **Floor Plans > Level 1**.
3. Select the **Massing & Site** tab to bring up the **Massing & Site** toolbar.
4. In the **Massing & Site** toolbar, select the **In-Place Mass** button to bring up the **Revit** warning dialog box. Click **Close** to bring up the **Name** dialog box.
5. In the **Name** dialog box, type a name for the **Conceptual Mass** and press the **OK** button to bring up the **Mass Family Editor**.
6. In the **Mass Family Editor**, select the **Inscribed Polygon** tool and position the cursor in the middle of the screen. Click once and move the cursor upwards. Type **20′** and press <**Enter**> on the keyboard (see Figure 15-26).
7. Immediately click **Create Form > Solid Form** from the **Modify | Place Lines** toolbar. You should see the **3D Control** arrows on top of the polygon (see Figure 15-27). This signifies that the polygon was extruded or given a default thickness.

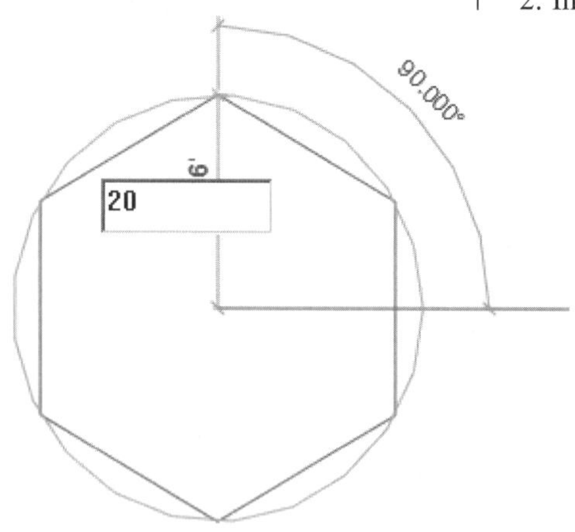

After you type 20', press the <Enter> key on the keyboard.

Figure 15-26

Extruding a mass

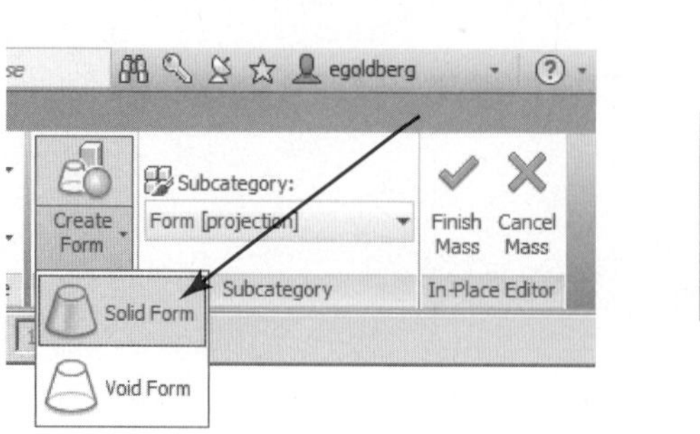

Figure 15-27

3D Control arrows on top of the polygon

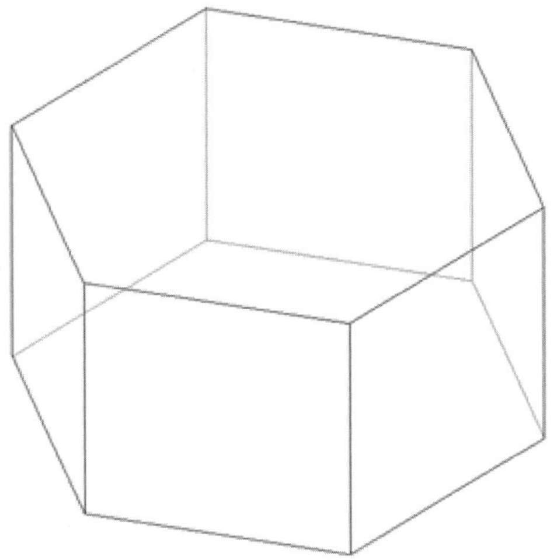

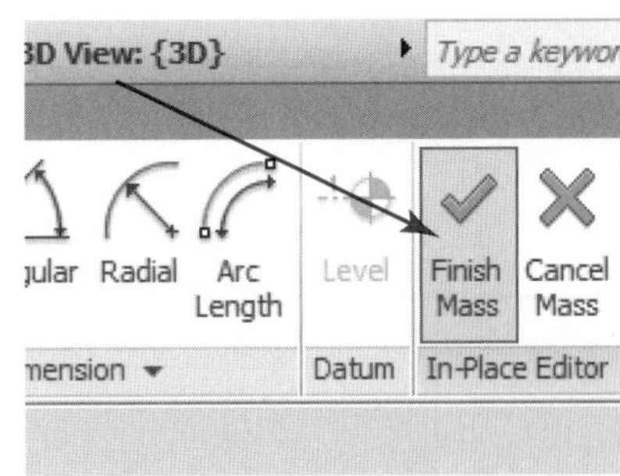

Figure 15-28

Press the **Finish Mass** button to create the **Mass**

8. Click the **Default 3D View** icon from the **Quick Access** toolbar.
9. Press the **Finish Mass** button to create the **Mass** (see Figure 15-28).
10. Edit the polygon by clicking an edge. A contextual menu is added to the **Modify | Mass** tab. Click the **Edit In-Place** button; this takes you back to the **Mass Family Editor**. Click the top right edge of the polygon to bring up its movement arrows (see the right side of Figure 15-29).

NOTE:

After you finish drawing a closed loop, you can click **Create Form** *right away* without even selecting the profile you just drew. This is regardless of what drawing tool you use from the **Draw** panel.

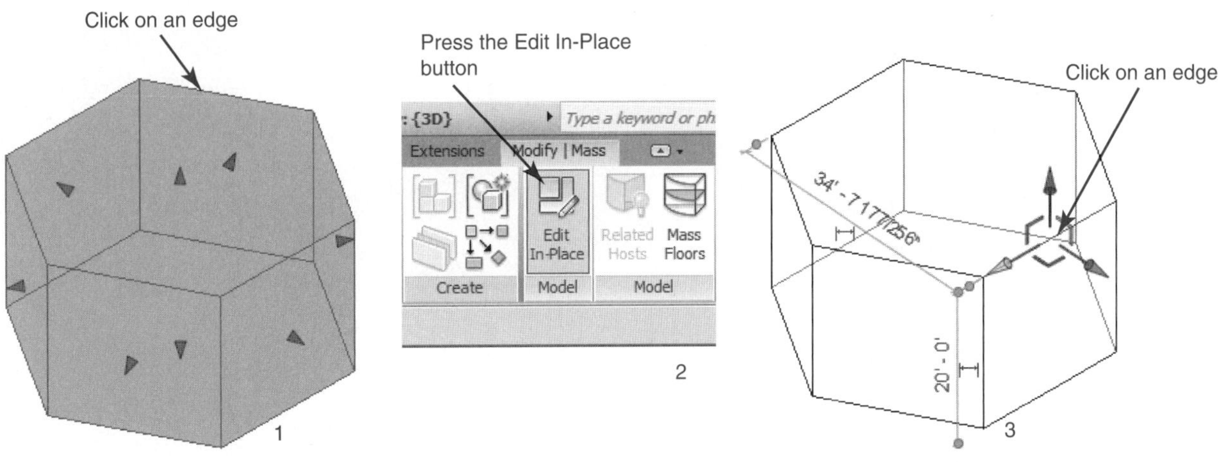

Figure 15-29

Edit the polygon by clicking an edge

In the **Mass Family Editor**, after you click an edge, surface, vertex, or point of a mass form, you will notice a group of colored arrows in the middle or center. This is called **3D Control**. By dragging its arrows or planar controls, you can manipulate a form directly (see Figure 15-30).

Depending on the shape of the object you are trying to manipulate, the meanings of the colors are as follows:

Blue arrow: This lets you drag an object along the global Z axis.

Red arrow: This lets you drag an object along the global Y axis.

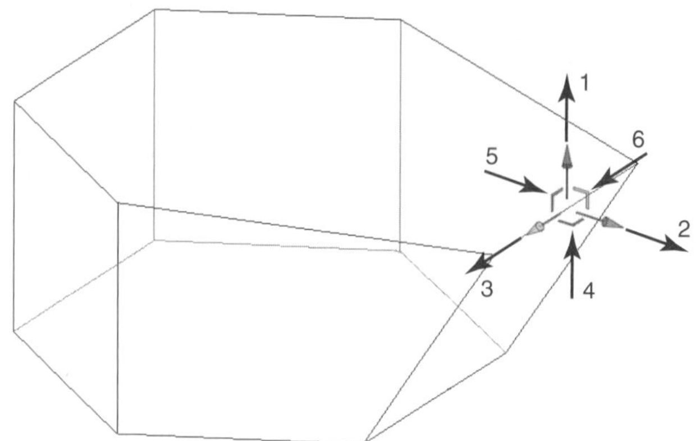

Figure 15-30

By dragging the **3D Control** arrows or planar controls, you can manipulate a form directly.

Green arrow: This lets you drag an object along the global X axis.

Blue planar control: This lets you drag an object in the Z plane.

Red planar control: This lets you drag an object in the Y plane.

Green planar control: This lets you drag an object in the X plane.

11. Press the <Esc> key on the keyboard, and then click the top surface of the polygon to bring up its **3D Control** arrows.
12. Click the blue arrow and drag it upwards until the temporary dimension indicates 30′.
13. In the **Modify | Form** Toolbar, select the **Finish Mass** button to create the **Mass**.
14. Save the project as **MASS SOLID EXTRUSION**. Do not close the file yet.

> **NOTE:**
>
> Sometimes it is hard to get the exact dimension while dragging the **3D Control** arrows. When this happens, click the temporary dimension instead, type **30′**, and then press the **<Enter>** key on the keyboard. You will now have a solid extrusion with a height of 30′ (see Figure 15-31).

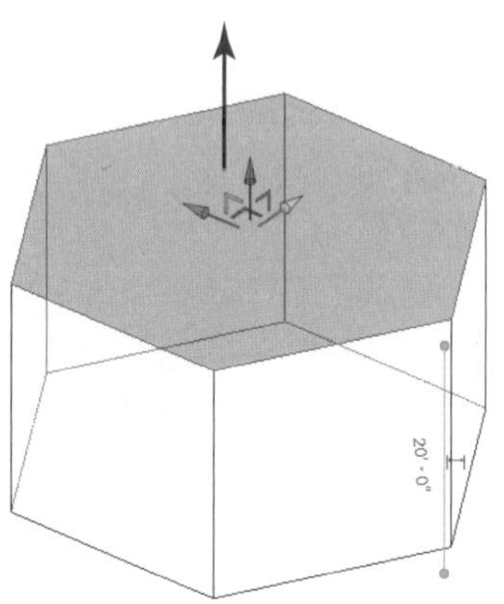

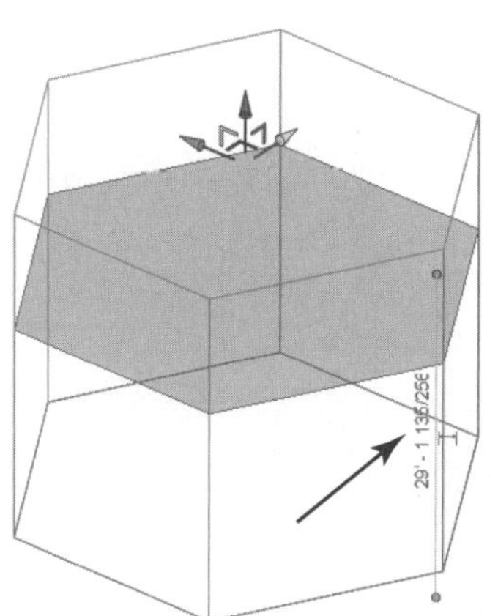

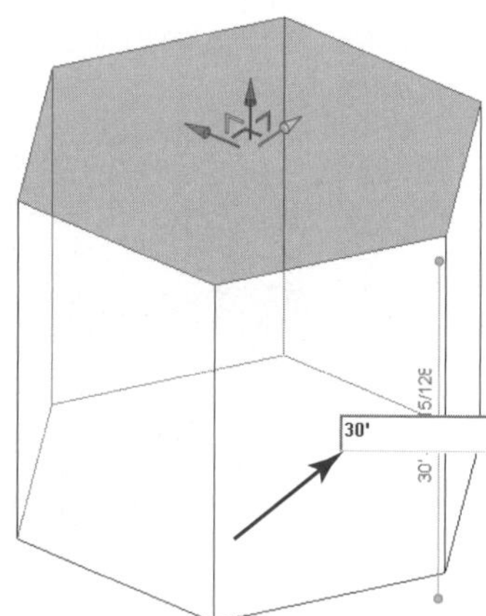

Figure 15-31

Clicking the temporary dimension to get the exact dimensions

EXERCISE 15-5 **SOLID & VOID MASS EXTRUSIONS**

Creating a Void Extrusion and Applying It to a Mass

A void is a **Mass** similar to a solid extrusion. However, its function is to *subtract* its volume from a solid extrusion.

1. Using the previous project file, click the edge of the polygon, then click **Edit In-Place** from the **Modify | Mass** contextual menu.

2. Click the front face of the mass extrusion to make it active.
3. Select the **Line** tool from the **Draw** panel. Position the cursor on the left side of the face.
4. When you see the triangular magenta snap indicator, click the mouse and drag the line to the right edge.
5. When you see the snap indicator, click again. Press the **<Esc>** key on the keyboard twice and your model line is drawn (see Figure 15-32).

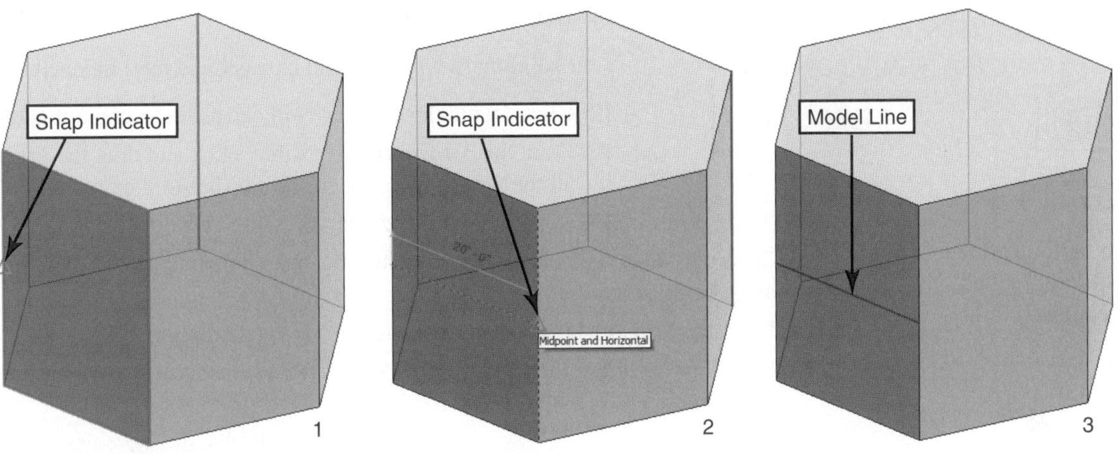

Figure 15-32

Snapping to the middle point of a model line

6. Select the **Circle** tool from the **Draw** panel. Position the cursor in the middle of the model line.
7. Click when you see the snap indicator and move the cursor away, then type **5′-0″** for the radius.
8. Press <**Enter**> on the keyboard.

You should see the circle you just drew in the middle of the model line (Figure 15-33).

9. In the **Modify | Lines** Toolbar, press the **Create Form > Void Form** button to bring up the **Intent Stack** (see Figure 15-33).

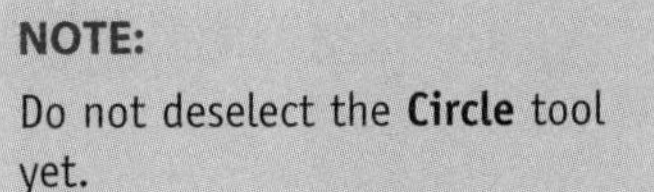

NOTE:

Do not deselect the **Circle** tool yet.

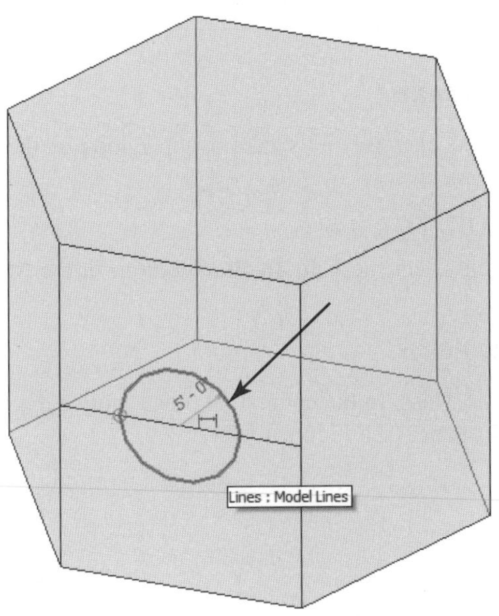

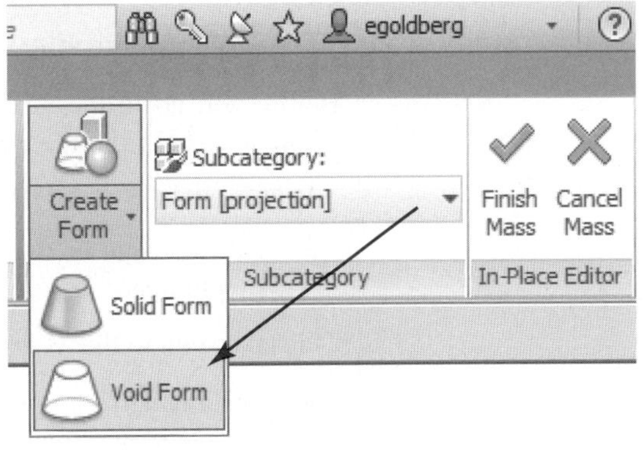

Figure 15-33

Press the **Create Form > Void Form** button

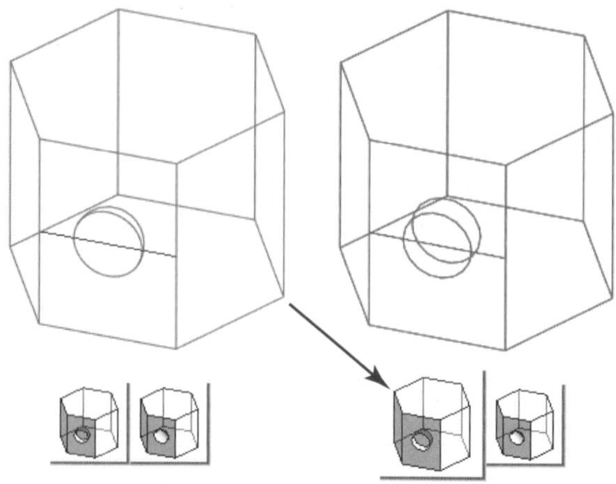

Figure 15-34

Void Form button and the **Intent Stack** (also called **Preview Frames**)

The **Intent Stack** should appear in close proximity to the Mass, giving a choice of two possible **Void** shapes.

10. Hover the cursor on the first frame (left) of the **Intent Stack**. The frame will enlarge to let you know when you are on top of it (see Figure 15-34).

Click on this frame. This will result in a recessed hole in the polygonal mass.

11. **Delete** the horizontal line you used to center the circle.

Your solid mass with the void extrusion is now finished.

12. Click inside the circular void extrusion to make it active.
13. Once the **3D Control** is visible, click and drag the green arrow all the way to the back surface of the solid extrusion.
14. Release the mouse and you will see a circular hole.
15. Press the **<Esc>** key once. You have just created a hole in the solid extrusion using a void extrusion.
16. Press the **Finish Mass** button to create the **Mass** (see Figure 15-35).
17. Save the file as **EXTRUDING A VOID FORM**.

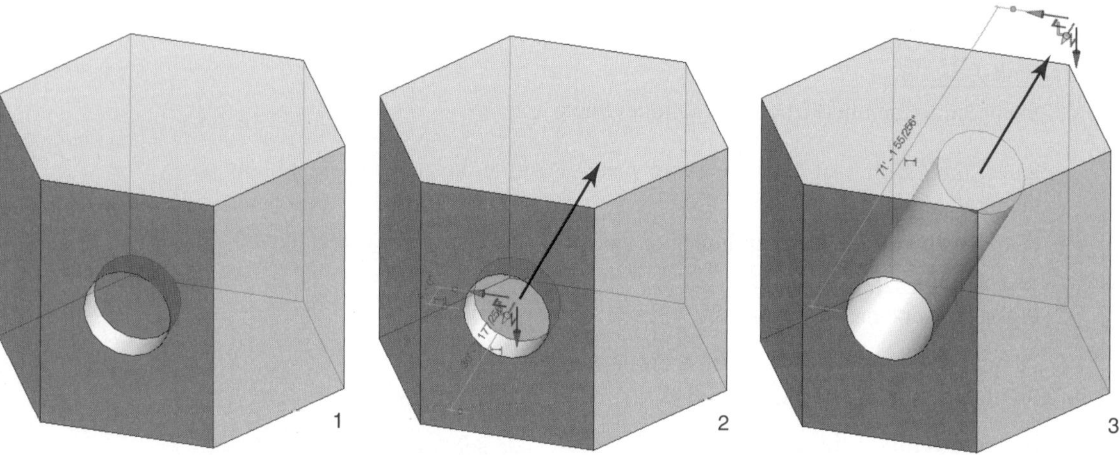

Figure 15-35

Extruding a void form

EXERCISE 15-6 THE FORM ELEMENT PANEL

Before you go to the next topic and exercise, let's take a quick look at the **Form Element** panel from the contextual menu.

1. Open the **EXTRUDING A VOID FORM** file.
2. Click the edge of the Mass and select the **Edit In-Place** button in the **Modify | Mass** toolbar.

This takes you to the **Mass Family Editor.**

3. Click any surface or edge of the Mass. In the contextual menu, notice the following tools in the **Form Element** panel (see Figure 15-36):

   X-Ray

   Add Edge

   Add Profile

   Dissolve

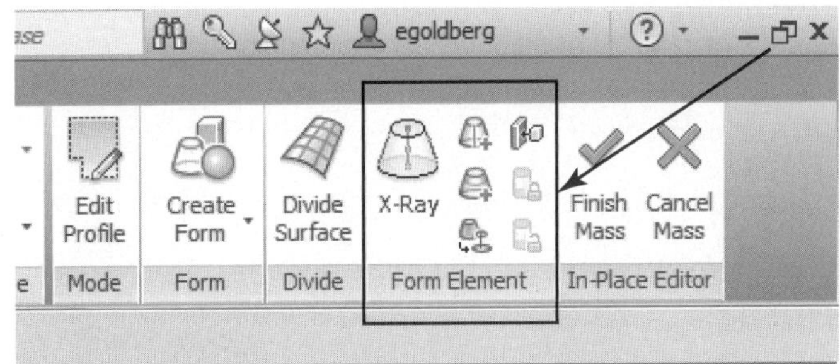

Figure 15-36

Form Element panel

Pick New Host

Lock Profiles

Unlock Profiles

These are additional **Form Element** tools that will help you change the shape of your mass.

EXERCISE 15-7 CREATING A LOADABLE FAMILY: SOLID & VOID EXTRUSIONS ON WORK PLANES

1. From the **Application** menu, select **New** > **Conceptual Mass** to bring up the **New Conceptual Mass - Select Template File** dialog box.
2. In the **New Mass - Select Template File** dialog box, double-click the **Mass.rft** template to enter the **Conceptual Mass** editor.

You are taken to the **Default 3D view** showing the work planes.

3. Click the **Center (Left/Right)** reference plane to make it active (see Figure 15-37).
4. Select the **Rectangle** tool from the **Draw** panel. Position the cursor on the top left side of the reference plane. The exact location is not important. Click once, then move the cursor downwards to the right until the temporary dimensions indicate 100′ × 100′.

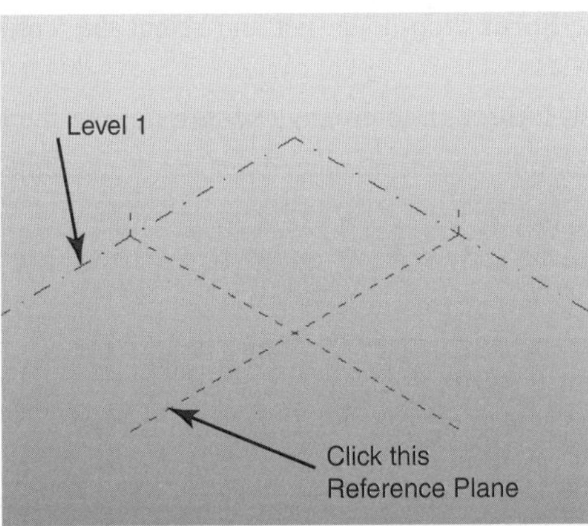

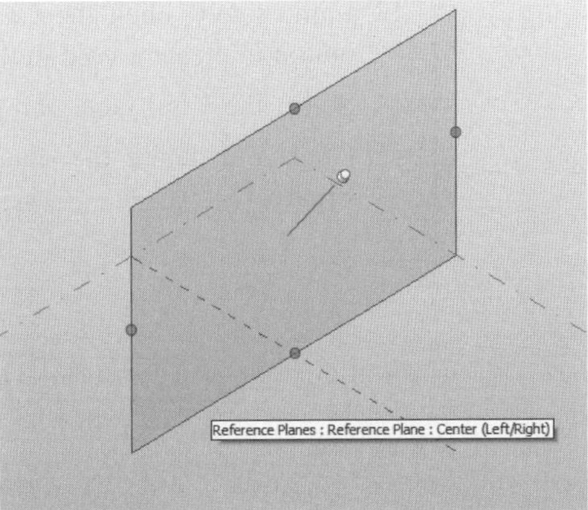

Figure 15-37

Default 3D view of a mass family; selecting a reference plane

5. Click the second point to finish your sketch.
6. Click the **Create Form > Solid Form** button right away without deselecting the **Rectangle** tool. This creates a solid extrusion with a default thickness of 40′ (see Figure 15-38).
7. Select the **Line** tool from the **Draw** panel.

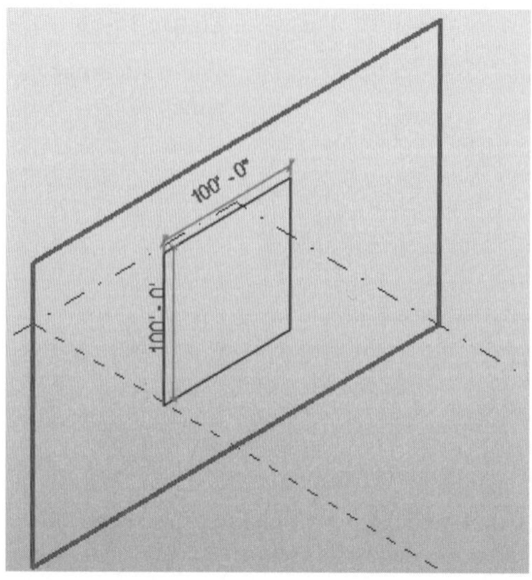

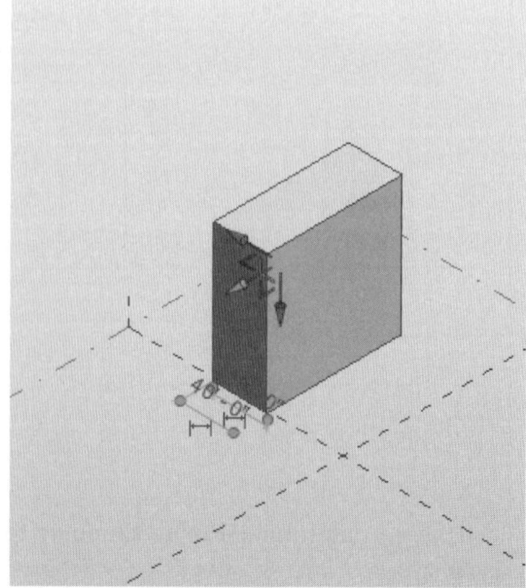

Figure 15-38

Drawing on the surface of a work plane

8. Position the cursor on the top left corner edge until you see the snap indicator, then click the first point.
9. Draw a line across the front surface from the top left edge to the bottom right edge. When you see the snap indicator, click one more time.
10. From the **Draw** panel, select the **Rectangle** tool. Position the cursor on the line, then click when the snap indicator appears.
11. Move the cursor to the lower right along the line and press <**Enter**> on the keyboard.

A **Rectangle** is now drawn on the square Mass.

12. Move the cursor to the lower right along the line and press <**Enter**> on the keyboard.
13. Immediately, click the **Create Form** drop-down list and select the **Void Form** button to create a void in the Mass.
14. Select the Void face, and push it through to create a square hole in the mass.
15. Click and delete the diagonal line you first placed on the Mass object (see Figure 15-39).

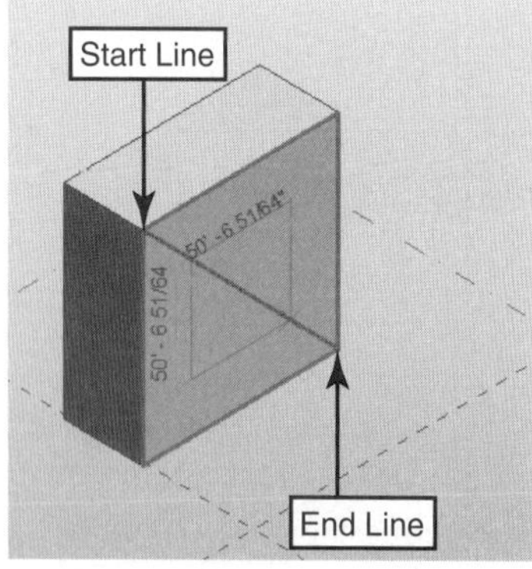

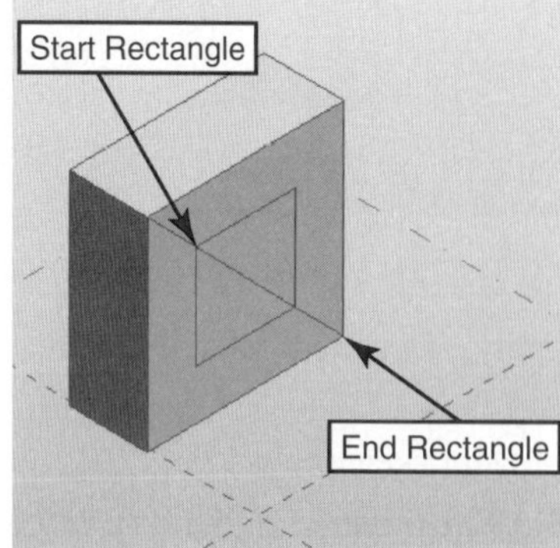

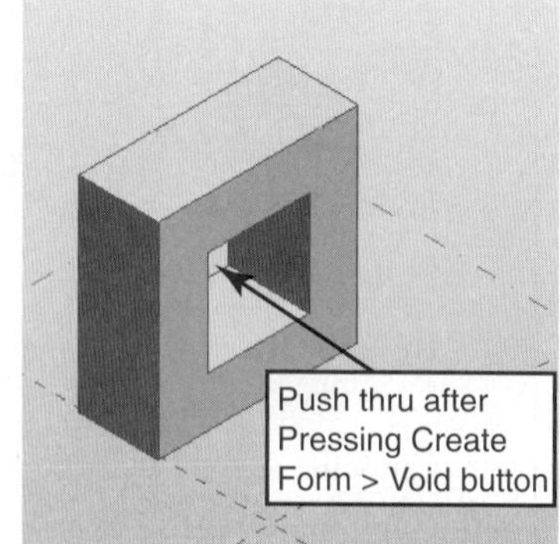

Figure 15-39

Drawing a model line on the surface of a work plane

16. Next, re-create the square Mass and Void on a different work plane.
17. Click the **Center (Front/Back)** reference plane to make it active.
18. Select the **Rectangle** button from the **Draw** panel.
19. On the **Center (Front/Back)** reference plane, again place a 100′ × 100′ rectangle.
20. After creating the rectangle, click the **Create Form > Solid Form** button right away without deselecting the **Rectangle** tool.
21. Duplicate the steps to re-create the square Mass with the rectangle Void on this plane by following the procedure outlined in steps 7 through 9 of this exercise (see Figure 15-40).

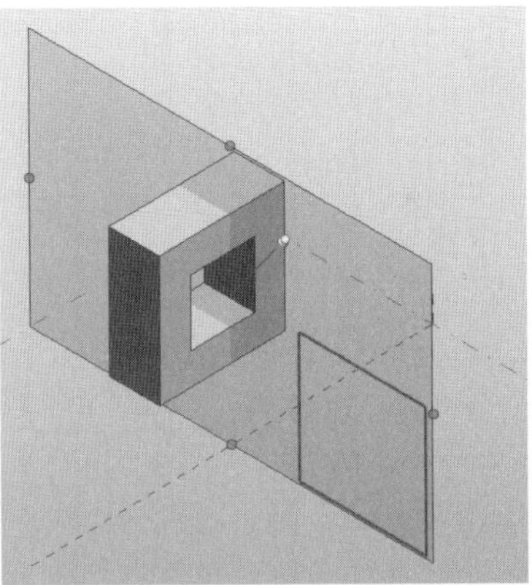

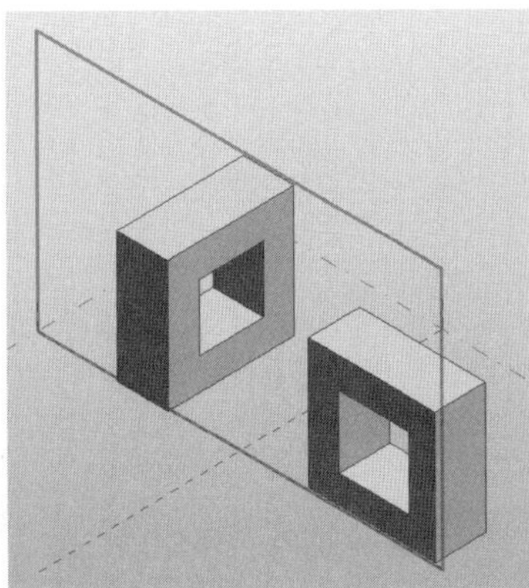

Figure 15-40

Duplicate the steps to re-create the square Mass with the rectangle Void

You now have two identical extrusions created on two different reference planes. Now, create a different extrusion on top of the **Level 1 Work plane.**

22. Click the **Level 1 Work plane** to make it active.
23. Select the **Rectangle** tool from the **Draw** panel.
24. Place a 100′ × 100′ rectangle on the **Level 1 Work plane.**
25. Click the **Create Form > Solid Form** button right away without deselecting the **Rectangle** tool.
26. Press the **<Esc>** key on the keyboard to end the command.

You now have a square solid Mass on **Level 1** with a default height of 40′-0″ (see Figure 15-41).

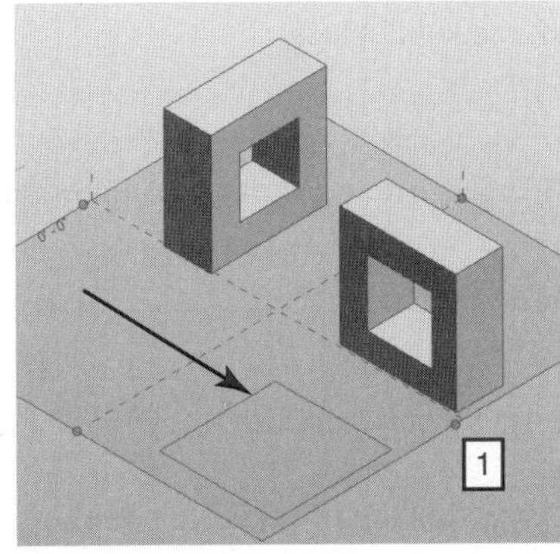

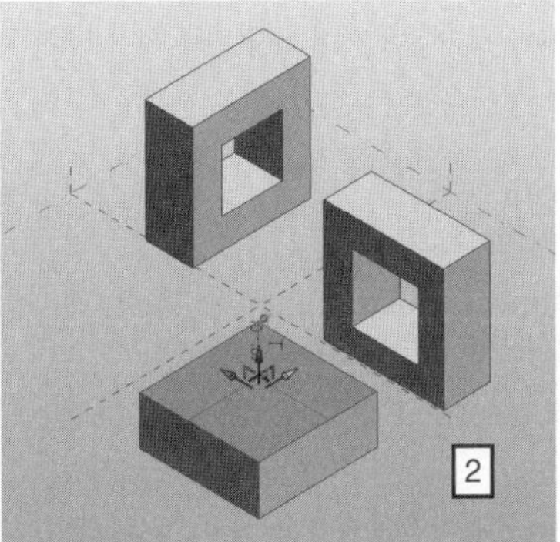

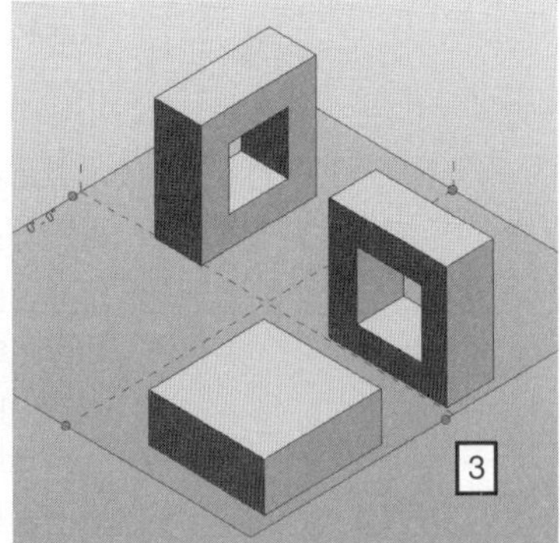

Figure 15-41

You now have a square solid Mass on **Level 1** with a default height of 40′-0″

27. Select the **Circle** tool from the **Draw** panel and hover on the top edge and face of the square Mass until the top face is selected.
28. Snap on the middle of the top face edge.
29. Move the cursor, type **32′-0″**, and press the <**Enter**> key on the keyboard.

You have just drawn a circle whose center is on the top edge of the square Mass.

30. Click **Void Form** from the **Create Form** drop-down list. This brings out the **Intent Stack**.
31. Click the right frame of the **Intent Stack**. The **Void** extrusion will subtract its shape from the solid **Mass** (see Figure 15-42).

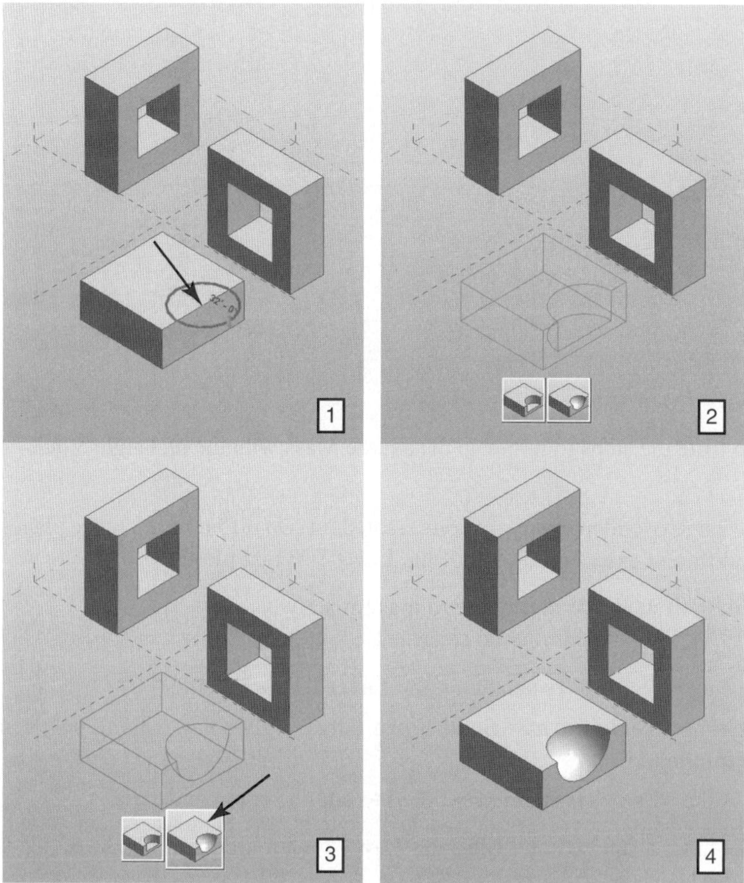

Figure 15-42

The **Void** extrusion will subtract its shape from the solid **Mass**

32. In the **Project Browser**, double-click **Level 1** under **Floor Plans** to bring it up in the **Drawing Editor**.
33. In the **Home** toolbar, click the **Reference Plane** button to bring up the **Modify | Place Reference Plane** toolbar.
34. Click the cursor at the intersection of the top left corner of the last Mass that was created.
35. Move the cursor towards the bottom right direction and make sure the angle indicates 45°.
36. Click a second point. Press the **<Esc>** key twice to deselect the reference plane tool.

37. Click the 45° angled reference plane you just drew to bring up its **Properties** dialog box.
38. In the **Properties** dialog box, under **Identity Data**, click the blank field to the right of **Name** and type **DIAGONAL REFER PLANE**.
39. In the **Properties** dialog box, click the **Apply** button.

The name of the **Reference Plane** will now appear at the starting point of the angled reference plane in the Floor Plan view (see Figure 15-43).

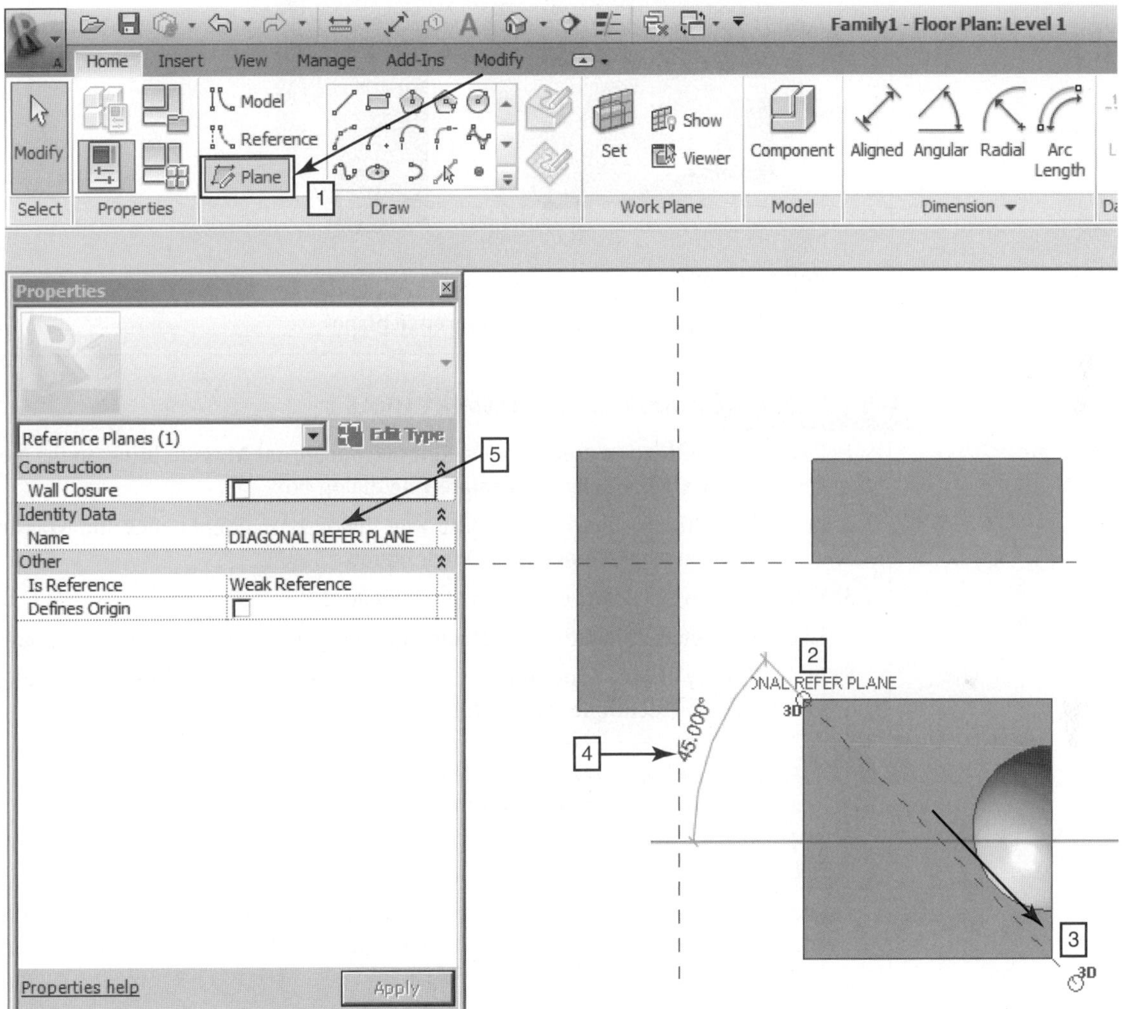

Figure 15-43

Angled reference plane

40. Change to the **Default 3D view**.
41. Orbit the view, and select the **DIAGONAL REFER PLANE** to make it active.
42. Select the **Rectangle** tool from the **Draw** panel and create an 88′ × 88′ rectangle.
43. Again, create a **Solid Form** from the rectangle.
44. Duplicate the steps to re-create the square Mass with the rectangle Void, but this time select **Solid Form** from the **Create Form** drop-down list to extrude the Rectangle. Follow the procedure outlined in steps 7 through 9 of this exercise (see Figure 15-44).

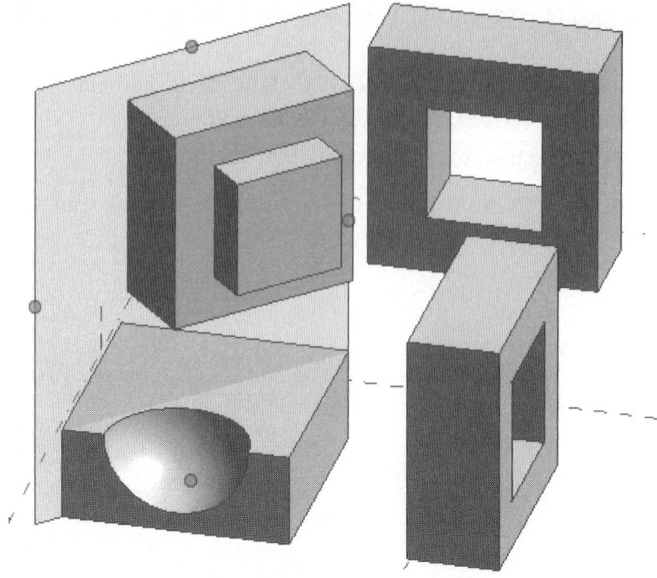

Figure 15-44

Solid **Mass** forms on different **Reference** planes

EXERCISE 15-8 USING THE FORM ELEMENT TOOLS

1. From the **Application** menu, select **New** > **Conceptual Mass** to bring up the **New Conceptual Mass - Select Template File** dialog box.
2. In the **New Mass - Select Template File** dialog box**,** double-click the **Mass.rft** template to enter the **Conceptual Mass** editor.
3. Select the **Level 1 Reference** plane to activate it.
4. Select the **Rectangle** tool from the **Draw** panel and place a 200′-0″ × 200′-0″ rectangle.
5. In the **Modify | Place Lines** toolbar, select the **Create Form > Solid Form** button to extrude the **Rectangle** into a **Mass.**

TIP: If you deselect any shapes before pressing the **Create Form > Solid Form** button, just reselect all the lines to create a **Mass** form.

6. The **3D Control** arrows appear.
7. Drag the blue arrow upwards, release the mouse, click the temporary dimension, and type **200′**. You now have a 200′ high square Mass (Figure 15-45).
8. Click the bottom edge of the right face.
9. Drag the red arrow in the right direction.
10. Release the mouse when the temporary dimension is approximately 300′-0″ (see Figure 15-46). The exact dimension is not important.
11. From the **Modify | Form Element** panel, select the **Add Edge** button (see Figure 15-47).
12. Place the cursor on top of the angled face and you will see an outline of a line as you move the cursor. Position it about one-third of the distance from the left edge and click.
13. The **Add Edge** tool should still be active.
14. Hover the cursor to the right about another third of the distance, then click.
15. Press the **<Esc>** key to end the command.

NOTE:
You may also access any of the **Form Element** tools from a pop-up contextual menu by right-clicking the mouse.

The **Mass** form will now have three divisions (see Figure 15-48).

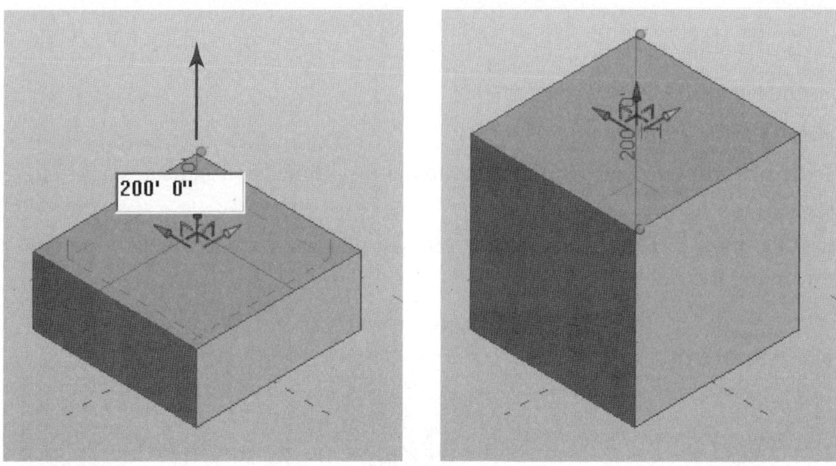

Figure 15-45

Extruding a profile

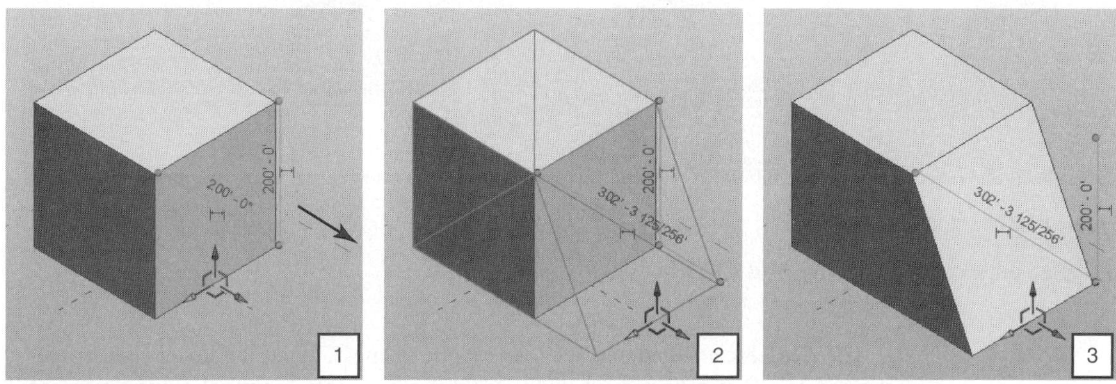

Figure 15-46

Release the mouse when the temporary dimension is approximately 300′-0″

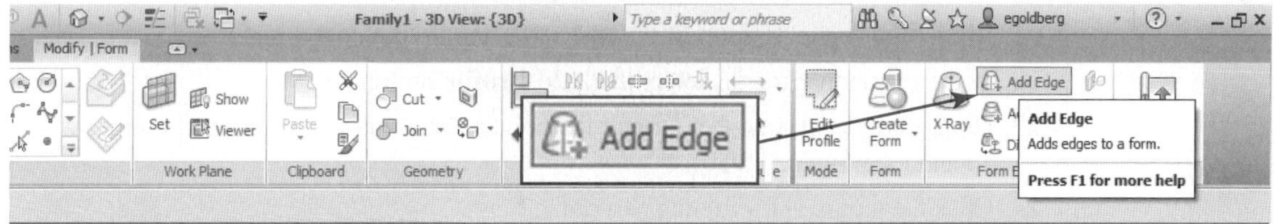

Figure 15-47

The **Add Edge** button

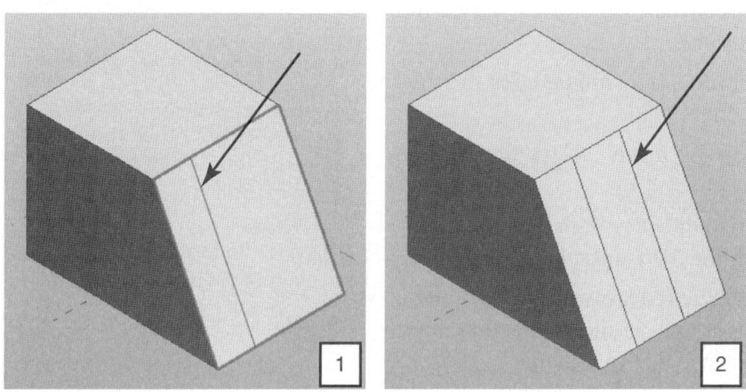

Figure 15-48

Adding edges using the **Add Edge** button

16. Hover the cursor on the top middle edge
17. Click and the **3D Control** arrows appear.
18. Drag the red arrow to the right until the temporary dimension indicates approximately 270′.
19. Release the mouse. The surface of the leftmost plane turns into a yellow-orange color (see Figure 15-49).

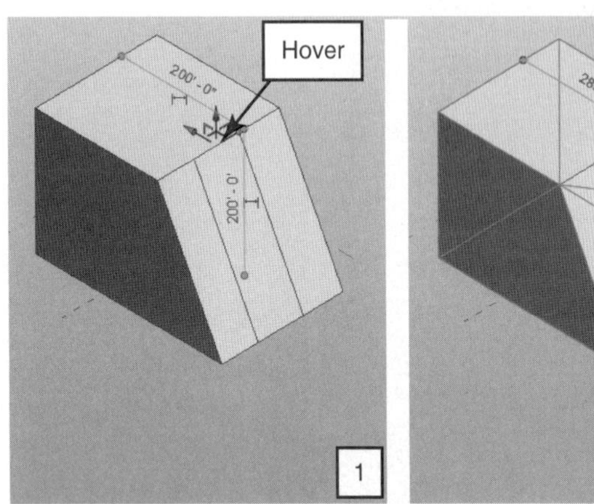

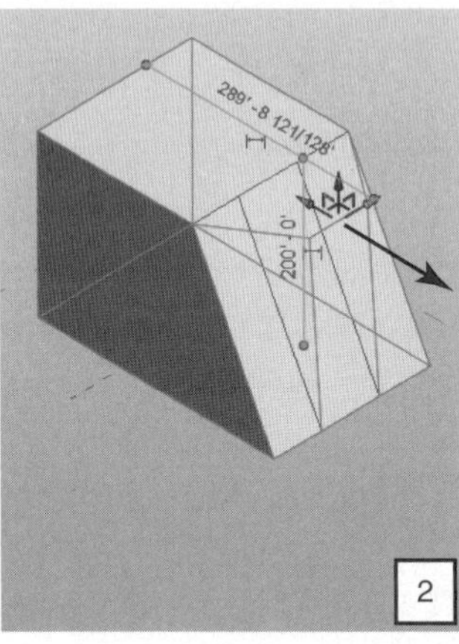

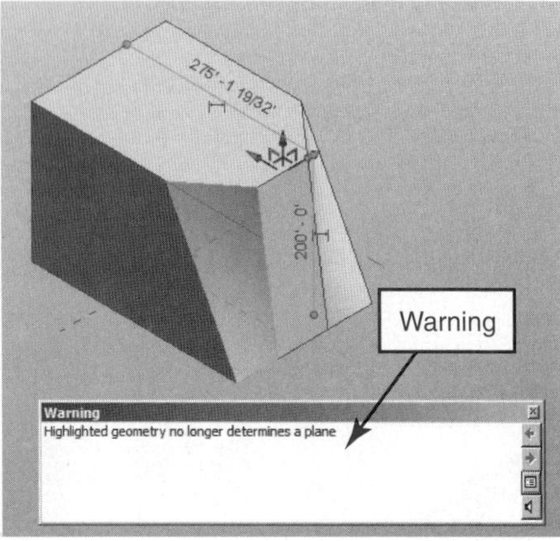

Figure 15-49

Editing an edge created with the **Add Edge** button

You will also hear a sound and see a text warning message on the lower right corner of your screen. Depending on what you just did, a one- or two-page **Warning** message will appear. The warning means that the curved yellow-orange surface is not lying on a plane. It is OK to ignore this warning.

20. Click on a blank area in the **Drawing Editor** to deselect the **3D Control**.
21. Right mouse click on top of the mass to bring up the contextual menu.
22. In the contextual menu, select the **Add Profile** button.
23. Hover the cursor anywhere along the height of the mass; a horizontal outline will appear (see Figure 15-50).
24. Click the mouse at the middle part of the Mass.
25. Press the **<Esc>** key to deselect the **Add Profile** tool.
26. Click on the narrow part of the edited face (this will be referred to as ***narrow panel*** for reference later on).
27. When it is selected, right mouse click to bring up the contextual menu.
28. In the contextual menu, select the **X-Ray** button.
29. Click the horizontal edge in the middle of the narrow panel; the **3D Control** arrows appear.
30. Click and drag the red arrow to the right until you see a slight arch in the **Trajectory** line. The exact distance does not matter.

NOTE:
The profile has disappeared. It is still there, but the default graphic display does not show it.

NOTE:
As the name implies, the **X-Ray** tool enables you to see through the mass. The visibility of the object becomes transparent and the profiles, edges, and vertices that make up the underlying structure of the mass become visible (see Figure 15-51).

After you release the mouse, the arched face of the narrow panel will change color. You will also hear a warning sound and get a warning message. Ignore it and just click on a blank area to deselect the mass and see the resulting shape (see Figure 15-52).

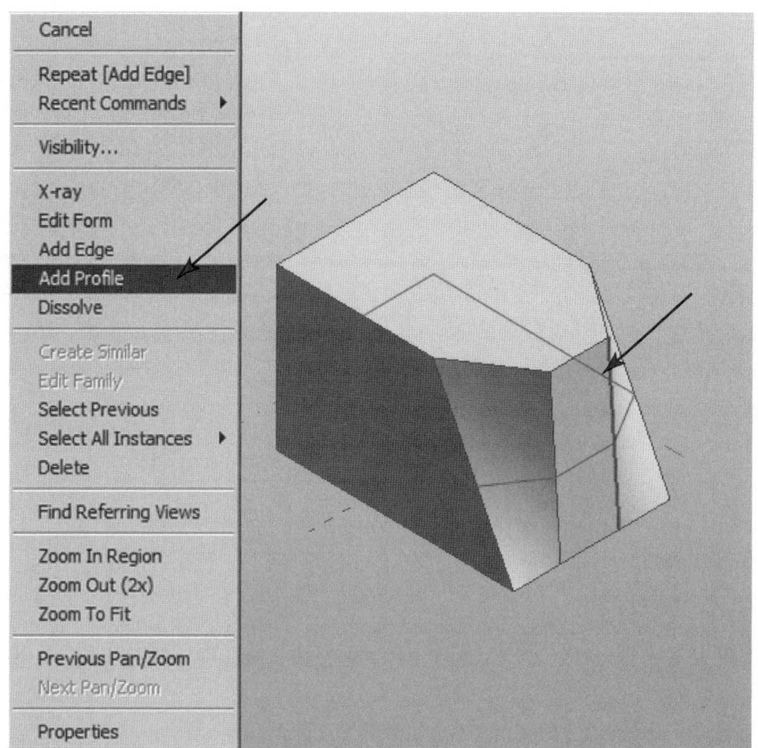

Figure 15-50

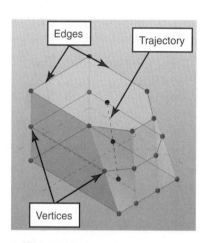

Adding profiles using the **Add Profile** button

Edges

Trajectory

Vertices

Figure 15-51

The **X-Ray** mode

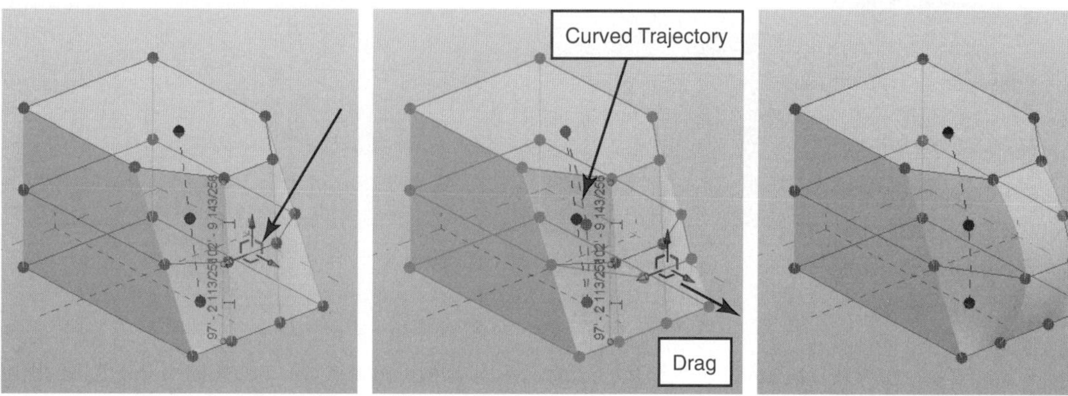

Figure 15-52

Selecting and moving a line in the **X-Ray** mode

31. Click the lower left vertex at the back of the mass.

The **3D Control** arrows will appear.

32. Click and drag the green **3D Control** arrow away from its location; the exact distance does not matter.
33. Click on a blank area in the **Drawing Editor** to see the result (see Figure 15-53).
34. Select the left surface of the panel.
35. Right mouse click to bring up its contextual menu.
36. In the contextual menu, unselect the **X-Ray** tool; this will turn the visibility of the **Mass** back to its opaque state.
37. Click in a blank area in the **Drawing Editor** to deselect the **X-Ray** tool and see the shape of the mass (see Figure 15-54).

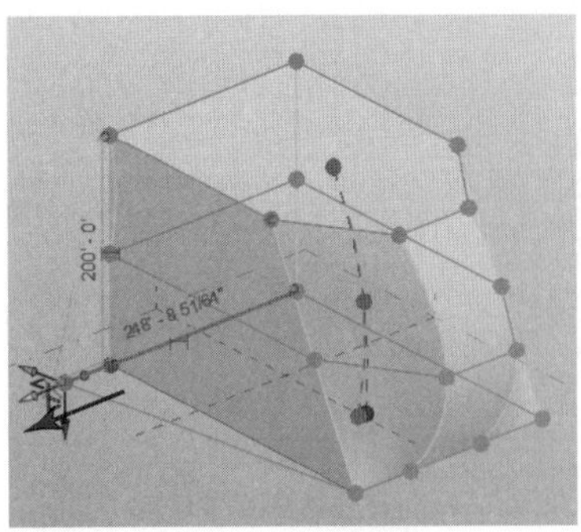

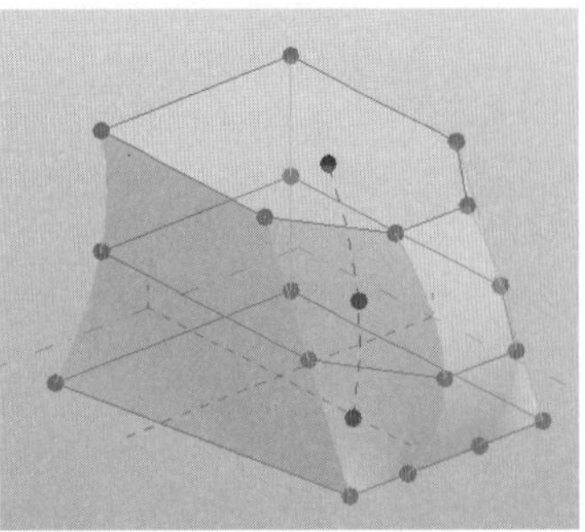

Figure 15-53

Moving a vertex point

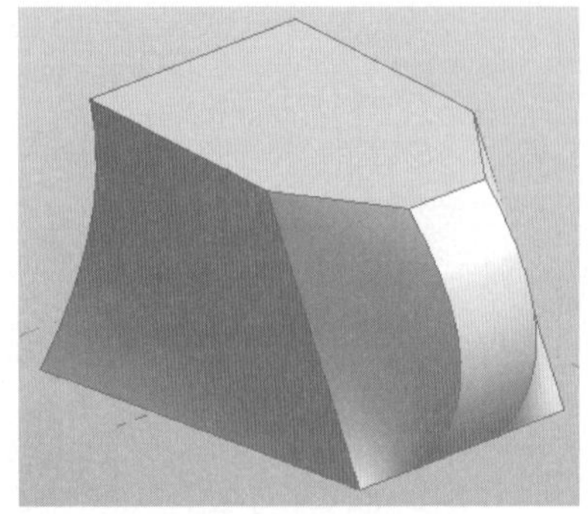

Figure 15-54

Deselect the **X-Ray** tool and see the shape of the mass

38. Once again, select any surface of the **Mass**.
39. Right mouse click to bring up the contextual menu.
40. In the contextual menu, select the **Dissolve** button.

The **Dissolve** tool removes all the surfaces, leaving only the skeleton or profiles that make up the **Mass.**

41. Click the edge of the topmost polygon (see Figure 15-55).

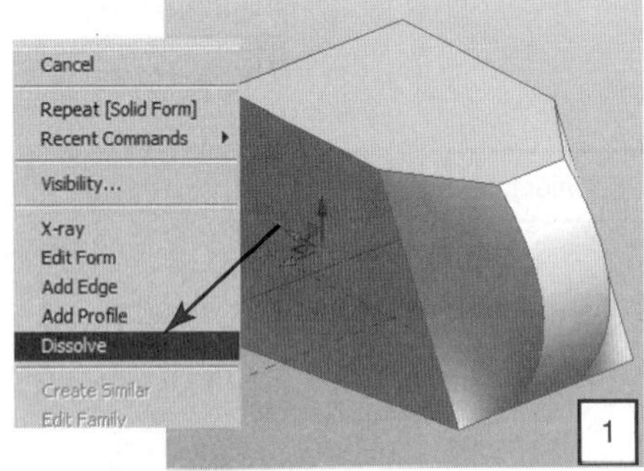

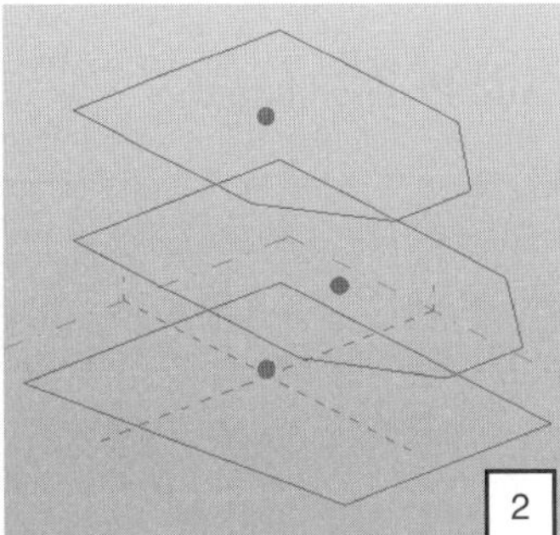

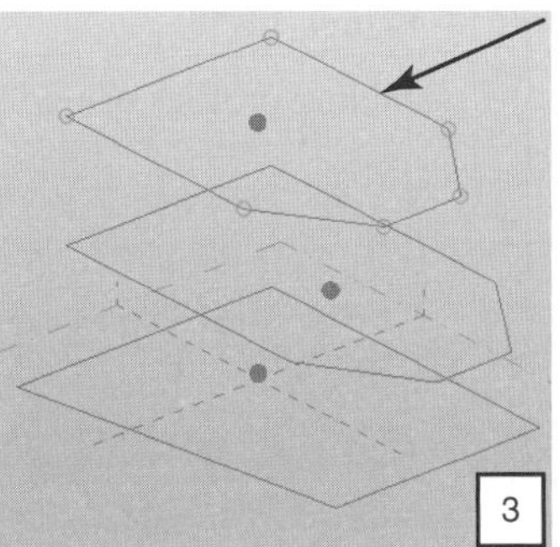

Figure 15-55

Using the **Dissolve** tool

The small dots in the corners of the selected polygon are called **Drag Line Ends.** They function as drag controls that can move and relocate in order to change the shape of the profile.

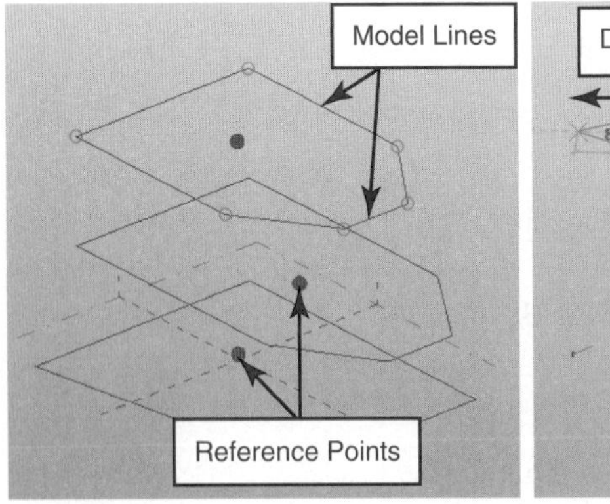

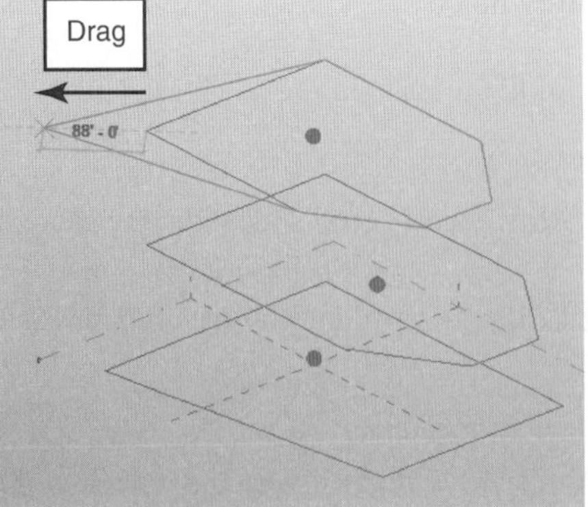

Figure 15-56

The underlying structure of a mass form after using the **Dissolve** tool

42. Click and hold the mouse on top of the top left **Drag Line End,** and drag it away from its location; the exact location is not important (see Figure 15-56).
43. Click on a blank area in the **Drawing Editor** to see the resulting shape.
44. Select the three polygons by selecting each one of them while holding down the **<Ctrl>** key.
45. With the three polygons selected, select the **Create Form** button to see the result (see Figure 15-57). The resulting shape is called a **Loft Form**.

46. Save your file as **FORM ELEMENT**, and then quit Revit.

The following are other types of **Forms** that you can create with the massing tools:

- **Extrusions**: solid and void
- **Lofts**: solid and void
- **Revolves**: solid and void
- **Sweeps**: solid and void
  - Swept Blend
- **Surfaces**

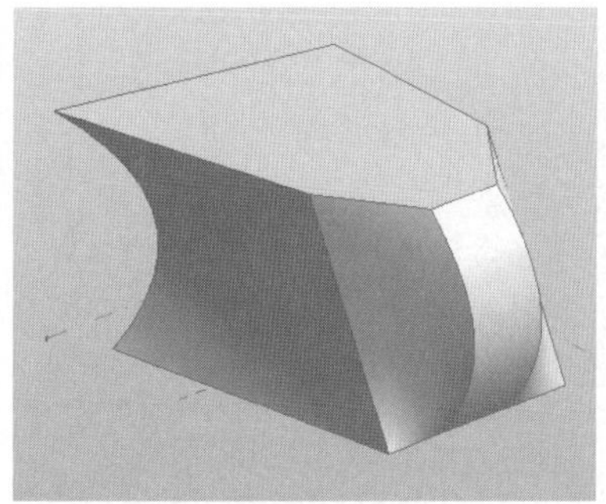

Figure 15-57

The resulting shape is called a **Loft Form**.

EXERCISE 15-9 CREATING A LOFT FORM

A **Loft** form is created by selecting two or more open or closed profiles. These profiles can be created on different levels associated with reference planes and reference lines. When all of them are selected and the **Create Form** button is clicked, a shape is created between the profiles.

In this exercise, you will create five different profiles at five **Levels.** Here are the dimensions of the profiles and heights of the **Levels** (see Figure 15-58).

Figure 15-58

Reference dimensions for the Loft exercise

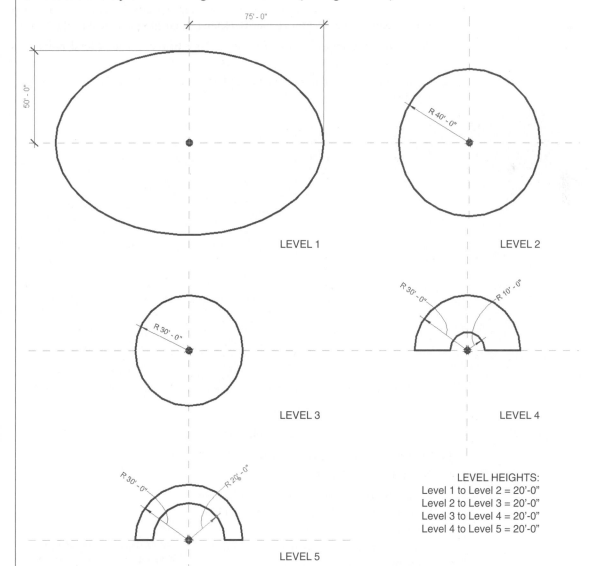

75' - 0"
50' - 0"
LEVEL 1
R 40' - 0"
LEVEL 2
R 30' - 0"
LEVEL 3
R 30' - 0"
R 10' - 0"
LEVEL 4
R 30' - 0"
R 20' - 0"
LEVEL 5

LEVEL HEIGHTS:
Level 1 to Level 2 = 20'-0"
Level 2 to Level 3 = 20'-0"
Level 3 to Level 4 = 20'-0"
Level 4 to Level 5 = 20'-0"

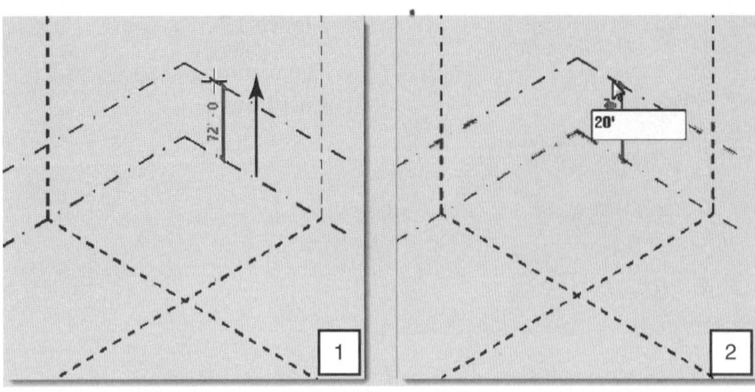

Figure 15-59

Creating a new **Level**

1. Start Revit.
2. From the **Application** menu, select **New > Conceptual Mass** to bring up the **New Conceptual Mass - Select Template File** dialog box.
3. In the **New Conceptual Mass Template File** dialog box, double-click the **Mass.rft** template to enter the **Conceptual Mass** editor.
4. In the **Conceptual Mass** editor, select the **Home** tab to bring up the **Home** toolbar.
5. In the **Home** toolbar, select the **Level** button.
6. Inside the drawing area, you will see the **Level** dashed line symbol and a temporary dimension following the cursor. Without deselecting the **Level** tool, type **20′** to create a second **Level.** Press the **<Esc>** key to end the command (see Figure 15-59).
7. Select the **Level** button again, and repeat the previous process creating four more levels—five levels total (see Figure 15-60).
8. Select **Level 1** to make it active.
9. From the **Draw** panel, select the **Ellipse** tool. Click three points to create an ellipse.
10. Click the first point at the intersection of the reference planes. Move the cursor on top of **Reference Plane: Center (Front/Back)** in the direction indicated by the arrow.
11. Don't click the mouse. Type **75′** and press <**Enter**>. The second point gets established.
12. Without moving the mouse, type **50′** and then press <**Enter**>. The third point gets established (see Figure 15-61).

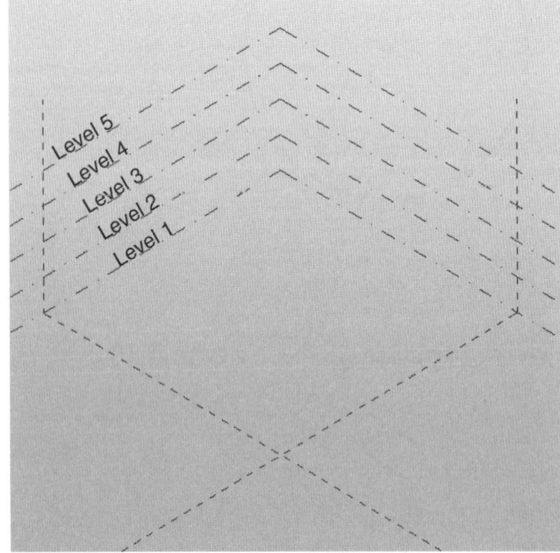

Figure 15-60

Creating the remaining levels

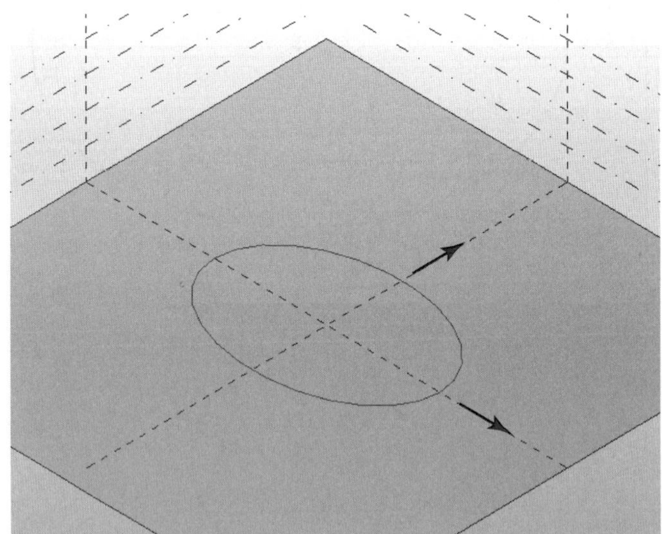

Figure 15-61

Drawing an **Ellipse** in 3D view

13. Press the **<Esc>** key twice to deselect the **Ellipse** tool.
14. Select the **Level 2 Reference Plane**.
15. In the **Modify** toolbar, select the **Workplane Viewer** button to bring up the **Workplane Viewer** (see Figure 15-62).
16. Select the **Level 2** reference plane from the **3D view** to make it active.
17. Expand the **Workplane Viewer**.

NOTE:

The **Workplane Viewer** is a working **View,** in **Plan,** of the presently selected **Workplane.**

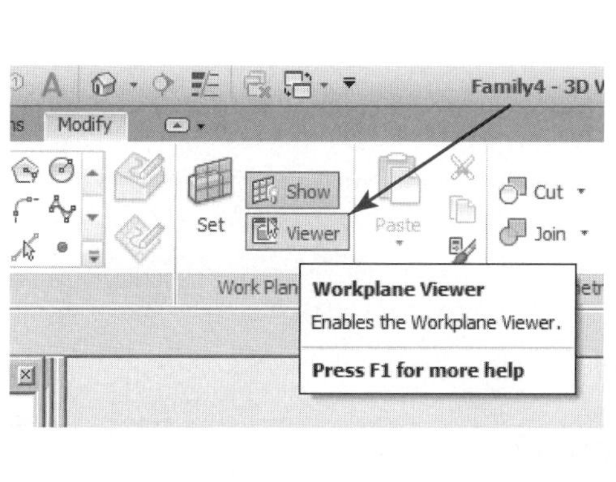

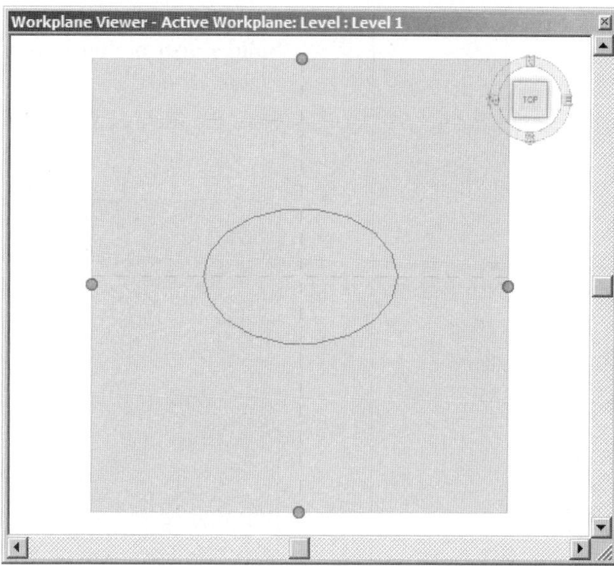

Figure 15-62

Workplane Viewer

18. Select the **Circle** tool from the **Draw** panel.

In the **Workplane Viewer,** the reference planes are seen on the first level only and are very dim on other levels. However, you can see alignment lines on **Level 2** when you hover the cursor over them.

19. Place the center of the **Circle** at the intersection of the reference planes in the **Workplane Viewer**, and create a **40′** circle.
20. Press <**Enter**> on the keyboard, and then press the <**Esc**> key twice.
21. Repeat this process, selecting each **Level**, and placing its respective curve (see Figure 15-63).

Figure 15-63

Curves placed on Workplanes

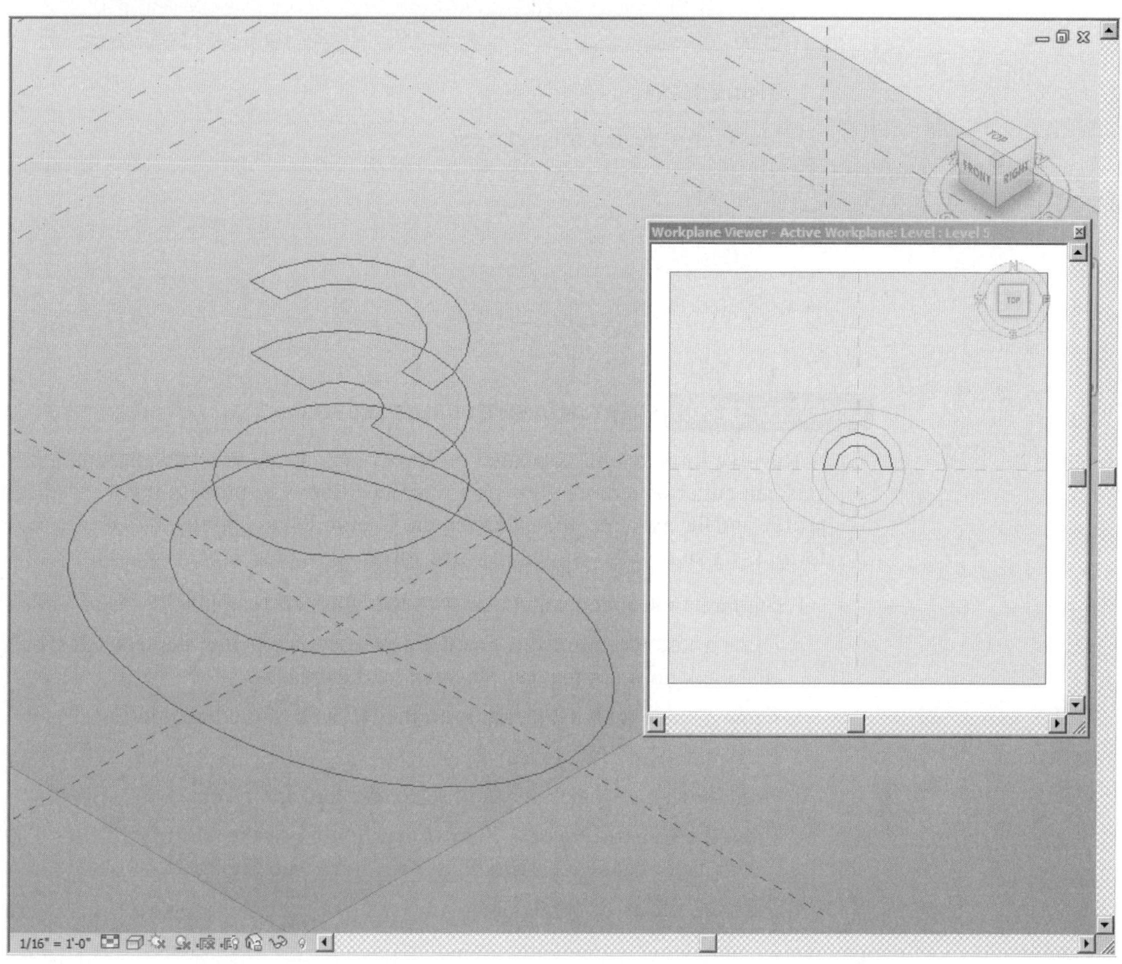

22. In the 3D view, select all the curves you placed, and press the **Create Form > Solid Form** button in the **Modify | Lines** toolbar to create the **Mass** form (see Figure 15-64).
23. Save the file as **LOFT FORM.rfa.**

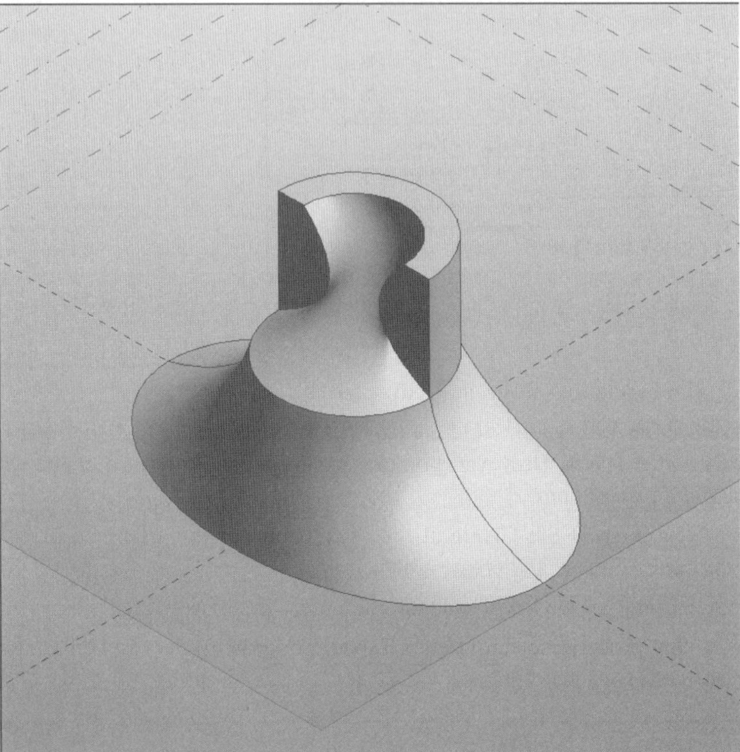

Figure 15-64

Mass form created from curves

EXERCISE 15-10 CREATING A SIMPLE REVOLVE FORM

A **Revolve** form is a mass created by revolving a shape or profile around an axis. The axis can either be a model line or a reference line. The process involves selecting the profile and the axis line, then clicking the **Create Form** command to create the revolve form. Let's start with a simple revolve form:

1. Start a new **Conceptual Mass** with the **Mass.rft** template.
2. Draw a line on top of the **Front/Back** reference plane; the exact location of the first click does not matter. This will be the axis line.
3. Draw a circle with a **20′** radius on the left side of the line you just drew.
4. Press the **<Esc>** key twice.
5. Hold down the **<Ctrl>** key and select the **line** and **circle.**
6. Press the **Create Form > Solid Form** button in the **Modify | Lines** Toolbar to create the donut-shaped **Revolve Mass** form (see Figure 15-65).
7. Save the file as **REVOLVE-1**.

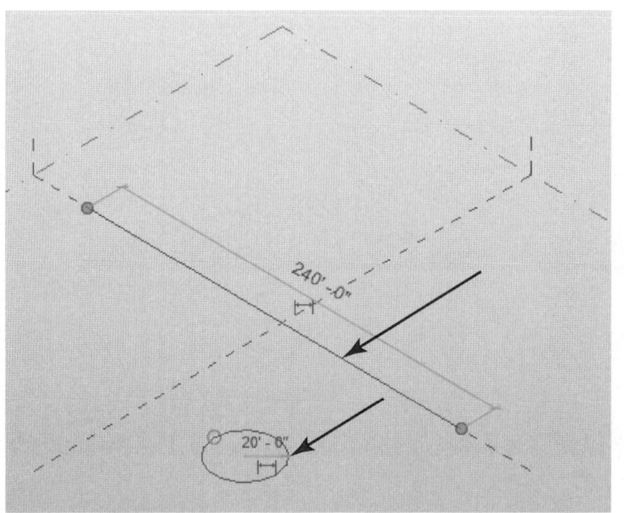

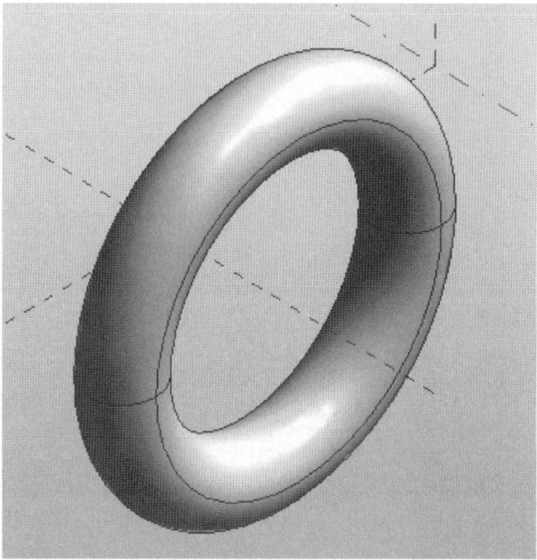

Figure 15-65

Press the **Create Form > Solid Form** button in the **Modify | Lines** toolbar to create the donut-shaped **Revolve Mass** form

EXERCISE 15-11 CREATING A COMPLEX REVOLVE FORM

1. Start a new **Conceptual Mass** with the **Mass.rft** template.
2. Select the **Workplane Viewer**.
3. Select the **Line** button from the **Home** toolbar.
4. In the **Workplane Viewer**, sketch a long axis line on top of the **Front/Back** reference plane, then press the <**Esc**> key.
5. With the **Line** tool still active, draw the polygon profile shown in Figure 15-66.

Figure 15-66

With the **Line** tool still active, draw the polygon profile

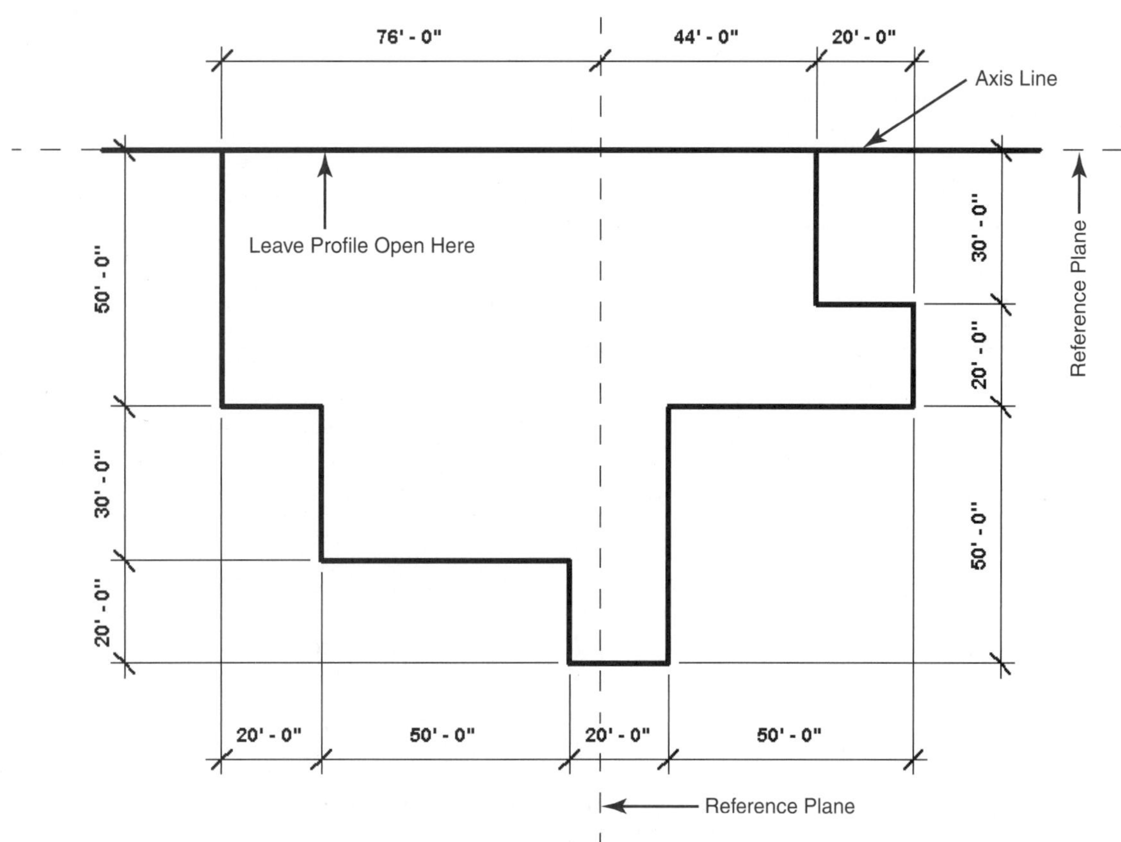

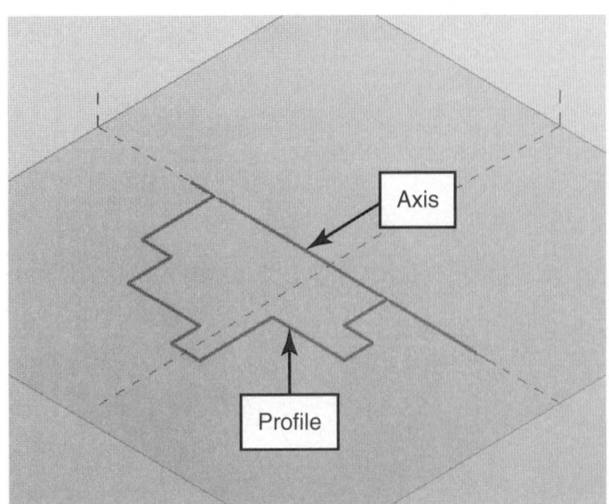

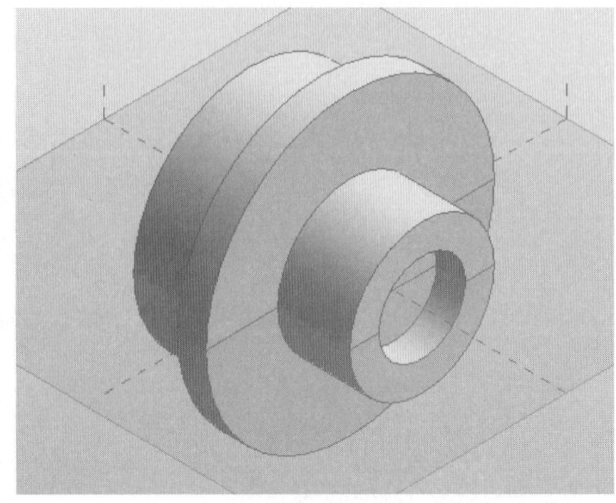

Figure 15-67

Creating a **Revolve** form

6. Switch to the **default 3D view**. Select the **axis** and the **profile**.
7. Select the **Create Form > Solid Form** button to create the **Revolve** form (see Figure 15-67).
8. Select any surface of the **Revolve** form to bring up the **Properties** dialog box.
9. In the **Properties** dialog box, under **Constraints>End Angle**, type **270**.
10. Press the **Apply** button and notice that the **Revolve** has changed its shape; it appears like a portion of the mass has been carved out (see Figure 15-68).

NOTE:

Profiles can be closed or open loops. For now, leave it open where it coincides with the reference plane. Later on, you will close the loop and observe the effect on the revolve form.

NOTE:

When you create a revolve, the default revolution of the profile around the axis is 360°. This can be changed so that you can create a section-like shape like a pie.

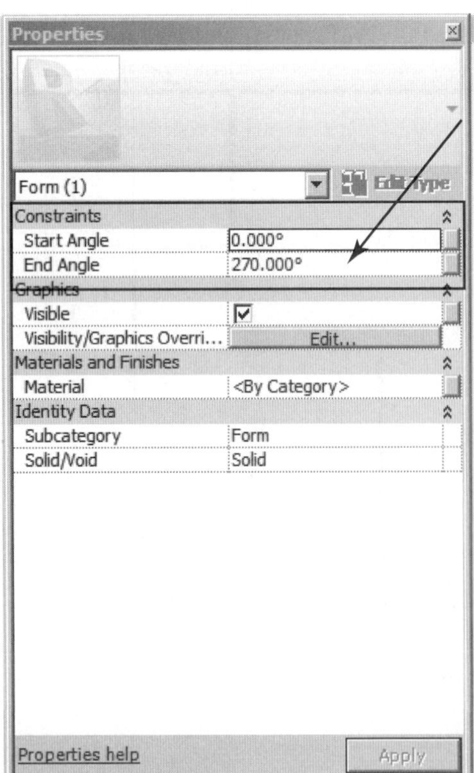

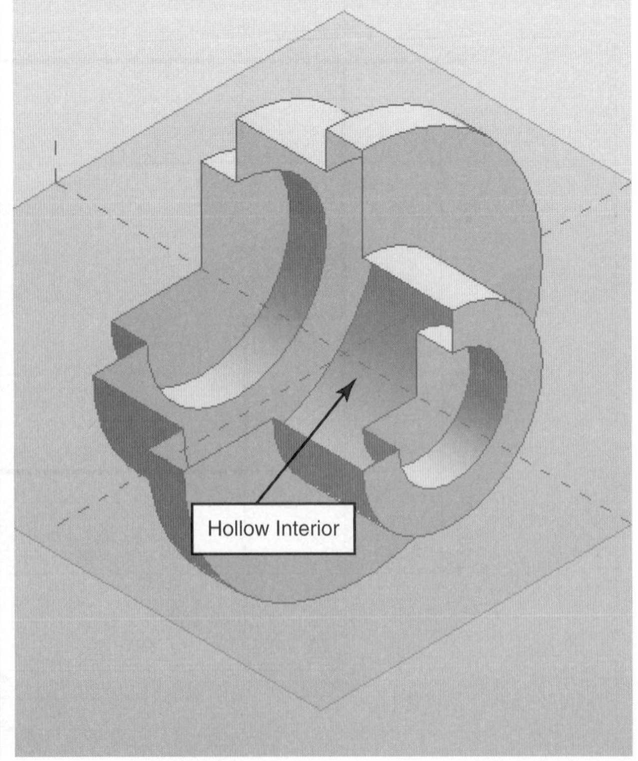

Figure 15-68

Changing the angle constraint of a revolve form

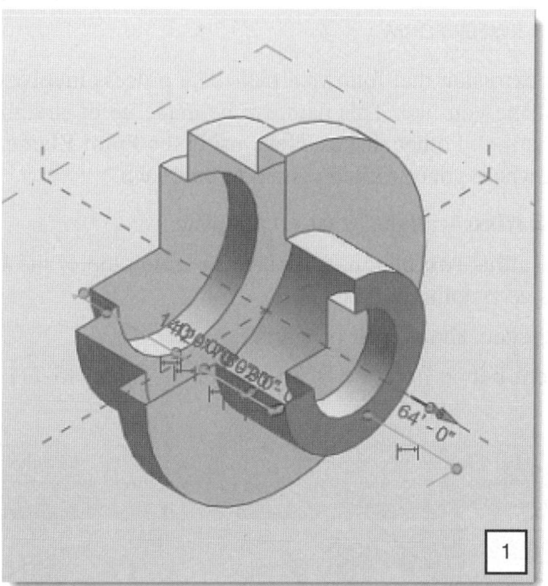

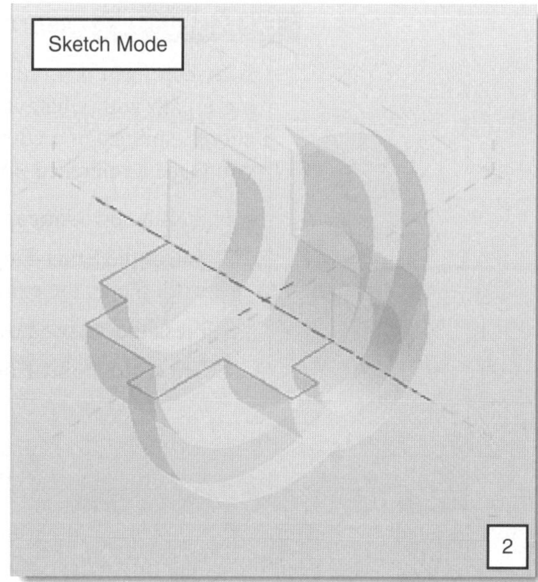

Figure 15-69

Editing the **Revolve** form

11. The cut section also appears hollow. You can make it look solid by closing the loop of the profile.
12. Select any of the surfaces of the **Revolve** form and click **Edit Profile**. You will be taken into the sketch mode (see Figure 15-69).
13. Draw a line to close the shape of the revolve profile.
14. Click the green check mark at the end of the **Modify | Edit Profile** toolbar to complete the **Revolve Mass**.
15. Press the **<Esc>** key to end the command (see Figure 15-70).
16. Save the file as **REVOLVE-2.rfa**

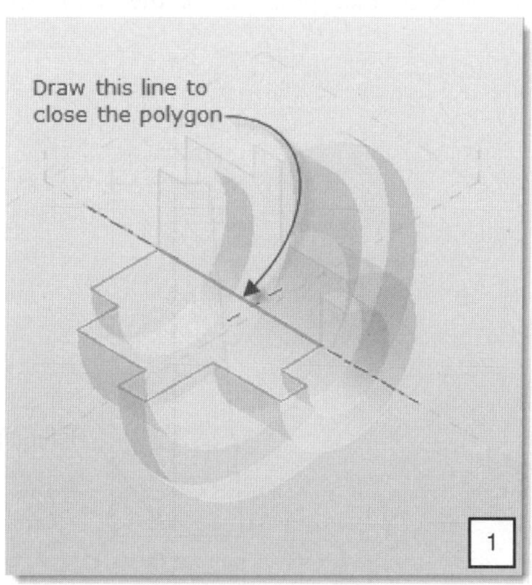

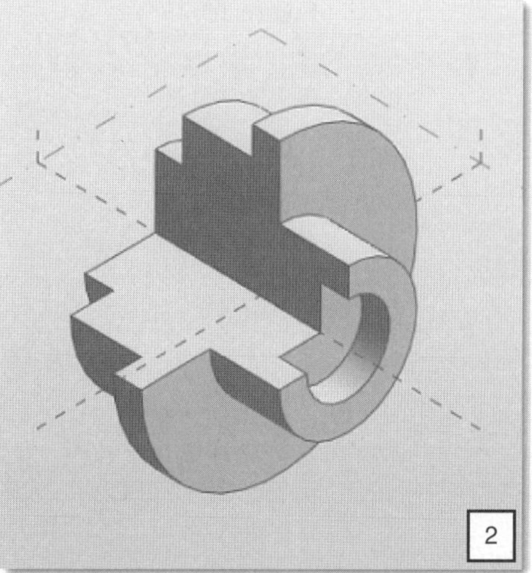

Figure 15-70

Closing the profile of a revolve form

EXERCISE 15-12 CREATING A SWEEP FORM

A **Sweep** form is a type of extrusion that follows a path. The process involves drawing a path with whatever shape you like. This path can be made up of straight lines, curves, splines, or a combination of other shapes. Next, using the **Point Element** tool, you place a reference point where your profile is going to be drawn.

1. Start a new **Conceptual Mass** with the **Mass.rft** template.
2. Select the **Start-End-Radius Arc** button, and place an arc on top of the **Level 1** work plane; the exact size is not important.
3. Press the **<Esc>** key; the tool should still be active.
4. Select the **Point Element** button from the **Draw** panel (see Figure 15-71).

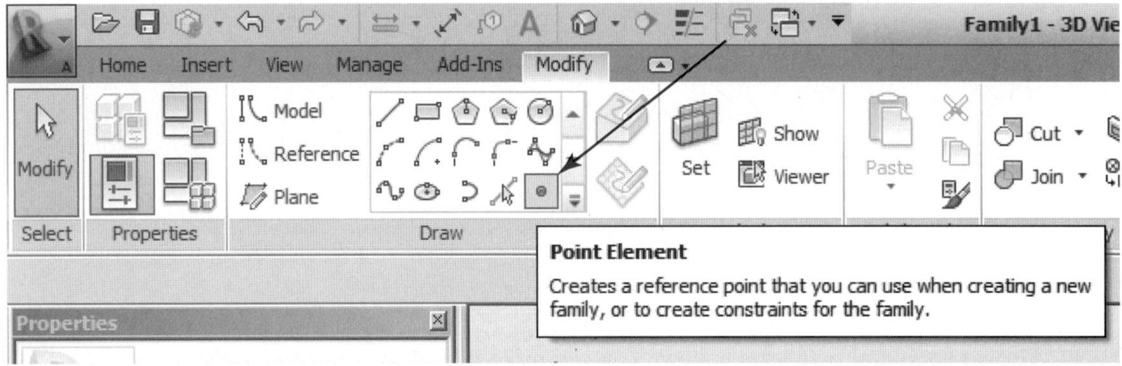

Figure 15-71

The **Point Element** button

5. Click the cursor at the starting point of the arc.
6. Press the **<Esc>** key, and a **Reference Point** will be established.
7. Click on the **Reference Point** you placed to show its **Reference Plane** (see Figure 15-72).
8. In the **Modify** toolbar, select the **Workplane Viewer** button to bring up the **Workplane Viewer**.
9. In the **Workplane Viewer**, at the Reference point, draw the shape shown in Figure 15-73.

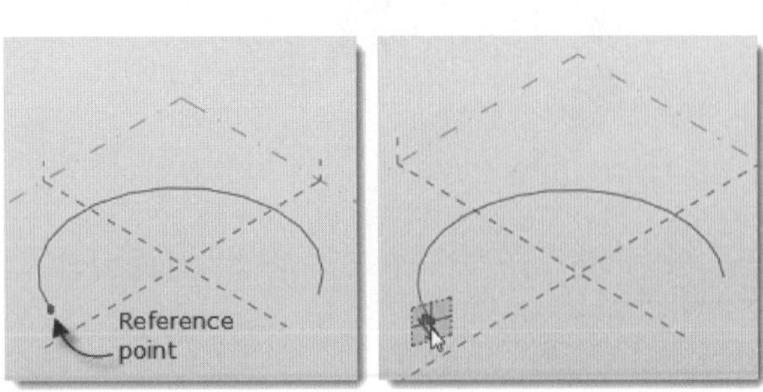

Figure 15-72

Placing a **Point Element** on a path

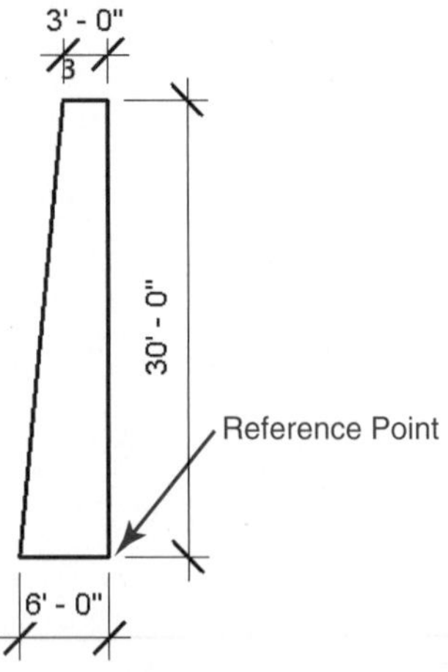

Figure 15-73

Creating the **Shape**

10. Return to the **Default 3D View**.
11. Hold down the **<Ctrl>** key and select both the profile and the arc path.
12. Press the **Create Form** > **Solid Form** button to create the **Sweep** (see Figure 15-74).
13. Save your file as **Sweep-1**.

> **NOTE:**
> If the shape you drew on the **Workplane Viewer** is reversed in 3D, return to the **Workplane Viewer,** change the view to left in the **ViewCube,** and redraw.

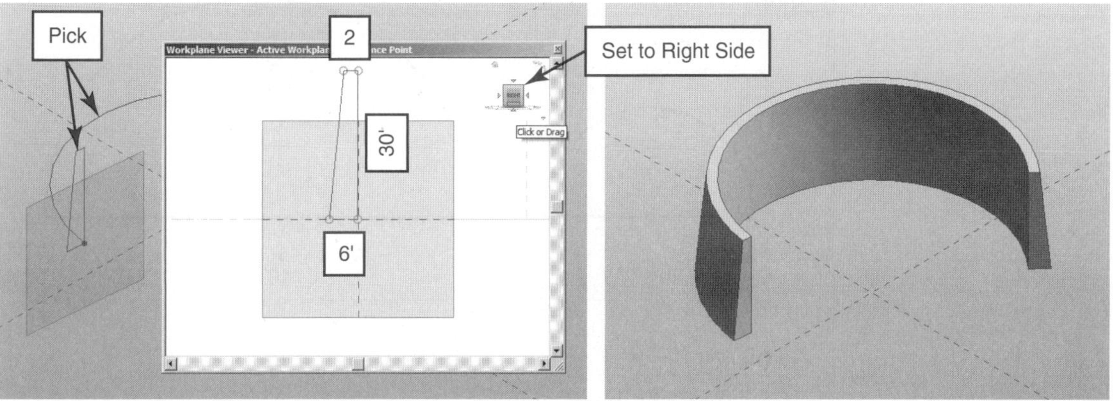

Figure 15-74

Press the **Create Form** > **Solid Form** button to create the **Sweep**

EXERCISE 15-13 CREATING A SWEPT BLEND FORM

A swept blend is a variation of the **Sweep** form. In this type of form, you can have more than one profile with different shapes that follow a path. The profiles are blended together to form a complex mass.

> **NOTE:**
> This exercise requires the use of the **Spline** tool to generate a smooth curved path. A spline is created by clicking a series of control points.

1. Start a new **Conceptual Mass** with the **Mass.rft** template.
2. Using the **Spline** tool from the **Draw** panel, draw a curved path in the order shown in Figure 15-75.

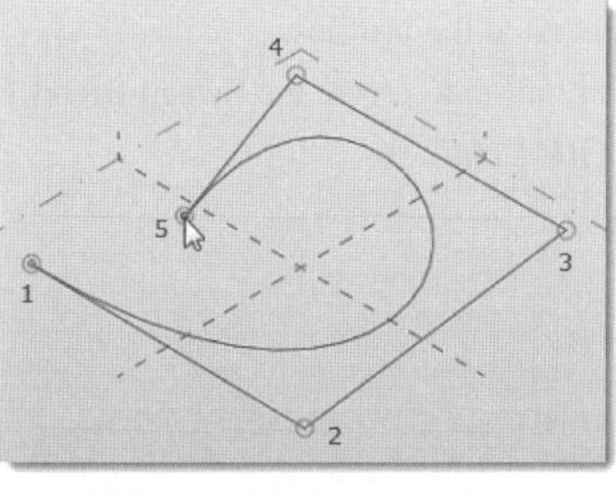

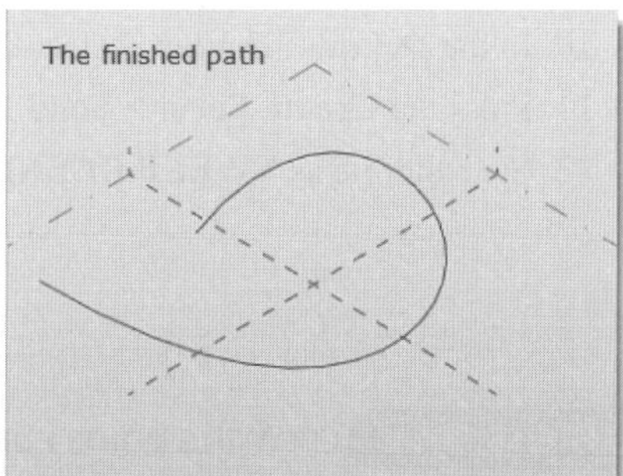

Figure 15-75

Drawing a curve using the **Spline** tool

3. Right-click and select **Cancel** to exit the tool after placing the last point. The exact locations of the points are not important.
4. Select the **Point Element** tool and click the first and last points of the path to place **Reference Points**.
5. Select the first **point element** to make it active.

6. In the **Modify** toolbar, select the **Workplane Viewer** button to bring up the **Workplane Viewer**.
7. In the **Workplane Viewer**, at the first Reference point, draw the **Profile 1** shape shown in Figure 15-76.

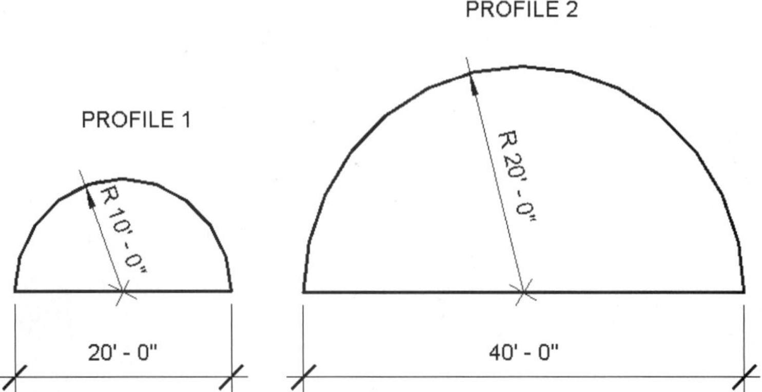

Figure 15-76

Sweep Blend Form profiles

8. Select the last **point element** in the path to make it active.
9. In the **Workplane Viewer**, at the last Reference point in the path, draw the **Profile 2** shape shown in Figure 15-77.

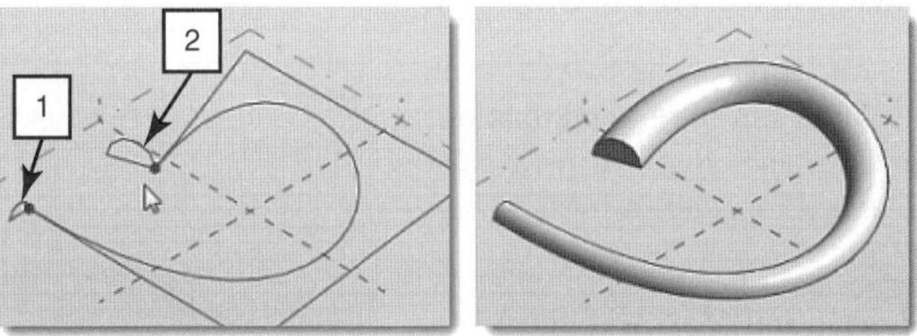

Figure 15-77

Create the **Sweep Blend Form**

10. In the **Default 3D View**, select the path and the profiles.
11. Press the **Create Form** > **Solid Form** button to create the **Sweep Blend Form.**
12. Save the file as **SWEEP BLEND FORM.rfa**

EXERCISE 15-14 CREATING VOIDS FORMS AND THE CUT GEOMETRY TOOL

There are times when you have to create a void away from the solid that you want to carve it from. However, overlapping the void to the solid to subtract it does not cut the solid automatically. In this situation, you have to use the **Cut Geometry** tool (**Modify | Form > Geometry**).

1. Start a new **Conceptual Mass** with the **Mass.rfa** template.
2. Activate the **Level 1** work plane.
3. Select the **Circumscribed Polygon** button.
4. In the **Options Bar**, type **4** for the number of **sides**.

5. Place the cursor at the intersection of the two vertical **Reference** planes.
6. Click and drag it on top of a reference plane and type **50′.**
7. Press the <**Enter**> key on the keyboard; this creates a square on the **Level 1** work plane (see Figure 15-78).

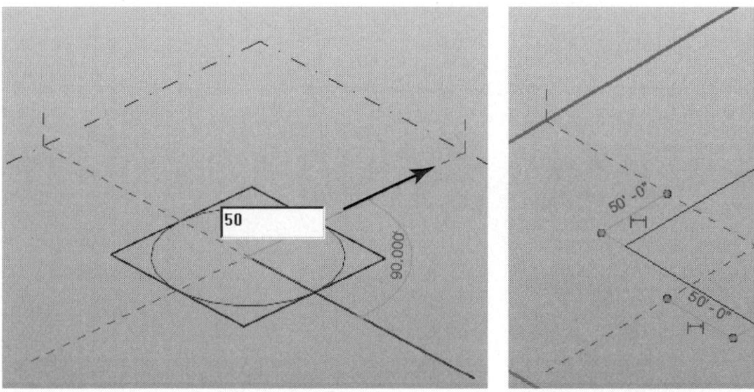

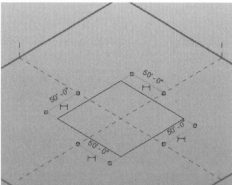

Figure 15-78

Drawing a square at its center in 3D view

8. Press the **<Esc>** key twice and select the **Center (Left/Right)** reference plane to make it active.
9. In the **Modify** toolbar, select the **Workplane Viewer** button to bring up the **Workplane Viewer**.
10. In the **Workplane Viewer**, at the first Reference point, draw an **80′** × **50′** triangle profile (see Figure 15-79.

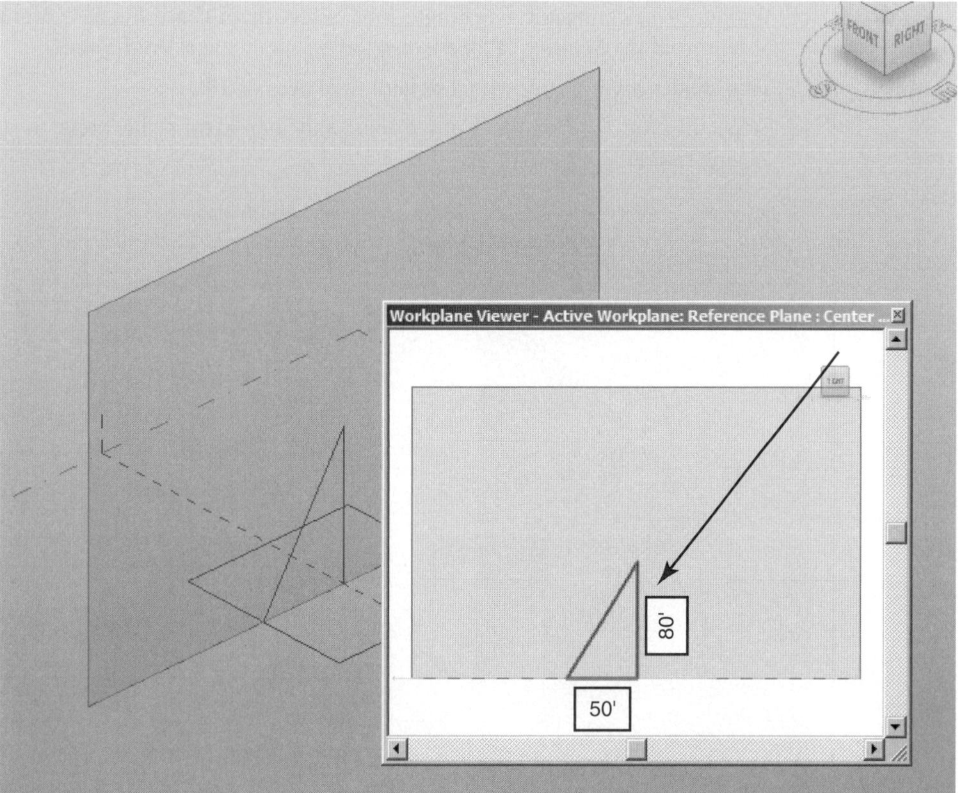

Figure 15-79

Creating a vertical profile in 3D view

11. Press the <**Esc**> key twice.
12. Hold down the <**Ctrl**> key and select the square and triangle profiles.
13. Select the **Create Form** > **Solid Form** button; the resulting form is a pyramid-shaped **Mass** (see Figure 15-80).

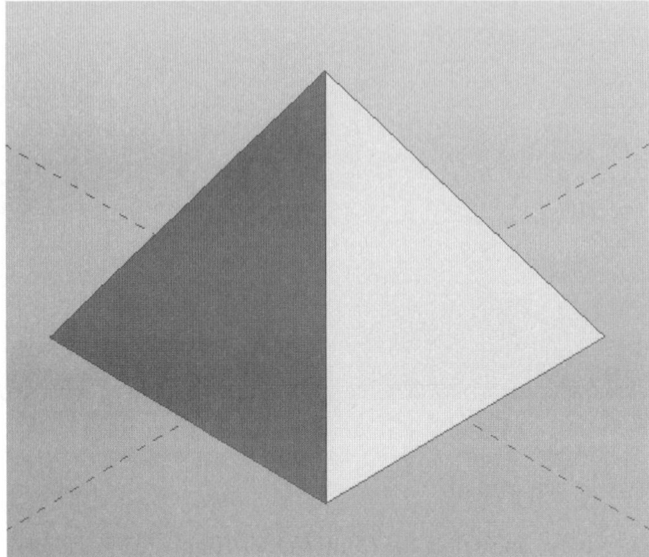

Figure 15-80

Creating a **pyramid** in 3D view

14. Activate the **Level 1** work plane again.
15. Select the **Rectangle** tool and place a **20′** × **40′** rectangle away from the pyramid.
16. Without deselecting the **Rectangle** tool, select the **Create Form** > **Void Form** button from the **Modify** | **Place Lines** toolbar to create a **Void Form**.
17. This creates a void form with a default thickness of **10′**.
18. Select the top face of the **Void Form**, and increase its thickness to **40′** (see Figure 15-81).

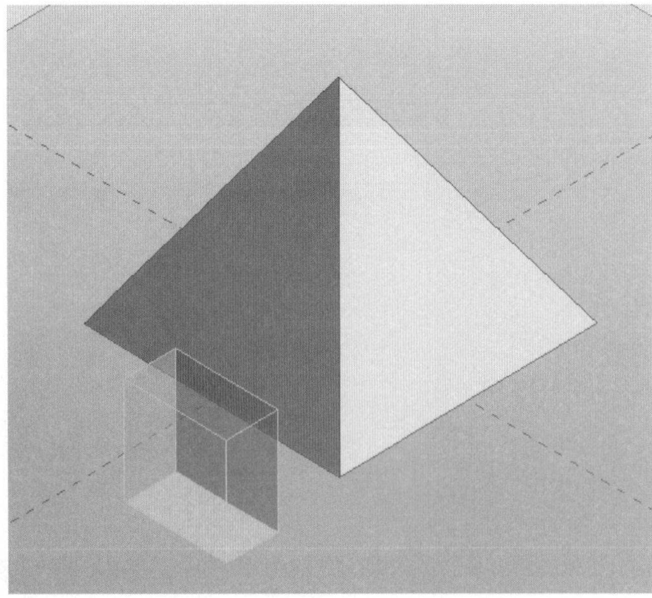

Figure 15-81

Select the top face of the **Void Form**

19. Select the entire **Void Form** by enclosing it in a selection box, and move it to the center of the pyramid.
20. This locates the void form in the middle of the pyramid.

Observe that the void did not automatically cut an opening on the pyramid.

21. Select the **Cut Geometry** button in the **Modify** toolbar.
22. Select the pyramid, and then select the **Void Form** to subtract it from the pyramid (see Figure 15-82).
23. Save the file as **VOID FORM OPENING.rfa**

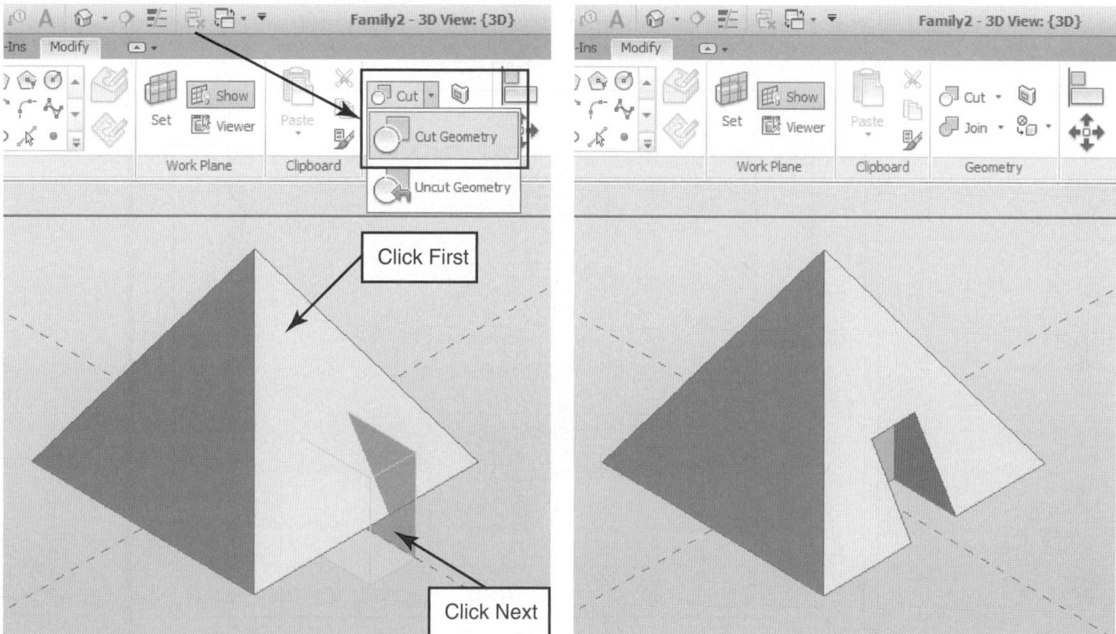

Figure 15-82

Using the **Cut Geometry** tool

EXERCISE 15-15 CONVERTING A MASS FORM INTO A BUILDING

A powerful feature of Revit is its ability to convert mass forms into building elements. After you create your mass forms as an **In-Place Mass** or **Loadable Mass Family**, you can transform them into building components that can be documented and eventually built. This is done through the tools found in the **Model by Face** panel of the **Massing & Site** tab.

1. Start a new drawing using the RAC 2012\Imperial Templates\default.rte template.
2. In the **Project Browser**, double click **Floor Plans > Level 1**.
3. Set the scale to **1/8″ =1′-0″**.
4. Create seven levels:
   a. Ground Floor : -1′-0″
   b. Level 1 : 1′-0″
   c. Level 2 : 12′-0″
   d. Level 3 : 23′-0″
   e. Level 4 : 36′-0″
   f. Roof : 48′-0″
   g. Top of Parapet: 51′

5. Change to **Level 1 Floor Plan**.
6. Select the **Massing & Site** tab to bring up the **Massing & Site** toolbar.
7. In the **Massing & Site** toolbar, select the **In-Place Mass** button.
8. A warning dialog will appear saying that **Show Mass** has been enabled.
9. In the warning dialog box, press the **OK** button to bring up the **Name** dialog box.
10. Enter **TEST BUILDING MASS** in the **Name** field, and press the **OK** button to enter the **In-Place Editor**.
11. In the **Home** toolbar, select the **Line** button in the **Draw** panel, and create the figure shown in Figure 15-83.

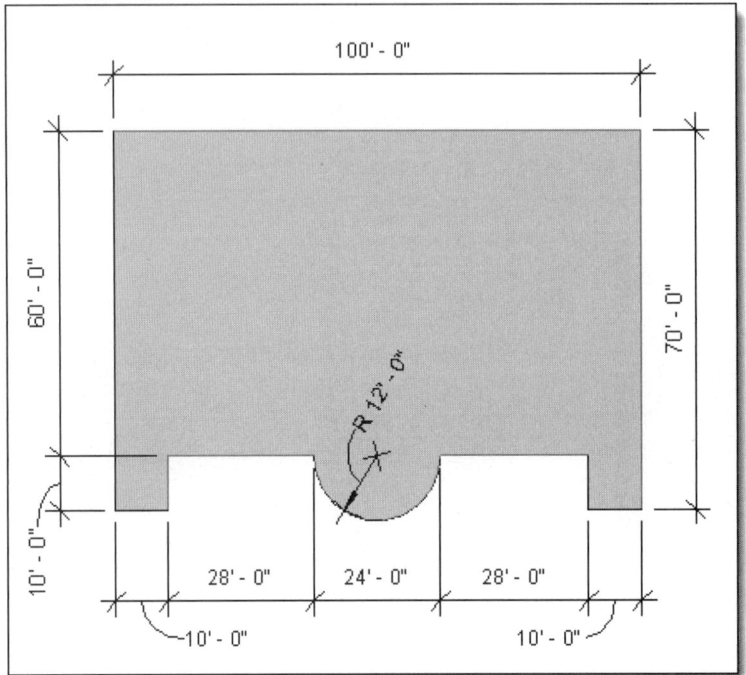

Figure 15-83

Dimension references for this exercise

12. Select the lines you just placed to bring up the **Modify | Lines** toolbar.
13. In the **Modify | Lines** toolbar, select the **Create Form > Solid Form** button to create the mass object and return to the **Modify | Form** toolbar.
14. Change to the **Default 3D View**.
15. Select the **top face** of the mass to activate its adjustment arrows.
16. Immediately change to the **East Elevation**.
17. With adjustment arrows active, drag the top of the **Mass** until it snaps onto the **Top of Parapet** level (see Figure 15-84).
18. Change back to the **3D** view.
19. In the **Modify** toolbar, select the **Finish Mass** button to create the **TEST BUILDING MASS** (see Figure 15-85).
20. Select the **Mass** to bring up the **Modify | Mass** toolbar.
21. In the **Modify | Mass** toolbar, select the **Mass Floors** button to bring up the **Mass Floors** dialog box.
22. In the **Mass Floors** dialog box, check the **Level 1** through **Level 4** check boxes, and press the **OK** button to create **Mass Floors** in your building mass (see Figures 15-86 and 15-87).

Figure 15-84

Drag the top of the **Mass**

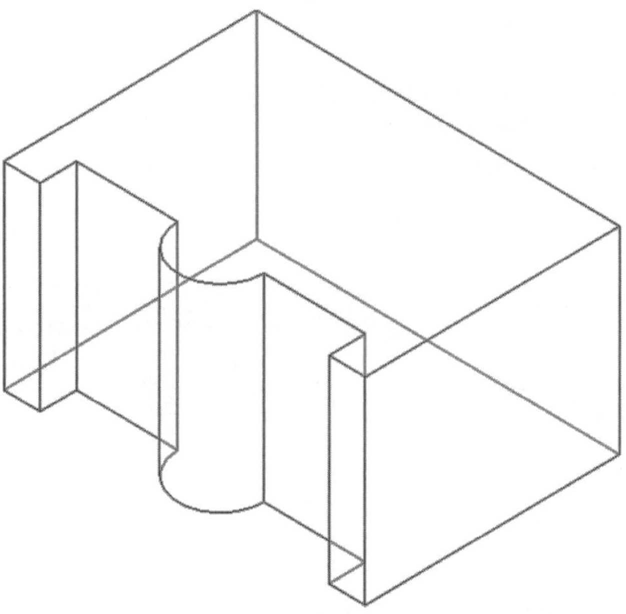

Figure 15-85

Drag the top of the **Mass**

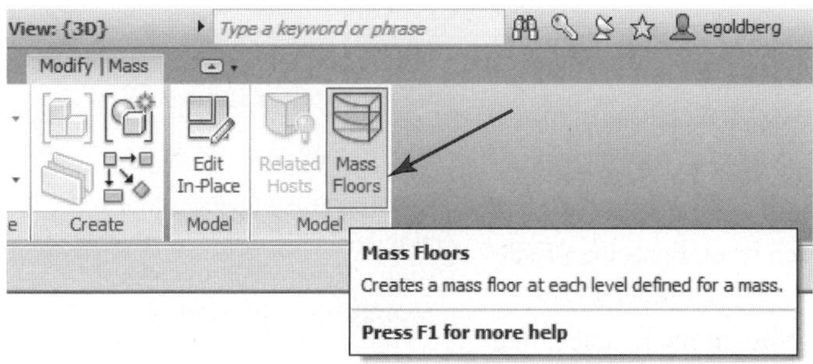

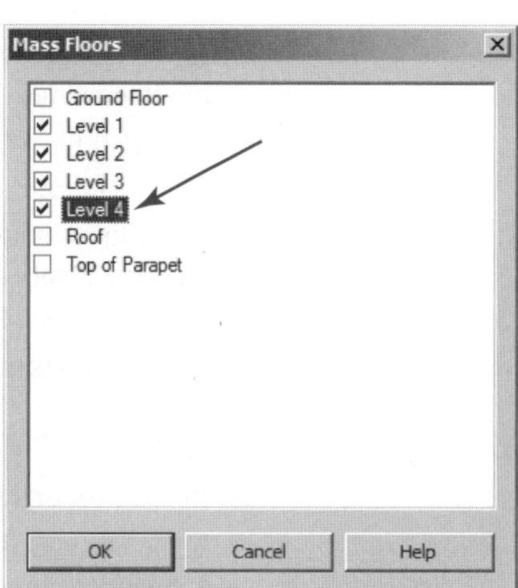

Figure 15-86

Select the **Mass Floors** button

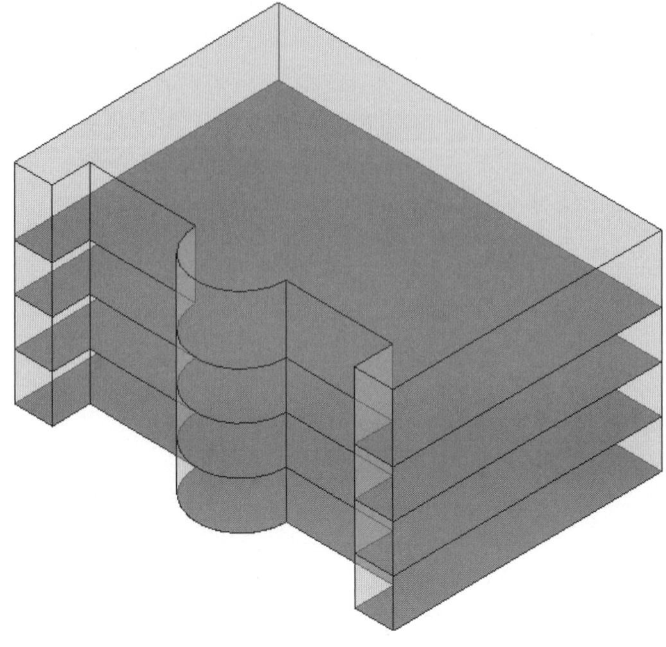

Figure 15-87

The created floor faces using the **Mass Floors** command

23. In the **Massing & Site** toolbar, select the **Floor > Floor by Face** button to bring up the **Modify | Place Floor by Face** toolbar.
24. In the **Modify | Place Floor by Face** toolbar, select the **Select Multiple** button (see Figure 15-88).

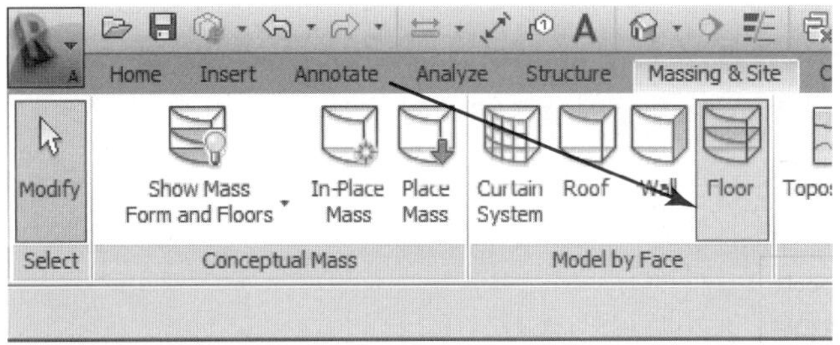

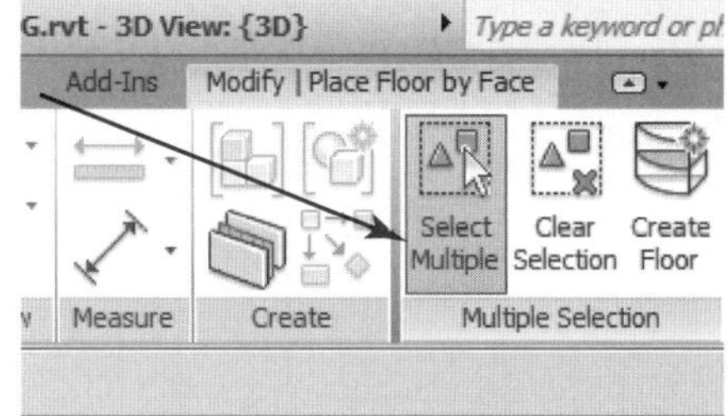

Figure 15-88

The **Floor > Floor by Face** button and the **Select Multiple** command from the contextual menu

25. Make sure the **Generic - 12″** wall is shown in the **Properties** dialog box.
26. Select all the **Mass Floors** faces.
27. In the **Modify | Place Floor by Face** toolbar, select the **Create Floor** button to create **12″ Generic Floors** on each level. Press the <Esc> key to end the command (see Figure 15-90).
28. In the **Massing & Site** toolbar, select the **Wall** button (or in the **Home** toolbar, select the **Wall > Wall by Face** button) to bring up the **Modify | Place Wall** toolbar.
29. In the **Properties** dialog box, select the **Basic Wall : Brick on Mtl. Stud** wall.
30. In the **Options Bar**, select the **Location Line** drop-down list and select **Finish Face: Interior** to create the walls outside the boundary of the floors (see Figure 15-91).

NOTE:

After each floor is selected, it will remain highlighted even without pressing the **<Shift>** key. The **Floor by Face** tool will highlight only the faces that were created using the **Mass Floors** button (see Figure 15-89).

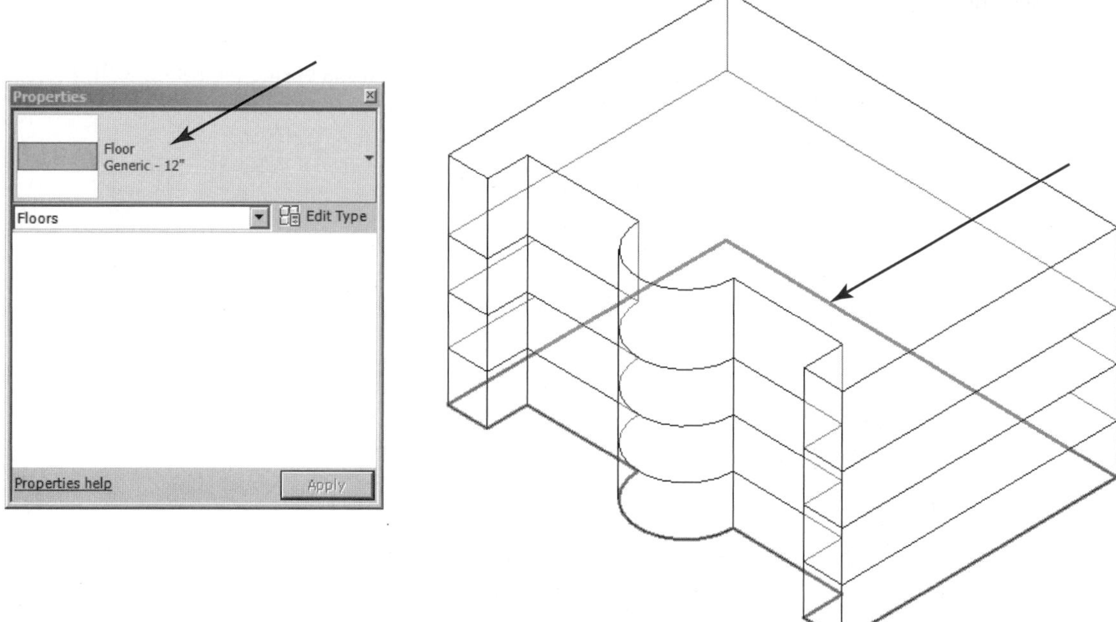

Figure 15-89

The **Floor type selector**

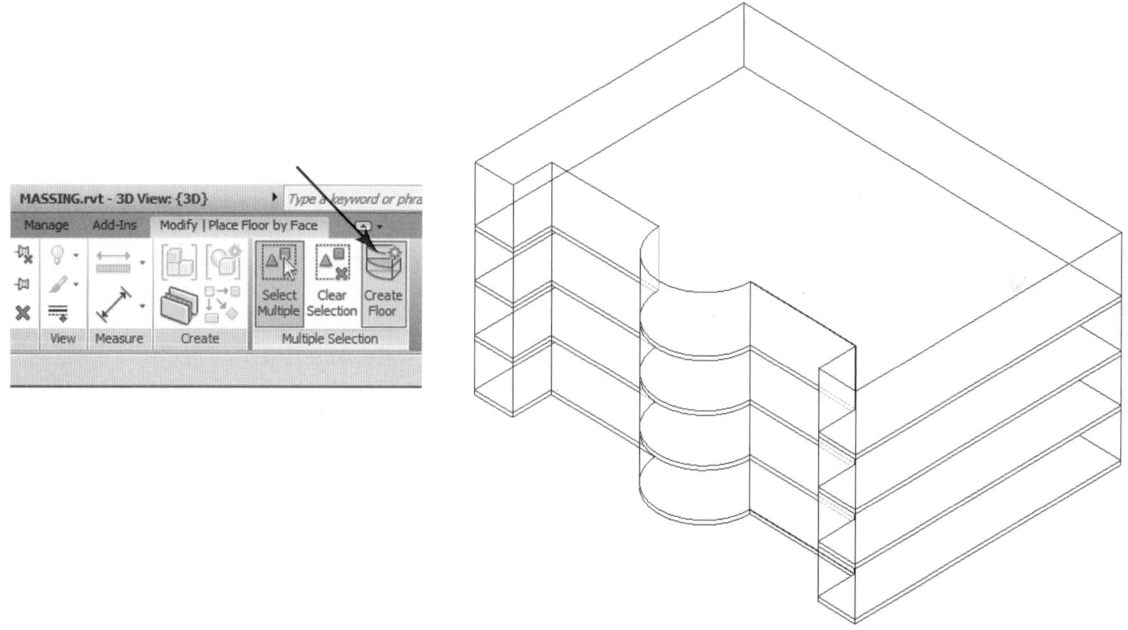

Figure 15-90

The **Create Floor** button; the floors now have thickness in them

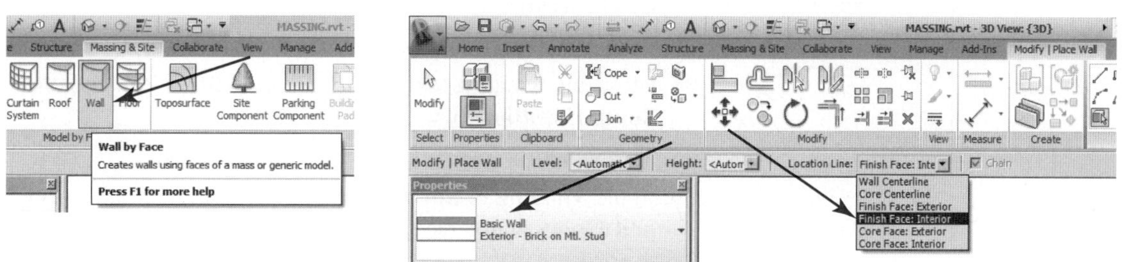

Figure 15-91

Using the **Wall by Face** command

31. Next, click all the exterior walls except the two walls beside the round wall. Press the <Esc> key when finished to end the command (see Figure 15-92).

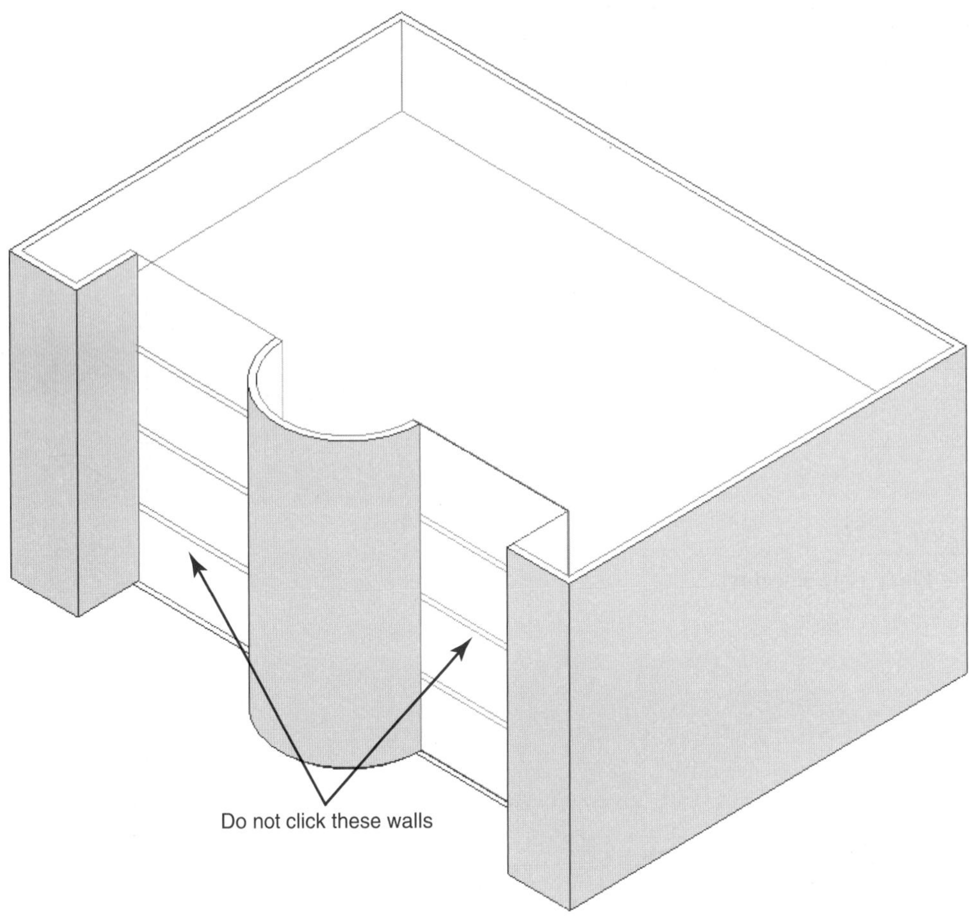

Figure 15-92

From the **Location Line** drop-down list, select **Finish Face: Interior**

The next step is to create the roof. The **Roof by Face** tool will highlight or recognize only the top or bottom surfaces of a mass form (not the floors created by the **Floor by Face** tool). In this exercise, the top surface of the mass is actually the **Top of Parapet** level. It is also where the side walls end. The problem is that you need a surface for a roof. The solution is to bring down the height of the solid mass (used for the **Top of Parapet** level) to the level of the roof. The walls that were already created are not associated to the mass anymore; therefore, they will not be affected.

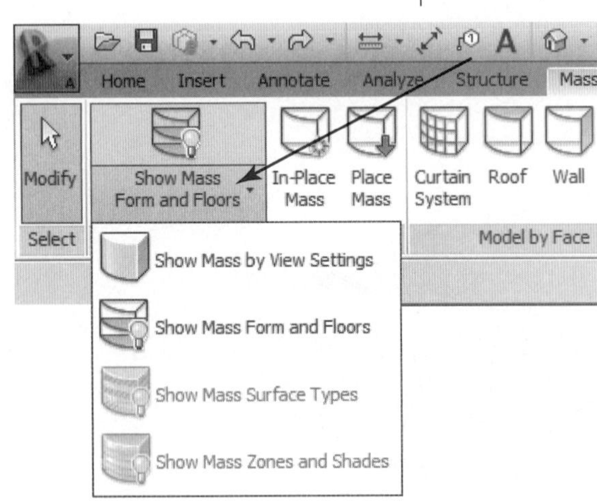

Figure 15-93

Show Mass Form and Floors button

32. **Double-click** the **South Elevation** view (any elevation can also be used).
33. Type **WT** (keyboard shortcut for **Tile Windows**).
34. Close all windows except the **Default 3D View** and the **South Elevation** view.
35. Two windows will now be visible on the screen.
36. In the **Massing & Site** toolbar, select the **Show Mass Form and Floors** button (see Figure 15-93).
37. Type **ZA** (keyboard shortcut for **Zoom All**).
38. Click a blank area on the **Default 3D view** to make the window active.

39. Select the solid mass by clicking the **inner** part of the parapet wall.
40. With the **Solid Mass** selected, click a blank area on the elevation view to make the window active.
41. Drag the top triangular control grip downward to the **Roof** level (see Figure 15-94).

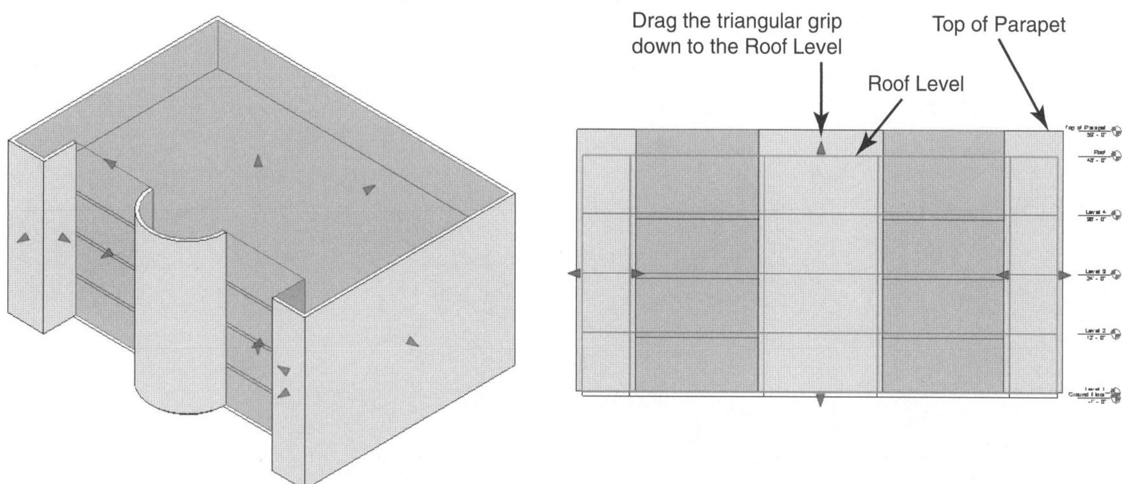

Figure 15-94
Creating a new face for the roof

42. Expand the **Default 3D View**.
43. In the **Massing & Site** toolbar, select the **Roof** button (or in the **Home** toolbar, select the **Roof** > **Roof by Face** button).
44. In the **Properties** dialog box, select **Generic - 9″** from the **Roof type selector**.
45. Hover the cursor over the top of the mass, and click when it highlights.
46. With the top surface highlighted, select the **Create Roof** button from the **Modify | Place Roof by Face** toolbar to create the roof.
47. Press the **<Esc>** key to end the command (see Figure 15-95).
48. Maximize the **Default 3D View** window and type **ZA**.
49. In the **Massing & Site** toolbar, select the **Curtain System** button.

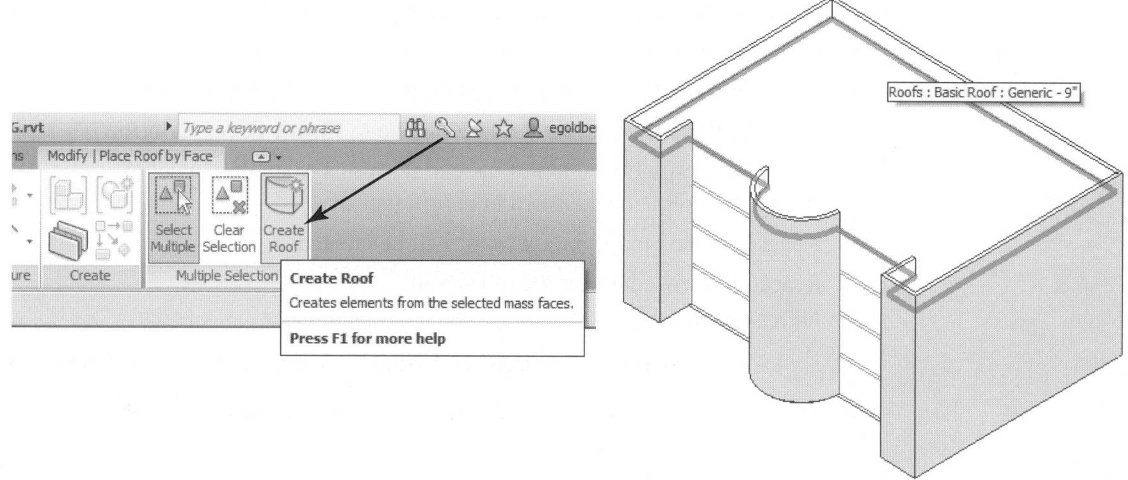

Figure 15-95
Using the **Create Roof by Face** command

50. In the **Properties** dialog box, select the **Curtain System 5′ × 10′** wall.
51. Select the left and right mass faces beside the round wall.
52. With the two faces selected, select the **Create System** button in the **Modify | Place Curtain System by Face** toolbar.

The selected walls change to curtain walls. Press the **<Esc>** key to end the command (see Figure 15-96).

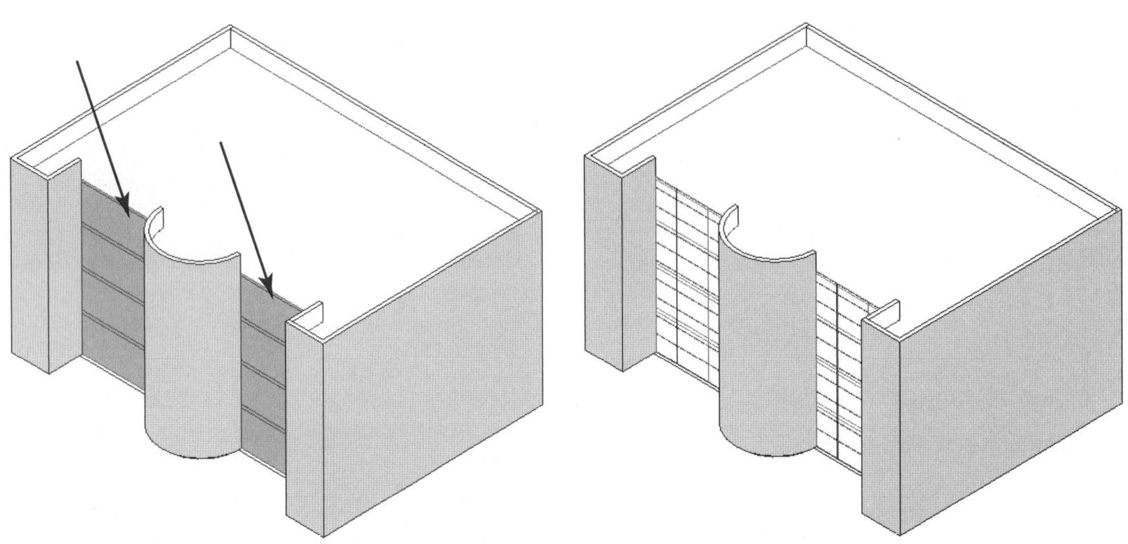

Figure 15-96

Using the **Curtain System by Face** command

Since the **Mass Form** was dragged down to the **Roof** level in Step 41, the curtain walls that were created ended on the roof level. What is missing now are the parapet walls on top of each curtain wall system. No problem. Just manually create the parapet walls.

53. In the **Massing & Site** toolbar, select the **Wall** button (or in the **Home** toolbar, select the **Wall > Wall by Face** button).
54. Select the **Pick Lines** tool from the **Draw** panel of the **Modify | Place Wall** toolbar.
55. In the **Options Bar**, make sure that the **Level** is set on **Roof**.
56. In the **Options Bar**, set the **Height** drop-down list to **Top of Parapet**.
57. In the **Options Bar**, set the **Location Line** to **Finish Face: Exterior**.
58. Hover the mouse on the top of the curtain wall system until a couple of lines consisting of a solid and a dashed blue line appear.
59. Select this line type; a parapet wall will be created.
60. Repeat this procedure for the other wall.
61. Press the **<Esc>** key twice to end the command (see Figure 15-97).
62. Switch to the **Realistic** view from the **Visual Style** button of the **View Control Bar**.

Notice the overlapping surfaces, and also notice that the curtain walls appear dark. That is because the **Mass Form** is still there.

63. Select the **Show Mass Form and Floors** in the **Massing & Site** toolbar; this button is an **on/off** switch that toggles the display of the mass.
64. Toggle the Mass Form **off**.

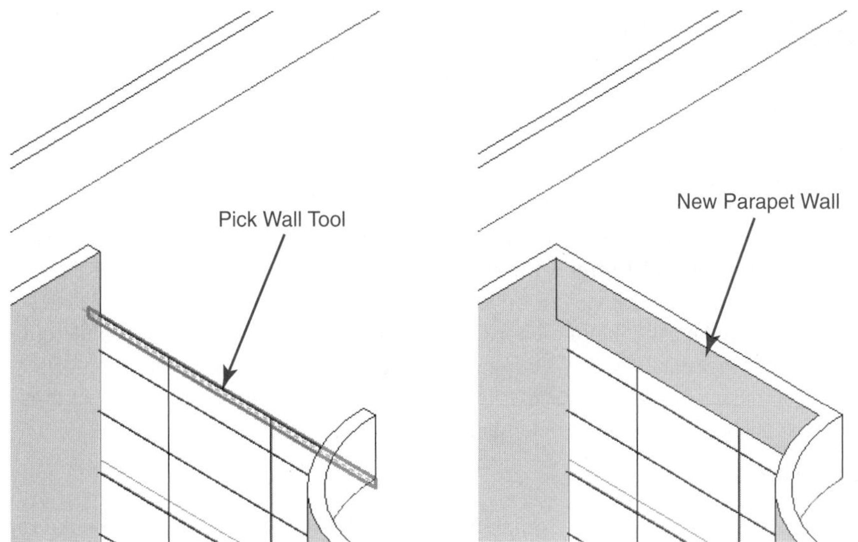

Figure 15-97

Creating a parapet wall using the **Pick Lines** tool

65. In the **View Control Bar**, click the **Shadows** button. This button toggles the shadows display to be **On** or **Off**.
66. Toggle the shadows **on** (see Figure 15-98).
67. Save the file as **CONVERTING A MASS FORM TO A BUILDING**.

Figure 15-98

Close-up view of the finished building

EXERCISE 15-16 DIVIDED SURFACE, PATTERNING TOOLS, AND ADAPTIVE COMPONENTS

Revit allows you to apply complex geometric shapes and patterns to surfaces through its **Divided Surface** tools. The patterns are line-based pattern representations that are helpful in visualizing building elements such as supporting structures, curtain walls, screens, skylights, and other complex surfaces. After you have chosen a grid or pattern scheme, you can then replace it with massing components such as mullions, structural components, and surface materials. This is done through another family template called **Curtain Panel Pattern Based.rft.** In this template, you can model the frames and members that make up the divided surface. Upon completion, load it back into your conceptual mass. The line-based scheme initially established will then be replaced by these components, thereby giving a more realistic graphic representation of the design. The beauty of this is that the vertical and horizontal spacing of the patterns can still change. The surface components loaded will update to the new spacing.

Adaptive Components

Another massing feature that complements the **Divided Surface** tool is the **Adaptive Components.** As their name implies, these are components that adapt or adjust to the shape of the mass into which they are loaded. They are particularly useful in creating complex components and irregular shapes that the **Divided Surface** tool cannot address. They pretty much work like the components created from the **Curtain Panel Pattern Based** family template. However, they are not tied up to a grid or a fixed framework. The **Adaptive Components** feature can also be used by itself to build components that grow or change their shape when your design changes.

Adding Constraint Parameters (instance)

1. Start a new **Conceptual Mass** with the **Mass.rft** template.
2. In the **Default 3D view**, set **Level 2** to the height of **120′-0″**.
3. Set the scale for **Levels 1** and **2** to **1/32″=1′-0″.**
4. Using the **Line** tools, draw the profiles in Figure 15-99 on **Levels 1** and **2.**
5. In the **Home** toolbar, select the **Align Dimension** button and place dimensions as shown in Figure 15-99.
6. After the dimensions have been placed, select the **100′-0″** dimension to bring up the **Options Bar**.

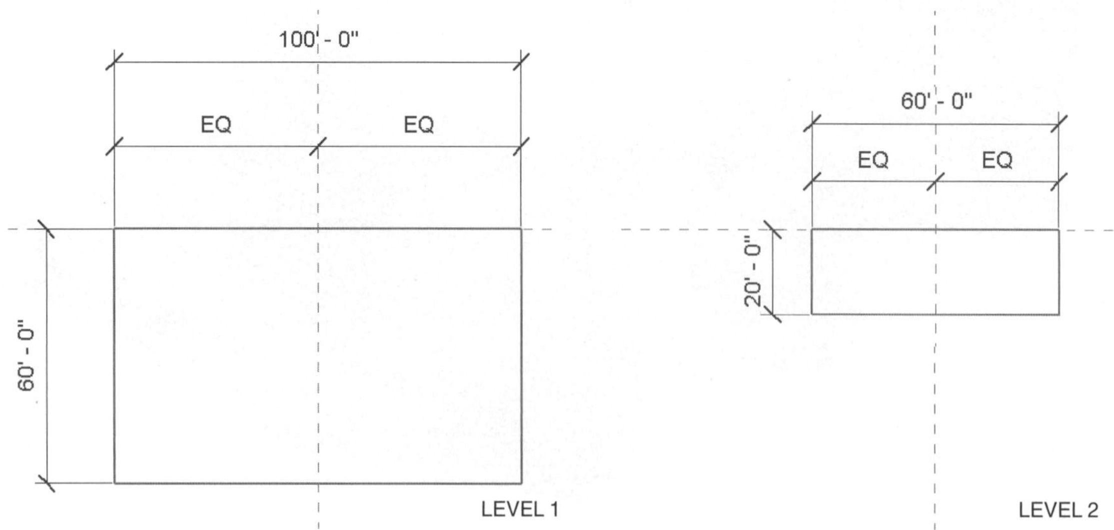

Figure 15-99

Dimension references for this exercise

7. In the **Options Bar**, select the **<Add parameter…>** from the **Label** drop-down list to bring up the **Parameter Properties** dialog box (see Figure 15-100).
8. In the **Parameter Properties** dialog box, enter **WIDTH_1 PROFILE** in the **Name** field and select the **Instance** radio button.
9. Press the **OK** button to return to the **Drawing Editor**.

Notice that the **100′-0″** dimension now reads **WIDTH_1 PROFILE = 100′-0″** (see Figure 15-101).

10. Repeat steps 6 through 8 of this exercise and add **Constraint** parameters to the remaining dimensions on both profiles (see Figure 15-102).
11. Switch to the **Default 3D view**.
12. Select the two profiles to bring up the **Modify | Form** toolbar.

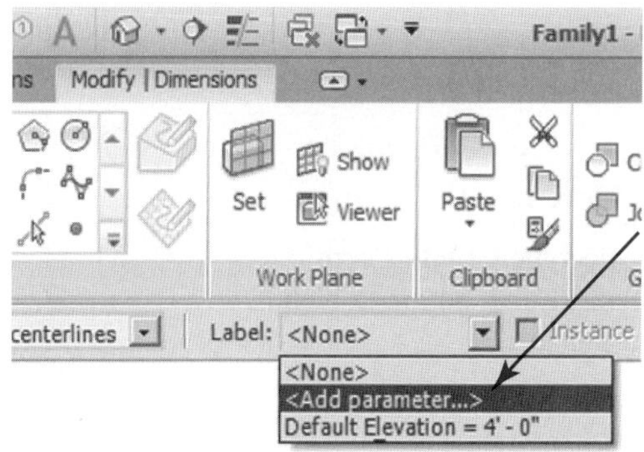

Figure 15-100

Select the **<Add parameter…>** from the **Label** drop-down list

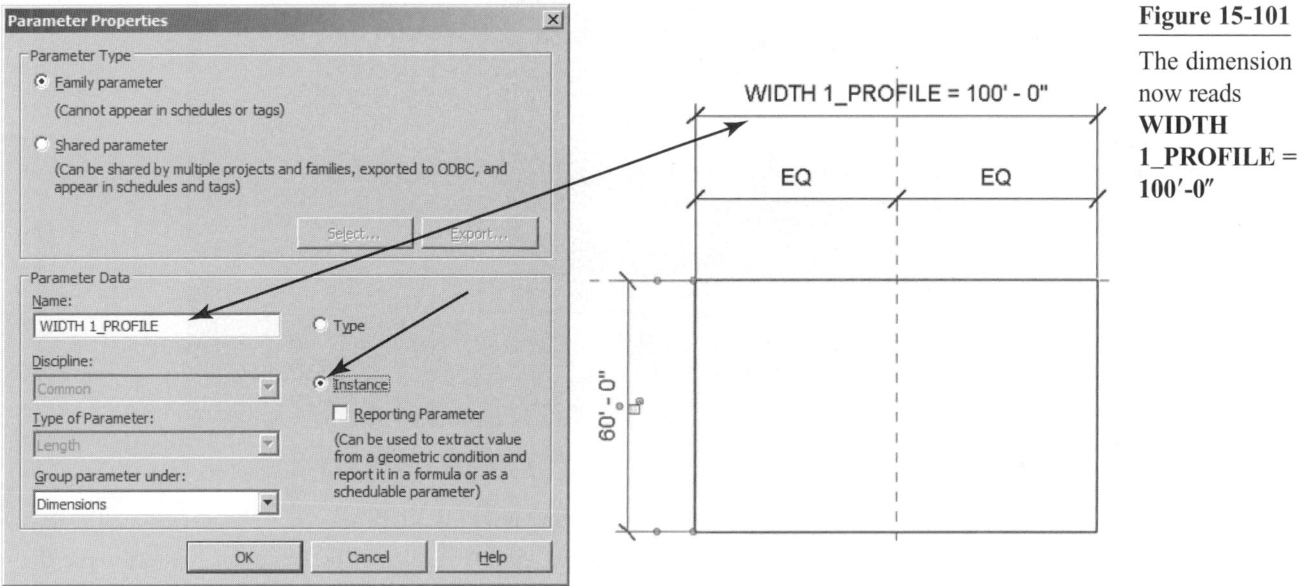

Figure 15-101

The dimension now reads **WIDTH 1_PROFILE = 100′-0″**

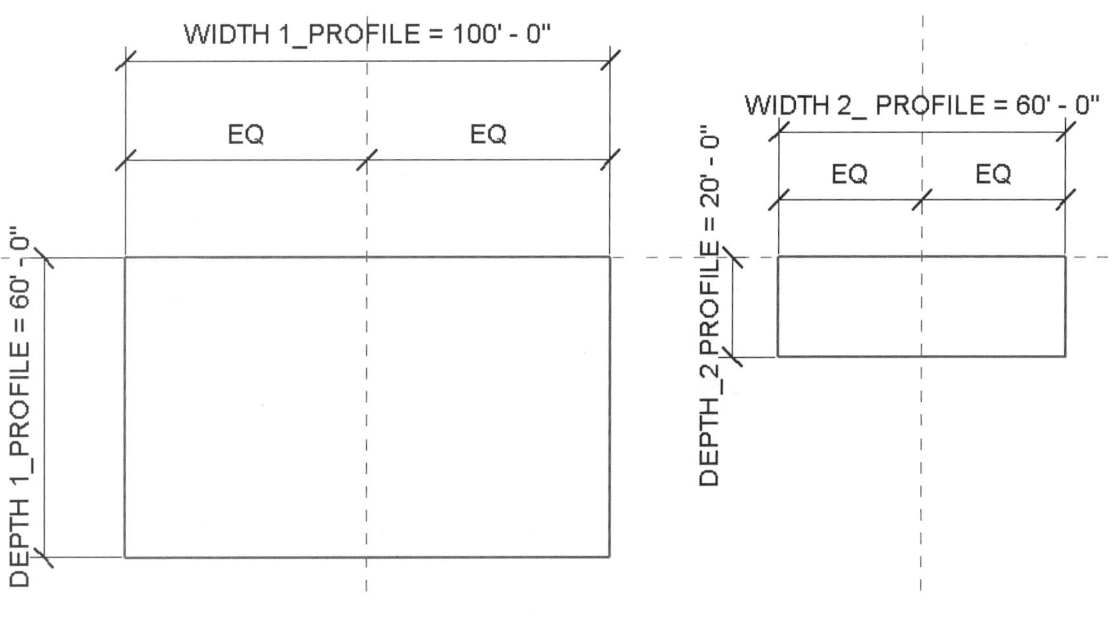

Figure 15-102

Add **Constraint** parameters to the remaining dimensions

13. In the **Modify | Form** toolbar, select the **Create Form > Solid Form** button to blend their shapes (see Figure 15-103).

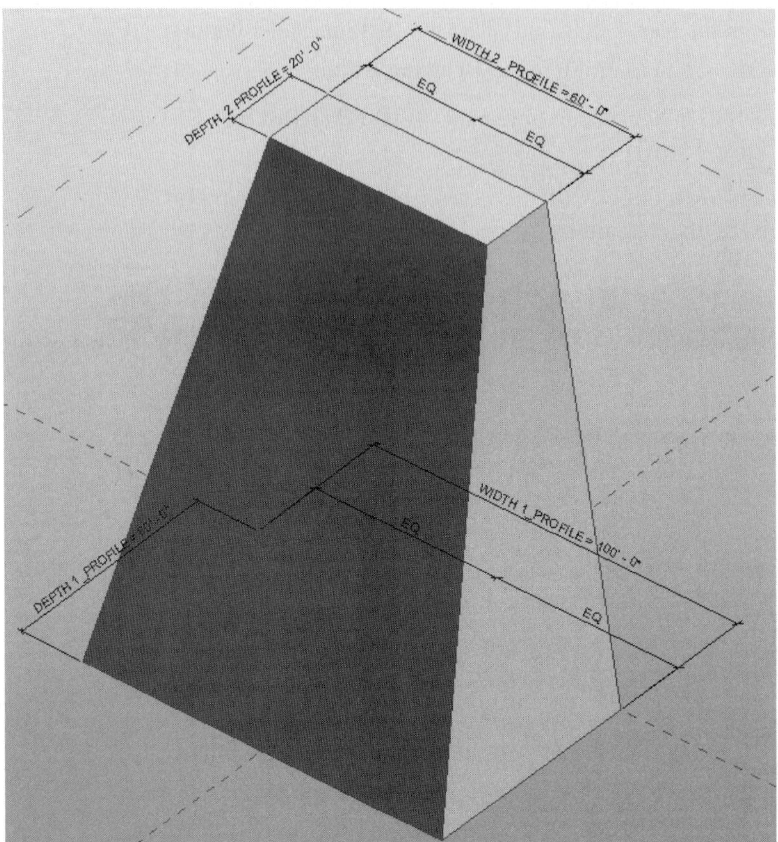

Figure 15-103

Select the **Create Form > Solid Form** button to blend the shapes

14. Change to the **South Elevation** view.
15. Select the **Align** tool from the **Modify** toolbar. You can also choose to type the keyboard shortcut **AL**.
16. Click the **Level 2** grid; hover the cursor on top of the mass. (Its top surface should highlight.)
17. Click it and an **open padlock** appears.
18. Click the top of the padlock to lock the surface to **Level 2**.
19. Press the **<Esc>** key twice to finish the command (see Figure 15-104).

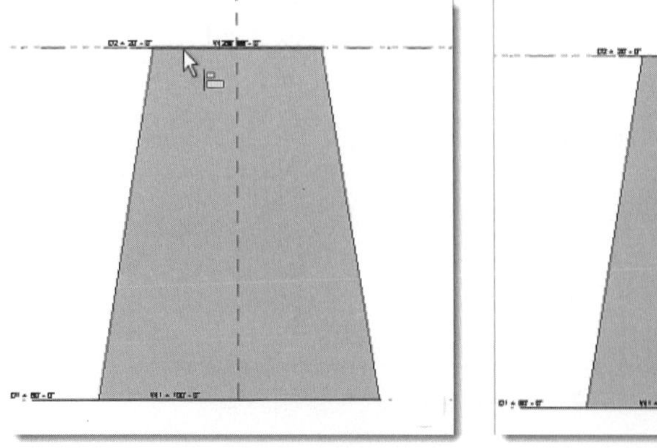
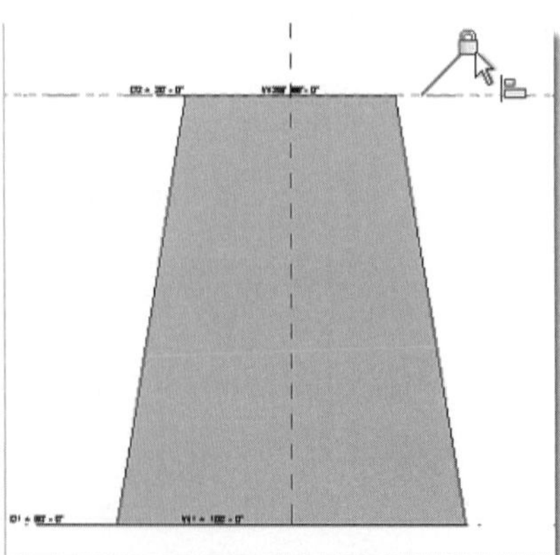

Figure 15-104

The extruded profiles; locking a surface to a level

20. Repeat steps 6 through 8 of this exercise and add a **Constraint** parameter to the height of the **Mass Form**, and name it **MASS HEIGHT**.
21. In the **Home** or **Modify** toolbar, select the **Family Type** button to bring up the **Family Types** dialog box.
22. In the **Family Types** dialog box, you can see all the assigned parameters for the **Mass Form** (see Figure 15-105).

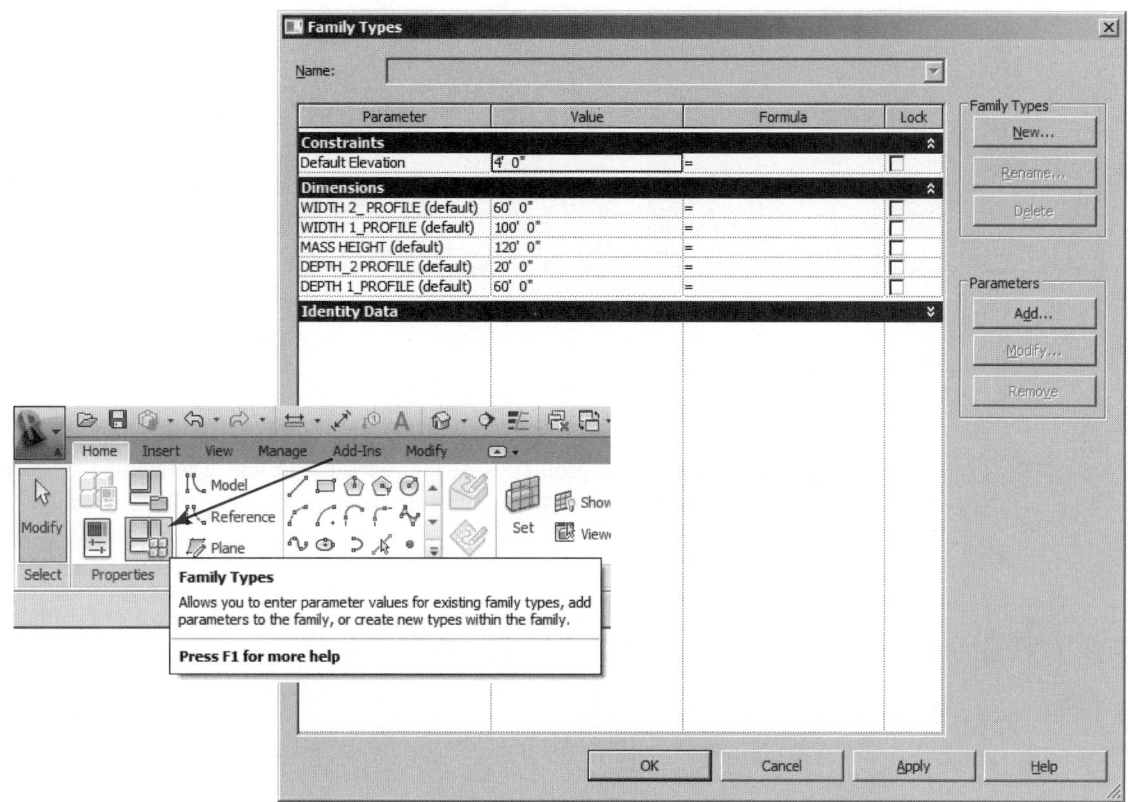

Figure 15-105

Family Types dialog box

23. In the **Family Types** dialog box, change the **MASS HEIGHT** value to **60′-0″** and press the **Apply** button.

Notice that the **Mass** changes height.

24. In the **Family Types** dialog box, change the **WIDTH 2_PROFILE** value to **10′-0″** and press the **Apply** button again.

Notice that the **Mass** again changes. This process is called **flexing** (testing) the parameters (see Figure 15-106).

25. Click **OK,** then press **<Ctrl> Z** twice to set the parameters back to their previous dimensions.
26. Save the file as **ADDING CONSTRAINT PARAMETERS rfa.**

Divided Surface and Patterning

27. Use the **ADDING CONSTRAINT PARAMETERS rfa**.
28. Click the front surface of the **Mass Form** to bring up the **Modify | Form** toolbar.
29. In the **Modify | Form** toolbar, select the **Divide Surface** button.

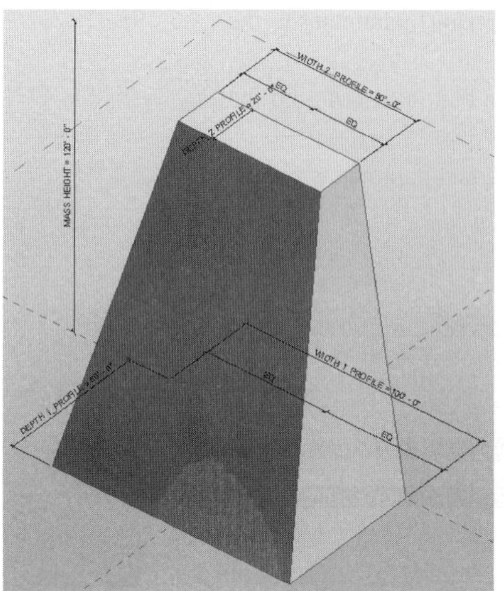

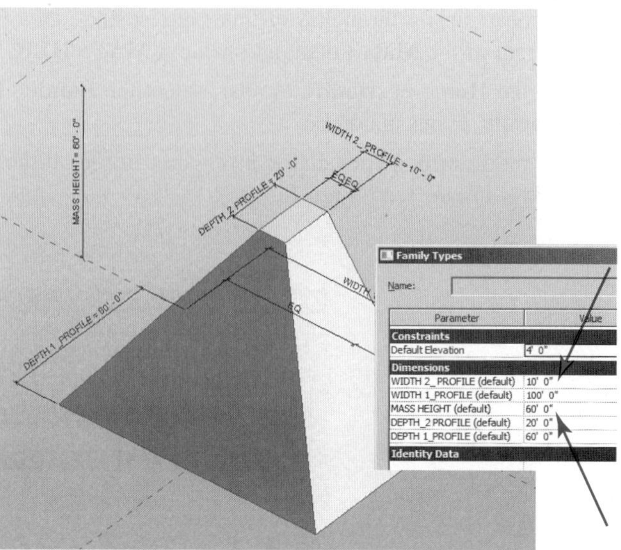

Figure 15-106

Testing (**flexing**) the parameters

30. The surface turns into a default grid pattern. The **Properties** dialog box also changes to reveal the properties of the default grid that was applied. The type selector becomes a **Pattern type selector** showing the name of the current grid as **No Pattern** (see Figure 15-107).

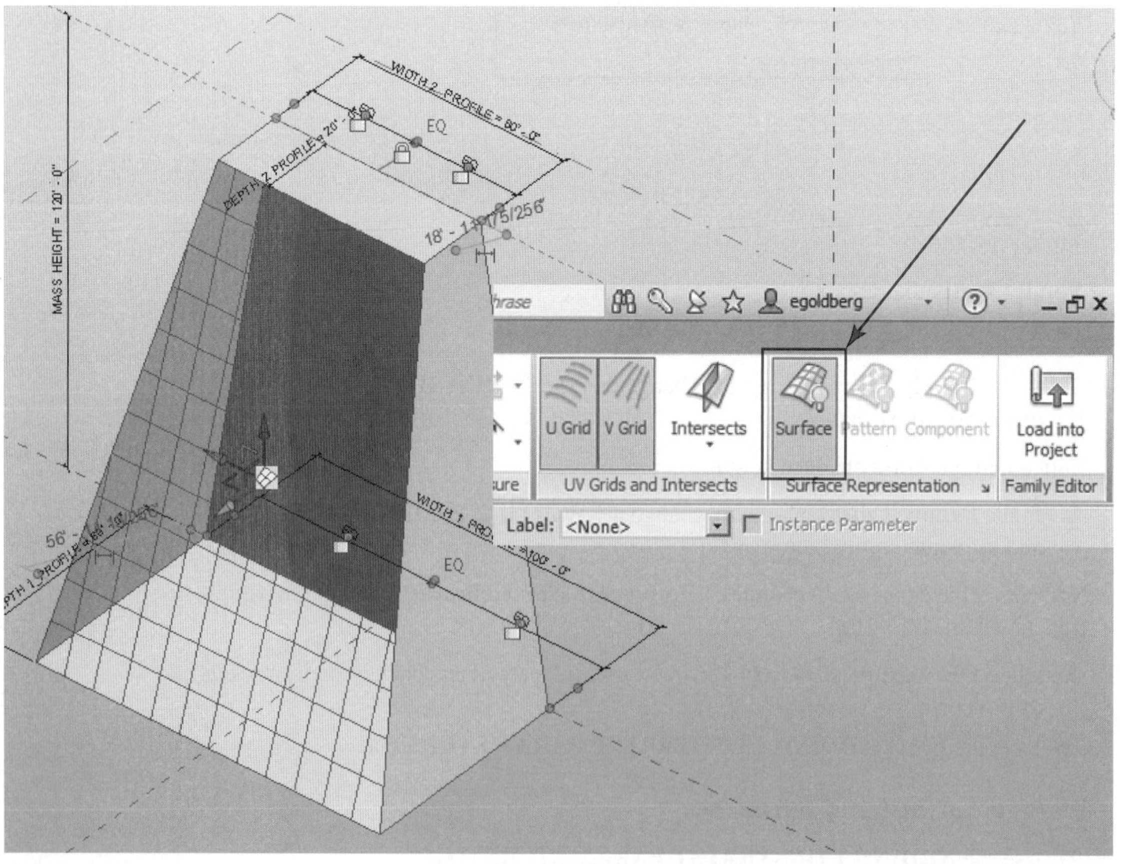

Figure 15-107

The **Divide Surface** button

31. In the **Properties** dialog box, select the **Pattern type selector** and select **Rectangle Checkerboard** from the drop-down list.
32. The surface pattern of the mass updates to this type of pattern (see Figure 15-108).

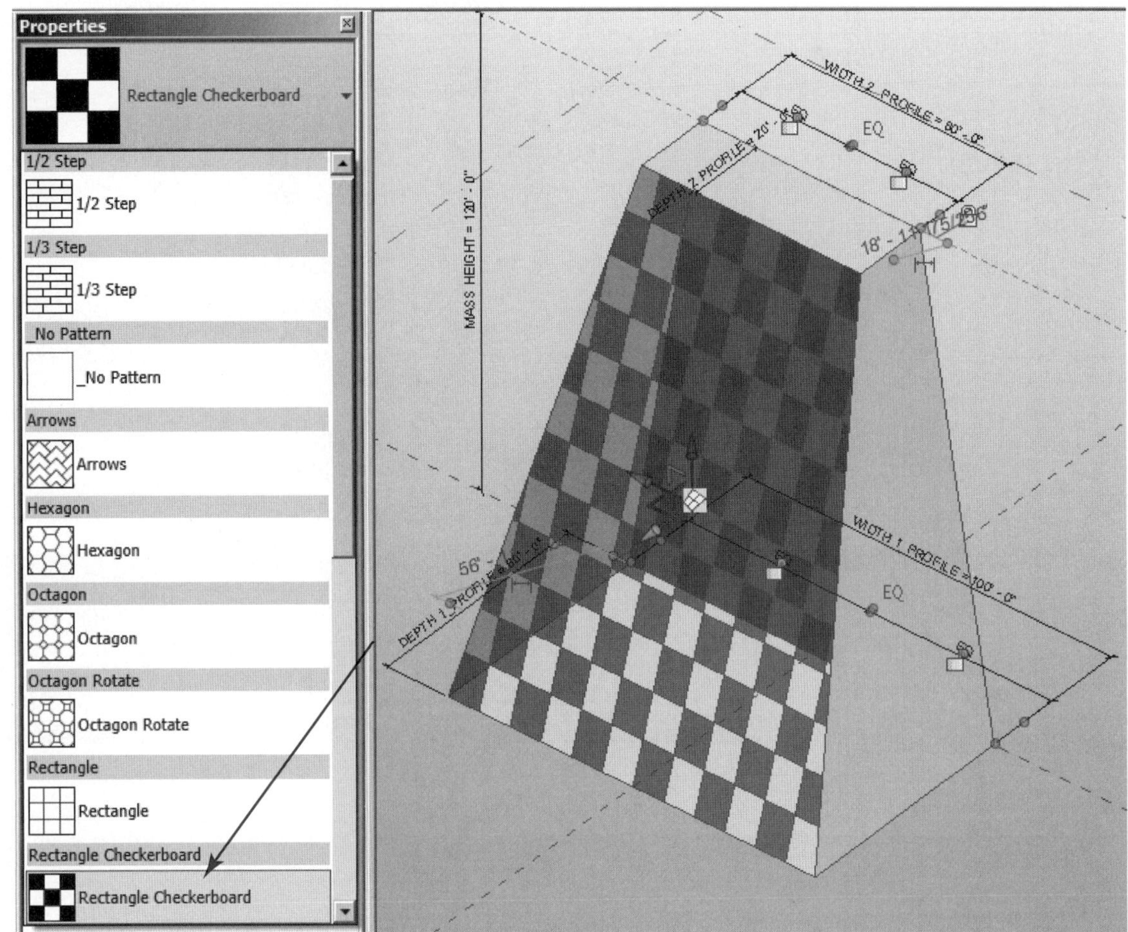

Figure 15-108

Selecting a new surface pattern; the updated surface pattern

33. In the **Properties** dialog box, you can change the number of **U** and **V** grids. You can also change them from the **Options Bar**.
34. While the surface is still selected, go to the **Options Bar** and change the **U Grid** number to **4**. Leave the **V Grid** number as **12**, then move the cursor inside the drawing area. The spacing of the **Rectangle Checkerboard** pattern will update (see Figure 15-109).

> **NOTE:**
> Instead of the XY coordinate system, a surface pattern uses a UV coordinate system. This serves as a guide in creating patterns on a surface. In the conceptual design environment, UV grids are comparable to XY grids.

35. Save the file as **MY DIVIDED SURFACE.rfa**, but leave it open.

Creating the 3D Model Representations of the Frames with Glass

36. From the **Applications** drop-down menu, select the **New > Family** button to bring up the **New Family - Select Template File** dialog box.
37. In the **New Family - Select Template File** dialog box, double-click **Curtain Panel Pattern Based.rft** (see Figure 15-110).

Figure 15-109

Changing the **U Grid** value; the updated surface pattern

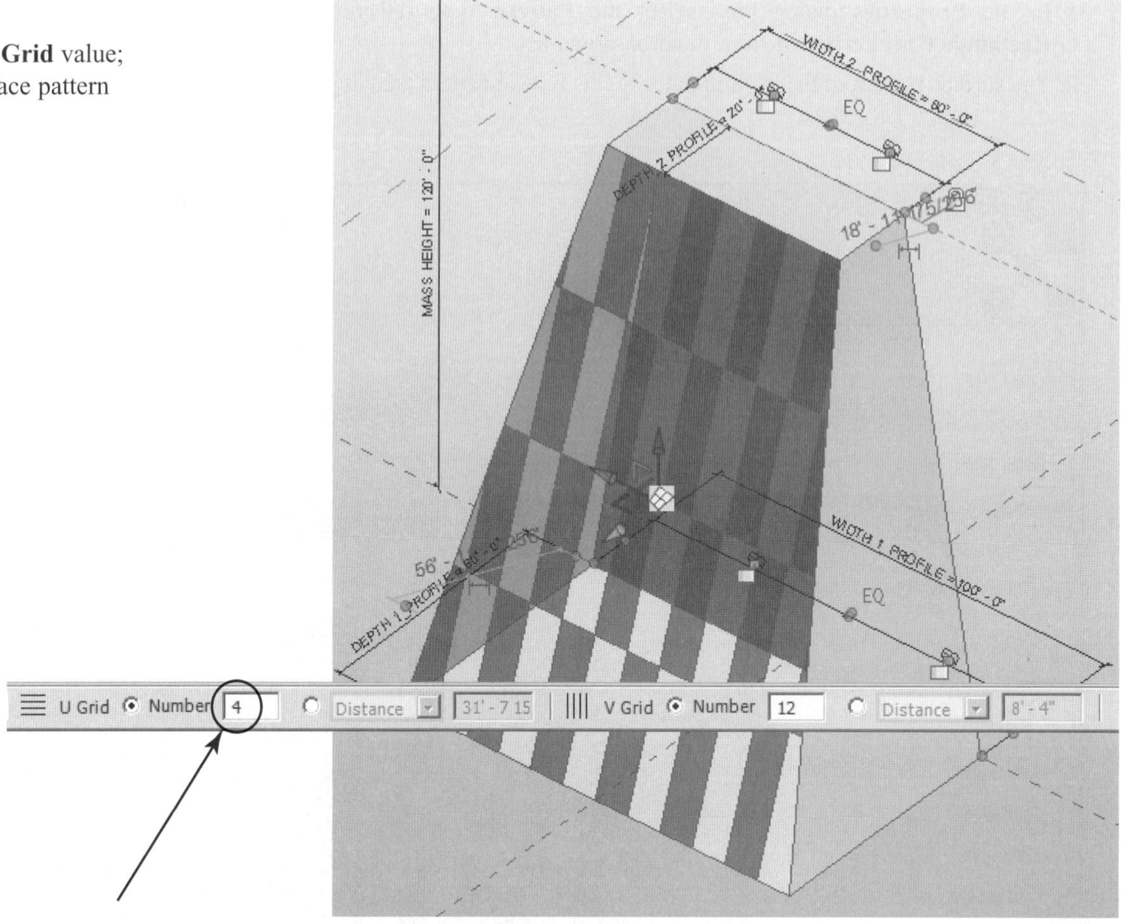

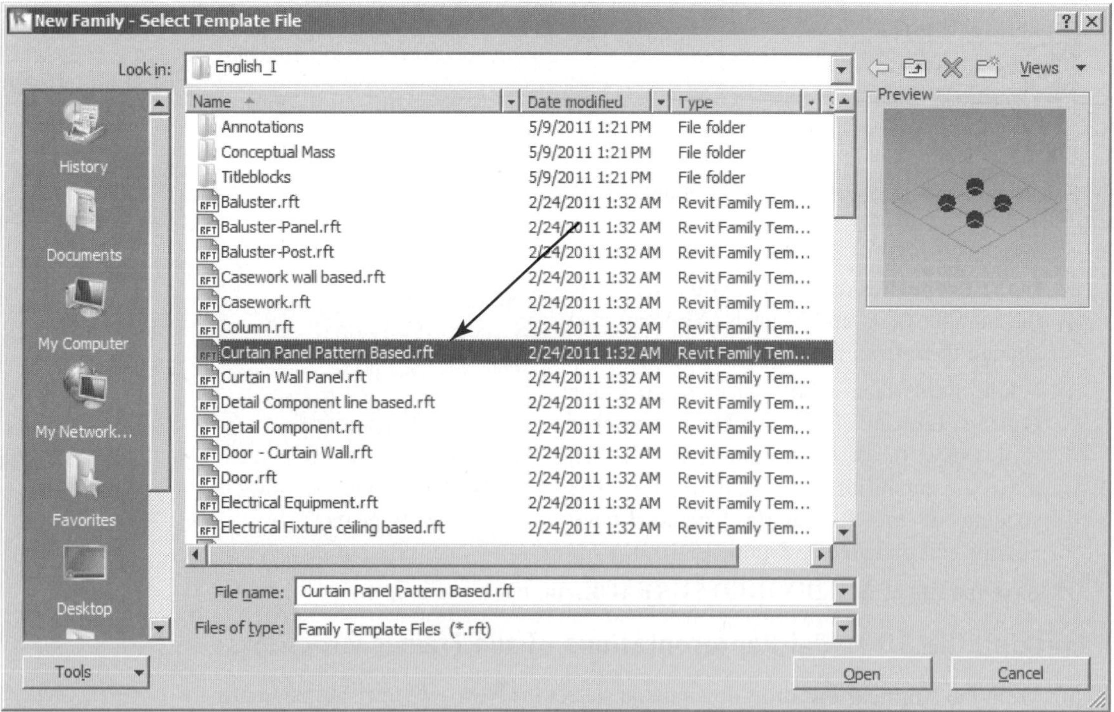

Figure 15-110

The **New Family - Select Template File** dialog box

38. This opens a template with a default grid framework containing the reference lines that make up the pattern.
39. Select the blue grid; the **Properties** dialog box changes to the properties of a **Rectangle** pattern (see Figure 15-111).
40. Click the **Pattern type selector** drop-down list and select **Rectangle Checkerboard**; the image now updates to the grid and reference lines framework of a **Rectangle Checkerboard** pattern.

NOTE:
The pattern in the 3D view didn't seem to change because the **Rectangle** and the **Rectangle Checkerboard** framework basically look the same. The only indicator that the type has been changed is through the name in the **Pattern type selector.**

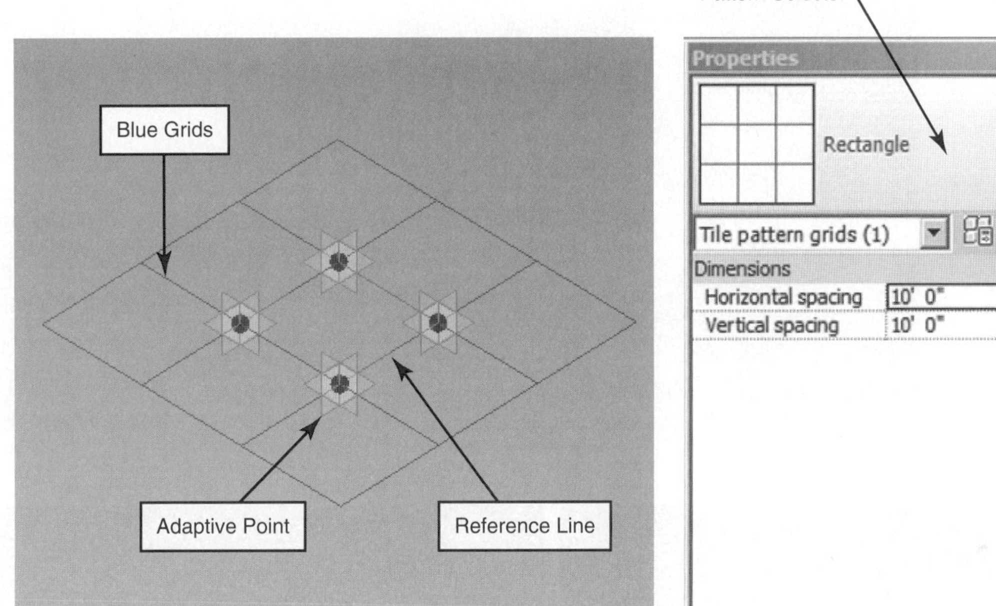

Figure 15-111
The **Curtain Panel Pattern Based Default 3D view** and the corresponding **Properties** dialog box

41. Select the **Point Element** tool from the **Draw** panel and place a **Reference** point in the middle of the top left reference line.
42. With the **Reference** point selected, in the **Modify** toolbar, select the **Workplane Viewer** button to bring up the **Workplane Viewer**.
43. In the **Workplane Viewer**, using the **Circumscribed Polygon** tool, draw a 4-sided polygon with a radius of **6″** (see Figure 15-112).
44. Hold down the **<Ctrl>** key and select the **profile** and the **square path.**
45. Select the **Create Form** > **Solid Form** button to create the **Frame** form (see Figure 15-113).

Next, create the glass inside the frame by using the edges of the frame to create a surface.

46. In the **View Control Bar**, change the **Visual Style** to **Wireframe**.
47. Select the bottom inside edge of the frame to select that edge.
48. Hold down the **<Ctrl>** key and select the other inside edges.

NOTE:
You will have to rotate the view of the frame to select the other edges.

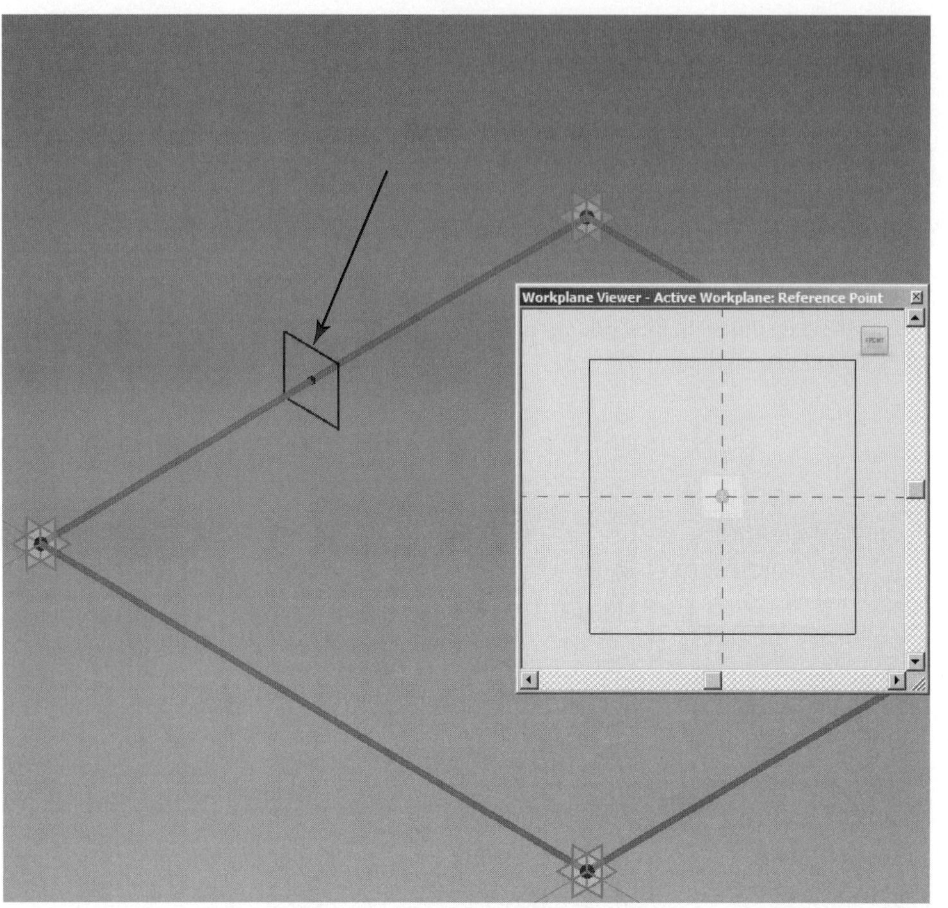

Figure 15-112

Creating a profile with the **Circumscribed Polygon** tool

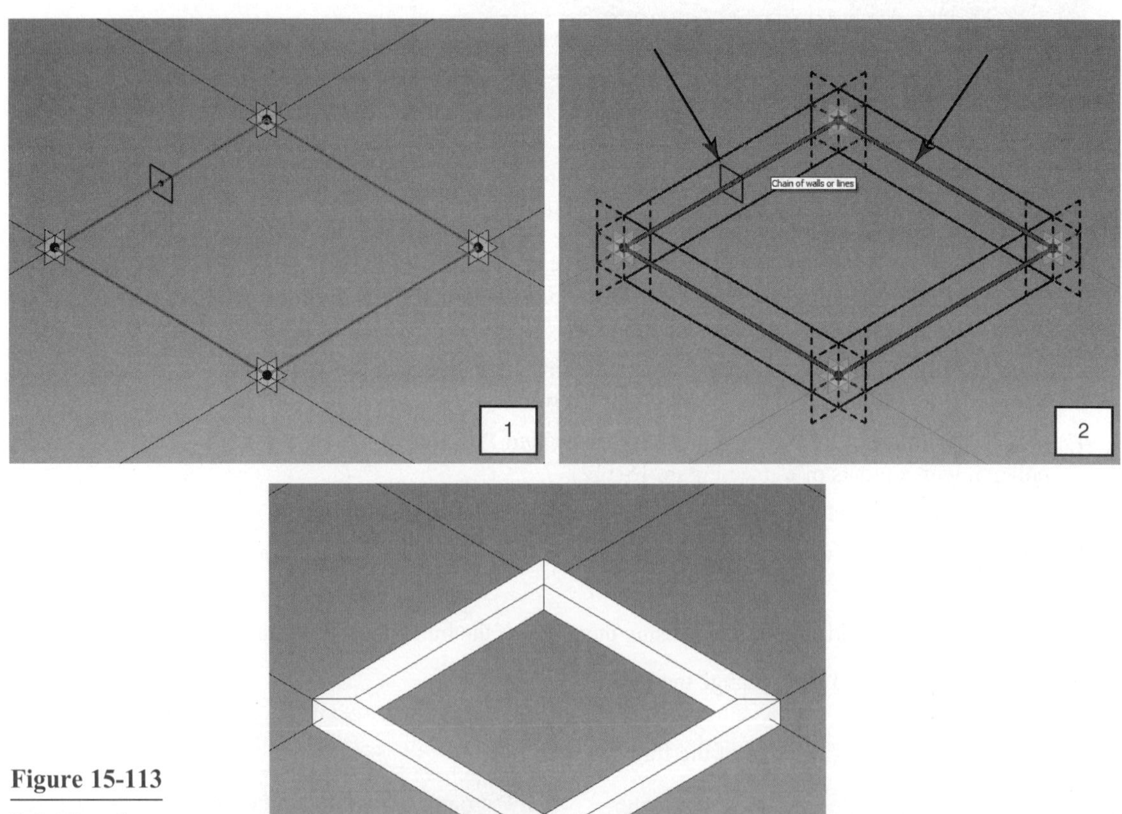

Figure 15-113

Selecting the square profile and square path

49. In the **Modify | Form Element** toolbar, select the **Create Form > Solid Form** button.
50. Select the **Flat Form** in the **Intent Stack** to create the glass pane with *no* thickness (see Figure 15-114).
51. Select the top of the **Flat Form** just created.
52. In the **Properties** dialog box, under **Materials and Finishes** and right beside the **Material** column, click the inner right edge of the text field.

NOTE:

The left frame of the **Intent Stack** could have been chosen, thereby creating a mass with a thickness on it.

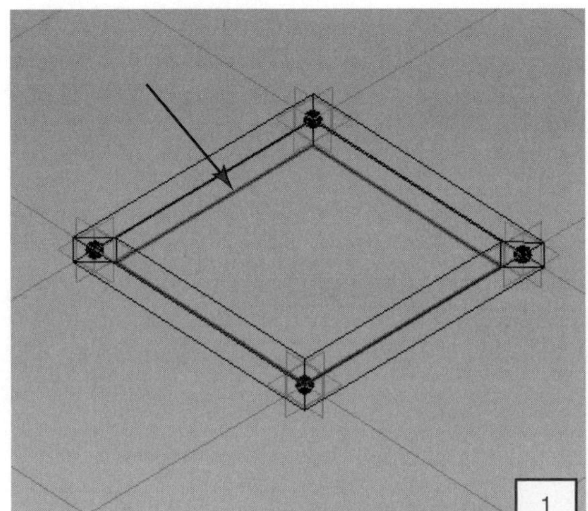

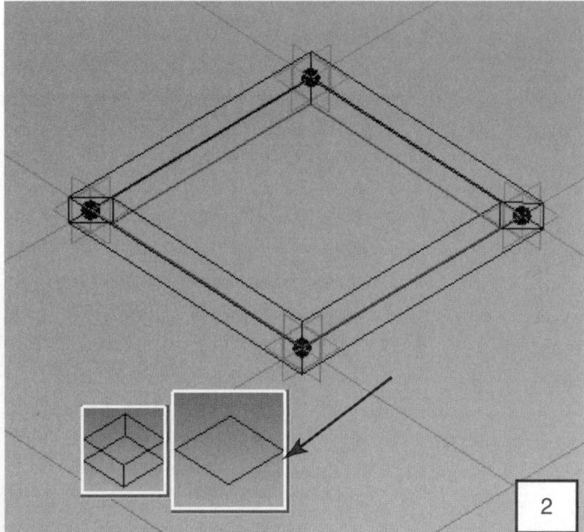

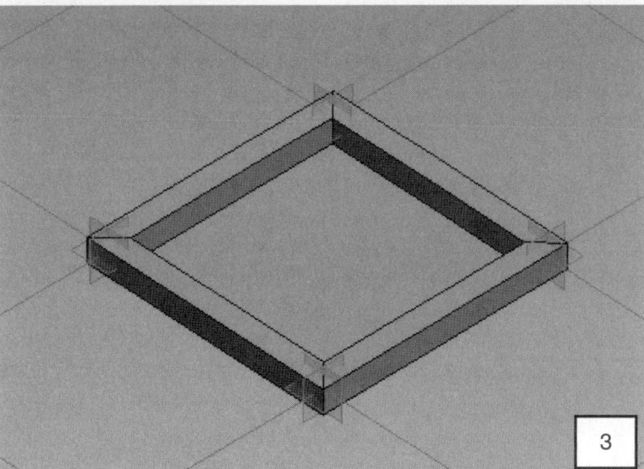

Figure 15-114

Creating the glass pane

53. This brings up the **Materials - Default** dialog box.
54. In the **Materials - Default** dialog box, select **Glass** from the **Materials** list and click the **OK** button to assign a glass material to the surface form inside the frame (see Figures 15-115 and 15-116).
55. Press the **<Esc>** key.
56. Save the file as **RECTANGLE CHECKERBOARD FRAME.rfa**.

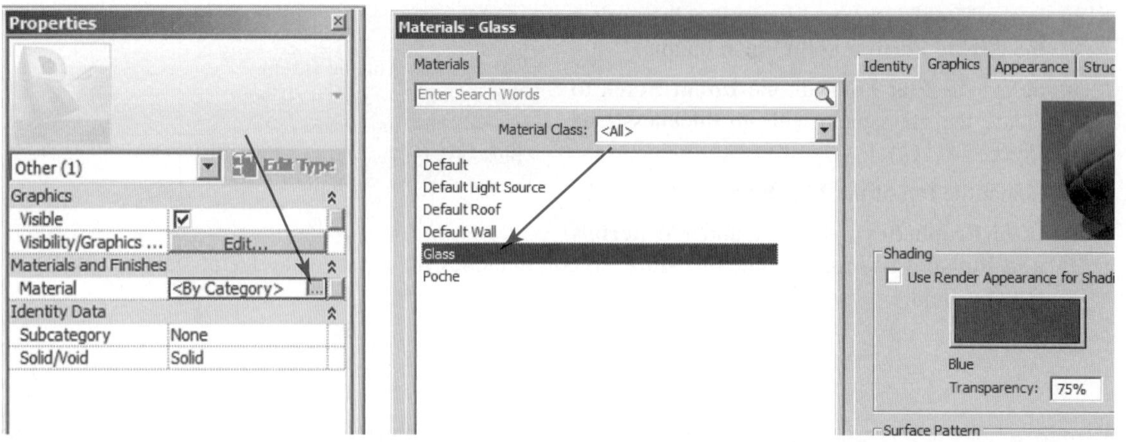

Figure 15-115

Selecting the mass and applying a **Glass** material to it

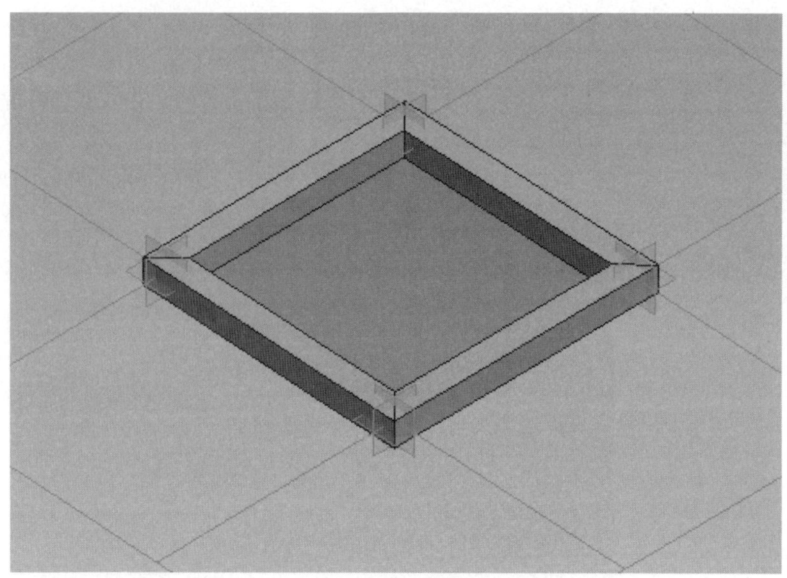

Figure 15-116

Frame and **Glass** panel

Loading the Frames into the Mass Model

57. In the **Home** toolbar**,** select the **Load into Project** button to bring up the **Load into Projects** dialog box.

This loads the **Rectangle Checkerboard Frame** family inside the parametric mass form **(MY DIVIDED SURFACE).** Make sure that you are in the **Default 3D view**. Notice that the front surface of the mass form didn't change. That is because the family was added to the drop-down list of the **Pattern selector.** *You still must select it* and apply it to the **Mass.**

58. Select the front surface of the mass. Click the **Pattern type selector** and scroll down to select the **Rectangle Checkerboard Frame**.

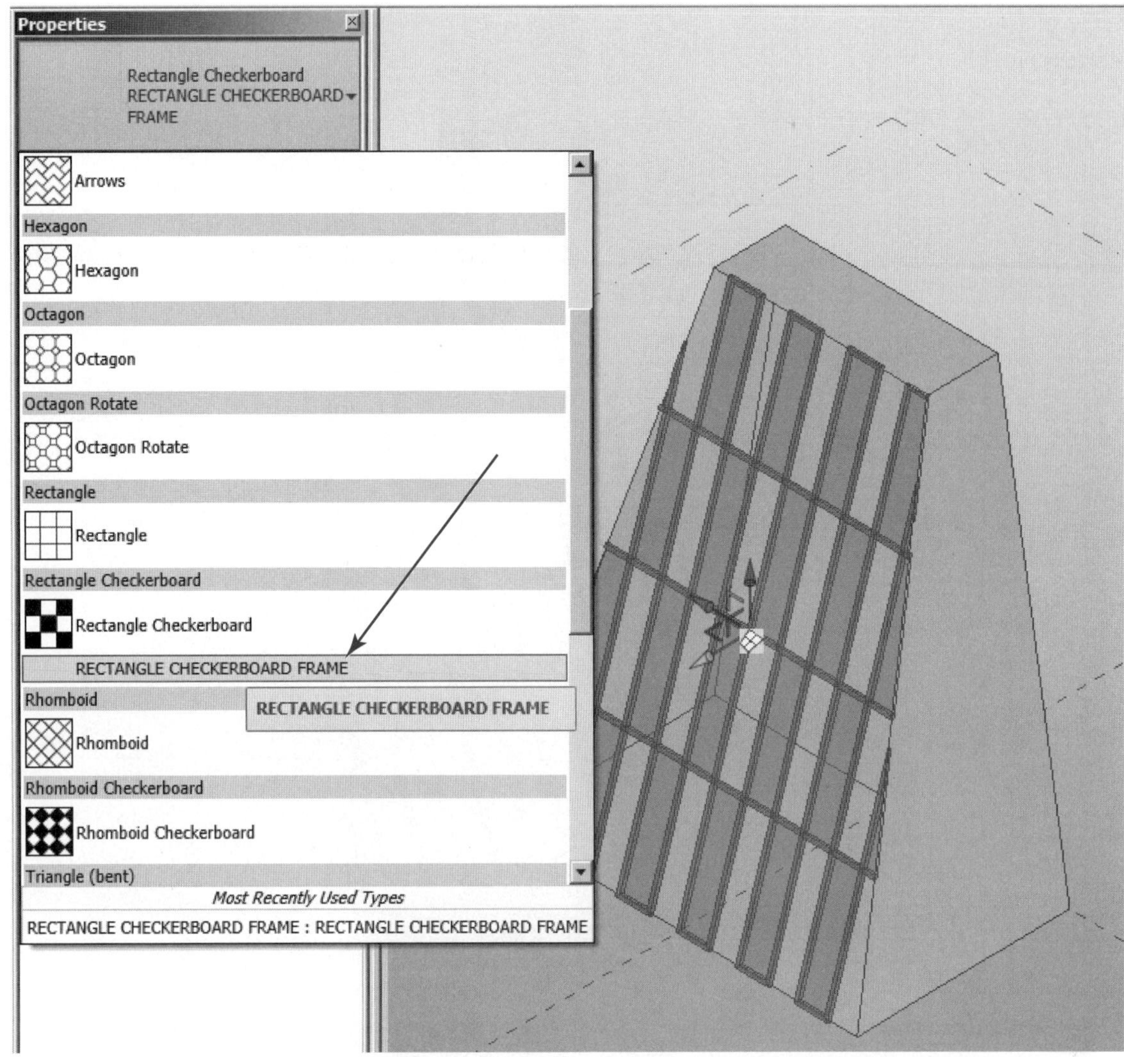

Figure 15-117

Loading the new **Curtain Panel Pattern Based** family

59. The **Mass** form now updates to show a curtain wall system with mullions (see Figure 15-117).
60. Zoom in close, and notice that the curtain wall lacks an overall frame (see Figure 15-118).

Creating the Exterior Frame with an Adaptive Component Family

This is where you can use the family. You can create a mullion to frame the entire curtain wall system, which will adjust if the values of the mass form parameters are changed. Here is how it is done:

61. From the **Application** drop-down menu, select **New > Family** to bring up the **New Family - Select Template File** dialog box.
62. In the **New Family - Select Template File** dialog box, double-click the **Generic Model Adaptive.rft** to bring it into the **Drawing Editor** (see Figure 15-119).

Notice that the configuration of the **Default 3D view** of this template is similar to the conceptual mass family. The difference is the color of the reference planes. In the **Generic Model Adaptive** family, the color of the two dashed intersecting reference planes is green.

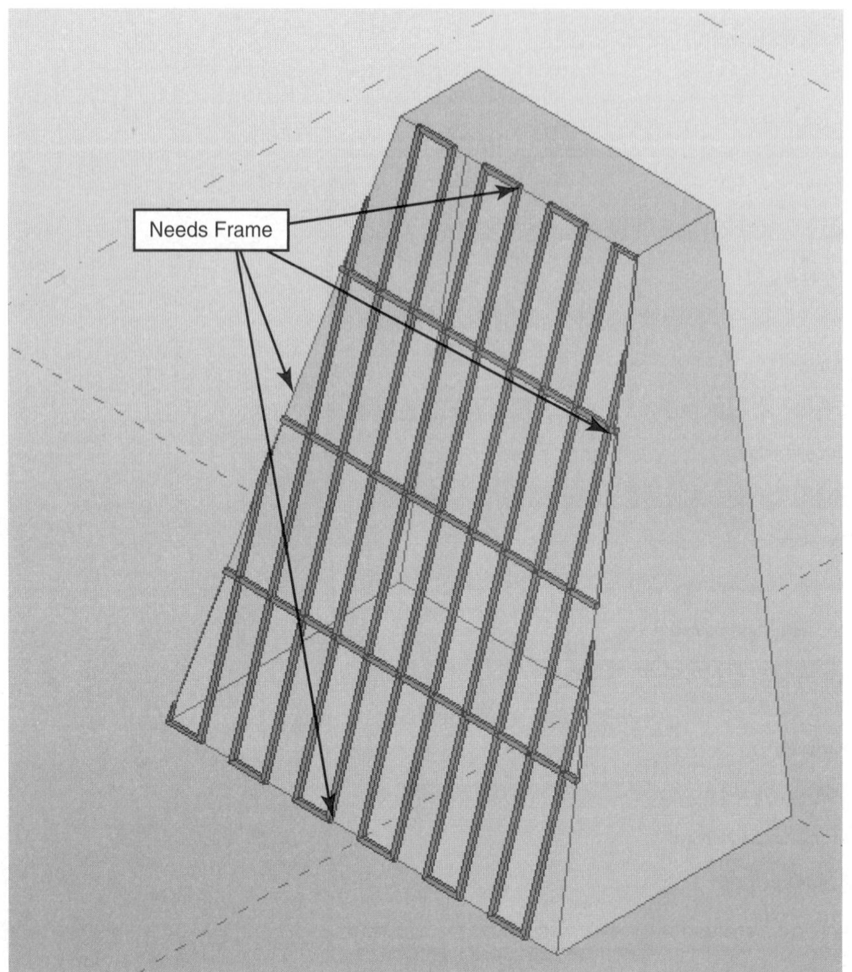

Figure 15-118

The curtain wall lacks an overall frame

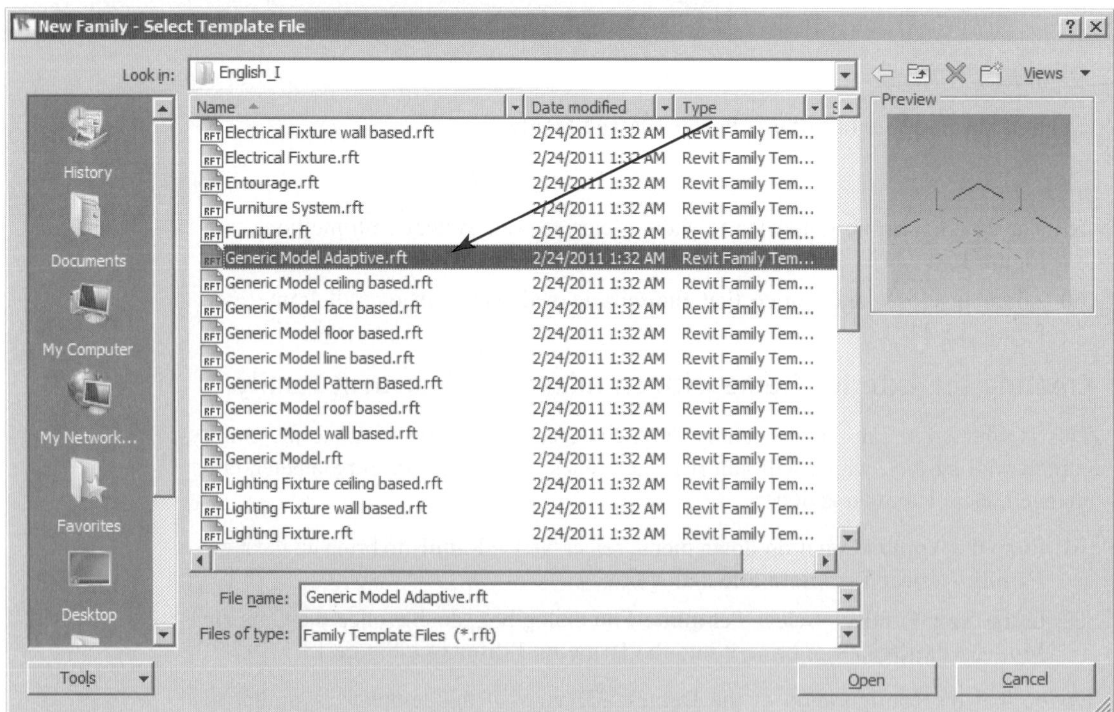

Figure 15-119

Double-click the **Generic Model Adaptive.rft**

63. In the **Home** toolbar, select the **Point Element** button in the **Draw** panel.
64. Place four **Point Elements** on the reference level in consecutive order; the exact locations of the points are not important.
65. Press the **<Esc>** key to complete the command.
66. Select all the points that were placed to bring up the **Modify | Reference Points** toolbar.
67. In the **Modify | Reference Points** toolbar, select the **Make Adaptive** button (see Figure 15-120).

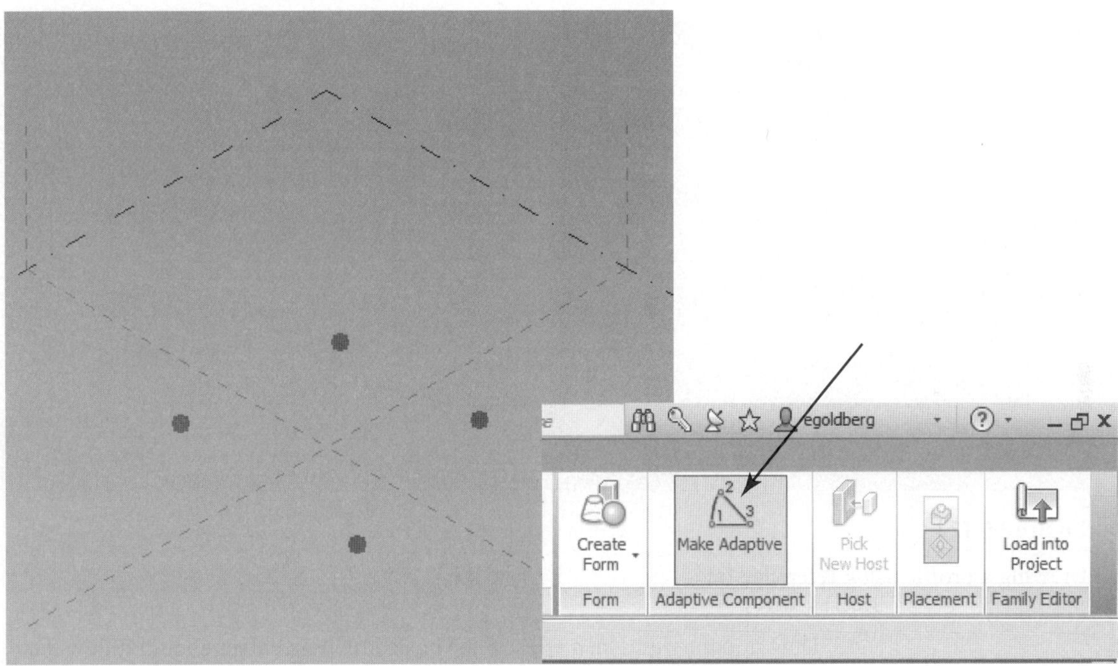

Figure 15-120

Select the **Make Adaptive** button

Notice that after the points are converted to **Adaptive** points, they each appear with three planar surfaces (X, Y, and Z) and a number on top. The number signifies the order in which they were placed (see Figure 15-121).

68. Press the **<Esc>** key to deselect the points.
69. In the **Home** toolbar, select the **Reference Line** button in the **Draw** panel.
70. In the **Options Bar**, put a check mark in the **3D Snapping** box.
71. The cursor will appear as a **black dot**.

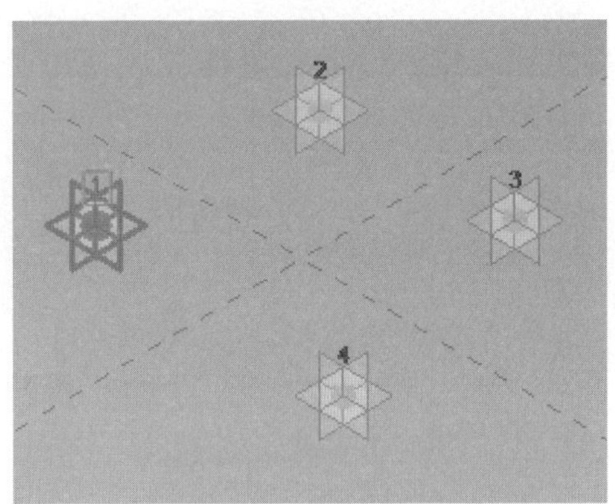

Figure 15-121

Point Elements converted to **Adaptive** points

72. Starting at the number **1** reference point and moving clockwise, connect all the points by clicking the cursor on top of each reference point. The cursor should snap to the points (see Figure 15-122).
73. Press the **<Esc>** key twice to end the command.
74. Zoom in and hover over the **3rd** point.
75. Press the <**Tab**> key until the **Reference** point is selected.

> **NOTE:**
> When a reference line connects to an adaptive point, its end vertex becomes hosted to that point. This means that when the adaptive point is moved, the reference lines connected to it will follow. Test to see if this works.

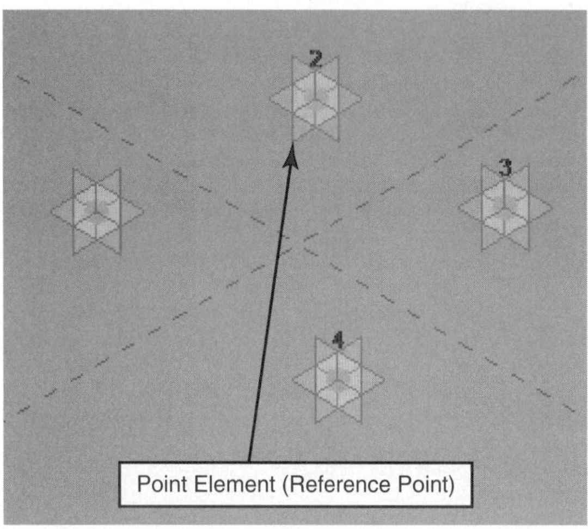

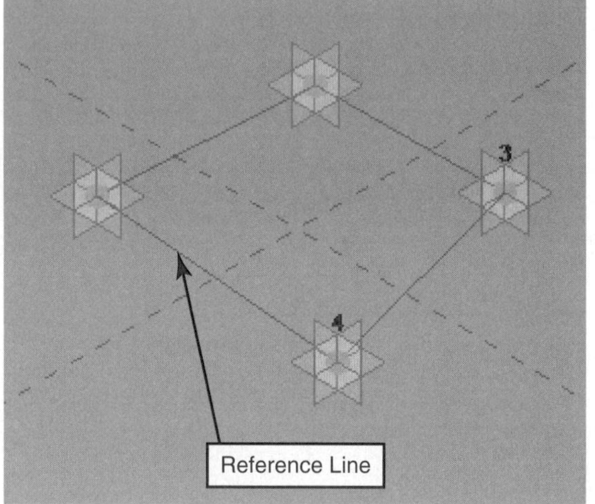

Figure 15-122

Drawing a profile using reference lines

76. Drag it to the right, then release; the hosted reference lines should follow the relocated point (see Figure 15-123).
77. Select the **Point Element** tool from the **Draw** panel and place a **Reference** point in the middle of the right reference line.
78. With the **Reference** point selected, in the **Modify** toolbar, select the **Workplane Viewer** button to bring up the **Workplane Viewer**.
79. In the **Workplane Viewer**, using the **Circumscribed Polygon** tool, draw a 4-sided polygon with a radius of **6″**.
80. Press the **<Esc>** key twice.
81. Hold down the **<Ctrl>** key, then select both the profile and the path.

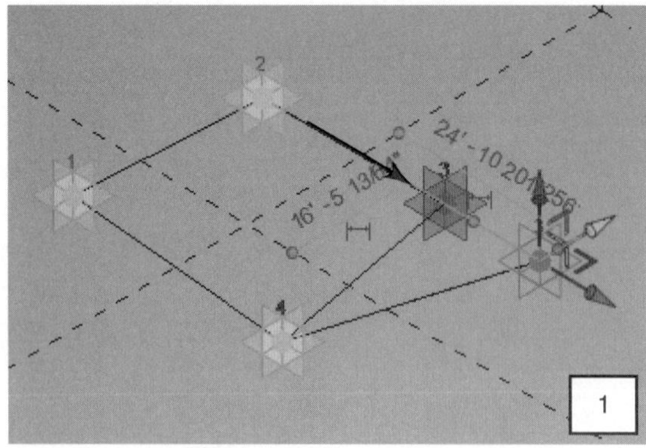

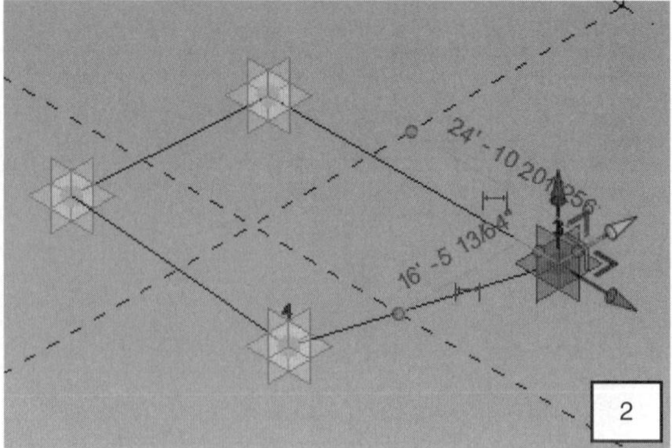

Figure 15-123

Moving an **Adaptive** point

82. In the **Modify | Form Element** toolbar, select the **Create Form > Solid Form** button to create the **Adaptive Component** family (see Figure 15-124).

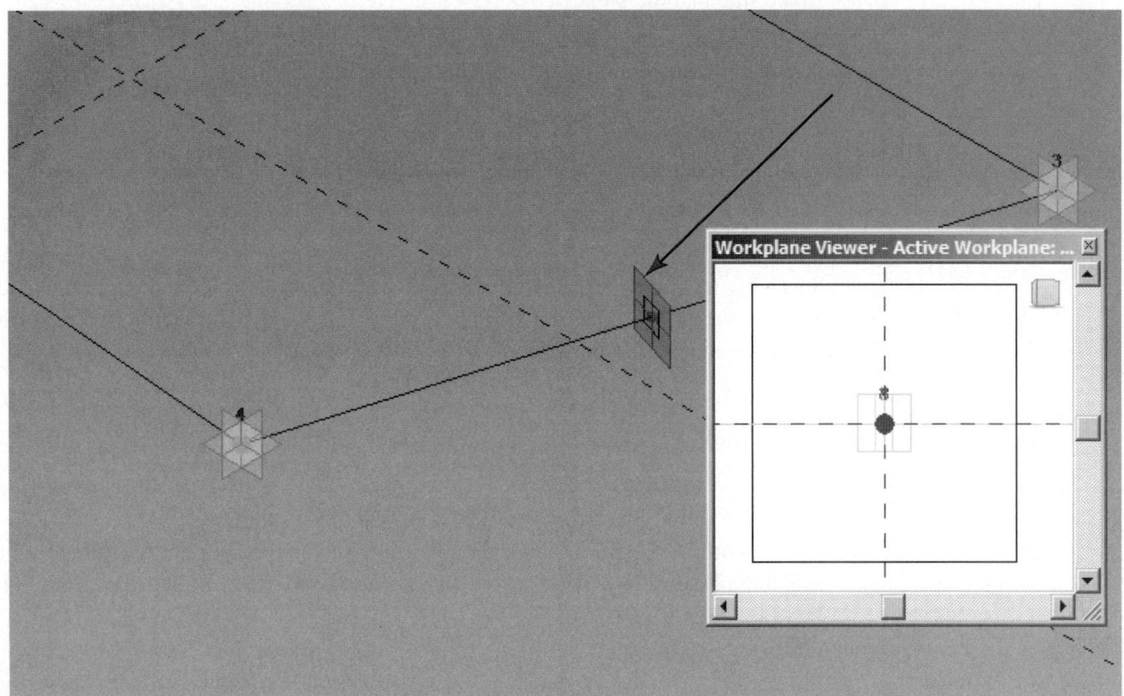

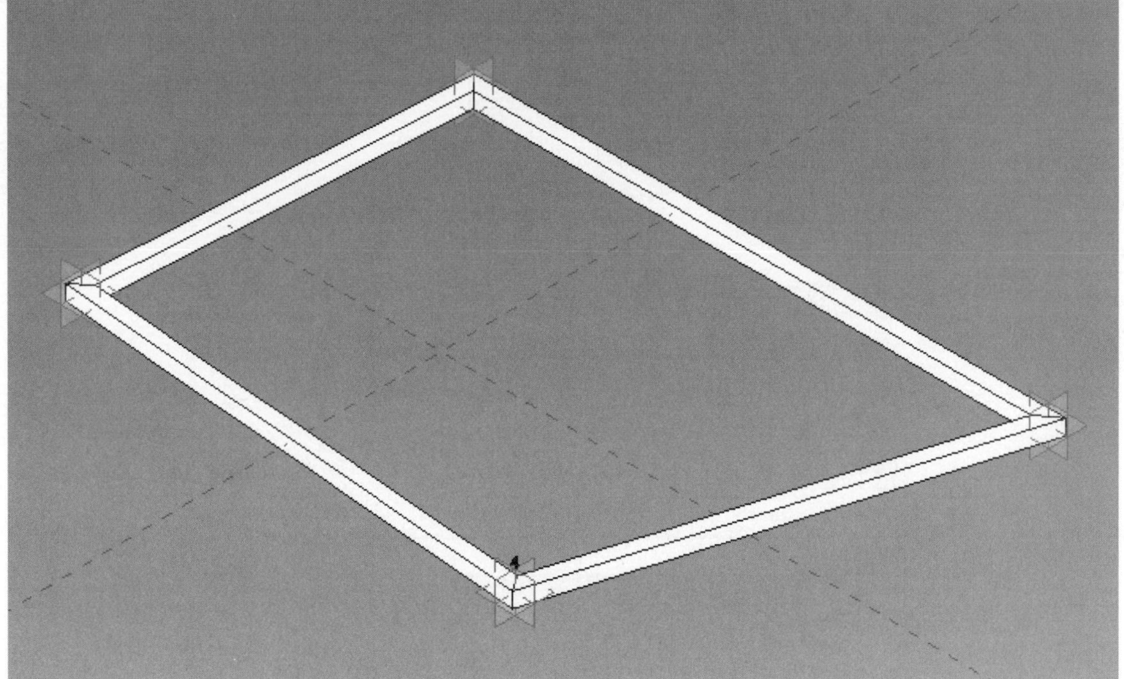

Figure 15-124

Extruding the profile and the path

83. Save the family as **EXTERIOR ADAPTIVE FRAME**.

Placing the Adaptive Frame

84. In the **Home** Toolbar, select the **Load into Project** button to bring up the **Load into Projects** dialog box.

85. In the **Load into Projects** dialog box, check the **MY DIVIDED SURFACE.rfa** check box.
86. Make sure that the **Default 3D view** is active.
87. Notice that a semi-transparent image of the **Adaptive Component** family is attached to the cursor; the **Adaptive** component is now ready for placement.

> **NOTE:**
> If the **MY DIVIDED SURFACE.rfa** does not appear in the **Load into Projects** dialog box, open that file and repeat step 85.

88. For now, press the <**Esc**> key to **deselect** the family.

Points of the **Frame** family are now going to be placed on the four corners of the **Mass** form. In certain situations, however, some components might obstruct your view when you are trying to place an **Adaptive** component. Changing the display temporarily will help to locate the placement points. This is done through the **Surface Representation** panel of the contextual menu.

89. Select the front surface pattern to bring up the **Modify | Divided Surface** toolbar.
90. In the **Modify | Divided Surface** toolbar, deselect the **Component** by clicking on top of it.
91. Next, select the **Surface** and **Pattern** buttons (see Figure 15-125).
92. In the **Modify | Divided Surface** toolbar, below the **Surface** and **Pattern** buttons, select the **Dialog Launcher** arrow to bring up the **Surface Representation** dialog box (see Figure 15-126).

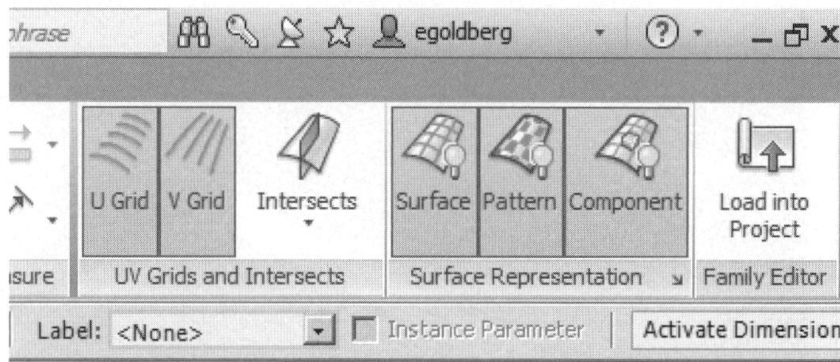

Figure 15-125

The **Surface** and **Pattern** buttons

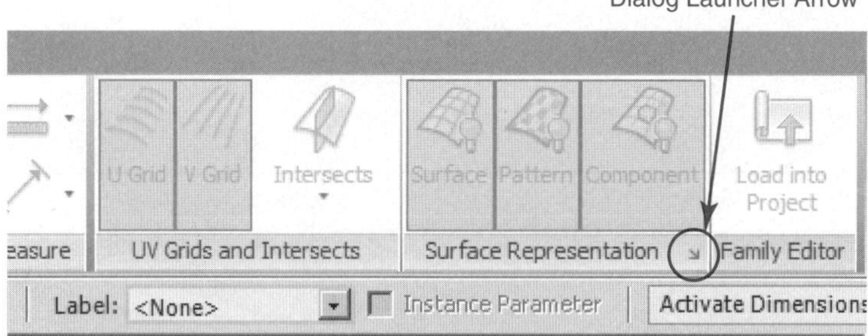

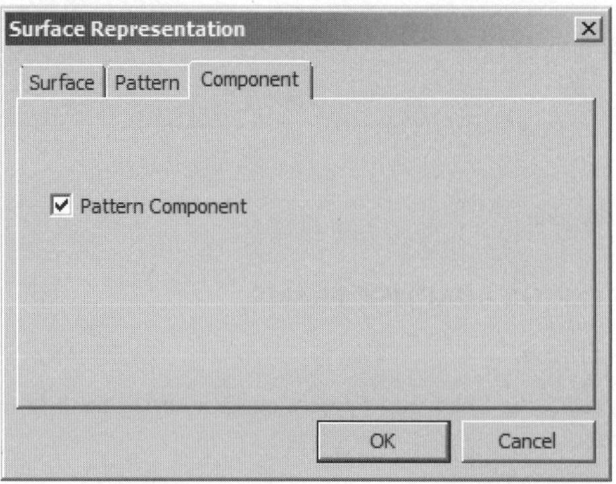

Figure 15-126

Loading an **Adaptive Component**; the **Surface Representation** panel

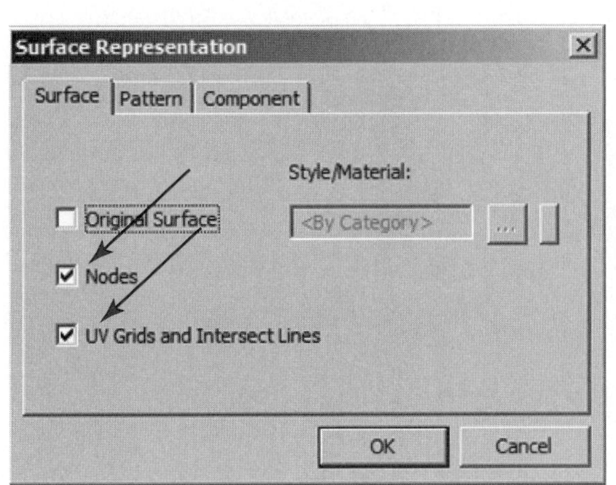

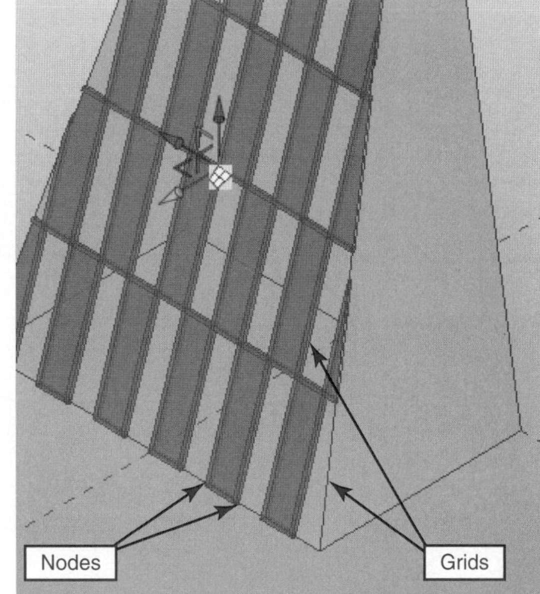

Figure 15-127

The **Surface Representation** dialog box

93. In the **Surface Representation** dialog box, select the **Surface** tab.
94. In the **Surface** tab, check the **Nodes** and **UV Grids and Intersect Lines** check boxes.
95. Click **OK**, and the surface pattern will display just the grids and nodes (see Figure 15-127).

> **NOTE:**
> When the **Frame** family was initially loaded, it automatically attached to the cursor for placement. However, when the family is deselected, the only way to load it back is to drag it from the **Project Browser.**

96. In the **Project Browser,** locate and expand the **Families** category.
97. In the **Families** category, expand the **Generic Models** category to locate the **Frame** family.
98. Drag the **Frame** family into the **Drawing Editor.** When the mouse is released, the **Frame** family will be attached to the cursor.
99. Click one corner, then click the rest of the corners in consecutive order; the image of the adaptive component will follow the mouse like a rubber band (see Figures 15-128 and 15-129).

> **NOTE:**
> It doesn't matter at which corner one starts as long as the points are clicked in consecutive order. When the snap indicator (little circle) appears, that means the cursor is on top of a node or vertex.

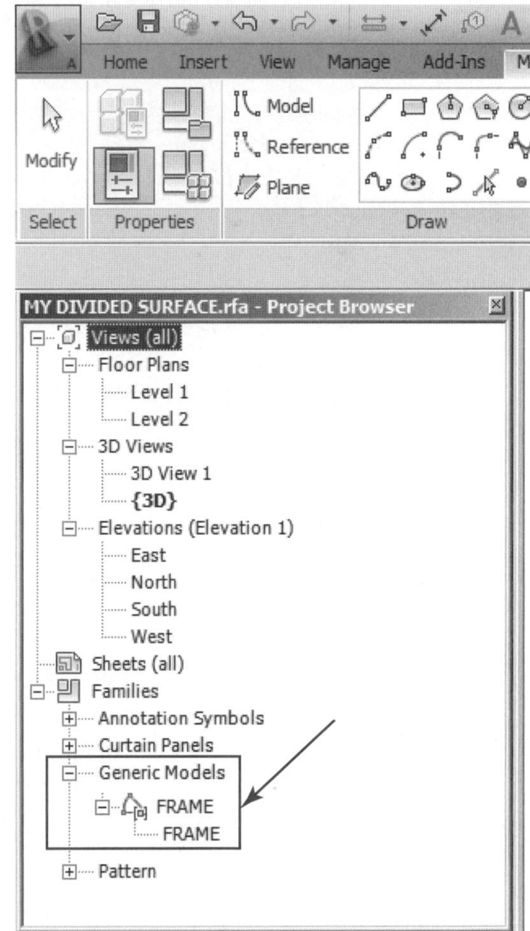

Figure 15-128

Loading an **Adaptive Component** from the **Project Browser**

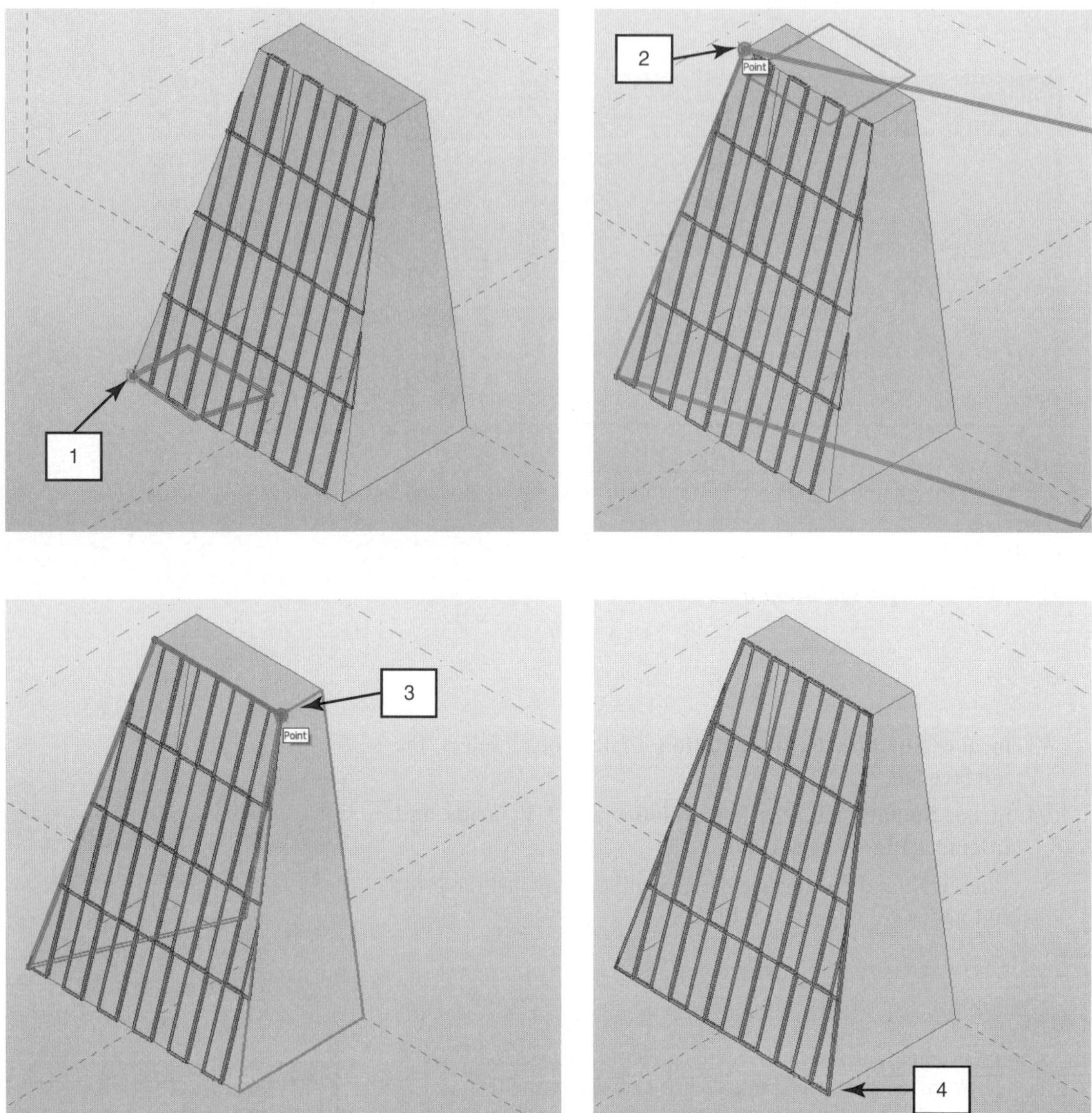

Figure 15-129

The adaptive component will follow the mouse like a rubber band

100. Press the **<Esc>** key a couple of times to see the result.
101. Select the front surface of the **Mass**.
102. In the **Modify | Divided Surface** toolbar, deselect the **Surface** and **Pattern** buttons.
103. Next, select the **Component** button.
104. Click on a blank area.

All the mullions and the overall frame will become visible (see Figure 15-130).

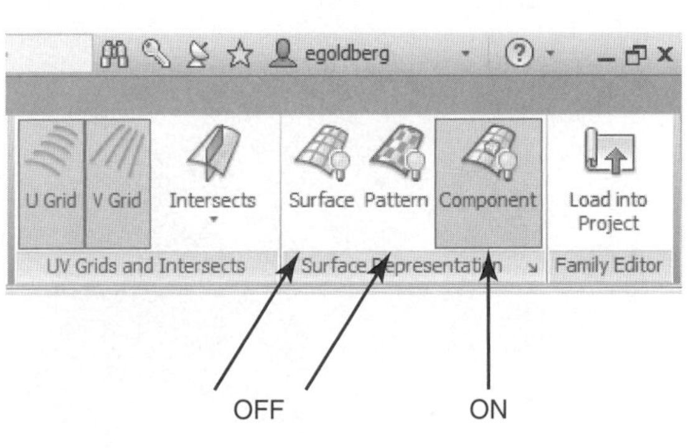

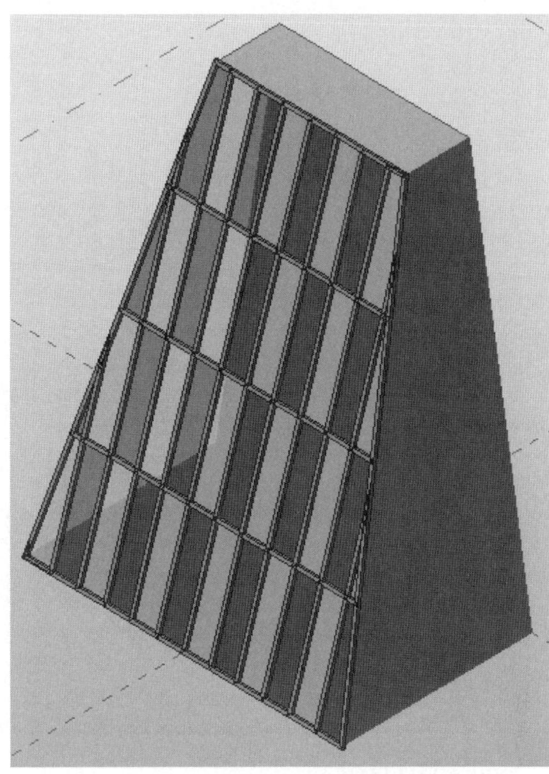

Figure 15-130

The **Curtain Wall System** updated

105. In the **Home** Toolbar, select the **Family Types** button and change the **MASS HEIGHT** value to **60′-0″** (see Figure 15-131).

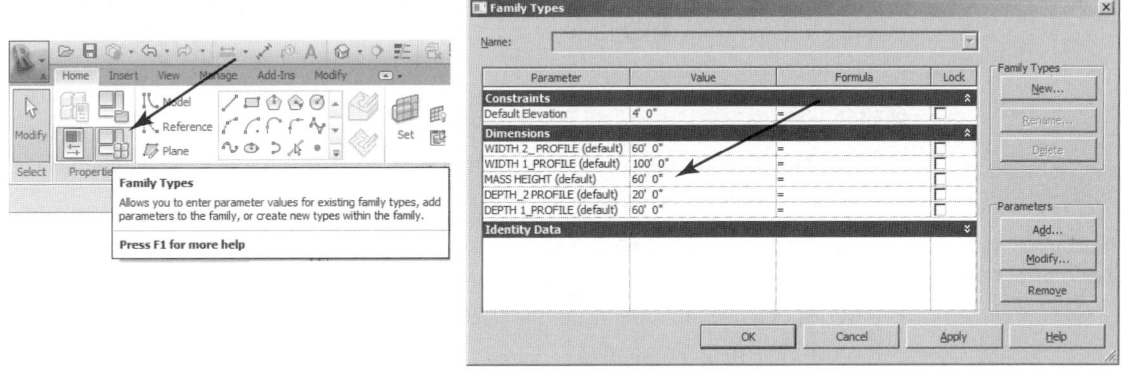

Figure 15-131

Change the **MASS HEIGHT** value to **60′-0″**

The surface pattern and the **Adaptive Component** will adjust to the new height (see Figure 15-132).

106. Save the file.

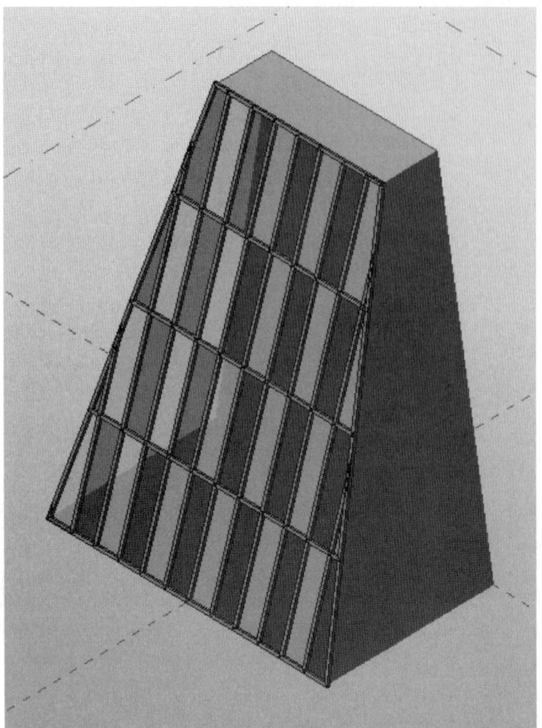

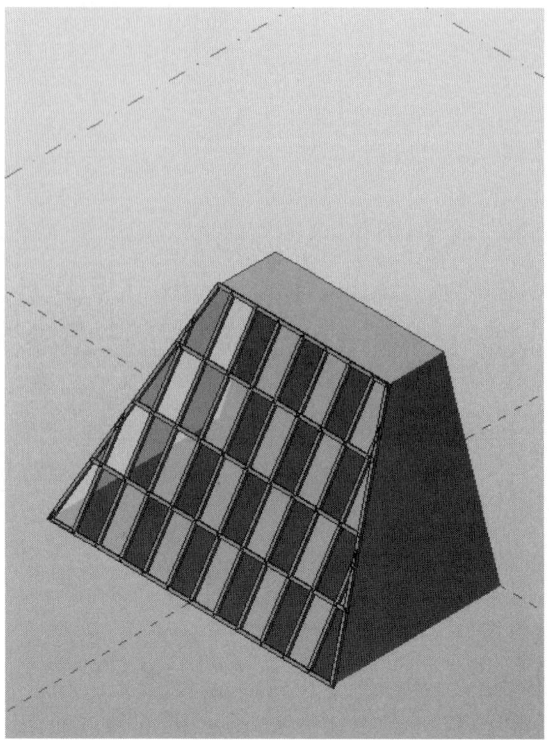

Figure 15-132

Surface pattern with an **Adapted Component** added; testing the height parameter

Site

Most architectural projects include site drawings. Revit Architecture 2012 has an excellent site creation tool called the **Toposurface** tool. This tool allows you to develop the site manually by entering elevation points or automatically by importing point data from your civil engineer's or surveyor's 3D files.

EXERCISE 15-17 **USING THE TOPOSURFACE TOOL**

The **Toposurface** tool is used to create a Revit 3D ground model when you have a 3D CAD topo file from your civil engineer.

To access student datafiles, go to **www.pearsondesigncentral.com.**

1. Download the **TEST SITE 1** file from **www.pearsondesigncentral.com**, and place it in a folder on your computer.
2. Start a new drawing using the RAC 2012\Imperial Templates\default.rte template.
3. In the **Project Browser**, double-click on the **Site** floor plan to bring it into the **Drawing Editor**.
4. Set the **Scale** to **1″ = 40′**.
5. Select the **Insert** tab to bring up the **Insert** toolbar.
6. In the **Insert** toolbar, select the **Import CAD** button to bring up the **Import CAD Formats** dialog box (see Figure 15-133).

TIP: You can use either **Link CAD** or **Import CAD**. **Link CAD** allows you to change the CAD drawing in AutoCAD and then update the CAD drawing in Revit through the **Manage Links** button in the **Insert** toolbar.

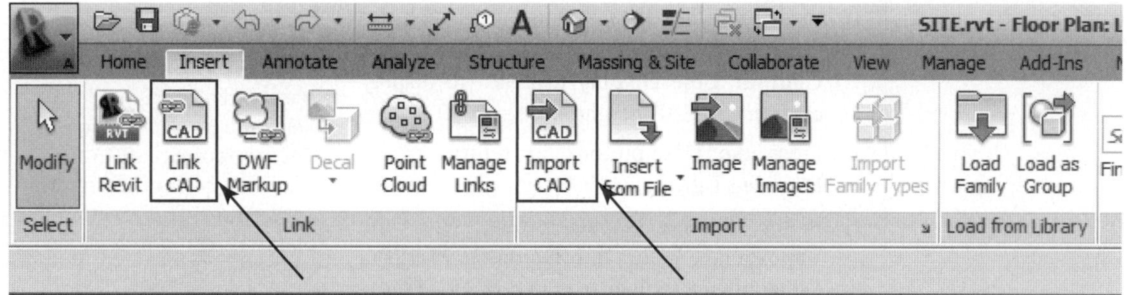

Figure 15-133

Import CAD button

7. In the **Import CAD Formats** dialog box, locate the **TEST SITE 1** file you downloaded, set the **Layer/Level Colors** to **Black and white**, select the **Manually place** radio button, set **Place at level** to **Level 1**, and then press the **Open** button to bring the **TEST SITE 1** file into your project (see Figure 15-134).

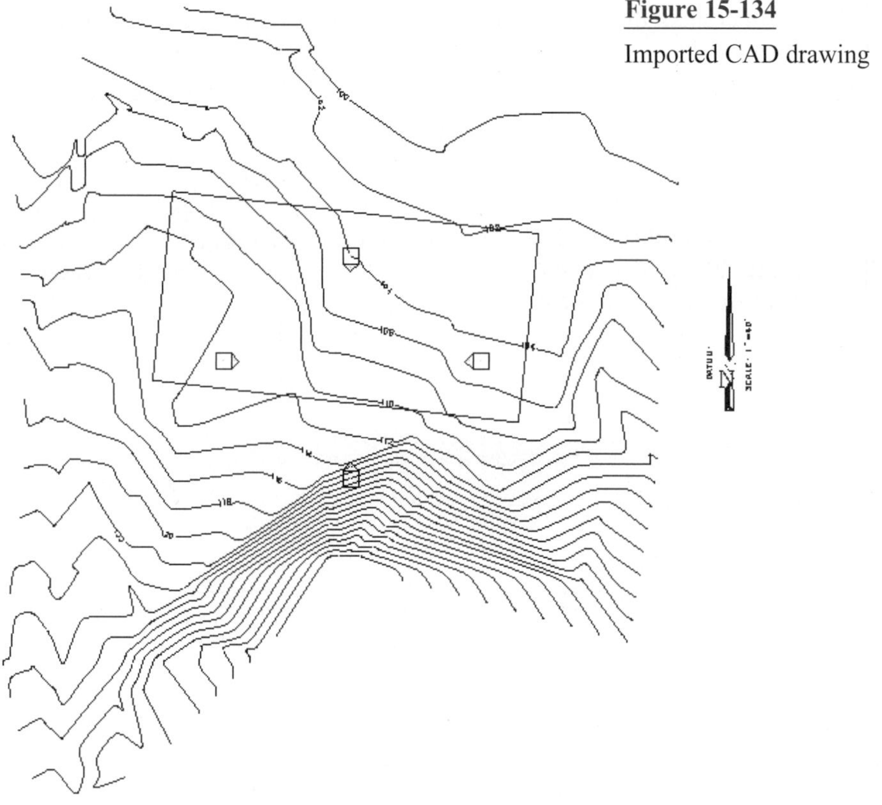

Figure 15-134

Imported CAD drawing

8. Select the **Massing & Site** tab to bring up the **Massing & Site** toolbar.
9. In the **Massing & Site** toolbar, select the **Model Site** panel arrow to bring up the **Site Settings** dialog box (see Figure 15-135).

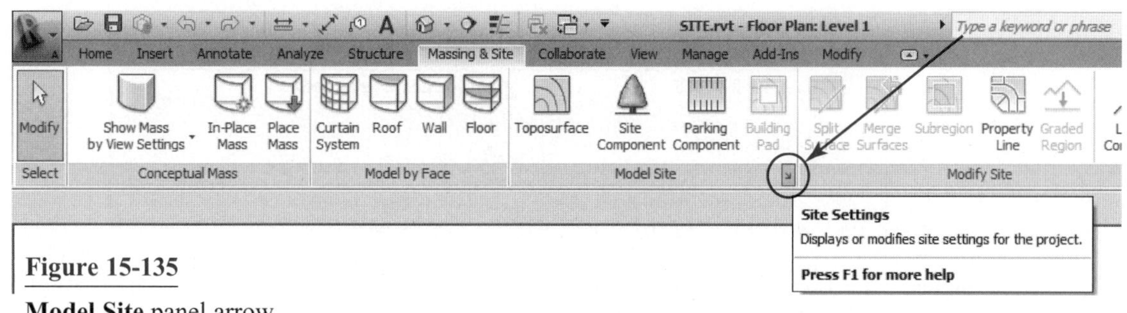

Figure 15-135

Model Site panel arrow

10. In the **Site Settings** dialog box, check the **At Intervals of:** check box, and set the **Contour Line Display** to **2′-0″** (to display contours at 2′-0″ heights).
11. Press the **OK** buttons to return to the **Drawing Editor**.
12. In the **Massing & Site** toolbar**,** select the **Toposurface** button to bring up the **Modify | Edit Surface** toolbar (see Figure 15-138).
13. In the **Modify | Edit Surface** toolbar, select the **Create from Import > Select Import Instance** button (see Figure 15-139).

NOTE:
If you want to change the pattern that displays when you cut a section through the **Toposurface** or change the rendering color of the surface, you can select the **Section Cut Material** button to bring up the **Materials** dialog box (see Figures 15-136 and 15-137).

14. Select the imported **TEST SITE 1** file in the **Site** view to bring up the **Add Points from Selected Layers** dialog box.
15. In the **Add Points from Selected Layers** dialog box, press the **Check None** button to clear all the check boxes, then check the **EG-EX** check box, and press the **OK** button to create the surface points (see Figure 15-140).
16. In the **Modify | Edit Surface** toolbar, select the **Finish Surface** button to return to the **Site** view, and create the **Toposurface**.
17. Type **VG** to bring up the **Visibility/Graphic Overrides for Floor Plan: Site** dialog box.
18. In the **Visibility/Graphic Overrides for Floor Plan: Site** dialog box, select the **Imported Categories** tab.

NOTE:
In the file sent by the civil engineer, all the intervals were placed on the **EG-EX Layer.**

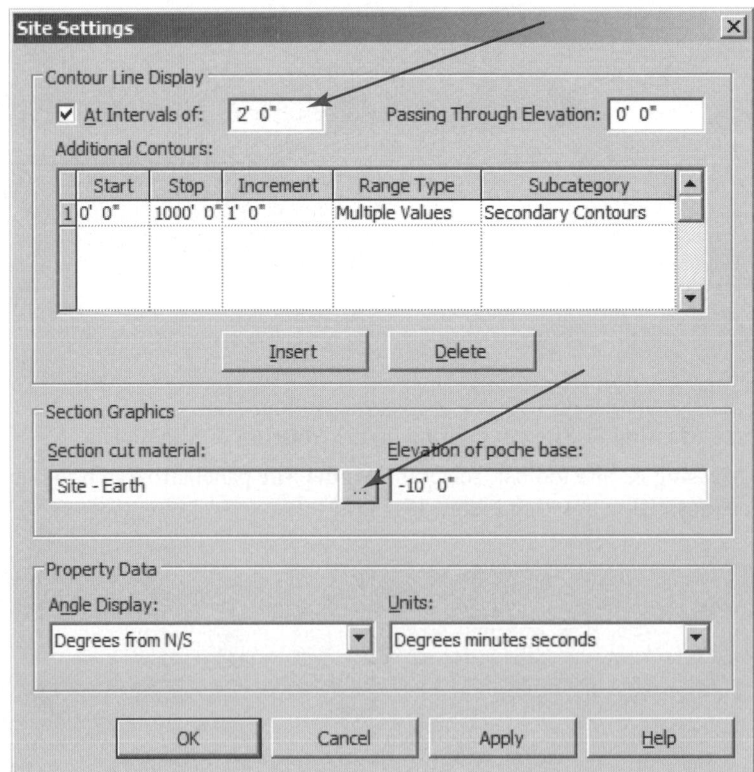

Figure 15-136
Site Settings dialog box

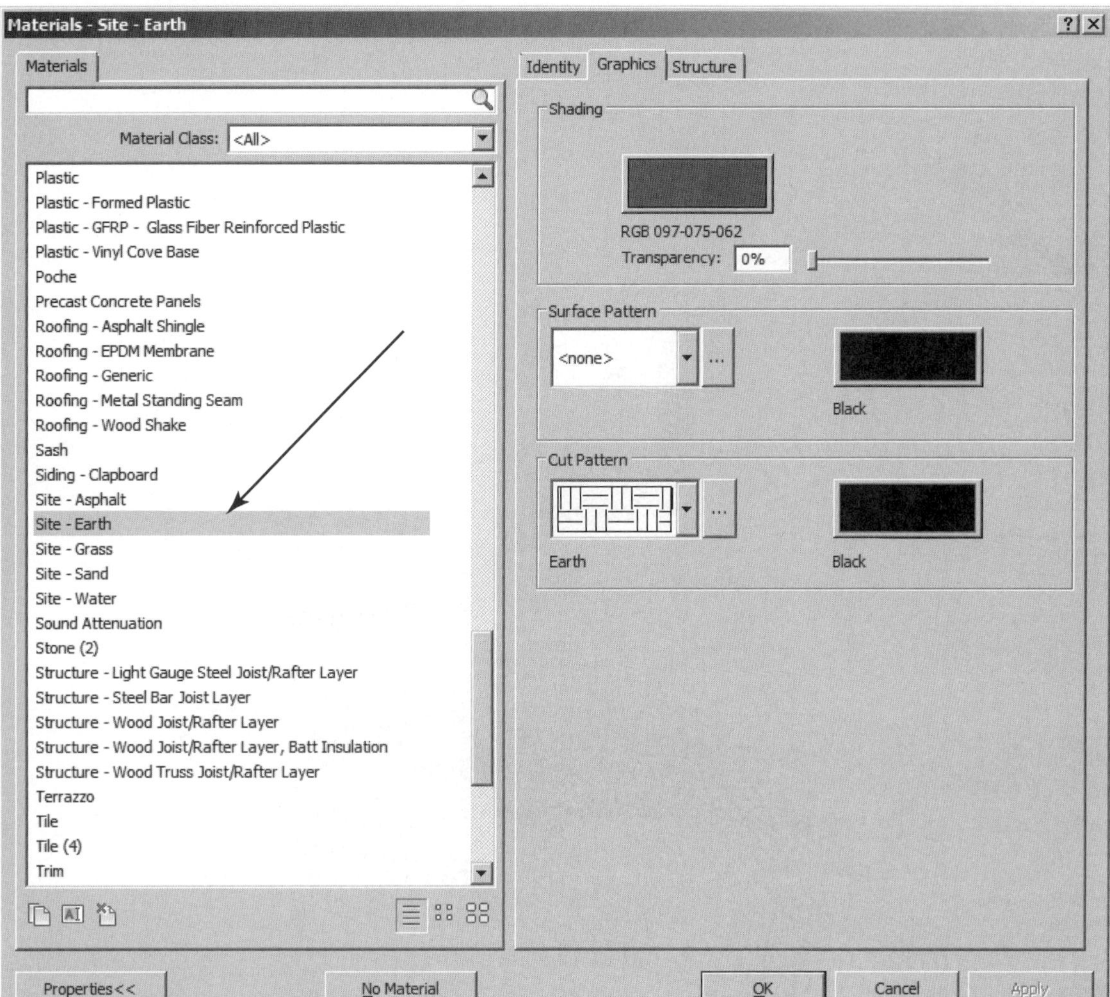

Figure 15-137

Materials dialog box

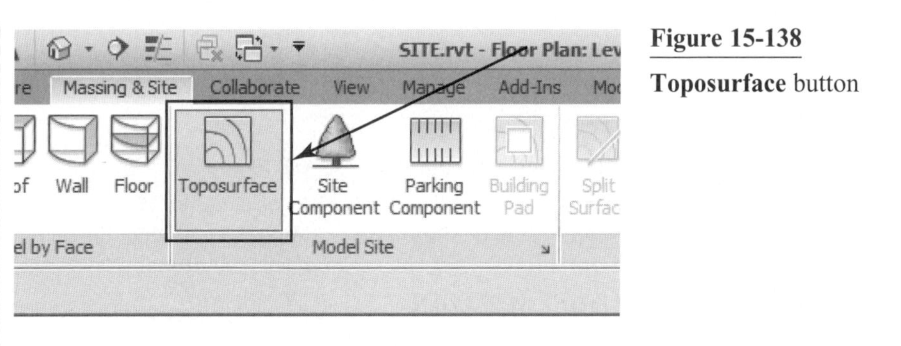

Figure 15-138

Toposurface button

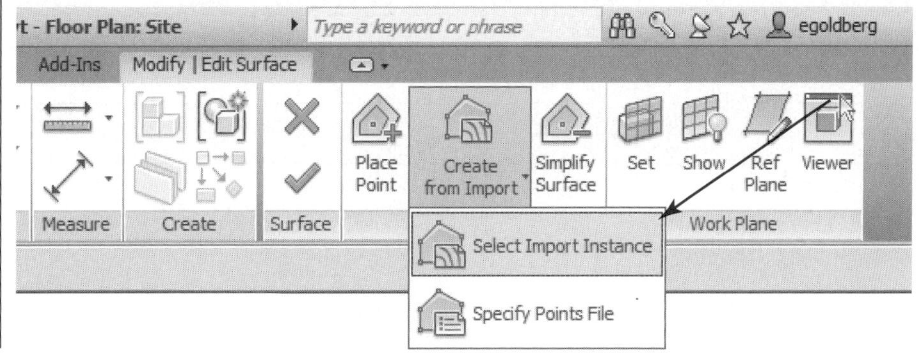

Figure 15-139

Create from Import > Select Import Instance button

Figure 15-140

Create **Surface** points

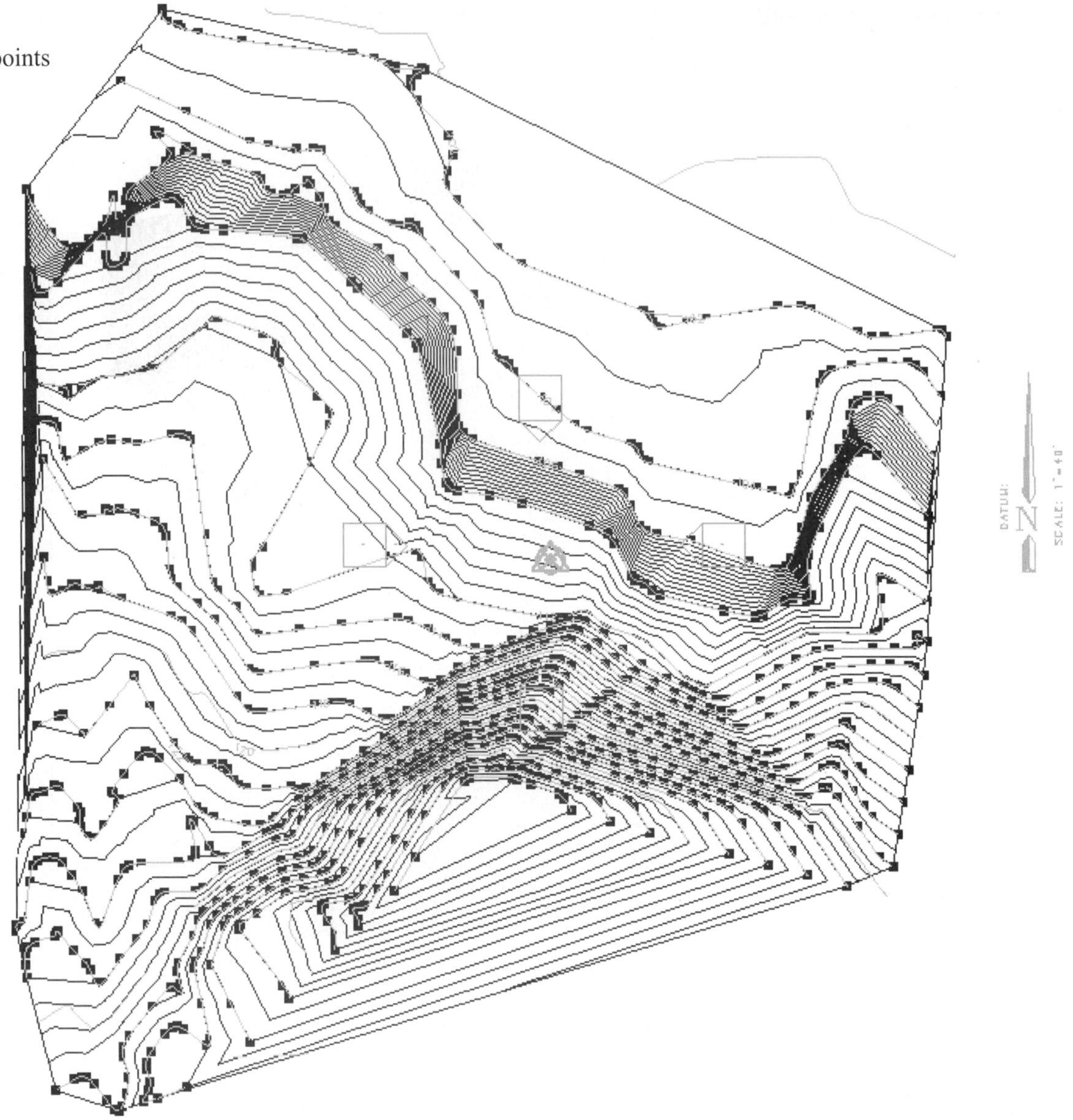

19. In the **Imported Categories** tab, uncheck the **TEST SITE 1** drawing to make it invisible, and press the **OK** button to return to the **Drawing Editor** (see Figure 15-141).
20. Save this file as **TOPOSURFACE TOOL**.

NOTE:

Unchecking the **TEST SITE 1** drawing will hide the CAD drawing in **Site** view (see Figure 15-142).

Figure 15-141

Visibility/Graphic Overides for Floor Plan: Site dialog box

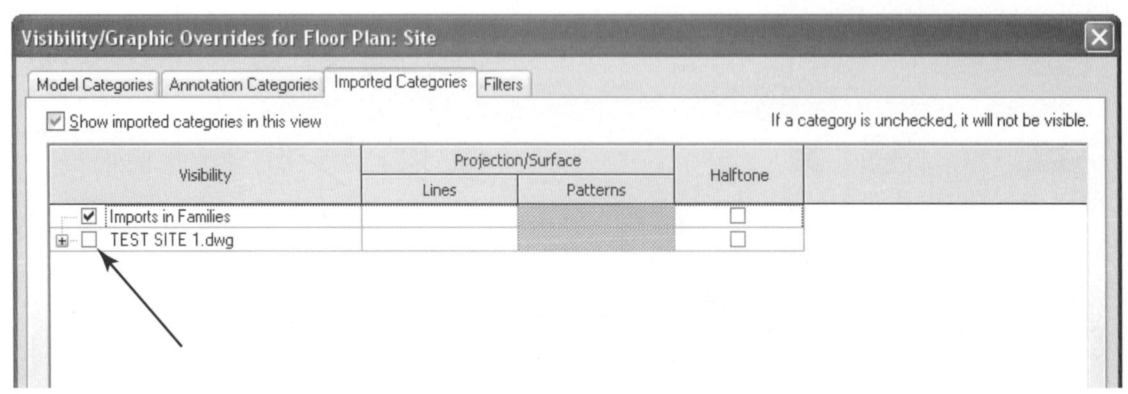

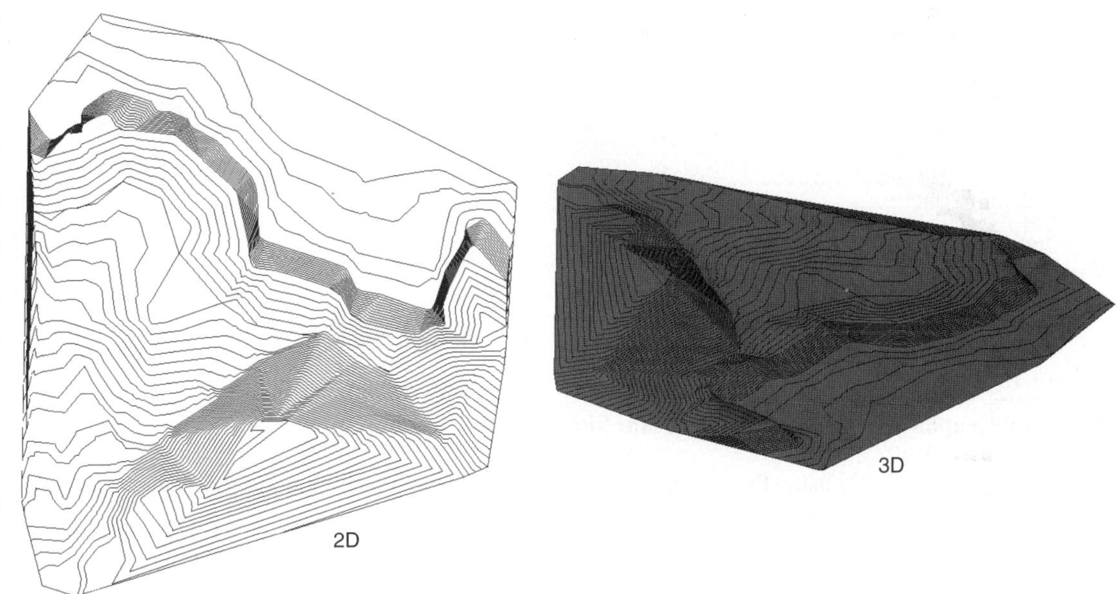

Figure 15-142

Unchecking the **TEST SITE 1** drawing will hide the CAD drawing in **Site** view

EXERCISE 15-18 USING THE PAD TOOL WITH THE TOPOSURFACE

The **Pad** tool is used to create a building pad for a building.

1. Using the previous exercise, change to the **East** view.
2. Drag **Level 1** to the lowest point on the **Toposurface (102′-0″)**.
3. Drag **Level 2** to the highest point on the **Toposurface (146′-0″)** (see Figure 15-143).

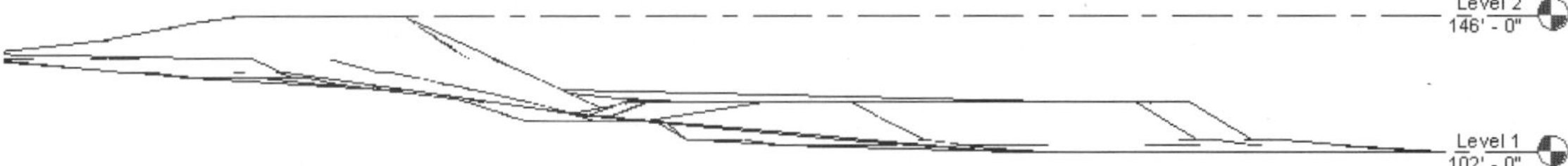

Figure 15-143

Lowest and highest points on the **Toposurface**

4. Change to the **Level 1** floor plan.
5. Type **VG** to bring up the **Visibility/Graphic Overrides for Floor Plan: Site** dialog box.
6. In the **Visibility/Graphic Overrides for Floor Plan: Site** dialog box, select the **Imported Categories** tab.
7. In the **Imported Categories** tab, check the **TEST SITE 1** drawing to make it visible, and press the **OK** button to return to the **Drawing Editor** (see Figure 15-144).

Notice that the **Toposurface** you created does not show in the **Level 1** floor plan.

8. Type **VG** to bring up the **Visibility/Graphic Overrides for Floor Plan: Site** dialog box.
9. In the **Visibility/Graphic Overrides for Floor Plan: Site** dialog box, select the **Model Categories** tab.
10. In the **Model Categories** tab, check the **Topography** check box.
11. Select the **Home** tab to bring up the **Home** toolbar.
12. In the **Home** toolbar, select the **Wall** button to bring up the **Modify | Place Wall** toolbar.

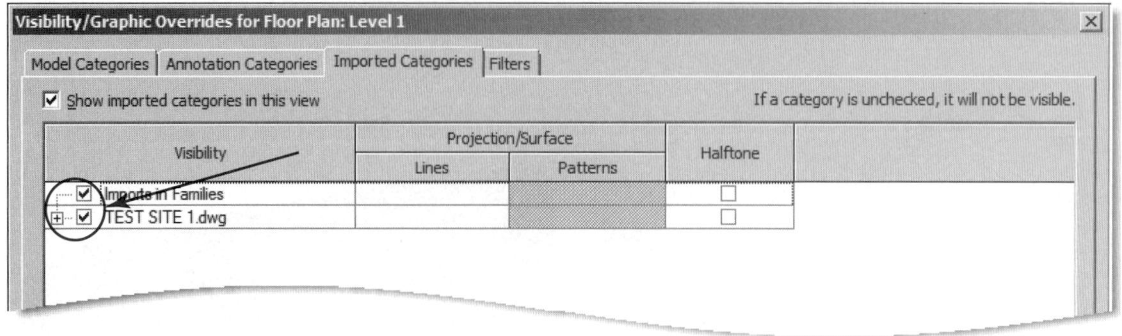

Figure 15-144

Visibility/Graphic Overrides for Floor Plan: Site dialog box

13. In the **Properties** dialog box, select **Basic Wall: Generic – 8″** from the **Properties** drop-down list.
14. In the **Modify | Place Wall** toolbar, select the **Pick Lines** button.
15. In the **Options Bar**, set the **Height** to **Level 2**, and **Location Line** to **Finish Face: Exterior**.
16. Pick on the lines of the rectangle in the **TEST SITE 1** CAD drawing to create a **40′** high enclosure.
17. Select the **Massing & Site** tab to bring up the **Massing & Site** toolbar.
18. In the **Massing & Site** toolbar, select the **Building Pad** button to bring up the **Modify | Create Pad Boundary** toolbar (see Figure 15-145).
19. In the **Modify | Create Pad Boundary** toolbar, select the **Pick Walls** button (see Figure 15-146).

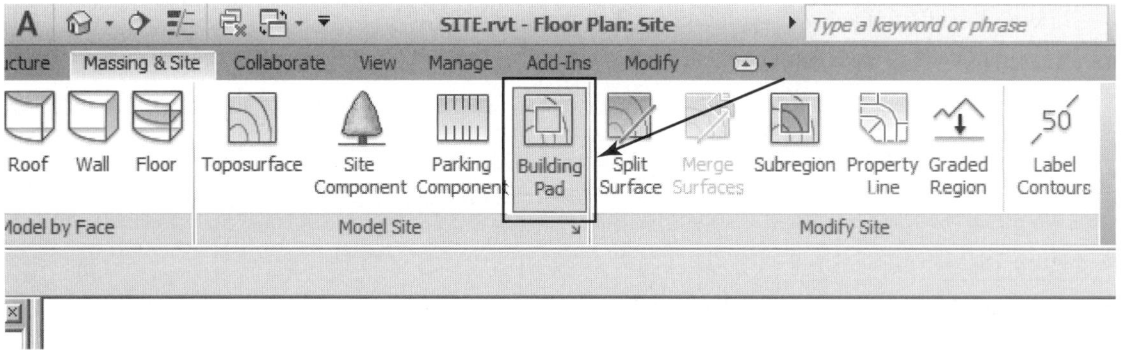

Figure 15-145

Building Pad button

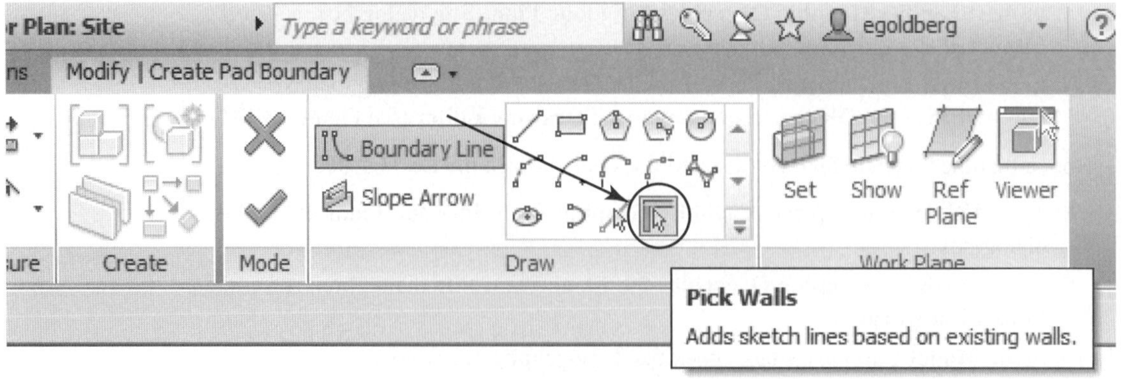

Figure 15-146

Pick Walls button

20. Pick the outside walls of the enclosure you previously created.
21. In the **Properties** dialog box, set the **Height Offset From Level** to **1′-0″**, and then press the **OK** button to return to the **Drawing Editor**.
22. In the **Modify | Create Pad Boundary** toolbar, select the **Finish Edit Mode** button to create the building pad.

You have now created the walls and building pad (see Figure 15-147).

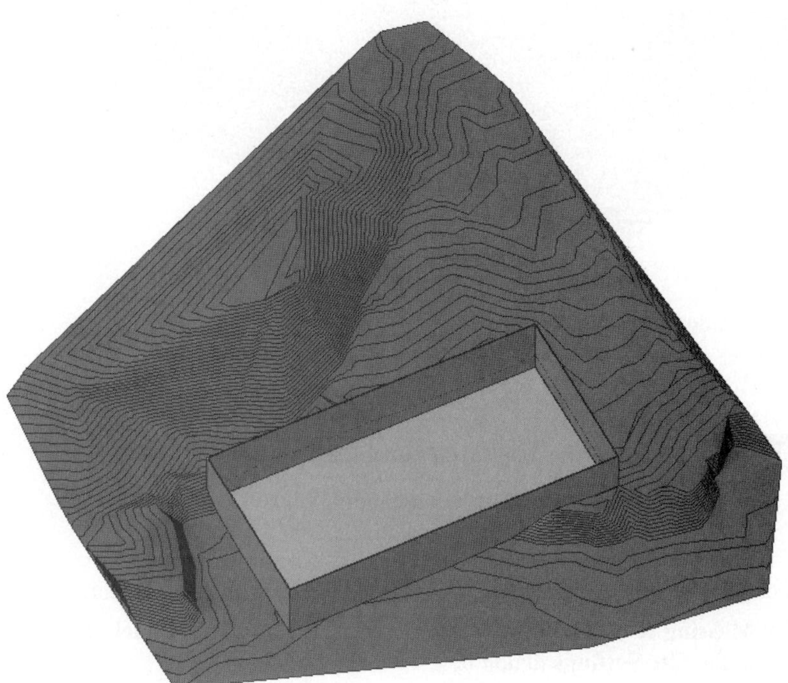

Figure 15-147
Walls and building pad

23. Change to **Level 2**.
24. Select the **Home** tab to bring up the **Home** toolbar.
25. In the **Home** toolbar, select the **Roof > Roof by Footprint** button.
26. The **Lowest Level Notice** dialog box will appear asking if you would like to move the roof to **Level 2**. Press the **Yes** button to bring up the **Modify | Create Roof Footprint** toolbar.
27. In the **Modify | Create Roof Footprint** toolbar, select the **Pick Walls** button in the **Draw** panel.
28. In the **Options Bar**, check the **Defines Slope** check box, and enter **2′-0″** in the **Overhang** field.
29. Pick the outside walls of the enclosure you previously created.
30. In the **Modify | Create Roof Footprint** toolbar, select the **Finish Edit Mode** button to create the roof.
31. Change to the **Default 3D View**, and select **Shading with Edges** from the **Model Graphics** button in the **View Control Bar**.
32. Select the **Shadows On** button in the **View Control Bar** (see Figure 15-148).
33. Save this file as **TOPOSURFACE.**

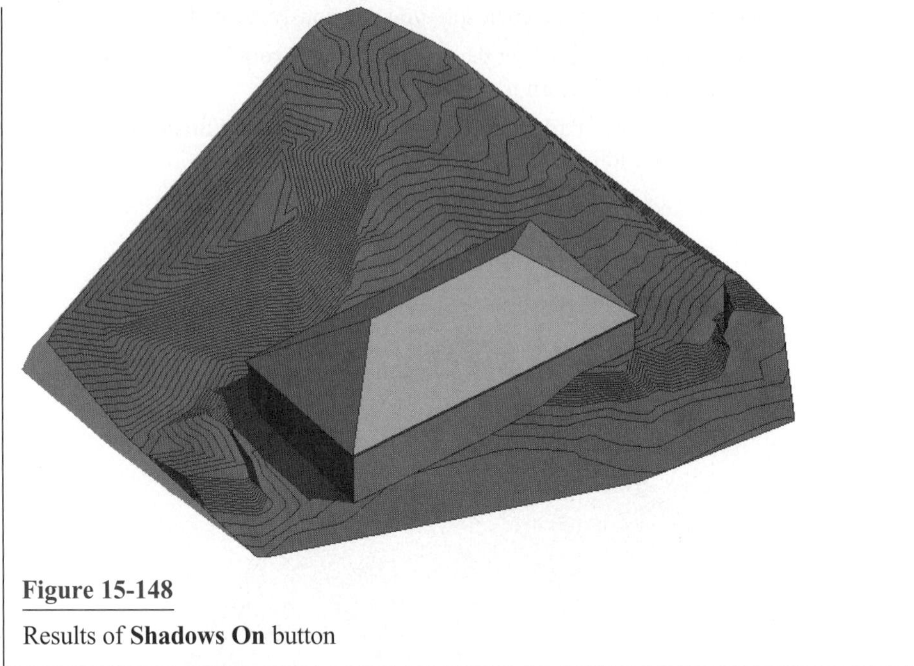

Figure 15-148

Results of **Shadows On** button

EXERCISE 15-19 **CREATING THE TOPOSURFACE BASE**

You have created a **Toposurface**, but it is not sitting on a base.

1. Use the previous file.
2. Select the **Massing & Site** tab to bring up the **Massing & Site** toolbar.
3. In the **Massing & Site** toolbar, select **Site Settings** from the **Model Site** panel to bring up the **Site Settings** dialog box.
4. In the **Site Settings** dialog box, select the **Section cut material** button to bring up the **Materials** dialog box.
5. In the **Materials** dialog box, select the **Cut Pattern** button to bring up the **Fill Patterns** dialog box.
6. In the **Fill Patterns** dialog box, select the **No Pattern** button, and then press the **OK** buttons to return to the **Drawing Editor** (see Figures 15-149 and 15-150).

Figure 15-149

Site Settings and **Materials** dialog boxes

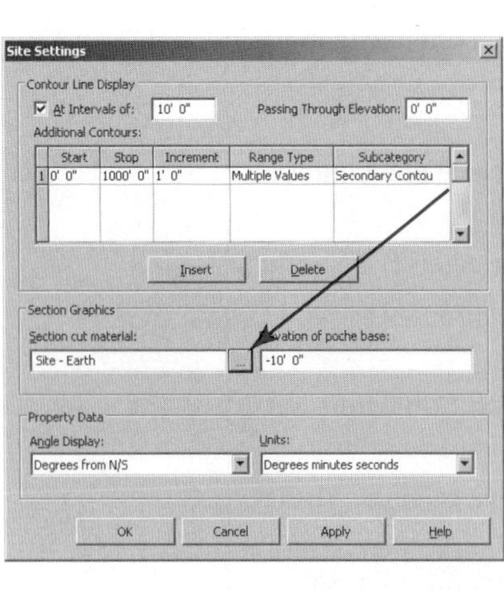

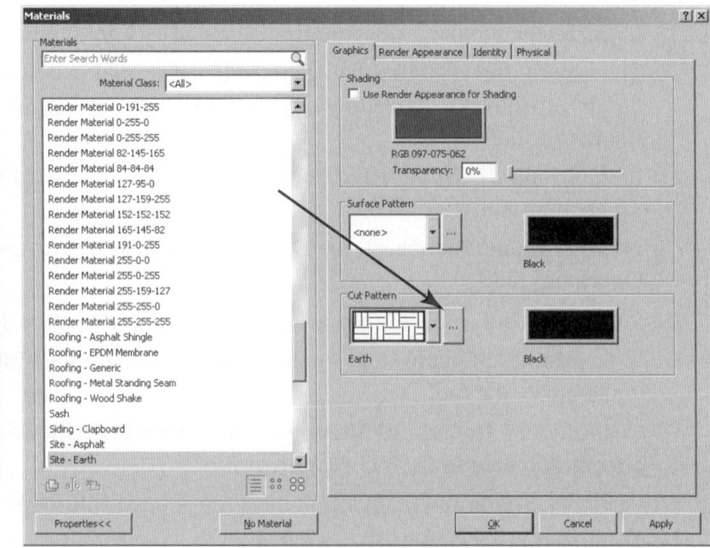

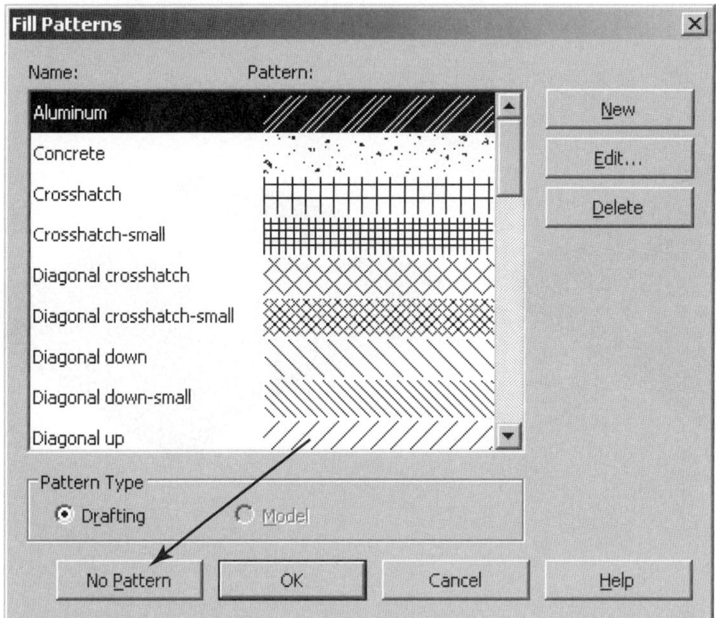

Figure 15-150

Fill Patterns dialog box

7. Change to the **Default 3D View**.
8. In the **Properties** dialog box, check the **Section Box** check box (see Figure 15-151).

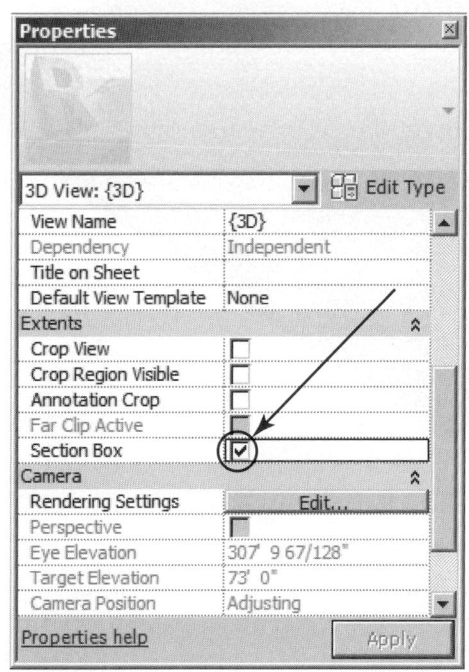

Figure 15-151

Section Box check box

The **Section Box** will appear around your toposurface and building.

9. Select the **Section Box**, and drag the handles to "crop" the **Toposurface**.
10. With the **Section Box** still selected, press the **Temporarily Hide/Isolate > Hide Element** button in the **View Control Bar** at the bottom of the **Drawing Editor** to hide the **Section Box** (see Figures 15-152 and 15-153).

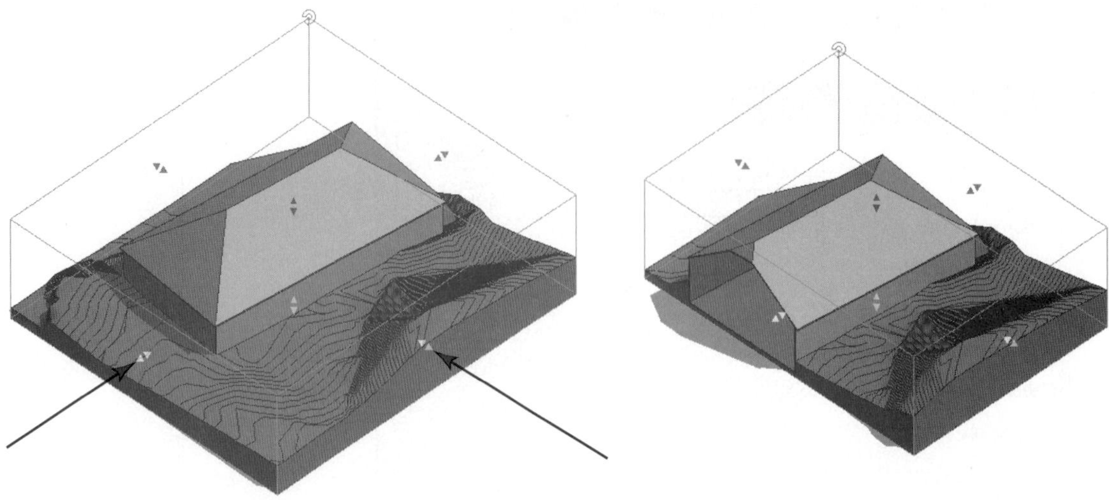

Figure 15-152
Hide the **Section Box**

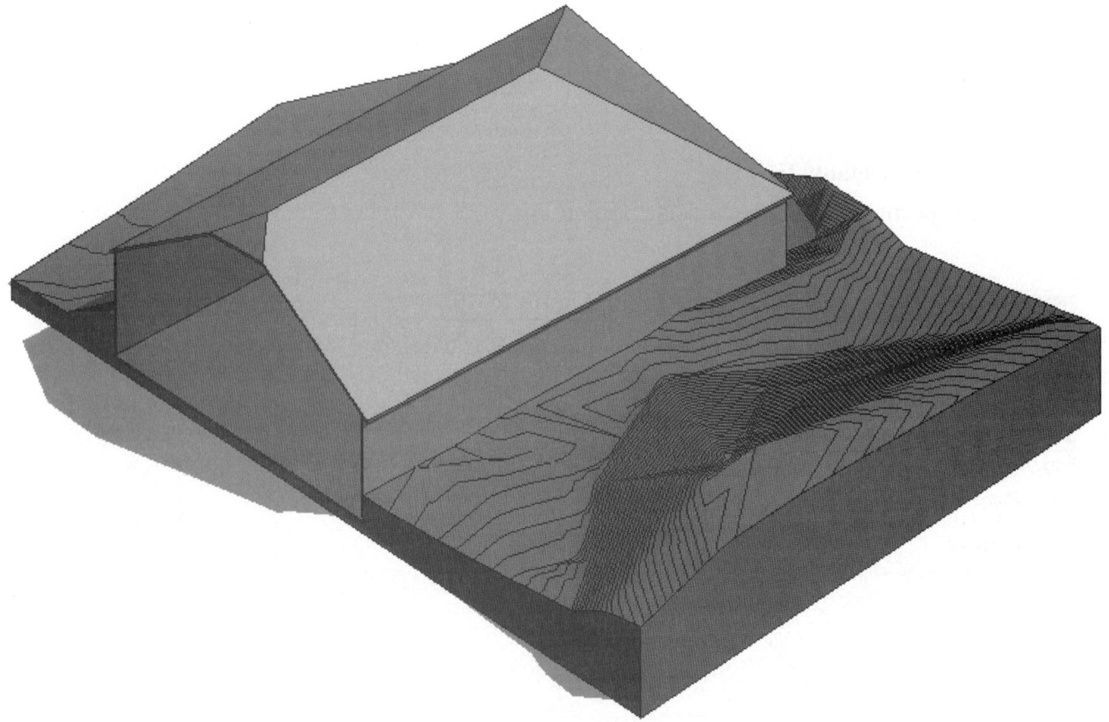

Figure 15-153
Hide the **Section Box**

11. Save this file as **TOPOSURFACE BASE.**

EXERCISE 15-20 CREATING A TOPOSURFACE WITH POINTS

1. Start a new drawing using the RAC 2012\Imperial Templates\default.rte template.
2. In the **Project Browser**, double-click on the **Site** plan to bring it into the **Drawing Editor**.
3. Change the **Scale** to **1″ = 1′-0″**.
4. Select the **Home** tab to bring up the **Home** toolbar.

5. In the **Home** toolbar, select the **Wall** and **Roof** buttons and create a simple **10′** high enclosure with a roof using the dimensions shown in Figure 15-154.

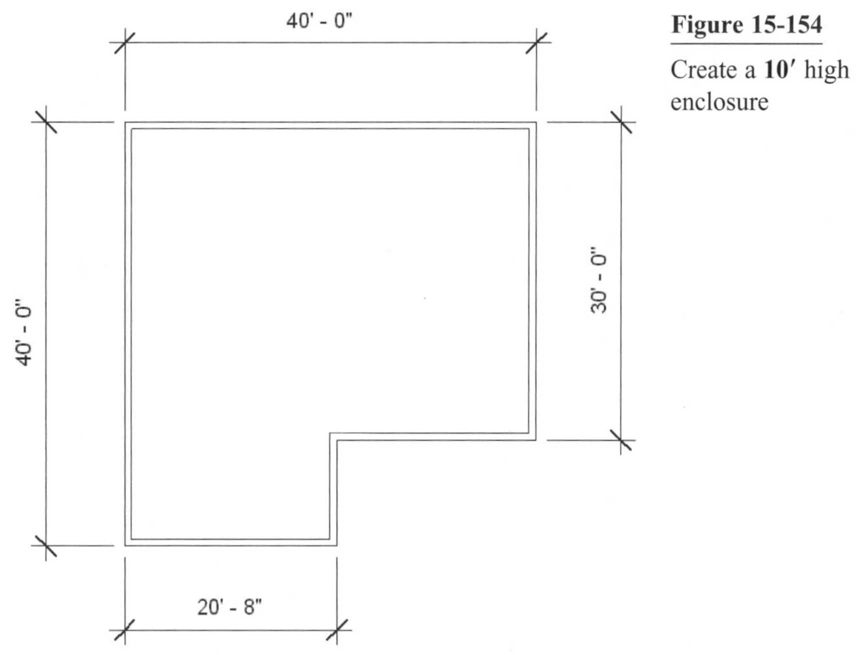

Figure 15-154

Create a **10′** high enclosure

6. Select the **Massing & Site** tab to bring up the **Massing & Site** toolbar.
7. In the **Massing & Site** toolbar, select the **Toposurface** button to bring up the **Modify | Edit Surface** toolbar.
8. In the **Modify | Edit Surface** toolbar, select the **Place Point** button.
9. In the **Options Bar**, set the **Elevation** to **0′-0″** (see Figure 15-155).

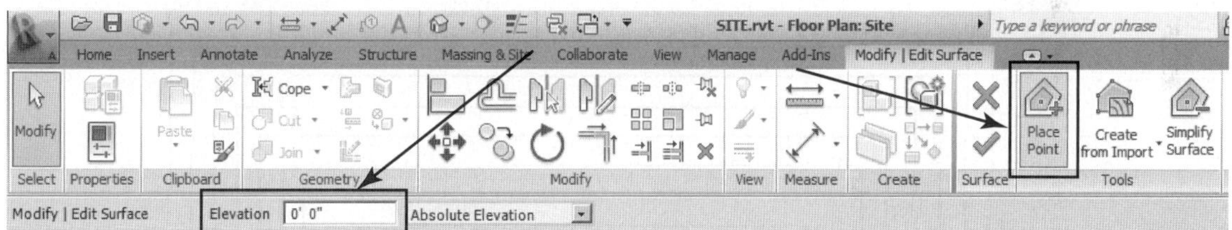

Figure 15-155

Set the **Elevation** to **0′-0″**

10. Place four points around the building as shown in Figure 15-156.
11. In the **Options Bar**, set the **Elevation** to **-4′-0″**.
12. Place more points as shown in Figure 15-157.

Notice that more increments appear between the levels than you created. That is because the **Site** settings are set to have **1′-0″** increments. To change these intervals, do the following:

13. In the **Massing & Site** toolbar, select the **Model Site** panel arrow to bring up the **Site Settings** dialog box.
14. In the **Site Settings** dialog box, check the **At Intervals of:** check box, set the **Contour Line Display** to **0′-6″**, and press the **OK** button to return to the **Drawing Editor**.

Notice that the increments have increased (see Figure 15-158).

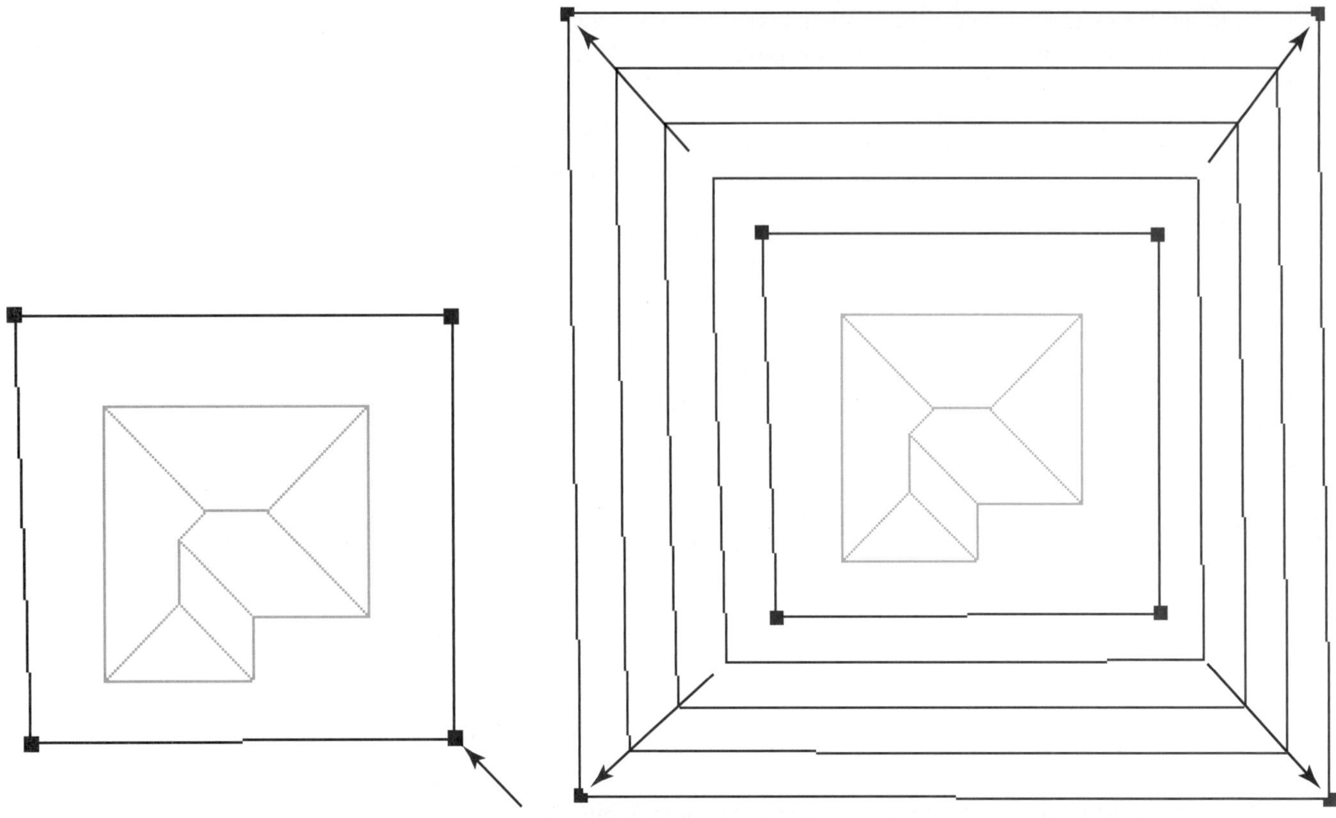

Figure 15-156

Place four points around the building

Figure 15-157

Place more points

Figure 15-158

Increments have increased

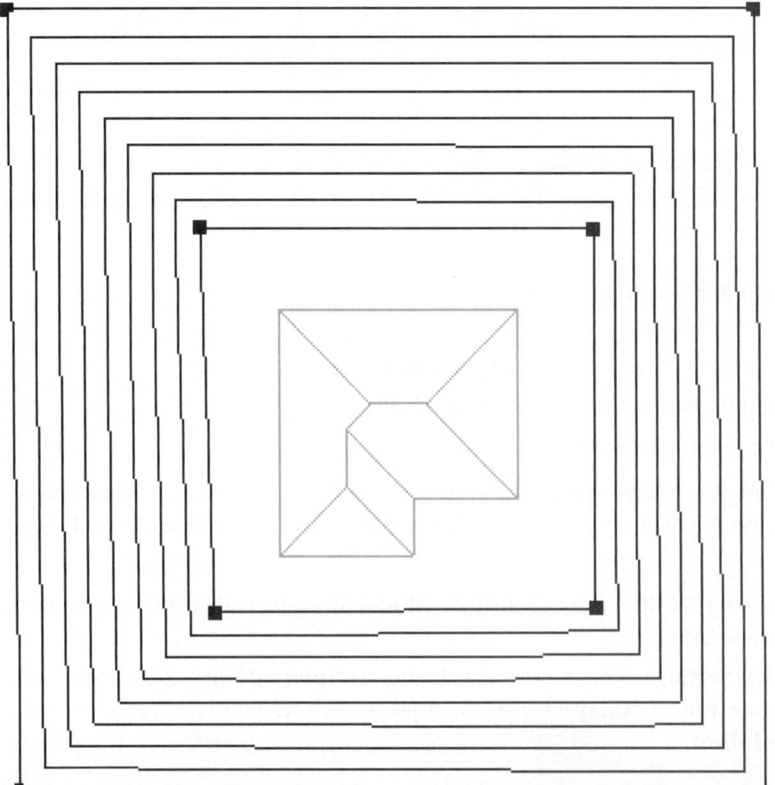

15. In the **Options Bar**, set the **Elevation** to **-8′-0″**.
16. Place more points.
17. In the **Modify | Edit Surface** toolbar, select the **Finish Surface** button in the **Surface** panel, and change to the **East Elevation** (see Figure 15-159).
18. Save this file as **TOPOSURFACE by POINTS**.

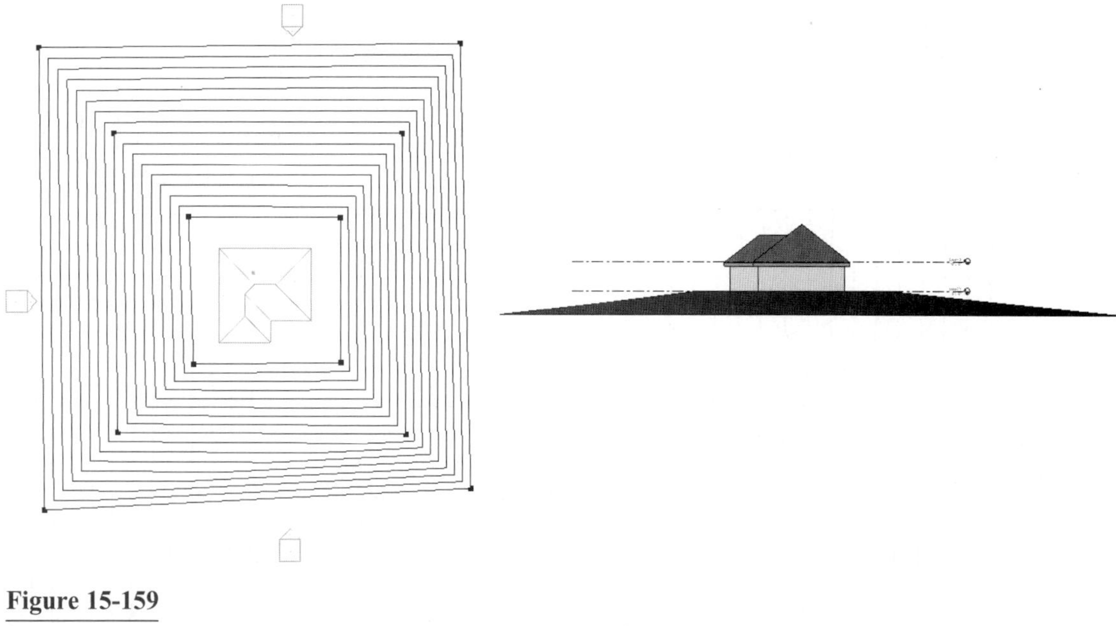

Figure 15-159

East Elevation

EXERCISE 15-21 **USING THE SPLIT SURFACE TOOL ON A TOPOSURFACE**

1. Using the previous exercise, change to the **Site** view.
2. Select the **Massing & Site** tab to bring up the **Massing & Site** toolbar.
3. In the **Massing & Site** toolbar, select the **Split Surface** button, and then click on the **Site** object in the **Drawing Editor** to bring up the **Split Surface** toolbar (see Figure 15-160).
4. In the **Modify | Split Surface** toolbar, select the **Rectangle** button in the **Draw** panel.
5. Place a **12′** wide rectangle as shown, and press the **Finish Edit Mode** button in the **Modify | Split Surface** toolbar to create the split surface (see Figure 15-161).
6. Select the split surface to bring up its **Properties** dialog box.

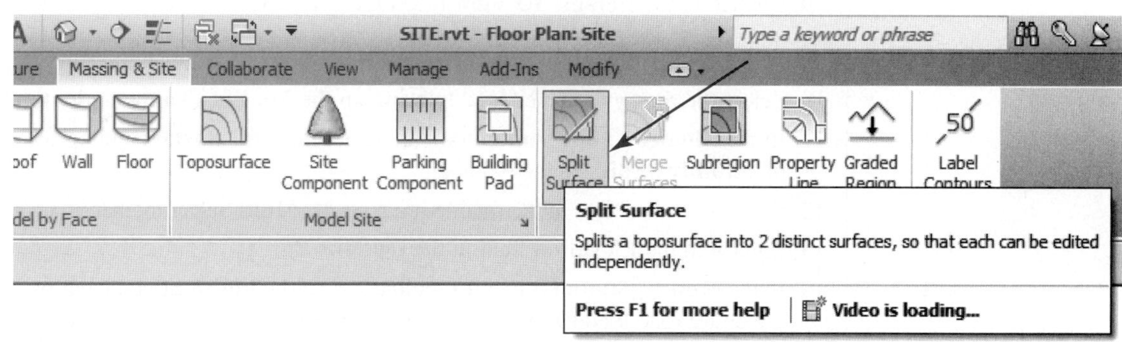

Figure 15-160

Split Surface button

Figure 15-161

Create the split surface

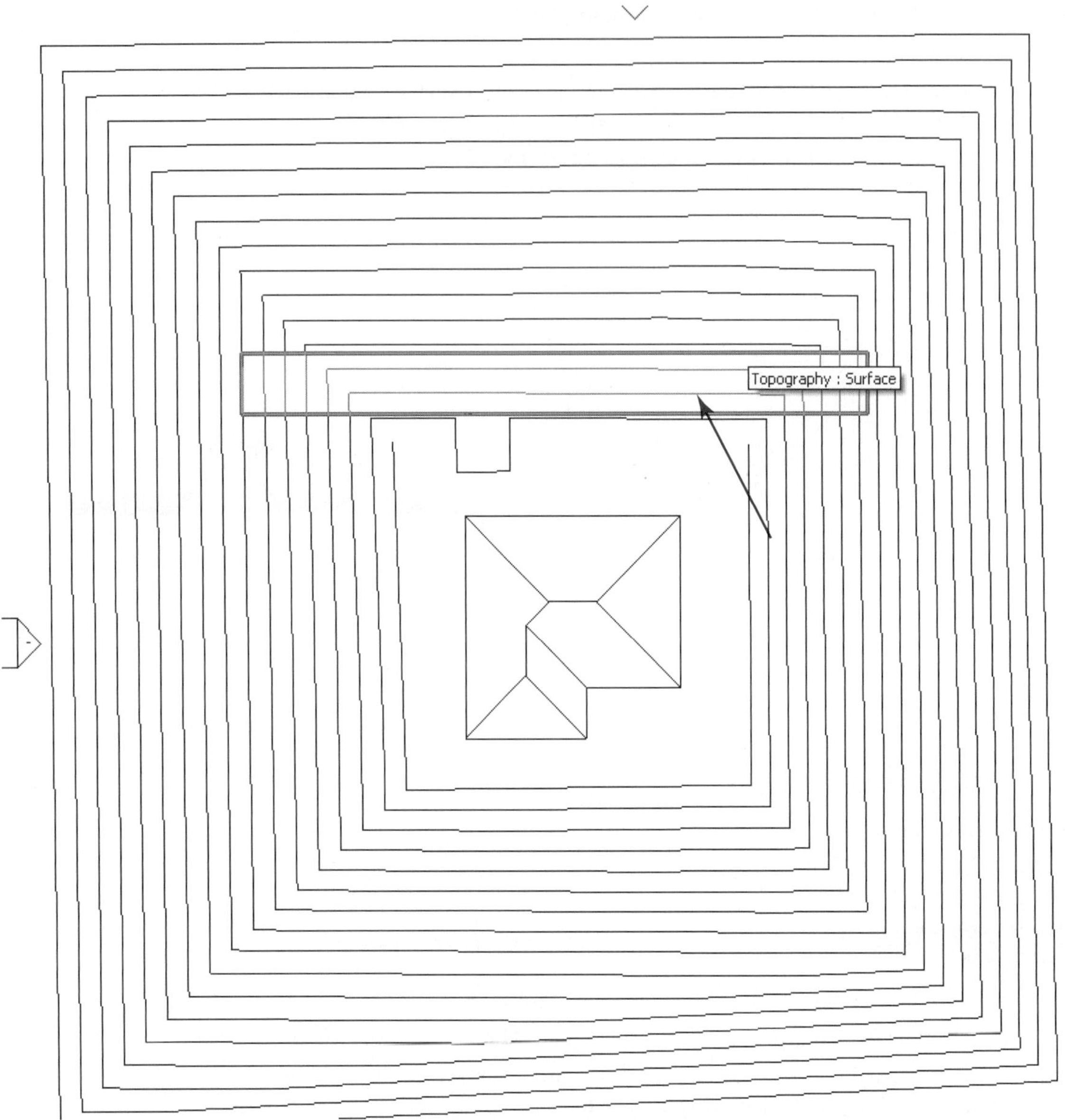

7. In the **Properties** dialog box, select the button to the right of the **Materials** field to bring up the **Materials** dialog box.
8. In the **Materials** dialog box, select **Site – Asphalt** and press the **OK** buttons to return to the **Drawing Editor**.
9. Change to the **Default 3D View** (see Figure 15-162).

The split surface (road) is not level, but it follows the contours. To fix this, do the following:

10. Select the road you just created to bring up the **Modify | Topography** toolbar.
11. In the **Modify | Topography** toolbar, select the **Edit Surface** button to bring up the **Modify | Edit Surface** toolbar.
12. Select all the vertices in the road to bring up the **Multi Select** toolbar.
13. Enter **0** in the **Elevation** field in the **Options Bar**.
14. In the **Modify | Boundary Point** toolbar, select the **Finish Surface** button to make the entire road **0** elevation (see Figure 15-163).
15. Select the **Site** toposurface to bring up the **Modify | Topography** toolbar.
16. In the **Modify | Topography** toolbar, select the **Edit Surface** button to bring up the **Modify | Edit Surface** toolbar.

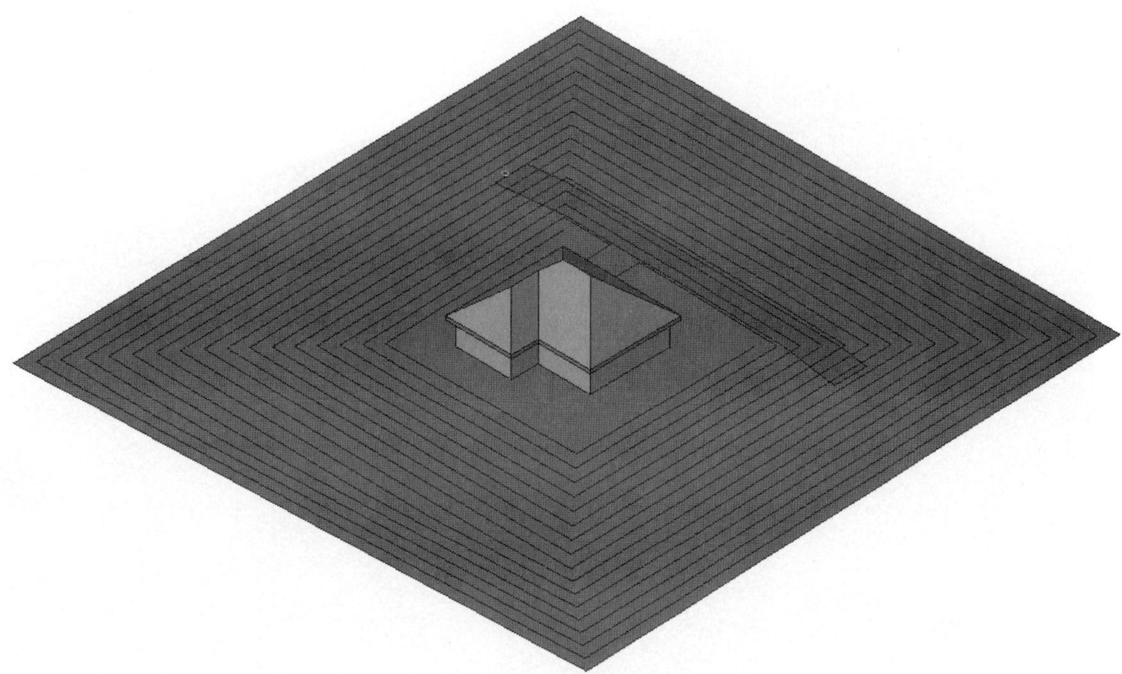

Figure 15-162
Create an asphalt road

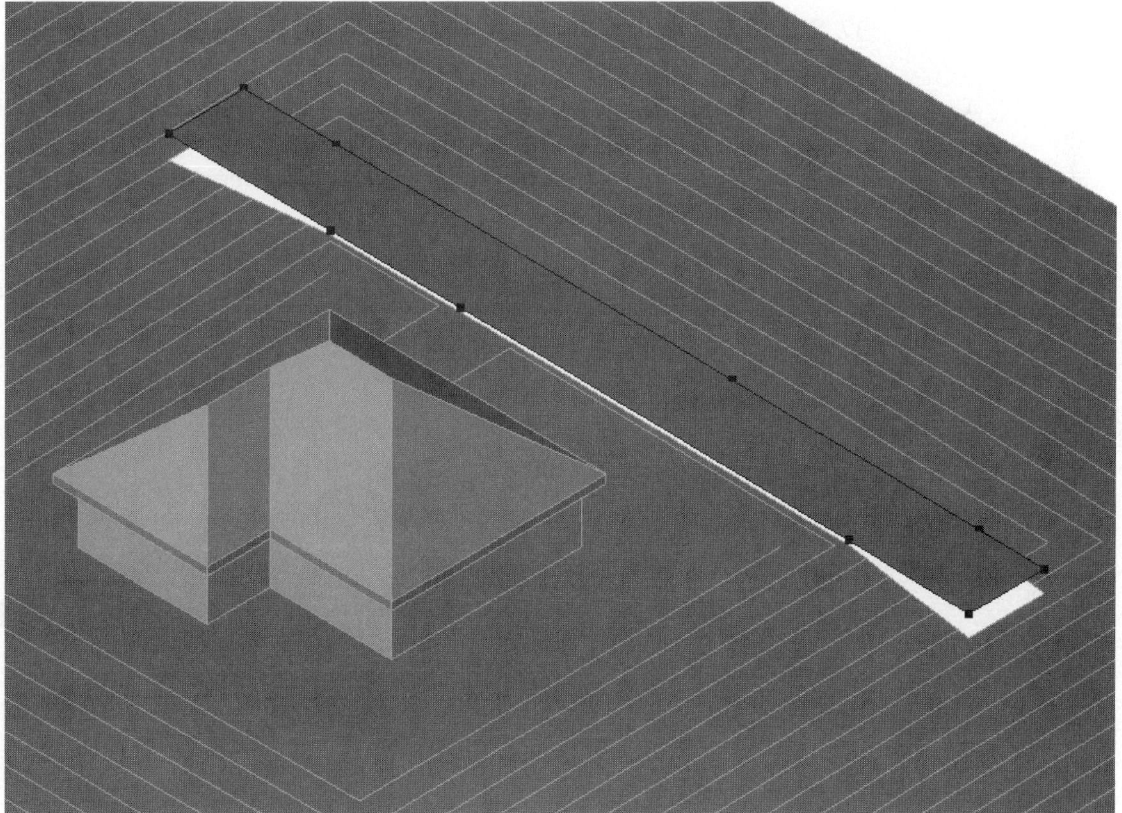

Figure 15-163
Entire road is **0** elevation

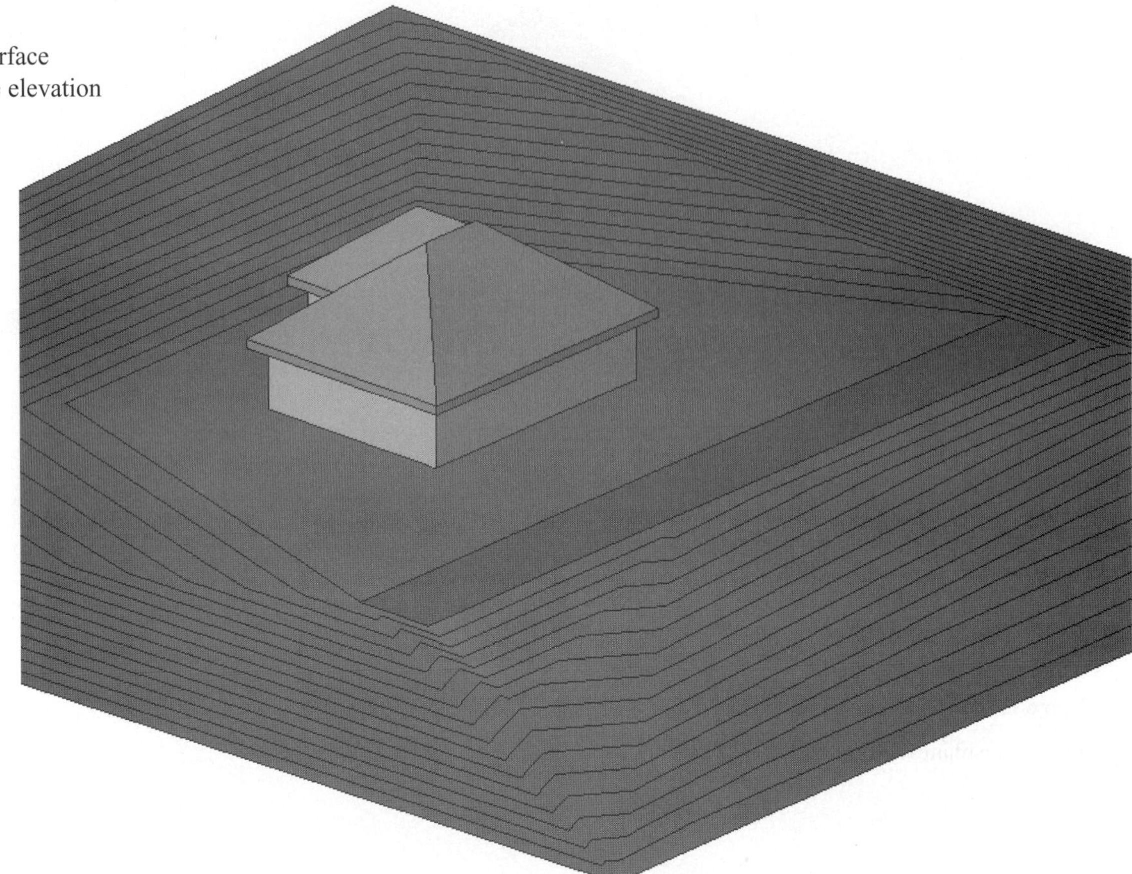

Figure 15-164

The **Site** toposurface edges match the elevation of the road

17. Select all the vertices adjacent to the road to bring up the **Multi Select** toolbar.
18. Enter **0** in the **Elevation** field in the **Options Bar**.
19. In the **Modify | Boundary Point** toolbar, select the **Finish Surface** button to make the **Site** toposurface edges match the elevation of the road (see Figure 15-164).
20. Select an empty spot in the **Drawing Editor**. In the **Properties** dialog box, check the **Section Box** check box.
21. Select the **Section Box**, and drag the handles to "crop" the toposurface.
22. With the **Section Box** still selected, press the **Temporarily Hide/Isolate > Hide Element** button in the **View Control Bar** at the bottom of the **Drawing Editor** to hide the **Section Box** (see Figure 15-165).
23. Save this file as **SPLIT SURFACE**.

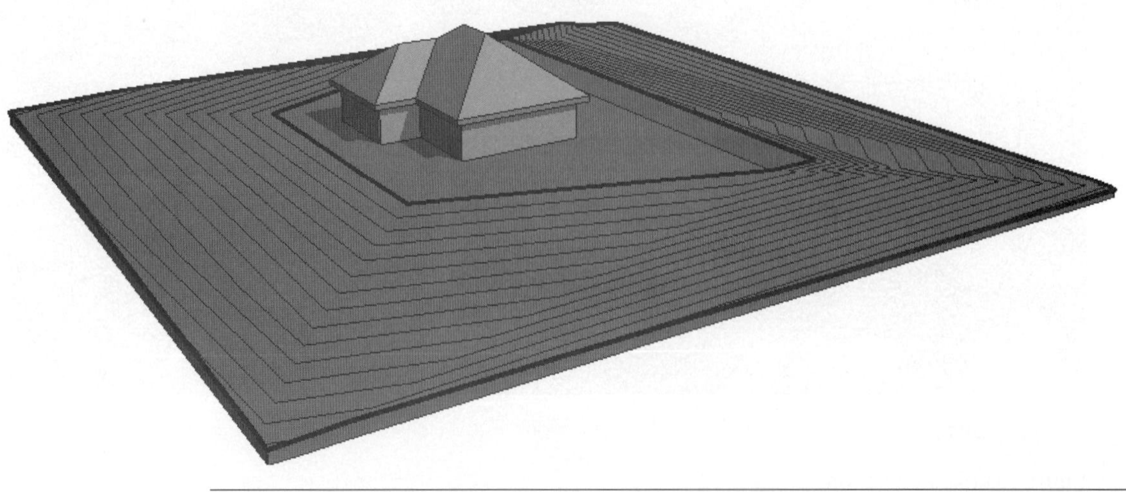

Figure 15-165

Hide the **Section Box**

EXERCISE 15-22 ADDING SITE COMPONENTS TO A TOPOSURFACE

1. Using the previous exercise, change to the **Site** view.
2. Select the **Massing & Site** tab to bring up the **Massing & Site** toolbar.
3. In the **Massing & Site** toolbar, select the **Site Component** button to bring up the **Modify | Site Component** toolbar (see Figure 15-166).

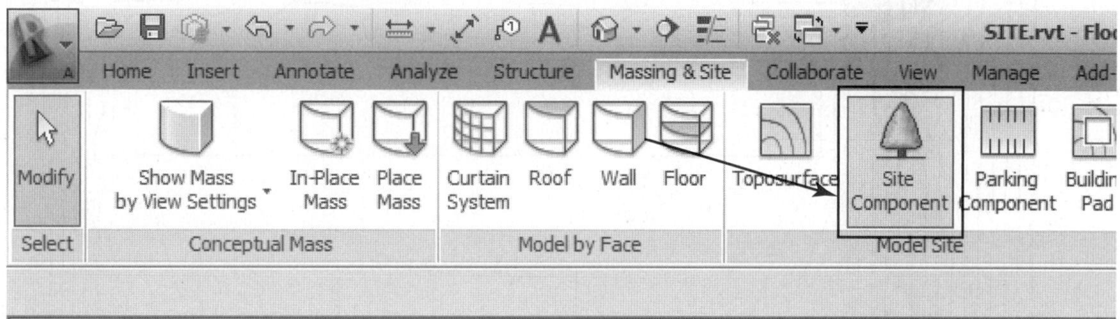

Figure 15-166

Site Component button

4. In the **Properties** dialog box, select **RPC Tree – Deciduous: Red Ash - 25′** from the **Properties** drop-down list.
5. Click on the **Site** object. Continue to place trees on the **Toposurface** as shown in Figure 15-167.
6. Change to the **East Elevation**.

Notice that the trees automatically attach to the level of the **Toposurface** upon which they were placed in **Site** view (see Figure 15-168).

7. Change back to the **Site** view.
8. In the **Massing & Site** toolbar, select the **Site Component** button to bring up the **Modify | Site Component** toolbar.
9. In the **Modify | Site Component** toolbar, select the **Load Family** button to bring up the **Load Family** dialog box.
10. In the **Load Family** dialog box, change to the **Imperial Library** folder.
11. In the **Imperial Library** folder, select and open the **Entourage** folder.
12. In the **Entourage** folder, double-click on the **RPC Beetle** to close the dialog box and return to the **Drawing Editor**.
13. In the **Options Bar,** check the **Rotate after placement** check box.
14. Click on the **Site** object to place and then rotate the car on the road.
15. Change to the **3D** and **North** views (see Figure 15-169).
16. Save this file as **SITE COMPONENTS**.

Figure 15-167

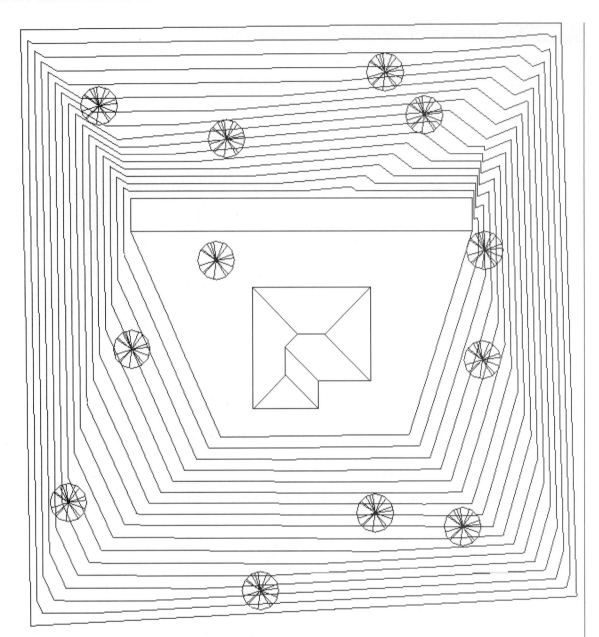

Place trees on the **Toposurface**

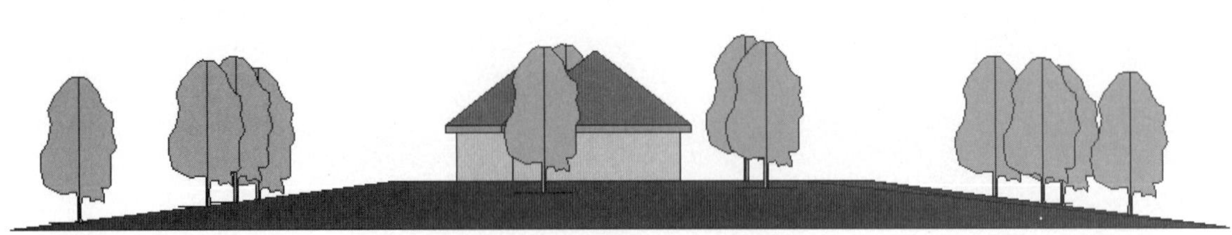

Figure 15-168

Trees automatically attach to the level of the **Toposurface**

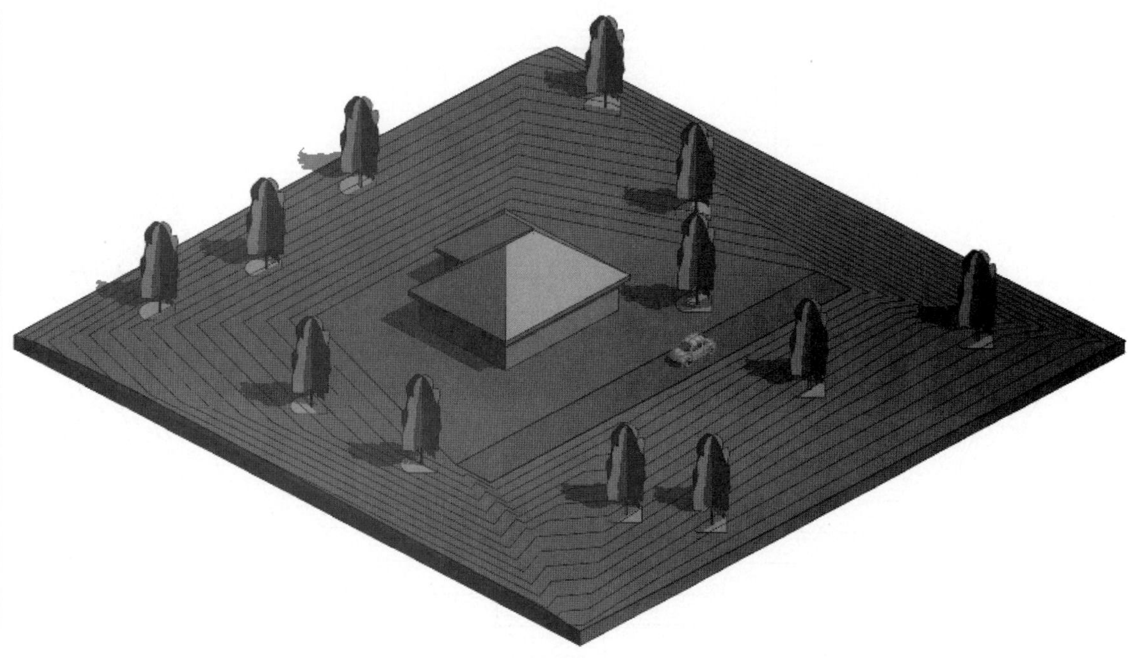

Figure 15-169

3D View

EXERCISE 15-23 **LABELING CONTOURS**

1. Using the previous exercise, change to the **Site** view.
2. Select the **Massing & Site** tab to bring up the **Massing & Site** toolbar.
3. In the **Massing & Site** toolbar, select the **Label Contours** button to bring up the **Label Contours** toolbar (see Figure 15-170).

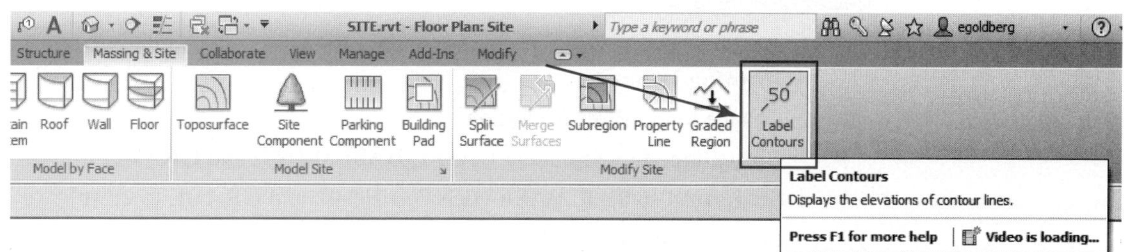

Figure 15-170

Label Contours button

4. Select the spot shown in Figure 15-171, drag downward, and click again to place the contour labels.
5. Save this file as **LABELING CONTOURS**.

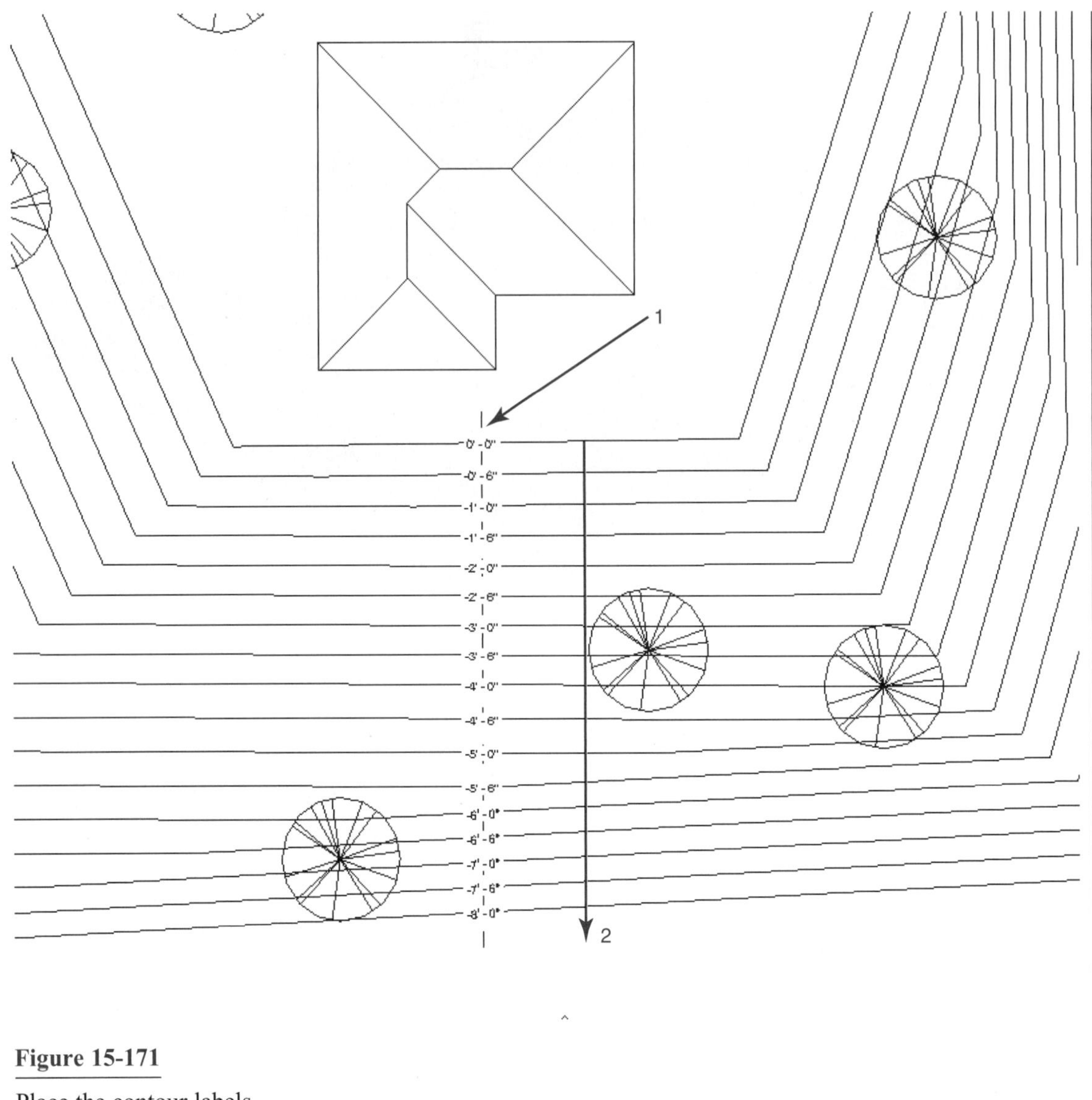

Figure 15-171

Place the contour labels

EXERCISE 15-24 **SLOPED BUILDING PADS**

1. Double-click on **Site** view in the **Project Browser** to bring the **Site** view into the **Drawing Editor**.
2. Change to the **West Elevation**.
3. Create three **Levels** named **Level 1, BASEMENT**, and **GRADE**.
4. Set **Level 1** to **0′-0″, BASEMENT** to **10′-0″,** and **GRADE** to **20′-0″**.
5. Select the **Massing & Site** tab to bring up the **Massing & Site** toolbar.
6. In the **Massing & Site** toolbar, select the **Toposurface** button to bring up the **Modify | Edit Surface** toolbar.
7. Create a **100′** × **100′ Toposurface** that is **20′-0″** high.
8. Double-click on the **BASEMENT** floor plan in the **Project Browser** to bring the **BASEMENT** view into the **Drawing Editor**.
9. In the **Massing & Site** toolbar, select the **Building Pad** button to bring up the **Modify | Create Pad Boundary** toolbar.
10. In the **Modify | Create Pad Boundary** toolbar, select the **Rectangle** button, and place a rectangle as shown in Figure 15-172.

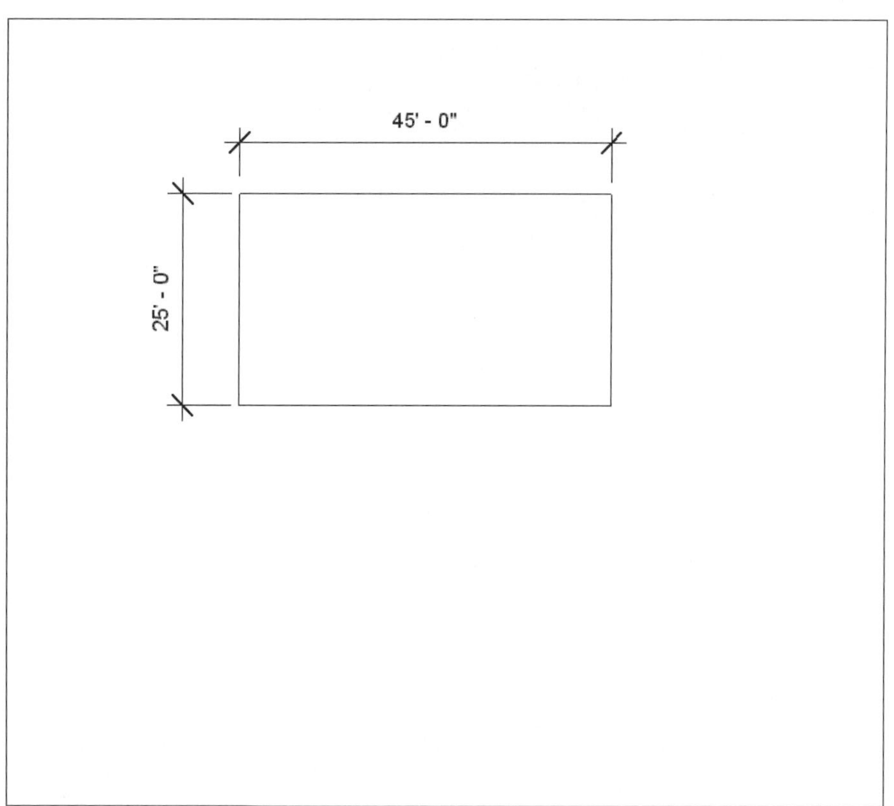

Figure 15-172

Place a rectangle

11. In the **Modify | Create Pad Boundary** toolbar, select the **Finish Edit Mode** button to create the pad.
12. In the **Massing & Site** toolbar, select the **Building Pad** button to bring up the **Modify | Create Pad Boundary** toolbar.
13. In the **Modify | Create Pad Boundary** toolbar, select the **Rectangle** button, and place a rectangle as shown in Figure 15-173.

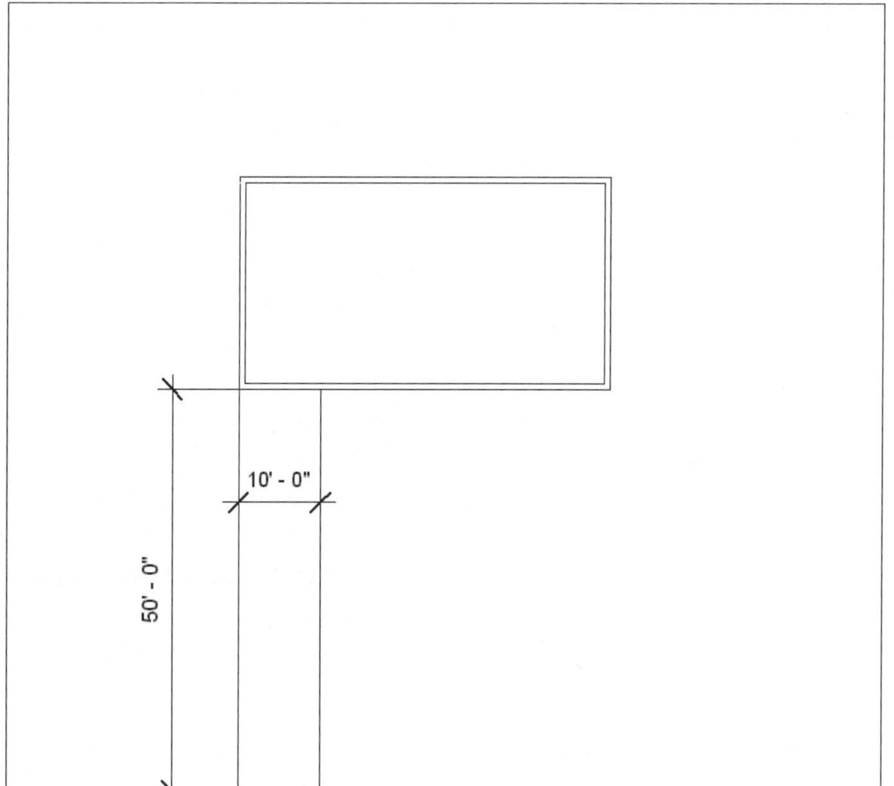

Figure 15-173

Place another rectangle

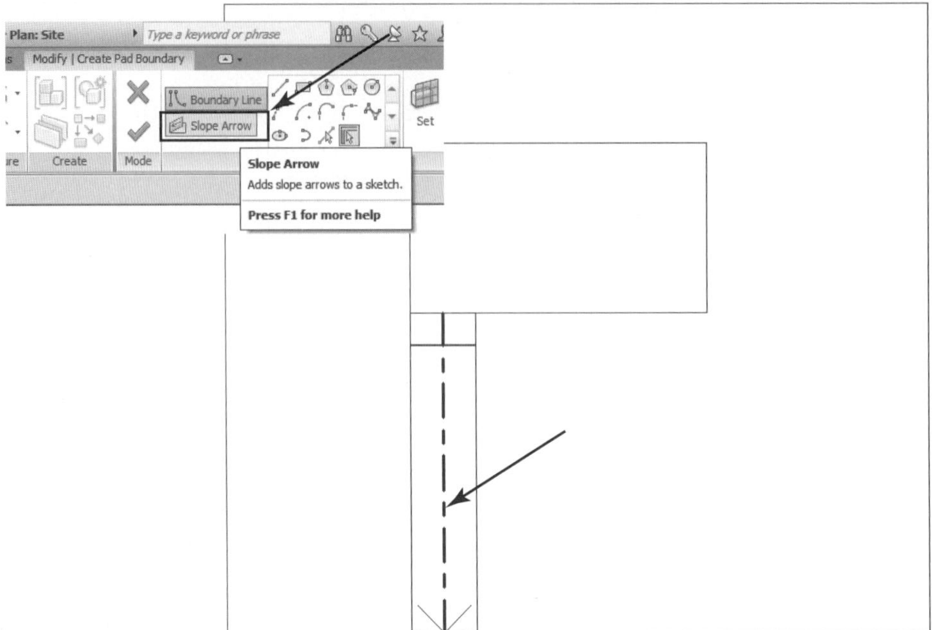

Figure 15-174

Slope Arrow button

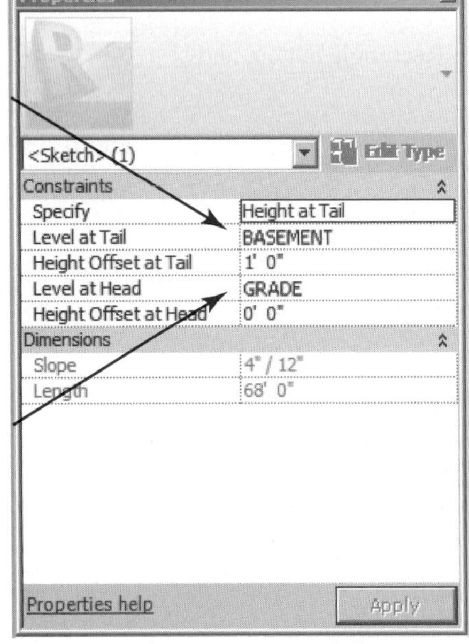

Properties for the Pad "Slope Arrow"

Figure 15-175

Properties dialog box

14. In the **Modify | Create Pad Boundary** toolbar, select the **Slope Arrow** button, and place it as shown in Figure 15-174.
15. Select the **Slope Arrow** to bring up its **Properties** dialog box.
16. In the **Properties** dialog box, set the **Level at Head** and **Level at Tail** to named levels. This is an easy way to control the **Slope Arrow** (see Figure 15-175).
17. In the **Modify | Create Pad Boundary** toolbar, select the **Finish Edit Mode** button to create the sloped pad.
18. Select the **View** tab to bring up the **View** toolbar.
19. In the **View** toolbar, select the **Section** button to bring up the **Modify | Section** toolbar.
20. Click in the **Drawing Editor**, drag downward, and then click again to place a **Section** callout (see Figure 15-176).
21. In the **Project Browser,** double-click on **Section 1** that you just created to bring the **Section 1** view into the **Drawing Editor** (see Figure 15-177).

Adding a building creates an excellent presentation (see Figures 15-178 and 15-179).

22. Save this file as **SLOPED BUILDING PADS**.

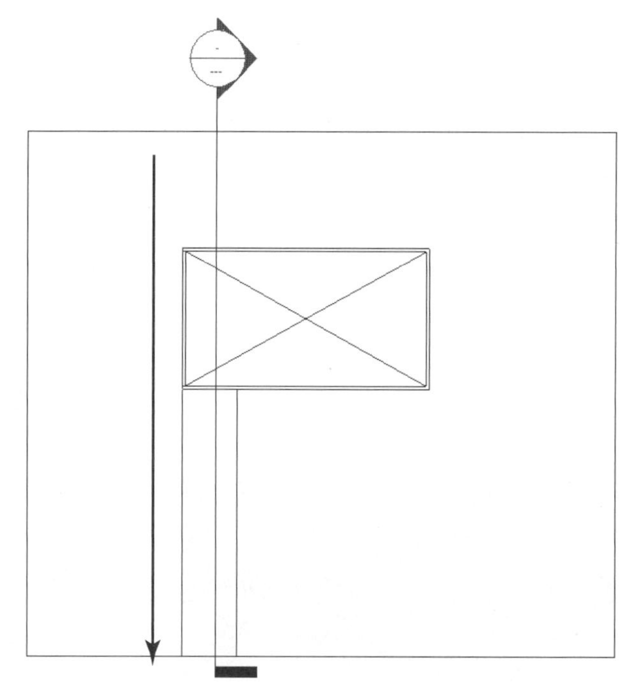

Figure 15-176

Place a **Section** callout

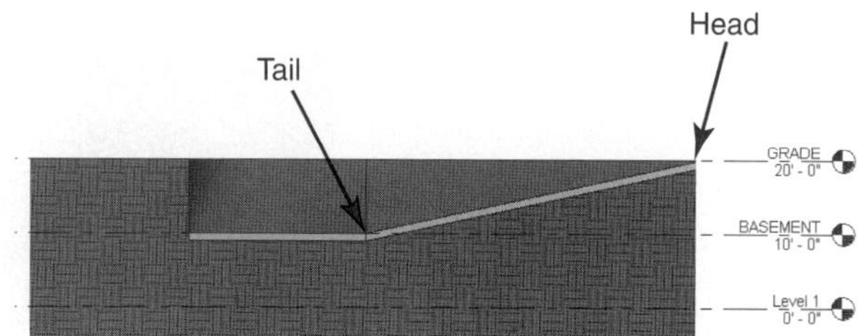

Figure 15-177

Section 1 view

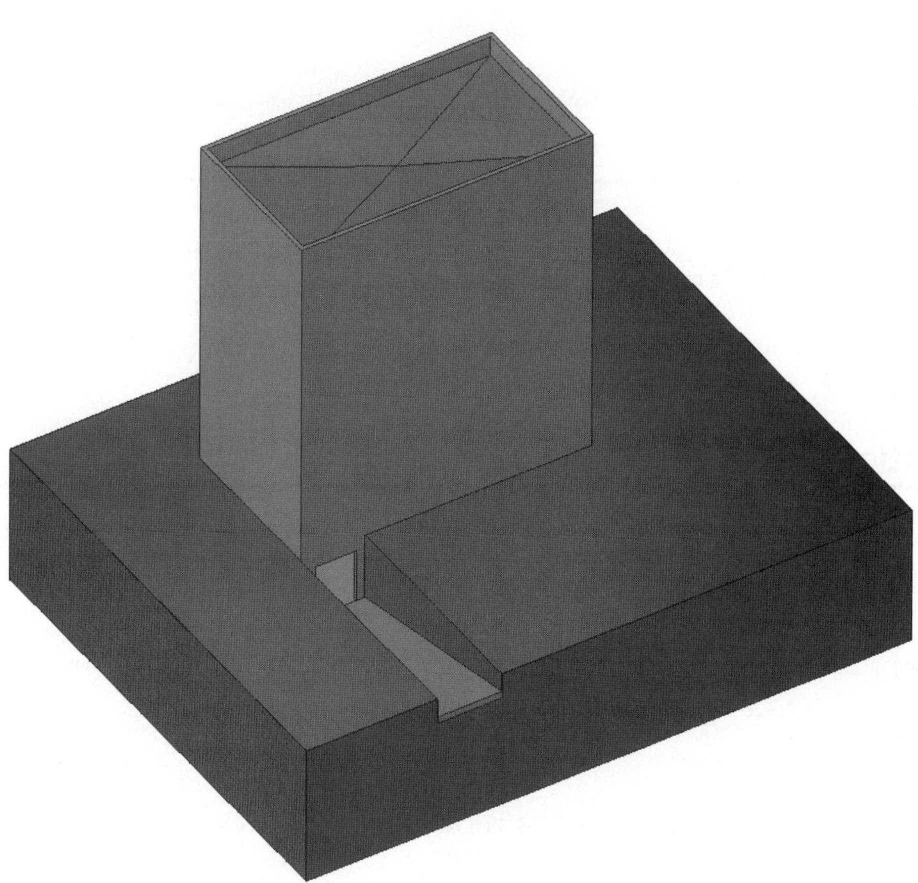

Figure 15-178

Add a building

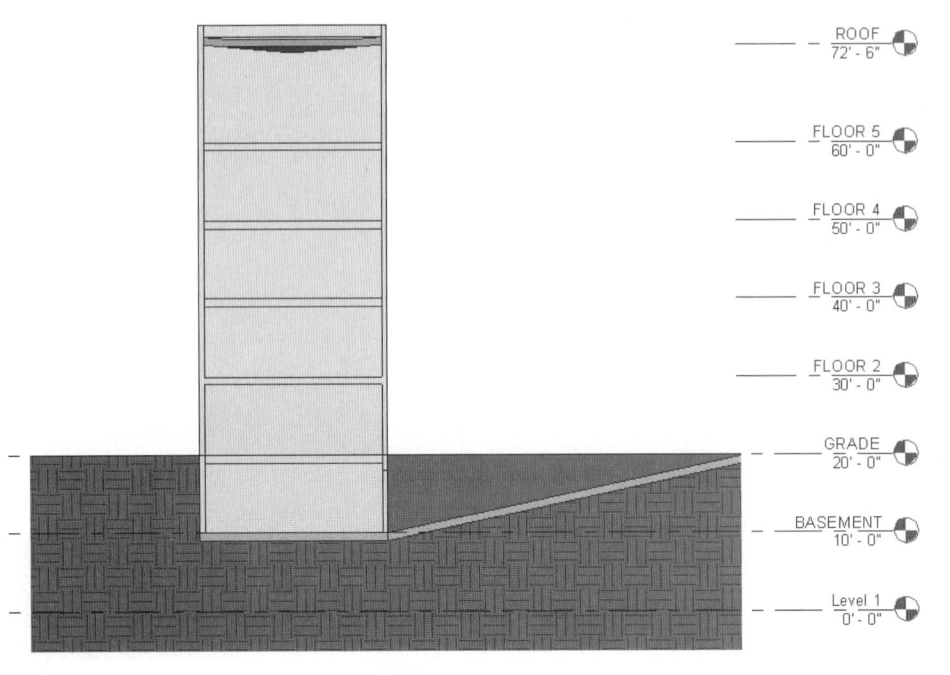

Figure 15-179

Building with a basement, floors, and roof

Chapter Summary

Mass Modeling has been presented with simple examples to demonstrate the power of the massing tools. With a little creativity, you can pretty much model any form you envision. It is up to you to take it to the next level and create complex shapes that once were impossible to create.

Chapter Test Questions

Multiple Choice

Circle the correct answer.

1. Massing can be approached in ________ way(s).
   a. 1
   b. 2
   c. 4
   d. 5
2. When you first open Revit, you will be taken to the ________ screen.
   a. Welcome
   b. Family editor
   c. Recent files
   d. In-Place family
3. To create a **Sweep** form, you need a profile and a
   a. Path.
   b. Void.
   c. Solid.
   d. Command.
4. In a **Revolve** form, you need a profile that revolves around a drawn
   a. Path.
   b. Reference line.
   c. Reference plane.
   d. Axis.

5. In order to extrude a profile, you need to select it and then click
   a. A blank area.
   b. A level.
   c. **Create form**.
   d. The **3D Control** arrows.

True or False

Circle the correct answer.

1. **True or False:** A surface form has no thickness.
2. **True or False:** You can extrude a line.
3. **True or False:** You can open a new mass family from the **Project Browser.**
4. **True or False:** To edit a mass form, you need to click a level, then click **Edit Profile**.
5. **True or False:** The work plane of a **Point Element** is parallel to the line where it is placed.

Questions

1. Which tool do you use to create a wall from a mass form?
2. What is a reference plane?
3. How does an **Adaptive Component** work?
4. How do you divide a surface of a mass?
5. Which tool do you use to see through a mass form?

CHAPTER

16 Views

CHAPTER OBJECTIVES

- Understand and use **Floor Plan** and **Reflected Ceiling Plan** (RFC) views.
- Learn how to create **Elevation** views.
- Learn how to create **Section** views.
- Learn how to create **Callout** views.
- Learn how to create **Drafting** views.
- Learn how to create **Camera** views.
- Learn how to animate with **Walkthrough** views.
- Know how to create and modify **Legend** views and **Legend** components.
- Learn how to create **Matchline** views.
- Learn how to create **Schedule** views.

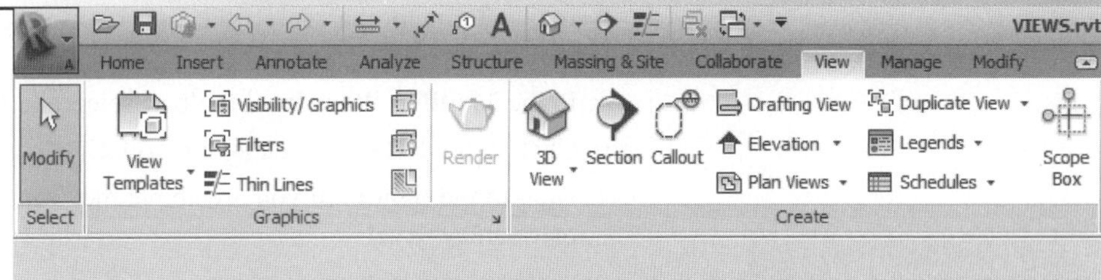

Introduction

Revit Architecture provides floor plans and reflected ceiling plans. It also includes many types of views, such as **Elevation**, **Interior Elevation**, **Drafting**, **Camera**, and **Walkthroughs**.

Floor Plans and Reflected Ceiling Plans

The **Floor Plan** view is the default view in a new project. Most projects include at least one floor plan. **Floor Plan** views are created automatically as you add new levels to your project. **Reflected Ceiling Plan** views are also created automatically as you add new levels to your project.

The default Revit Architecture 2012 template ships with two **Floor Plans** and two **Ceiling Plans** labeled **Level 1** and **Level 2** (see Figure 16-1).

Floor Plans and **Reflected Ceiling Plans** are connected to, and interactive with, the levels in **Elevation** view.

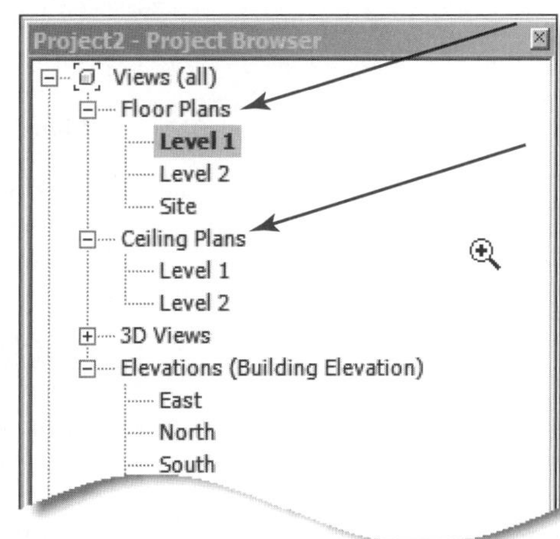

Figure 16-1

Revit 2012 ships with two **Floor Plan** and two **Ceiling Plan** views

EXERCISE 16-1 **CREATING NEW LEVELS AND FLOOR PLAN VIEWS**

1. Start a new drawing using the RAC 2012\Imperial Templates\default.rte template.
2. In the **Project Browser**, double-click on the **East Elevation** to bring it into the **Drawing Editor**.
3. Select the **Home** tab to bring up the **Home** toolbar.
4. In the **Home** toolbar, select the **Level** button to bring up the **Modify | Place level** toolbar.
5. In the **Modify | Place level** toolbar, select the **Line** button in the **Draw** panel.
6. Click to the left end and above **Level 2**.
7. Drag to the right until you are above the "roundel" of **Level 2**, and click again to place a new level.

TIP

You can also select a level, right mouse button click, and select **Create Similar** to create new levels.

Notice that the levels show up as new levels in the **Project Browser.** If you change the name of the levels in the **Elevation**, the levels change name in the **Project Browser** (see Figure 16-2).

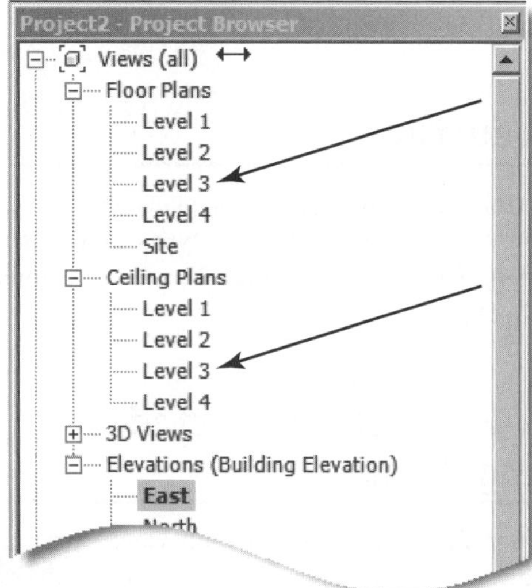

Figure 16-2

New level names are added to the **Project Browser**

Elevation Views

Elevation views are part of the default template in Revit Architecture. When you create a project with the template, four **Elevation** views are included: **North**, **South**, **East**, and **West**.

You can create additional **Exterior Elevation** views and **Interior Elevation** views. **Interior Elevation** views depict detailed views of interior walls and show how the features of the wall should be built.

The **Floor Plan** views in the default 2012 template contain four **Elevation** view **Cameras** labeled **North**, **East**, **South**, and **West**. They correspond to the **North**, **East**, **South**, and **West Elevations** in the **Project Browser** (see Figure 16-3).

Double-clicking on any **Elevation** view in the **Project Browser** will bring up that view in the **Drawing Editor** (see Figure 16-4).

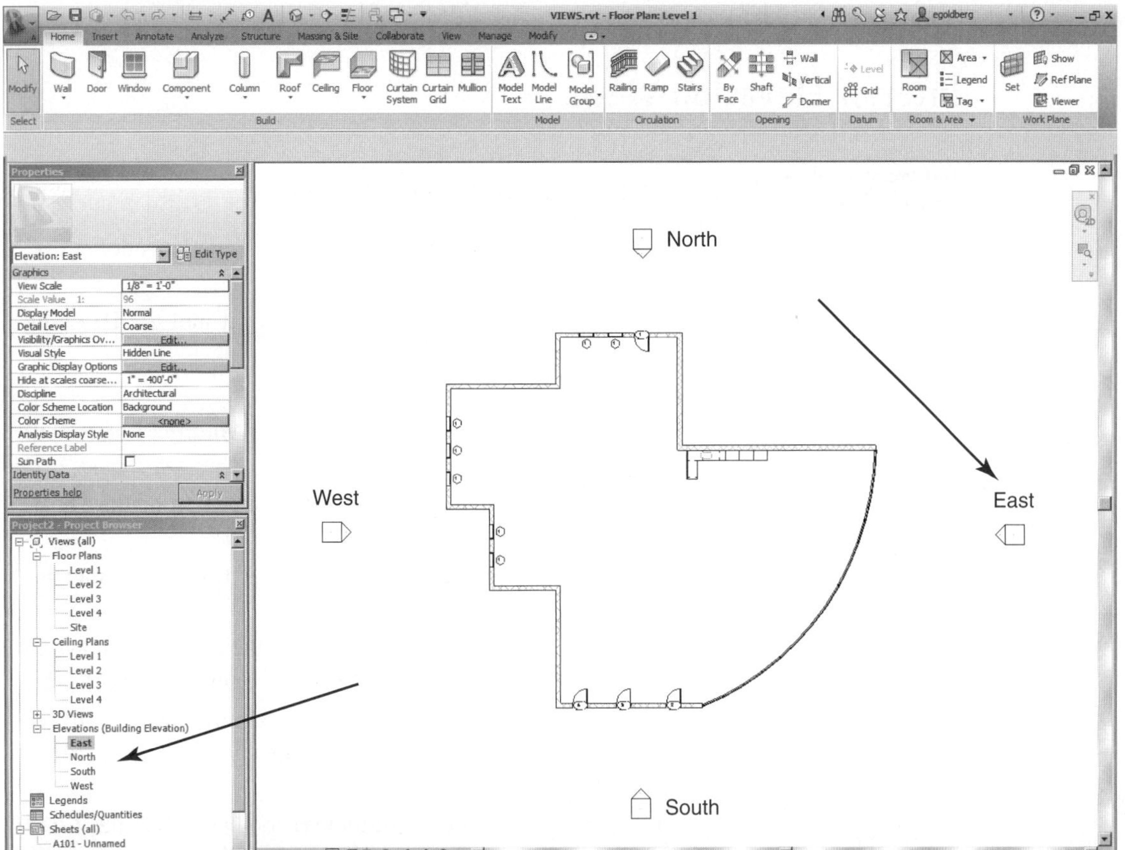

Figure 16-3

Four **Elevation** view cameras

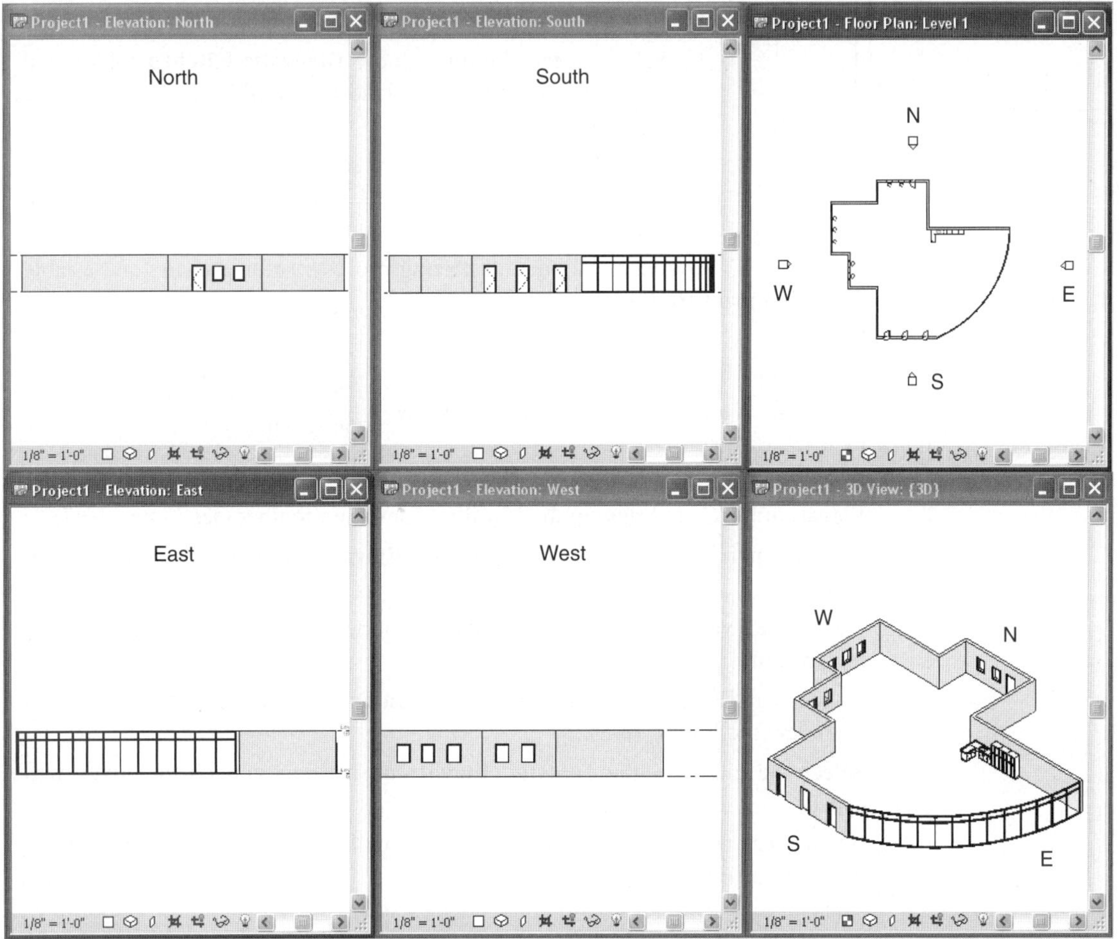

Figure 16-4

The **Drawing Editor**

Interior Elevation Views

EXERCISE 16-2 **CREATING NEW INTERIOR ELEVATION VIEWS**

1. Start a new drawing using the RAC 2012\Imperial Templates\default.rte template.
2. Double-click on **Level 1** in the **Project Browser** to bring it into the **Drawing Editor**.
3. Select the **Home** tab to bring up the **Home** toolbar.
4. In the **Home** toolbar, select the **Wall** button to bring up the **Modify | Place Wall** toolbar.
5. In the **Modify | Place Wall** toolbar, select the **Line** button from the **Draw** panel.
6. In the **Properties** dialog box, select **Basic Wall: Generic - 8″** from the **Properties** drop-down list.
7. Place the walls **10′-0″** high, and create the enclosure shown in Figure 16-5. Then press the **<Esc>** key to end the command.

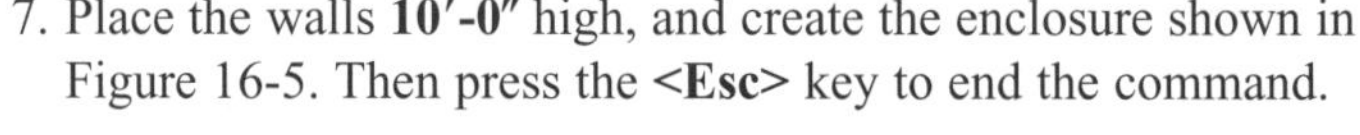

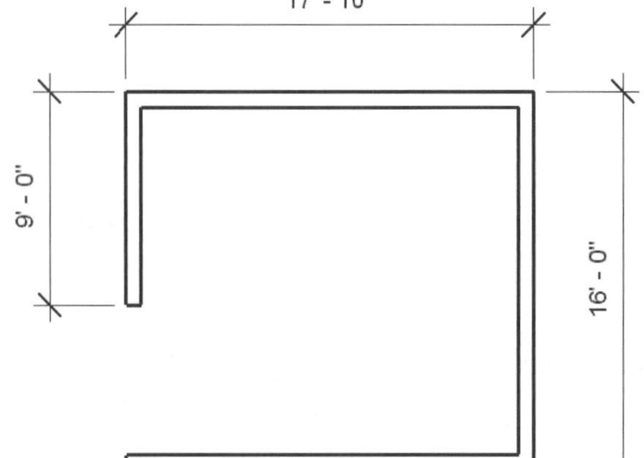

Figure 16-5

Create an enclosure

8. In the **Home** toolbar, select the **Component** > **Place a Component** button to bring up the **Modify | Place Component** toolbar.
9. In the **Modify | Place Component** toolbar, select the **Load Family** button to bring up the **Load Family** dialog box in the **Imperial Library** folder.
10. In the **Imperial Library** folder, open the **Casework** folder.
11. In the **Casework** folder, open the **Domestic Kitchen** folder.
12. Select all the **Families** in the **Domestic Kitchen** folder, and press the **Open** button to load the **Families** and return to the **Drawing Editor**.
13. In the **Properties** dialog box, select base cabinets, countertops, and upper cabinets from the **Change element** drop-down list, and place them in the enclosure you made.
14. Repeat the **Component** loading and placing process, loading chairs and a table from the **Furniture** folder.
15. Place two windows in the enclosure walls (see Figure 16-6).
16. Select the **View** tab to bring up the **View** toolbar.
17. In the **View** toolbar, select the **Elevation** > **Elevation** button to bring up the **Modify | Elevation** toolbar (see Figure 16-7).
18. In the **Properties** dialog box, select **Interior Elevation** from the **Properties** drop-down list.
19. Place the **Elevation** marker in the middle of your enclosure with the pointer pointing upward.
20. Notice that **Elevation 1-a** appears in the **Interior Elevations** of the **Project Browser** (see Figure 16-8).
21. Select the circle in the **Interior Elevations** marker, and check boxes will appear.
22. If you check the check boxes, new elevations will appear in the **Project Browser** (see Figure 16-9).

> **NOTE:**
>
> Chapter 6 covers **Components** in more detail.

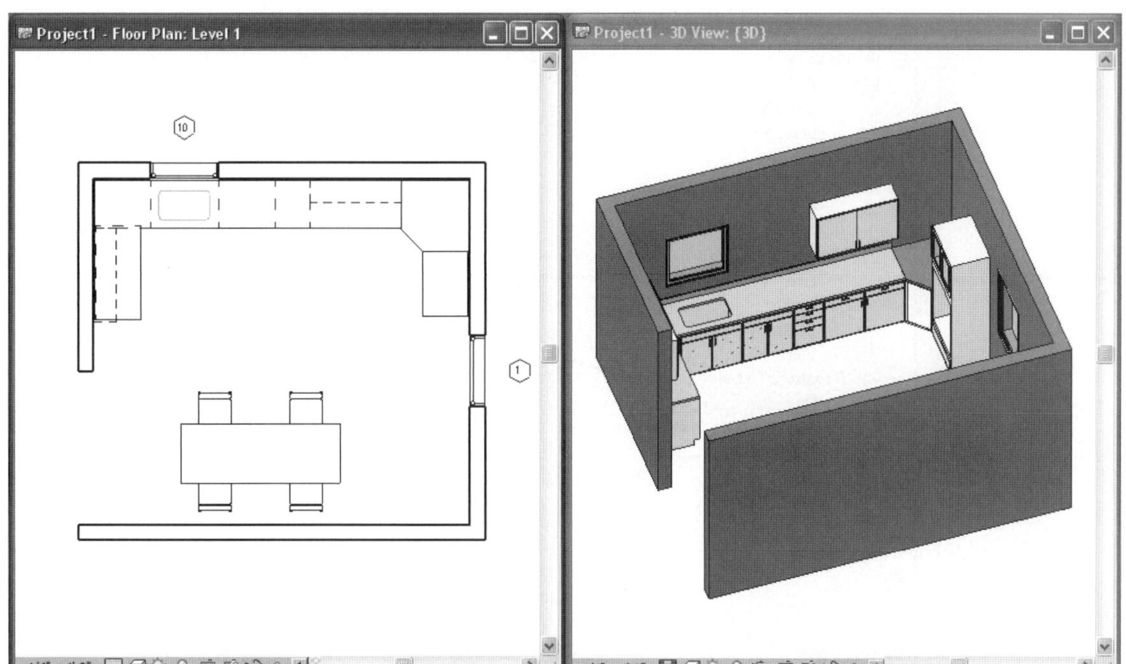

Figure 16-6

Place two windows in the enclosure walls

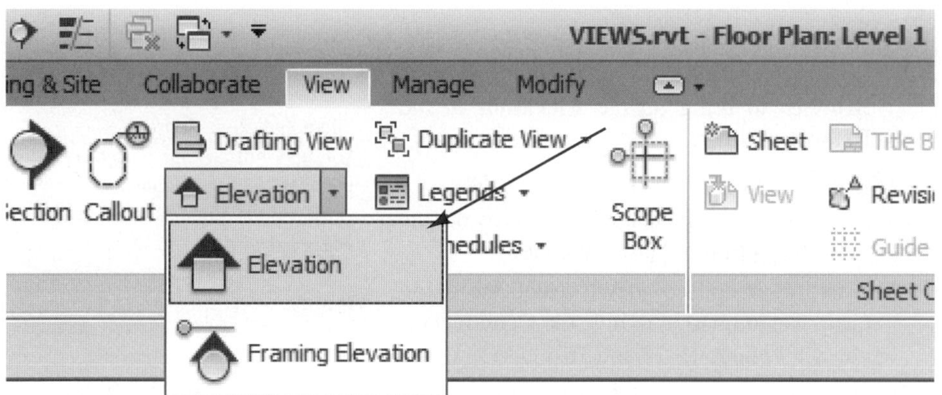

Figure 16-7

The **Elevation** > **Elevation** button

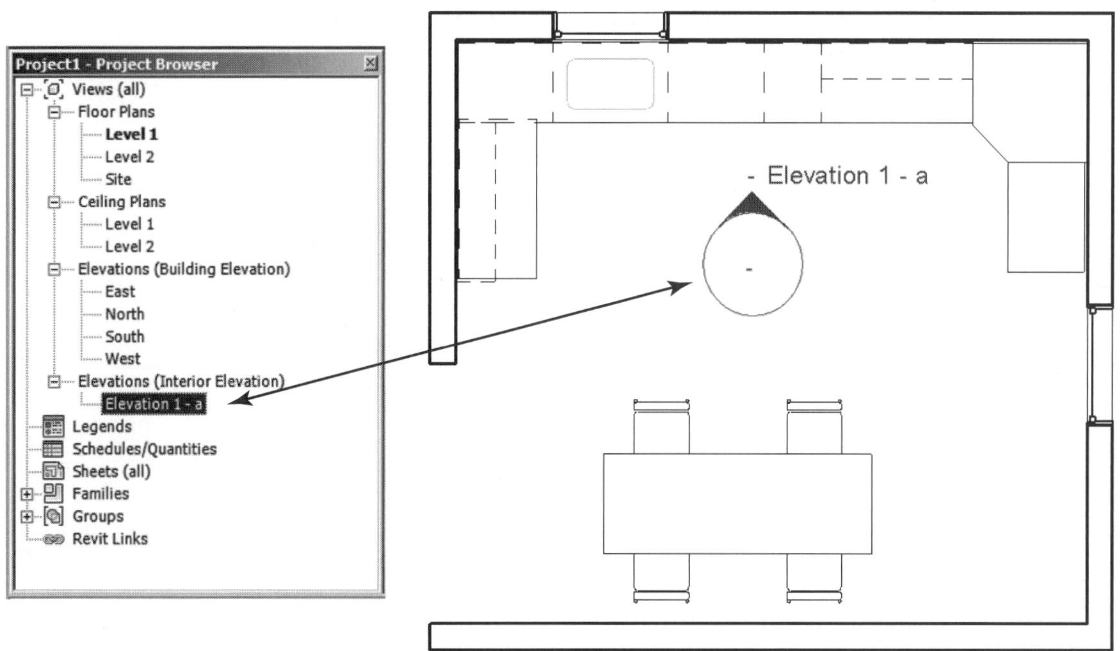

Figure 16-8

Interior Elevations in the **Project Browser**

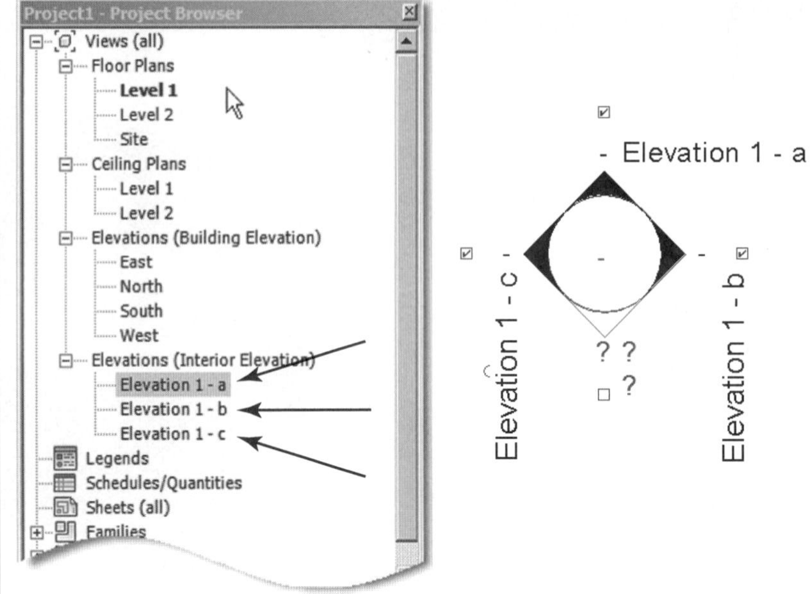

Figure 16-9

New elevations appear in the **Project Browser**

23. Double-click on **Elevation 1-a** in the **Project Browser** to bring up the **Elevation** in the **Drawing Editor**.

To control the **Crop** view, do the following:

24. Select the **Crop** rectangle, and move the arrows that appear to "crop" the view.
25. After cropping the view, select the **Hide Crop Region** button to hide the **Crop** rectangle (see Figures 16-10 and 16-11).

> **NOTE:**
> When the **Elevation** comes up, you may notice that it is surrounded by a rectangle. This is the **Crop** view and dictates what will be shown on the **Drawing** sheet when you drag the view to that sheet.

26. Double-click on **Level 1** in the **Project Browser** to bring it into the **Drawing Editor**.
27. Select the circle of the **Elevation** marker you placed in Step 19 to activate its adjustment.

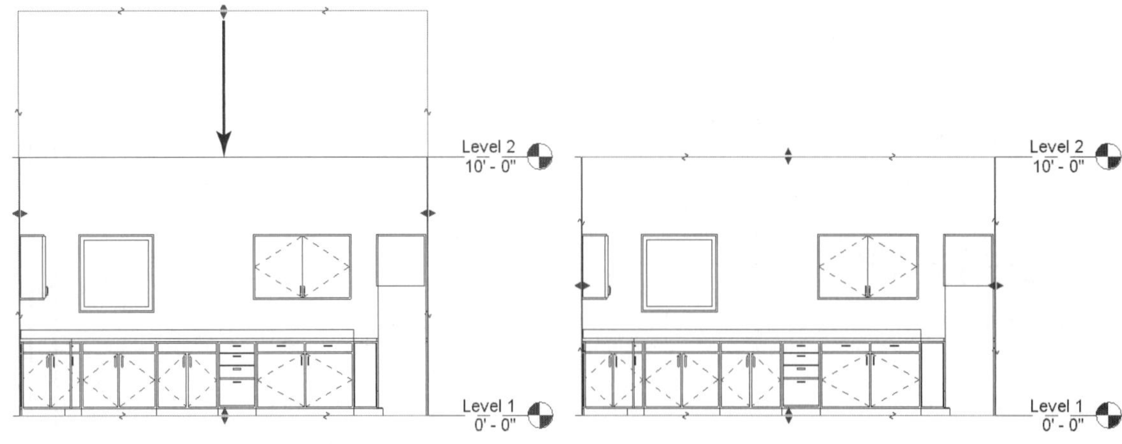

Figure 16-10

Select the **Crop** rectangle

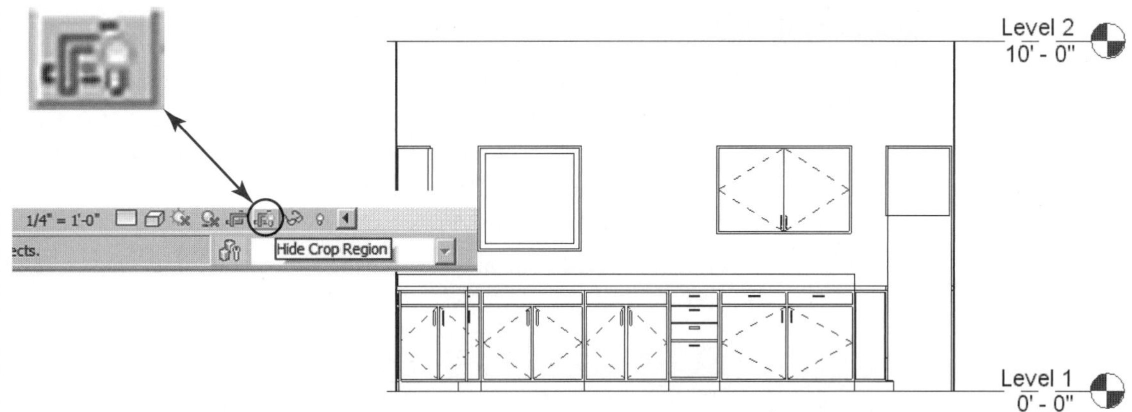

Figure 16-11

Hide Crop Region button

28. Check the check boxes opposite the elevations you wish to add, and then press the <Esc> key to create the new **Elevation** view.
29. Repeat Steps 24 and 25 to create all four views.
30. Click on one of the arrows in the **Elevation** marker to show the **Crop Region** in the **Floor Plan** view.
31. Adjust the **Crop Region** in the **Floor Plan** view to encompass the objects you wish to see in the **Elevation** view, and press the **<Esc>** key to complete the adjustment.
32. Double-click on **Elevation 1-a, Elevation 1-b, Elevation 1-c,** and **Elevation 1-d** that have been automatically created in the **Project Browser** to bring them up in the **Drawing Editor**.
33. Adjust the **Crop Region** for each elevation you created.
34. Save this file as **INTERIOR ELEVATIONS** (see Figure 16-12).

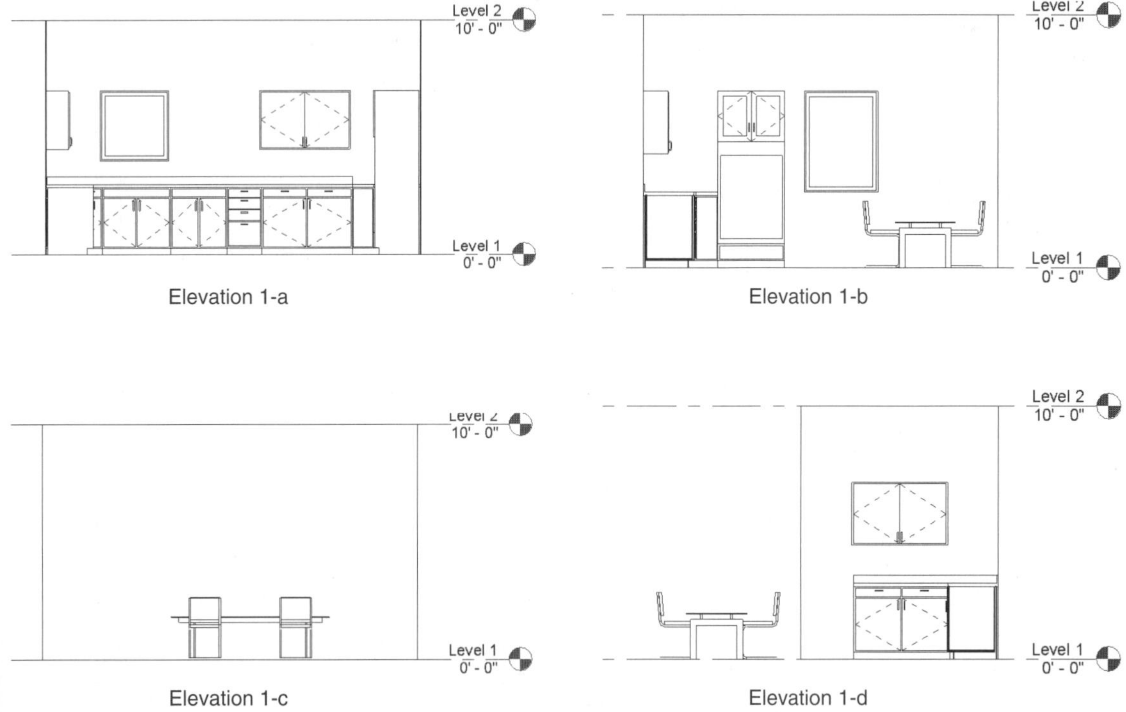

Figure 16-12

Interior Elevations floor plan

EXERCISE 16-3 CREATING NEW SECTION VIEWS

1. Using the previous exercise, double-click on **Level 1** in the **Project Browser** to bring it into the **Drawing Editor**.
2. Delete the **Elevation** marker, or delete **Elevation 1-a, Elevation 1-b, Elevation 1-c,** and **Elevation 1-d** from the **Project Browser**.
3. Select the **View** tab to bring up the **View** toolbar.
4. In the **View** toolbar, select the button to bring up the **Section** toolbar (see Figure 16-13).

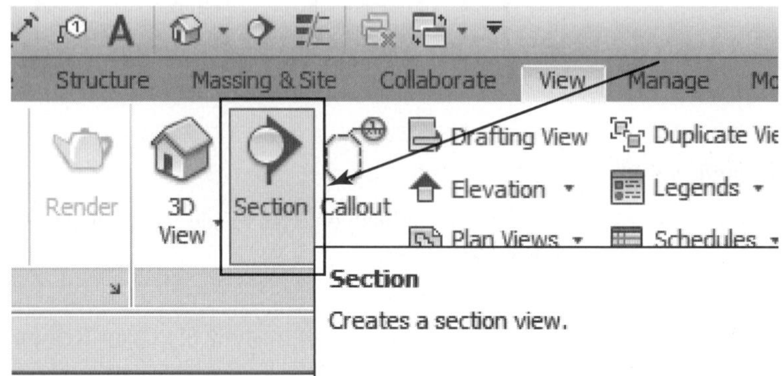

Figure 16-13

Section toolbar

5. Place a **Section** marker by clicking at the left of the enclosure, dragging to the right of the enclosure, and clicking again. Make sure the marker bisects the cabinets and counter (see Figure 16-14).
6. Click in an empty space in the **Drawing Editor** to end the **Section** command.

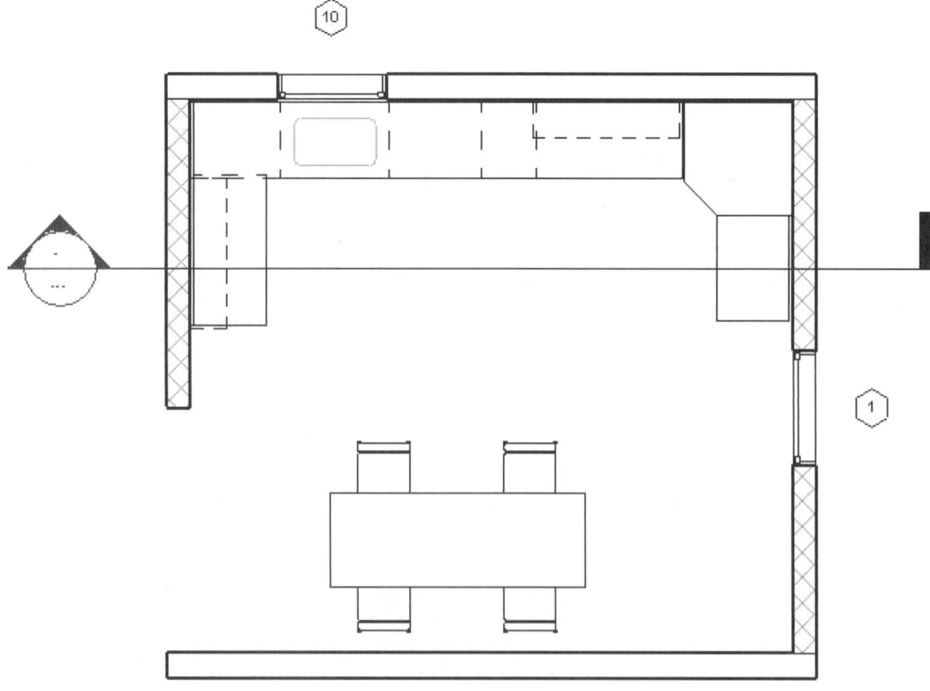

Figure 16-14

The **Section** marker bisects the cabinets and counter

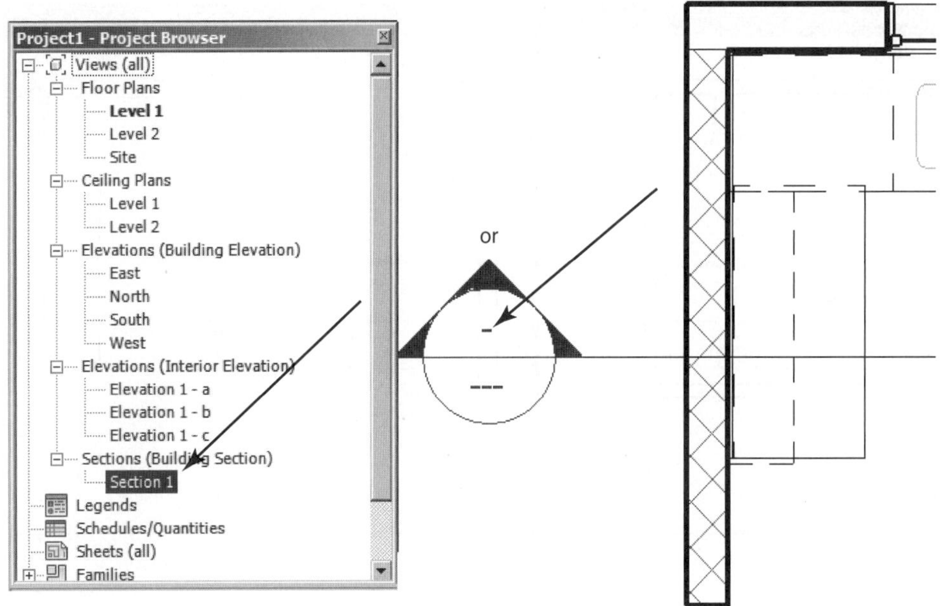

Figure 16-15

Bring **Section 1** into the **Drawing Editor**

7. Click the dashes in the head of the **Section** marker, or double-click **Section 1** that has appeared in the **Sections (Building Section)** tree in the **Project Browser**. This will bring the section into the **Drawing Editor** (see Figure 16-15).

A **Crop Region** will appear around the section; using the information you learned in the previous exercise, adjust and hide the **Crop Region**.

8. Close all views except **Level 1** and **Section 1**.
9. In the **View** toolbar, select the **Tile** button to tile the views side by side (see Figures 16-16 and 16-17).
10. Select and move the **Section** marker in the **Level 1** view, and notice how the **Section** view changes (see Figure 16-18).
11. Save this file as **SECTION VIEWS**.

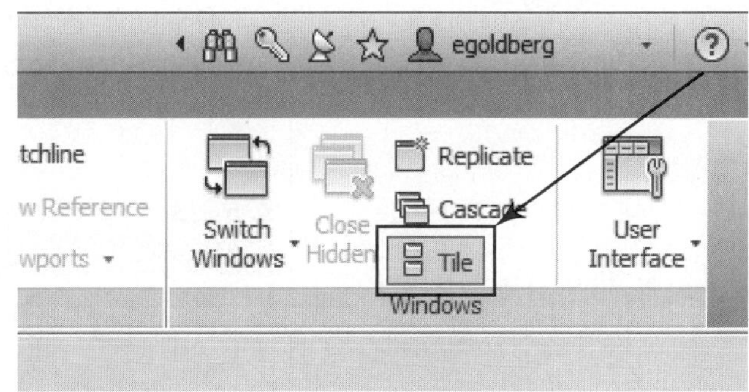

Figure 16-16

Tile button

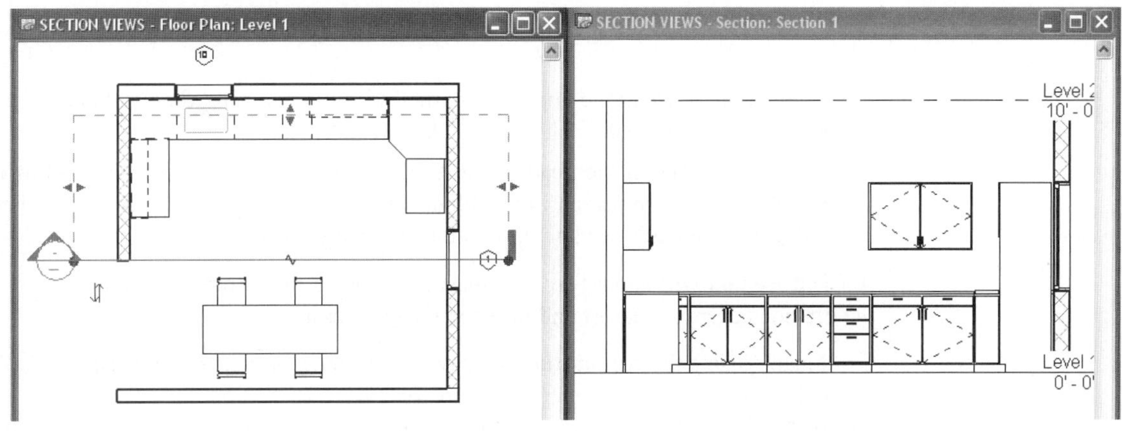

Figure 16-17

Section views

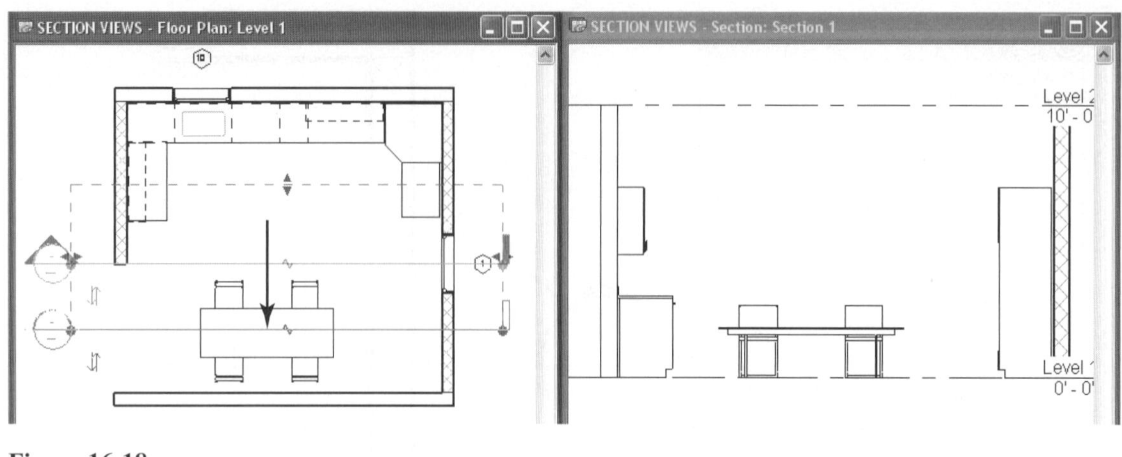

Figure 16-18

Move the **Section** marker

EXERCISE 16-4 **CREATING NEW CALLOUT VIEWS**

Callout views are used to show special areas in more detail.

1. Using the previous exercise, double-click on **Level 1** in the **Project Browser** to bring it into the **Drawing Editor**.
2. Delete the **Section** marker, or delete **Section 1** from the **Project Browser**.
3. In the **View** toolbar, select the **Callout** button to bring up the **Callout** toolbar (see Figure 16-19).

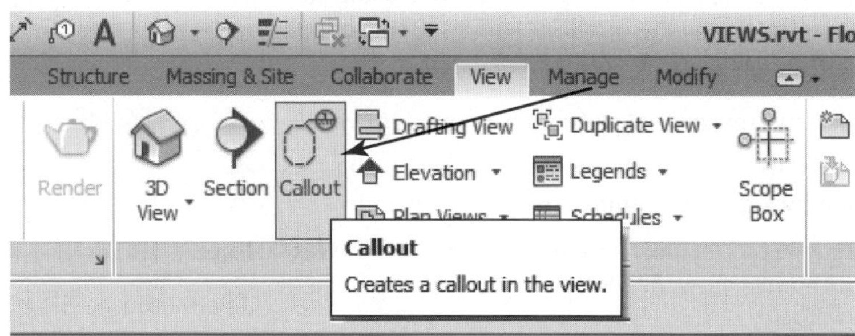

Figure 16-19

Callout button

4. Click your mouse at the upper left corner of your enclosure; drag and click again at the lower left location shown in Figure 16-20.
5. Click the dashes in the head of the **Callout** marker, or double-click **Callout of Level 1** that has appeared in the **Floor Plans** tree in the **Project Browser**. This will bring the **Callout** view up into the **Drawing Editor**.

A **Crop Region** will appear around the section; using the information you learned in the previous exercise, adjust and hide the **Crop Region**.

6. Finally, using the **Annotation** tools, you can change scale, add dimensions, put in extra insulation, and so on (see Figure 16-21).
7. Delete the **Callout** marker, or delete **Callout of Level 1** that has appeared in the **Floor Plans** tree of the **Project Browser**.
8. Again, select the **Callout** button from the **View** toolbar.

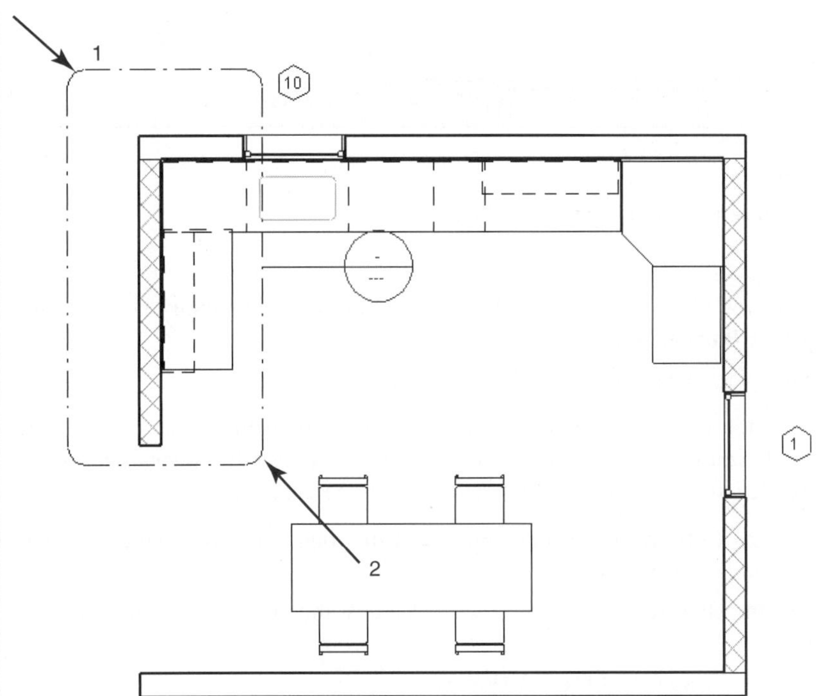

Figure 16-20

Click and drag from the upper left corner of the enclosure

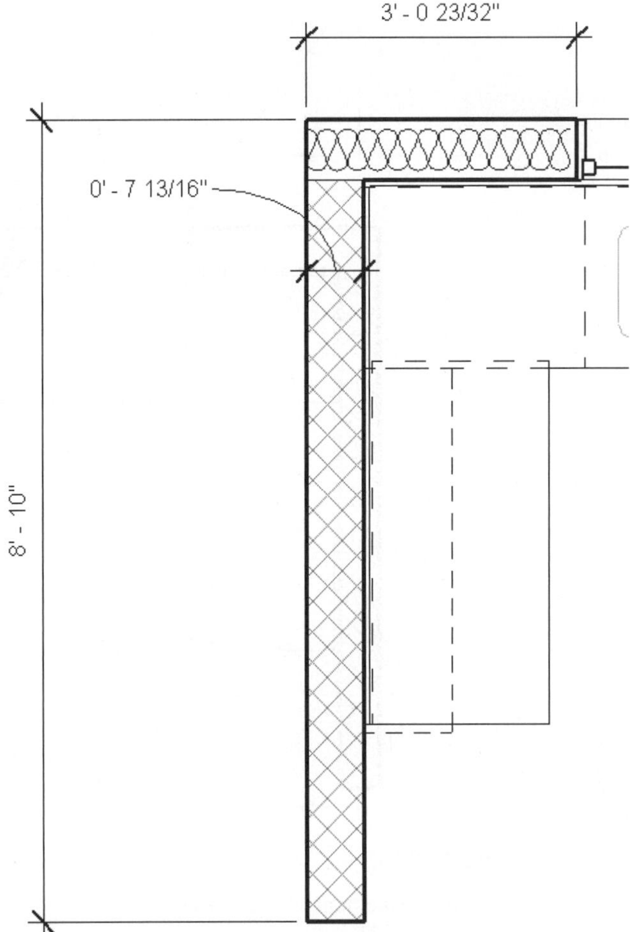

Figure 16-21

Use the **Annotation** tools to change scale, add dimensions, add insulation, and so on

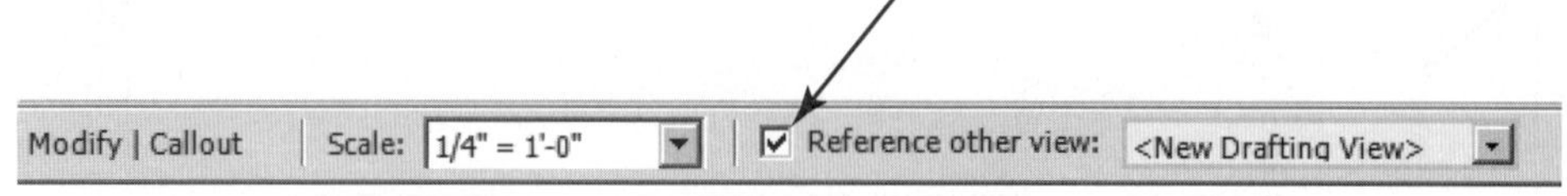

Figure 16-22

Check the **Reference other view** check box

9. Before you place the **Callout**, check the **Reference other view** check box in the **Options Bar** (see Figure 16-22).
10. Again, place a callout as you did in Step 4 of this exercise.

Notice that the **Level 1 Callout** now appears under **Drafting** views in the **Project Browser**. If you double-click on this callout in the **Project Browser**, you will get a **Drafting** view on which to draw 2D details and be referenced to the **Callout**.

11. Select the **Callout** marker line, and select the round grip to move the marker as shown in Figure 16-23.
12. Select the other round grips to move and adjust the placement of the marker (see Figure 16-24).
13. Save this file as **CALLOUT VIEWS**.

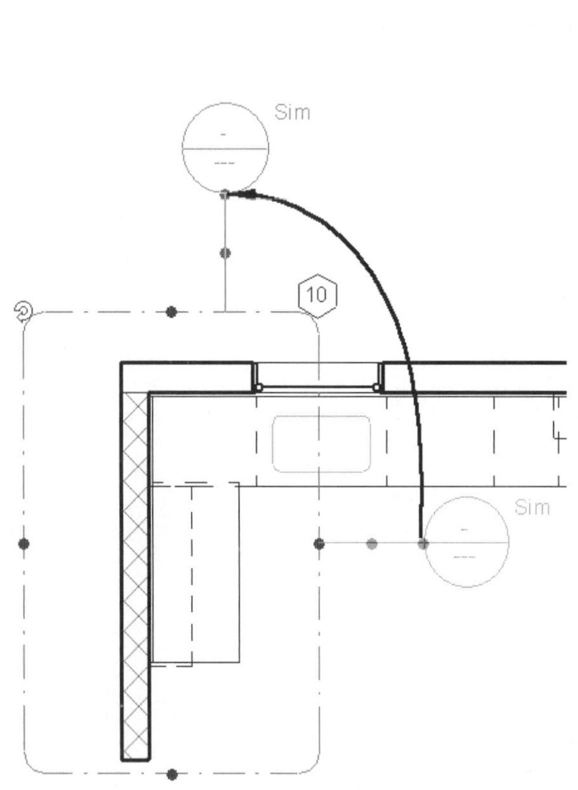

Figure 16-23

Select the round grip to move the marker

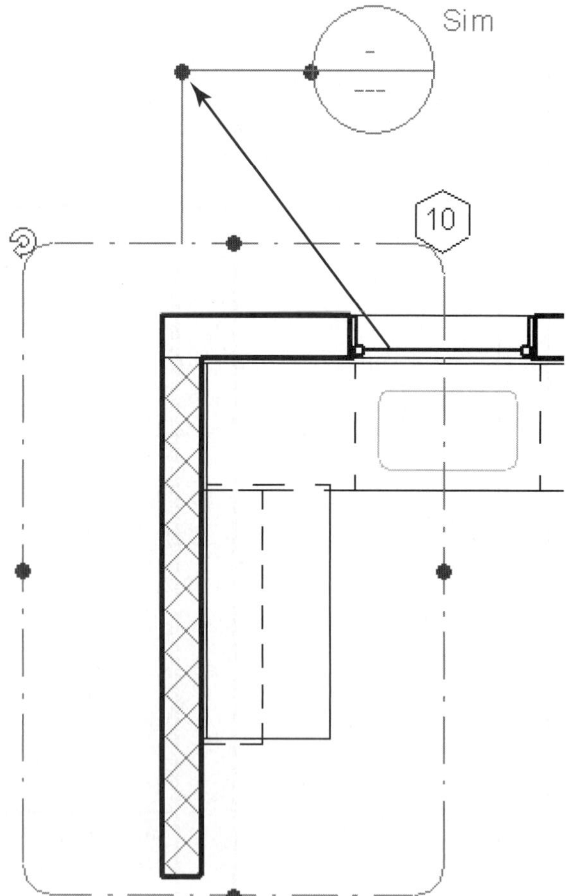

Figure 16-24

Adjust the placement of the marker

Drafting Views

During the course of a project, you may want to create details in a view that is not directly associated with the model. Rather than create a callout and then add details to it, you may want to create detail conditions where the model is not needed (for example, a carpet-transition detail, which shows where carpet switches to tile, or roof-drain details not based on a callout on the roof).

You create this unassociated, view-specific detail in a Drafting view. The Drafting view is not associated with the model. In a Drafting view, you create details at differing view scales (coarse, medium, or fine) and use 2D detailing tools: detail lines, detail regions, detail components, insulation, reference planes, dimensions, symbols, and text. These are the exact same tools used in creating a Detail view. However, Drafting views do not display any model elements. When you create a Drafting view in a project, it is saved with the project.

The use of the Drafting view is illustrated in Chapter 12.

Camera Views

Camera views are a variation of the **3D Default View (Isometric)**. The difference is that a **Camera** view is true perspective. Most typical architectural presentations and visualizations are done in this view.

EXERCISE 16-5 **CREATING NEW CAMERA VIEWS**

1. Using the previous exercise, double-click on **Level 1** in the **Project Browser** to bring it into the **Drawing Editor**.
2. Delete the **Callout** marker, or delete **Callout of Level 1** in the **Project Browser**.
3. In the **View** toolbar, select the **3D View > Camera** button (see Figure 16-25).

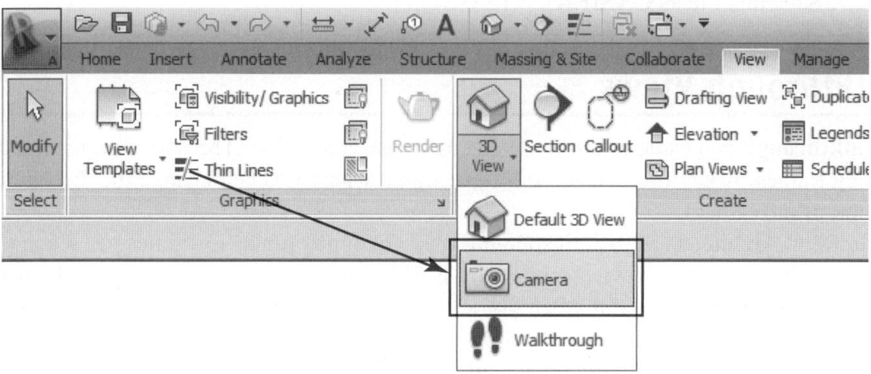

Figure 16-25

3D View > Camera button

4. Place a **Camera** by clicking at the left of the enclosure (to place the camera), and then clicking again in the center of the enclosure (to place the target).
5. In the **Project Browser**, expand the **3D Views** tree, and select **3D View 1** (the **Camera** view you just created), **RMB** (right mouse button click), and select **Rename** from the contextual menu that appears.
6. Change the name of **3D View 1** to **CAMERA**.
7. Close all views except **Level 1** and **CAMERA**.
8. In the **View** toolbar, select the **Tile** button to tile the views side by side.
9. In the **View Control Bar**, select **Shading with Edges** and **Shadows On** from the **Model: Graphic Style and Shadows** buttons at the bottom of the **Drawing Editor** (see Figure 16-26).
10. In the **CAMERA** view, select the **Crop Region**.

Figure 16-26

Use the **View Control Bar** to add shading and shadows

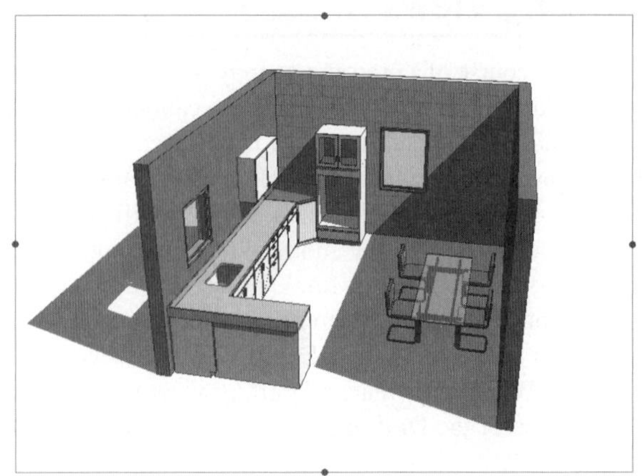

11. With the **Crop Region** in the **CAMERA** view selected, the camera will appear in the **Level 1** view.
12. Click in the **Level 1** view.
13. Move the camera, and the **CAMERA** view will change.
14. Change to the **CAMERA** view.
15. Place your cursor within the **Crop Region**, hold the **<Shift>** key, and depress the **middle** (roll button) on your mouse.
16. While holding these buttons, move your mouse to change the **CAMERA** view, and also move the camera in the **Level 1** view.
17. Save this file as **CAMERA VIEWS**.

NOTE:

You must activate the **Crop Region** in the **CAMERA** view before you can again see the **Camera** in the **Floor Plan** view.

Walkthrough Views

A **Walkthrough** is a camera that follows a path that you define. The path comprises frames and key frames. A key frame is a modifiable frame where you can change the direction and position of the camera.

In Revit Architecture 2012, the default **Walkthroughs** run at 15 frames per second. The default **Walkthrough** in Revit Architecture is 300 frames (pictures) or 20 seconds of playback. The key frame is a point when you click to change direction. The name "key frame" comes from the fact that the main animators (in Disney's time) were the people who made the key (or main) pictures, and their aides made the in-between pictures (tweens).

EXERCISE 16-6 **CREATING WALKTHROUGH VIEWS**

1. Start a new drawing using the RAC 2012\Imperial Templates\default.rte template.
2. In the **Project Browser**, double-click on the **Level 1 Floor Plan** to bring it into the **Drawing Editor**.
3. Select the **Home** tab to bring up the **Home** toolbar.
4. In the **Home** toolbar, select the **Wall, Door,** and **Window** buttons, and then create the enclosure shown in Figure 16-27. Make the walls **10′-0″** high, and vary their **Families**.
5. In the **View** toolbar, select the **3D View** > **Walkthrough** button to bring up the **Modify | Walkthrough** toolbar (see Figure 16-28).
6. Starting at the left, click approximately every **10′-0″** as you trace a path through the enclosure.
7. After the last click, in the **Modify | Walkthrough** toolbar, press the **Finish walkthrough** button to stop the path, and create the **Walkthrough** as shown in Figure 16-29.

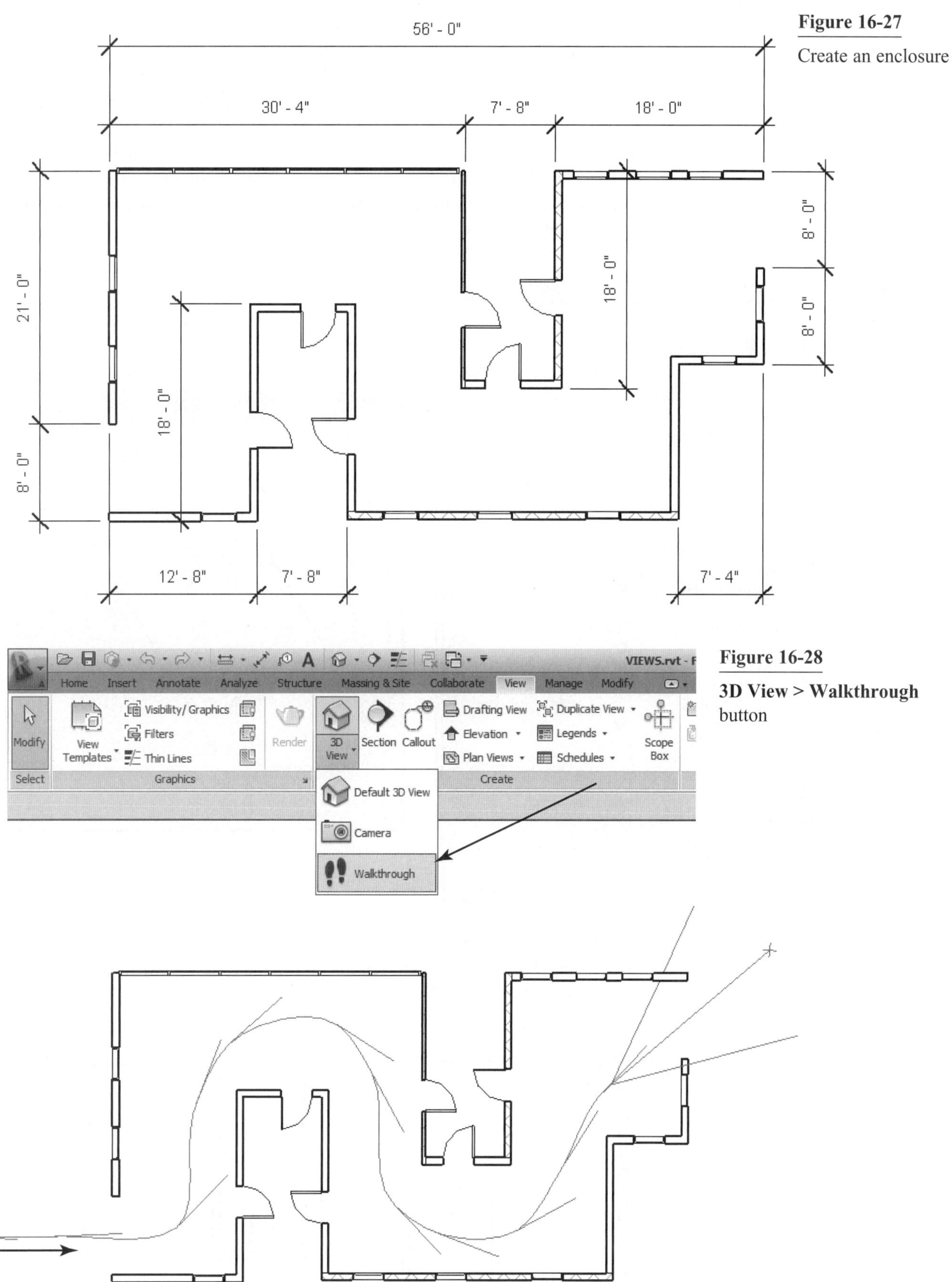

Figure 16-27

Create an enclosure

Figure 16-28

3D View > Walkthrough button

Figure 16-29

Create a **Walkthrough**

8. Expand the Walkthrough list in the Project Browser.
9. Right mouse click on the Walkthrough in the list and select Show Camera from the contextual menu.
10. In the **Drawing Editor**, select the **Walkthrough Path** to bring up its **Properties** dialog box.
11. At the bottom of the **Properties** dialog box, select the **300** button in the **Walkthrough Frames** field to bring up the **Walkthrough Frames** dialog box.
12. In the **Walkthrough Frames** dialog box, check the **Indicators** check box, leave the **Frame increment** at **30**, and press the **OK** buttons to return to the **Drawing Editor** (see Figure 16-30).

Figure 16-30

Properties dialog box and **Walkthrough Frames** dialog box

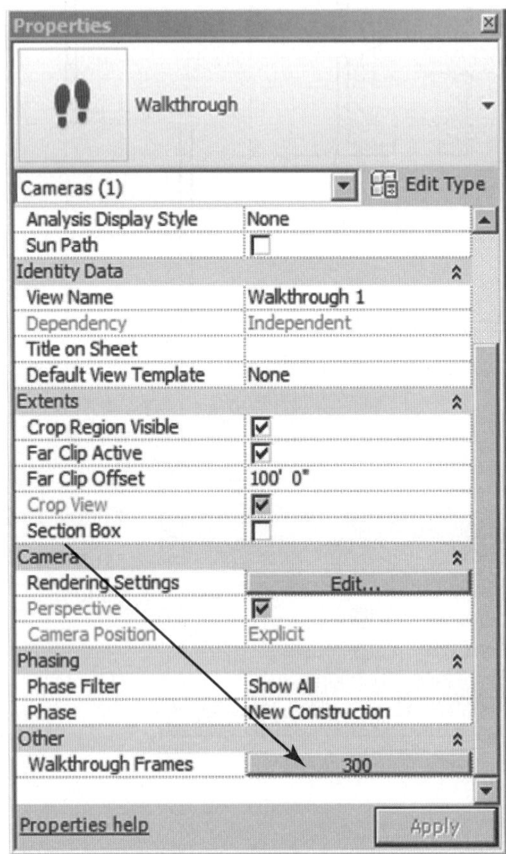

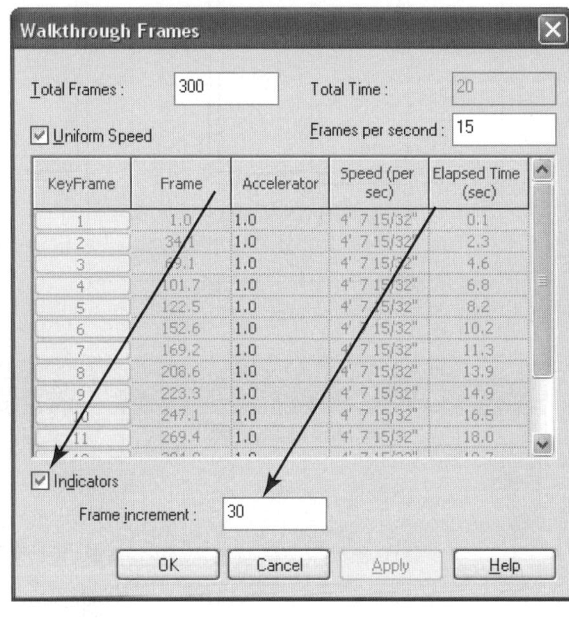

You can now see 10 of the frames in the **Level 1** floor plan (see Figure 16-31).

13. With the **Walkthrough Path** selected, select the **Edit Walkthrough** button in the **Modify | Cameras** toolbar.

Figure 16-31

Level 1 floor plan

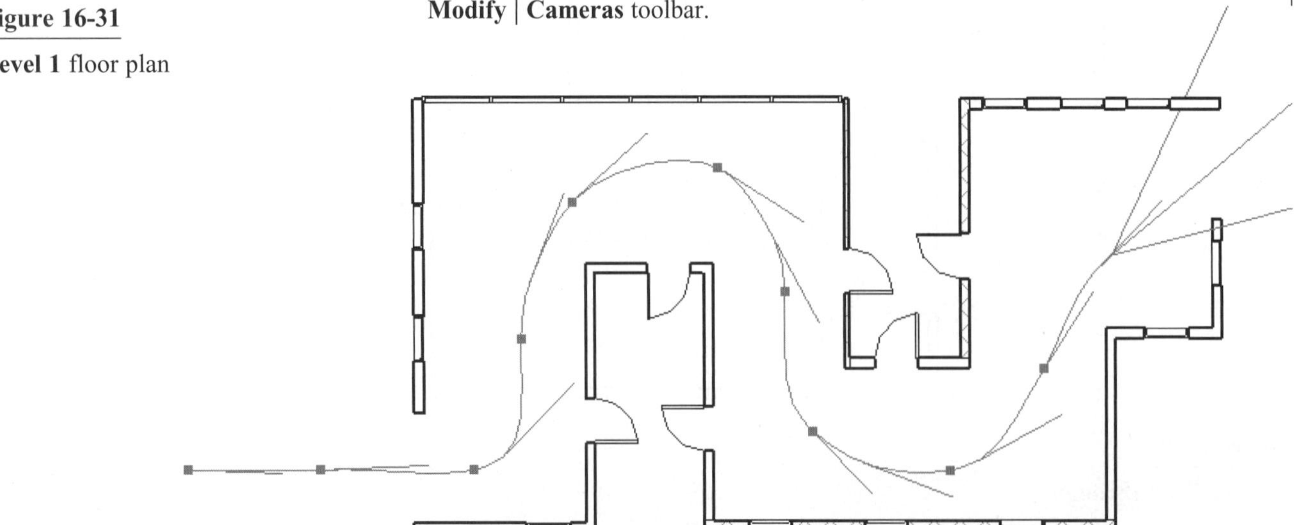

14. In the **Options Bar**, select **Path** from the **Controls** drop-down list (see Figure 16-32).

The **Key Frames** will now appear, and you can drag them to change the path. You can experiment with **Add Key Frame** and **Remove Key Frame** if you wish. Adding more **Key Frames** increases your control; decreasing **Key Frames** gives the program more control.

NOTE:
If your camera path disappears from view, **RMB** (right mouse button click) on **TEST WALKTHROUGH** in the **Project Browser,** and select **Show Camera** from the contextual menu that appears.

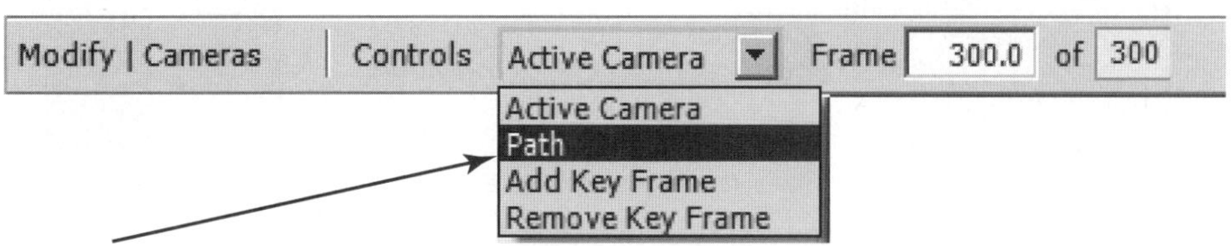

Figure 16-32

Controls drop-down list

15. In the **Properties** dialog box, uncheck the **Far Clip Active** check box.

Far Clip clips the picture in the distance from the **Camera** target and can be set to a distance. Turn this off (see Figure 16-33).

16. Select **Active Camera** from the **Controls** drop-down list.
17. Set the **Frame** to **1**, and leave everything else alone.
18. Click in an empty space in the **Drawing Editor**, and the **Revit** message, **"***Do you want to quit editing the walkthrough?***"** will appear; press the **Yes** button to return to the **Drawing Editor**.
19. Double-click on **Walkthrough 1** in the **Walkthroughs** tree in the **Project Browser** to bring up the perspective **Walkthrough** in the **Drawing Editor**.
20. Select **Shading with Edges** and **Shadows On** from the **Model: Graphic Style** and **Shadows** buttons at the bottom of the **Drawing Editor**.
21. In the **Project Browser**, **RMB** (right mouse button click) on **Walkthrough 1,** and select **Show Camera** from the contextual menu to bring up the **Modify | Cameras** toolbar.

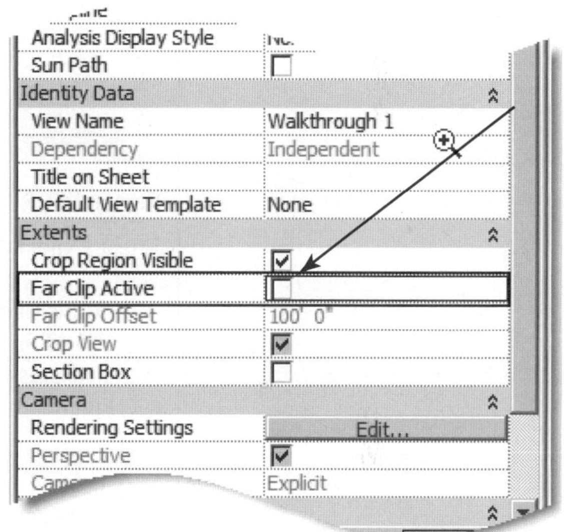

Figure 16-33

Turn **Far Clip Active** off

22. In the **Modify | Cameras** toolbar, select the **Edit Walkthrough** button to bring up the **Play** button.
23. Select the **Play** button to view the walkthrough animation (see Figure 16-34).

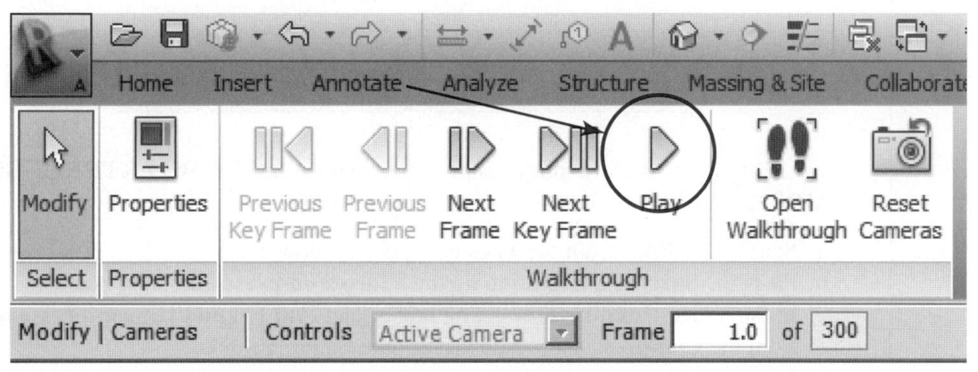

Figure 16-34

Play button

EXERCISE 16-7 MAKING AN AVI MOVIE FROM THE WALKTHROUGH

1. Once you have made the **Walkthrough**, select **Export > Images and Animations > Walkthrough** from the **Application** menu to bring up the **Length/Format** dialog box (see Figure 16-35).

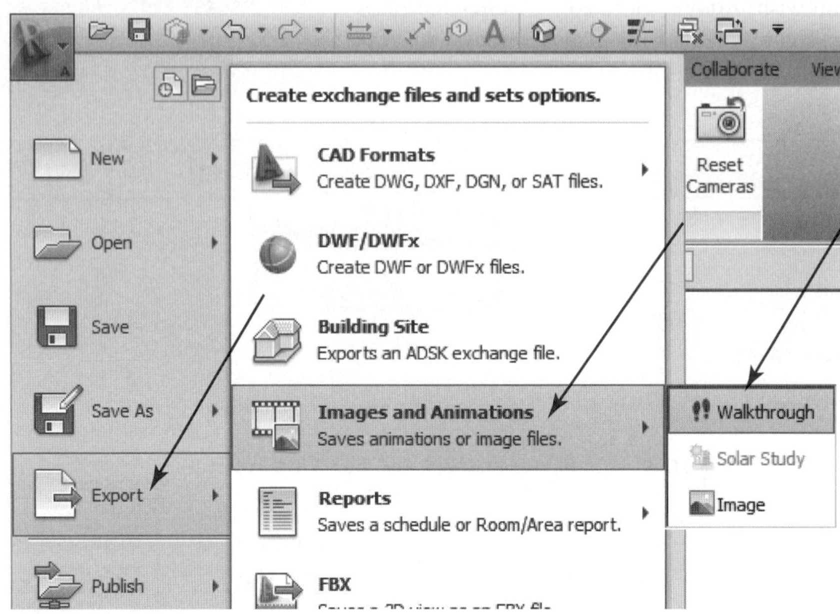

Figure 16-35

Select **Export > Images and Animations > Walkthrough**

2. In the **Length/Format** dialog box, select the **All frames** radio button, select **<Shading with Edges>** from the **Model Graphics Style** drop-down list, and then press the **OK** button to open the **Export Walkthrough** dialog box (see Figure 16-36).

Figure 16-36

Length/Format dialog box

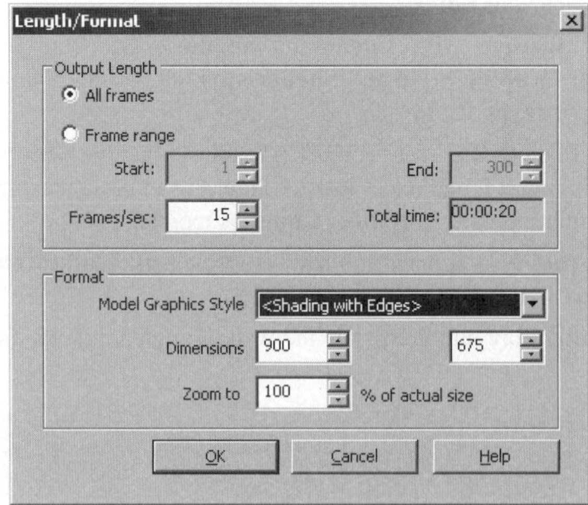

3. In the **Export Walkthrough** dialog box, name the file **WALKTHROUGH MOVIE**, and select a location on your computer to save the file.

   a. Select **AVI Files** from the **Files of type** drop-down list.
   b. Press the **Save** button to bring up the **Video Compression** dialog box.
   c. In the **Video Compression** dialog box, select **Full Frames [Uncompressed]** from the **Compressor** drop-down list (see Figure 16-37).

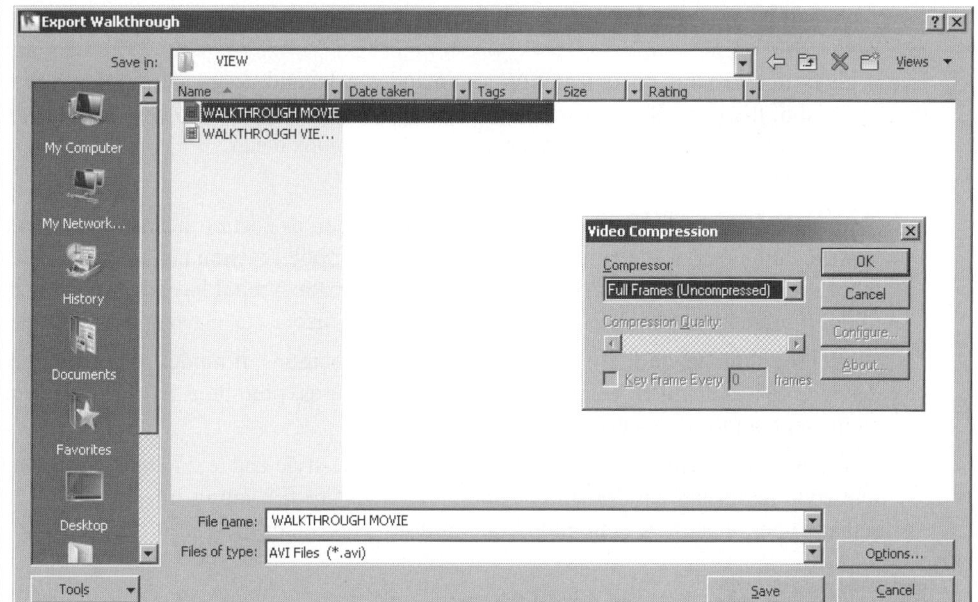

Figure 16-37

Video Compression dialog box

4. Press the **OK** button in the **Video Compression** dialog box to start the movie-making process; this should take about three minutes.
5. Go to the **Windows Desktop**, and open **My Computer**.
6. Go to the location where you saved the **Walkthrough AVI**.
7. Double-click on the **WALKTHROUGH MOVIE.avi** file.
8. The **Windows Media Player®** will open, and your movie will play (see Figure 16-38).

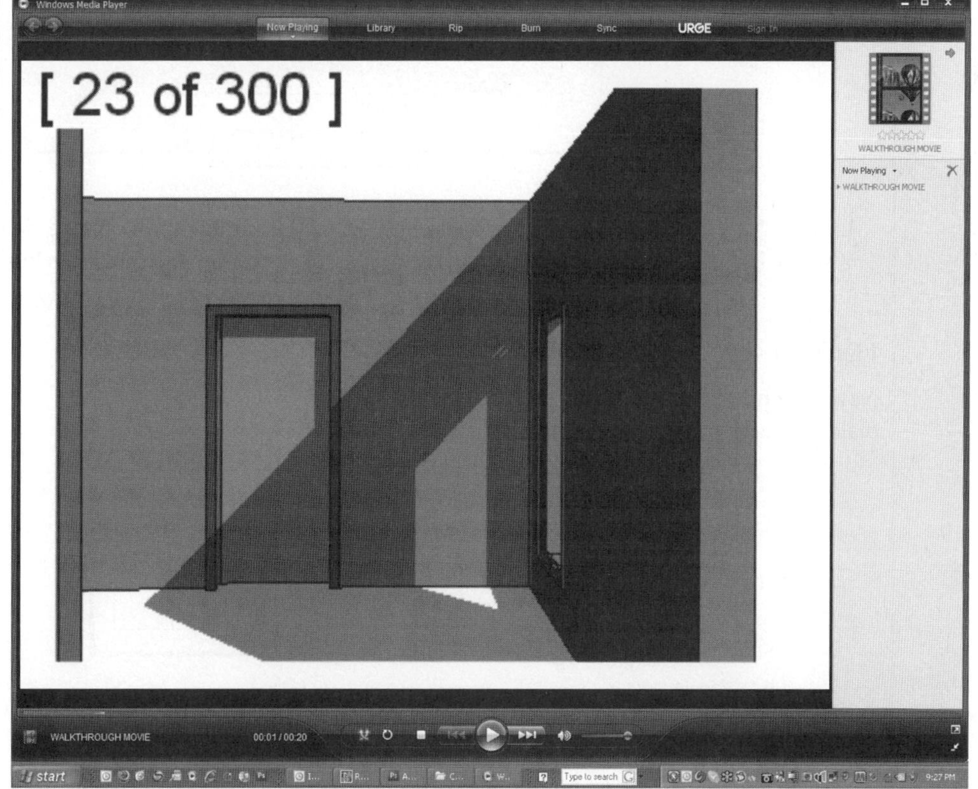

Figure 16-38

Windows Media Player®

9. Save this file as **WALKTHROUGH VIEWS**.

Legend Views and Legend Components

Every good architectural documentation set includes a legend. Legends provide a way to display a list of the various building components and annotations used in a project, making it easy for someone to understand what the various annotations mean.

Some typical legends include:

- **Annotation Legend:** Displays sheet annotations such as section heads, level markers, spot elevation marks, elevation symbols, keynote symbol, revision tag, element tags, and other symbols that do not represent model objects. Each symbol has an associated piece of descriptive text. All symbols are shown at printed size.
- **Model Symbol Legend:** Displays symbolic representations of model objects with some descriptive text. Typical elements are electrical fixtures, plumbing fixtures, mechanical equipment, and site objects.
- **Line Styles Legend:** Displays a line in a selected line style and text identifying what that line style represents on drawings. Among the uses are fire rating lines, property lines, setback lines, electric wiring, plumbing, utilities, and centerlines.

EXERCISE 16-8 CREATING A LEGEND VIEW

1. Start a new drawing using the RAC 2012\Imperial Templates\default.rte template.
2. Change to the **View** toolbar.
3. In the **View** toolbar, select the **Legends > Legend** button to bring up the **New Legend View** dialog box (see Figure 16-39).

Figure 16-39

Legends > Legend button

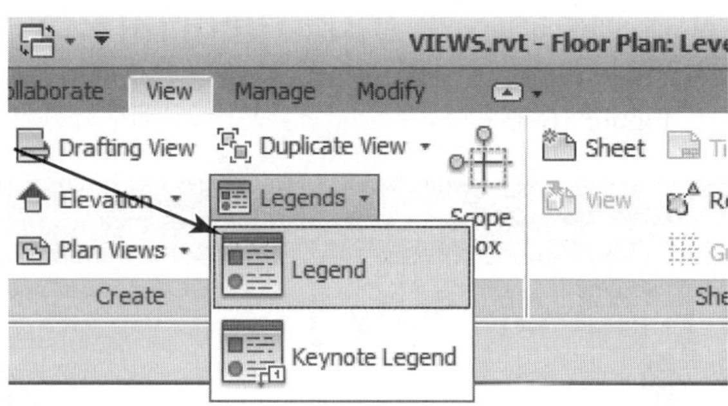

4. In the **New Legend View** dialog box, enter **TEST LEGEND** in the **Name** field, select **1/4″ = 1′-0″** from the **Scale** drop-down list, and press the **OK** button to bring up the **TEST LEGEND** view (see Figure 16-40).

Figure 16-40

New Legend View dialog box

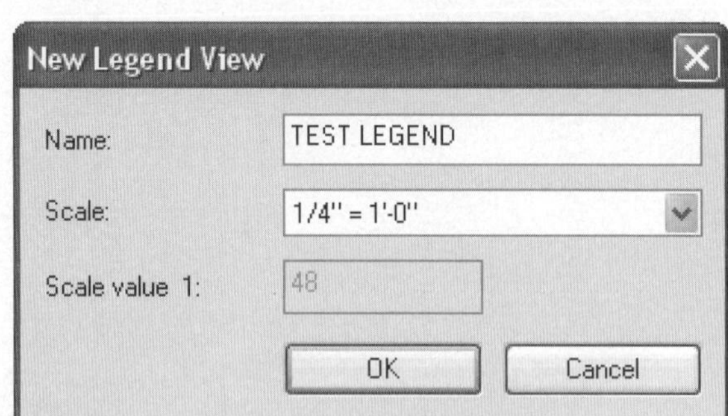

Notice that **TEST LEGEND** now also appears under **Legends** in the **Project Browser** (see Figure 16-41).

5. Change to the **Drafting** button in the **Design Bar**.
6. In the **Annotate** toolbar, select the **Component > Legend Component** button (see Figure 16-42).

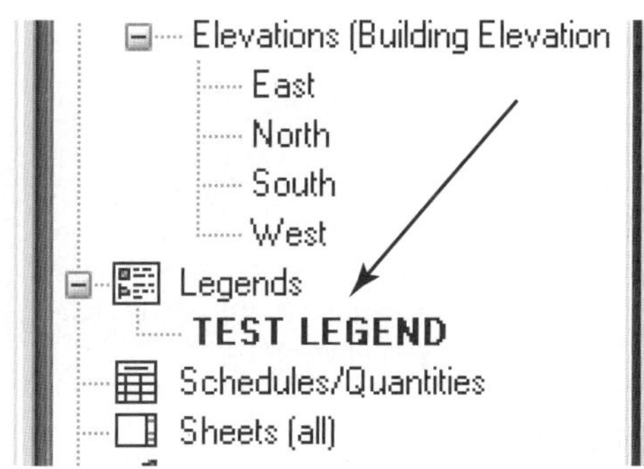

Figure 16-41

TEST LEGEND appears under **Legends** in the **Project Browser**

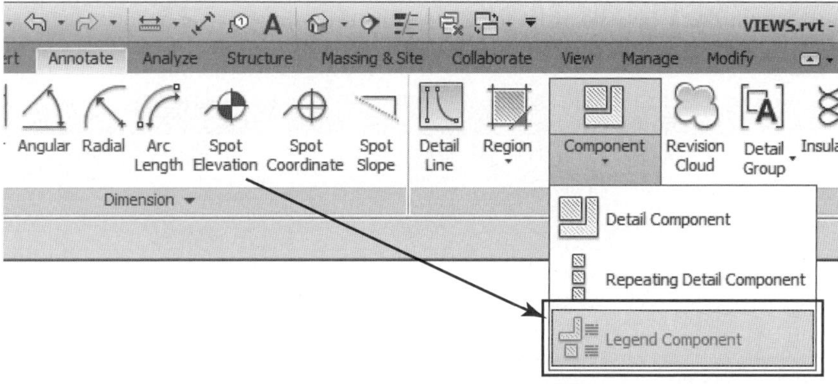

Figure 16-42

Component > Legend Component button

7. In the **Options Bar**, select **Doors: Single-Flush: 32″ × 84″** and **Floor Plan** from the **View** drop-down list.
8. Place the door in the **TEST LEGEND** view that is in the **Drawing Editor**.

> **NOTE:**
>
> When you select the **Legend Component** button, the **Options Bar** will also appear with **Family** and **View** options. All the **Families,** such as doors, windows, walls, annotations, and so on, that have been loaded in the project are available here (see Figure 16-43).

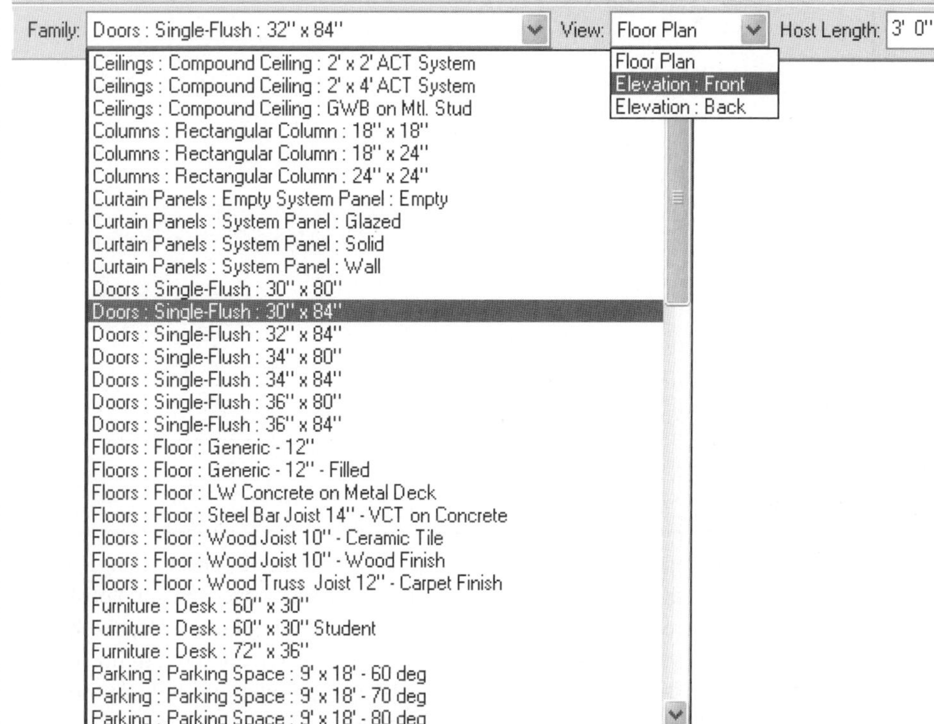

Figure 16-43

Family and **View** options

9. Repeat Step 7, selecting **Elevation: Front** from the **View** drop-down list, and placing the door elevation next to the **Floor Plan** view.
10. In the **Options Bar**, select **Walls: Basic Wall: Exterior – Brick and CMU on MTL Stud**.
11. Select **Section** from the **View** drop-down list.
12. Enter **8′-0″** in the **Host Length** field, and place the wall in the **TEST LEGEND** view.
13. In the **Annotate** toolbar, select the **Symbol** button.
14. Select different symbols from the **Properties** drop-down list and place them in the **TEST LEGEND** view.

NOTE:

You can dimension doors and windows in the **Legend** view, but not walls. If you change the parameters of an object in your project, their 2D views in the **Legend** view will also change (see Figure 16-44).

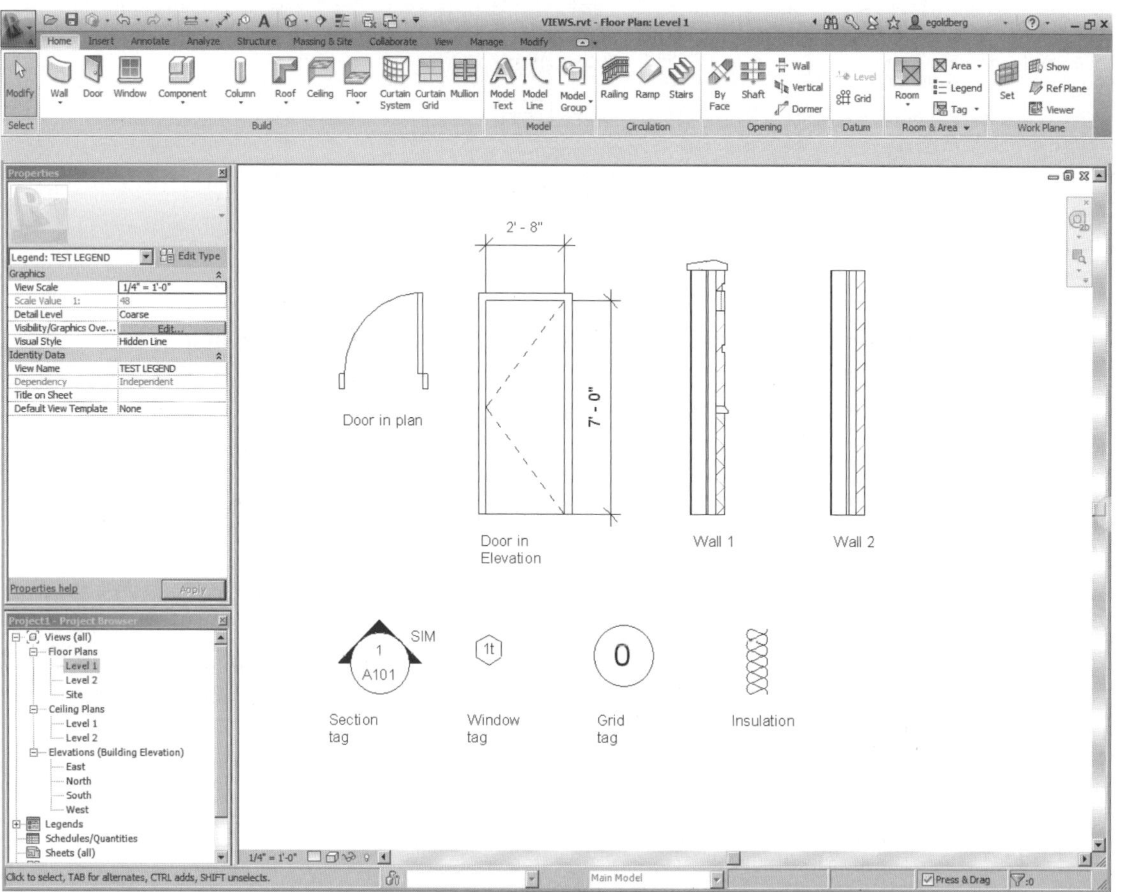

Figure 16-44

Legend view

15. Save this file as **LEGEND VIEWS**.

Matchlines

Matchlines are used when buildings are too big to be shown on one plot sheet. Using a **Matchline**, you can separate a building into several parts and spread the plans over several plot sheets.

In Revit Architecture 2012, **Matchlines** can be used in **Floor Plans, Callouts, Elevations,** and **Sections**. **Matchlines** have properties that can specify the top and bottom line constraints, thus giving them the ability to match different levels. These properties, though, are not available in **Elevation** and **Section** views since these properties do not apply in these views.

EXERCISE 16-9 CREATING A MATCHLINE VIEW

1. Start a new drawing using the RAC 2012\Imperial Templates\default.rte template.
2. Select the **Scale** to **1/4″ = 1′-0″**, and **Detail Level** to **Medium**.
3. Change to the **Home** toolbar.
4. In the **Home** toolbar, select the **Wall** button to bring up the **Modify | Place Walls** toolbar.
5. In the **Modify | Place Walls** toolbar, select the **Line** button.
6. Place **Basic Wall: Exterior – Brick on CMU** walls, **10′-0″** high to create the enclosure shown in Figure 16-45.

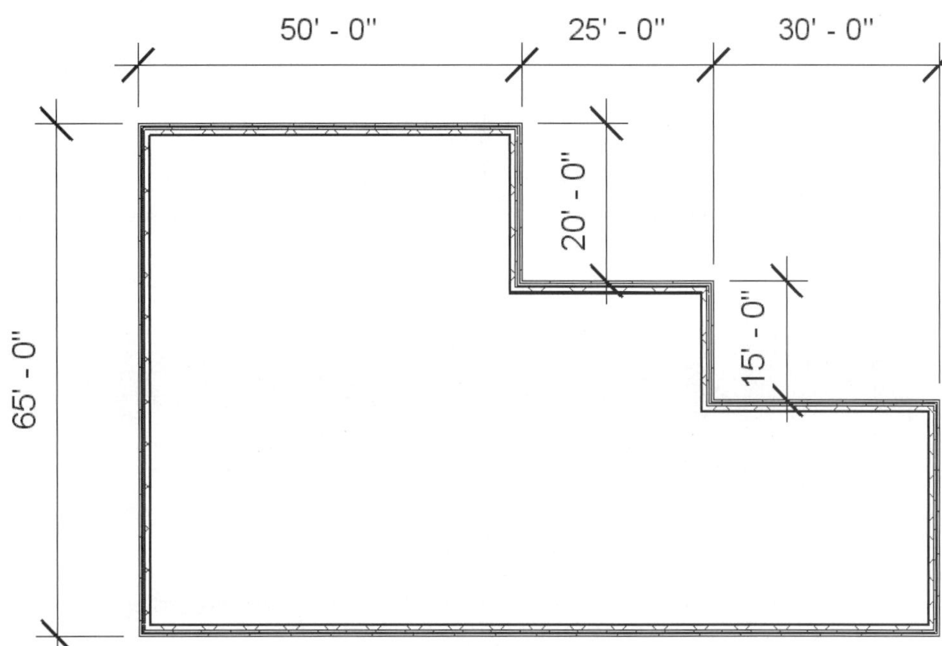

Figure 16-45
Create an enclosure

At **1/4″ = 1′0″** scale, this drawing might be too big to be contained on one 22″ × 34″ plot sheet. In the following steps, you will divide the floor plan into two sections that are electronically connected.

7. Change to the **View** toolbar.
8. In the **View** toolbar, select the **Matchline** button to bring up the **Modify | Create Matchline Sketch** toolbar (Figure 16-46).

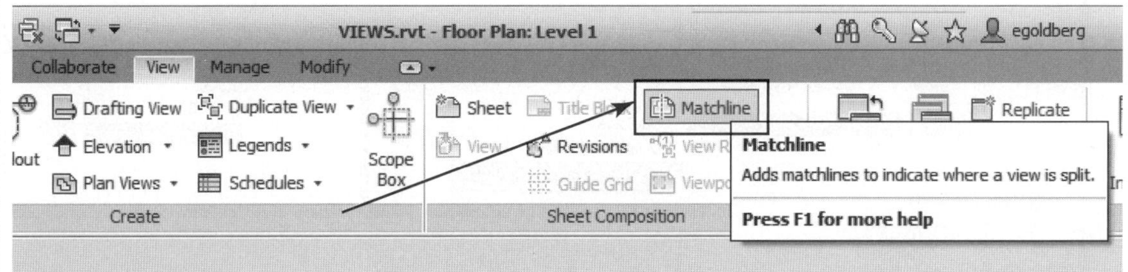

Figure 16-46
Matchline button

9. You are now in **Sketch** mode. Using the **Line** button from the **Draw** panel, create a **Matchline**, and press the **<Esc>** key to end the sketch.

10. Press the **Finish Edit Mode** button to return to the **Drawing Editor** (see Figure 16-47).
11. In the **View** toolbar, select the **Duplicate View > Duplicate as Dependent** button (see Figure 16-48).

This new **Dependent** view will appear in the **Project Browser** as **Dependent on Level 1** (see Figure 16-49).

Figure 16-47

Return to the **Drawing Editor**

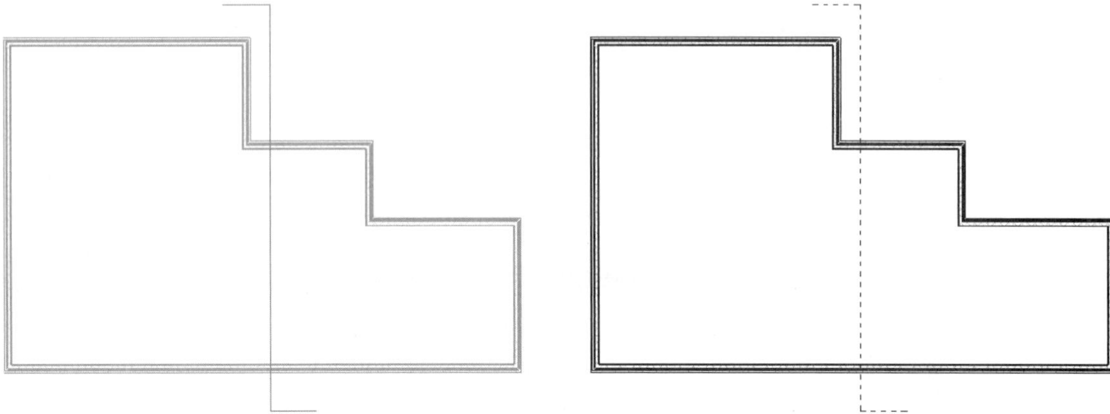

Figure 16-48

Duplicate View > Duplicate as Dependent button

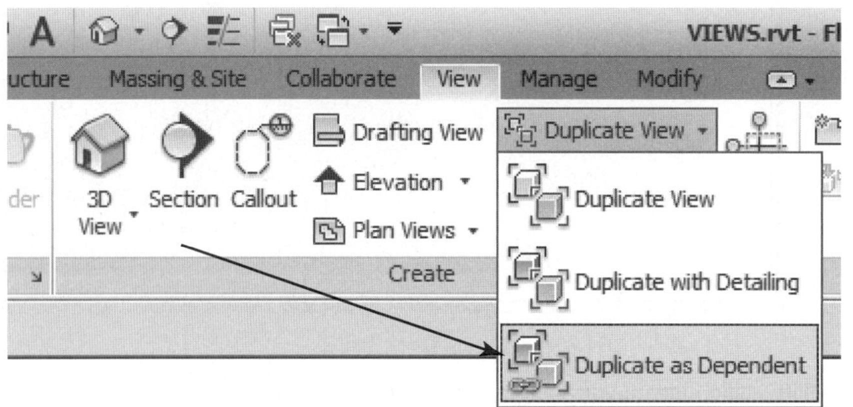

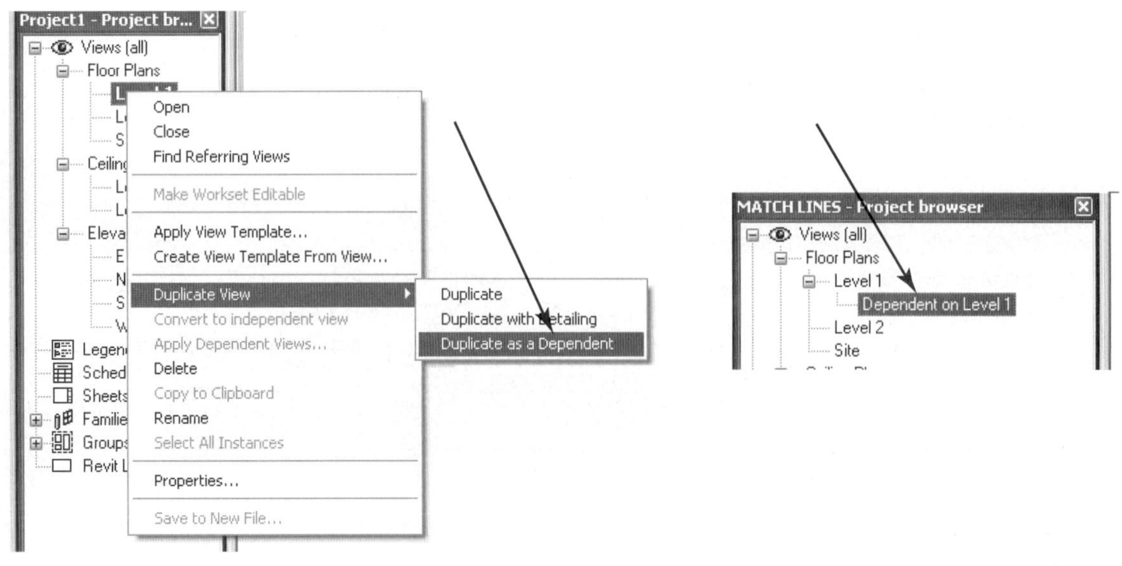

Figure 16-49

Dependent view will appear in the **Project Browser** as **Dependent on Level 1**

You now have two views of **Level 1**. Using the **Crop Regions**, you will crop opposite portions of the building on each view, and assign them sheet numbers.

12. Select the **Show Crop Region** button in the **View Control Bar** to turn the **Crop Region On**. (If the **Crop Region** is already **On**, the button will read **Hide Crop Region**.)
13. Select the **Crop Region** in the **Drawing Editor**, and move the right arrow grips to the left so that only the left portion of the floor plan is showing (see Figure 16-50).
14. Double-click on **Dependent on Level 1** in the **Project Browser** to bring it into the **Drawing Editor**.
15. Select the **Show Crop Region** button in the **View Control Bar** to turn the **Crop Region On**. (If the **Crop Region** is already **On**, the button will read **Hide Crop Region**.)
16. Select the **Crop Region** in the **Drawing Editor**, and move the left arrow grips to the right so that only the right portion of the floor plan is showing (see Figure 16-51).

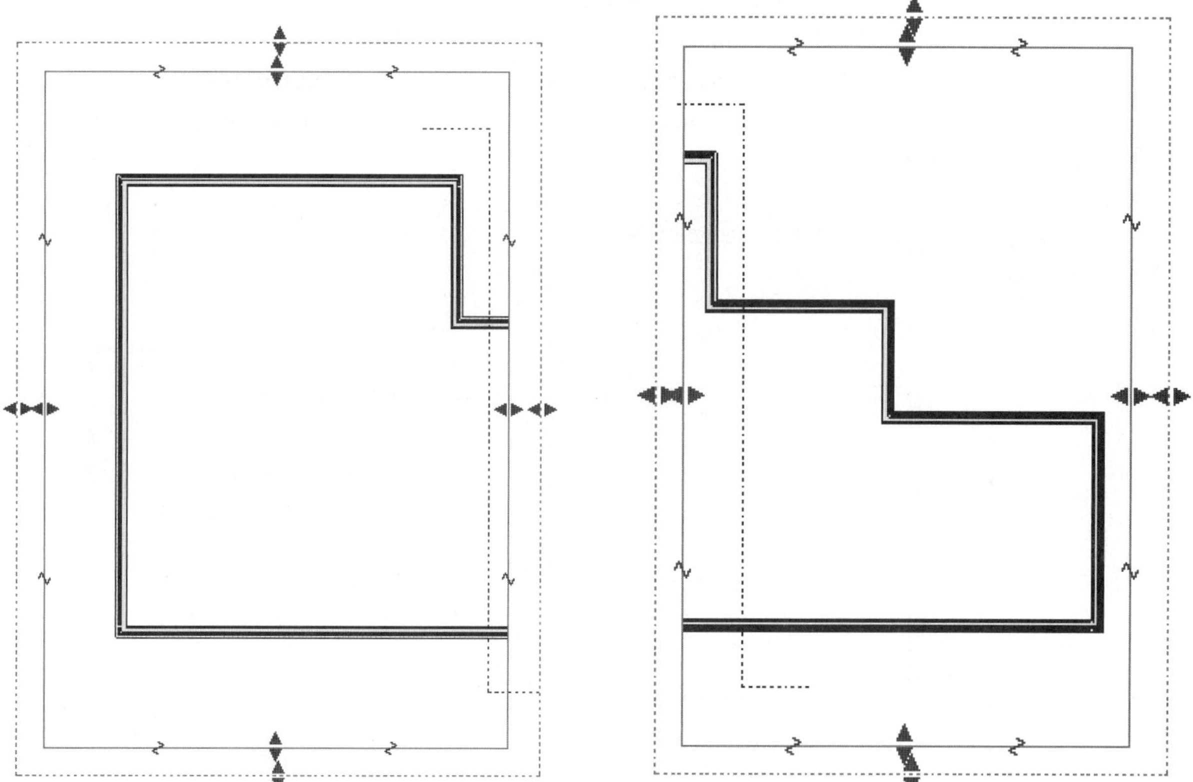

Figure 16-50

Move the right arrow grips to the left

Figure 16-51

Move the left arrow grips to the right

17. In the **View Control Bar**, select the **Hide Crop Region** button to turn the **Crop Region Off**.
18. Bring the **Level 1** floor plan view up into the **Drawing Editor**.
19. Select the **Hide Crop Region** button at the bottom of **Drawing Editor** to turn the **Crop Region Off**.

Now you must add a **View Reference** tag.

20. In the **View** toolbar, select the **View Reference** button (see Figure 16-52).

NOTE:

When placed on a **Matchline**, a **View Reference** will show which plot page contains the **Dependent** view.

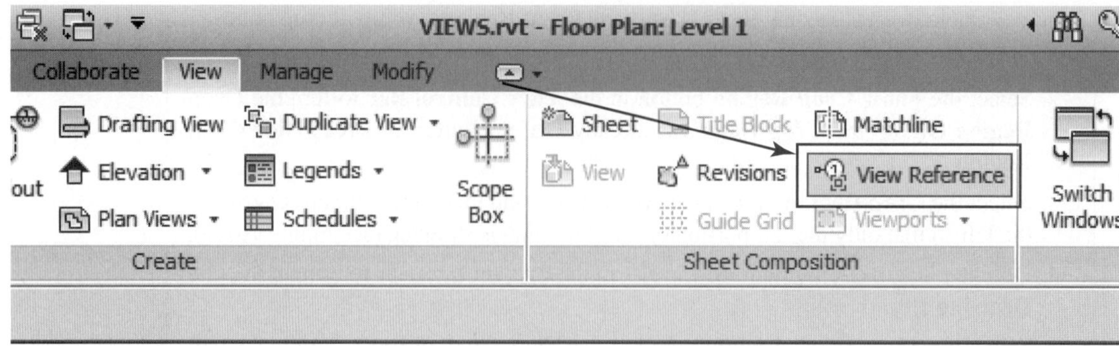

Figure 16-52

View Reference button

21. Place **View References** at the top and bottom of the **Matchline** you created.
22. Change to the **Annotate** toolbar.
23. In the **Annotate** toolbar, select the **Text** button.
24. Place the text **"Match Line"** above the **View References** you placed.
25. Repeat this process for the **Dependent on Level 1** view (see Figure 16-53).

Figure 16-53

Place the text **"Match Line"** above the **View References**

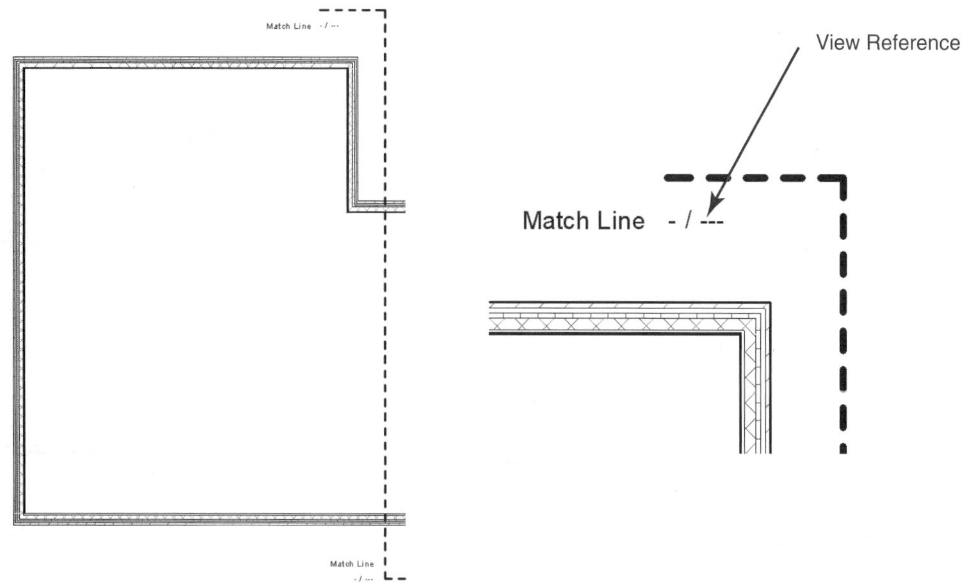

26. In the **View** toolbar, select the **Sheet** button to bring up the **New Sheet** dialog box (see Figure 16-54).
27. In the **New Sheet** dialog box, press the **Load** button to go to the **Imperial Library**.

Figure 16-54

Sheet button

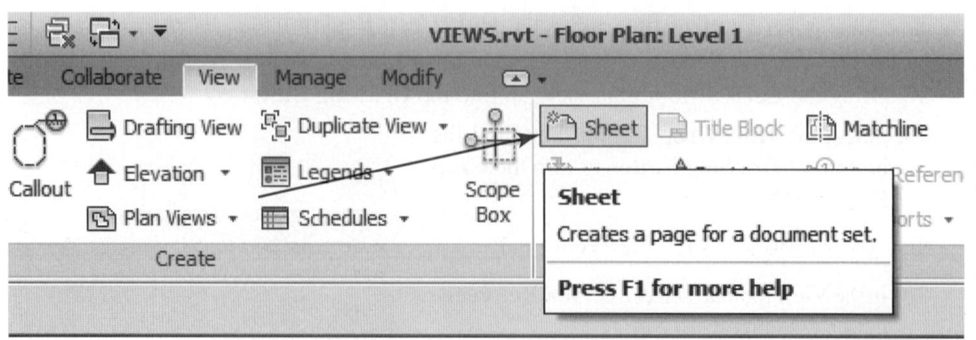

28. In the **Imperial Library**, open the **Titleblocks** folder, and open the **C17 × 22 Horizontal** family. You will then return to the **Select a Titleblock** dialog box.
29. In the **Select a Titleblock** dialog box, select the **C17 × 22 Horizontal** family, and press the **OK** button to bring up the first plot sheet.
30. Make sure the sheet number is **A101**; select and change it if necessary.
31. Select the **Level 1** view from the **Project Browser**, and drag it into plot sheet **A101**.
32. Again, select the **Sheet** button to bring up the **Select a Titleblock** dialog box.
33. Again, select the **C17 × 22 Horizontal** family, and press the **OK** button to bring up the second plot sheet.
34. Make sure the sheet number is **A102**; select and change it, if necessary.
35. Select the **Dependent on Level 1** view from the **Project Browser**, and drag it into plot sheet **A102**.

Open plot sheet **A101**, and notice that the **View Reference** reads **1/A102**. This means that the matching part of the drawing is **# 1** on page **A102**.

Open plot sheet **A102**, and notice that the **View Reference** reads **1/A101**. This means that the matching part of the drawing is **# 1** on page **A101** (see Figure 16-55).

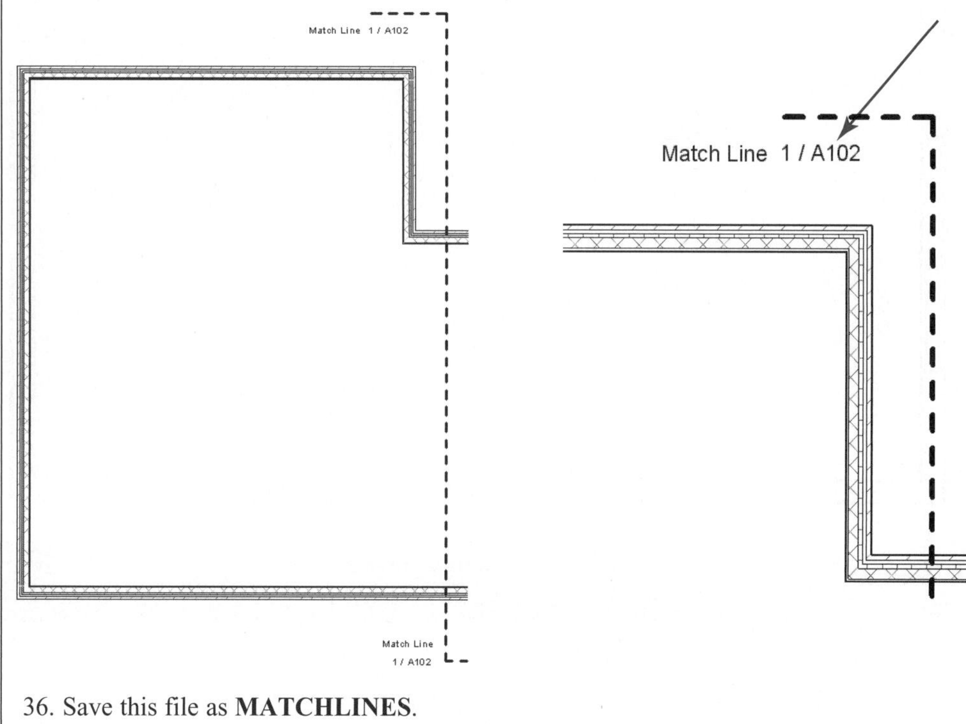

Figure 16-55

Plot sheet **A102 View Reference**

36. Save this file as **MATCHLINES**.

Schedule Views

A schedule is a display of information, extracted from the properties of elements in a project. A Revit Architecture schedule can list every instance of the type of element you have placed in the project.

EXERCISE 16-10 CREATING A SCHEDULE VIEW

1. Start a new drawing using the RAC 2012\Imperial Templates\default.rte template.
2. Select the **Scale** to **1/4″ = 1′-0″** and **Detail Level** to **Medium**.
3. Change to the **Home** toolbar.

4. In the **Home** toolbar, select the **Wall**, **Door**, and **Window** buttons. Load several different doors and windows.
5. Place **Basic Wall: Generic - 8″**, **10′-0″** high, and several doors and windows to create the enclosure shown in Figure 16-56.
6. Change to the **View** toolbar.
7. In the **View** toolbar, select the **Schedules > Schedule/Quantities** button to bring up the **New Schedule** dialog box (see Figure 16-57).

> **NOTE:**
> You can select and change the numbers in the **Window Tags**.

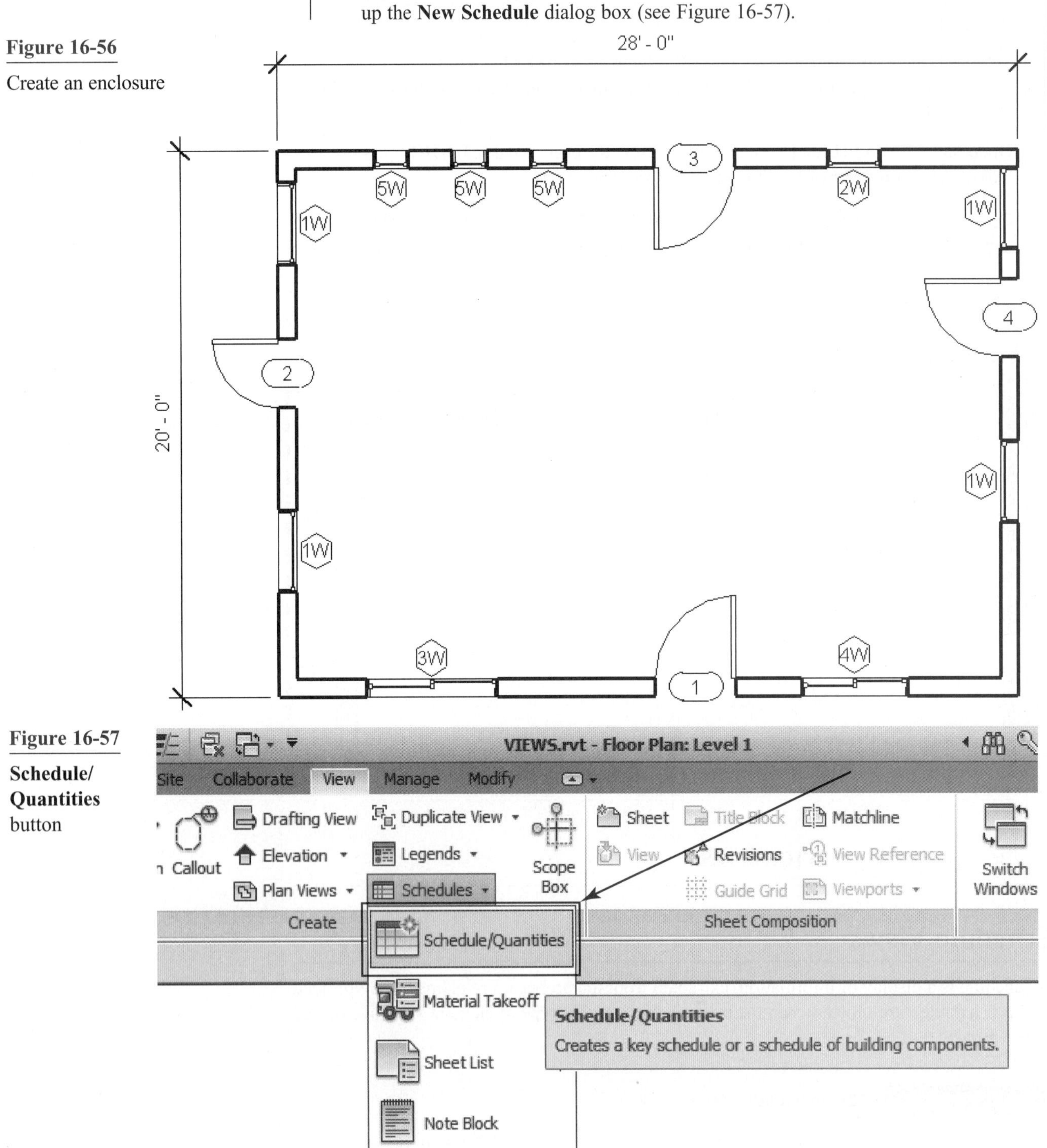

Figure 16-56

Create an enclosure

Figure 16-57

Schedule/ Quantities button

8. In the **New Schedule** dialog box, scroll down, select the **Windows** category, and press the **OK** button to bring up the **Schedule Properties** dialog box (see Figure 16-58).

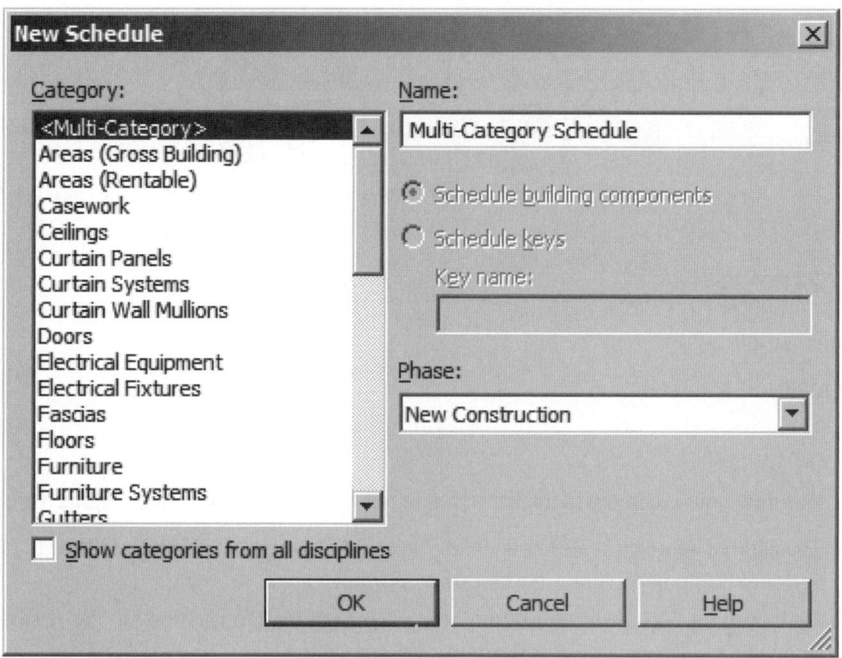

Figure 16-58

Schedule Properties dialog box

9. In the **Schedule Properties** dialog box, change to the **Fields** tab.
10. In the **Fields** tab, select **Count**, and press the **Add** button.
11. Repeat the **Add** process with **Type, Height, Width**, and **Type Mark**.
12. Press the **OK** button, and the **Window Schedule** will appear in the **Drawing Editor**. The **Modify Schedule/Quantities** toolbar also will appear (see Figure 16-59).

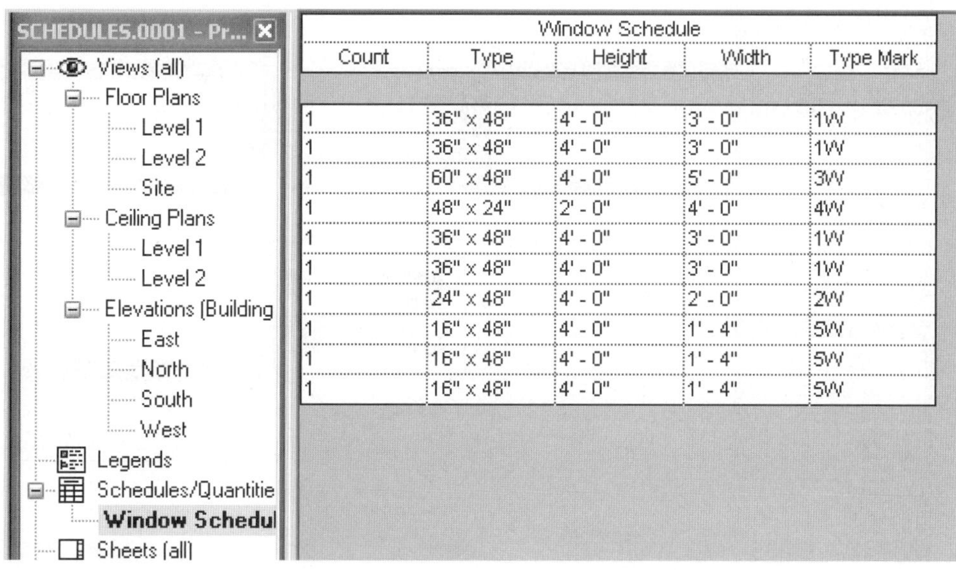

Window Schedule				
Count	Type	Height	Width	Type Mark
1	36" x 48"	4' - 0"	3' - 0"	1W
1	36" x 48"	4' - 0"	3' - 0"	1W
1	60" x 48"	4' - 0"	5' - 0"	3W
1	48" x 24"	2' - 0"	4' - 0"	4W
1	36" x 48"	4' - 0"	3' - 0"	1W
1	36" x 48"	4' - 0"	3' - 0"	1W
1	24" x 48"	4' - 0"	2' - 0"	2W
1	16" x 48"	4' - 0"	1' - 4"	5W
1	16" x 48"	4' - 0"	1' - 4"	5W
1	16" x 48"	4' - 0"	1' - 4"	5W

Figure 16-59

Window Schedule

13. Select one of the fields. In the **Modify Schedule/Quantities** toolbar, select the **Highlight in Model** button (see Figure 16-60).

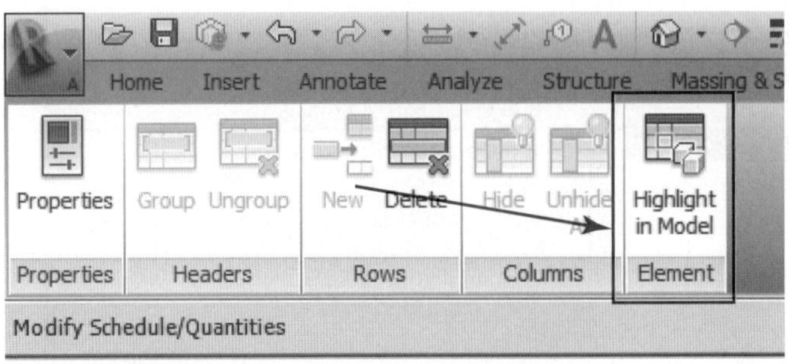

Figure 16-60

Highlight in Model button

The **Window** you selected will appear in red in the **Level 1** Floor Plan (see Figure 16-61).

14. The **Show Element(s) In View** dialog box will also appear. Press the **Show** button in the dialog box to show the **Window** in other views.
15. Double-click **Window Schedule** under **Schedules/Quantities** in the **Project Browser** to bring it into the **Drawing Editor** again.
16. Select a different **Window Size** from the **Type** drop-down list, and press the **Show** button again.

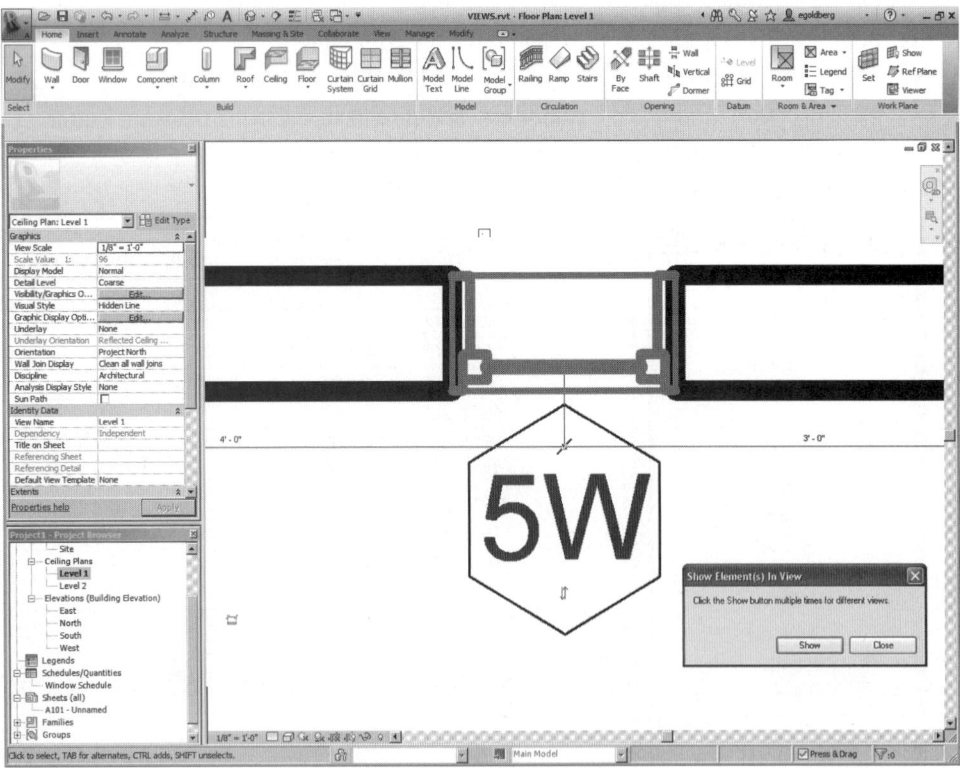

Figure 16-61

Window selected will appear in red

The **Window** will change in the **Level 1** floor plan, and add a new **Type Mark** number (see Figure 16-62).

17. Double-click **Window Schedule** under **Schedules/Quantities** in the **Project Browser** to bring it into the **Drawing Editor** again.

Window Schedule

Count	Type	Height	Width	Type Mark
1	36" x 48"	4' - 0"	3' - 0"	1W
1	36" x 48"	4' - 0"	3' - 0"	1W
1	60" x 48"	4' - 0"	5' - 0"	3W
1	48" x 24"	2' - 0"	4' - 0"	4W
1	36" x 48"	4' - 0"	3' - 0"	1W
1	36" x 48"	4' - 0"	3' - 0"	1W
1	24" x 48"	4' - 0"	2' - 0"	2W
1	16" x 48"	4' - 0"	1' - 4"	5W
1	16" x 48"	4' - 0"	1' - 4"	5W
1	36" x 72"	6' - 0"	3' - 0"	9

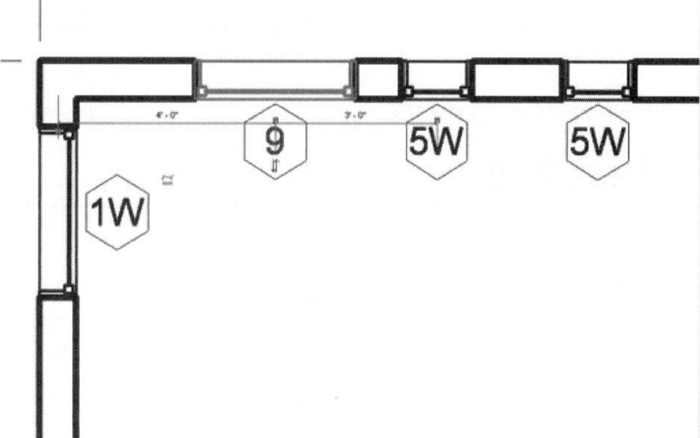

Figure 16-62

A new **Type Mark** number is added

18. In the **Properties** dialog box, press the **Sorting/Grouping** button to bring up the **Sorting/Grouping** tab in the **Schedule Properties** dialog box.
19. In the **Sorting/Grouping** tab, check the **Grand totals** and **Itemize every instance** check boxes (see Figure 16-63).

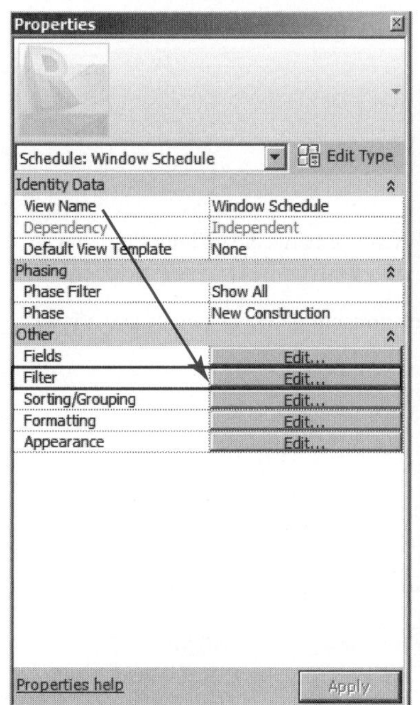

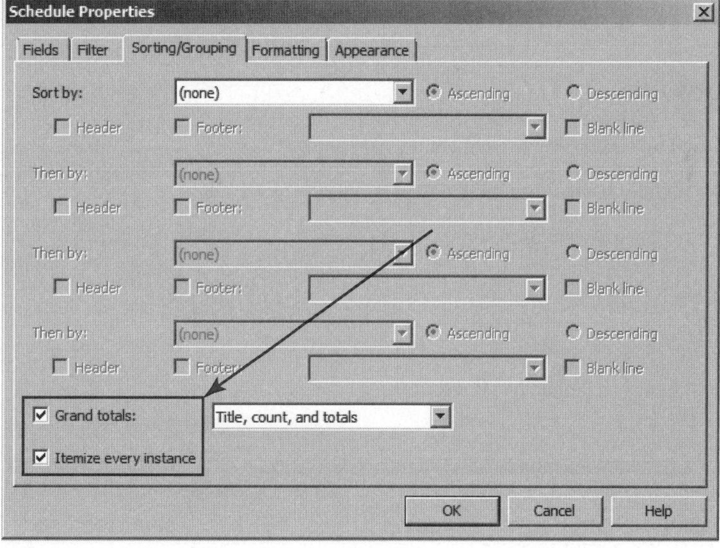

Figure 16-63

Grand totals and **Itemize every instance** check boxes

20. Press the **OK** buttons to return to the **Window Schedule**. The schedule will now show **Grand Total** plus the total count of windows.
21. Continue to change parameters in the different **Element Properties** tabs, and observe the changes in the schedule.
22. Save this file as **SCHEDULES**.

Chapter Summary

This chapter explained and demonstrated the different views available in Revit Architecture 2012. Also included in this chapter was a demonstration of how to make an animated **Walkthrough** and a **Matchline** view.

Chapter Test Questions

Multiple Choice

Circle the correct answer.

1. The **Matchline** tool
   a. Matches an existing line.
   b. Matches a **Dependent** view.
   c. Matches one drawing with another.
   d. All of the above
2. The **Camera** button is located under which button?
   a. **Callout**
   b. **Elevation**
   c. **3D View**
   d. **Plan** view
3. The **Drafting** view
   a. Can be used for 3D and 2D drafting.
   b. Can be used only for 3D drafting.
   c. Can be used only for 2D drafting.
   d. Cannot be used for annotation.
4. Which cannot be scheduled?
   a. **Windows**
   b. **Typography**
   c. **Wall Sweeps**
   d. **Annotation**
5. Which **Animation** file format is used for **Walkthroughs**?
   a. **.wav**
   b. **.mov**
   c. **.avi**
   d. **.3ds**

Questions

1. What are the default Revit Architecture 2012 views?
2. What is a **Callout** view used for?
3. What is a **Legend** view used for?
4. What is the difference between a **Floor Plan** and a **Reflected Ceiling Plan**?
5. What is the relationship between **Levels** and **Views**?

Exercise

Create the following Schedule headings.

Door Schedule						
Fire Rating	Head Height	Level	Mark	Manufacturer	Thickness	Width

Electrical Equipment Schedule						
Cost	Family	Model	Count	Type Mark	Wattage	Voltage

Gutter Schedule				
Profile	Material	Count	Length	Type

CHAPTER

17 Manage

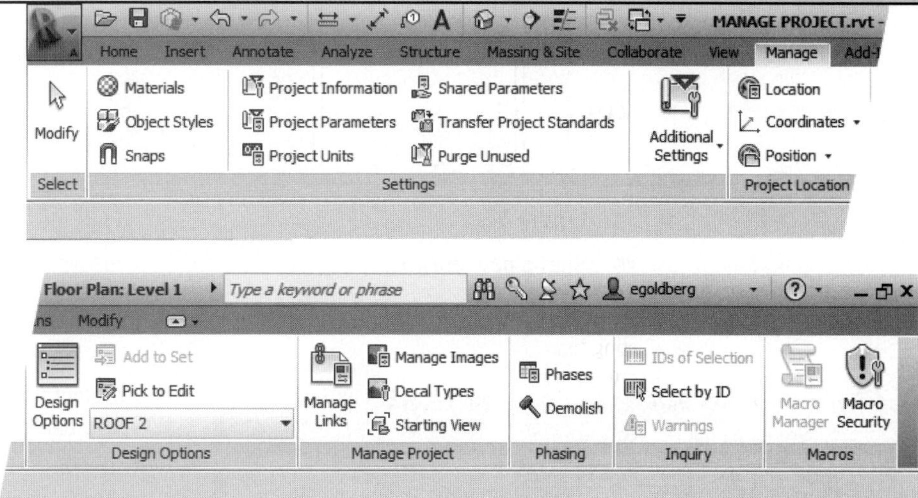

CHAPTER OBJECTIVES

- Learn how to use the **Design Options** tool.
- Learn how to use the **Manage Links** tool.
- Learn how to use the **Additional Settings** button.
- Learn how to use the **Materials** tool.
- Learn how to use the **Object Styles** button.
- Learn how to use the **Snaps** button.
- Learn how to use the **Project Information** button.
- Learn how to use the **Project Units** button.
- Learn how to use the **Purge Unused** button.
- Learn how to use the **Location** button.
- Learn how to use the **Phases** button.
- Learn how to use the **Demolish** button.

Introduction

In Revit Architecture 2012, the **Manage** toolbar contains tools for setting all of the project's defaults. These tools include, but are not limited to, changing or modifying the appearance of objects, materials, snaps, phasing, design options, and project information.

Manage Tools

Designers can choose from a variety of tools and buttons, such as **Design Options, Manage Links, Materials, Additional Settings, Object Styles, Snaps, Project Information, Project Units, Purge Unused, Location, Phases,** and **Demolish.** Using these tools gives you the ability to make changes quickly and easily.

EXERCISE 17-1 DESIGN OPTIONS TOOL

The **Design Options** tool gives you a method for storing design variations, which you can quickly retrieve or make permanent.

> **NOTE:**
> By now, you should be able to create simple structures.

1. Start a new drawing using the RAC 2012\Imperial Templates\default.rte template.
2. Create a simple structure similar to that shown in Figure 17-1.

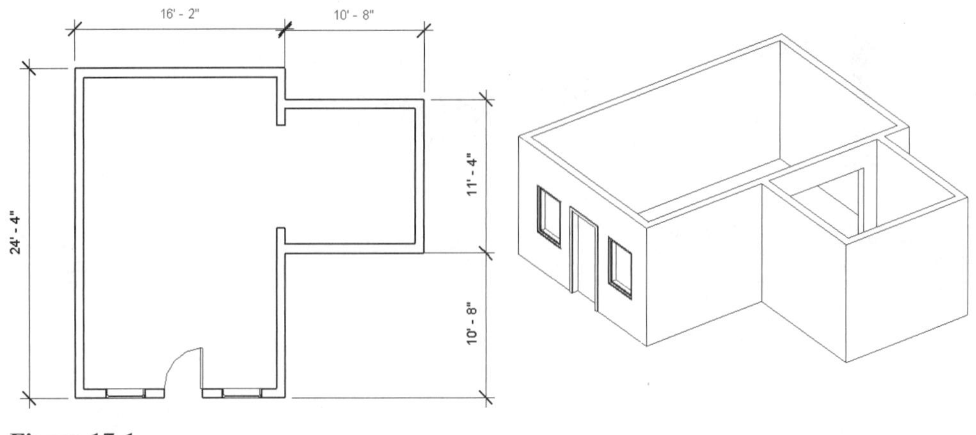

Figure 17-1

Start a new drawing

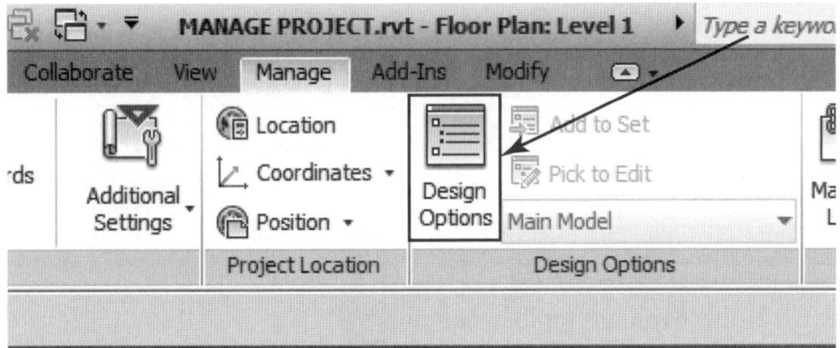

Figure 17-2

Design Options button

3. Select the **Manage** tab to bring up the **Manage** toolbar.
4. In the **Manage** toolbar, select the **Design Options** button to bring up the **Design Options** dialog box (see Figure 17-2).
5. In the **Design Options** dialog box, select the **New** button under **Option Set** to create **Option Set 1** and its **Option 1 (primary)**.
6. In the **Design Options** dialog box, select the **Rename** button under **Option Set,** and rename **Option Set 1** as **BUILDING**.
7. In the **Design Options** dialog box, select **BUILDING**, and then select the **New** button under **Option** to create an **Option Set**.
8. Rename the **Option Set** as **ROOF 1**.
9. Repeat Steps 7 and 8 to create **ROOF 2** (see Figure 17-3).
10. In the **Design Options** dialog box, select **ROOF 1**, and then select the **Edit Selected** button (see Figure 17-4).

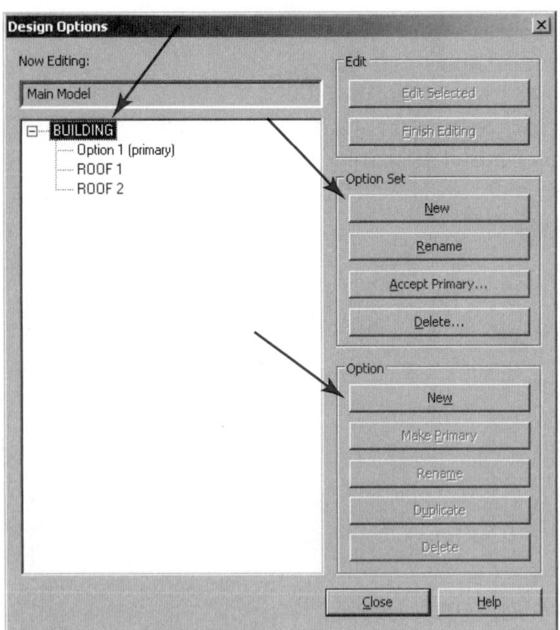

Figure 17-3

Design Options dialog box

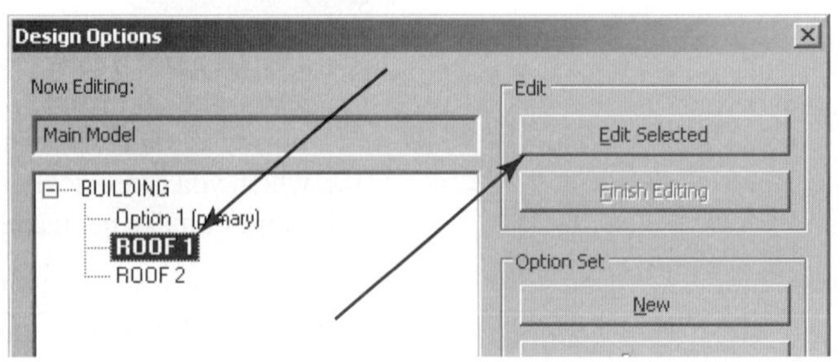

Figure 17-4

Edit Selected button

The building in the **Drawing Editor** will turn gray.

11. Using the **Roof** button in the **Home** toolbar, create a roof similar to that shown in Figure 17-5.

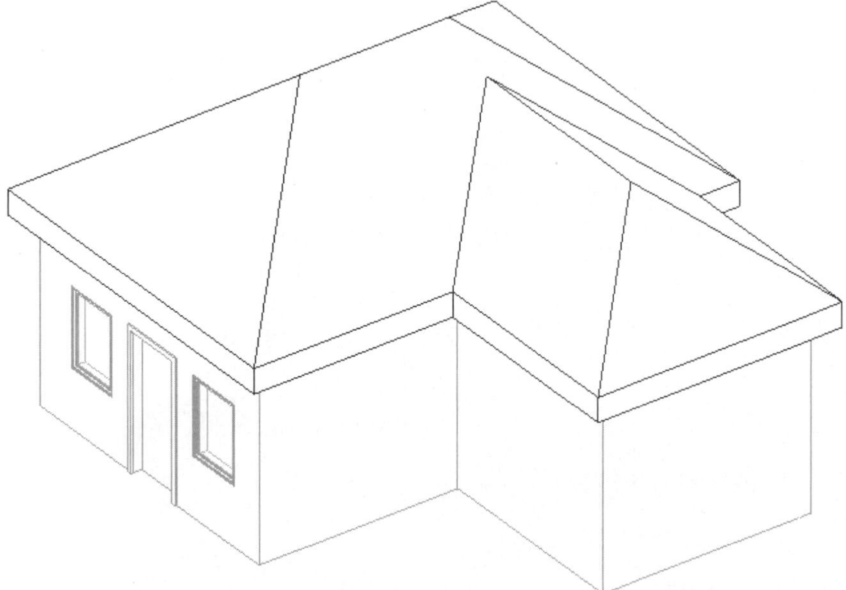

Figure 17-5

Create a roof

12. In the **Design Options** dialog box, select the **Finish Editing** button (see Figure 17-6).
13. Repeat Steps 10–12 for **ROOF 2**, creating a roof similar to that in Figure 17-7.
14. In the **Manage** toolbar, select the **Pick to Edit** button in the **Design Options** panel to bring up the different roof options you created (see Figure 17-8).
15. When you decide which option you wish to make permanent, select the **Design Options** button to bring up the **Design Options** dialog box.
16. In the **Design Options** dialog box, select the **Make Primary** button.
17. Finally, in the **Design Options** dialog box, select the **Accept Primary** button, and accept the **Revit** warning.

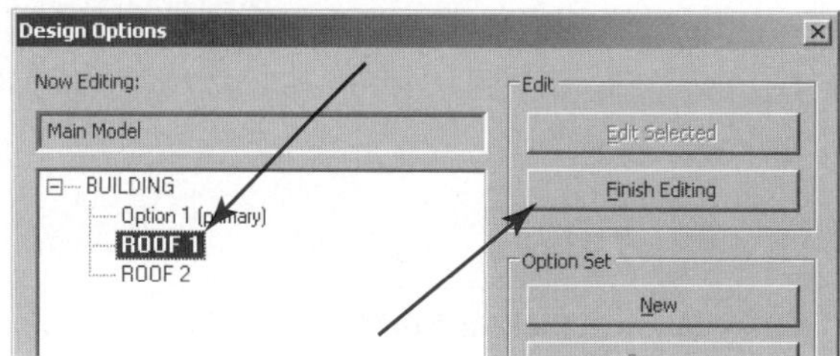

Figure 17-6

Finish Editing button

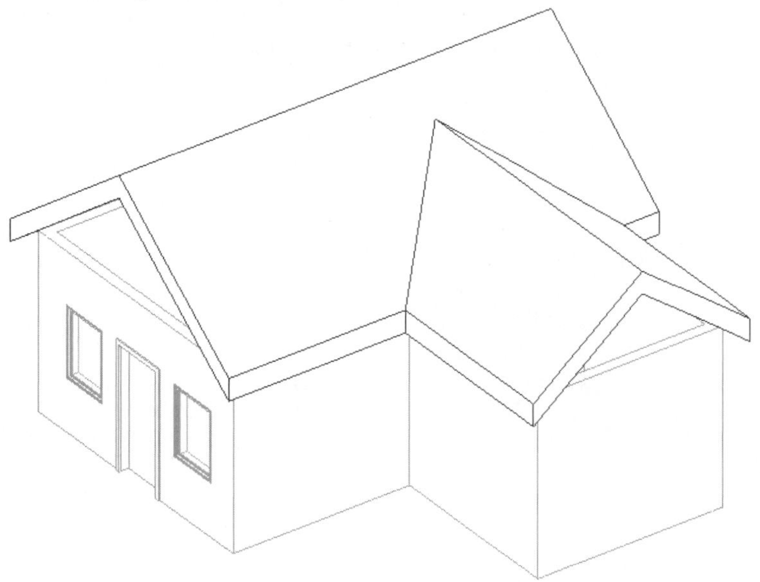

Figure 17-7

Create a second roof

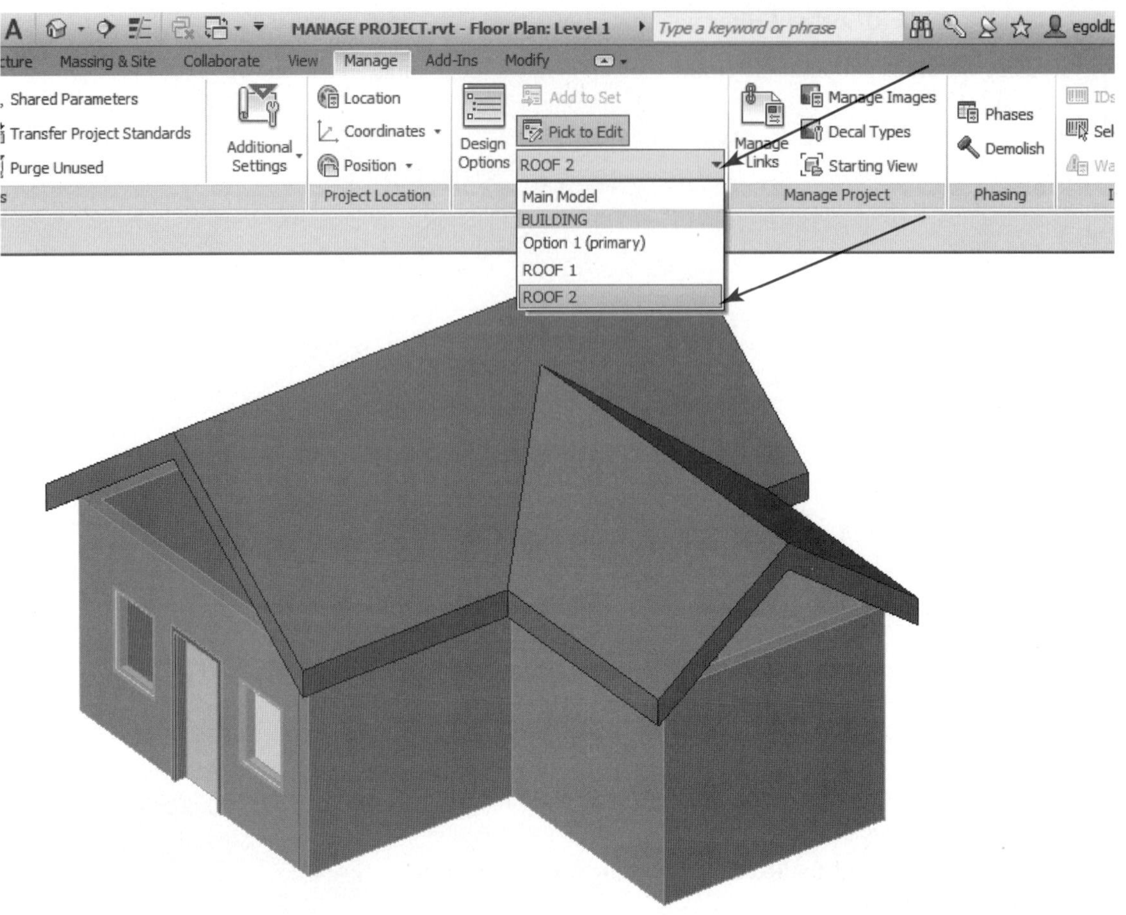

Figure 17-8

Pick to Edit button

18. You have now cleared the **Design Options** dialog box and created one building with the optional roof only (see Figure 17-9).

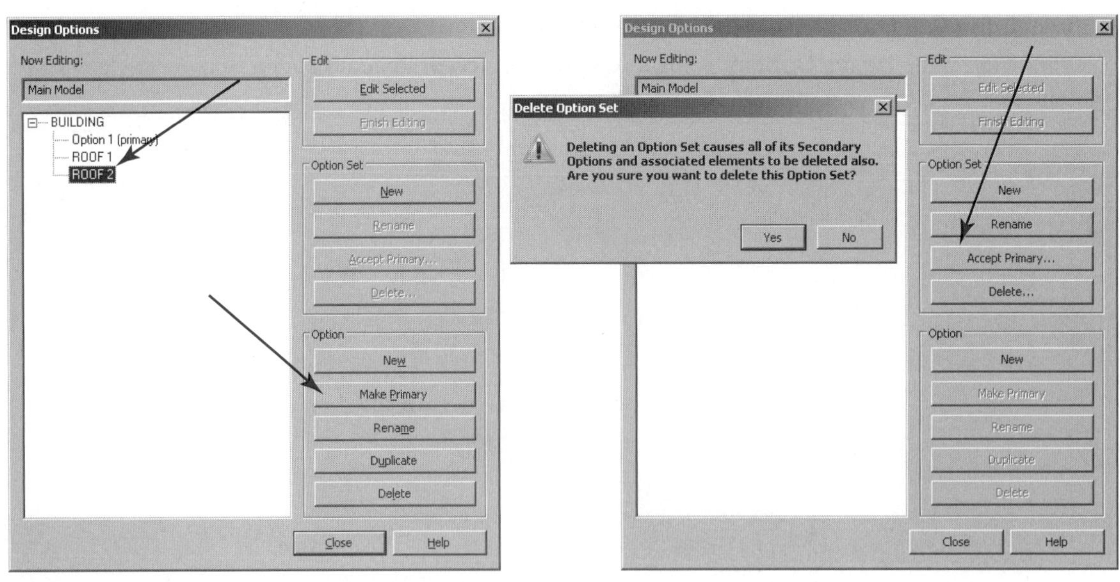

Figure 17-9

Delete Option Set warning

EXERCISE 17-2 MANAGE LINKS TOOL

The **Manage Links** tool allows you to import, reload, or remove electronic file links for Revit, CAD, and DWF markup files.

1. Use the **WALLS by PICK LINES** file created in Exercise 3-2 in Chapter 3.

The **WALLS by PICK LINES** file contains the **CARRIAGE HOUSE WALLS.dwg** file.

2. In the **Manage** toolbar, select the **Manage Links** button to bring up the **Manage Links** dialog box (see Figure 17-10).

Figure 17-10

Manage Links button

In the **Manage Links** dialog box, select the **CAD Formats** tab.

3. In the **CAD Formats** tab, select the **CARRIAGE HOUSE WALLS.dwg** file.
4. If any changes have been made to the DWG file, selecting the **Reload** button will reload the drawing.

This can be very helpful if you have a subcontractor who is sending you CAD underlays and may want you to incorporate the changes in your file. Please note that this does not change your Revit model.

Selecting the **Revit** or **DWF Markups** tabs will give you the ability to reload those file formats (see Figure 17-11).

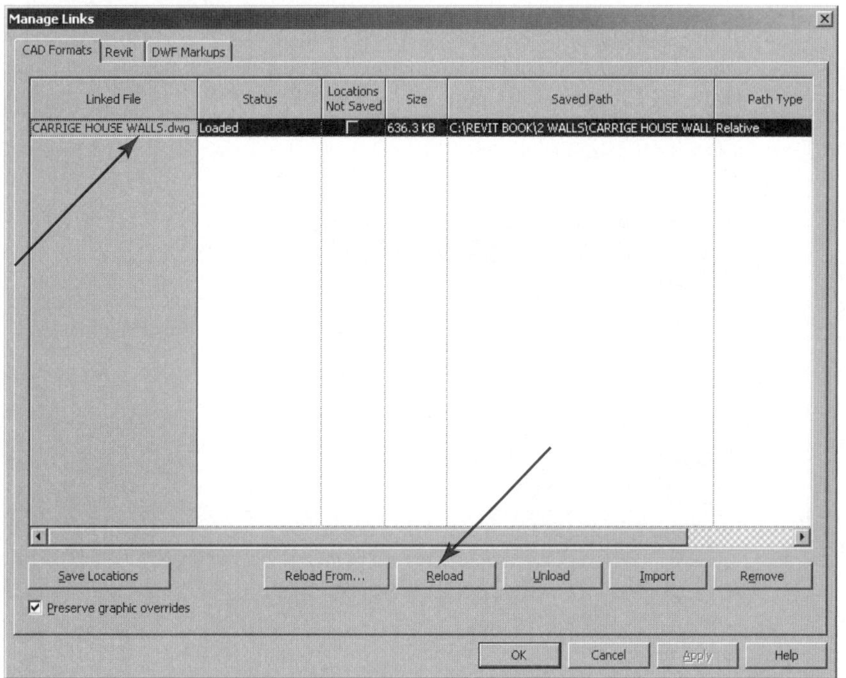

Figure 17-11

Reload file formats

EXERCISE 17-3 ADDITIONAL SETTINGS BUTTON

The **Additional Settings** button has fill pattern options; a **Render Appearance Library**; line style options; callout, elevation, and section tag settings; and temporary dimension options.

1. In the **Manage** toolbar, select **Additional Settings > Fill Patterns** to bring up the **Fill Patterns** dialog box. Here you can select and modify the patterns used in **Sections** and **Filled Regions** (see Figure 17-12).

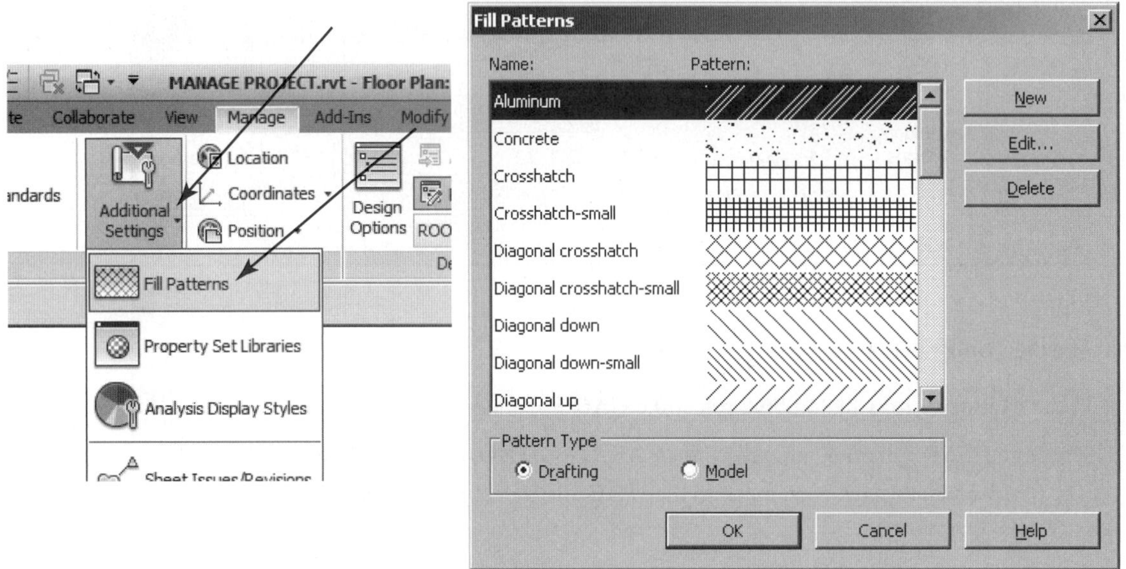

Figure 17-12

Fill Patterns button

2. In the **Manage** toolbar, select **Additional Settings > Property Set Libraries**. These libraries contain bitmap pictures that can be mapped onto surfaces from the **Material Library** (see Figures 17-13 and 17-14).

Figure 17-13

Render Appearance Library button

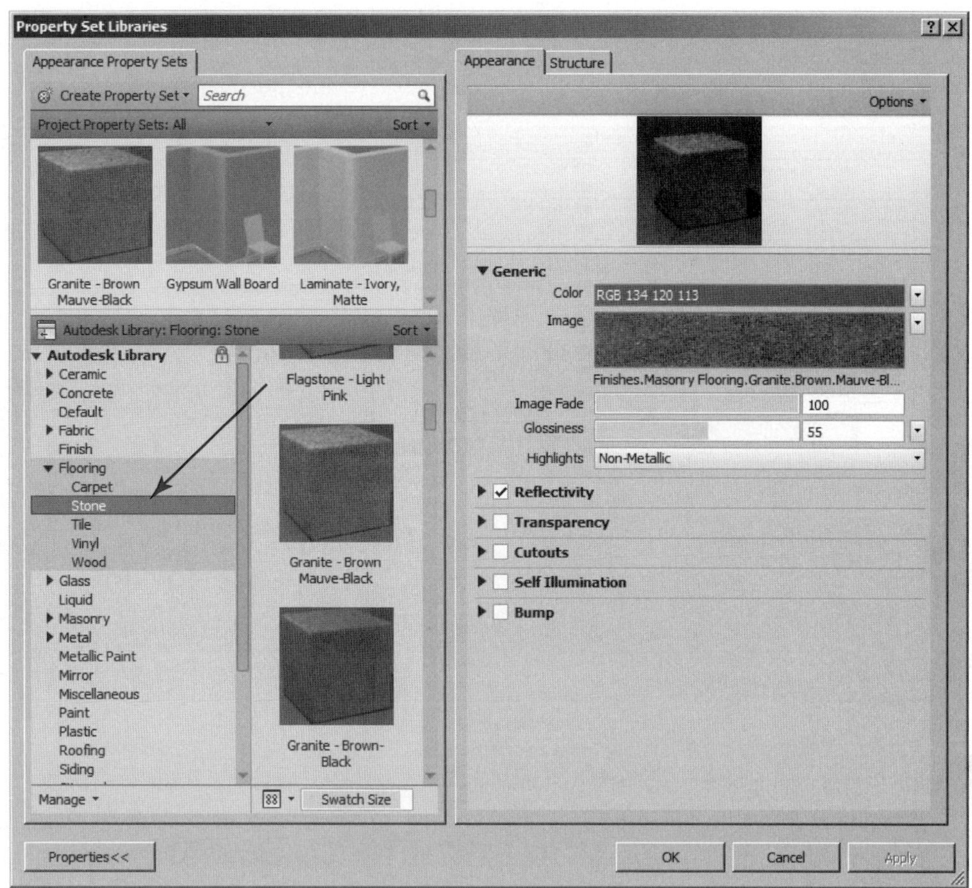

Figure 17-14

Material Library

3. In the **Manage** toolbar, select **Additional Settings** > **Line Styles**. This button brings up the **Line Styles** dialog box where **Line Weight** (thickness), **Color**, and **Line Pattern** are set (see Figures 17-15 and 17-16).

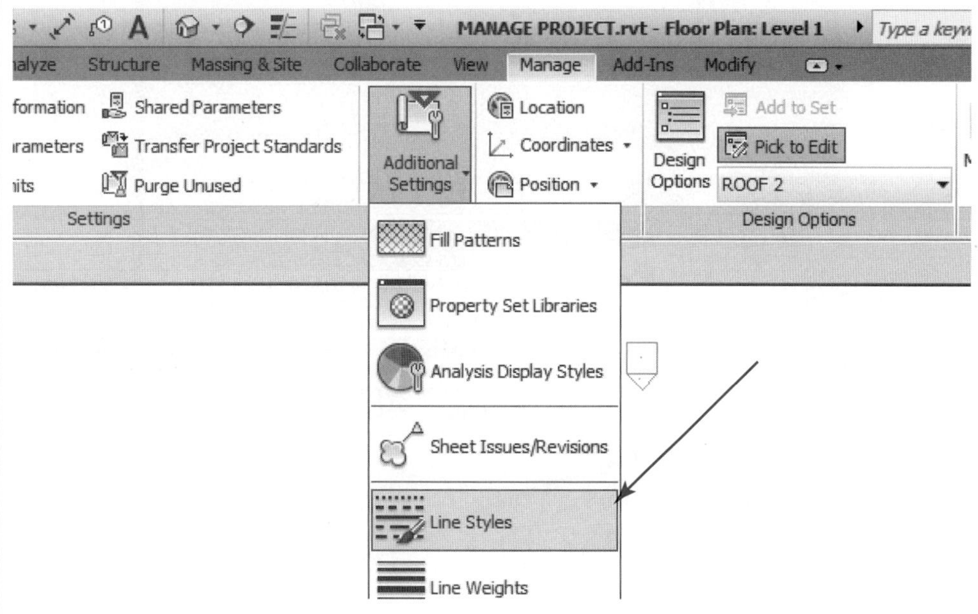

Figure 17-15

Line Styles button

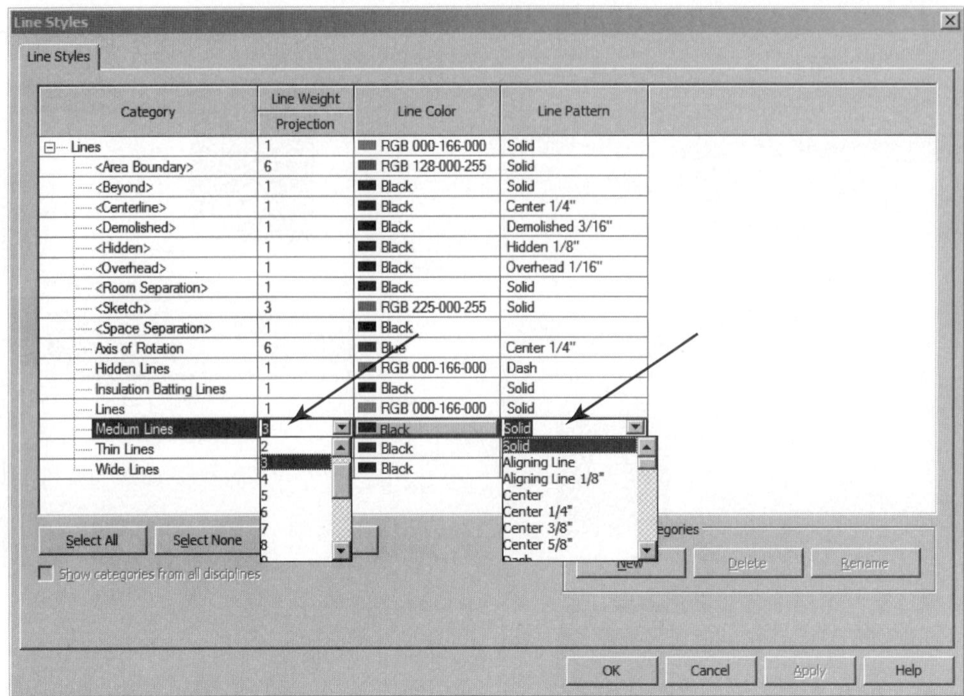

Figure 17-16

Line Styles dialog box

4. In the **Manage** toolbar, select **Additional Settings > Callout, Elevation, and Section Tags**. This button brings up the **Type Properties** dialog box where **Tags** and **Arrows** can be modified (see Figure 17-17).

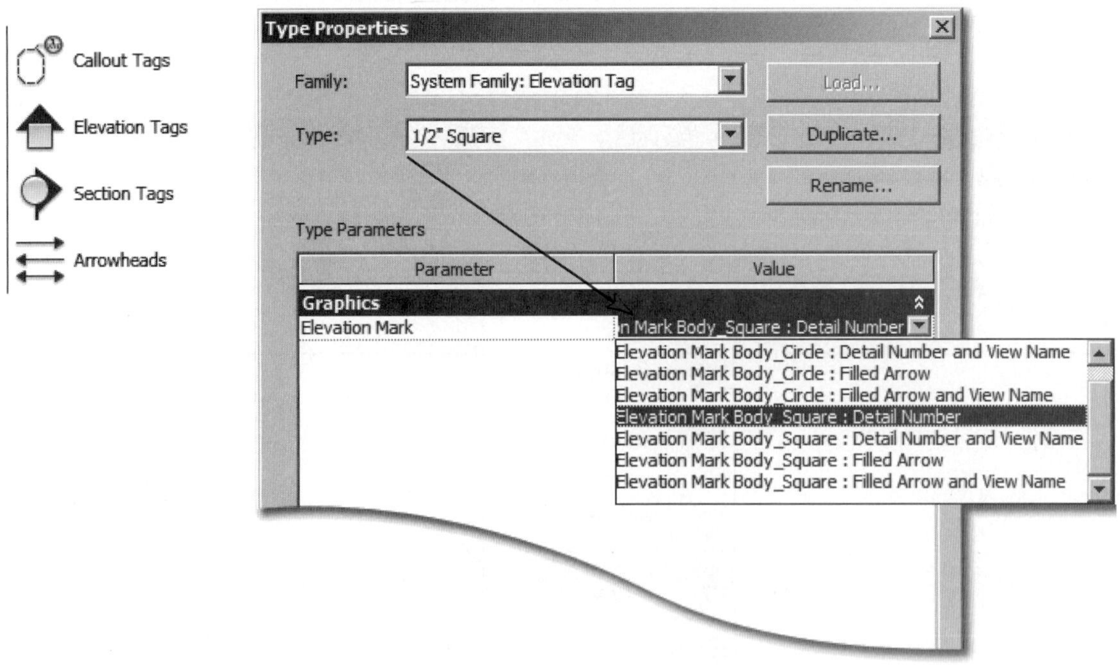

Figure 17-17

Type Properties dialog box

5. In the **Manage** toolbar, select **Additional Settings > Temporary Dimensions**. This button brings up the **Temporary Dimension Properties** dialog box where **Temporary Dimensions** start and end points are set (see Figure 17-18).

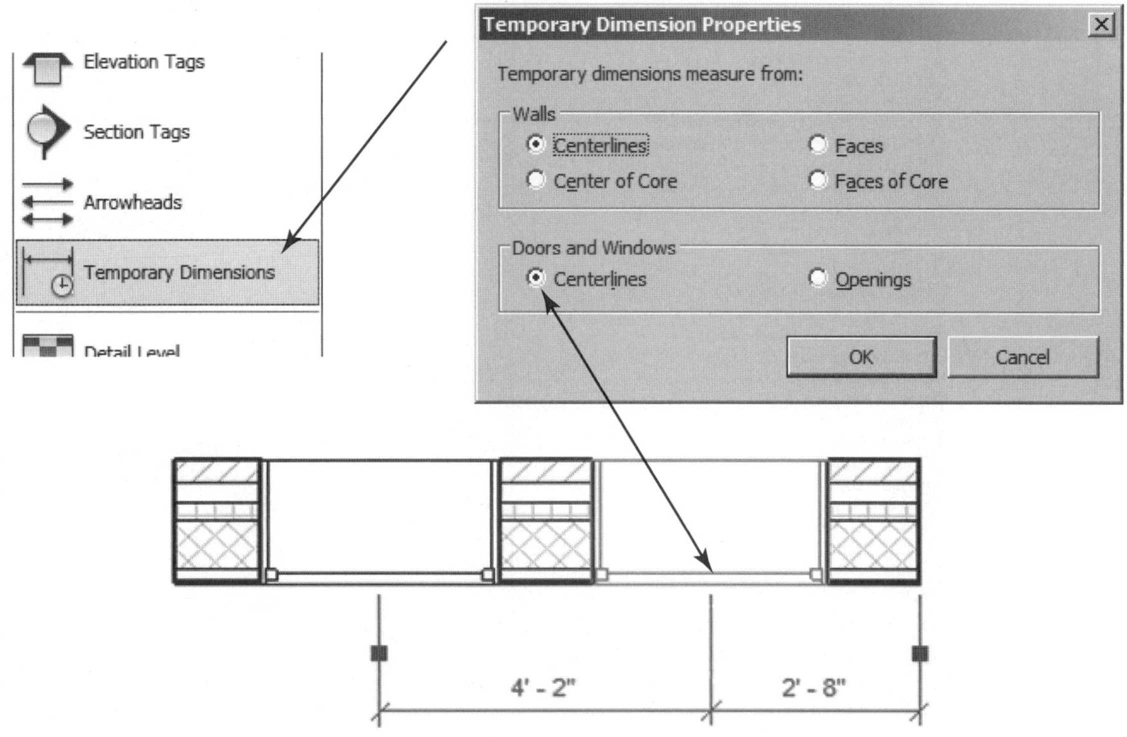

Figure 17-18

Temporary Dimension Properties dialog box

EXERCISE 17-4 MATERIALS TOOL

Select the **Materials** button in the **Manage** toolbar to bring up the **Materials** dialog box. Here you can modify material appearance as well as add new bitmap pictures. There are so many options that it is often best just to use the defaults. The best way to use this feature is to experiment and render the result (see Figures 17-19, 17-20, and 17-21).

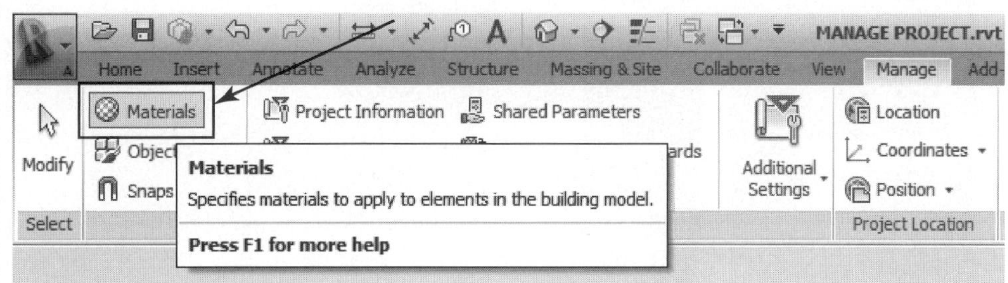

Figure 17-19

Materials button

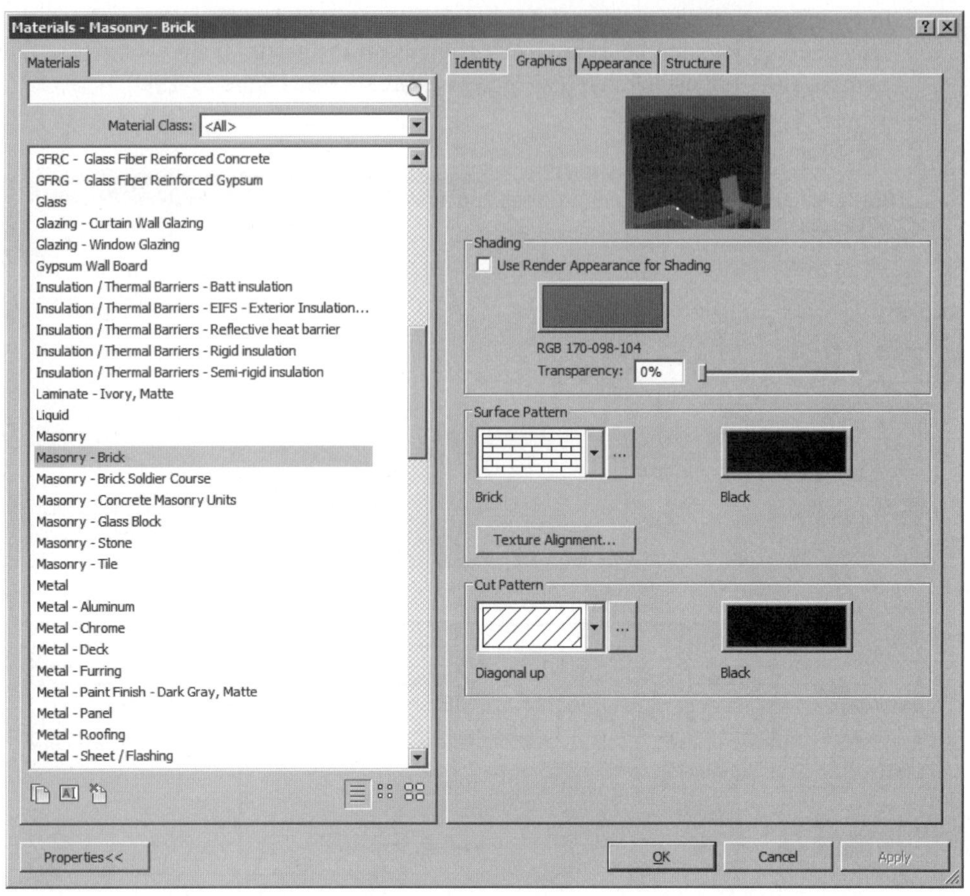

Figure 17-20

Materials dialog box

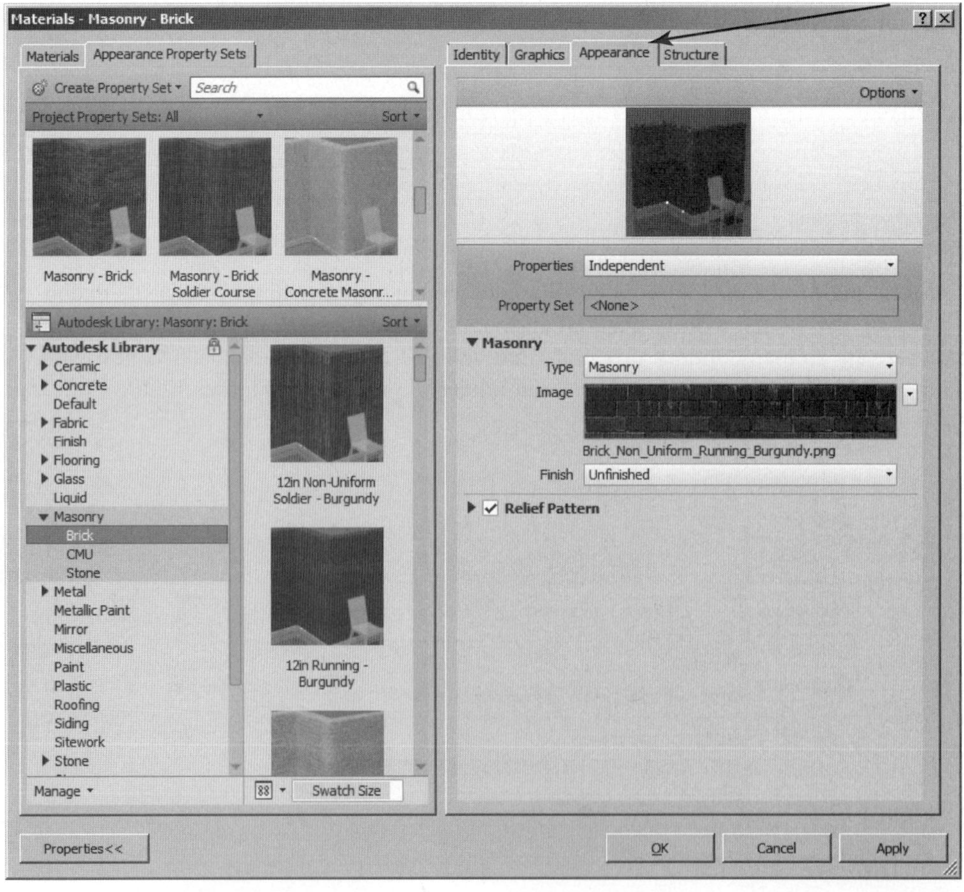

Figure 17-21

Render Appearance tab

EXERCISE 17-5 OBJECT STYLES BUTTON

Select the **Object Styles** button in the **Manage** toolbar to bring up the **Object Styles** dialog box. Here you can set the **Line Weight** (width), **Line Color, Line Pattern**, and **Material** for different objects such as Walls, Windows, and so on (see Figures 17-22, 17-23, and 17-24).

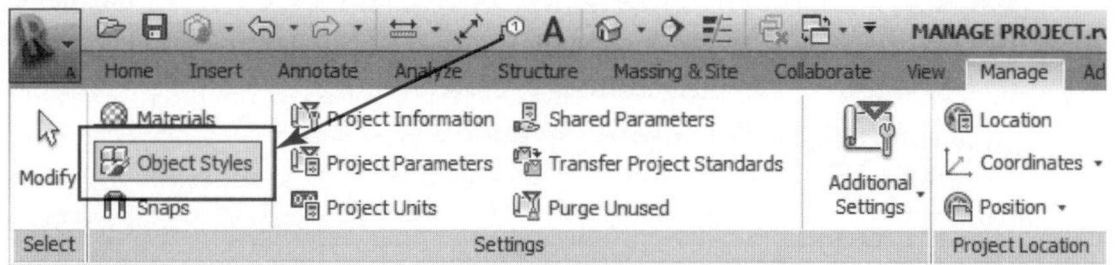

Figure 17-22

Object Styles button

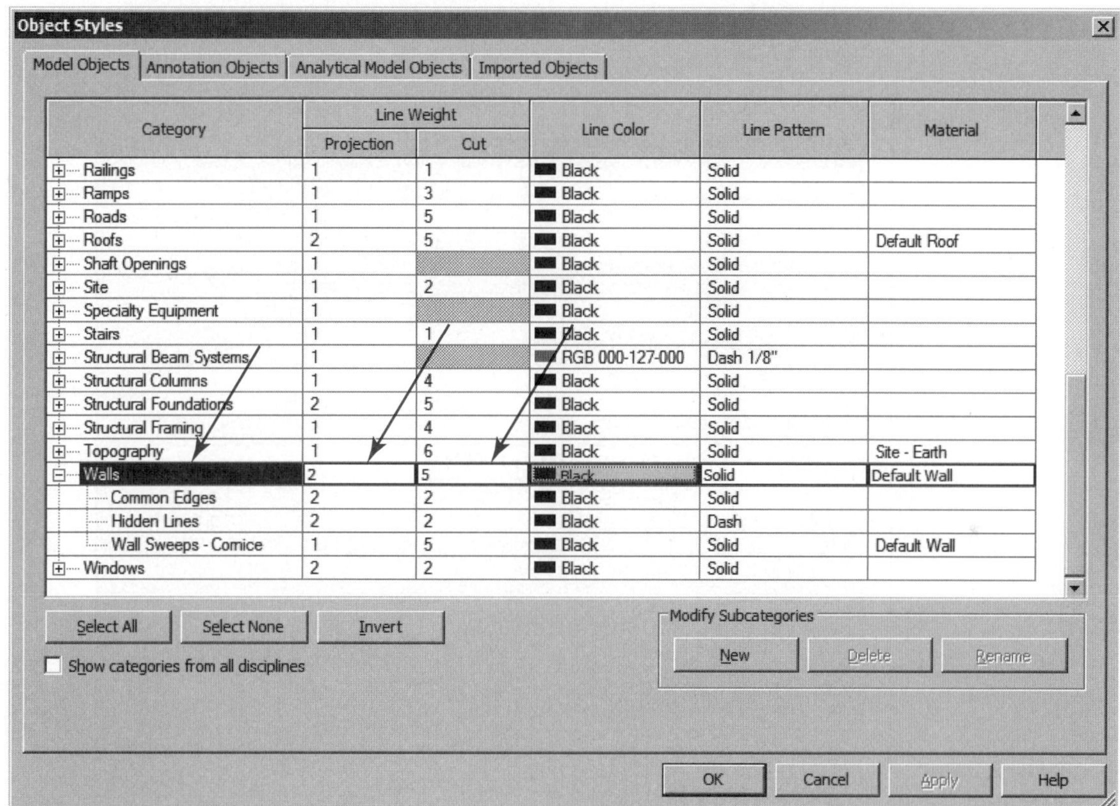

Figure 17-23

Object Styles dialog box

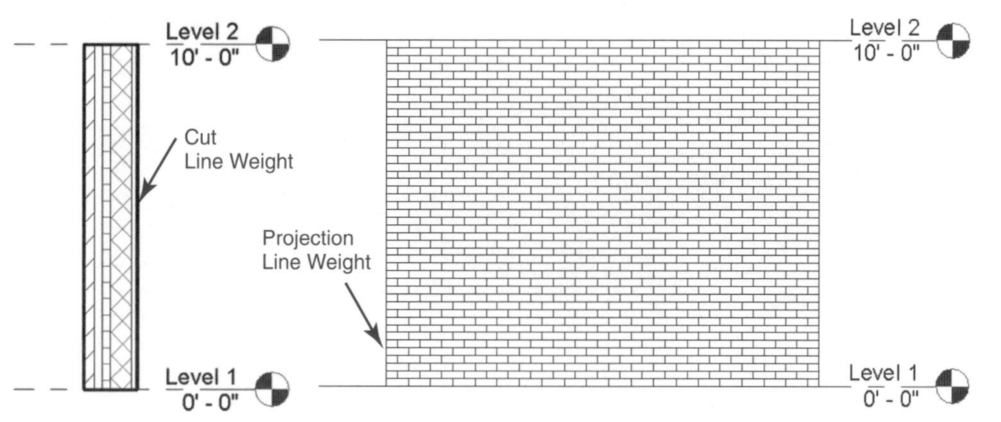

Figure 17-24

Drawing with **Cut Line Weight** and **Projection Line Weight**

EXERCISE 17-6 SNAPS BUTTON

Select the **Snaps** button in the **Manage** toolbar to bring up the **Snaps** dialog box. Here you can set the points at which an object will automatically snap. If you have enough computer power, turn them all on. Once they are on, pressing the <**Tab**> key will cycle through the **Snaps** when approaching an object within a command (see Figures 17-25 and 17-26).

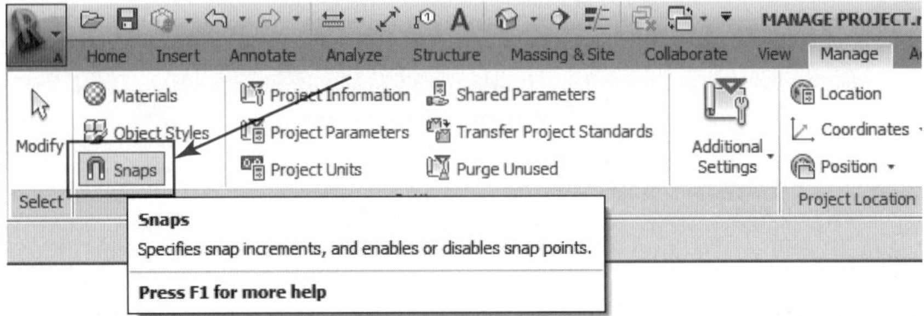

Figure 17-25

Snaps button

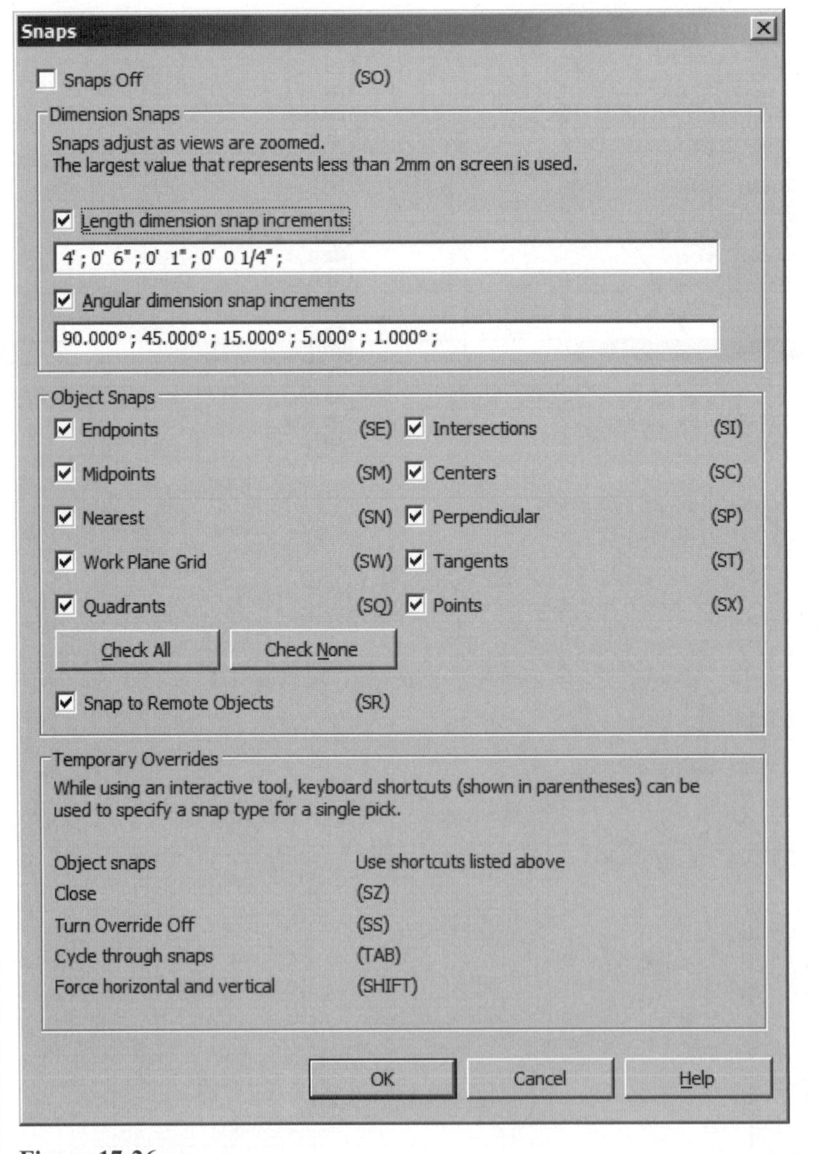

Figure 17-26

Snaps dialog box

EXERCISE 17-7 PROJECT INFORMATION BUTTON

Select the **Project Information** button in the **Manage** toolbar to bring up the **Instance Properties** dialog box for the project. Here you can set information that will appear on the title block of your Construction Document Sheet (see Figures 17-27 and 17-28).

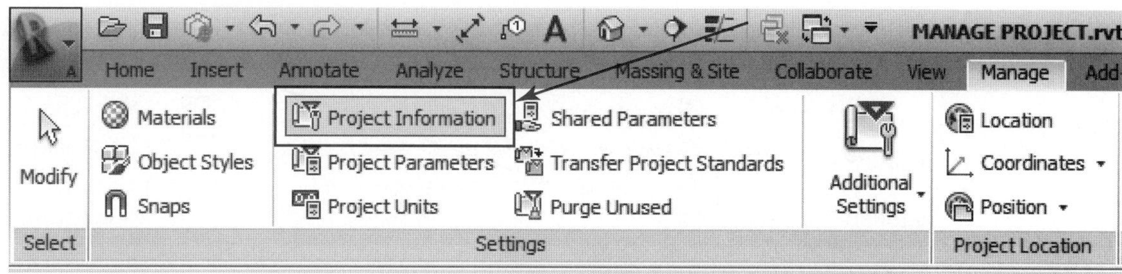

Figure 17-27

Project Information button

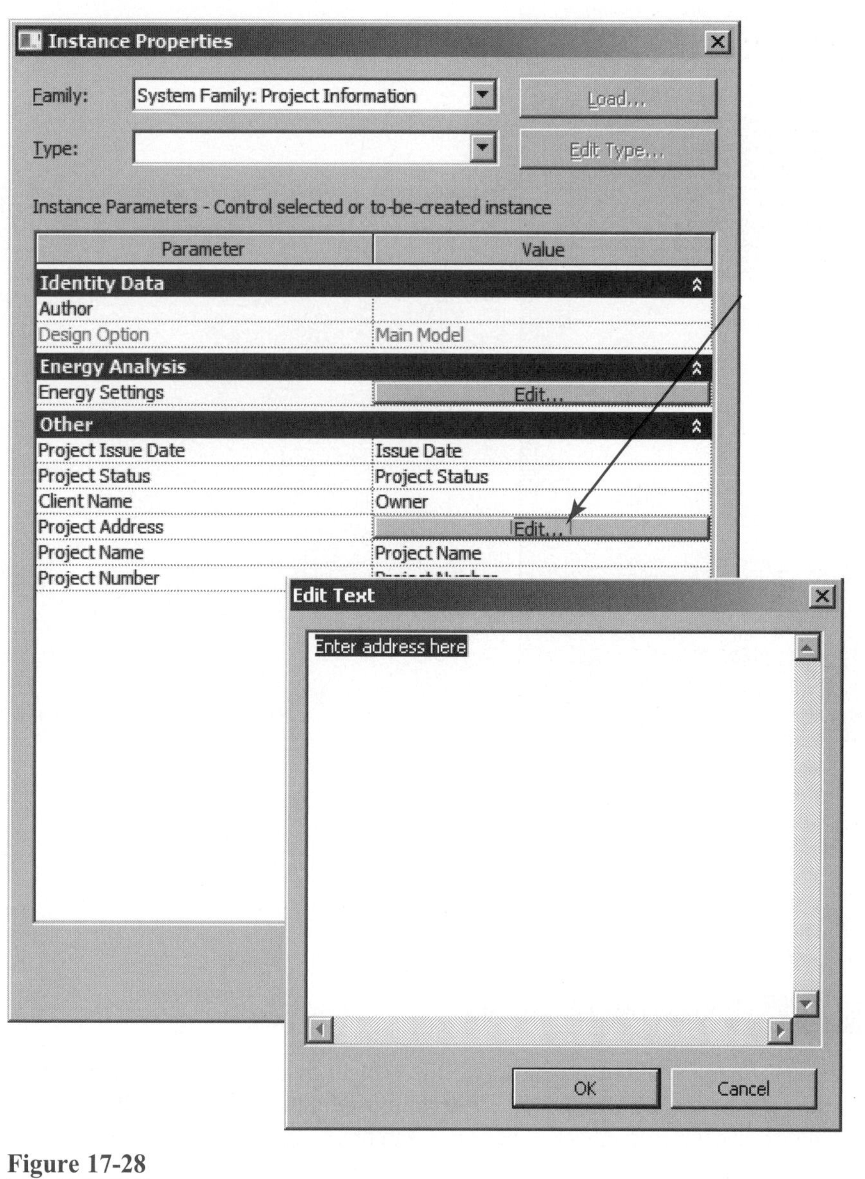

Figure 17-28

Instance Properties dialog box

EXERCISE 17-8 PROJECT UNITS BUTTON

Select the **Project Units** button in the **Manage** toolbar to bring up the **Project Units** dialog box for the project. Here you can customize the **Unit Format** (see Figures 17-29 and 17-30).

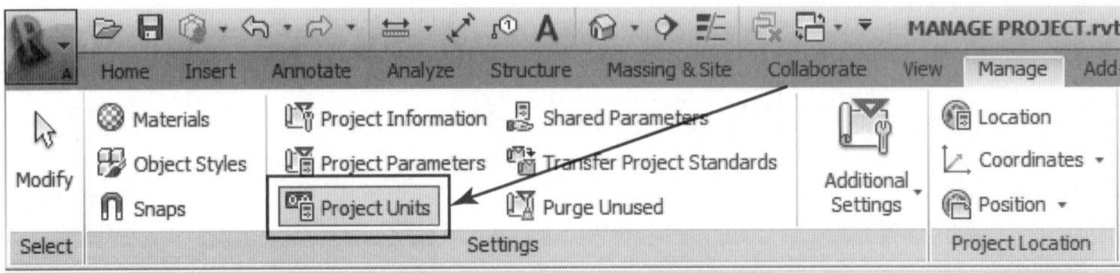

Figure 17-29

Project Units button

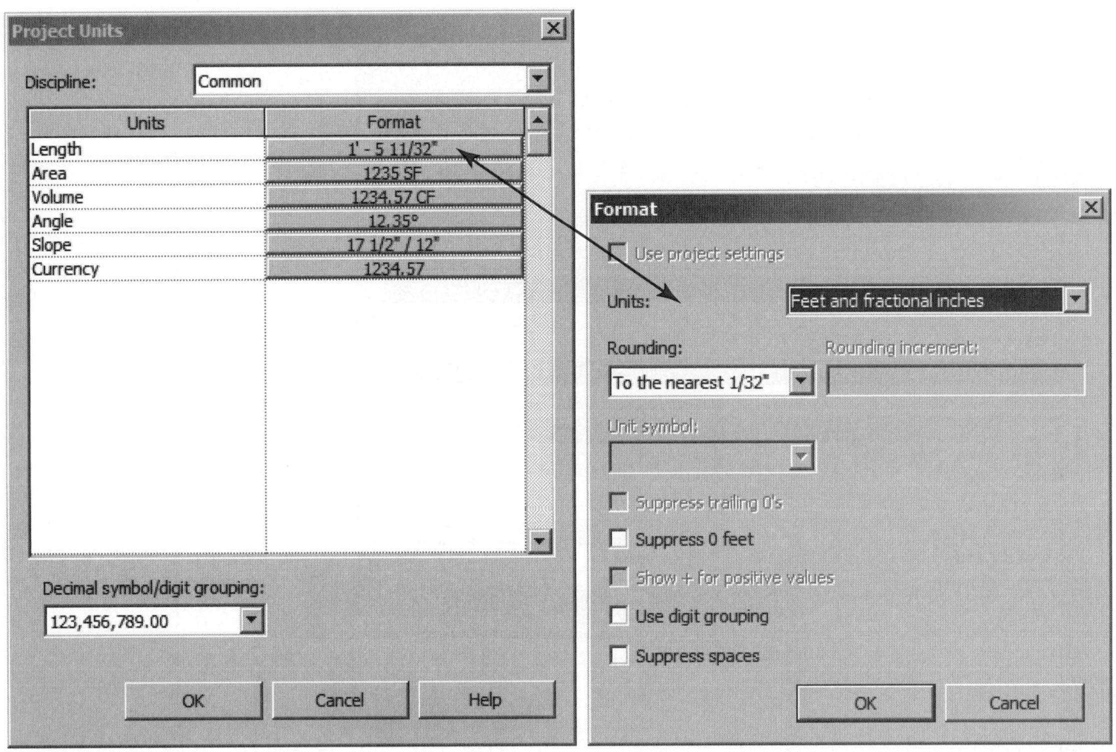

Figure 17-30

Project Units dialog box

EXERCISE 17-9 PURGE UNUSED BUTTON

Select the **Purge Unused** button to rid the project of unused **Families** and **Types**. Pressing this button will bring up the **Purge unused** dialog box. In the **Purge unused** dialog box, checking an object's check box and pressing the **OK** button will purge the objects. Doing this will make your project file more compact and easier to transfer electronically (see Figures 17-31 and 17-32).

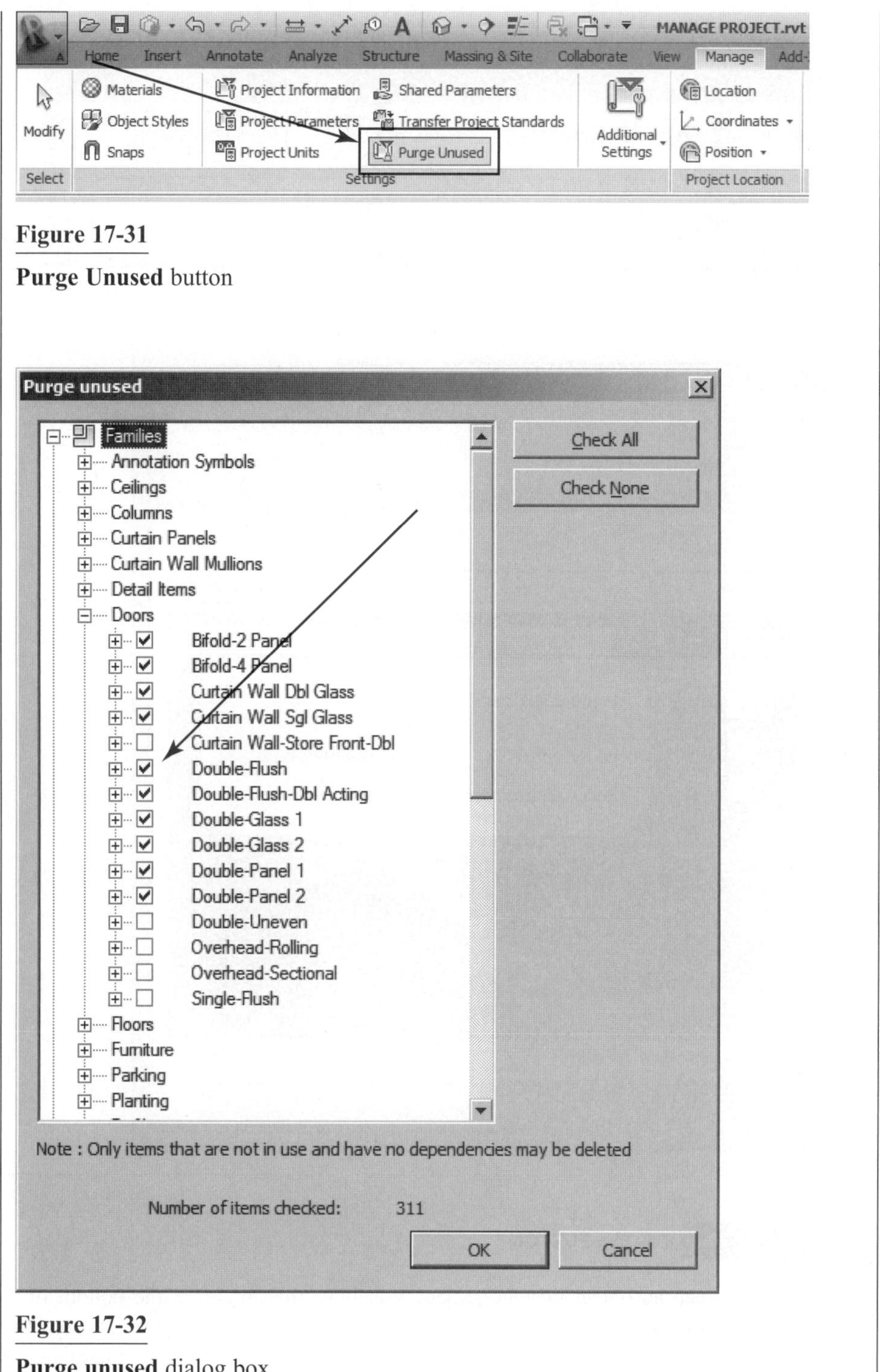

Figure 17-31

Purge Unused button

Figure 17-32

Purge unused dialog box

EXERCISE 17-10 LOCATION BUTTON

Select the **Location** button to establish the location of the project. Pressing the **Location** button brings up the **Location Weather and Site** dialog box. This location can later be used by the **Sun** and **Shadows** tools for renderings and for energy analysis (see Figures 17-33 and 17-34).

NOTE:

This requires an Internet connection.

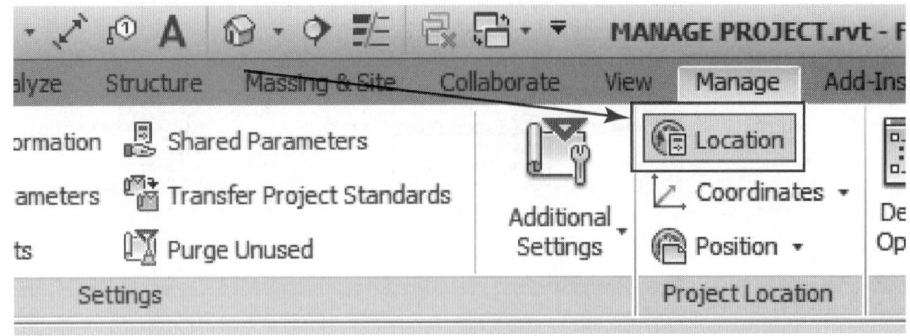

Figure 17-33
Location button

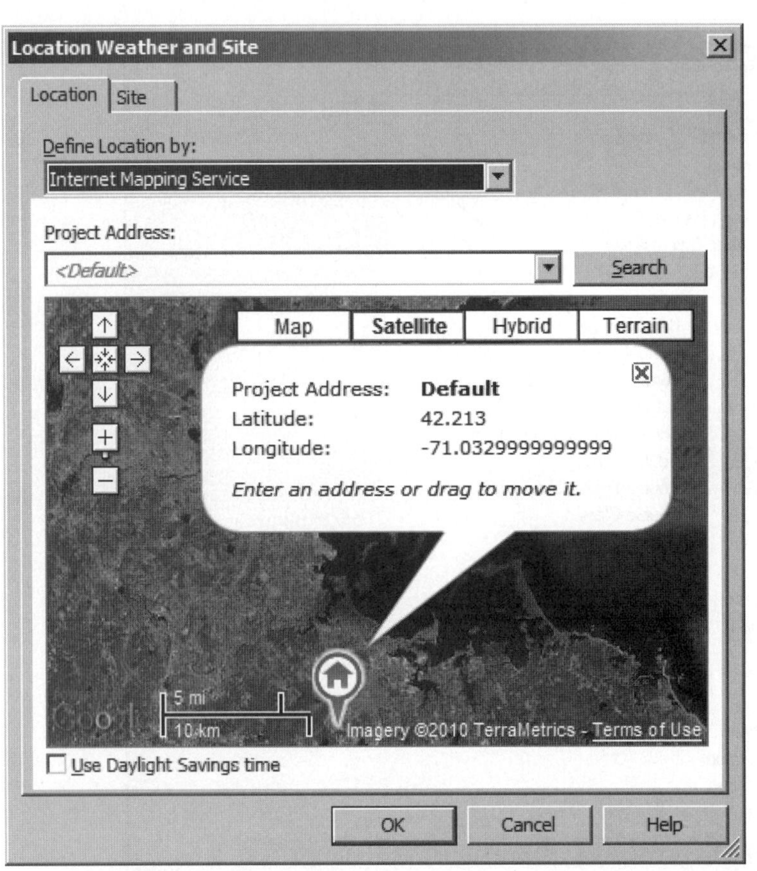

Figure 17-34
Location Weather and Site dialog box

EXERCISE 17-11 **PHASES BUTTON**

When you place an object in your project, you have the option, at the bottom of the object's **Properties** dialog box, to enter in which phase of the construction the object belongs. The **Phases** button brings up the **Phasing** dialog box where you can filter these objects for use in different phase sheets (see Figures 17-35, 17-36, 17-37, 17-38, and 17-39).

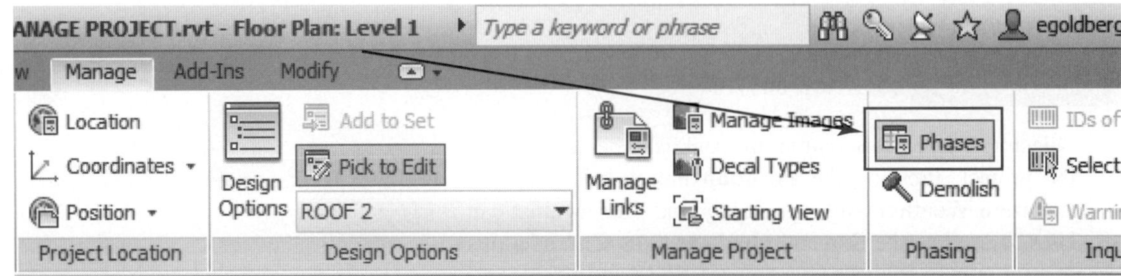

Figure 17-35
Phases button

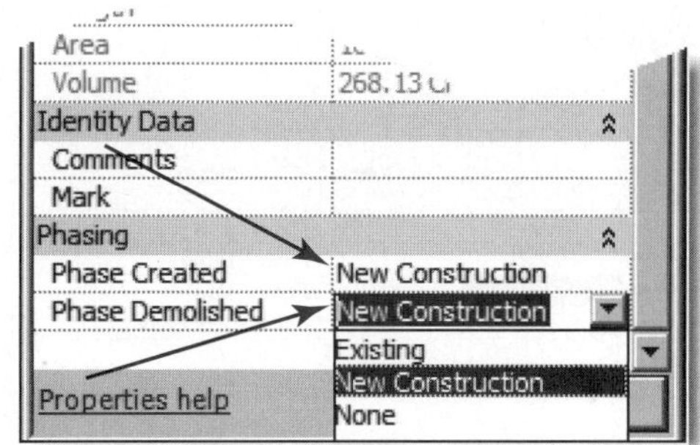

Figure 17-36

New Construction field

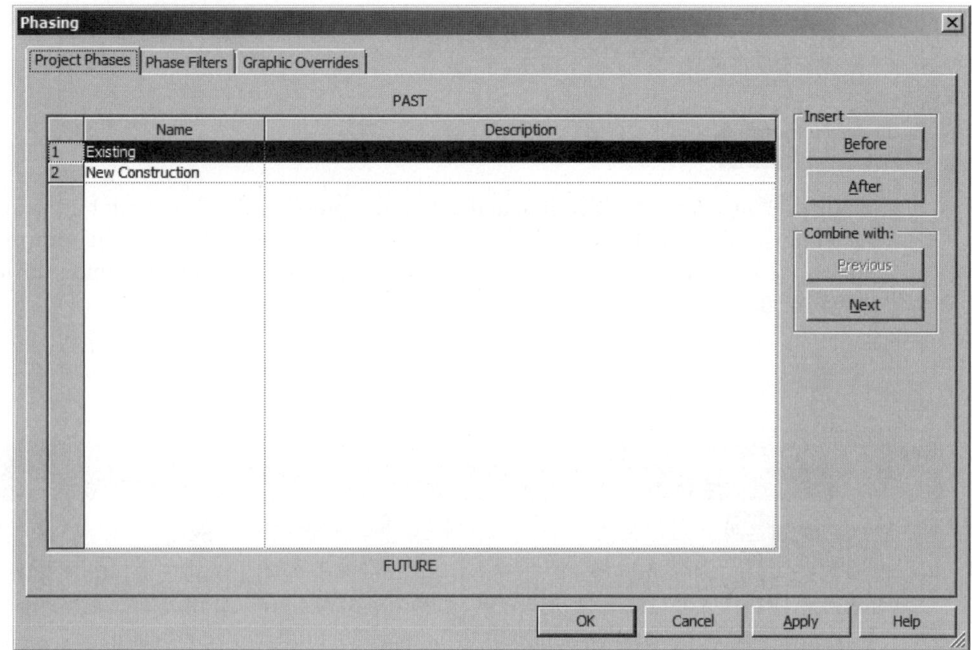

Figure 17-37

Project Phases tab

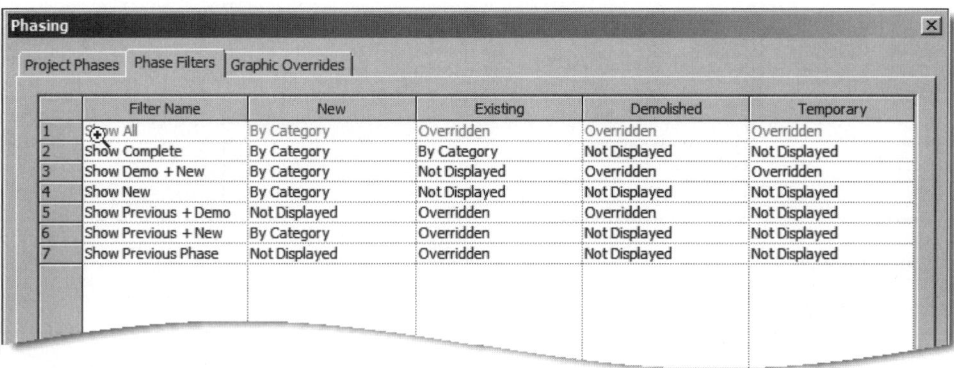

	Filter Name	New	Existing	Demolished	Temporary
1	Show All	By Category	Overridden	Overridden	Overridden
2	Show Complete	By Category	By Category	Not Displayed	Not Displayed
3	Show Demo + New	By Category	Not Displayed	Overridden	Overridden
4	Show New	By Category	Not Displayed	Not Displayed	Not Displayed
5	Show Previous + Demo	Not Displayed	Overridden	Overridden	Not Displayed
6	Show Previous + New	By Category	Overridden	Not Displayed	Not Displayed
7	Show Previous Phase	Not Displayed	Overridden	Not Displayed	Not Displayed

Figure 17-38

Phase Filters tab

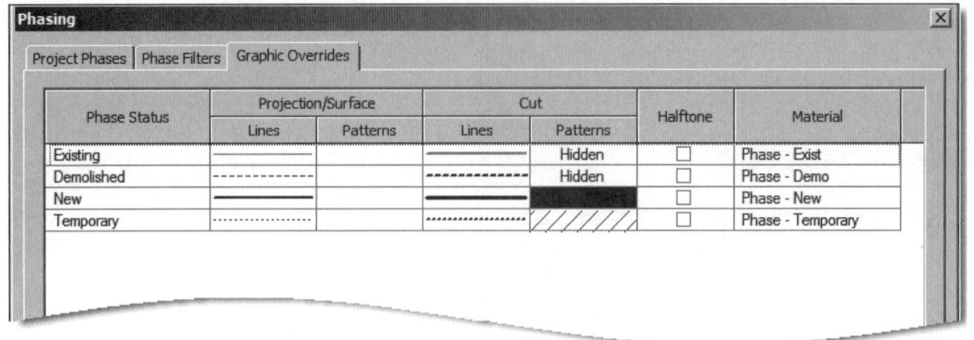

Figure 17-39

Graphic Overrides tab

EXERCISE 17-12 DEMOLISH BUTTON

When in Plan, Elevation, Section, and 3D views, pressing the **Demolish** button and selecting an object will create dashed lines in the drawing and record the information in the project. This information is used by the **Phases** tool (see Figures 17-40 and 17-41).

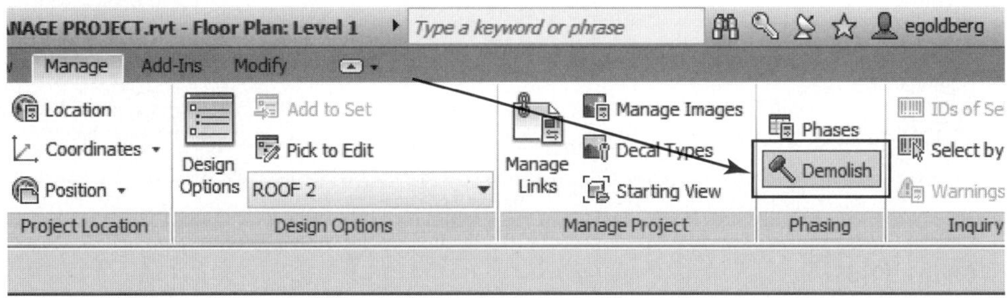

Figure 17-40

Demolish button

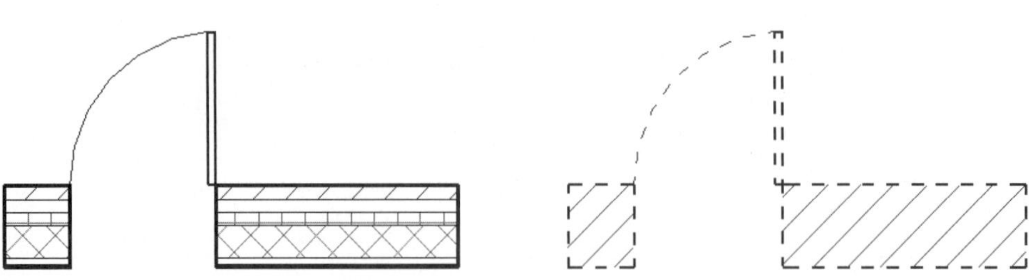

Figure 17-41

Dashed lines in a drawing

Chapter Summary

In this chapter, Revit Architecture 2012's **Manage** toolbar was investigated. This toolbar contains most of the project visual and information controls.

Chapter Test Questions

Multiple Choice

Circle the correct answer.

1. The **Fill Patterns** button controls
   a. The patterns used for materials.
   b. The patterns used for **Filled Regions**.
   c. The patterns used for text backgrounds.
   d. All of the above
2. The **Manage Links** tool manages the
   a. Linkage between objects.
   b. Linkage between imported files.
   c. Internet links.
   d. Linkage of bitmap images.
3. The **Demolish** tool
   a. Removes old files.
   b. Removes unused content.
   c. Demolishes content.
   d. Indicates what will be removed.
4. The **Phases** are
   a. **New, Existing**, and **Demolish**.
   b. **New** and **Existing**.
   c. **New, Existing**, and **None**.
   d. All of the above
5. What is not listed in the **Default Project Information**?
   a. Revision Date
   b. Project Name
   c. Project Number
   d. Client Name

True or False

Circle the correct answer.

1. **True or False:** You should not have all **Snap** check boxes turned on.
2. **True or False:** Purging unused content does not make a file smaller.
3. **True or False:** The **Render Appearance Library** allows you to adjust materials.
4. **True or False: Elevation Tags** are modified in the **Properties** dialog box.
5. **True or False:** Line color is controlled in the **Line Styles** dialog box.

Questions

1. What is the purpose of the **Object Styles** button?
2. What does **Line Weight** mean?
3. What does the **Temporary Dimensions** button control?
4. What is a bitmap?
5. What is the purpose of Revit's **Design Options** tool?

CHAPTER

18

Modify Toolbar

CHAPTER OBJECTIVES

- Learn how to use the <Tab> key.
- Learn how to use the **Match Type** tool.
- Learn how to use the **Join Geometry** tool.
- Learn how to use the **Cut Geometry** tool.
- Learn how to use the **Wall Joins** tool.
- Learn how to use the **Split Face** tool.
- Learn how to use the **Paint** tool.
- Learn how to use the **Align** tool.
- Learn how to use the **Copy** tool.
- Learn how to use the **Offset** tool.
- Learn how to use the **Mirror–Pick Axis** and **Mirror–Draw Axis** tools.
- Learn how to use the **Extend/Trim** tools.
- Learn how to use the **Split** tool.
- Learn how to use the **Linework** tool.
- Learn how to use the **Measure** tool.

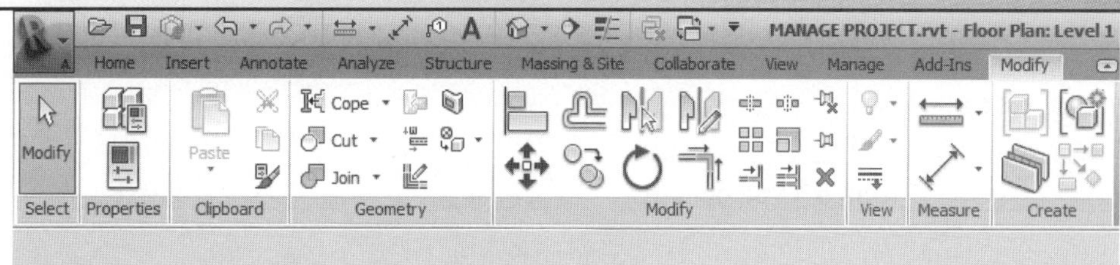

Introduction

In Revit Architecture 2012, the **Modify** toolbar contains tools for modifying lines and objects.

Modify Tools

The **Modify** tools are used for measuring, matching, changing line styles, assigning textures to surfaces, splitting objects, cutting objects in sections, and so on. Using the <**Tab**> key makes it easier and faster to perform these tasks.

EXERCISE 18-1 THE <TAB> KEY

Use the <**Tab**> key to perform the following tasks:

- Cycle through the prehighlighting of elements to select among ones that are close to one another.
- Prehighlight wall faces or wall centerlines when placing dimensions.
- Toggle between selecting a curtain wall or a glazed panel in a Plan view.
- Cycle through different snaps while creating walls and lines, placing components, and moving or pasting elements.

EXERCISE 18-2 MATCH TYPE

Use the **Match Type** tool when you want to change an object to the same parameters as an existing object. This also works with text (see Figures 18-1 and 18-2).

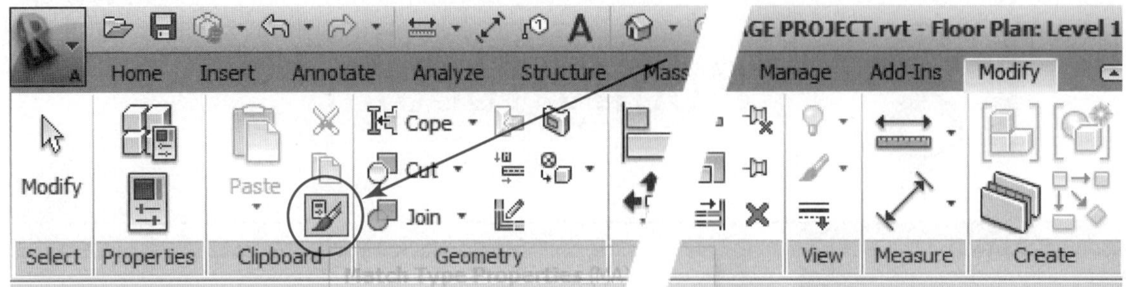

Figure 18-1

Match Type button

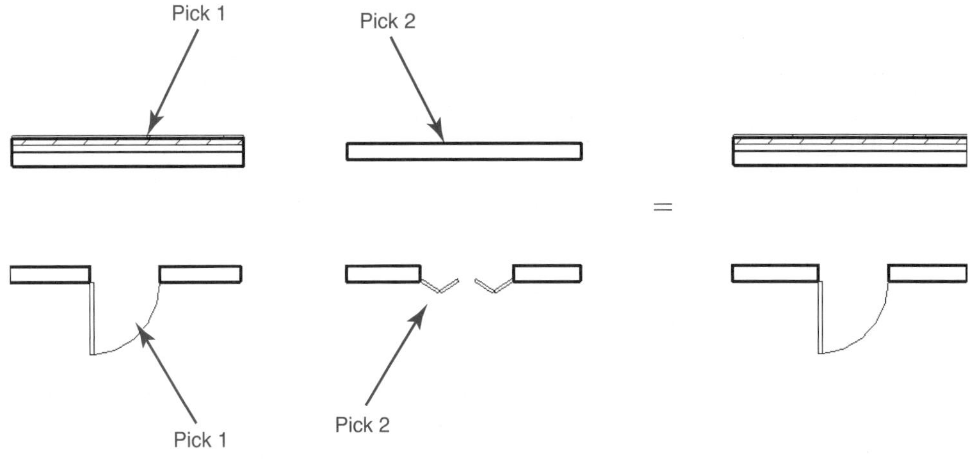

Figure 18-2

Use an existing object to change another

EXERCISE 18-3 JOIN GEOMETRY TOOL

Use the **Join Geometry** tool to create clean joins between two or more host elements that share a common face, such as walls and floors. You can also use the tool to join hosts and in-place families or to join hosts and project families. As shown in the following illustrations, the tool removes the visible edge between the joined elements. The joined elements then share the same line weight and fill pattern.

When you join geometry in the **Family Editor**, you create a union between different shapes. In a project, however, one of the joined elements actually cuts the other according to the following scheme:

- Walls cut columns.
- Structural elements cut host elements (walls, roofs, ceilings, and floors).
- Floors, ceilings, and roofs cut walls.
- Gutters, fascias, and slab edges cut other host elements. Cornices do not cut any elements.

To join geometry, follow these steps:

1. Click the **Modify** tab to bring up the **Modify** toolbar.
2. In the **Modify** toolbar, select the **Join Geometry** button in the **Geometry** panel.
3. If you want to join the first selected geometry instance to several other instances, select **Multiple Join** on the **Options Bar**. If you do not select this option, you must make a first and second selection each time.

4. Select the first geometry to join (for example, a wall face).
5. Select the second geometry to join to the first (for example, an edge of a floor).
6. If you selected **Multiple Join**, continue selecting other geometry to join to the first.
7. To exit the tool, press the **<Esc>** key (see Figures 18-3 and 18-4).

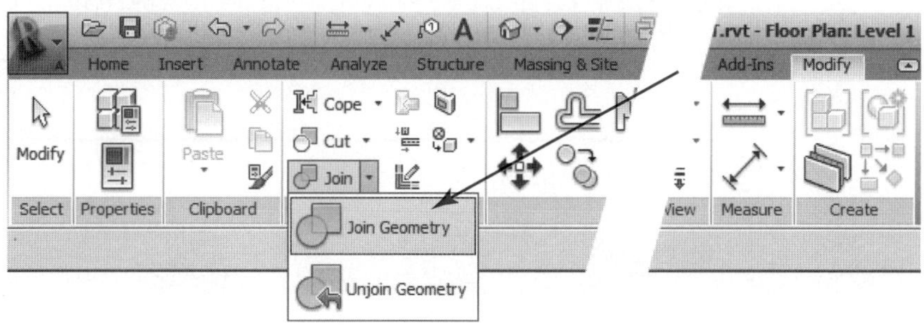

Figure 18-3

Join Geometry button

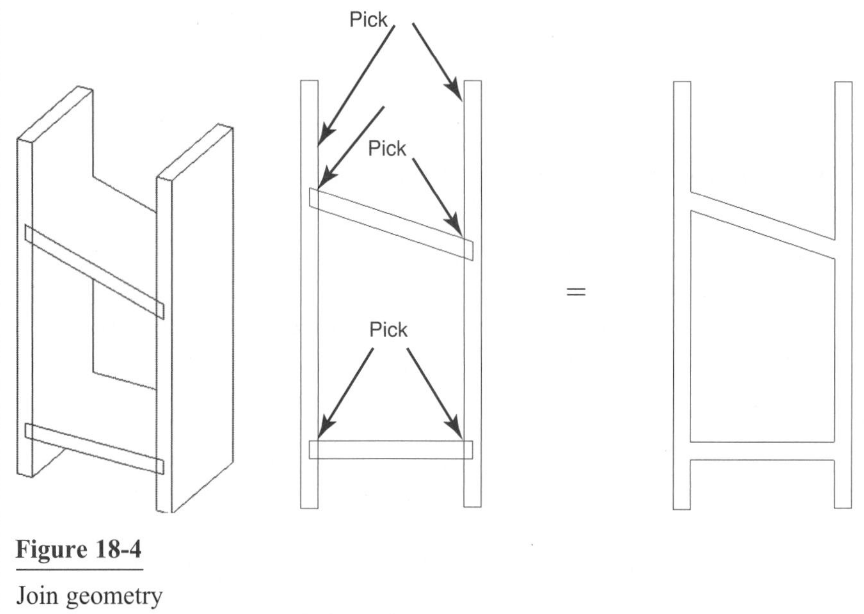

Figure 18-4

Join geometry

EXERCISE 18-4 CUT GEOMETRY TOOL

With the **Cut Geometry** tool, you can pick and choose which geometry gets cut and which does not, regardless of when the geometry was created.

1. Place two overlapping **Generic 8″ × 10″** high walls in the **Level 1** Floor Plan view as shown in Figure 18-5.
2. Click the **Modify** tab to bring up the **Modify** toolbar.
3. In the **Modify** toolbar, select the **Cut Geometry** button in the **Geometry** panel (see Figure 18-6).
4. Select the longer wall, and then select the shorter one.
5. Change to the **Default 3D View**.

NOTE:

The walls will turn orange in color, and a **Revit** warning will appear telling you to use the **Cut Geometry** tool.

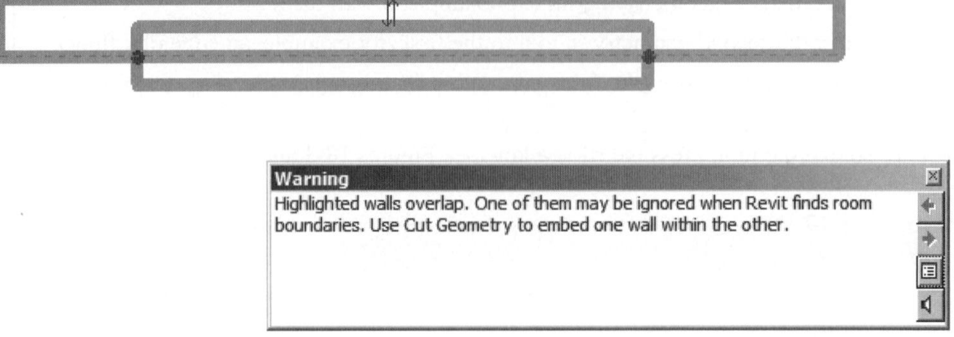

Figure 18-5

Place overlapping walls

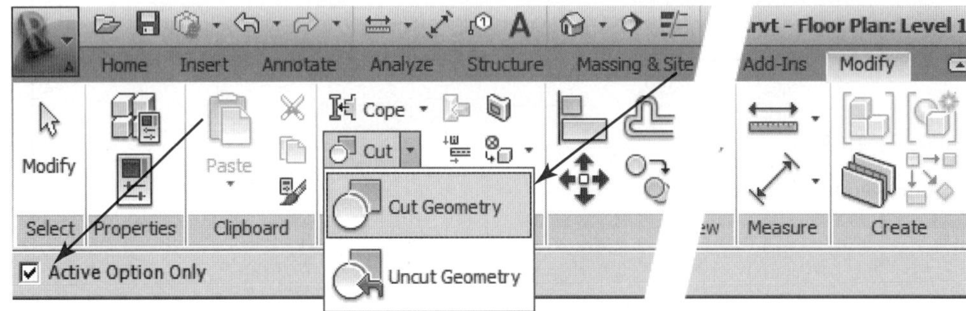

Figure 18-6

Cut Geometry button

6. In the **3D** view, select the shorter wall, and move its grips.
7. Deselect the grips by pressing the **<Esc>** key.
8. **RMB** (right mouse button click) on the shorter wall to bring up its contextual menu.
9. In the contextual menu, select **Hide in View > Elements** to hide the shorter wall (see Figures 18-7 and 18-8).

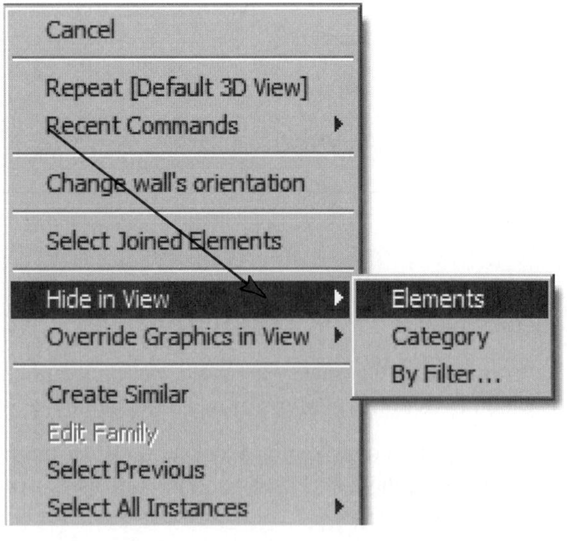

Figure 18-7

Hide in View > Elements option

TIP

If you want to unhide the object, click on the **Reveal Hidden Elements** button to show the hidden object, **RMB** on the revealed hidden object, and select **Unhide in View > Elements** from the contextual menu. Once the object has been unhidden, click again on the **Reveal Hidden Elements** button to unhide the object permanently (see Figure 18-9).

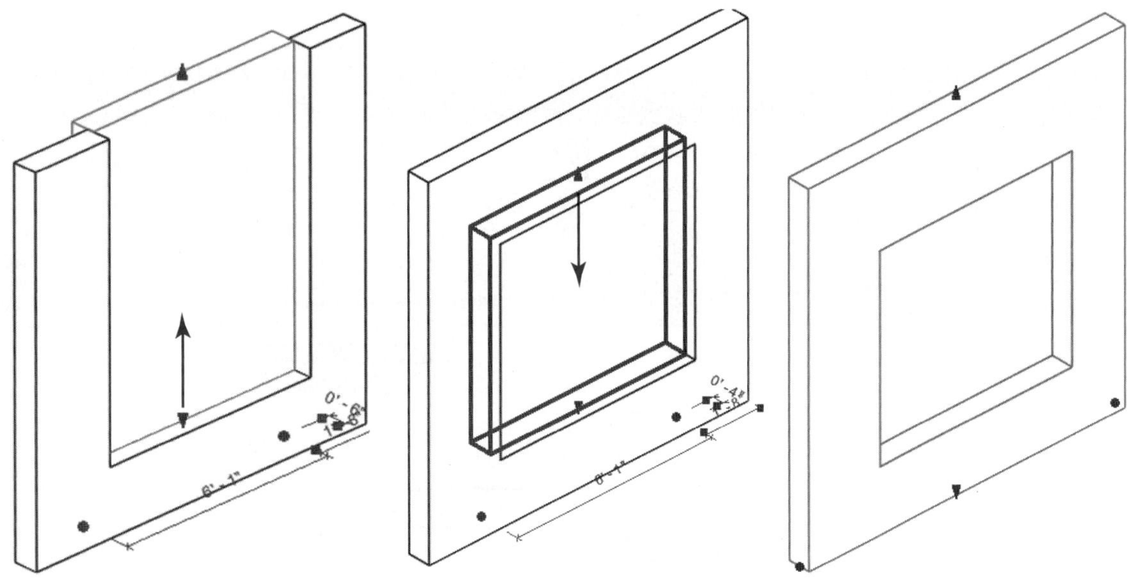

Figure 18-8

Hide the shorter wall

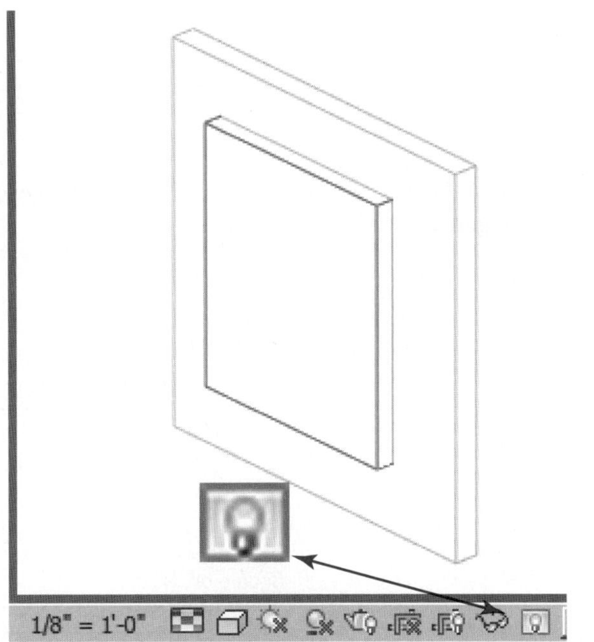

Figure 18-9

Reveal Hidden Elements button to reveal the hidden wall.

EXERCISE 18-5 **WALL JOINS TOOL**

When you create walls, Revit Architecture automatically joins them at their intersections. You can edit wall joins by selecting the **Wall Joins** button when necessary. For best results, edit wall joins in a Plan view (see Figure 18-10).

1. In the **Modify** toolbar, select the **Wall Joins** button in the **Geometry** panel.
2. Move the cursor over the wall join and click.

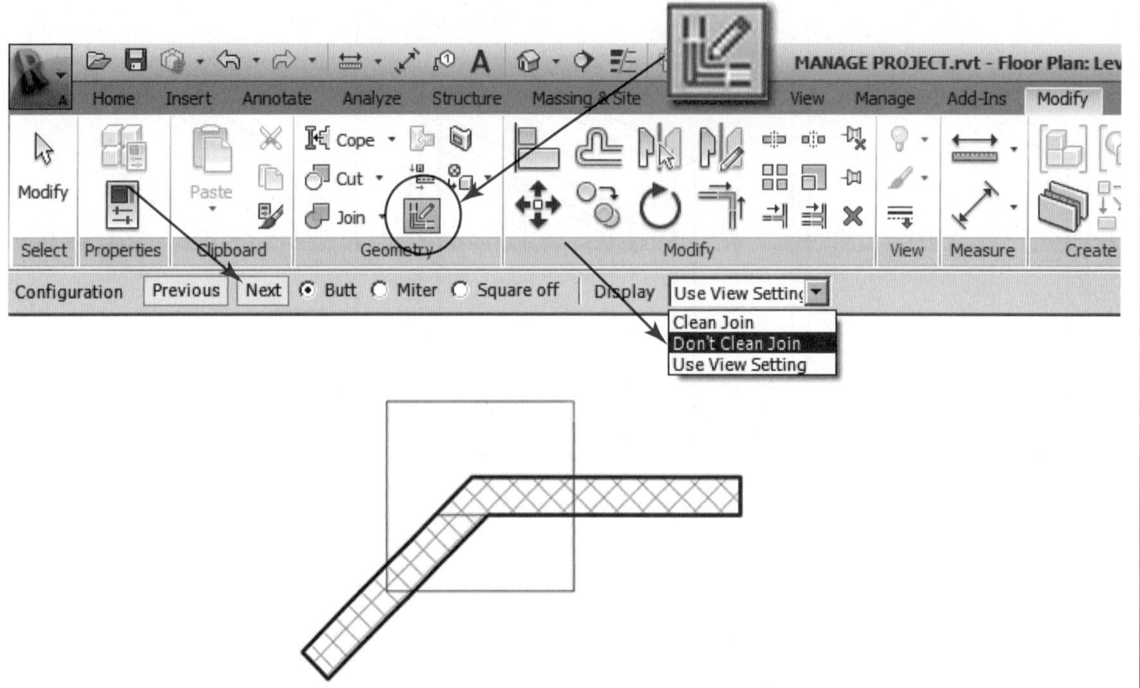

Figure 18-10

Wall Joins button

A square encloses the wall join.

3. On the **Options Bar**, select a **Join Type**, and then select the **Next** button to cycle through the **Join** options (see Figure 18-11).

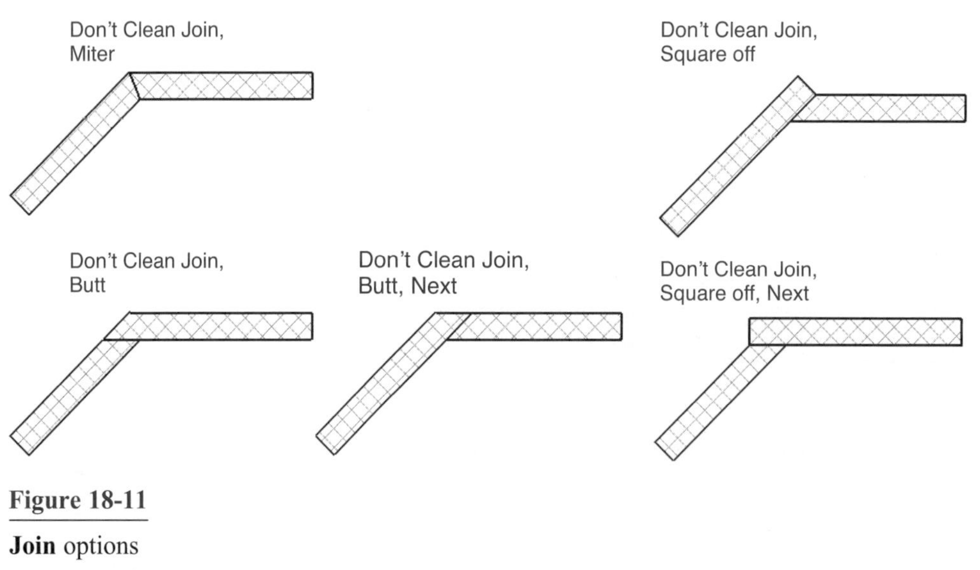

Figure 18-11

Join options

EXERCISE 18-6 SPLIT FACE TOOL

Use the **Split Face** tool to create a split in a wall.

1. In the **Modify** toolbar, select the **Split Face** button to bring up the **Modify | Split Face > Create Boundary** toolbar (see Figure 18-12).

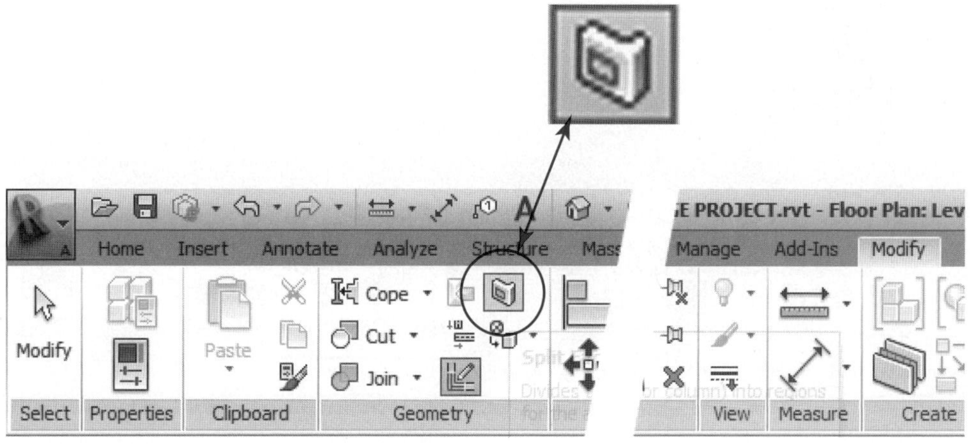

Figure 18-12

Split Face button

2. Select a wall (it will “gray out”).
3. Select a tool from the **Draw** panel (**Line**, **Arc**, and so on).
4. Draw an enclosed space on the wall, and then select the **Finish Edit Mode** button to create the split (see Figure 18-13).

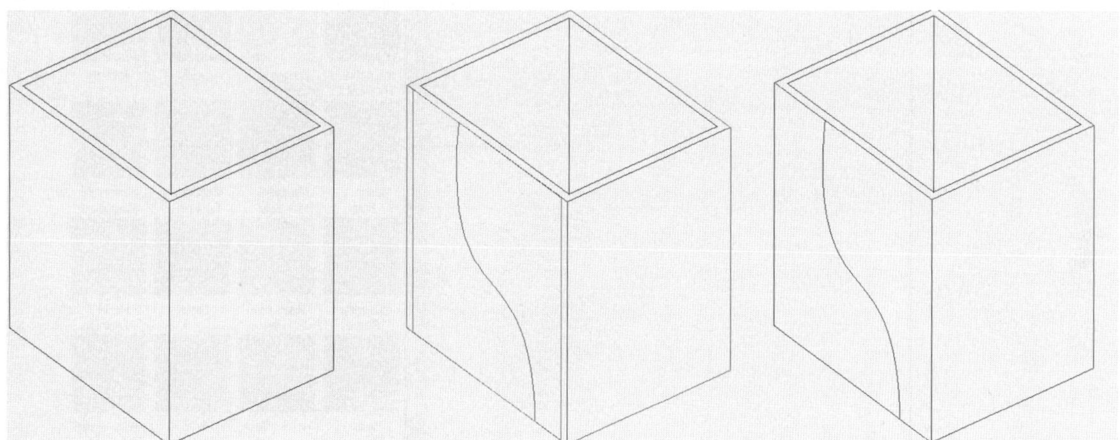

Figure 18-13

Split a wall

EXERCISE 18-7 PAINT TOOL

Use the **Paint** tool to “paint” patterns on a surface.

1. Use the previous exercise.
2. From the **Modify** panel, select the **Paint** button to bring up the **Modify | Paint** toolbar (see Figure 18-14).
3. Select the previous wall you split to bring up the **Paint** toolbar.
4. In the **Modify | Paint** toolbar, select **Masonry - Glass Block** from the **Material** drop-down list (see Figure 18-15).

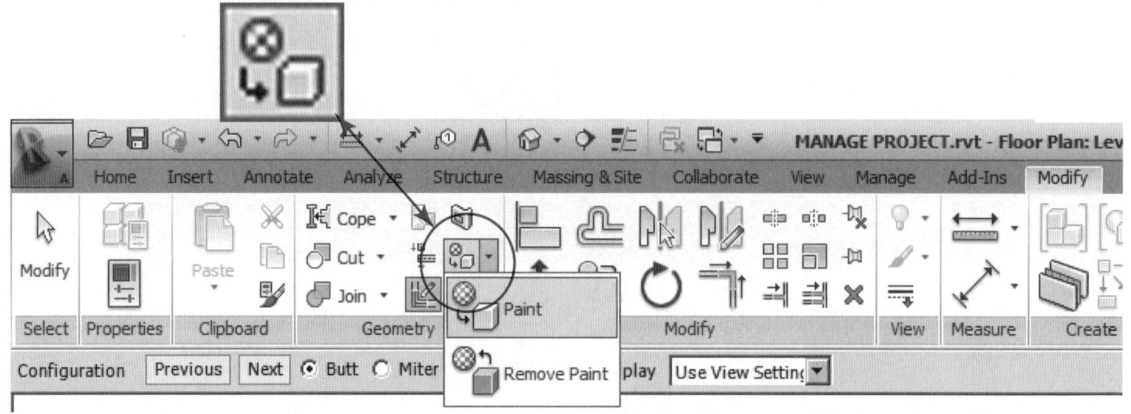

Figure 18-14

Paint button

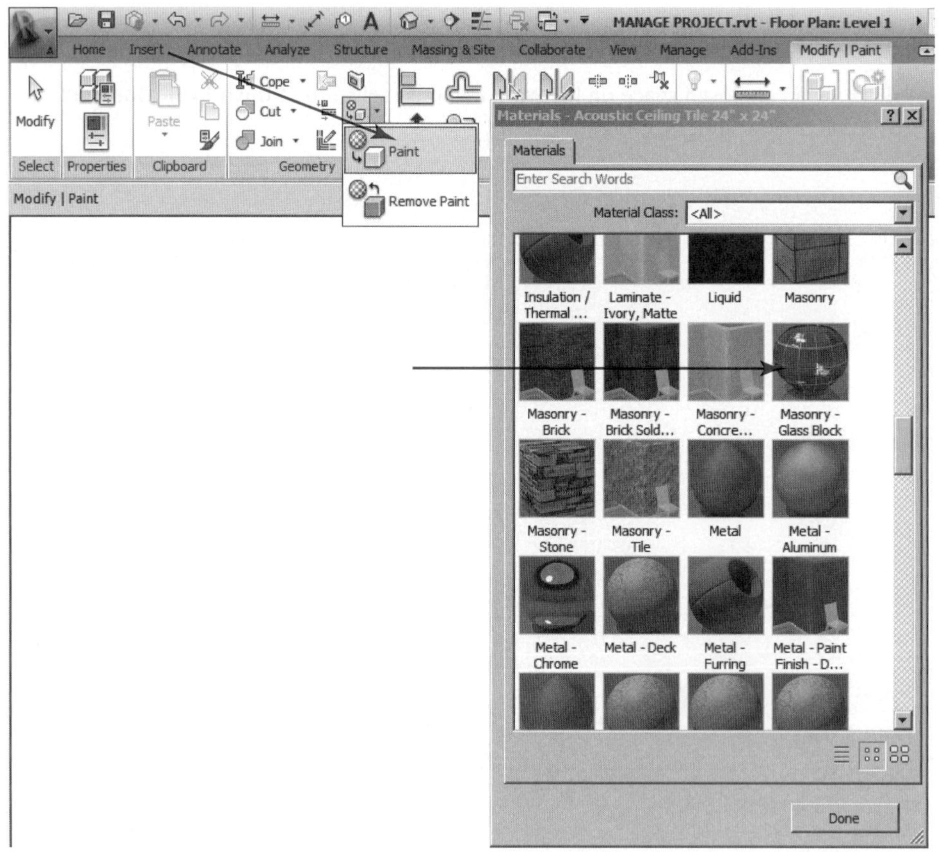

Figure 18-15

Select **Masonry - Glass Block**

5. Select a face to "paint" the pattern you have just selected (see Figure 18-16).

The **Paint** tool can be used to paint any face with a material (see Figure 18-17).

> **NOTE:**
> Elements that you can paint include walls, roofs, massing, families, and floors.

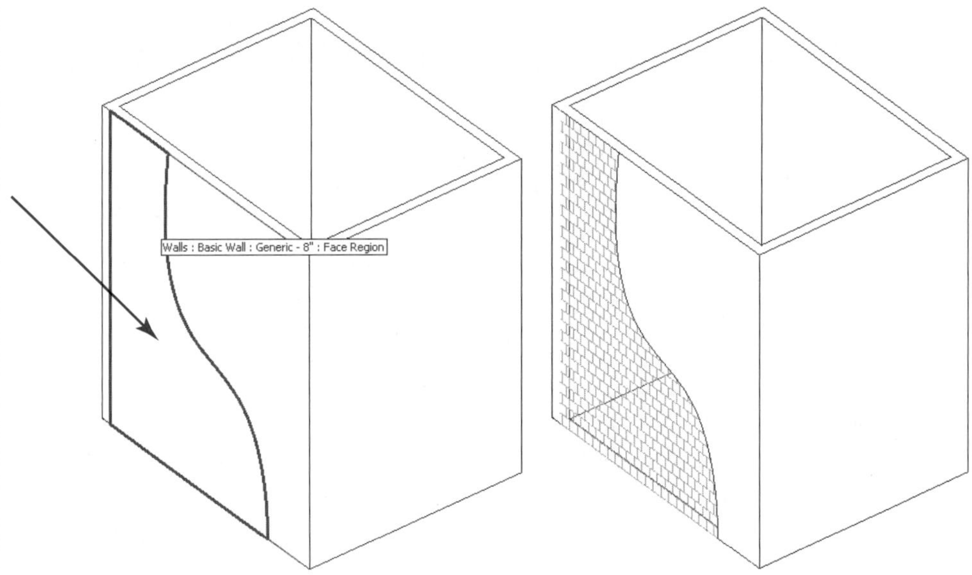

Figure 18-16

"Paint" a face

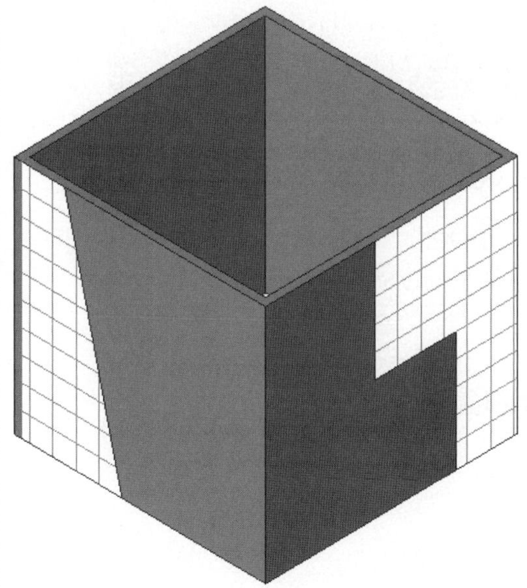

Figure 18-17

Use the **Paint** tool on any face

EXERCISE 18-8 ALIGN TOOL

Use the **Align** tool to align one or more elements with a selected element. This tool is generally used to align walls, beams, and lines, but it can be used with other types of elements as well. The elements to align can be of the same type, or they can be from different families. You can align elements in a Plan view or Elevation view only.

1. In the **Modify** toolbar, select the **Align** button (see Figure 18-18).

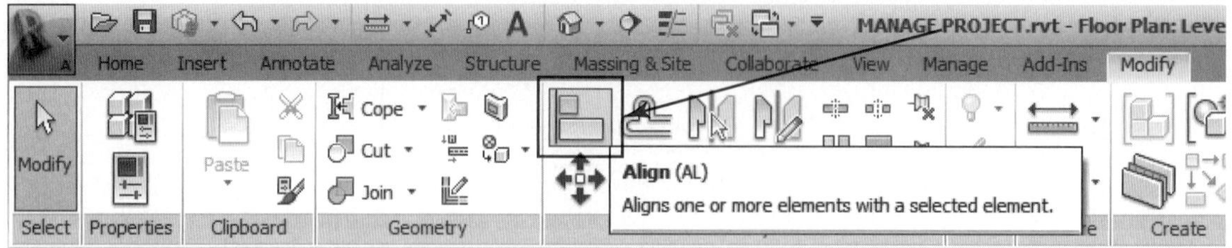

Figure 18-18

Align button

The cursor appears with the **Align** symbol.

2. On the **Options Bar**, select the desired options:
   - Select **Multiple Alignment** to align multiple elements with a selected element. (As an alternative, you can press the **<Ctrl>** key while selecting multiple elements to align.)
   - When aligning walls, use the **Prefer** option to indicate how selected walls will be aligned using **Wall faces, Wall centerlines, Faces of core,** or **Center of core.** The core options refer to walls that have multiple layers (see Figure 18-19).

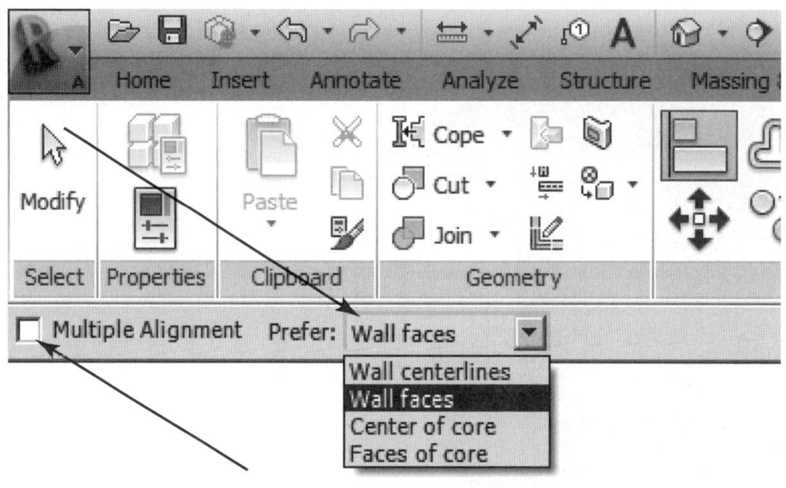

Figure 18-19

Multiple Alignment and **Wall faces** options

3. Select the reference element (the element to which other elements will be aligned).
4. Select one or more elements to align with the reference element.
5. If you want the selected elements to stay aligned with the reference element (if you later move it), click the **Padlock** symbol to lock the alignment. If the **Padlock** symbol has disappeared because you have done something else, click **Modify**, and select the reference element to make the symbol reappear.
6. To start a new alignment, press the **<Esc>** key once.
7. To exit the **Align** tool, press the **<Esc>** key twice (see Figure 18-20).

NOTE:

Before selecting, move the cursor over the element until the part of the element to align with the reference element is highlighted. Then click it.

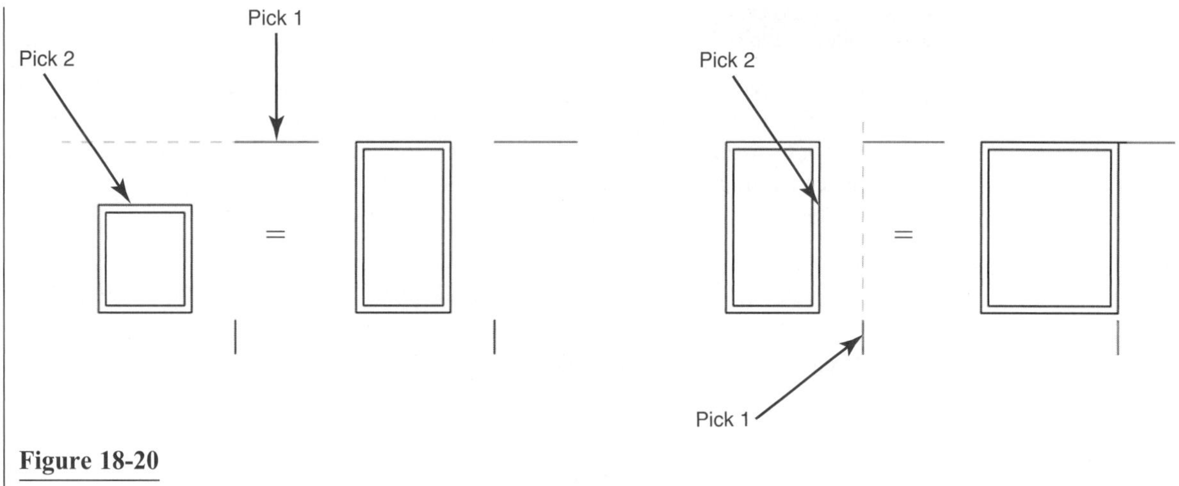

Figure 18-20

Align an element with a reference element

EXERCISE 18-9 **COPY TOOL**

The **Copy** tool copies one or more selected elements and allows you to place copies in the drawing immediately. It activates the **Move** tool with the **Copy** option selected.

The **Copy** tool is different from the **Copy to Clipboard** tool. Use the **Copy** tool when you want to copy a selected element and place it immediately (for example, in the same view). Use the **Copy to Clipboard** tool when you need to switch views before placing the copies.

1. Select one or more elements in the drawing area to bring up its **Modify** toolbar.
2. In the **Modify** toolbar, select the **Copy** button (see Figure 18-21).

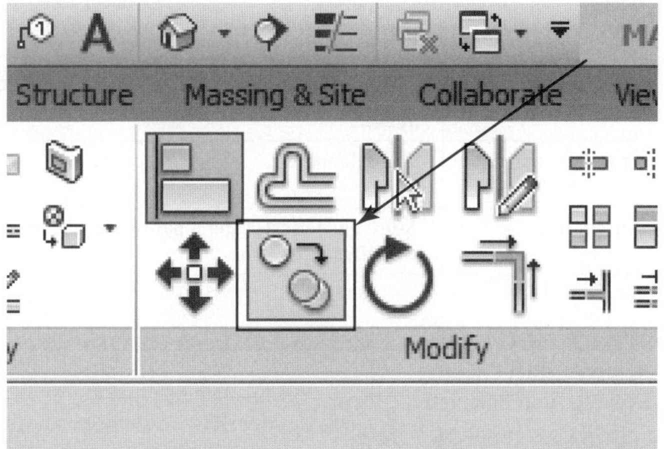

Figure 18-21

Copy button

3. Click once in the drawing area to set the start point, and begin moving away and clicking to copy the elements or objects at a new location.
4. Check the **Constrain** and **Multiple** check boxes on the **Options Bar** to constrain to **Vertical** and **Horizontal** only and to continue placing copies every time you click.
5. Continue placing more elements, or press <Esc> to exit the **Copy** tool.

NOTE:

Selecting a wall will bring up the **Modify | Wall** toolbar, selecting a window will bring up the **Modify | Window** toolbar, and so on. Although they are different toolbars, the **Modify** panel will always be in the same general location.

EXERCISE 18-10 OFFSET TOOL

Use the **Offset** tool to copy or move a selected model line, detail line, wall, or beam a specified distance perpendicular to its length. You can apply the tool to single elements or to chains of elements belonging to the same family. You can specify the offset distance by dragging the selected elements or by entering a value.

The following restrictions apply to the **Offset** tool:

- You can offset lines, beams, or braces in their own work planes only. For example, if you sketch a model line whose work plane is set to **Floor Plan: Level 1**, you can offset that line only in the Plan view plane.
- You cannot offset walls created as in-place families.
- You cannot offset elements in a view perpendicular to their move plane. For example, you cannot offset a wall in an Elevation view.

1. In the **Modify** toolbar, select the **Offset** button.
2. On the **Options Bar**, select how you want to specify the offset distance (see Figure 18-22).

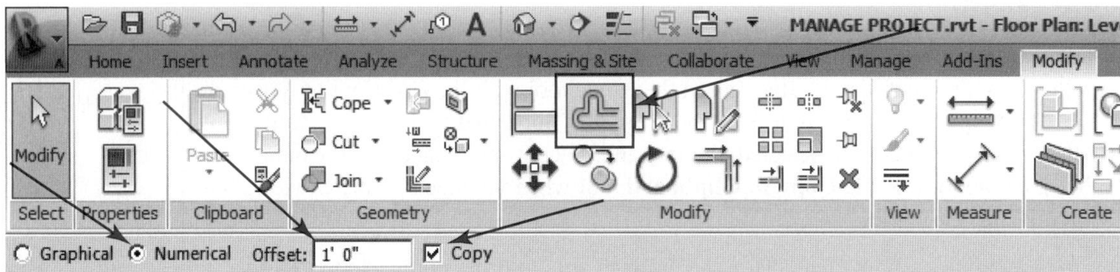

Figure 18-22

Offset button

If you want to...	Then...
Drag the selected element to the desired distance,	Select **Graphical.**
Enter a value for the offset distance,	Select **Numerical.** Enter a positive number in the **Offset** check box.

3. If you want to create and offset copies of the selected element, select **Copy** on the **Options Bar**. (If you selected **Graphical** in the previous step, pressing the <**Ctrl**> key as you move the cursor has the same effect.)
4. Select the element or chain to offset.

NOTE:

If you specified an offset distance using the **Numerical** option, a preview line displays at that distance from the highlighted elements on the side where the cursor is positioned.

EXERCISE 18-11 MIRROR–PICK AXIS AND MIRROR–DRAW AXIS TOOLS

The **Mirror** tool mirrors (reverses the position of) a selected model element, using a line as the mirror axis. For example, if you mirror a wall across a reference plane, the wall flips opposite the original. You can pick the mirror axis or draw a temporary axis.

Use the **Mirror** tool to flip a selected element or to make a copy of an element and reverse its position in one step.

1. Select the element or object to bring up its **Modify** toolbar.

You can select inserts, such as doors and windows, without their hosts.

2. In the **Modify** toolbar, select the **Mirror Pick Axis** or **Mirror Draw Axis** button. To select an existing line that represents the mirror axis, select the **Mirror Pick Axis** button. To sketch a temporary mirror axis line, select the **Mirror Draw Axis** button (see Figure 18-23).

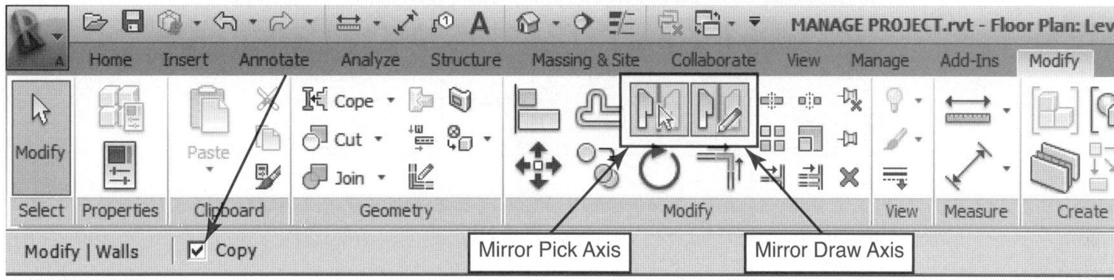

Figure 18-23

Mirror Pick Axis and **Mirror Draw Axis** buttons

The mirror cursor appears.

3. To move the selected item (rather than making a copy of it), uncheck **Copy** on the **Options Bar**.
4. Select or draw the line to use as a mirror axis.

You can pick only a line or a reference plane to which the cursor can snap. You cannot mirror a component around empty space.

EXERCISE 18-12 EXTEND/TRIM

Use the **Trim** and **Extend** tools to trim or extend one or more elements to a boundary defined by the same element type. You can also extend nonparallel elements to form a corner or trim them to form a corner if they intersect. When you select an element to be trimmed, the cursor position indicates the part of the element to retain. You can use these tools with walls, lines, beams, or braces (see Figures 18-24, 18-25, 18-26, and 18-27.)

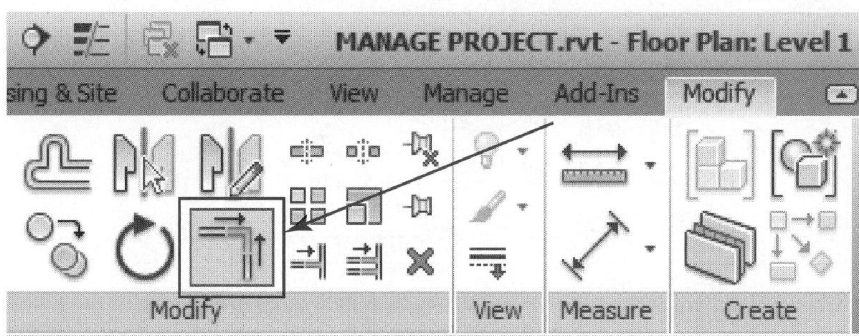

Figure 18-24

Trim button

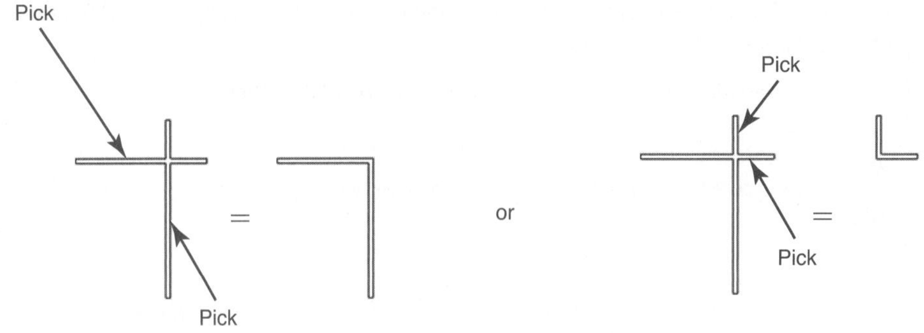

Figure 18-25

Trim an element

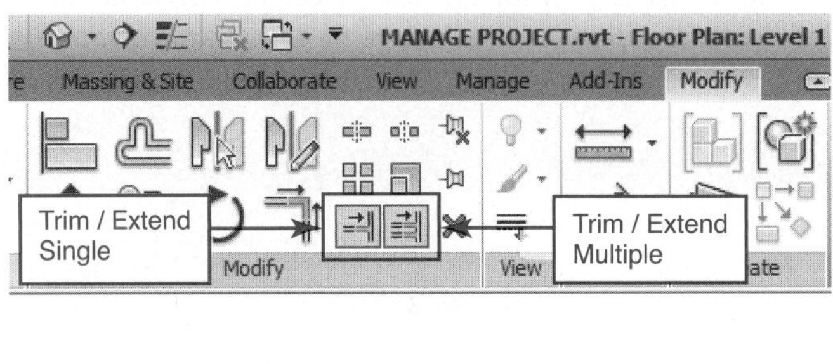

Figure 18-26

Extend Single and **Extend Multiple** buttons

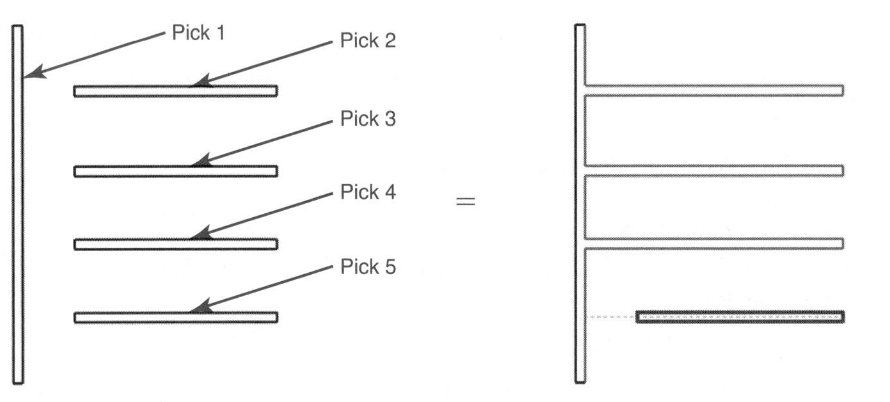

Figure 18-27

Extend multiple elements

EXERCISE 18-13 SPLIT TOOL

Use the **Split** tool to split an element. You can also split an element and insert a gap (see Figures 18-28, 18-29, and 18-30).

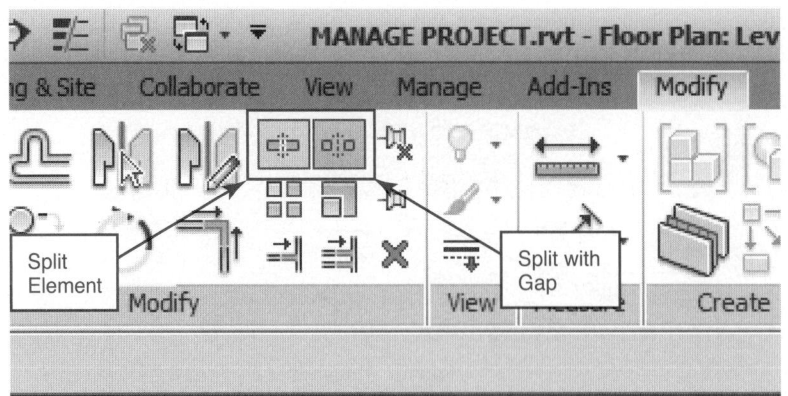

Figure 18-28

Split buttons

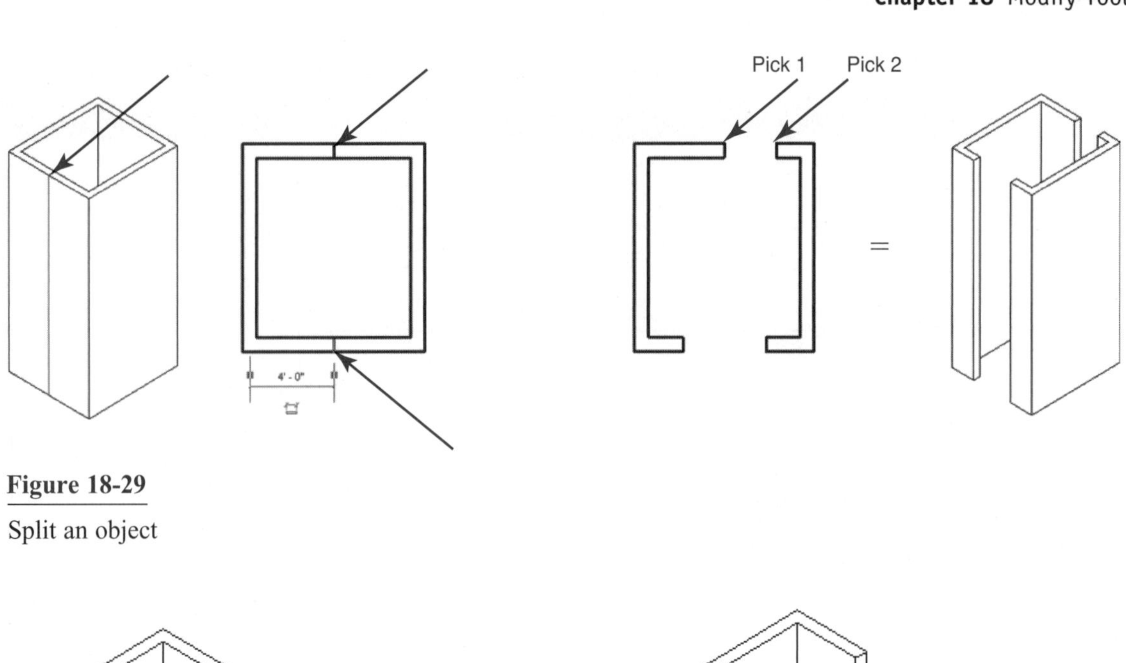

Figure 18-29

Split an object

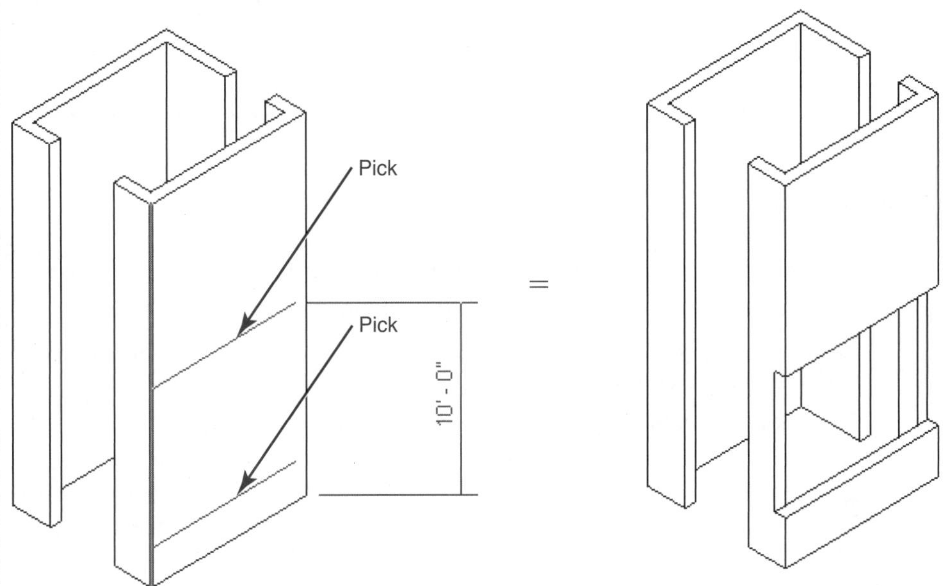

Figure 18-30

Split an object and insert a gap

EXERCISE 18-14 **LINEWORK TOOL**

The **Linework** tool does not create new model or detail lines in the view. Instead, it overrides the current line style of the selected line and applies a different line style.

You can use the **Linework** tool to change the line style of **Projection** edges of model elements, including silhouette edges and projection edges caused by **Plan Regions**.

1. Select the **Modify** tab to bring up the **Modify** toolbar.
2. In the **Modify** toolbar, select the **Linework** button in the **View** panel to bring up the **Modify | Linework** toolbar.
3. In the **Modify | Linework** toolbar, select the line style to apply to the edge from the **Line Style** drop-down list (see Figure 18-31).

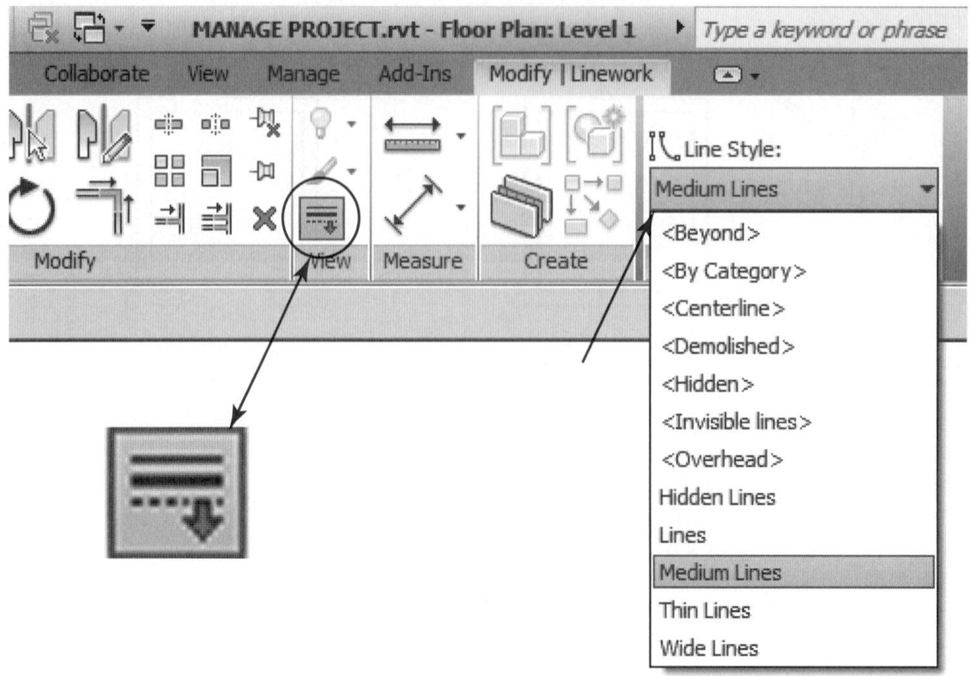

Figure 18-31

Linework button

4. In the drawing area, highlight the edge whose line style you want to change.
5. Click the highlighted edges to apply the selected line style.
6. Continue applying the selected line style to edges in the view, or select a new style in the **Line Style** drop-down list.
7. To exit the **Linework** tool, press the **<Esc>** key.

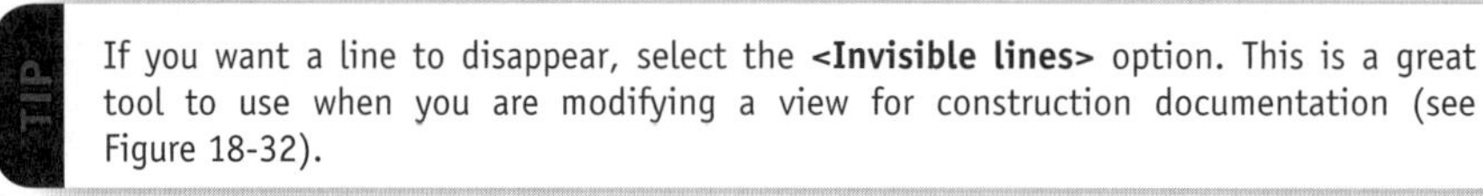

TIP: If you want a line to disappear, select the **<Invisible lines>** option. This is a great tool to use when you are modifying a view for construction documentation (see Figure 18-32).

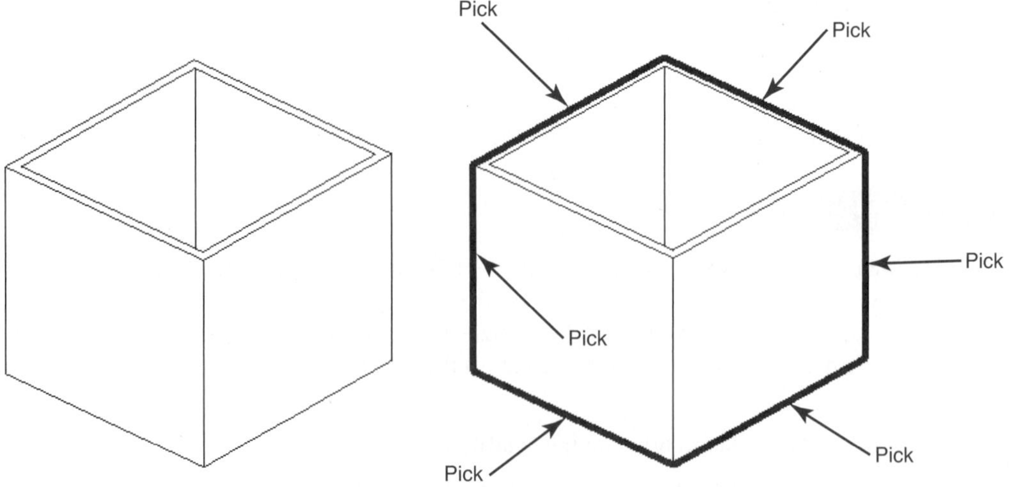

Figure 18-32

The **Linework** tool overrides the current line style

EXERCISE 18-15 **MEASURE TOOL**

Use the **Measure** tool to measure between two references or to measure along an element (see Figure 18-33).

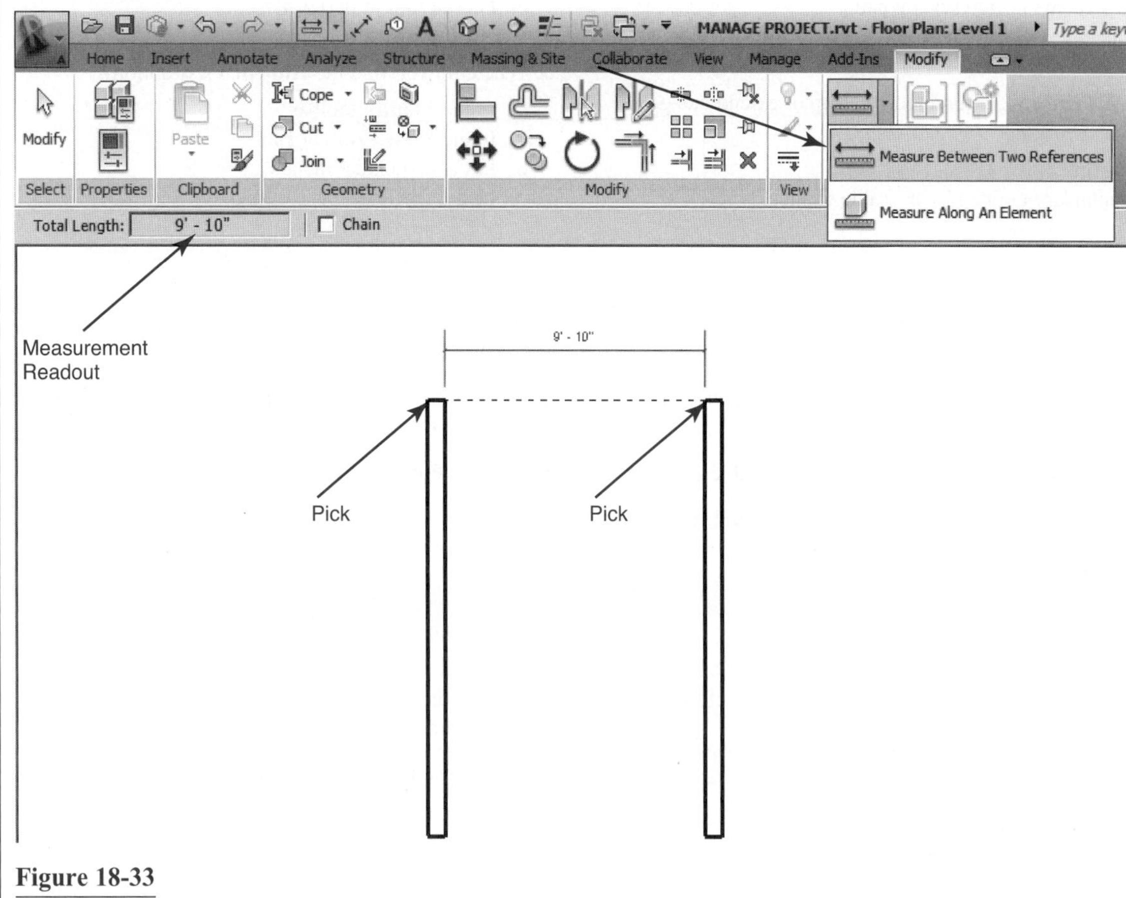

Figure 18-33

Measure tool options

Chapter Summary

This chapter discussed the tools used to modify **Objects** and **Elements**. These tools are very necessary when creating a 3D model or 2D construction documents. Among these are the **Match Type**, **Join Geometry**, **Cut Geometry**, **Wall Joins, Split Face**, **Paint**, **Align**, **Copy**, **Offset**, **Mirror**, **Extend/Trim**, **Split**, **Linework**, and **Measure** tools.

Chapter Test Questions

Multiple Choice

Circle the correct answer.

1. Which of the following is not true?
   a. Walls cut columns.
   b. Structural elements cut host elements (walls, roofs, ceilings, and floors).

c. Floors, ceilings, and roofs cut gutters.
d. Gutters, fascias, and slab edges cut other host elements. Cornices do not cut any elements.

2. The **Cut Geometry** tool
   a. Splits a face into two parts.
   b. Cuts geometry into several parts.
   c. Cuts one wall from another.
   d. None of the above
3. Use the **Trim** and **Extend** tools to trim or extend one or more elements to
   a. Any line.
   b. A boundary defined by the same element type.
   c. Walls, windows, and doors.
   d. All of the above
4. The **Match Type** tool
   a. Is used to match text.
   b. Is used to compare one wall with another.
   c. Is used to join two walls.
   d. None of the above
5. Where do you find the **Hide in View** option?
   a. In the **Modify** toolbar
   b. In the **View Control Bar**
   c. In the contextual menus
   d. Under the **Hide Face** button

True or False

Circle the correct answer.

1. **True or False:** You cannot offset elements in a view perpendicular to their move plane.
2. **True or False:** An edge cannot be made invisible.
3. **True or False:** Roofs can be extended with the **Extend/ Trim** tool.
4. **True or False:** The **Linework** tool overrides the current line style of the selected line.
5. **True or False:** You can mirror a component around empty space.

Questions

1. What tool is used to change the pattern faces of objects?
2. What tool is generally used to align walls, beams, and lines?
3. What does the **Split** tool do?
4. What is the difference between the **Copy** and the **Copy to Clipboard** tools?
5. What does the **Offset** tool do?

CHAPTER

19 Rendering

CHAPTER OBJECTIVES

- Learn how to render an exterior scene.
- Learn how to set up an exterior model for rendering.
- Learn how to set up the **Camera** view.
- Learn how to render an exterior scene.
- Learn how to render **Elevations**.
- Learn how to render an interior scene.
- Learn how to create grass with 3ds Max 9.
- Learn how to use RPC content.

Introduction

Visualization has always been important in the practice of architecture. Whether visualizations "sold" the project or just made it clear to the client, they became symbolic of architecture to the public. This chapter explains the tools in Revit Architecture 2012 to create these visualizations.

Mental Ray® Rendering Engine

Revit Architecture 2012 contains the "mental ray" rendering engine. In this author's opinion, Revit Architecture's rendering system is more than acceptable for most general presentation purposes; but for the best quality visualizations and animations, nothing beats Autodesk's 3D Studio Max platform. If you wish to integrate Revit Architecture with Autodesk® 3ds Max® or Autodesk® 3ds Max® Design to produce high-end renderings and add final details, these may be purchased separately.

- *3ds Max* is a professional 3D animation package that provides additional animation, modeling, and workflow functionality for the most complex problems in design visualization and visual effects.
- *3ds Max Design* is a 3D design visualization solution for architects, engineers, designers, and visualization specialists. It is designed for interoperability with FBX® files from Revit Architecture, preserving model geometry, lights, materials, camera settings, and other metadata from a Revit project. With Revit Architecture and 3ds Max Design working together, designers can extend the building information modeling process to include design visualization.

Before we start, it is best that you understand a few terms.

Rendering

The word *render* (according to the *Dictionary.com Unabridged (v 1.1)* website, http://Dictionary.com, accessed April 13, 2010) means "to represent; depict, as in painting: *to render a landscape.*" Computer rendering is used to create realistic and photorealistic visualizations, or *presentations*. These presentations can be made in either still or animated form. Typically, the operator will export the still presentations in .JPG or .TIFF file format. For animations, .MOV or .AVI formats are very popular and can easily be played back through the Internet or placed on CD or DVD.

mental ray®

mental ray is an Academy Award®–winning, high-performance, photorealistic rendering software. It produces images of realism for digital content creation and design in the areas of entertainment, product design, and data visualization. Its applications include visual effects for motion pictures, full-length feature animations, content creation for computer games, Computer Aided Design (CAD), product design and styling, architectural design, lighting design, fluid flow simulation, seismic data studies, and medical imaging. The mental ray features include patented and proprietary ray tracing and rasterizer algorithms. It supports 32-bit and 64-bit CPUs and Graphics Processing Units (GPUs) and parallel computer architectures, including networks of computers for maximum performance. The mental ray software combines the physically correct simulation of the behavior of light with full programmability for the creation of any imaginable visual phenomenon.

Texture Maps

Texture maps are bitmap (raster) images (such as a picture of bricks) that can be placed on objects, such as walls and so on. When these objects are rendered, these objects will appear to be made of these materials. By using texture maps effectively, you can render visualizations quickly and with great realism.

RPC®

RPC® stands for Rich Photorealistic Content, a term used to describe the software and content associated with ArchVision's award-winning Image-Based Rendering (IBR) technology. (RPC is also the file extension for this image-based content.) RPC is the first major commercial project in the evolution of image-based rendering technology. Since its introduction in 1998, the company's solutions have become the preferred method of incorporating complex objects into 3D computer graphics environments. Because RPCs rely on photo image data, the incredible richness of detail and quality of images far surpasses that of even the best computer-generated models.

Before starting a rendering, you must set up a render scene.

Rendering an Exterior Scene

EXERCISE 19-1 SETTING UP THE EXTERIOR MODEL

1. Select **File > Open** from the **Main** menu to bring up the **Open** dialog box.
2. Go to **www.pearsondesigncentral.com** and download the **Chapter 19 RENDERING MODEL.rvt** file.
3. In the **Project Browser**, double-click on the **Site** floor plan to bring it into the **Drawing Editor**.
4. In the **Home** toolbar, select the **Model Line** button to bring up the **Modify | Place Lines** toolbar.
5. In the **Place Lines** toolbar, select the **Rectangle** button and place a **280′ × 225′** rectangle around the building.
6. In the **Place Lines** toolbar, select the **Offset** button.
7. In the **Options Bar**, enter **5′** in the **Offset** field, and check the **Copy** check box.
8. Select the lines from the rectangle you placed, and offset them **5′** to create another rectangle **5′-0″** from the first rectangle (see Figure 19-1).
9. Change to the **Massing & Site** toolbar.
10. In the **Massing & Site** toolbar, select the **Toposurface** button to bring up the **Modify | Edit Surface** toolbar.
11. In the **Modify | Edit Surface** toolbar, select the **Place Point** button.
12. In the **Options Bar**, enter **0′-0″** in the **Elevation** field.
13. With the **Endpoint Snap (On)**, snap to the corners of the first rectangle you placed.

To access student datafiles, go to **www.pearsondesigncentral.com.**

NOTE:
When downloading, **RMB** (right mouse click) on the file, select **Save as Target**, and download the file to a convenient folder.

NOTE:
In order to see the shadows on the ground, you will need a ground plane. If you don't already have a toposurface for the model, you can create a flat ground plane with the **Toposurface** button.

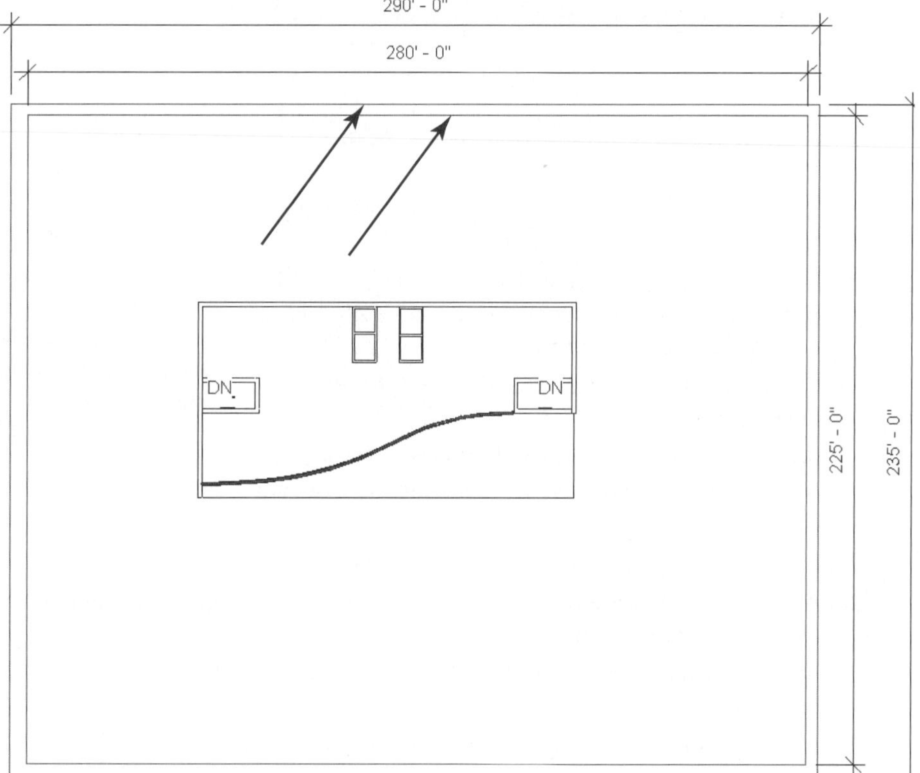

Figure 19-1
Create a rectangle

14. In the **Options Bar**, enter **–10′-0″** in the **Elevation** field.
15. With the **Endpoint Snap (On)**, snap to the corners of the offset rectangle you created.
16. In the **Modify | Edit Surface** toolbar, select the **Finish Surface** button to create the toposurface.
17. Change to the **Default 3D View**.
18. Select everything in the **Default 3D View**, and then select the **Filter Selection** button at the bottom of the interface to bring up the **Filter** dialog box.
19. In the **Filter** dialog box, select the **Check None** button to clear the check boxes, check the **Lines (Lines)** check box, and then press the **OK** button to return to the **Drawing Editor**.
20. Since the rectangles were the only lines, they have been selected; press the **<Del>** key to delete them.

NOTE:
The rectangles you created will be the only objects selected (see Figure 19-2).

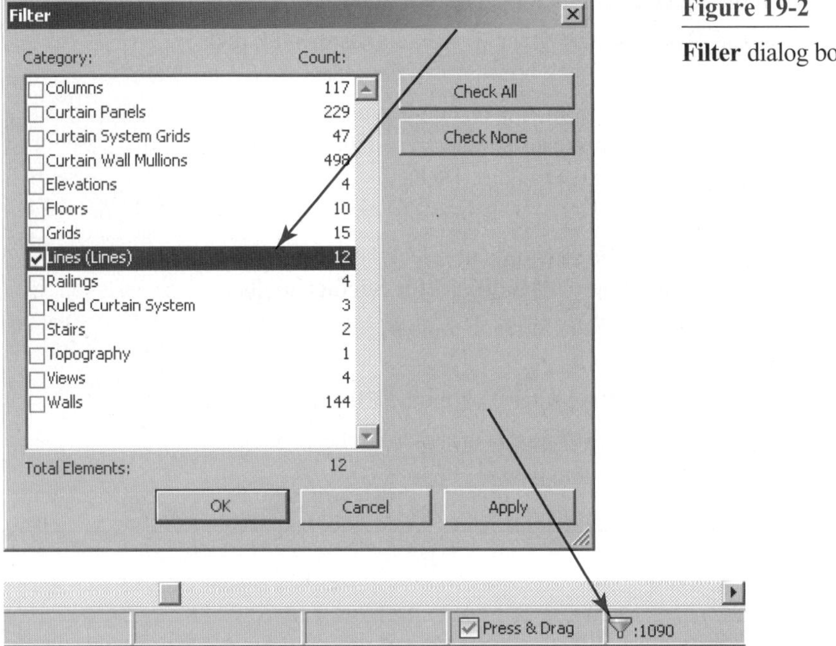

Figure 19-2
Filter dialog box

21. Using the information you learned in the Massing & Site chapter, split the toposurface, and create an asphalt road.
22. In the **Massing & Site** toolbar, select the **Site Component** button to bring up the **Load Family** dialog box for the **Imperial Library**.
23. In the **Imperial Library** folder, select the **Planting** folder, and open it.
24. In the **Planting** folder, select the **RPC Tree – Deciduous**, and then press the **OK** button to return to the **Drawing Editor**.
25. Press the **<Esc>** key twice to end the command.
26. Again, in the **Massing & Site** toolbar, select the **Site Component** button to bring up the **Site Component** toolbar.
27. In the **Site Component** toolbar, select the **Load Family** button to bring up the **Load Family** dialog box.
28. In the **Load Family** dialog box, select the **Imperial Library** folder.
29. In the **Imperial Library** folder, select the **Entourage** folder, and open it.

NOTE:
If no **Site Family** is loaded, a dialog box will appear asking if you would like to load one now.

30. In the **Entourage** folder, select the **RPC Beetle** (car), **RPC Male**, and **RPC Female**. Then press the **OPEN** button to return to the **Drawing Editor** (see Figure 19-3).

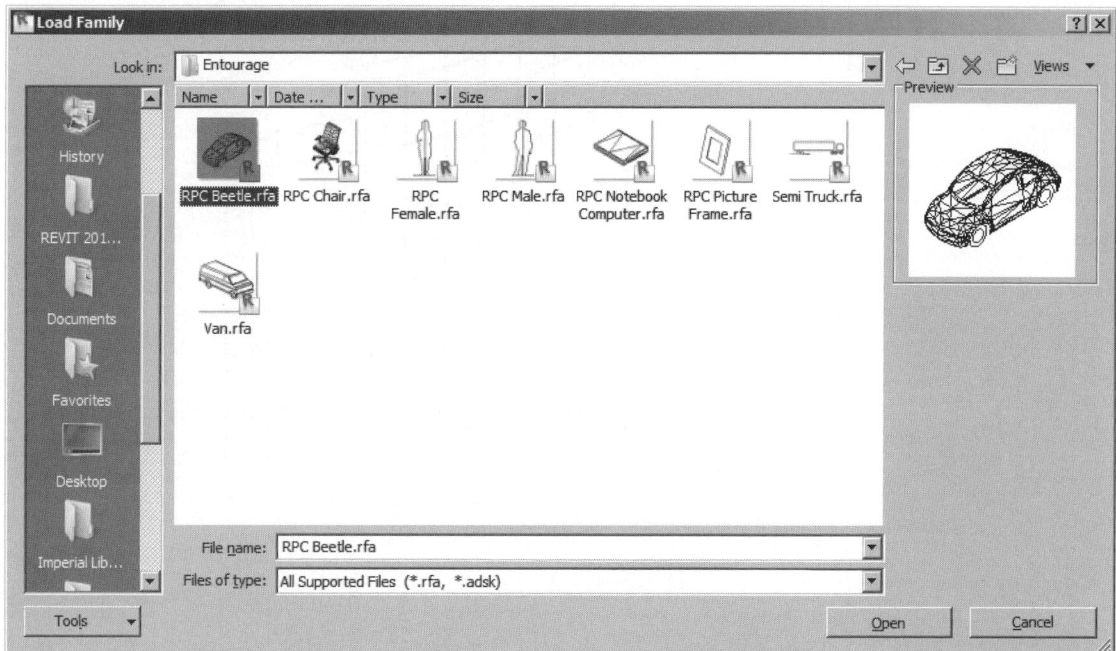

Figure 19-3

Entourage folder

31. Press the **<Esc>** key twice to end the command.
32. Change to the **Massing & Site** toolbar.
33. In the **Massing & Site** toolbar, select the **Site Component** button to bring up the **Site Component** toolbar.
34. In the **Site Component** toolbar, select **RPC Tree – Red Maple - 30′** from the **Change Element Type** drop-down list, and place trees as shown in Figures 19-4 and 19-5.

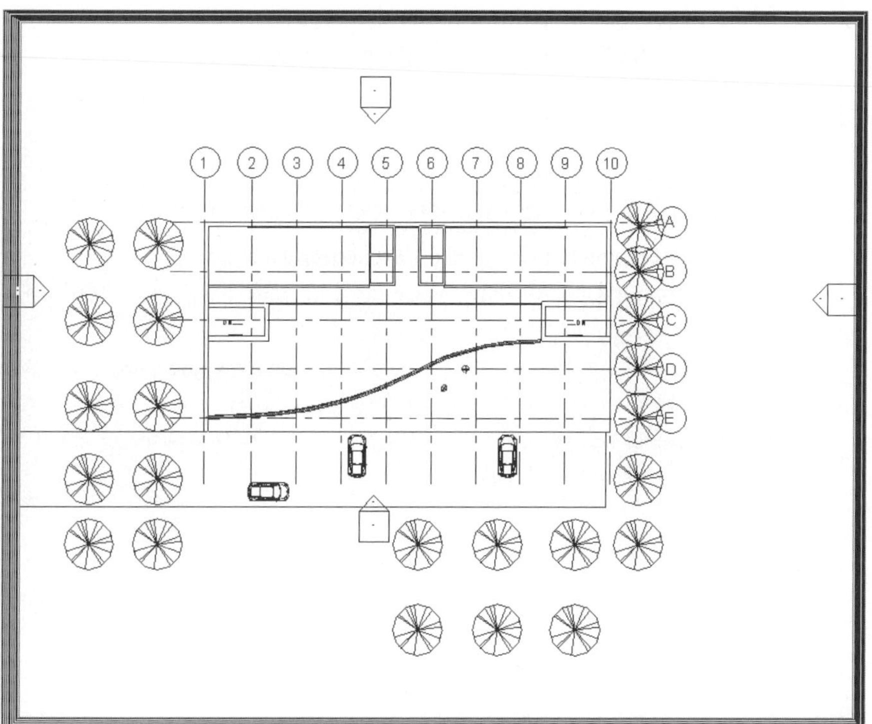

Figure 19-4

Place trees in drawing

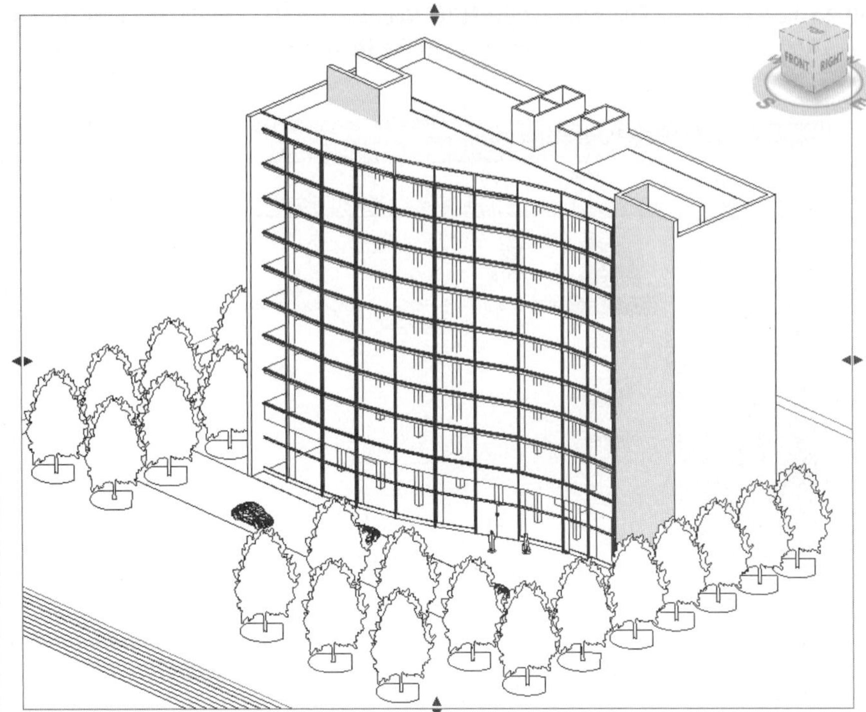

Figure 19-5

3D Drawing with trees, cars, and people

35. After placing trees, press the <**Esc**> key twice to end the command.
36. In the **Properties** drop-down list, select the **RPC Beetle** car, and place it on the road in your scene.
37. Press the <**Esc**> key twice to end the command.
38. Again, select the **Site Component** button from the **Massing & Site** toolbar.
39. In the **Properties** drop-down list in the **Properties** dialog box, select the **RPC Female** and **RPC Male**, and place them in your scene.

NOTE:

If any of the **RPC** content that you placed appears as a cube, do the following:

1. Select the **RPC** object to bring up the **Properties** dialog box.
2. In the **Properties** dialog box, select the **Edit Type** button to bring up the **Type Properties** dialog box.
3. In the **Type Properties** dialog box, select the **Render Appearance** button shown to bring up the **Render Appearance Library** dialog box (see Figure 19-6).
4. In the **Render Appearance Library** dialog box, select the person or object that you want to appear as the object.

40. Select the remaining RPC objects, and use the above process to change their appearance.

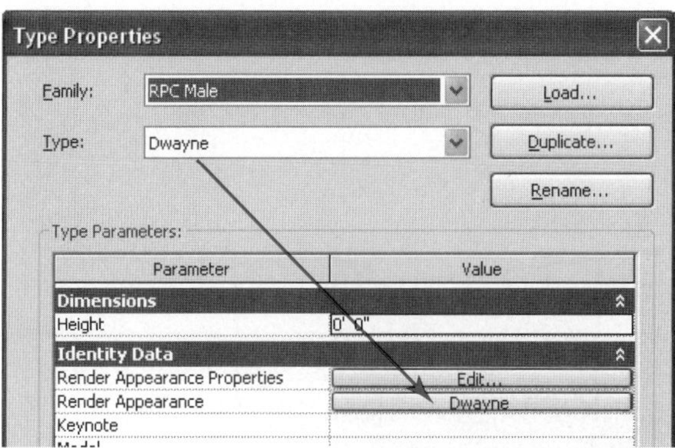

Figure 19-6

Type Properties and **Render Appearance Library** dialog boxes

NOTE:

For a fee, you can download many more RPC libraries of people, trees, automobiles, furniture, and so on, at **http://www.archvision.com.** The ArchVision website also has tutorials and helpful staff who will guide you through all the RPC content and its controls.

41. Save this file as **RENDERING MODEL**.

EXERCISE 19-2 SETTING UP THE CAMERA VIEW

1. Using the **RENDERING MODEL** file, change to the **Site** floor plan.
2. Select the **View** tab to bring up the **View** toolbar.
3. In the **View** toolbar, select the **3D View > Camera** button.
4. In the **Site** view, click your mouse where you expect the **Camera** to stand.
5. Drag to the point you expect to be the **Target** or view, and click your mouse again to create and open the new **3D View** (see Figure 19-7).
6. In the **Project Browser**, select the new **3D View**, **RMB**, and rename it to **PERSPECTIVE VIEW 1**.
7. Hold down the **<Shift>** key and the mouse wheel.
8. With the **<Shift>** key and mouse wheel held down, move your mouse to rotate the view.
9. Select the crop outline to activate its grips.

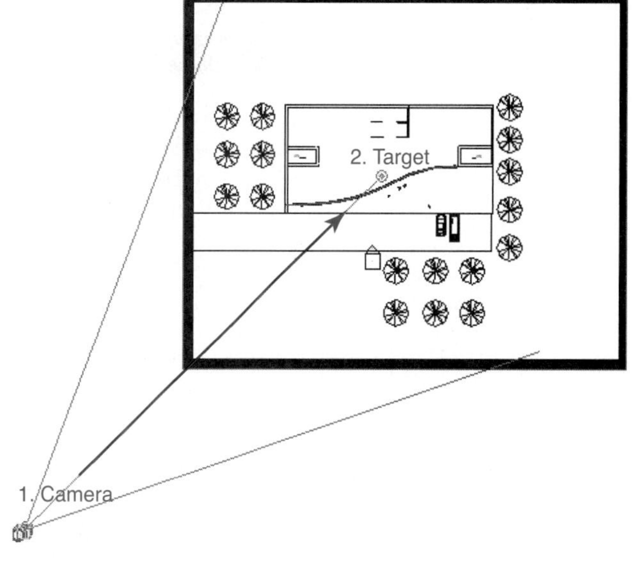

Figure 19-7

Camera and **Target** in **3D View**

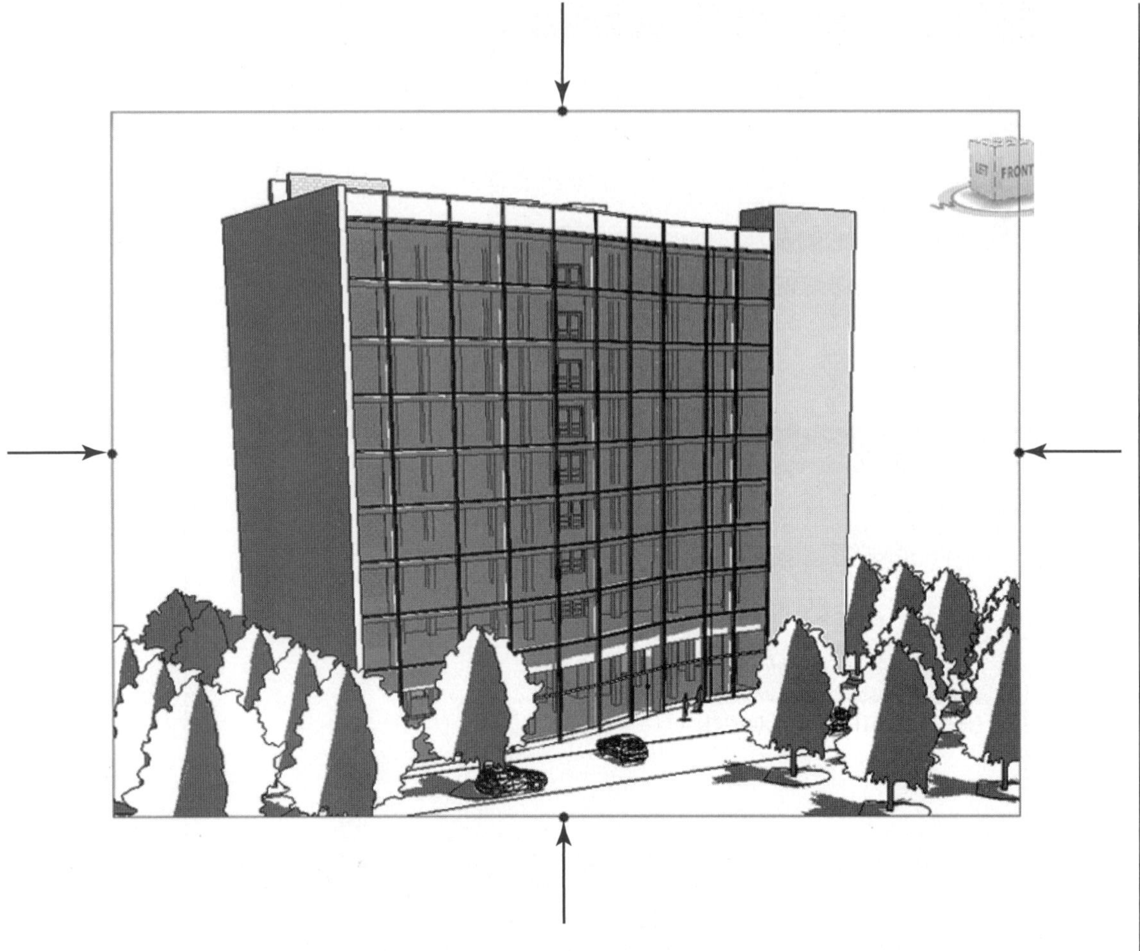

Figure 19-8

Perspective scene

10. Move the grips to frame the **PERSPECTIVE VIEW 1** (see Figure 19-8).
11. Save this file as **PERSPECTIVE SCENE**.

EXERCISE 19-3 USING THE SETTINGS DIALOG BOX TO CHANGE RESOLUTION

1. Using the **PERSPECTIVE SCENE** file, select the **Show Rendering** dialog button at the bottom of the **Drawing Editor** in the **View Control Bar**, to bring up the **Rendering** dialog box (see Figure 19-9).

NOTE:

The **Teapot** is the typical symbol for rendering because a teapot was the first digital object ever rendered.

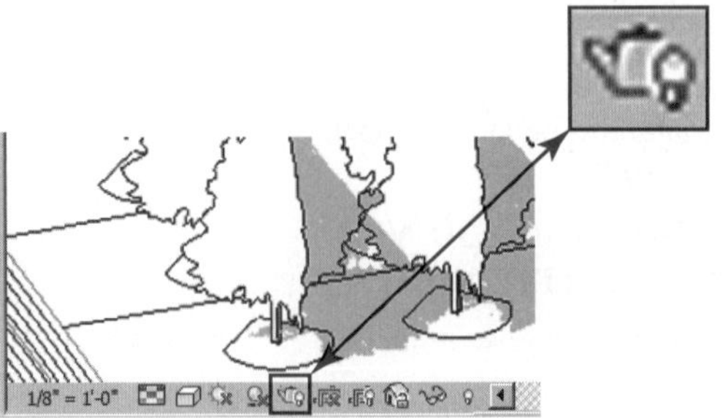

Figure 19-9

Show Rendering dialog button

2. The **Rendering** dialog box will now appear (see Figure 19-10).

Figure 19-10

Rendering dialog box

3. Make sure the settings are as shown in Figure 19-10, and press the **Render** button at the top of the dialog box.

In approximately one minute, a draft (low-resolution) rendering will appear in the **Drawing Editor** (see Figure 19-11).

NOTE:

Draft renderings are the quickest to create and are generally used to test lighting, material, and composition trials.

Figure 19-11

Draft rendering of drawing

4. In the **Rendering** dialog box, select the **Region** check box.

This causes a red rectangle to appear. Select it (see Figure 19-12).

5. Select the control points on the red rectangle, and adjust the rectangle to enclose the cars and people.
6. Press the **Render** button in the **Rendering** dialog box.

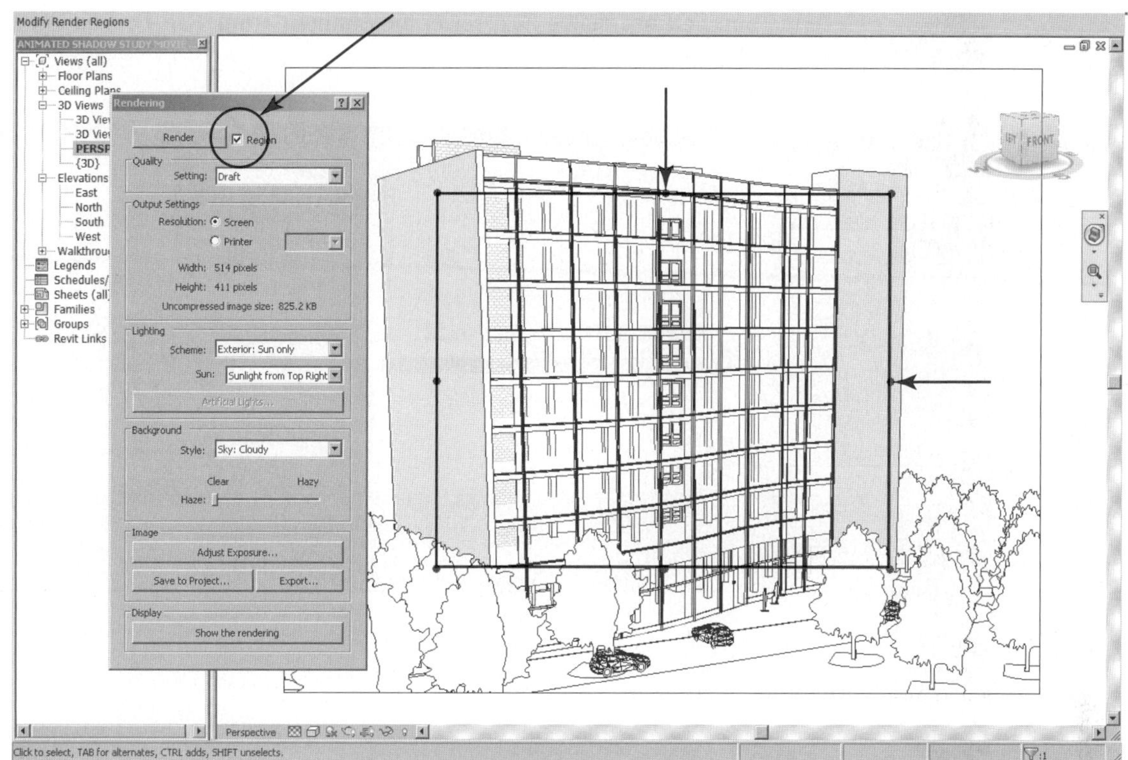

Figure 19-12

Select the red rectangle

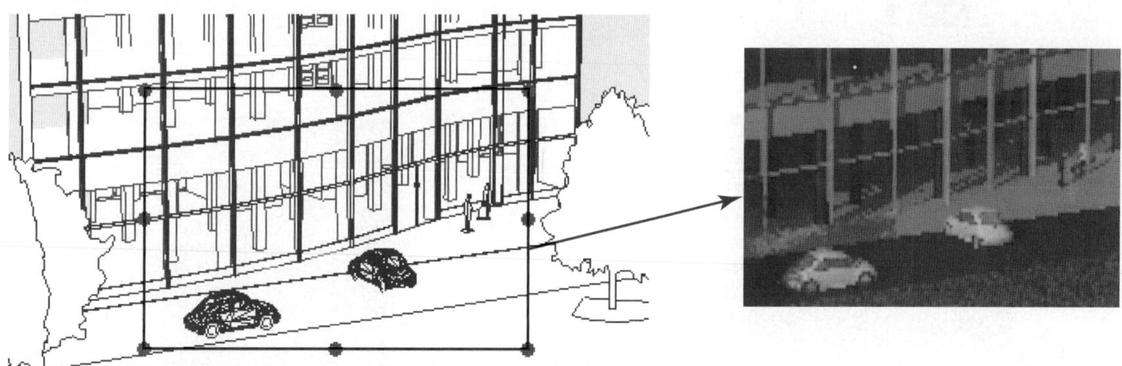

Figure 19-13

The area inside the selected rectangle is rendered

In 18 seconds, the area inside the rectangle renders. This method is used to quickly check a particular part of the rendering (see Figure 19-13).

7. Press the **Show Model** button at the bottom of the **Rendering** dialog box to return to the unrendered working model in the **Drawing Editor**.
8. In the **Rendering** dialog box, uncheck the **Region** check box.
9. In the **Rendering** dialog box, under **Lighting**, select **Exterior: Sun only** from the **Scheme:** drop-down list.
10. In the **Rendering** dialog box, select the **Sun Setting** button to bring up the **Sun Settings** dialog box.

11. In the **Sun Settings** dialog box, select the **Sunlight from Top Left** button (see Figure 19-14).

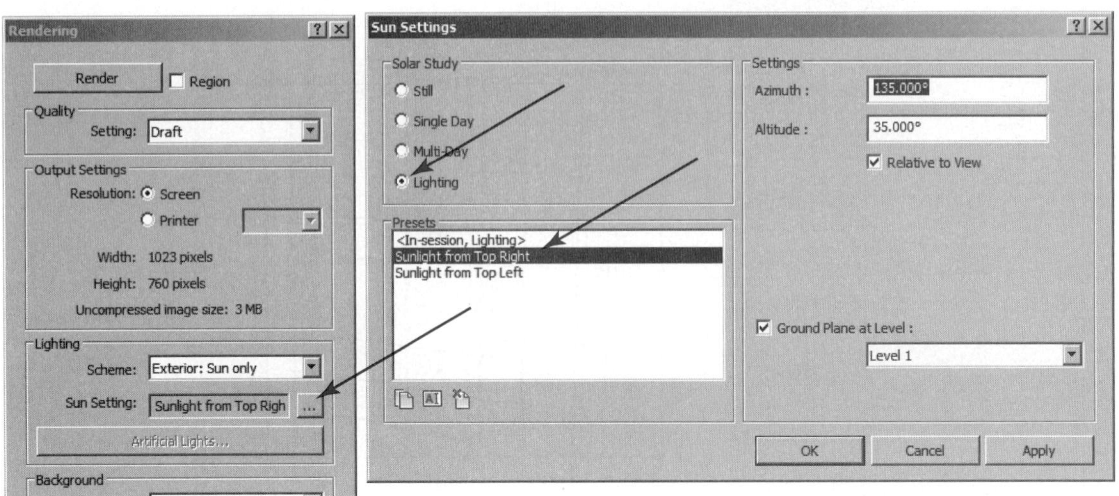

Figure 19-14

Rendering and **Sun Settings** dialog boxes

NOTE:

If you turn on the **Hidden Line** and **Shadows**, you can see the difference made by changing the direction of the **Sun.** Be sure to turn the **Shadows Off** if you are going to move the building or any content, because real-time shadowing slows down the computer (see Figure 19-15).

Sun from the Top Right

Sun from the Top Left

Figure 19-15

Changing the **Sun** direction

12. In the **Rendering** dialog box, change the **Quality** setting to **Medium**, and press the **Render** button.

In approximately three and one-half minutes, a **Medium** (resolution) rendering will appear in the **Drawing Editor**.

13. Select the **Export** button near the bottom of the **Rendering** dialog box to bring up the **Save Image** dialog box.
14. In the **Save Image** dialog box, save the rendering as **MEDIUM RENDERING.jpg** in a convenient folder on your computer (see Figures 19-16 and 19-17).

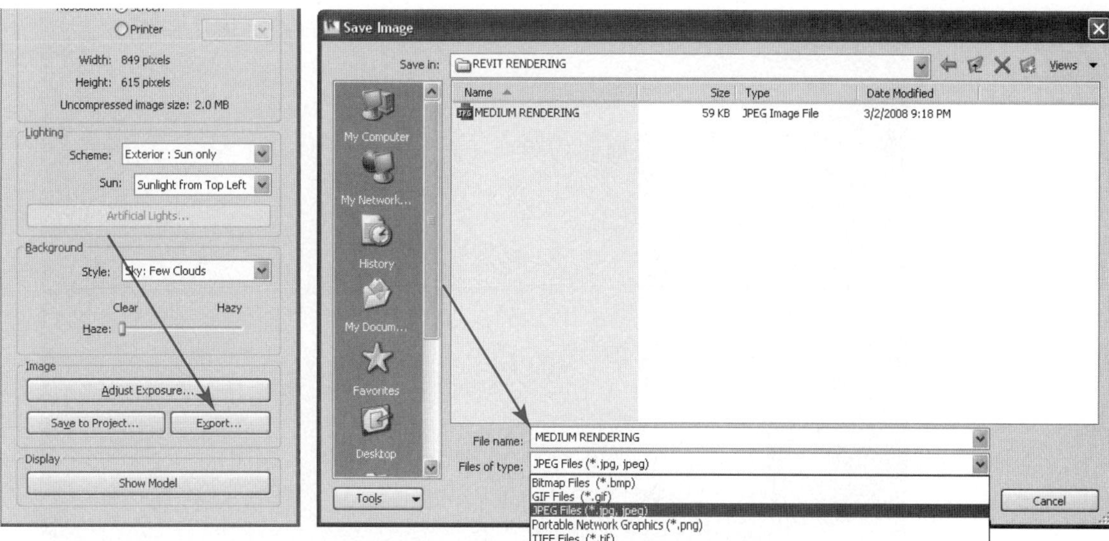

Figure 19-16

Export and save the image

Figure 19-17

Medium rendering of drawing

15. In the **Rendering** dialog box, select **Color** from the **Background** > **Style** drop-down list.
16. Again, in the **Rendering** dialog box, press the **Render** button; the background of the rendering is black (see Figure 19-18).
17. In the **Rendering** dialog box, select the **Adjust Exposure** button to bring up the **Exposure Control** dialog box.
18. Move the **Exposure Control** dialog box to the side, and slowly change the settings.

Figure 19-18

Change the color of the background

19. Press the **Apply** button, and notice the changes.
20. Continue to make adjustments until you have the presentation you like best, then press the **OK** button, and **Export** the rendering to your computer (see Figure 19-19).
21. Save this file as **RENDERED SCENE**.

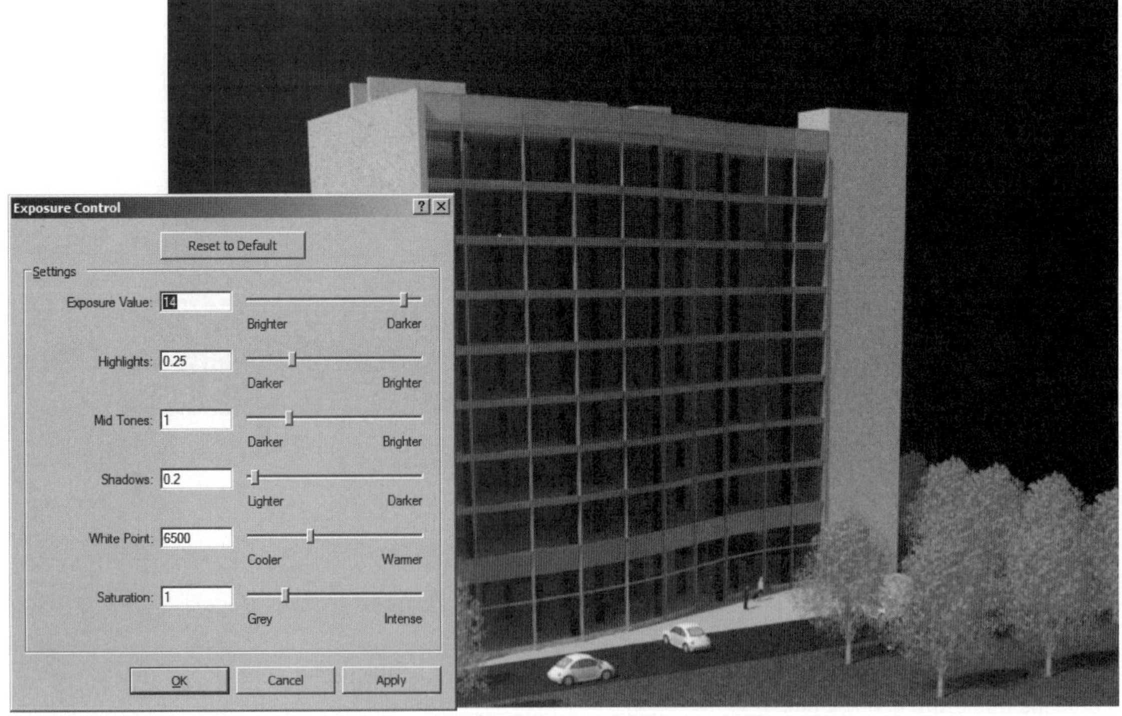

Figure 19-19

Make adjustments in the **Exposure Control** dialog box

EXERCISE 19-4 RENDERING ELEVATIONS

> **NOTE:**
> You cannot render **Elevation** views. In order to achieve an elevation rendering, you must do a "work around."

1. Using the previous exercise, change to the **Default 3D View** (not **Camera** view).
2. **RMB** on the **Face** of the **ViewCube** to bring up its contextual menu.
3. Select **Orient to View > Elevations > Elevation South** from the contextual menu (see Figure 19-20).

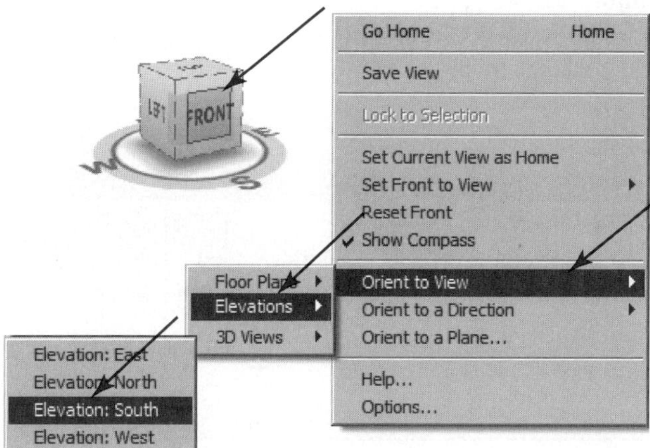

Figure 19-20

Select **Orient to View > Elevations > Elevation South**

4. Bring up the **Rendering** dialog box by pressing the **Teapot** icon.
5. Render the view with a **Background Style** of the **Color White** and **Quality Setting** of **Medium** (see Figure 19-21).

Figure 19-21

Rendered view with white background and medium quality setting

Select the **Export** button near the bottom of the **Rendering** dialog box to bring up the **Save Image** dialog box. In the **Save Image** dialog box, save the rendering as **ELEVATION RENDERING.jpg** in a convenient folder.

6. Save this file as **RENDERED ELEVATION**.

Rendering an Interior Scene

EXERCISE 19-5 **SETTING UP THE INTERIOR SCENE AND ADDING LIGHTING**

To access student datafiles, go to **www.pearsondesigncentral.com.**

1. Select **File > Open** from the **Application** menu to bring up the **Open** dialog box.
2. Go to **www.pearsondesigncentral.com** and download the **Chapter 18 INTERIOR MODEL.rvt** file.
3. In the **Project Browser**, double-click on the **Level 1 Ceiling Plan** to bring it into the **Drawing Editor**.
4. In the **Home** toolbar, select the **Ceiling** button to bring up the **Modify | Place Ceiling** toolbar (see Figure 19-22).

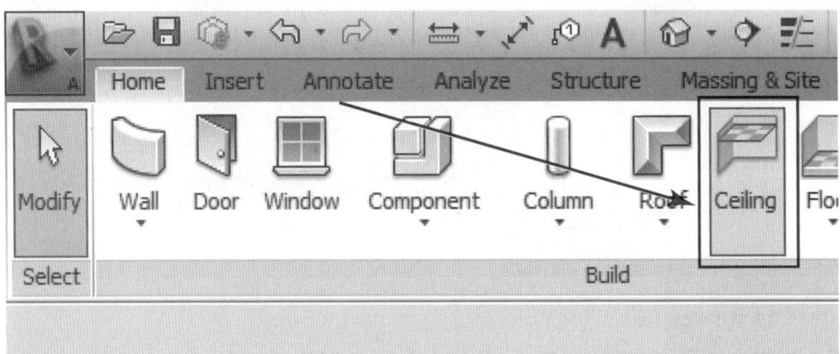

Figure 19-22

Ceiling button

5. In the **Properties** dialog box, select the **Compound Ceiling: 2′ × 4′ ACT System** from the **Properties** drop-down list.
6. Move your cursor over the ceiling (a red perimeter line will appear), and click within the ceiling boundary.

The ceiling will now appear.

7. Press the **<Esc>** key twice to end the command.
8. Select the ceiling grid you just placed to bring up the **Modify | Ceilings** toolbar.
9. In the **Modify | Ceilings** toolbar, select the **Move** and **Rotate** buttons, and adjust the grid (see Figure 19-23).

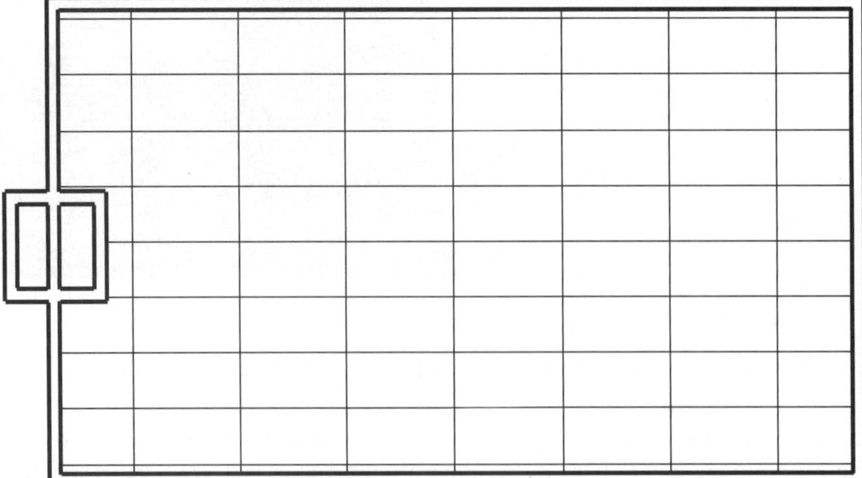

Figure 19-23

Adjust the grid with **Move** and **Rotate** buttons

10. Select everything in the project.
11. With everything selected, select the **Filter** funnel icon at the lower right of the **Drawing Editor** to bring up the **Filter** dialog box.
12. In the **Filter** dialog box, check only the **Ceilings** check box, and press the **OK** button to return to the **Drawing Editor**.

The **Ceiling** will now be selected; press the **<Del>** key to delete it.

13. In the **Home** toolbar, select the **Ceiling** button to bring up the **Modify | Place Ceiling** toolbar.
14. In the **Modify | Place Ceiling** toolbar, select the **Sketch Ceiling** button to bring up the **Modify | Create Ceiling Boundary** toolbar (see Figure 19-24).

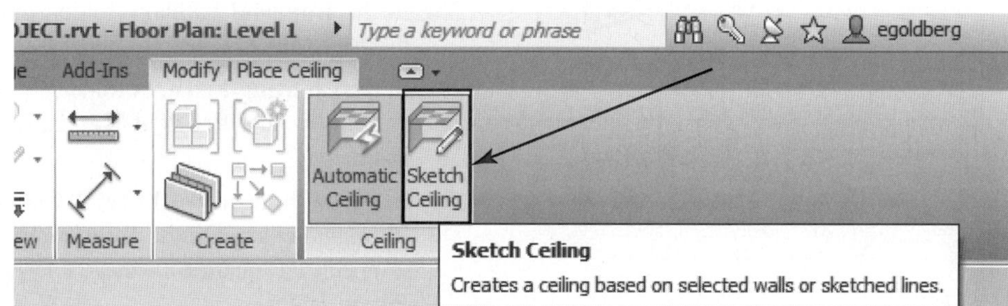

Figure 19-24

Sketch Ceiling button

15. In the **Modify | Create Ceiling Boundary** toolbar, you can use the **Draw** tools or the **Automatic Ceiling** button to create ceiling boundaries.
16. When you are finished creating a boundary, press the **Finish Edit Mode** button to make the ceiling.
17. In the **Project Browser**, double-click on the **Level 1** floor plan to bring it into the **Drawing Editor**.
18. In the **View** menu, select the **3D View > Camera** button.
19. Click your mouse where you expect the **Camera** to stand.
20. Drag to the point you expect to be the **Target** or view, and click your mouse again to create and open the new **3D View**.
21. **RMB** (right mouse button click), and rename the new **3D View** to **INTERIOR SCENE** (see Figures 19-25 and 19-26).

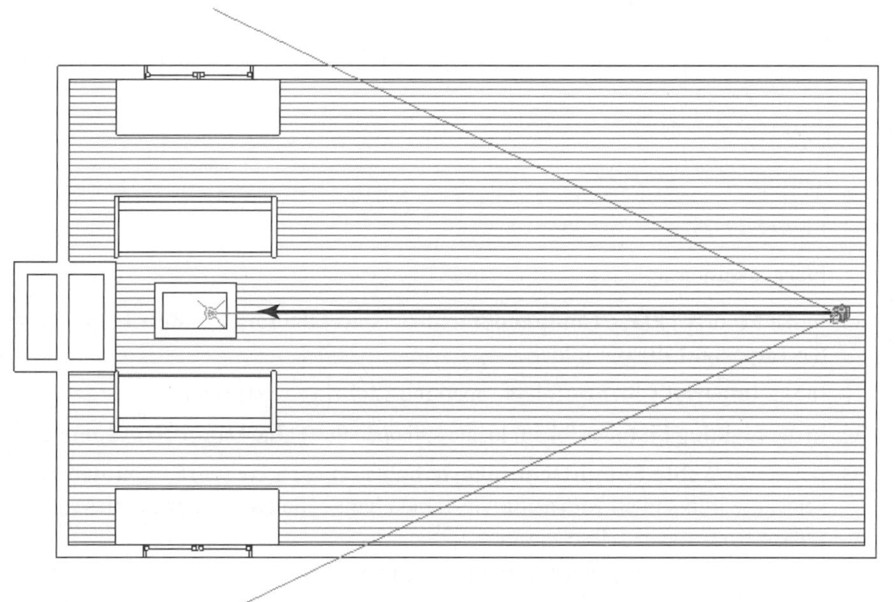

Figure 19-25

Select locations for **Camera** and **Target**

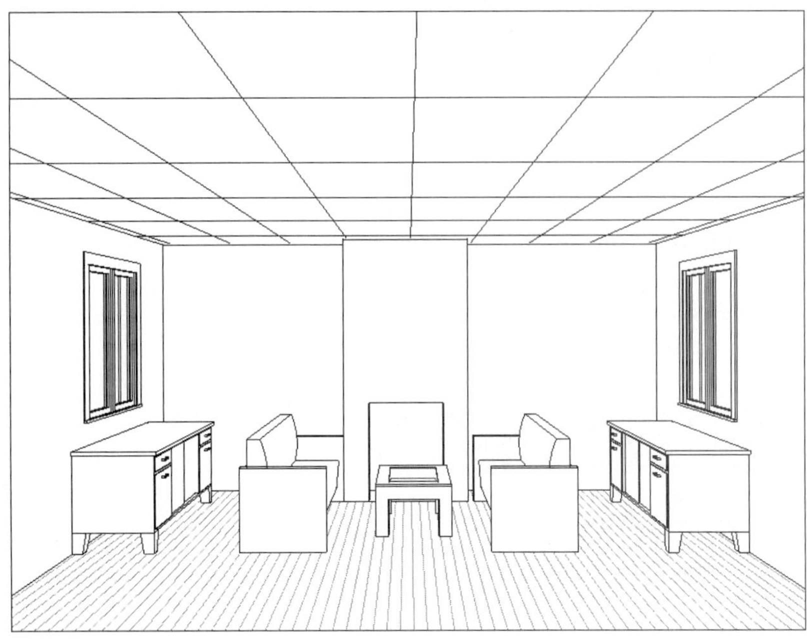

Figure 19-26

3D view of interior scene

22. Again, in the **Project Browser**, double-click on the **Level 1 Ceiling Plan** to bring it into the **Drawing Editor**.
23. Change to the **Home** toolbar.
24. In the **Home** toolbar, select the **Component** button to bring up the **Modify | Place Component** toolbar.
25. In the **Modify | Place Component** toolbar, select the **Load Family** button to open the **Imperial Library** folder.
26. In the **Imperial Library** folder, open the **Lighting Fixtures** folder.
27. In the **Lighting Fixtures** folder, locate and open the **Pendent-Hemisphere** light.
28. Place the light in the **Level 1 Ceiling Plan**, and change to the **Interior View** to check its location in the scene (see Figure 19-27).
29. Change back to the **Level 1** floor plan.

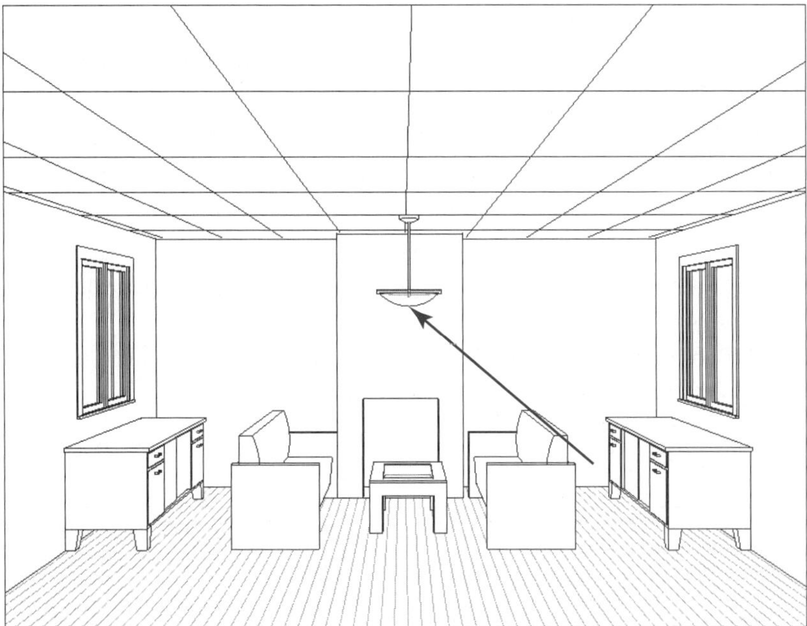

Figure 19-27

Place a ceiling light

30. In the **Modify | Place Component** toolbar, select the **Load Family** button to open the **Imperial Library** folder.
31. In the **Imperial Library** folder, open the **Lighting Fixtures** folder.
32. In the **Lighting Fixtures** folder, locate and open the **Table Lamp-Hemispheric** light.
33. Place two **Table Lamp-Hemispheric** lights on each credenza. You will have to select the lights in an **Elevation** view and change the element properties to a **2′-5″ Offset** from **Level 1** (see Figure 19-28).
34. Save this file as **SETTING UP THE INTERIOR**.

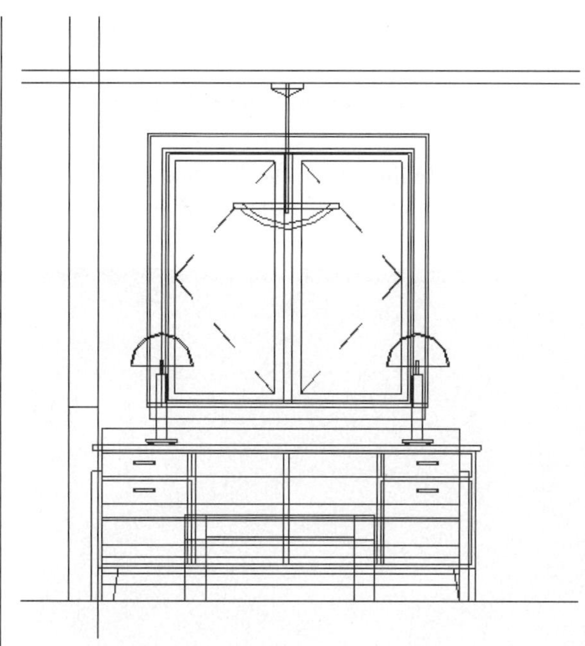

Figure 19-28

Place two **Table Lamp-Hemispheric** lights

EXERCISE 19-6 **RENDERING THE INTERIOR SCENE**

1. Using the **SETTING UP THE INTERIOR** file, double-click on **INTERIOR VIEW** in the **Project Browser** to bring it up in the **Drawing Editor** (see Figure 19-29).

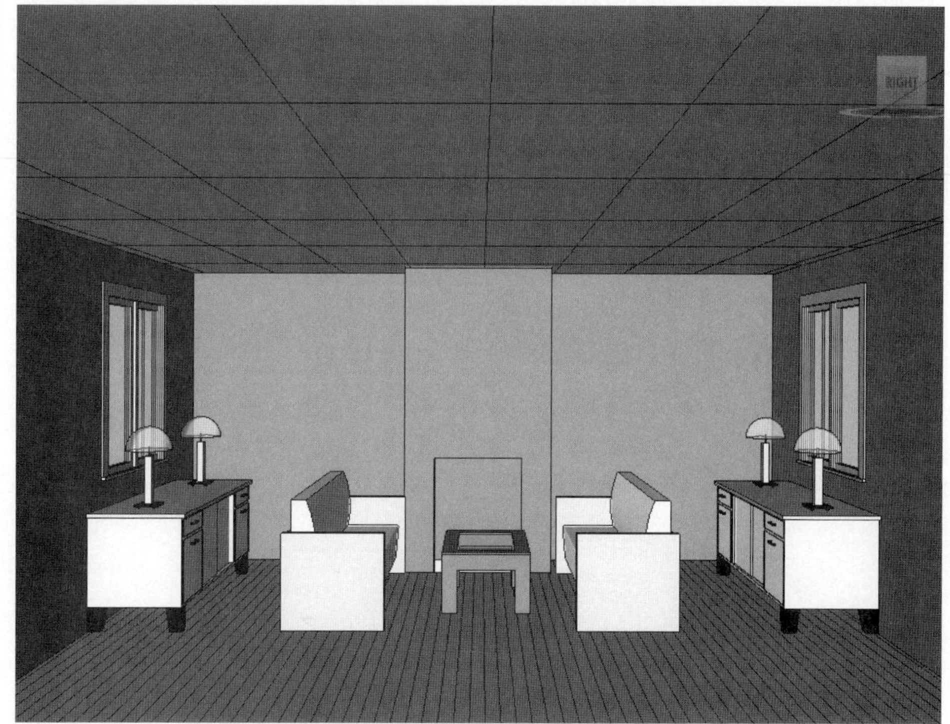

Figure 19-29

INTERIOR VIEW drawing

2. Select the **Show Rendering** dialog button at the bottom of the **Drawing Editor** to bring up the **Rendering** dialog box.
3. In the **Rendering** dialog box, select **Interior: Sun and Artificial** from the **Scheme** drop-down list.
4. In the **Rendering** dialog box, select **Medium** from the **Quality > Setting** drop-down list, and press the **Render** button to render the file (see Figure 19-30).

Figure 19-30

Rendered interior view

5. The rendering will be dark. To fix this, select the **Adjust Exposure** button in the **Rendering** dialog box to bring up the **Exposure Control** dialog box.
6. In the **Exposure Control** dialog box, change the exposures to those shown in Figure 19-31, and press the **Apply** button.

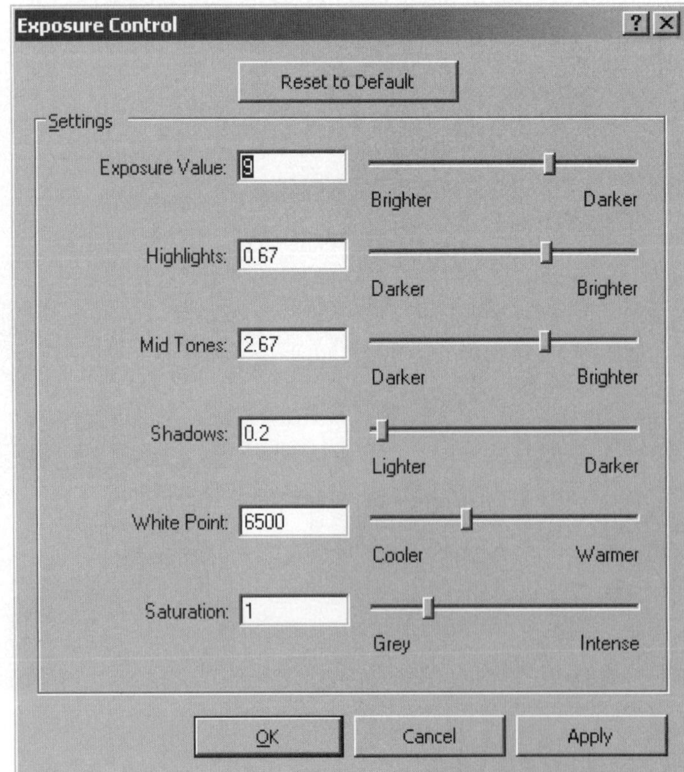

Figure 19-31

Exposure Control dialog box

7. In the **Rendering** dialog box, select the **Render** button to render the view; the rendering will now be lighter (Figure 19-32).
8. Select the **Export** button near the bottom of the **Rendering** dialog box to bring up the **Save Image** dialog box.
9. In the **Save Image** dialog box, save the rendering as **INTERIOR RENDERING.jpg** in a convenient folder.
10. Save this file as **RENDERED INTERIOR SCENE**.

Figure 19-32

Exposure changed to lighter

Although Revit Architecture has a good rendering system, 3D Studio MAX is much better. With its lighting capability and ability to Animate, it will give you many more options for your presentations and visualizations. Although the version of MAX demonstrated in this book is not the most recent, the principles and tools, except for the Grass tool, apply to all versions on MAX, MAX Design, and VIZ.

Rendering with 3D Studio Max

EXERCISE 19-7 CREATING AND PLACING MATERIALS IN AUTODESK 3DS MAX 9

1. Create a simple enclosure with walls, windows, doors, and roof in Revit Architecture 2012.
2. Change to the **3D View. DO NOT USE a FLOOR PLAN VIEW**
3. Select **Export** > **CAD Formats** > **DWG** from the **Applications Menu** to bring up the **Export CAD Formats** dialog box.
4. In the **Export CAD Formats** dialog box, press the **Export** button to bring up another **Export CAD Formats** dialog box.
5. In this second **Export CAD Formats** dialog box, save your file as an **AutoCAD 2007 DWG** file, name the file **REVIT CAD DRAWING**, and save it in a location on your computer.
6. Start **3DS MAX** (this tutorial uses 3DS MAX 9).
7. Select **File** > **Import** from the **Main** menu to bring up the **Select File to Import** dialog box.

You will get a Proxy Objects Detected dialog box telling you that there are custom objects in the drawing, press the Yes button to import the file anyway.

8. Next you will get the **AutoCAD DWG/DXF Import Options** dialog box, accept the defaults, and press the **OK** button to import the building.
9. Select the Zoom All button at the bottom right of the interface, and zoom all the viewports smaller. (see Figure 19-33)

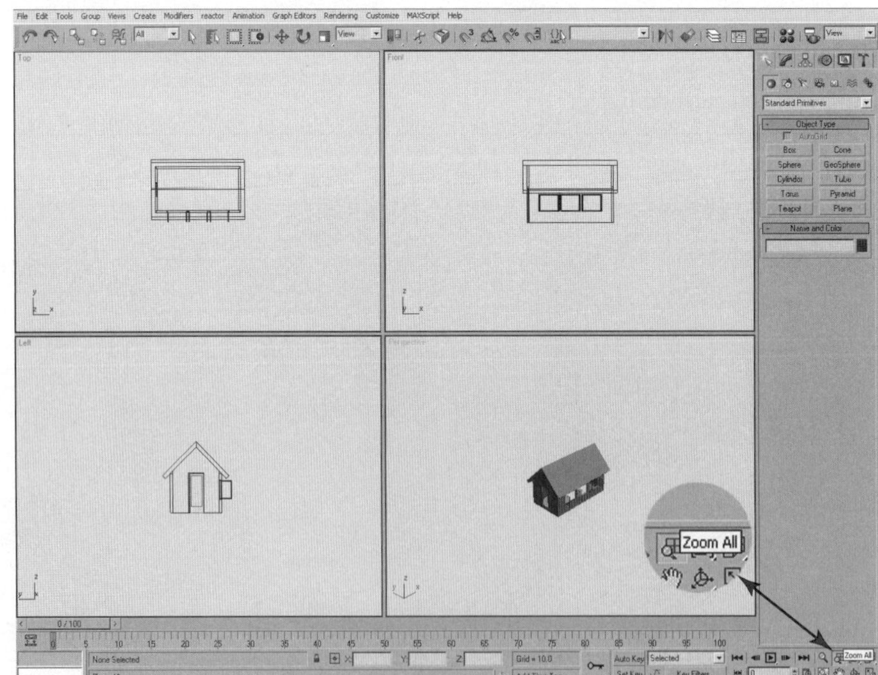

Figure 19-33

Zoom all the viewports smaller

10. Using the **Create** tools add a **Camera–Target** button, place a camera to the left of the building, and then drag and click its target at the center of the building.

11. After placing the camera, select the lower right viewport (Perspective), and press the **C** key on your keyboard to change it to the view thru the camera. (see Figure 19-34)

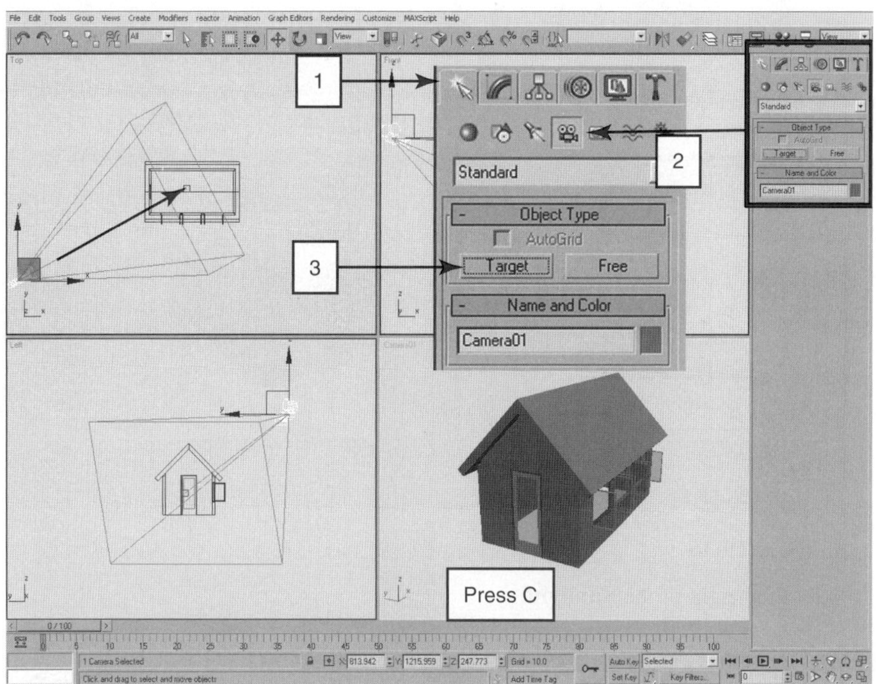

Figure 19-34

Change to the view through the camera

12. Select the **Camera** viewport, and using the **Navigation** tools **(Distance, Pan, and Rotate)** at the bottom right of the screen, adjust the view to the scene you wish. (see Figure 19-35)

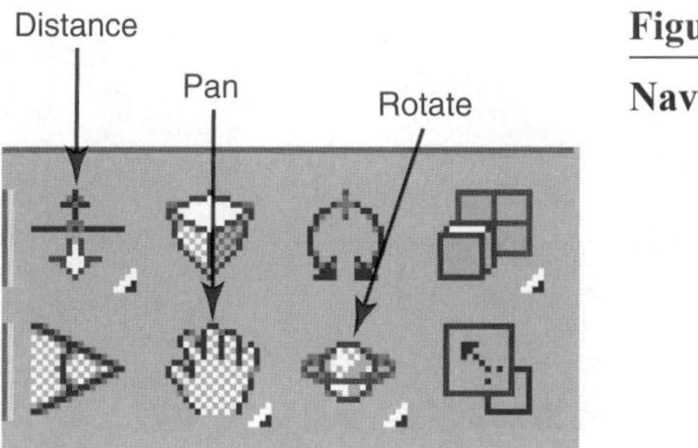

Figure 19-35

Navigation tools

13. Using the **System** tools, add a **Sunlight** button. Click and drag to set the **Compass**, and then drag your cursor upwards and click to set the height of the **Sunlight**. (see Figure 19-36)
14. Click in the **Top** view to make it the active view.
15. Using the **Create** tools, add a **Plane**. Be sure to click the color box, and set it to a green color. Make the box approximately 50′ × 50′, and set the Length Segs to 1 (see Figure 19-37)

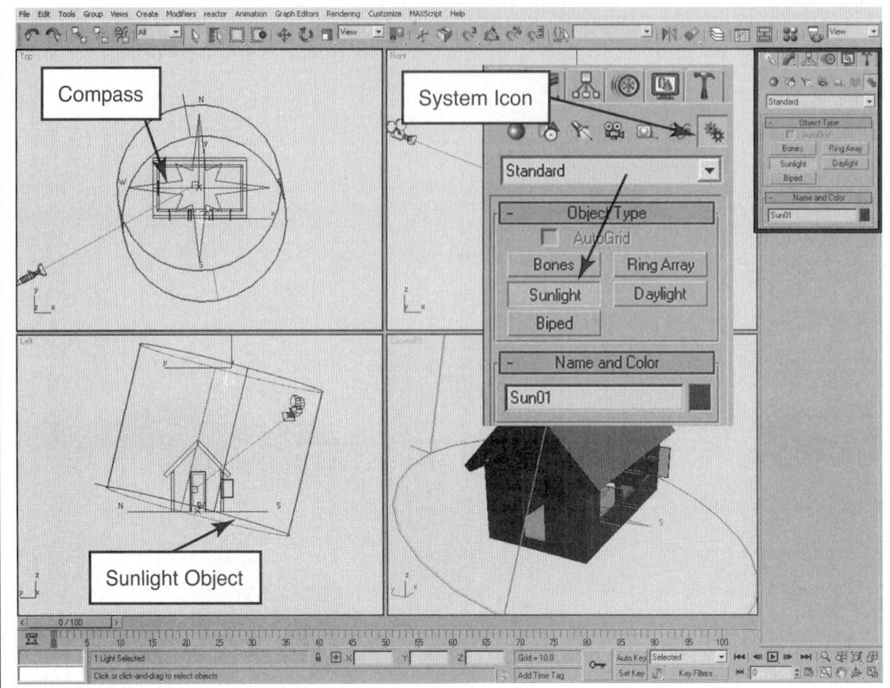

Figure 19-36

Set the height of the **Sunlight**

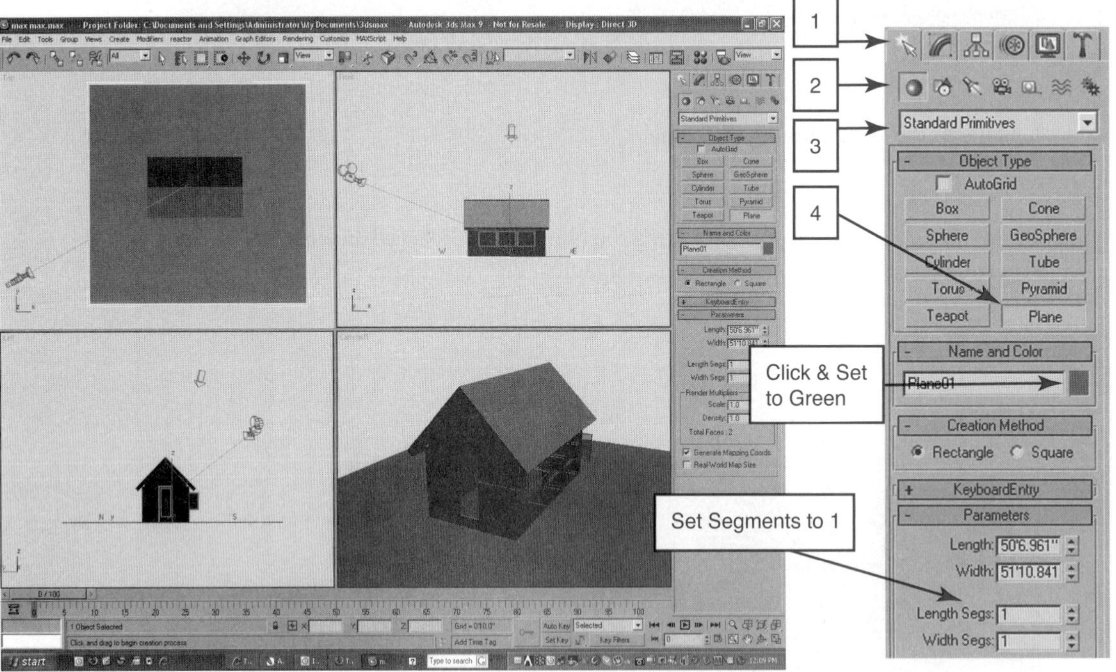

Figure 19-37

Create a green plane

16. Select the **Render** icon to bring up the **Render Scene** dialog box.
17. In the **Render Scene** dialog box, press the **Render** button to render the scene.

Notice that the rendering is dark; that is because the sunlight is coming from the back. (see Figure 19-38)

NOTE:

The Render Scene dialog box contains all the controls for size, Renderer, etc. For these tutorials, just use the defaults.

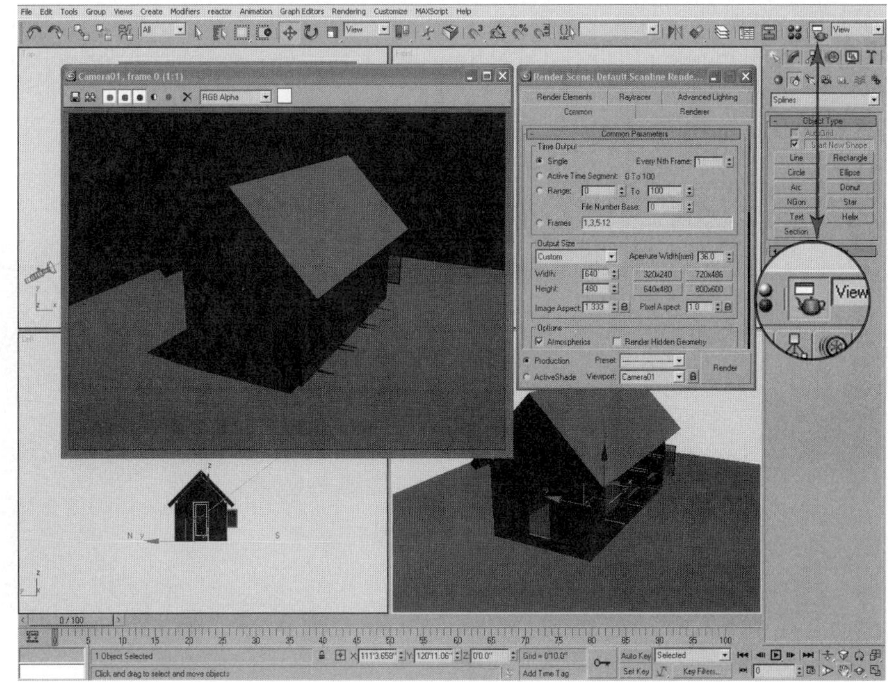

Figure 19-38

Render Scene dialog box

18. Select the **Sun** object, and then select the **Motion** icon in the upper right of the **MAX 9** interface to open the **Motion** parameters.
19. Adjust the **Latitude** and **Longitude** and watch how the light changes in the scene. This author set the **Latitude** to 75, and the **Longitude** to **56** for the default location. (see Figure 19-39)

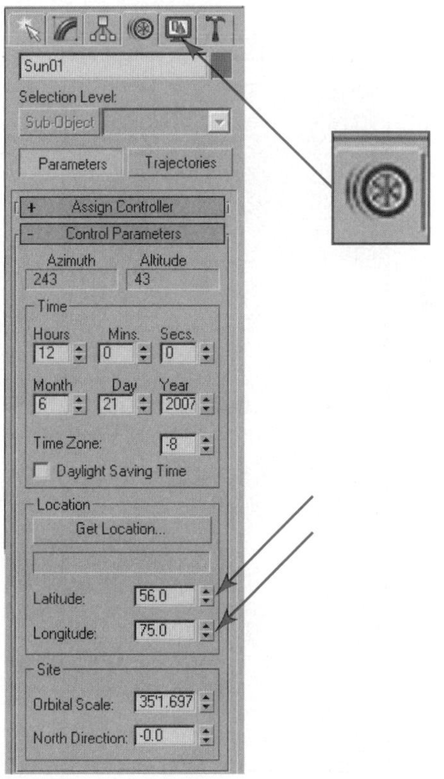

Figure 19-39

Motion parameters

20. Re-render the scene. It is better, but the shadows are too dark on the right side.
21. To fix this, select Lights – Omni from the Create panel, and place an omni light at the right side of the building.
22. Click in the Camera view, re-render, and save the file. **(see** Figure 19-40**)**

Figure 19-40

Re-render the file

EXERCISE 19-8 **CREATING AND PLACING MATERIALS IN AUTODESK 3DS MAX 9**

1. Select the **Material Editor** icon at the top right of the **MAX** interface to bring up the **Material Editor.**
2. In the **Material Editor**, enter **WALL MATERIAL** in the list shown in Figure 19-41

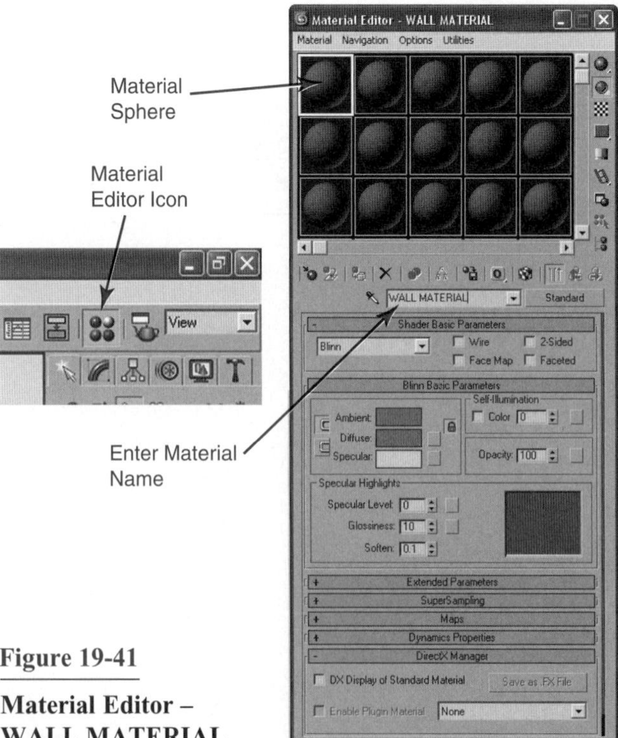

Figure 19-41

Material Editor – WALL MATERIAL

3. Expand the **Material** display shapes, and pick the Block shape.
4. Double click on the Material shape to expand it for better viewing. (see Figure 19-42)

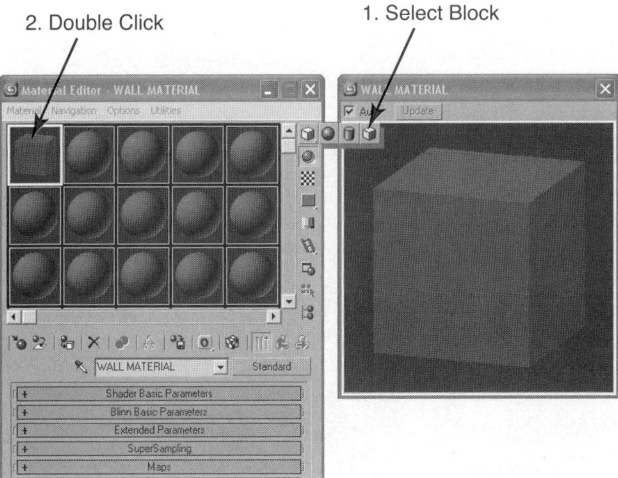

Figure 19-42

Expand Material shape

5. With the **WALL MATERIAL** shape selected, press the **Diffuse Color** button to open the **Material Map Browser** dialog box.
6. In the **Material Map Browser** dialog box, double click on **Bitmap** to bring up the **Select Bitmap Image** dialog box.
7. In the **Select Bitmap Image** dialog box, browse to the location where your bitmap pictures are stored (they are in the same place as was shown in the **AutoCAD Architecture Materials** tutorial earlier in this section).
8. In the **Select Bitmap Image** dialog box, select the **Masonry.Unit Masonry.Brick. Modular.Flemish Diagonal** bitmap, and press the **Open** button to place it in the **Material Editor. Repeat this process creating ROOF MATERIAL using the Thermal - Moisture.Roof Tiles.Spanish.Red** bitmap. (see Figure 19-43)

Figure 19-43

Select Bitmap Image dialog box

9. Select the **Show Map in Viewport** button, and drag **WALL MATERIAL** onto the walls. Repeat by dragging **ROOF MATERIAL** on to the roof. (see Figure 19-44)

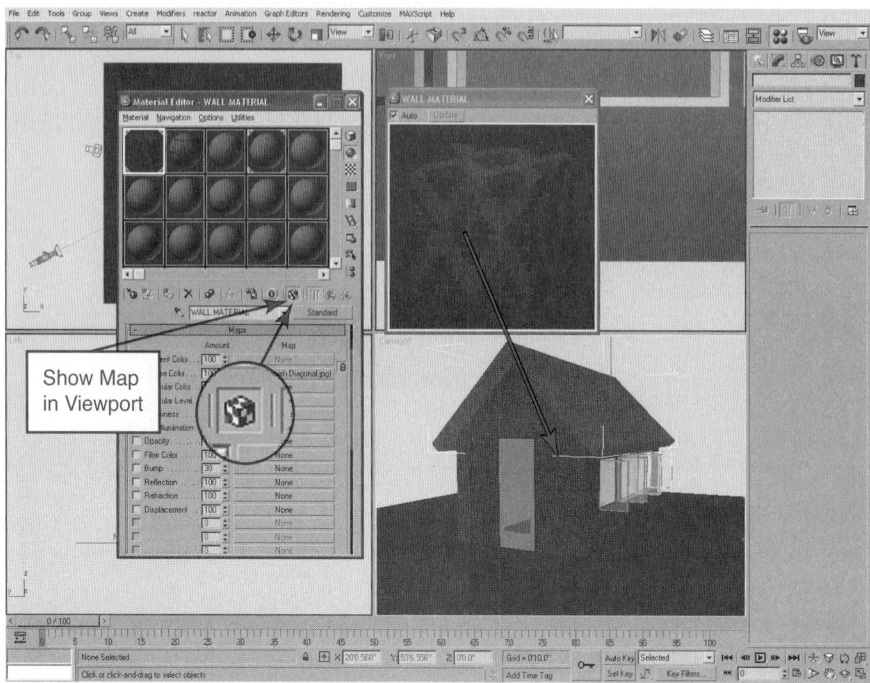

Figure 19-44

Show Map in Viewport button

10. Select a wall, and then select the **Modify** icon from the **Create** panel to bring up the **Modifier list.**
11. In the **Modifier** list, select the **MapScaler**.
12. Select the other walls and roof, and repeat step 11. (see Figure 19-45)

NOTE:

The WALL MATERIAL and ROOF MATERIAL do not look like the bitmaps you selected – they are too small. To correct this do the following:

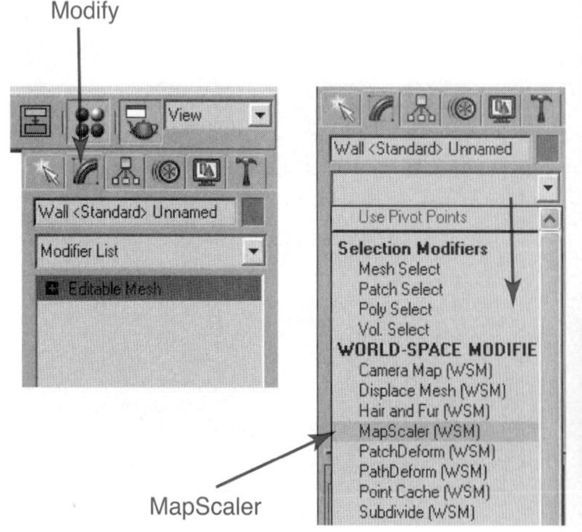

Figure 19-45

Modify wall and roof materials

13. Press the **Select by Name** icon at the top left of the **MAX** interface to bring up the **Select Objects** dialog box (you can select all the objects in your scene here).
14. In the **Select Objects** dialog box, choose **Roof Body**, and then press the **Select** button. (see Figure 19-46)

> **NOTE:**
> The Ends of the roof should not have ROOF MATERIAL. To correct this do the following:

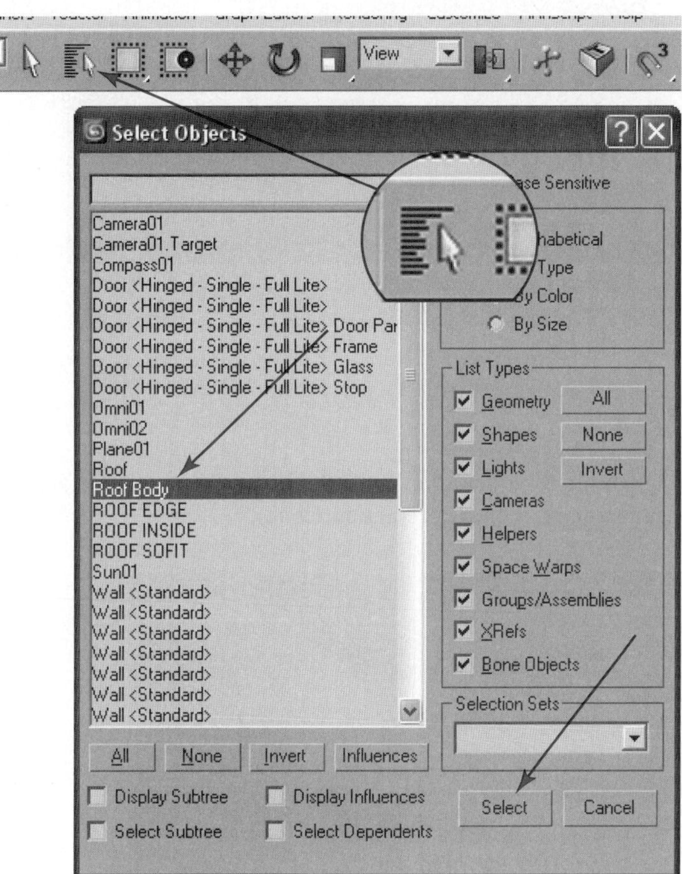

Figure 19-46

Select Objects dialog box

15. Select the **Modify** icon from the **Create** panel to bring up the **Modifier list.**
16. In the modifier list, select and expand **Editable Mesh.**
17. In the expanded **Editable Mesh**, select **Polygon**.
18. Select the edge of the roof (it will turn red), and then press the **Detach** button to bring up the **Detach** dialog box.
19. In the **Detach** dialog box, enter **ROOF EDGE**, and press the **OK** button.
20. Repeat steps **13-19**, and detach the other roof edges, and the inside of the roof – give each detached object a unique name such as **SOFIT**, etc. (see Figure 19-47)
21. Open the **Material Editor**, and create a new material called **ROOF EDGE MATERIAL**.

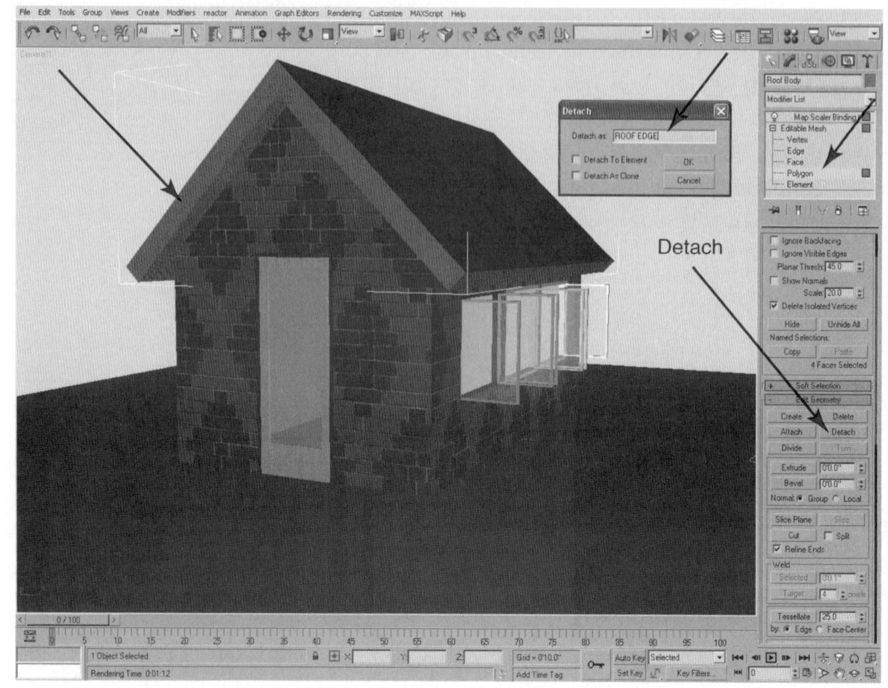

Figure 19-47

Detach dialog box

22. Click on the **Ambient** button to open the **Ambient Color** selector, and choose a color (the author chose white). (see Figure 19-48)

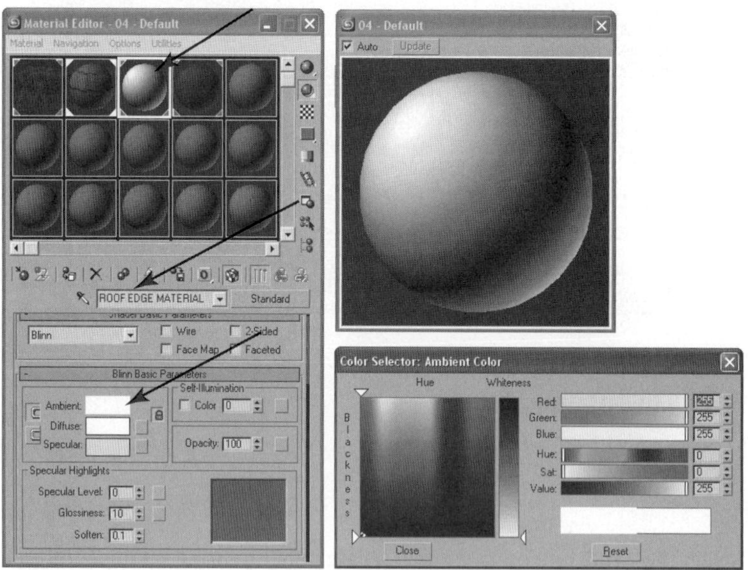

Figure 19-48

Ambient Color selector

23. Again, press the **Select by Name** icon at the top left of the **MAX** interface to bring up the **Select Objects** dialog box.
24. In the **Select Objects** dialog box, choose the new roof objects you created to select them.
25. With the new roof objects selected, press the Assign material to Selection icon to apply the **ROOF EDGE MATERIAL** to them. (see Figure 19-49)

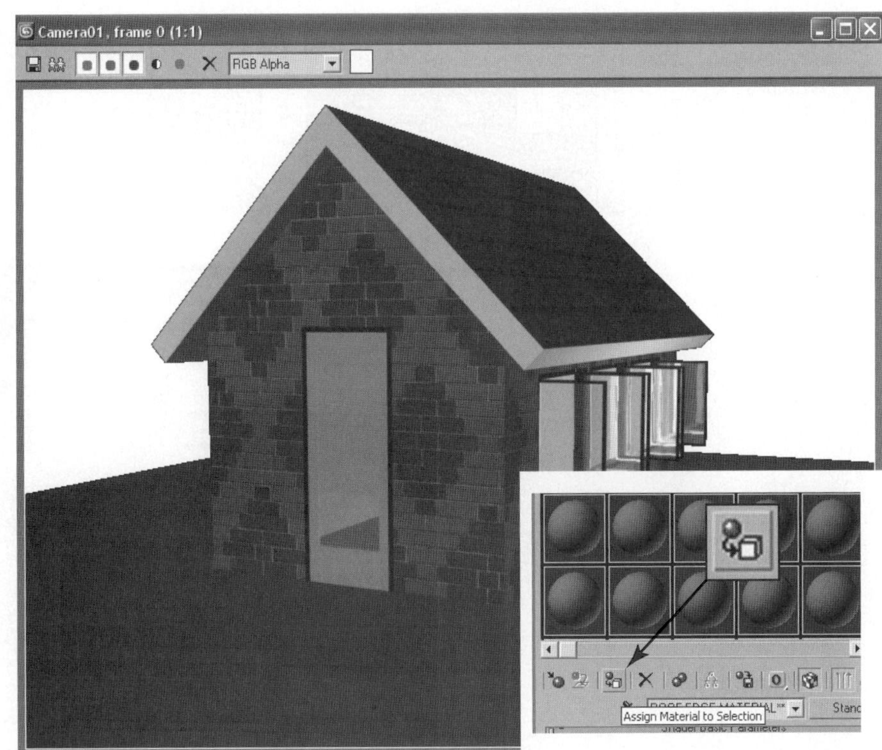

Figure 19-49

Assign Material to Selection icon

EXERCISE 19-9 **ADDING THE SKY IN AUTODESK 3DS MAX**

1. In the **Select Bitmap Image** dialog box, select the **Sky** picture you have created or found, and press the **Open** button to place it in the **Material Editor.**
2. Select **Rendering > Environment** from the **Main** menu to bring up the **Environment and Effects** dialog box.
3. In the **Environment and Effects** dialog box, select the **Use Map** check box, and then press the **Environment Map** button to bring up the **Select Bitmap Image** File dialog box.
4. In the **Select Bitmap Image File** dialog box, browse to the folder where you have placed a picture of the sky, and open the picture. (see Figure 19-50)

NOTE:

The Author took a picture of a cloudy sky with his digital camera and saved it in his textures folder. You can also search the internet for pictures, or purchase texture maps (pictures).

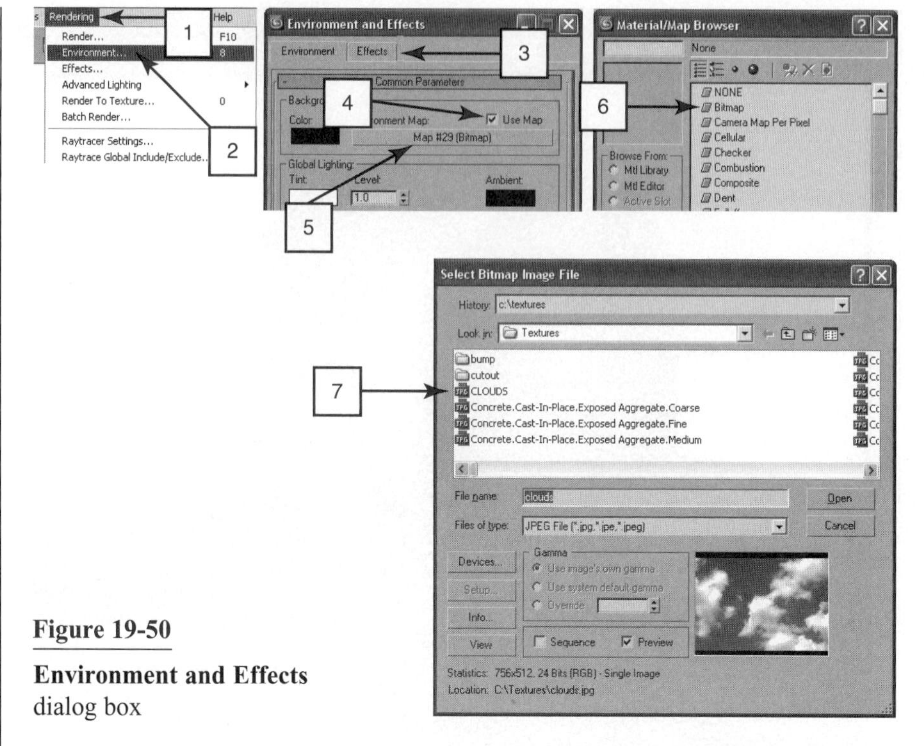

Figure 19-50

Environment and Effects dialog box

EXERCISE 19-10 CREATING GRASS IN AUTODESK 3DS MAX 9

3DS MAX 9 has a Modifier called **Hair and Fur**. It has this name because MAX is often used in the gaming industry, and it is used to apply hair and fur to people and animals. This is a very sophisticated modifier, and can be easily used to create realistic grass for architectural visualizations.

Hair and Fur only renders in the **Camera** view, so you will not see its effects in any other views. For architectural visualizations, this author suggests only attaching the **Hair and Fur** modifier to a **Plane** object.

Because this is a very sophisticated modifier, this tutorial has been simplified, Please check the help file for more in-depth information.

1. Select the **plane** that you created in step **13** of the **Visualization with 3DS MAX** tutorial.
2. Select **Modifiers > Hair and Fur > Hair and Fur (WSM)** from the **Main** menu to apply it to the selected **Plane**.
3. Select the **Modifier** icon in the **Create** panel to expose the **Hair and Fur** controls.
4. In the **Hair and Fur** controls, set the following:

   General Parameters

   a. Hair count = **30,000**

   b. Scale = **2** (height of grass)

   c. Rand Scale = **40** (40% random sizes)

   d. Root Thick = **4** (thickness of grass root)

   e. Tip Thick = **0.4** (thickness of grass tip)

   Material Parameters

   a. Tip Color = **make light green**

   b. Root Color = **make dark green**

Frizz Parameters

a. Make all the Frizz Parameters = **0**

(makes the grass vertical)

Multi Strand Parameters

a. Count = **3**

b. Root Splay = **.82**

c. Tip Splay = **1.82**

(see Figure 19-51)

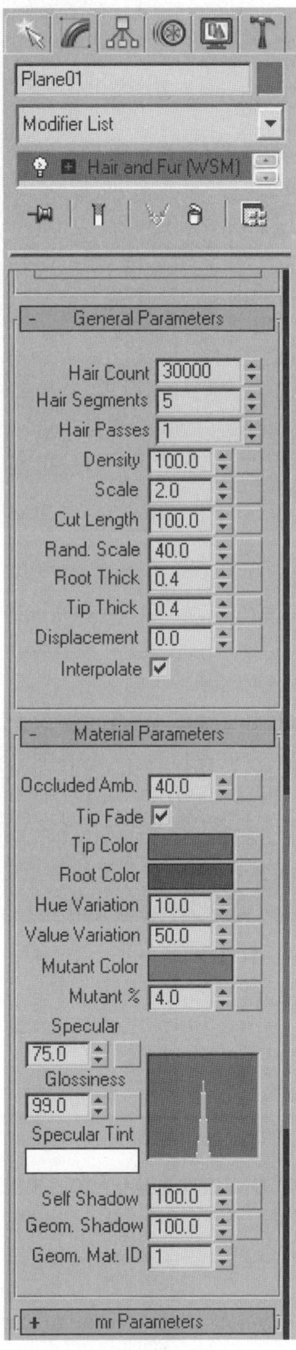

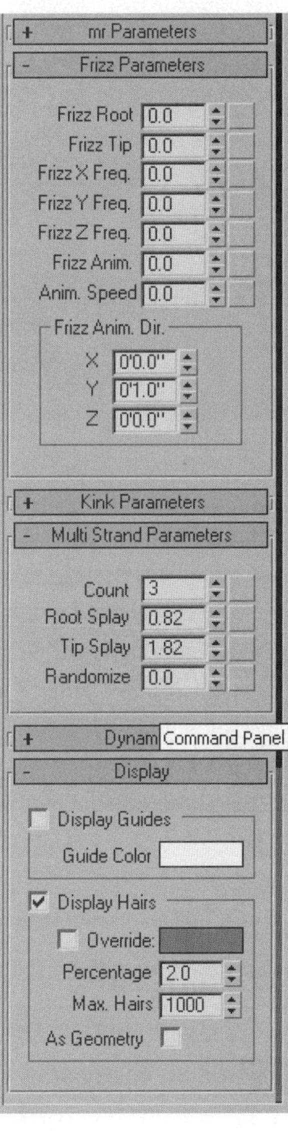

Figure 19-51

Set **Hair and Fur** controls

5. Render the picture (be patient, this render takes two passes), and save the file. (see Figure 19-52).

Figure 19-52

Render the picture

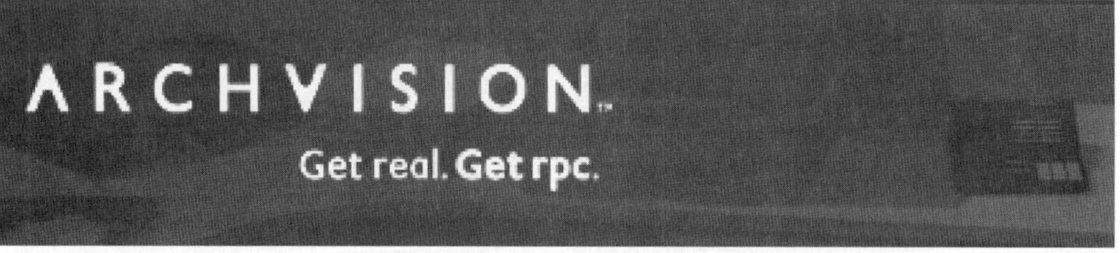

Using ArchVision™ RPC

EXERCISE 19-11 USING ARCHVISION™ RPC CONTENT IN AUTODESK 3DS MAX 9

1. Using your Internet browser, go to http://www.archvision.com.
2. At the first screen, select **Software Updates** from the **Support** drop-down to take you to the **Software Updates** screen.
3. In the **Software Updates** screen, download and install the **RPC 3.13** plug-in.

NOTE:

All software companies are always updating software. This plug-in was the latest release as of the writing of this book. (see Figure 19-53)

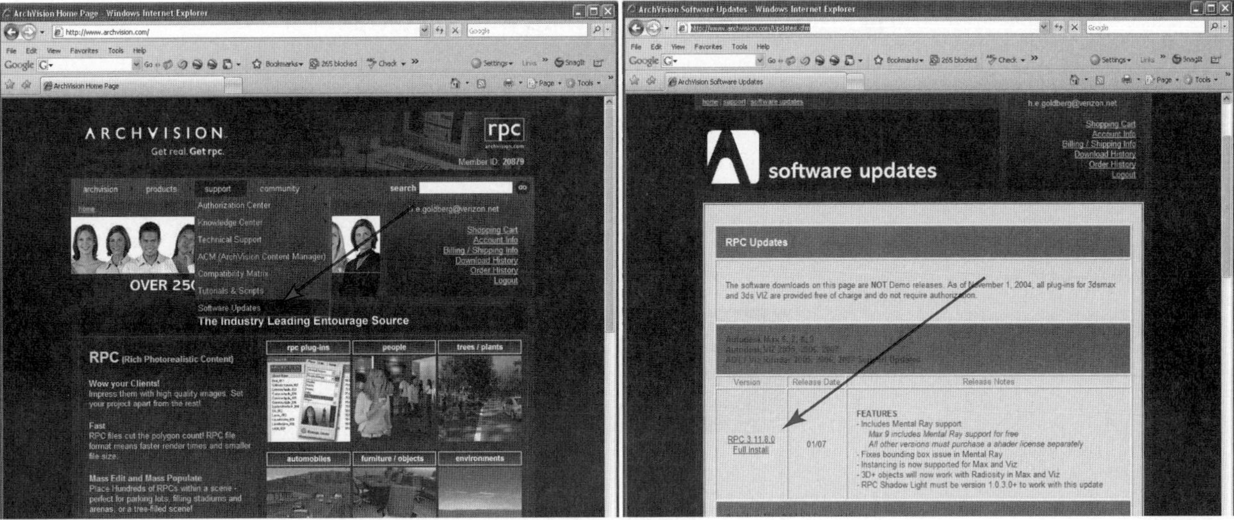

Figure 19-53

ArchVision™ website

4. Once you have installed the plug-in, select the **Geometry** icon in the **Create** panel, and then select **RPC** from the drop down list.
5. Once you have **RPC** from the drop down list, the **RPC** parameters will appear.
6. From the **RPC** parameters, select the RPC button, select content you want and then place and rotate it in your scene. (see Figures 19-54, 19-55 & 19-56)

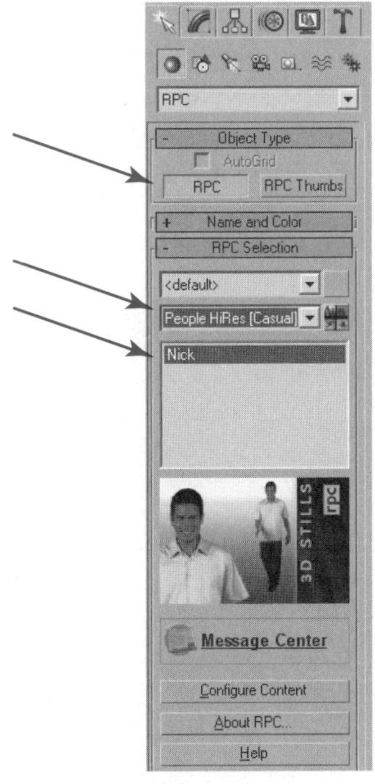

Geometry Button

RPC

Standard Primitives
Extended Primitives
Compound Objects
Particle Systems
Patch Grids
NURBS Surfaces
Doors
Windows
AEC Extended
Dynamics Objects
Stairs
RPC

Figure 19-54

Geometry button

Figure 19-55

RPC parameters

Figure 19-56

Rendered drawing

EXERCISE 19-12 **SHADOWING THE RPC CONTENT**

1. Select one of the **RPC** content objects you placed, and select **Mass Edit** from the **RPC** parameters to bring up the **RPC Mass Edit** dialog box.
2. In the **RPC Mass Edit** dialog box, select all the content, and then click under the **3D** column. When an S appears opposite the content, the object is set to shadow. (see Figure 19-57).

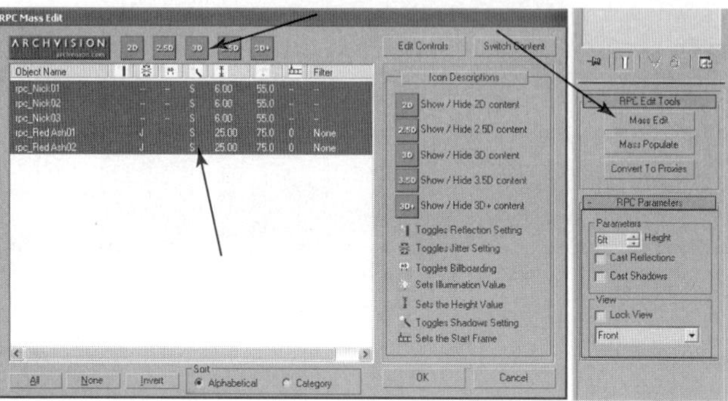

Figure 19-57

RPC Mass Edit dialog box

3. Press the **Select by Name** icon at the top left of the **MAX** interface to bring up the **Select Objects** dialog box (you can select all the objects in your scene here).
4. In the **Select Objects** dialog box, choose **Sun01**, and then press the **Select** button.

RPC content needs to be included in the **Sun** parameters to be seen. **Sun01** is the default name that was given when you first placed the **Sunlight** object.

5. With the **Sun01** selected, press the **Modify** icon in the **Create** panel.
6. In the **General Parameters**, check the **Shadows** check box, and then press the **Include** button to bring up the **Exclude/Include** dialog box.
7. In the **Exclude/Include** dialog box, make sure that the **Include** radio button is pressed, and that all the content in the scene is together on the **Include** side (see Figure 19-58).

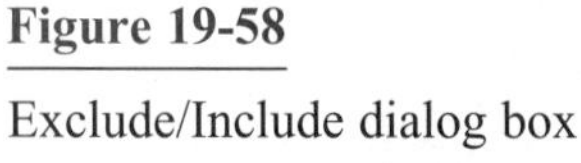

Figure 19-58

Exclude/Include dialog box

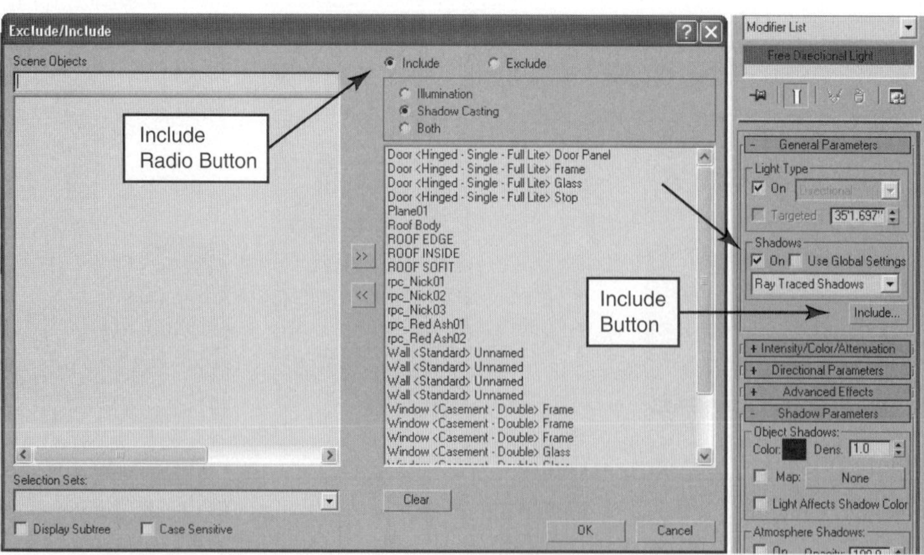

8. Finally, select **Rendering > Environment** from the **Main** menu to bring up the **Environment and Effects** dialog box.
9. In the **Environment and Effects** dialog box, select the **Effects** tab. (see Figure 19-59).

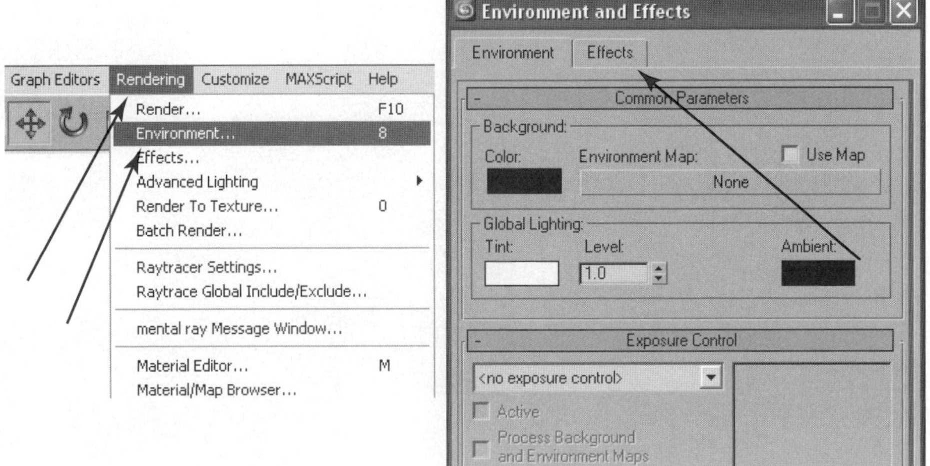

Figure 19-59

Environment and Effects dialog box

10. In the **Effects** tab, select Hair and Fur to bring up the **Hair and Fur** effects parameters.
11. In the **Hair and Fur** effects parameters, select the **GBuffer** radio button, and then press the **Custom** radio button under **Occlusion Objects.**
12. Render the scene. (see Figure 19-60).

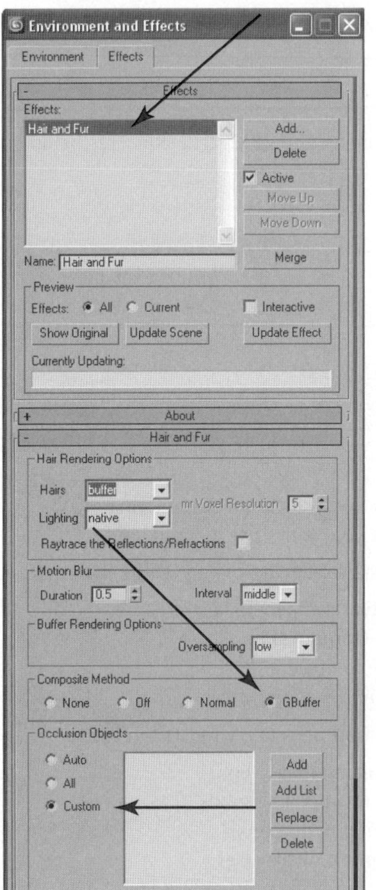

Figure 19-60

Hair and Fur Effects parameters

13. Render the scene and save the file. (see Figure 19-61)

Figure 19-61

Render the scene

Chapter Summary

This chapter explained and demonstrated how to render visualizations in Revit Architecture 2012. The concepts behind rendering were explained as well as how to use RPC content.

Chapter Test Questions

Multiple Choice

Circle the correct answer.

1. A texture map is
   a. A picture of a material.
   b. The location where textures are located.
   c. The color of a material.
   d. How shadows are mapped on a surface.
2. Which program reads .AVI files?
   a. Camtasia
   b. Windows Media Player
   c. Mac QuickTime Player
   d. All of the above
3. When should you use draft quality in Revit Architecture?
   a. When you want a presentation rendering
   b. When you want to illustrate the effect of the wind
   c. When you want a quick rendering result
   d. When you want to save a rendering
4. The **Show Rendering** dialog button is located in the
   a. **Application** menu.
   b. **View Control Bar**.
   c. **Home** toolbar.
   d. **Massing & Site** toolbar.
5. The **Sunlight** presets are located in the
   a. **Rendering** dialog box.
   b. **Sun Settings** dialog box.
   c. **Lighting** dialog box.
   d. **Sunlight Control Bar.**

True or False

1. **True or False:** The **Region** tool locates the **Region** in which the building is built.
2. **True or False:** You use the **Adjust Exposure** tool before creating a rendering.
3. **True or False:** Elevation renderings cannot be done in Revit.
4. **True or False:** Computer rendering is used to create realistic and photorealistic visualizations.
5. **True or False:** The 3ds Max modifier called **Grass** creates realistic grass.

Questions

1. Where did the concept of rendering come from?
2. Why does the **Teapot** icon symbolize rendering?
3. What commands are used to prepare a **Default 3D View** for rendering as an **Elevation** view?
4. What is mental ray?
5. Which button brings up the **Rendering** dialog box?

CHAPTER

20 Tutorial Project

CHAPTER OBJECTIVES

- Place a JPG logo in a template file.
- Create a plot sheet family from scratch.
- Set up the **Hillside House** project.
- Test the created plot sheet.
- Set up levels.
- Create the site.
- Create the foundation.
- Create the FIRST FLOOR framing and hardwood floor.
- Create the exterior walls.
- Create the exterior wall assembly.
- Place the FIRST FLOOR exterior walls.
- Create the SECOND FLOOR exterior walls.
- Create the SECOND FLOOR wing walls.
- Create the skylight side walls.
- Create the SECOND FLOOR floors.
- Create the stairway.
- Create the roof.
- Create the skylight roof.
- Create the bridge.
- Create the plot sheets.
- Create the interior walls.
- Place exterior doors and windows.
- Create the front and rear decks and their railings.
- Create the wall detail.
- Place wall tags.
- Create the door and window schedules.
- Create the kitchen and bath.
- Render the **Hillside House** project model.

Introduction

The purpose of this tutorial project is to illustrate the methodology for creating a set of construction documents in Revit Architecture 2012 while giving practical practice in using Revit Architecture 2012 tools.

For the tutorial project, this author has chosen a two-story hillside house. The project progresses through the design process to the construction documentation stage.

Creating a Project

Before starting the project, it will be necessary to create a customized plotting sheet that includes the company logo. Using Adobe® Illustrator®, Adobe® Photoshop®, CorelDRAW®, Paint Shop Pro™, Macromedia FreeHand®, Canvas™, or even Windows® Paint, create a JPG of your logo. Save the logo as **LOGO** in a new folder on your computer called **HILLSIDE HOUSE**. The logo the author created looks like that shown in Figure 20-1.

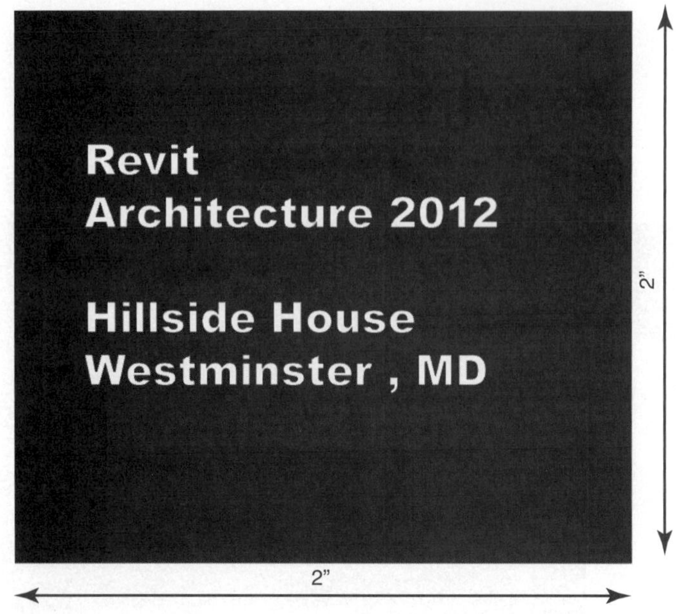

Figure 20-1

Company logo

EXERCISE 20-1 **PLACING THE LOGO IN THE TEMPLATE FILE**

Select **Open > Family** from the **Application** menu to bring up the **Open** dialog box in the **Imperial Library** folder.

1. In the **Imperial Library** folder, select and open the **Titleblocks** folder.
2. In the **Titleblocks** folder, select the **D 22 × 34 Horizontal** file, and press the **Open** button to bring it into the **Family Editor**.

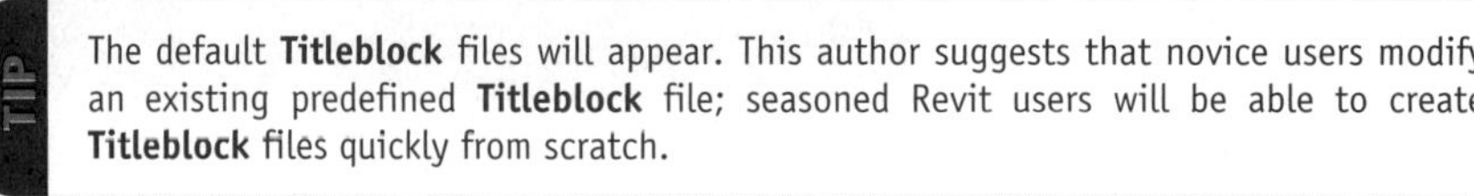

TIP

The default **Titleblock** files will appear. This author suggests that novice users modify an existing predefined **Titleblock** file; seasoned Revit users will be able to create **Titleblock** files quickly from scratch.

3. Select the **Insert** tab to bring up the **Insert** toolbar (see Figure 20-2).
4. In the **Insert** toolbar, select the **Image** button to bring up the **Import Image** dialog box.
5. In the **Import Image** dialog box, locate the **HILLSIDE HOUSE** folder, where you placed the **LOGO** JPG you previously created.

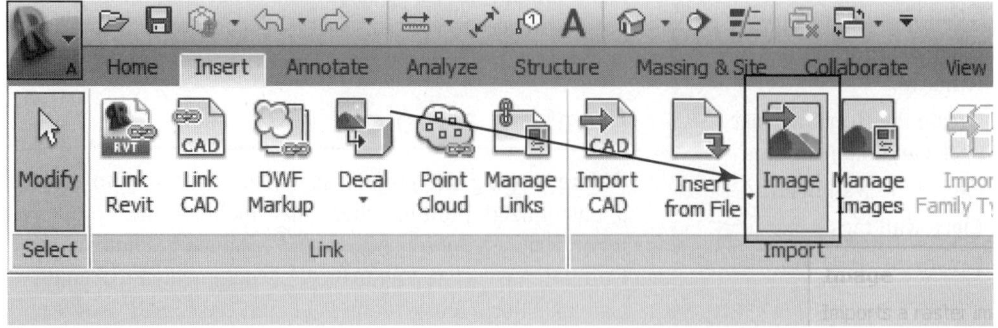

Figure 20-2

Insert toolbar

6. Select the **LOGO** JPG created, and press the **Open** button to bring the image into the **Drawing Editor**.
7. Place the logo in the drawing as shown in Figure 20-3.

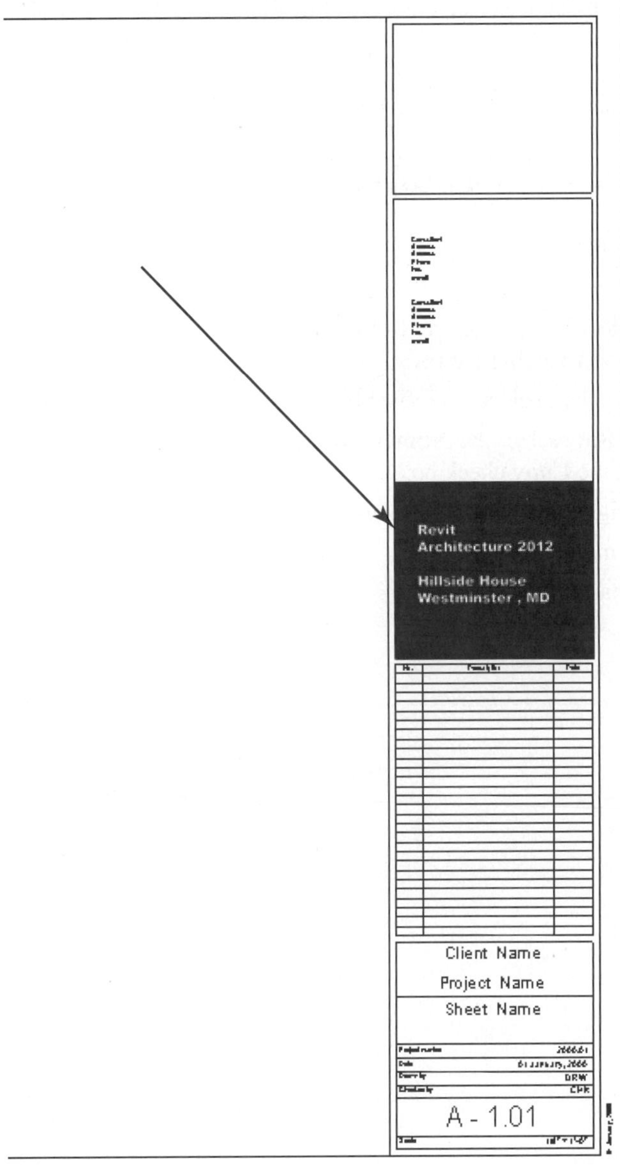

Figure 20-3

Insert the logo in the drawing

> **TIP** You can adjust the size of the **LOGO** JPG by selecting it and dragging on the corner grips.

8. Delete the default **Revit** logo from the top of the drawing.
9. Select **Save As > Family** from the **Application** menu to bring up the **Save As >** dialog box.
10. In the **Save As >** dialog box, save the file as **HILLSIDE HOUSE SHEET FAMILY**, and place it in the **HILLSIDE HOUSE** folder.
11. Close the file.

EXERCISE 20-2 CREATING A PLOT SHEET FAMILY FROM SCRATCH

1. Select **New > Title Block** from the **Application** menu to bring up the **New Title Block – Select Template File** dialog box.
2. In the **New Title Block – Select Template File** dialog box, locate the **Titleblocks** folder.

TIP

Unless you change the default paths, the **New Title Block – Select Template File** dialog box should open in the **Titleblocks** folder.

3. In the **Titleblocks** folder, select the **D-36 × 24.rft** file, and press the **Open** button to bring it into the **Drawing Editor**.
4. In the **Modify** toolbar, select the **Offset** button.
5. In the **Options Bar**, select the **Numerical** radio button, enter **1/2″** in the **Offset** field, and check the **Copy** check box.
6. Offset the top, right, and bottom margins of the D-36 × 24 template.
7. Offset the right margin **2-1/2″** again.
8. Offset the left margin **1-1/2″**.
9. Trim the lines (see Figure 20-4).

Figure 20-4

Offset the margins and trim the lines of the template

10. Add your **LOGO** JPG as you did in the previous exercise.
11. Add a **2″** horizontal line inside the **2″** title block to separate the drawing number.
12. In the **Home** toolbar, select the **Label** button to bring up the **Modify | Place Label** toolbar.
13. Click in the **Drawing Editor** to bring up the **Edit Label** dialog box (see Figure 20-5).

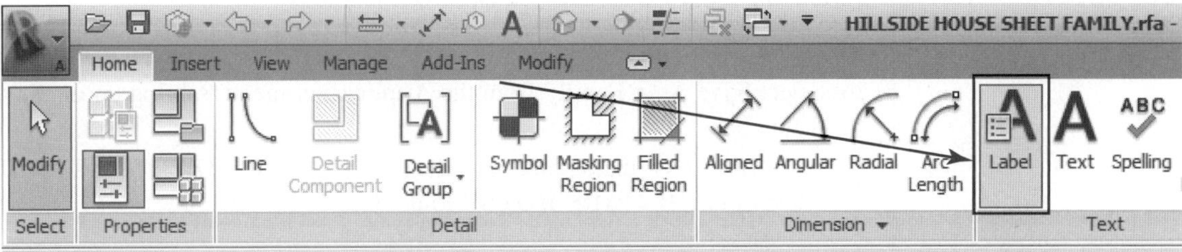

Figure 20-5

Label button

14. In the **Edit Label** dialog box, select **Sheet Number**, and then press the **OK** button to place the **Sheet Number** tag (see Figure 20-6).

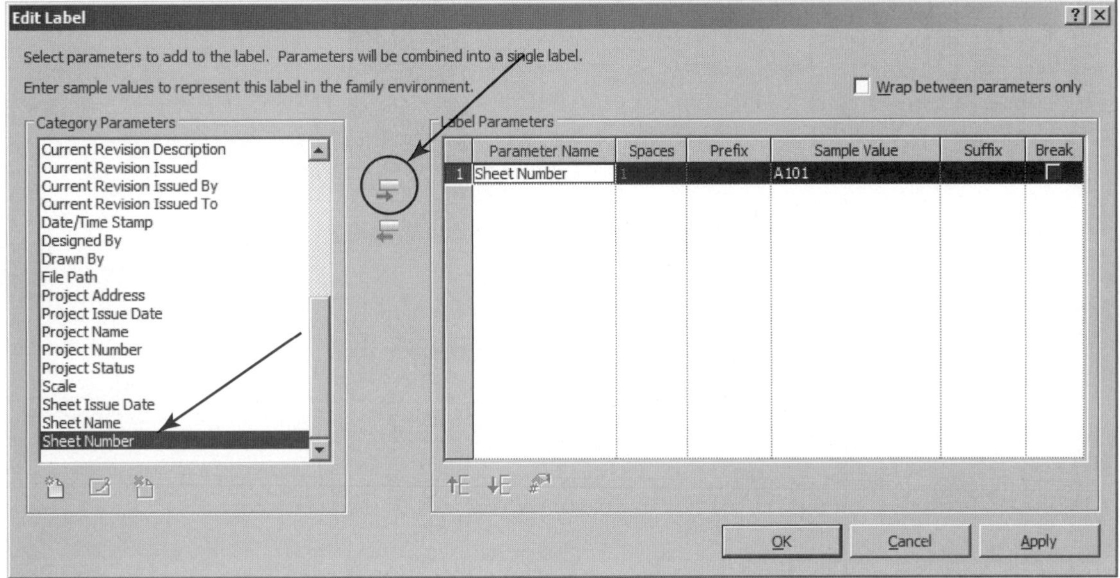

Figure 20-6

Edit Label dialog box

15. Move the **Sheet Number** tag into position at the bottom of the title block.
16. Again, in the **Home** toolbar, select the **Label** button to bring up the **Modify | Place Label** toolbar.
17. Click in the **Drawing Editor** to bring up the **Edit Label** dialog box in the **Drawing Editor**.
18. In the **Edit Label** dialog box, select **Project Name**, and then press the **OK** button to place the **Project Name** tag.
19. Rotate the **Project Name** tag, and place it in the title block.
20. Select the **Project Name** tag to bring up the **Properties** dialog box.
21. In the **Properties** dialog box, press the **Edit Type** button to bring up the **Type Properties** dialog box.
22. In the **Type Properties** dialog box, press the **Duplicate** button to bring up the **Name** dialog box.
23. In the **Name** dialog box, enter **3/8″ TAG**, and press the **OK** button to return to the **Type Properties** dialog box.
24. In the **Type Properties** dialog box, change the **Text Size** to **3/8″**, and press the **OK** buttons to return to the **Drawing Editor**.

25. Repeat the previous steps, placing tags and lines to create your own customized drawing sheet.
26. Select **Save As** > **Family** from the **Application** menu to bring up the **Save As** > dialog box.
27. In the **Save As** > dialog box, save the file as **CUSTOMIZED SHEET FAMILY.rfa** in your **HILLSIDE HOUSE** folder (see Figure 20-7).

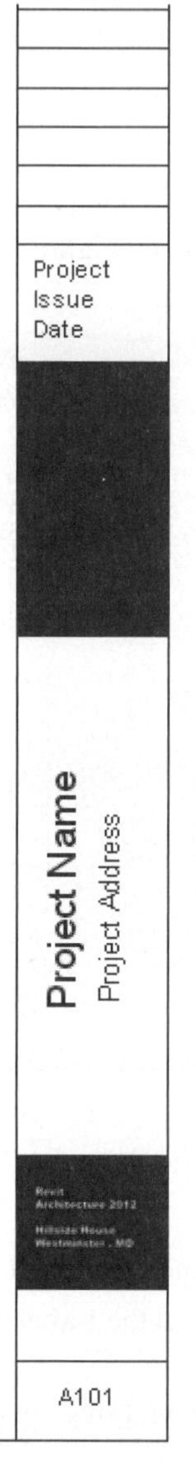

Figure 20-7

CUSTOMIZED SHEET FAMILY.rfa sheet

EXERCISE 20-3 SETTING UP THE PROJECT

1. Select **New** > **Project** from the **Application** menu to bring up the **New Project** dialog box.
2. Accept the defaults in the **New Project** dialog box, and press the **OK** button to create the new project.
3. Select **Save As** > **Project** from the **Application** menu to bring up the **Save As** > dialog box.

4. In the **Save As** > dialog box, name the file **HILLSIDE HOUSE PROJECT.rvt**, and save it as a **Project File** in the **HILLSIDE HOUSE** folder.
5. Select the **Manage** tab to bring up the **Manage** toolbar.
6. In the **Manage** toolbar, select the **Project Information** button to bring up the **Instance Properties** dialog box for the project (see Figure 20-8).

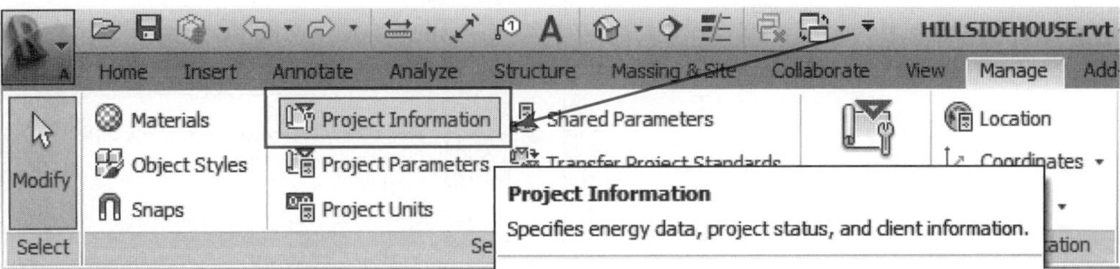

Figure 20-8

Project Information button

7. In the **Instance Properties** dialog box, select the **Edit** button opposite the **Project Address** field to bring up the **Edit Text** dialog box.
8. In the **Edit Text** dialog box, enter **Westminster, MD** as the address, and press the **OK** button to return to the **Element Properties** dialog box.
9. Fill in the rest of the information in the **Instance Properties** dialog box (see Figure 20-9).

Parameter	Value
Energy Analysis	
Energy Data	Edit...
Other	
Project Issue Date	Issue Date
Project Status	Project Status
Client Name	Owner
Project Address	Edit...
Project Name	HILLSIDE HOUSE
Project Number	2011

Figure 20-9

Instance Properties dialog box

NOTE:

Although not available for this project, which is a residence, the **Energy Data** button will set you up for export to gbXML. When this format is combined with the postal code of the project, sites such as Green Building Studio (http://www.greenbuildingstudio.com) will give you a general energy analysis of your commercial building. To set this up, do the following:

- In the **Instance Properties** dialog box, select the **Edit** button opposite the **Energy Data** field to bring up the **Energy Settings** dialog box.
- In the **Energy Settings** dialog box, select the **Building Type** and the button to the right of the **Location** field to bring up the **Location Weather and Site** dialog box.
- In the **Location Weather and Site** dialog box, enter the location and press the **Search** button to locate the site.
- In the **Location Weather and Site** dialog box, press the **OK** button to return to the **Energy Settings** dialog box.
- In the **Energy Settings** dialog box, press the **OK** button to return to the **Drawing Editor** (see Figure 20-10).

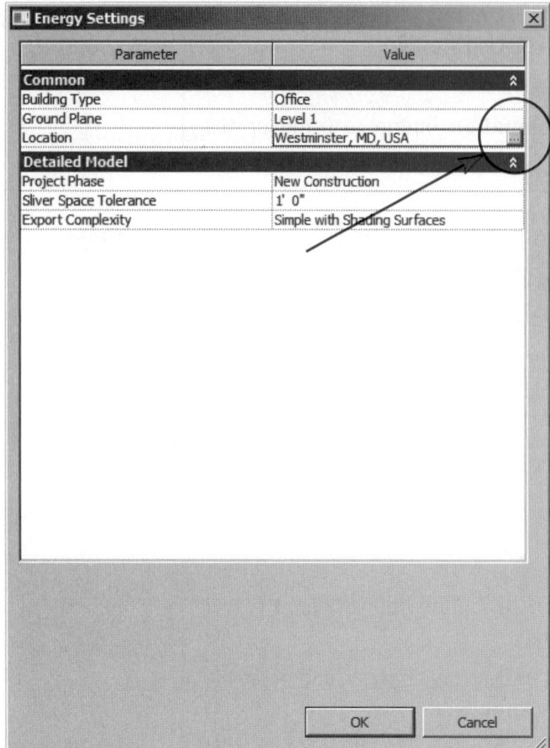

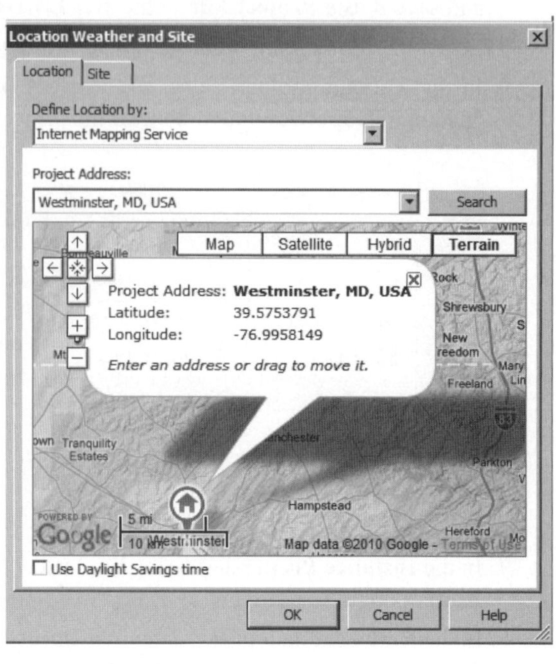

Figure 20-10

Energy Settings dialog box

10. Select **Save** from the **Application** menu to save the project.

EXERCISE 20-4 TESTING THE PLOT SHEET

1. Select the **View** tab to bring up the **View** toolbar.
2. In the **View** toolbar, select the **New Sheet** button to bring up the **New Sheet** dialog box (see Figure 20-11).

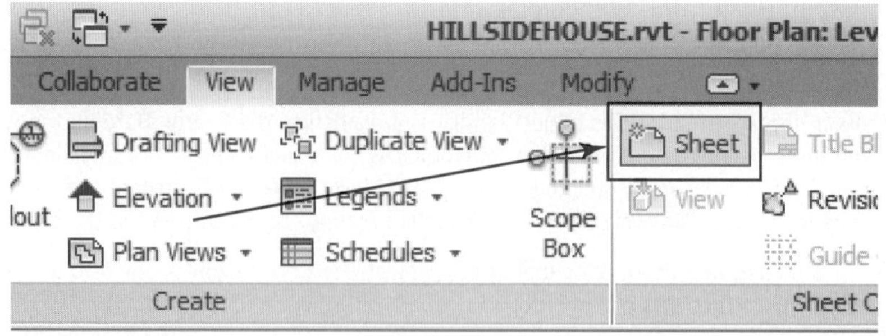

Figure 20-11

New Sheet button

TIP

You can also **RMB** (right mouse button) click on the **Sheets (all)** icon in the **Project Browser** to bring up the **New Sheet** button. Pressing this button will bring up the **New Sheet** dialog box (see Figure 20-12).

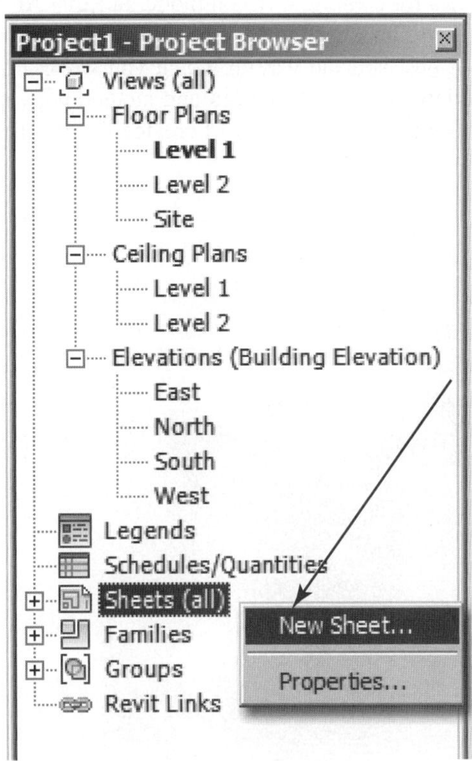

Figure 20-12

Project Browser

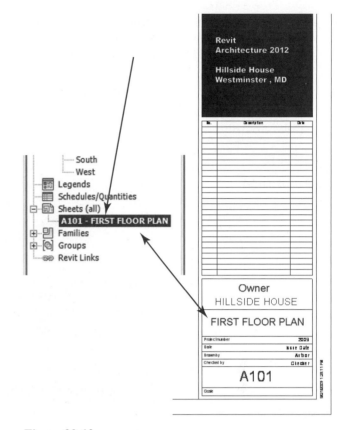

Figure 20-13

Rename the sheet and sheet number

3. In the **Select a Titleblock** dialog box, press the **Load** button, browse, and locate the **HILLSIDE HOUSE SHEET FAMILY** title block you previously created.
4. After the **HILLSIDE HOUSE SHEET FAMILY** title block appears in the **Select a Titleblock** dialog box, select it, and press the **OK** button to return to the **Drawing Editor**.

Notice that the plot sheet contains all the project information that you placed in the **Project Information** settings. Notice also that the plot sheet has a sheet number and that the plot sheet appears in the **Project Browser** under **Sheets (all)**.

You can now rename the sheet and sheet number, if you wish, either by clicking on those fields in the sheet itself or from the **Project Browser**. To rename inside the **Project Browser**, **RMB** (right mouse button) on the name of the sheet, and select **Rename** from the contextual menu that appears to bring up the **Sheet Title** dialog box. Rename and renumber it there (see Figure 20-13).

The Two-Story Hillside House Project

This project has been patterned after a real project that Rick Donally and I designed in 1978. It is located on a hillside overlooking the Bachman Valley and sits on 60 acres of farmland. The original concept was for the house to be built on an exterior exposed steel frame set on concrete piers, and the exterior walls were to be faced with plywood siding. The final building used a more conventional brick-and-block foundation with wood frame bearing walls and redwood siding. To take advantage of the site, Rick and I decided to place the building away from the ridge of the hillside and enter the second level by way of a bridge. This allowed us to place the living areas at the treetop level and access the lower bedrooms by an external stair. By doing this, the client (a bachelor at the time) could walk from his bedroom directly out to the ground level. For this project, I have simplified the building, but the main concepts still are evident. There are many methodologies for creating a virtual model in Revit Architecture 2012; this project uses one method. As you become more familiar with the program, you will discover the methods and tools that best suit the way in which you work. I hope you enjoy doing this project and enjoy experiencing both the design and methodology concepts. Figures 20-14 and 20-15 show pictures of the cardboard model I created for the client.

Figure 20-14

Cardboard model

Figure 20-15

Cardboard model

EXERCISE 20-5 SETTING THE LEVELS

1. Make sure that you have the **HILLSIDE HOUSE** as the current project.
2. In the **Project Browser**, double-click on the **East Elevation** to bring it into the **Drawing Editor**.
3. In the **Home** toolbar, select the **Level** button and make or rename **Levels** to match the settings shown in Figure 20-16.

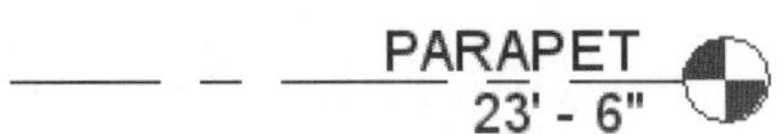

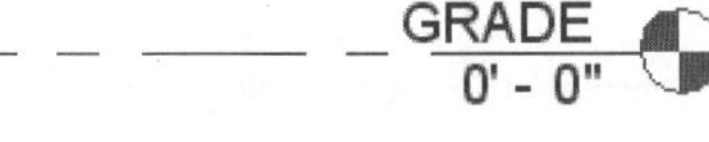

FIRST FLOOR
2' - 6"

GRADE
0' - 0"

SITE
-5' - 0"

Figure 20-16

Rename **Levels**

Name	Floor Elevation	Floor-to-Floor Height
PARAPET	23′-6″	0′-0″
SECOND FLOOR	11′-6″	12′-0″
FIRST FLOOR	2′-6″	9′-0″
GRADE	0′-0″	2′-6″
SITE	-5′-0″	5′-0″

EXERCISE 20-6 **CREATING THE SITE**

1. In the **Project Browser**, double-click on **Site** (under **Floor Plans**) to bring the **Site** plan into the **Drawing Editor** (see Figure 20-17).

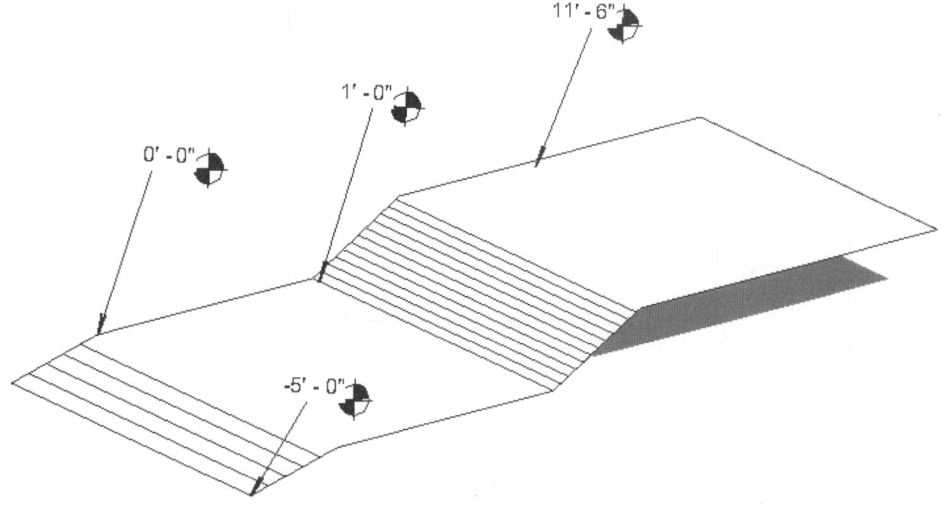

Figure 20-17

Site plan

2. Set the **Scale** to **1″ = 10′**.
3. Change to the **Annotate** toolbar.
4. In the **Annotate** toolbar, select the **Detail Line** button.
5. In the **Site** plan, place lines as shown in Figure 20-18.
6. In the **Massing & Site** toolbar, select the **Toposurface** button to bring up the **Modify | Edit Surface** toolbar.

NOTE:

Detail Lines are "view-specific"; they appear only in the view in which they are placed. For an example, a **Detail Line** placed in a floor plan will not appear in a **3D** view.

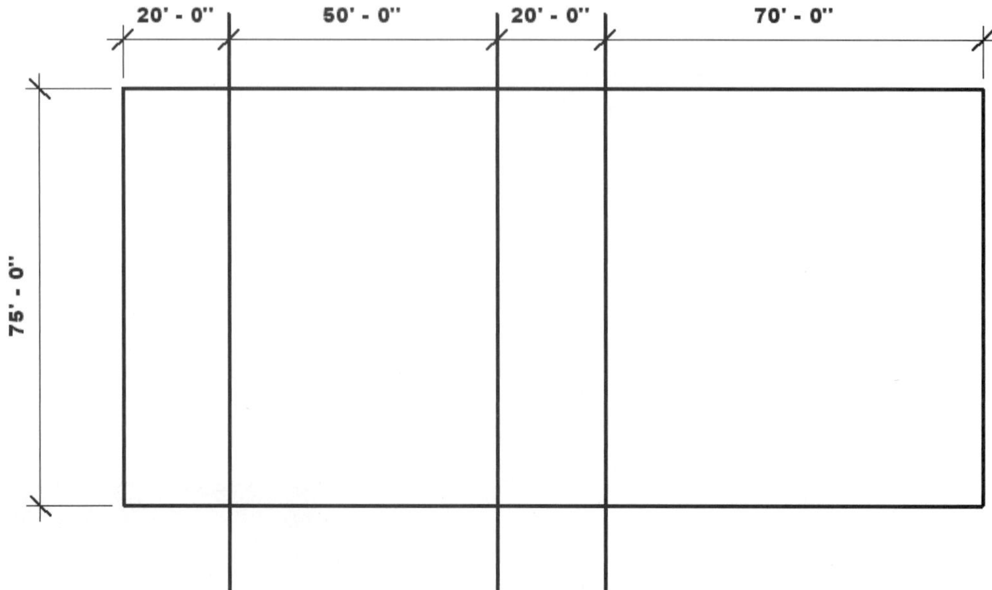

Figure 20-18

Place **Detail Lines**

7. In the **Modify | Edit Surface** toolbar, select the **Place Point** button.
8. In the **Options Bar**, set the **Elevation** to **-5′-0″**.

This will be the lowest point in your site.

9. Using the **Place Point** button, follow the diagram shown in Figure 20-19 while changing the **Elevations** in the **Options Bar** as you snap on the intersections of the lines you placed.

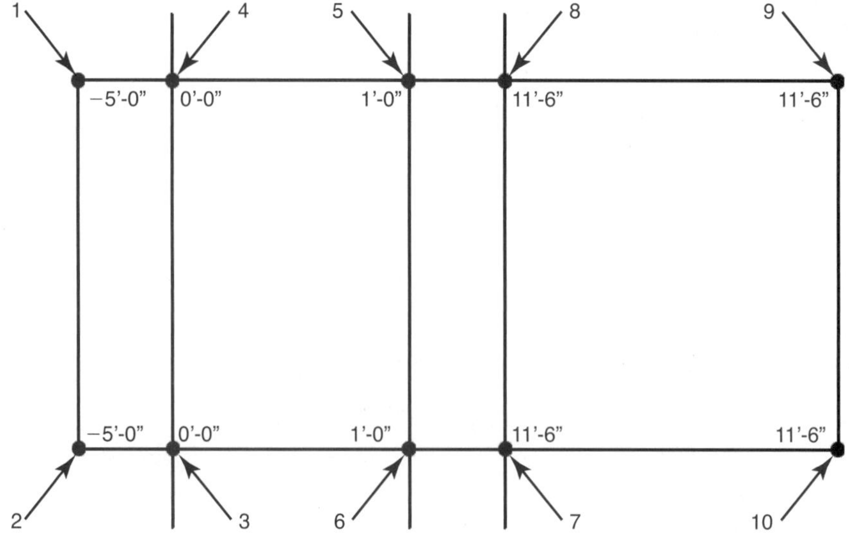

Figure 20-19

Change **Elevations** using **Place Points**

10. In the **Modify | Edit Surface** toolbar, select the **Finish Surface** button to complete the surface.
11. Select everything in the **Site** plan, and press the **Filter** button at the lower right of the **Drawing Editor** to bring up the **Filter** dialog box.
12. In the **Filter** dialog box, uncheck the **Topography** check box, and press the **OK** button to return to the **Drawing Editor** (see Figure 20-20).

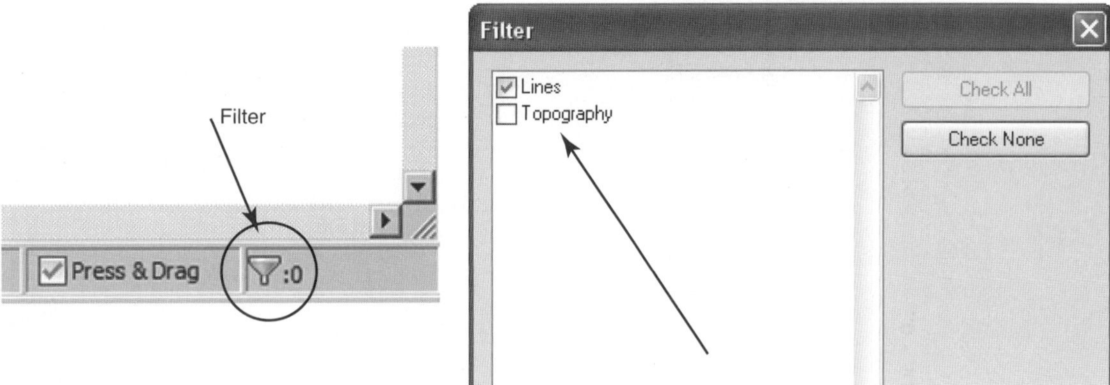

Figure 20-20

Filter button and dialog box

Now only the **Lines** have been selected.

13. With the **Detail Lines** selected, press the <**Del**> key to delete the lines, leaving only the toposurface.
14. Save the file.

Foundation Walls

EXERCISE 20-7 CREATING THE FOUNDATION WALLS

1. Set the **Scale** to **1/4″ = 1′-0″**.
2. Make sure you are in the **Site** plan.
3. Change to the **Home** toolbar.
4. In the **Home** toolbar, select the **Wall > Structural Wall** button to bring up the **Modify | Structural Place Wall** toolbar.
5. In the **Properties** dialog box, select **Basic Wall: Generic – 12″ Masonry** from the **Properties** drop-down list.
6. In the **Properties** dialog box, set the **Base Constraint** to **GRADE**, the **Base Offset** to **–1′-6″**, the **Top Constraint Up to level: FIRST FLOOR**, the **Top Offset** to **-1′-0 5/8″** (the height of the trusses plus the plywood floor), and then press the **OK** button (see Figure 20-21).

NOTE:

This will set the bottom of the foundation wall 1′-6″ below the grade.

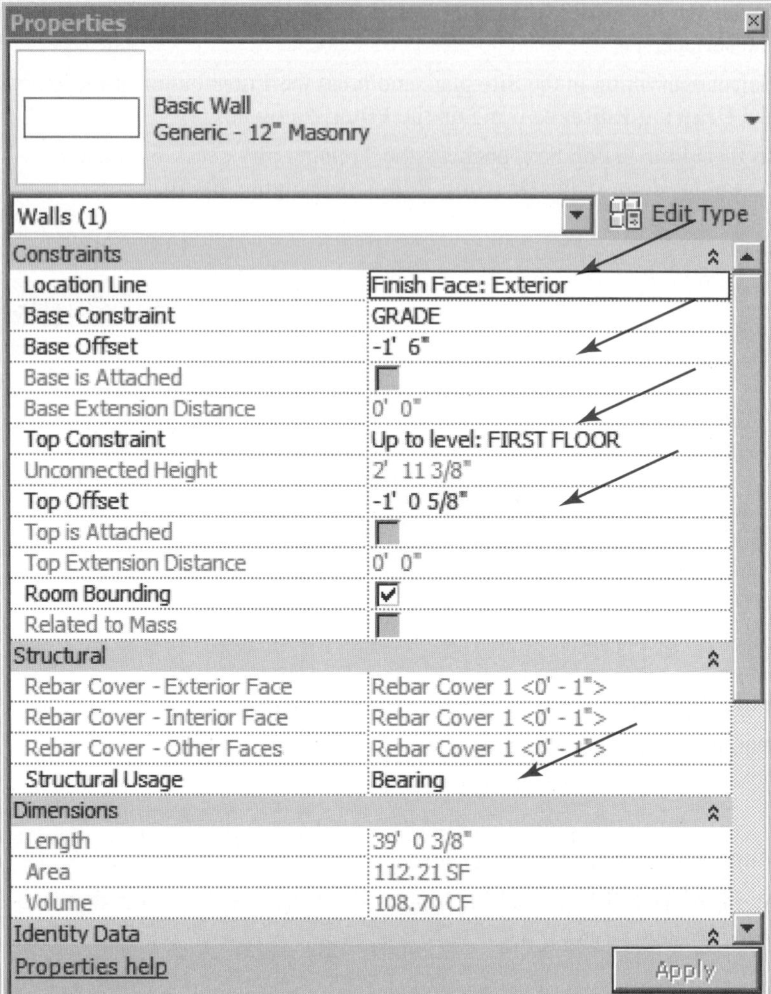

Figure 20-21

Properties dialog box

7. In the **Options Bar**, set the **Height** to **FIRST FLOOR**, and **Location Line** to **Finish Face: Exterior** (see Figure 20-22).

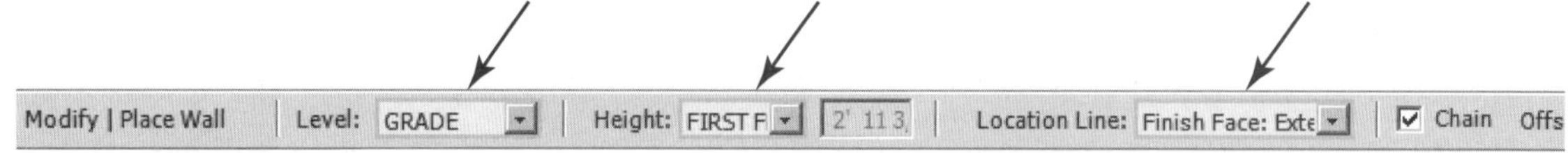

Figure 20-22

Options Bar

8. In the **Modify | Structural Place Wall** toolbar, select the **Rectangle** button from the **Draw** panel.
9. Place an enclosure as shown in Figure 20-23.
10. Change to the **Default 3D View** by selecting the **3D** button in the **Quick Access** toolbar (see Figure 20-24).
11. Hold down the **<Shift>** key while pressing the roller wheel on the mouse. Rotate the scene so that you can see the foundation below grade.
12. Select the **Home** tab to bring up the **Home** toolbar.

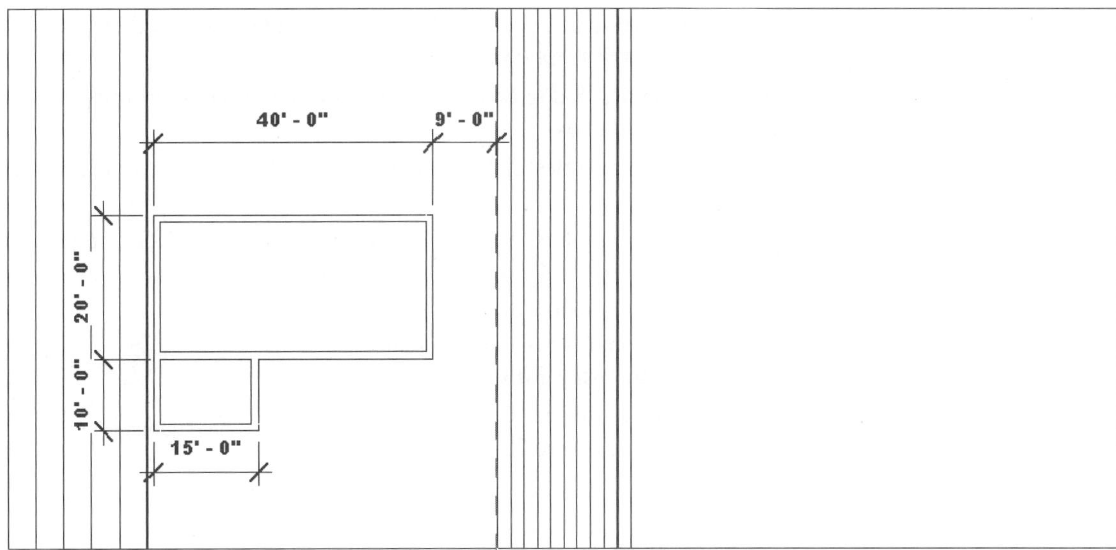

Figure 20-23

Place an enclosure

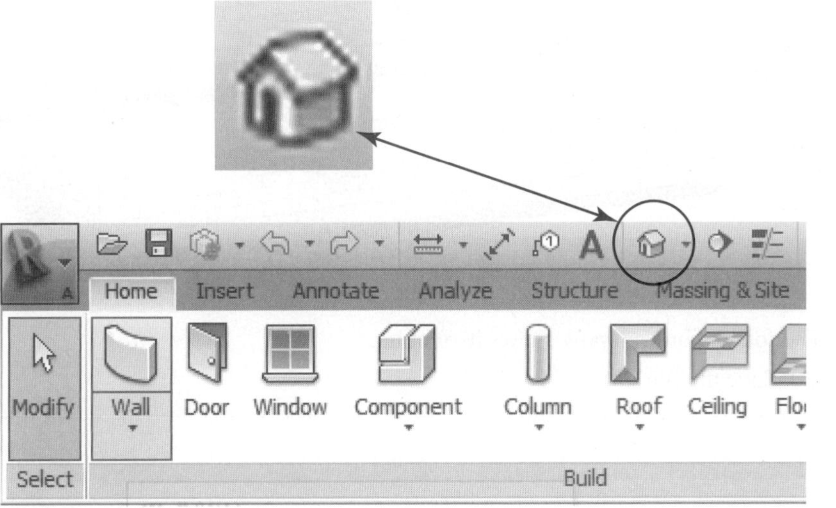

Figure 20-24

3D button

13. In the **Structure** toolbar, select the **Wall** button in the **Foundation** panel to bring up the **Modify | Place Wall Foundation** toolbar (see Figure 20-25).

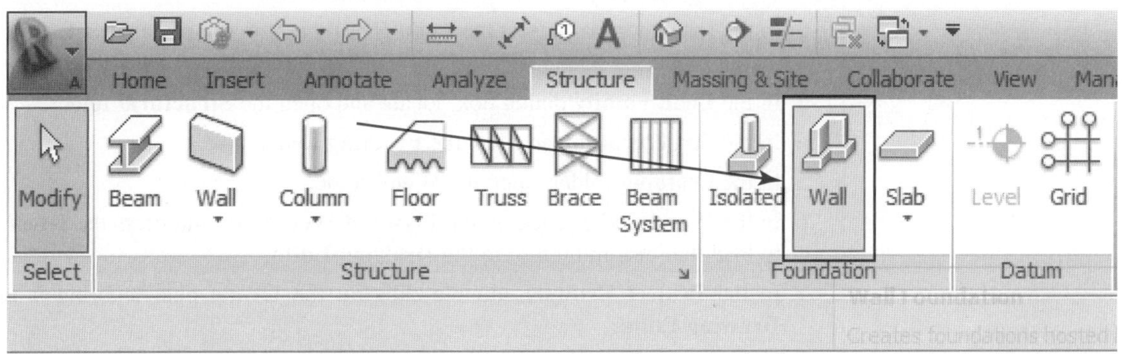

Figure 20-25

Wall Foundation button

14. In the **Properties** dialog box, select **Wall Foundation: Bearing Footing - 36″ × 12″** from the **Properties** drop-down list.
15. In the **Properties** dialog box, press the **Edit Type** button to bring up the **Type Properties** dialog box.
16. In the **Type Properties** dialog box, select the **Duplicate** button to bring up the **Name** dialog box.
17. In the **Name** dialog box, enter **20″ × 12″ STRIP FOOTING**, and press the **OK** button to return to the **Type Properties** dialog box.
18. In the **Type Properties** dialog box, change **Width** to **20″**, and press the **OK** buttons to return to the **Drawing Editor**.
19. Touch the bottom of each wall to place the strip footing (see Figure 20-26).

NOTE:

For this picture, the toposurface has been hidden.

Figure 20-26

Place the strip footing

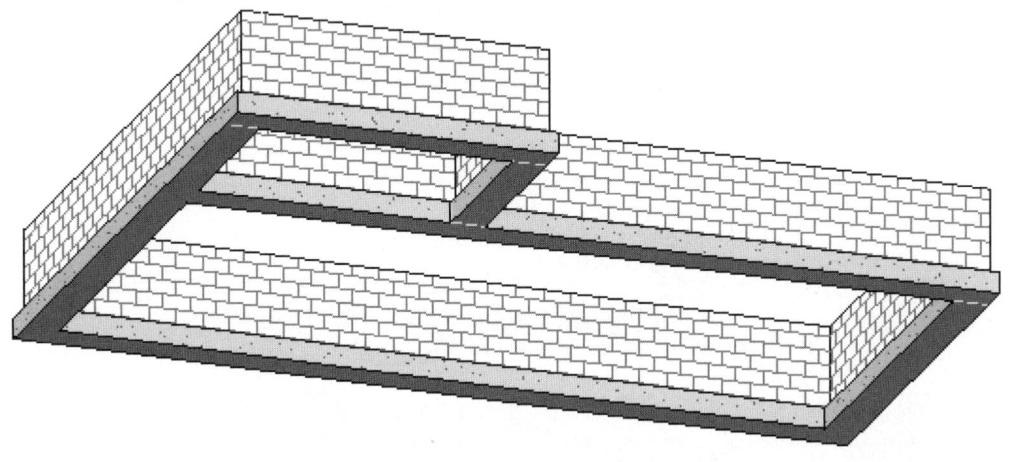

The foundation wall now shows its footing.

20. Save the file.

Framing and Floor

EXERCISE 20-8 CREATING THE FIRST FLOOR FRAMING AND HARDWOOD FLOOR

The First Floor framing is made from **1-3/4″ × 11-7/8″ Plywood Web joists @ 2′-0″ o/c.**

1. Select the **Insert** tab to bring up the **Insert** toolbar.
2. In the **Insert** toolbar, select the **Load Family** button to bring up the **Load Family** dialog box.
3. In the **Load Family** dialog box, locate and open the **Structural** folder.
4. In the **Structural** folder, open the **Framing** folder.
5. In the **Framing** folder, open the **Wood** folder.
6. In the **Wood** folder, click on the **Plywood Web Joist**, and press the **Open** button to load the joist and return to the **Drawing Editor**.
7. In the **Project Browser**, double-click on the **Grade** plan to bring it into the **Drawing Editor**.
8. Select the **Structure** tab to bring up the **Structure** toolbar.
9. In the **Structure** toolbar, select the **Beam System** button to bring up the **Modify | Create Beam System Boundary** toolbar (see Figure 20-27).

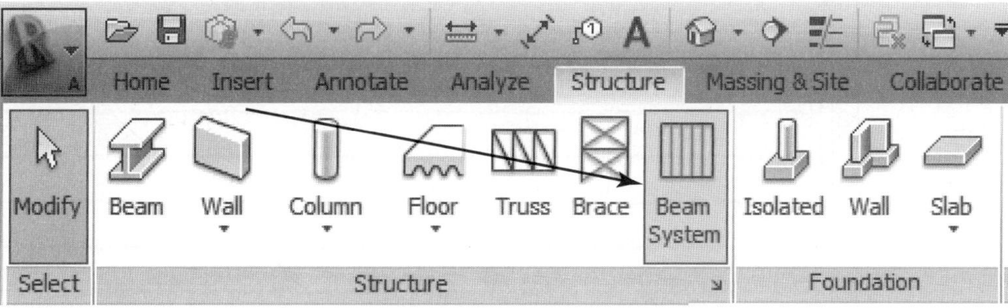

Figure 20-27

Beam System button

10. In the **Modify | Place Structural Beam System** toolbar, select the **Automatic Beam System** button.
11. In the **Properties** dialog box, set the **Elevation** to **2′-5 1/4″**, the **Layout Rule** to **Fixed Distance**, the **Fixed Spacing** to **2′-0″,** the **Justification** to **Beginning**, and the **Beam Type** to the **Plywood Web Joist: 1 3/4 × 11 7/8** that you loaded. Press the **OK** button to return to the **Drawing Editor** (see Figure 20-28).

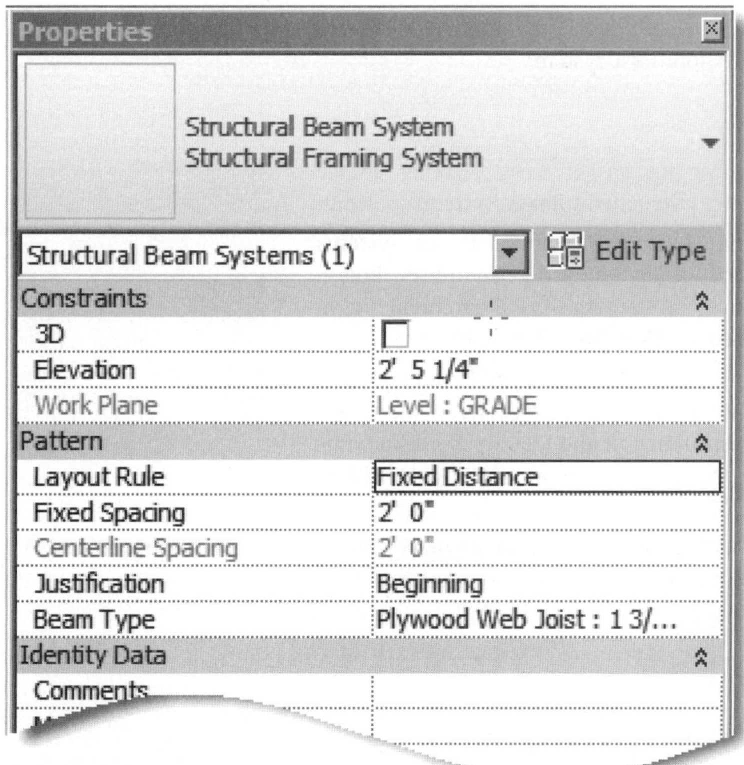

Figure 20-28

Properties dialog box

12. Click on the foundation, and dashed lines will appear. Click again to create the floor joist system (see Figure 20-29).
13. Press the **<Esc>** key to end the command.
14. Move your cursor over the foundation walls until the dashed line from the **Automatic Beam System** appears.

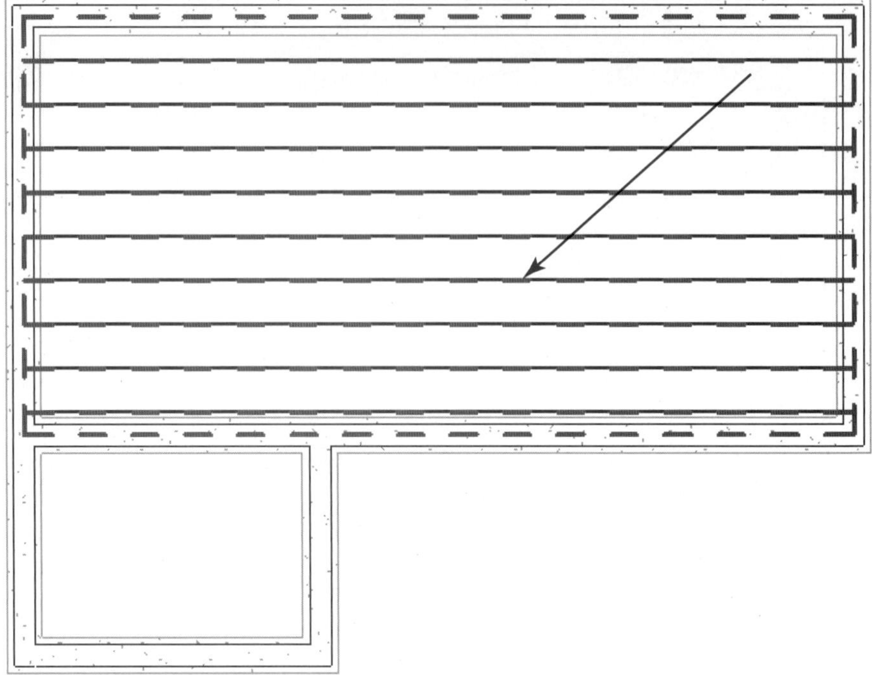

Figure 20-29

Create the floor joist system

15. Click on the dashed lines to bring up the **Modify | Structural Beam Systems** toolbar.
16. In the **Modify | Structural Beam Systems** toolbar, select the **Edit Boundary** button to bring up the **Modify | Structural Beam Systems > Edit Boundary** toolbar.
17. In the **Modify | Structural Beam Systems > Edit Boundary** toolbar, select the **Beam Direction** button and touch the left line; this sets the beam direction (see Figures 20-30 and 20-31).

NOTE:

The beams you placed will disappear, and a blue rectangle will appear in their place; this is the boundary. Also notice the double lines that indicate the direction of the joists (see Exercise 14-8 in Chapter 14).

18. In the **Modify | Structural Beam Systems > Edit Boundary** toolbar, select the **Finish Edit Mode** button to complete the joists and return to the **Drawing Editor**.
19. Set the **Detail Level** to **Medium** to see the joists.

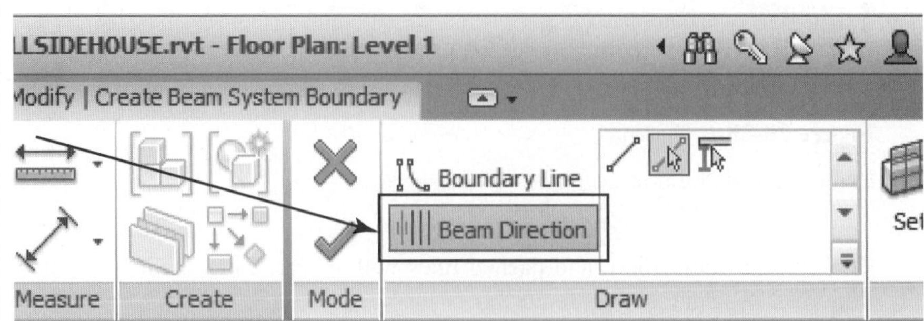

Figure 20-30

Beam Direction button

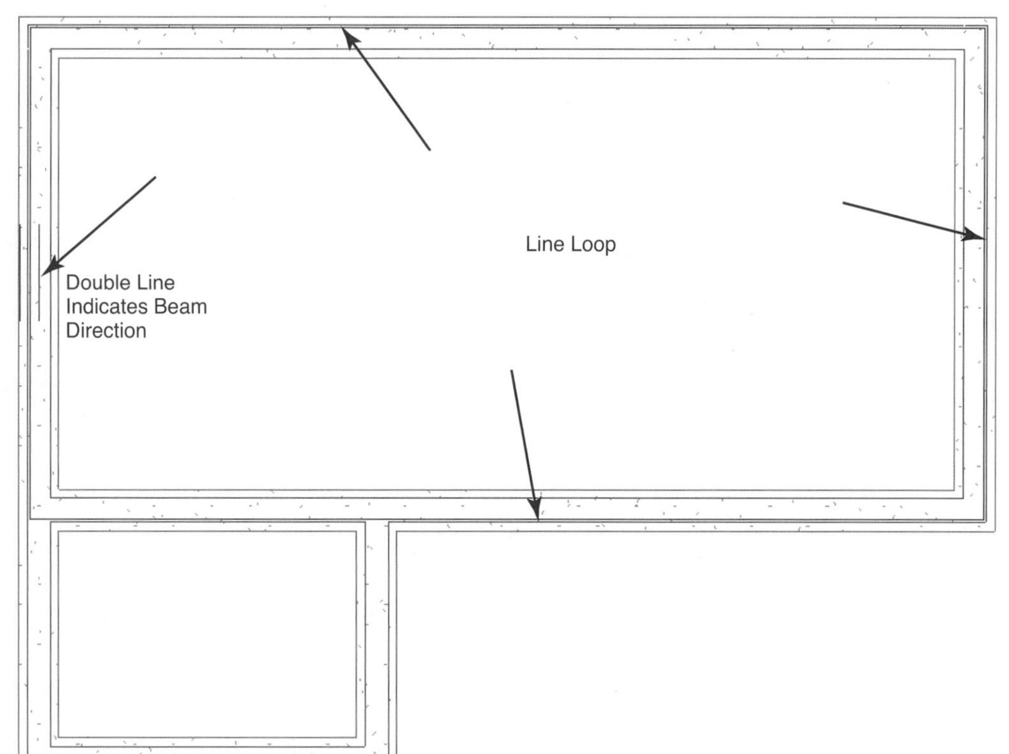

Figure 20-31

Setting the beam direction

The joists will stop at the inside of the foundation. To fix this, do the following:

20. Select all the joists to bring up their **Properties** dialog box.

TIP: This selection process is easier if you select one of the joists, **RMB**, and pick **Select All Instances > Visible in View** from the contextual menu that appears.

21. In the **Properties** dialog box, scroll down to the **Construction** section, and set the **Start extension** and **End extension** to **10-3/4″.** (This will extend the joists to the inside of the wall sheathing.)
22. Press the **OK** button to return to the **Drawing Editor**.

You may have to add joists. To do this, select the joist, click on the **Pushpin** to unconstrain it, and make a copy.

23. Press the **OK** button to return to the **Drawing Editor**.
24. Change to the **Default 3D View**. Set the **Detail Level** to **Medium**, and turn the **Shadows** to **On** (see Figure 20-32).
25. For the hardwood floor, double-click the **GRADE** view in the **Project Browser** to bring it into the **Drawing Editor**.
26. In the **Home toolbar**, select the **Floor > Floor** button to bring up the **Modify | Create Floor Boundary** toolbar.

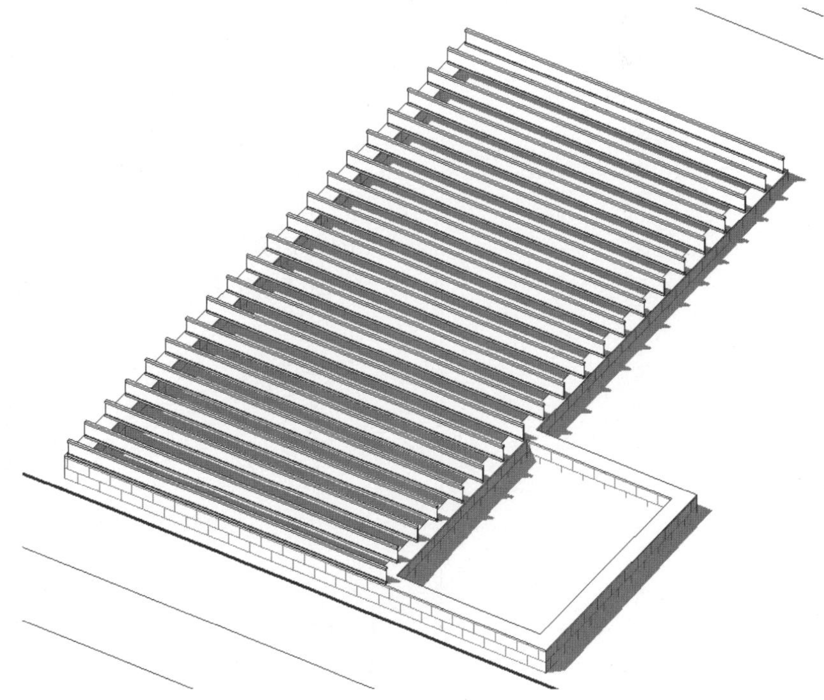

Figure 20-32

Set **Detail Level** and **Shadows**

27. In the **Properties** dialog box, press the **Edit Type** button to bring up the **Edit Type** dialog box.
28. In the **Edit Type** dialog box, select the **Generic – 12″** floor from the **Type** drop-down list.
29. In the **Edit Type** dialog box, press the **Duplicate** button to bring up the **Name** dialog box.
30. In the **Name** dialog box, enter **3/4″ HARDWOOD FLOOR**, and press the **OK** button to return to the **Type Properties** dialog box.
31. In the **Type Properties** dialog box, press the **Edit** button in the **Structure** field to bring up the **Edit Assembly** dialog box.
32. In the **Edit Assembly** dialog box, change the **Material** for **Structure [1]** to **Wood – Flooring**, and the **Thickness** to **3/4″**.
33. Press the **OK** buttons to return to the **Properties** dialog box.
34. In the **Properties** dialog box, set the level to **Grade**, and the **Height Offset From Level** to **2′-6″**.
35. Press the **OK** button to return to the **Drawing Editor**.
36. In the **Modify | Create Floor Boundary** toolbar, select the **Rectangle** button in the **Draw** panel.
37. Place the rectangle around the joists, and then press the **Finish Edit Mode** button to create the floor (see Figure 20-33).
38. Change to the **Default 3D View** to see the result.

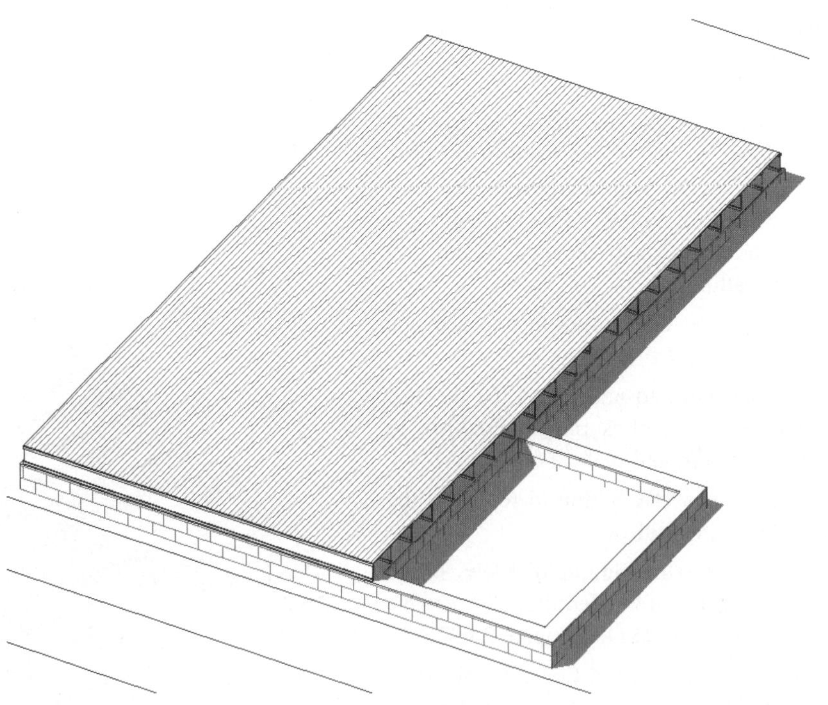

Figure 20-33

3D view of floor

39. Change to the **FIRST FLOOR** Plan view.
40. In the **View** toolbar, select the **Section** button.
41. Place a cross section and lateral section as shown in Figure 20-34.

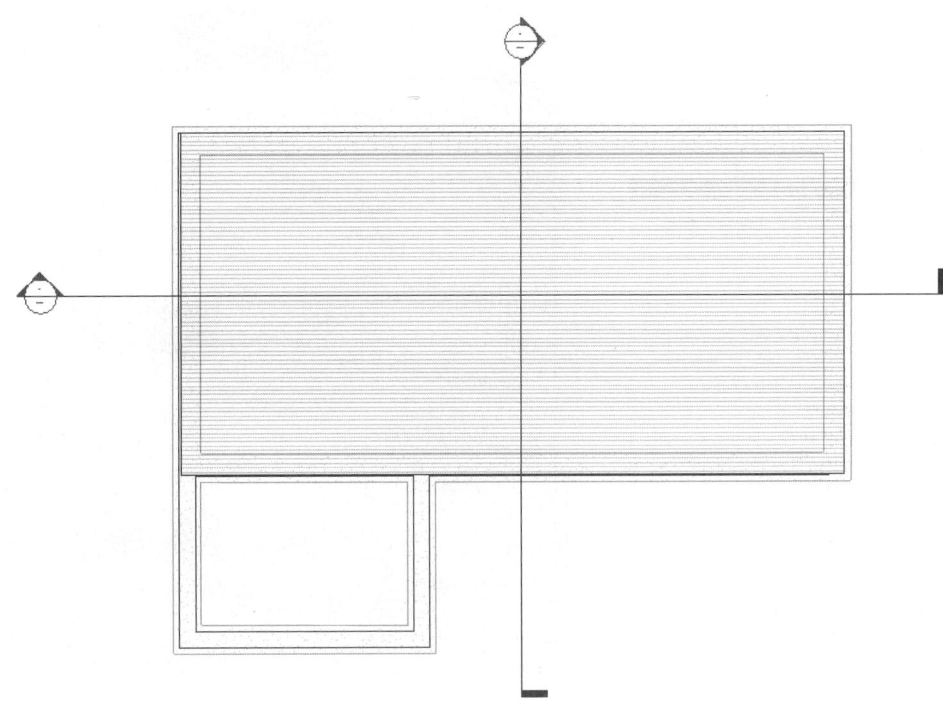

Figure 20-34

Place a cross section and lateral section

42. Save the file.

Exterior Walls

The exterior walls for the **HILLSIDE HOUSE** are 2″ × 6″ wood stud with a 1/2″ exterior sheathing, 3/4″ vertical wood plank, and 1/2″ gypsum wall board on the interior.

EXERCISE 20-9 **CREATING THE VERTICAL PLANK MATERIAL**

1. Select the **Manage** tab to bring up the **Manage** toolbar.
2. In the **Manage** toolbar, select the **Materials** button to bring up the **Materials** dialog box.
3. In the **Materials** dialog box, select **Finishes - Exterior – Siding - Clapboard** (see Figure 20-35).

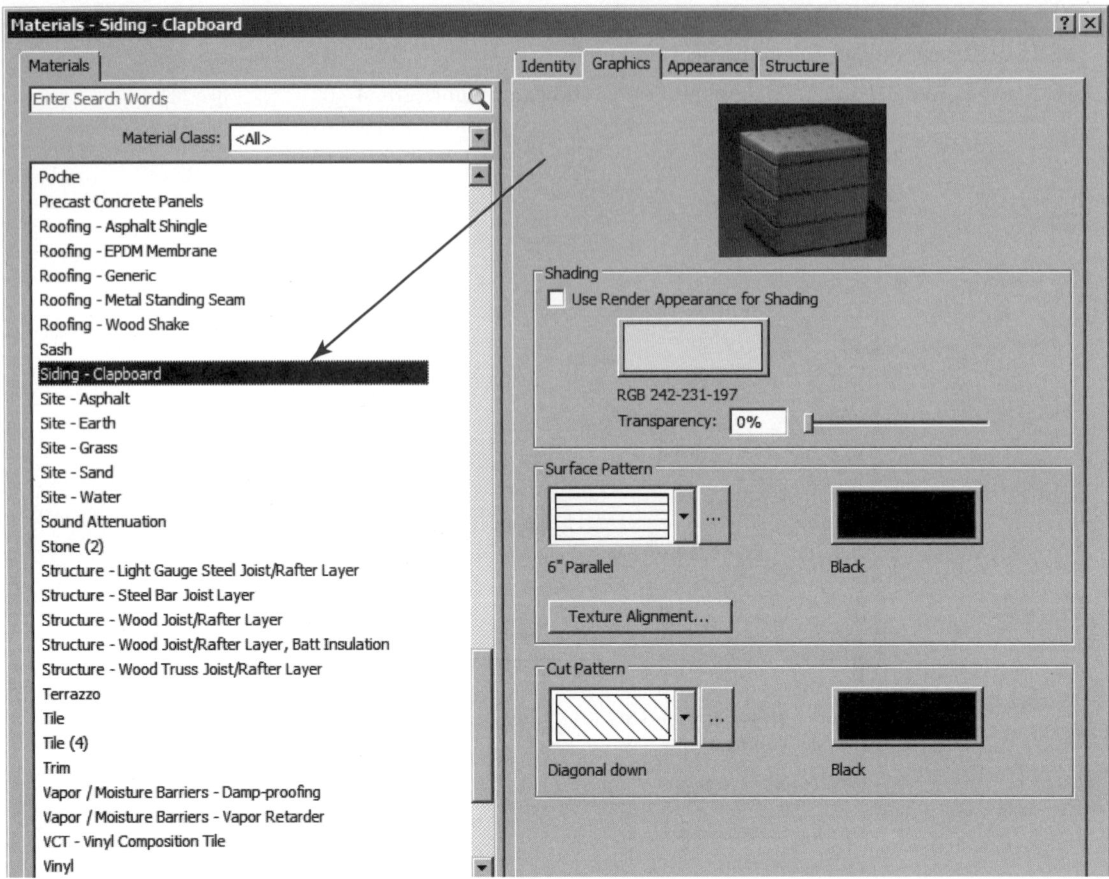

Figure 20-35

Materials dialog box

4. Click on the **Render Appearance** tab, and notice that the picture of the material is displayed on a cube (see Figure 20-36).
5. In the **Render Appearance** tab, select the drop-down list (1), then **Walls** (2), and finally (3) **mental ray – Production Quality** (see Figure 20-37).

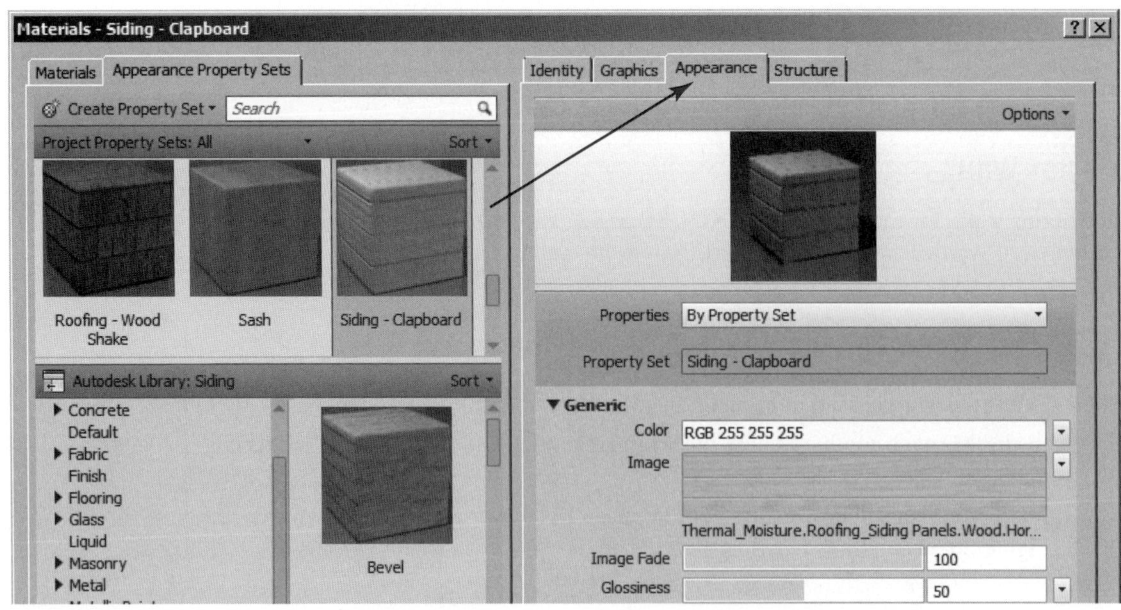

Figure 20-36

Render Appearance tab

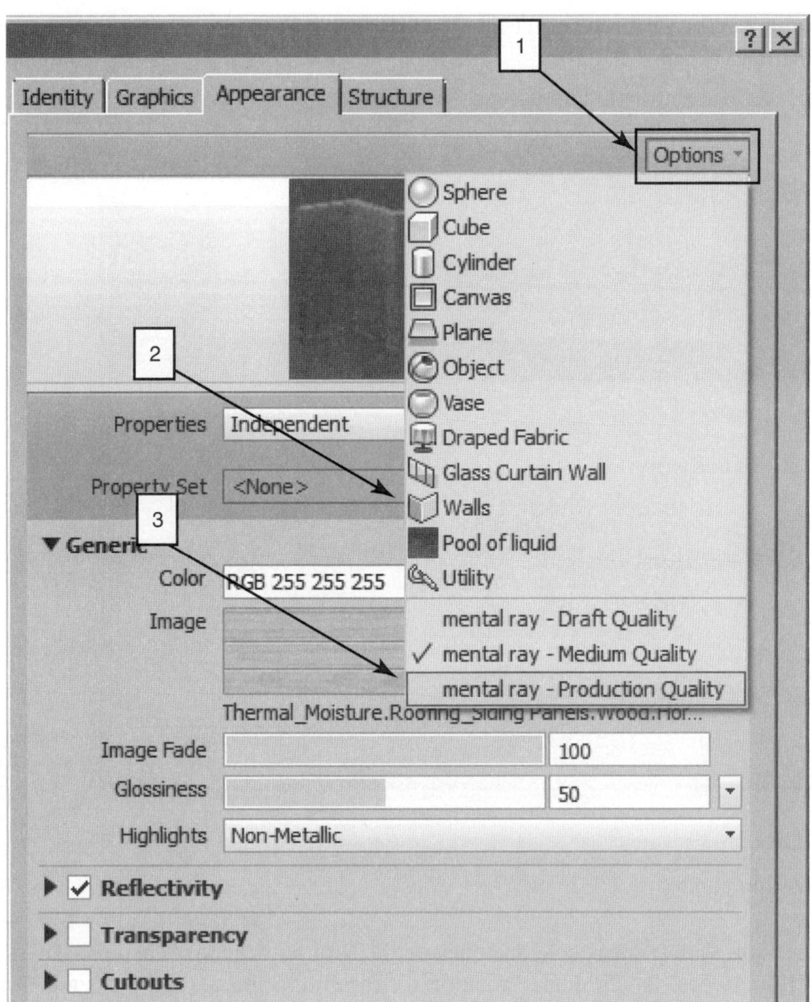

Figure 20-37

Select the **Render Appearance** drop-down list to view the options

The **Siding** is placed sideways, but the siding for this house needs to be vertical.

6. Click on the image of the siding to bring up the **Texture Editor** (see Figure 20-38).

Figure 20-38

Texture Editor

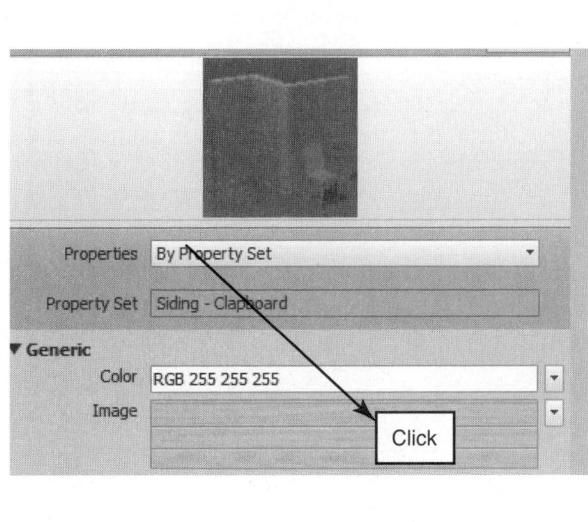

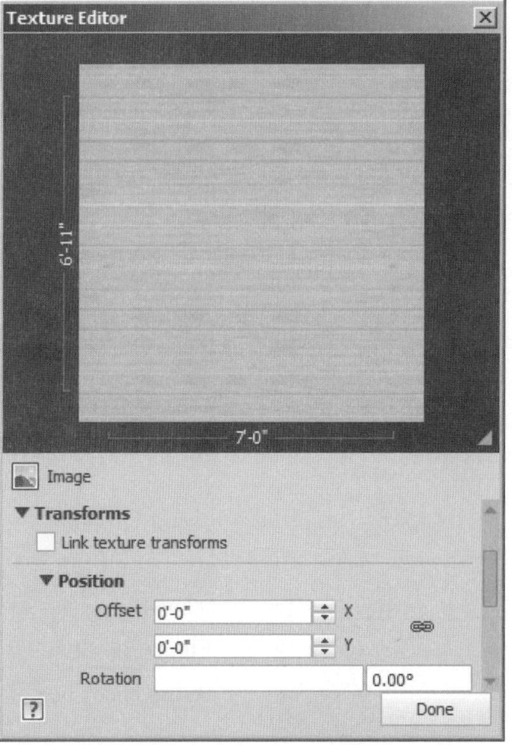

7. In the **Texture Editor**, select the **Transforms > Position** arrows to expose the **Position** controls.
8. Change the rotation to **90.00 degrees** (see Figure 20-39).

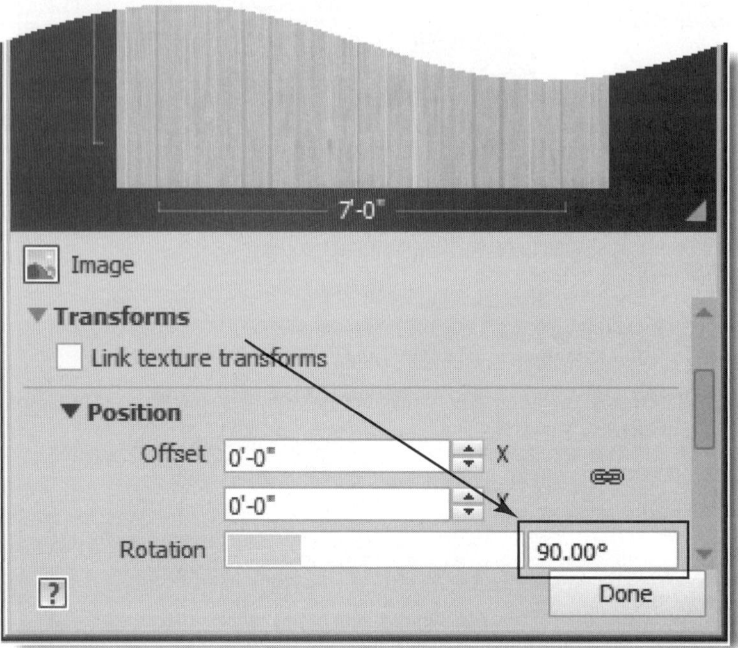

Figure 20-39

Position controls

9. Check the **Bump** check box, and click on the **Bump** image to bring up its **Texture Editor**. Repeat the 90 degree rotation for the **Bump** image, and press the **Done** button (see Figure 20-40).

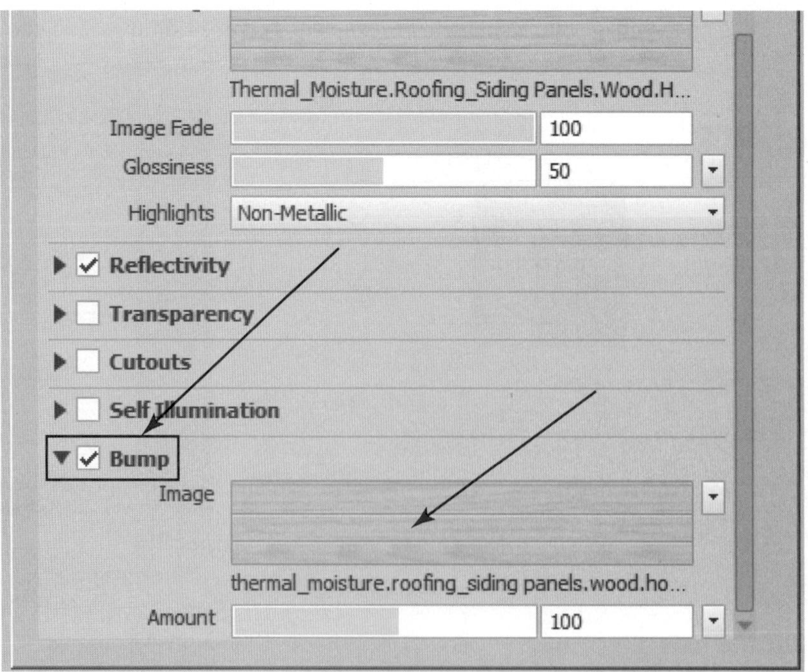

Figure 20-40

Bump check box

NOTE:

A **Bump** image (or **Bump Map**) is an image that causes a material to have a 3D texture. It is actually just a bitmap or raster image. If you increase its amount, the texture appears deeper. For this exercise, when the **Generic** image is rotated, the **Bump** must also be rotated, or the material will have horizontal and vertical lines. This is a good time to experiment with the different settings to see the result.

If you want to see a clearer view of the change in the material, change back to a cube (see Figure 20-41).

The **Material** will show when you are rendering, but you also need to set the surface texture when you are working.

10. Return to the **Graphics** tab in the **Materials** dialog box.
11. Click on the **Surface Pattern** button (which will be 6″ Parallel by default) to bring up the **Fill Patterns** dialog box.
12. In the **Fill Patterns** dialog box, press the **New** button to bring up the **Add Surface Pattern** dialog box.
13. In the **Add Surface Pattern** dialog box, enter **VERTICAL 6″ PARALLEL** in the **Name** field.
14. Set the **Line angle** to **90**, **Line spacing** to **6″**, select the **Parallel lines** radio button, and then press the **OK** buttons to return to the **Materials** dialog box (see Figure 20-42).

Figure 20-41

View of the change in the cube material

You have now modified the **Siding - Clapboard** material to be used for your exterior walls.

You have made all the materials with which to display your wall components; now you will create the wall assembly.

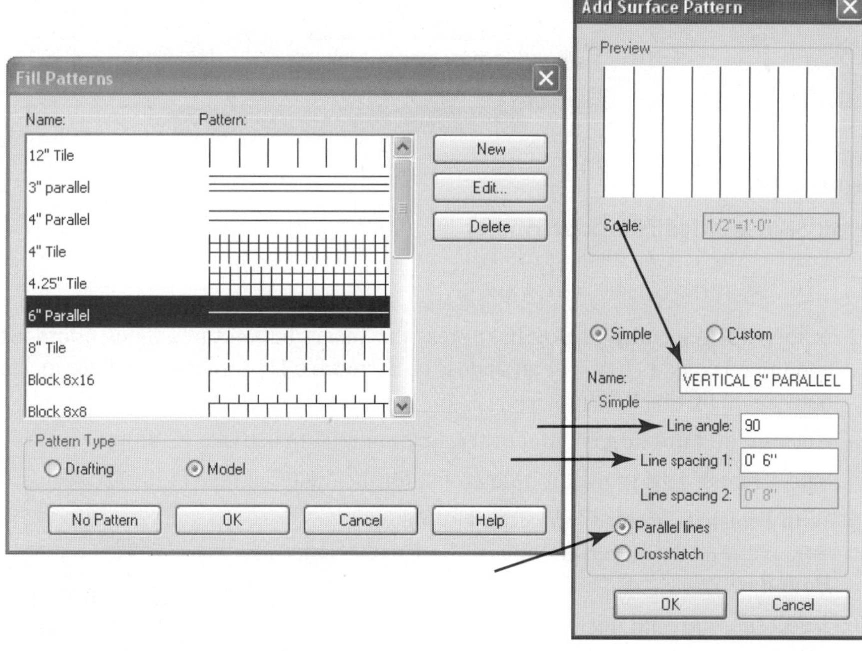

Figure 20-42

Fill Patterns and **Add Surface Pattern** dialog boxes

15. Save the file.

EXERCISE 20-10 **CREATING THE HILLSIDE HOUSE EXTERIOR WALL ASSEMBLY**

1. Double-click on **FIRST FLOOR** (under **Floor Plans**) in the **Project Browser** to bring the **FIRST FLOOR** plan into the **Drawing Editor**.
2. Change the **Scale** to **1/4″ = 1′-0″**.
3. Set the **Detail Level** to **Medium**.
4. Change to the **Home** toolbar.
5. In the **Home** toolbar, select the **Wall** button.
6. In the **Properties** dialog box, select the **Basic Wall: Generic - 6″** from the **Properties** drop-down list.
7. In the **Properties** dialog box, select the **Edit Type** button to bring up the **Type Properties** dialog box.
8. In the **Type Properties** dialog box, select the **Duplicate** button to bring up the **Name** dialog box.
9. In the **Name** dialog box, enter **HILLSIDE HOUSE EXTERIOR WALLS**, and press the **OK** button to return to the **Type Properties** dialog box.
10. In the **Type Properties** dialog box, press the **Edit** button in the **Structure** field to bring up the **Edit Assembly** dialog box.
11. In the **Edit Assembly** dialog box, press the **Preview** button at the lower left of the dialog box, and then make sure that the **View** is set to **Section: Modify type attributes** (see Figure 20-43).

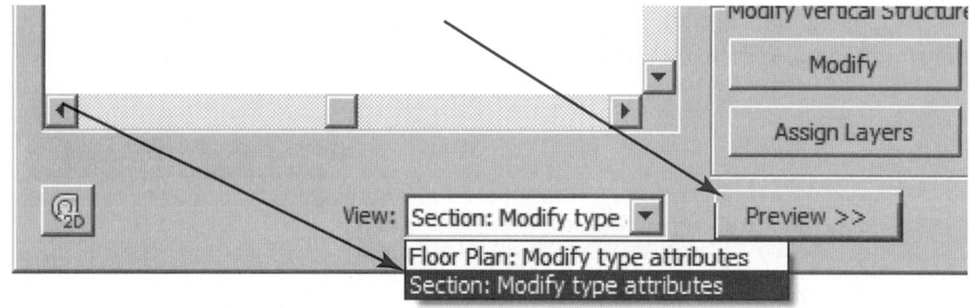

Figure 20-43

Select **Section: Modify type attributes**

12. In the **Edit Assembly** dialog box, press the **Insert** button three times in order to add three layers. (They will all appear as **Structure [1] Function** and are located between the **Core Boundaries**.)
13. Click in the **Function** column of the first material to activate its drop-down list.
14. Select **Finish 1** from the drop-down list for this material (see Figure 20-44).
15. With **Finish 1** selected, press the **Up** button to move it to the **Exterior Side** of the **Core Boundary**.
16. Select the **Material** next to **Finish 1** (usually **<By Category>**), and then press the button that appears at the right side of the column to open the **Material Library**.
17. In the **Material Library**, select the **Finishes – Exterior – Siding - Clapboard** material, and press the **OK** button to return to the **Edit Assembly** dialog box.
18. Click in the **Thickness** column, and set the thickness to **3/4″**.

NOTE:

What does the number **[4]** after **Finish 1** mean? It is the **Line Width** number.

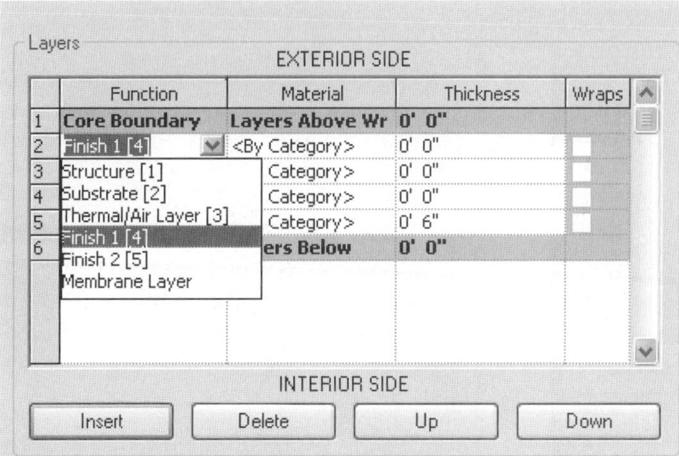

Figure 20-44

Function drop-down list

Notice that preview shows the exterior siding (see Figure 20-45).

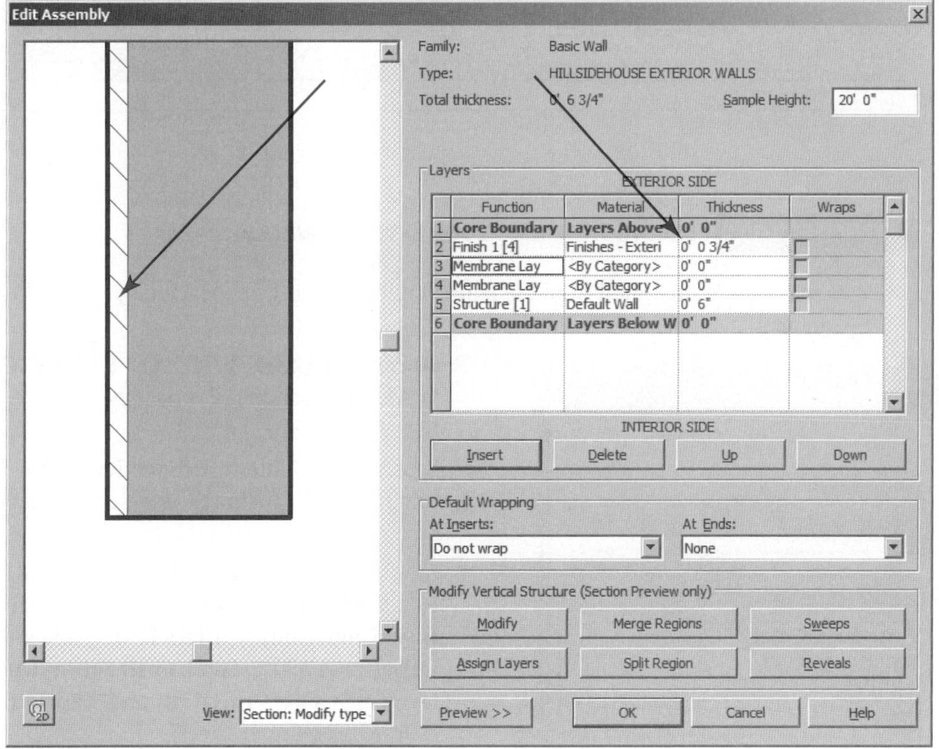

Figure 20-45

Preview shows the exterior siding

19. Repeat the process for the other layers.
20. Make **Structure [1]** the **5-1/2″** stud, with **Default Wall** material, and place it between the **Core Boundaries**.
21. Make the next layer **Substrate [2]** the **1/2″** sheathing, with **Wood - Sheathing** material, and place it above **Structure [1]** outside the **Core Boundary**.
22. Make the next layer **Finish 2 [5]** the inside **1/2″** gypsum board with **Finishes – Interior – Gypsum Wall Board** material, and place it below **Structure [1]** outside the **Core Boundary** (see Figure 20-46).
23. Press the **OK** buttons to return to the **Drawing Editor**.
24. Save the file.

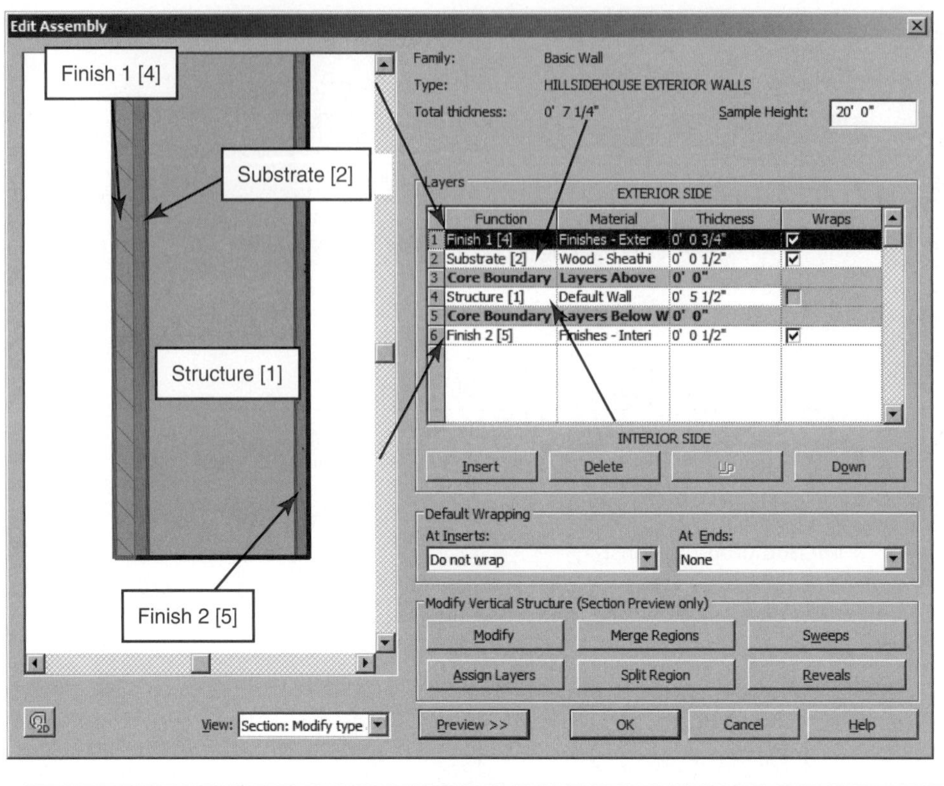

Figure 20-46

Edit Assembly dialog box

EXERCISE 20-11 PLACING THE FIRST FLOOR EXTERIOR WALLS

1. Select the **Wall** button from the **Home** toolbar to bring up the **Modify | Place Wall** toolbar.
2. Select **HILLSIDE HOUSE EXTERIOR WALLS** from the **Properties** drop-down list.
3. Select the **Element Properties** button to bring up the **Instance Properties** dialog box.
4. In the **Properties** dialog box, set the **Location Line** to **Finish Face: Exterior**, **Base Constraint = FIRST FLOOR**, **Base Offset = -1′-5/8″**, **Top Constraint = Up to level: SECOND FLOOR**, and **Top Offset = 0′-0″** (see Figure 20-47).
5. Press the **OK** button to return to the **Drawing Editor**.
6. Select the **Pick Lines** button.
7. Pick the foundation walls shown in Figures 20-48 and 20-49.
8. Select the **<Esc>** key to end the command.
9. Save the file.

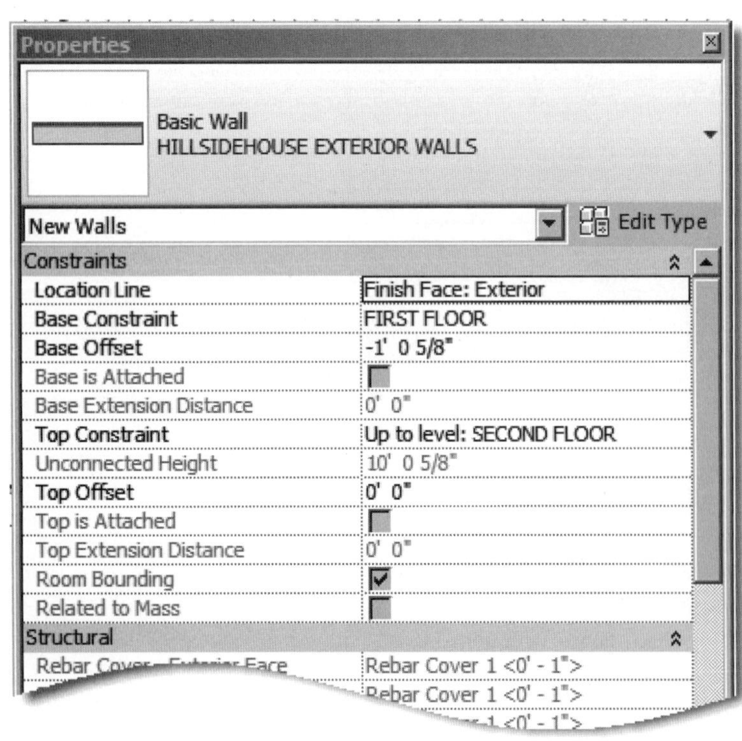

Figure 20-47

Properties dialog box

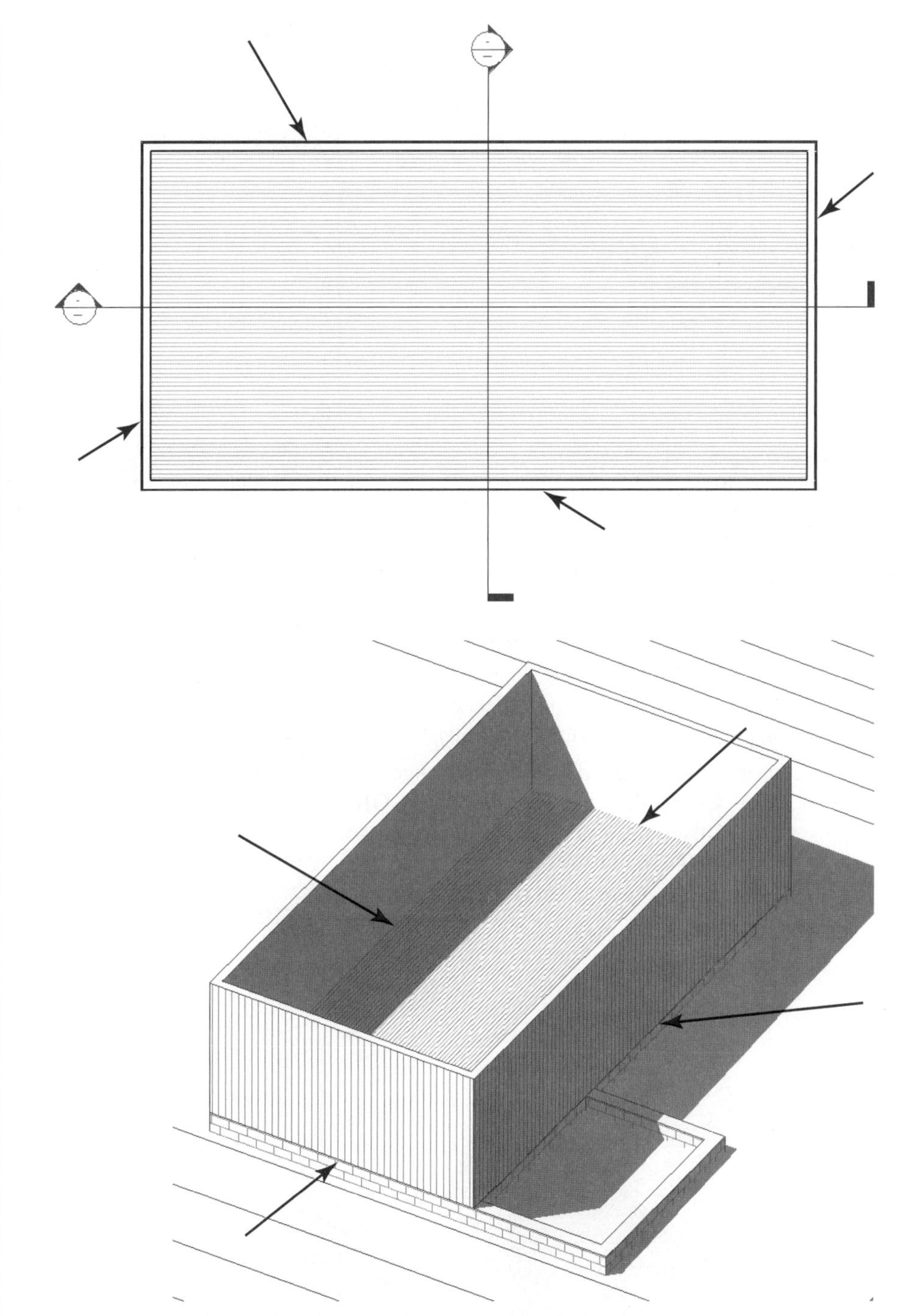

Figure 20-48
Pick foundation walls

Figure 20-49
3D view of walls

EXERCISE 20-12 CREATING THE SECOND FLOOR EXTERIOR WALLS

1. In the **FIRST FLOOR** plan view, select the **HILLSIDE HOUSE EXTERIOR WALLS** you just placed to bring up the **Modify | Walls** toolbar.
2. In the **Modify | Walls** toolbar, select the **Copy to Clipboard** button in the **Clipboard** panel to copy the walls.
3. In the **Modify | Walls** toolbar, select the **Paste > Aligned to Selected Levels** to bring up the **Select Levels** dialog box.
4. In the **Select Levels** dialog box, select **SECOND FLOOR**, and press the **OK** button to return to the **Drawing Editor** (see Figure 20-50).

> **NOTE:**
> You will get a warning that the walls will overlap. Don't worry. This is because the walls you are copying have a negative base offset. You will change this next.

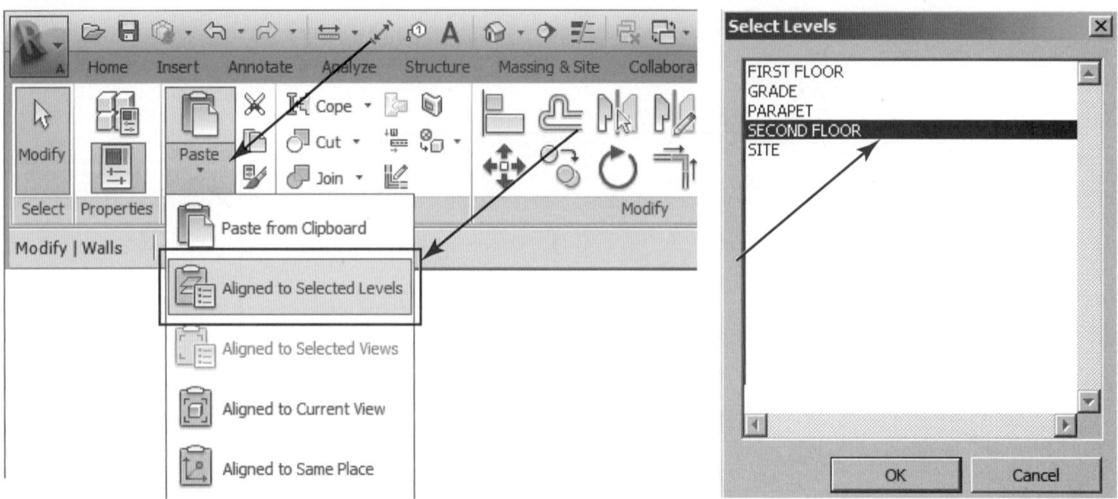

Figure 20-50

Select Levels dialog box

5. Select the **3D** button on the **Quick Access** toolbar to bring up the **Default 3D View** in the **Drawing Editor**.
6. Select the walls you just placed on the **SECOND FLOOR** to bring up the **Properties** dialog box for the walls.
7. In the **Properties** dialog box, change the **Base Constraint** to **SECOND FLOOR**, **Base Offset** to **0′-0″**, **Top Constraint** to **PARAPET**, **Top Offset** to **2′-0″**, and press the **OK** button to return to the **Drawing Editor**.
8. Save the file.

NOTE:

You are setting the **Top Offset** to **2′-0″** above the **PARAPET** level to form the 2′-0″ high parapet (see Figure 20-51).

Figure 20-51

Parapet

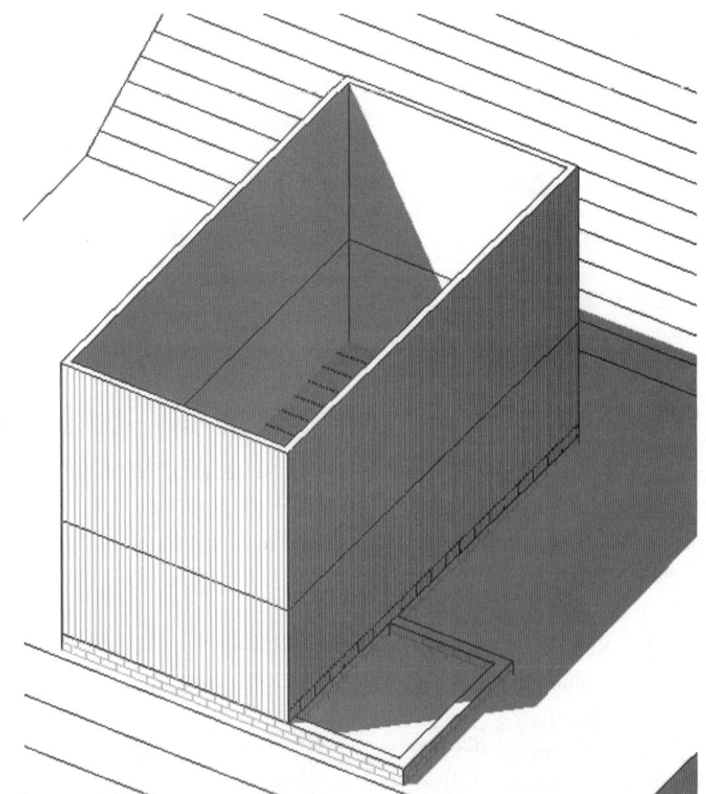

EXERCISE 20-13 CREATING THE SECOND FLOOR WING WALLS

> **NOTE:**
> The **SECOND FLOOR** wing walls are similar to the exterior walls except that they have sheathing and siding on both sides of the wall.

1. Double-click on **SECOND FLOOR** in the **Project Browser** to bring the **SECOND FLOOR** plan view into the **Drawing Editor**.
2. Change the **Scale** to **1/4″ = 1′-0″**.
3. Set the **Detail Level** to **Medium**.
4. In the **Home** toolbar, select the **Wall** button.
5. In the **Properties** drop-down list, select the **Basic Wall: HILLSIDE HOUSE EXTERIOR WALLS**.
6. In the **Properties** drop-down list, select the **Edit Type** button to bring up the **Type Properties** dialog box.
7. In the **Type Properties** dialog box, select the **Duplicate** button to bring up the **Name** dialog box.
8. In the **Name** dialog box, enter **HILLSIDE HOUSE EXTERIOR WING WALLS**, and press the **OK** button to return to the **Type Properties** dialog box.
9. In the **Type Properties** dialog box, press the **Edit** button in the **Structure** field to bring up the **Edit Assembly** dialog box.
10. In the **Edit Assembly** dialog box, press the **Insert** button one time in order to add one new layer above **Finish 2**.
11. Change the new layer to **Substrate [2]**, and **Finish 2** to **Finish 1 [4]**.
12. Set the new **Substrate [2]** material to **Wood - Sheathing**, **Thickness** to **1/2″**, and check the **Wraps** check box.
13. Set the new **Finish 2** material to **Finishes – Exterior – Siding - Clapboard**, **Width** to **3/4″**, and check the **Wraps** check box.
14. With the **Up** and **Down** buttons, move the layers, and press the **OK** button to return to the **Type Properties** dialog box.
15. In the **Type Properties** dialog box, change the **Wrapping at Ends** to **Exterior**, **Wall Function** to **Exterior**, and press the **OK** button to return to the **Properties** dialog box (see Figures 20-52 and 20-53).

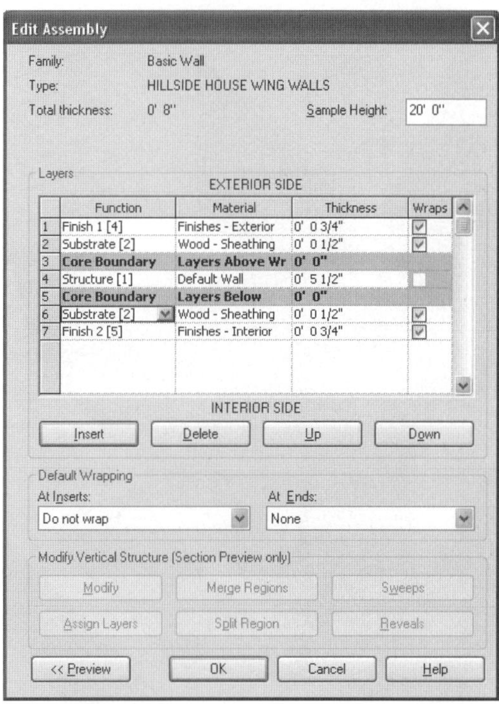

Figure 20-52

Edit Assembly dialog box

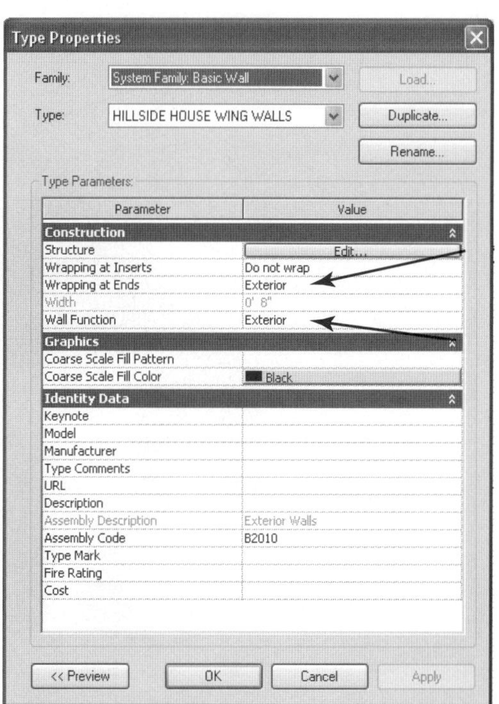

Figure 20-53

Type Properties dialog box

16. In the **Properties** dialog box, set the **Base Constraint** to **SECOND FLOOR**, **Base Offset** to **0′-0″**, **Top Constraint** to **PARAPET**, **Top Offset** to **2′-0″**, and press the **OK** button to return to the **Drawing Editor**.
17. Place **10′-0″** long **HILLSIDE HOUSE EXTERIOR WING WALLS** at the west side of the **SECOND FLOOR**, and **7′-0″ HILLSIDE HOUSE EXTERIOR WING WALLS** at the east side of the **SECOND FLOOR**.
18. Place **10′-0″** long **HILLSIDE HOUSE EXTERIOR WING WALLS** at the south side of the **SECOND FLOOR** to create the office enclosure (see Figures 20-54 and 20-55).
19. Save the file

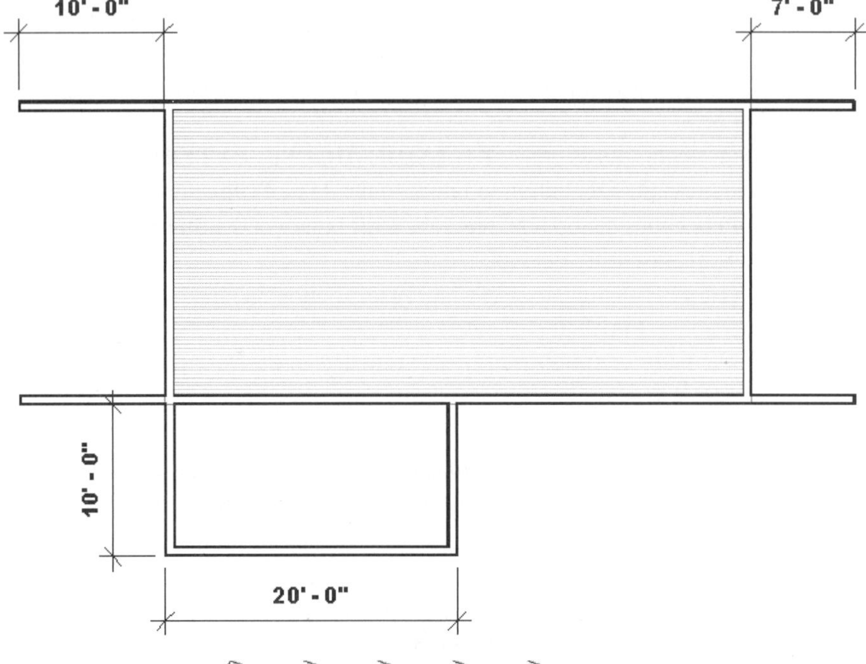

Figure 20-54
Create the office enclosure

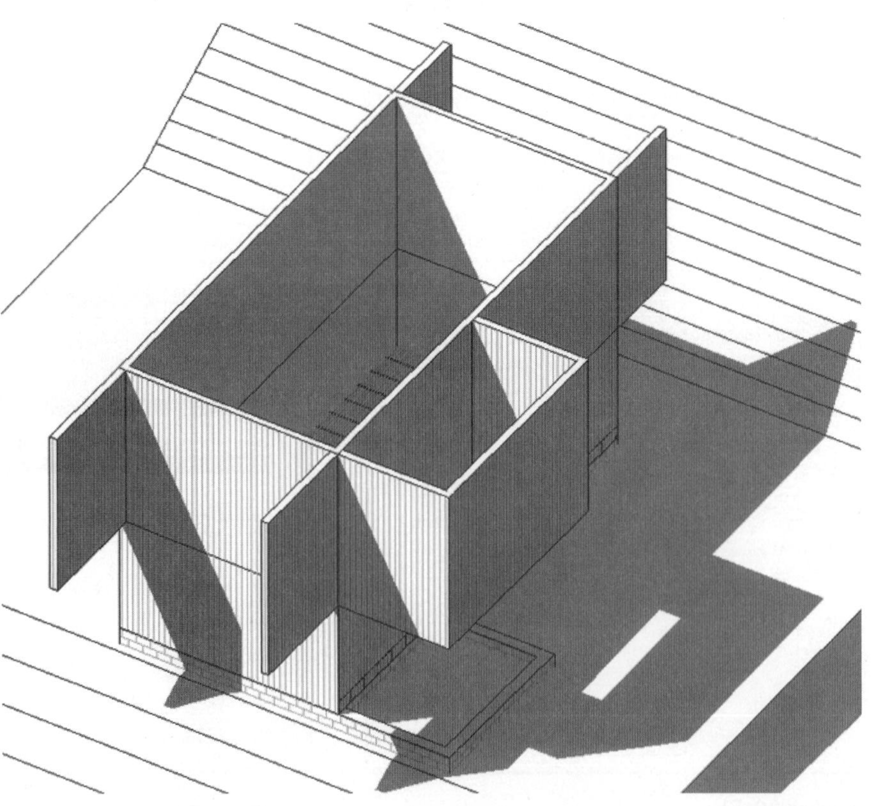

Figure 20-55
3D view of the office enclosure

EXERCISE 20-14 CREATING THE SKYLIGHT SIDE WALLS

1. Double-click on the **South Elevation** in the **Project Browser** to bring it into the **Drawing Editor**.
2. Select the south wall to bring up the **Modify | Walls** toolbar.
3. In the **Modify | Walls** toolbar, select the **Edit Profile** button to bring up the **Modify | Walls > Edit Profile** toolbar.
4. In the **Modify | Walls > Edit Profile** toolbar, select the **Line** button, and modify the top profile of the wall as shown in Figure 20-56.
5. After you have modified the wall profile, press the **Finish Edit Mode** button to complete the wall, and then repeat the same operation for the other side (see Figure 20-57).
6. Save the file.

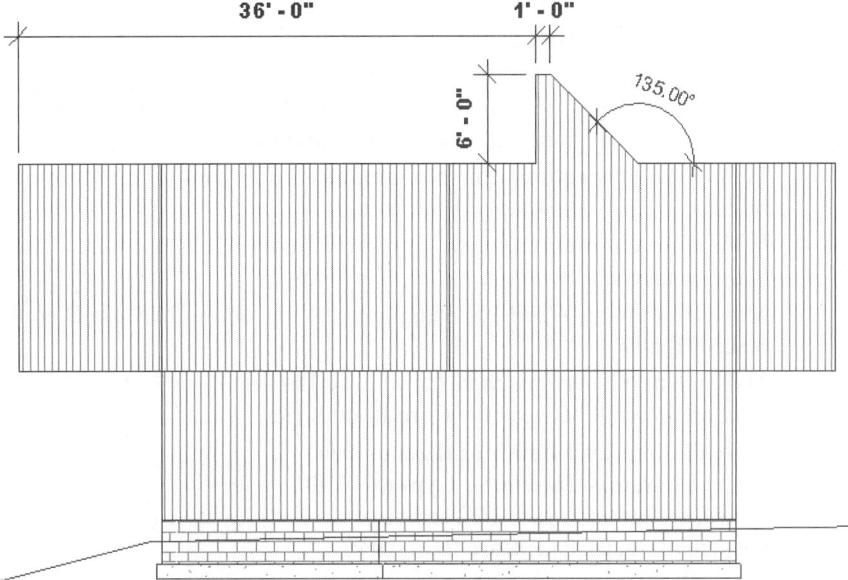

Figure 20-56

Modify the top profile of the wall

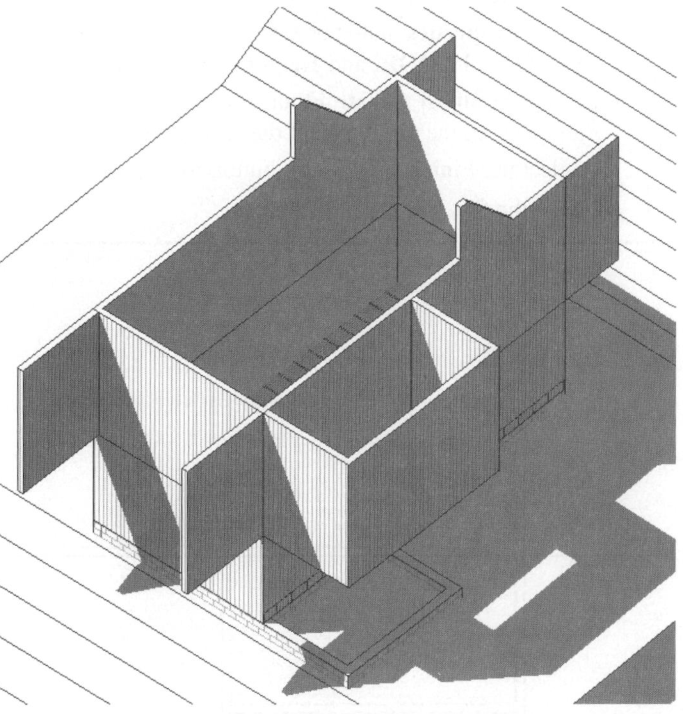

Figure 20-57

3D view of completed walls

Second-Story Floor

EXERCISE 20-15 CREATING THE SECOND FLOOR FLOORS

1. Double-click on the **SECOND FLOOR** plan view in the **Project Browser** to bring it into the **Drawing Editor**.
2. In the **Home** toolbar, select the **Floor** > **Floor** button to bring up the **Modify | Create Floor Boundary** toolbar.
3. In the **Properties** dialog box, select the **Edit Type** button to bring up the **Type Properties** dialog box.
4. In the **Type Properties** dialog box, select the **Basic Wall: 3/4″ HARDWOOD FLOOR** from the **Type** drop-down list.
5. In the **Type Properties** dialog box, select the **Duplicate** button to bring up the **Name** dialog box.
6. In the **Name** dialog box, enter **SECOND FLOOR 3/4″ HARDWOOD FLOOR**, and press the **OK** button to return to the **Type Properties** dialog box.
7. In the **Type Properties** dialog box, press the **Edit** button in the **Structure** field to bring up the **Edit Assembly** dialog box.
8. In the **Edit Assembly** dialog box, press the **Insert** button one time in order to add two new layers.
9. Move the existing **Wood Flooring** up to the top, above the **Core Boundary**, and make it **Finish 1**.
10. Make the next layer **Structure [1]** with the **Default Floor** material, **11-7/8″** thickness, and place it between the **Core Boundaries**.
11. Make the third layer **Finish 1 [4]**, set its material to **Finishes – Interior – Gypsum Wall Board**, set its thickness to **1/2″**, and place it on the bottom—outside the **Core Boundary**.
12. Press the **OK** buttons to return to the **Properties** dialog box.
13. In the **Properties** dialog box, set the **Level** to **SECOND FLOOR**, and **Height Offset From Level** to **0′-0″**.
14. In the **Modify | Create Floor Boundary** toolbar, select the **Pick Walls** button, and pick all the walls except the east and west wing walls.
15. Select the **Finish Edit Mode** button to complete the floor (see Figure 20-58).
16. Save the file.

NOTE:

For these exercises, you will use the **Floor** button, but you will not model the structure as you did on the first floor. Either method is fine, but with this second method, you will have to use detail components later to illustrate the framing in the **Section** views.

NOTE:

Trim the sketch lines as necessary, and make sure that they extend to the inside of the exterior sheathing.

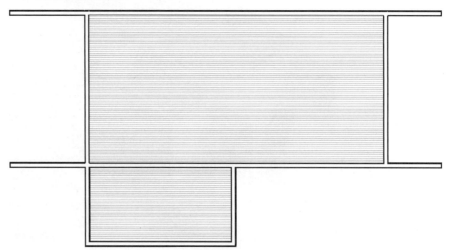

Figure 20-58

Second Floor drawing

Stairway

The stairway is tied to the exterior of the building so that it does not subtract from the area inside the house.

EXERCISE 20-16 CREATING THE STAIRWAY

1. Double-click on the **FIRST FLOOR** plan view in the **Project Browser** to bring it into the **Drawing Editor**.
2. Select one of the **HILLSIDE HOUSE EXTERIOR WALLS** to bring up the **Modify | Walls** toolbar.
3. In the **Modify | Walls** toolbar, select the **Create Similar** button to bring up the **Modify | Place Structural Wall** toolbar (see Figure 20-59).

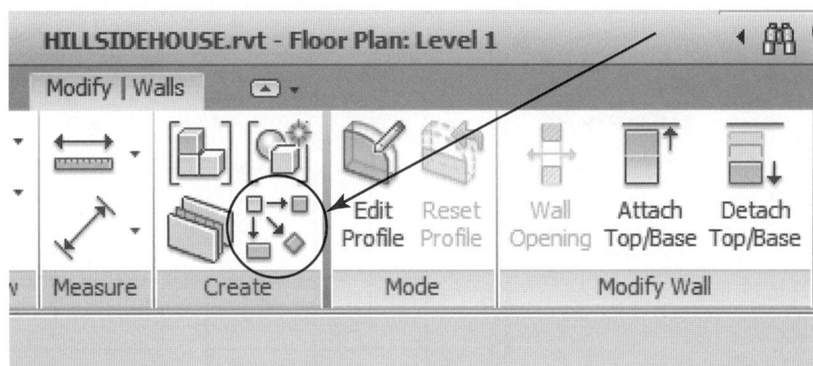

Figure 20-59

Create Similar button

TIP: You can get the same result by selecting the wall, **RMB**, and selecting **Create Similar** from the contextual menu that appears to bring up the **Modify | Place Structural Wall** toolbar.

4. In the **Modify | Place Structural Wall** toolbar, select the **Line** button, and place walls as shown in Figure 20-60.

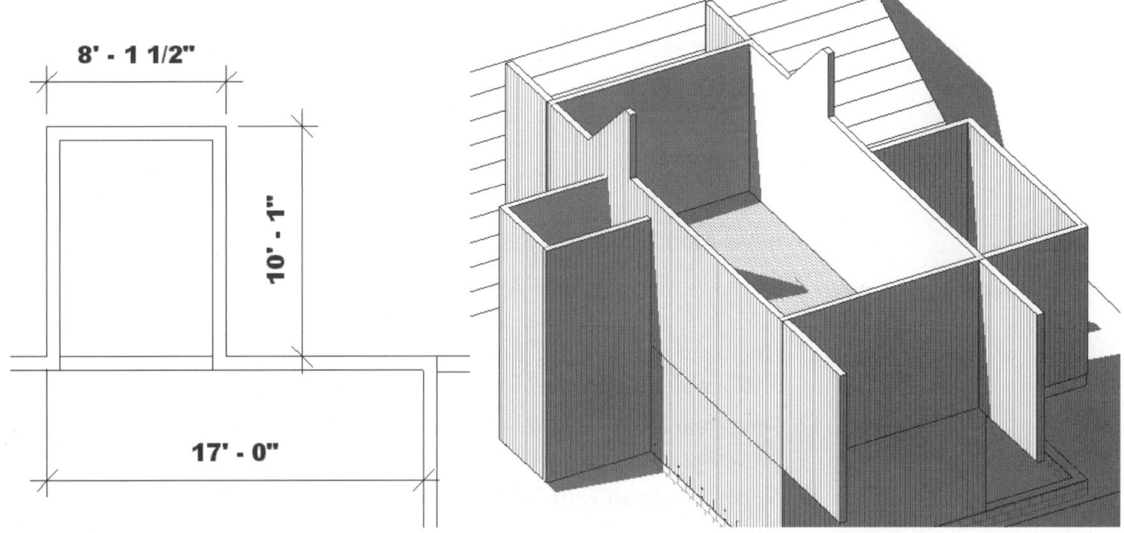

Figure 20-60

Place the **Stairway** walls

5. Select the walls you just placed to bring up the **Properties** dialog box.
6. In the **Properties** dialog box, set the **Top Constraint** to **PARAPET**, and the **Top Offset** to **0′-0″**.
7. Change to the **Home** toolbar.
8. In the **Home** toolbar, select the **Stairs** button to bring up the **Modify | Create Stairs Sketch** toolbar.
9. In the **Properties** dialog box, make the settings and check boxes shown in Figure 20-61.

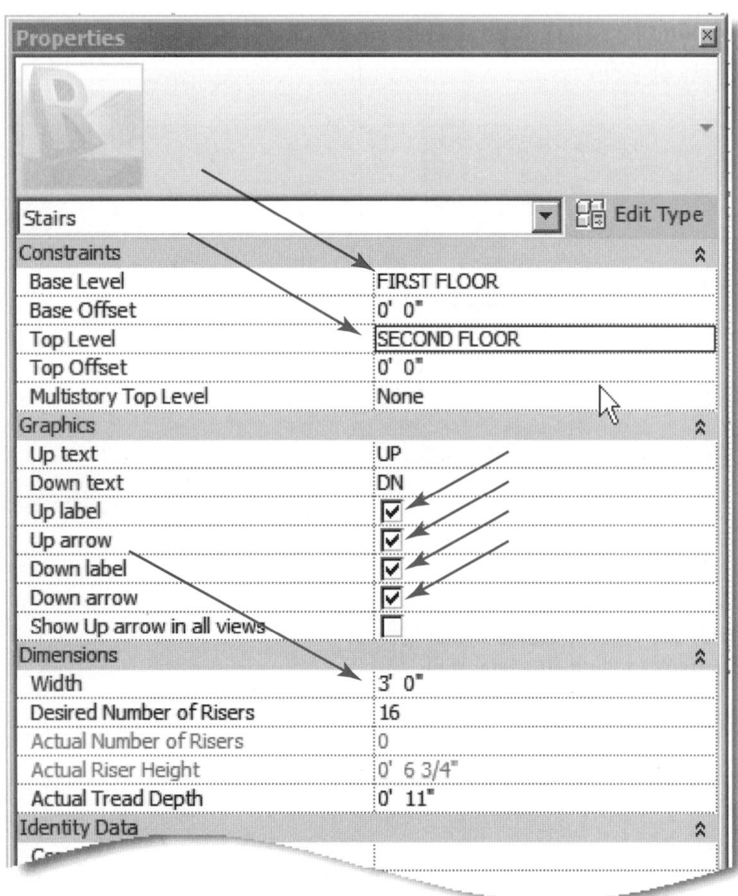

Figure 20-61

Properties dialog box

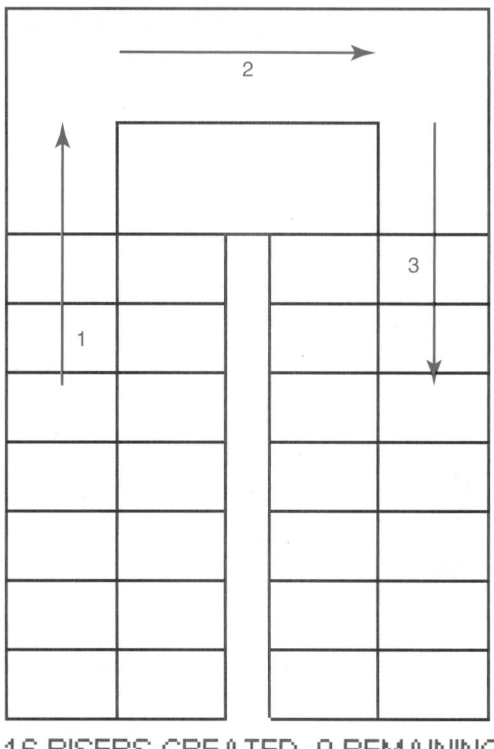

Figure 20-62

Create stair lines

10. In the **Modify | Create Stairs Sketch** toolbar, select the **Run** button.
11. Click and then drag your cursor upward until the message "*8 RISERS CREATED, 8 REMAINING*" appears, and click again.
12. Drag your cursor to the **East** (approximately **3′-6″**), and click again.
13. Drag your cursor down, and click again to create the stair lines (see Figure 20-62).
14. Select the **Finish Edit Mode** button to create the stair.
15. Delete the outside stair railing that is automatically created.

NOTE:

You will have to edit the distances between the runs to fit exactly inside the stairway. Instructions on how to do this are in the Stairs, Railings, and Ramps chapter.

16. Select the **Align** button from the **Modify** toolbar.
17. Click the left inside of the stairway wall, and then the left side of the stair.

Repeat using the **Align** button on the top inside of the stairway and the top of the landing. Doing this will align the stair inside the stairway (see Figures 20-63 and 20-64).

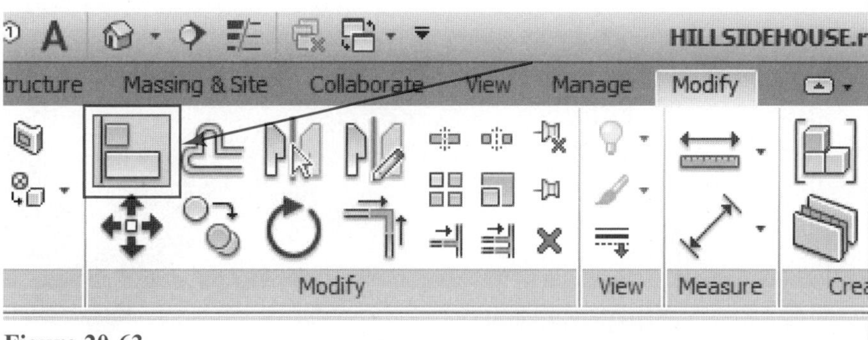

Figure 20-63

Align button

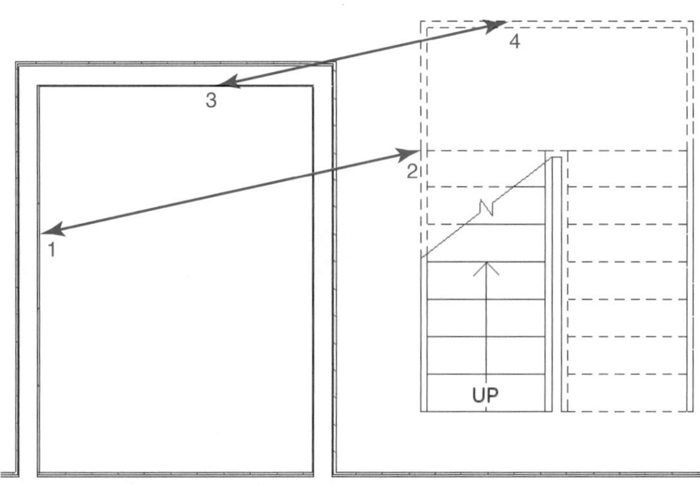

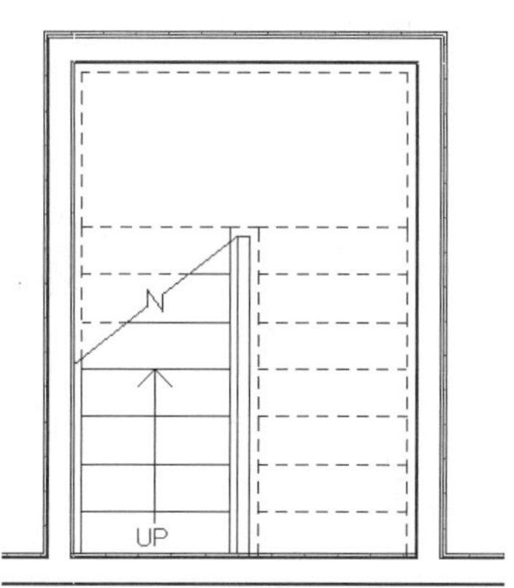

Figure 20-64

Align the stair inside the stairway

18. Double-click on the **West Elevation** in the **Project Browser** to bring it into the **Drawing Editor**.
19. Set the scale to **1/4″ = 1′-0″**, and the **Detail Level** to **Wireframe**.
20. Select the stairway walls to bring up the **Modify | Walls** toolbar.
21. In the **Modify | Walls** toolbar, select the **Edit Profile** button to bring up the **Modify | Walls > Edit Profile** toolbar.
22. Using the **Line** and **Split** buttons, modify the top and bottom of the stairway wall.
23. Press the **Finish Edit Mode** button to complete the wall.
24. Repeat for the opposite wall, and then adjust the rear wall of the stairway.
25. Change to the **Default 3D View** (see Figure 20-65).
26. Change to the **FIRST FLOOR** view.
27. Select the **Home** tab to bring up the **Home** toolbar.
28. In the **Home** toolbar, select the **Wall Opening** button (see Figure 20-66).

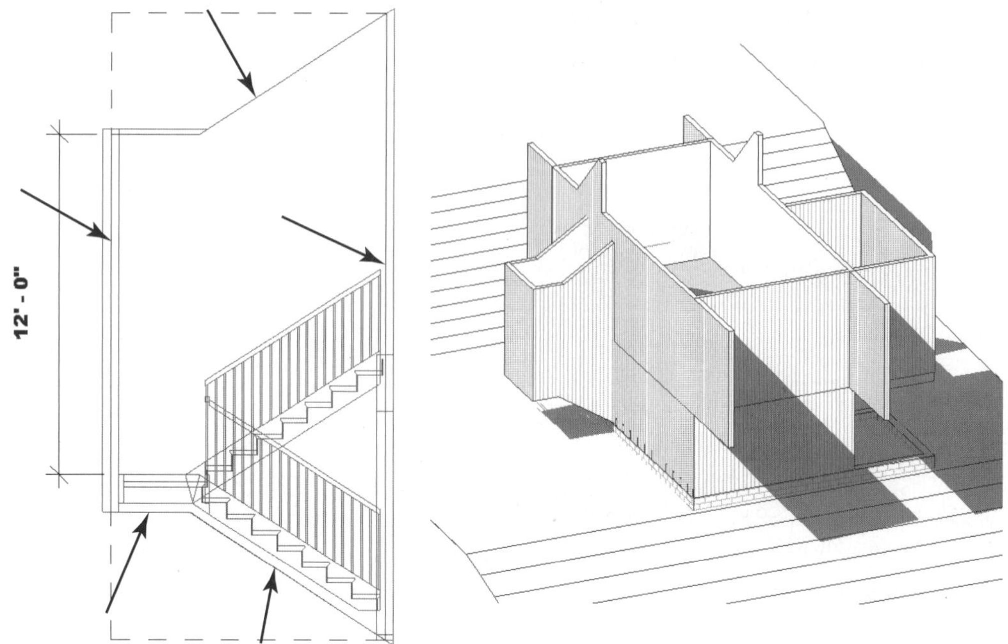

Figure 20-65

3D view of stairway

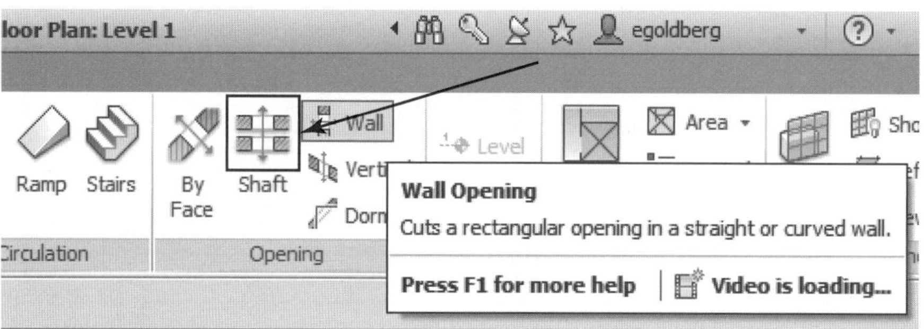

Figure 20-66

Wall Opening button

29. Select the wall between the stair and the wall.
30. Click again to set a start point, click again diagonally, and create a **3′-0″** wide opening leading from the stairway to the **FIRST FLOOR**.
31. Select the opening to bring up its **Properties** dialog box.
32. In the **Properties** dialog box, set the **Unconnected Height** to **7′-0″**.
33. Repeat Steps 30–32 for the **SECOND FLOOR,** making the second floor opening **6′-8″** wide × **7′-0″** high.
34. Change to the **Default 3D View**, and hide the outside walls of the stairway.
35. Select **Visual Style: Hidden Line**, and **Shadows On** from the **View Control Bar** (see Figure 20-67).
36. Save the file.

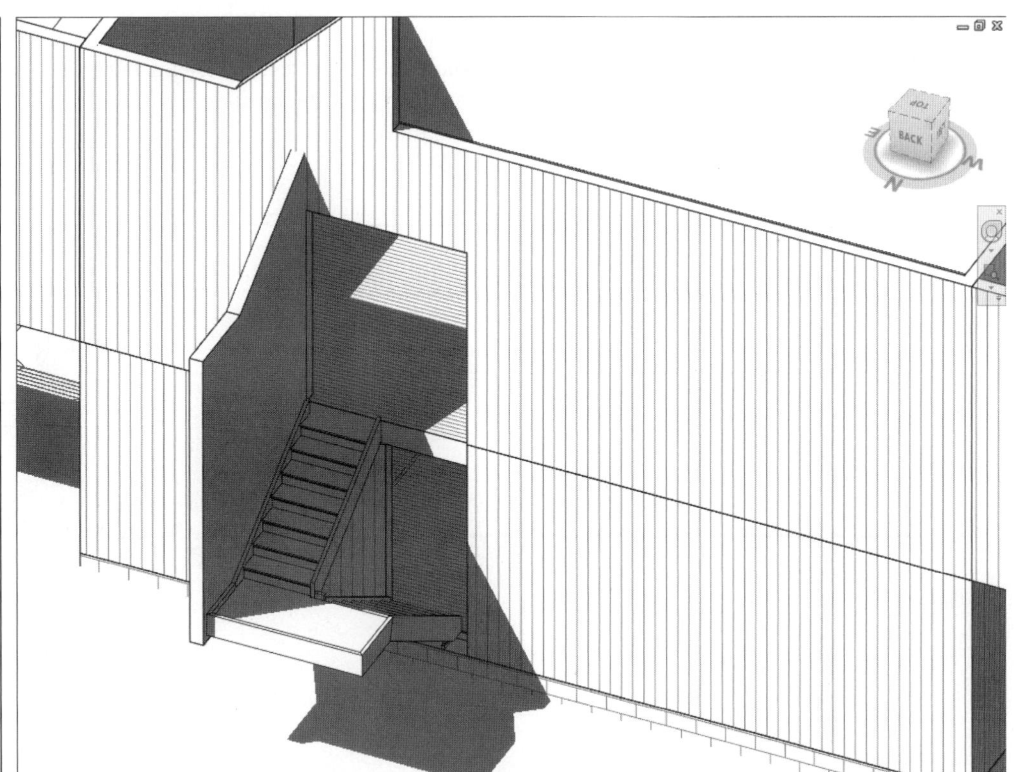

Figure 20-67

Hide the outside walls of the stairway

Roof and Skylight

EXERCISE 20-17 CREATING THE ROOF

1. Double-click on the **PARAPET** level plan to bring it into the **Drawing Editor**.
2. Change the **Scale** to **1/4″ = 1′-0″**.
3. Change to the **Insert** toolbar.
4. In the **Insert** toolbar, select the **Load Family** button to bring up the **Load Family** dialog box.
5. In the **Load Family** dialog box, locate the **Imperial Library** folder.
6. In the **Imperial Library** folder, locate and open the **Structural** folder.
7. In the **Structural** folder, locate and open the **Framing** folder.
8. In the **Framing** folder, locate and open the **Steel** folder.
9. In the **Steel** folder, select the **K-Series Bar Joist-Rod Web**, then select the **18K3** type, and press the **Open** button to return to the **Drawing Editor**.
10. Change to the **Structure** toolbar.
11. In the **Structure** toolbar, select the **Beam > Beam System** button to bring up the **Modify | Create Beam System Boundary** toolbar.
12. In the **Properties** dialog box, set the **Elevation** to **0′-0″**, **Layout Rule** to **Fixed Distance**, **Fixed Spacing** to **2′-0″**, **Justification** to **Beginning**, and **Beam Type** to **K-Series Bar Joist-Rod Web: 18K3**.
13. Press the **OK** button to return to the **Drawing Editor**.
14. In the **Modify | Create Beam System Boundary** toolbar, select the **Rectangle** button.

15. Place a rectangle.
16. In the **Create Beam System Boundary** toolbar, select the **Beam Direction** button, and click the left side of the rectangle to indicate the direction of the web joists (two small parallel lines) (see Figure 20-68).

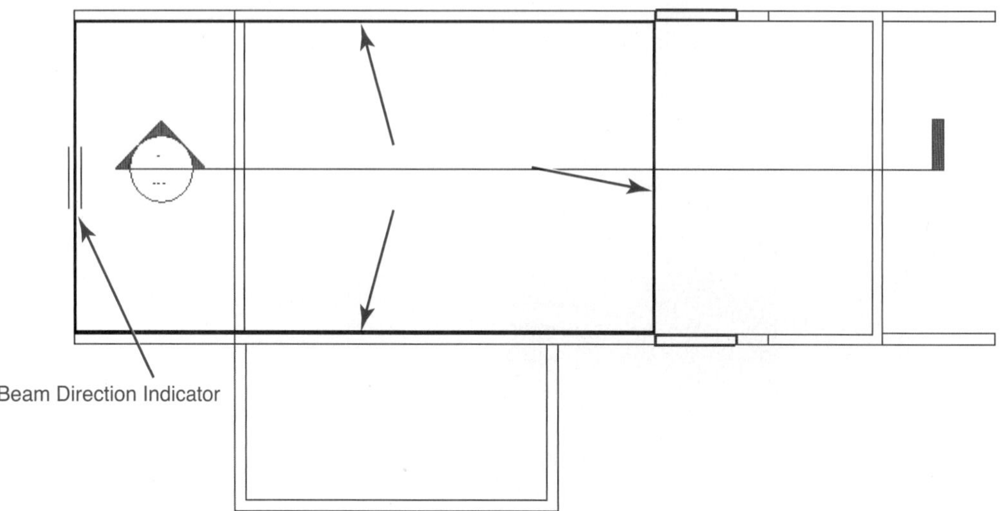

Figure 20-68

Place a rectangle and indicate the direction of the web joists

17. Select the **Finish Edit Mode** button to place the bar joists.
18. Press the **<Esc>** key to end the command.
19. Change to the **PARAPET** plan view.
20. In the **Home** toolbar, select the **Roof > Roof by Footprint** button to bring up the **Modify | Create Roof Footprint** toolbar.
21. In the **Properties** dialog box, press the **Edit Type** button to bring up the **Type Properties** dialog box.
22. In the **Type Properties** dialog box, select the **Generic – 12″** roof from the **Type** drop-down list.

NOTE:

If you have not made the side walls bearing walls, you may get a warning that the wall is a non-bearing wall; press the **Make Wall Bearing** button, and then press the **OK** button to create the roof joists (see Figures 20-69 and 20-70).

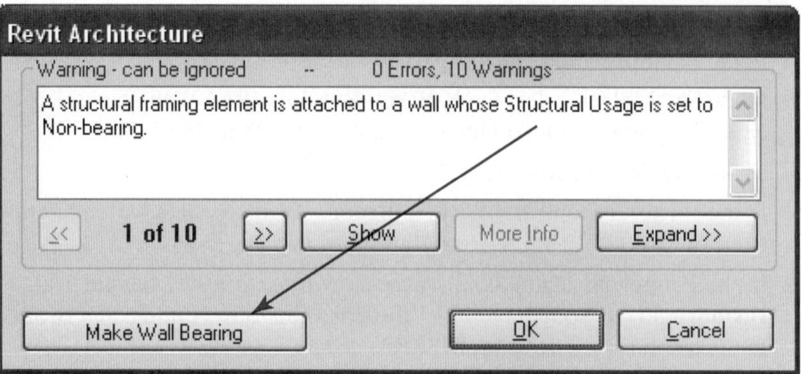

Figure 20-69

Wall Bearing warning

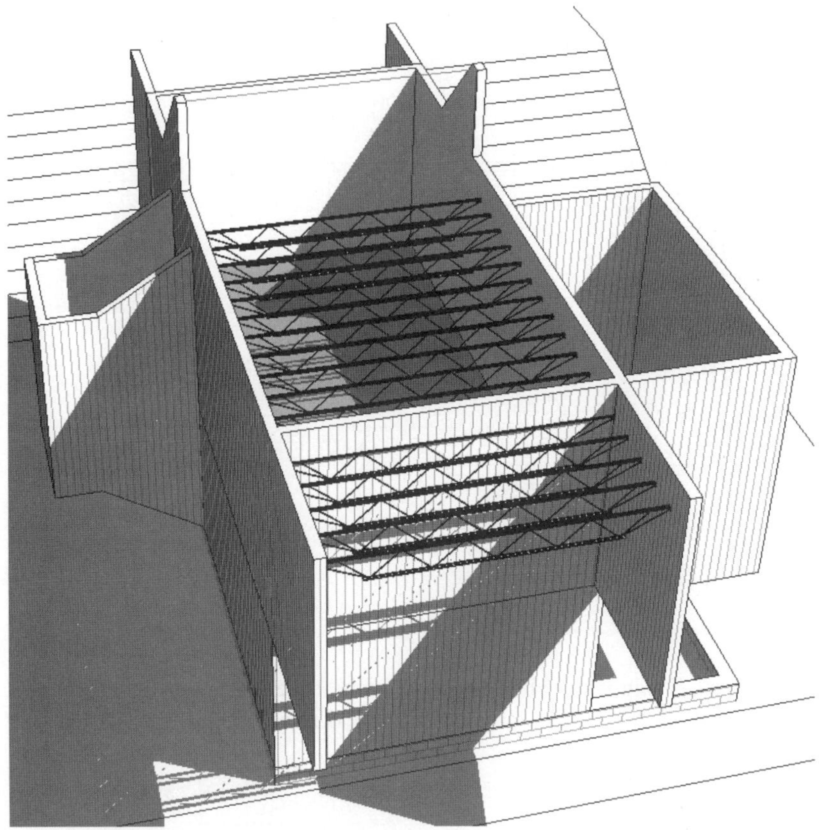

Figure 20-70

3D view of beams

23. In the **Type Properties** dialog box, press the **Duplicate** button to bring up the **Name** dialog box.
24. In the **Name** dialog box, enter **SECOND FL FRONT ROOF**, and press the **OK** button to return to the **Type Properties** dialog box.
25. In the **Type Properties** dialog box, press the **Edit** button in the **Structure** field to bring up the **Edit Assembly** dialog box.
26. In the **Edit Assembly** dialog box, select the **Insert** button, and add a new layer.
27. Press the **Up** button to move the new layer above and outside the **Core Boundary**.
28. Change the **Function** of the layer outside the **Core Boundary** to **Finish 1 [4]**.
29. Set the **Material** for **Finish 1 [4]** to **Concrete-Cast-in-Place Lightweight Concrete**, and **Thickness** to **0′6″**.
30. Set the **Material** for the **Structure [1]** to **Metal-Deck**, and set its **Thickness** to **0′2″**.
31. Check the **Variable** check box for **Finish 1 [4]**.
32. Press the **OK** buttons to return to the **Drawing Editor** dialog box.
33. In the **Modify | Create Roof Footprint** toolbar, select the **Rectangle** button.
34. In the **Options Bar**, uncheck the **Defines Slope** check box. This will allow a flat roof to be created.
35. Place a rectangle as shown in Figure 20-71, and press the **Finish Edit Mode** button to create the roof.
36. Change to the **Default 3D View**.
37. Select the roof you just created.

NOTE:

Checking the **Variable** check box for **Finish 1 [4]** will allow that finish to have a slope.

Figure 20-71

Place a rectangle to create a roof

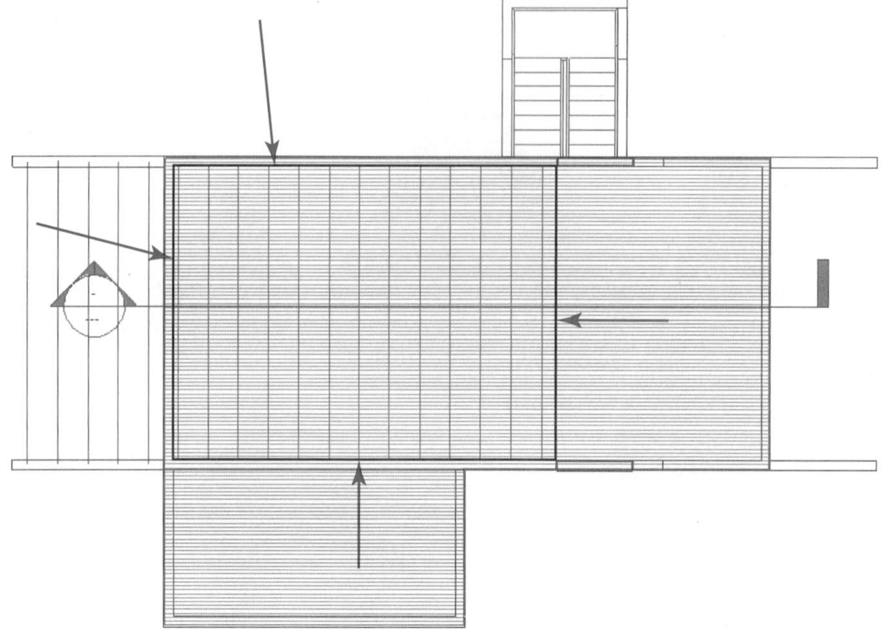

38. Press the **Temporary Hide/Isolate** button at the bottom of the **Drawing Editor**, and then select **Isolate Element** to isolate the roof (Figure 20-72).

Figure 20-72

Temporary Hide/Isolate button

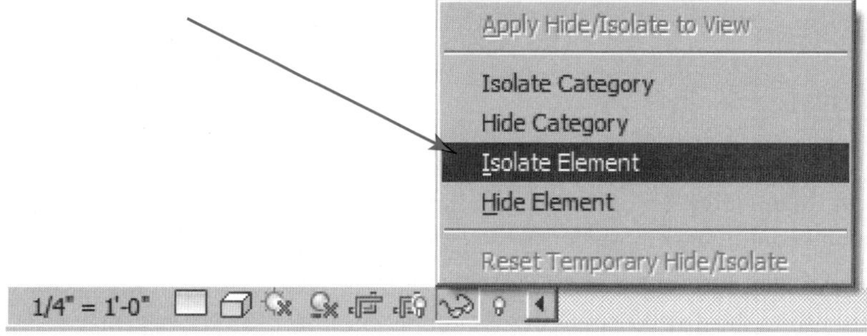

39. Select the isolated roof to bring up the **Modify | Roofs** toolbar.
40. In the **Modify | Roofs** toolbar, select the **Add Split Line** button (Figure 20-73).

Figure 20-73

Add Split Line button

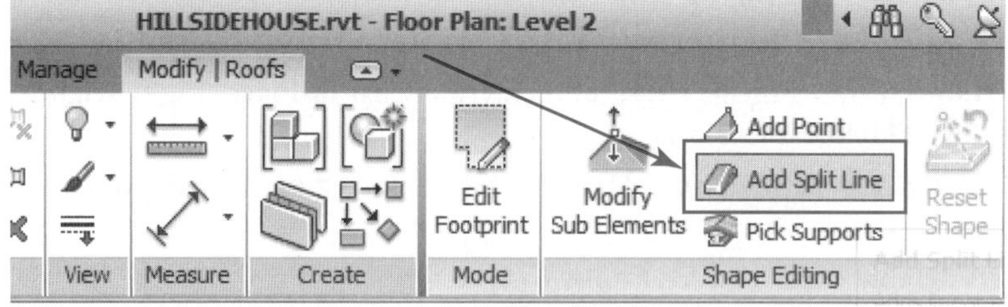

41. Draw split lines diagonally crossing the roof.
42. Select the **Modify Sub Elements** button.
43. Select the grip at the intersection between the split lines; enter **-0′-3″** in the **Elevations** field in the **Options Bar**, click outside the roof, and then press the **<Esc>** key to complete the command (see Figures 20-74 and 20-75).
44. Select the **Temporary Hide/Isolate** button at the bottom of the **Drawing Editor**, and then select **Reset Temporary Hide/Isolate** to unhide everything.
45. Double-click the **Section 1** view in the **Project Browser** to bring it into the **Drawing Editor**.

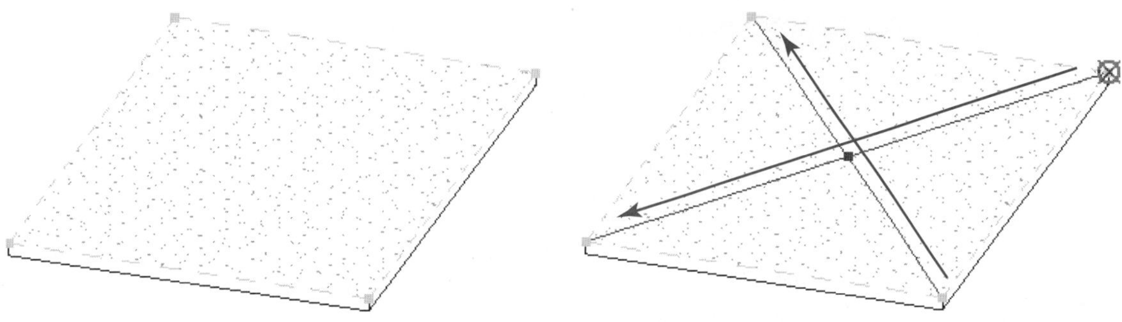

Figure 20-74

Select the intersection between split lines

In the **Section 1** view, you can see the cast-in-place concrete that slopes to the center of the roof. Eventually, a roof drain will be placed in the center of this roof, and it will exit through a pipe to the drain (see Figure 20-76).

46. Save the file.

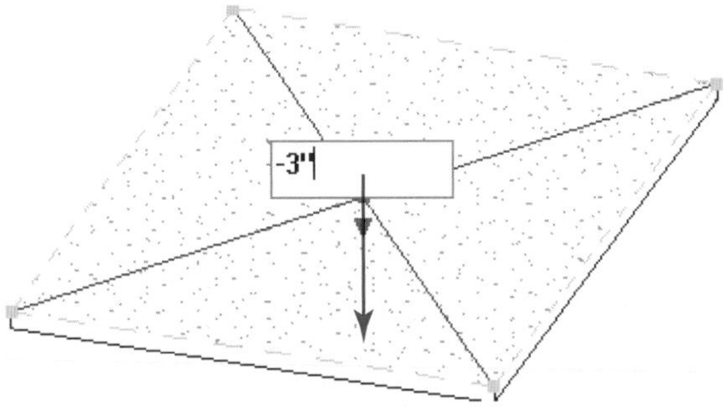

Figure 20-75

Enter **-0′-3″** in the **Elevations** field

Figure 20-76

Cast-in-place concrete slopes to the center of the roof

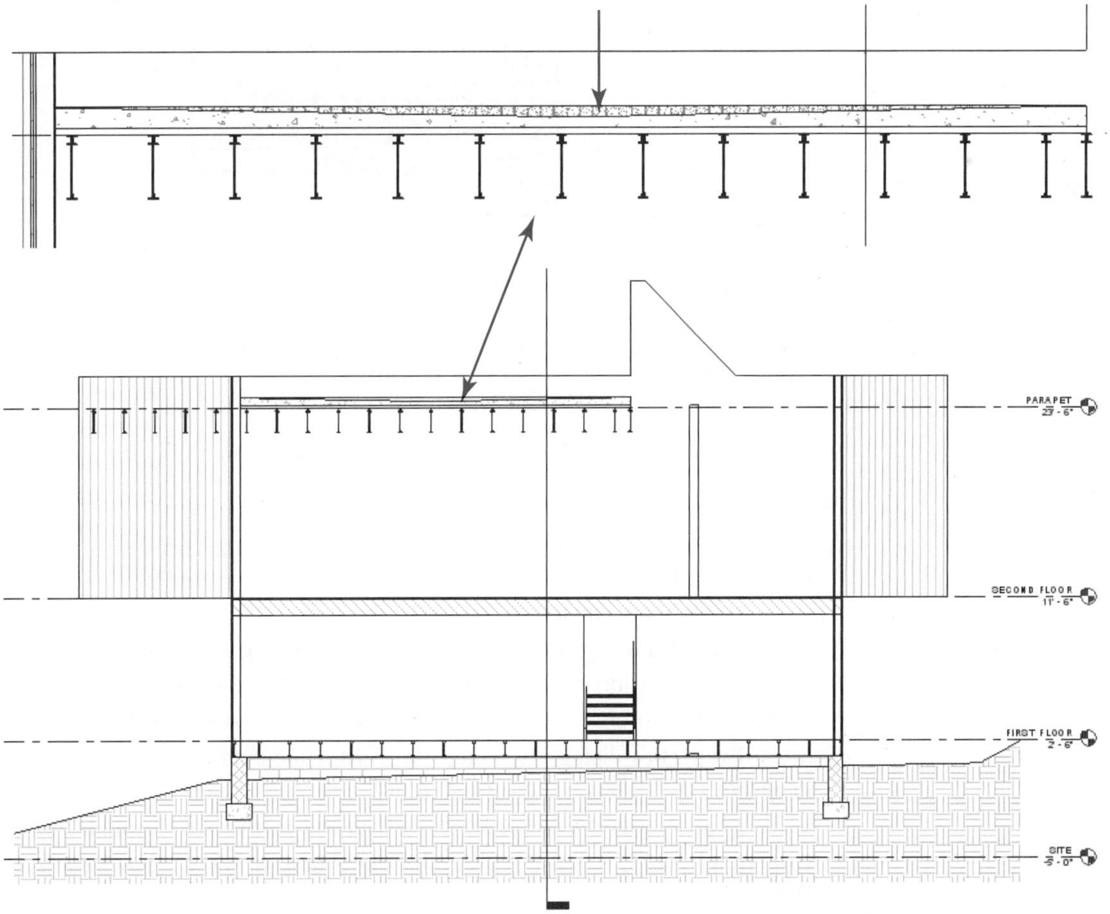

EXERCISE 20-18 CREATING THE SKYLIGHT ROOF

1. Double-click on the **PARAPET** level plan to bring it into the **Drawing Editor**.
2. Change to the **Home** toolbar.
3. In the **Home** toolbar, select the **Ref Plane** button to bring up the **Modify | Place Reference Plane** toolbar.
4. In the **Modify | Place Reference Plane** toolbar, select the **Pick Lines** button in the **Draw** panel.
5. In the **Options Bar**, enter **0′-1″** in the **Offset** field.
6. Pick the outside of the north and south exterior walls to place reference planes, and press the **<Esc>** key to end the command.
7. Select each reference plane to bring up its **Properties** dialog box.
8. Enter **NORTH** in the **Name** field for the north reference plane, and **SOUTH** in the **Name** field for the south reference plane (see Figure 20-77).

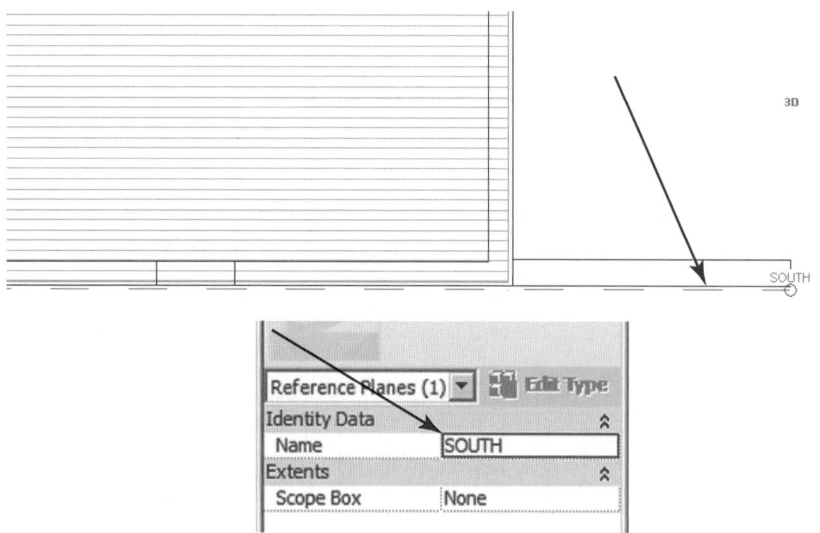

Figure 20-77

Reference Planes drawing and dialog box

9. In the **Home** toolbar, select the **Roof > Roof by Extrusion** button.

The **Work Plane** dialog box will appear.

10. In the **Work Plane** dialog box, select the **Name** radio button, select **Reference Plane: SOUTH** from the drop-down list, and then press the **OK** button to bring up the **Go to View** dialog box.
11. In the **Go to View** dialog box, select **Elevation: South**, and then press the **Open View** button to bring up the **Roof Reference Level and Offset** dialog box. Press the **OK** button to bring up the **Modify | Create Extrusion Roof Profile** toolbar.
12. In the **Properties** dialog box, select the **Edit Type** button to bring up the **Type Properties** dialog box.
13. In the **Type Properties** dialog box, select **Wood Rafter 8″ – Asphalt Shingle – Insulated** from the **Type** drop-down list, and press the **OK** button to return to the **Drawing Editor**.
14. In the **Modify | Create Extrusion Roof Profile** toolbar, select the **Line** button.

15. In the **Options Bar**, check the **Chain** check box, and set the **Offset** to **-0′ 8 3/8″** (thickness of the roof).
16. Trace the outline of the skylight walls as shown in Figure 20-78, and press the **Finish Edit Mode** button to create the roof.

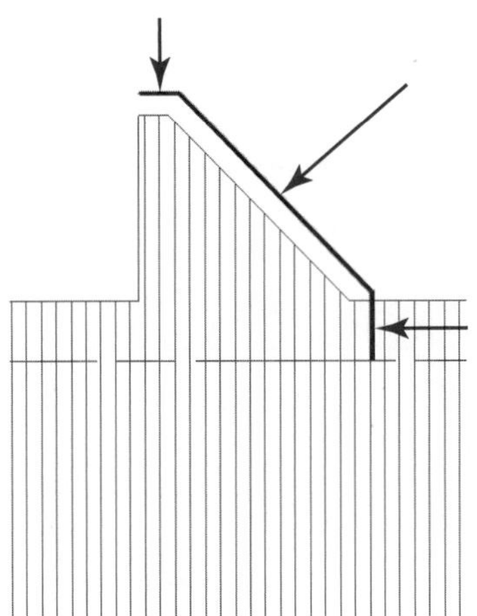
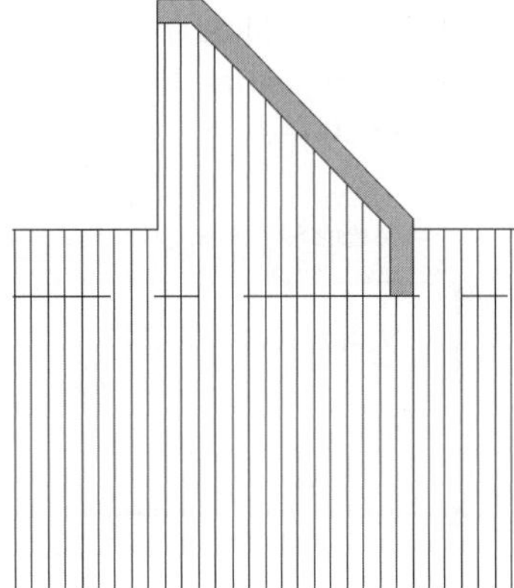

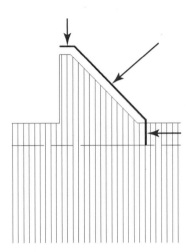

Figure 20-78

Trace the outline of the skylight walls

17. Press the <**Esc**> key to end the command.
18. Double-click on the **PARAPET** plan view to bring it into the **Drawing Editor**.
19. Select the roof you just placed to activate its grips.
20. Drag the north grip of the roof, and drag it until it snaps on the north reference plane.

You have now created the skylight roof (see Figure 20-79).

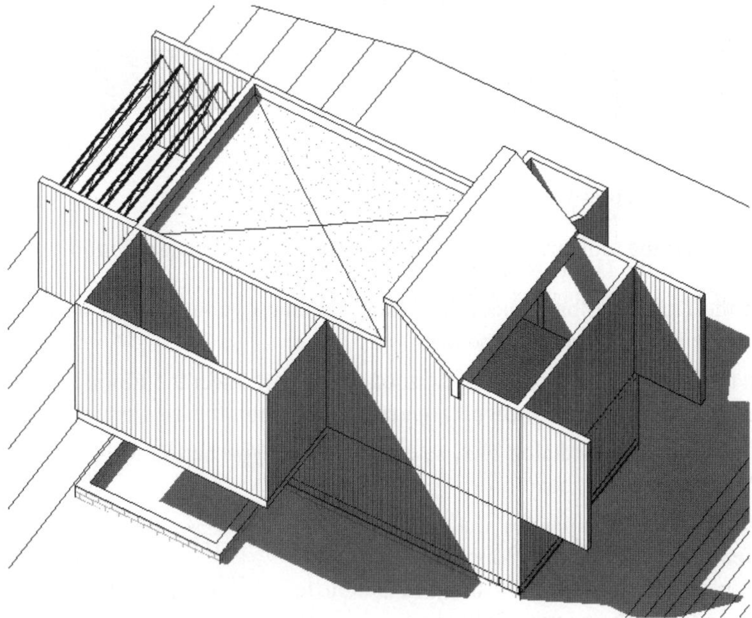

Figure 20-79

3D view of skylight roof

Bridge

EXERCISE 20-19 **CREATING THE BRIDGE**

1. Double-click on the **SECOND FLOOR** level plan to bring it into the **Drawing Editor**.
2. Change the **Scale** to **1/4″ = 1′-0″**.
3. Click in an empty space in the **SECOND FLOOR** level plan to bring up its **Properties** dialog box for the floor plan.
4. In the **Properties** dialog box, select **SITE** from the **Underlay** drop-down list (see Figure 20-80).

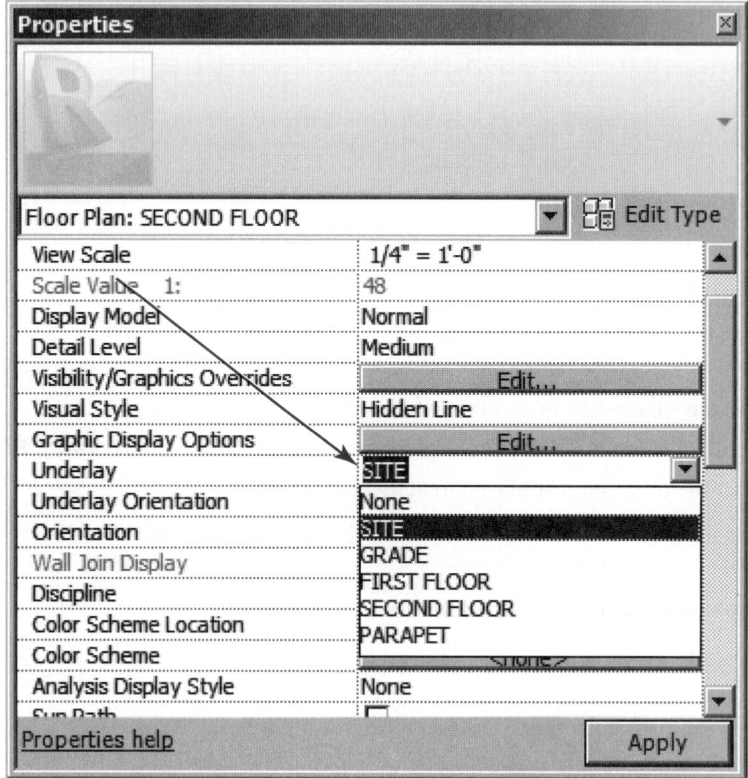

Figure 20-80

Underlay drop-down list

5. Change to the **Home** toolbar.
6. In the **Home** toolbar, select the **Floor > Floor** button to bring up the **Modify | Create Floor Boundary** toolbar.
7. In the **Modify | Create Floor Boundary** toolbar, select the **Floor Properties** button to bring up the **Instance Properties** dialog box for the floor.
8. In the **Properties** dialog box, select the **Edit Type** button to bring up the **Type Properties** dialog box.
9. In the **Type Properties** dialog box, select **Generic - 12″ Filled** floor from the **Type** drop-down list, and press the **OK** button to return to the **Properties** dialog box.
10. In the **Properties** dialog box, select **SECOND FLOOR** for the **Level**, and enter **-0′-10″** for the **Height Offset From Level**.

NOTE:

Step 10 is done because the bridge will have a 6″ step up to the rear deck, and the rear deck will be 4″ below the **SECOND FLOOR** level.

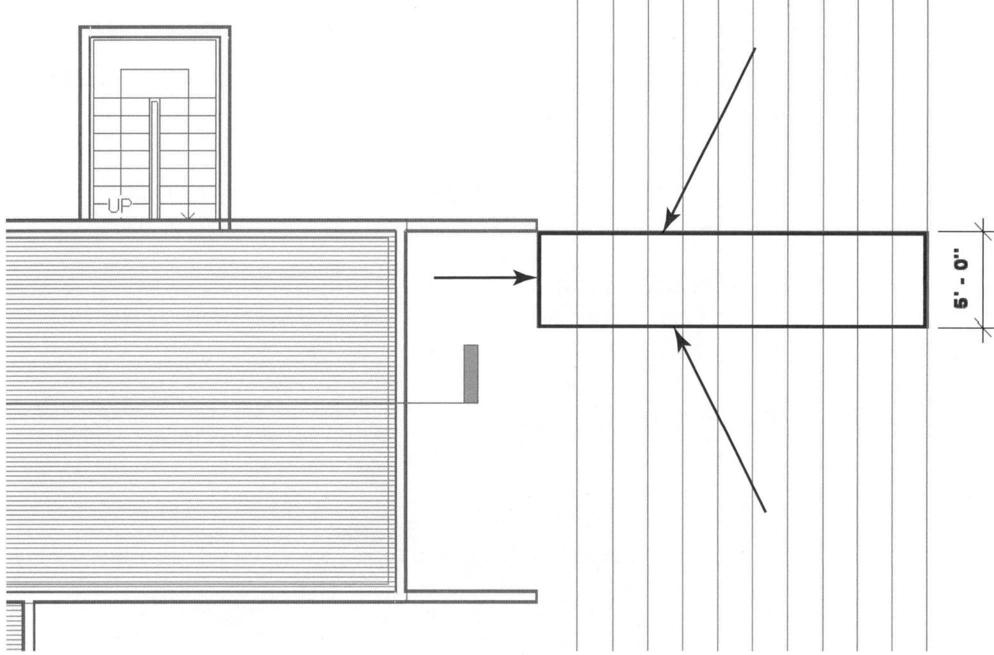

Figure 20-81

Place a **5′-0″** wide rectangle

11. Press the **OK** button to return to the **Drawing Editor**.
12. In the **Modify | Create Floor Boundary** toolbar, select the **Rectangle** button, and place a **5′-0″** wide rectangle that reaches from the upper edge of the site slope to the edge of the rear wing wall (see Figure 20-81).
13. Press the **Finish Edit Mode** button to create the deck, and press the **<Esc>** key to end the command.
14. Change to the **Home** toolbar.
15. In the **Home** toolbar, select the **Railing** button to bring up the **Modify | Create Railing Path** toolbar.
16. In the **Properties** dialog box, select the **Edit Type** button to bring up the **Type Properties** dialog box.
17. In the **Type Properties** dialog box, select **Handrail – Pipe** for the **Type**.
18. Press the **OK** button to return to the **Drawing Editor**.
19. In the **Modify | Create Railing Path** toolbar, select the **Pick New Host** button, and then select the bridge you created (see Figure 20-82).

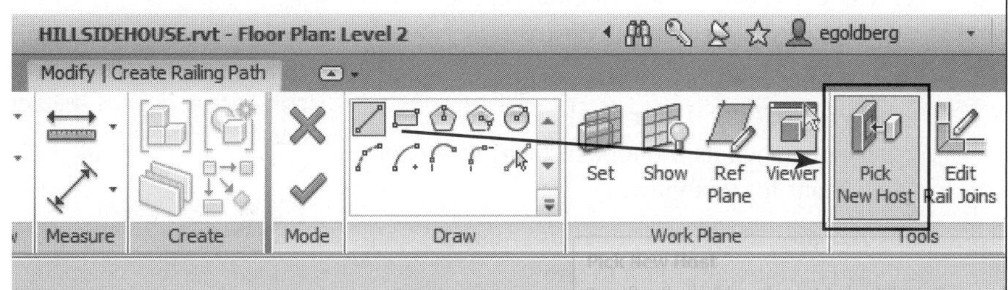

Figure 20-82

Pick New Host button

20. In the **Modify | Create Railing Path** toolbar, select the **Line** button, and place a line where the north railing will appear.
21. In the **Modify | Create Railing Path** toolbar, select the **Finish Railing** button to create the railing.
22. Repeat Steps 19–21 for the south railing.
23. Change to the **Default 3D View** to see the result (see Figure 20-83).

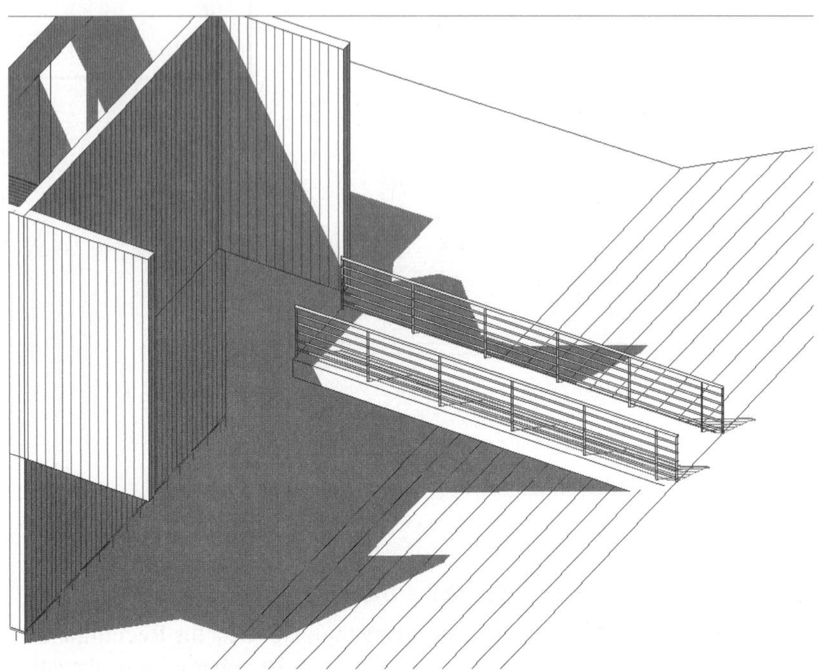

Figure 20-83
3D view of bridge

24. Save the file.

Plot Sheets

EXERCISE 20-20 CREATING THE PLOT SHEETS

The following is an example of how to set your views correctly.

1. Bring up the **FIRST FLOOR** plan view.
2. Press the **Show Crop Region** button at the bottom of the **Drawing Editor**.
3. Select the **Temporary Hide/Isolate** button in the **View Control Bar**, and hide anything in the view (such as the toposurface) that is not important for this view.
4. Move any of your **Elevation** markers into view (if you want them to show).
5. Change any **Underlay** to **None**.
6. Set your **Detail Level**, **Model Graphic Style** (shading), and **Shadows**.

NOTE:
Before you create the plot sheets, open up all your views. Make sure that they are set to the correct scale and that the crop regions are correct. The crop region defines the boundaries of a view.

NOTE:
If the **Crop Region** is already showing, the button tooltip will say *"Hide Crop Region"* (see Figure 20-84).

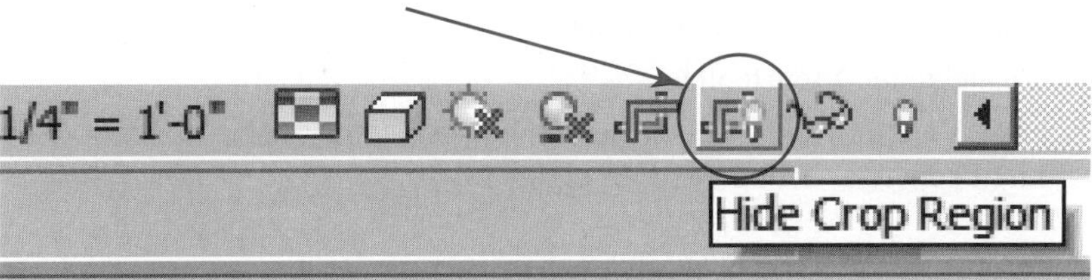

Figure 20-84

Show Crop Region button tooltip

7. Zoom out until you see the **Crop Region**.
8. Select the **Crop Region** to activate its grips.
9. Drag the **Crop Region** grips until the region frames the area that you want to show on your plot sheet (see Figure 20-85).

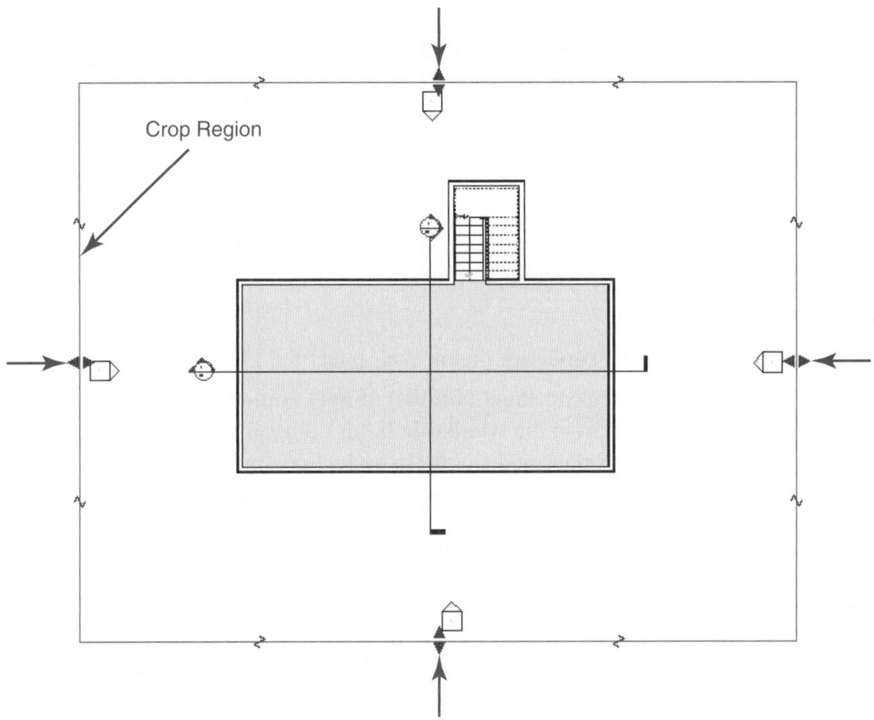

Figure 20-85

Select the area you want to show on your plot sheet

10. Press the **Hide Crop Region** icon (previously called **Show Crop Region**) at the bottom of the **Drawing Editor** to hide the region.

Once you have prepared all your views, you can proceed to place them on plot sheets.

11. Select the **Sheets [all]** icon in the **Project Browser**, **RMB**, and select **New Sheet . . .** to bring up the **Select a Titleblock** dialog box.
12. In the **Select a Titleblock** dialog box, press the **Load** button to bring up the **Open** dialog box.
13. In the **Open** dialog box, browse and locate the **HILLSIDE HOUSE SHEET FAMILY** that you created in Exercise 20-4.
14. Press the **OK** button to bring the sheet into the **Drawing Editor**.
15. In the sheet's title block, select the **Unnamed** field, and change it to **TITLE SHEET**.

16. Change the sheet number to **A100**.
17. Change to the **View** toolbar.
18. In the **View** toolbar, select the **Schedules > Sheet List** button to bring up the **Sheet List Properties** dialog box (see Figure 20-86).

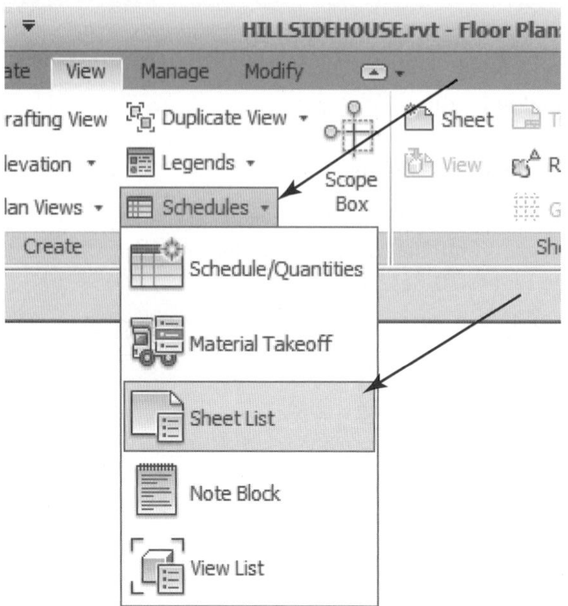

Figure 20-86

Schedules > Sheet List button

19. In the **Sheet List Properties** dialog box, select the **Fields** tab.
20. In the **Fields** tab, select **Sheet Number**, **Sheet Name**, **Drawn By**, **Checked By**, and **Approved By** from the **Available fields** column, and press the **Add** button to move them to the **Scheduled fields [in order]** column.
21. Press the **OK** button to create the **Drawing List**.
22. Double-click on **A100–TITLE SHEET** (under **Sheets [all]**) in the **Project Browser** to bring it into the **Drawing Editor**.
23. Select the **Drawing List** name in the **Project Browser**, and drag it into the **TITLE SHEET** in the **Drawing Editor** (see Figure 20-87).
24. Again, select the **Sheets [all]** icon in the **Project Browser**, **RMB**, and select **New Sheet . . .** to bring up the **Select a Titleblock** dialog box.

NOTE:

You will now be in the **Drawing Editor** with the **Drawing List** at the top of the screen. The **Drawing List** name will also appear in the **Project Browser** under **Schedules/Quantities.**

25. In the **Select a Titleblock** dialog box, the **HILLSIDE HOUSE SHEET FAMILY** will already be selected; press the **OK** button to bring the sheet into the **Drawing Editor**. The new sheet will be automatically numbered **A101**.
26. In the sheet's title block, select the **Unnamed** field, and change it to **SITE PLAN**.
27. Select **SITE** in the **Project Browser**, and drag it into the sheet you just created.
28. Create four more sheets labeled **FIRST FLOOR PLAN**, **SECOND FLOOR PLAN**, **ELEVATIONS**, and **SECTIONS**.
29. Drag the appropriate views from the **Project Browser** into the plot sheets.

The **Drawing List** on the **TITLE SHEET** will now show all the drawings you created.

NOTE:

You may have to go back to the **Views** and adjust their scale for the sections to **3/16″ = 1′-0″** to get them to fit on the plot sheet and also make the elevations **1/8″ = 1′-0″**.

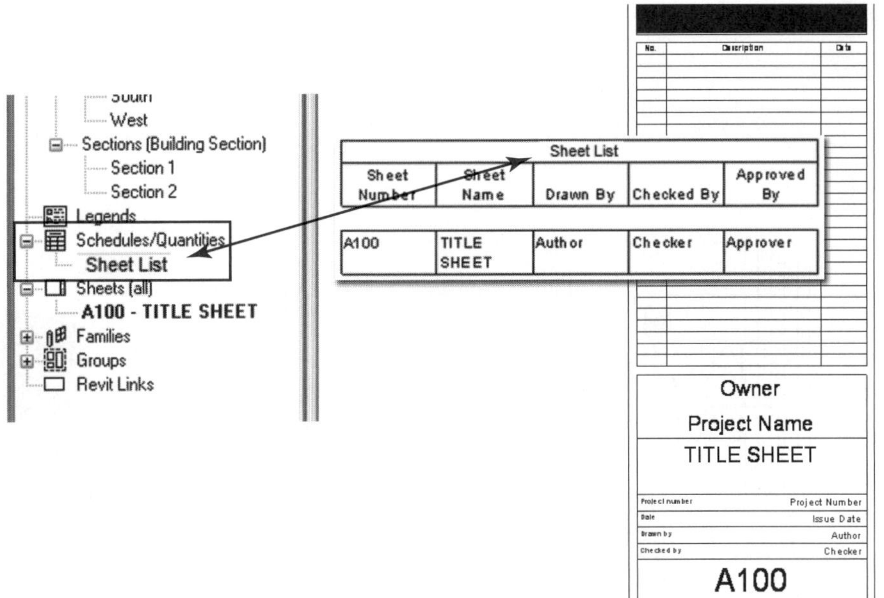

Figure 20-87

Create a **Sheet List**

You have now created the basic plot sheets. Now that you have created and saved the sheets, you can return to modifying the building model. All your changes will be updated on the sheets (see Figures 20-88, 20-89, 20-90, 20-91, 20-92, and 20-93).

30. Save the file.

> **NOTE:**
> If the line from a view title (under the view) in the sheet is too long, select that view, and then adjust the line. After you have adjusted the line, deselect the view, and then select the title and its line and move it.

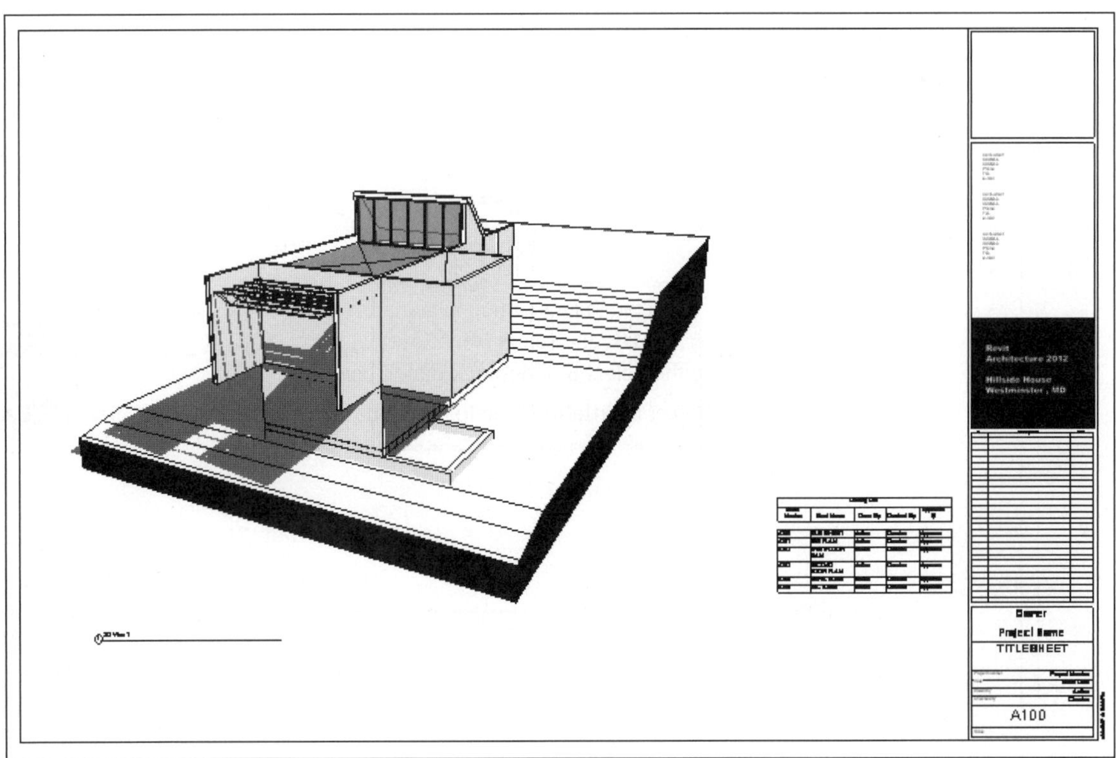

Figure 20-88

Title sheet

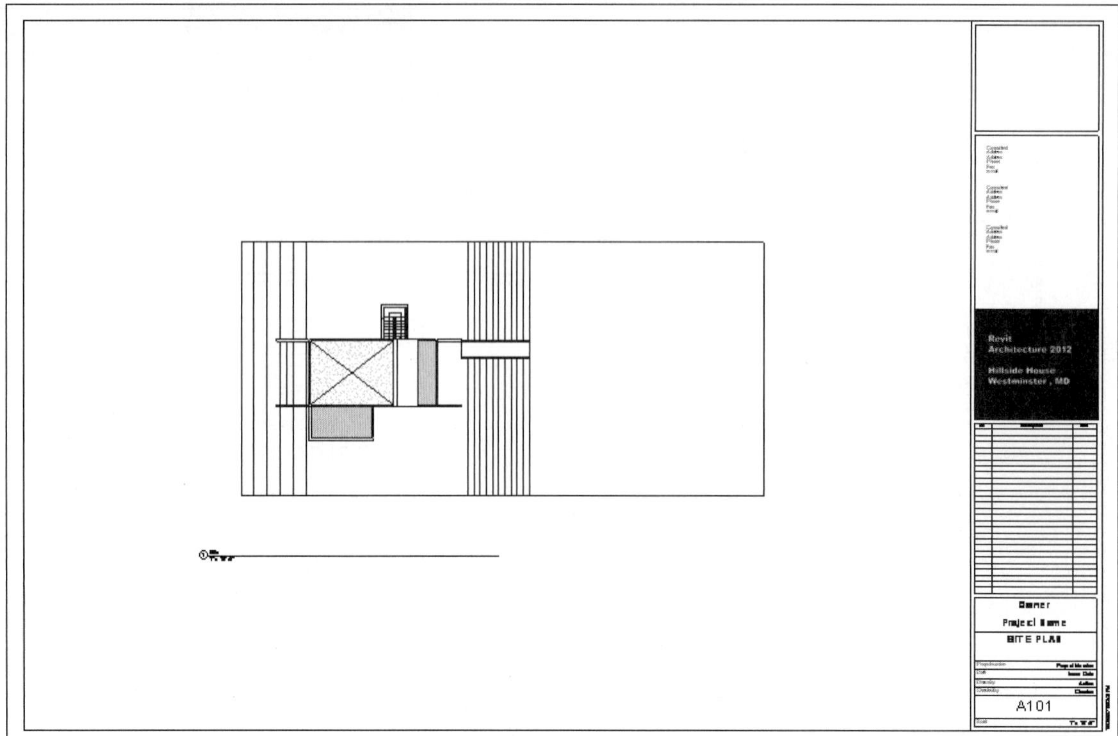

Figure 20-89

Site plan

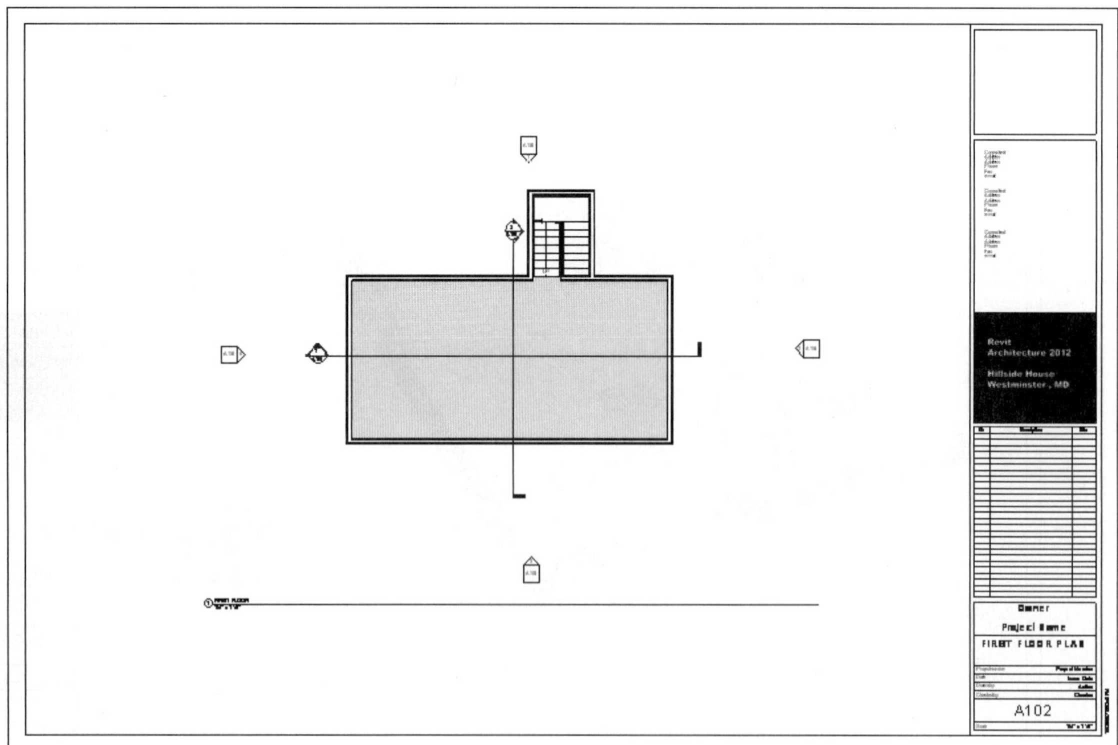

Figure 20-90

First Floor plan

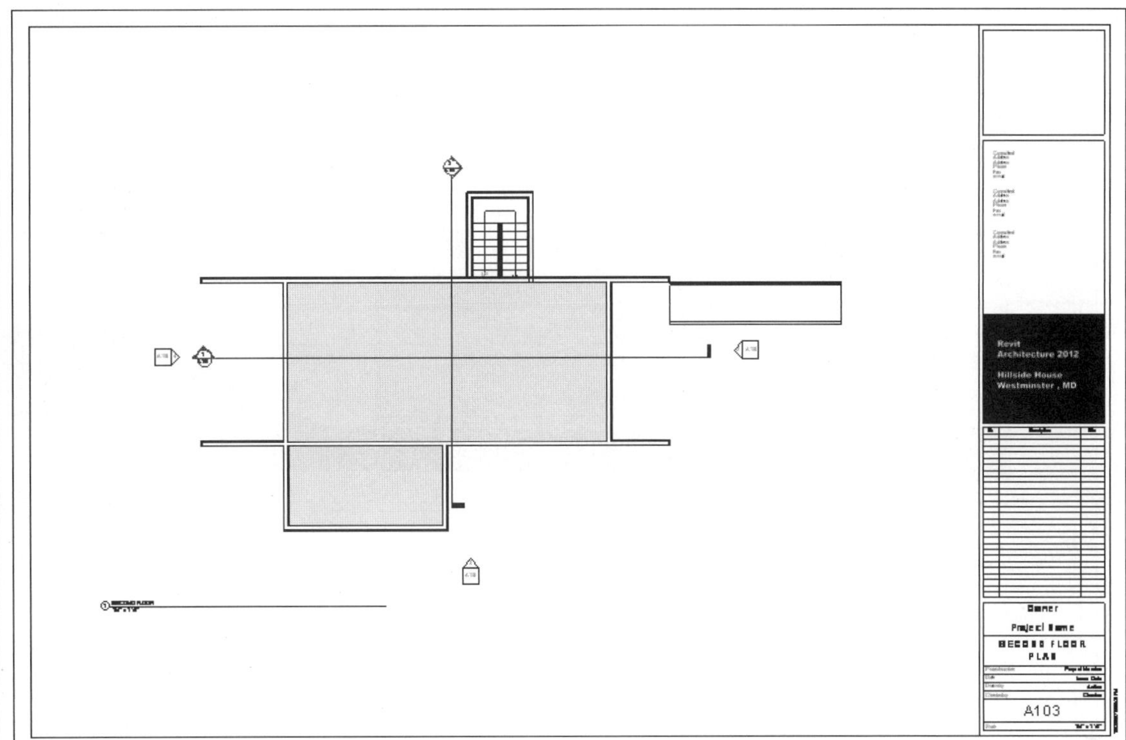

Figure 20-91

Second Floor plan

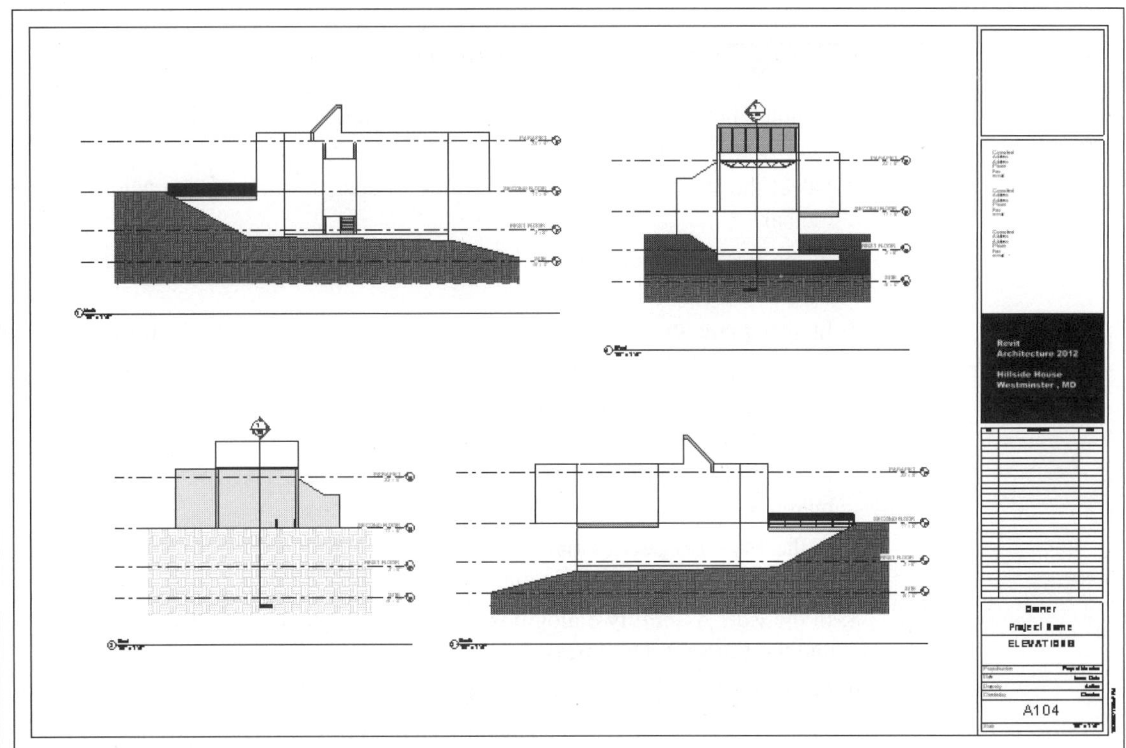

Figure 20-92

Elevations

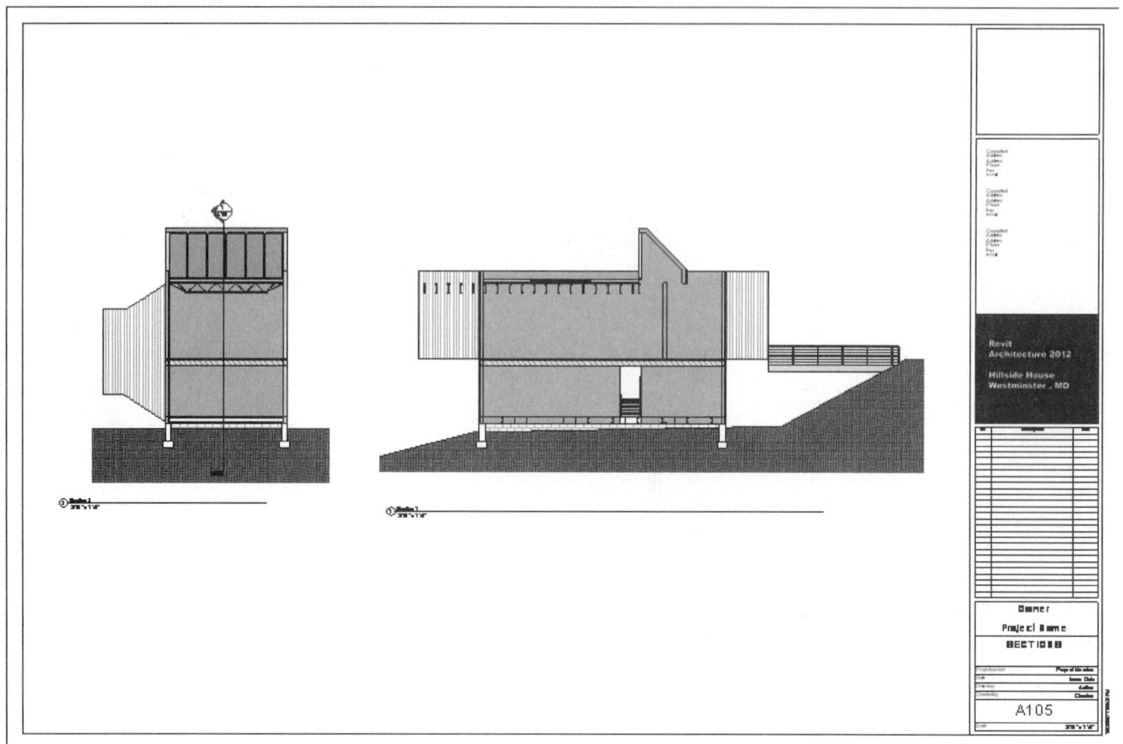

Figure 20-93

Section

Interior Walls

EXERCISE 20-21 CREATING THE INTERIOR WALLS

1. Double-click on the **FIRST FLOOR** plan view in the **Project Browser** to bring it into the **Drawing Editor**.
2. Select the **Wall** button from the **Home** toolbar to bring up the **Modify | Walls** toolbar.
3. In the **Properties** dialog box, select the **Edit Type** button to bring up the **Type Properties** dialog box.
4. In the **Type Properties** dialog box, select the **Basic Wall: Interior -4-7/8″ Partition [1-hr]** from the **Properties** drop-down list.
5. In the **Type Properties** dialog box, select the **Duplicate** button to bring up the **Name** dialog box.
6. In the **Name** dialog box, enter **INTERIOR 4 1/2″ WALLS**, and press the **OK** button to return to the **Type Properties** dialog box.
7. In the **Type Properties** dialog box, press the **Edit** button in the **Structure** field to bring up the **Edit Assembly** dialog box.
8. In the **Edit Assembly** dialog box, change the **Structure [1] Thickness** to **3-1/2″**, and the **Finish 2 Thickness** to **1/2″**.
9. Press the **OK** buttons to return to the **Drawing Editor**.
10. In the **Options Bar**, select **Unconnected** from the **Height** drop-down list, and enter **7′-10 7/8″**.
11. In the **Options Bar**, select **Finish Face: Exterior** from the **Location Line** drop-down list, and select the **Line** option.

12. Using the **INTERIOR 4 1/2″ WALLS** you just created, place walls and doors as shown in Figure 20-94.

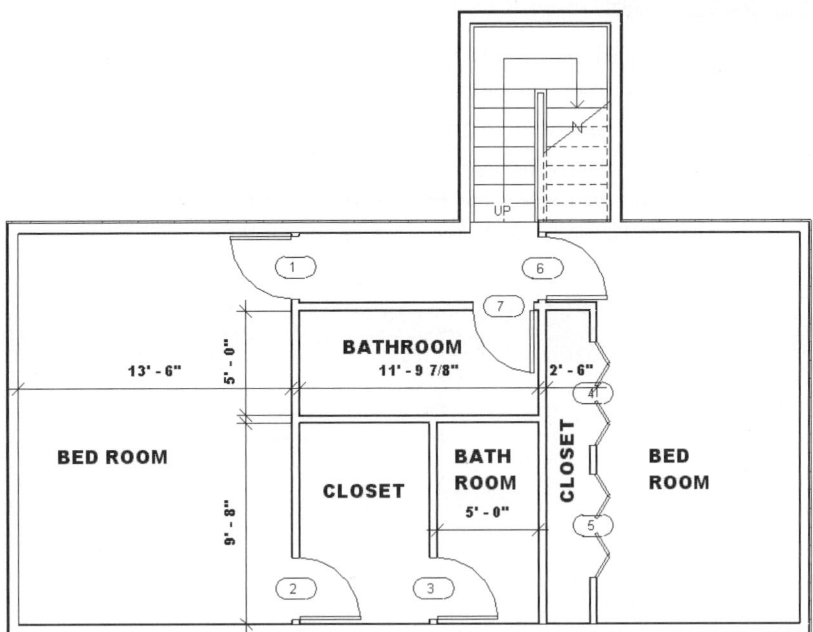

Figure 20-94

Place walls and doors in the First Floor drawing

13. Press the **<Esc>** key to end the commands.
14. In the **Project Browser**, double-click on the **SECOND FLOOR** plan view to bring up the **SECOND FLOOR** into the **Drawing Editor**.
15. In the **Home** toolbar, select the **Wall** button again to bring up the **Modify | Walls** toolbar.
16. Using the **INTERIOR 4 1/2″ WALLS** you previously created, in the **Properties** dialog box, change the **Height** to **9′-0″**, and place walls and doors as shown in Figure 20-95.
17. Save the file.

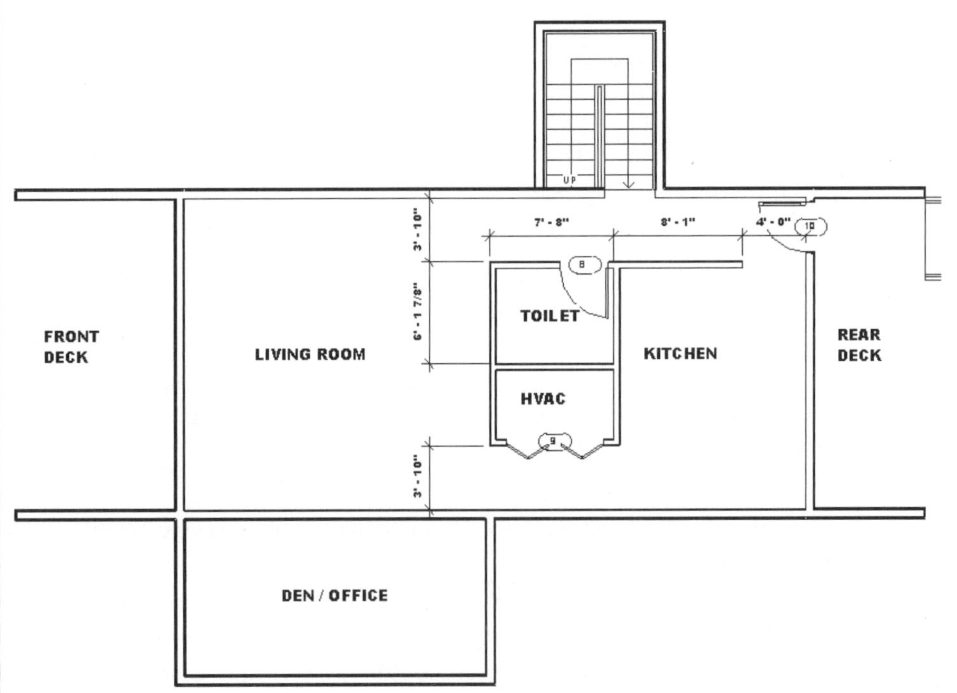

Figure 20-95

Place walls and doors in the Second Floor drawing

Exterior Doors and Windows

EXERCISE 20-22 PLACING EXTERIOR DOORS AND WINDOWS

1. Double-click on the **FIRST FLOOR** plan view in the **Project Browser** to bring it into the **Drawing Editor**.
2. Select the **Insert** tab to bring up the **Insert** toolbar.
3. In the **Insert** toolbar, enter "Casement Windows" in the **Autodesk Seek** search field, and then select the **Binocular** button to bring up the Autodesk Seek web page for Casement Windows (see Figure 20-96).

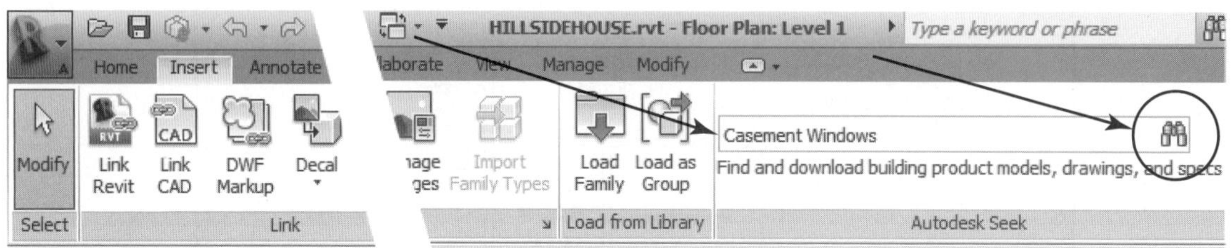

Figure 20-96

Autodesk Seek web page for Casement Windows

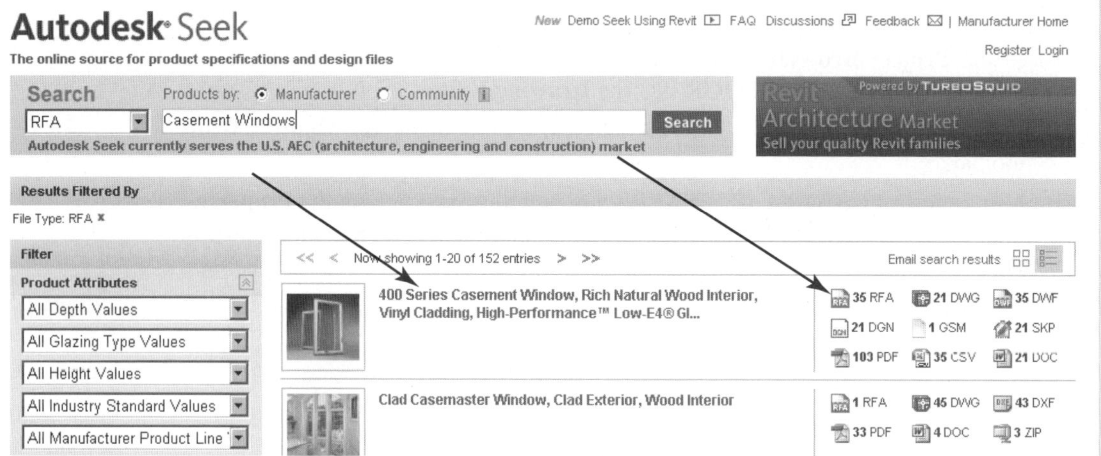

Figure 20-97

Manufacturer Windows web page

4. In the Autodesk Seek web page for Casement Windows, click on the **Andersen 400 Series Casement Window RFA** icon to bring up the Andersen web page (see Figure 20-97).
5. In the Andersen Windows web page, select the eye dropper to the right of the **Andersen Windows – 400 Series Casement C33 C335** and drag it to your **Drawing Editor** (see Figure 20-98).
6. Close the web library, and return to the **Drawing Editor**.
7. Select the **Windows** button in the **Home** toolbar to bring up the **Modify | Place Windows** toolbar.
8. In the **Properties** dialog box, select the **Casement – Triple w Trim 72″ × 48″** from the **Properties** drop-down list.
9. In the **Properties** dialog box, select the **Edit Type** button to bring up the **Type Properties** dialog box.

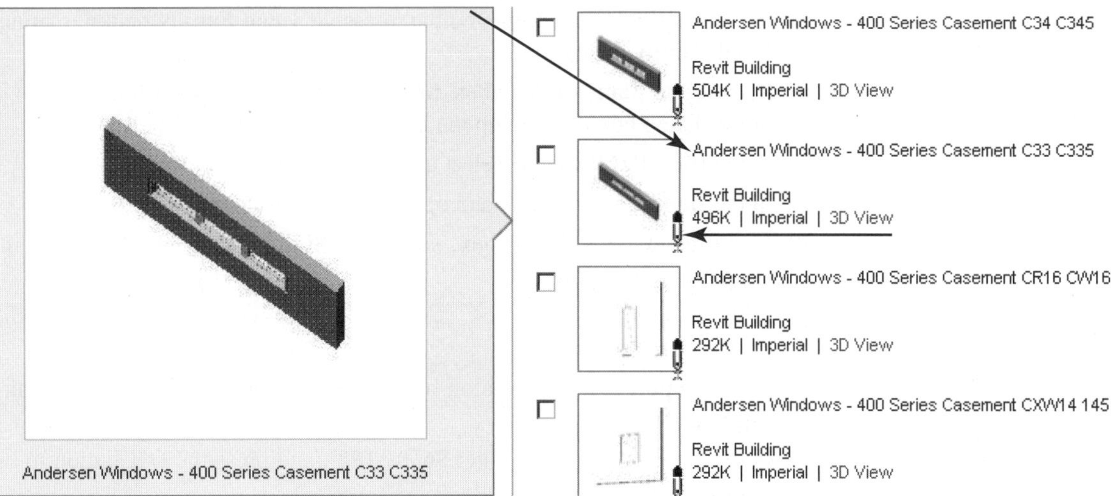

Figure 20-98

Use the eye dropper to select a window file from the Web

10. In the **Type Properties** dialog box, press the **Duplicate** button to bring up the **Name** dialog box.
11. In the **Name** dialog box, enter **96″ × 48″**, and press the **OK** button to return to the **Type Properties** dialog box.
12. In the **Type Properties** dialog box, change the **Width** to **8′-0″**, and press the **OK** buttons to return to the **Drawing Editor**.
13. Place windows in the front and back of the building as shown in Figure 20-99.

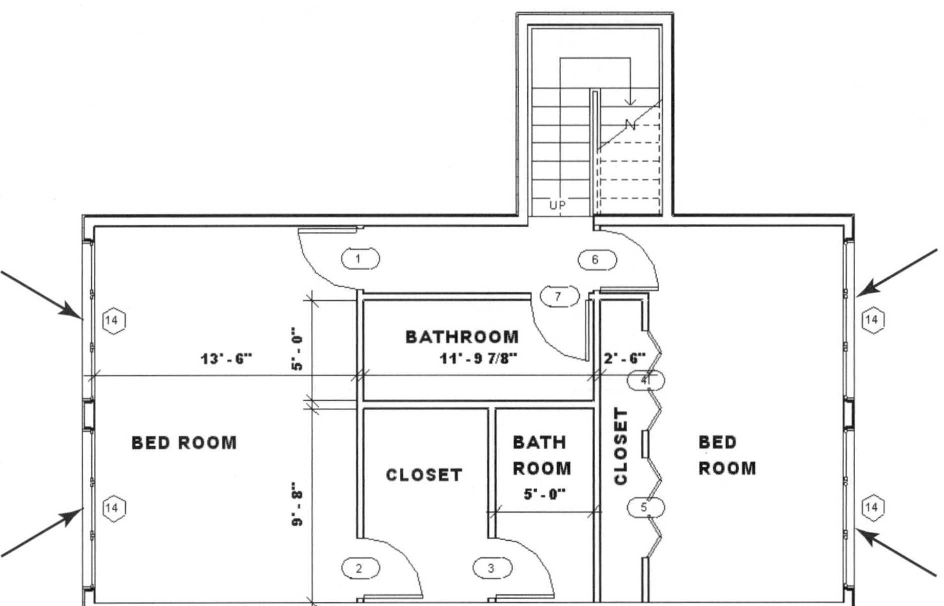

Figure 20-99

Place windows in the front and back of the building

14. Double-click on the **SECOND FLOOR** plan view in the **Project Browser** to bring it into the **Drawing Editor**.
15. In the **Home** toolbar, select the **Door** button to bring up the **Modify | Place Door** toolbar.

16. In the **Modify | Place Door** toolbar, press the **Load Family** button to bring up the **Load Family** dialog box.
17. In the **Load Family** dialog box, press the **Imperial Library** button at the left side of the dialog box to bring up the **Imperial Library**.
18. In the **Imperial Library**, select and open the **Doors** folder.
19. In the **Doors** folder, select and open the **Sliding-2 panel** door.
20. In the **Properties** dialog box, select the **Sliding-2 panel 72″ × 84″** from the **Properties** drop-down list.
21. In the **Properties** dialog box, select the **Edit Type** button to bring up the **Type Properties** dialog box.
22. In the **Type Properties** dialog box, press the **Duplicate** button to bring up the **Name** dialog box.
23. In the **Name** dialog box, enter **96″ × 108″**, and press the **OK** button to return to the **Type Properties** dialog box.
24. In the **Type Properties** dialog box, change the **Width** to **8′-0″**, the **Height** to **9′-0″,** and press the **OK** buttons to return to the **Drawing Editor**.
25. Place doors in the building as shown in Figures 20-100 and 20-101.
26. Save the file.

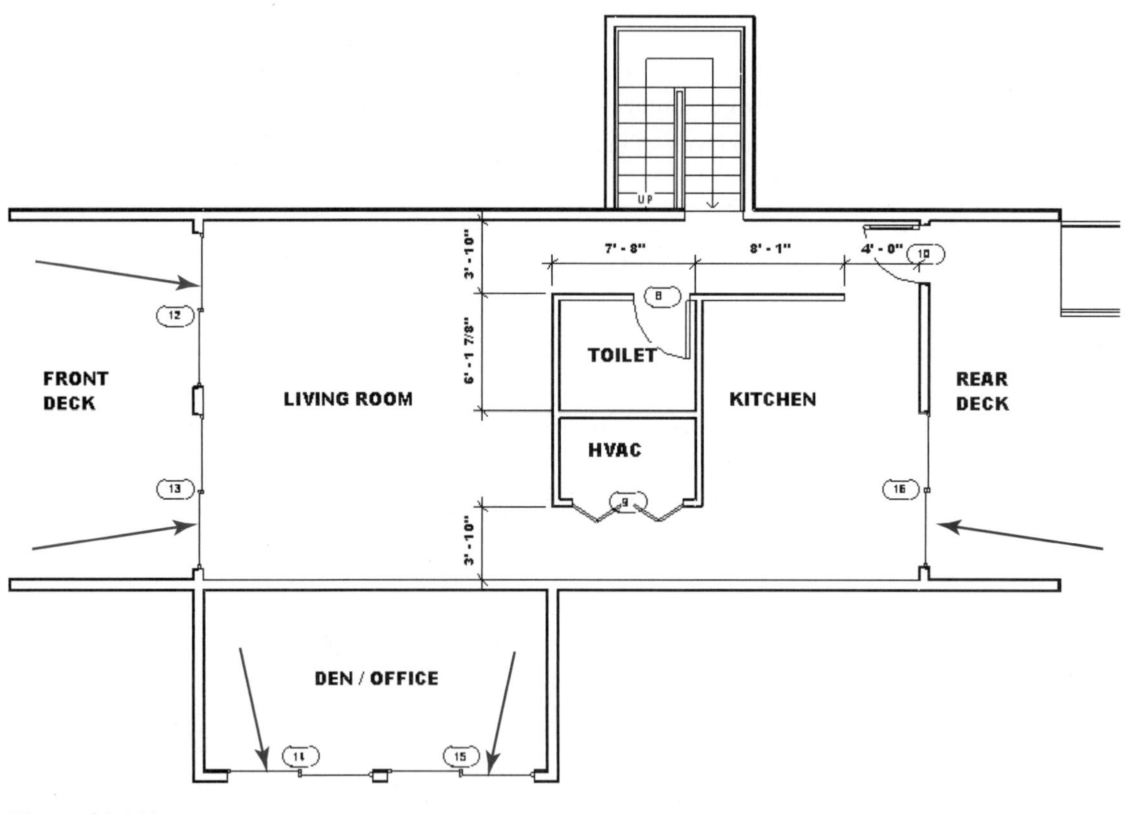

Figure 20-100

Place doors in the building

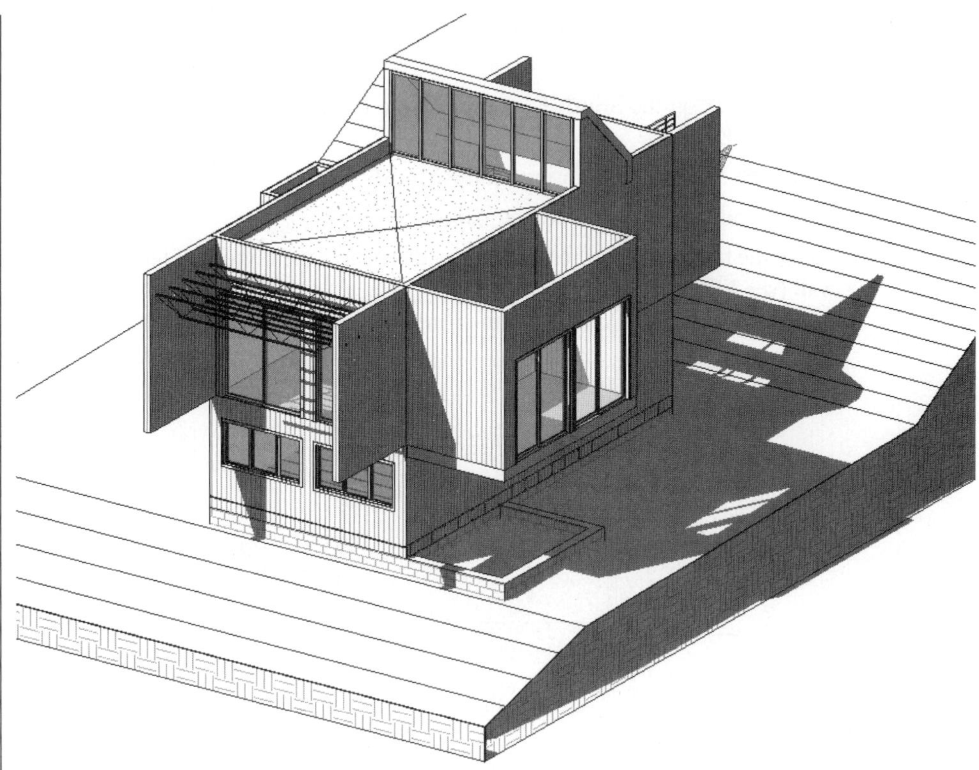

Figure 20-101

3D view of doors and windows

Decks and Railings

EXERCISE 20-23 CREATING THE FRONT AND REAR DECKS AND THEIR RAILINGS

1. Double-click on the **SECOND FLOOR** plan view in the **Project Browser** to bring it into the **Drawing Editor**.
2. In the **Home** toolbar, select the **Floor** > **Floor** button to bring up the **Modify | Create Floor Boundary** toolbar.
3. In the **Properties** dialog box, select the **Edit Type** button to bring up the **Type Properties** dialog box.
4. In the **Type Properties** dialog box, select **Wood Joist 10″ - Wood Finish** from the **Type** drop-down list.
5. In the **Properties** dialog box, select **SECOND FLOOR** from the **Level** drop-down list.
6. In the **Properties** dialog box, set the **Height Offset From Level** to **-0′ 4″** (this will set the deck 4″ lower than the **SECOND FLOOR**).
7. In the **Modify | Create Floor Boundary** toolbar, select the **Rectangle** button, and place a rectangle to form the front deck.
8. In the **Modify | Create Floor Boundary** toolbar, select the **Finish Edit Mode** button to create the deck.
9. At the Revit warning, "*Would you like walls that go up to this floor's level to attach to its bottom?*", press the **No** button.
10. Select the front deck you just created, **RMB**, and select **Create Similar** from the contextual menu to bring up the **Modify | Create Floor Boundary** toolbar again.
11. Repeat the floor creation process for the rear deck.

You will now need to make the bottom of the wing walls match the bottom of the decks.

12. Double-click on the **South Elevation** in the **Project Browser** to bring it into the **Drawing Editor**.
13. Select the **Modify** tab to bring up the **Modify** toolbar.
14. In the **Modify** toolbar, select the **Align** button.
15. Select the bottom of the front deck, and then select the bottom of the adjacent wing wall (see Figure 20-102).

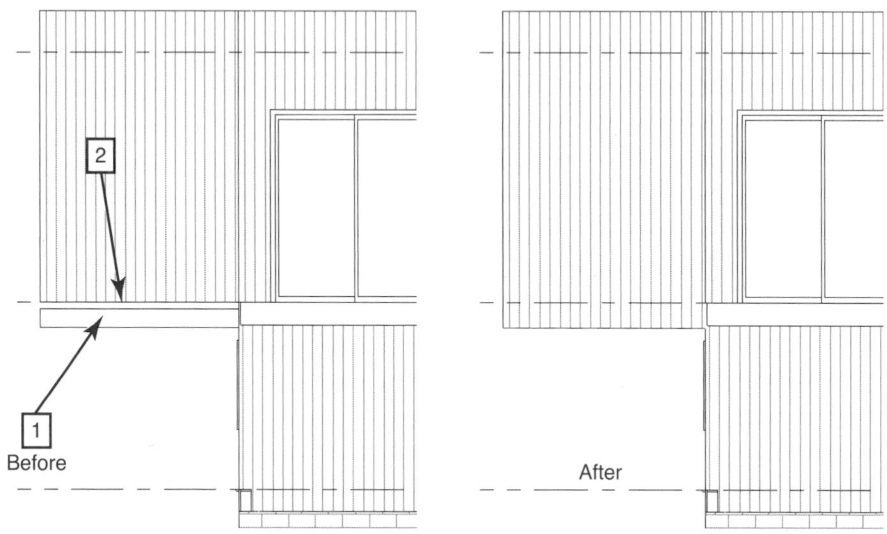

Figure 20-102

Align the bottoms of the front deck and the adjacent wing wall

16. Repeat this process for all the wing walls in all elevations.
17. Double-click on the **SECOND FLOOR** plan view in the **Project Browser** to bring it into the **Drawing Editor**.
18. Change to the **Home** toolbar.
19. In the **Home** toolbar, select the **Railing** button to bring up the **Modify | Create Railing Path** toolbar.
20. In the **Modify | Create Railing Path** toolbar, select the **Set Railing Host** button and select the front deck.
21. In the **Properties** dialog box, select **Handrail-Pipe** from the **Type** drop-down list, and press the **OK** button to return to the **Drawing Editor**.
22. Select the **Lines** button from the **Draw** panel, and place a line where the front rail will be.
23. In the **Modify | Create Railing Path** toolbar, select the **Finish Edit Mode** button to create the railing.
24. Repeat Steps 18–23 for the rear railing (see Figure 20-103).

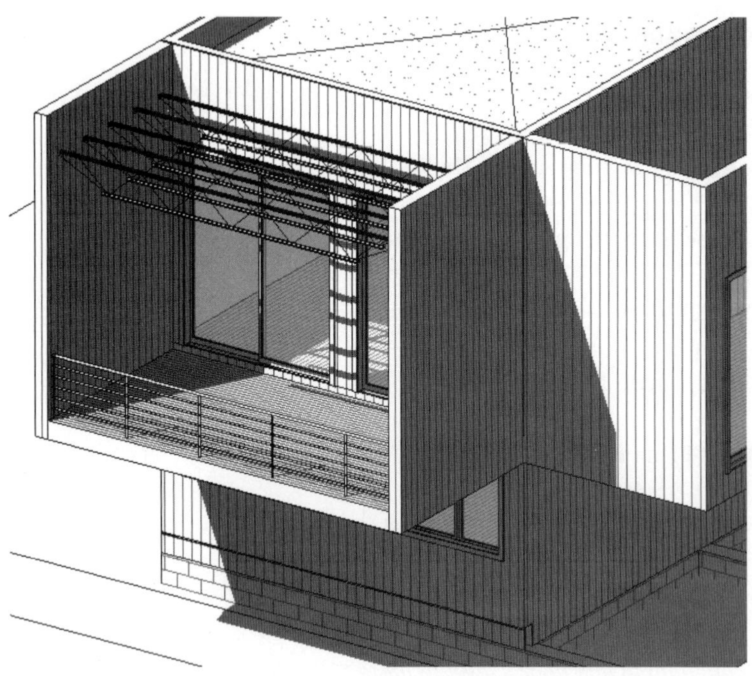

Figure 20-103

3D view of the railing

Wall Details

EXERCISE 20-24 CREATING THE WALL DETAIL

1. Double-click on **Section 1** in the **Project Browser** to bring it into the **Drawing Editor**.
2. Select the **View** tab to bring up the **View** toolbar.
3. In the **View** toolbar, select the **Thin Lines** button to make all the lines thin (see Figure 20-104).

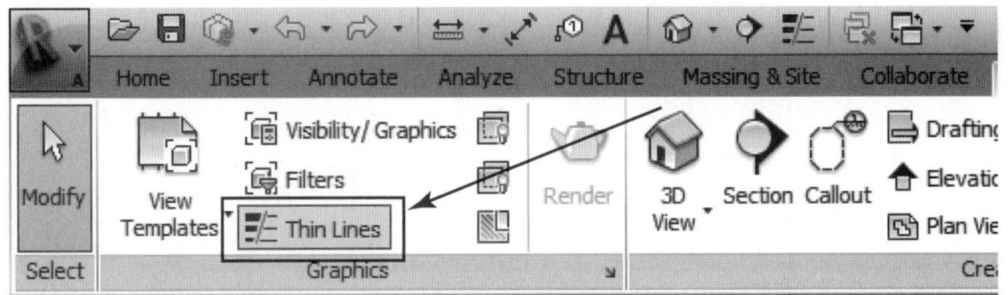

Figure 20-104

Thin Lines button

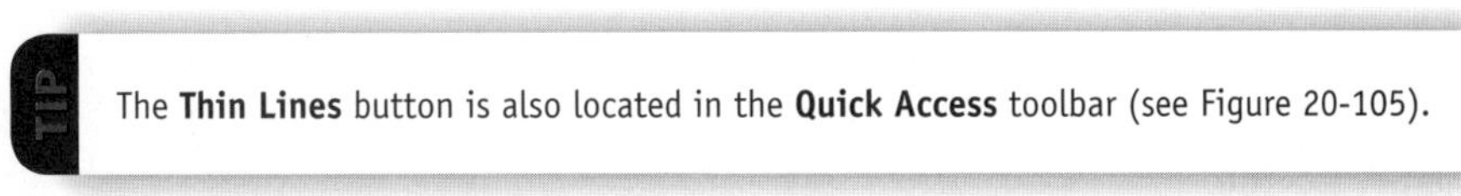

TIP: The **Thin Lines** button is also located in the **Quick Access** toolbar (see Figure 20-105).

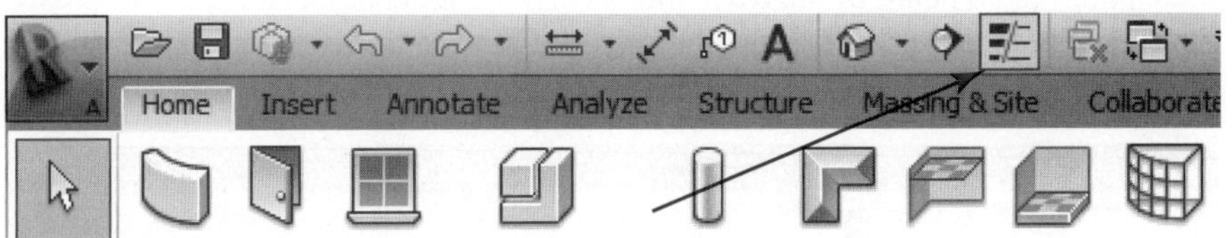

Figure 20-105

Quick Access toolbar

Notice that the stud and gypsum board of the front wall sits on the foundation and passes through the floor. This is not correct (see Figure 20-106).

To fix this type of condition, do the following:

4. Select the wall, to bring up its **Properties** dialog box.
5. In the **Properties** dialog box, select the **Edit Type** button to bring up the **Type Properties** dialog box.
6. In the **Type Properties** dialog box, press the **Edit** button opposite the **Structure** field to bring up the **Edit Assembly** dialog box.
7. In the **Edit Assembly** dialog box, select **Section: Modify type attributes** from the **View** drop-down list, and scroll the image so that you can see the bottom of the wall (see Figure 20-107).
8. In the **Edit Assembly** dialog box, select the **Modify** button, and then move your cursor over the bottom line of the structure within the **Core Boundary** (the stud), and click your mouse button.
9. A **Lock** symbol will appear; click the **Lock** to open it.
10. Repeat this process for the inside gypsum board adjacent to the stud (see Figure 20-108).

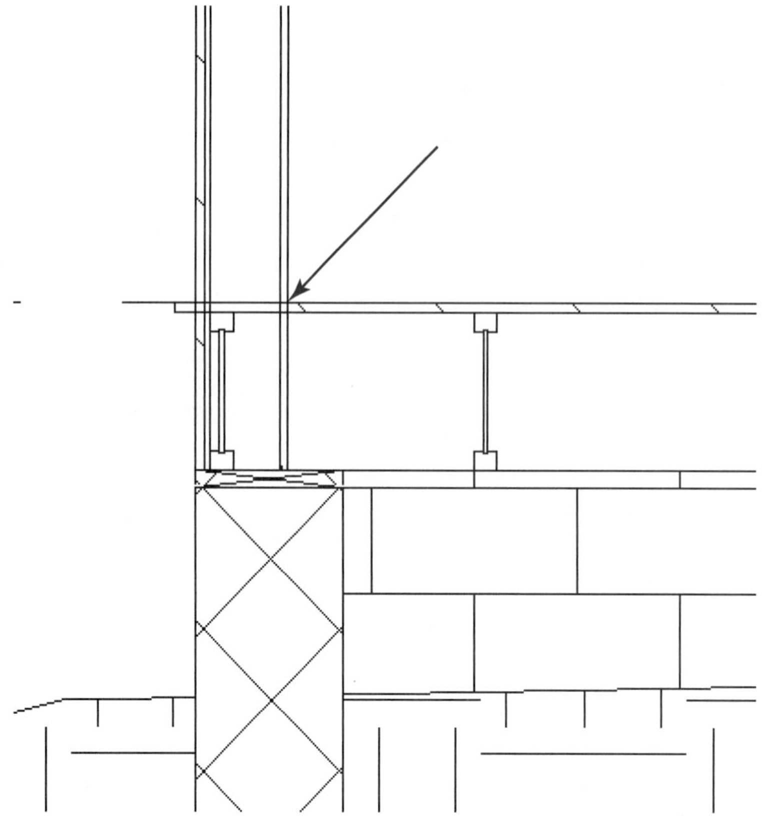

Figure 20-106

Stud and gypsum board of the front wall sits on the foundation and should not pass through the floor

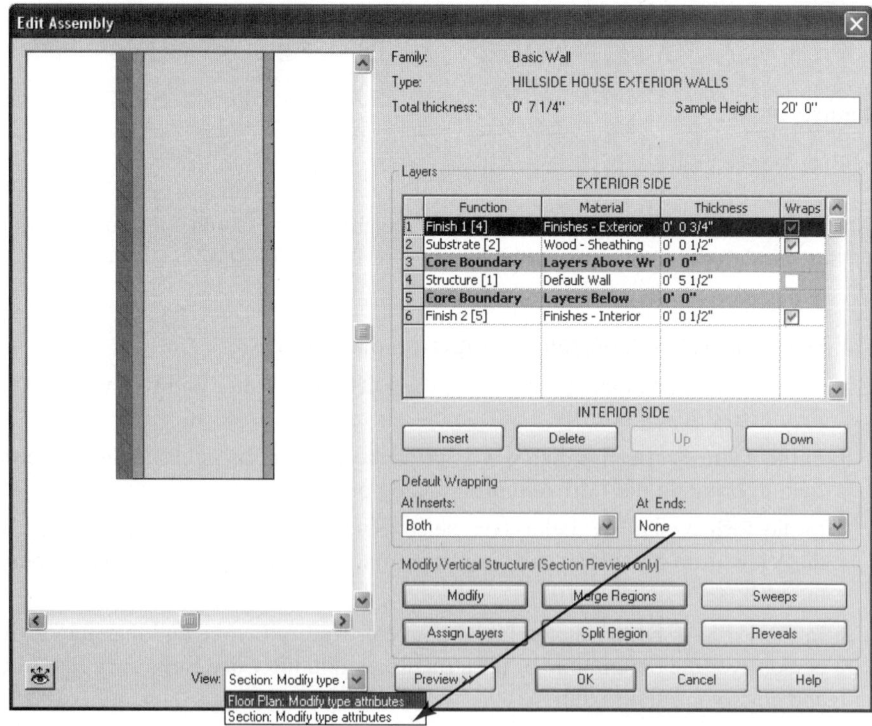

Figure 20-107

Edit Assembly dialog box

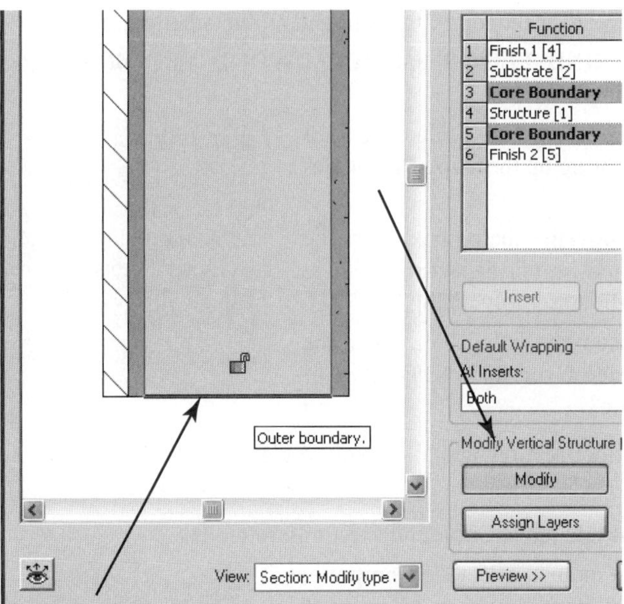

Figure 20-108

Unlock the bottom line of the structure

11. Repeat this process for the inside gypsum board adjacent to the stud.
12. Select the **OK** buttons to return to **Section 1** in the **Drawing Editor**.
13. Select the wall again, and notice that small blue arrows appear at the base of the wall.
14. Drag the wall rightmost arrow upward until the stud and gypsum board are sitting on top of the floor (see Figure 20-109).

NOTE:

Currently, you can do this operation only on two layers in a wall.

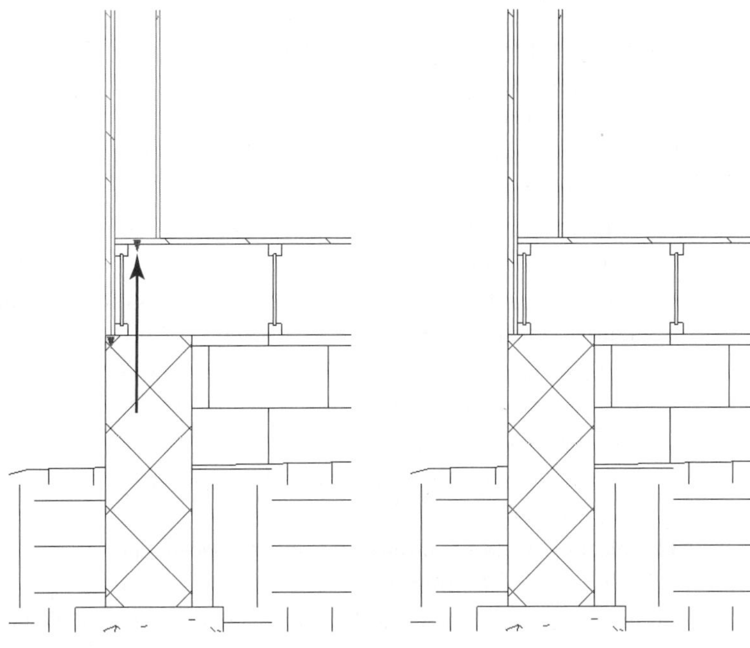

Figure 20-109

Small blue arrows in the **Section 1** drawing

15. Repeat this process for the top of the wall and all the other outer walls.
16. Select the **SECOND FLOOR 3/4″ HARDWOOD FLOOR** to bring up its **Properties** dialog box.
17. In the **Properties** dialog box, select the **Edit Type** button to bring up the **Type Properties** dialog box.
18. In the **Type Properties** dialog box, press the **Edit** button opposite the **Structure** field to bring up the **Edit Assembly** dialog box.
19. In the **Edit Assembly** dialog box, select the **Material** for each layer, and change its **Cut Pattern** to **None**.

NOTE:

Once you have modified a particular wall type in the **Edit Assembly** dialog box, you can move it to layers wherever that type of wall appears in your drawing. This modification will also appear in the 3D model.

This will clear the floor section, and allow you to place 2D detail components in this floor.

20. Select the **Annotate** tab to bring up the **Annotate** toolbar.
21. In the **Annotate** toolbar, select the **Component > Detail Component** button to bring up the **Modify | Place Detail Component** toolbar.
22. In the **Modify | Place Detail Component** toolbar, select the **Load Family** button to bring up the **Load Family** dialog box.
23. In the **Load Family** dialog box, press the **Imperial Library** button at the left side of the dialog box to bring up the **Imperial Library**.

NOTE:

For learning purposes, the first floor was modeled; the second floor was not modeled and will use 2D detail components to illustrate the structure in section.

24. In the **Imperial Library**, select and open the **Detail Components** folder.
25. In the **Detail Components** folder, select and open the **Div 06 - Wood and Plastic** folder.
26. In the **Div 06 - Wood and Plastic** folder, select and open the **06100-Rough Carpentry** folder.
27. In the **06100-Rough Carpentry** folder, select and open the **06170-Prefabricated Structural Wood** folder.
28. In the **06170-Prefabricated Structural Wood** folder, select the **Medium Load Wood Joist-Section**, and press the **Open** button to return to **Section 1** in the **Drawing Editor**.
29. In the **Properties** dialog box, select the **Edit Type** button to bring up the **Type Properties** dialog box.
30. In the **Type Properties** dialog box, press the **Duplicate** button to bring up the **Name** dialog box.
31. In the **Name** dialog box, enter **11-7/8″**, and press the **OK** button to return to the **Type Properties** dialog box.
32. In the **Type Properties** dialog box, change the **Web Diameter** to **1/2″** and the **Depth** to **0′ 11 7/8″**. Press the **OK** buttons to return to the **Drawing Editor**.
33. Place the 2D detail component of the wood joist in the drawing as shown in Figure 20-110.
34. Select the **Detail Component** you just placed, and select the **Array** button from the **Options Bar**.
35. In the **Options Bar**, press the **Linear** button, check the **Group And Associate** check box, and enter **20** in the **Number** field. Select the **Move To: 2nd** radio button, and check the **Constrain** (horizontal or vertical) check box (see Figure 20-111).

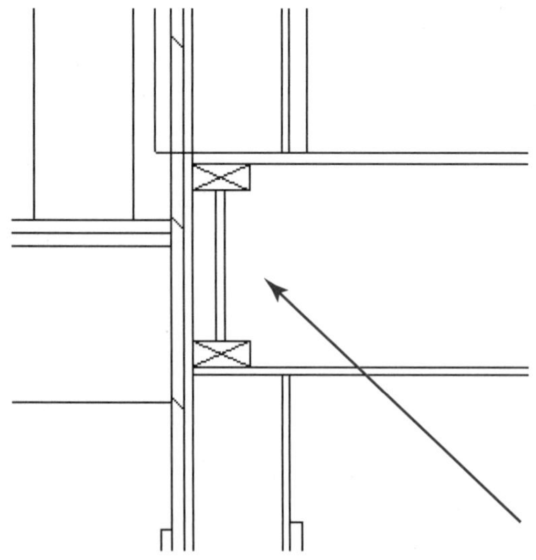

Figure 20-110

Place the 2D detail component of the wood joist

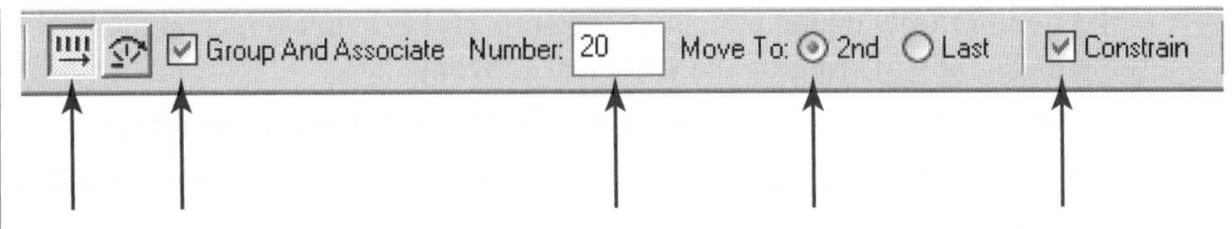

Figure 20-111

Linear button

36. Click on the center of the wood joist, drag to the right until the dimension reads **2′-0″**, and then click your mouse to array the joists.
37. Click in an empty spot in the drawing to clear the command.
38. Click on the center of the wood joist, drag to the right until the dimension reads **2′-0″**, and then click your mouse to array the joists.

NOTE:
You will have to copy the last wood joist and add it at the end because the last joist is less than 2′-0″ from the previous joist (see Figure 20-112).

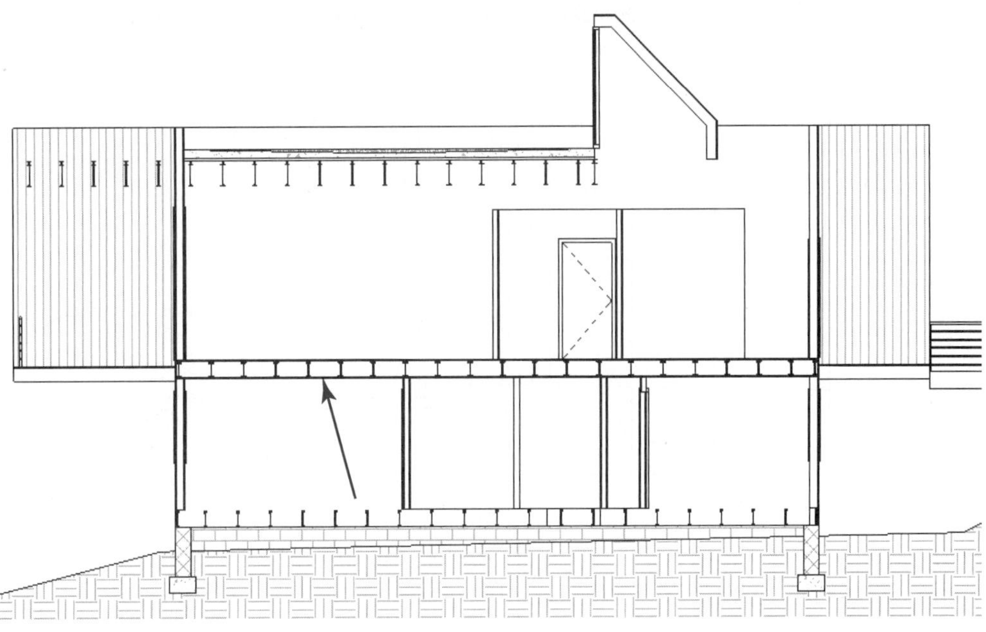

Figure 20-112

Wood joist in drawing

39. Click in an empty spot in the drawing to clear the command.
40. In the **Annotate** toolbar, select the **Component > Detail Component** button.
41. Again, in the **Annotate** toolbar, select the **Load Family** button to bring up the **Load Family** dialog box.
42. In the **Load Family** dialog box, press the **Imperial Library** button at the left side of the dialog box to bring up the **Imperial Library**.
43. In the **Imperial Library**, select and open the **Detail Components** folder.
44. In the **Detail Components** folder, select and open the **Div 06 - Wood and Plastic** folder.
45. In the **Annotate** toolbar, select the **Component > Detail Component** button.
46. Again, in the **Annotate** toolbar, select the **Load Family** button to bring up the **Load Family** dialog box.

47. In the **Load Family** dialog box, press the **Imperial Library** button at the left side of the dialog box to bring up the **Imperial Library**.
48. In the **Imperial Library**, select and open the **Detail Components** folder.
49. Again, in the **Detail Components** folder, select and open the **Div 06 - Wood and Plastic** folder.
50. In the **Div 06 - Wood and Plastic** folder, select and open the **06100-Rough Carpentry** folder.
51. In the **06100-Rough Carpentry** folder, select and open the **06110-Wood Framing** folder.
52. In the **06110-Wood Framing** folder, select **Nominal Cut Lumber-Section**, and press the **Open** button to return to the **Drawing Editor**.
53. In the **Properties** dialog box, select **Nominal Cut Lumber-Section: 2 × 6** from the **Properties** drop-down list.
54. In the **Options Bar**, check the **Rotate after placement** check box, place the detail component in an empty space in the drawing, rotate it, and click your mouse.
55. Move your mouse to the lower right of the **2 × 6**, and place it as a stud plate in the first and second floor walls in section.
56. Repeat this process, selecting lumber sections until you have detailed the walls and the decks (see Figure 20-113).

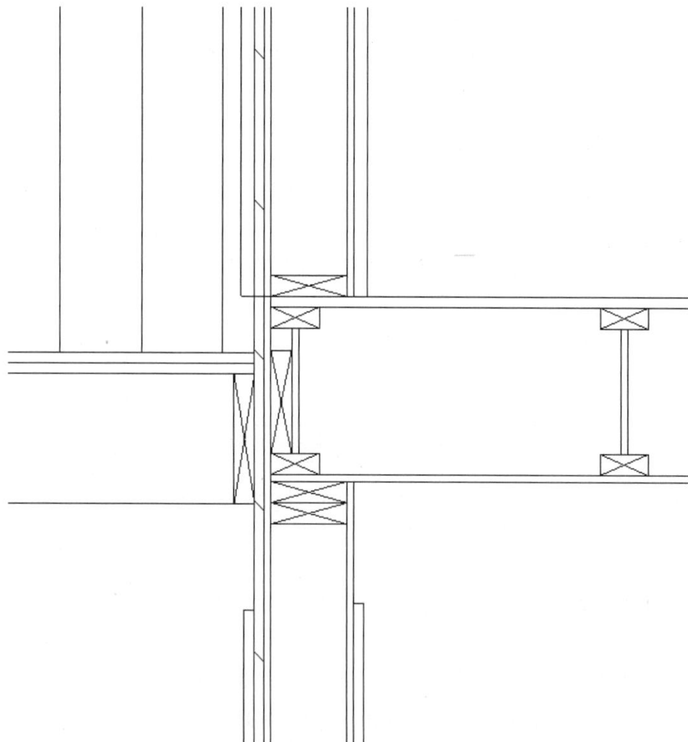

Figure 20-113

Detailed walls in drawing

57. Again, in the **Annotate** toolbar, select the **Component > Detail Component** button.
58. Locate and open the **05090 Metal Fastenings** folder in the **Detail Components** folder.
59. In this folder, select **A307 Bolts-Side**, and select **Open** to return to the **Drawing Editor**.

60. In the **Properties** dialog box, select **A307 Bolts-Side: 5/8″** from the **Properties** drop-down list, and place it.
61. In the **Annotate** toolbar, select the **Insulation** button.
62. In the **Options Bar**, enter **5-1/2″** in the **Width** field.
63. Click at the top bottom middle of the first floor wall plate, and click again at the middle of the bottom of the top plate of the wall (see Figure 20-115).

NOTE:

If you select the bolt after you place it, arrow grips will appear. Drag these to adjust the length of the bolt. This arrow grip convention for resizing is typical of many of the **Detail Components** (see Figure 20-114).

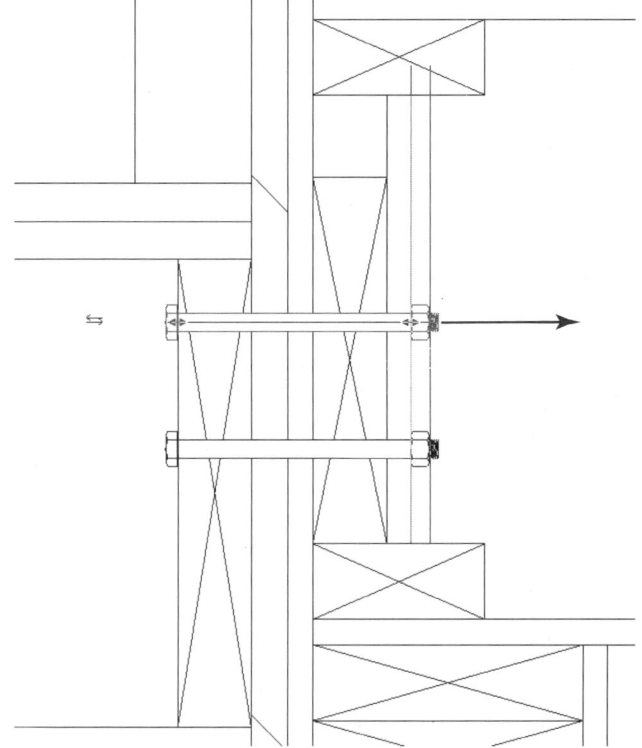

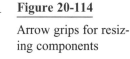

Figure 20-114

Arrow grips for resizing components

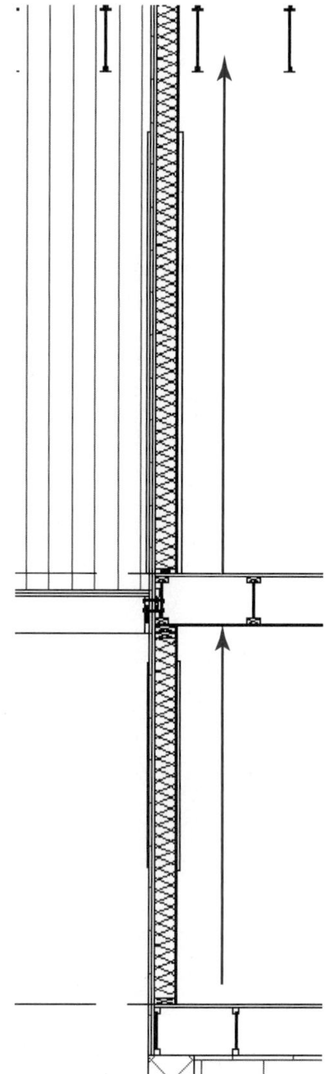

Figure 20-115

Add insulation in wall

64. In the **Annotate** toolbar, select the **Region > Filled Region** button to bring up the **Modify | Create Filled Region Boundary** toolbar.
65. In the **Properties** dialog box, select the **Edit Type** button to bring up the **Type Properties** dialog box.
66. In the **Type Properties** dialog box, select the **Duplicate** button to bring up the **Name** dialog box.
67. In the **Name** dialog box, enter **STONE FILL**, and press the **OK** button to return to the **Type Properties** dialog box.
68. In the **Type Properties** dialog box, select the **Fill Patterns** field to bring up the **Fill Patterns** dialog box.
69. In the **Fill Patterns** dialog box, select the **Sand** pattern, and press the **OK** buttons to return to the **Drawing Editor**.
70. In the **Modify | Create Filled Region Boundary** toolbar, select the **Line** button. Using various line options, draw the drainage field at the bottom of the foundation.
71. In the **Modify | Create Filled Region Boundary** toolbar, select the **Finish Edit Mode** button to create the sand-filled drainage field.

NOTE:

You can import any **Hatch** patterns from AutoCAD or AutoCAD Architecture.

72. Using **Detail Components**, complete the section.
73. Select the **View** tab to bring up the **View** toolbar.
74. In the **View** toolbar, select the **Callout** button.
75. In the **Options Bar**, select **1/2″ = 1′-0″** from the **Scale** drop-down field.
76. Drag the callout around the front wall as shown in Figure 20-116.

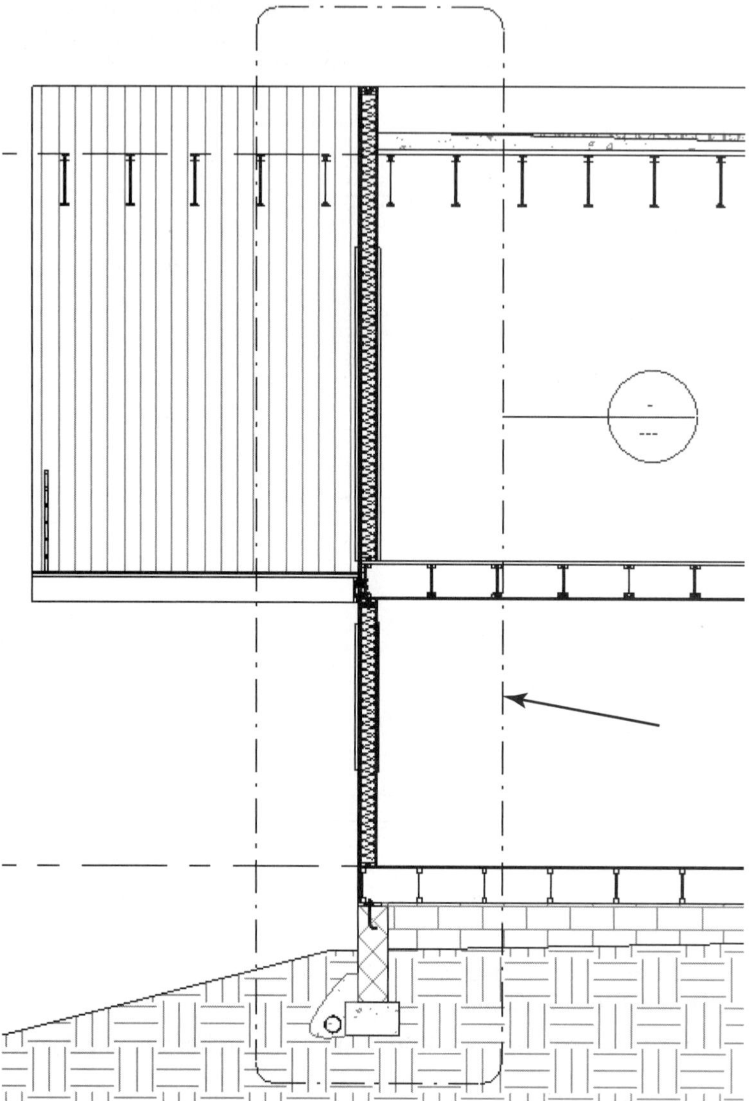

Figure 20-116

Drag the callout around the front wall

The callout will now appear as **Callout of Section 1** in the **Project Browser** (see Figure 20-117).

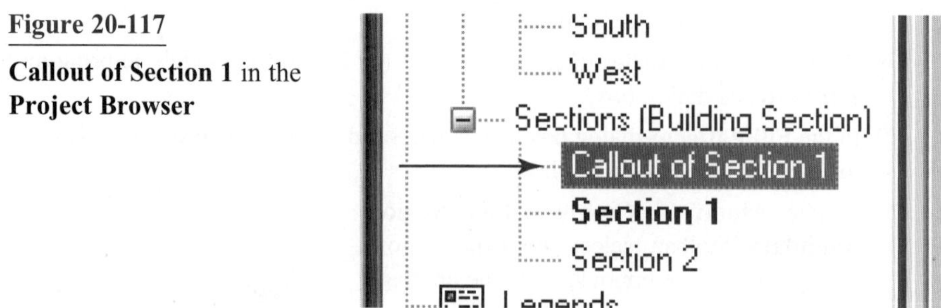

Figure 20-117

Callout of Section 1 in the **Project Browser**

77. Select the **View** tab to bring up the **View** toolbar.
78. In the **View** toolbar, select the **New Sheet** button to bring up the **Select a Titleblock** dialog box (see Figure 20-118).

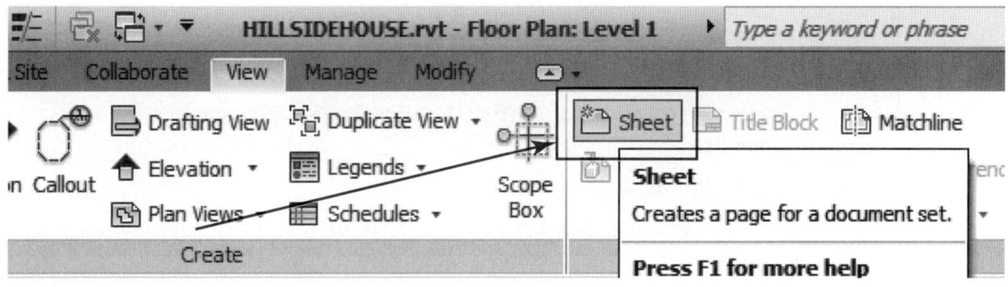

Figure 20-118

New Sheet button

79. In the **Titleblock** dialog box, press the **OK** button, and create a new sheet as you have done previously.
80. Name the sheet **DETAILS**.
81. In the **Project Browser**, select **Callout of Section 1**, and drag it into the **DETAILS** sheet.

NOTE:

The **Detail Components** will not be showing in the callout in the **DETAILS** sheet. There is a "work around" to fix this problem.

a. Double-click on **Section 1** in the **Project Browser** to bring it into the **Drawing Editor**.
b. Select everything in the front wall.
c. Select the **Filter** button to bring up the **Filter** dialog box.
d. In the **Filter** dialog box, uncheck everything except the **Detail Groups**, **Detail Items**, and **Insulation Batting Lines** (see Figure 20-119).

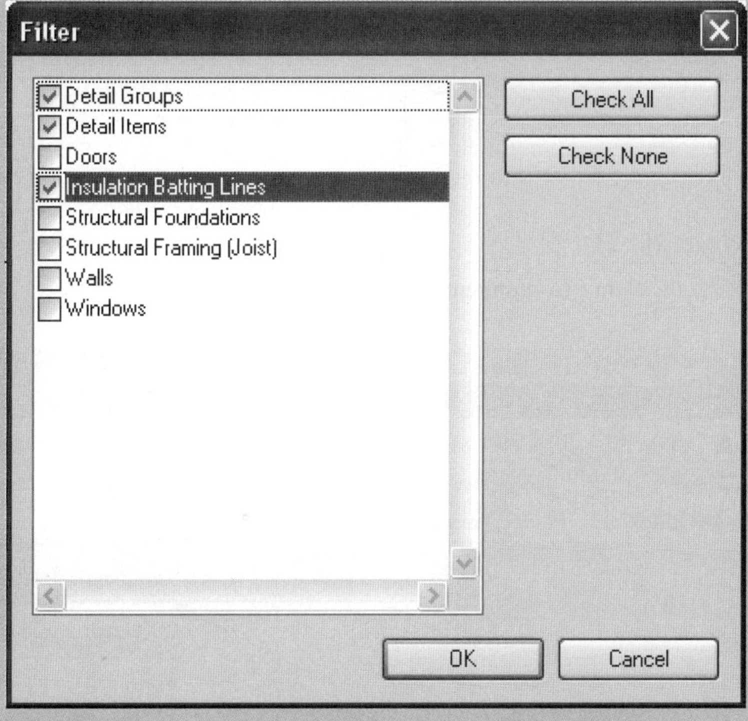

Figure 20-119

Filter dialog box

e. Press the **OK** button to return to the **Drawing Editor**, and select the checked items.
f. In the **Multi-Select** toolbar, select the **Copy to Clipboard** button.
g. Double-click on **Callout of Section 1** in the **Project Browser** to bring it into the **Drawing Editor**.
h. Select the **Modify** toolbar.
i. In the **Modify** toolbar, select the **Paste > Align to Same Place** button to copy all the **Detail Components** from **Section 1** into the callout.

82. Select the **View** toolbar again.
83. In the **View** toolbar, select the **Callout** button again, and this time make a **Callout of Section 1**.
84. This callout will be labeled **Callout [2] of Section 1**.
85. Make its scale **1-1/2″ = 1′-0″**.
86. As you did previously, copy and paste the **Detail Components** into **Callout [2] of Section 1** (see Figures 20-120 and 20-121).
87. Make sure **Callout [2] of Section 1** is in the **Drawing Editor**.
88. Change to the **Annotate** toolbar.
89. In the **Annotate** toolbar, select the **Keynote > Element Keynote** button to bring up the **Modify | Place Element Keynote** toolbar (see Figure 20-122).

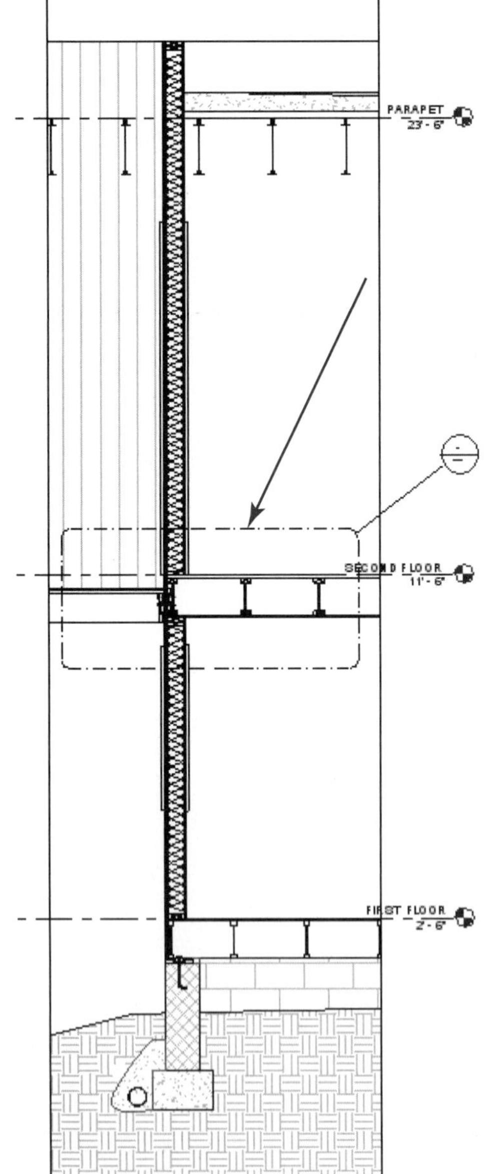

Figure 20-120

Copy the **Detail Components**

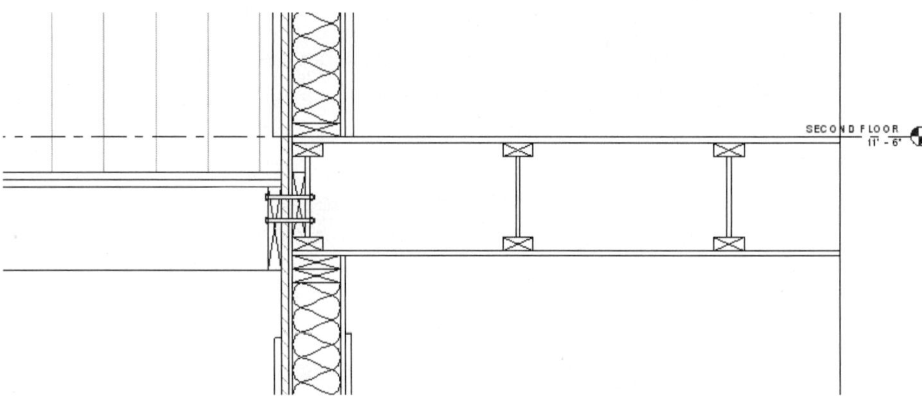

Figure 20-121

Paste the **Detail Components**

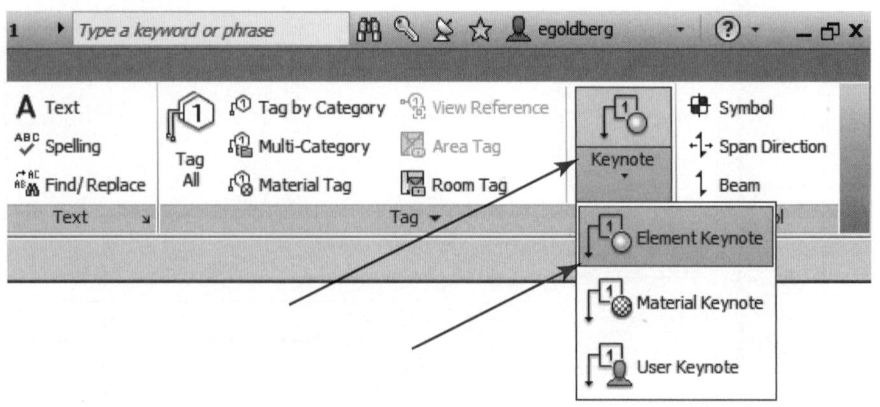

Figure 20-122

Keynote > Element Keynote button

90. In the **Properties** dialog box, select the **Edit Type** button to bring up the **Type Properties** dialog box.
91. In the **Type Properties** dialog box, select **Arrow Filled 15 Degree** from the **Leader Arrowhead** drop-down list, and press the **OK** button to return to the **Drawing Editor**.
92. In the **Modify | Place Element Keynote** toolbar, select **Keynote Tag: Keynote Text** from the **Change Element Type** drop-down list.
93. In the **Callout [2] of Section 1**, pick the batt insulation, drag to the right, and click twice to bring up the **Keynotes** dialog box.
94. In the **Keynotes** dialog box, select **07210.A3**, and press the **OK** button to return to the **Drawing Editor**.
95. Press the <**Esc**> key twice to complete the command and place the note.
96. Continue to add keynotes.

NOTE:
Once you have added a keynote for a particular material, you will not have to see its keynote thereafter; Revit will remember the material references for that keynote. You can also add keynotes to the keynote database. Please reference the Help guide for this information. You can also pre-add keynotes to a material by adding it in the **Type Properties** dialog box for a particular object (see Figure 20-123).

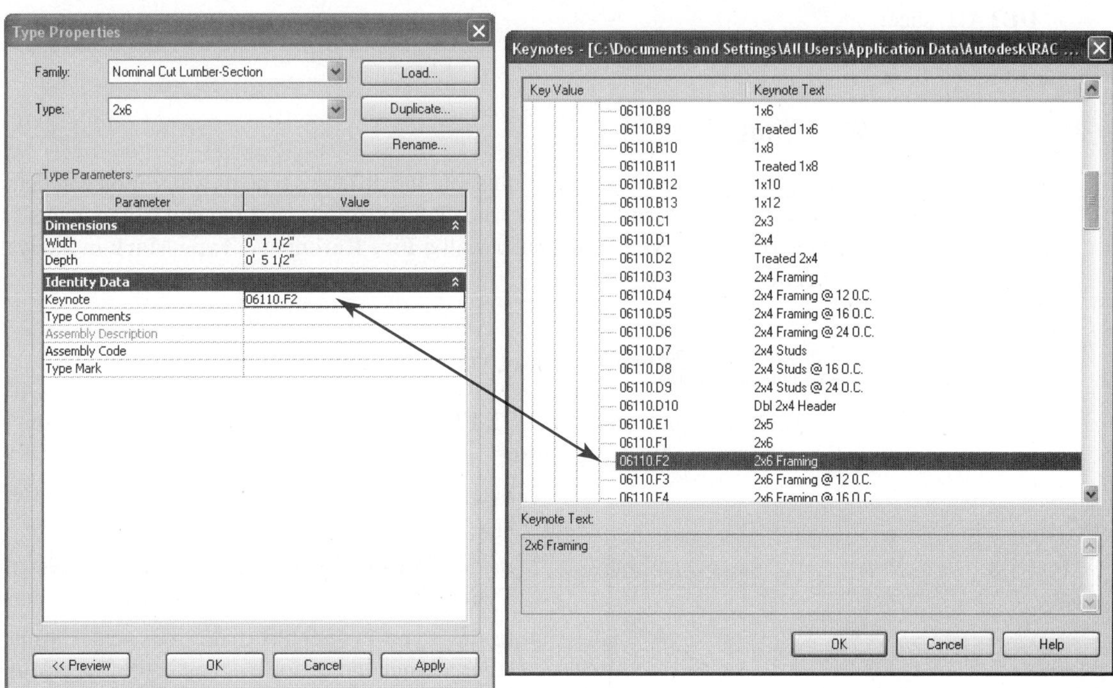

Figure 20-123

Type Properties dialog box

97. Double-click on the **DETAIL** plot sheet in the **Project Browser** to bring it into the **Drawing Editor**.
98. Drag the **Callout [2] of Section 1** into the **DETAIL** sheet (see Figure 20-124).
99. Save the file.

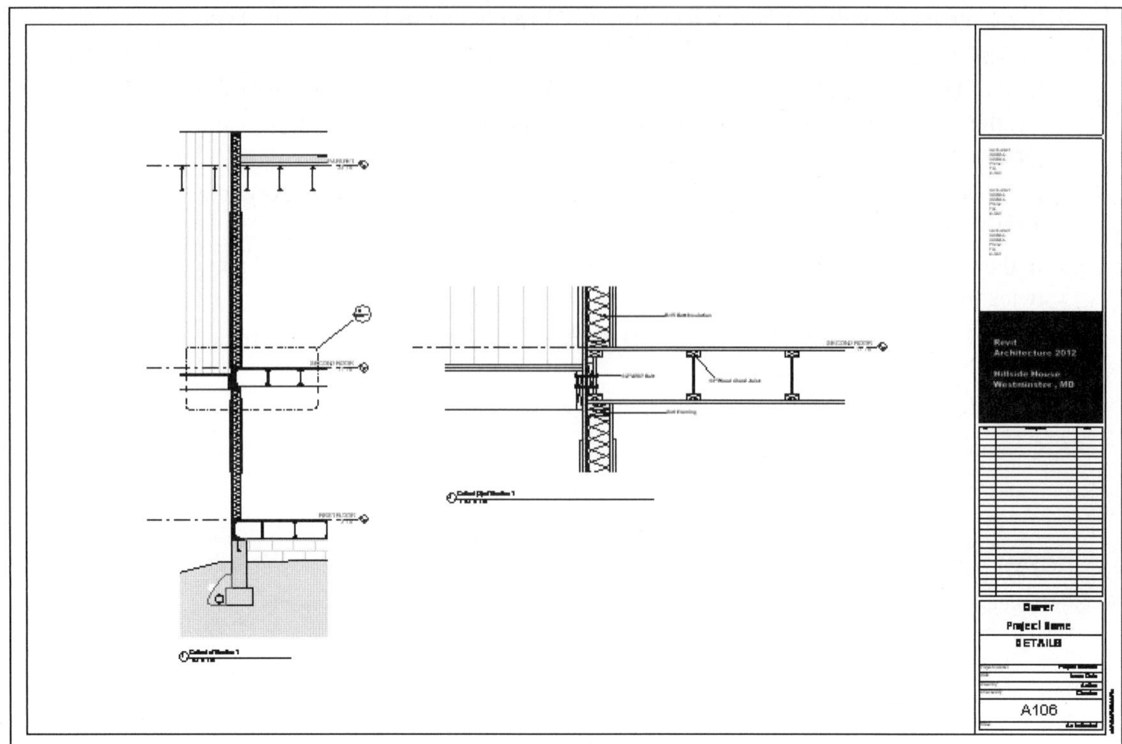

Figure 20-124

DETAIL sheet

Wall Tags

Wall tags are an excellent way to illustrate the different type of walls. You can detail the different walls in a **Legend View** (see the "Legend Views and Legend Components" section in Chapter 16). You give the particular wall a **Fire Rating** and **Type Mark** in the wall's **Type Properties** dialog box.

EXERCISE 20-25 PLACING WALL TAGS

1. Double-click on the **FIRST FLOOR** plan view in the **Project Browser** to bring it into the **Drawing Editor**.
2. Select a wall to bring up its **Element Properties** dialog box.
3. In the **Element Properties** dialog box, select the **Edit Type** button to bring up the **Type Properties** dialog box.
4. In the **Type Properties** dialog box, enter a number or letter of your choice for the type in the **Type Mark** field. If the wall is fire rated, enter the fire rating number in the **Fire Rating** field (see Figure 20-125).
5. Press the **OK** buttons to return to the **Drawing Editor**.
6. Change to the **Annotate** toolbar.
7. In the **Annotate** toolbar, select the **Tag > By Category** button to bring up the **Modify | Tag** toolbar.
8. In the **Options Bar**, set the tag to **Horizontal**, check the **Leader** check box, and enter **1/2″** in the **Leader** length field (see Figure 20-126).

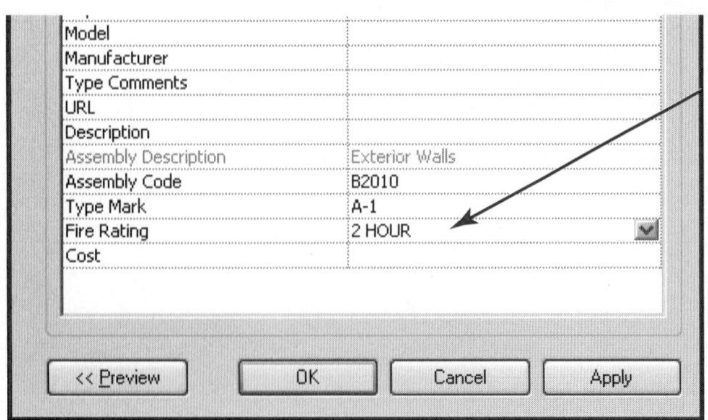

Figure 20-125

Fire Rating field

Figure 20-126

Modify | **Tag** options

> **NOTE:**
> You may have to adjust the **Leader** length to 1/4″ or 1/8″ on later drawings, but for this exercise, use the 1/2″ default. As with every tutorial in this book, it is a good idea to experiment and test all the options.

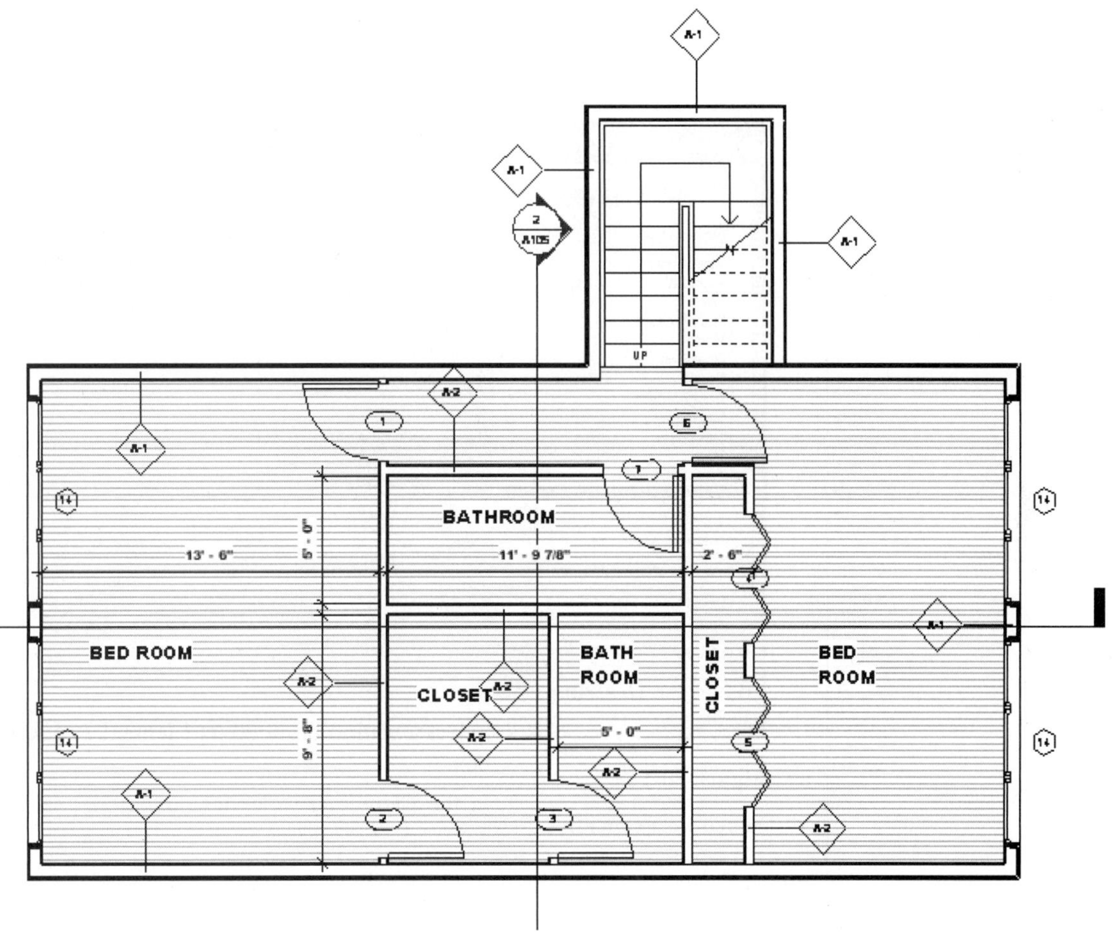

Figure 20-127

Place all the wall tags

9. Move your cursor over a wall, and a tag will appear. Click to place the tag.
10. Establish **Type Marks** in the **Type Properties** dialog boxes of all the different walls, and place all the wall tags (see Figure 20-127).

Door and Window Schedules

EXERCISE 20-26 CREATING THE DOOR AND WINDOW SCHEDULES

1. Change to the **View** toolbar.
2. In the **View** toolbar, select the **Schedule > Schedule/Quantities** button to bring up the **New Schedule** dialog box.
3. In the **New Schedule** dialog box, select **Doors** in the **Category** column, select the **Schedule Building Components** radio button, and press the **OK** button to bring up the **Schedule Properties** dialog box.
4. In the **Schedule Properties** dialog box, select **Width**, **Height**, and **Mark** from the **Available fields** column on the left side of the dialog box.
5. Select **Doors** from the **Select available fields from:** drop-down list.
6. Press the **Add** button to send these fields to the **Scheduled fields [in order]** column in the right side of the dialog box.
7. Press the **Move Up** and **Move Down** buttons to arrange the fields as shown in Figure 20-128.

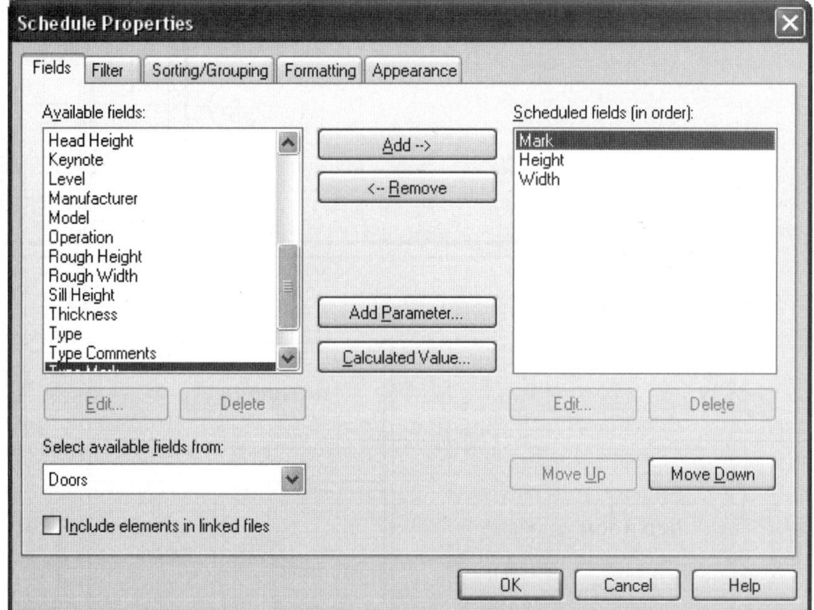

Figure 20-128

Schedule Properties dialog box

8. Press the **OK** button to create the **Door Schedule**. It will appear in the **Drawing Editor**, and its name will appear under **Schedules/Quantities...** in the **Project Browser** (see Figure 20-129).
9. Repeat Steps 1–8, creating a **Window Schedule** with **Type Mark**, **Height**, and **Width**.
10. Double-click on the **TITLE SHEET** in the **Project Browser** to bring it into the **Drawing Editor**.
11. Drag the **Door Schedule** and **Window Schedule** from the **Project Browser** into the **TITLE SHEET** (see Figure 20-130).

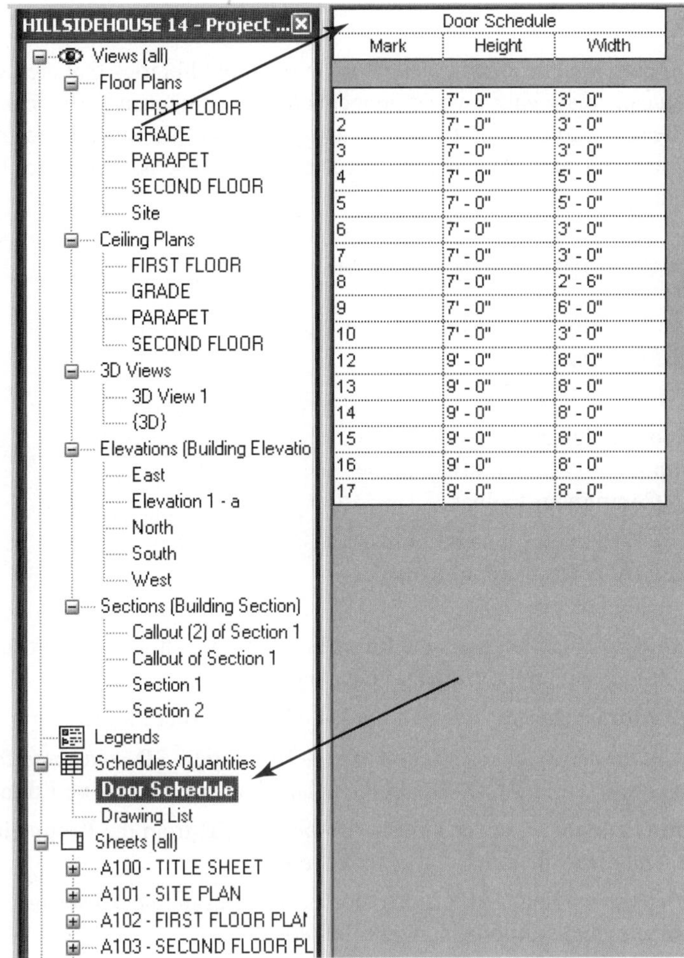

Figure 20-129

Door Schedule added under **Schedules/Quantities**

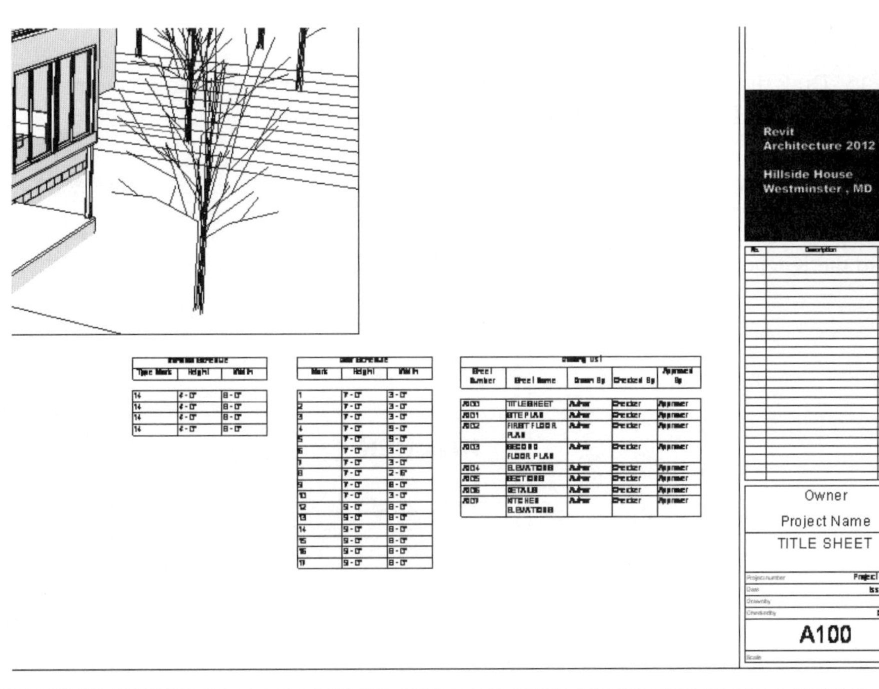

Figure 20-130

Door Schedule and **Window Schedule** added to the **TITLE SHEET**

Kitchen and Bath

Creating the kitchen and bath is quite simple using components and libraries that are available. Remember that you can create your own components or buy components from companies such as Autodesk Seek or Architectural Data Systems. As Revit increasingly becomes the standard in the architectural market, you can expect more manufacturers to offer their products as digital content.

EXERCISE 20-27 **CREATING THE KITCHEN AND BATH**

1. Double-click on the **SECOND FLOOR** plan view in the **Project Browser** to bring it into the **Drawing Editor**.
2. Change to the **Home** toolbar.
3. In the **Home** toolbar, select the **Component** > **Place a Component** button to bring up the **Modify | Place Component** toolbar.
4. In the **Modify | Place Component** toolbar, select the **Load Family** button to bring up the **Load Family** dialog box.

> **NOTE:**
> If no components are already loaded, you may get a Revit query asking whether you wish to load a component.

5. In the **Load Family** dialog box, press the **Imperial Library** button at the left side of the dialog box to bring up the **Imperial Library**.
6. In the **Imperial Library**, select and open the **Plumbing Fixtures** folder.
7. In the **Detail Components** folder, select **Toilet – Domestic - 3D**, and press the **Open** button to return to the **SECOND FLOOR** plan view in the **Drawing Editor**.
8. In the **Properties** dialog box, select **Toilet – Domestic - 3D** from the **Properties** drop-down list, and place the toilet in the **Toilet** room.
9. Repeat this process, loading and placing components from the **Casework** > **Domestic Bathroom** and **Domestic Kitchen** folders.
10. Change to the **View** toolbar.
11. In the **View** toolbar, select the **Elevation** > **Elevation** button.
12. In the **Options Bar**, set the scale to **1″ = 1′-0″**.
13. Place an elevation marker in the kitchen, and check the top and left check boxes in the marker to create two elevations.
14. Dimension the new elevations.
15. Drag these two new elevations from the **Project Browser** into a new plot sheet called **KITCHEN ELEVATIONS** (see Figures 20-131 and 20-132).

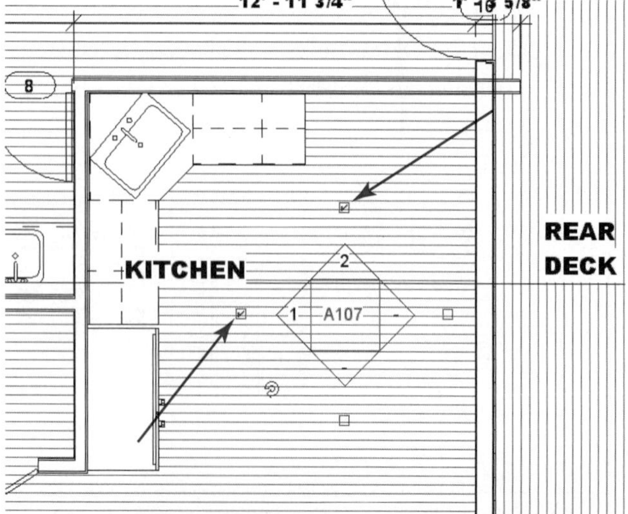

Figure 20-131

Add two new elevations to the Kitchen

Figure 20-132

KITCHEN ELEVATIONS sheet

Model Rendering

EXERCISE 20-28 RENDERING THE MODEL

1. Double-click on the **FIRST FLOOR** plan view in the **Project Browser** to bring it into the **Drawing Editor**.
2. Change to the **View** toolbar.
3. In the **View** toolbar, select the **3D View** > **Camera** button.
4. Click your mouse where you expect the **Camera** to stand.
5. Drag to the point you expect to be the **Target** or view, and click your mouse again to create and open the new **3D** view (see Figure 20-133).
6. In the **Project Browser**, select the new **3D** view, **RMB**, and rename it to **PERSPECTIVE VIEW 1**.
7. Change the **Detail Level** at the bottom of the **Drawing Editor** to **Fine**.
8. Hold down the **<Shift>** key and the mouse wheel.
9. With the **<Shift>** key and mouse wheel held down, move your mouse to rotate the view until you get a view you like.
10. Select the crop outline to activate its grips.
11. Move the grips to frame the **PERSPECTIVE VIEW 1** (see Figure 20-134).
12. Select the **Show Rendering Dialog** button in the **View Control Bar**.
13. In the **Rendering** dialog box, set the **Quality Setting** to **Medium**, **Light Scheme** to **Exterior: Sun only**, **Sun** to **Sunlight from Top Left**, and **Background** to **Very Cloudy**.
14. In the **Rendering** dialog box, press the **Render** button to start the rendering process.

The scene renders in a few minutes, depending on the settings.

Figure 20-133

Camera and **Target**

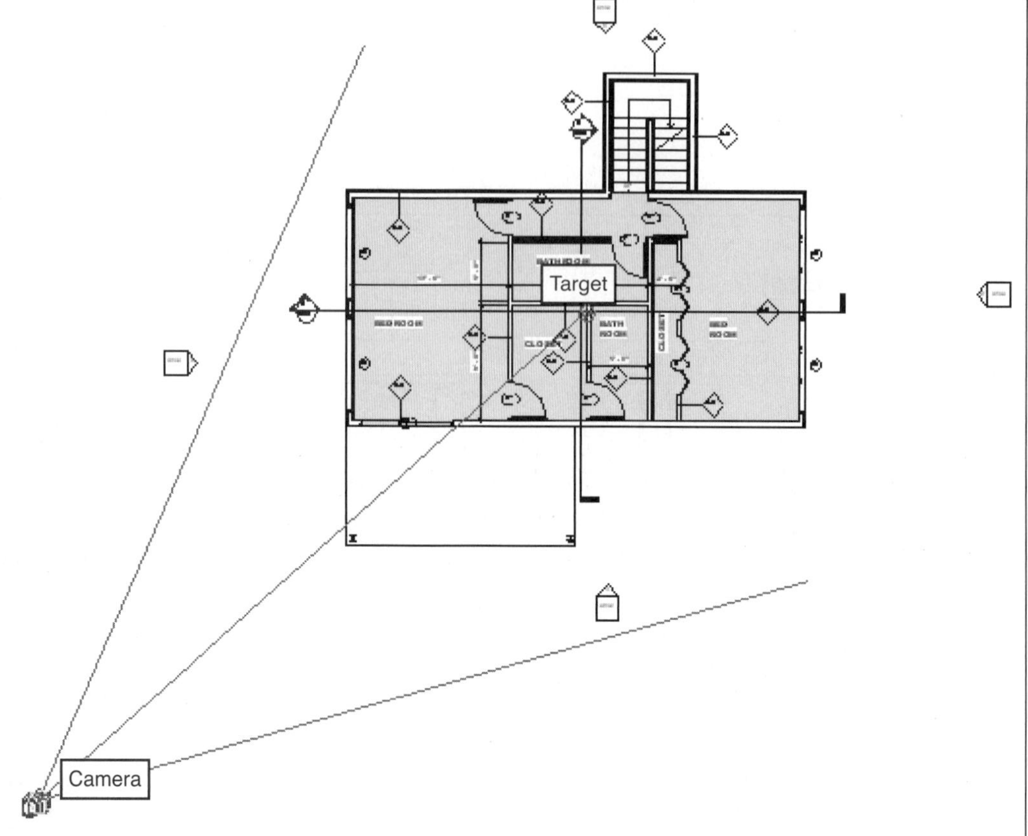

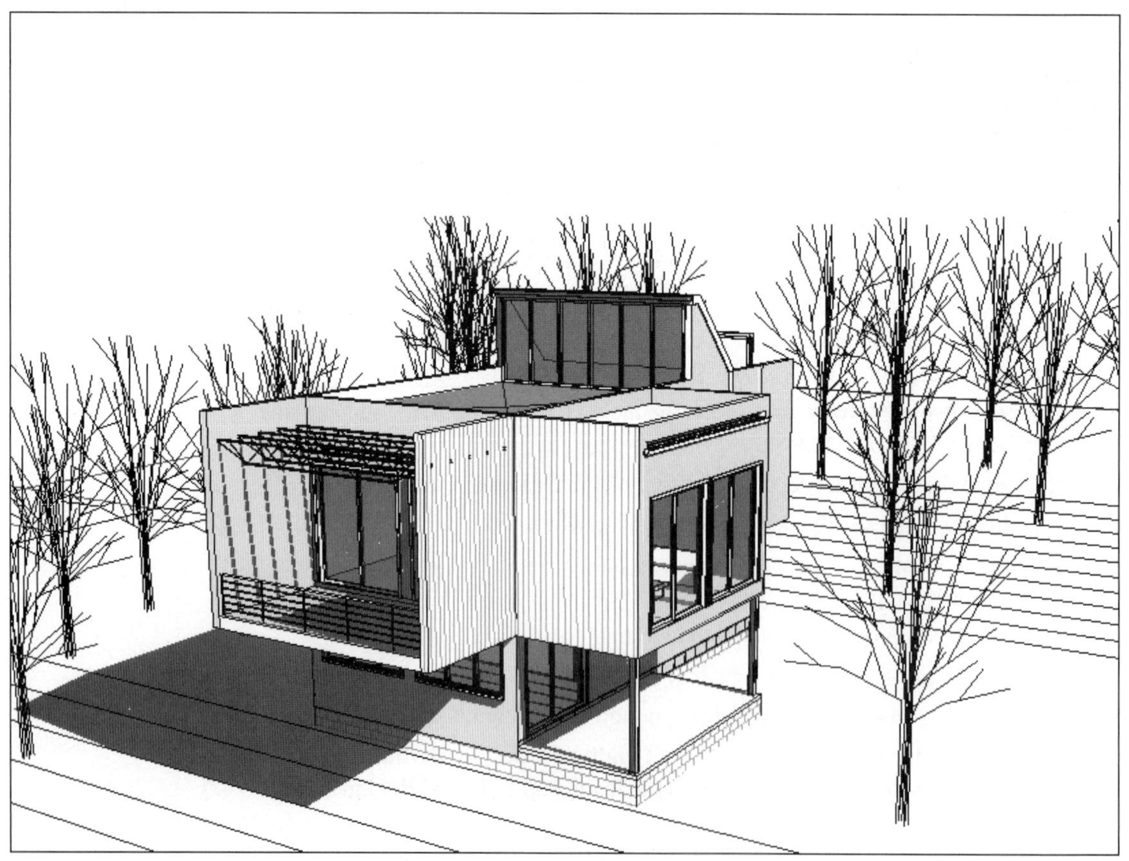

Figure 20-134

PERSPECTIVE VIEW 1

15. After the rendering process has finished, press the **Export** button in the **Rendering** dialog box, and save the image as **HILLSIDE HOUSE RENDER** in JPG (*.jpg,*.jpeg) file format (see Figure 20-135).

Figure 20-135

Save the image as **HILLSIDE HOUSE RENDER**

This is as far as we go; the rest is up to you. Once you have the methodology down, the system is really quite straightforward (see Figures 20-136 through 20-144).

16. Save the file.

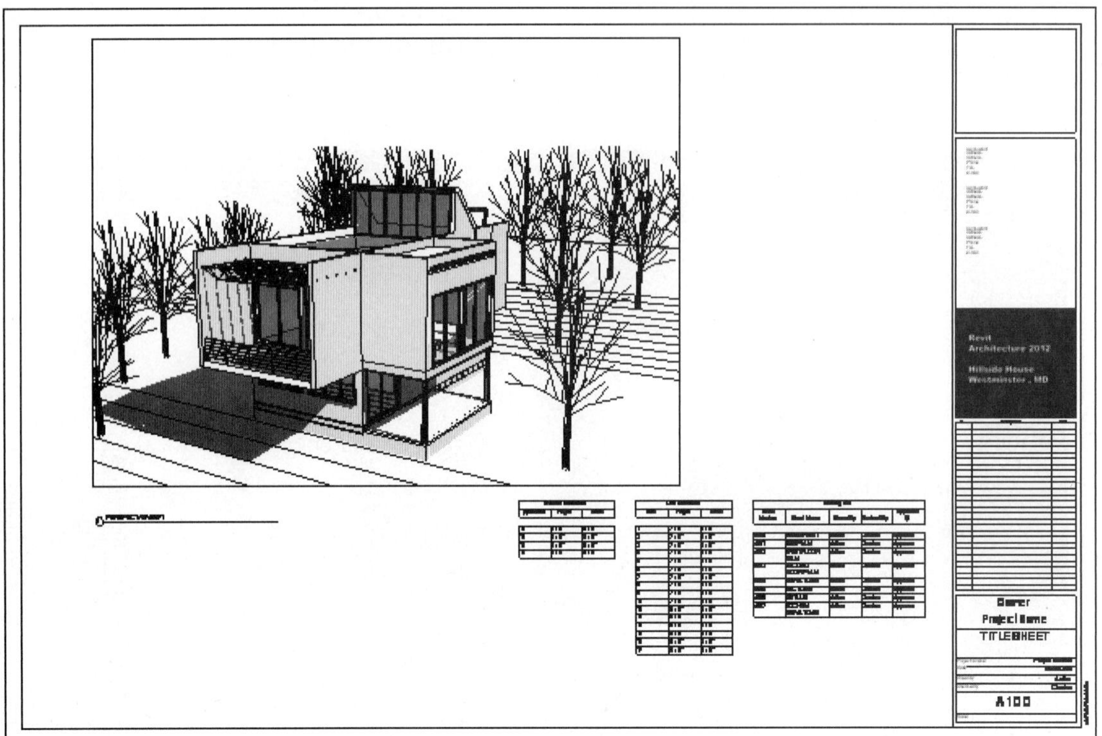

Figure 20-136

Title Sheet

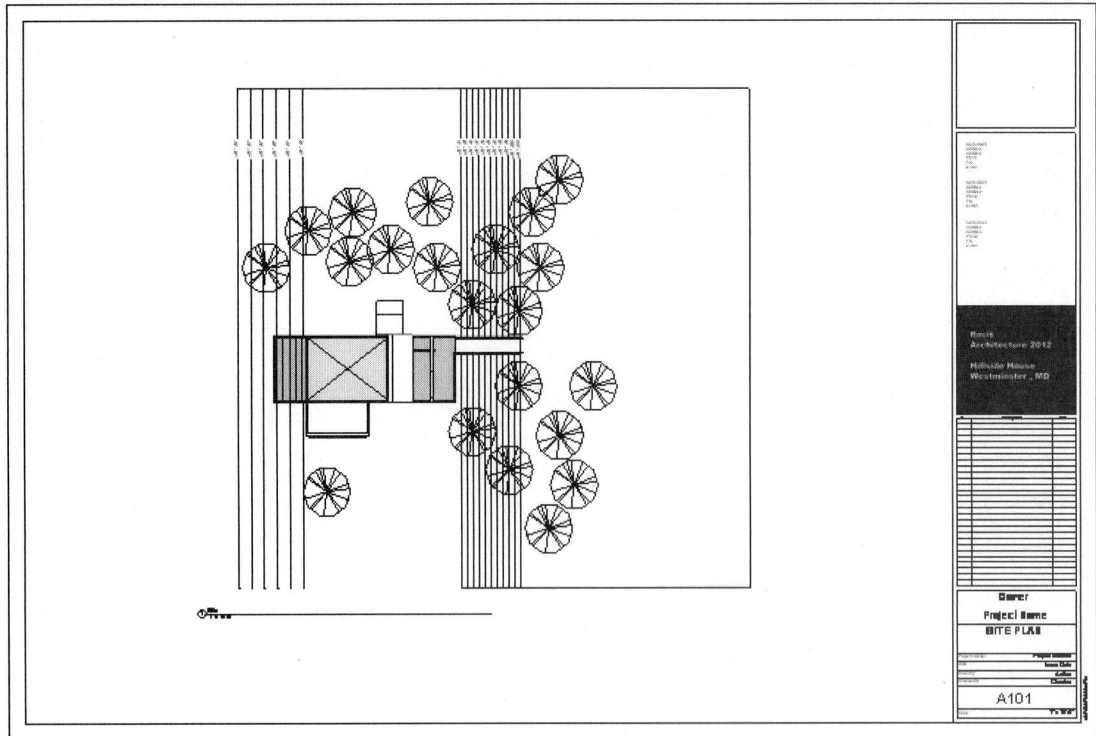

Figure 20-137

Site Plan

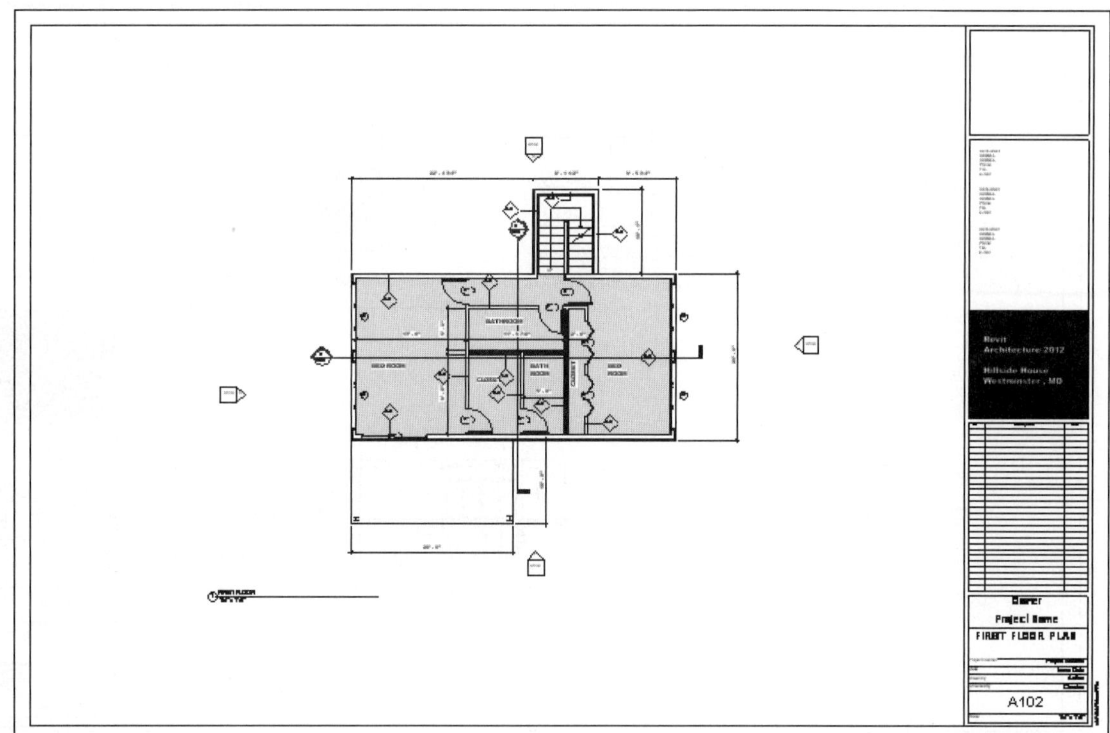

Figure 20-138

First Floor Plan

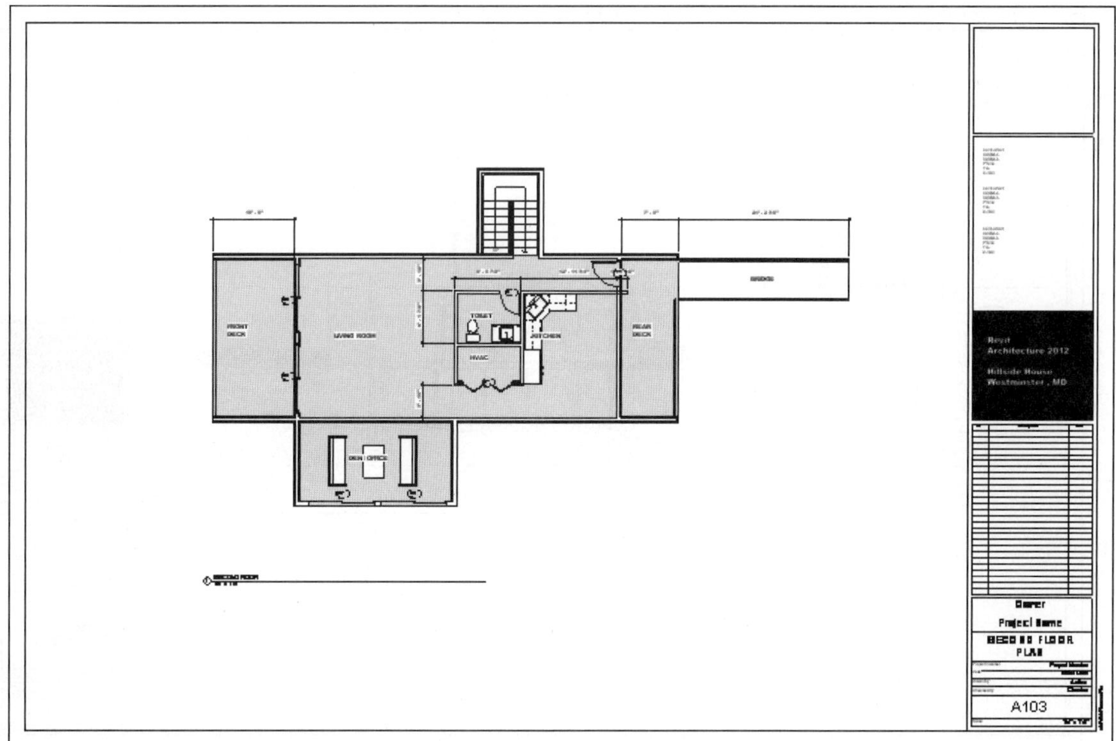

Figure 20-139

Second Floor Plan

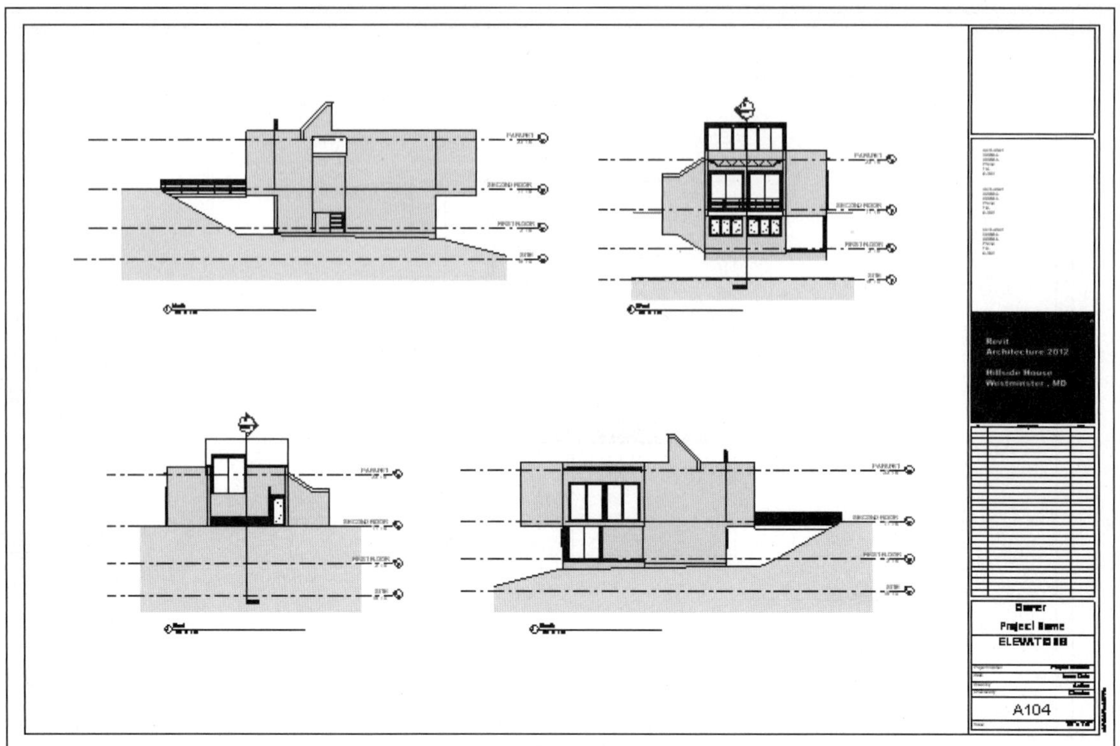

Figure 20-140

Elevations

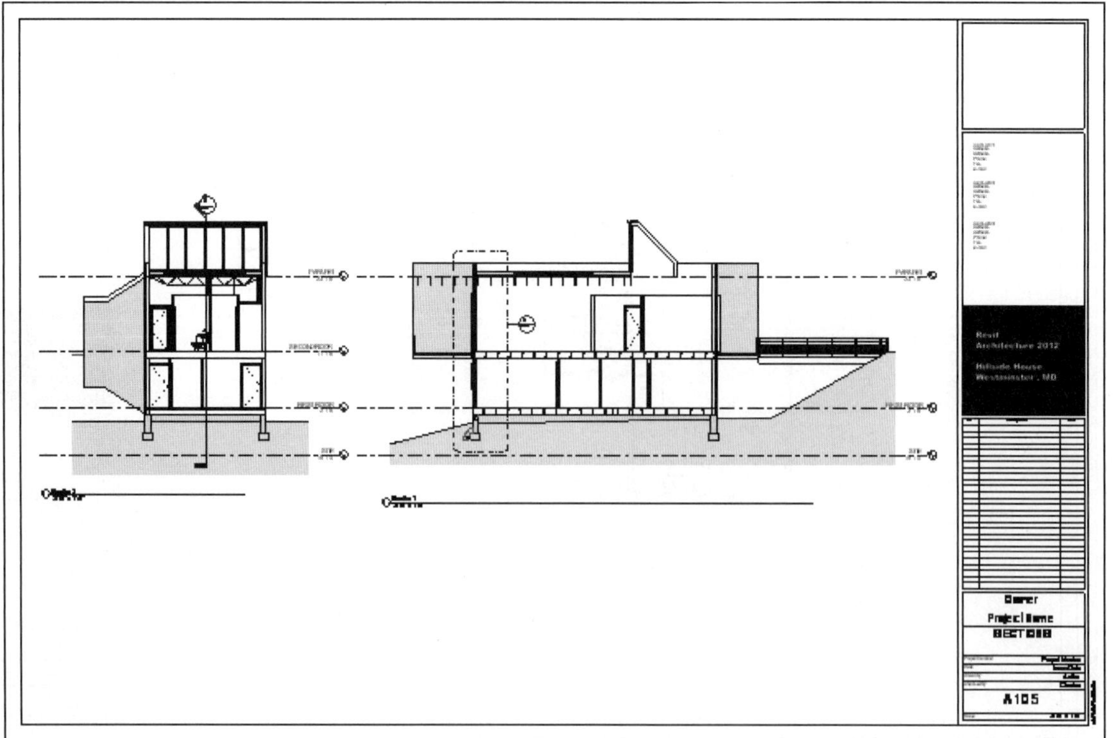

Figure 20-141

Sections

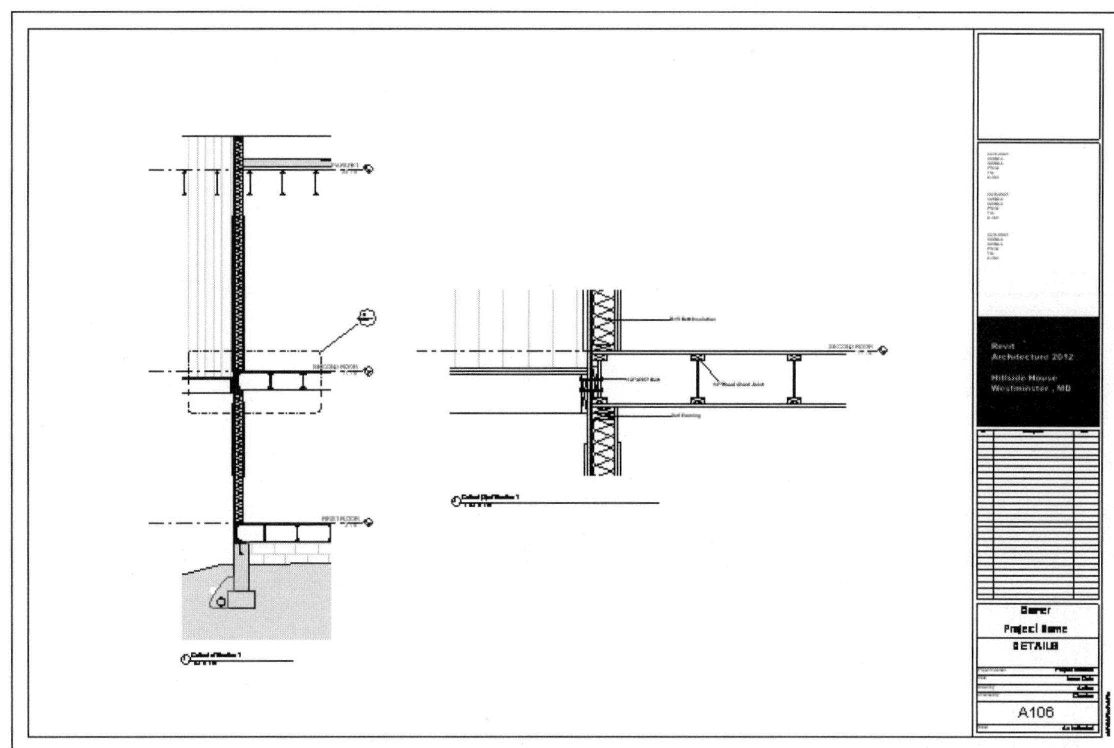

Figure 20-142

Details

Figure 20-143

Kitchen Elevations

Figure 20-144

Project Browser showing all views and sheets for the Tutorial Project

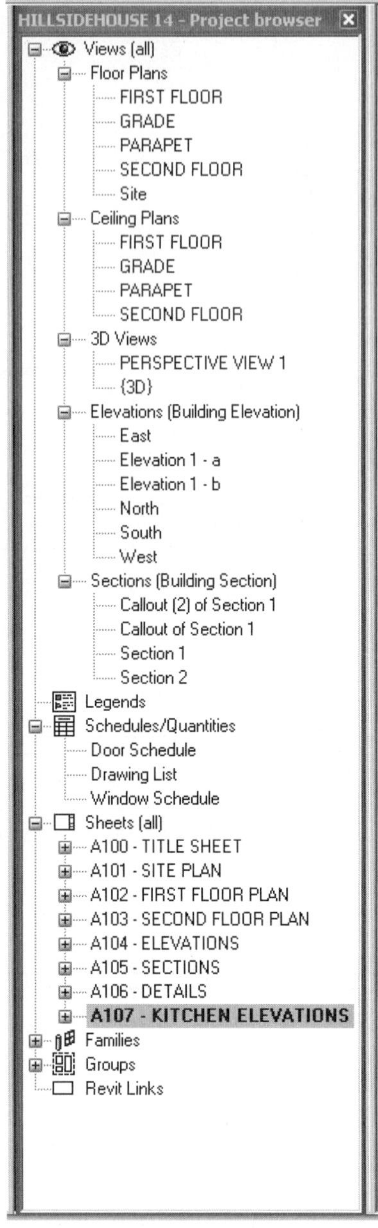

The following are examples of some of the author's projects (see Figures 20-145 through 20-152).

Figure 20-145

Rendered project of a storage facility office

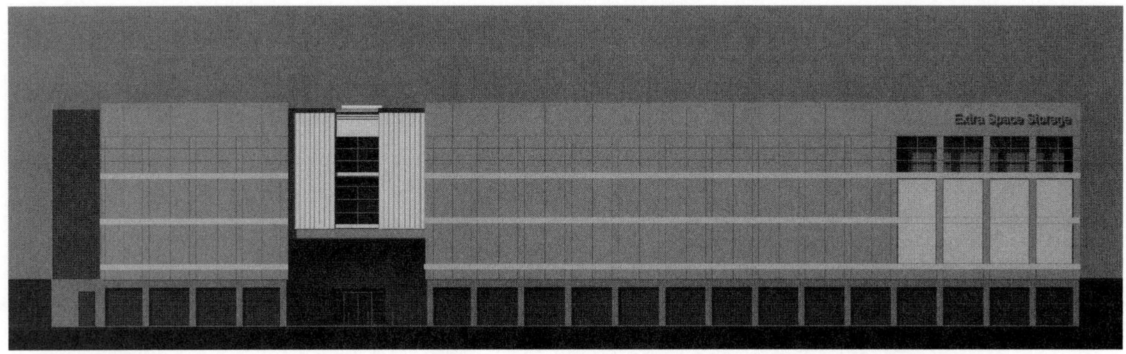

Figure 20-146

Rendered elevation of a four-story building

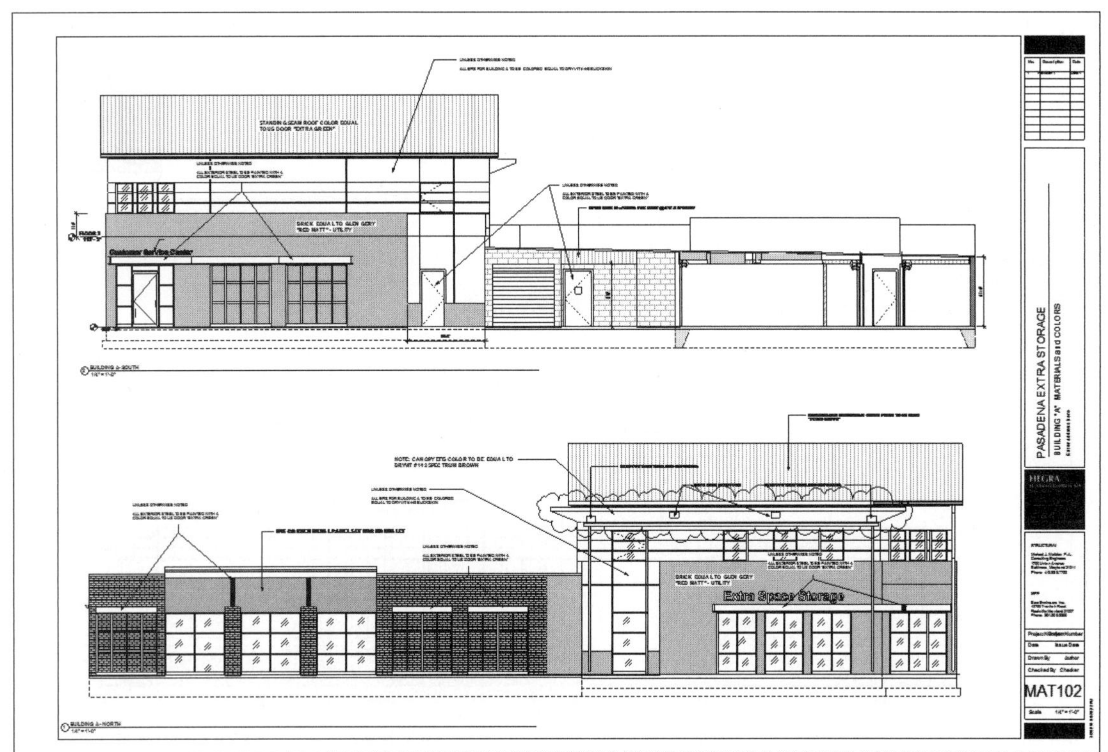

Figure 20-147

Two-story office elevations with **Material** definitions

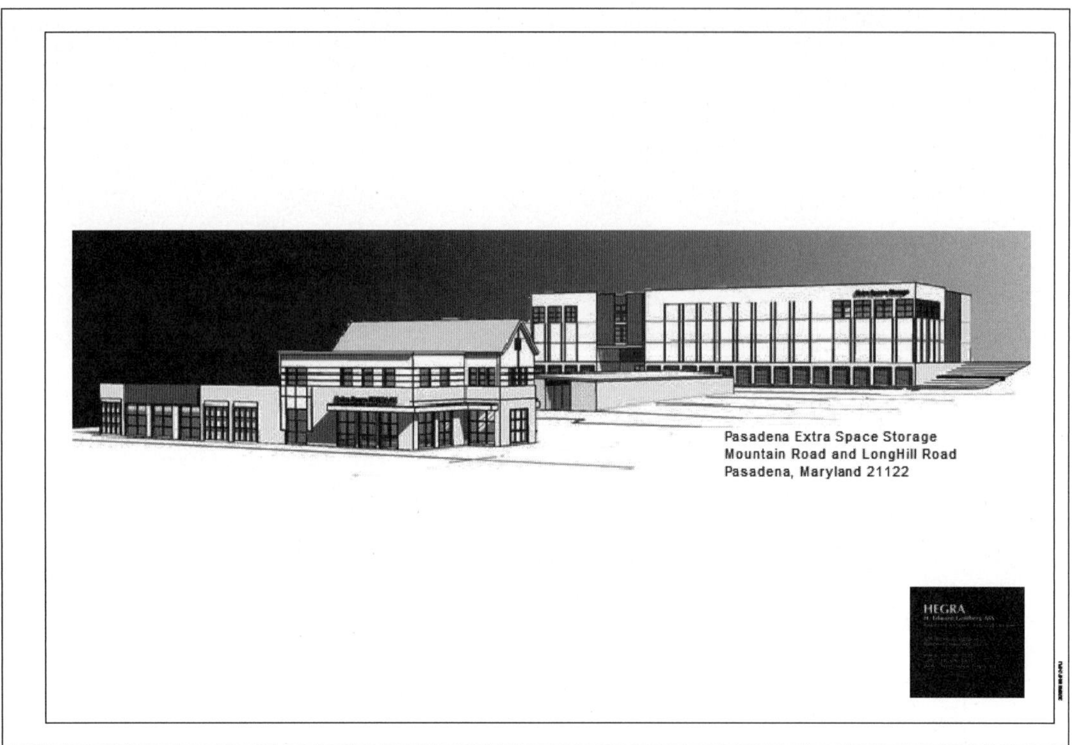

Figure 20-148

Title page with rendering modified in Adobe® Photoshop®

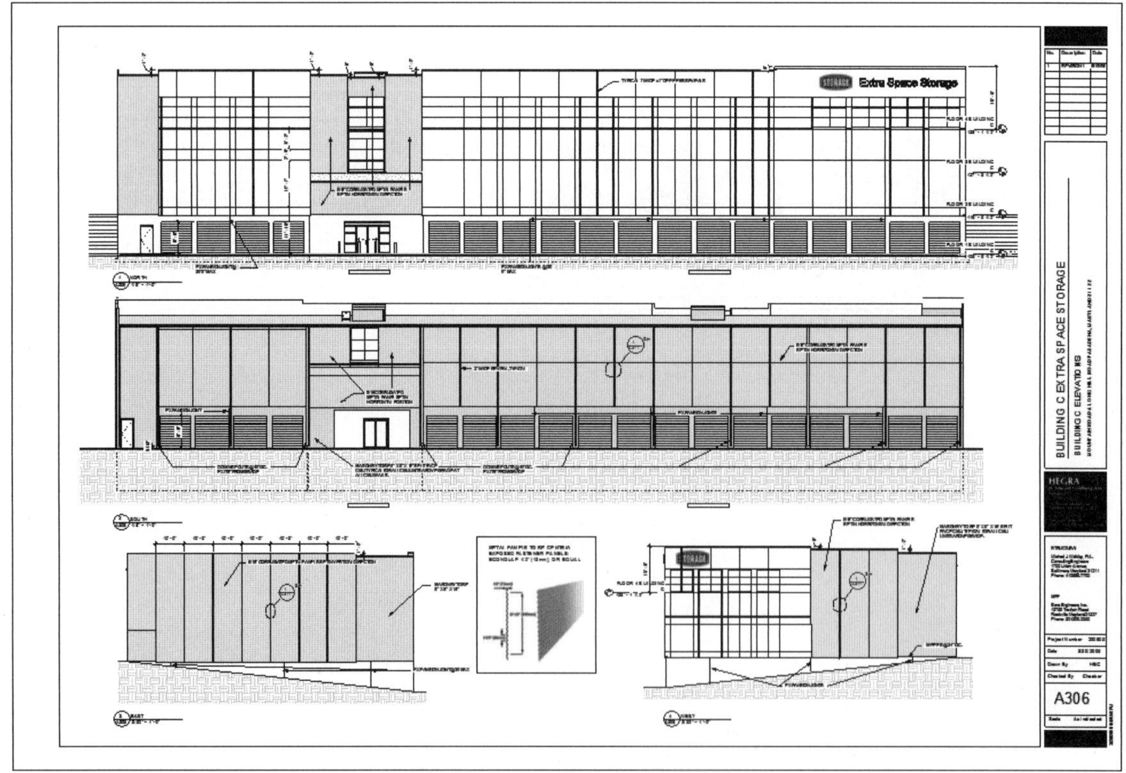

Figure 20-149

Four-story building elevations

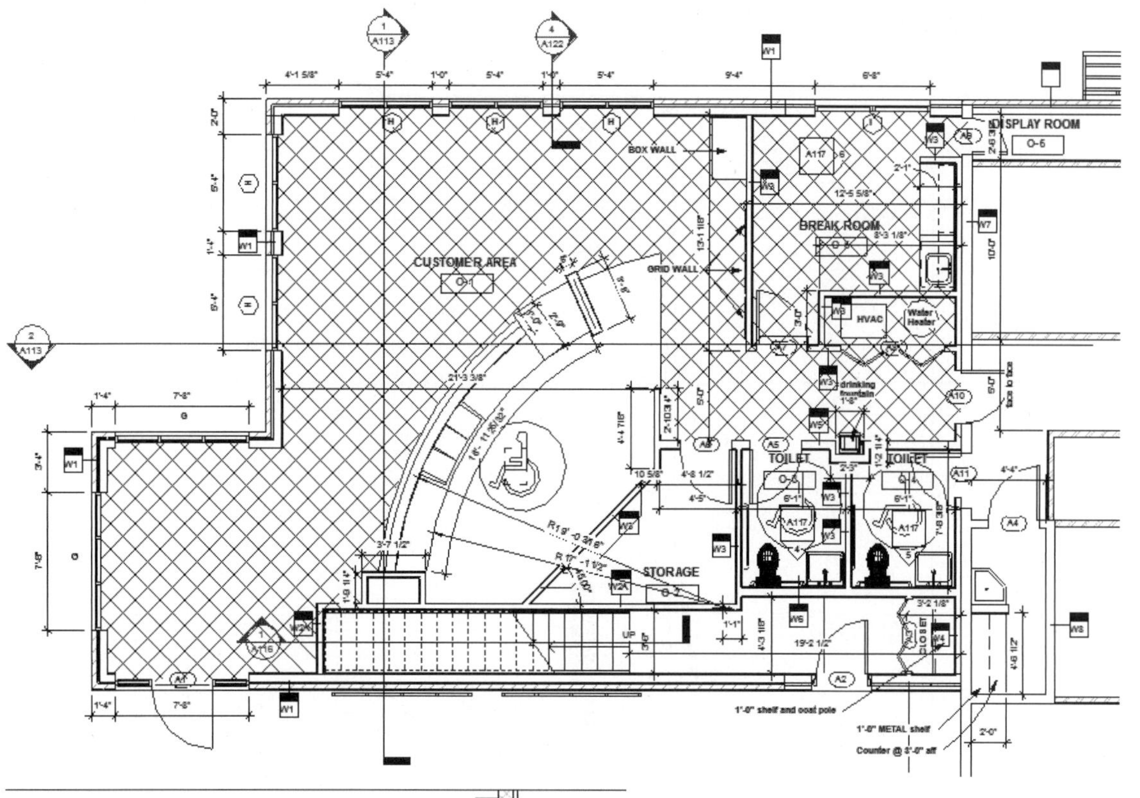

Figure 20-150

First Floor plan of storage office

DIAMOND PLATE STEEL TREADS AND LANDING, TYPICAL

FLOOR 4 BUILDING C 138' - 1 1/2"

FLOOR 3 BUILDING C 127' - 5 1/2"

FLOOR 2 BUILDING C 116' - 9 1/2"

W6 x 21

FLOOR 1 BUILDING C 106' - 9 1/2"

STAIR LATERAL SECTION 3/8" = 1'-0"

Figure 20-151

Four-story stair section

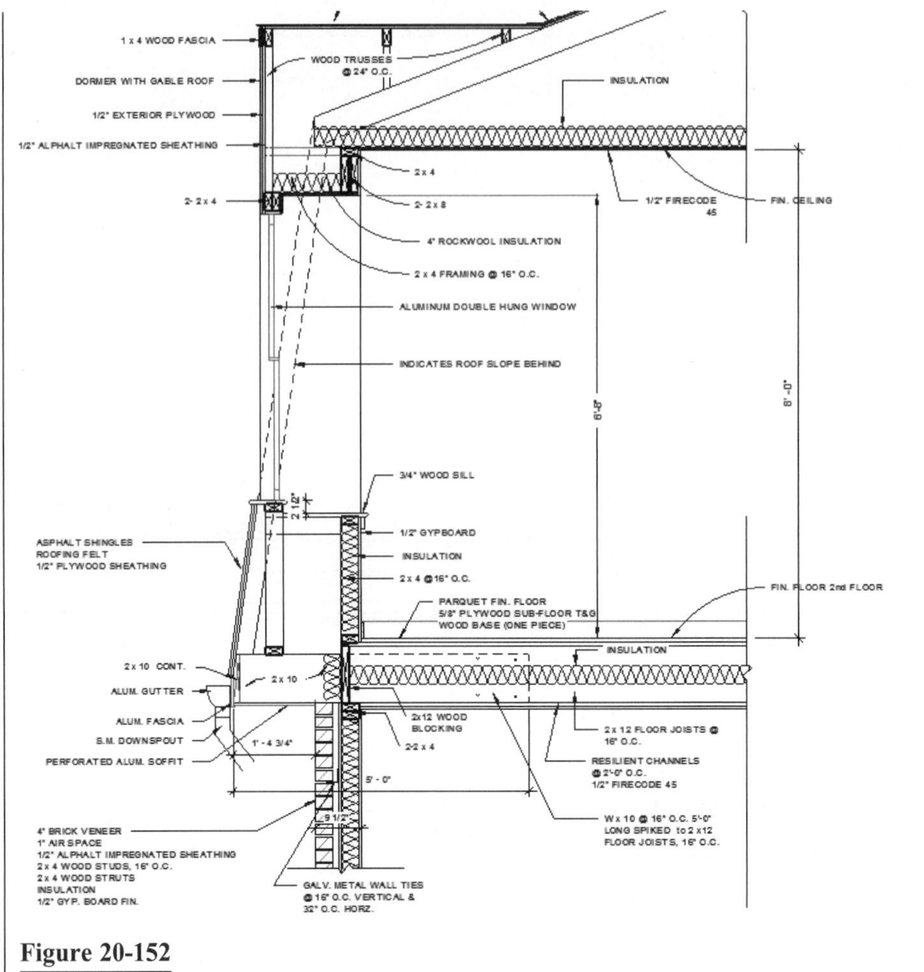
1 x 4 WOOD FASCIA
WOOD TRUSSES
@ 24" O.C.
DORMER WITH GABLE ROOF
INSULATION
1/2" EXTERIOR PLYWOOD
1/2" ALPHALT IMPREGNATED SHEATHING
2 x 4
2- 2 x 4
2- 2 x 8
1/2" FIRECODE
45
FIN. CEILING
4" ROCKWOOL INSULATION
2 x 4 FRAMING @ 16" O.C.
ALUMINUM DOUBLE HUNG WINDOW
INDICATES ROOF SLOPE BEHIND
6'-8"
8' -0"
3/4" WOOD SILL
2 1/2"
1/2" GYPBOARD
ASPHALT SHINGLES
ROOFING FELT
1/2" PLYWOOD SHEATHING
INSULATION
2 x 4 @16" O.C.
FIN. FLOOR 2nd FLOOR
PARQUET FIN. FLOOR
5/8" PLYWOOD SUB-FLOOR T&G
WOOD BASE (ONE PIECE)
INSULATION
2 x 10 CONT.
2 x 10
ALUM. GUTTER
ALUM. FASCIA
2x12 WOOD
BLOCKING
2 x 12 FLOOR JOISTS @
16" O.C.
S.M. DOWNSPOUT
1' - 4 3/4"
2-2 x 4
PERFORATED ALUM. SOFFIT
RESILIENT CHANNELS
@ 2'-0" O.C.
1/2" FIRECODE 45
5' - 0"
9 1/2"
W x 10 @ 16" O.C. 5'-0"
LONG SPIKED to 2 x12
FLOOR JOISTS, 16" O.C.
4" BRICK VENEER
1" AIR SPACE
1/2" ALPHALT IMPREGNATED SHEATHING
2 x 4 WOOD STUDS, 16" O.C.
2 x 4 WOOD STRUTS
INSULATION
1/2" GYP. BOARD FIN.
GALV. METAL WALL TIES
@ 16" O.C. VERTICAL &
32" O.C. HORZ.

Figure 20-152

Section through wood apartment building at second floor

Index

D

E

F

M

T

U

V

W

X